THE CAMBRIDGE HISTORY OF SOUTHEAST ASIA

VOLUME ONE

From Early Times to c.1800

THE CAMBRIDGE HISTORY OF SOUTHEAST ASIA

VOLUME ONE

From Early Times to c. 1800

edited by

NICHOLAS TARLING

CAMBRIDGE
UNIVERSITY PRESS

Published by the Press Syndicate of the University of Cambridge
The Pitt Building, Trumpington Street, Cambridge CB2 1RP, UK
40 West 20th Street, New York, NY 10011–4211, USA
10 Stamford Road, Oakleigh, Victoria 3166, Australia

Printed in Singapore by Kin Keong Printing Co.

National Library of Australia cataloguing-in-publication data:
The Cambridge history of Southeast Asia.
Bibliography.
Includes index.
ISBN 0 521 35505 2 (v. 1).
ISBN 0 521 35506 0 (v. 2).
1. Asia, Southeastern—History.
I. Tarling, Nicholas.
959

Library of Congress cataloguing-in-publication data:
The Cambridge history of Southeast Asia.
Includes bibliographical references and indexes.
Contents: v. 1. From early times to c. 1800—
v. 2. The nineteenth and twentieth centuries.
1. Asia, Southeastern—History. I. Tarling, Nicholas.
DS525.T37 1992   959   91-8808
ISBN 0-521-35505-2 (v. 1)
ISBN 0-521-35506-0 (v. 2)

A catalogue record for this book is available from the British Library

ISBN 0 521 35505 2 (v. 1).
ISBN 0 521 35506 0 (v. 2).

CONTENTS

MAPS

NOTE ON SPELLING

The spelling of proper names and terms has caused editor and contributors considerable problems. Even a certain arbitrariness may have not produced consistency across a range of contributions, and that arbitrariness contained its own inconsistencies. In general we have aimed to spell place-names and terms in the way currently most accepted in the country, society or literature concerned. We have not used diacritics for modern Southeast Asian languages, but have used them for Sanskrit and Ancient Javanese. We have used pinyin transliterations except for some names which are well known in English in the Wade–Giles transliteration.

NOTE ON GENDER IN SOUTHEAST ASIAN LANGUAGES

Southeast Asian languages do not distinguish the sexes in general. Many references to individuals or groups of people in ancient indigenous sources leave it unclear whether women are meant or included. For example, we usually do not know whether a certain function is occupied by a male or a female. Even words borrowed from Sanskrit (which has genders corresponding to sex) are sometimes applied without observing this correspondence: Queen Tribhuwanā (sic) or Tribhuwanottungadewī is called *mahārāja* (a masculine word). These languages do not distinguish between brothers and sisters, but they do between younger and older siblings.

There also seems to have been little discrimination between sexes as far as functions are concerned. There were not only queens reigning in their own right in ancient Java, but also 'prime ministers', such as Airlangga's Mahārastrī i Hino with a name ending in '-Dewī'. As to Kĕrtanagara's four daughters, it seems that this king had no sons—at least they are never mentioned. Therefore what the sources tell us about the daughters provides no evidence of matrilineal descent. Apparently, both lineages were equally important. In some ways ancient Indonesian society was less 'sexist' than our own still is.

ABBREVIATIONS

AP   *Asian Perspectives*, Honolulu.

BEFEO   *Bulletin de l'École Française d'Extrême-Orient*, Paris.

BIPPA   *Bulletin of the Indo-Pacific Prehistory Association*, Canberra.

BKI   *Bijdragen van het Koninklijk Instituut voor de Taal-, Land- en Volkenkunde*, 's-Gravenhage.

BSOAS   *Bulletin of the School of Oriental and African Studies*, London.

FMJ   *Federation Museums Journal*, Kuala Lumpur.

JAS   *Journal of Asian Studies*, Ann Arbor.

JBRS   *Journal of the Burma Research Society*, Rangoon.

JMBRAS   *Journal of the Malay/Malaysian Branch of the Royal Asiatic Society*, Singapore/Kuala Lumpur.

JRAS   *Journal of the Royal Asiatic Society*, London.

JSEAH   *Journal of Southeast Asian History*, Singapore.

JSEAS   *Journal of Southeast Asian Studies*, Singapore.

JSS   *Journal of the Siam Society*, Bangkok.

MAS   *Modern Asian Studies*, Cambridge, UK.

MQRSEA   *Modern Quaternary Research in Southeast Asia*, Rotterdam.

TBG   *Tijdschrift van het Bataviaasch Genootschap van Kunsten et Wetenschappen*, Batavia/Jakarta.

VKI   *Verhandelingen van het Koninklijk Instituut voor de Taal-, Land- en Volkenkunde*, 's-Gravenhage.

PREFACE

Two ideas came together in the project for a Cambridge History of Southeast Asia. One was the concept of the Cambridge Histories themselves. The other was the possibility of a new approach to the history of Southeast Asia.

In the English-speaking and English-reading world the Cambridge Histories have, since the beginning of the century, set high standards in collaborative scholarship and provided a model for multi-volume works of history. The original *Cambridge Modern History* appeared in sixteen volumes between 1902 and 1912, and was followed by the *Cambridge Ancient History*, the *Cambridge Medieval History*, the *Cambridge History of India* and others.

A new generation of projects continues and builds on this foundation. Recently completed are the Cambridge Histories of Africa and Latin America. Cambridge Histories of China and of Japan are in progress, as well as the New Cambridge History of India. Though the pattern and the size have varied, the essential feature, multi-authorship, has remained.

The initial focus was European, but albeit in an approach that initially savoured rather of the old Cambridge Tripos course 'The Expansion of Europe', it moved more out of the European sphere than the often brilliant one-author Oxford histories. But it left a gap which that course did not leave, the history of Southeast Asia.

Southeast Asia has long been seen as a whole, though other terms have been used for it. The title Southeast Asia, becoming current during World War II, has been accepted as recognizing the unity of the region, while not prejudging the nature of that unity. Yet scholarly research and writing have shown that it is no mere geographical expression.

There have indeed been several previous histories of Southeast Asia. Most of them have been the work of one author. The great work of the late D. G. E. Hall dates back to 1955, but it has gone through several editions since. Others include B. Harrison, *South-east Asia, A Short History*, London, 1954; Nicholas Tarling, *A Concise History of Southeast Asia*, 1966; and D. J. Steinberg, et al., *In Search of Southeast Asia*, 1971. The authors of these works faced difficult tasks, as a result of the linguistic diversity of the area; the extent of the secondary material; and the lacunae within it.

Given its diversity, Southeast Asia seemed to lend itself to the Cambridge approach. A magisterial single-volume history existed; others had also made the attempt. A single volume by several authors working together had also been successful. But a more substantial history by a larger number of authors had not been attempted.

The past generation has seen a great expansion of writing, but Southeast Asia's historiography is still immature in the sense that some aspects have been relatively well cultivated, and others not. The historical literature on the area has become more substantial and more sophisticated, but much of it deals with particular countries or cultures, and many gaps remain. A range of experts might help to bring it all together and thus both lay the foundation and point the way for further research effort.

The Cambridge approach offered a warning as well as an invitation. There were practical obstacles in the way of histories on the scale of the original European histories. They got out of hand or were never finished. A summation that was also to lead other scholars forward must be published within a reasonable time-span. It must not be too voluminous; it must not involve too many people.

Practical indications of this nature, however, coincided with historio-graphical considerations. There were some good histories of Southeast Asia; there were also some good histories of particular countries; but there was, perhaps, no history that set out from a regional basis and took a regional approach. This seemed worthwhile in itself, as well as establishing a coherence and a format for the volumes.

In almost every case—even when chapters are the work of more than one person—authors have been taken out of their particular area of expertise. They were ready to take risks, knowing that, whatever care they took, they might be faulted by experts, but recognizing the value all the same in attempting to give an overview. Generally contributors felt that the challenge of the regional approach was worth the hazardous departure from research moorings.

Authors invited to contribute recognized that they would often find themselves extended beyond the span of the published work which has made them well-known. The new history did, however, give them a chance—perhaps already enjoyed in many cases in their teaching—to extend into other parts of the region and to adopt a comparative, regional approach. The publishers sought a history that stimulated rather than presented the last word. Authors were the more ready to rely where necessary on published or secondary works, and readers will not expect equally authoritative treatment of the whole area, even if the sources permitted it.

At the same time, the editor and the contributors have had, like any historians, to cope with problems of periodization. That is, of course, always contentious, but particularly so if it seems to result from or to point to a particular emphasis. In the case of Southeast Asia the most likely temptation is to adopt a chronology that overdoes the impact of outside forces, in particular the Europeans. The structure of this history is not free from that criticism, but the contributors have sought, where appropriate, to challenge rather than meekly to accept its implications.

A similar risk is attached to the division of the material into chapters. The scope of a work such as this makes that all the more difficult but all the more necessary. Sometimes the divisions appear to cut across what ought to be seen as a whole, and sometimes repetition may result. That has been allowed when it seemed necessary. But it may still be possible to pursue certain themes through the book and not to read it merely in chronological sequence. Within the four major chronological divisions, chapters are in general organized in a similar order. The work may thus in a sense be read laterally as well as horizontally.

Some topics, including treatment of the arts, literature and music, have been virtually excluded. The focus of the work is on economic, social, religious and political history. But it will still be difficult to pursue the history of a particular people or country. The work does not indeed promise to offer this; though it offers guidance to those who wish to do this in its apparatus, the footnotes and bibliographic essay to each chapter, the historiographical survey, the list of bibliographies, and the index.

The regional approach has tested the authors, but it has also emphasized the deficiencies of the sources available. Much work has still to be done; much of the earlier life of Southeast Asia remains outside our reach. Each author found a different problem: too much material in one respect, too little in another.

The contributors come from Europe, Japan, Hong Kong, Southeast Asia, Australia and New Zealand, the USA. They have received help from other scholars, acknowledged in the notes to their chapters. The whole project benefited from a meeting of the contributors, held in Singapore with aid from the Sasakawa Foundation. In particular they received comment on their drafts from a number of Southeast Asian scholars at that conference, brought there with the aid of the Toyota Foundation. The editor expresses his grateful thanks to them, Dr Cheah Boon Kheng, Dr Abu Talib Ahmad, Professor Khoo Kay Kim, Dr Taufik Abdullah, and Dr Sombat Chantorn-vong, to Dr Kathirithamby-Wells, who became a formal contributor, and to Professor Wang Gungwu, who also attended. Other scholars have been of assistance to particular authors, such as Victor Lieberman, Ann Kumar, A. H. Johns, Taufik Abdullah, and Adrian Vickers.

Those to be thanked, indeed, are too numerous to mention. But the editor must record the encouragement, aid and support of Dr Robin Derricourt of the Cambridge University Press, and of his colleagues, Leonard and Barbara Andaya.

Nicholas Tarling
The University of Auckland

CHAPTER

1

THE WRITING OF SOUTHEAST ASIAN HISTORY

The writing of Southeast Asian history, as distinct from the history of its several parts, is a comparatively recent development. The first major history of the region as a whole, D. G. E. Hall's *A History of South-East Asia*, appeared only in 1955.[1] Hall's work, though describing itself as 'a bare outline, perilously compressed and oversimplified in many parts',[2] was a massive achievement, basing itself on the detailed work of other scholars and reflecting a knowledge of the critical issues of debate amongst them. Apart from urging that Southeast Asia be studied as an area 'worthy of consideration in its own right' and not as an appendage of India, China or the West, it offered no new conceptual or methodological approaches of its own. But in bringing together the fruits of existing scholarship it provided a kind of stocktaking of the state of that scholarship.

Since then the suitability of the region as a whole as an object of study has been more readily accepted. Cornell University had already established, in 1950, its Southeast Asia Program, and a number of other institutions in various countries followed suit. And, increasingly, comparative works focused on the region as a whole. Charles Fisher's social, economic and political geography (London, 1964) was entitled simply *South-east Asia*, and other works with a similar ambit followed: John F. Cady's *Southeast Asia: its Historical Development* (New York, 1964) and his *Post-War Southeast Asia* (Athens, Ohio, 1974) and Nicholas Tarling's *Southeast Asia: Past and Present* (Melbourne, 1966) are but a few examples. The very perception of Southeast Asia is, of course, a modern and external perception. Southeast Asians themselves, though aware of local, ethnic and cultural identities, did not, until very recently, perceive a Southeast Asian identity. And the external perception was, of necessity, somewhat contrived. The preface to *Governments and Politics of Southeast Asia*, edited by George McT. Kahin in 1959, still hesitated to see Southeast Asia as a significant unity. 'Southeast Asia is not an area of great political homogeneity. Politically as well as culturally its component states are more

---

[1] 2nd edn, 1964; 3rd edn, 1968; 4th edn, 1981. Brian Harrison's useful *South-East Asia: A Short History*, London, 1954, had appeared in the preceding year, but it was directed to the general reader and not to the specialist (Preface, v).
[2] Hall, *History*, Preface to the First Edition, v.

varied than those of Europe.'[3] And as late as 1971 six authors attempting an integrated and thematic history of the region entitled their work *In Search of Southeast Asia*.[4]

Hall's work, coming ten years after the end of World War II, constituted a watershed, embodying the changes in the direction of scholarship that had begun to make themselves felt after the war, and setting the stage for the expansion of Southeast Asian studies which followed. However, it was, of course, the war itself which changed the whole setting within which the region was studied, and it will be convenient, for the purposes of this chapter, to take that as a main dividing line in the development of the writing of Southeast Asian history.

Two further points must be made at the outset. First, in surveying writings about Southeast Asia's past, certain limits have been set. Attention will be confined to works that may be described as belonging to a modern, international tradition of historical enquiry. It would have been possible, in a chapter of this kind, to examine the different types of indigenous writing which contain views about, or presentations of, the past: *babads*, *hikayats*, chronicles of various kinds, literary works and inscriptions. One might have viewed these not merely as sources to be subjected to the critical scrutiny of modern historians, and examined for the light they might throw on past cultural configurations, but as historical writings in their own right, to be approached in their own terms and considered for their assumptions about the nature of the historical process. On the other hand it can be argued that—with the exception of Vietnam, whose dynastic historians did attempt to preserve a record of events— there was no genuinely historical tradition in Southeast Asia. For the most part the function of indigenous chronicles, even when they purported to deal with the course of events—the rise and fall of dynasties, battles, victories and defeats—was not to record a factual past but to perform other, largely moral, functions: to legitimize, to glorify, to assert unity or to express a perceived moral order of society. They might sometimes create a different past in the interests of the present, devising, for example, an appropriate lineage for a usurper. They might serve as part of the regalia of a ruler.[5] There are possible exceptions. One student of Javanese history draws a distinction between 'historical' and 'mythical' Javanese texts and takes the view that, where texts do purport to describe actual events, they are 'often more accurate than a survey of the secondary literature on

---

[3] Ithaca, 1959, Preface, v.

[4] David Joel Steinberg, David K. Wyatt, John R. W. Smail, Alexander Woodside, William R. Roff and David P. Chandler, ed. Steinberg, New York, 1971; 2nd edn, with additional author, R. H. Taylor, Honolulu, 1988.

[5] These issues were discussed at a seminar held in Canberra in 1976 at which an attempt was made to consider indigenous writings in their own terms. See Anthony Reid and David Marr eds, *Perceptions of the Past in Southeast Asia*, Kuala Lumpur, 1979. Contributors were of the view that these works could not be described as historical. As examples, see the essays of Charnvit Kasetsiri who contrasted religious and dynastic histories in Thailand with modern analytical history; Michael Vickery who argued that, in Cambodia, a recorded antiquity was necessary to validate kingship; and O. W. Wolters, who suggested that the function of eleventh-century Vietnamese texts was to assert the equality of Vietnamese and Chinese empires.

Javanese historiography might suggest'.[6] And it is possible, of course, to draw too sharp a contrast between the ritualistic function of texts and the purposes of the so-called 'scientific' historians. Scientific history, too, may justify or legitimize a later state of affairs and create a past to serve the needs of the present. The difference, reflecting a difference of intention, is that it can be called to account and criticized in terms of evidence and argument. It is, after all, perhaps a difference of degree. However, for the purposes of the present chapter it has been decided to regard traditional writings as amongst the sources for the study of Southeast Asia rather than as contributions to that study in their own right, and to confine attention to works based on a critical consideration of surviving sources and belonging to a modern scholarly tradition.

Second, it is not intended to offer here an exhaustive bibliographical survey. In the space available it is possible to refer to only a small minority of the significant works dealing with Southeast Asian history. What is proposed is rather an essay which will seek to identify the main character-istics of historical writing and to notice the principal shifts of focus, emphasis and modes of interpretation. Reference will be made to individ-ual works merely by way of example.

SOUTHEAST ASIAN STUDIES BEFORE WORLD WAR II

Before World War II the study of Southeast Asian history may be divided into two broad categories. There was first of all a concern with early history, with an attempt, in effect, to piece together from archaeological, epigraphical and literary sources, the outlines of a previously unexamined chronology. Second, attention was given to the activities of the European powers from the sixteenth century on, to the gradual creation of commer-cial and territorial empires in Southeast Asia and to the colonial policies pursued therein.

The first type of enquiry was severely constrained by the nature of the available evidence. It is only from about the fifth century CE that evidence exists to support some kind of genuinely historical perception of Southeast Asia. There are material remains deriving from before that period that allow tentative conclusions to be drawn about the indigenous prehistoric cultures of the region. Little can be known about original migrations. Stone tools, both chipped and polished, and bone artefacts give some evidence of palaeolithic and neolithic periods. There are tentative conclusions about the development of agriculture and about whether it was an indigenous development or was introduced from outside. The bronze drums discov-ered in the north Vietnamese village of Dong-son testify to the existence of a metal-working culture in about the fourth century BC. Megaliths and burial places provide evidence of a different kind. But the character and

---

[6] M. C. Ricklefs, *Jogjakarta under Sultan Mangkubumi, 1749–1792*, London, 1974, xix. A similar view is implied by Victor Lieberman whose study of Burma from the sixteenth to the eighteenth century draws heavily on indigenous sources: *Burmese Administrative Cycles: Anarchy and Conquest, c. 1580–1760*, Princeton, 1984, 6 and 271ff.

the scarcity of such remains meant that their interpretation required considerable speculation.

Even for the period where written sources and architectural monuments exist, there is considerable obscurity. According to de Casparis, the earliest known written materials in Southeast Asia are inscriptions on seals and other objects, discovered in south Vietnam and dated as belonging to between the second and fifth centuries CE[7] and the Vo-canh (Vietnam) inscription dated as third century. From about the fifth century epigraphical evidence becomes more plentiful, both on the mainland and in the archipelago, and this provides evidence of polities of substance. It is accompanied by monumental remains such as the ninth-century Buddhist stupa, the Borobodur, and the tenth-century Śaivite Lara Jonggrang complex at Prambanan in central Java, the splendours of Angkor from the ninth to the thirteenth century and of Pagan from the eleventh to the thirteenth century.[8] The evidence of organized power is there, but not a detailed political history of the kingdoms which created these monuments. On the basis of evidence of this kind, scholars have been free to debate such issues as, for example, the exact nature of early trading patterns or questions of political authority such as the Śailendra problem—the apparent simultaneous presence in central Java of both a Śaivite kingdom of the Sanjaya house and a Buddhist kingdom under the Śailendra dynasty (later to be rulers of Śrīvijaya in south Sumatra) in the eighth and ninth centuries—without a conclusive result.[9] Chronicles and other literary works have survived from about the fourteenth century.[10] In Java the more extended texts such as the *Pararaton*, the *Nāgarakĕrtāgama* and the *Babad Tanah Jawi* appear to contain details of political history. These works have survived only because they have been copied and recopied and, in their present form, they are therefore not documents of the period in which they were first written. In any case, for the reasons already suggested, they cannot be taken as reliable sources for the events they purport to describe.

For the second type of pre-war enquiry into the history of Southeast Asia, sources are much more abundant. Whereas students of early history had, perforce, to make what they could of very fragmentary evidence, students of the later period were able to draw on extensive sources provided by the writings of European observers and, in due course, by the colonial archives of the Western powers—Portuguese, Spanish, Dutch, French, British and American. To a European eye these appeared to provide sure ground for historical knowledge, though, as will become apparent, they have always presented their own problems of interpretation and perspective.

The two categories of enquiry shared certain features. The first of these has already been noticed: the almost universal tendency of historians to

---

[7] *Indonesian Paleography*, Leiden, 1975, 12.

[8] For Pagan see G. H. Luce, *Old Burma—Early Pagan*, 3 vols, New York, 1969–70.

[9] For a consideration of that debate and a suggested solution to the problem see J. G. de Casparis, *Inscripties uit de Çailendratijd*, I: *Prasasti Indonesia*, Bandung, 1950, and II: *Selected Inscriptions from the Seventh to the Ninth Century A.D. Prasasti Indonesia*, Bandung, 1956.

[10] de Casparis, *Indonesian Paleography*, 53.

focus on the constituent parts of Southeast Asia rather than to develop a perception of the region as a whole as a suitable object of study. This was perhaps inescapable where it was a matter of studying the activities of the imperial powers in the area. The very names, British Malaya, Netherlands India, French Indochina, indicated the territorial constraints of Western students of Southeast Asia.[11] Much of their work was concerned either with the broad goals of imperial policies or with administrative structures and methods, and such studies concentrated naturally on particular colonial dependencies. But the students of early history, too, focused for the most part on the past of the potential nations of the future, nations defined sometimes by the accidents of colonial rule, rather than on what might be described as 'natural' ethnic, linguistic or cultural entities cutting across the artificially established political boundaries. This represented, of course, the hindsight of nineteenth- and twentieth-century authors, though it is true that, by the eighteenth century, outside observers were bringing European notions of 'country' and 'state' and were imposing their own perceptions of the main political divisions of Southeast Asia. As examples taken almost at random may be cited the epigraphical work of G. H. Luce and Pe Maung Tin in Burma,[12] Georges Cœdès in Thailand and Cambodia,[13] and Cœdès, G. Ferrand, K. A. Nilakanta Sastri, F. D. K. Bosch and others in Indonesia.[14] In the field of archaeological studies and art history were Paul Mus' study of the Borobodur, the archaeological description of the same monument prepared by N. J. Krom while head of the archaeological service of Netherlands India, Bernet Kempers' work on Hindu-Javanese art, Stutterheim on Balinese art, Le May's history of Buddhist art in Siam, and Parmentier on Khmer art.[15] Textual and philological studies, too, followed the same pattern of local concentration, necessarily so in this type of enquiry because of the linguistic specialization required.[16]

[11] The literature is extensive. As examples one might cite J. L. Christian, *Modern Burma*, Berkeley, 1942; P. Le Boulanger, *Histoire de Laos Française*, Paris, 1931; A. Leclère, *Histoire du Cambodge*, Paris, 1914; G. Maspero, ed., *Un Empire Colonial Français: L'Indochine*, Paris, 1929–30; C. B. Maybon, *Histoire Moderne du Pays d'Annam*, Paris, 1920; V. Thompson, *French Indochina*, London, 1937; J. S. Furnivall, *Netherlands India*, Cambridge, UK, 1939; Clive Day, *The Dutch in Java*, New York, 1904; E. S. de Klerck, *History of the Netherlands East Indies*, Rotterdam, 1938; F. W. Stapel, ed., *Geschiedenis van Nederlandsch-Indië*, Amsterdam, 1939; L. A. Mills, *British Malaya 1824–1867*, Singapore, 1925.

[12] *Inscriptions of Burma*, published in the form of rubbings, 1933–9.

[13] *Recueil des Inscriptions du Siam*, Bangkok, 1924–9; *Inscriptions de Sukhodaya*, Bangkok, 1924; and *Inscriptions du Cambodge*, Hanoi, 1937–51.

[14] Cœdès, 'Le Royaume de Çrivijaya', BEFEO, 18 (1918), and 'Les inscriptions malaises de Çrivijaya', BEFEO, 30 (1930); Ferrand, 'L'Empire Sumatranais de Çrivijaya', *Journal Asiatique*, 11th series, 20 (1922), and 'Quatre textes épigraphiques malayo-sanskrits de Sumatra et de Banka', *Journal Asiatique*, 221 (1932); Sastri, 'Sri Vijaya', BEFEO, 40 (1940), and 'Takuapa and its Tamil Inscription', JMBRAS, 22 (1949); Bosch, 'De Inscriptie van Keloerak', *Tijdschrift van het Bataviaasch Genootschap*, 48 (1928).

[15] Mus, 'The Barabadur: Les origines du stupa et la transmigration', BEFEO, 32 (1923); Krom, *Barabadur: Archaeological Description*, The Hague, 1927; Kempers, *The Bronzes at Nalanda and Hindu-Javanese Art*, Leiden, 1930; W. F. Stutterheim, *Indian Influences on Old Balinese Art*, London, 1935, and other works; R. S. Le May, *A Concise History of Buddhist Art in Siam*, Cambridge, 1938; H. Parmentier, *L'Art Khmer Primitif*, Paris, 1927, and *L'Art Khmer Classique*, Paris, 1930.

[16] Editions and translations of major texts include, for Indonesia, J. J. Meinsma's Javanese edition of the *Babad Tanah Jawi* (1874), H. Kern's Dutch translation of the *Nāgarakĕrtāgama*

The same division of labour was apparent in works of synthesis, drawing together the detailed findings of scholarship. An example was the publication in 1926 of the first edition of N. J. Krom's monumental *Hindoe-Javaansche Geschiedenis* (Hindu-Javanese History) which represented a milestone in the study of early Javanese history. Based on the archaeological, epigraphical and textual work of earlier scholars as well as of Krom himself, it addressed questions that had been the subject of debate and aimed to present, in detail, what he believed to be the established record of that particular society. His methods and findings were later to be the subject of systematic criticism, specifically by C. C. Berg. For the time being, however, his work represented an important examination of earlier scholarship and the presentation of what was thought to be known about the history of Java.

There were important exceptions to the country-by-country study of the region. The publication of the first edition of Georges Cœdès' work, *Les États Hindouisés d'Indochine et d'Indonésie* in 1944[17] represented a culmination of his pre-war work and dealt in terms of cultures and political organization over a wider geographical area. Using the concept of 'Hinduization', he developed a broad analysis of Southeast Asian societies and polities and the ideas which supported them. The picture was one of inland kingdoms based on intensive wet-rice cultivation; they were hierarchical in character and sustained by ideas of cosmic order and of rulers embodying that order. But for the most part specialist historians focused on the past of what were to become the individual states of post-war Southeast Asia, and general historians, concerned not with the reading of a particular text or the interpretation of a particular inscription, still devoted themselves to the histories of the political entities created by the colonial era: G. H. Harvey's *History of Burma from the Earliest Times to the Beginning of the British Conquest* (London, 1925), W. A. R. Wood's *History of Siam* (London, 1926), H. G. Quaritch Wales' *Ancient Siamese Government and Administration* (London, 1934), E. d'Aymonier's *Le Cambodge* (Paris, 1900–4), C. B. Maybon's *Histoire Moderne du Pays d'Annam* (Paris, 1920), Richard Winstedt's *History of Malaya* (Singapore, 1935).

A second characteristic of most pre-war studies, whether of the earlier or the later periods of Southeast Asian history, was the tendency of scholars to see that history as shaped by influences external to the region rather than as the product of an internal dynamic. This was partly a consequence of the prior training of many scholars in either Indology or Sinology, which tended to lead them to see Southeast Asia from one or other of those perspectives; but it was perhaps more a consequence of the nature of the available sources. The presence, after about the fifth century CE, of the more extensive archaeological, epigraphical and architectural evidence

(1919), Krom's edition of the *Pararaton* (1920), and Olthof's translation of the *Babad Tanah Jawi* (1941); for Malaya, Winstedt's edition of the *Sejarah Melayu* (1938); for Burma, the translation by Pe Maung Tin and G. H. Luce of *The Glass Palace Chronicle* (1923); for Thailand, the translation of the *Annales du Siam* by C. Notton (1926–39).

17 Published under the title *Histoire ancienne des états hindouisés d'Extrême-Orient*. See Notes on the 2nd and 3rd Editions in the translation edited by Walter F. Vella, *The Indianized States of Southeast Asia*, Honolulu, 1968.

to which reference has already been made corresponds with the period when the cultural influence of India is so obviously apparent in the language and paleography of inscriptions, in the general style and the decorative detail of architectural remains, in the religious ideas of Hinduism and Buddhism and in other artistic forms such as the borrowing of the Sanskrit epics, the *Rāmāyaṇa* and *Mahābhārata*. So extensive were the signs of that influence that many saw it as the result of Indian emigration to, and colonization of, parts of Southeast Asia or of actual conquest, and wrote of Southeast Asia as 'Further India' or 'Greater India'.[18]

The character of this influence, and the way in which it was transmitted, formed a major subject of debate amongst pre-war students of Southeast Asia. A number of Indian scholars, R. C. Majumdar for example, advanced variants of the trade, colonization or conquest theories, even though Indian sources did not provide evidence of a colonizing process in Southeast Asia. And some European scholars argued in similar vein. C. C. Berg argued that Indianization was the result of conquest and settlement by Indian warriors, and N. J. Krom, in his *Hindu-Javanese History*, saw it as the result of the expansion of Indian trade and consequent settlement and intermarriage.[19] A contrary view, which emphasized indigenous impetus, was argued in different forms by other scholars. To take three examples, significant contributions of quite distinct kinds were published by Paul Mus in 1933, J. C. van Leur in 1934 and F. D. K. Bosch in 1946.

Mus, who had received his initial education in Indochina, and who was subsequently employed by the École Française d'Extrême-Orient in Hanoi, argued, with particular reference to earth cults in Champa, the existence of a common, primordial substratum of belief and culture in both Indian and Southeast Asian societies. Thus, when Hinduism and Buddhism became, as it were, available, there was a local basis in Southeast Asia for the acceptance of these beliefs and for their absorption into a local totality of belief.[20]

In 1934 van Leur, subsequently an official of the Netherlands Indies government (he was killed in the Battle of the Java Sea in 1942) published his doctoral thesis for the University of Leiden which applied new theoretical concepts to the study of Southeast Asian trade and which challenged the way in which scholars had approached the study of the region.[21] He insisted that Indian influence in Southeast Asia, and subsequently that of Islam, powerful though they may have been, were nevertheless comparatively superficial when seen in the context of the societies they were affecting—'a thin and flaking glaze' under which the

[18] e.g., R. C. Majumdar, *Ancient Indian Colonies in the Far East*, I, Lahore, 1927, II, Dacca, 1937–8.
[19] Berg, *Hoofdlijnen der Javaansche Literatuur-Geschiedenis*, Groningen, 1929; N. J. Krom, *Hindoe-Javaansche Geschiedenis*, The Hague, 1926.
[20] P. Mus, 'Cultes indiens et indigènes au Champa', BEFEO, 33 (1933), published as *L'Inde vu de l'Est: Cultes indiens et indigènes au Champa*, Hanoi, 1934; trans. I. W. Mabbett, and edited by Mabbett and D. P. Chandler as *India Seen From the East*, Monash Papers on Southeast Asia, no. 3, Clayton, 1975.
[21] Van Leur's thesis was published in 1934 under the title *Eenige beschouwingen betreffende den ouden Aziatischen handel* (Some Observations concerning Early Asian Trade). An English translation, 'On Early Asian Trade', was published, together with some of his other writings, in 1955 in a volume entitled *Indonesian Trade and Society*, The Hague and Bandung.

main form of an older indigenous culture continued to exist.[22] Van Leur rejected, first of all, hypotheses of Indian colonization and of cultural influence carried by trade, and advanced instead the idea of a deliberate Southeast Asian borrowing of ideas, artistic styles and modes of political organization as local polities of substance emerged. His view was based on arguments about the particular aspects of Indian culture that found a ready home in Southeast Asia and about the nature of early Asian trade which, according to some scholars, had been the bearer of that culture. In brief, he characterized Southeast Asian trade as a pre-capitalist, peddling trade which, by its nature, could not have been the means of transmitting those elements of Indian culture that were absorbed into the local scene. These were aspects of high culture—art, literature, ideas of power, sovereignty and kingship—and must therefore have been brought by brahmins, not by petty traders. Indian influence was a court matter and the process, in consequence, could only have been one of deliberate borrowing by Southeast Asian rulers seeking ideas, rituals and organization, not an example of general cultural diffusion. Second, the view that foreign influences did not transform indigenous culture but were a thin and flaking glaze imposed on it, followed from the idea of local initiative. The form of van Leur's analysis became the subject of renewed discussion after the publication of an English translation of his thesis in 1955.

F. D. K. Bosch's argument, advanced in a lecture at Leiden in 1946 which brought together the fruits of his pre-war work,[23] supported van Leur's general view. But whereas van Leur based his case to a considerable extent upon a conceptual analysis of Southeast Asian trade, Bosch had an eye to specific evidence. This included the absence of references to Indian conquest in any inscriptions; the character of linguistic borrowings; and the fact that signs of Indian influence were strongest in inland kingdoms, not coastal ones, as might have been expected if culture had been carried by commerce.

In spite of the growing conviction carried by these arguments, the idea of Greater India had considerable staying power and was reaffirmed in the synthesizing work of Cœdès in 1944 (his term was 'l'Inde extérieure'). His ideas about how Indian influence was conveyed were, however, not so very different from those of van Leur. He saw Indian influence as manifested not through conquest or colonization, but initially through trade; this laid the foundations for the subsequent transmission of the higher culture associated with the development of indigenous kingdoms able and ready to receive, or to take an initiative in acquiring, Indian conceptions of royalty, the sacred language of Sanskrit and the prescriptions of Hinduism.

The debate had many dimensions: the mechanics of transmission with which we have been concerned, the peculiar blend of Buddhism and Hinduism to be found in Southeast Asia, the question of passive acceptance as against active borrowing, of borrowed forms and local genius,[24]

[22] *Indonesian Trade and Society*, 95.
[23] Subsequently published as 'The Problem of the Hindu Colonization of Indonesia' in his *Selected Studies in Indian Archaeology*, The Hague, 1961.
[24] A notion later used by H. G. Quaritch Wales in his *The Making of Greater India*, London, 1951.

and these themes continued to be the subject of later argument. So did the more general issue: that of the 'autonomy' of Southeast Asian history. How is one, in the light of the available evidence, to judge the shaping forces of Southeast Asian culture? Is it indeed a matter of evidence? Or is it perhaps a matter of choice of perspective and framework and point of view? Do contending analyses contradict each other or do they present complementary points of view? In the post-war period, a new generation of scholars were to be less concerned with the details of the evidence than were their predecessors of the 1920s and 1930s, and more with the ways in which the process might be described.

The Indianization debate was so extensive because of the inconclusive nature of the evidence. China's impact on Southeast Asia was less a matter of controversy, perhaps because the record is established more clearly. That influence was felt directly through almost a thousand years of Chinese rule in Vietnam, but it had its effect beyond that. Chinese trade was carried on throughout the region as a whole, and Chinese political dealings with Southeast Asian kingdoms extended as far afield as the Indonesian archipelago. The fact that Chinese sources provide evidence of trading relations and of the receipt by China of tribute missions again means that a good deal of early Southeast Asian history is seen through Chinese eyes.

The penetration of Islam into the Malay peninsula and the archipelago from perhaps about the ninth century provided a further powerful external influence. Controversies about the coming of Islam, however, belong rather to the post-war period of Southeast Asian historiography.

For the period after 1500 the use of European sources has perhaps had an even more dramatic effect on the perspectives of historians. With the establishment of European trade monopolies and of an Asia-wide commercial network, followed by the acquisition of territory and the formation of directly ruled colonial dependencies, it seemed that Southeast Asian history had lost its autonomy. And colonial history, almost by its nature, was necessarily Eurocentric. Even if an attempt were made to read European sources 'against the grain' in an effort to recapture a Southeast Asian perspective, the issues they presented and the categories they used were inevitably those of the invader and not necessarily appropriate to the experiences of the region. Van Leur's analysis was relevant here, too, and one can hardly avoid quoting his famous remark, made with reference to Indonesian history, that 'with the arrival of ships from western Europe, the point of view is turned a hundred and eighty degrees and from then on the Indies are observed from the deck of the ship, the ramparts of the fortress, the high gallery of the trading house'.[25] In that sentence he caught the prevailing tendency of existing Southeast Asian historiography to interpret events after 1500 in terms of Western challenge and Southeast Asian response, and to imply his own contrary view that, at least until the nineteenth century, Europeans in Southeast Asia were fitting into Southeast Asia's existing political and economic patterns rather than making them over.

[25] Van Leur, *Indonesian Trade and Society*, 261.

It was characteristic of the pre-war study of Southeast Asia, then, to focus on the parts rather than the whole, and to see events as being shaped by external influences. A third feature of the pre-war study of Southeast Asia, both of the earlier and later periods, is that it was almost entirely the work of outside observers, European, Middle Eastern and Asian. In the nineteenth and twentieth centuries a number of indigenous Southeast Asian scholars emerged, but such individuals as R. Ng. Perbatjaraka and Hoesein Djajadiningrat in Netherlands India, U Tin in Burma, Tran Van Giap in Vietnam, and Prince Damrong in Thailand were themselves the products of Western education and were scholars in a modern international tradition.

Western students of Southeast Asia in the late nineteenth century were, of course, the latest in a long line of foreign observers of the region. Some of the earliest available information about Southeast Asia is in the form, not of local archaeological or epigraphic remains, but of written reports of travellers from elsewhere, whose accounts have served as sources for the later study of the trading patterns and the cultures of the area. Such accounts included those of the seventh-century Chinese traveller, I Ching (I Tsing), who is one of the sources for the existence of the kingdom of Śrīvijaya;[26] Marco Polo, who visited parts of Southeast Asia while at the Chinese imperial court and who returned to Europe by way of the Indonesian archipelago and the Malay peninsula in the late thirteenth century; Arab travellers such as Ibn Batuta in the early fourteenth century;[27] Pigafetta who accompanied Magellan;[28] the Portuguese, Tomé Pires, in the early sixteenth century;[29] John Jourdain, who visited India and the archipelago between 1608 and 1617;[30] and many others.

From the beginning of the sixteenth century, with the establishment of the Portuguese at Melaka (Malacca) and, later in the century, of the Spaniards at Manila, the period of European empire had begun—the 'Age of Vasco da Gama' as the Indian historian, K. M. Panikkar, has called it[31] — and reflective accounts of the societies and cultures they encountered become more abundant. A wide range of observers, such as Portuguese or Spanish missionaries, or those employed in the service of one or other of the European powers or engaged, sometimes, in the conduct of an official mission, produced significant works of reportage. Examples may be given almost at random. The Jesuit missionary, Alexander of Rhodes, published a history of Tonkin in 1651. Michael Symes, who represented the govern-

[26] See J. Takakusu, *A Record of the Buddhist Religion as practised in India and the Malay Archipelago, 671–695 by I Tsing*, Oxford, 1896. See also W. P. Groeneveldt, 'Notes on the Malay Archipelago and Malacca, compiled from Chinese sources', *Verhandelingen v. h. Bataviaasch Genootschap*, 39 (1876).

[27] See S. Lee, trans., *The Travels of Ibn Batuta in Asia and Africa, 1324–25*, London, 1829. See also G. Ferrand, *Relations de Voyages et Textes Géographiques Arabes, Persans et Turcs relatives à l'Extrême-Orient du VIII au XVIII siècles*, Paris, 1913–14.

[28] Lord Stanley of Alderley, trans., *The First Voyage Round the World by Magellan*, translated from the account of Pigafetta and other contemporary writers, Hakluyt Society, First series, no. 52, 1874.

[29] See A. Cortesão, ed. and trans., *The Suma Oriental of Tomé Pires*, London, 1944.

[30] William Foster, ed., The *Journal of John Jourdain, 1608–1617*, Hakluyt Society, Second Series, vol. XVI, Cambridge, UK, 1905.

[31] *Asia and Western Dominance*, London, 1953.

ment of India in two missions to Burma in 1795 and 1802 gave one of the first full accounts of the history, political system and society of that country in the published account of his first mission, *An Embassy to the Kingdom of Ava sent by the Governor-General of India in 1795*.[32] Thomas Stamford Raffles used his period as Lieutenant-Governor in Java between 1811 and 1816 to collect material for his *History of Java*.[33]

From the eighteenth century many European observers of Asia combined a philosophical interest in the exotic with a scientific temper. Asian and Pacific societies provided material for reflection on the nature of social evolution, perceived, sometimes, within the framework of contemporary romanticism. This coincided with the more general development of scientific enquiry and the establishment of divisions between emerging disciplines. Just as, in the observation of the natural world, botany, geology and geography began to establish themselves as distinct lines of enquiry, so one could perceive, in the study of other societies, the laying of the foundations of what were to become sociology and anthropology. In the nineteenth century such observations multiplied. Sir Arthur Phayre, who led a mission from the government of India in 1855 and subsequently became Chief Commissioner of British Burma, wrote the *History of Burma* (London, 1883), the first such work in English. Henry Yule, secretary to the 1855 mission, prepared the report of the mission and published Phayre's journal.[34] Francis Garnier's *Voyage d'Exploration en Indo-Chine* was an account of a journey up the Mekong under the command of Doudart de Lagrée, but it included what might be called philosophical observations on the customs observed and a vision of the Mekong as a way of entry to China.[35] Auguste Pavie, whose two missions to Luang Prabang between 1887 and 1892 helped to resist Siamese claims to part of Laos and to expand French control in Indochina, produced a massive account of his work.[36] These are but a few examples.

With the territorial expansion of the European powers and the rounding out of their colonial empires in the course of the late nineteenth and early twentieth centuries, a new class of colonial administrators emerged, many of whom engaged in the study of the societies in which they worked. For some this was an amateur interest, and the tradition of the scholarly amateur observer became a strong one. Many developed a high degree of professionalism and, as scholar administrators, they pioneered the archaeological, linguistic and historical study of Southeast Asia. Winstedt, Swettenham, Braddell and Wilkinson in Malaya, and Furnivall in Burma were distinguished examples. In the Netherlands Indies there emerged, at the end of the nineteenth century, a direct official interest in the study and

---

[32] London, 1800. For documents relating to his second mission, and for a defence of Symes' role, see D. G. E. Hall, ed., *Michael Symes: Journal of his Second Embassy to the Court of Ava in 1802*, London, 1955.

[33] London, 1817; published in facsimile by Oxford University Press, Kuala Lumpur, 1965.

[34] Hugh Tinker, ed., facsimile edn of Sir Henry Yule, *Narrative of the Mission to the Court of Ava in 1855*, Kuala Lumpur, 1968.

[35] *Voyage d'Exploration en Indo-Chine effectué pendant les années 1866, 1867 et 1868*, Paris, 1873, and the unofficial posthumous account published by Garnier's brother Leon, 1885. See also M. E. Osborne, *River Road to China: The Mekong River Expedition, 1866–73*, New York, 1975.

[36] *Mission Pavie*, Paris, 1898–1904.

preservation of antiquities, and scholars with a background in philology, Sanskrit and Indology were appointed to appropriate positions. Brandes was Government Philologist, Krom was President of the Archaeological Commission established in 1901 and, from 1913, head of the Archaeological Service which replaced it. Snouck Hurgronje was adviser to the government on Islamic affairs. But the amateur tradition was represented there also, for example, in G. P. Rouffaer whose extensive work earned a major tribute from Krom.[37] And after the introduction of the requirement that recruits to the colonial service receive an appropriate linguistic and cultural training, many officials had a more thorough preparation for extending that kind of interest in the field. There were significant differences in the kind of Indological training provided. The University of Leiden placed its emphasis on language, literature and sociology, while Utrecht was more interested in legal studies and in the nature, in particular, of customary law in Indonesian societies. These different emphases had certain policy implications. In practice the former emphasis became associated with reforming tendencies within the bureaucracy. There was a Leiden influence in the so-called Ethical Policy of 1900 which emphasized the responsibility of the metropolitan government to promote the welfare of its colonial subjects and which believed, too optimistically, in the possibility of effecting modernization and desirable social change by benign government action. The Utrecht approach, by contrast, tended to emphasize the social inertia of traditional social orders, the damage that could follow contact with the West, and the importance of shielding vulnerable societies from the worst effects of change.

Professional and amateur interests were supported by the growth of learned societies and their establishment of scholarly journals. In 1851 the Koninklijk Instituut voor Taal-, Land- en Volkenkunde van Nederlandsch-Indië (Royal Institute for Linguistics, Geography and Culture of the Netherlands Indies) was established at The Hague and its journal, the *Bijdragen* was, as it continues to be, a forum for the publication of scholarly work and debate. In the Indies the Batavia Genootschap van Kunsten en Wetenschappen (Batavian Society for Arts and Sciences), founded in 1788, provided a centre for scholars, officials and others with an interest in, amongst other things, the history and cultures of the Indies. Its *Verhandelingen* was launched in 1779 and its *Tijdschrift* in 1853. A similar highly significant role was played by a local organization in the Straits Settlements. In 1877 a Straits Asiatic Society was formed and within months it had arranged its affiliation with the Royal Asiatic Society (founded in 1826) and become the Straits Branch of the Royal Asiatic Society. In 1923 it was converted to the Malayan Branch and, in due course, after the formation of Malaysia, it became the Malaysian Branch (1964). Its distinguished journal went through similar metamorphoses.[38] The Burma Research Society and its journal (*Journal of the Burma Research Society*, 1911), the bulletin of the London School of Oriental Studies, later the School of Oriental and African

[37] 'Herdenking van Dr G. P. Rouffaer', BKI, 84 (1928).
[38] See the centenary volume of the Malaysian Branch of the Royal Asiatic Society, Reprint Series, no. 4, 1977.

Studies (1917), and the Siam Society and its journal (*Journal of the Siam Society*, 1904) provided further support for scholarly study and publication. Comparable roles were performed for French scholarship by the Societé Asiatique in Paris and the École Française d'Extrême-Orient in Indochina and their respective journals, *Journal Asiatique* (1822) and the *Bulletin de l'École Française d'Extrême-Orient* (1901).

The picture of Southeast Asia that had emerged from the work of these individuals, organizations and societies before World War II was clear enough in its main outlines, though highly debatable in its details. It was a picture of ethnic and cultural diversity, but some common patterns were also perceived. A broad distinction was made between societies based on intensive wet-rice cultivation, to be found in river valleys and on volcanic plains, and those in upland areas engaged in shifting slash-and-burn methods of agriculture. These societies participated to varying degrees in an extensive international trade, extending round the coasts of Asia from China to the Middle East. The picture was one of pockets of dense population where the economy allowed it, and of complex civilizations centred, in the so-called Indianized areas, on royal cities rather than on a perception of firm territorial boundaries. Indeed for the pre-colonial period it was seen as more appropriate to think of political centres rather than of states or kingdoms. Capitals were centres of the realm, reflective of a cosmic order, and shifted as dynasties rose and fell. Visible also were the influences of foreign religions—Hinduism, Buddhism, Theravāda and Mahāyāna, Confucianism, Islam and Christianity. Efforts were made to impose some sort of order on this diversity by classifying it in terms of dominant religious traditions—Confucian Southeast Asia (Vietnam), Theravāda Buddhist Southeast Asia (Burma, Thailand, Cambodiá), Muslim Southeast Asia (Malaya and Indonesia), Christian Southeast Asia (the Philippines)—rather than in ethnic terms, such as Thai, Burman, Mon, Malay, Khmer, etc., or in terms of patterns or dominant cultures as shaped by outside influences, such as Sinicized Southeast Asia, Hispanized Southeast Asia, Indianized Southeast Asia. The main difference between these attempts to group defining characteristics is that a cultural classification might see Indonesia as part of Indianized Southeast Asia, and link it with the Buddhist countries rather than with Malaya as part of Islamic Southeast Asia. For Cœdès, for instance, the features of Indonesia which justified such a linking were far more important than were religious links. As he said in the concluding sentence of *Les États Hindouisés*, it is 'the imprint of the Indian genius which gives the countries studied in this volume a family likeness and produces a clear contrast between these countries and the lands that have been civilized by China'.[39] And the whole is ultimately subjected to, and transformed by, the power of expanding Europe.

These perceptions were reflected in the conventional periodizations of Southeast Asian history: prehistory, Indian influence from, say, the fifth century CE to the thirteenth century, followed in the Malay peninsula and the Indonesian archipelago by the penetration of Islam and, in due course,

---

[39] Cœdès, ed. Vella, *Indianized States*, 256.

by the impact of Europe from the sixteenth century. In the works of colonial historians the effects of European empire were seen as so profound, at least by the end of the nineteenth century and the beginning of the twentieth—restructuring the economies of Southeast Asia, stimulating enormous social changes, establishing modern political systems, and bringing order and unity to the individual parts of the region—that they constituted a fundamental break in the continuity of Southeast Asian history.

It was a neat picture and, no doubt, it had its patronizing elements. The scholar administrators of the late nineteenth and early twentieth centuries belonged to a broad orientalist tradition which tended to see other cultures as objects of study—and perhaps as inferior objects. Some, who became deeply attached to the societies in which they worked, were attracted by the romanticism of the exotic. Others displayed a paternalistic conviction that their duty was to achieve the uplift of those they had come to rule. Even when scholarly study was based on respect for the local society rather than on a sense of superiority, there was likely to be an unquestioned assumption that the ultimate and inevitable outcome would be the transformation of that society by Western civilization. (There was, perhaps, a more open-minded acceptance of the patterns and values of other cultures on the part of eighteenth-century observers than on the part of their successors who belonged to the high imperialism of the late nineteenth century.)

This general outlook, and, in particular, a periodization leading up to the imperial present, served the interests of empire, and, in spite of the emergence of nationalist movements in some colonial dependencies, there seemed no reason why the processes set in motion by European rule should not continue indefinitely. Different powers had different views about the ultimate goals to be pursued in colonial policy. Self-government was at least the professed goal of Britain in Malaya and Burma, though, in the former case at least, it was not seen as likely to be an early outcome. In the Philippines the United States, having succeeded Spain after the war of 1898, did envisage a specific transition to independence. In the Indies the Dutch spoke of a planned development of Indies society and, again in an indefinite future, a degree of autonomy for the colony within an as yet undefined relationship with the Netherlands. The future 'East Indian Society' would have a place for a permanent European component. The French, pursuing their 'mission civilisatrice' (civilizing mission), looked to self-government of a different kind: the incorporation of the dependencies, in due course, within the framework of metropolitan France. Colonial nationalism did not appear to be inconsistent with these various perspectives for it, too, was part of the progressive forces perceived by colonial historians. Its élite leadership was itself a product of the modernizing process that imperialism had set in motion.

The basis of this way of looking at Southeast Asia was effectively destroyed between 1942 and 1945, and scholars after the war came to the study of the region in an entirely different setting from that of the past. They had different expectations, different preoccupations and found different answers to different questions. And they were present in much greater numbers than before.

SOUTHEAST ASIAN STUDIES SINCE WORLD WAR II

The tremendous expansion of Southeast Asian studies in the post-war years was hardly a surprising phenomenon. The Japanese occupation of most of the region had swept away the apparatus of colonial rule, and rendered impossible its simple restoration when the war was over. The struggles of new nations for independence, the attainment of that independence in the first instance by the Philippines, Burma and Indonesia and in due course by Malaya, the intensification of nationalist struggle in the French dependencies of Indochina, and changes in the surrounding areas of Asia—the establishment of India and Pakistan and, in 1949, the victory of the Chinese Communist Party—combined to evoke a concentrated study of the region in the West and to transform what it was that was being studied. The same developments stimulated the study of their history by the new nations of Southeast Asia themselves.

A mixture of imperatives was present. The emerging republics of the region required, as part of the creation of their identity, new perceptions of their past, perceptions going back beyond the intrusion of the Western powers and finding earlier roots in older pattens of culture and polity. For observers from outside Southeast Asia there were issues of policy which made a focus on the region not just a matter of scholarly investigation but a matter of practical urgency, arising from the changed distribution of power in the area. For the major powers these included what might be called Cold War issues. Southeast Asia was perceived in a global context. Political affiliations and questions of economic development, modernization and growth interlocked as the powers adjusted to the turbulence of what had appeared, in the past, to be a stable area, firmly under the benevolent rule of Western Europe and America. The Korean War and, in due course, the long-drawn-out trauma of Vietnam, accentuated the concern of Western students of Asia. The result was a massive expansion—one might almost say an explosion—of Asian studies in general, and Southeast Asian studies in particular, in the Western world.

The effect was apparent both in the expansion of institutional arrangements for the study of Asia and in changes in approach and in methods of study. In some cases these took the form of 'area studies' in which the methods of a variety of social sciences—sociology, anthropology, political science, economics—together with history, literature and philosophy, were brought together for the study of a defined area. In other cases the disciplines were preserved as providing distinctive methods of understanding. With differing emphases and styles of organization, a variety of programmes was developed in America, Canada, Britain, the Netherlands, and the Soviet Union; in Australia and New Zealand, which felt themselves to be in an exposed position on the edge of the region; and also in new or expanding universities in the countries of Southeast Asia itself.

Space does not allow a full catalogue, but some examples should be mentioned. In the West the United States was the powerhouse of the expansion and change of direction. Cornell University's Southeast Asia Program co-ordinated the study of the region at undergraduate and graduate levels, and its Modern Indonesia Project, supported by Rockefeller funds, launched a sustained research and publications programme. On a more modest scale Yale also developed a Southeast Asian emphasis and other universities, amongst them Berkeley, Michigan, Northern Illinois, Ohio, Washington, Wisconsin, followed suit. In Canada, the Department of Asian Studies in the University of British Columbia cast its net more widely and placed most emphasis on China and Japan, but Southeast Asia was included also. In Britain the London School of Oriental and African Studies (originally founded in 1917 as the School of Oriental Studies) expanded its activities; and after a committee of enquiry, appointed by the University Grants Committee, and chaired by Sir William Hayter, several new institutional initiatives were taken in order to strengthen Asian studies and to shift the emphasis from a traditional orientalist approach, concentrating on classical literature and philosophy, to a study of modern problems. St Antony's College, a new Oxford foundation, gave a special place to the graduate study of Asia. The University of Sussex established a School of African and Asian Studies, and its Institute of Development Studies (1966) gave some attention to Asia. For Southeast Asia the Centre of South-East Asian Studies at Hull and, later, the Board of Southeast Asian Studies at Kent were examples. In Australia, the establishment of the Research School of Pacific Studies, and later the Faculty of Asian Studies, at the Australian National University, of departments of Indonesian Studies at the Universities of Sydney and Melbourne, of the Centre of Southeast Asian Studies at Monash and the School of Modern Asian Studies at Griffith, and the placing of similar emphases at the University of Western Australia and at Flinders, reflected the same kind of interest.

At the same time Asian countries expanded the Southeast Asian emphases of existing universities—in the Ateneo de Manila, in Chulalongkorn and Thammasat University in Bangkok, for example—and founded new universities—Gadjah Mada University in Yogyakarta, the University of Malaya in Kuala Lumpur, the University of Singapore and others. In all of these, local circumstances and national interest dictated the placing of a Southeast Asian emphasis in undergraduate offerings and graduate programmes in the humanities and social sciences. The history of individual nations rather than of the region as a whole normally formed the main focus, but this was not always the case. The foundation in Singapore in 1968 of an Institute of Southeast Asian Studies represented an attempt to break the pattern. Set up by the government of Singapore as a research body, the institute had, amongst its other goals, the idea of giving fellowships to Southeast Asian scholars to enable them to study countries other than their own. In Japan a Southeast Asian focus was developed in, amongst other places, Waseda University in Tokyo and in Kyoto's Centre of Southeast Asian Studies, founded in 1963.

The institutional expansion was accompanied by the rejuvenation of old scholarly societies, the formation of new ones and the development of new avenues of publication. Earlier associations and their journals remained — the Koninklijk Instituut and its *Bijdragen*, the École Française and its bulletin, the Siam Society and the Malayan branch of the Royal Asiatic Society and their journals. Others changed their character. In America the Far Eastern Association transformed itself into the Association for Asian Studies in 1956, and its journal, the *Far Eastern Quarterly*, which had been launched in 1941, became the *Journal of Asian Studies*. This change meant both a shift from a Eurocentric perception of the 'Far East' and a widening of geographical scope to include the whole of Asia. In the Netherlands the journal *Indonesië*, launched in 1947 by the van Hoeve publishing house, was an important new organ of analysis, though it was to last for only ten years. The first issue of *Indonesia*, published by the Cornell Modern Indonesia Project in 1966, noted that Indonesian specialists had tended to confine themselves too narrowly within their respective disciplines, and aimed to publish articles covering a wide range of subject matter and methods of approach. It has continued to offer an avenue for innovative and provocative work, designed to 'stir discussion and criticism'. In Singapore the *Journal of Southeast Asian History* was launched in 1960. In 1969 it decided to widen its scope and changed its name to the *Journal of Southeast Asian Studies*. *Archipel*, published from 1977 under the patronage of the École Pratique dés Hautes-Études in Paris, provided a forum for the study of island Southeast Asia. And a variety of publication series also served the growing market: the Cornell Southeast Asia Program's Data Paper series, the Interim Report Series and the Monograph Series of the same university's Modern Indonesia Project, Yale's Monograph Series, Ohio's Centre for International Studies Series, the Monograph Series of Monash University, the Southeast Asia Publications Series of the Asian Studies Association of Australia, and many others.

While it would be true to say that the greater part of the new effort was directed to the study of the contemporary scene, the study of Southeast Asia's past also had its place in the radically altered environment.

Between 1956 and 1958 a series of seminars was held at the London School of Oriental and African Studies to survey the current state of historical writing about Southeast Asia. The seminars attempted an evaluation of what had been done in the pre-war years and in the first dozen years after the war, noticed some of the changes that were taking place, and posed questions for the future. Attention was drawn to a variety of special problems facing historians of Southeast Asia: the paucity and difficulty of the sources for the early history of the region; the multiplicity of indigenous languages, classical and vernacular, and of European languages also; the tendency of earlier scholars to concentrate on parts of the region without being fully aware of what was going on in other parts; and changes in perspective as new nations came into being.

It is interesting, thirty and more years later, to look back at the papers resulting from these seminars.[40] It would be fair to judge the outlook of the participants as compounded of a mixture of humility and confidence. They

---

[40] D. G. E. Hall, ed., *Historians of South-East Asia*, London, 1961.

were humble in the face of the sheer difficulty of the task, and were aware of the danger of bias of various kinds, whether arising from the Euro-centric perspectives of European historians in the past or from the South-east Asian perspectives of new nationalist historians. But bias was seen in comparatively simple terms, as something that, with care and goodwill, could be corrected or avoided. Hence the ground for confidence. Was it possible, asked the editor of the collected papers, 'to write a real history of South-East Asia before the coming of the European?' (p. 7). The expecta-tion appeared to be that it was possible. The problem here, however, was one of sources and whether they were such as to enable satisfactory knowledge to be achieved: a knowledge comparable, say, to that available for Greece and Rome. What was not questioned, but would certainly be questioned by historians of a later generation, was the very notion of a 'real history', a notion reminiscent of the confidence of Acton introducing the first *Cambridge Modern History*. In the same vein D. G. E. Hall, as convenor of the seminars, referred to a 'new enlightenment' in the approach of Western scholars to the study of the history of the region, revealed in a readiness to see Southeast Asia from a Southeast Asian centre rather than from outside, and in the search for an appropriate nomen-clature and for 'a periodization free from colonial implications' (p. 9). Hall referred also to the idea of scientific enquiry by which the 'real' history would be achieved. Indeed Southeast Asia's awareness of its own past and its 'first real notions of history' were largely the product of its contact with the scientific tradition of the West (p. 2). The historians who gathered in London at that time, though cautious about the problems of dealing with Southeast Asia's past, were certainly not plagued to any great extent by fundamental doubts about their craft.

Against that background one might judge post-war historical scholar-ship, as it continued after the date of the London seminar, as revealing, at first, a considerable confidence in the historical enterprise—a confidence very much in line with that of the historians' social-science colleagues in their onslaught on the problems of the modern world—but with a growing awareness of the sheer difficulty of securing any genuine under-standing of other cultures and other times. Such an attitude was not confined to the study of Southeast Asian history. It is possible to detect, in the profession of history in general in the latter part of the twentieth century, a sense of uncertainty and a recognition of the precarious nature of historical knowledge: a reflection, no doubt, of the scepticism of the age.

The initial mood of historians of Southeast Asia in the post-war years was certainly one of confidence, a confidence which must be seen against the background of the expansion of Southeast Asian studies in general to which reference has been made. That expansion, it was noted, involved changes in method as well as in focus. Since much of the motivation came from urgent issues of policy, a great deal of the effort was concentrated at first on the study of current political and economic issues: questions of political trends and political stability, the nature of emerging political systems, the conflict of ideologies, questions of economic development and distribution. To a great extent the methods used were, in consequence, those of the social sciences: economics, political science, sociology and anthropology. These were the disciplinary approaches that were regarded as likely to provide an understanding of the modern Southeast Asian world.

The same general outlook was to be found amongst historians. In the post-war period they were affected both by the methodological themes of their social-science colleagues and by the concern with the immediate problems of the post-war scene. On the methodological front they learned more and more to draw on the methods and the findings of neighbouring disciplines. In a seminal article of the early 1960s, H. J. Benda argued vigorously that historians must be social scientists as well, and should address themselves to the structure of Southeast Asian history as distinct from 'the mere charting of dynastic cycles or the chronicling of wars, as ends in themselves'.[41] He sought to establish a periodization based not merely on political developments but on major structural changes in the social, economic and political relationships of the region. In similar vein, W. F. Wertheim called on historians to apply the techniques of sociology in studying Southeast Asian history.[42] And J. H. Romein urged historians of Southeast Asia to adopt a comparative approach as a means of developing a more systematically scientific method and of coming to grips with such processes as nationalism, revolution and social change in Asian societies.[43] The fact that the countries of Southeast Asia had shared a broadly common experience of Western imperialism over the previous couple of centuries was, in itself, a stimulus to the development of comparative enquiries. It must be conceded that, in spite of a growing disposition to see Southeast Asia as a region, much of the post-war work in history and the social sciences continued to be directed to individual countries rather than to the region as a whole. However, most scholars were aware of comparative considerations even when focusing on one area, and that awareness did give substance to the idea of Southeast Asian history.

The emphasis on the need for historians to draw upon the techniques of neighbouring disciplines went, naturally enough, with a focus on recent history. Such a focus was, indeed, characteristic of a general approach to Southeast Asian history at least in the first two decades of the post-war period. Historians shared the general concern with the major political and international issues of the day and it was not unusual for them to direct their enquiries to the immediate background of the contemporary scene, to the point where the boundaries between disciplines, especially those between politics and history, tended to become blurred.[44] The work of

---

[41] 'The Structure of Southeast Asian History: Some Preliminary Observations', in JSEAH, 3 (1962), reprinted in Continuity and Change in Southeast Asia: Collected Journal Articles of Harry J. Benda, Yale University Southeast Asian Studies Monograph Series, No. 18, New Haven, 1972.

[42] 'The Sociological Approach', in Soedjatmoko, Mohammad Ali, G. J. Resink and G. McT. Kahin eds, An Introduction to Indonesian Historiography, Ithaca, 1965, 340ff.

[43] 'The Significance of the Comparative Approach in Southeast Asian Historiography', ibid., 380ff.

[44] For a discussion of these issues J. D. Legge, 'Southeast Asian History and the Social Sciences', in C. D. Cowan and O. W. Wolters, eds, Southeast Asian History and Historiography: Essays Presented to D. G. E. Hall, Ithaca and London, 1976.

George McT. Kahin, a political scientist with historical training, provided an example of a dominant style. Kahin carried out fieldwork in Indonesia in 1948 and 1949, formed close links with leading figures of the young republic, and was a first-hand observer of events as they unfolded during the closing months of the struggle for independence. This privileged position gave a sharpness and an immediacy to his study of the Revolution, but he added depth and analytical coherence by placing it in an historical context of Dutch rule, the rise of a nationalist movement and the impact of the Japanese Occupation.[45]

This became a familiar pattern. John F. Cady's *A History of Modern Burma* (Ithaca, 1958) devoted over half of its length to pre-war history. F. N. Trager's *Burma from Kingdom to Republic* (London, 1966) was subtitled 'a historical and political analysis', and dealt with British rule as the background to independence. The Cornell tradition of linking politics and history received further expression in a major textbook, *Government and Politics of Southeast Asia*, the seven authors of which wrote to a prescribed pattern in which a substantial historical chapter preceded an examination of the contemporary setting and the political processes of the individual countries of Southeast Asia.[46]

Given this style, it was sometimes difficult not only to distinguish historical writing from that of political scientists (such works, for example as J. H. Brimmell's examination of Southeast Asian communism or Ellen J. Hammer's account of the initial stages of the Indochina conflict),[47] but to distinguish either from the enormous body of works of serious reportage of, and comment on, the contemporary scene. One might mention, as distinguished examples of the latter, Bernard Fall's *Street Without Joy: Indochina at War, 1946–1954* (Harrisburg, 1961) or, from a decade later, Frances FitzGerald's *Fire in the Lake: The Vietnamese and the Americans in Vietnam* (Boston, 1972). Some of the writings on the borders of history, politics and the other social sciences were more concerned than others to develop, self-consciously, a conceptual analytical framework and this served to mark them off from narrative accounts. Herbert Feith, a political scientist, placed his political history of the first ten years of the Republic of Indonesia within a framework of contrasting leadership styles—solidarity-makers and administrators—and contrasting political cultures—Javanese aristocratic and Islamic entrepreneurial—as a means of explaining the instability of successive governments during the 1950s.[48] A specifically sociological approach was adopted by G. W. Skinner in his history of Chinese society in Thailand.[49] And other conceptual tools lay to hand: Fred Riggs' distinction between 'diffused', 'prismatic' and 'diffracted' societies;[50] Lucian Pye's exploration of personality traits in shaping leadership modes in transitional societies;[51] Karl Deutsch's attempt to define the

[45] *Nationalism and Revolution in Indonesia*, Ithaca, 1952.
[46] George McT. Kahin, ed., Ithaca, 1959.
[47] Brimmell, *Communism in South-East Asia*, London, 1959; Hammer, *The Struggle for Indochina, 1940–1955*, Stanford, 1955.
[48] *The Decline of Constitutional Democracy in Indonesia*, Ithaca, 1962.
[49] *Chinese Society in Thailand: an Analytical History*, Ithaca, 1957.
[50] *Administration and Developing Countries: The Theory of Prismatic Society*, Boston, 1964.
[51] *Politics, Personality and Nation Building: Burma's Search for Identity*, New Haven, 1962.

essential characteristics of nationalism;[52] John Kautsky's consideration of class formation;[53] and Clifford Geertz's notions of primordial loyalties, cultural 'streams' and agricultural involution.[54]

Not all historians were concerned with the contemporary scene and its immediate background, though most of those who directed their enquiries to earlier periods still tended to remain within the period of European contact with Southeast Asia. Walter Vella, A. L. Moffat and David Wyatt explored the successive reigns of Rama III, Mongkut and Chulalongkorn.[55] An historian, M. A. P. Meilink-Roelofsz, and an economic historian, Kristof Glamann, brought different tools to the study of trade in the Indonesian archipelago.[56] Wong Lin Ken surveyed the development of the Malayan tin industry and later R. E. Elson subjected the cultivation system in nineteenth-century Java to a new and close scrutiny.[57] Imperial history, in the sense of a focus on the motives and policies of the metropolitan powers, continued to be studied in the post-war period, especially the history of Britain in Malaya. Nicholas Tarling examined the circumstances surrounding the British interest in the Malay world in the late eighteenth and early nineteenth centuries.[58] Mary Turnbull traced the evolution of British policy in the Straits Settlements.[59] C. N. Parkinson and C. D. Cowan considered, from different angles, the reasons lying behind the British 'forward movement' in Malaya.[60] And a number of studies were devoted to the methods and character of British administration and to the economic history of the peninsula.[61]

Increasingly, historians writing of the nineteenth and early twentieth centuries were as ready to draw on the methods and conceptual schemes of neighbouring social sciences as were their colleagues who focused on more recent developments. Edgar Wickberg brought the skills of an

---

[52] *Nationalism and Social Communication*, New York, 1953.

[53] *Political Change in Underdeveloped Countries: Nationalism and Communism*, New York, 1963.

[54] *The Religion of Java*, Glencoe, 1962; *Agricultural Involution*, Berkeley, 1963; *Peddlers and Princes: Social Change and Modernization in Two Indonesian Towns*, Chicago, 1963; and *The Social History of an Indonesian Town*, Cambridge, Mass., 1965.

[55] e.g., Vella, *Siam Under Rama III*, New York, 1957; Moffat, *Mongkut, the King of Siam*, Ithaca, 1961; Wyatt, *The Politics of Reform in Thailand: Education in the Reign of King Chulalongkorn*, New Haven, 1969.

[56] Meilink-Roelofsz, *Asian Trade and European Influence in the Indonesian Archipelago between 1500 and about 1630*, The Hague, 1962; Glamann, *Dutch–Asiatic Trade, 1620–1740*, Copenhagen and The Hague, 1958. C. R. Boxer's two volumes, *The Dutch Seaborne Empire, 1600–1800*, London, 1965, and *The Portuguese Seaborne Empire, 1415–1825*, London, 1969, though magisterial works of maritime history, were more conventional in approach and style.

[57] Wong Lin Ken, *The Malayan Tin Industry to 1914*, Tucson, 1965; Elson, *Javanese Peasants and the Colonial Sugar Industry: Impact and Change in an East Java Residency, 1830–1940*, Singapore, 1984.

[58] *British Policy in the Malay Peninsula and the Archipelago, 1824–1871*, Singapore, 1957; *Anglo-Dutch Rivalry in the Malay World, 1780–1824*, St Lucia, Qld, and Cambridge, UK, 1962; and *Piracy and Politics in the Malay World*, Melbourne and Singapore, 1963.

[59] *The Straits Settlements, 1826–67: Indian Presidency to Crown Colony*, London, 1972.

[60] Parkinson, *British Intervention in Malaya, 1867–77*, Singapore, 1960; Cowan, *Nineteenth-Century Malaya: The Origins of British Political Control*, London, 1961.

[61] E. Sadka, *The Protected Malay States, 1874–1895*, Kuala Lumpur, 1968; Eunice Thio, *British Policy in the Malay Peninsula, 1880–1910*, Singapore, 1969; Khoo Kay Kim, *The Western Malay States, 1850–1873*, Kuala Lumpur, 1972; G. C. Allen and Audrey Donnithorne, *Western Enterprise in Indonesia and Malaya*, London, 1957; J. Norman Parmer, *Colonial Labor Policy and Administration: A History of Labor in the Rubber Plantation Industry in Malaya*, New York, 1960.

economic and social historian to his study of the Chinese community in the Philippines in the last fifty years of Spanish rule, observing its internal structure and consciousness and its relations with the surrounding society in a period of rapid economic and social change.[62] Daniel Doeppers' study of Manila between 1900 and the outbreak of World War II—a study in social mobility—focused on the city as 'a set of employment structures and as a stratified society', and buttressed its findings by close statistical analysis.[63] The Indonesian historian, Sartono Kartodirdjo, endeavoured to construct a taxonomy to distinguish between various categories of peasant unrest in Java.[64] In an exercise in economic geography, Michael Adas sought to provide a new framework of analysis of British rule in Burma by focusing on the 'Burma Delta'. This enabled him to develop Furnivall's notion of a plural society and, by using a demographic approach based on information drawn from the settlement reports of the Revenue Department, to integrate the role of the peasantry with that of traditional rulers, British administrators and a nationalist élite from the mid-nineteenth century.[65] Many other examples could be cited. The contributors to the book edited by A. W. McCoy and E. de Jesus, *Philippines Social History: Global Trade and Local Transformations* (Quezon City and Sydney, 1982), took as their starting point the intensive work done on Philippines regional history over the previous two decades, and brought the techniques of economic history and sociology to their assessment of late colonial Philippines society. In Thailand, Jit Poumisak offered a class interpretation of what he saw as Thai feudalism.[66] And following the students' uprising of 1973 a new emphasis could be seen in Thai historical studies, an emphasis on socio-economic history led by such scholars as Chattip Nartsupha, Chai-anan Samudavanija and Nidhi Aeusrivongse, and directed, in different ways, to the study of the structure of pre-capitalist society and culture.[67]

The post-war concentration on the nineteenth and twentieth centuries, taking place as it did within the context of a greatly expanded Asian studies 'industry', tended to overshadow the study of earlier periods, but did not entirely eclipse it. Early history continued to command the attention of distinguished scholars. Wang Gungwu's examination of early Chinese trading patterns in Southeast Asia, O. W. Wolters' study of early Indonesian commerce and of political rhythms in the Malay world in the fourteenth and fifteenth centuries, the epigraphic work of J. G. de Casparis, and Paul Wheatley's construction of the historical geography of the Malay peninsula before 1500, may be given as examples.[68] More

[62] *The Chinese in Philippine Life, 1850–1898*, New Haven and London, 1965.
[63] *Manila, 1900–1914: Social Change in a Late Colonial Metropolis*, New Haven, 1984.
[64] *Protest Movements in Rural Java*, Singapore, 1973.
[65] *The Burma Delta: Economic Development and Social Change on an Asian Rice Frontier, 1852–1941*, Madison, 1974.
[66] *The Real Face of Thai Feudalism Today*, 1957, trans. Craig J. Reynolds in *Thai Radical Discourse: The Real Face of Thai Feudalism Today*, Ithaca, 1987.
[67] Craig J. Reynolds, 'Marxism in Thai Historical Studies', JAS, 43, 1 (1983).
[68] Wang Gungwu, 'The Nanhai Trade: A Study of the Early History of Chinese Trade in the South China Sea', JMBRAS, 31 (1958); Wolters, *Early Indonesian Commerce: A Study in the Origins of Srivijaya*, Ithaca, 1967, and *The Fall of Srivijaya in Malay History*, London, 1970; de Casparis, *Prasasti Indonesia*; Wheatley, *The Golden Khersonese*, Kuala Lumpur, 1961.

recently, the early history of the region has attracted a growing number of younger scholars, such as Michael Aung-Thwin (Pagan), Pierre-Yves Manguin (Śrīvijaya), Nidhi Aeusrivongse (Angkor), and K. W. Taylor and J. K. Whitmore (ninth- and tenth-century Vietnam).[69] Many of the recent advances made in the study of early history have been, in effect, archaeological in character.[70] Archaeological enquiry using modern techniques has also begun to transform views about the prehistory of the region. The archaeological services of the individual republics of Southeast Asia have played an increasingly significant part in these enquiries and have contributed to a rethinking of the conclusions of pre-war studies and to a clearer perception of cultural development taking place over some thousands of years and predating influences from outside the region.[71]

MAJOR THEMES IN POST-WAR STUDIES

Against the background of these general remarks about the methods of approach and the focus of historical writing after World War II, some of the main themes that attracted the attention of historians may be indicated.

One of the most important of these took up the thread of the pre-war debates about the nature and significance of external influences, Indian, Islamic and European, on Southeast Asian societies. The publication, in 1955, of the English translation of van Leur's doctoral thesis and other writings under the general title, *Indonesian Trade and Society: Essays in Asian Social and Economic History* (The Hague and Bandung, 1955), captured the attention of historians. It revived the earlier debate but carried it in a somewhat different direction. Whereas the pre-war argument had focused largely on the processes of 'Indianization' and the extent to which it shaped, or was shaped by, local cultures, the new debate was conducted to a considerable degree at a more general and conceptual level. It was concerned with the notion of the 'autonomy' of Southeast Asian history.

The Indianization question as such was not, of course, ignored. A

---

[69] See articles by Michael Aung-Thwin, Nidhi Aeusrivongse, K. W. Taylor and J. K. Whitmore in Whitmore and K. R. Hall, eds, *Explorations in Early Southeast Asian History: The Origins of Southeast Asian Statecraft*, Ann Arbor, 1976; Pierre-Yves Manguin, 'Études Sumatranaises: I. Palembang et Sriwijaya: anciennes hypothèses, recherches nouvelles', BEFEO, 76 (1987); K. W. Taylor, *The Birth of Vietnam*, Berkeley, 1983; and articles by a number of scholars in David Marr and A. C. Milner, eds, *Southeast Asia in the 9th to 14th Centuries*, Singapore and Canberra, 1986.

[70] See, e.g. Alastair Lamb, 'Takuapa: The Probable Site of a Pre-Malaccan Entrepôt in the Malay Peninsula' in J. Bastin and R. Roolvink eds, *Malayan and Indonesian Studies: Essays Presented to Sir Richard Winstedt*, Oxford, 1964; E. Edwards McKinnon, 'Kota Cina: Its Context and Meaning in the Trade of Southeast Asia in the Twelfth to Fourteenth Centuries', Ph.D. thesis, Cornell University, 1984, and McKinnon and A. C. Milner, 'A Letter from Sumatra: A visit to some early Sumatran historical sites', *Indonesia Circle*, 18 (1978); C. C. Macknight, *The Voyage to Marege*, Melbourne, 1976; J. N. Miksic, 'From Seri Vijaya to Melaka: Batu Tagak in Historical and Cultural Context', JMBRAS, 60, 2 (1987).

[71] For an account of post-war archaeological findings see R. B. Smith and W. Watson eds, *Early South East Asia: Essays in Archeology, History and Historical Geography*, London and New York, 1979. See also Peter Bellwood, *Man's Conquest of the Pacific: The Prehistory of Southeast Asia and Oceania*, New York, 1979, and *Prehistory of the Indo-Malaysian Archipelago*, Sydney, 1985.

number of new contributions were made, notably by H. G. Quaritch Wales, Alastair Lamb, O. W. Wolters, I. W. Mabbett and others. Wolters, in his seminal work *Early Indonesian Commerce*, threw light on the nature of trade in the archipelago before the seventh century CE. He took as his point of departure Cœdès' rediscovery of Śrīvijaya.[72] Exactly where Śrīvijaya was based and what sort of a kingdom it was remained obscure, but Wolters attempted, through his notion of the 'favoured coast' of Sumatra, to show why the emergence of a maritime power in south Sumatra in the seventh century made sense. Though he was concerned only obliquely with the process of Indianization, it was an important part of his argument that 'the expansion of trade at that time was an indigenous and not an Indian achievement'.[73]

Wolters confronted the Indianization question more directly in a consideration of the processes by which Hindu influences were received in Cambodia. In an article of 1979 he substituted the notion of 'prowess' for that of descent and dynasty as a means of understanding political authority in seventh-century Cambodia, and proceeded to argue that prowess was able to make use of Hindu notions of authority. In this and other ways the Khmers were able to construe Hinduism in terms familiar to them within their own culture and to 'empathize' with it on the basis of an experience that was 'as much Khmer as "Hindu"'.[74] Elsewhere he introduced the idea of 'localization' to characterize the way in which external influences might be absorbed into the local scene and restated in a local idiom to the point where a local–external antithesis becomes irrelevant.[75]

The arguments about Indianization and the nature of the relevant evidence were brought together and surveyed convincingly by Mabbett, who argued that different categories had been confused by earlier participants in the argument.[76] Mabbett's contribution was to clarify the issues by sorting out the separate and distinct questions which are involved. These questions relate to the evolving patterns of Southeast Asian agriculture; the date at which wet-rice cultivation might have begun; the kind of political order which might have preceded the emergence of centralized kingdoms like Angkor; and the kind of interaction which might have developed between local custom and Sanskrit lore, not only in Southeast Asia but in India itself. Pointing out that the evidence was inconclusive, Mabbett proposed a distinction between arguments about the process by which Indian influence spread and those about the extent to which it could be said to have dominated local cultures, and he then proceeded to dissolve both types. After surveying the evidence presented by a wide range of scholars,[77] he pointed out that in fact no evidence exists about

[72] Cœdès, 'Le Royaume de Çrivijaya'.
[73] *Early Indonesian Commerce*, 247. Further discussion of the location of Śrīvijaya can be found in Bennet Bronson, 'The Archaeology of Sumatra and the Problem of Srivijaya', in Smith and Watson, eds, *Early Southeast Asia*, 406–26, and in Manguin, Études Sumatranaises'.
[74] 'Khmer "Hinduism" in the Seventh Century', Smith and Watson, 427.
[75] *History, Culture and Region in Southeast Asian Perspectives*, Singapore, 1984.
[76] 'The "Indianization" of Southeast Asia': I. Reflections on the Prehistoric Sources; II. Reflections on the Historical Sources, JSEAH, 8, 1 and 2 (1977).
[77] Amongst others, H. G. Quaritch Wales, H. A. Lamb, Paul Wheatley, W. G. Solheim II, R. D. Hill, L. Malleret, K. A. N. Sastri, K. C. Chang, B. Bronson.

process. All we have is evidence in Chinese, epigraphic and archaeological sources, of Southeast Asian polities already showing signs of Indian influence. And with regard to the second type of question he concluded that to oppose Indian imperialism and local autonomy is to present a false dichotomy, given the complexity of local patterns; the fact that in any case there was not a single, homogeneous 'India'; and that, in India itself, 'Sanskritization' was uneven and patchy.

While the search for evidence of process and character, and the analysis and discussion of that evidence, continued, the main interest of modern historians was captured by other aspects of van Leur's writings.

There were two features of his overall argument which were of particular interest in the late 1950s and early 1960s. First of all was the method by which he argued his case. The greater part of the pre-war discussion was concerned with the interpretation of particular items of evidence of an Indian presence, or the lack of items of evidence of conquest and settlement and, as we have seen, those who saw Indianization as a positive shaping process regarded India-based commerce as an important element in the transmission of that influence. Van Leur, by contrast, developed his conclusions not by examining existing evidence in detail, or by presenting new evidence, but on the basis of definitions of different types of trade. His thesis, indeed, was essentially a methodological discussion. At the centre of his argument was a definition of capitalism, not in terms of accumulation, investment and profit, but, more narrowly, as 'modern capitalism'—in terms of mass production based on a free market, a financial system involving stock market exchange, and a free market for sales—none of which, of course, applied to early Asian commercial activity.[78] Asian trade, he pointed out, was based on handicraft industry and was financed not by a capitalist class but by rulers or aristocrats, investing in individual voyages. From this conceptual framework followed the further concept: that of a peddling trade. Though trade was carried out over vast distances its actual conduct was in the hands of small traders— pedlars—who carried the goods, exchanged them, and formed foreign enclaves in the port cities of Southeast Asia.

The final conclusion formed part of the same conceptual rearrangement. It was a logical step to his view that commerce could not have been central to the transmission of high cultural forms; that the influence was therefore likely to have been the result of borrowings of those features of Indian culture which were of use in the emerging kingdoms of the region; and that India was therefore not imposing itself on indigenous cultures.[79] Southeast Asia becomes, not a passive recipient of external influences, but the active agent in the process. The conceptual device reversed, at one stroke, the framework within which the question was discussed.

The second feature of the post-war debate followed closely from this method of analysis. By changing sharply the terms of the debate, van Leur directed attention away from details of evidence and towards the more general notion of autonomy. If Indian influence were to be seen as

[78] *Indonesian Trade and Society*, 17.
[79] ibid., 103.

borrowed or absorbed, it allowed continuing independence and authority to local cultures which might otherwise be seen as subject to, or conquered by, external pressures.

If this argument could be applied to Indian influence and to the coming of Islam, might it not also be applied to the period of European penetration into the region? This question, which was especially the subject of discussion for a decade after 1955, had obvious value implications. A view of Southeast Asia as continuously 'in charge' of its own history appealed alike to nations concerned with the consolidation of their newly acquired independence and to outside observers who wished to think in terms of the autonomy of the region as an object of study.

Van Leur himself argued that European influence had indeed been overemphasized by earlier historians. He did so by using much the same conceptual tools as had supported his discussion of indigenous and selective borrowings of Indian culture. The Dutch East India Company in the seventeenth and eighteenth centuries was not unlike a merchant prince financing successive voyages, and its employees in the Indies were performing functions similar to those of the pedlars. To that extent it fitted the existing patterns of trade of the archipelago. Even as its power expanded and it was able to impose its own monopoly over the area, and acquired territorial footholds, it was still far short of being a sovereign ruler. Its relations with indigenous authorities, van Leur argued, were more like international relations than relations between ruler and subjects, a point later developed in detail by G. J. Resink.[80] At the very most it might be regarded as a paramount power, stronger than other individual polities but not entirely different from them in kind.

While van Leur's criticism of historians who looked at Southeast Asia through European eyes was readily accepted, and the idea of an Asia-centric history became a goal to be achieved by a sensitive approach to local cultures, his argument that the coming of the European made almost no difference, at least until the late eighteenth century, would seem an overstatement. The Dutch East India Company, to take the example that van Leur focused on, was an organization very different in size, in the scope of its operations and in power, from the pedlars whom he saw as the bearers of trade in the past. It was able to enforce its control over trade and, in due course, to acquire territorial influence as well. There is certainly much point in identifying those features of its activity which can be seen in terms of the earlier trade and in stressing elements of continuity with the pre-European period. But there is also point in drawing attention to elements of change and discontinuity. C. R. Boxer examined closely the impact of the Portuguese commercial system, and M. A. P. Meilink-Roelofsz saw considerable changes following from the intrusion of Portuguese and Dutch into the trade of the region. Even van Leur himself conceded that, by the end of the eighteenth century and the beginning of the nineteenth, the sheer power of the European intruders into Southeast

---

[80] 'Inlandsche Staten in den Oosterschen Archipel, 1873–1915', BKI, 116 (1960), translated as 'Native States of the Eastern Archipelago, 1873–1915', in Resink, *Indonesian History between the Myths*, The Hague, 1958.

Asia was such as to create a watershed in Southeast Asian history. And, since much of the work of modern historians has been directed to the study of the nineteenth and twentieth centuries, the period of greatest Western impact, it has been difficult for historians, either from within the region or outside it, to avoid interpretations couched in terms of European challenge and Southeast Asian response.

Difficult, but perhaps not impossible. The issues of perspective and autonomy became, for a time, a major focus for discussion. In 1961 John Smail, in an influential article, indicated a variety of meanings which the idea of Eurocentrism could have.[81] It could refer to the angle of the historian's vision: was the history of the region to be seen from the point of view of the outside observer or of the indigenous people? Or it could reflect the preferences and values of the historians: whose side were they on, as it were, in their account of events? Third, it could refer to a judgment of historical significance: what were the decisive factors in shaping the course of history? The three meanings, of course, often went together. If the angle of vision was that of the European intruder (and there was always a danger of this, given that the historian's sources were often those created by the intruder), it was perhaps likely that the value judgments would support the role played by the European and that the European would be placed in the foreground of the analysis as the shaper of events. Smail argued that the thought-world of modern scientific inquiry—both in the natural sciences and the humanities—was now a universal thought-world, and all serious historians, whether Western or Eastern, worked within it. In these circumstances his own concern was with the moral viewpoints and the perspectives of historians. By perspectives he seems to have meant judgments about causal significance. He noted that a new generation of nationalist historians had, in effect, reversed the moral position of the old colonial historians, 'exchanging one systematic bias for another', while preserving a perspective which tended to see the European still as the effective agent of change. By contrast Smail's aim was to achieve a morally neutral viewpoint and an Asiacentric perspective, an aim which might be achieved, he believed, by adopting a sociological method. If one focused on fundamental cultural patterns, the actions of the colonial ruler were likely to appear, if not superficial and transitory, at least less important. Local cultures were resilient, resistant to change, and readily able to absorb stimuli from outside. And even when the European intrusion had seemed most obviously to have promoted change—in stimulating the emergence of new élites or of urban working classes, for example—that could still be seen as part of a local evolution. His conclusion was that the antithesis between Eurocentric and Asiacentric was a false one. The goal should be, not the writing of an Asiacentric history, but the writing of an 'autonomous' history.

A retrospective look at this discussion makes it seem clearer that the question of perspective is very much a function of the issues that interest the historian and of the ways in which central questions are posed. The

[81] 'On the Possibility of an Autonomous History of Modern Southeast Asia', JSEAH, 2, 2 (1961).

motives and policies of metropolitan powers are a legitimate subject of enquiry and impose a different framework from that appropriate for studies of what happened in Southeast Asia during the period of European expansion. The debate, however, undoubtedly affected the way in which historians framed their questions. Even studies which continued to concentrate on the colonial period no longer saw it almost as a part of European history as their predecessors had tended to do. On the contrary, they reflected a deliberate attempt to achieve a shift of perspective. Milton Osborne, for example, attempted to see both sides of the colonial equation in dealing with French rule in Indochina.[82] So did David Marr, whose *Vietnamese Anticolonialism 1885–1925* (Berkeley, 1971) placed evolving Vietnamese political thought firmly in a local setting. Both drew on *quoc-ngu* (Vietnamese) as well as French sources. And in dealing with Thailand, the one country that avoided the fate of colonial rule, David Wyatt portrayed Chulalongkorn's educational reforms, not in terms of the initiative of a Westernized absolute monarch, but as a response to the West 'which flowed painfully but naturally out of Thai history, society and culture'.[83]

The coming of Islam to Southeast Asia, and its impact on the societies of the region, formed a further major theme of historians in the post-war period, though the discussion was conducted in different terms from those of the debate about Indianization and the autonomy of Southeast Asian history. Van Leur, of course, had extended his analysis of the nature of Indian influence, and the comparative superficiality of its impact, to cover the penetration of Islam, but he had done so more or less in passing and as a consequence of the methodological position he had adopted. The coming of Islam did not, in his eyes, constitute a new phase or period of Southeast Asian history. He argued that Muslim trade introduced no significant change in economic forms; and culturally he saw Islam as being received and absorbed, not imposed on those who were converted. In general, however, the arguments by which he supported these conclusions were less developed than those relating to Indianization; it was rather a matter of bringing it within his general conceptual framework than of presenting new evidence or revising the old.

There was no major challenge to that general picture in the 1950s and 1960s. Broadly, historians of Islam in Southeast Asia addressed themselves to three types of enquiry: to the diffusion points from which Islam reached the peninsula and archipelago; to the nature of its initial impact; and to the evolution of Islamic thought and organization in that environment.

The issues in the debate about the method of Muslim penetration were threefold: whether it was carried by traders from Gujerat in the thirteenth and fourteenth centuries; or whether an earlier source was to be found in South India; or whether Bengal was the principal point of origin. Amongst the participants in the discussion were G. E. Marrison and G. W. J. Drewes, who inclined to the view that Southeast Asian Islam

[82] *The French Presence in Cochin China and Cambodia: Rule and Response, 1859–1905*, Ithaca, 1969.
[83] *The Politics of Reform in Thailand*, vii.

came from the Coromandel coast of India.[84] By contrast, S. Q. Fatimi argued for Bengal as the diffusion point though he allowed that, at different times, different diffusion points might have played a part.[85]

Side by side with the question of origins went the second type of discussion: that concerned with the particular character of the Islam which established itself in Southeast Asia and the way in which it adapted to, or transformed, the local scene. Did it stimulate extensive social changes or was it, as van Leur asserted, adapted, domesticated and assimilated? There were obvious elements of change, both in belief and social order, with the coming of Islam. The almost universal observance of Islamic ritual in the societies converted, attendance at the mosque, the call to prayer, the fast, the pilgrimage, all appear to testify to a universal conversion. But it was an uneven conversion. The religion had a stronger foothold in those parts of the archipelago most directly involved in international trade—Aceh, the west coast of Sumatra, Melaka, the north coast of Java, Makassar—but the penetration of Islam in the inland agrarian society of Java, with its hierarchical tradition and its ability to blend Islam with older customary beliefs, was apparently less profound. This would seem to point to differences in Islam's transforming role. There were clearly incipient tensions between the new religion and an earlier tradition, which varied from place to place, and which became acute in certain areas from time to time.

Historians have stressed both continuity and change. A. H. Johns emphasized the role of members of Sufi orders in bringing to Southeast Asia a mystically tinged Islam. Sufi readiness to accept and use elements of non-Islamic culture was precisely what was important in making Islam acceptable in the Southeast Asian environment.[86]

However, while emphasizing the acceptability of Sufism, Johns was perhaps more concerned with the network of links connecting the city states of Southeast Asia with the centres of Islamic learning in Cairo, Medina and Mecca, and with diverse schools and a variety of influential teachers, than with the impact of the new religion on the society that received it. He noted the absence of a 'central, stable core of Islamic civilization and learning' within the region,[87] and drew attention to the theological and intellectual traditions of a wider Muslim world on which the Muslim leaders of Melaka, Aceh and other port cities were able to draw. He emphasized that it was 'not a single tradition, but a complex web'.[88] Within that diversity Sufism provided the main current until the rise of the Wahhabi movement in the eighteenth century stimulated a fundamentalist attempt to cut through 'the accretions and innovations' of the intervening centuries and return to what was seen as the original faith.

If Johns was concerned with the doctrinal world of the *ulamā* (learned

---

[84] Drewes, 'New Light on the Coming of Islam to Indonesia?' BKI, 124 (1968), 433ff. Marrison, 'The Coming of Islam to the East Indies', JMBRAS, 24 (1951).

[85] *Islam Comes to Malaysia*, Singapore, 1963, 53.

[86] 'Sufism as a Category in Indonesian Literature and History', JSEAH, 2, 2 (1961).

[87] 'Islam in Southeast Asia: Reflections and New Directions', *Indonesia*, 19 (1975) 33.

[88] ibid, 42. See also Johns, 'Islam in Southeast Asia: Problems of Perspective', in Cowan and Wolters, eds, *Southeast Asian History and Historiography*.

men), other writers have focused more on the processes by which Islam was accommodated. Soemarsaid Moertono explored the resilience and persistence of Hindu-Javanese forms and ideas even after the conversion of the inland Javanese kingdom of Mataram.[89] Amongst the populace Islam provided a base for resistance to oppression, but at the court level old Javanese elements continued. A. C. Milner, who also focused on kingship, stressed the way in which local rulers adopted Islamic ideas selectively, adopting those aspects with which they could 'empathize'— the Persian tradition of kingship, or the mystical idea of the 'perfect man'—and thus fitting them into the local scene, rather than transforming it.[90] This kind of compromise became more difficult to maintain with changes in the character of Islam and the growth of 'sharī'a-mindedness' in the nineteenth century.

The third type of enquiry—that concerned with the later evolution of Muslim thought and action—was prompted in part by the general concern of post-war students of Southeast Asia with the contemporary scene. Students of politics, sociology and economic development were drawn, amongst other interests, to examine, in particular, the current strength and the social and political role of Islam in Indonesia and Malaysia, where tensions between Muslims and non-Muslims, among different types of Muslim, and between Muslims and the state are a central part of today's political conflicts. While in Malaysia the state itself has sought an Islamization of society, in Indonesia Islam has provided a basis for opposition to the Suharto regime. But to distinguish between those two situations in such simple terms is to obscure the complexity, in both situations, of differences within the Islamic community. In West Malaysia there are shifting intra-élite rivalries within the Malay community, where at one time an aristocratic élite, centred round the courts of Malay rulers, was in incipient conflict with ulamā leaders, and at another time a Western-educated élite, nominally Muslim, nevertheless did not share the desire of religious leaders for a sharī'a-based political order. In Indonesia the picture is complicated by regional differences. Orthodox Islam (though what is orthodox might be a matter of dispute) has established itself more strongly in Sumatra, south Sulawesi and west Java than in central and east Java, and even in those regions there is some tension between strict observance and the pull of custom. In central and east Java a division exists between what might be called 'nominal' Muslims (abangan), whose religion has developed on the basis of a syncretist accommodation with earlier beliefs, and the santri community whose members profess a stricter adherence to orthodoxy. Differences of this kind have had an impact on political alignments and conflict. Whether the issues at stake are religious and theological, or whether economic and social conflicts have taken on a religious garb, may be a matter of debate, but either way the religious dimension remains a fact of modern politics.

Historians have played their part in this type of enquiry by focusing on nineteenth- and twentieth-century developments in Muslim thought and

[89] *State and Statecraft in Old Java: A Study of the Later Mataram Period, 16th to 19th century*, Ithaca, 1968.

[90] 'Islam and the Muslim State', in M. B. Hooker ed., *Islam in Southeast Asia*, Leiden, 1983.

action, concerning themselves with classical issues of Islamic debate and with conflicts between competing orthodoxies. The nineteenth century saw the development of fundamentalist doctrines stemming from the wider Muslim world, and challenging existing practice in one way or another. The Wahhābi movement, for example, originating in Arabia, attacked the compromises that Islam had made with custom and called for a return to the original simplicity and austerity of the faith. Towards the end of the century the Modernist movement, with its centre in Cairo, presented a challenge of a somewhat different kind. It, too, was concerned to strip the faith of the scholastic accretions which, it believed, had come to obscure the teachings of the prophet, but it also sought an accommodation between Islam and the forces of the modern world, believing that a purified—and rational—faith could be reconciled with science and contemporary thought.

Historians have tackled the question from a variety of angles. Christine Dobbin and Taufik Abdullah have considered the special circumstances of Minangkabau. Dobbin focused on revivalism in the eighteenth and early nineteenth centuries which culminated in the Padri movement.[91] Taufik Abdullah's concern was the relation of religion and custom in the early twentieth century. Minangkabau custom, in his argument, embodied the idea of interaction with peoples, ideas and mores outside the Minang-kabau heartland. Custom thus contained within itself the idea of its own transformation. Against that background he examined the conflict—in part generational, in part theological, and in part ideological—between reforming and conservative forces within the Islamic community.[92] Deliar Noer charted the growth of the Modernist movement in the twentieth century, the formation of the reformist organization, Muhammadiyah, in 1912, and the development of a political role for Islam in the closing decades of Dutch rule.[93] Though he did explore questions of doctrine—for example, the right of individual interpretation, and the role of reason—his particular focus was on the consequences of religious teaching for the exercise of political authority. A political role for Islam would, indeed, seem inevitable, given its absolute claims, summed up in Noer's view that Islam is 'both a religious and a civil and political society' (p. 1). Muslims are nevertheless likely to differ about how such claims should be implemented. W. R. Roff's study of the origins of Malay nationalism was concerned with the Islamic dimension of the emerging élites he was able to identify.[94] For Indonesia, B. J. Boland examined the way in which the relations of religion and the state took political form in the history of the independent repub-lic.[95] A special case was that of the Muslim community in the Philippines whose role was surveyed by C. A. Majul.[96]

[91] *Islamic Revivalism in a Changing Peasant Economy: Central Sumatra, 1784–1847*, London and Malmö, 1983.
[92] 'Modernization in the Minangkabau World: West Sumatra in the Early Decades of the Twentieth Century', in Claire Holt, B. R. O'G. Anderson and James Siegel, eds, *Culture and Politics in Indonesia*, Ithaca, 1972.
[93] *The Modernist Muslim Movement, 1900–1942*, Singapore and Kuala Lumpur, 1973.
[94] *The Origins of Malay Nationalism*, New York and London, 1967.
[95] *The Struggle of Islam in Modern Indonesia*, The Hague, 1971.
[96] *Muslims in the Philippines*, Quezon City, 1973.

While some scholars have focused on the political role of Muslims, others have directed their enquiry towards their economic activities. Clifford Geertz threw out the suggestion that the austerity of Islam, and its insistence on the equality of believers, made it an appropriate faith for an embryo bourgeoisie, and hinted at a comparison between the role of Islam in Southeast Asia and that ascribed by Weber to Protestantism in Europe—the role of sacralizing commercial behaviour and thus assisting the development of a commercial class.[97] This suggestion was taken up by at least one historian, Lance Castles, whose study[98] of the cigarette industry in Kudus, on the north coast of central Java, attempted to test the Geertz hypothesis. James Siegel's study of Acehnese traders discussed the Islamic notion of reason (*akal*) as possibly contributing to the individualism of a commercial class.[99]

On the whole it can be said that the main thrust of historical enquiry into Islam in Southeast Asia was directed to what could be described as the political and economic behaviour of Muslims in the present and more or less recent past, rather than to matters of doctrine and belief. And such a focus was, of course, in line with the general preoccupations of post-war scholarship.

Another subject of increasing interest to historians was the character of traditional authority and social order—of ruler and realm, state and statecraft, to borrow the titles of two significant contributions[1]—and of the ideas which appeared to support that authority.

As described by Robert Heine-Geldern in an influential article of 1942,[2] the classical states of Southeast Asia were in theory highly centralized, and embodied ideas, derived from Indian influence, of a divine kingship and of parallelism between the universe and the terrestrial order. The capital of the ruler was the magical centre of the realm, and at its centre, in turn, a temple or the royal palace, whose towers and terraces and orientation were designed in accordance with an elaborate symbolism, represented Mt Meru, the abode of the gods. As the kingdom was a microcosm of the universe so the king in his capital, a descendant of a god or an incarnation of a god—Śiva or Viṣṇu, Indra or Brahmā—maintained the harmony of the kingdom, matching the harmony of the universe. The political reality was, of course, very different from the doctrine of the exemplary centre and it was, no doubt, precisely because of the facts of balance and division that the theory was so firmly centralist in character. T. Pigeaud, writing of Java, emphasized the precarious nature of royal power and saw the

[97] *The Development of the Javanese Economy*, Boston, 1956, 91.
[98] *Religion, Politics and Economic Behaviour in Java: The Kudus Cigarette Industry*, New Haven, 1967.
[99] *The Rope of God*, Berkeley and Los Angeles, 1969.
[1] B. J. O. Schrieke, *Ruler and Realm in Early Java*, The Hague, 1957, being a collection of papers on which Schrieke was working at the time of his death in 1942; and Moertono, *State and Statecraft*.
[2] 'Conceptions of State and Kingship in Southeast Asia', *Far Eastern Quarterly*, 2, 1 (November 1942).

'perennial division and reunion of the realm' as an inherent part of the system.[3]

In the 1960s and early 1970s the interest in traditional political order and political theory sprang in part from the focus on recent and contemporary history. The political behaviour of the so-called 'new states' could be illuminated, perhaps, by the exploration of older forms and perceptions. That was essentially the thrust of B. R. O'G. Anderson's essay on 'The Idea of Power in Javanese Culture'.[4] Though probing traditional Javanese culture, and seeking to establish that that culture included a coherent political theory, its main concern was with the way in which these conclusions might sustain a better understanding of contemporary Indonesian politics, illuminating, for example, Sukarno's leadership style, the tension between centre and periphery, or the role of ideology in political action. Clifford Geertz's notion of the 'theatre, State', proposed in his *Islam Observed* (New Haven, 1968) and developed in his later study of the nature of the nineteenth-century Balinese principality,[5] served a similar function. Other studies, perhaps more strictly historical in character, have been concerned either to explore traditional concepts of authority for their own sake or to examine particular polities in particular periods.

As an example of the former approach, I. W. Mabbett re-examined conclusions about the nature of Khmer kingship by d'Aymonier, Finot, Cœdès and others, and asked whether the notion of divine kingship represented a literal or a metaphorical claim. He demonstrated the ambiguity of epigraphical references to the 'Devarāja', and of the expressions of that concept in ritual and in architectural forms.[6] He concluded that the symbolism of the Devarāja cult was a kind of language in which statements about the moral and political order were expressed. In similar vein, Hermann Kulke argued that the *devarāja* cult related to the worship of Śiva as king of the gods rather than to the worship of a god king, though kings may have been 'participants' in divine rule.[7]

In the second category are works such as M. C. Ricklefs' study of the reign of Sultan Mangkubumi in Yogyakarta, an account of the division of the realm and a consideration of Javanese ideas about the nature of the realm—and about its indivisibility.[8] In Ricklefs' account, the centralist nature of Javanese political theory masked, or was perhaps a response to, a reality in which power was in fact divided. Moertono's work was also directed to a particular period of Javanese history, the later Mataram period from the sixteenth to the nineteenth century. More sociological in approach and method was Akin Rabibhadana's examination of Thai social

---

[3] *Java in the Fourteenth Century: A Study in Cultural History: The Nagara-Kertagama by Rakawi Prapañca of Majapahit, 1365 AD*, The Hague, 1960, IV. 122.

[4] In Holt et al., eds, *Culture and Politics in Indonesia*.

[5] *Negara: The Theatre State in Nineteenth-Century Bali*, Princeton, 1980.

[6] 'Devarāja', in JSEAH, 10, 2 (1969).

[7] *The Devarāja Cult*, 1974, translated from the German, Ithaca, 1978. For further exploration of the question see J. Filliozat, 'Sur le Çivaisme et le Bouddhisme du Cambodge', BEFEO, 70 (1980), and Claude Jacques, 'The Kamraten Jagad in Ancient Cambodia', in Norobu Karashima, ed., *Indus Valley to Mekong Delta: Explorations in Epigraphy*, Madras, 1985.

[8] *Jogjakarta Under Sultan Mangkubumi, 1749–1792*, London, 1974.

order and its stratification according to formal and informal patron–client relations.[9] Victor Lieberman's account of dynastic cycles in Burma between the sixteenth and eighteenth centuries sought the explanation of the phenomenon of division and reunification in the administrative structure of the kingdom. Though sticking closely to his chosen case, Lieberman threw out the suggestion that there was a basic coherence in administrative processes throughout agrarian Southeast Asia and he concluded his work with a comparision of the Burmese case with those of Siam and Mataram.[10]

Part of the same general concern with social order and authority was the interest in peasant society and its occasional disturbances, uprisings and movements of resistance. These have sometimes been seen as early manifestations of nationalist revolt, but increasingly scholars have focused on the millenarian character of such movements and on the way they combined protest at specific grievances with elements of traditional belief and practice. For example the Javanese idea of a Just Ruler (*Ratu Adil*) who could restore harmony and prosperity to a disturbed society was a common element in the movements described by Sartono Kartodirdjo in his attempt to classify different types of peasant protest in Java. Sartono drew attention to the syncretistic nature of the ideologies to be found in his case studies where anti-extortion protests were apt to take on a messianic flavour, mixed with nativistic longings for a return to a pristine culture and with Holy War ideas.[11] Others have explored similar themes in other cases. Yoneo Ishii and Chattip Nartsupha have described the leadership of 'men of merit' and 'Holy Men' in revolts in Thailand.[12] David Chandler has observed a similar phenomenon in Cambodia,[13] and Reynaldo Ileto has shown how Catholic ideas were appropriated and incorporated into local ideology in the Philippines.[14] Michael Adas has attempted a bold comparative study, taking five different cases of millenarian revolts in Africa, India, Southeast Asia and Oceania. In the general setting of accelerated social change and dislocation under colonial rule, he emphasized the special role of prophetic leadership in shaping these revolts.[15]

These themes have been explored through a number of specific case studies, as in Sartono's study of the Banten Revolt in 1888;[16] and in the

---

[9] *The Organization of Thai Society in the Early Bangkok Period, 1782–1873*, Ithaca, 1969, and 'Clientship and Class Structure in the Early Bangkok Period', in G. William Skinner and A. Thomas Kirsch, eds, *Change and Persistence in Thai Society: Essays in Honor of Lauriston Sharp*, Ithaca, 1975.

[10] *Burmese Administrative Cycles*, 6 and 271ff.

[11] *Protest Movements*, Ch. 1. See also his 'Agrarian Radicalism in Java', in Holt et al., eds, *Culture and Politics in Indonesia*.

[12] Yoneo Ishii, 'A Note on Buddhistic Millenarian Revolts in North-eastern Siam', JSEAH, 6, 2 (1975), and Nartsupha, 'The Ideology of Holy Men Revolts in North East Thailand', in Andrew Turton and Shigeharu Tanabe, eds, *History and Peasant Consciousness in South East Asia*, Osaka, 1984.

[13] 'An Anti-Vietnamese Rebellion in Early Nineteenth-Century Cambodia: Pre-Colonial Imperialism and a Pre-Nationalist Response', JSEAH, 6, 1 (1975).

[14] *Pasyon and Revolution: Popular Movements in the Philippines, 1840–1910*, Quezon City, 1979.

[15] *Prophets of Rebellion: Millenarian Protest Movements against the European Colonial Order*, Chapel Hill, 1979.

[16] Sartono *The Peasants' Revolt of Banten in 1888*, The Hague, 1966.

study of H. J. Benda and Lance Castles of the Samin movement in Java.[17] In this as in other fields, historians have been influenced by anthropological studies such as James Scott's exploration of peasant order and resistance in Malaya.[18]

The autonomy debate, changing emphases in the approach to the study of Islam, the increasing interest in the remoter past, the focus on the nature of social structure and political authority were but some of the matters commanding the attention of historians. Of importance, too, was the study of emerging élites, their role in movements of nationalist resistance to colonial rule, the institutions developed for the government of new states, questions of ethnicity and class.[19] A Marxist framework of analysis has been employed by some Thai historians and by Vietnamese historians, though in both cases it has been shaped by indigenous perspectives.[20] Local history has also become an important field of enquiry. Carried out by graduate students, by their teachers and by enthusiastic amateurs, it can be expected, in time, to provide an extended base for comparative studies. While biography has not yet been a major feature of historical writing about Southeast Asia, there have been a number of examples both of comparatively recent political figures (Poeze's study of Tan Malaka and Dahm's of the formative years of Sukarno are examples)[21] and text-based studies of earlier figures.[22] And a significant new approach to the history of the region is provided by Anthony Reid's attempt to apply the methods of the French *Annales* School to the study of the region. Reid aims at a 'total history' of Southeast Asia of the kind represented by Fernand Braudel's study of the Mediterranean world.[23]

---

[17] 'The Samin Movement', BKI, 125 (1969), republished in H. J. Benda, *Continuity and Change*, New Haven, 1972.

[18] *The Moral Economy of the Peasant: Rebellion and Subsistence in Southeast Asia*, New Haven, 1976, and *Weapons of the Weak*, New Haven, 1985.

[19] The literature on nationalism is extensive. Examples, almost at random, are J. E. Ingleson, *The Road to Exile: The Indonesian Nationalism Movement, 1927–1934*, Kuala Lumpur, 1979; R. T. McVey, *The Rise of Indonesian Communism*, Ithaca, 1965; C. A. Majul, *The Political and Constitutional Ideas of the Philippine Revolution*, Quezon City, 1967; David Marr, *Vietnamese Anti-Colonialism*, Berkeley, 1971; W. R. Roff, *The Origins of Malay Nationalism*, New Haven and London, 1967; R. van Niel, *The Rise of the Modern Indonesian Elite*, The Hague and Bandung, 1960; Alexander Woodside, *Community and Revolution in Modern Vietnam*, Boston, 1976.

[20] Reynolds, 'Marxism in Thai Historical Studies'; J. K. Whitmore, 'Communism and History in Vietnam', in W. S. Turley, ed., *Vietnamese Communism in Comparative Perspective*, Boulder, 1980.

[21] Harry A. Poeze, *Tan Malaka: Strijden voor Indonesie's vrijheid*, I: *Levensloop van 1897 tot 1945*, The Hague, 1976; and Bernhard Dahm, *Sukarnos Kampf um Indonesiens Unabhangigkeit*, Hamburg, 1966, trans. Mary F. Somers Heidhues as *Sukarno and the Struggle for Indonesian Independence*, Ithaca, 1969. See also J. D. Legge, *Sukarno: A Political Biography*, London, 1972, 2nd edn, Sydney, 1985.

[22] Anne Kumar, *Surapati, Man and Legend: A Study of Three Babad Traditions*, Leiden, 1976, and Peter Carey's assessment, in his edition of the *Babad Dipanagara*, of Diponegoro's leadership in the Java War of 1825, *Babad Dipanagara: An Account of the Outbreak of the Java War, 1825–1830*, a transliteration and translation of the Surakarta Court version of the *Babad*, Kuala Lumpur, 1981.

[23] Reid, *Southeast Asia in the Age of Commerce, 1450–1680*, I: *The Lands Below the Winds*, New Haven, 1988. Braudel, *The Mediterranean and the Mediterranean World in the Age of Philip II*, trans. S. Reynolds, New York, 1976.

In the study of these and other themes it is possible to discern certain shifts in the way historians of the region have handled and presented their subject matter. It might be appropriate to speak of changing fashions of interpretation or of changing views as to what constituted a satisfactory explanation of events. This is not to say that there was any sharp dividing line between successive types of approach or between successive periods. What is in question is rather the subtle alterations of emphasis or focus that take place within a continuing discourse. Before exploring these further, however, it may be appropriate to give consideration, first, to political developments which helped to shape changing perspectives both of the present and of the past of the region. For the most part, Western students of the contemporary scene after World War II had optimistic expectations for the future of the new states that were emerging. For Indonesia it seemed possible that the transfer of sovereignty by the Dutch would open the way to a democratic independent future. A peaceful transition to independence for Malaya and the Philippines held similar promise, though prospects for Burma and Vietnam were more clouded. The emerging reality was, however, to be different. Indonesia's constitutional experiment 'declined', to use Feith's term; authoritarian tendencies were to appear in the Philippines; and Burma turned inwards to a particular version of socialism. These developments necessarily affected the perspectives of later students, with respect both to the character of the forces at work in the immediate post-war scene and to the longer historical processes which had produced those forces. But of overwhelming importance for a whole generation of observers was the direction taken by events in Vietnam. Just as World War II had created a dramatically new environment for the study of Southeast Asia by Western and indigenous scholars alike, so the Vietnam conflict altered the framework of enquiry and affected perceptions of the very foundations of scholarship.

The post-war conflict between the French, anxious to reassert their control over Indochina, and the Vietnamese nationalist movement in some ways paralleled Indonesia's struggle for independence, but there were special complicating factors, in particular the increasing intervention of the United States as Vietnam came to be seen more and more in global Cold War terms.

This is not the place to consider the course of the struggle, the issues involved or the bitterly divisive consequences for the United States and its allies, as opposing perceptions of the situation came into conflict with each other. Was American action a matter of supporting South Vietnam in its resistance to aggression from the North and, indeed, a defence of the free world? Or was intervention really a case of supporting one side in what was really a civil war within Vietnam? Were those differences in perspective insignificant in the light of the fact that the Hanoi regime was a communist régime supported by China? The fusing of ideological considerations and considerations of global balance was associated with fears of the consequences of a northern victory—the expectation that it would lead to the fall of the neighbouring dominoes. For our purposes here it is sufficient to notice the types of response evoked by the conflict from students of the region. There were committed approaches sympathetic to one side or the other in Vietnam. As examples could be cited Douglas Pike's detailed study of the organization and techniques of the NLF in South Vietnam, *Viet Cong* (Cambridge, Mass., 1966) which, in spite of its attempt to be dispassionate and 'affectively neutral', was clearly hostile to the NLF, and Jeffrey Race's *War Comes to Long An: Revolutionary Conflict in a Vietnamese Province* (Berkeley, 1972), which attempted a more sympathetic explanation of the resilence of the Viet Cong. The perspectives of these works carried implied judgments on the validity of American intervention. Other works focused more directly on the intervention itself. George Kahin and John W. Lewis launched a sustained criticism in their book *The United States in Vietnam* (1967). So did Gabriel Kolko in his later *Anatomy of a War* (New York, 1985). A slightly more sympathetic, though still critical, assessment of American policy was G. Lewy's *America in Vietnam* (New York, 1978). There were many significant works of reportage and of serious journalistic comment. Bernard Fall's *Street Without Joy* has already been mentioned. Robert Shaplen's *The Lost Revolution* (London, 1966) is another example. Other studies attempted to see the conflict against the background of French colonial rule. Donald Lancaster, for example, in *The Emancipation of French Indochina* (London, 1966), set the post-war struggle, occupying about three-quarters of the book, in the context of French rule in Indochina. Finally reference should be made to George Kahin's massive study of the steps by which America became locked into a position of continuing commitment, *Intervention: How America Became Involved in Vietnam* (New York, 1986). It is part of the framework of Kahin's approach that until 1966, where his story ends, there were other choices that might have been made.

The Vietnam War thus evoked a great deal of serious enquiry at a number of levels. Much of it may be described as scholarly analysis, of the contemporary scene or of the immediate background or of the longer-term history of the conflict and the setting in which it took place. And much of it was passionate criticism or defence of policy. Scholarly enquiry and passion are not necessarily mutually exclusive, and a considerable part of the scholarly work was indeed prompted by moral considerations and was directed to an examination of evidence bearing on the political issues. This was the rationale of the Committee of Concerned Asian Scholars and of its *Bulletin*. Such enquiry was thus linked closely to the currents of passion and bitterness that ripped through American campuses and moved other sections of American society.

As we have seen, the post-war expansion of Asian studies had reflected a general concern with issues of national and international policy. The Vietnam War provided a focus for those issues. But whereas, in the 1950s and 1960s, there was a confidence that the accumulation of knowledge of Southeast Asian countries could provide a sound and agreed basis for policy, by the late 1960s and early 1970s it would be true to say that observers were disposed, not only to criticize the thrust of Western policies towards Southeast Asia, but to call into question the basic assumptions on which those policies had rested. And associated with such criticisms was a recognition of the difficulty of acquiring any real understanding of the processes of change transforming Southeast Asia societies.

CHANGES IN INTERPRETATION

This leads us back to the suggestion that a gradual shift was to be observed, discernible perhaps from the early 1960s, in the interpretative modes of historians.

This is a complex matter, involving a variety of levels of analysis and interpretation. For the purposes of the present argument one may distinguish at least four aspects of the question. There have been, first of all, changes of perspective or changes in the angle from which the events of the past were perceived. Second, there have been changes in perceptions of what it was important to study, i.e. judgments about subject matter. Third, there have been changes in the categories of explanation—in ideas about what would constitute a satisfactory account of past events and processes. And finally there have been sharp and major changes in the actual circumstances of modern Southeast Asia which must affect the way in which the past is interpreted. Van Leur's realignment of concepts of Asian trade is a prime example of the first of these categories. The second category is well illustrated, for example, by Jean Gelman Taylor's posing of new questions about lineage and family relations in the mestizo society of the Indies which gave a different shape to the social history of the Indies in the eighteenth and nineteenth centuries, and by James Warren's essay in 'history from below' in his study of Singapore rickshaw drivers as an integral part of the society and economy of Singapore.[24] But it is intended to focus here on the third and fourth categories.

The readiness of many historians to adopt the conceptual models of the social sciences—of politics, or sociology or anthropology—in illuminating aspects of the region's past has already been noticed, and this was part of the shift taking place in modes of historical thought; but what is referred to here goes beyond specific methodological borrowing. It involves a general and growing disposition to move from interpretation in narrowly political terms toward a consideration of what were seen as more fundamental cultural patterns. The immediate problems of the post-war world which, as we have noticed, were important in stimulating the enormous expansion of Southeast Asian studies were seen, to a considerable extent, as political. They were to do, that is to say, with international balances of power, with the shape, character and politics of the 'new states' which affected that balance, with constitutional forms and leadership styles. And to a great extent they were explored at a political level: in terms of parties, emergent élites and political pressures, and of concepts such as statehood, nationalism, democracy, communism, with their implied comparisons with Western situations. These emphases were to change. As the new generation of scholars who came to the study of Southeast Asia gradually made their way, learning the necessary languages, acquiring through doctoral training and fieldwork a closer knowledge of the societies with which they were dealing, they came to a greater sense of difference rather than similarity, to an awareness of the deeper dimensions of local tradition

[24] Taylor, *The Social World of Batavia: European and Eurasian in Dutch Asia*, Madison, 1983; Warren, *Rickshaw Coolie: A People's History of Singapore, 1880–1940*, Singapore, 1986.

and culture and to a recognition of their effect upon patterns of political action. In attempting to come to grips with such levels of interpretation, students of the modern world perhaps also became more alive to the sheer difficulty of grasping the 'inwardness' of other societies and, philosophically, of dealing with the problem of knowing 'the other'.

These changes in the commonly accepted frameworks of interpretation may have been due, in part, to the influence of the particular social scientists specifically concerned with the interpretation of cultures, the anthropologists. Observers such as Clifford Geertz, through their exploration of the social context of political action in Southeast Asia, have done much to illuminate the contemporary scene in a way that is of direct relevance for the work both of political scientists and historians. For students of Indonesia the seminal work of Geertz was of particular importance. His notions of agricultural involution, shared poverty, primordial loyalties, *aliran* (cultural streams) and theatre state, though subject to criticism by later students, combined to alter the way in which political events were perceived and understood in their cultural setting. The extent to which such categories became part of the conceptual equipment of historians might be seen, for instance, in Benedict Anderson's interpretation of the first year of the Indonesian Revolution in terms of fundamental configurations of Javanese society;[25] in his essay, already noticed, on the Javanese concept of power; in Ruth McVey's exploration of the way in which the Indonesian Communist Party appealed to the Javanese peasantry through its ability to tap traditional perceptions;[26] in Heather Sutherland's account of the impact of colonial rule on the Javanese aristocracy;[27] or in Bernhard Dahm's study of Sukarno whom he saw, for all his appearance as the modern leader of a twentieth-century state, as displaying the characteristic traits and modes of thought of the Javanese culture from which he sprang.[28] It was clearly no longer possible to see Indonesian political interactions primarily in terms of parties, pressures and institutions. In a similar way David Marr's essay in the intellectual history of Vietnam, *Vietnamese Tradition on Trial, 1920–1945* (Berkeley, 1981), examined changes in Vietnamese outlooks and values, but also saw intellectuals as engaged in a dialogue with traditional ideas.

In broad terms, and in the light of what has already been said about the study of classical political theory and social order, it might be possible to describe the change in terms of an appeal to tradition as an explanatory factor, and an accompanying tendency to emphasize the inertia of tradition. Observers were increasingly disposed to switch their attention from the things that appeared to be in process of rapid change—political forces, in brief—to those that appeared to be stable, deeply rooted in the past and persistent. This focus, of course, fitted the emphasis placed, since the work of van Leur, on the essential autonomy of Southeast Asian history. If activities and institutions which seemed to owe most to the modernization

[25] *Java in a Time of Revolution*, Ithaca, 1972.
[26] *The Rise of the Indonesian Communist Party*, Ithaca, 1965.
[27] *The Making of a Modern Bureaucratic Elite: The Colonial Transformation of the Javanese Priyayi*, Kuala Lumpur, 1979.
[28] *Sukarno and the Struggle for Indonesian Independence*.

processes set in motion by European imperialism, and to have been carried further by the radical transformation of the post-colonial era, were, on closer analysis, still really embedded in profound traditional patterns, the colonial era itself could be regarded not only as an interlude in the longer history of the region, but as an interlude which did not fundamentally alter indigenous patterns. Something of this way of looking at things was present in Harry Benda's idea of 'decolonization', which was not just a matter of ending colonial rule but of ending also the way it was perceived by Western historians, and of rejecting the excessive weight of influence they had tended to ascribe to it.[29]

The appeal to tradition as providing an explanatory framework for the analysis of 'modern' conflicts, however, had its own difficulties. Modernity and tradition are abstract concepts and are likely to distort the complexity of reality if used as simple antitheses in the examination of present-day societies. The very notion of tradition implies a judgment made now about past patterns of belief and behaviour. It tends to imply, further, if not a static past, at least a stable and slowly changing past. The idea of the 'inertia' of tradition is an integral part of the notion. There are enormous conceptual and analytical problems here. What is to be regarded as 'the tradition' and what is to be seen as change must depend in part on where observers take their stand. In Southeast Asia, for example, were Indian influences from the second and third centuries onwards to be seen as external to a more basic local tradition? And what of Islam? As we have seen, van Leur was in no doubt that the 'sheen of the world religions' was a 'thin and flaking glaze'. But other observers would tend to see these elements as absorbed and made an integral part of Southeast Asia's own patterns. A similar argument could be brought to bear when assessing the rapid currents of change of the nineteenth and twentieth centuries. Should emerging élites be categorized unquestioningly as 'modern' or regarded as a part of a continuously evolving local adaptation? There are no absolute criteria to be applied. The contrast between tradition and modernity may sometimes serve a useful analytical purpose, but only for particular ends and within the framework of a particular enquiry. It must also be remembered that the application of these categories is made in the present and may, indeed, be seen as a modern construction—a modern perception of what was the case in a more or less distant past. To that extent the tradition becomes the creation of the modern observer.[30]

Perceptions of tradition went hand in hand, of course, with recognition of the enormous upheavals that were transforming Southeast Asian societies. Terms like 'underdeveloped' came to be replaced by 'developing' or 'transitional' as adjectives to describe societies such as these, and attention was given to particular elements of change and to the analytical modes which could best express them. Was class an appropriate analytical cat-

---

[29] 'Decolonization in Indonesia: The Problem of Continuity and Change', *American Historical Review*, 70 (1965).

[30] For a discussion of these issues see S. N. Eisenstadt, 'Reflections on a Theory of Modernization', J. C. Heesterman, 'Political Modernization in India' and J. R. Gusfield, 'The Social Construction of Tradition: An Interactionist View of Social Change', in J. D. Legge, Convenor, *Traditional Attitudes and Modern Styles in Political Leadership*, Sydney, 1973.

egory for Southeast Asian societies for example? To what extent was it useful to speak of new class formation? Were peasants in process of becoming proletarian as a result of the introduction of export commodities within a traditional agricultural framework? Were there signs of emergent middle classes within what were predominantly agricultural social orders?[31]

In a discussion of this kind it is necessary to distinguish between the 'real' changes occurring and investigators' perceptions of them, or at least to notice the theoretical necessity of such a distinction, even if, in practice, it is difficult to make with confidence. Questions such as those just listed cannot be taken as neutral and 'scientific' in character. They are loaded with values, and the way in which they are answered may reflect the attitudes of the observer rather than the reality that is observed. Even if that could be avoided, the use of a particular analytical framework might well influence what is seen and introduce its own unsuspected values. The placing of an analytical emphasis on the inertia of tradition, for example, may have the conservative effect of turning the attention of participants and observers alike away from elements of change. Similarly, to focus on the vertical divisions of society, divisions, perhaps, between ethnic groups or between competing regions, may be to play down elements of class conflict and emphasize the barriers in the way of any fundamental restructuring of society, and thus serve the interests of existing élites which are reluctant to accept changes that might possibly threaten their dominance. (And, of course, even to point this out may serve a purpose.)

Modern Thai historiography provides an example of the presence of such hidden perspectives. Thailand did not have to develop a nationalist history to cope with the colonial experience, and some recent Thai historians have argued that their predecessors, Prince Damrong amongst them, placed too much emphasis on the continuity of Thai history, and on the reforming role of the monarchy, perhaps to the point where the notion of continuity became one of the weapons whereby a traditional élite was helped to perpetuate its rule.[32] A similar view was argued by B. R. O'G. Anderson,[33] who drew attention to the emphasis placed by Western as well as Thai students on the uniqueness of Thai culture and on the role of the Thai monarchy, in the nineteenth and twentieth centuries, as a modernizing and national institution. That focus, said Anderson, had strong value implications. To view the monarchy as a modernizing institution is to regard it as performing a national role. He argued that the monarchy should be seen more properly as comparable with the *colonial*

---

[31] See, e.g., discussions of the nature of labour engaged in the sugar industry in Java and the Philippines: G. R. Knight, 'Capitalism and Commodity Production in Java', in H. Alavi ed., *Capitalism and Colonial Production*, London, 1982; Knight, 'Peasant Labour and Capitalist Production in Late Colonial Indonesia: The "Campaign" at a North Java Sugar Factory, 1840–1870', JSEAS, 19, 2 (1988); J. A. Larkin, *The Pampangans*, Berkeley, 1972; A. W. McCoy, 'A Queen Dies Slowly: The Rise and Decline of Iloilo City', in McCoy and De Jesus, eds, *Philippine Social History*. See also Rex Mortimer, 'Class, Social Cleavage and Indonesian Communism', *Indonesia*, 8 (1969).

[32] See Charnvit Kasetsiri, 'Thai Historiography from Ancient Times to the Modern Period', in Reid and Marr, 166.

[33] 'Studies of the Thai State: The State of Thai Studies', in Eliezer B. Ayal, *The Study of Thailand: Analyses of Knowledge, Approaches and Prospects in Anthropology, Art History, Economics, History and Political Science*, Athens, Ohio, 1978.

régimes of Southeast Asia, which were also modernizing régimes in their way, and not, as had been the case, as representative of the national leadership of a stable society. The Thai socialist, Jit Poumisak, challenged that perspective in 1957, and his work, said C. J. Reynolds, marked 'a seismic change in the semiotic code' by which Thai society was understood in both European and Thai historiography.[34] And after 1973, when Jit's work was rediscovered, other approaches, though still focusing on the continuity of Thai culture, did so for different purposes, using it either as a means of explaining Thailand's resistance to change or of emphasizing the adaptability of that culture and its capacity to incorporate external influences.[35]

Awareness of the presence of such value dimensions is a further element in the interpretative shifts that we are discussing. Historians and other social scientists became increasingly sensitive to the value positions and political assumptions embedded in what were apparently the most dispassionate of analyses, and that self-consciousness has simultaneously sharpened the tools of investigation and undermined some of the confidence with which those tools were formerly applied. Sometimes, of course, the values of investigators were proudly displayed. A new generation of nationalist historians, while anxious to maintain the rigorous standards of the discipline, were nevertheless naturally concerned to develop indigenous perspectives on the past, in order to sustain the identity of new nations. And it would be possible to describe most Western students of Southeast Asia in the early post-war period as representing a liberal orthodoxy. Reference has already been made to the way in which they were disposed to sympathize with the movements of emancipation to be observed in Asia and to be optimistic about the future political and economic progress of the new states once the imperial yoke had been thrown off. The rise of the theory of underdevelopment and dependency during the 1970s provided a further example of scholarly commitment to an open value position. The exponents of that approach were concerned with Third World poverty in general and argued in a variety of ways that there was an inbuilt and systematic inequality in the relations between underdeveloped and developed economies. This inequality could be removed, not, as orthodox growth theory had it, by aid and foreign investment but by alternative strategies aimed at achieving rural reform.[36] Such strategies, however, were unlikely to be chosen by existing power holders; the solution, in consequence, was conceivable only in a situation where the power of entrenched interests, anxious to

[34] *Thai Radical Discourse*, 139, 150.
[35] See Chatthip Nartsupha, 'Thai Studies by Thai Scholars since 1973', Paper presented to the 36th Congress of the Japan Association of Historians of Southeast Asia, 7 December 1986. Chatthip gives Chai-anan Samudvanija and Chusit Chuchart as examples of the first view and Nidhi Aeusrivongse as an example of the second. See also Reynolds, *Thai Radical Discourse*, 9–10, on the construction of continuities in Thai history.
[36] There is an extensive literature on underdevelopment/dependency theory (UDT). Major works include Andre Gunder Frank, *Capitalism and Underdevelopment in Latin America*, New York and London, 1969, M. Barratt Brown, *Essays on Imperialism*, Nottingham, 1972, Samir Amin, *Accumulation on a World Scale*, New York and London, 1974 and *Imperialism and Unequal Development*, New York and London, 1977, Immanuel Wallerstein, *The Modern World System*, New York, 1974.

preserve the status quo, had been broken. Dependency theory presupposed, that is to say, major social revolution. In other words, what appeared at first to be a technical criticism of conventional growth theory seemed on closer inspection to contain a moral criticism of existing orders of power and to represent a direct and frank advocacy of, possibly violent, political and social change.

Not all students of Southeast Asia have been as open and frank about their preferences, or as aware of them. Values may be concealed in the way questions are posed, in the analytical models by which they are explored, or in the vocabulary that is used to present them; and historians have become conscious, as a matter of course, that this is so, with profound consequences for their perceptions of their enterprise. In the past they were aware of the dangers of concealed bias, but there was nevertheless a conviction that, in spite of the dangers, truth was attainable in principle. More recently there has developed a sense that, since the meaning perceived in the events of the past is necessarily that of the observer, the notion of truth is hardly applicable. All one can hope to achieve are competing perceptions. The excitement which stimulating teachers like Benda managed to convey to their students as they set themselves to understand the world about them has, perhaps, given way to caution and hesitation.

The effect of these considerations will be the main focus of the remaining sections of this chapter.

DECONSTRUCTING SOUTHEAST ASIAN HISTORY

For Southeast Asian historians of Southeast Asia who were also, perforce, participants in the struggles of the day, the problem was yet more complex than for others. For Indonesian historians the nature of their dilemma was explored in considerable detail in a major seminar organized jointly by Gadjah Mada University and the University of Indonesia in 1957, which led, some years later, to the preparation of a stocktaking symposium designed to identify the problems of writing Indonesian history and to chart possible directions for the future. Contributions were made by Europeans, Asians and one American, and the papers were published by Cornell University Press.[37] In the concluding essay Soedjatmoko attempted to bring into focus the peculiar problems of the modern Indonesian historian and, by extension, the modern historians of other Southeast Asian nations. Like scientific historians in general they must have 'a loving concern with the past in all its uniqueness', but at the same time they are caught up in an emotional involvement in the present. Their interest in the past is expected to serve the needs of that present which, in Indonesia's case, means providing a nationalist perspective and perhaps inventing new myths—or at least images of the past—to sustain a sense of identity and self-understanding for the nation in the present. Yet the new

---

[37] Soedjatmoko, Mohammad Ali, G. J. Resink and G. McT. Kahin, eds, *An Introduction to Indonesian Historiography*, Ithaca, 1965.

images must be scientifically defensible.[38] Is this a contradiction in terms or can the two be reconciled? Soedjatmoko referred to the 'polyinterpretability' of historical reality and the elusiveness of the search for objectivity. And he drew attention to other problems. Historians of today are operating in a period of rapid change, 'of shifting historical images the world over'. In a transitional situation our awareness, even of the present from which the past is viewed, is constantly changing. In all that transience how can one pin down a pattern of meaning in the events of the past? In these circumstances historians, because of their professional training, have lost the historical innocence which would enable them to write the patriotic history that their society wants.

Soedjatmoko advanced a moderately optimistic response to this cluster of dilemmas. Historical knowledge is at best provisional, and historians have to accept that limitation and recognize that they can work only for a 'new, but still limited' understanding of their situation. In so doing they remain participants in the events of the day, with the freedom and the responsibility that entails. But a strict adherence to the disciplinary requirements of the study will help to save them from the distorting effects of the surrounding culture.

In this way Soedjatmoko attempted to reconcile the idea of scientific history with that of participation. Others have been less sure of the possibility of any such reconciliation, or rather have been acutely conscious of the cultural determinants of any perception of the past and, in consequence, of the imperfect and partial character of any historical account. If, as has been suggested above, traditional writings are cultural artefacts, the same can surely be said about so-called 'scientific' history. What is seen from a privileged vantage-point in the present, what is taken for granted and what is selected for comment, is necessarily shaped by interest, purpose and culture and, at a more general level, will reflect fundamental assumptions about how the world is constituted.

One critic of Western studies of Asia, Edward Said, has detected an all-embracing framework within which Asia has been observed, a framework which he called 'Orientalism'. By this he did not mean simply studies of an objectively existing East. Certainly, though arguing that the 'Orient' was almost a European invention, he allowed the real existence of an Orient; but he was concerned, not with that reality, but with the way in which it had been perceived, with the special place that Asia had occupied in European experience and imagination, with Orientalism as a discourse. For Said, Western perceptions were a way of coming to terms with—and managing—the East. Orientalism was a 'corporate institution' for dealing with the East, 'dealing with it by making statements about it, authorizing views of it, describing it, by teaching it, settling it, ruling over it'. In short Orientalism was 'a western style for dominating, restructuring and having authority over the Orient'.[39]

The idea of hegemony was central to Said's analysis, a hegemony which

---

[38] Indonesia's national history project attempted to give just such a combination of scientific method and national perspective. See Sartono Kartodirdjo, Djoened Poesponegoro, Nugroho Notosusanto, eds, *Sejarah Nasional Indonesia*, 6 vols, Jakarta, 1973.

[39] *Orientalism*, London, 1978, 3.

he claimed was expressed in the structure of the disciplines—history, language, sociology, economics and others—by which the Orient was examined and in the assumptions which informed those disciplines. For him the idea of hegemony was the defining characteristic of Orientalism— and simultaneously an empirical conclusion about it. In illuminating fashion he detected that hegemony in both academic and imaginative accounts, in language, in artistic conventions and in the categories by which Asian societies and cultures were analysed, carrying his account from the eighteenth century to the present day. There is no doubt that there is substance in his argument, though it might be said that it needs to be demonstrated more carefully, and argued case by case, rather than by the development of the all-embracing category of 'Orientalism', which is itself a value-laden weapon designed for a counterattack. Once it was defined, innumerable examples could be fitted into the general picture. It is a question whether Orientalism is one phenomenon, or many; and even Said admits the possibility of 'a scholarship which is not as corrupt . . . as the kind I have been mainly depicting'.[40] It would indeed be odd if European perceptions of Asia in the eighteenth century and those of the twentieth century were so uniform and unchanging as to be satisfactorily covered by the one term, or if the linguist's Orient of the twentieth century were really part of the same Orient as that of the economist or the historian or the political scientist. And are Western students of China part of the same phenomenon as Western students of India? And what of Indian students of Indonesia or Japanese students of Thailand? Working within an international tradition of scholarship, are they too Orientalists in Said's sense? One might well doubt whether all these parts do form part of the 'larger whole' to which he refers.[41]

However, in setting up the problem as he did, and in drawing attention to elements of cultural hegemony, Said did emphasize in a dramatic form the way in which all social and historical enquiry is likely to be culture-bound. The framework within which it is carried out is a constructed framework and is therefore open to deconstruction, and to the laying bare of the influences and the interests that have shaped it in one way rather than another, and of the political functions it may be seen to perform. In general terms he was giving one formulation of the problem of coming to terms with the 'other'. It is not merely a cultural 'other' that is in question, of course. Certainly cross-cultural studies present their own significant difficulties of symbols and meanings; but those difficulties apply by extension to attempts to understand subcultures within the one society, to understand classes or social groups other than one's own, to understand, for that matter, other individuals—and, of course, other times. As L. P. Hartley remarked, 'The past is a foreign country: they do things differently there.'

The uncertainties and hesitations arising from the recognition of those difficulties have been accentuated over recent years by developments in

---

[40] ibid., 326.
[41] ibid., 24. Said, p. 25, specifically warns Asian students of Asia against the dangers of employing the structure of cultural domination upon themselves and others.

the realm of literary theory, which were seen to have implications for the study of Asian texts: implications which went far beyond textual study in the narrow sense.

An example of a new approach to textual analysis was provided in the early post-war period by the work of C. C. Berg, who mounted a systematic criticism of the apparent certainties of early Javanese history as they had been presented by pre-war Dutch scholars. Berg's fire was directed especially at the work of Krom. In a series of articles, written from an essentially structuralist point of view, he argued that the so-called historical writings of Java, the fourteenth-century *Nāgarakĕrtāgama*, the possibly older *Pararaton* and the later *Babad Tanah Jawi*, were not works of history at all and could only be understood if read within the framework of the society which produced them.[42] Krom had assumed that such texts contained a substratum of fact. His method was to subject the texts to rigorous internal criticism but to proceed, nevertheless, on the assumption that they could provide evidence of an actual past. As Berg put it, his approach was 'to put aside intrinsically improbable assertions, in the case of conflicting assertions to select the most probable one, and to reject the others, for the time being'.[43] Instead, said Berg, the scholar should recognize the function—often the magical function—which the text performed, perhaps supplying a legitimate ancestry for a usurper, or transmitting myths about the past which sustained a subsequent world view. Following his own method, Berg advanced a radical reading of these texts and called into question the political history which Krom had been prepared to accept. He rejected, for example, the story of Airlangga's division of his kingdom between his two sons, he questioned the existence of the first two rulers of the thirteenth-century Singhasari dynasty in Java, and he argued that the *Nāgarakĕrtāgama's* account of the extent of the empire of Majapahit was no more than a display of geographical knowledge. In brief, the literary sources from which Krom drew much of his account of Hindu-Javanese history from the ninth to the mid-thirteenth centuries offered evidence not for events but only, if properly read, for the cultural configurations of Javanese society.

Notwithstanding their seminal effect on the assumptions underlying textual analysis, Berg's views did not entirely change the findings of scholarship. Later scholars have inclined to the view that Berg had overstated his case. F. D. K. Bosch, in an article in the *Bijdragen* in 1956, argued that, while the evidence for the political chronology accepted by Krom might be weak, firm evidence for Berg's alternative reading was lacking also.[44] He accused Berg of proceeding from an 'intuitive' brainwave on which he built 'an extremely unstable tower of hypotheses piled on top of each other'.[45] De Casparis, writing at about the same time, was equally

---

[42] 'Kartanegara, de Miskende Empirebuilder', *Orientatie*, 1950; 'De Sadang-Oorlog en de Mythe van Groot-Majapahit', *Indonesie*, 5 (1951); 'De Geschiedenis van Pril Majapahit', *Indonesie*, 4 and 5 (1950 and 1951); 'The Work of Professor Krom', in Hall, ed., *Historians*, 164ff.

[43] 'The Work of Professor Krom', in Hall, 167.

[44] C. C. Berg and Ancient Javanese History', BKI, 1956, 112.

[45] Bosch's critique, amongst other things, considered in detail the substance of Berg's argument with regard to the first two rulers of Singhasari and the extent of Majapahit's empire.

emphatic. Arguing from an epigrapher's point of view, he insisted that the reading of at least some inscriptions was really beyond doubt and that this kind of evidence could not be brushed aside so easily by an attempt at alternative hypotheses based on a 'weak or even imaginary foundation'.[46]

What is important for the present discussion, however, is the confidence with which Berg put forward his alternative readings. Clearly, both he and his critics saw themselves as concerned with what might be called matters of fact. What was the political chronology of thirteenth-century Java? Was Majapahit an extensive realm? And they shared a belief that, if handled properly, textual study could illuminate some sort of reality. They disagreed about what constituted proper handling; but that there was a reality to be discovered by an examination of this kind of evidence was not in question. Later theorists were to raise more fundamental doubts about such a possibility.

The theorists in question were those adopting structuralist and semiological approaches to the reading of indigenous texts. The structuralist and post-structuralist enterprise has operated simultaneously at a number of levels. In part it has been an exploration of the nature of language, signs and meaning, of the links between linguistic systems and social order, and of the ways in which meaning is encoded in symbol and metaphor. In part it has focused on the relationship between reader and text, suggesting in some formulations that meaning is a function of that relationship and cannot exist independently of it. The reader creates the reading and there is no further criterion of reality, no external meaning to be ascertained. And it has also implied conclusions about the nature of reality and the grounds of knowledge. The evolving discussion of these and related ideas by Saussure, Lévi-Strauss, Jakobsen, Barthes, Culler, Derrida and many others over the years has had revolutionary implications for literary criticism. It sharpened the awareness not only of students of literature but indeed of those engaged in considering human behaviour in whatever form. And amongst others it has influenced modern students of the textual sources of Southeast Asian history, whose work has come to represent a renewed interest in the early history of the region, in its literary forms and cultural expressions.

In focus and method the work of this later generation of textual scholars differs sharply from the largely contemporary concerns, and the social science modes, of the 1950s and 1960s. Even where the attention of historians in the immediate post-war period was directed to early history—to a consideration, for example, of the structure of authority of the classical kingdoms—they tended to deal in terms of such generalized categories as patrimonial states, bureaucratic élites, patron–client relationships, status systems, and social stratification, rather than examining the cultural expressions of those periods for their own sake. Moreover, as we have seen, their primary interest was often in the light that traditional order might throw on modern political behaviour. It differs also from the earlier 'Orientalist' tradition. At first glance the growing interest in textual study may appear as a swing back to the linguistic, literary and philosophical

[46] 'Historical Writing on Indonesia (Early Period)' in Hall, ed., Historians, 160.

concerns of classical scholarship, but, in fact, its application of structuralist theory has led it into new paths of enquiry. By an examination of basic formal patterns, inner relationships, codes and symbols embedded in the literatures, inscriptions and other records of the Southeast Asian past, it seeks to uncover meanings below the surface of the texts and to gain some perception of the cultural conventions and shared knowledge within which the creators of the sources unselfconsciously existed: to attain, that, is to say, insights into how these societies, perhaps unconsciously, saw themselves. And the language is now the language of image and myth, discourse, signs and symbols, codes and emplotment.

Examples of such an approach are provided by James Siegel's examination of Acehnese historical thinking, Shelley Errington's essay on assumptions about history in Malay writings, Anthony Day's exploration of Javanese concepts of time, prophecy and change, Michael Aung-Thwin's consideration of prophecies, omens and dialogue in Burmese historiography, A. C. Milner's study of the political ideas implied in certain Malay texts, Keith W. Taylor's use of texts to catch the voices of eleventh-century Vietnam, and Michael Vickery's attempt to discern the nature of state formation in Cambodia.[47] An example of the application of the same sort of approach to more recent history may be found in Craig Reynolds' consideration of modern Thai historiography.[48]

Of considerable importance in fostering this type of approach is the work of O. W. Wolters, whose attempt to detect the subtle implications that lie within the structure of thirteenth- and fourteenth-century Vietnamese texts is a model of its kind.[49] It is a hallmark of his work that he has been more concerned than many other practitioners are to stay strictly within the texts he is reading. In the application of the method, he seeks, as a matter of principle, not to appeal for explanation to matters outside the text or to use the text as evidence of a reality external to it.[50]

Though much of the work done under structuralist influence has been directed to the study of texts in the literal sense—chronicles, inscriptions, poems and other literary creations—the same type of approach may be applied to texts of a different kind, texts by analogy. Cultural traits, patterns of behaviour, events in the normally accepted sense of the term

[47] Siegel, *Shadow and Sound*, Chicago, 1979; Errington, 'Some comments on Style in the Meanings of the Past', in Reid and Marr; Day, 'Ranggawarsita's Prophecy of Mystery', in David K. Wyatt and Alexander Woodside, eds, *Moral Order and the Question of Change: Essays on Southeast Asian Thought*, New Haven, 1982; Michael Aung-Thwin, 'Prophecies, Omens and Dialogue: Tools of the Trade in Burmese Historiography', in Wyatt and Woodside; Milner, *Kerajaan: Malay Political Culture on the Eve of Colonial Rule*, Tucson, 1982; Taylor, 'Authority and Legitimacy in 11th-Century Vietnam' and Michael Vickery, 'Some Remarks on Early State Formation in Cambodia' in Marr and Milner, eds, *Southeast Asia*.

[48] *Thai Radical Discourse*.

[49] 'Possibilities for a Reading of the 1293–1357 Period in the Vietnamese Annals', in Reid and Marr; Wolters, *History, Culture and Region*; 'Narrating the Fall of the Ly and the Rise of the Tran Dynasties', *ASAA Review*, 10, 2 (November 1986); *Two Essays on Dai-Viet in the Fourteenth Century*, New Haven: Yale Southeast Asia Studies, 1988.

[50] Note his distinction between a 'textual' and a documentary approach to a text: Wolters, *History, Culture and Region*, 69. One might compare this with Victor Lieberman who also bases much of his work on textual analysis but who focuses more on the historical events evidenced by the texts than on the structure of the texts themselves: Lieberman, *Burmese Administrative Cycles*.

may also be regarded, in their own way, as texts to be read. They are like language, with internal relationships to be observed. Human actions themselves reflect the sign systems of those who perform them. To put it another way, culture is not merely 'like' language. It is in large measure shaped by its language, and indeed social behaviour is itself a language. There is no objective, external, 'innocent', world to be perceived. The student of society can only perceive the system of signs and language habits by which that society is encountered. These may be so private that an outside observer has little hope of really entering that society; and they may be distorted in the very process of being observed. But, by being attentive to the forms, the student of texts, both written and acted, may hope in some measure to penetrate the linguistic system and, as it were, to crack the codes within which meanings are concealed. Reynaldo Ileto's decoding of the language and gestures of peasant rebels in the Philippines, for example, was concerned with texts both written and acted.

Closely connected with the theoretical underpinnings of the textualist approach was the temper displayed in its practice. It involved careful, scrupulous and attentive consideration of words and actions. Wolters, in his study of thirteenth- and fourteenth-century Vietnam, makes a distinction between 'choosing to do something to the past' and 'doing something with the past'.[51] The former involves constructing the shape of the past, with the danger that the shape might 'be influenced by preconceptions of the nature of the past in question'. The latter involves 'following directions and messages provided by the linguistic and structural systems that generate the sources' meaning when they are read as texts'. One might question the validity of the distinction. (Might not preconceptions of the nature of the past affect one's perceptions of the directions and messages? And is not the reading of the messages in a sense a construction of the shape of the past?) Nevertheless the distinction does convey a sense of the care, subtlety and sensitivity with which the sources are to be studied.

The method has been fruitful, though the ideas that sometimes accompany it and underpin it may be disturbing. The idea that texts are self-regarding, that they are not referential—that they refer only to themselves and not to a reality outside themselves, and that they may be open to an infinite multiplicity of readings—may seem to lead to an absolute relativism. Are the patterns and structures to be discerned in texts objectively there or are they merely the constructs of the reader, and as such open to deconstruction? Is there such a thing as a valid reading? Or must there be, as Derrida argues, a constant deferment of judgment, a continuing deconstruction of the rhetoric that is always present in a text and in any reading of it? Is the textual scholar, including the student of texts by analogy, to be left, in the end, with an inescapable indeterminacy of meaning?

Questions of this kind have become part of the general methodological discourse of the human sciences and have contributed to a recognition on the part of historians in general, and not merely of historians studying cultures other than their own, of the enormous difficulties facing their

---

[51] *Dai-Viet in the Fourteenth Century*, ix.

enterprise. The difficulties are, of course, present in any enquiry in which human beings study themselves. Such a recognition has affected the fundamental assumptions on the basis of which historical study is conducted. For historians of Southeast Asia, the change of atmosphere which has taken place since the London seminars of the 1950s is apparent. No longer would they speak, with quite the same confidence, of the possibility of a 'real' history, whether of Southeast Asia or anywhere else, or of an attempt 'to arrive at a real world-history sense of values'.[52]

This is not the place to seek answers to the questions raised above, though a short response may be to suggest that many of the assertions that are to be found in structuralist theory are epistemological rather than practical assertions, concerned with the nature and grounds of knowledge rather than with the world as it may be perceived. Though students of history must certainly be aware of language as a social construct, and of the rhetoric built into their readings of texts, what matters, in the end, is how they might defend the statements that they make. They are anchored in the contingent world and must cope with it as best they can, describing and analysing it with the tools at their disposal. Even if they stay within the texts, the statements they make must be defended by reference to the texts. To that extent, and contrary to structuralist principle in at least some of its formulations, the texts are indeed referential. Historians may never succeed in capturing reality, but that is not to say that there is no reality to be captured.

The self-reflexive aspect of structuralist thought does not necessarily lead, it is suggested, to a paralysing relativism. Certainly the self-awareness it has brought, and the recognition of the difficulty of getting some kind of grasp of other cultures may appear to represent a retreat from the confidence which, according to the present argument, marked the study of Southeast Asian history in the early post-war years. But perhaps it should be described as an advance rather than a retreat? If it makes historians more cautious and self-critical than before, and more alert to the difficulties lying in the way of understanding other cultures, it leaves them still with the responsibility of grasping, as well as they can, the nature of the past of the societies with which they deal.

---

[52] Hall, ed., *Historians*, 7 and 9.

PART
ONE

FROM PREHISTORY TO c. 1500 CE

This section of the work gives an account of the region up to the fifteenth century of the Christian era. The opening chapter, drawing on archaeological, anthropological and linguistic evidence, is concerned with the prehistory of its peoples. The next three have parallels in subsequent sections of the work. An account of the political structures of the region is followed by accounts of its economic and social history, and of its religious experience and popular beliefs.

Chapter 2 considers the environment of the region through time and it then attempts to integrate data from a range of disciplines in order to deal with a broad range of hypotheses on its prehistory. It discusses the extent of distributional correlation among human biological groupings, cultures and languages before the rise of the first historical states.

This is the subject of Chapter 3. It begins with an account of the Vietnamese polity and of its unique relationships with the Chinese empire. It then considers the development of other Southeast Asian polities. A comparative approach is attempted, limited by the relative paucity of material. But that in itself is connected with the attitude to history prevailing in the several polities concerned, and in turn that is a guide to understanding their nature. Champa, it is concluded, is not a kingdom in the conventional sense of the word. The Khmer polity at Angkor, dependent on ricefields, differed again. Pagan is compared with Angkor. In the Irrawaddy basin, more culturally diverse and competitive, the need to affirm the ethical nature of political authority was the greater. Both polities came to an end at the time of the advent of the Tai peoples into lowland Southeast Asia. Tai polities emerged, including Lan Na, Lan Sang and Ayutthaya, the last of which was the most enduring.

The history of the Malay world is a modern reconstruction, based on Chinese and Arabo-Persian texts, inscriptions and archaeological evidence: the Malays preserved almost no memory of Śrīvijaya, the south Sumatra polity or polities of the seventh to the fourteenth centuries. Malay ambitions were limited by the advance of Siamese power on the peninsula and the rise of Majapahit in Java, and then revived with the development of Melaka as a new commercial entrepôt.

Either maritime trade, rice-growing, or both, formed the economic basis of these polities. These activities are described in Chapter 4, together with their relationship to the political dynamics of the various states. The chapter gives special attention to the Javanese kingdoms and to Majapahit, but it also discusses Angkor and Pagan, and the very different Cham and Vietnamese realms. Though more impersonal structures were emerging in Majapahit, their political economies remained rather similar than dissimilar to those elsewhere in the region.

Religion, though spiritually motivated, was also a basis of political power and resource mobilization. Indeed, as Chapter 5 shows, it was integrated with social and cultural life rather than being seen, as in modern Western societies, as something separate. The sources for its study are richer than for other aspects of Southeast Asian civilization, but are unequally distributed, in terms of region, period and social level. They show the assimilation of Indian culture and Indian religions and their adaptation to or accommodation of Southeast Asian beliefs and practices. They also show the divergent experience of mainland and archipelago. In the former, Theravāda Buddhism, disseminated from Burma, came to predominate. In Java, the worship of Śiva was the prevalent form of Hindu religion, while Mahāyāna Buddhism flourished in Sumatra, the Malay peninsula and western Kalimantan. Islam appeared in the region six centuries after its foundation, and Islamization was at first slow. The conversion of the ruler of Melaka at the beginning of the fifteenth century was a crucial step. By the end of the century Islam was firmly established in northern Sumatra, the peninsula, northern Java and western Kalimantan.

SOUTHEAST ASIA BEFORE HISTORY

Southeast Asia is a region of anthropological and archaeological complexity, remarkable for the sheer variety of cultural expression which it has nourished since very early times. Geographically, it comprises an environmental patchwork of highlands, lowlands and intervening seas extending across tropical latitudes for about 5000 kilometres southeastwards from Burma (Myanmar) to eastern Indonesia. Throughout this region were represented, before the appearance of the first historical records about 2000 years ago, societies of many socio-economic levels—from hunters and gatherers, through tribal agriculturalists, to socially ranked chiefdoms fully conversant with the manufacture of artefacts of bronze and iron. Cutting across these socio-economic levels were considerable variations in language and human biology, all reflecting many millennia of adaptation, innovation, colonization and contact between populations.

The prehistory of Southeast Asia is of importance to the world for several reasons. In terms of remotest human ancestry, the area holds important evidence for the expansion of hominids from Africa into Asia around one million years ago. It also witnessed the earliest known human sea crossings anywhere in the world—into the western Pacific and Australia beginning at least 40,000 years ago. Its northern regions may also hold the key to the domestication of rice, one of the modern world's most important plant foods, and the area as a whole may have witnessed the domestication of many other major species, including certain yams, aroids (especially taro), bananas, and perhaps sugarcane. Southeast Asia also provided the source-region and early environmental backdrop for the most extensive diaspora of a single ethnolinguistic group in the history of mankind—that of the speakers of Austronesian languages, who by the early centuries CE had spread more than halfway around the world to Madagascar and Easter Island.

Research in the prehistory of Southeast Asia is currently at an exciting stage, with new discoveries and interpretations appearing almost annually. It may thus be apposite to recall a tendency on the part of many scholars writing before the mid-1960s to regard the region in prehistory as little more than a backward appendage of the more advanced cultures of India and China. It is now clear that this view was far too simple, and that Southeast Asia has a prehistory as complex and as indigenously creative as any other major region of Eurasia. It also served, over a timespan of at least

40,000 years, as the ultimate source-region for the populations of Australia and the Pacific Islands; populations as diverse and as anthropologically significant today as the Aboriginal Australians, the Melanesians, the Micronesians and the Polynesians.

In order to write a coherent account of the prehistory of Southeast Asia, one which goes beyond the minutiæ of the archaeological record, it is necessary to consider the results of many separate disciplinary fields of study. A major task is to consider the environment of the region and to examine how it may have changed through time. Beyond this, in order to identify hypotheses of real human significance, one must compare and integrate data from the independent disciplines of biological anthropology, comparative linguistics, and archaeology. It will be evident that few immutable interpretations of the prehistoric record are accepted by all scholars, and one must instead deal with a broad range of hypotheses which reflect the disciplinary and cultural backgrounds of their authors as much as the mechanical calculations of scientific objectivity. There are, however, certain points of agreement, a major one being that there is considerable overlapping of human biological groupings, cultures and languages. Especially when one takes a broad geographic scale, it becomes impossible to construct watertight categories. Even a cursory survey of the ethnographic record reveals that people who appear biologically to be quite different may speak languages in the same family (for instance, Negritos and Southern Mongoloids in the Philippines), and peoples with strong physical similarities may be quite different in terms of language and cultural background.

Such circumstances, however, should not lead to the view that all biological, linguistic and cultural variation is entirely uncorrelated. This is not the case even in the modern world with its unprecedented rate of biological and cultural mixing, and it may be better to infer relatively high correlations, especially on a local scale, amongst the majority of the pre-urbanized populations who inhabited Southeast Asia before the rise of the first historical states. Individual explanations may then be sought for those contrary situations which obviously will occur from time to time in real life, as a result of the normal processes of contact and intermarriage which occur between adjacent human groups.

PRESENT-DAY ENVIRONMENTS OF SOUTHEAST ASIA

In a purely geographical sense, Southeast Asia falls conveniently into two parts: mainland, comprising China south of the Yangtze,[1] Burma (Myanmar), Thailand, Indochina and peninsular Malaysia; and island,

---

[1] It must not be forgotten that the incorporation of southern China into the political and cultural boundaries of Han Chinese civilization did not occur until the first millennium BC. South China before this was an integral part of Southeast Asia in cultural and linguistic terms, and many millions of speakers of languages in the Tai, Tibeto-Burman, Miao-Yao and Austroasiatic families still live north of the southern Chinese border today. It is impossible to understand the later stages of Southeast Asian prehistory without reference to southern China.

comprising Indonesia, East Malaysia, Brunei, the Philippines and Taiwan. Biogeographically, however, the major division lies much further to the east, since the islands of Sumatra, Java, Borneo, Bali and Palawan lie on the once-exposed continental Sunda Shelf (Sundaland), a geologically stable and now partly drowned extension of the Asian landmass (Map 2.1). During glacial periods of low sea-level, much of Sundaland was joined as dry land to the rest of Asia—a recurring circumstance with profound implications for the origins of the flora and fauna and the most ancient human inhabitants of the area.

To the east of Bali and Borneo, across Huxley's Line of biogeographers, lie the deep seas and islands of the Philippines and the region of Wallacea, the latter (Sulawesi, Nusa Tenggara and Maluku) named after the nineteenth-century naturalist Alfred Russel Wallace. This region has never been crossed by a continuous land connection: its colonization by plants, animals and humans required, for the most part, the crossing of ocean divides. Eastwards again, and mostly beyond the concern of this chapter, lies the continental Sahul Shelf which joins Australia and New Guinea.

In terms of geology and geomorphology, the major part of the mainland of Southeast Asia is formed by the roughly north–south trending basins of the Irrawaddy, Salween, Chao Phraya, Mekong and Red (Hong) rivers and their tributaries, and by the intervening areas of high relief such as the Truong Son spine of Indochina and the mountains which separate Thailand from Burma. The major environmental distinction within this region is therefore that between the low-lying and broad riverine plains and alluvial plateaux, the latter including the archaeologically-important Khorat Plateau of northeastern Thailand, and the intervening uplands. It is this environmental distinction which correlates most closely with the anthropological division of mainland Southeast Asian societies into the coastal/riverine civilizations of the lowlands and the inland/upland 'hill peoples'.

The land masses which lie on the Sunda Shelf proper, that is the Thai-Malay peninsula and the islands of western Indonesia, have survived the post-glacial rise in sea level as enclaves of varied relief which necessarily have much shorter river systems than the non-peninsular parts of the mainland. Although the distinction between riverine/coastal plains and interior uplands is still of major cultural importance, the major environmental differentiation in this zone lies between terrain which is stable and volcanically inactive (Malay peninsula, Borneo, eastern Sumatra) and that produced by the awe-inspiring Sunda–Banda volcanic arc. This spectacular alignment of volcanoes, which includes the famous Krakatoa between Java and Sumatra, has been wrought by subduction of the bed of the Indian Ocean around the southern side of Indonesia from western Sumatra, past Java and Bali, to Maluku. Further volcanic arcs run northwards through Sulawesi and the Philippines and onwards to Japan. Certain of these volcanic regions, with their fertile soils and monsoonal climates, support some of the greatest agricultural population densities on earth, while the geologically stable and relatively infertile interiors of Borneo and parts of eastern Sumatra until recently supported some of the sparsest.

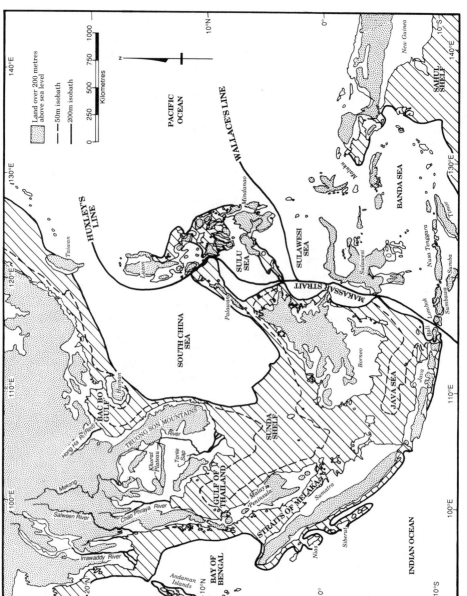

Map 2.1 The physical geography.

The biogeographical zone of Wallacea between the Sunda and Sahul Shelves is also partially the result of volcanic arc formation, here in open and deep seas rather than against a continental shelf in the way that the western part of the Sunda–Banda arc impinges on Sundaland. Hence the Wallacean islands are smaller than those of Sundaland, and have also been more isolated through geological time. The Philippine islands are similarly of volcanic origin and have apparently never been joined in entirety to the Asian mainland, with the exception of Palawan which lies on the Sunda Shelf. The absence of major land bridges joining these regions has caused distinctive flora and fauna to evolve, and may also have barred any eastward dispersal of hominids beyond Bali and Borneo prior to the Late Pleistocene.

The Climate and Vegetation of Southeast Asia

The whole of Southeast Asia lies within the tropics and is therefore in a zone of uniformly high temperature, except at high altitude. However, the annual pattern of rainfall in the equatorial zone is different from that in the flanking intermediate tropical zone (Map 2.2). The equatorial zone lies mainly in Indonesia and Malaysia within about five degrees of the equator (there is also a northwards extension in the eastern Philippines) and it has a non-seasonal climate with heavy rainfall occurring throughout the year. In contrast, the intermediate tropical (or intertropical) zone beyond is characterized by a 'winter' dry season which increases to almost half the year as one moves southwards towards Australia and northwards towards southern China.

The significance of this climatic zonation for human prehistory is considerable. The equatorial zone demonstrates several environmental features which might be deemed hostile towards easy human colonization, whether by foraging or agricultural groups.[2] Soils tend to be infertile clays, especially outside zones of recent volcanic activity, and most nutrients are cycled within the enormous rainforest biomass rather than in the topsoil. Equatorial forests present few edible wild plants or animals; numbers of species of course proliferate, but large stands of plant foods suitable for human consumption do not, and the fauna is also dispersed or arboreal, and difficult to hunt. Even with agricultural production, the labour of clearing forest in such constantly humid conditions with rapid weed growth did not encourage dense populations in preindustrial times, and many of the equatorial regions are still strikingly underpopulated today.

[2] It has recently been suggested that inland equatorial rainforest would have provided insufficient food for a human population to live by hunting and gathering alone. If this view is correct, much of the interior equatorial rainforest of Southeast Asia might have been totally uninhabited until the development of agriculture. The coastal zones, however, certainly did support some habitation according to the archaeological evidence, as did the interior of peninsular Malaysia (see page 129). The situation is therefore quite complex. See T. N. Headland, 'The wild yam question: how well could independent hunter-gatherers live in a tropical rain forest ecosystem?', *Human Ecology*, 15 (1987); R. C. Bailey et al., 'Hunting and gathering in tropical rainforest: is it possible?', *American Anthropologist*, 91 (1989); P. Bellwood, 'From Late Pleistocene to Early Holocene in Sundaland', in C. Gamble and O. Soffer, eds, *The Late Palaeolithic Global Record*, II, London, 1990.

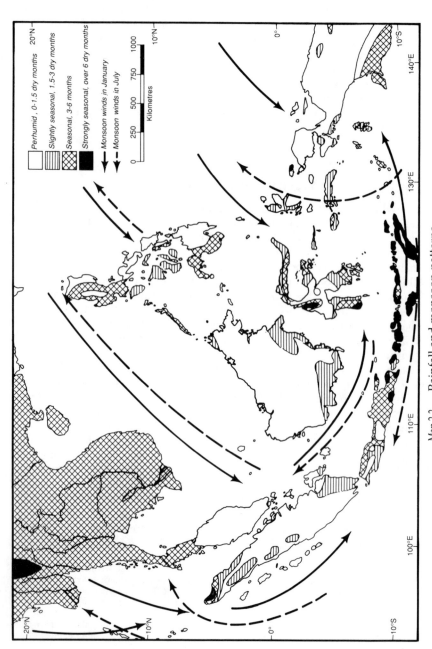

Map 2.2   Rainfall and monsoon patterns.

Perhumid , 0-1.5 dry months
Slightly seasonal, 1.5-3 dry months
Seasonal, 3-6 months
Strongly seasonal, over 6 dry months
Monsoon winds in January
Monsoon winds in July

Kilometres
0   250   500   750   1000

In contrast, those regions which lie within the intertropical zone, especially where the dry season is reliable and three months or more in duration, support more open monsoonal forests with a deciduous tendency during the driest periods. This zone, which of course exists both north and south of the equator, includes most of mainland Southeast Asia north of Malaysia, the islands of southeast Indonesia from Java to Timor, and parts of Sulawesi and the western Philippines. Many of these regions also have very fertile soils, and the resulting combination of good soil and sufficient dry season sun for the ripening of rice has led in some areas to intensive irrigation agriculture and the growth of dense populations. Even from the viewpoint of prehistoric hunting and collecting, the animal biomass of the intertropical zone, when not curtailed by island isolation and poverty of species, should have been higher than that of the equatorial rainforests. This observation would apply especially to the large browsing mammals of mainland Southeast Asia and the islands of Sundaland.[3]

The distributions of large mammals, however, and fauna and flora in general, are not determined simply by good soil and the incidence of rainfall. Southeast Asia straddles one of the most ancient zones of biogeographical transition in the world—that which has generally kept apart the placental mammals of Eurasia and the marsupial fauna of Australia and New Guinea. The Sunda Shelf islands west of Huxley's Line form the true eastern limit of Asia, and contain (ignoring instances of local extinction) Asian species such as cattle, deer, pigs, elephants, tigers, monkeys, gibbons, and orang utan. The only native placental mammals in Australia and New Guinea are species of rodents and bats which managed to reach these areas across sea gaps in pre-human times.

The islands of Wallacea have few endemic large mammals, and those which do occur are mostly of Sundaland as opposed to Australasian origin. Sulawesi, for instance, has the endemic pig-like *babirusa* and the buffalo-like *anoa*, and also three species of marsupial phalangers, small tree-dwelling mammals whose ancestors presumably island-hopped in pre-human times from the Sahul zone. The simple fact that Sundaland and Sahul-land were never directly joined by a continuous land bridge is obviously one of great importance for the story of human expansion eastwards.

THE CHANGING NATURE OF THE SOUTHEAST ASIAN ENVIRONMENT

The record of human settlement in Southeast Asia extends back in time for about one million years. During that time the landscapes and climates of the region have fluctuated considerably, according to the cyclical rhythm of changes associated with the Pleistocene glaciations in temperate

---

[3] For instance, wild *banteng* cattle occur at densities of 1–2 animals per hundred hectares in primary rainforest, but up to 10–15 animals per hundred hectares in savanna grasslands in eastern Java (where herds of up to 246 animals have been recorded). See P. Pfeffer, 'Fauna of humid tropical Asia', in *Natural Resources of Humid Tropical Asia*, Paris: Unesco, 1974.

latitudes. Some understanding of the magnitude of these changes is necessary before the human prehistoric record can be presented. The data will be discussed according to the standard chronological subdivisions of Early Pleistocene (c.1.6 million to 700,000 years ago), Middle Pleistocene (700,000 to 125,000 years ago) and Late Pleistocene (125,000 to 10,000 years ago). The Late Pleistocene corresponds to the last interglacial and last glacial periods, and is succeeded by the Holocene, the present period of warm interglacial climate within which all human developments beyond the Palaeolithic appear to have taken place.

It is now known, as a result of the study of pollen sequences and the documentation of changing oxygen isotope ratios in the shells of marine micro-organisms, that approximately seven episodes of temperate latitude glaciation have occurred since the beginning of the Middle Pleistocene. Others, perhaps of lesser magnitude and shorter duration, extend back into the Pliocene. True glacial low points in temperature were quite short (c.10,000 years), as were true interglacial high points. For example, the generalized 'shape' of the last full glacial cycle (which is the one best understood) consisted of a very rapid rise out of the penultimate glacial into the last interglacial, and then a very long-term and erratic downward slide in temperature from the last interglacial (c.120,000 years ago) into the last maximum cold stage (c.18,000 years ago). The phenomenon of rapid amelioration of the climate in post-glacial phases is particularly important since the last one was clearly associated, perhaps via increasing temperature and rainfall and a greater degree of rainfall seasonality, with the origins of cereal and tuber agriculture.

In tropical Southeast Asia, of course, true continental glaciations did not occur, although ice caps are known to have expanded dramatically in the high mountains of New Guinea, and to a much lesser extent on Mount Kinabalu in Sabah and some of the high volcanoes in Sumatra. Tree lines and vegetation zones were correspondingly depressed, in some cases by more than 1500 metres of altitude. The main results of glaciations for humans in the Southeast Asian tropics would have been a lowering of average annual temperature,[4] a major decrease in annual rainfall, changes in vegetation patterns, and a lowering of sea level to as much as 130 metres below the present as enormous quantities of water became progressively trapped in the high-latitude ice sheets. The sea-level changes would probably have had dramatic effects on human migration and expansion, and they will be examined first.

The Sunda Shelf is the largest area of shallowly submerged continental shelf on earth. When it was almost fully exposed as dry land during glacials it would have formed a subcontinent over four million square kilometres in extent. The terrestrial deposits which now form the beds of the South China and Java Seas give ample evidence of this, as do several

---

[4] By up to 8 degrees Celsius in highlands, but probably much less in lowlands and at sea level. See J. R. Flenley, 'Late Quaternary changes of vegetation and climate in the Malesian mountains', *Erdwissenschaftliche Forschung*, 18 (1984); D. Walker and Sun Xiangjun, 'Vegetational and climatic changes at the Pleistocene-Holocene transition across the eastern tropics', in *The Palaeoenvironment of East Asia from the Mid-Tertiary*, I, Centre of Asian Studies, University of Hong Kong, 1988.

drowned river valleys and frequent records of mangrove pollen in cores drilled into the sea bed. Full exposure of the shelf, however, so that all the islands which now rise from it were joined together by dry land extending to the shelf edge, need not have been a particularly common circumstance. The last time it occurred was for a few millennia around 18,000 years ago, prior to that around 135,000 years ago,[5] and then possibly at intervals of between 90,000 and 120,000 years back into the Middle Pleistocene (Figure 2.1). Drowning of the Sunda Shelf to the level of the present ocean surface would have occurred at similarly spaced intervals, with the most recent peaks occurring at 6000, 125,000 and possibly about 210,000 years ago. Sea level was probably slightly higher than now about 6000 years ago, following a very rapid post-glacial rise which drowned about two million square kilometres of low-lying Sundaland terrain in about 8000 years.

Prior to half a million years ago there is far less agreement about cycles of Sundaland submergence and emergence. Not only may the cycles of sea-level change have differed in amplitude and chronology, but the geological and faunal records are both open to differing interpretations. Some authors favour a fairly continuous emergence and continental character for Sundaland until about 500,000 years ago, and others stress the significance of episodes of island isolation, especially for Java.[6] Despite these uncertainties it is apparent that during the Middle and Late Pleistocene the sea level would have oscillated for most of the time between 20 and 80 metres below the present level. This prompts some very important observations in respect of human dispersal.

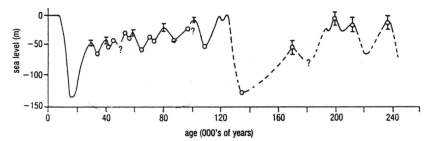

Figure 2.1   A sea-level curve for the past 250,000 years based on data from the Huon Peninsula, northeastern Papua New Guinea.

Redrawn from J. Chappell and N. J. Shackleton, 'Oxygen isotopes and sea level', *Nature*, 324 (1986), 137–40.

[5] Sea-level changes have been well studied for the Pleistocene in Australia and New Guinea, and these results may generally be applied to Southeast Asia, despite some variation in isostatic crustal movements. For current views, see J. Chappell and N. J. Shackleton, 'Oxygen isotopes and sea level', *Nature*, 324 (1986); and chapters in M. J. Tooley and Ian Shennan, eds, *Sea Level Changes*, Oxford, 1987.

[6] See discussion in my *Prehistory of the Indo-Malaysian Archipelago*, Sydney, 1985 (hereafter PIMA), 30–1. For the view that Java was an island around one million years ago, see J. M. Leinders, F. Azis, P. Y. Sondaar and J. de Vos, 'The age of the hominid-bearing deposits of Java', *Geologie en Mijnbouw*, 64 (1985). A contrary view based on faunal composition is expressed by L. R. Heaney, 'Zoogeographic evidence for Middle and Late Pleistocene land bridges to the Philippine Islands', MQRSEA, 9 (1985).

The Malay peninsula, Sumatra and Java, for instance, would all be joined to each other and to Asia at a sea level of 20 metres below present. Borneo would be joined as well at 50 metres below present. This means that Java and Sumatra may have been joined to Asia for well over half and possibly even 90 per cent of Middle and Late Pleistocene time, Borneo for perhaps less.[7] However, when high sea levels did separate islands they certainly led to a dramatic increase in the rate of extinction of terrestrial mammals.[8] One can only guess what biological effects they would have had on the sparse populations of *Homo erectus*, who presumably would have lacked the ability to cross sea to maintain their links with the Asian gene pool to which they originally belonged.

Within Wallacea the fluctuating Pleistocene sea levels would not have produced any major land bridges, although most of the Philippine islands excluding Palawan could have been joined together as one or two major islands in the Middle Pleistocene, as may some of the Nusa Tenggara chain from Lombok eastwards. However, it seems that neither of these regions was ever joined by dry land to Sundaland during the timespan of hominid settlement in the region, despite many past claims for various land-bridge possibilities.[9] At present, all indications are that the first hominids to cross Huxley's Line did so by crossing sea, and the available evidence suggests that these first intrepid migrants were members of the modern species *Homo sapiens* at a date around or a little prior to 40,000 years ago.

The other effects of glaciation in the tropics referred to above, namely reduced rainfall and a consequent change from closed rainforest to more open vegetation, would have had effects on human dispersal additional to those caused by changes in sea level. Since human foragers can maintain only very small numbers in rainforests,[10] pre-agricultural human ranges and population densities in equatorial Southeast Asia might have been much greater during full glacials than in interglacials. There is evidence from many disciplines which suggests that Southeast Asian climates during periods of glacial low sea level were drier than now, and that rainfall was perhaps significantly reduced in some parts of the area now occupied by ever-wet rainforest.[11] Major results of such changes might

---

[7] These estimates are reflected to some extent in the percentages of endemic mammal species which these islands support today. Only 4.5 per cent of the terrestrial mammal species of Malaya are endemic, while the percentages for Sumatra, Java, Borneo and Palawan are, respectively, 10.3, 23.0, 32.5 and 63.3. Sulawesi terrestrial mammal species are 100 per cent endemic. See C. Groves, 'Plio-Pleistocene mammals in Island Southeast Asia', MQRSEA, 9 (1985).

[8] See L. R. Heaney, 'Biogeography of mammals in Southeast Asia: estimates of rates of colonization, extinction and speciation', *Biological Journal of the Linnean Society*, 28 (1986).

[9] For recent arguments against land bridges to the Philippines (excluding Palawan) and Sulawesi during the Pleistocene, see L. R. Heaney, 'Zoogeographic evidence . . . ', MQRSEA, 9 (1985) and G. Musser, 'The mammals of Sulawesi', in T. C. Whitmore, ed., *Biogeographical Evolution of the Malay Archipelago*, Oxford, 1987. The Pleistocene mammal faunas of these islands and of Nusa Tenggara to as far east as Timor include a variety of mammals ranging in size up to the elephant-like stegodonts. Their dispersal, which may long predate that of humans, can be explained by invoking Late Pliocene (rather than Pleistocene) land bridges, or they may have swum across short sea gaps. See PIMA, 23–6.

[10] See footnote 2, above.

[11] See, for instance, R. J. Morley and J. R. Flenley, 'Late Cainozoic vegetational and environmental changes in the Malay archipelago, in Whitmore, ed., *Biogeographical Evolution*; W. S.

have been corridors of relatively open forest or parkland vegetation, crossing Sundaland from the northern hemisphere into the southern. Such corridors would help to explain how the earliest *Homo erectus* pioneers managed to reach Java, given that this species has no record of rainforest adaptation during its evolution in Africa. However, there is no evidence that the great belt of rainforest which now occupies most of the Malay peninsula, Borneo, Sumatra and Sulawesi was ever completely broken up or replaced. It has always existed, but perhaps not always as extensively as it does today.

HUMAN PREHISTORY: THE FIRST MILLION YEARS

Remains of early humans of the species *Homo erectus* have been recovered extensively in Java and China, and to a lesser extent in northern Vietnam;[12] in this section the focus will be mainly on Java (Map 2.3). There is a general consensus amongst biological anthropologists that the early evolution of humanity took place in Africa, and that hominids expanded into the tropical latitudes of Asia around one million years ago. The species *Homo erectus* was fully developed in East Africa by at least 1.6 million years ago, and there is no compelling evidence at present for any existence outside Africa of earlier hominids of the genus *Australopithecus*.

By 750,000 years ago *Homo erectus* had spread into temperate climatic zones in Europe and China, and the species as a whole underwent some degree of geographical differentiation, at least in terms of cranial variation. Research with respect to the species as a whole has concentrated on interpreting this observed regional variation, and explaining the slow pre-*sapiens* chronological tempos of biological and cultural evolution. An even more significant question concerns genetic continuity: were Asian *Homo erectus* populations the direct ancestors of modern Asians, or were they replaced and consigned to an eventual fate of extinction by incoming modern *Homo sapiens*, ultimately from Africa? The origin of modern humans is one of the most contentious and important issues in anthropology today, and the Southeast Asian fossil record has potentially much to contribute to this debate.

Before examining current opinions on the issue of continuity versus replacement, it is necessary to review some of the facts, especially for Java, confused and disputed as they may be. The modern discovery of 'Java Man' began in 1891 when Eugene Dubois found part of the skull-cap of *Homo erectus* (for many years better-known as '*Pithecanthropus*') in deposits cut by the Solo River at Trinil, central Java. Other locations which have

Broecker et al., 'New evidence from the South China Sea for an abrupt termination of the last glacial period', *Nature*, 33 (1988); Earl of Cranbrook, 'The contribution of archaeology to the zoogeography of Borneo', *Fieldiana, Zoology*, 42 (1988).

12 Teeth and partial jaws of *Homo erectus* are believed to occur in a fossiliferous cave breccia in the cave of Tham Khuyen in northern Vietnam, but no detailed report is available. See Le Krung Ha, 'First remarks on the Quaternary fossil fauna of northern Viet Nam', *Vietnamese Studies*, 46 (1978); R. L. Ciochon and J. W. Olsen, 'Palaeoanthropological and archaeological research in the Socialist Republic of Vietnam', *Journal of Human Evolution*, 15 (1986).

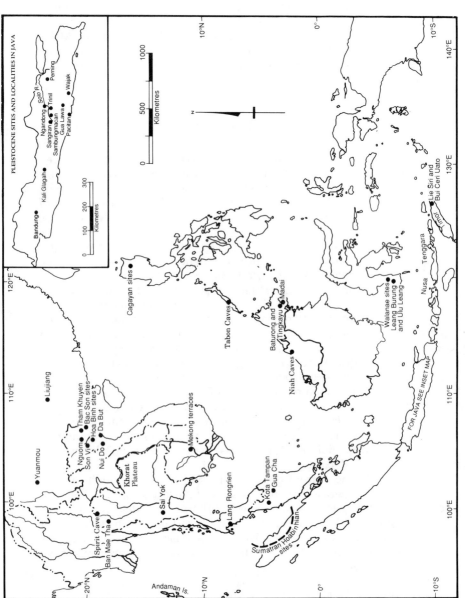

Map 2.3   Major Pleistocene and early Holocene sites.

PLEISTOCENE SITES AND LOCALITIES IN JAVA

Bandung
Kali Glagah
Ngandong
Solo R.
Sangiran
Sambungmacan
Trinil
Perning
Gua Lawa
Pacitan
Wajak

Kilometres
0   100 200 300

Yuanmou
Liujiang
Tham Khuyen
Nguom
Bac Son sites
Son Vi
Hoa Binh sites
Nui Do
Da But
Khorat Plateau
Sai Yok
Mekong terraces
Lang Rongrien
Spirit Cave
Ban Mae Tha
Kota Tampan
Gua Cha
Sumatran Hoabinhian sites
Andaman Is.

Cagayan sites
Tabon Caves
Baturong and Tingkayu
Madai
Niah Caves
Walanae sites
Leang Burung and Ulu Leang
Nusa Tenggara
Lie Siri and Bui Ceri Uato
Timor

FOR JAVA SEE INSET MAP

N

Kilometres
0   500   1000

10°N
0°
10°S

120°E
110°E
100°E
110°E
130°E
140°E
20°N
10°N
0°
10°S

yielded human fossils this century include Ngandong and Sambung-macan, also on the Solo River, Perning near Mojokerto in eastern Java, and the important site of Sangiran where the Cemoro River, a small tributary of the Solo, has cut into an anticlinal dome exposing layers dating from the Pliocene to the Middle and Late Pleistocene.

Sangiran holds the most reliable information recovered so far on the dates, faunal and environmental associations of the Javanese hominids. The deposits provide excellent environmental conditions for fossilization and begin with Pliocene marine and estuarine sediments at the base, grading up through lacustrine, fluvial and volcanic deposits which probably span most of the Pleistocene. A major phase of uplift and erosion set in during the Late Pleistocene causing an erosional disconformity, above which lie Late Pleistocene river terrace gravels. Sangiran has recently been subjected to a detailed programme of interdisciplinary research, and the major lithostratigraphic divisions recognized are shown in Figure 2.2, together with their apparent correlations with the earth's magnetic rever-sal record.[13] The absolute chronology is supported by fission track and potassium-argon dates on volcanic materials and fluorine measurements on animal bones. It is sufficient here to state that the major *Homo erectus* finds from the sites of Sangiran, Trinil and Perning are agreed by most authorities to date between about 1.3 and 0.5 million years ago, with a maximum (but perhaps unlikely) age of around 1.7 million years. The Ngandong and Sambungmacan remains are considerably younger and fall very close to the transition to *Homo sapiens*.

The faunal sequence presented in Figure 2.2 is currently disputed. The traditional view, as developed by von Koenigswald and Hooijer, suggests that the Jetis 'Sino-Malayan' fauna (Late Pliocene–Early Pleistocene) already contained ancestral species of gibbon, orang utan, elephant, cattle, deer, pig, hippopotamus, tiger, bear, panther and dogs of the *Cuon* genus, as well as the now-extinct *Stegodon* and, of course, *Homo erectus*. This traditional scheme has recently been criticized and rearranged[14] into a new scheme which places a number of these species later in time, especially the rainforest forms such as gibbon and orang utan, which are claimed to have appeared in Java only during the last interglacial period. These problems have arisen because of uncertainties about the exact find-places of animal

[13] Reported in N. Watanabe and D. Kadar, eds., *Quaternary Geology of the Hominid Fossil Bearing Formations in Java*, Bandung: Geological Research and Development Centre, 1985. Other references used in compiling Figure 2.2 are D. A. Hooijer, 'The Middle Pleistocene fauna of Java', in G. Kurth, ed., *Evolution und Hominization*, Stuttgart, 1968; S. Sartono, 'the stratigraphy of the Sambung Mekan site in Central Java', MQRSEA, 5 (1979); A. Sémah, 'A preliminary report on a Sangiran pollen diagram', ibid., 7 (1982); S. Matsu'ura, 'A chronological framing for the Sangiran hominids', *Bulletin of the National Science Museum, Tokyo*, Series D, 8 (1982); F. Sémah, 'Le peuplement ancien de Java: ébauche d'un cadre chronologique', *L'Anthropologie*, 90 (1986); G.-J. Bartstra et al., 'Ngandong Man, age and artifacts', *Journal of Human Evolution*, 17 (1988); G. Pope, 'Recent advances in Far Eastern Palaeoanthropology', *Annual Review of Anthropology*, 17 (1988).

[14] By J. J. M. Leinders et al., 'The age of the hominid-bearing deposits of Java: state of the art', *Geologie en Mijnbouw*, 64, (1985). The traditional scheme is still supported strongly by G.-J. Bartstra, 'The vertebrate-bearing deposits of Kedungbrubus and Trinil, Java, Indonesia', ibid., 62 (1983); and by D. A. Hooijer, 'Facts and fiction around the fossil mammals of Java', ibid., 62 (1983).

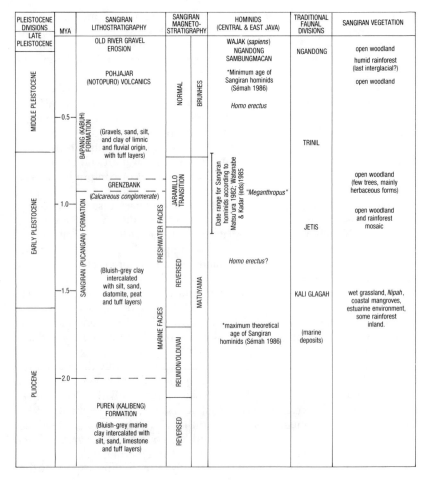

MYA=millions of years ago

Figure 2.2   The Sangiran sequence of geological formations, hominids, faunas and vegetations since the Late Pliocene.

bone assemblages—a problem which also applies to the find-places of many of the human fossils, which were originally collected by villagers rather than by professional scientists. It need hardly be stressed that the study of human evolution in Java is still affected by a great deal of stratigraphic and chronological disagreement.

The oldest Javanese fossil hominids come from the upper part of the Sangiran (or Pucangan) formation at Sangiran, whereas the majority from Sangiran, and also the crania from Trinil and Perning, appear to belong to the overlying Bapang (or Kabuh) beds. The oldest specimens are the most robust, and the species overall has an average cranial capacity of about 950 cubic centimetres, thick skull bones, a broad face with large teeth and a low skull broadest at its base. Stature perhaps ranged up to 160 centimetres, weight to 80 kilograms, and the species had an upright posture and bipedal gait quite similar to modern humans. Sexual dimorphism in size and musculature is generally assumed to have been greater than amongst ourselves.

Although most fossils found in Java fit comfortably within the acceptable morphological limits of *Homo erectus*, there has been sporadic but continuing debate with respect to the mandible fragments of a particularly massive-toothed hominid found close to the Grenzbank layer in Sangiran. These were originally named *Meganthropus*, and several authorities during the past twenty years have claimed Australopithecine affinities for them. Most today consider them to be within the range of tooth-size allowable for *erectus*. Nevertheless, the African evidence has shown how two separate hominid lines could and did exist contemporaneously in the same part of the continent for about one million years (*Homo* and the robust Australopithecines). So while it seems very unlikely that Australopithecines *sensu stricto* did reach Indonesia, mainly because the fossil record begins there too late in time, the possibility of two successive *erectus* immigrations cannot yet be ruled out entirely. Indeed, the whole question of population replacement arises in a far more controversial context in the transition from *erectus* to *sapiens*.

The great mystery over *Homo erectus* in Southeast Asia concerns its fate. The view most widely accepted until recently has been that formulated originally by Weidenreich, and more recently supported by A. G. Thorne and M. Wolpoff,[15] that the Javanese remains all belong to a recognizable and regional morphological lineage which lies in the ancestral line of at least some of the *Homo sapiens* populations of early Australian prehistory. The Chinese fossils may likewise be considered to lie in the direct ancestry of the modern Mongoloids of eastern and Southeast Asia. Wolpoff has more recently claimed, in partial support of this view, that *Homo erectus* across the Old World underwent specific evolutionary changes during the 1.5 million years of its existence. These changes include increasing brain size, reductions in muscularity and tooth size, and decreasing sexual dimorphism. They suggest that the species was not a static and extinct dead-end outside Africa and that it could have evolved into, or at least transmitted many genes to, modern populations over many regions of the Old World.[16]

The major opposition to the regional continuity school comes from those who favour a punctuational or 'Noah's Ark' model of evolution; in their view, the ancestors of modern *sapiens*, ultimately derived from an *erectus* population in Africa, spread out over the Old World at some uncertain time before about 40,000 years ago.[17] In this view, speciation is regarded as

---

[15] 'Regional continuity in Pleistocene hominid evolution', *American Journal of Physical Anthropology*, 55 (1981); Wolpoff, 'Human evolution at the peripheries: the pattern at the eastern edge', in P. V. Tobias, ed., *Hominid evolution: past, present and future*, New York, 1985.

[16] M. Wolpoff, 'Evolution in *Homo erectus*: the question of stasis', *Paleobiology*, 10, 4 (1984). See also A. Fisher, 'The emergence of humanness', *Mosaic*, 19, 1 (1988).

[17] R. L. Cann, M. Stoneking and A. C. Wilson, 'Mitochondrial DNA and human evolution', *Nature*, 325 (1987); C. B. Stringer and P. Andrews, 'Genetic and fossil evidence for the origin of modern humans', *Science*, 239 (1988); G. P. Rightmire, '*Homo erectus* and later Middle Pleistocene humans', *Annual Review of Anthropology*, 17 (1988).

a local rather than a continent-wide event; novel adaptations arise locally, and their bearers then spread more widely. This model regards *Homo erectus* as static in an evolutionary sense and, except in Africa, without genetic issue.

This debate has, of course, been of importance for many years in Europe, a region which may (like Southeast Asia) be regarded as a fairly remote peninsula of the Eurasian super-continent. In Europe the debate is over replacement of Neanderthals by modern humans versus the possibility of genetic continuity. It is significant to note that the debate changes in character with the area under consideration; Neanderthal replacement and extinction seem to be favoured explanations in France, but not necessarily in eastern Europe where transitional forms between Neanderthals and modern humans are claimed by several researchers. Unfortunately, in Southeast Asia there is simply insufficient fossil evidence to allow a proper evaluation of the two theories, and it may be simplistic to regard them as all-or-nothing alternatives. Indeed, there are biologists who favour both a radiation of modern humans into Southeast Asia and some degree of genetic assimilation of pre-existing populations;[18] one can hardly deny that both processes have operated on an enormous scale within the recent millennia of agricultural and colonial population expansion. But the recent human experience has involved one species capable of interbreeding throughout its range; one can only guess if this would have been true for late *erectus* and incoming *sapiens* populations in China and Java, for whom the remoteness of common ancestry might have been much greater than that which binds modern populations.

It is my suspicion, albeit without the benefit of formal proof, that Asian *Homo erectus* was not simply replaced without issue. The morphological similarities of the cranium and skeleton which link *erectus* in Java and China with the younger *sapiens* populations of the eastern Old World are hard to explain simply as the identical results of natural selection on successive and unrelated species, although the 'Noah's Ark' model in its purest form demands such an explanation. Furthermore, the youngest remains of *Homo erectus* from Java, those from Ngandong and Sambungmacan, show clear signs of evolution beyond the earlier series from Sangiran and Trinil. The eleven crania found together with a dense accumulation of animal bones in the lower part of the Late Pleistocene terrace at Ngandong, recently dated by the uranium-thorium method on bone to about 100,000 years ago,[19] have large (1160 cubic centimetres) and broad braincases and yet are clearly the direct and regional descendants of the earlier Javanese populations in terms of skull morphology and facial robusticity. They are, however, sufficiently advanced for some authors to regard them as early *sapiens*, and they are the first Javanese hominids for whom there is strong circumstantial evidence for stone-tool use. It is therefore not impossible that tool-using hominids approaching the *sapiens*

---

[18] For instance, G. Brauer, 'The "Afro-European *sapiens* hypothesis", and hominid evolution in East Asia', in P. Andrews and J. L. Franzen, eds., *The Early Evolution of Man*, Frankfurt: Senckenberg Institute, 1984.

[19] G.-J. Bartstra, S. Soegondho and A. van der Wijk, 'Ngandong man: age and artefacts', *Journal of Human Evolution*, 17 (1988).

grade, living some 60,000 years before the first truly modern populations in Southeast Asia, should have been at least partially ancestral to their ultimate successors.

Like the debate over the fate of *Homo erectus*, the issue of the cultural standing of this species in Southeast Asia is also very contentious. There are no known primary living sites older than about 40,000 years in Southeast Asia, and all of the *erectus* fossils from Java have been found in situations suggesting secondary deposition, without direct and unequivocal associations with stone tools. For instance, the Ngandong remains occurred with very large numbers of animal bones in a situation which suggests movement by river action,[20] and the earlier fossils all come from alluvial or lacustrine deposits. Hence the Sangiran and Trinil hominids have no stone tools in proper association, and debates about the tool-using abilities of these particular hominids are unlikely to be productive at the present time.[21]

However, it is clear that, like the other pre-*sapiens* populations of Africa and Eurasia, the Javanese hominids favoured fairly open parkland or monsoonal forest landscapes with high mammal biomasses, and generally avoided the equatorial rainforests. The much fuller archaeological records of Africa and China clearly indicate stone-tool use and meat-eating throughout the timespan of *Homo erectus*, and back beyond two million years ago in East Africa, although there is still considerable debate over whether the meat was hunted or simply scavenged from carnivore kills. The Southeast Asian evidence cannot yet contribute to this debate, and one analyst has recently suggested that the teeth of the Java fossils suggest a vegetarian rather than a meat diet.[22] This could explain the absence of stone tools, if the absence is real. On the other hand, stone tools are certainly found in association with Middle Pleistocene hominid fossils in India and China, so a complete absence of them in Java would be unprecedented. Only further fieldwork is likely to solve this problem.

Despite the absence of stone tools in direct association with any Southeast Asian pre-*sapiens* hominids, there have been numerous discoveries of tools in geological contexts for which Middle Pleistocene dates have been claimed. None of these claims is secure, but a brief review is warranted. Most of these industries are based on large pebble and flake tools which have become popularly known as 'chopper/chopping-tools'. They contrast in a very general way with the Acheulian handaxe industries of Africa, Europe and India, although it must be remembered that bifacial handaxes often do occur in the chopper/chopping-tool industries, especially in Vietnam and Java. The problem in the past, however, has been that researchers have often assumed that large and crude tool industries of this type are necessarily 'Lower Palaeolithic' and of Early or Middle Pleistocene age. Modern research has shown that they need have no particular

[20] A. P. Santa Luca, *The Ngandong Fossil Hominids*, New Haven, 1980.
[21] R. P. Soejono, 'New data on the Palaeolithic industry in Indonesia', *Congrès Internationale de Paléontologie Humaine*, Pretirage Tome 2, Nice, 1982, states that a single stone tool has been excavated from Bapang (Kabuh) deposits at Ngebung near Sangiran. A single find such as this clearly needs more confirmation.
[22] P. F. Puech, 'Tooth wear, diet and the artifacts of Java Man', *Current Anthropology*, 24 (1983).

chronological focus—they can indeed be Holocene in many instances—and in no case is an antiquity older than Late Pleistocene absolutely secure.

On the mainland of Southeast Asia pebble-tool industries of this type have been reported from many sites over the years; from the terraces of the middle Irrawaddy in Burma (the 'Anyathian' industry), from the Mekong terraces of Cambodia, and from sites such as Nui Do in Thanh Hoa Province of northern Vietnam. None of these assemblages has absolute dates, but it has recently been claimed that stone tools found at Ban Mae Tha in Lampang Province, northern Thailand, originate from beneath a basalt flow dated by the potassium-argon method to between 600,000 and 800,000 years ago.[23] If the claims are correct these tools would certainly be the oldest dated ones in Southeast Asia, but this still requires confirmation. The only other important mainland industry once thought to date from the Middle Pleistocene, the so-called 'Tampanian' pebble and flake industry from Kota Tampan in Perak, Malaysia, is now believed to date only to about 30,000 years ago.[24] Hence, it may well turn out to be an early facies of the Hoabinhian, to be described below.

In island Southeast Asia the best-known of these chopper/chopping-tool industries is the Pacitanian, recovered from non-fossiliferous colluvial and alluvial valley deposits in south central Java. This industry, which contains handaxes, steep-edged scrapers and 'horsehoof' cores as well as large flake tools, is now believed, as a result of geological research by G.-J. Bartstra, to be less than 50,000 years old. This researcher, however, has recently suggested that a much smaller flake industry found in water-rolled condition in Late Pleistocene river gravels at Ngebung near Sangiran and at Ngandong may represent the handiwork of the late *Homo erectus* population represented by the fossils from Ngandong and Sambungmacan.[25] These tools are, potentially at least, the oldest in Indonesia.

Elsewhere in the islands, pebble and flake industries have also been attributed to periods before the Late Pleistocene from the Cagayan Valley in northern Luzon and the Walanae valley in south Sulawesi. Clearly, if these attributions are correct, then views about the seaborne dispersal of early hominids across Huxley's Line would be revolutionized. Regrettably, however, the data are not secure, and the same applies to the many industries of this type reported down the Nusa Tenggara chain from Lombok to Timor,[26] in some cases in apparent but probably secondary association with the bones of stegodonts.[27] The reasons for all this uncertainty over the dating of Southeast Asian stone tools are fairly clear: no

[23] G. Pope, 'Evidence of Early Pleistocene hominid activity from Lampang, northern Thailand', BIPPA, 6 (1985); P. Sorensen, 'The prehistory of Thailand', in C. Flon, ed., *The World Atlas of Archaeology*, London, 1985.
[24] Zuraina Majid and H. D. Tjia, 'Kota Tampan, Perak', JMBRAS, 61, 2 (1988).
[25] 'Sangiran, the stone implements of Ngebung, and the Palaeolithic of Java', MQRSEA, 9 (1985); G.-J. Bartstra et al., 'Ngandong Man' *Journal of Human Evolution*, 17 (1988).
[26] For recent discoveries in Wallacea see R. P. Soejono, 'Stone tools of Palaeolithic type from Lombok', *Man and Culture in Oceania*, 3 (1987).
[27] However, since many of the Lesser Sundas would have been visible from one another, starting from Bali across to Lombok, it is clear that the possibility of pre-*sapiens* settlement as far east as Timor must be considered seriously. The water gaps would have been narrower during glacial periods.

cave deposits are known with an antiquity greater than about 40,000 years, perhaps due to the very rapid rate of limestone solution and erosion in the humid tropics. All the industries just described come from open sites, mainly alluvial, where secondary deposition has frequently occurred and where no absolute dating method has so far been applicable. It is not surprising, therefore, that the archaeological record in Southeast Asia takes on a remarkable clarity after 40,000 years ago—from this time onwards there are stratified cave deposits with ample opportunity for radiocarbon dating. Figuratively at least we enter a world of light, inhabited by tool-making and ocean-crossing members of our own species, *Homo sapiens*. The record takes on recognizable and meaningful links with the present, and begins to relate sensibly to the origins of living peoples.

ANCESTORS FOR THE LIVING

The archaeological record of stone tools does, of course, continue on from the industries just described into the recent past. Before describing it, however, the peoples of Southeast Asia themselves, descendants of the early *sapiens* populations of the eastern Old World, must be introduced. The question of the origins of *Homo sapiens* in Asia, whether directly from local *erectus* predecessors or by a replacement radiation, has been discussed above. What should be stressed here is that the task of documenting the origins of modern human physical differentiation is a biological one which depends on studies of genetic characteristics, ancient and recent skeletal materials (especially crania), and comparative studies of phenotypic features in modern populations. Linguistic and archaeological reconstructions of prehistory can give only ambiguous hints about biological differentiation, and it is important that the results of the three disciplines be granted the independence which they deserve.

The great majority of the 400 million inhabitants of Southeast Asia today belong to a biological grouping which may be termed Southern Mongoloid. There is a degree of variation within this population, expressed most visibly in darkening skin pigmentation and increasing face and jaw size as one moves from north to south, and also from west to east within Indonesia. The only indigenous populations in Southeast Asia who are outside the Southern Mongoloid grouping are the Negritos of central peninsular Malaysia and the Philippines, and the Melanesians focused in and around New Guinea. Much of eastern Indonesia, especially Maluku and Nusa Tenggara, is an area of gentle biological gradation between Southern Mongoloids and Melanesians. There is no sharp boundary here, although major phenotypic differences are apparent if one compares populations from opposite ends of the cline, such as Timorese and Balinese.

The cline which links Indonesians and lowland Melanesians probably represents the results of gene flow over many millennia through intermarriage between populations who were ultimately of different origin. The opposite hypothesis, that the observed cline represents the results of evolutionary processes of natural selection operating on a once-unified and geographically static population, is much less satisfactory. This is because one would have to explain which selective factor could have produced such relatively lightly-pigmented and straight-haired Southern Mongoloid populations in tropical latitudes, especially along the equator in Indonesia, when elsewhere at this latitude in the Old World, and particularly in Melanesia and Africa, the trend is generally for very dark pigmentation and curled hair.[28] Indeed, there are strong but complex grounds for regarding the Southern Mongoloids as mainly the heirs to a population expansion from southern China and northern mainland Southeast Asia, for the most part within the past seven thousand years of agriculture and consequent population growth. Evolution never ceases, however, and new clines form constantly as new populations enter a region, or as existing ones adapt to new evolutionary circumstances. It would be most unwise to claim that the Southern Mongoloid populations migrated southwards in one vast, identical and unchanging wave, even though the writings of some earlier authorities suggest that they visualized such a scenario.

The most acceptable model for Southeast Asian biological prehistory therefore postulates a gradual and complex replacement of an indigenous Australo-Melanesian population by expanding Southern Mongoloids. The Negritos, who have probably undergone localized and independent selection for their relatively short stature, are thus the only Southeast Asian survivors of the original Australo-Melanesian continuum outside the eastern Indonesian clinal zone. The early expansion of the Southern Mongoloid population was due in part to the demographic advantages provided by an agricultural as opposed to a foraging economy, together with the inter-island mobility encouraged by the development of advanced seagoing and navigational skills.

The Negritos are thus of great significance in Southeast Asia: they seem to represent the modern members of an Australo-Melanesian population which may once have occupied much of the region, perhaps even to as far north as Cambodia and Taiwan if some admittedly ambiguous historical records are taken into consideration. Today, they occupy only the Andaman Islands, parts of peninsular Malaysia and Thailand, and parts of the central and northern Philippines. Most of the Philippine Negritos have now adopted sporadic agricultural practices and all have adopted, within recent millennia, Austronesian languages from neighbouring cultivators. The Semang of Malaysia, while still primarily hunter-gatherers and forest collectors-for-trade, have at some time adopted Austroasiatic languages related to ancestral Mon and Khmer. The few remaining Andamanese, some of whom live in virtual island isolation, are the only ones to have

---

[28] On the general correlation of skin pigmentation with latitude see G. L. Tasa et al., 'Reflectometer reports on human pigmentation', *Current Anthropology*, 26 (1985). The only other large indigenous equatorial population which has not developed dark skin pigmentation is that in the Americas. Since the ancestors of these American Mongoloids crossed from Asia at least 10,000 years ago, it is clear that differences in skin pigmentation may take tens of thousands of years to develop; see J. S. Friedlaender, ed., *The Solomon Islands Project*, Oxford, 1987, 357. Likewise, Australia has been settled for at least 40,000 years by a dark-pigmented population of ultimate tropical Indonesian origin, but it seems that only a slight loss of pigmentation occurred in the cool temperate south of the continent and Tasmania.

retained a relatively pure foraging economy together with their original languages, unrelated to any outside major grouping.

The major point about the Negritos, one which has often been over-looked, is that none live close to the equator. As far as can be detected, the inland equatorial rainforests of Sumatra, Borneo and possibly Sulawesi seem to have been virtually uninhabited, except within reach of coastal resources, until they were entered by the ancestors of the present South-ern Mongoloid agricultural inhabitants. The Negritos, therefore, may stem ultimately from the larger Australo-Melanesian populations who inhabited the more widespread monsoonal forest environments of the Pleistocene intertropical zone. The relatively short stature characteristic of modern Negritos may be the result of adaptation to the warmer and more humid climatic conditions of the Holocene, adaptations mediated by the lowered availability of protein and the value of small body size for easy movement in closed rainforests.

Modern genetic data also help to support the above picture of recent (mainly post-Pleistocene) Southern Mongoloid expansion in Southeast Asia. Blood groups alone are no longer considered reliable indicators of population origins owing to their tendency to undergo rapid changes in frequency, but there are other genetically controlled systems which seem to be much more stable in this regard, perhaps because their frequencies reflect mutation alone and not the biasing effects of selection and drift. These, therefore, may record aspects of shared ancestry between popula-tions rather than just similar environmental adaptations. Population-specific variants which appear to distinguish Asian Mongoloids (including Southern Mongoloids) from Aboriginal Australians and Melanesians occur in the transferrin, immunoglobulin, and Gc serum protein systems, the Diego red cell and human leukocyte antigen systems, and the mito-chondrial genome.[29] In addition, the transferrin variants seem to undergo a clinical change of frequency along the Nusa Tenggara chain which corresponds with the visible phenotypic situation in eastern Indonesia.

Abnormal haemoglobin E is also common amongst Southeast Asian populations as far east as Timor and virtually absent beyond; Melanesians have other genetic abnormalities which give resistance to malaria, such as thalassemia, G6PD deficiency and the ovalocytosis red-cell variant. Unlike the genetic variants discussed above, the genes for these abnormalities must have been highly susceptible to natural selection when carriers first entered a malarial region. However, as pointed out by R. L. Kirk,[30] once the effective protective gene was established, the chance of a new muta-tion entering the population would be reduced, so in this respect a high frequency of haemoglobin E could be an important and ancient marker for many Southeast Asian Mongoloids, dating back at least to the period of agricultural expansion into tropical latitudes.

---

[29] See R. L. Kirk, 'Human genetic diversity in south-east Asia and the western Pacific', in D. F. Roberts and G. F. de Stefano, eds., *Genetic Variation and its Maintenance*, Cambridge, 1986; A. V. S. Hill and S. Serjeantson, eds., *The Colonization of the Pacific: a Genetic Trail*, Oxford, 1989.

[30] 'Human genetic diversity', 116.

Another interesting observation about Indonesian genetics has been made by A. Sofro.[31] His analysis of genetic distances based on eighteen polymorphic loci shows that Indonesian populations fall into western and eastern clusters, with the Bimanese of Sumbawa occupying an approximate mid-point, and that the eastern cluster reflects the most internal variation. This may be a very important observation, since the Melanesian region to the east seems to have been a focus of early agricultural development and a presumed centre of genetic gravity since at least the early Holocene. One might expect that Australo-Melanesian populations were always denser in Holocene times in eastern Indonesia than in the west, hence the impressive length and complexity of the Mongoloid–Melanesian cline in the east.

Despite the many important observations which can be made from genetic evidence, however, the most direct evidence for ancient human ancestry comes not from the living, but from the dead. Skeletal remains are often poorly dated, fragmentary, and frankly ambiguous when questions of population origin are under consideration, but they certainly cannot be ignored. Skeletal remains tend to add complexity to the picture; nowhere is there clear-cut evidence from them for rapid population replacement, and we must allow for millennia of intermarriage and local evolution. The important concept is that human biological history of Southeast Asia has involved not a swift replacement of some populations by others, but a gradual southwards and eastwards shift in the structure and centre of gravity of a cline between Southern Mongoloids and Australo-Melanesians.

As discussed above, there is considerable disagreement amongst biological anthropologists concerning the presence or absence of continuity from *erectus* to *sapiens* in East and Southeast Asia. In China the arguments for a continuous local evolution of Mongoloids are quite strong, and many linking skeletal remains of Late Pleistocene age are now reported. In Southeast Asia the oldest cranial and mandibular remains which can be referred to as putatively Australo-Melanesian come from Niah Cave in Sarawak and Tabon Cave on Palawan (Philippines), both dated loosely within the range 40,000 to 20,000 years ago. In addition, a very large series of skeletal remains of Australoids *sensu stricto* dates from about 30,000 years ago and onwards in Australia.

No Pleistocene fossils from Southeast Asia have yet been claimed as unequivocally Mongoloid, although the Late Pleistocene skulls from Wajak in Java are stated to have certain Mongoloid facial features by T. Jacob.[32] In addition, it has recently been claimed that certain Australian and Southeast Asian skulls of Late Pleistocene age have affinities with some contemporary or older Chinese skulls, such as that from Liujiang in Guangxi.[33] The basic conclusion to be drawn from this is that not all 'Mongolization' of Southeast Asia necessarily occurred with the develop-

[31] 'Population Genetic Studies in Indonesia', Ph.D. thesis, Australian National University, 1982.
[32] *Some Problems Pertaining to the Racial History of the Indonesian Region*, Utrecht, 1967.
[33] M. H. Wolpoff, X. J. Wu and A. G. Thorne, 'Modern *Homo sapiens* origins . . . ', in F. H. Smith and F. Spencer, eds., *The Origins of Modern Humans*, New York, 1984.

ment of agriculture in the Holocene, and some gene flow from more northerly sources may well have been entering the region long before the end of the Pleistocene. Unfortunately, available data do not allow greater specificity.

During the Holocene there is an increasingly widespread occurrence of Southern Mongoloid skeletal material during the past 7000 years, except in regions such as the central Malay peninsula and eastern Indonesia where modern populations still demonstrate a great deal of Australo-Melanesian inheritance. An overall reduction in tooth size in Southeast Asia seems also to be associated with these changes, presumably linked with the availability of softer foods through agricultural processing.[34] This gene flow trend has been gradual, however, and even in regions as far north as northern Vietnam and southern China the prevailing phenotype in early Neolithic times appears to have been considerably less Mongoloid than is the case today. Indeed, it is quite clear that a great deal of the Mongoloid expansion which is evident in Southeast Asia, whether replacing Australo-Melanesian hunter-gatherers or assimilating populations of 'Proto-Malays',[35] has taken place squarely within the historical period. It is still happening today, as Filipino agriculturalists impinge on the hunting territories of Negritos and Indonesian transmigrants leave Java for the hinterlands of Irian Jaya and Maluku.

Apart from the timing of Mongoloid gene flow into Southeast Asia, another important question concerns its general source-region. Simple geographical logic would of course point to adjacent parts of southern China, as well as northern Southeast Asia itself. This logic is supported by the dental analyses of Turner, who has proposed that the dentitions of Southeast Asians (including Negritos) belong, in terms of tooth morphology, to a grouping termed Sundadont. He distinguishes Sundadont teeth from those of Sinodonts (north-east Asian Mongoloids) and Australo-Melanesians, and points out that all prehistoric teeth from Southeast Asia, even the most ancient such as those of the Niah and Wajak skulls, are Sundadont. Hence, no case for a southerly expansion of northeast Asian Mongoloids can be seriously entertained, and the teeth of Aboriginal Australians and Melanesians clearly began to diverge away in morphological terms from their Southeast Asian Sundadont cousins at least 40,000 years ago. Since Sundadont teeth were probably universal throughout southern China during the Late Pleistocene and early Holocene, all sources of direct gene flow into Southeast Asia are likely to lie south of the Yangtze River.[36]

In summarizing this section, the main features of Southeast Asian

[34] C. L. Brace, 'Tooth size and Austronesian origins', in P. Naylor, ed., *Austronesian Studies*, Ann Arbor, 1980.

[35] The terms 'Proto-Malay' and 'Deutero-Malay', as used by previous generations of physical anthropologists, mean little in the light of modern knowledge of Southeast Asian prehistory. They suggest two separate Mongoloid strata, a concept unsupported by any other evidence.

[36] See C. G. Turner II, 'Teeth and prehistory in Asia', *Scientific American*, February 1989. For a related view emphasizing evolution within Southeast Asia, see D. Bulbeck, 'A re-evaluation of possible evolutionary processes in Southeast Asia since the Late Pleistocene', BIPPA, 3 (1982).

biological evolution within *Homo sapiens* populations may be presented as follows:

1 The population of Southeast Asia around 40,000 years ago may have been predominantly Australo-Melanesian, with some Southern Mongoloid features developing in the northern part of the region. Founders moved away to settle Australia and New Guinea at this time, if not before, and these have since evolved in relative isolation from their Southeast Asian contemporaries.

2 The continuing populations of Southeast Asia underwent widespread cranial and facial gracilization, due partly to local selection and partly to southerly gene flow from regions of Mongoloid development in southern China. Southerly populations probably remained predominantly Australo-Melanesian in many aspects of phenotype until well into the Holocene.

3 During the Holocene, and especially within the past 7000 years, continuing southerly and easterly expansions of Southern Mongoloid populations have occurred. Today these movements can most easily be identified in the linguistic and historical records of peoples speaking Austroasiatic, Tai-Kadai, Tibeto-Burman and Austronesian languages. Perhaps the most significant of them can be postulated to have occurred during the early millennia of agriculture, when expansionary processes began which ultimately were to carry people of Mongoloid affinity right across the Indian and Pacific Oceans, to places as far as Madagascar and Easter Island.

THE ARCHAEOLOGICAL RECORD—LATE PLEISTOCENE TO MID-HOLOCENE

Radiocarbon dating can be utilized from about 40,000 years ago. From that time down to the appearance of agriculture, mainly between 6000 and 3000 years ago depending on locality, the archaeological record is focused on tools of flaked stone and circumstantial evidence for a fairly mobile foraging lifestyle. The record is a simple one in lithic terms, since blade and microlithic tools did not appear in the region until well into the Holocene. Furthermore, the rising sea levels of the post-glacial period have probably destroyed the vast majority of coastal sites which may have existed prior to about 9000 years ago, especially in the western part of Sundaland.

The artefact assemblages to be described in this section belong to a period when the hunting and collection of food, as opposed to systematic agricultural production, may be presumed to have been the sole form of subsistence. The transition to the latter mode was in most regions relatively sharp, the implication being that most of the original hunters and gatherers of Southeast Asia were assimilated fairly rapidly in areas favourable for cultivation. In some regions they may have developed or adopted cultivation practices themselves, but the archaeological record alone is generally ambiguous on this point. Whatever the mechanisms behind this economic change, it is clear that the remnant hunters and gatherers who survive today have undergone considerable contact with agriculturalists and can give only very ambiguous information about life in the Late Pleistocene.[37]

For instance, the Negritos have probably survived assimilation only because they occupy remote and relatively unproductive environments which until recently were of little interest to expanding agriculturalists. The only Negritos who may be considered relatively uninfluenced by contact with alien cultural traditions are the Little Andamanese, but even these had probably acquired pigs and pottery manufacture by about 2000 years ago, and like all other Negrito groups had stopped making stone tools well before European contact.[38] The Philippine Negritos have virtually all adopted some kind of cultivation, albeit reluctantly,[39] and the Semang of Malaysia have also been in contact with neighbouring cultivators for millennia, although they have been able to retain a mobile hunting and collecting lifestyle more successfully than their Philippine counterparts. It would be presumptuous, therefore, to assume that these groups can reveal very much about the details of Late Pleistocene life in Southeast Asia, apart from the generalizations which one might make about the likelihood that societies of that time were egalitarian, of low population density, and built around small numbers of independent and mobile nuclear families.

The situation is even less helpful with the Southern Mongoloid hunters and gatherers. These include Austronesian-speaking groups such as the Punan of interior Borneo, Kubu of Sumatra and Tasaday of Mindanao,[40] and the Austroasiatic-speaking Yumbri of northern Thailand and Shompen of Great Nicobar. With these there are some very grave questions to be asked concerning the lengths of time for which their present lifestyles, dominated by hunting and gathering, have been practised. The Punan and Kubu, for instance, must almost certainly be derived from original populations of cultivators. Their ancestors possibly entered the forests gradually and voluntarily, partially as hunters and partially as collectors of forest products for trade.[41] These groups may well have little to tell us about 'pristine' and pre-agricultural hunting and gathering in the region.

The conclusion to be drawn is that Late Pleistocene life can be reconstructed only from Late Pleistocene data. The linguistic and ethnographic records cannot be extended back this far, and comparative cultural observations of present-day peoples are likely to have little relevance. It is also becoming more apparent that Late Pleistocene people inhabited environments which

[37] See T. N. Headland and L. A. Reid, 'Hunter-gatherers and their neighbours from prehistory to the present', *Current Anthropology*, 30 (1989).

[38] Z. Cooper, 'Archaeological explorations in the Andaman Islands', BIPPA, 6 (1985).

[39] T. Headland, *Why Foragers do not Become Farmers*, University Microfilms International, 1986. A reluctance amongst hunters and gatherers to develop agriculture if they can exchange or work in return for cultivated produce is also reported from Africa; see J. D. Clark and S. A. Brandt, eds., *From Hunters to Farmers*, Berkeley, 1984, 5.

[40] The Tasaday, according to many recent media statements, are reputed to be fakes. I think it may be better to regard them as the last survivors of a short-lived and relatively unsuccessful attempt to colonize what was once a large block of rainforest, without investing the labour input demanded by agriculture.

[41] For a clear statement of this argument see C. L. Hoffman, 'Punan foragers in the trading networks of Southeast Asia', in C. Schrire, ed., *Past and Present in Hunter Gatherer Studies*, Orlando, 1984.

were often very different from those of today, and which probably underwent dramatic changes over fairly short periods of time. Some of these changes have already been discussed; they include sea-level fluctuations, changes in vegetation and rainfall, and animal extinctions. At 40,000 years ago the sea level was around 50 metres below present; sufficient to join Borneo, Sumatra and Java to the Asian mainland. By 18,000 years ago the sea was at its lowest, perhaps 130 metres below the present level, and Sundaland would have been exposed as a vast and probably rather dry subcontinent with a vegetational cover comprising less rainforest than now, but probably more seasonal monsoon forest and mangrove. With the coming of the Holocene the rainfall increased, and equatorial rainforests expanded to occupy virtually the whole of the equatorial region.

The results of these changes on humans are still rather obscure. It has been suggested, for instance, that the rapidly rising sea levels of the period between 18,000 and 6000 years ago would have forced people to migrate away from Sundaland, eastwards into the Pacific, as they lost their lands.[42] However, as pointed out by F. L. and D. F. Dunn,[43] the coastlines of Sundaland increased in length by about 46 per cent as the sea level rose from minus 120 metres to the present level, so the conditions for coastal occupation may actually have improved and people could have survived individual episodes of rapid inundation by simply retreating inland. Thus the changes in sea level need not have impacted directly on sparse groups of human foragers, although there may have been other indirect and minor impacts.

As one example, the terminal Pleistocene severing of land links to Borneo, combined with increasing forest cover as the climate became warmer and wetter, seems to have led to a number of local animal extinctions (tiger, Javan rhinoceros, dhole, tapir and possibly giant pangolin) and probably also many instances of species reduction in size.[44] The earlier shift into drier conditions leading up to the last glacial maximum may also have taken a toll of forest animals; the orang utan made its final appearance on the Asian mainland in cave deposits in northern Vietnam about 18,000 years ago,[45] and may have succumbed to the cool, dry and relatively deforested conditions of this period. The precise timings and reasons for animal extinctions in Southeast Asia are poorly understood, but most zoologists favour natural causes rather than over-hunting by humans; all the evidence for this period suggests that human populations were fairly sparse, and for the most part avoiding the

[42] J. Gibbons and F. Clunie, 'Sea level changes and Pacific prehistory', *Journal of Pacific History*, 21 (1986); and reply by P. Bellwood, 'The impact of sea level changes on Pacific prehistory', *Journal of Pacific History*, 22 (1987).
[43] 'Maritime adaptations and exploitation of marine resources in Sundaic Southeast Asian prehistory; MQRSEA, 3 (1977).
[44] Earl of Cranbrook, 'The contribution of archaeology to the zoogeography of Borneo', *Fieldiana, Zoology*, 42 (1988); L. R. Heaney, 'Mammalian species richness on the Sunda Shelf', *Oecologia*, 61 (1984).
[45] Ha Van Tan, 'The Late Pleistocene climate in Southeast Asia; new data from Vietnam', MQRSEA, 9 (1985).

rainforests until the Holocene, by which time better methods of trapping might have allowed more hunting success.

In general, it must be accepted that there is no convincing evidence of any major impact of the Late Pleistocene environmental changes on the human cultures of Southeast Asia, a clear contrast with the situation in many temperate zones of Europe and Asia. This contrast, however, may simply reflect poor knowledge of Southeast Asia compared with the rest of the Old World, and also the relatively inimical conditions for survival there of the Late Pleistocene archaeological record.

This record, as it is currently understood, comprises a very basic flake industry, with sundry core and pebble-tool components, which occurs virtually everywhere from about 40,000 years ago until well into the metal-using period (variously between c. 2000 BC and the first millennium CE). Basic forms were also carried east by some of the early settlers of Australia and New Guinea. This fundamental flake industry is diversified in some places with elaborations such as biface, prepared-core, blade and micro-lithic technologies (Figure 2.3), but overall patterning is hard to discern; Southeast Asia does not have widespread horizon-marking tool forms, and the flaked-stone industries of the region still tell little about any zones of stylistic or ethnic differentiation which may have existed during the pre-agricultural period. Neither do they record in any clear fashion the Holocene economic changes centred on agriculture.

The basic flake industry occurs chiefly on fine-grained rocks such as chert, jasper and obsidian in the islands of Southeast Asia, and generally on coarser-grained rocks of river pebble origin on the mainland. Most flakes are unretouched and simply used as struck, and they occur together with a range of cores (sometimes of a distinctive horsehoof shape which also occurs commonly in Australia and New Guinea), pebble tools, and debitage. The well-known 'Hoabinhian' stone tool industries of mainland Southeast Asia are focused more on pebble-tool production, but these are almost entirely a Holocene phenomenon, as are the blade and microlith industries of Java and Sulawesi.

On the Southeast Asian mainland the oldest reliably-dated flake industry (excluding those listed above as possibly connected with *Homo erectus*) comes from basal layers dated between 37,000 and 27,000 years ago at Lang Rongrien cave in Krabi Province, southern Thailand. These tools occur with remains of land tortoises and rodents, but marine shells are absent; the cave is twelve kilometres inland now, and was probably much further inland during lower sea-level conditions. Above this tool-bearing layer is a layer of roof-fall 1.5 metres thick, and the cave appears not to have been inhabited again until Hoabinhian pebble tools first appeared about 9600 years ago.[46] The older Lang Rongrien industry lacks pebble tools (although the sample is very small), but these are present in the lower layers of Sai Yok cave in Kanchanaburi Province, where pebble tools and horsehoof or 'flat-iron' shaped cores occur towards the base of the

[46] D. Anderson, 'A Pleistocene–early Holocene rock shelter in Peninsular Thailand', *National Geographic Research*, 3 (1987).

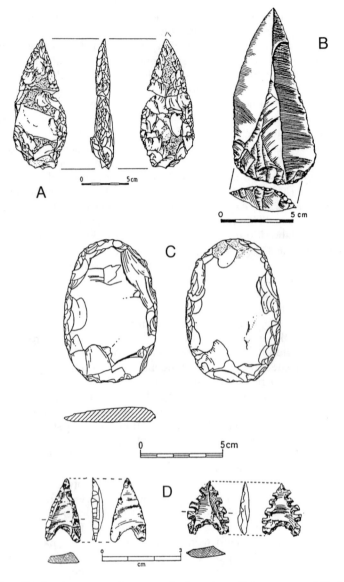

Figure 2.3   Distinctive types of stone tools from Late Pleistocene and Holocene Southeast Asian assemblages.
A.   Late Pleistocene chert biface from Tingkayu, Sabah, northern Borneo.
B.   Late Pleistocene chert blade with faceted striking platform from Leang Burun shelter 2, south Sulawesi.
C.   Early Holocene Hoabinhian pebble biface from Gua Cha, Kelantan, Malaysia.
D.   Mid-Holocene Maros Points (top) and backed microliths (below) from Ulu Leng shelter, south Sulawesi.

B and D, courtesy Ian Glover, Institute of Archaeology, London; C courtesy Adi Haji Taha, National Museum, Kuala Lumpur.

4.75 metre sequence. Although Sai Yok has no absolute dates, a Late Pleistocene antiquity may be expected.[47]

In northern Vietnam an industry termed the Sonviian is reported from open sites on elevated terrain around the inland edge of the Red River deltaic plains, and also from several caves where it is stratified beneath Hoabinhian layers. Sonviian pebble tools tend to be flaked peripherally, rather than over the whole of one or both faces as were many later Hoabinhian tools, and in Nguom rock shelter in Bac Thai Province they are dated between about 23,000 and 18,000 years ago. They occur here with bones of pig, cattle, porcupine, macaque monkey, and also the locally-extinct orang utan.[48] Below the true Sonviian industry as recognized by Vietnamese archaeologists there is a layer in Nguom shelter with only small flakes, but as with Lang Rongrien the sample size appears to be small. More evidence is needed before it can be accepted that a small flake industry preceded a large pebble one in Southeast Asia—a sequence which would be entirely the reverse of that in most other regions of the Old World.[49]

After about 13,000 years ago these earlier mainland industries graded into a fairly classic form of pebble-tool Hoabinhian in many regions, and widespread evidence for rainforest occupation, particularly in the Thai-Malaysian peninsula, commenced. To this we will return, after a brief survey of Late Pleistocene industries in island Southeast Asia, where the record is seemingly more variable than on the mainland. Flake-tool industries of Late Pleistocene data are now known from many sites, including the Niah Caves in Sarawak, the Madai-Baturong region in Sabah, Tabon Cave on Palawan, and Leang Burung shelter 2 in southern Sulawesi.

Inside the huge 60-metre-high West Mouth of the Niah Caves in Sarawak an industry of flake and pebble tools, together with bone spatulae and points, appears to date back to between 30,000 and 40,000 years ago.[50] The early modern skull from the lower levels of this site has been referred to above; this is potentially the oldest of this evolutionary grade so far recovered from Southeast Asia, although its date is not very secure. Niah is also of interest because it has produced edge-ground axes made on pebbles which may be over 10,000 years old; these represent an important technological innovation which also appeared, presumably independently, in Late Pleistocene contexts in Japan, northern Australia and the New Guinea Highlands. The edge-grinding of axes might also go back into the terminal Pleistocene in the Bacsonian of northern Vietnam, and it is

---

[47] It is impossible to give a reference for every archaeological site mentioned from here onwards. Further descriptions for most will be found in PIMA, and P. Bellwood, *Man's Conquest of the Pacific*, Auckland, 1978; also C. Higham, *The Archaeology of Mainland Southeast Asia*, Cambridge, UK, 1989.

[48] Ha Van Tan, 'The Late Pleistocene climate'.

[49] It should be noted, however, that Bartstra has recently claimed this to be the case for Java, with small flakes from Ngebung predating the larger pebble and flake Pacitanian industries; 'Sangiran, the stone implements of Ngebung, and the Palaeolithic of Java', MQRSEA 9 (1985).

[50] Z. Majid, 'The West Mouth, Niah, in the prehistory of Southeast Asia', *Sarawak Museum Journal*, 32 (1982).

of interest that the appearance of this technology long predates the appearance of systematic agriculture in this part of the world. In most other regions of the Old World such tools are normally found in agricultural contexts.

The West Mouth has also yielded a large series of human burials in flexed or sitting postures dated between 14,000 and 8000 years ago. Some of these were coated with haematite, one had a rhinoceros femur as a pillow, and another was apparently buried with an edge-ground pebble tool. As with Hoabinhian burials on the mainland of Southeast Asia, a fully extended burial posture is rare and only becomes dominant in the later agricultural stage. The cave inhabitants were also able to hunt or scavenge meat from no less than fifty-eight species of mammals, including primates, carnivores, and herbivores ranging in size from small rodents to rhinoceros and cattle. The economy here was clearly opportunistic: anything available was caught and eaten, although pigs, porcupines and monkeys were the most common animals, perhaps reflecting their easier availability. The fauna suggests that, while there may have been more open glades within the forest during the Late Pleistocene, the region around Niah was essentially under rainforest not too different from that of today. This means that some degree of occupation in near-coastal equatorial rainforest is of great antiquity in this part of Sundaland. As yet there is no evidence for any long-term interior rainforest occupation by pre-agricultural foragers, as already noted.

Further north in eastern Sabah recent archaeological research has focused on a series of caves and open sites in the Madai and Baturong limestone massifs and the Tingkayu valley, slightly inland from Lahad Datu Bay.[51] The Tingkayu open sites are believed to have been situated near the outlet of a lava-dammed lake of 75 square kilometres which existed between 28,000 and 17,000 years ago, and include a well-preserved working floor for a wide range of pointed or ovate bifacially-flaked tools made on slabs of chert (Figure 2.3A). Unfortunately these sites cannot be directly dated, and they contain nothing apart from the debitage left by biface manufacture. However, the tools are so far unique in Southeast Asia, with only distant and possibly coincidental parallels in Late Pleistocene northeast Asia and Japan. They remain something of a mystery.

Following the draining of the Tingkayu lake, the Sabah biface industry occurred no more, and caves in the Baturong and Madai massifs contain a simple industry of chert flakes and cores dating between 18,000 and 7000 years ago. These tools occur in freshwater shellfish middens (marine species were absent until the coastline moved inland towards its present position early in the Holocene), together with bones of pig, deer, cattle, porcupine, orang utan, monkey, rat, snakes and reptiles. Bones of the Javan rhinoceros and dhole, both now extinct in Borneo, occur in layers dating to about 10,000 years ago, and from this period there is also a number of large hollowed anvils or mortars with smoothly ground surfaces.

[51] P. Bellwood, *Archaeological Research in South-eastern Sabah*, Sabah Museum Monograph 2, Kota Kinabalu, 1988.

On Palawan Island in the southern Philippines a chert flake and pebble industry similar to that from the Sabah sites has been excavated from several of the Tabon caves. This seems to have commenced at least 30,000 years ago, and like that from the Sabah sites is unassociated with marine shellfish until the Holocene; the Tabon caves would have been at least thirty-five kilometres from the sea during the last glacial maximum. Another assemblage of definite Late Pleistocene age is that from the rock shelter of Leang Burung 2 in the Maros limestone region of southern Sulawesi, north of Ujung Pandang (Makassar). Here layers dated to between approximately 30,000 and 20,000 years ago have produced a few elongated blade-like flakes with faceted striking platforms (Figure 2.3B), representing a prepared-core technology similar to the Levalloisian of western Eurasia.[52] In this case the development seems to be localized and independent, as does a similar appearance of the technique in north-western Australia at a much later Holocene date, about 4000 years ago. Some of the Leang Burung flakes also have silica glosses on their cutting edges, perhaps resulting from the cutting of grasses or rattans, and haematite pieces are present, perhaps witnesses to some long-vanished tradition of artistic expression.[53]

Apart from the above, the only other well-reported industry which commenced during the Late Pleistocene consists of steep-edged scrapers and knives made on flakes and thick blades at least 13,000 years ago in eastern Timor. This is associated with a rather sparse Wallacean faunal assemblage of bats, extinct giant rats and reptiles,[54] together with plant fragments of Job's tears (a perennial cereal), betel vine and *Areca* nut (the ingredients of betel chewing), and candlenut (*Aleurites*). There is no reason, however, to assume that these plants were domesticated rather than simply collected and perhaps protected in the wild.

Holocene Stone Industries and the Transition to Agriculture

The Late Pleistocene industries of Southeast Asia give an impression of uniformity with sporadic localized innovation. During the Holocene the picture becomes more variable in the islands, with the appearance of localized microlithic and blade technologies. Such small tool classes seem to have been absent on the mainland of Southeast Asia, where the pebble-tool industries generally termed Hoabinhian attained a seemingly universal distribution. The Hoabinhian, however, may have witnessed the

[52] I. Glover, 'Leang Burung 2', MQRSEA, 6 (1981).

[53] Some of the Maros caves have negative hand stencils outlined with red pigment, and drawings of pig or babirusa also occur. While these are undated, there seems no reason why some hand stencils at least should not be Late Pleistocene. See H. R. van Heekeren, *The Stone Age of Indonesia*, The Hague, 1972, 118–20.

[54] The fauna of some of the Lesser Sunda Islands today includes non-native mammals such as macaque monkey, civet cat, pig, deer (*Cervus timorensis*) and porcupine. The marsupial phalanger also occurs archaeologically on Timor. The archaeological record for Timor, and zoological opinions in general, suggest that all these animals were introduced during the agricultural period (post–3000 BC). However, some of the non-domesticated species could have been introduced by earlier hunting and gathering populations. See G. Musser, 'The Giant Rat of Flores and its Relatives East of Borneo and Bali', *Bulletin of the American Museum of Natural History*, 169 (1981); I. Glover, *Archaeology in Eastern Timor*, Terra Australis II, Canberra, 1986.

development of edge grinding in Vietnam by the beginning of the Holocene.

It is important to note that these industries in some (but certainly not all) regions of both mainland and island Southeast Asia continued with little morphological change well into the era of agriculture and pottery, occasionally even into the first millennium CE, as perhaps in inland parts of Cambodia-Thailand and southern Sulawesi. One suspects here that the hunting and gathering populations who originally developed these flaked-stone industries continued to use them until they were eventually assimilated to an agricultural lifestyle, or until stone was replaced by iron for tools and weapons. The early agricultural populations appear to have used flaked-stone tools on a much lesser scale than their hunting and gathering predecessors, and concentrated more widely on the manufacture and use of ground-stone tools, especially adzes and knives.

On the mainland of Southeast Asia, from Burma and southern China southwards to Malaysia and parts of northern Sumatra, the dominant industry from about 13,000 years ago until the arrival of agriculture is termed the Hoabinhian, after discoveries made in the 1920s in the former Hoa Binh (now Ha Son Binh) Province of northern Vietnam.[55] The Hoabinhian has acquired a certain notoriety amongst Southeast Asian archaeologists because of claimed associations with the origins of agriculture and pottery manufacture. These associations still lack definite proof, mainly because most of the data come from poorly excavated and probably disturbed cave deposits. The term Hoabinhian also hides a great deal of local and regional variation which still remains to be documented; the use of such a term for all early Holocene assemblages of mainland Southeast Asia from beyond the Tropic of Cancer almost to the equator does not imply technological homogeneity, or that the makers were necessarily closely related in linguistic or biological terms. Indeed, the only clear observations about Hoabinhian identity come from the Malay peninsula, where the Hoabinhian foragers were almost certainly the ancestors of the Austroasiatic-speaking Negritos, and in part also of the Senoi agriculturalists. Whether the Hoabinhian also has a place in the ancestry of other mainland groups such as the Vietnamese, Thais and Burmese is simply unknown, given the difficulty of determining how much population expansion and replacement occurred throughout the region with the spread of agriculture. What is clear, however, is that many skulls from Hoabinhian sites have been accorded a degree of Australo-Melanesian affinity by Vietnamese, French and Indonesian researchers,[56] and these observations, while often vague, can hardly be ignored.

One of the most significant points about the Hoabinhian is that it seems to represent the colonization of the wet Holocene rainforests of the Malay

---

[55] Detailed and referenced surveys of the Hoabinhian can be found in PIMA, 162–75; Bellwood, *Man's Conquest*, 64–71; Higham, *Archaeology*, 31–65; Ha Van Tan, Nouvelles recherches préhistoriques et protohistoriques au Viêt Nam', BEFEO, 68, (1980); Ha Van Tan, 'The Hoabinhian in the context of Viet Nam', *Vietnamese Studies*, 46 (1978).

[56] See, for instance, Nguyen Lang Cuong, 'An early Hoabinhian skull from Vietnam', BIPPA, 7 (1986–7); S. Budisampurno, 'Kerangka manusia dari Bukit Kelambai Stabat, Sumatera Utara', *Pertemuan Ilmiah Arkeologi ke-III*, Jakarta, 1985.

peninsula and northern Sumatra. It also suggests a considerable increase in population density in certain more northerly zones of seasonal rainfall distribution, especially western Thailand and northern Vietnam. Demographically, therefore, it appears to represent some degree of success in the forging of new adaptations to post-glacial environments. However, there are also areas where archaeological survey has failed to find any occupation of this period, for instance the Khorat Plateau of northeastern Thailand, which for some unknown reason appears to have been almost uninhabited when settled by agriculturalists after 5000 years ago.

In terms of basic archaeological data, evidence for Hoabinhian occupation and burial activities occurs mainly in limestone caves and shelters. There are also a few coastal shell middens dating from after 8000 years ago in northern Sumatra, western peninsular Malaysia and northern Vietnam; any older than this would have been destroyed by rising sea levels. Many of the sites with marine shell deposits, both caves and open middens, occur well inland today, and this presumably reflects the higher sea levels during the middle Holocene combined with the massive effects of coastal and estuarine aggradation caused by subsequent forest clearance for agriculture. Many of the Sumatran middens, for instance, lie on an old shoreline 10–15 kilometres inland and are totally buried under alluvium. A few other non-midden inland and riverine open sites have also been reported from Sumatra, the Malay peninsula and northern Thailand.

Hoabinhian tools are characteristically made on flat, oval or elongated river pebbles flaked around their peripheries and over one or both surfaces. Bifaces dominate in parts of the Malay peninsula (Figure 2.3C), and unifaces (so-called 'Sumatraliths') elsewhere. They occur sporadically with other flake tools, grindstones, bone points and bone spatulae. In one region of northern Vietnam north of Hanoi there is an interesting regional variant of the Hoabinhian known as the Bacsonian which has a marked emphasis on the edge-grinding of pebble tools. This seems to have commenced about 10,000 years ago. Hoabinhian burials are mostly flexed or contracted, and often dusted with haematite; definite instances of the placement of grave goods are rare.

In the upper levels of many Hoabinhian cave sites there are also potsherds; these are plain or impressed with vines or mats in Vietnam, cord-marked in most other areas. There are problems in explaining the presence of pottery amongst presumably mobile foraging societies. Cave disturbance, for instance, cannot be invoked as the sole explanation, since pottery does appear to be well tied to a Bacsonian context in the shell midden of Da But, Thanh Hoa province (7000 years ago), and it may also date to about 8000 years ago in the upper layer of Spirit Cave in northwestern Thailand (but see page 97). There also seems to be an overlap in time between pottery and Hoabinhian tools at certain caves in Cambodia and the Malay peninsula, although at the site of Gua Cha in Malaysia there was a much sharper change from the aceramic Hoabinhian to a Neolithic layer with richly furnished burials about 3300 years ago. The overall picture is by no means simple, and the big question remains: did the makers of the Hoabinhian stone industry play any role in the development of agriculture and Neolithic technology in mainland Southeast Asia?

This is not a question which can be easily answered. It is clear from most sites that the Hoabinhians were hunters. Bones of a wide range of mammal species are found; pig and deer predominate, but large mammals including elephant, rhinoceros and cattle occur as well, as of course do small ones like rats and squirrels. None of these species appear to have been domesticated, although bones of dog, certainly a non-native and domesticated introduction into Southeast Asia from the Indian subcontinent or China, are reported from the Da But midden. Plant remains, on the other hand, are scarce, with the most important coming from early Holocene contexts in Spirit Cave, northwest Thailand. These include parts of food plants (almond, and possibly some legumes), stimulants (betel nut), poisons (butternut kernels), and other useful plants including bamboo and gourd. No remains of cereals such as rice or millet were found, although rice does occur in the nearby Banyan Valley Cave in contexts which postdate 5500 years ago, and hence may reflect contact with adjacent agriculturalists. In general, none of the plant remains found in early Holocene Spirit Cave can be proved to be from domesticated plants, and it seems that they may belong to a stable and broad-spectrum hunter-gatherer adaptation which may have lasted in this remote region to the first millennium CE, albeit with earlier sporadic contact with lowland agricultural groups.[57]

The Hoabinhian thus poses many questions for future research, not least concerning the existence of regional facies, its role (if any) in agricultural developments, and its role in the ancestry of the modern cultures and populations of the region. At the present time it exists as little more than a classificatory pigeonhole for pebble tools; it clearly merits far more serious attention.

In island Southeast Asia there is no true pebble-tool Hoabinhian beyond northern Sumatra, although variants have been claimed for Taiwan and Luzon. In most regions the flake industries of Late Pleistocene type, as exemplified in sites such as the Tabon, Niah and Madai caves, simply continued without technological change until flaked stone gradually faded away with the development of polished Neolithic adze technology and eventually metal tools. Holocene industries of this continuing type have been reported from regions as far apart as southern Sumatra, Java, northern Luzon, northern Sulawesi, Flores and Timor, and also eastwards into New Guinea and the western Pacific.

As a variation on this basic theme there was an emphasis in parts of the Philippines, Sulawesi and Java on the production of small blades and blade-like flakes after about 7000 years ago. By far the best-known elaboration along these lines is the microlithic technology which appeared in the Toalian industry of southern Sulawesi from about 8000 years ago, also in parts of Java, and from 6000 years ago across much of the Australian continent. This distribution has to be explained to some extent by diffusion, but whether the microlithic tool forms were first developed within

[57] For discussions of the Spirit Cave evidence, see C. Gorman, 'The Hoabinhian and after', *World Archaeology*, 2 (1971); D. E. Yen, 'Hoabinhian horticulture', in J. Allen et al., eds, *Sunda and Sahul*, London, 1977; Higham, *Archaeology*, 45–61.

Southeast Asia or introduced from some outside region remains unknown. The Toalian, the most important of these industries in Southeast Asia, occurs in caves, rock shelters, and in open sites on slightly raised alluvial deposits in the southwestern peninsula of Sulawesi. The best sequence comes from the excavated shelter of Ulu Leang in the Maros limestone district, where small elongated or geometric-backed microliths appeared after 8000 years ago, to which were added remarkable and distinctive hollow-based and serrated projectile points ('Maros points') after about 6000 years ago (Figure 2.3D).[58] Other artefacts found in Toalian levels include glossed flakes, small bipolar cores, bone points, and possible bivalve shell scrapers. Pebble tools and edge-ground tools seemingly do not occur in this region, but it must be remembered that the microliths make up only a small percentage of the total of flaked stone in Toalian sites —the background core and flake industry continued throughout with little change. The Toalian also continued in a morphologically simplified form in the southern part of the south Sulawesi peninsula until about 1000 CE. It is quite possible that hunters and gatherers survived in this remote region until well after this time, although in Ulu Leang itself, further north in the Maros region, rice appeared in a level dated to 500 CE, perhaps indicating exchange with nearby agriculturalists. Plain potsherds also became quite numerous in Ulu Leang in association with Toalian tools after about 4000 years ago.

The Toalian economy involved the hunting of native Sulawesi mammals—phalanger, macaque monkey, civet cat, *anoa*, *babirusa* and pig (*Sus celebensis*). In perhaps contemporary (mid-Holocene?) deposits in the cave of Gua Lawa in central Java were found bones of cattle, elephant, water buffalo, clouded leopard, pig and deer, together with bone points, bone spatulae, and hollow-based but unserrated arrowheads similar to the Maros points. Backed blades, points and geometrics have also been reported in obsidian from the Bandung region in western Java, and an overall picture emerges of bands of hunters with microlith-tipped projectiles (arrows or spears) roaming the open monsoonal forest landscapes of Java, southern Sulawesi, and probably many of the Lesser Sunda Islands before and during the gradual spread of agricultural communities throughout the region.

No signs have yet appeared of any such industries north of the equator or in the equatorial rainforests of Sumatra, Borneo, central Sulawesi or New Guinea, and in this respect southern Indonesia had its closest early and mid-Holocene cultural affinities with Australia. All this began to change as Austronesian-speaking agriculturalists expanded right through and ultimately dominated the whole of island Southeast Asia, just as the speakers of Austroasiatic languages appear to have replaced or assimilated many of the original Hoabinhian foraging communities of mainland Southeast Asia. To this new era, and to the agricultural foundations of all complex societies in Southeast Asia, we now turn.

[58] I. Glover and G. Presland, 'Microliths in Indonesian flaked stone industries', in V. N. Misra and P. Bellwood, eds, *Recent Advances in Indo-Pacific Prehistory*, New Delhi, 1985.

THE RISE AND EXPANSION OF AGRICULTURAL
COMMUNITIES

With the rise of agriculture, the Southeast Asian archaeological record takes on a new level of complexity, owing to the increasing range of technological and economic categories of evidence which survives. Fairly obvious examples include pottery, remains of houses and villages, elaborate burial practices, bones of domesticated animals, and the tools and plant remains associated with agriculture. This does not mean that early agricultural societies were necessarily more complex in all respects than foraging ones, but they have left behind, at least in the Southeast Asian context, an archaeological record which is more suitable for the making of inferences about culture, history and lifestyle. The record of agricultural societies is also closer to us in time and can be related more easily to the linguistic and ethnological records of present-day populations.

As well as having increased material complexity, agricultural populations also tend to have much greater population densities than hunters and gatherers—by factors of ten or more with even the simplest systems of shifting cultivation, and factors of hundreds with the very intensive wet-rice systems of the historical civilizations. Early agriculturalists created more substantial and more numerous archaeological sites than foragers, an obvious fact which is very evident in the Neolithic and Early Metal phase records of Thailand and Vietnam. In the equatorial zone, however, ancient open sites can be notoriously difficult to locate in the densely-vegetated conditions, and far less evidence about the actual settlements of early agriculturalists is available.

Why did human societies first adopt agriculture, evidently independently in several parts of the world, just after the beginning of the Holocene? There is no simple answer to this question, but there are some logical observations which can be emphasized. By the time that agricultural techniques were successful enough to support the considerable increases of population evident in the Neolithic records of China and mainland Southeast Asia, the system as a whole would have required an annual cycle of labour investment and settlement stability very different from that practised by contemporary foragers. Unless the incentives or pressures for accepting such social and economic upheaval were strong, it is hard to understand why successful early Holocene foragers who had sufficient food and experienced no pressure on their resources would have wanted to change. Modern hunter-gatherers in Southeast Asia generally resist the total adoption of agriculture unless shrinking land resources leave them with few other options, and many hunters and gatherers of the Holocene probably did not switch their economies simply because concepts of food production entered their lives. Modern ethnography also suggests that those who did ultimately adopt agriculture would hardly have done so via 'affluent forager' leisure-time experimenting.

Despite the complexities behind the acquisition by foragers of an integrated and successful agricultural lifestyle, the fact remains that some of them, in certain localities such as western Asia, central and southern

China, the New Guinea highlands and the Mexican and Peruvian high-lands, did at one time develop agriculture from an economic base of hunting and gathering. There is an important distinction to be made here between the concepts of primary indigenous development in isolation, and secondary adoption through various processes of borrowing. Agri-culture has only rarely been adopted by borrowing with conscious and willing intent—if the ethnographic record is any guide—and could have developed indigenously out of a foraging economic base only in regions where suitable high-yielding plants occurred, and where human societies were perhaps nudged towards a greater investment in cultivation by various stress factors. These might have included seasonal uncertainty of wild food supplies, reductions in food supplies caused by environmental changes, and even crude population growth. True and primary develop-ments of agriculture did not occur commonly, but once they had occurred the populations behind them were offered substantial demographic advantages over their foraging neighbours. Hence some of the great ethnolinguistic expansions of prehistoric times—of the Indo-Europeans, Bantu, and in Southeast Asia the speakers of Austroasiatic and Austro-nesian languages—occurred when populations who had recently devel-oped systematic and productive methods of agriculture expanded slowly, but continuously and inexorably, into territories held only by foragers. Such processes are continuing today on a much smaller geographical scale as the last of the foraging peoples across the world face historically unprecedented pressures to give up their old ways of life.

In most of Southeast Asia (excluding southern China and possibly coastal northern Vietnam) there is no evidence to suggest that any primary development of agriculture occurred, and it seems basically to have been introduced by people already acquainted with the cultivation of rice, millet and other subtropical crops like yams, taro and sugarcane. They also kept domesticated pigs, chickens, dogs, and perhaps cattle. All evidence to hand suggests that this expansion into Southeast Asia commenced mainly from the coastal regions of southern China. However, it is very important to emphasize that many tropical fruits and tubers native to Southeast Asia were brought into cultivation systems as they expanded southwards, and existing foraging populations may well have contributed useful knowledge of such plants to agricultural groups. Futhermore, recent research indicates that a separate and primary centre of plant cultivation, perhaps associated with such crops as taro, sugarcane, pandanus and Australimusa bananas, was developing in the New Guinea highlands by at least 6000 years ago. The agricultural developments in this region had no apparent impact on Southeast Asia beyond the eastern part of Indonesia, but they did have the crucial result for Pacific prehistory of making New Guinea mainly impervious, presumably for demographic reasons, to Austronesian colonists.

The view which I state here clearly ignores the possibility of an early and indigenous stratum of agriculture in Southeast Asia based purely on fruits and tubers, which was favoured at one time by a number of geographers and ethnologists. I find it impossible to identify any evidence for such a stratum west of New Guinea and the Pacific islands (where cereals were

not grown in prehistoric times), and in the absence of such supporting
evidence it seems wiser at this time to focus on the importance of the
high-yielding annual cereals, particularly rice. It is rice which has yielded
the bulk of the positive archaeological record for ancient agriculture in
Southeast Asia.

The annual cereals—in particular wheat, barley, maize, rice and the
millets—have formed the economic bases for the great majority of
the densely-populated complex societies on record. Annual cereals have
by definition evolved in subtropical or temperate regions with alternating
wet and dry (or warm and cold) seasons of growth and dormancy. They
tend to have large grains, and—after selection for increased grain size and
yield, loss of shattering habit when ripe, and synchronous ripening—they
are capable of yielding very large quantities of nutritious food per unit of
land. Rice (*Oryza sativa*) and foxtail millet (*Setaria italica*) were first cultivated from annual forebears in China, the latter north of the Yangtze where it
supported the oldest Chinese Neolithic cultures from 6000 BC onwards.
According to current archaeological evidence, rice was first cultivated
somewhere in the lower Yangtze region under the warmer climatic conditions of the early Holocene,[59] and it was supporting the inhabitants of
impressive timber villages such as Hemudu in Zhejiang Province by
5000 BC. The wealth of technology associated with these developments in
central coastal China includes pottery, carpentry, stone adzes, wooden
and bone agricultural tools, boats, paddles, spindle whorls for weaving (of
cotton?), matting and rope, together with the evidence for domesticated
pigs, dogs, chicken and possibly for cattle and water buffalo. This all
suggests changes away from a former forager lifestyle, which can only be
described as revolutionary.

The problem, however, is that the Chinese archaeological record does
not yet tell in fine detail how and why these developments took place. The
absence of convincing evidence for agriculture anywhere in the world
during the Pleistocene suggests very strongly that the post-glacial climatic
amelioration had a role to play, perhaps in allowing a radiation of large-
grained annual cereals throughout many zones of Eurasia between about
15 and 35 degrees north latitude.[60] Foraging populations perhaps began to
utilize and depend upon these wild cereals for food, until situations
of stress obliged them to systematize cultivation practices in order to
maintain regular supplies. In the case of southern coastal China, the stress
factors may have been related to periodic temperature coolings during
the early Holocene[61] which caused a lowering of yield or even a local

[59] Average annual temperatures were 2–4 degrees Celsius warmer than now over much of
China between 6000 and 2000 BC: K. C. Chang, *Archaeology of Ancient China*, New Haven,
1986, 74–9.
[60] According to R. O. Whyte, annual cereals evolved around the fringes of central Asia with
increasing dry-season stress and higher temperatures around the end of the last glaciation:
'Annual crops of South and Southeast Asia', in Misra and Bellwood eds, *Recent Advances*.
Recent palynological research in Yunnan provides some support for this view; see
D. Walker, 'Late Pleistocene–early Holocene vegetational and climatic changes in Yunnan
Province, southwest China', *Journal of Biogeography*, 13 (1986).
[61] According to Yang Huairen and Xie Zhiren, 'Sea level changes in east China over the past
20,000 years', in R. O. Whyte, ed., *The Evolution of the East Asian Environment*, Hong Kong,
1984, there were cool stages from pollen evidence at 8200 and 5800 BP.

disappearance of wild rice stands. We really do not know the answers here, however, and precise causal explanations for agricultural origins in all parts of the world still remain elusive.

Once successful cereal agriculture was established, with a stable annual round of cultivation activities and storage techniques, then expansion of the system began. Here we come to an area of some disagreement, since agricultural expansion has been related by some authors to population pressure. It must be stated, however, that large-scale pressure of people on land is not evidenced in the archaeological or pre-modern ethnographic records for Southeast Asia or even southern China. It cannot even be invoked to explain renowned ethnographic cases of agricultural expansion such as that of the Iban of Sarawak, where the opening of new lands last century offered status as well as more cultivation space for ambitious and warlike young men. The same, of course, applied to the great Pacific migrations of the Polynesians, if we are to believe some of their legends. New frontiers, new wealth and the chance to escape difficulties at home have always been attractive lures, as recent colonial history attests.

The reason why early rice cultivation spread very quickly, at least in the intermediate tropical zone where it yielded best,[62] was perhaps that the swampy and alluvial environments most suited to it (and also to the taro tuber) were of limited geographical extent. Under conditions of low population density people might have preferred to seek new natural swamps along rivers which flooded during the wet season, rather than to create their own by laborious processes of damming, bunding and water transport. Rice and taro, therefore, may both have been grown in natural wet fields of a simple and seasonal kind from the very beginning, and dry-land shifting cultivation in most areas may be a secondary development.[63] Swamps and low-lying seasonally flooded alluvial soils, particularly in thickly forested habitats, can also produce higher and more stable yields than dry swiddens without markedly higher labour inputs.[64] Environments of this kind were perhaps actively sought by early Neolithic colonists, with or without the stimulus provided by localized population pressure on resources.

Before leaving this background discussion of agricultural origins and dispersals, it is necessary to emphasize the major shifts which took place in agricultural economies as they expanded southwards towards the equator, and on into the Pacific islands. The agricultural economy which developed in southern China and northern mainland Southeast Asia, and which came eventually to dominate the intermediate tropical regions both north

---

[62] Prehistoric rices probably grew best in intermediate tropical latitudes for a complex series of reasons connected with photoperiodicity (i.e. growth cycles are synchronized with changes in day length), the need for reliable dry-season sun for ripening, and increased grain size and protein content in these environments. Humid equatorial climates were probably unsuitable for rice until considerable selection within the species had taken place. See discussion with references in PIMA, ch. 7.

[63] See T. T. Chang, 'The ethnobotany of rice in Island Southeast Asia', AP, 26 (1988); Joyce White, 'Origins of plant domestication in Southeast Asia', in D. Bayard, ed., *Southeast Asian Archaeology at the XV Pacific Science Congress*, Dunedin, 1984.

[64] For example, see M. R. Dove, *Swidden Agriculture in Indonesia*, Berlin, 1985, 299; C. Padoch, 'Labor efficiency and intensity of land use in rice production: an example from Kalimantan', *Human Ecology*, 13 (1985).

and south of the equator, was focused on the cultivation of cereals such as rice, foxtail and other millets (*Panicum* and *Echinochloa*), and the perennial Job's tears. Cotton (*Gossypium arboreum*[65]), sugarcane, greater yam (*Dioscorea alata*) and perhaps taro (*Colocasia esculenta*) were also of considerable importance in these latitudes.

Within the equatorial zone of Indonesia and Malaysia, however, the prevailing climatic conditions were clearly unsuitable for the cultivation of the photoperiodic rices introduced by early Austronesians. The result was that rice declined to relative insignificance, and was indeed never taken into the Pacific islands, with the minor exception of the Marianas (which, not surprisingly, are outside the equatorial zone). The later prehistory of equatorial Southeast Asia was focused more on the cultivation of millet, tubers (yams, taro and other aroids), sago palms for starch, and tree fruits such as coconut, banana and breadfruit.[66] Rice is now dominant in many parts of equatorial Indonesia, but there are indications that this dominance may have developed subsequent to the initial millennia of agriculture as the rice plant itself became better adapted to equatorial conditions. On the other hand, some of the intermediate tropical islands of the southern hemisphere, such as Java and Bali, would have been suited to rice from the very beginning, as soon as the plant was transmitted to them through the equatorial zone.

THE ARCHAEOLOGY OF EARLY AGRICULTURAL SOCIETIES

Societies with a Neolithic mode of technology appeared almost everywhere in lowland and coastal regions of Southeast Asia between approximately 4000 and 1000 BC (Map 2.4), except in those ever-decreasing territories which remained the preserve of hunters and gatherers. Bronze became widespread in the northern part of mainland Southeast Asia during the second millennium BC, and iron after 500 BC; both first appeared together towards the end of the first millennium BC in Malaysia and island Southeast Asia. In this section I will discuss those cultures and assemblages which can be termed Neolithic[67] before turning to the essen-

---

[65] See R. K. Johnson and B. G. Decker, 'Implications of the distribution of native names for cotton (*Gossypium* spp.) in the Indo-Pacific', AP, 23 (1983).

[66] P. Bellwood, 'Plants, climate and people; the early horticultural prehistory of Indonesia', in J. J. Fox, ed., *Indonesia: the Making of a Culture*, Canberra, 1980.

[67] The term 'Neolithic' is no more than a convenient pigeon-hole, implying the existence of agriculture and the absence of metal, and should not be taken to refer to any particular grade of cultural evolution. Many Neolithic societies (such as the Maya) were undoubtedly far larger and more complex than many metal-using ones in Southeast Asia. However, circumlocutions such as 'Era of Early Agriculture' or 'Pre-Metal Agricultural Period' beg many questions and serve no useful purpose. D. Bayard, 'A tentative regional phase chronology for northeast Thailand' in Bayard, ed., *Southeast Asian Archaeology*, and Higham, *Archaeology*, have recently divided the archaeology of non-peninsular mainland Southeast Asia into four General Periods lettered A to D, but the cultural characteristics used for these periods cannot yet be applied in equatorial regions such as Malaysia or Indonesia. I will therefore retain a traditional terminology which will be more appropriate for the non-specialist reader.

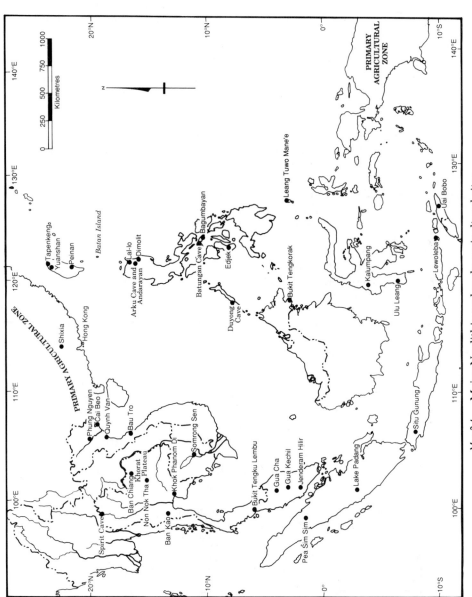

Map 2.4 Major Neolithic and early agricultural sites.

tial linguistic record which allows them to be interpreted in a culture-historical framework. These Neolithic assemblages are oldest in southern China and the northern parts of Southeast Asia, and they seem to become younger in age as one moves southwards and eastwards through Indonesia. New Guinea appears to have been the focus of an independent origin of agriculture as old as that in China.

The wealth of southern Chinese coastal cultures in Neolithic times has already been alluded to in connection with the site of Hemudu in Zhejiang Province. The quantity of rice found here should be emphasized; not only were rice husks used for tempering pottery, but the site also yielded a waterlogged layer of husks, grain, straw and leaves up to fifty centimetres thick. Much further south, at Shixia in Guangdong Province, rice remains have been found in cooking pits and store pits, and apparently used as a temper for building daub, in a 3-hectare settlement site dating to about 3000 BC.[68] It is apparent that the whole southern coast of China became inhabited by pottery-using and rice-cultivating peoples between 5000 and 3000 BC, and even earlier dates are quite conceivable.[69]

Recent research in the coastal regions of northern Vietnam has yielded a number of sites, often shell middens, with a rather confusing array of Neolithic material culture dating from the fifth millennium BC onwards.[70] This includes pottery with pointed or round bases, decorated by cord-making, red-slipping, basket or mat impressions, or incision. Untanged or shouldered stone adzes, flexed burials, and bones of deer, cattle, pig and dog are also found in some of these sites, but it is not clear whether any of these animals were domesticated (presumably pigs and dogs were). Few data about subsistence are available, although the situation improves slightly with the Phung Nguyen culture of the middle Red River valley above Hanoi, dated to the late third or early second millennium BC. This, the immediate precursor of the first bronze-using cultures in northern Vietnam, does have evidence for the cultivation of rice, together with a broader range of material culture. This includes stone arrowheads and knives, baked clay spindle whorls and bow pellets, and pottery with incised and comb-stamped decoration which Vietnamese archaeologists consider to be directly ancestral to the pottery of the Dong-son civilization of the first millennium BC.

More information is available about the prehistory of Thailand than any other country in Southeast Asia, mainly because a succession of large

[68] A. E. Dien et al., eds, *Chinese Archaeological Abstracts*, Los Angeles: University of California Institute of Archaeology, 1985, II. 121–3.

[69] For instance, pottery, generally associated with agricultural rather than foraging societies, could be as much as 12,000 years old in southern Japan and nearby Jiangsu Province in central coastal China. W. Meacham, 'C-14 dating of pottery', *Journal of the Hong Kong Archaeological Society*, 11 (1984–5), discusses several dates as old as 5000 BC for pottery in Hong Kong and Macao. C. L. Brace et al. have also suggested that the smallness of south Chinese tooth sizes favours very early agricultural origins in this region: 'Prehistoric and modern tooth size in China', in F. H. Smith and F. Spencer, eds, *The Origins of Modern Humans*, New York, 1984.

[70] Relevant sites include Quynh Van, Bau Tro and Cai Beo. See Ha Van Tan, 'Nouvelles recherches'; and 'Prehistoric pottery in Viet Nam and its relationships with Southeast Asia', AP, 26 (1988). Cord-marked pottery has apparently been found with edge-ground ('Bacsonian') tools dating from about 5000 BC in the Da But shell mound (see page 87).

multidisciplinary projects have occurred there in recent years. However, general understanding has been confused by suggestions that agriculture and bronze-working arose in Thailand at very early dates, earlier perhaps than anywhere else in the world.[71] Recent research has placed these discoveries in their proper contexts, and although sporadic disagreements still erupt it is now clear that some of the earlier claims were exaggerated. One of these claims was that plant remains recovered from contexts dated prior to 7000 BC in the Hoabinhian layers of Spirit Cave in northwest Thailand were domesticated—a claim since rendered unlikely by the botanical analyses of Yen.[72] Spirit Cave also produced, from an upper layer, pottery with cord-marked or net-impressed decoration, some with a resin surface coat, together with untanged stone adzes and slate knives. The date of 6000 BC originally published for these items would make them the oldest of their kind by at least a millennium in Southeast Asia, but similar artefacts found with remains of rice (believed to be wild) in the nearby Banyan Valley Cave date only to some time after 3500 BC. Given the difficulties of dating artefacts from shallow cave deposits such as those in Spirit Cave it seems that the date for the Neolithic assemblage from the site will have to be held in abeyance for the time being, at least until more data are available to allow a surer assessment. As noted above, Higham's general view of the sequence represented by the northwest Thailand cave sites is that they represent a broad-spectrum foraging economy which may have survived well into the first millennium CE,[73] albeit perhaps with contact with nearby agriculturalists after about 3500 BC.

This rather negative conclusion, however, certainly does not apply to the broad and fertile floodplains which cross the Khorat Plateau of north-east Thailand. Agricultural societies were firmly established here by about 3000 BC, evidently in a region which was almost totally devoid of any preceding settlement by foragers if the results of recent archaeological surveys are accepted at face value. The first of these sites to be excavated, in 1966 and 1968, was Non Nok Tha, a low mound on the western side of the Khorat Plateau which contained many extended burials spanning both the Neolithic and Early Metal phases. The older graves contained untanged adzes, shell beads, and cord-marked and rare painted pottery, and also yielded bones of domesticated cattle, pig and dog together with rice husks used as a temper for the pottery. The dates proposed by the main excavator of the site suggested an initial settlement during the fourth millennium BC. This date has since been challenged, but a foundation of the site during the third or second millennium BC still seems likely.[74]

The results from Non Nok Tha were soon paralleled by the excavations

---

[71] See summaries in Bellwood, *Man's Conquest*, 161–5; W. G. Solheim II, 'Reworking Southeast Asian prehistory', *Paideuma*, 15 (1969).

[72] C. Gorman, 'Hoabinhian: a pebble-tool complex with early plant associations in Southeast Asia', *Science*, 163 (1969); Yen, 'Hoabinhian horticulture; as in footnote 57.

[73] *Archaeology*, 61.

[74] For a preliminary excavation report see D. T. Bayard, *Non Nok Tha: the 1968 excavations*, Dunedin, 1972. On chronology, see D. Bayard, 'A tentative regional phase chronology for northeast Thailand', in Bayard, ed., *Southeast Asian Archaeology*. Higham favours a commencement date for Non Nok Tha only in the second millennium BC ('The Ban Chiang culture in wider perspective', *Proceedings of the British Academy*, 69 (1983) 249).

at the more famous site of Ban Chiang about 120 kilometres to the northeast. Ban Chiang rose to prominence in the 1970s owing to the appearance on the antiquities market of very fine red-on-buff pottery dug illegally from graves: pottery which is now dated at about 2000 years ago. The lower occupation of the site, however, commenced by at least 3000 BC. While the exact cultural contents of these lower layers are uncertain (they certainly did not contain bronze, which appears in this site after 2000 BC), likely components include extended and flexed burials, infant burials in pottery jars, the pottery with fairly elaborate cord-marked, incised and burnished decoration.[75] Significant economic information from the site includes, as from Non Nok Tha, evidence for rice chaff temper in sherds, and bones of domesticated pig, dog, chicken, and cattle (probably of gaur or banteng stock, rather than the Indian zebu). There is also a very wide range of hunted and collected meat resources, including shellfish, turtles, crocodiles, and mammals ranging in size up to large deer and rhinoceros.[76] These people probably practised rice cultivation in low-lying and seasonally flooded soils, but analysis of their skeletal remains by M. Pietrusewsky indicates that their life expectancy was fairly short, averaging only thirty-one years for a sample of 112 individuals.[77] The analyses also indicated a likelihood that malaria was a significant disease by this time.

Despite problems in interpreting the sites of Non Nok Tha and Ban Chiang, they are both of great potential significance for the period prior to the appearance of bronze, which enters the record in northeast Thailand at some time between the late third millennium and 1500 BC (the precise date for the appearance of cupreous metallurgy in Thailand is still uncertain). Indeed, Ban Chiang is still the only excavated site in northeast Thailand for which there is a base deposit which is pre-bronze but putatively agricultural. It seems reasonable to assume that the earliest inhabitants during the late fourth millennium BC were migrants into the region, which appears to have been only very sparsely inhabited up to that time. They brought in a fully agricultural economy and Neolithic technology, the latter different only in a few stylistic details from contemporary assemblages in southern China and Vietnam. Unhappily, the Thailand sites have yielded only very limited evidence for settlement or house plans;[78] this was not the fault of the excavators, but reflects the fact that ephemeral timber architecture rarely survives in readily-identifiable post-hole patterns in the tropics, a circumstance which puts this region at an

[75] Joyce White, *Ban Chiang*, Philadelphia, 1982; *A Revision of the Chronology of Ban Chiang*, University Microfilms International, 1987; 'Ban Chiang and charcoal in hypothetical hindsight', BIPPA, 8 (1988).

[76] C. Higham and A. Kijngam, 'New evidence for agriculture and stock-raising in monsoonal Southeast Asia', in Misra and Bellwood, eds, *Recent Advances*.

[77] 'The ancient inhabitants of Ban Chiang', *Expedition*, 24, 4 (1982). For Ban Chiang rice (which still had certain wild characteristics) see D. Yen, 'Ban Chiang pottery and rice', *Expedition*, 24 4 (1982).

[78] Presumably these people lived in nucleated villages, and the Ban Chiang mound may indeed represent a prehistoric village with an uncertain area of at least 3.5 and possibly as much as 8 hectares. Non Nok Tha, however, might have had a more specialized function as a cemetery for several small and scattered settlements; see R. N. Wilen, *Excavations at Non Pa Kluay, North-east Thailand*, Oxford, 1989, 152–4.

archaeological disadvantage compared with more temperate environments in China and Europe. In terms of the natures of these societies it can only be emphasized that grave goods give no clear indications of the existence of ranking or stratification prior to the mid-second millennium BC, by which time bronze was in common circulation.

Meanwhile, of course, there remains the question of where the first agricultural inhabitants of northeast Thailand came from. My own preference is for the coastal regions of northern Vietnam and southern China, but Higham has recently suggested that movements inland occurred from an early centre of agricultural development, sedentism and population growth around the head of the Gulf of Thailand.[79] No agricultural sites have yet been found here which predate 2000 BC, but new reports suggest their presence a little further north near Lopburi by the late third millennium.[80] Evidence for an increase in charcoal and grass pollen from cores taken near the site of Khok Phanom Di suggests that some incipiently agricultural activities could have been practised in the region as early as the fifth millennium BC.

The huge habitation and burial mound of Khok Phanom Di[81] is one of the richest and most impressive pre-bronze sites ever excavated in Southeast Asia, although it may have a parallel in the remarkable but poorly-recorded site of Somrong Sen in Cambodia, excavated earlier this century. Khok Phanom Di is 200 metres in diameter and has almost seven metres of archaeological deposit dating between 2000 and 1400 BC. When first occupied it lay on an estuary close to a mangrove shore, perhaps with freshwater ponds where wild rice grew, but today the site is far inland as a result of a slight fall in sea level combined with alluviation resulting from inland forest clearance for agriculture. The basal of the three major excavated levels yielded 104 burials (mostly extended) in clusters, some wrapped in barkcloth and dusted with red ochre. Grave goods of this phase included shell beads and bracelets, stone adzes, and well-crafted pottery of which the finest vessels have black burnished surfaces and horizontal zones of incised decoration. The people grew or collected rice, which occurs as husk temper and impressions in pottery, used harpoons and fishhooks of bone, and ate large quantities of marine foods such as fish, shellfish, crabs and turtles.

In the middle level of Khok Phanom Di, dating presumably to early in the second millennium BC, a number of richly-provided burials made an appearance. Two women were buried under an apparent mortuary hut with a floor which was replastered forty-three times. Another woman was buried under a large pile of the clay cylinders from which pots are made, together with strings of beads—120,000 shell disc beads in total—over her chest, and lots of fine pottery vessels. Evidently she was a potter of high

[79] Archaeology, 86–7.
[80] Here with copper-casting crucibles and slag, perhaps the earliest dates for metallurgy in Thailand if the dates are correct. See V. Pigott and S. Natapintu, 'The Thailand Archaeometallurgy Project: 1984–7', paper presented to Conference on Ancient Chinese and Southeast Asian Bronze Age Cultures, Kioloa, Australia, February 1988.
[81] C. Higham et al., 'Khok Phanom Di: the results of the 1984–5 season', BIPPA, 7 (1986–7); Higham, Archaeology, 65–89; C. Higham, 'Social organisation at Khok Phanom Di, central Thailand, 2000–1500 BC', Arts Asiatiques, 44 (1989).

status. A child, perhaps a member of the same family, was buried near her with similar high-status goods. These wealthy burial assemblages could indicate that the society was perhaps ranked on a genealogical basis, and females in particular appear to have enjoyed high positions. Individual burial zones seem also to have been used by members of the same family through several generations, according to skeletal analyses. But while this picture of burgeoning Neolithic wealth could indicate an attractive source region for a gradual fissioning of population inland to the Khorat Plateau, the main problem is that the dates are simply too late in time. An independent development of rice cultivation by foragers at this latitude is certainly not impossible, but more evidence to support such a hypothesis is clearly essential.

Apart from the sites mentioned there are few other coherent Neolithic cultures known from the northern mainland of Southeast Asia. Burma, Cambodia and Laos offer few data which can be incorporated into a modern archaeological narrative. Southern Vietnam belongs to the Austronesian story, to which we will return. The long peninsula of southern Thailand and Malaysia, however, does have an intriguing and very widely spread series of Neolithic assemblages dating between about 2000 and 500 BC. These have been termed the Ban Kao culture after the site of this name in Kanchanaburi Province, and the pottery of this culture does have some similarities with that from Khok Phanom Di, which lies only about 200 kilometres to the east of Ban Kao.

The burial assemblage from Ban Kao itself dates from the middle of the second millennium BC; it comprises extended burials with a range of grave goods, including untanged stone adzes, barbed bone harpoon or spear points, shell beads and bracelets, and finely made cord-marked pottery with an unusual predilection for high pedestal or tripod supports. The habitation layers of the site have also produced many other important categories of Neolithic technology, including shouldered adzes, stone bracelets, bone fishhooks and combs, and baked clay barkcloth beaters and spindle whorls (the latter for spinning, possibly cotton thread?). One site south of Ban Kao has yielded the post-holes of a small house with a raised floor, and there is some evidence that these people may have had domesticated pigs, chicken and cattle. So far there is no direct evidence for rice, but its presence must be assumed given its importance at Khok Phanom Di.[82]

Perhaps the most remarkable point about the Ban Kao culture is its expansion southwards for 1500 kilometres into central peninsular Malaysia. Pottery of Ban Kao type has been found right down the peninsula to as far as Selangor, occasionally with other distinctive artefact types such as T-sectioned stone bracelets and stone cylindrical barkcloth beaters. The most striking type of Ban Kao vessel is a carinated cooking pot supported on cord-marked tripod legs. Complete or broken examples of such tripods have now been found at about twenty sites overall, from Ban Kao itself right down to Jenderam Hilir in Selangor, where many such tripods found during tin-mining operations have recently been radiocarbon dated to the

---

[82] For a good illustrated summary of Ban Kao see P. Sorensen, 'Agricultural civilizations', in C. Flon, ed., *The World Atlas of Archaeology*, London, 1985.

early second millennium BC.[83] At the cave of Gua Cha in Kelantan the upper layers contained extended burials with excellent pottery of Ban Kao type (but here without tripods), together with stone bracelets and adzes, shell bead necklaces and a cylindrical stone barkcloth beater. This Gua Cha assemblage dates to around 1000 BC, and intruded fairly sharply over an earlier Hoabinhian assemblage of bifacial pebble tools.[84] Another cave in Bukit Tengku Lembu, Perlis, produced similar pottery in association with a sherd believed to be Northern Black Polished Ware from India (mid to late first millennium BC), although this site was destroyed by fertilizer diggers and the exact associations of the artefacts found are unclear. Nevertheless, if all the dates[85] are taken at face value it appears that the Ban Kao culture as a whole may date from 2000 BC to the late first millennium BC.

Explanations for the Ban Kao culture in anthropological and historical terms will necessarily be rather complex, given the very high degree of anthropological and biological variation still found in the peninsula. Prior to 2000 BC the region was occupied by Hoabinhian foragers who may be considered ancestral to both the Semang Negritos and perhaps to a lesser degree the Senoi, who have a greater degree of Southern Mongoloid biological affinity than the Semang. The southward expansion of the Ban Kao culture, most probably by movement of people rather than by trade or superficial diffusion, appears to have led to three major introductions into southern Thailand and Malaysia: agriculture, Austroasiatic languages, and gene flow of Southern Mongoloid origin. The Semang have clearly at some time in their past adopted Austroasiatic languages, and the languages of both the Semang and the Senoi populations are today classified in a subgroup termed Aslian which retains distant relationships with Mon and Khmer.[86]

The ancestry of the Senoi, if this historical reconstruction is accepted, may thus be quite closely correlated with the expansion of the Ban Kao Neolithic culture. Continuity from local populations cannot be ignored, however, and skeletons from both Hoabinhian and Neolithic contexts at Gua Cha show no marked signs of any phenotypic population change across the cultural boundary. Presumably, therefore, the skeletons from

[83] Leang Sau Heng, 'A tripod pottery complex in Peninsula Malaysia', in I. C. and E. A. Glover, eds, *Southeast Asian Archaeology 1986*, Oxford, 1990; P. Bellwood, 'Cultural and biological differentiation in Peninsular Malaysia; the last 10,000 years', paper presented at 2nd International Conference on Malay Civilization, Kuala Lumpur, August 1989.

[84] For a reanalysis of the earlier results obtained from this site by G. de G. Sieveking, see Adi Haji Taha, 'The re-excavation of the rockshelter of Gua Cha, Ulu Kelantan, West Malaysia', FMJ, 30 (1985).

[85] Owing to its chronological isolation, I am not here accepting the fourth millennium BC date for pottery from the shelter of Gua Kechil in Pahang. See F. Dunn, 'Radiocarbon dating of the Malayan Neolithic' *Proceedings of the Prehistoric Society*, 32 (1966).

[86] For a good discussion of Asian linguistic prehistory, see G. Benjamin, 'Austroasiatic subgroupings and prehistory in the Malay Peninsula', in P. N. Jenner, et al., eds, *Austroasiatic Studies*, Honolulu, 1976; 'In the long term; three themes in Malayan cultural ecology', in K. Hutterer, A. T. Rambo and G. Lovelace, eds, *Cultural Values and Human Ecology in Southeast Asia*, Ann Arbor, 1985; 'Ethnohistorical perspectives on Kelantan's prehistory', in Nik Hassan Shuhaimi, ed., *Kelantan Zaman Awal*, Kota Bharu, 1987. From my own theoretical viewpoint it is quite unnecessary to postulate that Austroasiatic languages were spoken in the peninsula in Hoabinhian times, and no traces of earlier pre-Austroasiatic languages remain.

both periods at Gua Cha can be considered ancestral Senoi, although this is a remote site and one might expect the evidence for biological change to be a little sharper in more accessible and densely populated coastal regions. Whatever the exact situation, it is clear that, prior to the first arrival of Austronesian-speaking peoples in peninsular Malaysia, perhaps during the first millennium BC, the populations of the lowlands were firmly established in an agricultural mode of production.

Island Southeast Asia

The archaeological record of Neolithic societies in the islands of Southeast Asia, like that of the mainland, seems to commence increasingly later in time as one moves generally southwards. The pattern of agricultural expansion into the islands should correlate to a high degree with the pattern of expansion of the Austronesian-speaking peoples, simply because these are today the only occupants of the area, apart from some small groups of Papuan-speakers in Halmahera and the eastern part of Nusa Tenggara (especially Timor). However, the pattern of Austronesian expansion can be reconstructed formally only from linguistic and not from archaeological evidence, and the linguistic aspects of the historical narrative will be covered in the following section. The archaeological record is necessarily rather unspecific on ethnolinguistic matters, but it does give a very important record of dates, material culture and economic adaptations to equatorial latitudes.

In southern China, it will be recalled, societies with rice cultivation and highly developed Neolithic technological characteristics existed in coastal regions south of the Yangtze from about 5000 BC onwards. The plentiful evidence for rice in some of these cultures must be emphasized, as too should many features of artefact design and economy which characterize a great many Neolithic cultures in island Southeast Asia and Oceania. These include the use of a red slip to decorate pottery, bent knee-shaped adze handles, untanged or stepped stone adzes, art styles emphasizing the uses of spirals and circles, and domestication of pigs, dogs and chickens. The list can be continued with items of less widespread distribution such as the cord-marking of pottery, pottery pedestals with cut-out decorations, baked-clay spindle whorls, slate reaping knives and slate spear points, all common or present in the Neolithic cultures of southern China, Taiwan and the northern Philippines, but increasingly rare further south.[87]

I should make my opinions on the significance of southern China clear from the outset, however, since I do not wish to suggest that all Austronesian-speaking peoples of island Southeast Asia and Oceania descend from Neolithic populations in this region, both linguistically and

[87] In the Chinese context I am here referring particularly to the Hemudu, Majiabang and Liangzhu cultures of the southern Lower Yangtze region; the record further south on the Chinese coast is more attenuated. Interestingly, layer 4 at Hemudu (c. 5000 BC) has produced a pottery stove, now on display in the Zhejiang Provincial Museum, almost identical to ethnographic examples used by the Bajaus of the southern Philippines and Sabah. The Bajaus use their stoves on boats; perhaps the people of Hemudu did likewise, since the site has produced a wooden paddle and a pottery boat model.

genetically, via some kind of sealed impervious tube. It is obvious that the past 5000 years have seen much interaction between different populations throughout the whole region from China to Melanesia, and also continuous biological and cultural change on a local scale. The main significance of southern China, and one which becomes ever firmer as the archaeological record unfolds, is that it was the zone where first developed the Neolithic technological and economic 'package' which fuelled all later population expansions into mainland and island Southeast Asia. It is quite possible that no more than a few families actually moved out of this region across to Taiwan, but those that did clearly began a process which had profound long-term cultural repercussions.[88]

The Neolithic cultures of Taiwan, from which ultimately were to be derived those in the islands to the south, commenced at some uncertain time between 5000 and 3500 BC,[89] with no apparent later survival of the preceding Hoabinhian-like flaked-stone assemblages of the island. The oldest Neolithic assemblages belong to the Tapenkeng culture, and they include cord-marked pots with incised rims, untanged and stepped stone adzes, polished slate spear points and a possible stone barkcloth beater. No plant remains have yet been reported from early Tapenkeng contexts, but rice remains and impressions are known from at least two other Taiwanese sites which probably predate 2000 BC. A pollen core from Sun-Moon Lake in the mountainous centre of the island also records an increase in grass pollen, perhaps as a result of agricultural clearance, from about 2800 BC onwards. The Austronesian-speaking peoples who survive in highland Taiwan still cultivate millet, yam, taro, sugarcane and gourd, and these must all, like rice, be of considerable antiquity as cultivars.

After about 2000 BC the archaeological assemblages of Taiwan seem to have divided into two separate style zones. That of the western side of the island retained a strong Chinese affinity, but the Yuanshan culture of eastern Taiwan is of more significance for island Southeast Asia since it reveals many characteristics found in the early Neolithic assemblages of the Philippines. Cord-marking had faded away by the early Yuanshan as a method of finishing pottery surfaces, and most decorated Yuanshan vessels are either slipped in red or brown, or decorated with incised or dentate-stamped patterns. Slate reaping knives and spear points; untanged, stepped or shouldered stone adzes; stone barkcloth beaters; and spindle whorls of baked clay are also characteristic of the Yuanshan culture, which seems to occur to as far south as Batan Island, between Taiwan and Luzon. The most dramatic Yuanshan discovery, however, has occurred recently as a result of railway construction in the town of Peinan in southeast Taiwan. No less than 1025 stone cist graves for extended burials have been excavated, often under the stone-paved floors of what appear to have been houses with walls and yards constructed of slate slabs.

[88] W. Meacham, 'On the improbability of Austronesian origins in South China', AP, 26 (1988), has suggested that no early Neolithic archaeological links existed between Taiwan and the south Chinese mainland. I have published a detailed reply to this: 'A hypothesis for Austronesian origins', AP, 26 (1988).

[89] Dates for island Southeast Asian Neolithic cultures have recently been reviewed by M. Spriggs, 'The dating of the Island South East Asian Neolithic', Antiquity, 63 (1989). See also PIMA, 214.

The contents of the Peinan graves are quite astonishing. They include perforated rectangular or curved slate reaping knives, tanged or straight-based slate spear points, stone fishing-net sinkers, baked-clay spindle whorls and bracelets, and a fine range of footed and handled pottery of Yuanshan affinity with occasional incised or punctate decoration. Nephrite split earrings are also common, including the important ling-ling-o type with four circumferential projections which has a remarkable distribution from southern Thailand, through southern Vietnam, and across to the Philippines, Sarawak, Taiwan and the Guangdong region of southern China.[90] The excavators of the Peinan site[91] date the graves to between 3000 and 500 BC, although the most reliable radiocarbon determinations seem to cluster around 3000 years ago.

The southwards expansion of agricultural subsistence into the equatorial latitudes of island Southeast Asia is not as clearly traceable as it is in Taiwan or southern China. This is partly because the perhumid environmental conditions are more inimical to coherent preservation of archaeological remains, and also because the nature of the agricultural economy itself changed. Plants like rice and cotton were not initially taken beyond intermediate tropical latitudes (if current archaeological and botanical evidence can be relied upon); as a result, many important artefact types such as stone reaping knives and baked-clay spindle whorls were simply dropped from cultural inventories.[92] The same applies to stone adzes, perhaps because early systems of tuber and fruit horticulture did not require such complete land clearance as the light-demanding cereals. The result of all these changes was that from the central Philippines southwards into Indonesia and east Malaysia the Early Neolithic archaeological record consists mainly of pottery, flaked-stone tools, very rare adzes, and little else. Indeed, the firmest evidence for the spread of agricultural communities into island Southeast Asia comes from the comparative study of the Austronesian languages, rather than from the primary archaeological record.

The archaeological evidence, however, does show very clear links between Taiwan and the northern Philippines, where many sites of the third and second millennia BC have been found with red-slipped pottery which resembles that of the Yuanshan culture.[93] They include Dimolit on the eastern coast of Luzon, where the postholes of two ground-level

---

[90] Most of these objects date from the first millennium BC, although it is quite possible that some are earlier. See H. Loofs-Wissowa, 'Prehistoric and photohistoric links between the Indochinese Peninsula and the Philippines', *Journal of the Hong Kong Archaeological Society*, 9 (1980–1).

[91] Wen-Hsun Sung and Chao-Mei Lien, *An Archaeological Report on the 9th–10th Terms of the Excavation at the Peinan Site. Taiwan*, Taipei: Department of Anthropology, National Taiwan University, 1987.

[92] Spindle whorls are reported from late prehistoric contexts in Mindanao, but this seems to be about their southerly limit. A shift towards the use of barkcloth amongst early agricultural communities presumably occurred in the equatorial zone, although by the first millennium CE the backstrap loom would have been known to most populations and the growing of cotton would perhaps have been extended to regions such as Borneo, where its production occurs on a local scale today.

[93] See B. Thiel, 'Austronesian origins and expansion; the Philippines archaeological data', AP, 26 (1988).

houses were excavated, each about three square metres in size; Arku Cave in the Cagayan Valley, which has also yielded shell bracelets, baked-clay spindle whorls, and shell and stone ling-ling-o earrings; the Lal-Lo shell middens near the mouth of the Cagayan Valley; and the Andarayan site near Arku Cave, which has produced rice-husk temper in red-slipped pottery dated by the accelerator radiocarbon method to the mid-second millennium BC.[94] In general, these assemblages support a hypothesis of a Neolithic settlement of Luzon from Taiwan, by people with rice (doubtless amongst other crops), commencing perhaps in the early third millennium BC.

Beyond Luzon, a horizon of plain or red-slipped pottery (otherwise undecorated) appears to continue southwards during the late third and early second millennia BC. It can be traced with reasonable certainty in the Bagumbayan site on Masbate and the Edjek site on Negros (both central Philippines), the Leang Tuwo Mane's shelter in the Talaud Islands, the Ulu Leang shelter in southern Sulawesi (where it occurs at c. 2500 BC with a continuing Toalian industry of Maros points), and the Uai Bobo 2 shelter in eastern Timor.[95] All of these assemblages are rather limited in artefact variety compared to those of Taiwan and northern Luzon, and, as already stressed, generally lack stone adzes (many have continuing flake industries in association) or any evidence for rice cultivation or weaving. One stone adze and four of *Tridacna* shell, however, were found in a burial of the third millennium BC in Duyong Cave on Palawan Island, but unfortunately this burial had no pottery in association. Another point of some interest is that the introduction of pig into Timor about 2500 BC may have been associated with the arrival of the first pottery-using peoples, as also might the introduction of wild populations of phalangers, civet cats and macaque monkeys.[96]

The archaeological record, therefore, suggests that pottery-using peoples, circumstantially with varied agricultural economies, settled large parts of island Southeast Asia during the third millennium BC. The archaeological record alone cannot prove the existence of agriculture but, when the palynological record is considered in support, the hypothesis of an expanding agricultural population becomes convincing. This record of forest clearance and burning comes mainly from cores drilled in highland swamps in Java and Sumatra.[97] Unfortunately these regions have no archaeological records in direct association, but the results are of great

[94] See B. E. Snow et al., 'Evidence of early rice cultivation in the Philippines', *Philippine Quarterly of Culture and Society*, 14 (1986).

[95] References for all these sites will be found in PIMA, 223–30.

[96] But see also footnote 54, above; the wild species together with *Rattus exulans* (the Polynesian rat) could have been introduced by hunters and gatherers prior to the arrival of agriculture, and the available radiocarbon dates do not allow an exact resolution of the chronology. The overall result of so many new animal arrivals was the eventual extinction, by perhaps 1500 years ago, of the large native murid rodents of the island.

[97] See B. K. Maloney, 'Man's impact on the rainforest of West Malesia; the palynological record', *Journal of Biogeography*, 12 (1985); J. Flenley, 'Palynological evidence for land use changes in Southeast Asia', ibid., 15 (1988). Unfortunately, cultivated cereals, tubers and fruits do not produce pollens which are generally identifiable to species, so the pollen record can normally identify only the activities of forest clearance and burning. In addition, foragers as well as agriculturalists can burn forest, although rarely in the humid tropics.

interest nevertheless. For instance, a pollen core from Pea Sim Sim swamp near Lake Toba in northern Sumatra (1320 metres above sea level) indicates that some minor forest clearance could have started as early as 4500 BC, but the major phase, evidenced by an increase in large grass pollen, began during the first millennium BC. The Lake Padang core from central Sumatra (950 metres above sea level) indicates swamp vegetation clearance and burning by about 2000 BC, and there is evidence here for an increasing protection of the useful *Arenga* tree palm species by 2000 years ago. At Situ Gunung in western Java there is an increase of pandanus and fern spores, perhaps indicating forest clearance, at about 3000 BC.

The overall pollen record seems to suggest some intermittent forest clearance in Sumatra and Java starting during the fourth and third millennia BC, with an intensification after about 3000 years ago. Since these records are all from highland areas it may be reasonable to expect that cultivation in coastal lowlands began slightly earlier, but this remains uncertain. It is also apparent that the Pea Sim Sim dates for initial forest clearance are a little earlier than would be expected from the archaeological record alone. Given the evidence from the Malay peninsula and Indonesia generally, it seems unlikely that systematic forest clearance for agriculture would have begun in Java and Sumatra much prior to 2500 BC, but new data could change this view.[98] It is not impossible that Sumatra was settled by agricultural groups from southern Thailand or Malaysia before Austronesian settlement commenced.

The archaeological record has now been considered to the eve of bronze working on the Southeast Asian mainland, variously between 2000 and 500 BC, and to the end of a rather loosely defined 'Early Neolithic' phase in island Southeast Asia, at approximately 1500 BC. After this date in the eastern island regions, especially the Philippines, Sulawesi, Sabah and Timor, new Neolithic fashions in pottery and other artefacts developed which had links with contemporary cultures extending almost 5000 kilometres into the Pacific. Before examining these later cultural phases, however, it is necessary to clarify the record of early agricultural expansion, both on the mainland and in the islands, by considering the evidence from comparative linguistics.

THE LINGUISTIC RECORDS

As I have stated elsewhere,[99] the record from comparative linguistic research is essential for tracing the origins and subsequent histories of populations defined according to linguistic criteria. The concept of a group of people who share a common language for essential day-to-day communication is an important one, given that the main channels of trans-generational transmission of a language flow via birth and kinship. In

---

[98] For instance, Flenley ('Palynological evidence' 186) claims a decline of forest before 4800 BC from the Lake Diatas core from Sumatra, followed by forest recovery and then further disturbance at about 2500 BC.

[99] 'The Great Pacific Migration', *Yearbook of Science and the Future* (1984); 'A hypothesis for Austronesian origins', AP, 26 (1988).

small-scale societies the possession of a common language gives people one of their most important guarantees of group membership.

While a great many individual languages associated with major political units have been learnt deliberately by millions of non-native speakers (for instance, Latin, Malay, Spanish and English), these secondary learning processes cannot explain the great extents of certain major language families (as opposed to single dominant languages) across millions of square kilometres of the earth's surface. Many of these very wide distributions can best be explained as the results of demographic expansions which occurred after agriculture was first developed in different parts of the world. This explanation, of course, is unlikely to be universal for all language families, and it is clear that major language similarities can also develop through various processes of areal diffusion, as perhaps happened with the languages of the Aboriginal Australian hunters and gatherers. However, such processes are not convincing as sole explanations of the enormous and deep-seated geographical extensions of language families such as Austronesian,[1] Austroasiatic or Sino-Tibetan (Maps 2.5, 2.6).

There are two important corollaries in terms of the geographical patterning of languages which arise from this theoretical viewpoint. One is that areas where agriculture developed in a primary sense should also be areas where there is high linguisitic diversity, expressed in terms of the existence of more than one major language family. The second is that there should also be in such areas a high degree of lingusitic diversity between the individual languages within the families themselves.[2] Southern China, for instance, contains languages in four separate families (excluding Chinese), these being Austroasiatic (now confined to parts of Yunnan), Tai-Kadai, Miao-Yao, and Tibeto-Burman (a branch of the larger Sino-Tibetan family). In addition, each of these language families also has its area of greatest diversity in the general region of southern China and immediately-adjacent parts of northern Southeast Asia. The Tai languages offer an especially clear example of this, since Thai itself has expanded southwards into most of what is now Thailand within historical times.[3] The focus of Tai linguistic diversity occurs today north and east of Thailand, in Laos, northern Vietnam and southern China.

Within the Southeast Asian region there are two language families which appear to represent a primary dispersal of agricultural populations

---

[1] W. Meacham ('On the improbability', 93) has recently suggested that Austronesian languages arose by a process akin to areal diffusion from a stage of 'New Guinea-like linguistic diversity' over most of island Southeast Asia. I am unable to visualize such a process, given that very intricate patterns of linguistic diffusion via trade in New Guinea itself have certainly never had such a homogenizing effect.

[2] The reason for this is that those populations who developed agriculture first will have been able to resist linguistic assimilation, owing to their increasing population sizes, for the longest periods of time: diversity correlates to a large extent with time depth of development. It should be emphasized, however, that the concept of 'diversity' requires very careful definition: attempts by linguistics in the past to define it in terms of lexicon alone (via the technique of lexicostatistics) have not always met with convincing success. In addition, the reverse corollary to the one stated here, that areas of high linguistic diversity are necessarily areas of agricultural origin, can easily be shown to be untrue.

[3] Tai is the name of the language subgroup to which Thai, the modern national language of Thailand, belongs.

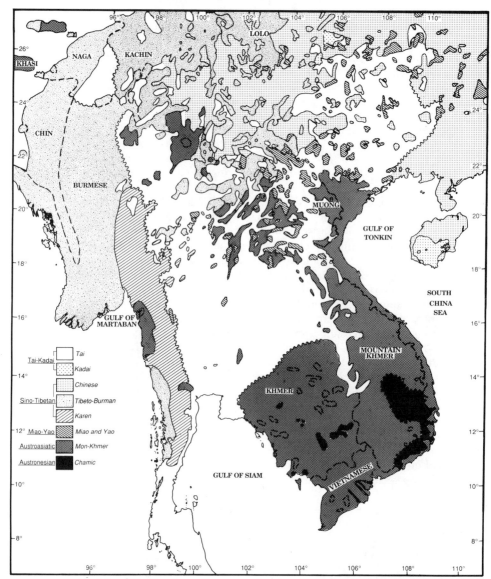

Map 2.5   Distribution of language families and major languages.

through landscapes which were mostly occupied previously only by foraging groups. These are the Austroasiatic and Austronesian families. The other two major families represented in the region, Tibeto-Burman and Tai-Kadai, undoubtedly also underwent initial expansion at the same time, but the greatest expansions of these occurred when the Burmese and Thai languages were distributed over very large areas due to historical conquests and processes of state formation within the last millennium. Khmer and Vietnamese, both members of the Austroasiatic family, also expanded historically for similar reasons, as have Malay and Javanese within the Austronesian family.

The Austroasiatic language family, the most widespread and also the most geographically fragmented in mainland Southeast Asia, includes approximately 150 languages in two major subgroups: Mon-Khmer of Southeast Asia, and Munda of Northeastern India.[4] The Mon-Khmer subgroup is the largest and contains Mon, Khmer, Vietnamese and—besides many other tribal languages—the far-flung outliers of Khasi in Assam, the Aslian languages of Malaya, and Nicobarese. The Munda languages of Bihar, Orissa and West Bengal are even more far-flung, which probably explains their divergence over time (at least four millennia?) into a separate first-order subgroup of Austroasiatic.

To date, no one has attempted to write a combined account of Austroasiatic prehistory from the linguistic and archaeological perspectives, but it is probable that many of the prehistoric sites of northeast Thailand, such as Non Nok Tha and Ban Chiang, were inhabited by speakers of Austroasiatic languages which eventually fell victim to the assimilatory tendencies of the historical Thai kingdoms after the thirteenth century CE. Another observation of great interest is that the reconstructed vocabulary of Proto-Austroasiatic suggests a knowledge of rice,[5] a circumstance in perfect accord with the Neolithic archaeology of the region from northeast India across to southern China and northern Vietnam. The possibility that Austroasiatic languages were also once spoken very widely in southern China, with linguistic traces even as far north as the Yangtze River,[6] is also worthy of note; it is quite apparent that a once-continuous distribution of Austroasiatic languages over most of mainland Southeast Asia, and even across into the Nicobars and possibly northern Sumatra, has been broken up by the historical expansions of the Chinese, Tai, Vietnamese, Burman and Austronesian (Malay and Cham) peoples.

It is not possible at this stage of research to make any sensible correlations between the Tibeto-Burman or Miao-Yao languages and the archaeological record, mainly owing to the lack of archaeology in the regions

---

[4] G. Diffloth, 'Austro-Asiatic languages', *Encyclopaedia Britannica*, 15th edn, Macropaedia, 2, 1974; 'Asian languages and Southeast Asian prehistory', FMJ, 24 (1979). See also M. Ruhlen, *A Guide to the World's Languages*, Stanford, 1987, 156. The Andamanese languages do not belong to Austroasiatic or any other major family and have presumably been evolving in isolation since far back in the Pleistocene.

[5] A. and N. Zide, 'Proto-Munda cultural vocabulary: evidence for early agriculture', in P. N. Jenner, et al., eds, *Austroasiatic Studies*, Honolulu, 1976, II. 1295–334.

[6] The word 'Yangtze' (Yangzi) itself is even of Austroasiatic origin according to J. Norman and T.-L. Mei, 'The Austroasiatics in ancient South China, some lexical evidence', *Monumenta Serica*, 32 (1976).

of concern. The Tibeto-Burman subgroup, which includes such major languages as Burmese, Chin, Naga and Kachin (with Karen belonging to a separate but co-ordinate subgroup of Sino-Tibetan), has a more north-westerly centre of gravity than Austroasiatic and may reflect for the most part a more recent record of expansion. The Miao-Yao languages of southern China are still expanding into the Golden Triangle region of northern Thailand today, and in prehistoric times were perhaps confined to north of the Chinese border. The Tai-Kadai and Austronesian groups, however, can provide much more detailed information, and the Austro-nesian languages have witnessed decades of intensive archaeological and linguistic research which gives them an interdisciplinary relevance almost equal to that of the Indo-European languages.

Let us look first at the distributions of these two language families. The Tai-Kadai (or Daic) family includes Thai itself, Lao, Shan of northern Burma, and many languages in the Guizhou and Guangxi provinces of southern China. The Kelao language of Guizhou and Li of Hainan Island form the Kadai subgroup. The distribution of this language family allows one to infer an origin zone in southeastern China; it was presumably once much more widespread there before being overlain, especially in Guang-dong province, by Chinese.

The Austronesian family is far more widespread (Map 2.6), although it has never been represented on the southern Chinese mainland. The history of the Austronesian languages reflects one of the most phenomenal records of colonization and dispersal in the history of humanity. Austro-nesian languages are now spoken in Taiwan, parts of southern Vietnam, Malaysia, the Philippines, and all of Indonesia except for the Papuan-speaking regions of Irian Jaya and parts of Timor, Alor, Pantar and Halmahera. In southern Vietnam the Austronesian Chamic languages probably replaced earlier Austroasiatic languages, and have been replaced in turn by Vietnamese expansion down the coast after the release of the latter from Chinese domination in the tenth century CE. Everywhere else in the Austronesian world (including the Pacific islands and Madagascar) the Austronesian languages show few signs of post-expansion replace-ment, mainly because they have suffered no linguistic competition from non-Austronesian languages, with the singular and important exception of the Papuan languages of western Melanesia. This region has seen very rapid rates of linguistic interdigitation and change, undoubtedly because the Papuan-speaking peoples were the only ones beyond the mainland of Asia to develop their own indigenous systems of food production and demographic resistance to later colonists.

Because of the wealth of comparative research carried out on the Austronesian languages, it is possible to draw some very sound conclu-sions, using purely linguistic evidence, concerning the region of origin of the family, the directions of its subsequent spread, and also the vocabu-laries of important early proto-languages, particularly Proto-Austronesian and its close successor Proto-Malayo-Polynesian. The Malayo-Polynesian languages do not include those of Taiwan, but incorporate the vast remaining distribution of the family from Madagascar to Easter Island.

If we commence at the earliest time, it is necessary to refer to the

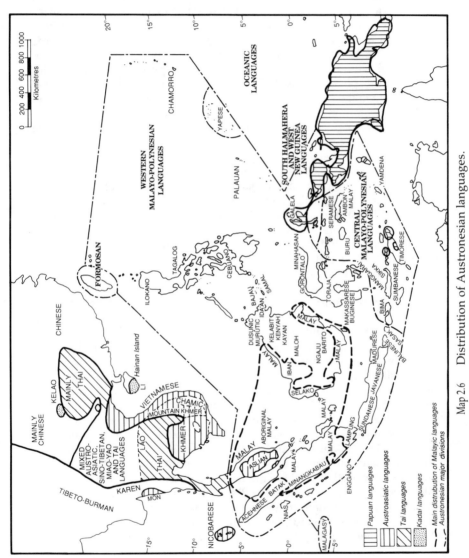

Map 2.6   Distribution of Austronesian languages.

MAINLY CHINESE

TIBETO-BURMAN

KAREN

MIXED AUSTRO-ASIATIC, SINO-TIBETAN, MIAO-YAO AND TAI LANGUAGES

MON

KELAO

MAINLY THAI

CHINESE

Hainan Island

LI

LAO

THAI

VIETNAMESE

CHAMIC

MOUNTAIN KHMER

KHMER

NICOBARESE

ASLIAN

ACEHNESE

BATAK

NIAS

MINANGKABAU

ENGGANO

MALAY

MALAGASY

ABORIGINAL MALAY

MALAY

MALAY

MALAY

LAMPUNG

MALAY

SUNDANESE

JAVANESE

MADURESE

BALINESE

SASAK

BIMA

SUMBANESE

TIMORESE

SIKA

MANGGARAI

FORMOSAN

ILOKANO

TAGALOG

CEBUANO

DUSUNIC

MURUTIC

IDA'AN

BAJAU

SAMAL

KELABIT

KENYAH

KAYAN

IBAN

MALOH

SELAKO

NGAJU

BARITO

MALAY

MALAY

MALAY

TORAJA

GORONTALO

MAKASSARESE

BUGINESE

MINAHASAN

GALELA

SERAMESE

BURU

AMBON MALAY

YAMDENA

WESTERN MALAYO-POLYNESIAN LANGUAGES

CHAMORRO

YAPESE

PALAUAN

OCEANIC LANGUAGES

SOUTH HALMAHERA AND WEST NEW GUINEA LANGUAGES

CENTRAL MALAYO-POLYNESIAN LANGUAGES

Kilometres
0   200   400   600   800   1000

20°

15°

10°

5°

0°

5°

15°

10°

5°

0°

5°

Papuan languages

Austroasiatic languages

Tai languages

Kadai languages

Main distribution of Malayic languages

Austronesian major divisions

hypothesis of P. Benedict, recently given strong support by L. R. Reid,[7] that the Tai-Kadai and Austronesian languages form a superfamily called Austro-Tai, with a common ancestral language or chain of languages (Proto-Austro-Tai) once spoken on the southern Chinese mainland. Benedict has recently attempted to include the Miao-Yao language family in Austro-Tai, and has also suggested a number of important vocabulary reconstructions for Proto-Austro-Tai, including terms for field, wet field (for rice or taro), garden, plough, rice, sugarcane, the betel nut complex, cattle, water buffalo, axe, and canoe. If Benedict is correct, and no convincing refutation has yet been presented, then one has to consider seriously the possibility that the initial expansions of these two great language families (or three with Miao-Yao) began among Neolithic rice-cultivating communities in south China. It may be no coincidence that the Austroasiatic languages also originated in the same general region. The archaeological record, of course, agrees very well with these reconstructions of linguistic dispersal, and even provides a date range between 5000 and 3000 BC; comparative studies of unwritten languages are quite unable by themselves to provide acceptable absolute dates since there is no universal rate of linguistic divergence between all pairs of languages.

Moving beyond Austro-Tai into Austronesian, the reconstruction of overall linguistic prehistory which is most acceptable today, and which fits best with all independent sources of evidence, is that favoured by R. Blust.[8] This is based on a postulated family tree of subgrouping relationships with a connected hierarchy of proto-languages extending from Proto-Austronesian forwards in time (see Figure 2.4). Reduced to its essentials, this reconstruction favours a geographical expansion beginning in Taiwan (the location of Proto-Austronesian), then encompassing the Philippines, Borneo and Sulawesi, and finally spreading in two branches, one moving west to Java, Sumatra and the Malay peninsula, the other moving east into Oceania.

A wealth of linguistic detail can, of course, be added to this rather bare framework, but I will restrict myself to some points of broad historical and cultural significance. During the linguistic stage termed Proto-Austro-Tai (c.4500 BC?) it would appear that some colonists with an agricultural economy moved across the Formosa Strait to settle in Taiwan. Here they established the Initial Austronesian languages, increased their population and occupied many regions of the island, until, after perhaps another millennium (c.3500 BC?), their linguistic descendants made the first moves into Luzon. This movement to the Philippines precipitated the break-up of the Initial Austronesian linguistic continuum in Taiwan into two major subgroups, Formosan and Malayo-Polynesian, and corresponds with the Proto-Austronesian stage of linguists.[9] The Proto-Austronesian vocabulary

---

[7] See Benedict, *Austro-Thai Language and Culture*, New Haven, 1976; G. Thurgood, 'Benedict's work: past and present', in G. Thurgood, J. A. Matisoff and D. Bradley, eds, *Linguistics of the Sino-Tibetan Area: the State of the Art*, Canberra 1985; Reid, 'Benedict's Austro-Tai hypothesis; an evaluation', *AP*, 26 (1988).

[8] 'The Austronesian homeland; a linguistic perspective', *AP*, 26 (1988). See also PIMA, 102–29.

[9] Austro-Tai likewise split into its two major 'subgroups' (now of course regarded as separate language families) of Tai-Kadai and Austronesian when populations became separated by

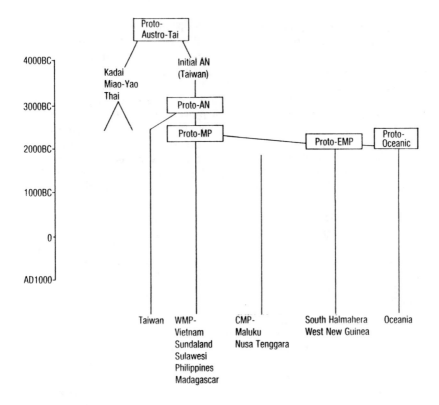

Figure 2.4   A family 'tree' (here shown inverted) for the Austronesian languages.

AN = Austronesian; MP = Malayo-Polynesian; WMP = Western Malayo-Polynesian; CMP = Central Malayo-Polynesian; EMP = Eastern Malayo-Polynesian.

indicates an economy well suited to marginal tropical latitudes, with cultivation of rice, millet, sugarcane, presence of domesticated dogs and pigs, and the use of canoes. This listing, of course, refers only to what has survived linguistically in terms of recognizable shared inheritances, and many other items recognizable in the archaeological record (such as pottery and domesticated fowls) do not have such well-documented linguistic histories.

As a result of further colonizing movements through the Philippines into Borneo, Sulawesi and Maluku, the Malayo-Polynesian subgroup eventually separated into its several constituent Western and Central-Eastern subgroups. The divergence of Central-Eastern Malayo-Polynesian commenced in Maluku or Nusa Tenggara, and this group also contains all

the Formosa Strait. Austronesian languages have never been spoken in southern China, for the simple reason that they did not begin to differentiate from Austro-Tai until after founder populations of speakers moved into isolation in Taiwan.

the Austronesian languages of the Pacific islands, apart from some in western Micronesia. The vocabulary of Proto-Malayo-Polynesian, a linguistic entity which may have been located in the general region of the lands bordering the Sulawesi Sea, is of great interest because it contains a number of tropical economic indicators which were absent in the earlier Proto-Austronesian stage. These include taro, breadfruit, banana, yam, sago and coconut, and their presence reflects the shift away from rice towards a greater dependence on tubers and fruits in equatorial latitudes.

The record of the initial expansion of the Western Malayo-Polynesian languages into Java, Sumatra and Malaya may be masked partly by the expansions of the Malayic and Javanese languages within the past fifteen hundred years. B. Nothofer believes that the oldest Austronesian settlement of this region is represented today by the languages spoken in the small islands off the west coast of Sumatra and in the northern Sumatran highlands (his Barrier Island-Batak group).[10] There is also evidence in the Aslian languages for borrowing from now-extinct Austronesian languages in the Malay peninsula.[11] Evidence from the pollen record in the Sumatran highlands (pages 105–6) could also be taken to indicate an initial expansion of Austronesian agriculturalists before 1000 BC, but this correlation can only be surmise.

Most of the major Western Malayo-Polynesian languages, however, including those of the Malayic subgroup (Malay, Minangkabau, Iban, and several other languages of Sumatra and western Borneo), together with Acehnese, Chamic, Javanese and Balinese, have been separating only since the first millennium BC or later.[12] A great deal of the expansion of Malay as a lingua franca around the coasts of Borneo and into eastern Indonesia has occurred since the seventh century with the development of major trading states such as Śrīvijaya and Melaka, and dialects of Malay now dominate almost the whole of peninsular Malaysia. This phenomenon of linguistic levelling is to be expected in a region which has witnessed a succession of major political formations at the state level, just as it has occurred in the histories of Thai and Vietnamese.

In eastern Indonesia the degree of linguistic diversity is greater than in the western regions, perhaps reflecting the lesser degree of political integration in this area in historical times. Another cause of diversity, especially close to New Guinea, has been a process of strong mutual influence between languages in the Austronesian and Papuan families; these processes have been particularly important in Melanesia itself, and have led to such rapid lexical diversification that some linguists have even claimed western Melanesia to be the homeland region of Proto-

---

[10] 'The Barrier Island languages in the Austronesian family', in P. Geraghty, L. Carrington and S. A. Wurm, eds, *Focal II: Papers from the Fourth International Conference on Austronesian Linguistics*, Canberra, 1986.

[11] G. Benjamin, 'Ethnohistorical perspectives on Kelantan's prehistory', in Nik Hassan Shuhaimi, ed., *Kelantan Zaman Awal*, Kota Bharu, 1987.

[12] Blust, 'The Austronesian homeland', 57. On the Malayic languages see the papers by Blust, Nothofer and Adelaar in M. T. Ahmad and Z. M. Zain, eds, *Rekonstruksi dan Cabang-Cabang Bahasa Melayu Induk'*, Kuala Lumpur, 1988; K. A. Adelaar, *Proto-Malayic*, Alblasserdam, Netherlands, 1985.

Austronesian.[13] This opinion, however, does not agree with the results of comparative phonological or grammatical research.

The completeness of Austronesian domination in island Southeast Asia is as striking as its inability to make any sizeable impact on the linguistic situation in the island of New Guinea. It is this domination in island Southeast Asia which makes so clear the conclusion that the archipelago cannot have supported any major agricultural population, if indeed any at all, before the period of Austronesian colonization. Even the Philippine Negritos, who have obviously been able to resist major assimilation until very recently, were converted to Austronesian speech from some unknown original languages quite early in the Austronesian sequence.[14] However, the Austronesians seem also to have borrowed a number of taboo concepts from the Negritos,[15] so the acculturation process was not entirely one-way.

The linguistic picture presented here of the origin and dispersal of the Austronesian languages clearly has some fairly convincing points of overlap with the archaeological record in its broadest sense. There is always an element of circularity in linguistic reconstruction, in that the reconstructions of proto-language vocabularies depend precisely on the shape of the family tree; if there are errors in the formulation of the latter, they will clearly affect the former. The family tree championed by most modern linguists, however, does have independent support from the Neolithic archaeological record in island Southeast Asia as it is currently understood, and this is not true for other hypotheses, such as that of an Austronesian homeland in Melanesia, or an Austronesian route of major expansion through the Malay peninsula into Indonesia. The identification of a homeland region in south China and Taiwan, however, does not mean that all worthwhile features of Austronesian prehistory evolved in this region and then spread southwards in a monolithic wave. The expansion process was highly complex, and the Austronesian lifestyle as a whole probably owes as much to the past 5000 years of adaptation and change in island Southeast Asia and the Pacific islands as it does to its original Proto-Austronesian roots.

THE EARLY METAL PHASE

Having described the evidence for the expansion of agricultural societies over much of Southeast Asia, I now examine the developments that occurred between the introduction of bronze, initially perhaps during the earlier second millennium BC in northern Thailand and Vietnam, and the spread of Indic and Chinese influences through parts of the region from about 2000 years ago. The period of gradation from prehistory into

[13] For instance, I. Dyen, 'A Lexicostatistical Classification of the Austronesian languages', International Journal of American Linguistics, Memoir 19, 1965.
[14] L. A. Reid, 'The early switch hypothesis: linguistic evidence for contact between Negritos and Austronesians', Man and Culture in Oceania, 3 (1987).
[15] R. A. Blust,'Linguistic evidence for some early Austronesian taboos', American Anthropologist, 83 (1981).

history is poorly documented in Southeast Asia, and many societies which were completely without historical records continued well into the last two thousand years in remote regions. These included not only foragers, but also metal-using agriculturalists in remote mountainous interiors. This means that no early historical 'horizon' extends right across the region, and I do not propose to adhere to a fixed termination date for prehistory in this chapter.

In the interests of simplicity I will simply refer to the late prehistoric metal-using phase across Southeast Asia as the 'Early Metal phase', a term which is intended to have no more than technological connotations. On the mainland of Southeast Asia north of the Thai-Malayan peninsula there clearly was a separate 'Bronze Age' which lasted to the coming of iron, after which bronze and iron continued in use side-by-side. In island Southeast Asia, however, bronze and iron appeared together from about 500 BC onwards. I will also describe later in this section certain Late Neolithic assemblages from the eastern regions of island Southeast Asia which are contemporary with the use of bronze on the mainland.

A number of other general observations about the Early Metal phase will be made here, before the archaeological record is considered in more detail. First, Southeast Asia had no early period when only copper was in use; bronze (an alloy of copper and tin) was present from the beginning, and although pure copper items have been identified from various times and places seem to have been rare. There is indeed no good evidence to suggest that bronze was invented independently in Southeast Asia, and a Chinese source is likely but still unproved. It must be remembered that the Yellow (Huang He) River Neolithic cultures (such as the Yangshao) were possessed of a high-temperature kiln technology for firing pottery from about 5000 BC onwards, and in recent years there have been reports of both copper and bronze industries from contexts of the third millennium BC in Gansu Province, western China.[16] However, the problem of the origin of bronze-working in eastern Asia, one which has provoked lively debate in recent years, still defies a clear solution.

The value of bronze to those societies which acquired it was not restricted simply to technological improvements. The metal also became associated with concepts of status and wealth, for obvious reasons connected with the skills, labour resources and trading connections all required for its production and ownership. Bronze, all over Southeast Asia, does appear to have had a significant correlation with the rise of ranked societies in pre-Indic times, and weapons, vessels and ornaments of the metal were probably exchanged between regional élites for purposes of alliance and intermarriage. Iron, which appeared widely after 500 BC, was clearly easier to obtain and manufacture. Yet, while not such a prized symbol of status as bronze, it did play a different but equally important role, mainly by improving the efficiency of productive labour, especially in agriculture and war. It is not surprising, therefore, that several authors

---

[16] K. C. Chang, *The Archaeology of Ancient China*, 143, 282; An Zhimin, 'Some problems concerning China's early copper and bronze artefacts', *Early China*, 8 (1982–3); Sun Shuyun and Han Rubin, 'A preliminary study of early Chinese copper and bronze artefacts', ibid., 9–10 (1983–5).

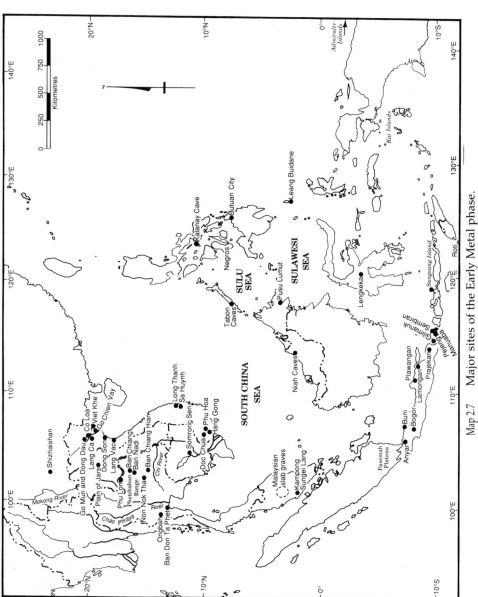

Map 2.7   Major sites of the Early Metal phase.

have correlated the arrival of iron with significant rises in the complexity
and extent of pre-Indic or pre-Chinese political integration in Thailand
and Vietnam.

Iron, like bronze, has uncertain origins in Southeast Asia. Again a
Chinese source seems most likely, albeit with the proviso that contacts
between littoral Southeast Asia and India after about 200 BC are now being
increasingly documented, and some transfer of technology from India
cannot entirely be ruled out. Although much Chinese iron was cast after
about 400 BC, it is apparent that the simpler smelting methods used in
Southeast Asia were present there, as also in India, from the early part of
the first millennium BC.[17]

With the coming of metal and the continuing increases in population
numbers and cultural complexity throughout Southeast Asia, the archaeological record necessarily becomes more detailed, especially in terms of the
categories of artefacts represented and the stylistic variations found within
them. The record is therefore more difficult to summarize briefly, and in
this final section I will concentrate on particular sites or cultures which are
relatively well understood, perhaps at the expense of complete regional
coverage.

Northern Thailand

On the Khorat Plateau of northern Thailand the agricultural societies
represented in the lower layers of Ban Chiang appear to have continued
their general lifestyle with no sharp change after the appearance of bronze,
which probably had little immediate impact on agricultural production.
The best record of such societies for the period after 1500 BC comes from
the burial and habitation mound of Ban Na Di, about twenty kilometres
southwest of Ban Chiang.[18] The lowest layer of this site dates to the late
second millennium BC, and contains bronze from the beginning. This
seems to have been brought in ready-smelted, the copper possibly from
a source such as that recently investigated at Phu Lon, near Nong Khai on
the Mekong River, where high-quality malachite ore was obtained from
excavated shafts and smelted on site during the first millennium BC.[19] The
inhabitants of Ban Na Di cast the copper and tin alloy (the tin perhaps from
northwest Thailand or Laos) using both the lost-wax technique and bivalve
moulds of baked clay or stone. Items produced included socketed axes,
spearheads, bracelets, beads, fishhooks, bells and bowls. The metal was

[17] See J. Needham, 'Iron and steel technology in East and Southeast Asia', in T. A. Wertime
and J. D. Muhly, eds, *The Coming of the Age of Iron*, New Haven, 1980. As in India and China,
many Southeast Asian iron tools or weapons were carburized by intentional heating in
charcoal followed by quenching, in order to increase the hardness and strength of the edge.

[18] C. Higham and A. Kijngam, *Prehistoric Investigations in Northeastern Thailand*, Oxford, 1984;
C. Higham, 'Prehistoric metallurgy in Southeast Asia', in R. Maddin, ed., *The Beginning of
the Use of Metals and Alloys*, Cambridge, Mass., 1988; J. Pilditch, 'The typology of the Ban Na
Di jewellery, *Proceedings of the International Conference on Thai Studies*, Canberra, 1987, II.
277–90; B. Vincent, *Prehistoric Ceramics of Northeastern Thailand*, Oxford, 1988.

[19] V. Pigott, 'Pre-industrial mineral exploitation and metal production in Thailand', *MASCA
Journal*, 3 (1986); S. Natapintu, 'Current research on ancient copper-base metallurgy in
Thailand', in Pisit Charoenwongsa and Bennet Bronson, eds, *Prehistoric Studies: the Stone and
Metal Ages in Thailand*, Bangkok. 1988.

melted in open hearth-type furnaces, probably with the assistance of bellows with clay nozzles, and poured from crucibles made of clay tempered with rice chaff. Similar chaff-tempered crucibles have been reported from other sites in both the Khorat Plateau and the Chao Phraya Basin, in the latter region with prolific evidence for copper ore preparation and casting at recently excavated sites in the Khao Wong Prachan Valley.[20]

Many burials were also found in cemetery groupings in Ban Na Di, often wrapped in mats or, in the case of one child, placed under a crocodile skin. The grave goods included bronze items, small shell beads (7850 found with one burial alone), trochus-shell bracelets, and stone bracelets with T-shaped cross-sections almost identical to specimens found in contemporary sites of the Ban Kao culture far to the south (page 100). Some of these bracelets had been deliberately cut into pieces and then reassembled with bronze wire, perhaps as their owners grew from youth into adulthood. Large numbers of unbaked clay figurines of cattle, pigs, dogs, other animals and humans were also found in the graves, together with cord-marked and painted pottery similar to that found in the Middle Period layers of Ban Chiang. A remarkable finding from contexts of the early to mid-first millennium BC at Ban Na Di is of silk impressions in the corroded surfaces of bronze items; whether the silk was made in Thailand or imported from China still remains unknown.

Iron made its first appearance in Ban Na Di at about 300 BC, as in the site of Ban Chiang Hian some 150 kilometres to the south, and probably also in Ban Chiang itself. Artefacts made of iron include neck rings, spearheads, bracelets and knives, and in the same iron-bearing layers at both Ban Chiang and Ban Na Di were found elaborately carved clay rollers similar to those found at Somrong Sen in Cambodia. While the functions of these items are disputed, I suspect they were strung as ornaments over body and clothing; other more exotic explanations include the view that they were used in systems of accounting.[21] The early iron-bearing layers in Ban Chiang have also produced the remarkable red-painted pottery with its outstanding repertoire of curvilinear designs, a style which seems to have been absent from Ban Na Di despite the geographical closeness of the two sites.

In economic terms, the pre-iron period at Ban Na Di, Ban Chiang and Ban Chiang Hian continued the Neolithic pattern, with evidence for domesticated cattle, pigs, fowl and dogs, together with the cultivation of rice in seasonally flooded fields in alluvial lowlands, perhaps bunded to encourage water retention. True canal irrigation to allow double cropping has not been suggested for this period, so only one harvest was probably taken per year, as remains the case generally today in this region. It has been suggested, however, that rice fields were perhaps used on a more

[20] According to V. Pigott ('Prehistoric copper production in Southeast Asia; new evidence from central Thailand', paper presented to the Circum-Pacific Prehistory Conference, Seattle, August 1989) the Khao Wong Prachan sites, which could date as early as the late third millennium BC, have produced copper slag and ore, crucibles, ceramic casting moulds (some for cup-shaped or conical ingots of copper), and several burials with copper artefacts.

[21] W. J. Folan and B. H. Hyde, 'The significance of the clay rollers of the Ban Chiang culture, Thailand', AP, 23 (1980).

permanent and intensive basis in the iron-using period, together with domesticated water buffaloes for trampling and possibly even plough traction (although metal ploughshares are known only from northern Vietnam). Whatever the details of agricultural change might have been, it does seem likely that more intensive production was developing during the first millennium BC in order to stabilize yields through good and bad years, and to feed the increasing populations in the fertile riverine lowlands.

In the more mountainous zones the picture may have been different from that on the alluvial plains. So far, no major signs of agricultural settlement predating the introduction of iron have been found in the Phetchabun Range west of the Khorat Plateau, despite intensive survey and excavation programmes there by three separate teams.[22] This could suggest that most agricultural settlement before about 500 BC was focused in the low-lying alluvial basins, and that the 'hill-tribe' phenomenon of mainland Southeast Asia—the expansion into high altitudes from the north of shifting agriculturalists—is a relatively recent development mainly limited to the historical period.[23]

The transition to a common use of iron in northern Thailand, or from General Period B to General Period C in the regional terminology favoured by Bayard and Higham,[24] may have witnessed a number of important social and economic changes. I have referred already to increases in the efficiency of labour and food production, and Higham has also suggested that these developments may have caused a shift from a gently ranked lineage type of social organization, evidently with a fairly elaborate network of exchange of prestige goods, to one with truly stratified classes and a ruling echelon controlling considerable amounts of wealth, labour and perhaps military force and tribute. Such a shift may be recognizable in changes in settlement sizes; while pre-iron settlements on the Khorat Plateau appear to have averaged around three hectares in size and to have been relatively independent of each other in social terms (as suggested by a marked regionality in pottery styles), those of General Period C were evidently ranked in size, with an upper echelon of 'central places' in some cases exceeding twenty hectares in size. Some of these very large settlements may have been partly encircled by 'moats', perhaps for water storage as much as defence, although none have yet been thoroughly investigated archaeologically.[25] Some degree of political aggrandizement may also have occurred during this period, with political influences from the Chi Valley of the central Khorat Plateau moving northwards to correlate with relatively sharp shifts in pottery styles at sites such as Ban Na Di and Ban Chiang.

---

[22] See D. Bayard, *The Pa Mong Archaeological Survey Programme, 1973–5*, Dunedin: Otago University Department of Anthropology, 1980; J. Penny, *The Petchabun Piedmont Survey*, University Microfilms International, 1986; S. Rutnin, 'Prehistory of Western Udon Thani and Udon region, northeast Thailand', *Proceedings of the International Conference on Thai Studies*, Canberra, 1987, III, part 2.

[23] This interpretation assumes that the site of Spirit Cave does not reflect early agricultural activities; see page 88.

[24] See footnote 67, above.

[25] Many moated sites are described from aerial photographs by E. Moore, *Moated Sites in Early North East Thailand*, Oxford, 1988.

It is worth noting also that these developments towards greater levels of political integration in northern Thailand appear to have occurred quite independently of any influences from India or China. For instance, glass and precious stone beads, fairly sure indicators of trade contact with India, do not seem to be present in Khorat Plateau sites much before 200 BC and do not become common until after 1 CE. However, it would be most unrealistic to think that the inland regions of Thailand were totally isolated from the outside world before this time. For instance, one indication of a very widespread exchange of metallurgical knowledge during the first millennium BC is provided by a number of bimetallic artefacts of both bronze and iron found in many sites across Southern and Eastern Asia. Ban Chiang has yielded two spearheads with iron blades and cast-on bronze sockets; similar bimetallic artefacts, including iron daggers with copper or bronze hilts, have also been reported from mid to late first millennium BC contexts as far apart as Mahurjhari in Madhya Pradesh, Shizhaishan and related sites in Yunnan, Gilimanuk in Bali, Prajekan in east Java and Dong-son in northern Vietnam. A bimetallic axe is even reported from a late Shang dynasty context in China. While the real meaning of these unusual artefacts in terms of trade or the diffusion of metal-working techniques is not yet clear, it does seem unlikely that they represent totally independent centres of innovation.

Northern Vietnam

Bronze working in Vietnam, as in Thailand, seems to have commenced during the early to middle second millennium BC. Items such as arrow-heads, spearheads, knives, fishhooks and socketed axes were first manu-factured in the Dong Dau phase, beginning about 1500 BC, and certain new forms such as shaft-hole sickles appeared in the Go Mun phase, after 1000 BC.[26] The site of Doc Chua in southern Vietnam has also yielded socketed axes, spearheads and sandstone bivalve moulds from layers contemporary with Dong Dau in the north. The most outstanding metal assemblages from Vietnam, however, belong to the bronze- and iron-using phase named after the major settlement excavated at Dong-son, in Thanh Hoa Province. The Dong-son repertoire with its splendid bronze drums marks the apogee of indigenous Southeast Asian metalworking achieve-ment, despite the fact that northern Vietnam itself was politically influ-enced by China from the mid-third century BC onwards, and eventually became a Chinese protectorate in 111 BC and a province of the Han empire in 43 CE.

The roots of the Dong-son metallurgical style appear to go back into the decoration on Neolithic and Early Metal phase pottery in Vietnam, and to the invention, perhaps a little before 600 BC, of the unique shape of drum which characterizes the style. These roots seem to be fundamentally Southeast Asian, although it has long been known that some of the motifs on the drums are paralleled on late Zhou bronzes of the middle Yangtze region, and some interaction with outside centres of metalworking is only

[26] Ha Van Tan, 'Nouvelles recherches'.

to be expected. The classical Dong-son bronze drum itself, however, termed the Heger type I by art historians was clearly not a form borrowed from Zhou or Han China; it seems to have been developed in either Yunnan or northern Vietnam by about 500 BC. This is a matter of some debate at present, and it appears that a recently-identified pre-Heger I type, considered the main ancestral form by some authorities,[27] might have appeared first in Yunnan. Despite this, the major centre of manufacture of the true Heger I drums seems to have been located in northern Vietnam; a divergent tradition evolved in Yunnan whereby many of the drums were modified into lidded cowrie containers and provided with three-dimensional scenes of human activities on their tops. These are amongst the most evocative and outstanding examples of bronze casting in non-Chinese East Asia, and portray scenes which include human sacrifice, horse riding, offering of allegiance to a lord, women weaving with back-strap looms, house models, and many species of animals.[28]

The cultural heart of the Dong-son world from perhaps 400 BC onwards was the Red River valley and adjacent coastal regions of Vietnam. The Heger I drums, of which more than two hundred are known from throughout Southeast Asia (apart from a total absence in Borneo, north-eastern Indonesia and the Philippines),[29] have flat tympana, bulbous upper sides and splayed feet, and were cast in one piece, complete with their decoration, by the lost-wax method. The largest are almost one metre high, and can weigh up to 100 kilograms. The decorative zones which encircle these drums are full of remarkable detail, showing friezes of birds, deer and other animals, warriors with feather headdresses, houses with raised floors, and a range of intricate running geometric patterns. The upper sides of the drums contain scenes of warriors in long boats, sometimes with a drum in a cabin or being beaten amidships. These were originally interpreted by Victor Goloubew in 1929 as boats to take the dead into the afterlife, using analogies from recent art and beliefs in south-eastern Kalimantan which he believed represented a survival of Dong-son traditions. This interpretation has recently been supported in the most recent authoritative survey of Heger I drums by Bernet Kempers,[30] but it must not be assumed that these drums were made only for funerary purposes, despite their common occurrence in burials. H. Loofs-Wissowa has recently surveyed a number of possible functions, including the possibility that they were bestowed as legitimizing 'regalia' on local chiefs

[27] Eiji Nitta, 'Pre-Heger I bronze drums from Yunnan', *Shiroku*, 18 (1985); D. Hollman and D. H. R. Spennemann, 'A note on the metallurgy of Southeast Asian kettle-drums', BIPPA, 6 (1985); M. von Dewall, 'New evidence on the ancient bronze kettle-drum of South East Asia from recent Chinese finds' in B. Allchin, ed., *South Asian Archaeology 1981*, Cambridge, UK, 1984; P. Sorensen, 'The kettledrums from the Ongbah Cave' in Sorensen, ed, *Archaeological Excavations in Thailand: Surface Finds and Minor Excavations*, London, 1988.

[28] See J. Rawson, ed., *The Chinese Bronzes of Yunnan*, London, 1983.

[29] 133 have been found in Vietnam alone according to Nguyen Duy Hinh, 'The birth of the first state in Vietnam', in Bayard, ed., *Southeast Asian Archaeology*, 185. A. J. Bernet Kempers (*The Kettledrums of Southeast Asia*, Rotterdam, 1988) mentions 55 from island Southeast Asia, and many others are known from elsewhere in Southeast Asia and southern China, especially Yunnan.

[30] *Kettledrums of Southeast Asia*.

by a religious authority in northern Indochina.[31] The distribution of these Heger I drums through the countries of Southeast Asia and right along the Sunda Chain almost to New Guinea is a truly remarkably phenomenon, to which I will return.

The manufacture of the Heger I drums, as noted above, was by the lost-wax method, most recently reviewed and described by Bernet Kempers. The wax model was evidently made around a hollow clay core, and the standardized geometric and animal decoration was impressed into the wax by using incised stone moulds, so that the designs appeared in low relief on the drum surfaces. The more detailed figurative designs, such as the houses with people and drums inside, appear to have been carved into the wax individually, and thus emerged incised rather than in relief in their final cast forms. Some of the Indonesian drums have four frogs cast in relief on their tympana, but these seem to be rather rare in mainland Southeast Asia, a circumstance which may reflect manufacture to order, to suit local tastes and preferences.

The oldest drums are generally considered to be the most naturalistic in their decoration: excellent examples include those from Ngoc Lu and Hoang Ha in northern Vietnam (Figure 2.5). In many later ones some of the standardized zonal decoration became highly schematized, and the feathered warriors broke down into almost illegible networks of lines and eye motifs. Surprisingly, however, this did not happen with the figurative scenes, which were incised in remarkable detail until the end of the tradition, as shown by the Sangeang drum from Indonesia, which may have been made as late as the third century CE. The Sangeang drum also shows figures in houses in Han Chinese and Indian (Kushan?) costumes, and one from the Kai Islands near New Guinea has an inscription in Chinese characters which also dates to about the third century CE. The significance of these historical connections, of course, is that many of the Heger I drums were made in Vietnam when it was fully a province of the Chinese empire, unless (and this has never been demonstrated) some of the later centres of Heger I manufacture moved southwards into Fu-nan or Java. Even if they did, the fact remains that many drums were still being traded in Indonesia well into the period of early Indian political and religious influence, so the Dong-son stylistic distribution cannot be considered entirely prehistoric in time.

The range of other Dong-son bronze goods, excavated from such sites as the pile-dwelling village of Dong-son itself on the lower Ma River, and more recently from burials at Viet Khe, Lang Ca and Lang Vac, includes bowls and situlae, miniature drums and bells, a range of mostly socketed tools and projectile points, bracelets, belt hooks, and some remarkable daggers with hilts cast as human figures in the round. As in Yunnan the techniques of lost-wax casting of human and other figures merit great admiration, and a clay crucible capable of holding twelve kilograms of molten bronze was found in the Lang Ca cemetery. The

---

[31] 'The distribution of Dongson drums: some thoughts', in P. Snoy, ed., *Ethnologie und Geschichte*, Wiesbaden, 1983.

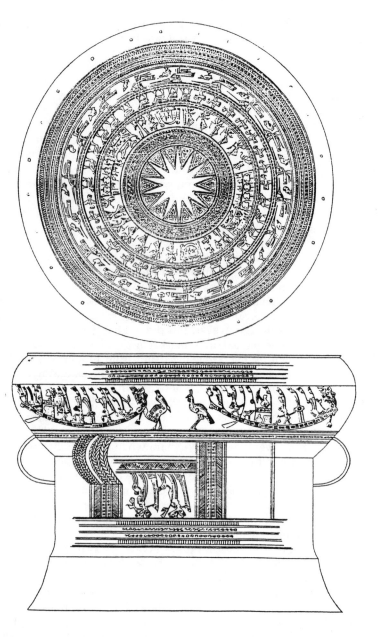

Figure 2.5   An early type of Heger I drum from Ngoc Lu, northern Vietnam.
The tympanum is decorated with concentric bands showing birds, deer,
warriors with head-dresses and perhaps loin-cloths, houses with raised floors
and saddle-shaped roofs, possible reed-ornamented shrines, pairs of people
pounding rice, and what may be raised floors with drums stored on posts
beneath. The sides show boats carrying warriors and drums.
From A. J. Bernet Kempers, *The Kettledrums of Southeast Asia*, Rotterdam, 1988, plate 11.30 a and c.

earthen-ramparted enceinte of Co Loa[32] near Hanoi, six square kilometres in extent, which was the traditional capital of the Au Lac kingdom from 257 BC, has also yielded a 72-kilogram bronze drum with over 100 socketed bronze ploughshares inside.

Iron artefacts are generally rare in northern Vietnam. The site of Dong-son has produced some spearheads, and a Chinese cast-iron hoe claimed to be associated with a radiocarbon date of about 400 BC was found at the site of Go Chien Vay. Indeed, it is quite possible that much Dong-son iron was imported from China, together with many bronze items including a Warring States sword from Viet Khe, and Han dynasty coins, a sword and mirror from Dong-son itself. The pottery from Dong-son sites also has strong parallels with the Geometric paddle-impressed pottery of this period in southern China, and constant interaction between this region and Vietnam can probably be taken for granted after about 300 BC.

The social and historical evidence for the Dong-son phase suggests, of course, the existence of a stratified society, perhaps under the rule of a single state centred on Co Loa if we are to believe traditional history. Indeed, the Au Lac kingdom of the third century BC had a traditional predecessor in the Van Lang kingdom, which may have commenced as early as the seventh century BC.[33] The burial sites themselves reveal marked stratification in the distribution of wealth; one burial at Viet Khe, for instance, included more than one hundred bronzes, and a few wealthy people seem to have been buried in coffins of lacquered wood; the Viet Khe burials are radiocarbon dated to between 550 and 350 BC. There is also evidence in Chinese records to the effect that canal-irrigated rice fields were present in northern Vietnam before 111 BC, which suggests the possibility of intensive double-cropping. In addition, a Chinese census of 2 CE records a population of almost one million people in northern Vietnam, and this in turn suggests that the population prior to the period of Chinese political control may also have been very large; large enough, perhaps, to demand some degree of centralized government.

Elsewhere on the mainland of Southeast Asia the archaeological record of the Early Metal phase is not as well known as in northern Vietnam or Thailand. For Burma and Cambodia the record is virtually blank, and while Laos has the splendid monuments of the Plain of Jars (at least those which have survived recent military activity) it appears that no systematic research has been done there since the 1930s.[34] The stone jars themselves, averaging about 1.5 metres in height, appear to have been used for burial purposes during the first few centuries CE. Heger I drums have been reported from scattered localities across Cambodia, Thailand, and down into the Malay portion of the peninsula where one, buried under a plank within a possible burial mound at Kampong Sungei Lang in Selangor, has been radiocarbon dated rather loosely to between 500 BC and 200 CE. The Malayan drums, like the Indonesian ones, have generally high lead and tin

---

[32] Details about Co Loa are regrettably few, but a plan of the site can be found in L. Bezacier, *La Viêtnam: de la Préhistoire à la Fin de L'Occupation Chinoise*, Paris, 1972, fig. 121.

[33] K. Taylor, *The Birth of Vietnam*, Berkeley, 1983.

[34] An account of the Plain of Jars can be found in my *Man's Conquest*, 195–8. For the results of recent bombing see P. T. White, 'Laos', *National Geographic*, 171, 6 (1987).

contents and seem to be relatively late in the typological sequence.

The later prehistory of peninsular Malaysia, however, as well as that of the Chamic province of southern Vietnam, belongs properly with the Early Metal phase of island Southeast Asia. To this world, the heartland of the Austronesians, we now turn.

THE LATE NEOLITHIC AND EARLY METAL PHASES IN THE AUSTRONESIAN WORLD

The late prehistoric archaeological record from the islands of Southeast Asia differs markedly from that of the northern mainland. The record in Thailand and Vietnam consists almost entirely of large settlement and burial sites which encourage debate on such matters as the rise of social complexity, the growth of settlement hierarchies and the evolution of skills in metalworking. The mainland tradition of tight settlement nucleation in a relatively dry environment with good conditions for site preservation (despite the common occurrence of leaching, bioturbation and agricultural disturbance) has clearly aided research into these questions.

In the islands, however, especially those with equatorial climates, the record has only rarely yielded coherent settlement and social evidence, despite the relatively frequent discovery and excavation of cemetery assemblages. Large, stable and nucleated settlements seem to have been rare in these latitudes in both prehistoric and historic times, and conditions for survival of a fine-grained archaeological record outside caves are poor. Perhaps because of this, interpretations of island Southeast Asian late prehistory tend to focus more on supra-settlement phenomena such as population expansion, style diffusion and trade. The history of social complexity before the Indic civilizations is basically unknown; so far none of the relevant prehistoric burial assemblages have been analysed or published in sufficient detail for many observations to be made. We are thrown back on the evidence from comparative linguistics to suggest that some Austronesian societies on the eve of Indic state formation were at least lightly ranked, especially in Java where Austronesian chiefly titles such as *ratu* or *raka* are presumed to have been retained from prehistoric times.[35]

This need not, of course, suggest that all societies of 2000 years ago in island Southeast Asia were actively developing systems of ranking. It is likely that the relatively egalitarian type of bilateral society which still exists in parts of the Philippines, Borneo and the remoter parts of Indonesia was also well represented in late prehistoric times, especially in regions of low population density. Indeed, it may be that the most intensive Indian contacts were attracted to islands such as Bali and Java precisely because they did have the highest levels of rice production, the largest populations and the greatest degrees of social stratification, just as they have had throughout much of historical time.

[35] J. Wisseman-Christie, 'Raja and Rama: the classical state in early Java', in L. Gesick, ed., *Centers, Symbols and Hierarchies*, New Haven, Yale University Southeast Asian Studies Monograph 26, 1983, 9–44.

The Late Neolithic

We now return to continue the Neolithic record in the central and eastern parts of island Southeast Asia (the record for the western part of Indonesia in this phase is still uncertain), by repeating the main points of pages 102–6. A horizon marked by the quite sudden appearance of plain or red-slipped pottery can be followed, generally during the third millennium BC, through the southern Philippines into Sulawesi and to as far as Timor. According to linguistic observations, this most probably records the expansion of speakers of Austronesian languages with agriculture through this part of the archipelago—a process which appears to have taken place fairly rapidly, perhaps covering the 3500 kilometres from Taiwan to Timor in less than one millennium. It is likely that this initial expansion was a rapid coastal process, followed by much later 'filling in' of island interiors, a process which still of course continues today.

After about 1500 BC there are hints of change, both in island Southeast Asia and in Melanesia, which was first settled by pottery-making peoples a little before this date. In my *Prehistory of the Indo-Malaysian Archipelago*, chapter 8, I have termed the phase between about 1500 and 200 BC (when metal first appeared in dated contexts in island Southeast Asia) the Late Neolithic, mainly in recognition of an apparent shift in pottery decoration towards an increasing use of geometric and curvilinear zoned incision, and away from the earlier plain or simple red-slipped styles. This shift is by no means well plotted in time and space and does not occur in all sites, but it is my opinion that the Late Neolithic phase in central and eastern island Southeast Asia was connected in some way with a very important episode of Austronesian expansion into the Pacific islands.

The pottery evidence is intriguing, with a wide range of incised, punctate and stamped styles of decoration documented after 1500 BC in the Philippines (sites in the Cagayan Valley on Luzon, Batungan Cave on Masbate, and the Tabon caves on Palawan), western Sulawesi (the Kalumpang site with its remarkable repertoire of decorated pottery), eastern Timor (several cave assemblages), and perhaps the coastal site of Lewoleba on Lomblen (Lembata) Island between Flores and Alor.[36] Kalumpang itself is not dated, but some of the pottery resembles that found in the first millennium BC levels of the Bukit Tengkorak cave site in Sabah (to be described below), and it occurs together with a range of stone adzes, a stone barkcloth beater, slate projectile points like those found commonly in Taiwan, and some possible stone reaping knives. The caves in eastern Timor have also yielded a small but interesting collection of shell and stone artefacts dating approximately from the Late Neolithic phase as here defined. These include shell one-piece fishhooks, beads and bracelet fragments, and, after 500 BC, an unusual industry of tanged stone points.

Some of the pottery and shell artefacts in the sites just listed have parallels of a generalized kind with artefacts characteristic of the Lapita cultural complex in the western Pacific. The Lapita story involved the

---

[36] For details see ibid.; I. Glover, *Archaeology in Eastern Timor*, 211; D. D. Bintarti, 'Lewoleba, sebuah situs masa presejarah di Pulau Lembata' in *Pertemuan Ilmiah Arkeologi*, ke—IV. vol. IIa, Jakarta: Pusat Penelitian Arkeologi Nasional, 1986, 73–91.

colonization of a 5000-kilometre spread of islands from the vicinity of New Guinea through to Samoa during the late second millennium BC. The islands of western Melanesia, particularly New Guinea, the Bismarck Archipelago and the Solomons, had already been settled by Melanesian populations during the Late Pleistocene, whereas the islands from Santa Cruz through to Tonga and Samoa in western Polynesia were now reached for the first time. Although no true Lapita sites have yet been found west of Papua New Guinea, there can be little doubt from linguistic and biological evidence that the makers of Lapita pottery were the ancestors of the Austronesian-speaking peoples of Melanesia and Polynesia, and thus to a major extent of island Southeast Asian derivation.

The most remarkable features of Lapita assemblages include striking dentate-stamped or incised pottery, a range of tools, body ornaments and fishhooks made of shell, and a far-flung exchange network involving obsidian from sources in the Admiralty Islands and New Britain. These features, especially the early Lapita decorated pottery, may reflect conscious innovation by a population of highly mobile colonists settling the fringes of a western Melanesia already inhabited by food producers of equal or greater population density. Perhaps the Lapita communities needed to emphasize consciously their cultural identity vis-à-vis other unrelated Melanesian populations through the use of a kind of tattoo-style decoration on their pottery, and almost certainly on their bodies as well.[37]

The immediate origins of the Lapita colonists of Melanesia clearly lay somewhere in the eastern part of island Southeast Asia, presumably amongst populations who had already abandoned the cultivation of rice under equatorial conditions and who had developed an economy based on tubers, fruits, marine resources, and the domesticated triad of pigs, dogs and fowls. Archaeologically, there are no specific regions or assemblages which can be isolated as definite ancestors for Lapita, and it is likely that the Lapita complex as a whole developed many of its most distinctive style characteristics during the actual process of expansion through the Melanesian region. Nevertheless, one recent discovery in east Malaysia has cast a clearer light on the question of Lapita relationships with island Southeast Asia, and this comes from the Bukit Tengkorak rock shelter in Sabah, northern Borneo. The shelter yielded, from a layer dated between approximately 1000 and 300 BC, sherds of red-slipped and incised pottery, shell beads and a fishhook fragment, an agate microblade industry used mainly for drilling shell and, most surprising of all, numerous flakes of obsidian from the Talasea source on New Britain in western Melanesia.[38] The finding of Talasea obsidian on Borneo doubles the extent of distribution of this commodity, which is now reported from Sabah to Fiji, a distance of 6500 kilometres. While the people of Bukit Tengkorak themselves probably had no direct involvement at all in Lapita origins, they were certainly part

[37] Most peoples of Polynesia, island Melanesia and Micronesia (and indeed most Austronesians) practised tattooing until recently, although the custom seems to have been rare amongst the Papuan-speaking populations of western Melanesia.
[38] See P. Bellwood and P. Koon, 'Lapita colonists leave boats unburned! The question of Lapita links with Island Southeast Asia', Antiquity, 63 (1989).

of the network of communities which was in touch in some way with the distant arena of colonization far to the east.

The whole Lapita saga provides one of the most exciting arenas for research in the Pacific region at present, mainly because it represents one of the fastest episodes of prehistoric human colonization on record. The rate of Neolithic colonization across Europe has recently been estimated to have occurred at an average of approximately one kilometre per annum.[39] I estimate, from current archaeological evidence, that the rate from Taiwan to Timor was possibly three kilometres per annum, allowing 1000 years for initial agricultural settlements to expand, and a phenomenal thirteen kilometres per annum from the Admiralty Islands to Tonga, allowing 300 years for settlement expansion as indicated by the Lapita radiocarbon dates. Of course, one can hardly make a direct comparison of a continental area such as Europe with an area of small islands such as Melanesia beyond New Guinea, but the figures are striking nevertheless. Finally, it is interesting to note that this very rapid rate of colonizing movement for early Polynesian-related populations in the western Pacific is supported to some extent by the results of recent genetic research.[40]

The Early Metal Phase

The remainder of the prehistoric record in southern Vietnam, peninsular Malaysia and island Southeast Asia falls into the Early Metal phase. In the last two regions it appears that copper, bronze and iron made their appearances together, between perhaps 500 and 200 BC according to dated finds from Malaya, Java, Sabah, the Philippines, Timor, and the Admiralty Islands of Melanesia.[41] The immediate source for the introduction of metalworking techniques into these southern regions is unknown, if indeed there was a single source, but the very broad distribution of Heger I drums throughout peninsular Malaysia and the Sunda Chain suggests that northern Vietnam played a large role in the dissemination of bronze-working technology. In addition, there are other items of possible Dong-son manufacture from Indonesia, of which the finest is perhaps a male statuette from Satus near Bogor in western Java which resembles the figurines on Dong-son anthropomorphic bronze dagger handles.[42]

While it is not known exactly how the tradition of bronze casting first became established in the island regions, it is clear that flourishing local industries were established in at least Java and Bali by early in the first millennium CE. These industries were responsible for the numerous 'swallow-tail' socketed bronze axes of Java, the splendid series of Pejeng style bronze drums from Java and Bali, the series of spiral-decorated bronze flasks and clapperless bells from Cambodia, peninsular Malaysia

[39] A. J. Ammerman and L. L. Cavalli-Sforza, *The Neolithic Transition and the Genetics of Populations in Europe*, Princeton, 1984.

[40] See A. Hill and S. Serjeantson, eds, *The Colonization of the Pacific: a Genetic Trail*, Oxford, 1989.

[41] For the Admiralty find see W. Ambrose, 'An early bronze artefact from Papua New Guinea', *Antiquity*, 62 (1988).

[42] PIMA, fig. 9.10.

and western Indonesia, and the flamboyant and unique ceremonial axes of Roti. The Pejeng drums, unlike the original Heger I specimens, were made in two pieces with mantles and tympana cast separately by the lost-wax method. Negatively-incised moulds such as the ones found at Manuaba in Bali were used to form the relief decoration on the wax surface, and the Manuaba stone mould pieces have a human face motif precisely like those around the side of the massive drum from Pejeng itself. During excavations by I. W. Ardika in 1989, the site of Sembiran in northeastern Bali produced a small fragment of a mould for casting a Pejeng type drum, here in association with Indian Rouletted Ware of the first two centuries CE (see page 133). In addition, villagers some years ago dug up a Pejeng-style drum in the nearby village of Pacung, which also seems to have been buried close to a horizon which has produced Rouletted Ware.[43] A local manufacture of bronze drums and other bronze artefacts in Bali from at least 2000 years ago is thus confirmed.

In terms of the introduction of ironworking techniques into island Southeast Asia we should look perhaps not to Dong-son, where evidence for local ironworking is sparse, but instead southwards to the Sa Huynh tradition of southern Vietnam. The Sa Huynh culture can circumstantially be associated with the Austronesian-speaking settlement of Vietnam from Borneo, perhaps late in the second millennium BC.[44] The Sa Huynh pottery from southern Vietnam has definite similarities with that of the Late Neolithic and Early Metal phases in the Philippines and Borneo, as stressed in many papers by W. G. Solheim II.[45] In addition, the evidence that jar burial was already in vogue in the Tabon Caves in the Philippines and in Niah Cave in Sarawak by the beginning of the first millennium BC, as well as at the Long Thanh site in Nghia Binh Province, southern Vietnam, does suggest that important cultural contacts were occurring across the South China Sea at this time. These contacts may have assisted the Chams to settle their portion of mainland Southeast Asia, and perhaps to interact on an equal basis with the previously-established Austro-asiatic-speaking inhabitants, many of whom would certainly have been fully-fledged rice agriculturalists by this time.

The Sa Huynh jar burial tradition is best known from Early Metal phase sites in southern Vietnam which presumably long postdate the period of initial Chamic expansion. They date to the period between about 600 BC and 500 CE, and probably overlap considerably with the foundation of the

---

[43] Ardika is currently writing his Ph.D. thesis at the Australian National University on these discoveries. On locally-manufactured Indonesian bronzes generally, see H. R. van Heekeren, *The Bronze-Iron Age of Indonesia*, The Hague, 1958; PIMA, 282–9. The Pacung drum is described by J. McConnell, 'Preliminary report on a newly found bronze drum from Bali, Indonesia', *Indonesia Circle*, 40 (1986). A Heger I and Pejeng-type drum were both placed vertically and base to base at the site of Lamongan in eastern Java in order to contain a child skeleton with gold beads, a bronze vessel and lots of other bronze and iron artefacts; this circumstance of course confirms a certain degree of contemporaneity for the two forms: D. D. Bintarti, 'Analisis fungsional nekara perunggu dari Lamongan, Jawa Timur', *Pertemuan Ilmiah Arkeologi ke-III*, Jakarta: Pusat Penelitian Arkeologi Nasional, 1985.

[44] According to Blust ('The Austronesian homeland', 57), the Chamic languages are most closely related to those of western Borneo. Acehnese of north Sumatra is also closely related to Chamic.

[45] For instance, 'Pottery and the Malayo-Polynesians', *Current Anthropology*, 5 (1964).

Indic state of Champa. Good examples include Sa Huynh itself, Hang Gon and Phu Hoa, all open (non-cave) jar burial sites which have produced large lidded burial jars containing fragmentary human bone (some possibly cremated), small accessory vessels with finely-executed incised and shell-edge stamped decoration, stone ling-ling-o earrings, and glass and carnelian beads which may be of Indian origin, thus confirming a proto-historical date for much of the material. The Sa Huynh sites have also produced many iron artefacts, mostly socketed tools of various kinds, but including a few bracelets, bells and small vessels of bronze. An iron sword of possible Chinese manufacture was also found at Hang Gon.[46]

The significance of the Sa Huynh tradition of southern Vietnam is thus its presumed association with an Austronesian settlement from Borneo or some nearby area, and then its secondary role in the acquisition of iron metallurgy and perhaps the transmission of this crucial aspect of technology back into island Southeast Asia. One rather puzzling observation, however, is that southern Vietnam at this time had very few significant contacts with the Dong-son world and its immediate predecessors to the north. Only two Heger I drums have ever been found in this part of the country, and the main links of Sa Huynh as far as iron metallurgy is concerned seem to have lain more to the west, with the contemporary iron-using societies of southern Thailand and Malaysia. As noted above (page 118) the origins of iron-working in Southeast Asia generally still remain something of a mystery.

The earliest iron-using societies of peninsular Malaysia are well represented in Perak, Pahang and Selangor, where a number of slab graves and other find-places have produced an unusual industry of long-necked iron tools with shaft holes for handles. There are also contemporary assemblages in western Thailand from Ongbah Cave and Ban Don Ta Phet. Both at Ongbah and at Kampong Sungei Lang in Selangor the iron industry was associated in burial contexts with the remains of Heger I drums, and Ban Don Ta Phet has produced a fine range of Indian agate and carnelian beads which appears to date from the final centuries BC, thus reinforcing the observation that much of what passes for 'Early Metal phase' in the archaeological record does, in fact, overlap well and truly with the beginnings of Indian contact.[47]

This observation is even more true for the islands of Southeast Asia, where the nebulous beginnings of 'history' occupied a labyrinthine spatial and temporal trajectory. This circumstance makes it difficult to order the record systematically; normal practice is to classify objects of Indic inspiration as 'Classical', and objects which lack such pedigree as 'prehistoric'. In reality, however, the Indic traditions were centred on courts and temples, and many peasant and tribal populations undoubtedly continued to use traditional types of artefacts for centuries after the first appearance of historical records and inscriptions. The result is that many assemblages

---

[46] See my *Man's Conquest*, 191–4, with references; also H. Fontaine and Hoang Thi Than, 'Nouvelle note sur le champ de jarres funeraires de Phu Hoa', *Bulletin de la Societé des Études Indochinoises*, 51 (1975); H. Fontaine, 'A note on the Iron Age in southern Vietnam', *Journal of the Hong Kong Archaeological Society*, 8 (1979).

[47] I. C. Glover, *Early Trade between India and South-East Asia*, Hull, 1989.

of late prehistoric appearance, even from islands such as Sumatra, Java and Bali where Indic states developed fairly rapidly, are likely to be contemporary with nearby historical civilizations.

In this final section we will pass over such problems, and examine a number of quite striking, if localized, expressions of late prehistoric and early historic cultural activity which seem to represent fully indigenous Southeast Asian traditions. These occur especially around the Sulu and Sulawesi Seas and in various places along the Sunda Chain. Many in the latter region fall under the general heading of 'megalithic cultures', a category which has lent itself to some rather bizarre hyper-diffusionist thinking in the past, but which still offers many interesting questions for interpretation.

The most famous megalithic traditions of Southeast Asia are, of course, known only from the ethnographic record. They occur in northern Sumatra (the Bataks), Nias, the Nusa Tenggara islands (especially Sumba, Flores and Timor), and parts of interior Sulawesi and Borneo.[48] Such cultures are rightly famous for the wealth of funerary and prestige ritual associated with the stone monuments which they have constructed in the recent past, and there can be no doubt that such practices in some form go back deeply into the Austronesian past in both Southeast Asia and in the Pacific islands. This is suggested by the existence of many prehistoric megalithic complexes in the region, of which the oldest seem to be the slab graves and associated house structures of south-eastern Taiwan (page 103). Most other examples belong to the Early Metal phase and, while none can be linked in any coherent way with the megalithic traditions of ethnographic times, there can be little doubt that many served similar prestige-related and funerary functions.

Perhaps the most striking Indonesian complex of prehistoric large stone monuments lies around Pageralam on the Pasemah Plateau of southern Sumatra. This includes large underground slab-lined burial chambers, some of which were once decorated on their inside surfaces with polychrome paintings of humans and buffaloes; a series of remarkable carved standing stones and boulders; and a range of more utilitarian carved stone items such as mortars and troughs. The slab-lined burial chambers contained a few glass beads and fragments of bronze and iron, and the most interesting of the carved boulders show men wearing a variety of ornaments and items of clothing, such as bracelets, anklets, necklaces, earplugs, helmets with peaks at the rear, loincloths, and tunics. Two of these carvings, the Airpurah and Batugajah reliefs, show men carrying or holding Heger I drums, a circumstance which could suggest a date for the whole complex during the early first millenium CE.

Further to the east, the slab graves of parts of Java and the unique lidded sarcophagi carved out of volcanic ash in southern Bali have also produced assemblages of both iron and bronze, together with glass and carnelian beads of kinds likely to have originated in India. The Balinese sarcophagi in particular have a very wide range of bronzes in association, and are

---

[48] For recent surveys see J. Feldman, ed., *The Eloquent Dead*, Los Angeles, 1985; J. P. Barbier and D. Newton, eds, *Islands and ancestors; indigenous styles of Southeast Asia*, New York, 1988; Janet Hoskins, 'So my name shall live', BKI, 142 (1986).

surely in themselves indicators of a complex and stratified society which, like that of contemporary Java, seems to have attracted Indian traders from perhaps as early as 2000 years ago.

Some recent and rather dramatic evidence of this has come to light in the form of sherds of Indian Rouletted Ware of the first and second centuries CE found in northwest Java (the Buni complex of sites) and at Sembiran in northeast Bali. The Buni finds include at least one complete vessel of Rouletted Ware which appears to have been retrieved, together with complete locally-manufactured vessels, from burials discovered by local villagers. The Sembiran finds come from habitation levels buried beneath more than three metres of alluvium just behind the beach on the narrow coastal plain which fringes the northeastern part of Bali. They are especially important because they have been excavated scientifically by Indonesian archaeologists under the direction of I. W. Ardika.

The artefacts recovered at Sembiran, from a presumed trading station visited by Indian as well as Indonesian vessels, include many sherds of Indian pottery of types paralleled precisely at Arikamedu, an Indo-Roman trading station near Pondicherry in south India. They include not only Rouletted Ware, but also the very distinctive Arikamedu type 10 stamped ware.[49] One sherd has three characters in Kharoshti script scratched on its surface. There are also a small fragment of blue glass which might have been intended for bead-making, a gold bead, and many small monochrome glass beads of various colours (mainly reds, greens, blues and yellows) which are presumably of Indian origin; these are still undergoing chemical investigation. In addition, the Sembiran finds are associated with the bronze drum mould fragment and perhaps also the Pejeng type drum from nearby Pacung, as described on page 130.

Although the Sembiran Indian finds are so far unique in Bali, the important burial assemblage of Gilimanuk in the western part of the island has produced a lot of very similar Early Metal phase local pottery, as well as an Indian type of gold foil funerary eye cover similar to ones also reported from Buni in northwest Java.[50] When all these finds are put together, they hint very strongly at the oldest direct evidence from Southeast Asia for the trade in spices which linked the Roman empire, India and Southeast Asia in the first centuries of our era.[51] They also give a

---

[49] For the Buni finds see M. J. Walker and S. Santoso, 'Romano-Indian rouletted pottery in Indonesia', AP, 20 (1977). The Sembiran research by I. W. Ardika (see also footnote 43) is a project currently under completion at the Australian National University. On Arikamedu and the Indo-Roman trade in general, see R. E. M. Wheeler, A. Ghosh and K. Deva, 'Arikamedu', Ancient India, 2 (1946); V. Begley, 'Arikamedu reconsidered', American Journal of Archaeology, 87 (1983); J. I. Miller, The Spice Trade of the Roman Empire, Oxford, 1969. Rouletted Ware may generally date between 150 BC and 200 CE in India. Concerning spices and timbers possibly involved in the trade, none have survived in the Sembiran excavations but Miller's investigations point to cinnamon, cloves, nutmegs, sandalwood and many other tropical tree products, all known to Roman authors of the first century CE.

[50] R. P. Soejono, 'The significance of excavations at Gilimanuk (Bali)', in R. B. Smith and W. Watson, eds, Early South East Asia: Essays in Archaeology, History and Historical Geography, London and New York, 1979.

[51] Although certain mainland Southeast Asian sites such as Chansen, Ban Don Thapet and Oc-eo have evidence for some form of Indian contact from the first century CE, Sembiran differs because of the quantity of Indian sherdage found there. This implies an actual Indian trader presence which cannot be so easily inferred from 'luxury' items such as beads or seals.

picture of flourishing Early Metal phase societies from western Java across to Bali sharing a similar range of local pottery styles, rich in iron and bronze, and having access, at least in coastal locations, to certain Indian status markers—fine pottery, glass and carnelian beads, and gold accoutrements. The evidence indicates that this was occurring perhaps 300 years before the first Sanskrit inscriptions in Indonesia, and perhaps even 600 years before the first surviving stone temples, so these societies are still essentially within prehistoric time. Their economic bases are still uncertain, although one could make an informed guess that the combination of wet-rice grown in bunded *sawahs* and the buffalo for ploughing were by now well established in both islands.[52]

Further to the east the Early Metal phase is best understood around the Sulu and Sulawesi Seas, where many assemblages dating between about 200 BC and 1000 CE have been excavated both in caves and in open sites. A distinctive feature of this region was the popularity of jar burial, usually involving the placing of secondary burials in large jars together with small and finely decorated accessory vessels, bronze and iron objects, glass and cornelian beads, shell bracelets, and (particularly in the Philippines) occasional earrings of the ling-ling-o type. Jar burials also occur quite frequently in Java and Bali, but usually in association with other primary earth burials as at the Anyar, Plawangan and Gilimanuk sites. Also worthy of mention are the impressive groups of stone burial jars and stone statues in central Sulawesi; although these are still undated, recent excavations around some of the stone jars at a site called Lengkeka in the Bada Valley have produced paddle-impressed pottery and iron fragments, thus suggesting a date in the Early Metal phase.[53]

The most important jar burial sites around the Sulawesi and Sulu Seas include the cave of Leang Buidane in the Talaud Islands, the caves of Pusu Semang Tas and Pusu Lumut in eastern Sabah, and a large number of sites in the central and southern Philippines, including Kalanay Cave on Masbate and several of the Tabon caves on Palawan. Most of these jar burial assemblages were smashed in antiquity and the bones and grave goods inextricably intermixed. It seems that most jars contained only one secondary burial, and the human remains, where studied, are always similar to those of the present Southern Mongoloid populations. Most of these sites date mainly within the first millennium CE; some have very specific kinds of Indian beads which can be traced back as far as 200 BC in the subcontinent itself; and virtually all have iron and bronze objects. Baked-clay bivalve casting moulds for axes were found in Leang Buidane and Pusu Lumut, evident signs that local casting was being carried out during this period, although perhaps using imported metal in the form of scrap or ingots.[54]

One remarkable open jar burial site at Magsuhot on Negros Island is

---

[52] For some discussion of this see N. C. van der Meer, *Sawah Cultivation in Ancient Java*, Canberra, 1979.

[53] H. Sukendar, *Laporan Penelitian Kepurbakalaan di Sulawesi Tengah*, Jakarta: Pusat Penelitian Arkeologi Nasional, 1980.

[54] For general descriptions of these sites see PIMA, 304–17; and P. Bellwood, *Archaeological Research in South-eastern Sabah*, Kota Kinabalu, 1988.

unique and deserves special mention. Three large burial jars were placed side by side in a large pit lined with broken sherds, associated with two baked-clay figurines of a woman and a calf, as well as the bones of a woman and two children. A jar weighing fifty-two kilograms was buried separately in an adjacent pit with no less than seventy small accessory vessels in association, and was connected to the ground by a tube of stacked pots, apparently to allow the pouring of libations or some kind of communication with the dead. All bone, unfortunately, seems to have dissolved in this particular jar (a common fate in open sites in the tropics), but it did contain an iron knife and some glass beads, and the pottery is generally of the first millennium CE Kalanay type characteristic of the central Philippines.[55]

Since the late prehistory of the Philippine-Sabah-Sulawesi region is best known from burials, as indeed is that of the remainder of Indonesia, little information has been recovered which can be related directly to matters of economy and food production. Such economic evidence as has been recovered is of varying reliability, and it would be less than honest to claim any clear knowledge of agricultural crops and techniques or settlement details during this period. What is clear, however, is that most of the Early Metal phase assemblages of island Southeast Asia, including those of southern Vietnam, share so many idiosyncratic features of artefact style and burial ritual that we must be seeing the results of some very frequent inter-island contact and trade, already well developed before any direct impact from the Indian, Chinese or Islamic traditions. My own expectation is that most of this contact between islands, especially in the Philippines, Borneo and eastern Indonesia during the first millennium CE, was probably following inter-island links established as much as two thousand years earlier when Lapita colonists first sailed their canoes into the western Pacific.

No chapter on prehistory is ever complete, and this one has had to leave out a large range of topics which fall on the borderline of history during the second millenium CE. Such topics, which have immediate roots in late prehistory, include the rise and expansion of the Malays and Makassarese, both of whom now have good archaeological pedigrees,[56] and the rise of trade entrepôts in the Philippines, as revealed by archaeological research on Chinese trade wares in Luzon and Cebu. Another late prehistoric find of great importance made recently is that of the remains of eight edge-pegged and sewn-plank boats of the early second millennium CE, together with evidence for local gold working at Butuan City on Mindanao.[57]

Finally, it is clear that the commencement of historical records, however important they may appear from our twentieth-century vantage point, did

---

[55] R. Tenazas, 'A progress report on the Magsuhot excavations . . .', *Philippine Quarterly of Culture and Society*, 2 (1974).

[56] On pottery associated with Malay expansion, see P. Bellwood and M. Omar, 'Trade patterns and political developments in Brunei and adjacent areas, AD 700–1500', *Brunei Museum Journal*, 4, 4 (1980). On the archaeology of the rise of the Gowa-Tallo kingdom (Makassar), see D. Bulbeck, 'Survey of open archaeological sites in South Sulawesi, 1986–7', BIPPA, 7 (1986–7).

[57] For the Philippines, see K. Hutterer, 'The evolution of Philippine lowland societies', *Mankind*, 9 (1974); J. Peralta, 'Ancient mariners of the Philippines', *Archaeology*, 33, 5 (1980).

not correlate with any sudden change in the daily lives of the vast majority of Southeast Asian people. Neither, as I have shown, are historical records alone sufficient to explain many of the deep-seated cultural, biological and linguistic characteristics which make Southeast Asia such a fascinating arena for study.

BIBLIOGRAPHIC ESSAY

Those looking for recent overviews of the prehistory of Southeast Asia will find them in two books recently published: P. Bellwood, *Prehistory of the Indo-Malaysian Archipelago*, Sydney, 1985, and C. Higham, *The Archaeology of Mainland Southeast Asia*, Cambridge, UK, 1989. Both authors have published shorter summaries in the *Journal of World Prehistory* (Bellwood, 'The prehistory of Island Southeast Asia', 1 (1987); Higham, 'The later prehistory of Mainland Southeast Asia', 3 (1989)).

Older general works, now rather outmoded but still useful, include the two books on Indonesia by H. R. van Heekeren (*The Stone Age of Indonesia*, The Hague, 1972, and *The Bronze-Iron Age of Indonesia*, The Hague, 1958). There is also the general survey by P. S. Bellwood, *Man's Conquest of the Pacific*, Auckland, 1978. Several volumes of conference papers covering many regions and topics across Southeast Asia have also been published in recent years; the most useful include R. B. Smith and W. Watson, eds, *Early South East Asia: Essays in Archaeology, History and Historical Geography*, New York, 1979; V. N. Misra and P. S. Bellwood, eds, *Recent Advances in Indo-Pacific Prehistory*, New Delhi, 1985; D. Bayard, ed., *Southeast Asian Archaeology at the XV Pacific Science Congress*, Dunedin, 1985; and K. C. Chang et al., eds, *Anthropological Studies of the Taiwan Area*, Taipei, 1989.

The most active journals devoted mainly or wholly to Southeast Asian prehistory and archaeology include *Asian Perspectives* (Hawaii), *Bulletin of the Indo-Pacific Prehistory Association* (Canberra), *Jurnal Arkeologi Malaysia* (Kuala Lumpur) and *Modern Quaternary Research in Southeast Asia* (Groningen). Other useful publications include *Amerta* and *Berita Penelitian Arkeologi* (Jakarta; both in Indonesian), *Federation Museums Journal* (Kuala Lumpur), *Journal of the Hong Kong Archaeological Society*, *Philippine Quarterly of Culture and Society* (Manila), *Sarawak Museum Journal* (Kuching) and the *SPAFA Digest* (Bangkok).

CHAPTER

3

THE EARLY KINGDOMS

The historical record for Southeast Asia begins with the arrival of Chinese soldiers and officials along the shores of the South China Sea towards the end of the third century BC. Archaeological evidence reveals the existence of many polities distributed across the terrain of Southeast Asia at that time.

VIETNAM

The one most directly encountered by record-keeping Chinese officials lay in the plain of the Hong (Red) River, in what is today northern Vietnam. Han Chinese armies conquered this area in the first century CE and, by the end of the third century, the efforts of Chinese frontier administrators and leading local clans had produced a relatively stable provincial polity, sensitive to Chinese imperial interests while at the same time representing a local system of power capable of taking initiative on behalf of its own interests when Chinese dynastic power was weak or in transition.

In the sixth century, provincial leaders renounced the overlordship of feeble Chinese dynasties, but in the early seventh century they gave no effective resistance to the arrival of Sui and Tang dynastic authority. During the seventh and eighth centuries, Tang administrators established the Protectorate of An Nam in northern Vietnam; the Protectorate was a type of frontier polity designed for remote, strategic areas inhabited by non-Chinese peoples. Establishment of the Protectorate of An Nam was accompanied by the absorption of the local ruling class into the hierarchy of imperial officialdom. So long as Tang dynastic power remained strong, the region remained relatively peaceful. But the late eighth and the ninth centuries were a time of political instability, with newly emergent local powers struggling for supremacy as partisans or opponents of an increasingly ineffective Tang rule; by the end of the ninth century, the imperial court was reduced to sending military expeditions into the region simply to maintain the integrity of the frontier.

One significant development during the Tang era was that the site of modern Hanoi became the political centre of the Vietnamese lands. The earliest-known political centres in the Hong River plain were along the northwestern and northern edge of the plain; by the seventh century,

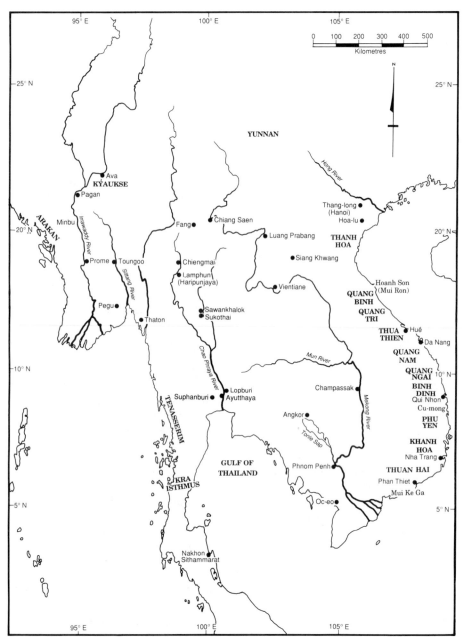

Map 3.1   Early mainland kingdoms.

the settlement of the plain had advanced to the point where Hanoi became the seat of authority. The centre of the Vietnamese polity would thereafter remain at Hanoi except during relatively brief periods of transition. Hanoi lies at the centre of the riverine network that links it to all parts of the roughly triangular-shaped plain; it is situated on the Hong River just beyond tidal influence.

In the tenth century, after the fall of Tang, efforts by ruling-class people in Vietnam to establish a monarchy failed, despite success in defeating an expedition from the Southern Han dynasty at Canton in 939. By the 960s, peasant armies led by a rustic named Dinh Bo Linh imposed a modicum of order from their headquarters at Hoa-lu, a natural redoubt among the rocky outcroppings that mark the southern edge of the Hong River plain. Early in the eleventh century, an emerging aristocratic leadership, allied with the Buddhist monkhood, moved the royal court to the site of modern Hanoi, which they named Thang-long; they proclaimed the Ly dynasty and established the realm of Dai Viet. Subsequent Chinese dynasties were unsuccessful in their efforts to enforce a lasting conquest of the Hong River plain, and the Viets emerged as custodians of the political and strategic wisdom accumulated during the previous centuries of participation in China's imperial system.

The Viet kings who ruled at Hoa-lu from the 960s until 1009 asserted their authority over all the localities inhabited by Viets and gained Chinese recognition of their regional authority. These two achievements were fundamental prerequisites for establishing a Viet polity, yet they were not enough, and Hoa-lu kingship was transitional. In the 960s, Dinh Bo Linh gained military supremacy over the plains of northern Vietnam, suppressing the claims and ambitions of several rivals; in 980–1, Le Hoan defeated a Sung Chinese expeditionary force, thereby earning Chinese acknowledgment of him as a vassal. But these were primarily military accomplishments. The extent to which they were translated into long-term diplomatic gains was due to the efforts of Buddhist monks employed by these rustic warriors of Hoa-lu.

The monks understood that the achievements of Hoa-lu were precarious because the Hoa-lu kings ruled chiefly by threat of violence, and the death of each one was followed by a war of succession. The monks made themselves indispensable to the volatile warrior-kings as learned experts capable of dealing with China and as mobilizers of labour, wealth, and popular opinion in the most populous parts of the Hong River plain, where Buddhist temples and monasteries were numerous. The monks perceived that the military achievements of Dinh Bo Linh and Le Hoan would not endure without corresponding achievements in political organization and cultural development; they further perceived that the kind of authority at Hoa-lu, limited by a warlord mentality, was incapable of moving toward these larger goals. Using their skills of persuasion, introducing their protégés into positions of influence and authority, and shaping public sentiment, the monks eventually succeeded in effecting a relatively peaceful transfer of power to a clan that was either allied with the Buddhist leaders or was simply their secular arm.

Ly Cong Uan was born in 974; raised and educated by monks as a temple orphan, he acquired a reputation as a devout Buddhist, a student of history, and a soldier. When an unpopular king died at Hoa-lu in 1009, he was commander of the palace guard. Advised and assisted by his patron, the monk Van Hanh, and by the efforts of the entire Buddhist establishment, he was proclaimed king by general acclamation and, in 1010, shifted the capital to the site of the Tang-era administrative centre, renamed Thang-long, surrounded by the temples and paddyfields of the Hong River plain.

During the nineteen years of his reign (1009–28), Ly Cong Uan (known posthumously as Ly Thai To) appears to have successively entertained three preoccupations. During the early years, he built his capital, organized the tax system, and led soldiers to the southern and northern frontiers of his realm, subduing rebels and upland tribespeople. After establishing suitable relationships with the terrestrial powers, he showed an interest in establishing proper relationships with the supernatural powers, patronizing the Buddhist religion and local cults, thereby cultivating a cultural basis for his authority. During his final years, he appears to have withdrawn from public life to meditate and to prepare for death, delegating authority to his talented sons, especially to his eldest son and designated heir, Ly Phat Ma.

There is considerable evidence that Ly Cong Uan was governed by an idea of restoring harmonious relationships between rulers and ruled, and between rulers and the supernatural powers. He criticized the Hoa-lu kings for ignoring 'the will of heaven', 'plundering and injuring' the people, and he pronounced the judgment that during the reigns of his predecessors 'all things in creation were improper'.[1] He affirmed a golden age during the Shang and Chou dynasties of antiquity, when rulers respected both heaven above and the people below, and he affirmed his intention to restore that state of affairs in his own lifetime. He was remembered as both devout in his attention to religion and merciful in his attention to the common people. He repeatedly cancelled tax debts or remitted tax due. Four of the six taxes he is recorded as having collected covered items of trade with the peoples in the upland areas (salt, rhinoceros horn, elephant tusk, aromatic wood, lumber, fruit, flowers). Lowland taxes were levied on ponds (fish and pearls), fields (rice), and mulberry trees (silk), and it appears that these taxes were collected only in the royal estates that surrounded the capital, leaving the agrarian wealth of most of the country in the hands of local powers.

Vietnamese historians remembered him as having 'made the people happy' and as having made 'far-sighted plans' for a stable dynastic institution.[2] Although he took vigorous action along the frontiers, attacking 'rebels' and establishing trading relations, he appears to have tolerated the prerogatives of local clans so long as they remained loyal; this was undoubtedly a 'happy' improvement for local clans in comparison with the rough-shod Hoa-lu régime. In preparing his son Ly Phat Ma to be his successor, he arranged for him to reside outside the gates of the capital so that he would be familiar with the common people, and sent him to lead

---

[1] Ngo, Si Lien, comp., *Dai Viet su ky toan thu*, Tokyo 1984–6, ban ky 2, 207–8.

soldiers against frontier peoples. In fact, it appears that Ly Cong Uan was not a strong personality and was very much under the influence of his mentor Van Hanh, who preceded him in death by only three years. Yet he played his assigned role with competence, and his place in history grew with the fortunes of the dynasty of which he became the founder.

Ly Phat Ma (posthumously known as Ly Thai Tong, r. 1028–54) was born in the year 1000 and had been carefully groomed to be a king. Many omens and portents are associated with his birth and youth, suggesting that, far from being simply an heir of his father, he had a destiny of his own. His achievement was to institutionalize Ly dynastic power, and he is accordingly understood as the greatest of the Ly kings and as one of the greatest kings in all Vietnamese history. A study of his 26-year reign is, among other things, a study of a complex and intelligent mind in the process of growth. More than any other ruler in early Vietnam, Ly Phat Ma is revealed in the sources as a living personality interacting with his advisers in a dynamic relationship of mutual stimulation. While Ly Cong Uan had proclaimed but one reign title during the years of his rule, Ly Phat Ma successively proclaimed six reign titles, each representing a phase in his intellectual growth and a corresponding style of leadership.

During the first five years of his reign, Phat Ma was relatively dependent upon advisers inherited from his father. He watched his father's officers put down an uprising by two of his brothers contesting his accession, and led an expedition against a third rebellious brother at Hoa-lu. After his succession was assured, he supervised court appointments, a reorganization of the palace guard, and a reform of the monkhood, these being three of the four main hierarchies at the capital; the fourth hierarchy was that of the palace women. In addition to attending to the ceremonial duties of kingship, he also led soldiers to pacify the southern and northern borders. He ably maintained his patrimony but did not show much of his own mind.

In 1034, Phat Ma changed his reign title in response to 'auspicious omens'[3] and for the next five years revealed a personalized style of authority that at times astonished and offended his officials. He insisted that his officers address him in a more exalted form. He ignored convention and promoted a favourite concubine to royal status, thereby provoking a rebellion, which he crushed. He reorganized administration on the borders and built ocean-going junks. He apparently attempted to reform the system of justice and prisons at Thang-long by placing it under the protection of the cult of a tenth-century hero. He ignored the objections of his advisers and insisted on personally conducting the spring ploughing ceremony. He captured the leaders of a rebellious clan in the northern mountains and publicly executed them at Thang-long, publishing an edict full of self-righteous pride and indignation. When, in 1039, his advisers requested that the reign title be changed, he argued heatedly with them, ordered them to cease the discussion, and acquiesced only after they had 'obstinately' insisted.[4] During these years, Phat Ma was running ahead

[2] ibid., ban ky 1, 188–9, and ban ky 2, 207.
[3] ibid, ban ky 2, 224.
[4] ibid., 228.

of his officials, exploring his own capacity for initiative, and refusing passively to accept their advice.

The argument of 1039, according to what survives in the sources, was about whether good government was the result of personal leadership or the observance of proper procedure. Phat Ma insisted that good government depended upon his own efforts as king, and resisted what he saw as a move by his officials to appropriate some of the initiative he had won in recent years. For their part, the officials were apparently simply endeavouring to take up the slack between their ruler's vigorous personality and the ramshackle administration with which he was trying to rule. Their argument over changing the reign title was their way of gaining Phat Ma's attention. Phat Ma's strong personal leadership had advanced beyond his court's institutional capability to follow. His advisers saw this sooner than he did. They did not want to restrain him so much as to increase the institutional efficiency of the government in order that it would support his vigorous style rather than fall apart under the rude tugs of his breakneck pace.

Phat Ma apparently came to understand his officials' point of view, and there followed a period of institution building, of concern with law and organization. The system of justice and prisons in Thang-long was reorganized along more practical lines, in contrast to the earlier attempt to improve it by appealing to the cult of a deceased hero. The hierarchy of palace women was reorganized, provoking an unsuccessful uprising, and was probably an effort to reduce influence from the clans of these women; palace women, except for those born into the royal family, were both tokens and facilitators of the relationships existing between their families and royal authority. An assembly of monks was convened after a period of lavish royal acts of Buddhist piety, apparently as a way of bringing the monkhood into a more explicit collaborative role with the court. The most distinctive endeavour of this era, however, resulted in the publication of the Minh-dao ('clear way') law book in 1042.

According to the edict announcing the new law book, the old laws, almost certainly of Tang origin or inspiration, were oppressive and fostered injustice. The new laws were written by officials charged by Phat Ma to 'deliberate about what was suitable to the contemporary age'.[5] The Minh-dao law book has not survived, but nine edicts dated within a few months of its publication have survived and may suggest some of the problems addressed by it. Most of these edicts are aimed at increasing the throne's control over the human and material resources of the state. They concern military discipline, the annual oath of loyalty to the king required of all officials and soldiers, theft of livestock from royal estates, the unlawful selling of taxpaying males into slavery, corrupt tax collectors, famine relief, the rights of ruling-class men to protect their women, and a definition of pardonable and unpardonable crimes, the latter being offences against royal authority.

The Minh-dao reign period, although short (1042–4), was significant because, at this time, Phat Ma's unusual ability as a leader was joined with

[5] ibid., 231.

a supportive and responsive institutional framework. His officials no longer stood back in astonishment as they had in earlier years. Now they were harnessed to his vigorous style of leadership by a more rationalized and disciplined scheme of government. Phat Ma and his advisers had translated his outstanding personal energy into a more energetic government at all levels of administration. An institutional foundation was raised capable of bearing the strains of a strong hand. An episode attributed to the year 1043 has Phat Ma visiting a ruined temple and causing a sagging pillar to straighten by mere thought; court officials subsequently 'composed a rhyming narrative to publish this extraordinary supernatural event'.[6] A few months later, amidst preparations for war, Phat Ma's battle shield moved of its own accord as it hung in a public hall; his officials advised him that this was 'a sign that divine beings have secretly united all classes of things to respond to your will'.[7] These stories suggest that Phat Ma had not stopped doing astonishing things, but rather that his officials had stopped being astonished by them.

The main activity of the Minh-dao era, made possible by the recently achieved institutional capabilities, was preparation for a seaborne expedition 950 kilometres south to the city of the Cham king, whose punishment was thought by Phat Ma to be necessary for the proper exercise of his authority along the southern coasts. Ships were built, soldiers trained, weapons put in readiness, rice stockpiled, coins minted, rebels chastised.

The expedition to Champa in 1044, led personally by Phat Ma, was a great success. Phat Ma returned laden with plunder, inaugurating a period of general well-being and prosperous ease. Taxes were reduced, foreign merchants were accommodated, markets were opened in the mountains.

A new reign period was proclaimed in 1049, marking a decline in Phat Ma's personal vigour and a new reliance on ceremonial formalities. This coincided with the rebellion of a vassal on the northern frontier and the uncovering of a conspiracy at court. These events appear to have turned Phat Ma's thoughts toward his own mortality and the fact that, no matter how great his achievements had been, he could not live forever, nor could he find permanent solutions to all the problems of government. He began to take personal comfort in religion, dreaming of the Bodhisattva Avalokitesvara and having the 'One-Pillar Temple' (Chua Mot Cot) built with elaborate gardens and fishponds. His final years were occupied with promoting and bestowing gifts upon meritorious officials, putting his family affairs in order, and, finally, a few months before his death in 1054, handing authority to his 31-year-old son Ly Nhat Ton.

Ly Phat Ma established the Ly dynasty upon an institutional foundation that endured for more than a century. All later Ly kings stood in his shadow. His personal style of leadership embodied a new independence from the constraints imposed by the anarchy and disunity that were revealed in the tenth century with the breakdown of the Tang heritage of government. Phat Ma's son and heir, Ly Nhat Ton, was the first Vietnamese king of the post-Tang era to enjoy an uneventful succession, a

[6] ibid., 232.
[7] ibid., 233.

clear indication that Phat Ma had firmly established a dynastic institution.

Ly Nhat Ton (posthumously known as Ly Thanh Tong, r. 1054–72) was a competent steward of his father's achievements, which he endeavoured to re-enact, but he did not advance beyond them. He further institutionalized and formalized the power gathered by Phat Ma, but tended to rest securely upon it, finding few opportunities to exercise initiative. Yet, benefiting from what his father had done, he entertained a grander conception of his power than any previous king. Surviving evidence does not afford a well-rounded view of his personality, as it appears to do for his father. His lavish building projects were criticized as wasteful and oppressive by later historians, who nonetheless praised his compassionate attitude toward the common people. What is clear from the sources is that he was a sophisti-cated and cultured man who was at once a scholar and a judge, a musician and a warrior, a devout Buddhist and a ruthless dynast. Furthermore, his imperial pretensions and fearless approach to the northern border attract-ed the concerned attention of the Sung court of China.

Chinese sources identify Ly Nhat Ton as the Viet king that dared to claim imperial status, which for the Chinese was a direct challenge to their view of the world. This Chinese perception may simply be a piece of historiographical debris from the Sino-Vietnamese war of the 1070s, a formula for justifying a later decision to send soldiers against Dai Viet. But even if this be so, there is corroborating evidence from the Vietnamese side that Ly Nhat Ton adopted many of the formalities of China's imperial court, from the official name of the realm, to the attire of his officials, to the ranks and titles conferred upon officials, upon members of the royal family, and upon the royal ancestors. It appears that it was Ly Nhat Ton who first conferred upon Ly Cong Uan and Ly Phat Ma posthumous titles derived from Chinese dynastic usage. But aside from these academic particulars, it was during the reign of Ly Nhat Ton that the Sino-Vietnamese border became the scene of confrontation.

During the reign of Ly Cong Uan, a buffer zone inhabited by upland tribespeople separated the lands under Thang-long's effective control and Sung border jurisdictions. Ly Phat Ma extended his power over this buffer zone through military conquest and marriage alliance with local chieftains, bringing Thang-long's power face to face with Sung's border outposts. The Sung court took a relatively passive attitude toward Phat Ma's success in eliminating the buffer of local chieftains, for it was then more concerned with Sung's northern frontier and did not want to provoke trouble in the south. But some Sung border officials took a more positive attitude and agitated for military action against Thang-long while secretly training local military units and sheltering refugees, including army deserters, from the Viet side of the border. The seeming contradiction between the benign pronouncements of the Sung court and the devious policy of some Sung border officials provoked Ly Nhat Ton to launch a punitive attack across the border in 1059, declaring his 'hate' for 'Sung's untrustworthiness'.[8] After a year or so of attacks and counter-attacks, in which the local Sung officials fared poorly, a parley between Sung and Vietnamese envoys

[8] ibid., ban ky 3, 242.

produced a temporary calm as some activist Sung officials were dismissed and the Sung court officially accepted Thang-long's explanation of events. But new incidents soon occurred, and Sung border officials went so far as to conspire with Champa to put pressure on Thang-long. However, official Sung policy remained opposed to any provocative action in the south. Consequently, during the 1060s, Sung border officials were divided in their opinions: some conspired to engineer a military expedition against Thang-long, while others denounced these efforts as foolhardy. Meanwhile, Nhat Ton allowed his subordinates to maintain pressure on the border and seems not to have understood the inherent danger in Sino-Vietnamese relations. This volatile border situation would not explode until after Ly Nhat Ton's death; he seems not to have given it much thought as his attention was focused elsewhere.

Ly Nhat Ton's chief preoccupation during the first twelve years of his reign was to father a son. Year after year, he orchestrated prayer recitations at shrines and temples throughout the land in quest of an heir. Finally, in 1066, a son, Ly Can Duc, was born to a concubine of commoner origin, the Lady Y-lan. This event was the watershed of Nhat Ton's reign. Before this, he was essentially waiting, seemingly constrained by the fear of dying without issue. With the birth of Ly Can Duc, he sprang into action, and the remaining six years of his life were an echo of his father's vigorous style. He decided to re-enact the crowning achievement of his father, the expedition to Champa. Both tactically and psychologically, Nhat Ton's 1069 expedition to Champa was a duplication of Phat Ma's expedition of 1044. The ritual of preparation, the omens, the itinerary were virtually identical to those recorded for Phat Ma. One difference was that while the Cham King was killed in 1044, his life was spared in 1069. Phat Ma had been asserting Thang-long's power and no quarter was given; Nhat Ton was simply reaffirming Thang-long's power and there was space to extend mercy to a defeated king.

Behind these expeditions to Champa lay a contest for maritime pre-eminence in the South China Sea. Thang-long was quick to perceive the importance of sea power and of dominating the southern coasts. Although agriculture defined power, trade adorned it, and Vietnamese chronicles record eleventh-century contacts with merchants from other parts of Southeast Asia, in particular Java. Ly Nhat Ton paid an enormous sum to a Javanese merchant for a pearl that 'glowed in the dark'.[9] Champa was in a position to block the access of Thang-long to the markets of the south seas and apparently attempted to do so. The Vietnamese took to the sea with alacrity and did not shrink from the rigour of long-distance military expeditions.

The reigns of Ly Cong Uan, Ly Phat Ma, and Ly Nhat Ton comprise a distinct era not only in the development of Vietnamese political organization but also in the development of Vietnamese culture and intellectual life. These kings mobilized the material resources available to them in ways that are not entirely clear from the sources. Their highly personalized style of rule was reinforced from the 1040s by a rudimentary dynastic

[9] ibid., 244.

FROM PREHISTORY TO c. 1500

institution, which appears to have been a court-based command hierarchy for governing royal estates, managing soldiers, and administering the frontiers where the soldiers were assigned; royal authority over regional Vietnamese leaders appears to have been based on mutual consent, reinforced with the threat of punitive action. Oaths of loyalty were sworn annually to the king, and all the kings held elaborate birthday celebrations to feast and reward the important people in their realm. Perhaps as important as threats, oaths, and rewards was the development of a common Vietnamese cultural point of view, a process in which the first three Ly kings played large roles.

Each of these kings took an interest in local spirit cults and was keen to bring them under the umbrellas of royal patronage and the Buddhist religion. They cultivated an image of themselves as men of virtue capable of interceding with supernatural powers on behalf of their followers. Furthermore, the virtue of these kings was understood as a positive force arousing supernatural powers to bring prosperity and martial success to the kingdom. After centuries of Chinese dynastic overlordship, this was a time of self-discovery when local traditions were assembled to form a common Vietnamese tradition associated with the Ly dynastic achievement. The process of exploring the limits of Vietnamese cultural sensibilities reveals a confident, self-absorbed attitude that was matched by expanding military power. This era of formulating a royal definition of what it meant to be Vietnamese came to an end in the 1070s with a serious military encounter with China and the awareness of limits imposed by this encounter.

When Ly Nhat Ton died in 1072, new policies at the Sung Chinese court were being initiated by Wang An-shih, an activist who promoted like-minded officials throughout the Sung bureaucracy and disdained traditional policies as 'passive'. Although his leadership provoked resistance and severe factional conflict, he was trusted by the emperor. He had endorsed aggressive policies formulated by activist officials on China's western border and elsewhere to 'nibble away' the power of upland tribal chieftains; these policies had been successful. He apparently perceived the Vietnamese border as a similar case, and so endorsed preparations for military operations by activist officials there.[10]

Ly Can Duc was enthroned in 1072 at the age of six, a clear indication that the dynastic concept had been effectively institutionalized. As Sung military preparations progressed on the border, the Vietnamese military commander, Ly Thuong Kiet, decided to make a pre-emptive strike; in 1075, he launched a surprise attack on Sung border provinces by both land and sea. The Sung fleet, several cities, and accumulated military supplies were destroyed by the Vietnamese before they withdrew. The Vietnamese were aware of the factional conflict in China, and left placards designed to appeal to Wang An-shih's enemies in the Sung bureaucracy.

Wang An-shih, surprised and angry, was stung into hastily organizing a punitive expedition against Thang-long, brushing aside cautionary admonitions advanced by his bureaucratic rivals. The Sung expedition of 1076–7,

---

[10] Kawahara Masahiro, 'Richō to Sō tono kankei (1009–1225)' [Relations between the Lý dynasty and the Sung], in Yamamoto Tatsurō, ed., *Betonamu Chūgoku kankeishi* [A history of international relations between Vietnam and China], Tokyo, 1975.

unlike Chinese campaigns before the tenth century, was led by officers on a short bureaucratic leash without sufficient preparation or the authority to take initiative. The Sung fleet failed to penetrate Vietnamese waters; the army was stalled at a river several miles northeast of Thang-long and withdrew after three months of fighting. After a few years of negotiations, Sung and Vietnamese officials agreed upon a common border, which has remained essentially unchanged to the present day.

This war forced the Chinese to recognize Thang-long as a special type of vassal that could not be 'nibbled away'; it forced the Vietnamese to recognize China as a power best left unprovoked. The border, clearly drawn across the terrain and understood by the Vietnamese as both a limitation and a protection, was an unusual feature of organizing political space in Southeast Asia, where traditional borders were never so firmly fixed. An awareness of this border, the importance of defending it and of maintaining relations with the power beyond it, became a large part of Vietnamese cultural consciousness from this time.

Without the personal authority of an adult king, Vietnamese leaders, at the height of the war crisis during the years 1075–7, legitimized court appointments by a series of 'examinations' to select suitable men from among those who could read and write; these examinations appear to have been a ritual of appointment in a time of emergency, and there is no further evidence of them after the 1080s. The leaders of the court at this time, Ly Dao Thanh (d. 1081), an official who had first risen to prominence under Ly Phat Ma, and his protégé Le Van Thinh, responded to Ly Can Duc's minority by trying to formalize the dynastic institution. Eventually, however, Ly Can Duc cut short this trend, banishing Le Van Thinh in 1096 and reaffirming the personalized style of leadership that was expected of Ly kings.

Ly Can Duc reigned until his death in 1127. He was childless, and, during the last years of his life, the maternal clan of his designated heir, a nephew, gained ascendancy at court. Thereafter, the Ly kings were simply figureheads for their mothers' clansmen and custodians of the cultural synthesis achieved by the early Ly kings. At this time, Vietnamese sources emphasize the role of loyal ministers rather than virtuous kings. In the twelfth century, Thang-long successfully resisted Khmer invasions in the south and promoted its status at the Southern Sung court of China. But internally, the Ly dynastic consensus that depended upon the strong personal leadership of kings faded into a series of confrontations between the maternal clans of potential kings, who controlled different regions of the realm. By the beginning of the thirteenth century, Dai Viet was in a state of chronic civil war.

The Ly dynasty made three major contributions to traditional Vietnamese culture. First, Buddhism was affirmed as the measure of civilized behaviour for both kings and subjects. Second, a pantheon of indigenous 'Vietnamese' spirits was identified as guardians of royal power. Third, a Vietnamized version of Chinese political theory was developed to affirm that Thang-long was the seat of a 'southern emperor' who ruled the 'southern kingdom' by heavenly mandate; the mandate of the 'northern emperor' of China extended only to the border, and the border was under the protection of 'Heaven' and the supernatural powers of the land.[11] The tributary relationship with China was nurtured as the only alternative to confrontation and war.

The Tran clan eventually succeeded in subduing all their enemies and proclaiming a new dynasty in 1225. This clan was from the coast of the Hong River plain, and an important element in their military success was their naval power, which enabled them to dominate the riverine channels of the plain. The architect of the Tran dynasty was Tran Thu Do. Although he never took the throne, he dominated the Tran clan during the period of its establishment as a dynasty. He endeavoured to remedy the weaknesses of the Ly political system that had allowed the Tran to seize power, and he achieved an unprecedented degree of centralized control over the royal clan, the court and administration, and the economy.

To avoid the danger of maternal clans intruding with their ambitions into the court, the Tran kings were to take queens only from the Tran clan; for four generations, Tran kings made queens of their cousins or, in one case, a half-sister. To avoid the dangers of a royal minority or a succession dispute, Tran kings abdicated the throne to their chosen adult heirs upon the death of their predecessors, thereafter ruling as 'senior' kings. At the peak of Tran power, kings made decisions in consultation with their uncles, brothers, and cousins, thereby fostering solidarity within the royal clan. The Tran dynasty eventually began to collapse when these rules were no longer observed.

To break the power of regional clans, Tran clan members were made lords of strategic areas, and a trend of royal estates growing at the expense of local powers in the Hong River plain gave the Tran control of a higher percentage of the rice surplus than had been available to the Ly. The Tran were so successful in eliminating potential rivals in the Hong River plain that, when dynastic power began to fade in the late fourteenth century, it was a clan from the Ma River plain, further south, that stepped forward to claim the throne.

In the 1230s, the Tran began using an examination system to recruit officials to staff a larger, more disciplined, adminstrative service than had existed under the Ly. The examination system was inevitably modelled upon Chinese precedents, and aspiring candidates prepared themselves by studying the classics, histories, and literature of China. Although the Tran were devout Buddhists and espoused their version of the Ly cultural achievement, from this time there began to appear a small but articulate class of literati, drawn from an emerging class of wealthy landowners, who cultivated an image of learning, loyalty, and competence derived from their classical, Confucian, education. When the royal clan faltered in the fourteenth century, this class strove to maintain order and eventually emerged in the fifteenth century as spokesmen for royal authority, definers of public morality, and guardians of the court.

The kind of centralizing policies pursued by Tran Thu Do became an asset to the generation of Tran clan leaders that followed him when Thang-long was challenged by military encounters with Mongol-Yuan forces.

---

[11] Ngo Si Lien, ban ky 3, 249.

Mongol forces conquered Yunnan in the mid-1250s and attempted to enter Dai Viet to encircle Southern Sung. The Tran resisted during the dry season of 1257–8 and forced Mongol forces to retire to Yunnan. After Khubilai Khan conquered Southern Sung in the late 1270s, he sent envoys to Thang-long demanding submission. The Vietnamese resisted this demand. At this time, the Tran king commissioned a history to be written demonstrating that he had inherited an imperial status equivalent to the Chinese emperor and was therefore not obligated to submit to the conqueror of the Chinese emperor.[12] The Tran court was also interested in the pantheon of Vietnamese spirits thought capable of turning their supernatural power against invaders, and when hostilities ceased in the late 1280s these spirits were recognized with imperial appointments.

When Mongol-Yuan forces flooded into Dai Viet in 1284 from four directions, the Tran were ably led by a group of princes, the most prominent being Tran Quoc Tuan (also known as Tran Hung Dao). After six months of fighting, during which Thang-long was abandoned to the invaders, a series of battles was fought along the lower Hong River in which the Vietnamese prevented a link-up between a Mongol army that had landed in Champa and marched north and the Mongol forces that had arrived directly from China. In the last of these encounters, the southern Mongol army was destroyed and its commander killed. The Mongol forces subsequently withdrew. In 1287–8, a final Mongol-Yuan invasion was defeated after Vietnamese naval forces seized the Mongol supply fleet. Mongol forces were trapped when they attempted to withdraw, and suffered defeats in battles that entered Vietnamese lore.

In the generations following the Mongol wars, the Tran clan gradually lost its taste for leadership. There is evidence of social unrest in the fourteenth century that is not yet well understood; a series of rebellions broke out, beginning in the 1340s. Tran Minh Tong, who ruled from the 1320s until his death in 1357, married a Tran kinswoman, but also had sons by two women of the Ho clan, the leader of which, Ho Quy Ly, thereby began to insinuate himself into the court. Tran Minh Tong's successor, reputedly decadent and incompetent, had no children and failed to abdicate in favour of a designated heir. Upon his death in 1369, a succession dispute resulted in the royal kinsmen of Ho Quy Ly gaining control of the throne. The ensuing two decades formed a time of acute crisis as the Chams, led by one of their most remarkable kings, known to the Vietnamese as Che Bong Nga, repeatedly ravaged the kingdom and sacked Thang-long. Not until the 1390s, after the death of Che Bong Nga, was Ho Quy Ly able to restore order.

Ho Quy Ly presided over the collapse of the aristocratic Buddhist world of the Ly and Tran dynasties and the initial stirrings of the literati-gentry class. He appealed to the classical histories to justify his authority, finally proclaiming his own dynasty in 1400. Striving to bring an end to prolonged disorder, he gained a reputation as a harsh and arbitrary ruler, and many

---

[12] O. W. Wolters, 'Historians and Emperors in Vietnam and China: comments arising out of Le Van Huu's History, presented to the Tran court in 1272', in Anthony Reid and David Marr, eds, *Perceptions of the past in Southeast Asia*, Singapore, 1979.

members of the Vietnamese ruling class resisted him.[13] The Yung-lo
emperor of Ming China did not ignore the opportunity to intervene, and,
in 1406, Ming armies, posing as restorers of the Tran dynasty, occupied
Dai Viet, capturing Ho Quy Ly after a series of battles. Ming officials
endeavoured during the course of the following two decades to transform
Dai Viet into a Chinese province. However, their policies were hindered
by three contradictions that ultimately led to failure.

First, there was a strategic contradiction in the Ming policy of sinicizing a
frontier era; efforts to sinicize a resisting population undermined the
order and security that was the goal of frontier policy. Second, there was a
bureaucratic contradiction between the ideal of civilizing barbarians that
was used to justify the occupation and the underworld of exploitation
that characterized the actual attempt of Ming officialdom to govern
the Vietnamese; the quality of Ming personnel available to be sent to the
Vietnamese lands subverted the stated goal of the occupation. Finally,
there was a fiscal contradiction between the private fortunes being made
by corrupt officials and the local government deficit that was a continual
drain on the imperial treasury; imperial troops were enforcing opportunities for private enrichment while revenue shortfalls required annual
subsidies from the central government. These contradictions, combined
with a new Vietnamese resistance movement that could not be overcome
without major new investments, led to the abandonment of the occupation
policy within a few years after the death of the Yung-lo emperor in 1424.
The Chinese were constrained to recognize that, while Vietnam was
within reach of Chinese armies, it was beyond the reach of China's
sinicizing influence. The lesson for the Chinese of their effort to occupy
Vietnam was that tributary relations represented a higher wisdom than did
a policy of conquest and assimilation.[14]

Vietnamese resistance to the Ming occupation eventually gathered
behind the leadership of Le Loi, a wealthy landowner from Thanh Hoa, in
the plain of the Ma River, south of the Hong River plain. Raising his
standard of resistance in 1418, he survived a series of Ming operations
against him and was eventually joined by a swelling entourage of talented
Vietnamese, most prominent of whom was Nguyen Trai, destined to be
recognized as a great statesman and the most gifted poet of his age. By the
end of 1426, Ming forces, including recently arrived reinforcements, were
besieged in Thang-long. Two Ming relief armies were defeated and turned
back in 1427. In 1428, surviving Ming forces were allowed to evacuate, and
Le Loi proclaimed the Le dynasty.

Le Loi died after only five years as king. He was succeeded by a son and
a grandson, both of whom reigned as minors under regencies dominated
by men who had served as Le Loi's officers during the anti-Ming resistance. A regicide and failed coup by a prince in 1459 led to the accession of
another grandson of Le Loi in 1460. The new king was Le Thanh Ton, and
his relatively long reign, to 1497, would be remembered as one of the most

---

[13] John K. Whitmore, *Vietnam, Ho Quy Ly, and the Ming (1371–1421)*, New Haven, 1985.
[14] Alexander B. Woodside, 'Early Ming Expansionism (1406–1427): China's abortive conquest
of Vietnam', *Papers on China*, 17.

famous in all of Vietnamese history. Agrarian, legal, and ideological reforms of earlier Le reigns culminated in the reign of Le Thanh Ton with the establishment of a bureaucratic form of government that became the model for Vietnamese rulers during the ensuing five centuries. This was an unprecedented age of scholarship and literature: important works of poetry, folklore, history, law, and government were written and have survived. It was also an age of military power, as expeditions into Laos and against Champa in the 1470s resulted in territorial acquisitions. The paradox of Le Thanh Ton's reign is that, although it was notable for its bureaucratic achievements, within ten years of his death the dynasty was plunged into a crisis of leadership from which it never emerged.

The Ming occupation and the establishment of the Le dynasty are conventionally understood as signposts of deep and significant change in Vietnamese history. The effects of the occupation were not casual. In addition to the physical destruction of Buddhist temples and much of the literary heritage of the Ly and Tran dynasties, there was also an experience among educated Vietnamese of psychological challenge, of being forced to redefine what it meant to be Vietnamese. The aristocratic Buddhist order of Ly and Tran had been swept away. The new ruling class was a mix of militarized clans from the southern provinces and of gentry literati educated with ideas of neo-Confucian rationalism and activism. Vietnamese society appears to have been disoriented by the decades of violence attending the collapse of Tran and the Ming occupation; and this is generally seen as giving meaning to the efforts of the early Le kings to enact a broad range of reforms leading to an altogether new conceptualization of government under Le Thanh Ton.

But Le Thanh Ton's reign was followed by a crisis that was more profound than the crisis that preceded the founding of the Le dynasty, for it led to something new in Vietnamese history: prolonged civil wars, internal divisions, and an expanding southern frontier. There are good reasons for seeing the collapse of Le leadership in the early sixteenth century as a more significant marker of discontinuity than the troubles attending the collapse of Tran. Le Thanh Ton had more in common with earlier Vietnamese kings than he had with any Vietnamese king that followed him. He ruled a realm that would have been recognizable to Ly and Tran kings in its geographical extent and in its dynastic integrity. Vietnamese rulers in later centuries would never again enjoy the security of such a well-defined space and of such unambiguous claims upon the loyalty of all Vietnamese.

Yet a comparison of Le Thanh Ton with the Ly and Tran kings is deceptive, for it risks ignoring the possibility that Le Thanh Ton's bureaucratic achievements were an indication of weakness rather than of strength: an indication that the popular cultural foundations of Vietnamese kingship, as developed under the Ly and Tran, had crumbled and that authority was thereafter rationalized within a ruling-class culture that lacked a solid base in the indigenous society. Constructing a bureaucracy may have been an effort to gain objective control over a society with which the ruling class no longer enjoyed a subjective sympathy. Such an approach would make Le Thanh Ton a transitional figure, a remarkable man in whom intelligence and energy, rather than institutional achievements, were the source of authority.

Comparing the Dai Viet case to other Southeast Asian polities of that time raises a serious problem. The quantity of information available about people and events at Thang-long is greatly out of proportion to what is known about Champa, Angkor, Pagan, the early Tai kingdoms, Śrīvijaya, and Majapahit. At least two responses can be made to this state of affairs. Attention can be focused upon a conjectural reconstruction of events and cultural trends that is understood as standing apart from disparities in the quantity and character of sources available for each polity. This approach is seemingly 'scientific', and furthermore 'democratic', but it is also relatively superficial and eschews any curiosity about whether or not the nature and amount of evidence available about a certain piece of the past may reveal a history of a particular kind. Any comparative exercise about histories of particular kinds will move beyond the collation of 'data' to the question of what history 'means' in each context.

Does the quantity and quality of information available about a particular polity in the past carry a message above and beyond the 'bare facts'? Does Vietnamese history, for example, mean something different from Khmer history in the respective Vietnamese and Khmer cultural traditions? If we answer these questions in the affirmative, as I am inclined to do, then how does this affect comparative analysis? This topic will appear jejune for those whose eyes are fixed on 'facts' and nothing more. But the 'facts' of one polity may turn out to be part of a well-developed historiographical tradition that has been shaped by a centuries-long process from one generation to the next in service to a particular historical point of view; whereas the 'facts' of another polity may come out of a very different process and experience, or may turn out to be part of a twentieth-century scholarly reconstruction of bits and pieces without the matrix of a shared living memory. We must ask, are these different kinds of 'facts' comparable? If they are, then the comparison is truly academic, which may be as far as it can be taken. But if they are not, then we are authorized to ask what exactly is being compared—relatively abstract models of polities in the past, or 'histories' of these polities. 'Histories' imply a point of view established by historical experience that lends a criterion for assigning value to stories remembered and recorded about the past, and this includes the collective decision about whether or not stories about the past should be or will be remembered or recorded.

History of a particular kind was relatively important to the Vietnamese, perhaps because they had no choice but to hold up their end of a relationship with China that demanded serious attention to the past. Judging by what has been remembered and recorded about Champa, Angkor, Pagan, the early Tai kingdoms, Śrīvijaya, and Majapahit, history of the Vietnamese kind was less important to these polities; this does not mean that history was less important in the cultural perspectives of these polities, but it could mean that their history meant something different from what Vietnamese history meant to the Vietnamese. Vietnamese history was largely an argument about the Sino-Vietnamese relationship, a story with a clear and urgent purpose, the acceptance of which was an important part of being Vietnamese. Have the Chams, Khmers, Burmans, Tai-speakers, Malays, and Javanese made a similar use of history, or have they been governed by entirely different notions of what history is 'for'? With this question in mind, let us turn to narratives of Champa, Angkor, Pagan, the early Tai kingdoms, Śrīvijaya, and Majapahit.

CHAMPA

Champa is a generic term for the polities organized by Austronesian-speaking peoples along what is now the central coast of Vietnam. Chinese perceptions of these polities have been preserved and have ascribed to Champa greater coherence and continuity than other evidence will support. What is generally understood as Cham history is a twentieth-century rationalization of scraps of evidence from inscriptions and Chinese sources. The time has come to set this rationalization aside and to take a fresh look. It immediately becomes apparent that the very concept of Champa must be redefined. Rather than signifying a 'kingdom' in the conventional sense of the word, Champa should more properly be understood as an archipelagically-defined cultural-political space. Two clues will provide entry into this unusual case, one geographical and one cultural-linguistic.[15]

The land of Champa at its maximum extent stretched along the central coast of what is now modern Vietnam from the Hoanh Son massif (Mui Ron) in the north to Phan Thiet (Mui Ke Ga) in the south, a distance of almost 1000 kilometres. Champa was comprised of small island-like enclaves defined by the sea and the mountains. It was the closest that a continental terrain could approximate the morphology of an archipelago. The 'islands' were relatively isolated from the continent by a thick band of mountains to the west, open to the sea on the east, and separated from each other by lines of mountains that ran out into the sea. Bearing this in mind, it is no accident that this is the one place (apart from the Malay peninsula, which approximates a large island), where Malayo-Polynesian peoples appropriated continental terrain.

The peoples of Champa, the lowland Chams and the upland Rhade and Jarai, are ethnolinguistically Malay. Their organization of political space can best be understood as a form of Malayo-Polynesian polity, quite different from the polities we are accustomed to find in continental settings or even on densely-populated islands such as Java. Political authority in traditional Malayo-Polynesian culture grew out of maritime nomadism; it was accordingly dispersed, with a preference for small groups enjoying relative freedom to move about as they pleased. The land of Champa offered opportunities for this type of organization, being broken up into many small coastal enclaves with an extended mountainous hinterland.

Champa can be best understood as a kind of archipelago where ambitious leaders repeatedly established centres of authority, simultaneously

---

[15] My understanding of Champa and of new directions in Cham studies is indebted to discussions with Nora Taylor. She bears no responsibility for my errors.

and in different places. In lieu of constructing a schematic and meaningless 'narrative' of Cham 'history', I propose to look at five regions that may be understood as 'island-clusters' within the larger archipelago. The evidence sits more comfortably in such a framework than it does in the conventional category of a unified kingdom.

Beginning in the north, Quang Binh, Quang Tri and Thua Thien Provinces correspond with what the Chinese called Lin-yi. Lin-yi, as something in the vicinity of Hué, held the attention of Chinese record-keepers from the late second century to the mid-fifth century, after which the Chinese appear to have applied the name to something further south in the vicinity of Da Nang. The outstanding feature of Lin-yi from the Chinese point of view was that it appeared out of the debris of the crumbling southern border of the Han empire and was a source of incessant frontier raids until 446 when a Sino-Vietnamese expedition destroyed its centre at Hué. The Chinese continued to apply the name Lin-yi to something they perceived further south for another three centuries. Instead of presuming that 'the Chams moved their capital further south', it appears more likely that whatever had been happening in this region was in some unknown way altered after 446 and that regions further south simply continued along lines of development already established.

The so-called Lin-yi that existed from the late second century to 446 cannot be verified with architectural or inscriptional evidence. According to the Chinese sources, this region was the southernmost frontier jurisdiction of the Han empire for three centuries before someone identified as a son of a local Han magistrate proclaimed himself king in the waning years of the Han dynasty. For the next two and a half centuries, the dominant feature of this Lin-yi is that its kings appear to have defined their ambitions in response to the rhythms of dynastic power in China; they seem to have been preoccupied with the Sino-Vietnamese frontier and with opportunities for plunder and expansion beyond that frontier. This perception can be attributed to the priorities of Chinese annalists. In fact, warfare along the border during this time increased in times of Chinese dynastic strength, when Sino-Vietnamese armies were most active, and decreased when Chinese dynasties were weak and least able to project military power into the far south.[16] This suggests that warfare may have been as much a factor of initiative from the north as from the south. The border was unstable and powers both in the north and in the south endeavoured to maximize their control of terrain. The modern territories of Quang Binh, Quang Tri and Thua Thien would in fact be a contested frontier zone until the fifteenth century when the arena of contention shifted further south.

After 446, Sino-Vietnamese annalists perceived kings of polities beyond the southern border as being situated in the vicinity of the modern city of Da Nang, in the modern province of Quang Nam. These annalists stopped using the name Lin-yi after 758, and from 875 began to use the name Chan-ch'eng, understood as equivalent to Champāpura or 'City of Champa'. This region is rich in architecture, statuary, and inscriptions in Sanskrit and Cham. The major archaeological sites are Mi-son, Dong Duong, and

---

[16] K. W. Taylor, *The Birth of Vietnam*, Berkeley, 1983, 106–9, 115–18.

Tra Kieu, each of which represents a distinctive artistic tradition.[17] The name Amarāvatī has been applied to some of the artistic remains by French scholars on the basis of a presumed relationship with the Indian style of that name. The name Indrapura has also been applied to this region. The task of absorbing the vast amount of archaeological evidence already found and still being found has barely begun. Inscriptions reveal a rhythm of political life centred on an aspiring leader's ability to erect a linga and to protect it from rivals.[18] According to the usual reading of the Sino-Vietnamese annalists, Cham–Viet warfare in the late tenth century led to the abandonment of the Quang Nam region as an arena for aspiring Cham kings, though in fact the annalists can be read as being ambiguous on that point.[19] This coincided with the appearance of a new Vietnamese kingdom separate from the Chinese imperial system and may suggest that the process by which the Vietnamese established their position of separation with regard to China also involved the assertion of a greater measure of military ascendancy in the south. However, inscriptional evidence reveals that Cham kings continued to be active in this region into the late twelfth century,[20] and the Sino-Vietnamese annalists themselves do not deny that this territory belonged to Cham kings until the late fifteenth century.

From the eleventh to the fifteenth centuries, Vietnamese annalists locate the kings they call Cham in the vicinity of the modern city of Qui Nhon. The Cham capital, often identified by the name Vijaya, was twice sacked by Vietnamese seaborne armies in the eleventh century as part of the process by which the Vietnamese were developing their dynastic space and exploring the limits of their maritime power. In the twelfth and early thirteenth centuries, Khmer armies, with Angkor at the peak of its power, repeatedly occupied parts of the Cham territories and endeavoured to establish an overlordship over the Cham kings; Cham kings remained active, however, and even managed to sack Angkor in 1177. In the late thirteenth century, Chams and Viets allied against the Mongol-Yuan invasions; the momentum of this alliance eventually led to the visit of a Vietnamese king to Champa in the early fourteenth century, and the marriage of a Vietnamese princess to the Cham king. According to Viet-namese annalists, however, territorial quarrels over the region of Quang Binh, Quang Tri and Thua Thien eventually led to hostilities, and, during the era of Tran dynastic decline in the late fourteenth century, as we have seen, an able Cham king, known to the Vietnamese as Che Bong Nga, repeatedly invaded and plundered the Vietnamese lands, thrice sacking the Vietnamese capital. Following the death of Che Bong Nga in 1390, Ho Quy Ly, and then the fifteenth-century Le kings, presided over new assertions of Vietnamese power in the Cham territories. In 1471, according to Vietnamese annalists, a Vietnamese army seized the Cham capital at Vijaya and the Vietnamese annexed everything north of what is today the southern border of Binh Dinh Province.

[17] Jean Boisselier, *La Statuaire Du Champa*, Paris, 1963.

[18] L. Finot, 'Notes d'epigraphie: les inscriptions de Mi-son', BEFEO, 4 (1904), inscriptions no. 4, 12, 14, & 15.

[19] G. Cœdès, *The Indianized States of Southeast Asia*, ed. Walter Vella, trans. Susan Brown Cowing, Honolulu, 1968, 124–5; Ngo Si Lien, ban ky 1, 189–94 passim.

[20] Finot, 'Les inscriptions de Mi-son', inscription no. 25.

The status of the region of Quang Binh, Quang Tri and Thua Thien during the thousand years after the so-called kings of Lin-yi ceased to rule there in the fifth century and until an unambiguous and final Vietnamese authority appears to have been established in the fifteenth century has yet to be carefully studied. It was clearly a border zone in which Viet and Cham peoples mingled. The Vietnamese annalists claim that northern portions of this region were annexed in the eleventh century and southern portions were obtained by marriage alliance in the early fourteenth century. But Ho Quy Ly's campaigns against Champa at the turn of the fifteenth century reveal that this was still a contested area. Similarly, the status of the Quang Nam region after the tenth century and until the Vietnamese annexation of 1471, has yet to be clearly understood. This was recognized by the Vietnamese as Cham territory, and Cham kings continued to rule from there, some of them emplaced by Khmer armies, but overall it appears to have been a less propitious place for Cham kingship after the tenth century than it had been before.

This should not lead to the conclusion that the Quang Binh, Quang Tri and Thua Thien region after the fifth century and the Quang Nam region after the tenth century were simply absorbed by Cham polities further south. On the contrary, it is more likely that, exceptional periods of Cham leadership aside, such as the case of Che Bong Nga, regional leaders exercised a kind of autonomous authority appropriate to local circumstances. The information from the Vietnamese annals about Cham–Viet relations must be treated carefully, for surely it reflects presumptions about interstate relations derived from experience with Vietnam's northern neighbour. Vietnamese-style historical narrative was not adequate to describe the relatively diffuse, personalized kind of authority that must have characterized Cham political experience.

The Vietnamese annexation of the coast down to Cu-mong in the late fifteenth century was not the end of Champa. A fourth Cham region centred in the vicinity of the modern city of Nha Trang, in the modern province of Khanh Hoa, had been the home of kings from the beginning of Cham history and has archaeological and inscriptional evidence comparable to the Quang Nam region in terms of chronology, quantity, and sophistication. Scholars sometimes apply the name Kauthara to this region. Sino-Vietnamese annalists recorded what appears to have been a perception of this region in the eighth and ninth centuries under the name Huan-wang. Cham kings ruled here until the end of the seventeenth century. Thereafter, Cham kings continued to rule under Vietnamese overlordship in what is the modern province of Thuan Hai until 1832.[21] In this region, often referred to by scholars as Panduranga, Cham kings had been ruling for centuries. The majority of Chams living in Vietnam today are in Thuan Hai.[22]

One of the wonders of Cham history is that a Malayo-Polynesian people was able to compete for space in a continental environment for so long. The archipelagic, maritime nature of this continental terrain is one way to

[21] Po Dharma, *Le-Panduranga (Campa) 1802–1835, ses rapports avec le Vietnam*, Paris, 1987.
[22] Vien khoa hoc xa hoi thanh pho Ho Chi Minh, *Nguoi Cham o Thuan Hai*, Thuan Hai, 1989.

understand this. Another dimension that deserves further consideration is the participation of the upland peoples in the Cham story. Temples and other archaeological remains can be found in the mountains, at least one king ruled from the mountains, and there is evidence of close relations between upland and coastal leadership groups. Much scholarly attention has been spent on lists and genealogies of kings as metaphors for a kingdom, but now it is clear that there were many kings ruling simultaneously in different places. Who were these kings? They were never called Cham; rather, they were called kings of Champa. It is in fact difficult to get a clear sense of who the Chams were. Judging from surviving Cham populations, we are encouraged to speak of there being several kinds of Cham peoples. And it is increasingly clear that the participation of peoples from the mountains, the Rhade and the Jarai, as soldiers and even kings, is more than a possibility. Furthermore, the significance of Champa as a network, or series of networks, of ethnic, religious, political, and commercial relationships connecting the Cham territories with the Malay world of peninsular and insular Southeast Asia is still poorly understood. There is in fact much evidence from Champa that has yet to be studied; what is meant by Champa appears to be on the threshold of a major revision.[23] The construction of Cham history will have a significant impact upon the development of Vietnamese historiography, which is at present in a preliminary phase of making space for Cham voices to be heard in the earlier history of the terrain now part of Vietnam.

ANGKOR

Turning to the lower Mekong basin, we find a very different historical experience from that of the Viets or the Chams. Here there was no experience with the soldiers and officials of a neighbouring empire, nor the awareness of boundaries, in terrain and in culture, that such an experience produced among the Viets and Chams. Information about the outside world available to Khmer leaders arrived as news about Hindu gods and forms of Hindu and Buddhist devotion as well as cosmological notions of political space that were expounded in the Sanskrit language. This news arrived, we assume, chiefly by way of maritime trade, and encouraged openness and receptivity toward distant contacts and awareness of being part of a borderless world. Early Khmer leaders learned to justify their authority by placing it in a universal context of devotion that could fully absorb the religious aspirations and compel the loyalty of their followers. In a process of developing the theory and practice of an increasingly centralized political space, warfare among rival hegemons was rationalized as corresponding to deified moral conflict on a universal scale. The emergence of the Angkor polity from the ninth century represents the accumulated political and cultural wisdom from generations of efforts to organize a political order in a relatively diffuse socio-economic environment.

Unlike the Viets, who developed their polity in a relatively confined

---

[23] Finot, 'Les inscriptions de Mi-son', inscription no. 21. T. Quach-Langlet, 'Le cadre géographique de l'ancien Campa', in *Actes du seminaire sur le Campa*, Paris, 1988, 36.

locale that was densely populated from an early time, and the Chams, whose ambitions were for the most part defined by coastal enclaves, other peoples in Southeast Asia inhabited more expansive landscapes where human settlement remained an important variable for a longer time. The Khmers inhabited the lower Mekong basin, which included the Tonle Sap, or Great Lake, a natural reservoir for the annual monsoon floods of the Mekong. During the earliest, or pre-Angkorean, centuries of Khmer history, there was no fixed centre, nor can it even be said that there was a single Khmer polity. Khmer leaders strove to promote and enforce their authority by demonstrations of battlefield and devotional prowess, the effectiveness of which seldom had any enduring value beyond their individual lifetimes.[24] However, in the ninth century, Khmer political life became centred at Angkor. Angkor is located near the northwest shore of the Tonle Sap, with good water transport from all the ricefields in the drainage basin of that lake as well as the lower Mekong plain. At the same time, it is well situated for land contact with the basins of the Mun and Chao Phraya, where more ricefields could be found. Once Khmer settlement had exploited the rice-growing potential of this region to a minimally-necessary level, and once Khmer leaders found ways of organizing their authority over much of this region, Angkor was the favoured site as long as agriculture remained the primary source of wealth. Pre-Angkorean and post-Angkorean Khmer centres were located to the east and south, along the Mekong with direct access to the sea and the commerce-generated wealth that this access afforded; but Angkor depended upon rice.

The establishment of the Angkorean polity is associated with the career of Jayavarman II during the first half of the ninth century. Prior to this time, there was a multiplicity of polities in the lower Mekong basin, relatively small and transitory realms representing the personal achievements of particular individuals rather than institutionalized political systems. Chinese record-keepers organized their information about these polities in the shape of two successive kingdoms, which they called Fu-nan, from the second to the sixth centuries, and Chen-la, from the sixth through to the eighth centuries. The Chinese perception of a change from 'Fu-nan' to 'Chen-la' in the sixth century appears to correspond to a transition from coastal or riverine entrepôts linked to the trade route between India and China to a more inland focus upon ricefields.

The earliest known maritime trade route between India and China followed the coasts, except for land transit across the Kra isthmus and transit through the natural and man-made channels of the lower Mekong plain. The archaeological site of Oc-eo, in southern Vietnam near the Cambodian border, appears to have been situated at a strategic junction of canals that linked the Gulf of Siam with the main channels of the Mekong.[25] Oc-eo was an entrepôt from the second to the sixth centuries, and is generally associated with the 'Fu-nan' era of pre-Angkorean history. But, beginning in the fourth century, an all-sea route was pioneered

[24] O. W. Wolters, 'Khmer "Hinduism" in the seventh century', in R. B. Smith and W. Watson, eds, *Early South East Asia: Essays in Archaeology, History and Historical Geography*, London and New York, 1979.
[25] Paul Wheatley, *Nagara and Commandery*, Chicago, 1983, 119–46.

between India and China via the Straits of Melaka (Malacca); by the sixth century this was the preferred route, and the old coastal route was neglected.[26]

In Cambodia, this shift in the trade route coincided with the appearance of conquerors from the mid-Mekong region in the north, the brothers Bhavavarman (who was active during the last half of the sixth century) and Mahendravarman (who was active during the first decade of the seventh century). They did not unite all of the Khmer lands under their rule, but their activities covered more of the Cambodian landscape than those of any previous aspiring hegemon. Furthermore, their careers were oriented toward the inland rice-growing areas of the Mekong basin rather than toward the old coastal entrepôts. Their conquests did not survive their deaths, but, later in the seventh century, the king remembered as Jayavarman I briefly reassembled his version of their conquests. Thereafter, until the eighth century, local Khmer leaders pursued their ambitions without any successfully laying claim to a hegemonic role.

The conquests of Bhavavarman, Mahendravarman, and Jayavarman I reveal an unprecedented interest in northwestern Cambodia, the future site of Angkor, and this suggests that conquerors were beginning to understand the significance of rice, in contrast to international commerce, and to value a site that would allow them to control areas where rice could be or already was being grown.[27] Jayavarman II began his career in the southeast of modern Cambodia, but his conquests were not completed until he had established himself near the future site of Angkor. This locality would remain the seat of Khmer kings for the next six centuries. On a nearby mountain, Sanskrit-educated priests performed a ceremony in the year 802 that nullified all prior oaths of vassalage and proclaimed Jayavarman II a universal monarch.

Jayavarman II is believed to have died in 850 and to have been succeeded by his son Jayavarman III, who reigned until his death in 877. Very little information survives about these two kings. They were followed by Indravarman, who reigned from 877 to 889, and his son Yaśovarman I, who reigned from 889 to around 900. There is no firm evidence that these kings were related to the two Jayavarmans, though later genealogists endeavoured to establish a connection. We have no information about the method of determining succession, but most probably the ability to lead soldiers and gather followers was an important part of enforcing one's claim to rule. Some kind of institutionalized officialdom was developed, apparently to oversee agrarian workers on behalf of the temples established throughout the realm by royal charter, but this did not include any strict notion of dynasty. Genealogies and claims of blood relationship with previous kings were part of the legitimizing process, but the mechanism of succession remained sensitive to the ability of claimants to assume command at Angkor.[28]

[26] O. W. Wolters, *Early Indonesian Commerce: A Study of the Origins of Sri Vijaya*, Ithaca, 1967, 71–85.

[27] O. W. Wolters, 'North-western Cambodia in the seventh century', BSOAS, 37, 2 (1974).

[28] Michael Vickery, 'The reign of Sūryavarman I and royal factionalism at Angkor', JSEAS, 16, 2 (1985).

Yaśovarman I was the first king to reside at the actual site of Angkor, and is known as a great builder. He built sanctuaries at Angkor as well as about one hundred monasteries throughout the realm, each apparently serving as a royal outpost in the locality where it was located. These monasteries were for monks who variously worshipped the three chief deities of Angkor: Śiva, Viṣṇu, and Buddha. All three cults favoured royal power and benefited from the patronage of kings.

Evidence permits only a few observations about the economic, social, and political organization of the Angkorean polity. It is certain that the economy was based upon wet-rice agriculture, that temples were prominent custodians of land and peasants, and that royal authority was expressed through a relatively well-developed hierarchy that included priests and religious sanctions. The degree of centralized control enjoyed by the kings over temples, ricefields, and available labour can only be conjectured, but it was sufficient to realize large building and excavation projects and, periodically, to sustain long-distance military expeditions. Judging from the vicissitudes of Angkorean history, it appears that, whatever the mechanism of hierarchical control available to the kings, orderly conditions and glorious deeds were more the result of their personal abilities than of an institutionalized command system.

Yaśovarman's death was followed by the unremarkable and relatively brief reigns of two of his sons. In the 920s, a brother-in-law of Yaśovarman, known as Jayavarman IV, established himself as king on a site about one hundred kilometres northeast of Angkor. In the 940s, Rājendravarman, identified in genealogies as a nephew of both Yaśovarman and Jayavarman IV, gained ascendancy and resided at Angkor, where he is credited with many architectural achievements. He appears to have been something of a conqueror, and is thought to have plundered a Cham temple near the modern city of Nha Trang. His accomplishments must have been considerable, because it appears that he was able to arrange that after his death, in 968, a high court dignitary, possibly a greatgrandson of Yaśovarman, ruled on behalf of his son, Jayavarman V, who did not complete his studies until 974. Inscriptional evidence indicates that, during the reign of Rājendravarman and Jayavarman V, a group of powerful families, typically claiming kinship by marriage with previous kings, succeeded in entrenching themselves near the centre of authority. Very little is known of Jayavarman V's reign. He apparently presided with success over the hierarchy of loyalties built up by his predecessors. But his death in 1001 was followed by a war of succession in which his nephew was pushed aside by another royal claimant who, in 1006, was in turn defeated by Sūryavarman I.

Sūryavarman I appears to have begun his career in northeastern Cambodia. His exact relationship with previous kings is unclear, but he established a successful claim to the throne, the concept of usurper not being appropriate to the Khmer situation. Sūryavarman I is known for extending his authority over the Lopburi region of the lower Chao Phraya plain in modern Thailand. Other than that, very few details survive from his reign, the most notable being the oath-taking ceremony of 1011, the earliest surviving evidence of such a ceremony in Cambodia. Some scholars believe that Sūryavarman I showed special favour to a Buddhist cult, but, if so, this seems not to have prejudiced the Śaivite and Vaiṣṇavite cults. It is generally assumed that Sūryavarman I was a strong ruler under whose leadership the Khmers expanded to the north and west. He died in 1050 and was succeeded by one of his sons, Udayādityavarman II.

The sixteen-year reign of Udayādityavarman II was marked by three major rebellions and military pressure from the Chams. Despite this evidence of warfare during his reign, Udayādityavarman II contributed one of the great Śaivite temples at Angkor, the Baphuon, as well as the large artificial lake known as the Western Baray with a Vaiṣṇavite temple. He was succeeded by a brother, Harshavarman III, of whom little is known. The last half of the eleventh century appears as a time when the kings of Angkor were challenged by aspiring local powers. Perhaps this development is related to the rise of families of high dignitaries in the tenth century whose ambitions could be woven into royal authority only by a strong figure such as Sūryavarman I.

In 1080, kingship was claimed by a family thought to have been established in northern Cambodia; some scholars believe that the descendants of Sūryavarman I continued to resist this family from a base in southern Cambodia for over thirty years. In 1113, Sūryavarman II, described as a grandnephew of the leader of the northern family, defeated two kings, one of whom may have been his great-uncle, to claim the throne.

Sūryavarman II is famed as a great conqueror. For several years his soldiers dominated the northern Chams, whom he recruited as allies in a series of unsuccessful invasions of Dai Viet. The Khmers communicated with the northern Cham territories through mountain passes from the Mekong Valley, and, interestingly, the southern Cham territories appear not to have felt the power of Sūryavarman II. Lopburi, which appears to have shaken off Khmer overlordship after the reign of Sūryavarman I, was again placed under the authority of Angkor. Evidence of unsuccessful Khmer attacks on the Mon polity at Haripunjaya, near modern Chiengmai in northern Thailand, may be dated to the general time of Sūryavarman II. There are indications that Sūryavarman II was also active in the Mun River basin and adjacent portions of the Mekong basin in modern Laos and Thailand.

The most famous of all Angkorean edifices, the Angkor Wat, was built by Sūryavarman II as his personal funerary temple. It reveals devotion to the cult of Viṣṇu at a time when Viṣṇu cults were also prominent in India and Java. This may reflect an alert interest in intellectual and religious trends in the Sanskritic world and a continuing sensitivity to the cultural authority of this world. At the same time, Sūryavarman II successfully conducted diplomatic relations with the Southern Sung court of China, posing as a vassal and promoting trade. Sūryavarman II disappears from the evidence around 1150, after which Angkor suffered internal discord and Cham raids for thirty years.

Sūryavarman II's immediate successors are undistinguished. The first of them, Dharaṇūrndravarman II, a cousin of Sūryavarman II, was married to a granddaughter of Sūryavarman I. This marriage produced the king later known as Jayavarman VII. Jayavarman VII's early career was spent on the sidelines as other contenders struggled for supremacy. In the 1170s, a trend of Cham raids, perhaps facilitated by Angkor's internal difficulties, culminated in 1177 when a Cham water-borne expedition sacked Angkor.

In the wake of this event, with the Khmer lands at the mercy of the Chams, Jayavarman VII stepped forward to lead resistance to the invaders. In the 1180s, he completed the expulsion of the Chams and established his authority at Angkor. In the 1190s he began to send expeditions into Champa, with the eventual result that Champa was ruled as a province of Angkor for nearly twenty years in the early thirteenth century. At the same time, Jayavarman VII sent armies to the north and west; there is evidence of his authority as far north as the modern site of Vientiane.

In addition to his conquests, Jayavarman VII is known for the many impressive buildings completed during his reign, including temples dedicated to each of his parents, and the Bayon, a Mahāyāna Buddhist temple in the centre of the Angkor Thom walled enclosure designed at that time. He is also credited with the building of roads, 121 rest houses, and 102 hospitals throughout Angkorean territory. Jayavarman VII favoured Mahāyāna Buddhism, and this, along with his reported conquests, the apparently hasty construction of his monuments, and the seemingly intense level of activity that characterized the thirty to forty years of his rule, has contributed to his reputation as an improviser in an age of decay, a man of energy searching for some new form of thought and organization capable of pushing the Angkorean polity into a fresh trajectory. But the momentum imparted to the Angkorean polity by Jayavarman VII appears to have come from his personality rather than his organizing achievements, and he has the distinction of being the last important king of Angkor. The manner in which his reign came to an end is unknown, but it is generally dated around 1220, when the Chams threw off Khmer overlordship.

Angkorean history in the eleventh, twelfth, and thirteenth centuries reveals a pattern of strong kings followed by disorder. Sūryavarman I, Sūryavarman II, and Jayavarman VII all enjoyed relatively long and distinguished reigns. All three were apparently men of unusual ability. But they were unable to translate their personal achievements into any sort of long-term institutional stability, as, for example, Ly Phat Ma had been able to do at Thang-long during the 1030s and 1040s. The reasons for this are probably related to the relative lack of threat perceived by the Khmers and the accompanying lack of incentive to affirm orthodox patterns, whether in terms of religious thought or of royal succession. The Chams did not pose the same order of threat to the Khmers as Chinese dynasties did to the Vietnamese. When the formation of Thai polities in the Chao Phraya and Mekong basins posed a higher level of threat to Angkor in the thirteenth century, the Khmers adapted with fundamental economic and cultural changes; they did not respond as if they had irrevocably invested themselves in any particular political or cultural heritage.

Following the Mahāyāna Buddhist fervour of Jayavarman VII, there was a brief revival of royal Śaivism, but by the end of the thirteenth century Theravāda Buddhism had spread widely among the Khmers, opening a new post-Angkorean age in Khmer culture. The building of monuments came to an end. Sanskrit inscriptions were replaced by Pāli scriptures; the old brahmanical priestly class was replaced by peripatetic monks with begging bowls. Beginning in the late thirteenth century, Thai military pressure posed serious problems; by the late fourteenth century, the site of Angkor could only with difficulty be defended against Ayutthaya. Rice-fields were neglected as trade and commerce grew in importance as a source of wealth. During the first half of the fifteenth century, Khmer kings abandoned Angkor in favour of sites further east and south, in the vicinity of modern Phnom Penh, with greater access to the maritime trade routes that were being invigorated at that time in response to new commercial initiatives from China.

The end of Angkorean history came not with a dramatic collapse but rather as a reorientation of the Khmer polity: from dependence on rice-fields to greater reliance upon wealth generated by trade and commerce; from continental empire to maritime entrepôt; from a religious culture that was priestly to one that was monastic. It is incorrect to attribute the abandonment of Angkor simply to Tai pressure. For one thing, the pattern of Angkorean history reveals an unstable and seemingly irremediable reliance upon personality that made it progressively more difficult for an aspiring ruler to enforce his royal claims. The final abandonment of Angkor in the 1430s appears to have resulted from conflicts that cannot be strictly defined as resulting from either internal rivalry or external interests, but were rather a more complicated aspect of the relationship that had developed between Ayutthaya and Angkor. Angkor had for centuries served as the focus of hierarchy in the lower Chao Phraya and Mekong basins. This was a political fact for the new Thai polity of Ayutthaya as well as for the Khmers; and Ayutthaya kings, no less than the Khmer kings, endeavoured to appropriate Angkorean traditions. Furthermore, the attraction of a site more accessible to seaborne foreign merchants appears to have been at least as important as the distraction of a site vulnerable to a rival power. Ayutthaya and Phnom Penh resembled one another both in their focus upon maritime trading contacts and in their investment in the legacy of Angkor.[29]

The appropriation of Angkor by modern Khmers as an important part of their history is based upon relatively recent reconstructions of the past. Between the days of Angkor and the twentieth century were generations of Khmers for whom Angkor, if not unknown, was nonetheless without the significance now attached to it.[30] Unlike the case of the Viets, who never abandoned Thang-long despite successive efforts by Chinese dynasties to wrest it away, the Khmer world offered options that did not require the retention of Angkor. Exercising the option to relocate the Khmer polity, both geographically and culturally, offered the possibility of leaving behind a particular historical experience. That this experience should be retrieved in modern times reflects a case of shrinking options. In a world of multiplying predators, the Khmers have begun to need Angkor.

[29] Michael Vickery, 'Cambodia after Angkor, the chronicular evidence from the 14th to 16th centuries', 2 vols, Ph.D. thesis, Yale University, 1977, 1. 513–22.
[30] Michael Vickery, 'Some remarks on early state formation in Cambodia', in David G. Marr and A. C. Milner, eds, *Southeast Asia in the 9th to 14th centuries*, Singapore, 1986.

PAGAN

A historical experience that may be usefully compared with those of the Viets and Khmers occurred in the Irrawaddy basin. Here, the selection of items from the cultural repertoire of ancient India was not the same as the news that made a difference to the Khmers. The universalized vision of authority that was credible among the Khmers, relatively isolated from alien threats in the lower Mekong basin, was too catholic, too indiscriminate, and too amoral for the political and intellectual process that evolved in the Irrawaddy basin. There the mood was more culturally diverse and competitive, and the need to affirm the ethical nature of political authority was accordingly greater. The Sarvāstivādin Buddhism of the Pyus and the Theravāda Buddhism of the Mons and the Burmans provided a more clearly defined programme for moral action and a correspondingly greater emphasis upon means for demonstrating merit to vindicate one's place in society. The cities of the Pyus, the Mons, and the Burmans shared a single lowland geo-strategic site, were vulnerable to mountain-based powers, were in close land contact with the borderlands of the Indian world (the Arakanese and Bengali coasts and the Assam basin), and were in regular maritime contact with the eastern coast of the Indian subcontinent and with Sri Lanka. The rulers of Pagan who aspired to unite these cities under their authority from the eleventh century claimed a superior measure of merit as defined by the religious ideas that united the different ethnocultural (and socio-economic) patterns of that time and place. They showed an ability to synthesize, to affirm a centre amidst the clamour of competing languages (Pyu, Mon, Burman), competing economies (the trading cities of the monsoon coast and the ricelands of the dry zone in the north), and competing enemies (Pagan history tells of invasions from both the mountains and the sea). This focus came to be based upon a well-developed notion of a moral centre as defined by the Pāli canon of Theravāda Buddhism. In contrast, the Angkorean achievement contained fewer contradictions, being measured less by the moral quality of the ruler than by the amoral power of the god whom the ruler worshipped.

A casual visitor to Pagan may be puzzled by such impressive architectural remains in the midst of what is essentially a desert in the dry zone of northern Burma, shielded from the monsoon rains by the surrounding mountains. Its location on the Irrawaddy River, however, is roughly equidistant from the regions of Minbu downriver and Kyaukse upriver. Minbu and Kyaukse emerged in early times as important rice-producing areas through the development of extensive irrigation systems. Pagan was the ideal site to concentrate the rice surplus of these two regions. Pagan's success as the first documented polity to extend its authority throughout the Irrawaddy basin is primarily a measure of the ability to mobilize the agrarian resources of Minbu and Kyaukse made possible by its location. Lower Burma, Arakan, and Tenasserim were all significant centres of trade and culture, but the history of Pagan reveals that, in that time and place, an inland agrarian polity was better able to concentrate people and wealth than were coastal entrepôts.

The history of Pagan reveals an interesting comparison with Angkor from at least three vantages. Like Angkor, Pagan was an inland agrarian polity that enforced its authority over coastal areas; both Angkor and Pagan are impressive centres of monumental architecture; and the history of each came to an end contemporaneously with the advent of Tai peoples into lowland Southeast Asia. Pagan history is much shorter than Angkorean history, but, for the better part of three centuries, these two polities gave direction to most of the intellectual and material resources of mainland Southeast Asia.

Pagan reportedly appeared as a walled city in the mid-ninth century. The kings of Pagan were Burmans, relatively recent arrivals in the Irrawaddy basin, which had been inhabited for several centuries by Pyus and Mons. The Burmans appear to have gained entry into the basin in conjunction with expeditionary operations of the kingdom of Nanchao, located in modern Yunnan, which early in the ninth century seems to have broken the power of the Pyus. In the ninth and tenth centuries, Pagan developed as a regional power in northern Burma, while further south a Mon kingdom, based at Thaton, was in maritime contact with Sri Lanka and the Indian subcontinent and was a centre for both overseas trade and Buddhism.

The history of Pagan as a major polity began with the reign of Anawrahta, dated from 1044 to 1077. He is famous for his conquests, the most important being Thaton, in 1057, which resulted in a massive infusion of Mon culture into Pagan. Burmese historiography has portrayed Anawrahta as a king whose conquests were motivated by his piety, either to gain possession of Buddhist relics and scriptures or to spread the Buddhist religion. His conquests included parts of Tenasserim and Arakan, and he is credited with an expedition into Yunnan; his votive tablets have been found throughout the Irrawaddy basin. But more significant than the extent of Anawrahta's conquests was the impact of Mon culture upon the Burmans after their conquest of Thaton and the removal of Mon ruling-class people and other skilled elements of the Mon population to Pagan.

Evidence suggests that Anawrahta's conquest of Thaton may have been in response to Khmer conquests in the lower Chao Phraya basin during the reign of Sūryavarman I, which disturbed the Mon populations there and threatened lower Burma. One result of Anawrahta's activities in lower Burma and the peninsula was to bring Pagan into the maritime trading network that linked the coasts along the Bay of Bengal. In the 1060s and 1070s, Anawrahta maintained friendly contact with the Sri Lankan conqueror Vijayabāhu I, including exchanges of monks and Pāli Buddhist texts. The larger world opened up by Anawrahta's conquests was for a century defined by the imagination of Pagan's kings; evidence of serious external threat and internal contradiction does not appear until the last half of the twelfth century.

The second prominent king of Pagan was Kyanzittha, who ruled from 1084 to around 1112. Remembered as a somewhat disreputable prince with a talent for leading soldiers, Kyanzittha suppressed a Mon uprising that had claimed the life of Anawrahta's son and successor. He was a great admirer of Mon culture and has left inscriptions in the Mon language as well as art and architecture in the Mon style. The Mons appear to have dominated the religious and intellectual life of Pagan at this time, and their language was widely used among ruling-class people. The language of the Pyu continued to be a cultural force as well, seemingly as the repository for the legacy of the Pyu cities of earlier times. Pāli became the language of scripture and liturgy as the Theravāda monkhood flourished under royal patronage. The Burmans themselves learned to write their language in a Mon script. Their initial contribution was, of course, military, for it was their battlefield prowess that had made of Pagan an assembly of such diverse cultural elements; but the story of Pagan eventually is concerned with how the Burmans assimilated these elements and went on to establish a Burman cultural tradition. The reign of Kyanzittha is generally understood as the time when this process of assimilation began to reach a level of maturity; the term 'synthesis' is often applied to cultural developments inspired by Kyanzittha's leadership. A fitting symbol for Kyanzittha is the Myazedi pillar, erected near the end of his reign, with identical inscriptions in four languages: Burman, Mon, Pāli, and Pyu.

The Shwezigon stupa and the Nanda temple were completed during Kyanzittha's reign; both are jewels in the rich architectural legacy of Pagan and both reveal an effort to direct popular religious sentiment toward Theravāda Buddhism through what can be described as architectural pedagogy. It was at this time that Theravāda Buddhism was implanted at the centre of Burmese cultural life.

Kyanzittha was succeeded by a grandson, Alaungsithu, who ruled for more than half a century, into the late 1160s. Alaungsithu presided over the beginning of a transition away from the conventions of Mon culture toward the expression of a distinctive Burman style. The temples built during this time include the last examples of Mon architecture at Pagan as well as the earliest efforts to construct Burman-style temples, the most famous example of which is the Thatbyinnyu.

Surviving evidence portrays Alaungsithu as a peripatetic king travelling extensively through his realm, building monuments and nurturing Buddhism with acts of piety. His travels also included punitive expeditions to Arakan and Tenasserim. Efforts by Pagan to control Tenasserim appear to have threatened trade between Angkor and Sri Lanka and to have elicited a Sri Lankan raid. Evidence suggests that Alaungsithu enjoyed a prosperous reign.

Narapatisithu, who reigned from around 1173 until 1211, was the last of the important kings of Pagan. By this time, according to the most recent study of Pagan, a contradiction in the system of land control required attention. The legitimacy of Pagan's kings had become dependent upon their ability to demonstrate superior merit by endowing temples and monasteries with tax-exempt lands. In the late twelfth century, land was no longer readily available for this purpose, and the revenue base of the kings had shrunk relative to the monastic lands. The authority of the throne being thus threatened by the growing wealth of the monks, Narapatisithu carried out an ecclesiastical reform as an acceptable means of depriving the monkhood of its wealth by way of 'purifying' it. The monkhood was pronounced corrupt, its ordination was declared invalid, and its possessions were confiscated. Monks were sent to Sri Lanka to be properly ordained, and returned with the recognized authority to ordain a new, 'purified' monkhood. Narapatisithu's successful reform of the monkhood allowed him to increase the amount of land available for taxation, and brought Pagan to the peak of its power.[31]

Narapatisithu's reign appears to have been a time of general peace and prosperity. Many great temples and other monuments were built. Art, architecture, and inscriptions reflected a confident Burman idiom. Mon influence was not as significant as it had been a century earlier.

The problem of land control that Narapatisihu had temporarily solved reappeared after his death as kings continued to transfer land to the monkhood to demonstrate the merit upon which their legitimacy and moral authority was based. Narapatisithu's successors, however, were unsuccessful in their attempts to reform the monkhood, and their ability to direct events began to fail as the monkhood found ways to protect its wealth. As royal authority shrank, outlying areas began to go their own way. A new Mon kingdom was established at Pegu in 1281. A king appeared in Arakan.

This unwinding of the internal hierarchy of Pagan was already in an advanced stage when Tai peoples known as Shans began to enter the lowlands from the mountains to the east and north. They were enticed by the opportunity offered by Pagan's weakness, and stimulated by the Mongol conquest of Yunnan in the 1250s and by subsequent Mongol expeditions in the direction of Pagan beginning in the late 1270s. When Mongol expeditions penetrated into the Irrawaddy basin and reached as far as Pagan during the period 1283–1301, Shan chieftains provided the leadership that eventually forced the Mongols to evacuate the lowlands, and the kings of Pagan were forced into a subordinate, mainly ceremonial, role. Pagan was thereafter of only local significance as a political centre.

After a period of disorder attending the assertion of Shan military and political leadership in northern Burma during the first half of the fourteenth century, Burmanized Shans established a regional polity at Ava, on the Irrawaddy River adjacent to the irrigated ricelands of Kyaukse. At the same time, Burmans fleeing from these disorders established a polity at Toungoo, further south on the Sittang River. Meanwhile, the Mon kingdom at Pegu prospered as a centre of commerce on the southern coast, an independent kingdom developed in Arakan, and Prome, in the central Irrawaddy basin, endeavoured to assert regional autonomy against both Ava and Pegu. The Pagan polity was thus partitioned among several regional powers. For the next two centuries, these powers pursued their ambitions through cycles of diplomacy and warfare.

The kings of Pagan appear to have comprised a dynasty in a sense that was not true at Angkor. Succession to Pagan was usually from father to son, while succession at Angkor included a wider horizon of brothers, uncles, nephews, cousins, and others with distant claims of kinship to earlier kings. Wars of succession appear to have been as common at Pagan as they were at Angkor, yet at Pagan these conflicts appear to have taken

[31] Michael Aung-Thwin, *Pagan: the origins of modern Burma*, Honolulu, 1985, 169–98.

their course within a more strictly defined circle of claimants than at Angkor. The reason for this may be related to the role of the monkhood at Pagan as a parallel hierarchy with an interest in stable royal authority.

On the other hand, the dynastic concept at Pagan was never institutionalized to the extent that it was at Thang-long, where, in the thirteenth century, royal marriage policy, the practice of royal abdication, and rules governing the status of collateral lines produced a highly controlled, relatively conflict-free version of dynastic organization. In addition to a politically active monkhood, Thang-long political life was also influenced by a group of officials educated in Chinese political thought and by the necessity of presenting to Chinese dynasties an image of stable dynastic rule consonant with Chinese ideas about good government. The Vietnamese dynastic concept was conditioned by the imperatives of a relatively intense tributary relationship with China that were not felt in other Southeast Asian polities.

The history of Pagan is not a twentieth-century reconstruction to the extent that Angkor's is; it is also not integrated into a continuous historiographical tradition to the same extent as that of Dai Viet. Although the vicissitudes of Burman, Mon, Shan, and Arakanese interaction offered a repertoire of possibilities that have given Burmese history its great variety and interest, the cultural achievement of Pagan has endured as a compelling, according to some the definitive, statement of what it means to be Burmese. This is different from both the case of Angkor, whose cultural achievements were not continued by later generations of Khmers, and Dai Viet, whose ideological, if not cultural, orientation was transformed without loss of continuity in the historico-political tradition. The greatest moments of Pagan's history grew out of a syncretic attitude that made space for non-Burman peoples; the effort by Burmans to appropriate Pagan appears to have led to alienation of the Mons and subsequent loss of lower Burma. Ethnic conflict should probably be placed beside the problem of land control in analysing Pagan's collapse. This makes ironic the idea of Pagan as the paradigm of what it means to be Burmese.

AYUTTHAYA

In the thirteenth century, the outer edge of authority enjoyed by Angkor and Pagan recoiled from the ambitions of Tai-speaking chieftains. The Tai peoples had for many generations inhabited the valleys leading from the Southeast Asian lowlands to the Yunnan plateau. They were peripheral participants in the Tibeto-Burman-led realm of Nanchao that, from its headquarters in Yunnan, mobilized upland peoples in the eighth and ninth centuries. By the eleventh and twelfth centuries, Tai leaders were organizing new centres of authority in the valleys of the upper Mekong as well as offering their military skills to lowland rulers. The Mongol conquest of Nanchao in the 1250s led to major Mongol expeditions against Dai Viet and Pagan. Angkor was too far off to experience such direct Mongol attention, but the Tai leaders of the upper Mekong were not, and in the space between Mongol activism and Angkorean passivity these leaders assembled conquests and jostled for status.

The most prominent of these northern Tai leaders was Mangrai, born in 1239 at Chiang Saen where, in 1259, he began his career as a ruler, subsequently shifting to Fang. He formed alliances with neighbouring Tai rulers, and in 1281 he conquered the kingdom of Haripunjaya at Lamphun, thereby suppressing the last Mon-Khmer outpost in the region. When Pagan collapsed in 1289, Mangrai sent an expedition to the Irrawaddy, established relations with the Shan there, and formed a marriage alliance with the new ruler of Mon Pegu. In the 1290s he began building a city at Chiengmai to be the centre of his realm. For nearly two decades he led resistance to Mongol pressure from the north. He is credited with a book of laws inspired by Buddhist norms of civilized behaviour. He died in 1317, and has been remembered as the founder of the kingdom of Lan Na. Mangrai's career vibrates with creative energy and is comparable to that of his ally and most illustratious contemporary, Ramkamhaeng of Sukothai.

Ramkamhaeng's grandfather had, in the 1240s, overthrown the regional Angkorean outpost in the central Chao Phraya plain, Sukothai. The Mon-Khmer population of this area had already been modified by generations of Tai settlers. When he became king of Sukothai in 1279, Ramkamhaeng initiated a policy of gathering vassals that eventually allowed him to claim suzerainty from Luang Prabang in the north to Nakhon Sithammarat in the south and from Vientiane in the east to Pegu in the west. The success of this enterprise owed much to Ramkamhaeng's battlefield reputation; accordingly, Ramkamhaeng's military and political achievements did not survive his lifetime. More enduring were the cultural developments stimulated by Ramkamhaeng's authority in the area of religion, literature, and sculpture. The type of Tai culture destined to be generalized under the rubric Siamese or Thai can be distinguished from this time at Sukothai. Ramkamhaeng died in 1298, and the far-flung bonds of vassalage that he had pulled together at Sukothai quickly unravelled. His successors ruled a small, local power that was absorbed by Ayutthaya within a century and a half.

The vigorous responses of Mangrai and Ramkamhaeng to the opportunities of their age were an indication of even more significant possibilities closer to the Angkorean heartland. Their ambitions were exercised along the periphery of Angkorean influence, but their cities created large inland markets that attracted the interest of littoral merchants. This was a time when Chinese merchants, enjoying the cosmopolitan atmosphere of the Mongol-Yuan dynasty, were especially active in the region. Chinese potters immigrated to Sawankhalok near Sukothai, which became a major centre of ceramics production. Within a few years, Chinese merchant interests in the lower plain of the Chao Phraya played a role in the founding of Ayutthaya.

By the mid-thirteenth century, the Angkorean administrative centre in the lower Chao Phraya plain, Lopburi, had become independent of Angkor. By the end of the century, the western parts of the plain were under the control of Tai rulers who bowed to Ramkamhaeng but after his death looked for other options; most prominent among these were those who

ruled from Suphanburi. Ayutthaya, located between Lopburi and Suphanburi on an island in the Chao Phraya, offered the prospect of an entrepôt to
those with commercial skills and resources. The initiative for establishing a
new kingdom at Ayutthaya is attributed to a man from a Chinese merchant
family named U Thong who managed to marry into the ruling families of
both Lopburi and Suphanburi. In 1351, he founded Ayutthaya as a united
kingdom of Lopburi and Suphanburi, taking the name Ramathibodi and
ruling until his death in 1369. This achievement is generally understood as
a bringing together of the Angkorean-style administrative skills of the
Mons and Khmers of Lopburi, the manpower and the martial skills of
the Tais of Suphanburi, and the wealth and commercial skills of the local
Chinese merchant communities.

One of the earliest discernible priorities of Ramathibodi was confrontation with Angkor. The border between Ayutthaya and Angkor was in
dispute, as was control of the people who lived in the borderlands. There
is evidence indicating that the Ayutthayans briefly seized Angkor during
the time of Ramathibodi. This reveals that, at its inception, Ayutthaya was
fighting to appropriate the claim to regional overlordship that had been
held for many generations by Angkor. It would be only sixty years before
the logic of Ayutthaya's advantage as an entrepôt of maritime commerce
would lead to the abandonment of Angkor.

The urgency of Ramathibodi's contest with Angkor was not shared by
the king who followed him, Borommaracha I (r. 1370–88), who was from
Suphanburi and accordingly perceived Sukothai as a greater threat and a
more natural enemy than Angkor. As former vassals of Sukothai, the Tai of
Suphanburi were keen to appropriate Ramkamhaeng's claim to supremacy
among the Siamese Tai. Borommaracha I appears to have focused all his
energies upon the goal of subduing Sukothai, yet without conclusive results.

The next two rulers were a son of Ramathibodi, Ramesuan (r. 1388–95),
and a grandson, Ramaracha (r. 1395–1409); these kings were from Lopburi
and they resumed Ramathibodi's policy of pressing against Angkor while
paying less attention to Sukothai. While it appears that the Ayutthayans
under Ramesuan may have succeeded in sacking Angkor a second time,
Tai Ayutthayans wanted a more assertive policy toward Sukothai; at least
this is how historians have understood the coup of 1409 when Ramaracha
was forced to flee and a son of Borommarcha I gained the throne.

The new king was Intharacha (r. 1409–24), and under his leadership
Sukothai was decisively reduced to vassalage. With the Sukothai affair
settled, the Ayutthayans were finally prepared to turn their full attention
to Angkor. Intharacha's son and successor, Borommaracha II (r. 1424–48),
sent an expedition to sack Angkor in 1431, after which, as we have seen, it
was abandoned by Khmer kings. The next rival on the horizon was Lan
Na, and in the 1440s Borommaracha II initiated a policy of attempting to
reduce the kings at Chiengmai.

The successors of Mangrai had maintained a resilient system of military
and administrative control and, in the reign of Ku Na (1355–85), established the basis for a distinctive regional cultural identity, called Tai Yuan
or Northern Tai. Ku Na was unusually well-educated for a king; he
promoted a scholarly sect of Buddhist monks that, for many generations,

became the leading religious, literary, and cultural influence in the region.

Ku Na's successors were troubled by factional strife for more than half a century, although they managed to pull together enough soldiers to repel Ming Chinese invasions in 1404 and 1405. Not until around 1450 did King Tilokaracha or Tilok (r. 1441–87), secure internal order. Tilok has been remembered as Lan Na's greatest king because during his long reign the kingdom was stable and prosperous; alien threats were successfully dealt with; and new symbols of cultural glory were raised, most famous of which was the Maha Chedi Luang, a massive Buddhist reliquary at Chiengmai.

Tilok's most famous enemy was Borommatrailokanat or Trailok, remembered as one of the greatest of Ayutthaya's kings (r. 1448–88). Trailok pursued the policy of attacking Lan Na that had been set by his father, Borommaracha II. Tilok and Trailok duelled repeatedly during their long reigns. The Ayutthaya–Lan Na warfare of this time is often labelled a stalemate, yet this is not precisely true, for it was decisive in that Lan Na successfully repelled Ayutthayan armies and grew stronger and more cohesive in the process; the Ayutthayan threat surely facilitated Tilok's efforts to enforce more centralized authority from Chiengmai and reinforced a Tai Yuan cultural identity separate from the Sukothai-Ayutthaya version of being Tai. Tilok never entertained the idea of conquering Ayutthaya, so he can be seen as having been successful in a way that Trailok was not, for Trailok failed in his endeavours to conquer Lan Na. Far from being inconclusive, this warfare determined that Lan Na would continue as a regional power beyond the reach of Ayutthaya for centuries to come.

Even more than his vain efforts to subdue Lan Na, Trailok is remembered for administrative reforms that began a process of extending bureaucratic control over labour. This can be interpreted as, at least partially, a result of his mobilizations against Lan Na. The progressive elaboration of the system of labour control conceived during his reign became the basis for the regenerative if not enduring strength of Ayutthaya in following centuries. One idea was essentially a hierarchical numbering system that was applied to everyone from the lowest slave to the king; this fixed each individual's rights and obligations under the law. Another idea was the division and subdivision of officialdom into units charged with specific functions. It is not clear to what degree these ideas were implemented during the reign of Trailok; but the significance of initiating such a reform is very great. It meant that the traditional Tai practice of personal patron-client relationships would henceforth be interacting with a more bureaucratic and impersonal system of control. Very likely, the administrative reforms of Trailok were inspired by the legacy of Angkor.

In addition to Lan Na and Ayutthaya, a third Tai power appeared at this time among the Lao along the middle Mekong. Ramkamhaeng had claimed Luang Prabang and Vientiane as vassals. Legends tell of the son of a former king of Luang Prabang in exile at Angkor named Fa Ngum who conquered his way up the Mekong valley to become King of Lan Sang at Luang Prabang in 1353. Fa Ngum departed from Angkor on his fateful venture in the same year that Ayutthaya was founded by Ramathibodi, but there appears to be no connection to be drawn between these episodes without excessive conjecture, except that the shrinking Angkorean frontiers and the collapse of Ramkamhaeng's network of vassalage offered opportunities to men of imagination and daring.

Lan Sang never achieved the level of organization enjoyed by Lan Na or Ayutthaya. It covered a huge area, from Luang Prabang in the north to Champassak in the south and most of what is today northeastern Thailand. It never advanced far beyond a simple mechanism for mobilizing soldiers. Fa Ngum's successor, Un Hüan (r. 1373–1416) successfully managed marriage alliances with Lan Na and Ayutthaya, but his death was followed by a quarter-century of factional conflict, coinciding with the disorders in Lan Na. Relative peace was restored during the reign of Sainyachakkaphat (1442–79), a contemporary of Tilok and Trailok.

In the 1470s, Le Thanh Ton of Dai Viet was endeavouring to establish more direct administrative control over his vassals among the Tai chieftains of Siang Khwang (Plain of Jars or Tran-ninh Plateau). These chieftains were two-headed birds who also posed as vassals of Lan Sang. When Vietnamese demands became too vexing, they appealed to Sainyachakkaphat, whose assistance emboldened them to rebel openly against Le Thanh Ton. The Vietnamese responded with a large expedition that seized Luang Prabang and sent Sainyachakkaphat fleeing westward. The Vietnamese subsequently withdrew as a younger brother of Sainyachakkaphat named Suvanna Banlang (r. 1479–86) organized resistance and restored order in Lan Sang. This was the only time before the twentieth century that Vietnamese armies marched beyond the mountains down to the mid-Mekong plain. The fact that Dai Viet was exceptionally strong during the reign of Le Thanh Ton helps account for this episode. But it also reveals the strategic significance of Siang Khwang to both Viet and Lao kings. The rulers of Siang Khwang would continue to balance their loyalties between Viet and Lao authority into modern times.

We have glimpsed the early Tai kingdoms in the formative stage of their development. What resulted from the first few generations of Tai leadership in the valleys of the Mekong and Chao Phraya rivers were two inland kingdoms, Lan Na and Lan Sang, and Ayutthaya. Lan Na was destined to experience many years of Burmese vassalage before eventually being incorporated into the nineteenth-century empire of the Chakri kings of Bangkok. Lan Sang eventually devolved into small regional powers who in varying degrees felt the touch of Bangkok's supremacy prior to the arrival of the French. Only Ayutthaya would continue to prosper and, despite recurring troubles with Burmese empire-builders, make good its claim to leadership among the Tai peoples of the region. This claim, however, was made possible by reasons beyond the Tai frame of reference. In appropriating the administrative legacy of Angkor, Ayutthaya moved beyond the skill of juggling vassals that was the glory of Sukothai. In linking up with the commercial networks of resident Chinese, Ayutthaya stepped beyond the narrow options of an inland valley economy. The syncretic achievement that marked the rise of Ayutthaya is similar to that which marked the rise of Pagan, but while the Burmese lost patience with the ambiguities of syncretism, the Ayutthayans continued to cultivate a cosmopolitan outlook. Modern Thai historiography is anchored in perceptions of the

Ayutthayan experience and in the assertion that this experience established a claim of authority among Tai peoples that continues to deserve honour.

ŚRĪVIJAYA

So far we have considered the histories of mainland polities whose sense of space was defined by mountains, plains, and sometimes coasts. When we shift our attention down the Malay peninsula to the islands beyond, terrain fades into the sea, and the history of the Malay peoples that we situate there has come to signify our understanding of the rhythms of maritime commerce that passed between western and eastern Asia, both changing and being changed by the region. The history we are talking about is a modern reconstruction based mainly upon Chinese and Arabo-Persian texts, a few inscriptions, and, increasingly and most promisingly, archaeological evidence. The Malays themselves have preserved virtually no memory of what we now call Śrīvijaya, a generic term for the succession of thalassocracies centred in southeastern Sumatra from the seventh to the fourteenth centuries. Affirming a particular version of the past was never an urgent priority in a culture with a relatively diffuse awareness of authority, where the sea offered countless options for people who were at home in boats and where agriculturalists were dispersed in many small riverine enclaves.

The earliest trade routes passed through the region overland or, if by water transport, along the coasts, save for Kra isthmus portages. This situation changed from the fourth century as the Malays responded to opportunities for direct maritime trade between southern China and western Asia via the Straits of Melaka. These opportunities have been conventionally explained by the division of China and the consequent growth of southern Chinese interest in seaborne access to west Asian markets, but this is a passive indicator. Malay initiatives in exploiting the possibilities also bear scrutiny. The Malays participated as carriers and also by substituting local products for established items of trade. The process of political organization set in motion among Malay leaders by this new source of wealth reached a critical phase during the last half of the seventh century when rulers near Palembang, on the Musi river of southeastern Sumatra, achieved a position of paramountcy.

Three inscriptions dating from the 680s and testimony of I Ching, the Chinese pilgrim, dating from the 670s to the 690s reveal a prosperous entrepôt where ships going to and coming from China and India gathered while waiting for the winds to change. The ruler was a great patron of Buddhism, and a large international community of monks resided nearby; Chinese monks came here to study with Indian teachers. In a more prosaic vein, ships with fighting men were being sent to intimidate potential rivals along the Straits of Melaka and of Sunda. During the first half of the eighth century, the ruler of Śrīvijaya sent several missions to China; beyond whatever commercial significance these missions may have had, they were primarily demonstrations of diplomatic prowess in the arena of Malay politics.[32] These smudges of evidence from the late seventh and early eighth centuries have been the object of much study and speculation. Their significance for the purposes of our narrative is that they reveal the emergence of the Palembang-based Śrīvijayan polity as a pyramidal network of loyalties among Malay rulers; these rulers were united by a common interest in wealth to be gained from the passage of merchant ships through the region.

Very little is known about Śrīvijayan history but all indications are that something like what we have just described continued to exist as the dominant political force on the Malay peninsula, Sumatra, and western Java for most of the next five hundred years. In the mid-ninth century, a ruler of Śrīvijaya was a prince of the Śailendra line that had ruled in central Java during the preceding century; evidence suggests that this monarch financed the building of a Buddhist monastery at Nālandā in Bengal. In the late tenth century, Śrīvijaya was challenged by Javanese invasions, in response to which it appears that a Śrīvijayan expedition destroyed the Javanese capital in 1016. During this time, the Cōḷa dynasty of Tamil Nadu in southern India developed a fleet and took an interest in Southeast Asia; in 1025, a Cōḷa expedition sacked the Śrīvijayan capital and raided other Malay centres. The earliest evidence of Chinese merchants appearing in Southeast Asia aboard their own ships comes from the tenth century. These sparse bits of information have given rise to theories about diplomatic relations during the tenth and eleventh centuries among the rulers of Tamil Nadu, Śrīvijaya, Java, and China.

The underlying plot of this tale seems to be that the benefits to Śrīvijaya of its supervision of commerce through the region inspired acquisitive instincts among other powers. The Cōḷas oversaw commerce in the western waters of the Bay of Bengal. The Javanese directed commerce in the Java Sea and points east. But opportunities in these areas were peripheral in comparison with Śrīvijaya's splendid position at the throat of the trade routes. Śrīvijaya could not be destroyed by its rivals, but it could be plundered and, for short periods of time, pressed into vassalage. Any power that could dominate the Straits of Melaka stood to benefit enormously from the commerce that passed through. What appears to be new from the tenth century is that the politics of control in the straits was no longer simply a Malay affair; other powers were now in a position to challenge and modify Śrīvijaya's hegemony at the centre of regional trade routes.

What ultimately affected the fate of Śrīvijaya more than military expeditions from Java or southern India was the growing presence of Chinese shipping. The importance of China to the international market ensured that Chinese ships were treated well, even without a Chinese threat of force. But the expansion of Chinese shipping, particularly during the twelfth century when Southern Sung looked south for trade with west Asia, greatly reduced the importance of Malay shipping, and with it the leverage of Malay rulers upon the flow of commerce. The effect of

[32] O. W. Wolters, 'Restudying some Chinese writings on Srivijaya', *Indonesia*, 42 (1986).

increased Chinese shipping was to disperse authority in the Malay world. Rather than there being a single Malay overlord, as the Śrīvijayan ruler had been, several local ports were now able to stand independently of other Malay powers by dealing directly with the Chinese. As the Śrīvijayan system of paramountcy unravelled, the position of Palembang receded to the level of other ports with access to the Straits of Melaka. In the twelfth century, rulers claiming the Śrīvijayan tradition of authority were located at Jambi, northwest of Palembang on the Batang Hari River, closer to the straits.

In the thirteenth and fourteenth centuries, new regional powers further reduced the options of Malay rulers. Sukothai and then Ayutthaya expanded Siamese military activities down the Malay peninsula, ultimately reaching the Straits of Melaka. A new expansionary momentum arose from Java in the thirteenth century and reached a peak in the fourteenth century under the leadership of Majapahit. Malay ambitions were ultimately squeezed out of the Śrīvijayan tradition by the weight of Ayutthaya and Majapahit. Siamese and Javanese expeditions competed to throw nets of vassalage over the Malay rulers of the straits region. This situation changed rapidly when Ming Chinese fleets patrolled Southeast Asian waters at the beginning of the fifteenth century, sponsoring the rise of Melaka and providing a new focus for Malay political activity.

The founder of Melaka, a Malay prince known as Parameśvara, first appears as a vassal of Majapahit at Palembang. In the 1390s he sought to escape Javanese overlordship by shifting to Tumasik (modern Singapore); recent archaeological work in Singapore reveals the late fourteenth century as an especially prosperous time for commercial activity.[33] Tumasik, however, was too exposed to Ayutthaya, and Siamese pressure forced Parameśvara to shift to Melaka, where he presided over a rebirth of Malay political authority under the protection of the Chinese. Parameśvara's close relations with China were the key to his success in competing with Ayutthaya for space on the Malay peninsula.

The newly established Ming dynasty of China took an unprecedented interest in Southeast Asia, and it supported this interest with large naval patrols during the first two decades of the fifteenth century. Parameśvara of Melaka took full advantage of this opportunity to place himself under Chinese protection. He welcomed the Chinese fleets, sent envoys to China, and in 1411 personally went to the Chinese capital to demonstrate his loyalty. Melaka quickly became a new version of the Śrīvijayan model of a Malay-led international entrepôt. Its relationship with China provided protection from Ayutthayan claims, and Majapahit, in the fifteenth century, was already in decline. Melaka established its supremacy over other centres of Malay authority along the coasts of the peninsula and the northeastern coast of Sumatra, thereby guaranteeing control of all trade passing through the straits. Firm relationships were developed with Gujerati and Tamil merchants having access to Western markets and with the north Javanese ports that enjoyed access to Maluku (the Moluccas),

---

[33] John N. Miksic, *Archaeological research on the 'forbidden hill' of Singapore: excavation at Fort Canning 1984*, Singapore, 1985.

the spice islands to the east. For the next century, Melaka was the central entrepôt for trade in and through Southeast Asia. Even after the Ming fleets ceased patrolling, the momentum of Melaka's initial emergence did not soon diminish, revealing both an increasingly diffuse political environment in the Southeast Asian archipelago and the relative advantage of Melaka's position as the regional entrepôt. Melaka also enjoyed effective leadership; in particular, Tun Perak, brother-in-law of one of Parameśvara's successors, has been remembered among Malays as a hero of the first order for his battlefield prowess against the Siamese during the last half of the fifteenth century.

During the fifteenth century, Islam was adopted by the rulers of Melaka, and from there it spread to other parts of the region. The founding of Melaka and the emergence of Islam mark the beginning of Malay history as it has been traditionally remembered in recent centuries. The Malay annals are informed by an Islamic historiographical perspective and do not consider the pre-Islamic Malay past to be of interest. While Malay history, as a collective memory, can thus be said to begin with Melaka, evidence allows us to say that Melaka was a new version of a very old tradition of behaviour among Malay rulers, a tradition of concentrating the benefits of trade.

The case of Melaka further shows a network of authority within which foreigners played functional roles in governing foreign merchant communities and overseeing port activities. Malay merchants were always at a disadvantage, because, unlike vulnerable rich foreigners, they could pose a political threat to Malay rulers from within their own society and were accordingly targets of suspicion and discrimination. Paradoxically, the supervision of commerce by Malay rulers could not lead to a commercial ethos among the Malays without undermining indigenous Malay authority.[34]

Śrīvijaya's role in Southeast Asian history as a regional entrepôt arose from conditions of geography more than from any quality particular to the Malays. Śrīvijaya was the result of Malay nautical skill and organizing initiative, and of opportunity. But history has shown that the exercise of leadership in the Śrīvijayan mode has not been confined to the Malays; Singapore can be understood as a modern version of the Śrīvijayan achievement of using a favourable location to concentrate commercial wealth.

MAJAPAHIT

The island of Java became the demographic centre of insular Southeast Asia because of its large fertile plains and rainfall suitable for growing rice. The earliest Javanese centres that have left a conspicuous mark on the landscape were located in upland plains, valleys, and plateaux nestled among the volcanic peaks of south-central Java. But population growth, the search for land suitable for ricefields, and efforts to escape from the cramped contradictions of political life as it developed in that region

[34] A. C. Milner, *Kerajaan*, Tucson, 1982, 14–28.

eventually shifted the focus of political authority eastward into the plains of the Solo and Brantas Rivers. Majapahit was admirably located to concentrate the rice surplus of the Brantas River plain and of the island of Madura. The rise of Majapahit from the end of the thirteenth century reveals that human settlement had by then reached a level sufficient to enable political authority to enact the logic of available terrain.

Evidence sufficient to begin a narrative of political events in Java dates from the first half of the eighth century when a ruler known as Sanjaya appears as a conquering Śaivite king who established himself at Mataram in south central Java. Kings who associated themselves with his achievement appear to have spent the next century as vassals of a line of Mahāyāna Buddhist kings called Śailendra. The Śailendras are credited with the Borobuḍur, a huge stupa-like monument of terraces built upon a hill in the Kedu plain. The walls of the terraces are covered with bas-relief sculpture illustrating Mahāyāna texts in a distinctive Javanese style based upon Guptan prototypes; this suggests a pedagogical intent. Aside from their architectural accomplishments, virtually nothing is known of the Śailendras, though there are indications that they were active not only in Java but also in Sumatra and along the coasts of what are today Cambodia and Vietnam. They were expelled from Java in the mid-ninth century by a Śaivite king of Sanjaya's line known in inscriptions by at least three names, the most common being Pikatan.

Later inscriptions describe Pikatan's career according to a three-phase pattern of hermit-like ascetic preparation, warfare leading to victory, and withdrawal from worldly affairs into ascetic resignation. The careers of later important Javanese kings were also remembered in terms of this pattern, which suggests a tradition of seeing the coercive violence necessary for political achievement as a manifestation of divine energy concentrated in certain individuals who then restore cosmic harmony through renunciation. The Śaivite temple complex at Prambanan, built by Pikatan or one of his successors and variously dated to the late ninth or early tenth century, appears to be a Śaivite answer to the Borobuḍur as a pedagogical centre.

Java in the eighth and ninth centuries thus presents two lines of kings, one Mahāyāna Buddhist and one Śaivite, each credited with the construction of impressive monuments whose dimensions were never again matched by later generations. The Borobuḍur and Prambanan were clearly designed to attract attention, to inspire awe, and to lend material substance to stories suitable for mass indoctrination. This suggests a time in which new religious ideas were being popularized and manpower was being mobilized with an unprecedented degree of central direction and cultural focus.

Evidence suggests that the structure of political authority at that time was essentially a realm of competing localities. The builders of the Borobuḍur and the Prambanan were apparently the two most prominent of these local powers. Their architectural achievements probably represent an enjoyment of momentary ascendancy over neighbouring powers.[35] Political ambitions appear to have gained religious sanction through association with the spread of Buddhist or Śaivite thought.

[35] Jan Wisseman-Christie, 'Negara, Mandala, and Despotic State: images of early Java', in Marr and Milner, eds, *Southeast Asia*.

In the tenth century, literature, drama, and music developed rapidly to produce a Javanized Hindu worldview that included both Buddhism and Śaivism and evolved into modern times with a remarkable degree of continuity. What appears to be religious dissonance in the eighth and ninth centuries should more correctly be interpreted as an early phase of Javanizing non-indigenous religious symbols from more than one source. By the end of the tenth century, Sanskrit texts were being translated into Javanese.

In the mid-tenth century, the royal seat was shifted eastward into the Brantas River plain where rulers could command a larger base of ricefields. The change of locale may also have been an important factor in the process of harmonizing Buddhism and Śaivism with a Javanese perspective. This new vantage afforded wider horizons, with access to the Java Sea and contact with Bali, Maluku, Sumatra, and the peninsula. As Javanese rulers began to explore this larger world, they appear to have come into conflict with the maritime trading polity of Śrīvijaya based in southeast Sumatra. In 1016, the Javanese polity was overtaken by some kind of military disaster, generally assumed to have been related to the rivalry with Śrīvijaya. Java appears to have thereupon fallen into a state of disorder until the rise of Airlangga, son of a Balinese king and a Javanese princess, who was active from the 1020s until his death in 1049.

Airlangga is remembered as one of the great kings of early Java. His career is recorded in conformity with the pattern of ascetic meditation, warfare with victory, and renunciation that has already been noted with reference to Pikatan. After suppressing local powers so as to reaffirm royal authority, he established a place for Java in the regional maritime world. Śrīvijaya having been humbled by an expedition from Cōḷa India in 1025, Airlangga obtained a marriage alliance with the ruler of Śrīvijaya, and Javanese ports thereafter began to emerge as maritime trading centres. Airlangga patronized Śaivites, Mahāyāna Buddhists, and people known in a generic fashion as 'ascetics', while he personally favoured Viṣṇu. Old Javanese literature flourished.

Before his death, Airlangga divided his realm between his two sons. Very little information survives about events during the remainder of the eleventh century, the twelfth century, and into the first two decades of the thirteenth century. By the late twelfth century, the eastern portion of Airlangga's realm, known as Janggala, had been absorbed by the western portion, known as Kaḍiri (originally Panjalu). Old Javanese literature continued to develop, with the writing of epic poems and Javanese versions of stories based upon episodes in the *Mahābhārata*. Javanese ports established commercial relations with spice-producing islands in Maluku and attracted merchants from Gujerat. This period of about a century and a half is generally referred to as the time of Kaḍiri; more is known of cultural and commercial developments than of political events.

Kaḍiri was overthrown in 1222 by a man called Ken Angrok, meaning 'he who upsets everything'. The legends and stories which contain information about Ken Angrok indicate a hero of lowly birth who flouted conventional rules of behaviour, thereby revealing his superior destiny. He attacked Kaḍiri, posing as the champion of Janggala, which Kaḍiri had swallowed a generation or two before; he set his capital in Janggala. The kingdom he established has been remembered as Singhasari, the name later given to his capital. He died in 1227, but his career marked the beginning of what, a century and a half later, became the prologue in the historical memory of Majapahit.[36]

During the Singhasari era of the thirteenth century, the process of Javanizing non-indigenous cultural influences entered an advanced stage in both poetry and bas-relief sculpture. The cultural basis of what, in the following century, became Majapahit was achieved at this time. The most famous king of Singhasari and the king who appears to have first perceived the possibilities that later became Majapahit was Kĕrtanagara (r. 1268–92).

Kĕrtanagara was an aspiring empire builder whose achievements stimulated the rise of Majapahit. He endeavoured to assert Javanese supremacy over a declining Śrīvijaya and despatched naval forces around the Java Sea. The extent of his conquests is not clear, but his ambitions included the islands of Madura and Bali as well as Java. In him can be detected for the first time the idea of a great archipelagic empire ruled by Javanese, which came to be expressed in the term *nusantara*. He practised a form of Śaivite-Buddhist Tantrism that he may have understood as a means of entering a new, more potent arena of spiritual power commensurate with his unprecedented ambition.

Kĕrtanagara was murdered and supplanted by a vassal in 1292, but in the following year his son-in-law, later known as Kĕrtarājasa, gained control and established his capital at Majapahit. Kĕrtarājasa's seizure of power was facilitated by the arrival of a Mongol expeditionary force, with which he first allied against his father-in-law's murderer, and which he subsequently drove back into the sea.

Kĕrtarājasa and his successors stood in the tradition of empire conceived by Kĕrtanagara, and, for the next hundred years, Majapahit claimed hegemony over most of insular and peninsular Southeast Asia. This claim was largely rhetorical: at the peak of its power in the mid-fourteenth century, Majapahit dominated eastern Java, Bali, and Madura, while exercising a punitive influence over western Java, portions of southern Borneo, Celebes, and Sumbawa. Majapahit was also capable for a time of projecting its power into the Straits of Melaka. But the moment of glory for Majapahit was relatively brief and depended upon the vision, determination, and skill of a single man, the minister Gaja Mada who conducted affairs from around 1330 until his death in 1364.

The first two reigns of Majapahit, that of Kĕrtarājasa (1293–1309) and his son Jayanagara (1309–28), appear to have been mostly occupied with suppressing rebellions and asserting military control over eastern Java. Jayanagara died without a male heir, so the throne was assigned to a daughter of Kĕrtanagara who had also been a wife of Kĕrtarājasa. She took no public role, however, and her eldest daughter was chosen to act as a regent on her behalf. This daughter, in 1334, gave birth to a son who

---

[36] Theodore G. Th. Pigeaud, *Java in the 14th century. A Study in Cultural History*, The Hague, 1962, III. 45ff.

became king in 1350, called Rājasanagara or Hayam Wuruk. Such an intricate arrangement of formal authority suggests a strong hand in the background, the hand of Gaja Mada.

The details of Gaja Mada's activities are known but imprecisely. It is clear that he conquered Bali; there is a story about how he trapped and killed a visiting Sundanese king; and there are indications that he ordered the compilation of a law book and established some kind of administrative system; but all else is obscure. The momentum of his achievements appears to have continued through to the end of Rājasanagara's reign, in 1389. The glory of Majapahit is celebrated in an epic poem, the *Nāgarakĕr-tāgama*, written in praise of Rājasanagara in 1365.

After Rājasanagara's death, Majapahit rapidly declined in importance, torn by warfare between rival lords and challenged by the rise of Melaka for control of regional entrepôt trade. Evidence from the fifteenth century is sparse and incoherent, but it is clear that by the beginning of the sixteenth century Majapahit had fallen to the level of a local polity, and shortly thereafter ceased to play any significant role in the affairs of Java. Majapahit faded from view as Muslim polities on the north coast of Java appeared and seized the initiative.

Early Javanese history is much richer than this brief narrative can convey. The relative seclusion of Java from the purview of predatory powers appears to have allowed Javanese rulers the luxury of savouring cultural and religious diversity and the intricate symbolisms that embraced this diversity. An island surrounded by islands, Java was the centre of its own world, able to define itself without the mutual pushing and shoving that shaped continental historical identities. Of course, Java and neighbouring islands contained a diversity of local perspectives, but there appears to have always been space for these perspectives within the larger Javanese tradition. The early encounter of Buddhism and Śaivism, represented in the Borobuḍur and Prambanan, was a critically important event in the formation of Javanese culture. Subsequently, space was made for Islam in the Javanese tradition with relatively little disruption. Perhaps these synthesizing achievements were possible because none of the new religions embodied a non-Javanese political or military threat.

The vision of Javanese paramountcy over the islands that inspired the rulers of Majapahit, and which is enshrined in the term *nusantara*, has in modern times been realized to a degree far beyond the capabilities of those rulers. In the twentieth century, Majapahit became the historical model and legitimation for the dreams of Javanese leaders. Its moment of glory has been frozen in the imaginations of recent generations as an enduring goal to achieve and preserve.

The diverse narratives we have constructed remind us that the attempt to schematize early Southeast Asia history is bound to be unrewarding. The peoples of Southeast Asia experienced a remarkable range of options in organizing their societies and polities. The choices they exercised upon these options reveal a region that continues to resist any convincing simplification. Southeast Asia's imperviousness to all-encompassing historiographical agendas that endeavour to construct a total regional vision of the past may be an indication of what is less perceptible under the heavy layers of scholarship in which our knowledge of other parts of the globe is embedded, or it may reflect distinctive regional conditions. Historians of Southeast Asia benefit from the lack of a coercive interpretative tradition. My intention in writing this essay has been to strengthen resistance to any such tradition.

BIBLIOGRAPHIC ESSAY

For many years the standard references for early Southeast Asian history have been G. Cœdès, *The Indianized States of Southeast Asia*, ed. Walter F. Vella, trans. Susan Brown Cowing, Honolulu, 1968, and D. G. E. Hall, *A History of Southeast Asia*, 4th edn, Macmillan, 1981. Although scholarship has advanced beyond these works, nothing has yet appeared with which to replace them as serviceable introductions. The most important and up-to-date discussion of conceptual themes in early Southeast Asia is O. W. Wolters, *History, Culture, and Region in Southeast Asian Perspectives*, Singapore, 1982. Collections of essays that are worthy and have significant implications are R. B. Smith and W. Watson, eds, *Early South East Asia: Essays in Archaeology, History and Historical Geography*, London, 1979, and D. G. Marr and A. C. Milner, eds, *Southeast Asia in the 9th to 14th Centuries*, Singapore, 1986. Other useful summaries of evidence are P. Wheatley, *Nagara and Commandery*, Chicago, 1983; C. Higham, *The Archaeology of Mainland Southeast Asia*, Cambridge, UK, 1989; and K. R. Hall, *Maritime Trade and State Development in Early Southeast Asia*, Honolulu, 1985.

An introduction to early Vietnamese history as far as the tenth century is K. W. Taylor, *The Birth of Vietnam*, Berkeley, 1983. For excellent discussions of methodological issues in reading early Vietnamese texts and of Vietnamese Buddhism, see O. W. Wolters, *Two Essays on Dai Viet in the Fourteenth Century*, New Haven, 1988. J. K. Whitmore, *Vietnam, Ho Quy Ly, and the Ming*, New Haven, 1985, is a study of the late fourteenth and early fifteenth centuries. There is no single scholarly treatment of early Vietnam in the English language; readers of French may consult Lê Thanh Khôi, *Le Viêt-Nam, Histoire et Civilisation*, Paris, 1955.

For Champa, J. Boisselier, *La Statuaire du Champa*, Paris, 1963, remains very useful. Cham inscriptions were studied by L. Finot in BEFEO, 4 (1904). Recent works of note on Cham studies are P. Y. Manguin, 'L'introduction de l'Islam au Campa', BEFEO, 66 (1979); D. Lombard, 'Le Campa vu du sud', BEFEO, 76 (1987); Po Dharma, *Le Panduranga (Campa) 1802–1835, ses rapports avec le Vietnam*, Paris, 1987; Centre d'Histoire et Civilisations de la Peninsule Indochinoise, *Actes du Seminaire sur le Campa organisé a l'University de Copenhague le 23 Mai 1987*, Paris, 1988; Po Dharma and P. D. LaFont, *Bibliographie Cam et Campa*, Paris, 1989, and Vien khoa hoc xa hoi thanh pho Ho Chi Minh, *Nguoi Cham o Thuan Hai*, Thuan Hai, 1989.

Any study of Angkor continues to rest upon the inscriptions, for which see G. Cœdès, *Inscriptions du Cambodge*, 6 vols, Hanoi, 1937–56. For an early synthesis, see L. P. Briggs, *The Ancient Khmer Empire*, Philadelphia,

1951. A brief narrative can be found in D. P. Chandler, *A History of Cambodia*, Westview, 1983. H. Kulke, *The Devaraja Cult*, Ithaca, 1978, advanced discussion of religion and politics at Angkor. E. Moran, 'Configuration of Time and Space at Angkor Wat', *Studies in Indo-Asian Art and Culture*, vol. 5 (1977), advanced understanding of the architectural features of Angkor Wat. Several articles by O. W. Wolters have proposed new ways of reading evidence, in particular 'Yayavarman II's Military Power: The Territorial Foundations of the Angkor Empire', JRAS, (1973), 'North-Western Cambodia in the Seventh Century', BSOAS, 37, 2 (1974), and 'Khmer "Hinduism" in the Seventh Century', in Smith and Watson, *Early South East Asia*. On Sūryavarman I, see M. T. Vickery, 'The Reign of Sūryavarman I and Royal Factionalism at Angkor', JSEAS, 16, 2 (1985). On the collapse of Angkor, see M. T. Vickery, 'Cambodia after Angkor, the Chronicular Evidence from the 14th to 16th centuries', Ph.D. thesis, Yale University, 1977.

For Pagan, most of the inscriptional evidence is available in G. H. Luce and Pe Maung Tin, *Inscriptions of Burma*, 5 vols, Rangoon, 1933–56. A classic introduction to Pagan studies is G. H. Luce, *Old Burma–Early Pagan*, 3 vols, New York, 1969–70. See P. J. Bennett, *Conference Under the Tamarind Tree: Three Essays in Burmese History*, New Haven, 1971, for discussions of the immediate post-Pagan period. For a stimulating synthesis of Pagan history based upon a model of interaction between ideology and economics, see Michael Aung-Thwin, *Pagan: The Origins of Modern Burma*, Honolulu, 1985.

For the early Tai kingdoms, one cannot do better than to consult D. K. Wyatt, *Thailand: A Short History*, New Haven, 1984.

On Śrīvijayan history, see O. W. Wolters, *Early Indonesian Commerce*, Ithaca, 1967, and *The Fall of Srivijaya in Malay History*, Ithaca, 1970. For a recent review of the state of Śrīvijayan scholarship, see O. W. Wolters, 'Restudying some Chinese Writings on Srivijaya', *Indonesia*, 42 (1986). On Śrīvijayan archaeology, see P. Y. Manguin, 'Étude Sumatranaise N. 1, Palembang et Srivijaya: ancien hypothese recherches nouvelles', BEFEO, 76 (1987).

For Javanese inscriptions see J. G. de Casparis, *Prasasti Indonesia II: Selected Inscriptions from the Seventh to the Ninth Century A.D.*, Bandung, 1956. On the Borobuḍur, see L. Gomez and H. W. Woodward, Jr, eds, *Barabuḍur: History and Significance of a Buddhist Monument*, Berkeley, 1981. Other important studies of early Java are J. G. de Casparis, 'Pour une histoire sociale de l'ancienne Java principale au Xème s.', *Archipel*, 21 (1981), and J. W. Christie, 'Raja and Rama: The Classical State in Early Java', in L. Gesick, ed., *Centers, Symbols, and Hierarchies: Essays on the Classical States of Southeast Asia*, New Haven, 1983. For Majapahit, see T. G. Th. Pigeaud, *Java in the Fourteenth Century*, 4 vols, Hague, 1962.

4

ECONOMIC HISTORY OF EARLY SOUTHEAST ASIA

In the pre-nineteenth-century world, the Southeast Asian region was eulogized as a land of immense wealth; developments there were of crucial importance to the entirety of world history in the pre-1600 period. Writers, travelers, sailors, merchants, and officials from every continent of the eastern hemisphere knew of Southeast Asia's wealth, and by the second millennium of the Christian era, most were aware of its power and prestige. By contrast, the early history of Southeast Asia and its international significance is not appreciated in the contemporary age.

In the early centuries CE Indians and Westerners called Southeast Asia the 'Golden Khersonese', the 'Land of Gold', and it was not long thereafter that the region became known for its pepper and the products of its rainforests, first aromatic woods and resins, and then the finest and rarest of spices.[1] From the seventh to the tenth centuries Arabs and Chinese thought of Southeast Asia's gold, as well as the spices that created it; by the fifteenth century sailors from ports on the Atlantic, at the opposite side of the hemisphere, would sail into unknown oceans in order to find these Spice Islands. They all knew that Southeast Asia was the spice capital of the world. From roughly 1000 CE until the nineteenth-century 'industrial age', all world trade was more or less governed by the ebb and flow of spices in and out of Southeast Asia.

Throughout these centuries the region and its products never lost their siren quality. Palm trees, gentle surf, wide beaches, steep mountain slopes covered with lush vegetation, birds and flowers of brilliant colours, as well as orange and golden tropical sunsets have enchanted its visitors as well as its own people through the ages. Indeed, it is said that when in the last years of the sixteenth century the first Dutch ship arrived at one of the islands of the Indonesian archipelago, the entire crew jumped ship, and it took their captain two years to gather them for the return trip to Holland.

---

[1] Paul Wheatley, *The Golden Khersonese: Studies in the Historical Geography of the Malay Peninsula before A.D. 1500*, Kuala Lumpur, 1959.

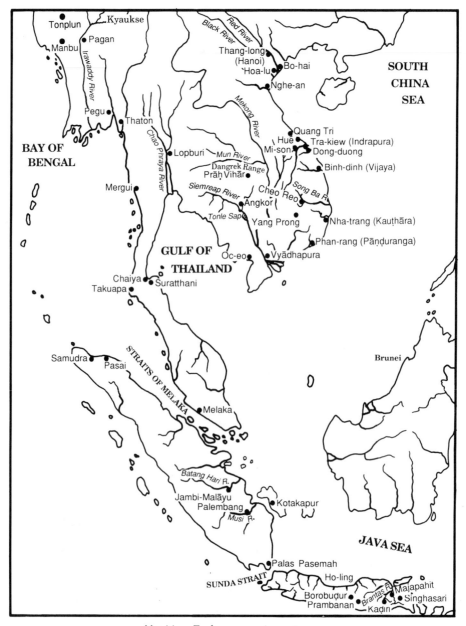

Map 4.1   Early economic centres.

EARLY ECONOMIC DEVELOPMENT

The story of economic development in early Southeast Asia begins long before the Christian era. Southeast Asia had already been for centuries a region with a distinct cultural identity. By the early Christian era, Southeast Asia had skilled farmers, musicians, metallurgists, and mariners. Even though they had no written language, no large urban concentrations, and no bureaucratic 'states' of recognizable proportions, they were nevertheless a highly accomplished people who had already assumed a significant role in the cultural development of the southern oceans of the eastern hemisphere.

Their expertise was in three general areas. First, they were innovative farmers. It is possible that Southeast Asians were the first to domesticate rice and to develop wet-rice cultivation. Early archaeological data for rice culture, as early as 2000 BC, have come from Southeast Asian sites (notably northeastern Thailand), and archaeologists have found evidence of a rice plant that could be classified as an intermediate stage between wild and domesticated rice that has been dated to 3000 BC. But they were never a rice monoculture. In addition to rice, they also harvested a number of other crops, including sugarcane, yams, sago, bananas, and coconuts. And they apparently were among the first (if not the first) to domesticate the chicken and the pig.

It may be that Southeast Asians independently discovered bronze and developed their own sophisticated metallurgical techniques based on the special qualities of bamboo. Since the trunk of this plant grows in hollow segments, they were able to use it to fashion a fire-piston that produced the heat required to liquefy metal. Archaeologists have dated bronze objects uncovered in northeast Thailand to 1500 BC, and iron bracelets and spearheads to about 500 BC. By 200 BC many peoples in the region possessed a sophisticated metal technology that included bronze, brass, tin, and iron. Beautiful large bronze ceremonial drums from Dong-son (in modern Vietnam) could be found all over Southeast Asia. That these drums were so widely dispersed throughout the region is clear evidence that there existed an extensive and efficient exchange mechanism within the Southeast Asian world prior to any significant trade with imperial India or China.

Their third area of expertise, that of sailing, may explain in part how these drums, among other things, became so widely dispersed. The people of the maritime realm were the pioneers of early watercraft developed on the southern oceans. From before the historic period, they knew how to ride the monsoons, the seasonal winds that pulled on to the continent during the hot months of the Central Asian summer and pushed away during the cold Central Asian winter. This basic rhythm of the Central Asian bellows offered an opportunity that the seaborne nomads of Southeast Asia seized. They sailed thousands of kilometres from their homes, navigating by means of swell and wave patterns, cloud formations, winds, birds and sea life. This sophisticated and complex knowledge was passed orally from generation to generation. They measured their peoples by 'boatloads', and on the slightest pretext, boatloads would leave islands where they were already concentrated and sail off to set up new communities on uninhabited islands, so that these 'Malayo-Polynesian' peoples eventually stretched halfway around the globe, from Madagascar on the East African coast to Easter Island in the Pacific.

They were the nomads of the Southern Ocean, and they played a role in history that in some ways resembles that of the nomads of the northern steppe. They were prime movers in the links created between larger centres, as well as potential impediments to those links once they were created. Exactly when this far-reaching maritime activity began is unknown, but 'Malay' (*Kunlun*) sailors were known in China by the third century BC, and there is evidence that they were settling along the East African coast by the first century CE. By the time of the Roman empire, there were permanent communities of Malayo-Polynesian speaking peoples on the coast of Malagasy, where they remain to this day.[2]

The Malay sailors did not cover these routes empty-handed, and in the process of sailing across the thousands of kilometres of southern ocean from Africa to Easter Island, they moved the specialties of one place to others. Cinnamon, a product that originally came from the South China coast, may also have reached the markets of India on the vessels of these sailors, and the markets of Southwest Asia and the Mediterranean through Malay trading stations in East Africa. The Roman historian Pliny, writing in the first century CE, described cinnamon traders between Africa and Asia who rode the winds 'from gulf to gulf'. Pliny describes their craft as 'rafts'. What he was no doubt referring to was the double outrigger canoe of the Malays. This same craft is still used today along the routes that these ancient mariners sailed. The cinnamon they brought was then traded north by the Africans until it reached Ethiopia, where the Europeans obtained it.

Bananas, too, may have made this journey from Southeast Asia to India to Africa with the Malays, and then spread across the continent to West Africa along internal, overland trade routes. But it was not only food that made the journey. The tuning scales of the Malayo-Polynesian xylophone also spread over the African continent and can still be heard today in West Africa, more than halfway around the world from their islands of origin.

Since Malay sailors were known in China by the third century BC, it was probably not long after that that they began to sail through the Straits of Melaka (Malacca) and Sunda into the Indian Ocean and on to India; and thus it is quite possible that the Southeast Asians themselves were responsible for the earliest contacts between Southeast Asia and South Asia. Historians do not know exactly when the first Indian ships went to Southeast Asia, but many believe that it was sometime in the last two centuries BC. It has been suggested that during the Mauryan period India's supply of gold had come from Siberia, from the northern reaches of Central Asia, but that after the Mauryans had fallen, the movements of

[2] Keith W. Taylor, 'Madagascar in the Ancient Malayo-Polynesian Myths' in Kenneth R. Hall and John K. Whitmore, eds, *Explorations in Early Southeast Asian History, The Origins of Southeast Asian Statecraft*, Ann Arbor, 1976. On early Southeast Asian seamanship, see Pierre-Yves Manguin, 'The Southeast Asian Ship: An Historical Approach', JSEAS, 11, 2 (1980).

steppe nomads cut them off from these sources and forced them to look elsewhere. It was then, they think, that merchants from India began to sail into Southeast Asian waters, looking for the 'Islands of Gold'.[3]

The early Southeast Asian population shared a relatively common physical geography, wherein ample and readily available productive land was available to support the basic economic needs of the indigenous society. The exceptions were the several dry and infertile islands of the eastern Indonesian archipelago, like Timor and northern Maluku (the Moluccas). Southeast Asia had no substantial grasslands, no pastoral tradition, and thus low dependency upon animal protein; meat and milk products had little importance in the traditional diet. Houses were constructed from the seemingly inexhaustible local supply of wood, palm, and bamboo; they were usually elevated on poles above the annual floods of the lowlands, and human and animal predators in the highlands. The ease of building and rebuilding and the abundance of unoccupied fertile land meant that the population was inherently mobile. Indeed, the shortage of labour relative to land produced a social pattern in which additional labour rather than land became the object of competition.

Traditional household-based production in early Southeast Asia consisted of clearing woods, planting, weeding, harvesting, cooking, feeding pigs and chickens, and fishing. Men and women performed daily chores according to local tradition, but everyone participated in food production. As more stratified societies emerged, productive activities became more differentiated. Work was often assigned by local leaders ('big men/women', chiefs, or religious élites who tended to distance themselves from food production) to their social subordinates, as well as to prisoners of war and debt slaves. When states began to emerge there was a corresponding dissociation of a small or large group of state élite, inclusive of religious functionaries; courtiers; musicians, dancers, and dramatists; as well as craftsmen and traders.

Millet, or dry rice, was highly adaptable and predates Southeast Asian wet-rice as the staple grain. The late Roman-era geographer Ptolemy's reference to *Yāvadvīpa* probably equates with *Yawadvipa*, 'millet island'. But millet (dry) and *sawah* (wet) cultivation were incompatible; as *sawah* agriculture spread, millet production was displaced.[4]

Initially, millet probably was produced in the uplands, by means of what is commonly called 'slash-and-burn' or 'shifting' cultivation. Shifting cultivation of rice was ideal for sloping highland areas with adequate drainage. It required little labour, and was able to produce a substantial surplus relative to the size of the workforce. A new patch of forest was cleared and burned each year. Planting normally consisted of using pointed sticks to make holes, into which two or three grains were placed. Nutrients added to the soil in the initial burn-off were washed away by rain within two seasons, thus necessitating the shifting cultivation cycle. Slash-and-burn

[3] Paul Wheatley, *Nagara and Commandery: Origins of the Southeast Asian Urban Traditions*, Chicago, 1983.
[4] N. C. van Setten van der Meer, *Sawah Cultivation in Ancient Java: Aspects of Development during the Indo-Javanese Period, 5th to 15th Century*, Canberra, 1979; Paul Wheatley, 'Agricultural Terracing', *Pacific Viewpoint*, 6, 2 (1965).

regions could usually produce a stable food supply, but their populations were not usually as spatially confined as were their lowland neighbours. Fields, rivers, and lake productive centres might be some distance apart rather than coincident, thereby making their aggregate revenue potential less. Local migration cycles, together with the relatively low yield per hectare, limited highland population density to twenty to thirty persons per square kilometre, and made it difficult to collect surplus for urban development or for export.

Transition from upland shifting to settled lowland rice cultivation may have been induced by population pressure, but was more likely due to a supportive physical environment. It is generally believed that wet-rice cultivation was becoming common in the early Christian era, although surviving records can definitively substantiate only that wet-rice agriculture in permanent fields was practised in eastern Java and the Kyaukse area of Burma by the eighth century. On the mainland (Cambodia, Thailand, and Burma), seed was more commonly broadcast on a bunded and ploughed floodplain, and grew quickly and needed little work. In Java, however, the transplanting method came to be preferred; this gave higher yields per land used, though not the highest per labour input. By either the broadcast or seedling method, a Southeast Asian lowland wet-rice farmer could normally expect an annual output of twenty to twenty-five bushels of grain per acre. In early times one rice crop proved adequate to supply local needs, although a second could be harvested, if weather and irrigation facilities permitted and there were incentive to produce a surplus for external consumption.

On Java, seed was annually sown in small seedling beds at the approach of the rainy season. While seedlings took root, farmers and family prepared nearby fields; they weeded and broke up soil with wooden, stone, or metal-tipped hoes until the monsoon rains soaked the earth. Then seedlings were transplanted by hand, with enough space between for each plant to grow. As the crops matured, farmers repaired the local irrigation system and regulated the flow of water as rains reached their peak. As water receded, fields were drained, and the sun ripened the grain. At harvest, the entire community worked side-by-side. Javanese women harvested using a finger-knife that cut only one stalk at a time, rather than use a sickle, which might offend the local rice spirit and thus jeopardize future production. During the subsequent dry season, fields were cleared, tools repaired, and feasts, festivals, and marriages were celebrated.

Sawah cultivation was effectively maintained only where dissolved volcanic matter was brought into the fields with irrigated water, in rich alluvial plains, or where fertilizer (such as water-buffalo excrement) was added. Initial Southeast Asian wet-rice may have been cultivated without ploughs, but by the late first millennium CE water-buffaloes were being driven into the irrigated fields to make the land suitable for the reception of seeds or seedlings. Ploughing with wooden or metal-tipped ploughs puddled the flooded soil and turned it into a creamy mud; it also produced a dense layer of soil at a depth of 30–50 centimetres, which reduced the percolation of irrigated water. As the water-buffalo worked the fields, their droppings added to soil fertility.

In *sawah* regions there were three food staples: rice, fish, and coconut. Rice might be affected by periodic disease and plagues; mice plagues are shown in Borobuḍur and Angkor Wat reliefs. But fish (from rivers, tanks, or *sawah* fields) and coconut (when properly maintained) were virtually free of pests and diseases. Rice was eaten by preference. Reliance upon other staples was looked down upon except during rice famines when *sawah* cultivators could normally turn to tubers (taro, which grew in *sawah* areas) and yams (which were gathered from nearby forests or were grown in the rain-fed fields), as well as to sago palms, which were another stable source of starch. The three staples were supplemented by a wide variety of vegetables, pigs, and fowl that could not be stored. Properly prepared, rice and fish—which was usually dried or fermented and was the major garnish to rice—could be stored more than a year; coconuts (the source of fruit, sugar, oil and palm wine) could not be stored as long, but were available at three-month intervals.

Sawah agriculture could thus support a high population density and high yields from small areas—a field of one hectare (2½ acres) could well support a household. But large population centres in the early *sawah* regions were the exception. Small housing clusters (one house and one field, or several houses and nearby fields) were more practical for flooding and draining of the fields. Too much water flow would damage the dykes, while too little would result in algae growth. Rights to occupy and use land were characterized by long-term commitment to a soil plot.

Such a stable food source was ideal to feed non-food-producers, i.e. state functionaries and traders. There is thus a general coincidence of *sawah* cultivation and state development in early Southeast Asia. *Sawah* cultivators could occupy the same lands for generations; because they had little need to move, they were ideal producers of surplus. Taxing the early small and scattered productive units must have been a time-consuming task for emergent states, yet *sawah* cultivators could not easily escape their revenue cesses. Leaving their fields uncontrolled was not an option among *sawah* cultivators, except just after harvest, and developing new lands for cultivation (bunding, etc.) might take several seasons. But early armies and state bureaucratic corps were not large enough constantly to threaten *sawah* producers. Instead, would-be élites had to offer inducements, such as protection (although this was not always needed in areas where population centres were geographically isolated from their neighbours or foreigners, as in central Java, Angkor, and Pagan). More commonly material rewards (foreign luxury goods) or ideological rewards (titles, temples) were bestowed to secure food and labour from subordinate *sawah* cultivators.

Control of water was important in dry areas, but in regions where rainfall was plentiful, or where there were too many rivers useful for irrigation, an élite would have had to employ too many functionaries to control a water system. Even in eastern Java, where there was a stronger seasonality than western Java, water control as the basis of the indigenous agrarian system does not seem to have been a major factor, although rulers based in east Java did build hydraulic networks that gave them better control of agricultural production. One incentive to develop this control was the more significant position that long-distance trade assumed in the east Java economy, particularly the rice-based trade to the eastern Indonesian archipelago via the Solo and Brantas Rivers. In contrast, in central Java, overland transport from the Kedu plain heartland to north coast harbours was more difficult.

Early Southeast Asian trade involved highland hunters and gatherers who exchanged their forest products (woods, bamboo, lacquer) and services with lowland rice cultivators. Salt from the coast was a key commodity in this upland–lowland exchange. Another type of exchange network encompassed hinterland populations and coastal peoples; the hinterland supplied local agricultural or forest products that were in turn dispensed externally to international traders. Coastal-based traders returned goods of foreign origin or specialized services (for example, transport) to the hinterland producers. In exceptional cases merchants worked from a coastal base to organize the necessary trade mechanisms that allowed them to extract local products from their hinterlands. In normal trade, agricultural and imported commodities entered the markets and trading system either laterally, through direct barter between producers and consumers, or vertically, through political or religious institutions or developing hierarchical commercial networks, and only rarely through monetized commercial transaction.

As is the case today, women assumed a significant role in the local market systems. Chinese sources report that women were in charge of trade in Khmer territories as well as elsewhere in the region.[5] While males normally dominated port-based and large-scale wholesale trade, there are counter examples. The most notable is that of Nyai Gede Pinateh, a Muslim from Palembang, China, or the Khmer realm who was the harbour master (*syahbandar*) of the major port of Gresik on the north Java coast around 1500; between 1405 and 1434, two queens ruled over Pasai just before Melaka eclipsed the Sumatra coast port as the paramount port of trade in the Straits of Melaka.[6]

Because land was plentiful in the Southeast Asian region, and additional labour was always in demand, women enjoyed a high degree of economic and social status—certainly by contrast with the low economic and social status of Chinese and Indian women. Our ability precisely to define the role of women in early Southeast Asian society is clouded by the epigraphic records that were preponderantly recorded on Indic temples, and were initiated by an élite who were emulating Indic culture. True to the Indian epics and religions that promoted male superiority and female dependency, there are infrequent references to women, and the inscriptional vocabulary is male or universal generic. A discrepancy between court ideal and reality is conspicuous in contemporary temple reliefs that portray everyday life, wherein females are participants in scenes that involve not only agriculture and home, but also market, trade, diplomacy, warfare, entertainment, literature, and even statecraft.

[5] Paul Pelliot, *Mémoires sur les coutumes du Cambodge de Tcheou Ta-Kouan*, Paris, 1951, 20; and J. V. G. Mills, *Ying-yai Sheng-lan of Ma Huan (1433)*, Cambridge, 1970, 104.
[6] M. A. P. Meilink-Roelofsz, *Asian Trade and European Influence in the Indonesian Archipelago between 1500 and about 1630*, The Hague, 1962, 108.

In everyday life, male work included ploughing, felling trees, hunting, metalwork, house building, statecraft, and formal (Indic or Sinic-based) religion; females transplanted, harvested, grew vegetables, prepared food, wove cloth, made pottery, and marketed local produce. Because of their control over birth and crop growth, women were believed to have magical powers relative to fertility. Women were deemed to have special capacity to mediate between mankind and the spirit world, and were called upon to heal the sick, and to change unfavourable weather conditions.

A common feature of the early Southeast Asian socio-economy was the practice of bilateral kinship. In determining inheritance, for instance, equal value was accorded the maternal and paternal lines, and sons and daughters usually received equal rights to their parents' estates (including land). The value of daughters was never questioned in early Southeast Asia. Bride wealth passed from male to female at marriage (the reverse of the European dowry custom), and it was normal practice for a married couple to reside with the family of the bride. Contemporary iconography as well as the earliest literary records portray the marriage ritual as involving the escort of the male, with his bride price, to the residence of the female for the marriage ceremony. Should the husband leave his wife, the bridal wealth, as well as their mutual resources (including their land), remained in her possession. From the perspective of the woman's family an absent husband created no substantial hardship, as the abandoned wife and children were quickly assimilated into the family work unit.

While the conjugal relationship tended to be strong, and the woman's predominance in the family gave her a major sense of responsibility for its survival, divorce was relatively easy. The Chinese envoy Chou Ta-kuan, reporting daily life in the Khmer realm around 1300, writes, 'If the husband is called away for more than ten days, the wife is apt to say, "I am not a spirit; how am I supposed to sleep alone?"'[7] Another display of the power and autonomy of women was the widespread practice among men of painful surgical implants of penis balls to enhance the sexual pleasure of their women. For example, two fifteenth-century temples near modern Surakarta in Java display lingas with three or four small ball implants.[8] The Chinese Muslim Ma Huan (1433) provides the earliest written record, reporting that among the Thai:

> when a man attained his twentieth year, they take the skin which surrounds the *membrum virile*, and with a fine knife . . . they open it up and insert a dozen tin beads inside the skin; they close it up and protect it with medicinal herbs . . . The beads look like a cluster of grapes . . . If it is the king . . . or a great chief or a wealthy man, they use gold to make hollow beads, inside which a grain of sand is placed . . . They make a tinkling sound, and this is regarded as beautiful.[9]

In the Khmer state, inheritance of the throne of the Angkor-based realm has been shown to be neither patrilocal nor matrilocal. Although males held monarchical authority, when they assumed power they would record

---

[7] Chou Ta-kuan (1297) in Pelliot, *Mémoires*, 17.
[8] W. I. Stutterheim, *Gids voor de oudheden van Soekoeh en Tjeta*, Surakarta, 1930, 31.
[9] Ma Huan (1433) in Mills, 104.

their official descent from either their father's or their mother's family, dependent upon which genealogical faction was most critical to their successful acquisition of the throne. With considerable royal polygamy, wherein marital alliances to regionally-powerful families were an important source of political stability, there were numerous offspring who might step forward to assert their claims of rightful descent, backed by their armed maternal relatives. That this was the case is documented in the frequent epigraphic references to the female links of Khmer monarchs, and corresponding failure in such cases to mention the male lineage.[10]

THE AGE OF FU-NAN: THE EMERGENCE OF THE SOUTHEAST ASIAN POLITICAL-ECONOMY IN THE EARLY CHRISTIAN ERA

The first known polity to emerge in Southeast Asia was a place the Chinese called Fu-nan. Its seaport at the present-day town called Oc-eo, was originally located in the Mekong River delta in what is now Vietnam, very near the Cambodian border, at the point where the Gulf of Thailand coast recedes closest to the river. Its capital Vyādapura was near Ba Phnom in what is now Prei Veng Province, Cambodia. Although Fu-nan's date of origin is obscure, it is usually dated from the first century CE. During this century there was an unprecedented Roman market for Asian goods, especially Chinese silk, and, most importantly, the enhancement of a maritime route between India and China that passed through Southeast Asia.

That this first Southeast Asian polity emerged several hundred kilometres north of Java and the straits region was due to the fact that prior to about 350 CE the international traffic between India and China avoided the trip around the 1600-kilometre length of the Malay peninsula. Travellers on their way to China ended their voyage around the Bay of Bengal at the Isthmus of Kra, the peninsula's narrowest point, and moved their goods overland to the Gulf of Thailand where their maritime journey resumed.

Although it might seem strange at first glance that Fu-nan emerged on the eastern shore of the Gulf of Thailand, on the opposite shore from the Kra and the portage, there was a most important reason. What distinguished Fu-nan's site from a number of other small coastal enclaves around the Gulf of Thailand was its agricultural productivity. The area around Oc-eo is the only place near the coast west of the Mekong where a particular kind of topography and soil enabled its people to grow significant amounts of rice with the existing pre-canal irrigation wet-rice methods of cultivation—they used the natural flooding of the river to water their rice fields. The ability to amass ample amounts of rice and other foodstuffs for themselves as well as for those who arrived on the ships gave them a

---

[10] A. Thomas Kirsch, 'Kinship, Genealogical Claims, and Societal Integration in Ancient Khmer Society: An Interpretation', in C. D. Cowan and O. W. Wolters, eds., *Southeast Asian History and Historiography*, Ithaca, 1976, 190–202. I have found similar bilateral succession patterns among the rulers of Śailendra-era Java. See Kenneth R. Hall, *Maritime Trade and State Development in Early Southeast Asia*, Honolulu, 1985, 110–11.

crucial advantage over would-be coastal entrepôts on the gulf that did not have such productive hinterlands.

But it was not simply the feeding of passers-by that made rice important. Oc-eo was nestled on a coastline that offered sailors protection from the troubled seas at the tip of southern Vietnam. Because of the winds, the travellers could not simply pass through. For half the year, when the winds blew off the continent, one could sail to Southeast Asian ports from either China or India. But one could not go on to either one until the winds had shifted and begun to blow toward the continent. Thus, the ships all tended to arrive at the same time and leave at the same time, regardless of which way the travellers were going. Indeed, their arrivals and departures became so predictable that the local people began to call them 'the migratory birds'. Furthermore, they were often obliged to remain in port, sometimes for as long as five months, waiting for the winds to shift. This meant that the Southeast Asian port often had to feed the travellers for months on end. It was this reality that ensured that a port's access to agricultural surpluses was one of the most important variables in its success.

Given the number of travellers coming from India and the length of time they were in port, it is not surprising that a cultural dialogue of profound importance to Southeast Asia generally developed between Fu-nan and India. The local explanation and legitimation of this dialogue are found in a legend that was already old when Chinese visitors recorded it in the 240s CE. According to this legend, the process began when a local princess (whom the Chinese called Lin-yeh) led a raid on a passing ship of unspecified nationality. The ship's passengers and crew managed to defeat the raiders and make a landing. One of the passengers was Kauṇḍinya, an Indian brahmin. And Lin-yeh subsequently married him, after he drank of the local waters. Thereafter Fu-nan set about to attract merchant ships by providing facilities and harbour improvements. The couple inherited the realm, which consisted of several settlements principally along the Mekong, each with its own local chief. Seven of these they transferred to the realm of their son, and the rest they retained as their own domain.

One cannot take legends of this sort too literally. There was already an ancient myth among the Malayo-Polynesian peoples that described a marriage between a sky-god and a foam-born princess (or sometimes a princess born from a bamboo shoot), and this story seems to be an updated version of that legend. There may never have been such a marriage. What this myth explains is that the rulers of Fu-nan began a cultural dialogue with India, and that the political integration of larger domains was contemporary with this dialogue.

It is important to note that the Malay princess married this foreigner and thus established for him a place within local society, and that he 'drank the waters', which suggests that he took an oath of loyalty to the local ruler, i.e. he entered his service, or that he in some way assisted in the development of the local wet-rice agriculture system. There is also an important moral to this story, that good things come not from attacking and plundering passing ships, but from befriending and servicing them.

Such a legend might also have been useful in maintaining good relations with both Indian traders and religious pilgrims, since it emphasized a friendly link between local rulers and Indian brahmins. It might also have been used to legitimize Fu-nan's expansion. Chinese accounts report that by the beginning of the third century, Fu-nan had conquered the entire northern rim of the gulf, all the way from the Mekong delta to the Isthmus of Kra, and a legend that claimed a special, Indian origin for its rulers would have been useful in distinguishing it from those it subordinated.

By the second or third century CE, Fu-nan was both rich and powerful, and foreign visitors were numerous. Not only were there Indians and Chinese, but by the third century Persian Gulf sailors from the Sassanid empire in Persia could also be found in Fu-nan. The third-century Chinese visitors, Kang Tai and Zhu Ying, were impressed and reported back to their ruler that the people of Fu-nan

> live in walled cities, palaces, and houses. . . . They devote themselves to agriculture. In one year they sow and harvest for three [i.e., they leave it in and it will grow back three years before they have to replant]. [Customs] taxes are paid in gold, silver, pearls, and perfumes . . . There are books and depositories of archives and other things. Their characters for writing resemble those of the Hu [a people whose alphabet was of Indian origin].[11]

Fu-nan was also importing goods brought to it by Malay sailors from other Southeast Asian ports. Copper and tin were transported downriver from the uplands of modern Thailand to supply the workshops of Oc-eo in Fu-nan, where, according to the results of excavations, there was no lack of raw materials.[12]

Fu-nan appears to have reached the peak of its fortunes sometime in the fourth century, prior to the instigation of a competitive, all-sea route from India to China that went through the Straits of Melaka. Although Fa Xian's early-fifth-century account is the earliest record of a traveller going through the straits region and laying over in the northwestern Indonesian archipelago for five months, he makes it clear that the route was not new when he took it; historians have dated this new route to China to about 350 CE.

Even during the time of Fu-nan's best years there had been a number of ports in the Sunda Strait region, east of the Straits of Melaka, that had already assumed some importance, and sailors from these ports had frequented the ports of Fu-nan. They were also engaged in a direct trade with India. The third-century visitors from China heard, for example, that in 'Zhiaying' (on the southeastern coast of Sumatra) there was a king who imported horses from the Yuezhi (the Kushana realm of northwestern India) and that in 'Sitiao' (central Java), there was a fertile land that possessed cities with streets.[13] Sanskrit inscriptions carved in stone on the east coast and Hindu and Buddhist archaeological remains on the west coast of Borneo indicate that ports there, too, were already engaged in a dialogue with India.

---

[11] Quoted in P. Pelliot, 'Le Fou-nan', BEFEO, 3 (1903) 252.
[12] O. W. Wolters, *Early Indonesian Commerce: A Study of the Origins of Sri Vijaya*, Ithaca, 1967, 52.
[13] ibid., 62–61.

These southern sailors had also played a large part in the introduction of Southeast Asian products to the international markets. Originally neither the Indians nor the international traders using the ports of Fu-nan were interested in Southeast Asian specialties. The traders at Fu-nan went to China in order to exchange Mediterranean, Indian, Middle Eastern, and African goods (items such as frankincense and myrrh, other plant resins, and other substances used to manufacture perfumes and incense) for China's silk. But, given the opportunity that the presence of the international transit trade at Fu-nan created, sailors from the Sunda Strait area responded with entrepreneurial skill and began to introduce their own products, beginning with those that might be construed as substitutes for products destined for the China market. Sumatran pine resins were substituted for frankincense, and benzoin (a resin from a plant related to the laurel family, also known as benjamin gum) was substituted for bdellium myrrh.

But it was not long before the sailors from the western Indonesian archipelago introduced their own unique products to the ports of Fu-nan and India. One of the most important was camphor, a resin that crystallized in wood and that was valued as a medicine, as incense, and as an ingredient in varnish. Throughout the ages the most highly prized camphor has been that of Barus, a port on Sumatra's northwestern coast. Aromatic woods such as gharuwood and sandalwood (a specialty of Timor) became important commodities, and the fine spices of Maluku also began to appear in international markets at this time. Charaka, who is believed to have been the court physician of the northwest Indian monarch Kanishka at the end of the first century CE, mentions in his medical text cloves, for example, as does one of the plays written by the Gupta court poet Kālidāsa, which was more or less contemporary with Fa Xian's travels.[14]

As long as the sailors from the ports near the straits brought their goods that were destined for the China market into Fu-nan's ports, they were no threat to the interests of Fu-nan. However, by the fourth century CE they had begun to bypass Fu-nan and were taking their products directly to China; if they stopped at any ports on the way, they were not those of Fu-nan but ports on the eastern coast of Vietnam. 'Malay' sailors had for centuries known the way to China, and once the Chinese market for their products made it worth their while to make the trip, they went. They could bring back goods from China to their own ports and could, furthermore, pass these along to Western marketplaces via their own Sunda Strait entrepôt.

During the fifth century, due to disturbances on the overland caravan routes still used by the majority of the silk traders, the maritime route became even more significant. And although some of the increased traffic still used the ports of Fu-nan, it was the ports of the Sunda Strait region that were the primary beneficiaries.[15]

After the fall of the Han dynasty in the third century CE, China was divided; and in the fourth century northern China was overrun by nomadic steppe peoples. This caused a massive flight of population from the north

[14] ibid., 66.
[15] O. W. Wolters, 'Studying Srivijaya', JMBRAS, 52, 2 (1979).

to the south. Since those who could afford to relocate were usually the more privileged, this group predominated among the refugees. Some historians claim that as many as 60 to 70 per cent of the northern upper classes moved south of the Yangtze River. These people had well-established tastes for the products that came from the West—from India, Southwestern Asia, the eastern Mediterranean, and the East African coast.

Prior to 439 this southern market had been supplied, for the most part, by the overland routes. Goods had continued to come overland through northern China to the south even after the fall of the Han dynasty and the steppe invasion. However, after 439, this source of foreign products was completely blocked when the Gansu corridor, the major road from China's population centres to the western boundaries, was captured by a hostile northern kingdom, and Chinese in the south for the first time were completely cut off from what they called 'the western regions'.

South China, however, did not wither on the vine. On the contrary, it witnessed an unprecedented commercial development. It could be defended more easily than the northern plains, since its rice paddies inhibited horse-riding steppe invaders, and it became the seat of two successful Buddhist kingdoms, the Liu Sung dynasty (420–79) and the Southern Qi (Nan Ch'i) (479–502). This China market was irresistible, and the seamen of the Sunda Strait region rose to the challenge, picking up the goods from the West in India and Sri Lanka, bringing them through Southeast Asia and then delivering them to this southern Chinese market.

These southern Chinese, too, developed a desire for Southeast Asian products, and not only for the resins and aromatic woods of the rainforest. China became an inexhaustible market for rhinoceros horn which was used as a tonic in China, guaranteed to overcome the male fear of sexual inadequacy in middle and old age, and as a bedroom charm in Japan. The Chinese also became important purchasers of kingfish and other bird feathers, as well as tortoiseshell, among other exotic things. And, by the late fifth or early sixth century, Chinese consumers were well acquainted with pepper and other spices, including cloves, nutmeg, and mace, items that they valued not only for their flavour, but for their medicinal properties as well.

The competition from the south, from the seamen of the ports of the Sunda Strait region, eventually deprived Fu-nan of its predominance in the international trade, and by the sixth century its realm was contracting. Its vulnerability was exposed in the middle of the sixth century when it was taken over by Zhenla, a name given by the Chinese to the Khmer people who lived along the middle reaches of the Mekong River. Although some traders continued to use the Kra portage, its special position was gone.

THE AGE OF THE ŚRĪVIJAYAN MARITIME EMPIRE
(670–1025)

Among the most significant factors in the rise of the Melaka-Sunda Strait region as the pre-eminent Southeast Asian maritime trade centre was its rulers' political acumen: their ability both to consolidate their own Sumatran hinterland and to dominate rival ports and thus indirectly their hinterlands. This control enabled the emergent Śrīvijaya polity to concentrate the agricultural, forest, and ocean products of the Indonesian archipelago in its own ports, both those goods that came by sea from neighbouring islands in relatively small ships carrying some twenty-five to fifty people, and those goods that moved downriver by way of mountain trails and the tributaries of Sumatra rivers. The creation of this realm was a political feat achieved not simply by force but, of equal importance, by the adroit merging of both local Malay and imported and adapted Buddhist symbols of power and authority.

The founders and rulers of the Śrīvijayan realm were local Malay chiefs who ruled the port area that the Chinese Buddhist pilgrim I Ching visited in the latter part of the seventh century on his return voyage from India, now generally accepted to have been at or near the modern city of Palembang, a port city in southeastern Sumatra.[16] It was this area that became the core of Śrīvijayan hegemony. In the traditional Malay view of the world there was a powerful duality, a landscape dominated by high and steep mountains and seas whose horizons seemed unreachable. Both the mountain heights and the depths of the sea were the loci of powerful forces that shaped the lives of the people, forces that were both generous and devastating. The same volcanoes that provided the most fertile land could and did on occasion destroy the villages that grew up on them. The sea, too, was a bountiful provider and a major means of communication, but its storms could also destroy the lives and livelihood of those dependent upon it.

In traditional Malay belief, both the source of the river waters and the home of the ancestral spirits were high on the mountain slopes; the highest reaches of the mountains were thus thought of as holy places and the source of beneficent forces that bestowed well-being upon the people. The Śrīvijayan king drew upon these beliefs as he took the title 'Lord of the Mountain'. He was also 'Lord of the Isles', and able to commune with the 'Spirit of the Waters of the Sea', a dangerous force that had to be propitiated and whose powers had to be absorbed by the king. It was for this purpose that the king blithely threw gold bricks daily into the Palembang estuary.

The critical link between these two forces of mountain and sea were the rivers, for they were the channels through which the rainwater that fell on the mountains flowed down, ultimately to merge with the sea. These river basins contained the earliest polities of island Southeast Asia, and shaped the political dynamic between them. The king's magical powers, closely associated with fertility, were also linked with the river. The magic of the association between the king and the water was so strong that it was dangerous for the king to bathe in ordinary water for fear of causing a flood. His bath water had to be treated with flower petals before it was safe. And there were other fertility taboos. On a specific day each year the

---

[16] E. Edward McKinnon, 'A Note on the Discovery of Spur-Marked Yueh-Type Sherds at Bukit Seguntang Palembang', JMBRAS, 52, 2 (1979) 35.

king could not eat grain. If he did, there might be a crop failure. Nor was he able to leave his realm, for if he did, the sun's rays might go with him, the skies would darken, and the crops would fail.

Palembang's significance as a port probably dates back to the prehistoric period when the metal culture of the mainland was spread about by the Malay sailors from the more easterly islands.[17] Sailors moving down the 1600-kilometre length of the Malay peninsula to the islands would have found both Palembang on the Musi and Jambi-Malāyu on the Batang Hari River were near the tip of the peninsula. As river-mouth ports, they offered the sailors access not only to those people who lived near the coast but indirectly to Sumatra's sizeable hinterland and to all those who lived along the banks of these two rivers' many tributaries. Thus, both of these ports probably began as small trading centres near the mouths of rivers that linked the peoples of the mountains with the sailors of the seas. There the sailors could exchange their goods, including metals, for the produce of the island.

When the international trade began to grow between the Fu-nan region and India sometime around the first century CE, these Sumatran ports emerged as small political centres that concentrated the resources of their river's drainage basin near the coast in order to attract traders. They could then use imported goods to enhance their own resources and as gifts or trade goods to be exchanged for the products of their hinterland. Since the maritime realm of Southeast Asia possessed many river systems that were separated by mountains, this dynamic led to the creation of many small riverine polities based at their mouths. These coastal centres tended to look back toward the mountains and forward to the sea, but they did not look kindly to their sides; they saw their neighbouring river systems as rivals and enemies. And some of them by about 350 CE had already begun their dialogue with Indian culture.

For centuries there had been many independent ports and polities in the southern maritime realm, but in the early part of the seventh century, one of them, Śrīvijaya, emerged victorious in a contest to dominate the others and thus become the core of an emergent state system. Why it was the local ruler of Palembang who became the paramount power in the region is not immediately apparent. Although its location about halfway between the Straits of Melaka and the Sunda Strait was significant, there were a number of other ports that enjoyed locations with similar advantages. Nor was either of the two major southeastern Sumatran ports, Palembang and its chief rival Jambi-Malāyu, located near those places that produced the items most desired by international traders. Camphor, the Sumatran forest product most sought after in this early period, came from more northern and western parts of the island. Although some pepper was locally grown, it was also a product of west Java across the Sunda Strait. Sandalwood, another product popular from the earliest period, came from Timor, which was about 2500 kilometres to Sumatra's east. The cloves, nutmeg, and mace that would eventually become the maritime realm's most famous

---

[17] R. B. Smith and W. Watson, eds, *Early South East Asia: Essays in Archaeology, History and Historical Geography*, London, 1976.

products came from other islands that were equally far away to the east.

Further, archaeological data currently available indicate a general absence of intensive rice cultivation near the early Sumatran ports. Unlike Java, where centres of power were in the vicinity of production centres, Sumatra's early downriver ports depended upon less direct means of collecting food and upland products. Unless food was imported from Java, which seems unlikely until later times when the volume of trade increased substantially, early Sumatra entrepôts would have drawn upon lower river basin deep-water rice (*lebak*) and tidal irrigated rice (*pasang surut*) to feed transients. Palembang's hinterland consisted of the Pasemah Highlands and the upper Musi, areas well-known today for their rice and very similar in natural conditions to Java's wet-rice areas; volcanic activity in these regions supplied fertile material for rice cultivation. Megalithic archaeological remains in south Sumatra come from Pasemah in what are now ricelands. One carved stone depicts a man riding on an elephant and carrying a drum of the Dong-son type. Such a stone monument, or at least its inspiration, may have been a present to Pasemah populations in return for their products. Bronze bowls and bells found in the same area suggest early foreign relations and downriver contacts. Similarly, in the Jambi-Malāyu upriver heartland, stone sculptures of the early Christian era depict male figures standing on somebody, a traditional Indonesian symbol of power, which would also indicate downriver contact.[18]

There were, no doubt, numerous factors that accounted for Palembang's victory over its rivals, but one of them probably was the agricultural productivity of the fields in the valleys of the Musi River and its tributaries. Although none of the river-mouth ports of the island realm had agricultural resources comparable to those of Fu-nan in the Mekong delta, Palembang did have the unusually wide, slow, and silt-rich Musi River behind it, a better agricultural base than any of its competitors had. A local legend claimed that civilization was founded at Palembang only after the waters of the various rivers were weighed, and it was determined that those of the Musi were heaviest. Obviously its founders were searching for a silt-laden river that could be depended upon continually to deposit the fertile silt on fields adjacent to the river. Today, the best rice land in the area is quite near modern Palembang, at Bukit Seguntang. It is on and around this hill that some of the richest finds of archaeological remains from the Śrīvijayan period have been made, and this hill appears to have been the location of the ceremonial centre described in the account of I Ching where 1000 priests resided and where gold and silver Buddhas were offered golden vessels shaped like lotus flowers. These bowls were known to be a specialty of Śrīvijaya, and as late as 1082 there is a Chinese record of Śrīvijayan envoys bringing lotus bowls filled with pearls and other precious objects as presents for the Sung emperor.[19]

Palembang also offered a fine natural harbour and a river that was

---

[18] F. M. Schnitger, *The Archeology of Hindoo Sumatra*, Leiden, 1937.

[19] Recent aerial photographic surveys of the Palembang region surrounding Bukit Seguntang reveal the existence of earth dock networks which substantiate that the Bukit Seguntang area was the centre of early commerce. Hermann Kulke and Pierre-Yves Manguin have graciously shared this information.

navigable for long distances. Even in the nineteenth century, the largest ocean-going steamers had no difficulty in reaching the city, which is 80 kilometres inland from the mouth of the Musi. Even above Palembang the river and its tributaries remain navigable by small boats for many miles. This gave the Palembang area unusually good access to the Sumatran hinterland and the island's valuable forest products.

In terms of indigenous understanding, the initial motivation for conquest most likely emerged from internal Malay politics, an attempt to unite the surrounding Malay peoples, and not necessarily from a desire to control the straits. The earliest image we have of the Śrīvijayan founder comes from a stone inscription dated 683 CE. What is revealed is a traditional Sumatran war chief, a local ruler who after assembling the surrounding chiefs and their forces, selected from 20,000 a force of 2000 men, which he led against Jambi-Malāyu, the rival to the north and the only other important river system on this strategic coast. Śrīvijaya defeated its rivals; the ruler had proved himself in battle, and thus he could claim in this inscription to possess supernatural power that allowed him to bestow prosperity upon his new subjects.

> The king expressed his concern that all the clearances and gardens made by them [his subjects] should be full [of crops]. That the cattle of all species raised by them and the bondsmen they possess should prosper . . . that all their servants shall be faithful and devoted to them . . . that, wherever they may find themselves, there be in that place no thieves, no ruffians and no adulterers . . . that there arise among them the thought of Bodhi [wisdom] and the love of the 'Three Jewels' [the Buddha, the Doctrines, and the monkhood].[20]

I Ching's account of Śrīvijaya suggests that Palembang's subjugation of Jambi-Malāyu and thus the Batang Hari River system occurred between 671 and 685 CE.

The realm that Śrīvijaya ultimately commanded can be divided into three parts: the core area around Palembang; its Musi River hinterland, upriver and downriver; and those river-mouth ports and their hinterlands that had previously been its rivals. In each of these three parts, the manner in which they ruled was somewhat different. The urban core centred at Palembang was directly administered by the monarch and his family. The monarch was assisted by royal judges, revenue collectors, land administrators, and various other officials. The king referred to the cultivators of the royal domain as 'my bondsmen', and they were also the nucleus of his imperial army.

The second part of the empire, the Musi River hinterland, was ruled by more indirect means, through alliances with local chiefs who swore allegiance to the kings at the Palembang core. This relationship between the royal centre and its upriver and downriver hinterland was based on what was in reality a mutual self-interest. These relationships had to be consolidated and could not be neglected or abused, for it did sometimes happen that peoples in the hinterland took over river-mouth ports and made them their own. The relationship between coast and hinterland was crucial since it was necessary to maintain the downriver flow of manpower

---

[20] Quoted in Hall, *Maritime Trade*, 163.

(with its military implications), agricultural resources (which could provision the port), and forest products such as the resins that were exported overseas, in order to uphold the royal centre's special position.

Although Śrīvijaya was not reluctant to use military means when it had to, it more often secured hinterland alliances through the offering of benefits, material and spiritual, to all who attached themselves to its centre. In return for their loyalty and their products, the leaders of these upriver and downriver populations received redistributions of wealth and provision of goods derived from the trade route, as well as the prestige and the reflected power of the Śrīvijayan centre. And the king's Buddhist advisers also played a strategic role in the hinterland. The king sent them out from the centre to make periodic contact with the local élite; to encourage them to hold local religious ceremonies and social pageantry that honoured both the king and the Buddhist faith; and to persuade them to participate in the royal cults at the centre, where public and religious edifices proliferated, and where oath-taking ceremonies were held.

At the same time that the Śrīvijayan centre offered benefits, it also resorted to traditional oaths and threats of dire consequences to those who broke them. One of the stone inscriptions found in the Śrīvijayan hinterland combined the traditional Malay water oath with Buddhist images of power. On the upper edge of the stone was a seven-headed snake, an Indian motif that evokes the cobra as protector of the Lord Buddha. This image may have been particularly effective in the Malay world, since Malay rulers, too, prior to any Buddhist presence, invoked the power of snakes to protect themselves and their realms. Below the snake was an oath of loyalty to the king, and below the oath was a funnel. During the oath-taking ceremony, water was poured over the snakes and the oath, and then drained out through the funnel. The water must have been drunk by the oath-takers, for the text said, in part, that anyone who was insincere in the oath would be killed by the water he drank (literally, his insides would rot). On the other hand, if the oath-taker remained faithful, he would receive not only a secret formula for the final (Buddhist) liberation of his soul, but also the pledge, 'You will not be swallowed with your children and wives', a reference either to snakes, which it was believed could swallow men, or to the possibility of being swallowed up by flood waters.[21]

In dealing with the third part of the Śrīvijayan realm, the other river-mouth ports and their hinterlands, the element of force played a much larger role. Although Indian-inspired formalities and techniques were employed and material advantages were shared, the crucial element in Śrīvijaya's control was force. Arab accounts claim that the Śrīvijayan monarch had bewitched the crocodiles in order to ensure safe navigation into the realm's ports, but the truth of the matter was that they had bewitched the sea nomads of the straits region.

During the heyday of Fu-nan, foreign sailors had feared Śrīvijaya's waters. Strong currents and hidden rocks and shoals made the straits area dangerous, and so did these sea nomads. They often engaged in piracy

---

[21] ibid., 166.

and preyed upon any merchant ship that happened to come their way. The Śrīvijayan monarchs, unable to suppress these nomads, essentially bought them out. The kings made an agreement with some of them that in return for a portion of the port's revenues, they would not raid the ships at sea. The kings could also use their seaborne allies to patrol the local waters and ensure the safe movement of trading vessels. They could also enlist their services as peaceful carriers in the trade. But in order to succeed in this manoeuvre, the kings had to have sufficient trade goods and revenues to make it worth the sailors' while, which meant that they had to attract a steady stream of foreign traders into their ports. If their ability to provide on a regular basis were ever to decline, the sailors could strike new alliances with rival ports, or revert to piracy. Śrīvijaya's rulers depended upon this navy in order to ensure Palembang's predominance and its development as the major international port and the central treasury for the entire realm.

Śrīvijaya's power overseas was also marked by monasteries patronized by its kings and by inscriptions. One 775 CE inscription on the east coast of the Malay peninsula commemorated the dedication by a Śrīvijayan king of a Buddhist monastery at the site, and also referred to the king as 'the patron of the snakes', a more traditional image of power. Śrīvijayan inscriptions with Buddhist elements can also be found at various strategic points along the Sumatran coast, including two places that overlook the Sunda Strait between Sumatra and Java.

Śrīvijaya's success was, no doubt, related to its good location on a major international trade route, its fine harbour, its 'heavy' and navigable river, and the political and economic talents of its rulers. But it may well be that the most important secret in Śrīvijaya's success was something not yet discussed: its curious relationship with the Buddhist Śailendras, a royal lineage located well outside Śrīvijaya's realm in central Java. Not only did the royal family of Śrīvijaya intermarry with the Śailendras; for public purposes, especially in India, they seem to have preferred to emphasize their descent from the Javanese lineage, rather than their more powerful Sumatran ancestors.

The marriage between the two was certainly convenient. During the days of Śrīvijaya, central Java was the most productive rice bowl in the island realm, and Śrīvijaya's ability to control the international trade that was crucial to its power was dependent upon its ability to provision the ships and feed the travellers who remained in its ports while waiting on the winds. While it is most likely that Palembang's agricultural resources were superior to those of any other river-mouth port within its realm, it is unlikely that they were equal to this task. Thus, any picture of Śrīvijaya would be incomplete without a view of the temple realm of central Java, the realm to which the Śailendras belonged.

THE TEMPLE REALM OF CENTRAL JAVA (570–927)

Central Java, generally known as Mataram, was already home to distinguished and important polities by 570 CE, a hundred years before the rise of Śrīvijaya. Indeed, some historians would trace the development of important centres back to the first centuries CE. Chinese dynastic records suggested that Sitiao, a place of fertile land and cities with streets reported by Fu-nan's third-century Chinese visitors, was in central Java. Ho-ling, based in central Java, was one of two fifth-century Java coastal centres with which the Chinese court interacted (Ho-lo-tan in the Tarum River basin near modern Jakarta was the other).[22]

When in the seventh century the kings of Śrīvijaya created their polity, they subordinated and incorporated into their realm a number of previously independent river-mouth ports on the northern and western coasts of Java, but they made no effort to include the rest of the island. In particular, they made no effort to subordinate central Java and its Kedu Plain, a unique and valuable part of the maritime realm. The relationship that developed between Śrīvijaya and central Java was a mutually advantageous, symbiotic linkage between a state dependent on the control of international trade and a rice-plain that remained somewhat distant from that trade.

The Kedu Plain was created by repeated volcanic eruptions; its rich soil and its size, combined with the region's year-round growing season, created an interior rice bowl unrivalled in the maritime realm of Southeast Asia. The prosperity of the rice plain, especially during its heyday in the eighth and ninth centuries, was related to the market for rice created by those Southeast Asian ports that serviced the international traders, and yet the rulers of this plain remained remarkably aloof from that trade. The Merapi-Perahu Mountains isolate the area from the ports on Java's north and east coasts, and its rivers flow south, away from the routes of international trade. Its royal centres and its pilgrimage sites always remained distant even from the small local ports on the nearby southern coast.

The relationship between the village-based producers of the rice plain and international traders was always indirect and mediated by other communities more directly related to international commerce. Local produce reached the international ports only through an intricate, multi-layered system of markets. The farmers and artisans of the villages took their produce, principally rice, salt, beans, and dyestuffs, to a periodic farmers' market that came to them every so many days, according to a fixed schedule. There they could find merchants who travelled with this market from place to place. The travelling merchants bought the local produce and passed it along in exchanges with intermediary wholesalers. Then merchants from the ports of Java's north coast purchased the produce from the wholesalers and sold it to merchants who travelled the seas, who delivered it to the ports where international merchants congregated. There were thus at least four layers of merchants and of markets between central Java's rice producers and the international traders.[23]

[22] W. J. van der Meulen, S. J., 'In Search of Ho-ling', *Indonesia*, 23 (1977).
[23] Jan Wisseman-Christie, 'Negara, Mandala and Despotic State: Images of Early Java' in David G. Marr and A. C. Milner, eds, *Southeast Asia in the 9th to 14th Centuries*, Singapore, 1986, 80–3. Wisseman-Christie argues that the Javanese trade system today is very similar to that of at least the tenth century. The key participant is the *bakul*, a market-based trader who buys from farmers and pedlars and sells both locally and to carriers moving on to other

Because this marketing system provided the international ports with the provisions they needed and did not compete with them for the international trade, the river-mouth ports, up to and including Śrīvijaya, had never felt a need to subordinate central Java. Furthermore, this same system acted as a buffer between the land-based élites on the rice plain and the region's merchants; the latter congregated in ports frequented by international traders and thus allowed the social coherence of the rice plain to remain largely undisturbed and its population's orientation to remain internally focused.

Clifford Geertz once described the attitude of Bali's post-1600 élites toward international trade, a description that is apt for central Java as well.

> [International trade] was connected to political life eccentrically—through a set of extremely specialized institutions designed at once to contain its dynamic and to capture its returns. The lords were not unmindful of the material advantages to be got from trade; but they were not unmindful either that, in reaching for them, they risked the very foundations of their power. Grasping by habit, they were autarchic by instinct, and the result was a certain baroqueness of economic arrangement. [24]

That there was no direct relationship between the élites of central Java and the international traders did not inhibit in any way their enthusiastic incorporation of Indian religions, ideas, architecture, or arts or crafts. Quite the opposite: they were just as enthusiastic users of things Indian and, compared to other places in the maritime realm, their monuments and their aesthetics tended to be more orthodox, more like those of India. The most spectacular results of this enthusism for Indian ways were the great temples of central Java.

During the heyday of Śrīvijaya, from the early eighth century until the middle of the tenth century, central Java witnessed a construction boom. In a little more than 200 years, the mountain-sides and plains of central Java were covered with monuments (mostly temples) of exquisite design and execution. This construction apparently began with a Hindu temple complex on the Dieng Plateau high in the mountains, and culminated with another Hindu temple complex at Prambanan. In between, in both time and space, was the Buddhist monument called Borobuḍur, which was built by the Śailendras, the closest allies of Śrīvijaya.

The temple boom of central Java marked the growing importance of a different sort of polity in Southeast Asia. While Śrīvijaya represents the river-mouth port system, with its dynamic of inter-port rivalry, the development of central Java points to the emergence of rice-plain polities whose political dynamics were quite different from those of the river-mouth ports.

One might expect that political centralization would have been relatively easier to accomplish on a rice plain than in the steep rainforest-covered

markets. The *bakul* is both a wholesaler and retailer, bulking goods for more distant markets, and breaking down lots that arrive from the outside. Wisseman-Christie argues that the *bakul* allowed the Javanese trade system to operate in the absence of large urban-supply markets. Jan Wisseman-Christie, 'States without Cities: Strategies of Decentralization in Early Java', *Indonesia* (Oct. 1991).

[24] *Negara: The Theater-State in Nineteenth Century Bali*, Princeton, 1980, 87.

valleys where the riverine states of the island realm emerged. Travel and communication across this plain were easier, and presumably a political network, like the marketing network that knitted it together, would have faced few physical obstacles. Nevertheless, political integration was not as easy as the plain's geography would suggest, for a great number of local élites, based in what have been called eco-regions, were firmly entrenched.

In the various phases of wet-rice growing, the need for water varies widely. When the crop is first planted, the fields must be flooded. But as it matures, the fields are gradually drained and are allowed to dry out by the time of the harvest. Thus, it was advantageous for all those whose water came from the same stream to co-ordinate their planting, to stagger it through the year so that not everyone was drawing off water at the same time. The need for co-ordination led to the creation of 'eco-region' water boards, organizations made up of representatives from all those villages that used the same source of water. The village leaders who participated on these water boards, members of special lineages, played a highly responsible role in the everyday lives of the people, and this gave them great power.

These eco-regions shared not only the same water, but the same gods, and the jurisdiction of the local water-board tended to overlap the jurisdiction of the local shrine. The behaviour of the gods, like the behaviour of the farmers, was shaped by the human planting cycles, for they came down to inhabit their shrines only on special days, usually related to the planting schedule. Both the operation of this intricate irrigation system and the habits of their gods instilled in the Javanese people an acute awareness of complex cyclical intersections based not so much on the cycles of heavens as on the cycles of the earth, the human-made intersections of ricefield and river.

Throughout the heyday of central Java, the heads of those lineages in charge of the eco-region water boards were always the most important political actors. The roots of the irrigation-based eco-regions grew deep and held tenaciously, and the political élites of these relatively small units were anxious not to give up their own local prerogatives even though they themselves might entertain notions of expansion that required others to relinquish theirs. For any one of them to distinguish himself from the others and emerge as king was not a simple matter, for their resource bases and their lineage-based legitimacies were similar.

The kingdoms that began to form on the central Javanese rice plain sometime in the sixth century were essentially alliance structures in which one local eco-region lineage managed to elevate itself over a larger area, to establish its superiority as a royal lineage, and to establish a centre with which other local eco-region lineages were willing to ally. Thus, these aspiring leaders had somehow to acquire a superior legitimacy that would distinguish them from the others and enable them to prevail. It was in this respect that the Indian religions and their temples came to play such a significant and prominent role in central Javanese statecraft. Those who became Hindus or Buddhists could claim a relationship to higher gods, a relationship fitting for higher kings.

In the same manner that local shrines marked the centres of eco-region networks, it was the remarkable temples and monuments of Indian inspiration that were to mark the new larger spiritual (and political) network that subsumed the local shrines and the networks they represented. The temples and the monuments served as centres where a king could demonstrate his spiritual superiority, his connection to these higher gods and to a higher knowledge, through elaborate rituals and state ceremonies conducted by Buddhist or Hindu holy men. Indeed, the sculpture that covered the walls of the temples was evidence of a higher learning and a principal means of imparting that knowledge to the people. The temples and especially the Borobuḍur, with its explicit Buddhist message, and the Prambanan complex, which exposed subsequent rulers' devotion to a syncretic Hindu tradition, were thus 'teaching' devices.

Moreover, the temples enjoyed the practical benefits that came from the special learning that the holy men possessed. The Sanskrit writing skills of the court-based priests had secular uses such as bookkeeping that assisted in the administration of the temples and the larger realms they represented. And they provided the kings with a royal Sanskrit vocabulary that assisted them in magnifying their status relative to that of other local leaders. The Śailendras in the eighth century were the first rulers in Java to adopt the title *Mahārāja*, the Sanskrit word for Great King, and to proclaim themselves rulers of a Javanese state.[25]

The purpose of the temples was to honour royal lineages, as well as the higher gods, but they were built by regional coalitions, each local constituent contributing a part of the complex. Much of the funding came from donations that bestowed religious merit upon the donors. Brahmins or monks laid out the temple designs and supervised. Royal 'bondsmen' moved the stones and did the rough shaping and chipping. Professional artisans then carved the statues and reliefs. In no case did royal labour demands exceed the king's customary labour rights. The sculptors' work demonstrates an exuberant creativity. Humorous improvisations can be found on many central Javanese monuments, including the two largest at Borobuḍur and Prambanan.

The temple complexes and royal centres grew to be the centres of a political-religious redistribution system that operated apart from the ordinary market. Temples usually had rights to a share of local production and local labour, and thus became collectors and marketers of agricultural produce, and could use the labour to construct not only religious edifices, but bridges, dams, or roads that contributed to the well-being of the temple, as well as the community. Like the temples, the kings, too, were the recipients of tribute (often rice) from their allies, tribute that they could exchange for imported goods that came from the north coast ports. These

[25] Earlier rulers, including the early monarchs of Śrīvijaya, ruled *bhumi*, a sphere of authority or realm, which was a more ambiguous statement of territorial authority than *rajya*. The earliest dated eighth-century Sailendra inscriptions speak of the *rajya*/state, ruled by a *maharāja* who defeated neighbouring *rāja*. The *rajya*/state was administered by a well-established hierarchy of state ministers, local lords, and superintendents of subordinate areas who linked the central court with intermediary, territorially-defined administrative units and villages. See, for example, the Kalasan Sanskrit inscription of 778, as discussed in Hermann Kulke, 'The "City" and the "State" in Early Indonesia', *Indonesia* (Oct. 1991).

rare and precious items, such as gold, silver, and textiles, especially Indian cottons, were then redistributed with great ceremony by the kings to their allies.

The kingdoms of central Java relied on alliances, often cemented by marriage, and on mutually beneficial exchange relationships. The kings never became superior landholders. Nor were their realms bureaucratic or highly institutionalized states that deprived local units of their separate identities. Theirs was a 'ritual sovereignty' marked by the temple complexes and the patronage of monks and priests steeped in Indian learning who endowed the king with sacred powers and reinforced an aura of divine majesty. They created ceremonial centres, centres of religion, art, and learning that drew their allies and held them in their orbit.

The Śailendras were only one of the kingly lineages of central Java. They were predominant from about 760 to 860, and it was during this time that they constructed the Borobuḍur, which became the focal point of the Śailendra monarchs' cult of legitimacy. They were different from other central Javanese royal lineages in large part because they, like their allies the rulers of Śrīvijaya, were patrons of Mahāyāna Buddhism rather than Hinduism.

When the Śailendras lost their predominance to a Hindu lineage of kings in the middle of the ninth century, royal refugees from the Śailendra realm went to Sumatra where they became incorporated into the Śrīvijayan royal house. Their arrival coincides in time with a Śrīvijayan decision to endow the funds for a monk's abode at the Nālandā pilgrimage centre in northeastern India. The inscription on this building recorded the benevolence of the Śrīvijayan monarch in a place where it would be visible not only to Indians, but to a wide variety of international visitors. In the early eleventh century another monk's abode was endowed by Śrīvijayan monarchs at Nāgapaṭṭinam, the centre of the Śaivite Hindu Cōḷa realm that was located on India's southeastern, Tamil-speaking Coromandel coast. What is most curious about these two endowments is that, in both cases, the royal donors of Śrīvijaya chose to identify themselves as Śailendras, even after this Javanese lineage had taken refuge on Sumatra.

The Śailendras had prevailed in central Java for a hundred years. After their demise, other royal lineages, patrons of Hinduism, including the builders of the Prambanan temples, replaced the Śailendras as hegemons of central Java, and they, too, came to enjoy a commercial relationship with Śrīvijaya. Indeed, temple building in the area did not slow until about 900 CE. Neither the ascendancy of Śrīvijaya nor the heyday of central Java came to an end until the early eleventh century. And it was a combination of three events that occurred almost simultaneously that marked the end of their great epoch.

First, Śrīvijaya's hegemony over trade within the maritime realm of Southeast Asia was challenged by a new power that had emerged in east Java, and from 990 to 1007 there was periodic war between the two. Then in 1025 Śrīvijaya suffered a devastating attack from the Cōḷas, based in South India. And in that same year a king based in east Java consolidated his authority over central Java and by 1037 had apparently severed his realm's ties to Śrīvijaya. Thereafter, both Śrīvijaya and the temple realm of central Java were overshadowed by the expanding power of a new realm based in east Java.

During this era there were significant increases in the volume of trade and more sailors (especially Chinese) were penetrating the archipelago; a single Southeast Asian entrepôt could no longer dominate trade. International traders were moving toward the sources of supply. Java, and especially east Java, was better suited to facilitate this new level of commerce. With its rivers that flowed from the heartland to the north coast, east Java could more adequately provide the rice for export that was required in an exchange for spices from the eastern archipelago.

EAST JAVA, 927–1222

When Marco Polo, a merchant of Venice, the port city that had grown rich while marketing Asian spices in Western Europe, travelled through Southeast Asia in the last decade of the thirteenth century, he was convinced that Java was unspeakably rich.

> [Java] is of surpassing wealth, producing . . . all . . . kinds of spices, . . . frequented by a vast amount of shipping, and by merchants who buy and sell costly goods from which they reap great profit. Indeed, the treasure of this island is so great as to be past telling.[26]

The Java that Marco Polo described was neither the realm of Śrīvijaya nor that of central Java. He was speaking of east Java, the site of kingdoms that replaced Śrīvijaya in international importance in the early part of the eleventh century, in spite of the fact that they were located somewhat east of the routes that the traffic between India and China usually took. It was not their location, but their control of spices that drew international traders to them. Contrary to what Marco Polo and many other foreigners thought, east Java was not a producer of spices. The greatness of the centres that developed there was ultimately based on their ability to stockpile rice, which they traded for the spices and other rainforest products harvested in the other parts of the eastern archipelago.

It was in east Java that, for the first time in the island realm, kings emerged who combined within one realm a trading position equal to that of Śrīvijaya with a control over agricultural resources comparable to those of central Java, and who furthermore created what was tantamount to a monopoly on the marketing of the fine spices, the rarest and most expensive. Along with this eastward shift in the geographical locus of power came changes in economic and political structures, and in aesthetics and worldview that marked a major transition in the political-economy of early Southeast Asia.

East Javanese polities grew up within the basin of the Brantas River. This is an unusually long river in the island realm, since it practically encircles a tangle of mountains before finding its way to the sea. Its headwaters

[26] Henry Yule, trans., *The Book of Ser Marco Polo*, London, 1903, 272–4.

converge on the slopes of Mount Arjuna and flow from there in a clockwise direction, first south, then west, then north, and finally east to the sea. As a result, it was rather more unruly than the straighter streams of the plains of central Java.

But of equal significance, the Brantas, unlike the rivers of central Java, empties on the island's northeast coast. Although its ports were a long way from the Straits of Melaka and Sunda where the transit traffic between India and China flowed, its waters did in the end flow north into the Java Sea. In fact, it was ideally situated to play a strategic role in the growing trade in fine spices, since it was located at an intermediate point between what is now called Maluku (the Moluccas), islands that included those where these spices were harvested, and the Straits of Melaka, where these spices had met the international trade routes during the time of Śrīvijaya's hegemony. It is quite possible that the earlier marketers of these spices had stopped off in East Java's ports to take on provisions on their way to the ports of Śrīvijaya, thus creating an east Javanese interest in the trade.

That the distribution of these spices could fall under what amounted to monopoly control by the east Javanese was due to the fact that the trees from which these fine spices came could be found in one place, and one place only, at the far eastern end of the hemisphere. There were three spices in particular that were of great importance to east Java: cloves from the clove tree; and nutmeg and mace, both from the nutmeg tree. Before 1600 the clove tree, an evergreen of the tropical rainforest, grew only on five tiny volcanic islands immediately off the western coast of Halmahera: Ternate, Tidore, Motir, Makian, and Batjan. The spice that we call cloves is the dried unopened flower-bud of this tree. The nutmeg tree, also a tropical evergreen, was equally rare. It grew only on some of the Banda Islands (of which there are ten), which occupy a total of forty-four square kilometres in the midst of the Banda Sea. What we call nutmeg is the kernel found inside the seed, and the spice known as mace is the thin membrane of a chewy rind that covers the kernel.

Given the value of these spices throughout the hemisphere, it is remarkable that prior to the modern period, the trees were never transplanted to other locations. No doubt, this was not from any lack of trying. The islanders kept a close watch on visitors to make sure that they did not smuggle out any plants or seeds; even if a few managed to get out, they apparently did not take root in foreign soils. The seeds of these trees do not remain viable for long. Probably of most importance, these trees require highly-skilled tending to make them produce, and they are particular about where they will grow and under what conditions. One common saying declares, 'nutmegs must be able to smell the sea, and cloves must see it'.

Furthermore, the winds conspired to keep international traders from meeting the real Spice Islanders, the sailors who brought the spices from Maluku. Those who delivered the spices sailed home with their cargoes of rice and other goods on the same west wind that delivered the international traders. While the international traders were in Java waiting for the wind to shift, these Spice Islanders were at home, 1600 kilometres east of Java.

They would return to Java with their precious cargoes of nutmeg, mace, and cloves, on the same east wind that carried the international traders back toward home. The winds thus kept these two groups apart, which no doubt worked to the advantage of the rulers of east Java and may have contributed to the mistaken notion that all spices were produced on Java.

Unlike the rulers of central Java, the monarchs of east Java sat in proximity to coastal ports, and became directly involved in stimulating the international trade. A 927 inscription found at Palebuhan describes a river-mouth port called Goreng Gareng (not yet located) and a local ruler, in what was essentially a frontier area, intent both on developing a port under royal patronage and on enticing farmers into his realm. Already in these early years, 135 vessels were based at the king's port, and he was sending not only Javanese port merchants, but also foreign merchants from Sri Lanka (Sinhalese), southern India, and Burma into the country-side to collect taxes.

Since the new east Javanese kingdom began to compete for a share in international commerce and for the rice surpluses of central Java, its relationship with Śrīvijaya soon became hostile. Between 990 and 1007 there was periodic war between the two, a matter that was settled not by east Java, but by the Cōḷas when they decimated Palembang in 1025. On the other hand, the issue of hegemony over central Java was settled by King Airlangga.

Airlangga (c.991–1049), eulogized as the founder of a new world, ruled for more than thirty years, from 1016 to 1049. His capital was at a place called Kahuripari. Since most of the inscriptions concerning him are found in the delta region around modern Surabaya, historians are confident that this royal centre was somewhere on the Brantas River delta, about 60 or 80 kilometres from the river's mouth, although its exact location has not yet been determined.

Airlangga's first acquisition outside east Java was the island of Bali, which he had managed to subordinate by 1025. Bali, located just two kilometres off the east coast of Java, was an important rice producer. Although it lacks Java's flat plains, it does have good volcanic soil, and rice was planted on the terraced hillsides. The relationship between east Java and Bali must have already been one of long standing, for Airlangga, who grew up in east Java, was the child of a royal marriage between an east Javanese princess and a Balinese prince.

According to tradition, his hegemony over central Java was achieved only after a struggle with 'demons' in central Java, a struggle that lasted from 1025 to 1037. These 'demons', like the kingdoms of central Java, were portrayed as allies of Śrīvijaya. But Airlangga, who generally relied on Javanese versions of Hindu images of statecraft, was able to overcome the demons due to the powers of meditation he developed only after an initial retreat. Like Arjuna in the Javanese version of the *Mahābhārata*, he was able to concentrate his mind and his powers on the defeat of his enemies. Airlangga also saw himself as an earthly manifestation of the Indic god Viṣṇu, who had appeared to Arjuna as Kṛiṣṇa. Although his direct admin-istration was probably limited to the lower reaches of the Brantas River, he had by 1037 established a 'new Mataram', and at least a ritual hegemony over both Bali and central Java.[27]

Another aspect of Airlangga's greatness lay in his successful damming of the Brantas River. Although its basin has rich volcanic soil, farmers had apparently remained reluctant to settle there because of periodic floods. An inscription of 1037 reveals that the river had burst its dykes, flooded villages, and impeded the progress of ships up the river to the royal port. Not only was there devastation and hardship for the people, but the king was losing revenue. Local villages were unable to deal with the problem; and thus, Airlangga assumed the responsibility. He decided upon a royal project that constructed dams at strategic points on the river. The dams not only reduced the hazard from floods, but also enhanced the possibilities of irrigation. Some sources suggest that Airlangga then transferred vanquished peasant population from central to east Java, presumably to populate the basin.

The water control project also provided a better harbour for international shipping at the royal port of Hujung Galah, a site that is presumed to be in the vicinity of Surabaya. The new port facilities serviced a growing international trade. It was not long before east Java had gained a dominant position in the international spice market, a market that grew to include most of the eastern hemisphere.

Airlangga thus transformed what had been disadvantages within his realm into advantages. The solution to the initial problems that the basin faced required more extensive organization and thus required a greater degree of direction by a supra-local authority. As a result, those monarchs based in the east were able to assume powers beyond those possible for their counterparts based in central Java to achieve. The increasing centralization is also reflected in a tradition that claims that Airlangga codified Javanese law by drawing together the various regional traditions into one 'Javanese' code, although it is no longer extant.

The international economic climate was favourable. The Tang dynasty in China had fallen in 906, but by 960, a few decades before Airlangga's birth, the Sung dynasty had once again united China; and, unlike previous empire-wide dynasties, it was more oriented toward its southern, commercial coast. Technological innovations also contributed to an increase in China's commercial and maritime interests, and after 1127 this trend accelerated even more when the Sung dynasty lost much of the north to invaders and moved its capital to Hangzhou, south of the Yangtze River. China's orientation toward the southern oceans would not be reversed until about 1430. It was during the Sung dynasty that Chinese porcelain gained an overseas market comparable to the one silk enjoyed, and large

---

[27] Kulke, regards Airlangga as an exception to the normal patterns of early Javanese statecraft. Through military conquest, not administrative accomplishment, Airlangga established a more direct Javanese royal authority than had previously been the case, and was appropriately the first Javanese monarch to have the title *ratu cakravartin*, 'universal monarch', bestowed upon him in epigraphic references. See also Wisseman-Christie, 'Negara, Mandala and Despotic State', 74–5. Majapahit-era monarchs assumed the title *bhatara* ('god'), which was appropriate to their enhanced status.

quantities began to move out on the maritime routes of the Southern Ocean.

Prior to the rise of east Java, the Abbasid Caliphate at Baghdad had been experiencing grave difficulties in controlling its empire. Ever since the latter part of the ninth century, the Persian Gulf area experienced rebellions and civil wars, a problem that compounded the difficulties on the routes from the Indian Ocean to the Mediterranean since the Red Sea area had been disturbed for even longer. However, by 973, the Fatimid Caliphate (909–1171, a Shi'ite power first based in present-day Tunisia) had secured its hold over Egypt and thus brought peace to the Red Sea route. Thus, once again the spices had good access to the Mediterranean market.

During the time of Airlangga, east Java's ports grew in importance. Like earlier east Javanese kings, he gave royal charters (metal plates that recorded agreements between the king and his subjects) to port-based merchants who participated in indigenous exchange networks that traded between the ports and the hinterland. Local market lists indicate that non-prestige goods of foreign origin, specifically metals and dyes, were traded for local products, especially rice, which the traders brought back to the port.

The charters also provided for what was essentially a royal tax on commerce, since they ensured that the king would receive his share of any commercial profits. Indeed, the largest percentage of royal charters issued during the tenth to twelfth centuries concerned port or coastal settlements in the Brantas delta region. Java's port-based merchants also played a role in collecting the king's tax on local agriculture since they also served as tax farmers, a role apparently no longer played by foreign merchants after the time of Airlangga.

The kings used their revenues to promote trade. Much was invested in the development of additional farmland in order to produce the all-important rice surpluses. The monarch provided for foreign visitors' lodging, harbourage, and board, expenses that he could afford since he received a percentage of all the gold, silver, and other metals paid in exchange for the merchandise in his ports. Royal revenues were also drawn upon to pay soldiers and seamen who went out in the monarch's name to force the subjugation of formerly autonomous coastal and hinterland religions, and to police the realm, to eliminate pirates and bandits who might prey on travellers or villagers. This security was an important factor in the traders' decision to use a certain port or not. For example, during this era the Chinese were aware that they could get a superior variety of pepper (or a better price) in the Sunda Strait region, but did not bother to go there since it had a reputation for brigandage.

Airlangga and the east Javanese kings who followed him also used their share of the realm's wealth to enhance their sovereignty, remitting tribute for the construction of temples, the performance of ritual, and the patronage of scholars, all to enhance the monarch's superior status and the centre's prestige. During this era there was a shift in the legitimization of the centres of power and their returns to their subject populations from huge religious buildings to much smaller ones, and from religious returns to prestige goods. It appears that east Java's kings controlled the importation of prestigious foreign goods and redistributed these luxury items throughout their realm, including the hinterland, through alliance-making or other sorts of gift-giving. Chinese sources indicate that quantities of these goods were shipped to Java and quantities of contemporary Chinese ceramic sherds have been found throughout the realm, and yet these goods are not mentioned in local market-related inscriptions. The most likely explanation for this apparent contradiction is that the kings controlled luxury goods such as Chinese ceramics and used them as political capital.

One of the puzzles in early Javanese history is why east Java between the ninth and thirteenth centuries—where population, wealth, and transport infrastructures were sufficient to have produced permanent urban centres beyond the coast—did not develop large-scale hinterland centres of permanent trade. One explanation, as we have seen, is that the Javanese wet-rice economy functioned most efficiently when its population was clustered in small productive communities that were encompassed within decentralized eco-regions. Another explanation is that royal policy purposefully nourished this decentralization. That this was the case at the inception of east Java hegemony is reflected in the inscriptions that record royal initiatives, such as those of Airlangga, that amplified the state revenue base, by means of state-encouraged development of previously uncultivated peripheral lands as well as taxable trade. Between 900 and 1060, for example, there were more than forty new enclaves established by direct royal intervention in the developing Brantas delta region.[28] While the economic returns from the development of the Brantas delta are undeniable, these and other royal initiatives were ultimately undertaken to promote the king's authority vis-à-vis other élites and rival institutions during an era in which monarchs based in east Java were asserting their sovereignty over their previously decentralized polity.

In the period from the ninth to the thirteenth century, prior to the establishment of the Majapahit state, royal grants known as sīma ('tax transfers') were the centrepiece of the royal offensive. These were not gifts of land: Javanese monarchs did not normally have local land rights, and even their tax rights were subject to social restraint. When title to land was to be transferred, that land was purchased first from those villages affected. Sīma were thus transfers of all or a denoted portion of the income rights (there was frequently a ceiling placed on the amount of tax the state was willing to forgo) due to a superior political authority from designated land.

Sīma grants were a means of encouraging territorial expansion and the pioneering of previously uncultivated peripheral areas, but they were also a means by which farmers and non-farmers were incorporated and subordinated to the prevailing agrarian order. Sīma land, which was designated to provide prescribed income to a religious institution—especially ancestor temples that honoured past monarchs, members of local élites or village ancestors—as well as a favoured individual or group, was considered to be outside the administrative authority of the king. In addition to sīma tax

---

[28] There were undoubtedly more for which no epigraphic records remain. See Wisseman-Christie, 'States without Cities'.

transfers made by those claiming monarch status, regional authorities (*rakai*) also issued *sīma* charters that ceded their rights to tax (usually with the approval of an 'overlord' king), and normally relinquished their local administrative rights over *sīma* land coincident with a monarch's tax transfers. Yet a ceremony that dedicated the *sīma* tax transfer, whether that of a king or a regional authority, emphasized that the grantee was expected to remain loyal to the Javanese state. This ritual involved an oath in which the recipient pledged fidelity, and it culminated with the pronouncement of a curse by a religious official threatening those present who were not faithful to the monarch. Usually a great public festival was held in honour of a new *sīma* foundation. These ceremonies and festivals must have served as a means of redistributing wealth that might otherwise have been used in ways disruptive to society—and to the king's sovereignty. *Sīma* were held in perpetuity, as evinced by inscriptional records of court cases in which *sīma* rights granted by defunct ruling families were upheld.[29]

Sīma grants were thereby used to free designated lands from numerous demands for taxes and services. In an age in which tax-farming was the norm, *sīma* grants also prohibited various tax collectors and officials, who were often also working for local magnates and village authorities, from entering *sīma* domains to extract payments on their own or others' behalf. Thus, while on the surface *sīma* 'tax transfers' would seem to have entailed the relinquishing of royal power locally, they instead subtracted a portion of the wealth directly available to a local élite (who were, however, compensated for their lost income with 'presents' of gold, silver, or cloth) and established a stable institutional foothold from which east Javanese rulers could attempt to extend their political and economic power beyond their shifting centres of royal power.

The *sīma* tax transfer system also acted as a brake on the growth of population clusters in the hinterland. Non-farmers, including merchants, were incorporated into rural communities rather than advancing the evolution of separate commercial enclaves. In a clear assertion of royal authority, *sīma* charters included limits on the amount of trade that could be carried on by resident professionals free of state taxes, as well as the number of professionals who could operate free-of-tax in a *sīma* community.[30] The *sīma* tax concessions would have encouraged economic activity in a community until it reached the tax transfer ceiling. But this would have also discouraged professional commercial activity beyond that ceiling. The *sīma* system thus reduced the level of local competition, and also ensured the dispersal of professional trading activity. Farming communities were themselves similarly affected by the prevailing state revenue collection system that taxed larger communities more heavily, which also encouraged community division rather than consolidation. Rather than demonstrating an increasing concentration of population, the epigraphic records of this age document the proliferation of small residential clusters; instead of forming larger housing assemblies, numerous villages subdivided into

[29] Wisseman-Christie, 'Negara, Mandala and Despotic State', 72; J. G. de Casparis, 'Pour une histoire sociale de l'ancienne Java, principalement au Xième S.', *Archipel*, 21 (1981) 128–30.
[30] Wisseman-Christie, 'States without Cities'.

hamlets and developed multiple sets of officials who were incorporated into an increasingly hierarchical state administrative structure.

When Airlangga died in 1049, his realm was divided between two of his sons and Bali was left again to its own devices. This decision to divide the empire was later blamed on the counsel of one of the king's advisers, a Hindu ascetic known as Bharada. In the east was Janggala/Singhasari and in the west Panjalu/Kaḍiri.[31] This bipolarity remained until the thirteenth century, for almost 200 years. That the realm was divided, however, did not in any way inhibit the further development of east Java's commercial position. It grew to be one of the world's richest lands, as bullion, gold and silver vessels, silk, and the world's best porcelain, lacquerware, chemicals, and metal manufacturers poured in.

Compelling testimony regarding the commercialization of Java comes from a 1225 report by Zhao Rugua, the Commissioner of Foreign Trade at the Chinese port of Quanzhou. He indicates that during the Sung Dynasty (960–1279) the Chinese were buying so much spice (especially pepper) from eastern Java that copper coinage was flowing out of the country at an alarming rate. Zhao reported that Java's own coins were mixtures of silver, tin, lead, and copper, and that, like Chinese coins, they had square holes in the middle so that they could be strung together (it is not clear whether Java was using Chinese coins or making coins similar to those of China). Finally, in an effort to protect its currency, the Chinese government banned trade with Java. The Javanese traders, however, tried to circumvent this prohibition by saying that they came from 'Sukadana' (*Su-ki-tan* in Chinese), a name that they apparently made up.[32]

SINGHASARI (1222–1292) AND MAJAPAHIT (1293–1528)

Majapahit was the last and the greatest of the empires in the pre-1500 Southeast Asia island realm. Its kings came to possess a degree of central control in East Java that went beyond previous precedent, and they furthermore created a state centre that established varying degrees of hegemony over central Java and an overseas realm almost three times the size of what had been Śrīvijaya's, a realm that included all the islands that are now Indonesia's, and more. The roots of Majapahit and its ambitions were in Singhasari. The Singhasari ruler Viṣṇuvardhana (r. 1248–68) had subordinated the Kaḍiri population centre and thereby become the pre-eminent political authority in east Java, a position Singhasari's rulers maintained until 1292. But it was his son Kĕrtanagara (r. 1268–92) who laid the foundations for Majapahit. Indeed, the *Nāgarakĕrtāgama*, an epic poem and chronicle composed in 1365 by the Buddhist monk Prapanca in order to glorify the rulers of Majapahit, actually begins its story with the reign of

---

[31] The alleged division of the whole of eastern Java by Airlangga into Janggala and Panjalu has been shown to be only a division of his own core realm in the delta region: Boechari, 'Sri Maharaja Garasakan, a new evidence on the problem of Airlangga's partition of his kingdom', *Madjalah ilmu-ilmu Sastra Indonesia*, 4 (1968).

[32] F. Hirth and W. W. Rockhill, *Chau Ju-kua: His Work on the Chinese and Arab trade in the twelfth and thirteenth centuries, entitled Chu-fan-chi*, St Petersburg, 1911, 78, 81–3.

this mysterious and highly controversial Singhasari king. Kĕrtanagara, who came to the throne only after destroying 'a wicked man', claimed to have been initiated into secret Tantric rites that gave him extraordinary powers against demonic force. And in order to maintain these powers, he was obliged to bring on his own ecstasy through Tantric rituals involving the consumption of intoxicating drink and the performance of sexual acts.

Although a later fifteenth-century chronicler hostile to Tantric rituals characterized him as a drunkard who was brought to ruin by his lust, the *Nāgarakĕrtāgama* described him as a saint and ascetic, free of all passion. To end despair (and the difficulties that Airlangga's legendary division of the realm seem to have caused), Kĕrtanagara erected a statue depicting himself as Aksubhya, the meditative Buddha, on the spot where Bharada (the ascetic blamed for the partition of the meditating Airlangga's kingdom) had lived. He also confirmed his father's patronage and synthesis of the indigenous Javanese religious traditions (Śaivite, Hindu, Mahāyāna Buddhist, and Tantric). Viṣṇuvardhana's ashes were divided between two shrines; at one he was worshipped as an incarnation of Śiva, at the second as Amoghapāśa, the Bodhisattva of Compassion. The *Nāgarakĕrtāgama* viewed Kĕrtanagara's religious purification of Java as the cause of his and his descendants' glory as divine kings and reuniters of the realm.

Indeed, Kĕrtanagara would need all the powers he could summon, for it was he, and then his son-in-law, who would face the Mongols, the Central Asian conquerors whose steppe cavalries had overrun much of the continents of Asia and Europe. By the time that Kĕrtanagara came to power in 1268, southern China and mainland Southeast Asia had already suffered the invasion of these armies. Nanchao, an independent kingdom in what is now China's southern Yunnan Province, had been invaded in 1253, setting in motion a stream of refugees. The Thais felt the brunt of the refugees; they expanded out, infringing upon what had been Burmese Pagan to the west and Cambodian Angkor to the east. They then started to expand down the Malay peninsula into territory that east Java's rulers at Singhasari considered to be within their sphere of interest.

The Mongols followed up their occupation of Nanchao with an invasion of Vietnam in 1257 (an invasion that the Vietnamese resisted for some twenty-seven years, after which they forced the Mongols out). And in 1267, the year before Kĕrtanagara came to power, Khubilai Khan made a direct attack on the Southern Sung. There followed an invasion of Burma in 1271 (where sporadic fighting did not end until 1300), and in 1274 for the first time the Mongols took to the seas and launched a naval attack against Japan.

In 1275 Kĕrtanagara made east Java's first significant move overseas, after both Thai expansion on to the Malay peninsula and Khubilai Khan's naval attack on Japan. He sent an expedition to occupy Jambi-Malāyu, the old Sumatran port that had been Śrīvijaya's first conquest. Up to this point in time, there is no record of an east Javanese presence in the straits region. At most, their concern had been to keep the Straits of Melaka open for international shipping.

However, that attitude soon changed. In 1271 Khubilai Khan had established the Mongol version of a Chinese dynasty, the Yuan; and in

1276 the Southern Sung capital, Hangzhou, fell to his armies. Apparently ports in Sumatra lost no time in applying to the new Yuan dynasty. In 1277 Palembang, in 1281 Jambi-Malāyu, and in 1282 Samudra-Pasai (a pepper depot on the northern tip of the island) sent envoys to Khubilai's capital. Presumably they were seeking Mongol recognition as special ports of trade with China, the old preferred-port status that Śrīvijaya had enjoyed.

These Sumatran appeals to the Mongol ruler of China were followed by the first sustained expansionist phase in east Java's history. After subjugating Bali in 1284, Kĕrtanagara again sent his armies westward, and by 1286 he had established Javanese hegemony over the straits region. It was in that year that he erected a statue of his father at Jambi-Malāyu.

Khubilai Khan, however, was not pleased by Javanese hegemony in the straits. In 1289 he sent envoys to Kĕrtanagara to confront him and demand that the tribute missions be sent from Java to the Khan's capital. Kĕrtanagara replied by disfiguring and tattooing the faces of the Mongol envoys, and sending them back in this disgraced fashion. His impudence so enraged Khubilai Khan that the Mongol sent 1000 warships to chastise Java.

However, before the fleet arrived, the previously subordinated ruler of Kaḍiri defeated Singhasari in 1292, and during the occupation of the royal residence of Singhasari, King Kĕrtanagara died. After this calamity in the last months of 1292 or early 1293, Kĕrtanagara's son-in-law Raden Vijaya cleared a new capital site from the forest, and named it Majapahit. This royal city, which gave its name to the realm, was located about fifty kilometres upriver from Surabaya, a little southeast of present-day Majakerta (near where Airlangga's capital had been).

When the Mongol warships arrived, the son-in-law managed to persuade them that Singhasari was gone and that since Kĕrtanagara had died, which was punishment enough, that they should help him chastise Kaḍiri's ruler instead. It was only after he had destroyed his local rivals and enemies with the help of the expeditionary army, that he turned on the Mongols and forced them to evacuate from Java.

After the founder of Majapahit defeated the Mongols in 1293, not only did Java manage to make peace with the Mongols and re-establish commercial relations with China; it also acquired, at the opposite end of the hemisphere, an expanding market of great significance, that of Western Europe. After undergoing an agricultural and commercial revolution and crusading in the eastern Mediterranean for some two hundred years, the Western Europeans had begun to consume meat in quantity, and had developed a taste for and subsequently a need for Asian spices to flavour dried or salted meat and preserved vegetables and fruits.

Venice was the principal supplier of this market. The city-state had taken over much of Byzantium's Mediterranean trade, had developed a sea route to Flanders and England, and eventually controlled about 70 per cent of Western Europe's spice market. And as a result of the Pax Mongolica, Venetian merchants, like the family of Marco Polo, had created their own trade links to the East. But the principal suppliers of Venice were the Mameluke rulers of Egypt (1250–1511) who had held the Mongols back and once again secured the Red Sea route to the Mediterranean.

The realm of Majapahit was to meet this demand and be changed in the process. Java's own marketing network benefited from the growth in international demand, the internal peace and security provided by Majapahit's hegemony, and from the kings' efforts to remove obstacles between hinterland producers and ports.

The relationship between Majapahit's kings and its merchants grew so close that some sources, both local and foreign, considered Java's spice merchants to be little more than the monarch's 'trade agents'. Although this was an exaggeration, it was certainly true that the kings were paid for the use of the ports, controlled the bullion and luxury goods that flowed in, and received a share of the profits made from the exchange and transportation of local and international products.

By 1331 the kings at Majapahit had secured all of eastern Java as well as the island of Madura. Placing his own relatives or, in a few cases, deserving members of the court at the head of each of these 'provinces', the king maintained firm control at the centre. By 1343 Bali had been secured, and thereafter was ruled by Javanese princes. In 1347 the kings began subordinating ports to their north and east, a process that culminated with their ritual hegemony over places as far away as the southern Philippines and New Guinea.

Majapahit was apparently content with the situation in the straits region until 1377. Although it had on occasion punished local rulers who became too ambitious (such as a Sunda Strait ruler in 1357), it does not seem to have made any attempt to establish a presence there until 1377. Exactly what prompted the king to move then is not clear, but it may have been the threat of a new alliance between ports in the Straits of Melaka and China. In 1368 the Chinese had succeeded in expelling the Mongols and had established the Ming dynasty. In 1371 this new dynasty had sent an imperial invitation to Palembang, whose rulers had responded with a tribute mission to China. Majapahit's 1377 expedition against these ambitious ports was apparently successful, for soon thereafter representatives of the ports in the straits region were participating in its central ceremonies.

Indeed, Majapahit was able to establish a close relationship even with Samudra-Pasai, a pepper depot that lay beyond the Straits of Melaka. A chronicler of that polity remembered the east Java centre at its height.

> The [Majapahit] Emperor was famous for his love of justice. The empire grew prosperous. People in vast numbers thronged the city. At this time every kind of food was in great abundance. There was a ceaseless coming and going of people from the territories overseas which had submitted to the king, to say nothing of places inside Java itself. Of the districts on the coast, from the west came the whole of the west, from the east came the whole of the east. From places inland right down to the shores of the Southern Ocean the people all came for an audience with the Emperor, bringing tribute and offerings . . . The land of Majapahit was supporting a large population. Everywhere one went there were gongs and drums being beaten, people dancing to the strains of all kinds of loud music, entertainments of many kinds like the living theatre, the shadow play, masked-plays, step-dancing, and musical dramas. These were the commonest sights and went on day and night in the land of Majapahit.[33]

[33] A. H. Hill, 'Hikayat Raja-Raja Pasai', JMBRAS. 32, 2 (1960) 161.

Thus, by 1377 Majapahit's realm included ports and their hinterlands from the furthest tip of Sumatra in the west to New Guinea in the east and as far north as the southern islands of the Philippines. The 'navy' with which it exercised its sovereignty over this far-flung peoples was based in ports on Java's north coast; the sailors were paid by the monarchs for their good behaviour and their transportation services. They were essentially mercenaries of trade as well as maritime security, and they served Majapahit only so long as it provided their most profitable opportunity.

The international traveller who came to Majapahit in the latter part of the fourteenth century, at the peak of its glory, would approach on a merchant ship, riding the west wind, and first enter the core region of the realm at the port of Surabaya, a town of about a thousand families (including some that were Chinese). But Surabaya, on the coast, was not the centre of either trade or politics. To reach Majapahit's centres one had to take a small boat from Surabaya up the Brantas River through the flat and fertile delta region.

After going some thirty or fifty kilometres, one would come to Canggu, a ferry crossing and a marketplace. From Canggu it was a half-day's walk further up the river to the 'twin cities', Majapahit and Bubat, a market city located on a wide plain to Majapahit's north. To its east ran the royal highway, and to its north, the Brantas River.

It is unclear from available archaeological and literary evidence whether Bubat (and Canggu, too) was a permanent market centre or a centre of trade that was periodically occupied at times coincident with the Majapahit agricultural and ritual cycle. The *Nāgarakĕrtāgama* tells us that most foreigners would stay at Bubat, a cosmopolitan city of many quarters (ethnic neighbourhoods), of which those of the Chinese and the Indians were most notable. Bubat's market was a square, surrounded on three sides by tall and splendid buildings, panelled with carvings of scenes from the Indian epic, the *Mahābharata*. Here traders from India, China, and mainland Southeast Asia, from the kingdoms of Cambodia, Vietnam, and Thailand among others, gathered to do business with the Majapahit monarch's representatives. Here is where the Majapahit realm's spices and other goods met the goods of China, India, and parts west.

Although it was a market, Bubat had taken on some of the character of a ritual capital due to its relationship to the monarchy. The *Nāgarakĕrtāgama* refers to Bubat as 'the crossroads, sacred, imposing'.[34] And it was here that Majapahit's own suppliers, traders, and artisans gathered, along with the foreign merchants. They came not only to do business, but also to pay homage to the king.

Bubat assumed special prominence as the centre for the celebration of the Caitra festival. This comprised a succession of ceremonies which were critical to Majapahit's sovereignty, and which exemplified the Majapahit state's economic and social life. This festival was held in March or April, soon after the wind had shifted and begun to blow from the west, bringing the international traders.

---

[34] Th. G. Th. Pigeaud, *Java in the Fourteenth Century: A Study of Cultural History*, The Hague, 1960–3, III. 9.

After initial ceremonies at the Majapahit centre, in which both Hindu brahmins and Buddhist monks prayed for the royal house's prosperity, the princes paraded in golden attire. Brahmins offered the king holy water in finely made ewers, and the scholars, nobles, and judges of the realm moved in stately procession to the beat of ceremonial drums and the blare of conch shells and trumpets, and to the praises of singers and poets. Thus, the court 'came down' for the first seven days of the Caitra festival to participate in public amusements and in ceremony.

At Bubat the men and women of the royal court and their visitors could enjoy all that was offered—not only the music, dancing and drama, but games and gambling and trials of combat. From the special viewing stands, the royal personages and their honoured guests, the holy men, their allies from within the realm, and foreign visitors and traders from many lands, watched as the Javanese fought with weapons, or demonstrated their skills at unarmed combat, or engaged in an elaborate tug-of-war.

But it was not only entertainment that was offered up to the king. It was here in Bubat that the king received various collections in kind and in cash. The court's right to a share of the local specialties produced throughout the realm ensured his supply of rice, salt, sugar, salted meats, cloth, oil, and bamboo. The international traders, too, brought gifts for the king, and thus the king amassed a mountain of both necessities and luxuries.

The king, however, did not hoard all these goods or try to keep them all for himself and the court. A king was measured by his generosity, and the Majapahit ruler was expected to redistribute these goods. Some were given as gifts in return for the services of the artisans who contributed their labour to the festival's preparations (such as those who had built the reviewing stands), and to the musicians and poets and other performers who contributed to the festival's success. Others would be consumed at the feasts that ended the festivities. A portion of local and imported luxury goods (such as silk and porcelain) would be distributed to the king's allies, and thus dispersed throughout the realm. In essence, it was the king's wealth and power that created his prestige and drew his tributaries to him: they expected something in return, something which they deemed equal to their own importance. At the close of the ceremonies at Bubat, as the moon of Caitra waned, the princes of the realm received the representatives of common village communities, and sent them away, too, with presents of clothing and food.

The seven days at Bubat were followed by seven more days of festivities at the royal centre of Majapahit. Here the royal family and its allies, including local village élites, gathered for ceremonies and speeches. These made clear that while the Majapahit monarch ruled both a wet-rice and maritime realm, it was his association with the Javanese wet-rice tradition that was critical to his legitimacy. One main theme in the speeches was the importance of both the farmers and the royal military. Neither the royal house nor the market towns could survive without the produce of the village. Java's international position was based on its rice, the major commodity sought by the harvesters of spice. It was for rice that the Spice Islanders came to Java. Thus, the livelihood of the farmers had to be protected.

On the other hand, the royal court had to have revenue; it had to be supplied. Without the court, its military and its many allies, rival trading centres based on other islands might come to attack. That the commercial élite recognized the importance of the king's military is indicated by the generous contributions (8000 copper cash per day) that market heads made to the commander-in-chief of Majapahit's forces.

The ceremonies culminated in a community meal that once again marked out the relationships between the centre and its allies. Those closest to the royal line were served on gold plates and ate their fill of mutton, water buffalo, poultry, game, wild boar, bees, fish, and ducks. Those of lesser rank and relationship, including the commoners, were served on silver dishes, and offered 'meats innumerable, all there is on the land and in the water', including those that the high-ranking did not eat, worm, tortoise, mouse, and dog.

Along with this food came prodigious quantities of alcoholic beverages made from the fruits of various sorts of palm trees, from sugar and from rice, and one and all drank until they were drunk, 'panting, vomiting, or bewildered'. And along with the food and drink came the best in entertainment, singers and dancers, and a musical play enacted and sung by the princes of the realm and the king himself.

The speeches of the princes at the royal centre of Majapahit also addressed the necessity of maintaining those public works that were under government protection, some of which were built and maintained by the centre, and others by central persuasion of local élites. Among the projects mentioned in these speeches were dams, bridges, fountains, market places, and tree planting.

Also among the royal projects were roads that served as a link with those important locations that lacked a riverine connection with the capital. The road network intersected with the rivers and generally ran perpendicular to them. Wherever the roads crossed the rivers, there were ferries to move carts across.[35] The ruler and his retinue periodically travelled along this road network, making royal progresses to receive the personal homage of the various royal subordinates. In these places he performed royal ceremonies that the local élite had to pay for (an indirect form of taxation). Nevertheless, the money or goods paid for services and supplies went to local people.

Special reference is made to tradesmen and women who accompanied the royal progresses and who camped in open fields near the court's lodging at the conclusion of each day's journey. These carts and tradesmen are well represented in the Majapahit era's temple reliefs. And even when the kings were not travelling, the roads were used to transport rice and other goods. The *Nāgerakĕrtāgama* speaks of 'caravans of carts' along Java's roads and of crowded highways. But the use of the road network was seasonal because of the monsoon rains. Movement on the roads was concentrated in the drier season from March to September. This same epic describes travel on the roads in the wet season: 'The road . . . over the whole length then was difficult, narrow. There followed rains. The incline

[35] There were at least seventy-nine ferry crossing 'districts' in east Java: ibid., II. 215–19, 227–47.

being altogether slippery, several carts were damaged there, colliding one with another.'[36] Thus, in the rainy season the bulk of Javanese rice was conveyed by river from the hinterland to the coast, and foreign goods moved upriver in return.

According to the epigraphical evidence, in the 1330s, shortly before the kings of Majapahit began to consolidate their far-flung maritime empire, they also began to consolidate the royal centre's control over the resources and the people of east Java. The two processes of annexation and the extension of effective hegemony were almost simultaneous.

The trend toward systematic annexation and integration within the Brantas River basin had begun as early as the tenth century, when the early kings had used port merchants and foreigners as royal tax-farmers to ensure that hinterland rice reached the royal port. Airlangga had carried the process a step further when he dammed the Brantas River, and expanded the use of *sīma* tax transfer grants; he thereby enabled east Java's kings to reduce the residual power of local agricultural élites. Apparently Airlangga also dispensed with the use of foreigners as tax-farmers, and used only local port merchants to collect the king's share from the villages in the royal domain. During the Majapahit period, even the tax-farmers were eliminated. Payments of rice due to the royal government were collected by state ministers within the royal domains, and local allies were obliged to deliver their own part of the king's share directly to him.[37]

As is typical in other early Southeast Asian political-economies, even in periods in which a strong central authority existed, the king's supply of agricultural produce came largely from his own domains and the amount of tribute rice expected from allies remained small. For the most part, rice from outside the royal domain continued to move to Java's ports through market mechanisms, not taxation or tribute. Because of their income from the commercial sector, it was not necessary for Majapahit's monarchs to confront the foundation of local autonomy and prosperity by increasing their collection of agricultural produce from their allies. To increase its demands on the agrarian sector, the state would have had to infringe further upon the most basic political rights and socio-economic powers of these entrenched local élites. When the kings sought to enhance royal revenue and authority, they pursued not a larger share of the realm's agricultural resources, but control over wealth generated outside the agricultural sector. They were content to tax local commerce and non-agricultural production; to promote the cause of merchants, artisans, and élite who could best assist in facilitating the flow of goods to and from Java's north coast ports; and in general, to encourage the development of Java's economy.

The principal means by which the Majapahit kings enhanced the royal treasury and royal power was by the issuing of royal charters that redefined the local tax system. Renewed interest in *sīma* tax transfers during the Majapahit era offers testimony to the state's efforts to extend its

---

[36] Quoted in ibid., III. 23; IV. 497.

[37] Kulke, 'The "City" and the "State" in Early Indonesia'; and J. G. de Casparis in Sartono Kartodirdjo, ed., *Papers of the 4th Indonesian-Dutch History Conference*, Yogyakarta, 1986, I. 3–24.

authority. Inscriptions explain that the state was giving attention to previous *sīma* grants because the original documents had become unreadable, and there was a legitimate need to reissue *sīma* charters. Since there is no evidence that the initial *sīma* tax remissions were altered, there must have been great symbolic importance associated with the Majapahit monarch's confirmation and recertification of the *sīma* charters bestowed by previous rulers.

A new class of *sīma* charters was also issued. These 'investment *sīma*' were coincident with the increase in the number of wealthy families who lacked hereditary landholding rights. These families bought land, built family temples on it, and then applied (with a lump-sum payment) to have the sanctity of their family temple (as well as the legitimacy of their landholding status) validated. Their family temple assumed a subordinate position within a royal ritual network, and their land was declared perpetually tax-exempt. In these charters the Majapahit ruler normally retained a portion of his tax rights (instead of relinquishing almost all his revenue rights, as had been the practice among previous monarchs), and divided the remainder between the temple and the petitioning family. *Sīma* grants of the Majapahit era thereby created a family trust that strengthened the status and position of the newly powerful—the establishment of an ancestor temple and its reception of *sīma*-holding status sanctified the family's élite status. These new *sīma* charters not only confirm the enhanced power of the Majapahit state (and a more public and visible monarchy), but also document a less rigid social hierarchy.[38]

Other royal charters reveal an accelerating trend toward relieving specified non-farmers (mostly merchants and artisans in the eastern part of Java) of their former obligations to local land-based élites by transferring them to royal tax-paying roles. These new royal taxpayers, as a result, gained a revised relationship with the king and his court that was no longer completely mediated by local authorities. Local authorities were thus deprived of some of their non-agricultural revenue as well as their authority over non-agricultural populations.

The Canggu Ferry Charter of 1358 and three charters (dated 1336, 1391, and 1395) addressed to the two neighbouring towns of Bililuk and Tanggulnam suffice to demonstrate how this was accomplished.[39] Prior to the ferry charter of 1358, the people who operated the ferries had no relationship with the royal court. They had been viewed as constituents of the local landed élite, and had paid their taxes to them. The new royal charter, however, relieved them of any obligation to pay taxes or tribute to the local authorities, and instead required them to deliver a quantity of textiles directly to the king and to make a substantial contribution of flowers and cash to help pay for royal ceremonies.

Their new status as royal taxpayers independent of local authorities was only part of the agreement. The charter required them to make a contribution of goods and money for Bubat's Caitra festival, a contribution that entitled them to participate in it along with the royal lineage and its

---

[38] Wisseman-Christie, 'Negara, Mandala, and Despotic State', 73.
[39] Pigeaud, passim.

distinguished guests. This was an unprecedented recognition, indeed, a display of their economic, political, and military importance in controlling transport in east Java.

The charters from Bililuk and Tanggulnam reveal that the townspeople engaged in making salt (from saline streams), refining sugar, packing water-buffalo meat, pressing oil, and manufacturing rice noodles, and that in the local market they purchased four kinds of spices (probably used in large quantities by the meat packers), iron ware, ceramics, rattan, and cloth.

There were also textile workers who bought cotton cloth and dyes. Most likely they were manufacturing batiks, materials dyed by an elaborate process that was indigenous to Indonesia and predated any Indian influence. There are written references to it in the literature of east Java. Batiks are made by painting designs on a material (now mostly cotton) with wax—the Javanese originally used beeswax. The cloth is then dipped into a dye. Only the unwaxed areas are able to pick up that particular colour. Once that colour has set, the old wax is removed and a new design is painted, and the cloth is dyed in a different colour. This process is repeated until an intricate and many-coloured design is completed. To this day, batiks remain one of the most beautiful products of island Southeast Asia.[40]

Prior to the granting of the royal charters, the local artisans and merchants had been subject to a local 'chief of trade', a representative of the local landed élite. Because he supervised the market in which they purchased their supplies and sold their products, they were obliged to make contributions to him on thirteen different occasions. One obligation concerned contributions that they should make toward his travel and transport costs; five refer to their obligations regarding any births, marriages, or deaths in his family; and seven concerned obligations such as entertaining his guests.

The royal charters abolished all of these obligations, and in their place instituted a fixed tax that was to be shared by both the king and the 'chief of trade'. Although the king probably had received some portion of the artisans' produce previously as a part of the local authorities' contributions to the royal centre, the king would now enjoy direct royal collection of what he considered his share. That the royal tax was a fixed amount also had the benefit of eliminating what had been arbitrary and unpredictable assessments levied by a representative of the local élite.

The royal charters issued to communities throughout east Java often required that local resources be used to pay for or provide the supplies for locally performed ceremonies that honoured the monarch and displayed his powers. Local authority had long been linked to local ceremony, and the king thus ensured that local people would be exposed to ritual enactments of royal power as well. Often the resources due to the king (goods or money) were designated as contributions to royal ritual at the capital, in which representatives of the local community were required to participate.

A temple network, in which local temples became ritual subordinates to

---

[40] W. Warming and M. Gaworski, *The World of Indonesian Textiles*, London, 1981.

those temples that were administered by royal abbots and priests, was one innovation that provided additional infrastructure and extended the effective core area of the ruler's authority. The first evidence of this consolidation is provided in the account of Kĕrtanagara, noted above, who reconfirmed the special privileges granted to religious domains by his father Viṣṇuvardhana. As explained in Kĕrtanagara's inscriptions, this was done to separate the 'holy domains' of the 'clergy of all kinds' from the 'lands of royal servants'. This would initiate the independence of the holy domains 'in order to render the more firm the Illustrious Great King's sitting on the jewel lion's throne, being considered as the one sunshade of all Java, as the exalted deity among all the honored [neighbouring divinities] of the land of Janggala and Pangjalu'. This realm-wide ritual network is verified a century later in the *Nāgarakĕrtāgama*'s 1365 description of the ancestor commemoration rites (*śrāddha*) performed for the queen Rājapatni at her funeral temple at Bayalangu. The *Nāgarakĕrtāgama* account mentions at least twenty-seven interconnected royal temples that were strategically placed throughout the extended imperial core, and had been established in the hundred years between the mid-thirteenth century and the time the *Nāgarakĕrtāgama* was written.[41]

That increased centralization was manifested in royal rituals is not surprising, given the propensity toward ceremony in early Southeast Asian states. As well as any political leaders today, the kings understood the use of rituals in which they could claim that their special powers, their relationship to illustrious ancestors and to higher gods, was at the root of local prosperity. They could display their families, their allies, and their strategic constituents as well as their own superior rank. Furthermore, there was another equally important political advantage to this method of centralization. It served to defuse possible resistance. Since donations and contributions to these ceremonies bestowed religious merit and the ceremonies ensured general prosperity, it was awkward for local authorities to refuse such levies.

Although new revenues generated by the agreements in the charters did not immediately add substantial income to the royal treasury, they promoted an indirect increase in revenue. Once an artisan community's obligations were fixed on an annual basis by royal decree, it was able to retain a greater or at least a more predictable share of its production. This gave the artisans an incentive to increase production, since any amount produced over the fixed assessment could be sold by them for their own profit. The flow of these goods into coastal ports and their exchange for goods of foreign origin increased the king's revenues, since it was this commerce that was directly taxed by the monarch.

New levels of demand emanating from hinterland and coastal towns for Java's rice, along with the growing foreign demand for spices that were acquired with Java's rice exports, had the effect of encouraging the production and sale of rice surpluses. As demand expanded, local peasants had an opportunity to increase their incomes. There is no doubt that the rice economy of eastern Java as well as the older region of central Java

---

[41] Kulke, 'The Early and Imperial Kingdom' in Marr and Milner, 16–17.

prospered. The wide distribution and heavy concentration of Chinese ceramics in archaeological sites that date to the Majapahit era, literary and epigraphic references to local consumption of commercial products of nonlocal origin, and archaeological evidence of monetarized exchange at all levels of the Javanese economy, suggest that the desire and the ability to consume imported or luxury goods had spread beyond the élite during this era.[42]

The availability of these 'foreign' goods also provided peasant cultivators with incentives to produce more rice. However, given the importance of religious ritual in early Javanese society, Javanese peasants may not have been responding to new economic opportunity simply for the sake of their own personal or family consumption. Religious ceremonies and temples, too, might have provided incentives. New or expanded sources of incomes may have made it possible for many outside the élite to become sponsors of religious ceremony for the first time. Investment of surplus income in temple construction or religious ritual, especially that directly associated with the king, bestowed significant merit upon the donor and enhanced the status of the benefactor within the traditional system.

The fact that some of the new royal taxes specified in the charters were payable in cash rather than in kind reveals the growing monetarization of the Javanese economy, a consequence of Java's commercial prosperity as a major international centre of trade. Chinese goods and copper cash continued to flow into Java; Mediterranean gold moved through the Middle East and India to Java, along with major export items from these regions. By the time of Majapahit, copper coins (either Chinese or similar to China's) had become the local currency not only in Java but in Sumatra's ports as well. Precious metals such as gold and silver were rarely used to facilitate exchange or make payments (a practice that had been common in the pre-Majapahit period). In Majapahit's realm gold and silver remained important not as currencies but as commodities and merchandise for the market.[43]

THE SOUTHEAST ASIAN MARITIME REALM, c.1500

Those forces that ultimately weakened Majapahit's control of its realm and the eclipse of its far-flung hegemony were both subtle and large. In short, the Javanese were too successful. The growth and development of the international spice business had fuelled Java's expanding commercial and political pre-eminence from the eleventh to the latter part of the fourteenth century, but the further development of that same market precipitated its

---

[42] Hall, 242–50. R. S. Wicks, 'Monetary Developments in Java Between the Ninth and Sixteenth Centuries: A Numismatic Perspective, *Indonesia*, 42 (1986). It is here implied that the Javanese society would have widely responded to such an opportunity to improve his income. This assumption is somewhat controversial, as scholars also argue that the typical Southeast Asian peasant had other priorities than economic goals in his life. See William C. Scott, *The Moral Economy of the Peasant*, New Haven, 1976; and Samuel L. Popkin, *The Rational Peasant: The Political Economy of Rural Society in Vietnam*, Berkeley, 1980.

[43] Wicks, op. cit.

decline, since the spice business grew so great that Majapahit could not contain it. By the early sixteenth century, north Sumatran pepper ports were exporting between 15,000 and 20,000 *bihars* of pepper annually, primarily to China, while the Malabar coast of western India was exporting 20,000 *bihars* of its own and Indonesia's pepper annually to the West. Coastal trading communities proliferated within and without the realm of Majapahit, and ports over which it had held sway became increasingly independent and boisterous. As a mark both of their growing independence and of their newly forged international links, the coastal communities of this Sanskritic island world converted to Islam.

In the first decade of the fifteenth century, a series of Chinese imperial embassies established direct contact with north Sumatran pepper sources. The Ming Dynasty became concerned about security in the strait, and even undertook to police it, with the permission of Majapahit (which was in no position to deny such a request). In 1405 China sent out a fleet under the admiral Ch'eng Ho, a Yunnanese Muslim, to clean out a Chinese pirate nest that had grown up at Palembang; this mission he successfully accomplished.

In that same year the Admiral approached the ruler of Melaka (Malacca), a new port that had been founded only three years before, in 1402. Melaka was on the western coast of the Malay peninsula, on what we now call the Straits of Melaka. Its ruler was a prince who claimed descent from a southeastern Sumatran royal lineage that had been defeated and forced into exile by Singhasari's 1275 attack on the port at Jambi-Malāyu. He offered Melaka a special relationship with China; this relationship protected it for decades, until China's maritime position was abruptly abandoned in the 1430s. Melaka immediately thereafter established a relationship with the commercial communities in Java's ports, and became a distribution point not only for Sumatran, but for Javanese trade goods as well. Thereafter, it was no longer necessary to go to Java for the fine spices. This new port grew rapidly in significance and soon began to return to the straits area the significance that it had had in the days of Śrīvijaya, before the triumph of east Java. Furthermore, the years 1405 and 1406 were marked by a civil war at the heart of the Majapahit realm; from that point on east Java's home base was wracked by political dissension, and the island's power overseas waned.

By 1410 Majapahit had lost its hegemony to the west of Java and by 1428 it had lost control over the western part of Java. By the middle of the fifteenth century, commercial communities in the realm's ports had succeeded in depriving Majapahit's rulers of their control over much of the international trade and much of their political realm besides. But the final battle did not come until 1513 when a coalition of Javanese coastal communities attacked the core area of the realm. By 1528 Majapahit's centre was taken, and the royal family was forced to flee and take refuge on Bali. With the exception of those who lived on Bali and a few other small islands, all those who had been Majapahit's would kneel and pray toward Mecca, the sacred centre of Islam on the Arabian peninsula.

Thus, one could say that the hemisphere-wide access of Majapahit's spice trade was its undoing. And the spices, like the islands themselves, had developed a siren quality that was irresistible. So strong was their allure that men at the opposite end of the hemisphere were willing to sail out into totally unknown oceans in order to find them. It was Iberian-sponsored sailors seeking the Spice Islands who were responsible for the sole possession of the western hemisphere by the Atlantic nations of Europe and also for the circumnavigation of Africa that led to the presence of Atlantic shipping in the Indian Ocean. Since these two feats were responsible for beginning the process by which the global balance of power was altered, one could say that their success was not only their own undoing, but the undoing of the entire balance of power in the hemisphere.

The coastal communities that defeated Majapahit and established the new Mataram state based in central Java were Muslim, but this was by no means an indication that any foreign Muslim power was behind this transition. The Muslims who overthrew Majapahit were local people, not foreigners, and few of their grievances against the old realm were religious in nature. Nor did the motivation to convert to the Islamic faith come from outside the realm, but from within it.

Although Muslim traders, both Arabs and Iranians, had been in Southeast Asia ever since the earliest days of Islam in the seventh century, their religion did not have any immediate impact on the Southeast Asian peoples. Indeed, from the seventh to the tenth centuries, few in Southeast Asia converted to Islam, even though this was the time of Śrīvijaya's hegemony when traders from the Islamic Caliphates predominated on the routes between the Arabian Sea and China, and the Caliphates' *dinar* had become the currency of choice in Śrīvijaya's ports. It was only after the decline of both the Caliphate and Śrīvijaya, and the rise of Islamic mysticism and Turkish and Mongolian power, that Islam began to have appeal to Southeast Asian islanders.[44]

It was Merah Silu, the local ruler of Samudra-Pasai, a small polity in northern Sumatra that controlled both a pepper-producing hinterland and a coastal port, who first converted to Islam at roughly the same time that Majapahit was founded, in the last decade of the thirteenth century. This aspiring leader had first established his credentials, military and economic, in the hinterland near the headwaters of the Pasangan River, and it was from this base that he conquered the coast. Thereafter, according to local tradition, he was converted to Islam, not by a foreign merchant but by his own dream. In this dream none other than the Prophet Mohammed came to convert him and gave him the name Malik al-Salih. When he awoke he could recite the Koran and the Islamic confession of faith. Some forty days later, as Mohammed had prophesied in his dream, a ship arrived from Mecca carrying a Muslim holy man who would serve his realm. It also carried the Sultan of Ma'bar, the major pepper-producing region on India's Malabar coast, and one of the principal places from which pepper was exported to the West.[45]

Samudra-Pasai soon after its conversion became a major centre of

[44] Meilink-Roelofsz, *Asian Trade and European Influence*, 103–15; L. C. Damais, 'L'epigraphie Musulmane dans le Sud-Est Asiatique', BEFEO, 54, 2 (1968).
[45] Kenneth R. Hall, 'The Coming of Islam to the Archipelago: A Reassessment' in Karl L. Hutterer, ed., *Economic Exchange and Social Interaction in Southeast Asia: Perspectives from Prehistory, History, and Ethnography*, Ann Arbor, 1977, 213–31.

Islamic studies, the first within the island realm, but for the first hundred years of its existence, neither this port nor the gradual spread of its religion to other ports had much impact on Majapahit's power. During the fourteenth century when Majapahit extended its hegemony out over the seas, representatives of Samudra-Pasai were among the participants in the ceremonies at its centre, probably because Samudra-Pasai was supplying Majapahit's ports with pepper destined for China.

However, eventually the new and growing ports began to resent what they felt was the unwarranted control of Majapahit. Then the Muslim faith offered them not only a sense of community but a new legitimacy as well. By the end of the fourteenth century, Islam had spread throughout the maritime realm, even to the ports on Java's northern coast (and, apparently, even to a few members of the royal family), and had become a symbol of autonomy, and ultimately a rejection of the aristocratic lineage and special religious connections claimed by Majapahit's rulers.[46] But the irony of it is that today it is only necessary to look at those places in Southeast Asia that are now Muslim to know where ports once loyal to Majapahit were.

THE TEMPLE-BASED POLITICAL-ECONOMY
OF ANGKOR CAMBODIA

Among historians who study Southeast Asia's pre-1500 history, there is substantial disagreement on what constituted a 'state'. Is the standard a unified bureaucratized polity that is consistent with traditional Western understanding of what an advanced civilization should be? This view is reinforced by the accounts of Chinese historians, whose dynastic histories contain highly flattering views of their southern neighbours' accomplishments (and consider several of the early Southeast Asian civilizations to have possessed state systems that were similar to their own). Or could an institutionally weak, yet integrated, society still be considered a major civilization?

One standard by which early Southeast Asian states are measured is the number of stone temple complexes they left—the more impressive the archaeological remains, the more prosperous and accomplished was the state; or so the reasoning goes. Thus, the massive temple complexes of central and eastern Java, as well as Angkor (Cambodia) and Pagan (Burma) on the mainland suggest that accomplished political systems were responsible for their construction, through a central administration that mobilized a realm's wealth and manpower to create these architectural wonders. But historians now are coming to find that broad levels of social, economic, and political integration were not necessary for such construction, and that

---

[46] The Majapahit state, basically decentralized and agrarian, was inadequately prepared to deal with the wealthy commercial enclaves that it had inadvertently created. The Majapahit rulers had tried to derive maximum benefit from the export of agricultural products without adequately reforming their internal administrative structure and practices.

the building of impressive religious edifices does not necessarily demon-strate the political and economic accomplishments of a society.

In the Angkor era—at its height from the ninth to the thirteenth centuries—inscriptions proclaimed the king as the creator and director of public works that were designed to ensure prosperity. These works irrigated some five million hectares, and were constructed around the Khmer capital at Angkor and in a number of regional domains under Khmer authority. Without this hydraulic system, the water supply was irregular and thus limited agricultural productivity.

Traditional conviction among the Khmer populations was that their monarch was the source of his subjects' economic welfare. The *nāga*, the water spirit, was widely portrayed in Khmer art, and was a central figure of popular religion. Chou Ta-kuan, Mongol envoy to Angkor in 1296, reported that the Khmer people believed that their ruler slept with a *nāga* princess, and that the result of their union was the country's prosperity.[47] This report implies that the Khmer monarch enjoyed a ritual relationship with the spirit of the soil that released the fertility that guaranteed the earth's productivity. In this same tradition Yaśovarman I (r. 889–910) constructed an artificial lake (*baray*) northeast of his new capital city of Yaśodharapura (Angkor) at the end of the ninth century. According to the inscription reporting this event, the king wished to 'facilitate an outlet for his abundant glory in the direction of the underworld'.[48] This underworld, also depicted as the place from which Khmer monarchs judged the dead, was the abode of the *nāgas*, the source of fertility.

A 1980 examination of the Angkor era water-management system demonstrates that Yaśovarman's lake was not a critical source of water for the Angkor region's agricultural production in a technical sense, though as the focus of Khmer religion, it was important symbolically in the Khmer system of 'theocratic hydraulics'.[49] Archaeologists have assumed that water seeped through the dyke base of Yaśovarman's lake (which meas-ured 6.5 kilometres long by 1.5 kilometres wide) into collector channels outside the dyke, which subsequently carried the water to surrounding fields. But studies conducted in the late 1970s found that Angkor-era agriculture was based instead on bunded-field transplanted wet-rice culti-vation that allowed the planting of approximately fifty million fields. In the Angkor region floodwaters would slowly rise from the Great Lake, the Tonle Sap, to its tributaries, but would rapidly recede after the rainy season. A network of dams and bunds diverted and retained the receding floodwaters of the Great Lake after the rainy season. The Khmer lacked the technology to build large-scale dams that could have allowed an integrated region-wide hydraulic system; instead they depended on a network of small, simple earthworks on minor streams to retard and spread flood-waters into clay-based ponds, which stored the water for later use.

[47] Chou Ta-kuan, *Notes on the Customs of Cambodia translated from the Shuo-fu*, trans. Paul Pelliot (trans. from French into English by J. G. d'Avery Paul), Bangkok, 1967, 31.

[48] A. Barth and A. Bergaigne, 'Inscriptions Sanskrites du Cambodge et Campa' in *Académie des Inscription et Belles-Lettres, Notices et extraits des manuscrits de la Bibliothèque du roi et autres bibliothèques* [henceforth ISCC], 27, Paris, 1884, 1893, 407.

[49] W. J. van Liere, 'Traditional Water Management in the Lower Mekong Basin', *World Archaeology*, 11, 3 (1980) 274.

Archaeological evidence demonstrates that Angkor itself was not a major centre of this water-management network but rather the hill Phnom Kulen, which was located upriver from Yaśovarman's lake some fifty kilometres northwest of Angkor. Phnom Kulen was near the headwaters of the Siemreap (river), which flowed from that area through Angkor to the Tonle Sap. A network of small earth dams regulated the flow of water downstream from Phnom Kulen to Angkor.

One striking feature of the water-management network at Phnom Kulen is that its dams, in addition to their effectiveness in managing water, were all constructed running east–west and north–south. Similarly, throughout the Angkor region Khmer temples were constructed at the intersection of moats and roads which were oriented east–west and north–south; this was done purposely to project the image of the heaven on earth (*maṇḍala*) that had been initiated by Khmer monarchs. In addition to being consistent with Indian and Khmer cosmological focus on east–west and north–south, the water-management network was consecrated by the traditional symbols of fertility. A number of linga phallic symbols were carved in the rocky riverbed at the mountain source, suggesting the sanctity of the water that flowed from the mountain region to Angkor. It is significant that Jayavarman II (r. 802–50) consecrated his *devarāja* cult (an emblem of the unification of the Khmer realm) at Phnom Kulen, which became the original 'Mount Mahendra', the centre of the Khmer heaven on earth, prior to the establishment of his new capital downriver at Hariharalaya and the consecration of a new Mount Mahendra there.[50] The original Mount Mahendra at Phnom Kulen was thus not only a source of legitimacy for later monarchs who drew upon the protective powers of Jayavarman's *devarāja* cult, but it was also seen quite correctly as the source of the Angkor region's water supply, a fact that enhanced the possibilities for success for the monarch's subjects.

Khmer inscriptions and archaeological evidence well reflect the growing religious sophistication of Khmer society in the Angkor era. The sacred language and symbols of 'Hindu' religious philosophy proclaimed the king's glory and abilities. The king was filled with life-sustaining energy derived from 'Hindu' and indigenous deities, as divinity flowed from the heavens or from the earth and permeated him, endowing him with the power to dispense 'purifying ambrosia' or other less abstract forms of prosperity upon his subjects. While local deities and spirits protected the monarch and his subjects, 'Hindu' gods suffused Khmer monarchs with their superior creative and purifying energy, enhancing further the prospects for prosperity in this and other worlds.

The principal concern of the leaders of early Khmer society was the establishment and endowment of local temples, for which they accrued religious merit and economic return. Key figures in the foundation of these early temples were consensual leaders of local populations, rather than persons claiming royal authority. Inscriptions recording such activities emphasize the religious prowess rather than the physical might of the local élites who were establishing the temples. Regional leaders held official

[50] G. Cœdès, *The Indianized States of Southeast Asia*, ed. Walter F. Vella, trans. Susan Brown Cowing, Honolulu, 1968, 100–3; Hermann Kulke, *The Devarāja Cult*, Ithaca, 1978.

titles; the power of the landed élites was recognized by those claiming the
authority to rule over the Khmer people by the bestowal of titles on these
pre-existing leaders, giving them 'new' authority as district officers in
the state administration. In such a way the landholders, the regional
economic, social, and political leadership, were integrated into an emerging state system.

The actions taken by landed élites involved the worship of local and
'state' divinities to 'acquire merit' and to 'exhibit devotion'. Inscriptions
celebrated the presentation of gifts made to the temple by local leaders as
part of their worship, and the wealth of those making the gifts was
stressed and donations were carefully calculated. The landed élites who
were responsible for this epigraphy emphasized the giving of gifts to
temples as the foremost means to ensure the prosperity of society.

The Khmer aristocracy concentrated economic resources under a temple's administration, whether to acquire the merit associated with such
donations, to allow for a more efficient management of an élite's resources,
or to avoid the revenue demands of those political élites claiming rights
to a share of the local landed élite's possessions. The foremost method
of accomplishing this goal was to donate land to temples. Boundaries of
donated lands were clearly defined in the inscriptions, usually associated
with place names—perhaps a village, an estate, a pond, or the riceland of
another landholder. Past and present holders of the assigned lands were
enumerated, along with the mode of the property's acquisition and its
price if acquired by purchase; the land's productivity (rice yield) was even
estimated. Inscriptions reporting assignments of populated land gave the
parcel's current occupants and spelled out what portion of the occupants'
production was assigned to the temple. If the land was unpopulated, a
labour force was assigned the task of working the newly donated lands.
These labourers were counted—males, females, females with children—
and their ethnic identity (e.g. Mon or Khmer) was recorded.

It is not uncommon to discover that the relatives of donors of such land
endowments were members of the priesthood servicing the local temple,
who became managers of the assigned property. In many instances the
donor family rather than the temple staff managed family land assigned to
a temple, the temple receiving only a designated share of the income.
What was transferred by donors was not 'ownership' of land, but the right
to income from land. Control over labour and production rather than
ownership of land was critical for the development of early Southeast
Asian states. To Khmer élites, 'landholding' meant rights to the production and labour service of the inhabitants of a parcel of land rather than
absolute possession of it. In land donations to temples, only certain rights
over the land were transferred; while inhabitants of the assigned land
normally continued to farm the land, the recipient temple collected much
or all of their production. Donated property was usually subject to a
combination of claims, those of the temple receiving the donation as well
as those of the donor's family, who retained certain personal rights to the
property—for example, the right to a share of the land's production as
well as administrative or political rights over the inhabitants.

The economic diversity of local temples is reflected in the variety of donations 'for the service of the property' assigned: domesticated animals, goats, buffaloes, cattle, coconut palms, fruit trees, areca nuts, betel leaves, clothing, a threshing floor, plus numerous individual objects, are examples. The type and size of gifts to temples indicate not only economic specialization within early Khmer society in order to create such wealth, but also the developing institutional capacity to utilize and administer this production. An economic system was emerging, centred in the temple. The assignments of land and its production by Khmer aristocrats turned temples into local storage centres; goods deposited in temple storehouses were a source of social and economic power, reinforcing the prestige of the temples' primary benefactors, the local landed élites, who influenced the redistribution of the temples' stores in support of their followers (including those working for the temple).

The concentration in temples of the authority to manage local resources had a significant impact on the process of local political integration. The implication of such centralization for economic control is reflected in epigraphic references to the 'joining together for the enjoyment of the gods', whereby a single landholder, or several, shifted a share of the income (goods and services) destined to one god or temple to that of another, or amalgamated the administration of one temple's lands with that of another.[51] Through these actions, a pattern of subordination of one local deity to another as well as one local temple to another began to emerge in Khmer society. Regional temple networks came to be sustained and controlled by a secular, landed élite who transferred income from their lands or donated material goods and services to temples in the network.

During the Angkor era amalgamation (miśrabhoga) arrangements were normally not undertaken without the approval of the king himself, but in pre-Angkor society private landholders and not a royal authority dominated the concentration of economic resources and the amalgamation of temple administration. Prior to the ninth century Khmer monarchs were concerned only with recruiting as their allies the local landed élites who had initiated such transfers and consolidations, confirming the transactions rather than challenging them. Royal edicts, although expressing concern for land, never claim that the monarchy's authority over land superseded that of the local landed élites.[52]

An inscription of the Angkor-era ruler Jayavarman IV (r. 928–41) speaks of a Khmer monarch's concern for land, forbidding the careless grazing of buffaloes that might destroy good riceland.[53] But in expressing concern, Jayavarman IV still had to take an indirect approach and respect the landholding rights of the local élites. In this instance Jayavarman ordered a royal official to notify the region's political leader (a khloñ viṣaya—a district

---

[51] M. C. Ricklefs, 'Land and the Law in the Epigraphy of Tenth Century Cambodia', JAS, 26, 3 (1967) 411–20.

[52] See O. W. Wolters, 'North-Western Cambodia in the Seventh Century', BSOAS, 37, 2 (1974) 383; and 'Jayavarman II's Military Power: The Territorial Foundation of the Angkorian Empire', JRAS (1973) 21–30. Wolters argues that in early Cambodian history local chiefs dominated. The early Khmer 'state', Wolters holds, was a temporary entity based upon the success of periodic independent leaders. See also Michael Vickery, 'Some Remarks on Early State Formation in Cambodia' in Marr and Milner, 95–115.

[53] G. Cœdès, Inscriptions du Cambodge, Hanoi, 1937–42, Paris, 1951–66, VI. 115.

chief) of his wishes; the local leader in turn decided to acknowledge the edict by permitting it to be published in his district. Clearly it was the regional chief's option to acknowledge Jayavarman IV's concern for the local lands; it would appear that the chief equally had the option of ignoring this expression of royal interest. Thus, while Angkor-era kings had a greater involvement in land transfers and assignments, early Khmer rulers could only express interest in the transfers of income and management rights of lands that were part of a regional élite's domain. Even in later times the nonroyal private sector, dominated by landed regional élites, was still strong and functional.

Within the Khmer realm religious foundations (i.e. temples) of powerful local families, who also held official titles in the Khmer state's administration, became a means of integrating the land and its production into the structure of the state. Family temples and their properties were subordinated to central temples placed strategically throughout the realm. A portion of the production collected by private temples was channelled to the state temples. In return, the priests of local family temples received validation through periodic participation in the rituals of the central temples. Local family cults also became legitimized via their worship by Khmer monarchs and their subordination to royal cults. In these times temples were not just religious centres but important links in the state's economic and political network. Religion supplied an ideology and a structure that could organize the populace to produce, tap this production, and secure a region's political subordination, without the aid of separate secular economic or political institutions.

Sūryavarman I's reign (1002–50) represents a critical phase in the development of an integrated Khmer economic and political order, with the Khmer temple network assuming a major role in the developmental process. The prosperity of families in the Khmer realm—a prosperity based upon control over the production of land and manpower—came to depend more and more upon royal favour. This new pattern demonstrates the intensified integration of the regional aristocracy into the Khmer state as 'bureaucrats'.[54] They were given official bureaucratic titles; their authority over land and manpower was recognized; and they were charged with responsibility for the expansion of the Khmer state's economic base. Along with this recognition, however, went the responsibility of sharing their land's production with the state. Land transferred to aristocratic families was assigned specifically for the benefit of family temples, whose staffs assumed responsibility for supervising its development. Because they were subordinated to royal temples, these family temples had to share the local production received with the central temples and thus with the Khmer kings who had made the original assignment.

What developed through this pattern of land assignment and development was a network of private and temple landholding rights that was

[54] Michael Vickery, 'The Reign of Sūryavarman I and the Dynamics of Angkorean Development', paper presented at the Eighth Conference of the International Association of Historians of Asia, Kuala Lumpur, 1980. Vickery notices a 'rapid bureaucratic expansion' in Angkor in the tenth century, which thus preceded Angkor's final 'imperial breakthrough' in the eleventh-century reign of Sūryavarman.

subject to the supervision of the monarchy. Angkor's society was élite-dominated. The king held the power to maintain élites with patronage and at the same time needed to prevent or neutralize the emergence of rival power centres. Élites were linked to the royal court through the Khmer temple network, if not through the bestowal of royal favour. Angkor's rulers were capable of reducing local power centres to subordinate provinces of their government, but in the process of awarding territorial grants or property right transfers they were not able to dispense landholding rights at will. The landed élites subject to the Khmer state did have independent rights and were not subject to the constant demands of the state. In the Angkor era, although local autonomy was assaulted—sometimes with a good deal of energy—the landed aristocracy retained power. The Khmer state system was not highly centralized or 'bureaucratic', nor was it a 'feudal' order in which the king assigned bureaucratic duties to a landed élite who derived their landholding rights and status as a consequence of the king's favour. Records of land assignments to families and their temples during the Angkor era reflect constant friction between the centre and its periphery and provide evidence about the nature of the relationship between the Khmer monarch and his regional élites.[55]

'Ownership' of land in the Khmer realm was thus embedded in a system of rights held by related people. The king in theory held the final authority to validate landholding rights, although this authority was not normally exercised—Sūryavarman I's initiatives were unusual; the Khmer monarch thus assumed the role of patron placing land under the 'exclusive' control of favoured families and their temples. The aristocracy, drawing their livelihood from the land, theoretically owed their continued prosperity directly or indirectly to royal favour.

In their epigraphic records Khmer monarchs reveal two purposes in their dealings with the land endowments of local temples: on the one hand they intervened where possible to limit the power of potential rivals, and on the other hand they desired to enhance the economic strength of their supporters. Avoiding possible conflict, Khmer kings rarely intervened in local temple affairs unless there was a direct threat to royal interests, but adeptly employed their right to assign their supporters' income rights to unsettled lands; rights to previously settled land left vacant could be solicited from the king by a family, the land rights of extinct lineages could be reassigned, and landholding rights to unpopulated and overgrown land

---

[55] On the application of the term 'feudal' to Khmer statecraft, see I. W. Mabbett, 'Kingship in Angkor', JSS, 66, 2 (1978). The ability of Khmer monarchs from the time of Jayavarman II to Sūryavarman II to wage apparently massive warfare demonstrates the strength and unity of the Khmer state, despite the impression that day-to-day government did not seem to be concerned with anything more extensive than securing the material needs of the centre or mediating local disputes and interests. Mabbett notes that Khmer monarchs created special posts with ceremonial functions and prospects for future favours in order to attract members of traditional landed élites. Khmer kings accommodated powerful kinship groups, each with its own network of relatives and dependants, by giving them administrative responsibilities, while the monarch monopolized divine authority. Subordinate Khmer élites thus flourished under a strong monarch. The Khmer system offset the absence of a strong centralized professional bureaucracy and dynastic institutions that were monopolized by a distinct 'royal family'. See also Mabbett, 'Varṇas in Angkor and the Indian Caste System', JAS, 36, 3 (1977).

could be assigned. Families with existing estates were sometimes encouraged to resettle in new territories.

The extension of agriculture into previously uncultivated lands and the construction of hydraulic networks to facilitate the production of rice surpluses were central to the development schemes of Khmer kings and their subordinates. Khmer temples at the state and regional levels fulfilled three economic functions in the agricultural development process. First, they were centres of investment ('banks'), the source of investment capital and management; donors' gifts were redistributed to individuals or groups of peasant and bondsman cultivators as capital investments (e.g., seeds, livestock, and land to be cultivated), which stimulated the agrarian sector. Second, temples were repositories of technological information and knowledge, directly or indirectly supporting scholars, astrologers, and artisans whose expertise and literacy could be drawn upon by cultivators. Third, Khmer temples were supervisory agencies that involved agricultural labourers in the development process, offering sufficient returns to encourage them to remain on the land.

As noted, lands assigned to temples for development were often unpopulated, requiring the assignment of a labour force (men, women and children are enumerated in the inscriptions) with no previous claim to the land's production. This workforce might be acquired by moving a population, possibly war captives (men and women), from an area peripheral to the state's core domain to the lands to be developed. Labourers assigned to develop new lands were incorporated into the local economic and social system by temples. Lone peasant cultivating families could not easily have borne the economic burdens of shortfalls in production as they brought new land into production or implemented agricultural technology associated with the construction of irrigation projects. Temples, however, could mobilize their storage and redistributive mechanisms to meet the subsistence needs of the labourers in such an event, drawing from material resources assigned for this purpose by kings or regional élites. Temples were also in charge of agricultural development, engaging diggers, scribes, managers, and other specialists, combining the technical expertise and human resources necessary for the extension of agriculture. Furthermore, temples offered labourers emotional security; workers sought not only personal economic profit but also worked for the spiritual gain derived from service to a temple's deity.

If land assigned to a temple was not to be administered by the temple staff, the heads of the family or other members of the lineage might act as property managers on the temple's behalf, utilizing income from the land to erect buildings, construct hydraulic projects, secure additional labour to work the land, or in general ensure that the land's productivity would increase. The dominant landholding families thus also benefited from the development of temple land and the accumulation of wealth by the family temple. This income was tapped for redistribution by the family to its supporters in various forms. Relationships between élite families and the temple were rarely questioned by Khmer monarchs, who instead attempted to obtain a share of the wealth accumulated locally by the right their central temples had to a percentage of the local temples' income. However, income from local temples covered only a small percentage of the royal temples' expenses, and this revenue sharing was more symbolic than critical to the financial well-being of the state temples.

That only limited demands were placed on local family temples is conveyed in the accounts of the Khmer royal temples. The Ta Prohm temple's rice needs during the reign of Jayavarman VII (1181–1218) were said to be 6589 kilograms daily for cooking and 2,512,406 kilograms annually.[56] This rice fed the temple's personnel, who included 18 high priests, 2740 officiants, and 2632 assistants—among whom were 615 female dancers, 439 learned hermits who lived in the temple monastery (aśrama), and 970 students. A total of 12,460 people lived within the walls of the temple compound. The sum of rice consumed annually was thus 2,512,406 kilograms, of which only 366,800 kilograms were delivered by villages assigned to the temple and 42,157 kilograms from royal storehouses, together covering less than one-fifth of the temple's rice consumption. Villages assigned to the central temple supplied rice through their local family temples, but in comparison to the total amount of production annually drawn by local temples from their assigned lands, the annual payment of roughly 90 kilograms of rice that these family temples were obliged to pay to a central temple was insignificant. The central temple's primary source of income was the temple's own assigned lands worked by 'bondsmen' (knum) at the behest of Khmer monarchs and state élites. State-level central temples thus functioned economically in a fashion similar to the local family temples, but on a much larger scale.

Following the twelfth-century inscription of Jayavarman VII in his Prah Khan temple complex describing the Khmer realm as being composed of 306,372 subjects, male and female, inhabiting 13,500 villages, one historian calculated that Khmer subjects were producing roughly 38,000,000 kilograms of hulled rice annually for 20,000 gold, silver, bronze, and stone gods. Each worker supplied an average of 120 kilograms of hulled rice, or 60 per cent of his productivity.[57] The potential of the flow of production to and the concentration of economic resources in Khmer temples is demonstrated in the Ta Prohm inscription's enumeration of the temple's stores, which contained a set of golden dishes weighing more than 500 kilograms; a silver service of equal size; 35 diamonds; 40,620 pearls; 4540 gems; 523 parasols; 512 sets of silk bedding; 876 Chinese veils; a huge quantity of rice, molasses, oil seeds, wax, sandalwood, and camphor; and 2387 changes of clothing for the adornment of temple statues.

The revenue demands of central temples upon local family temples thus appear to have had more political and social than economic importance. Royal interest in local temples, aside from guaranteeing the financial well-being of allies and limiting the economic resources of potential rivals, was more concerned about a local temple's ritual being in harmony with that of

---

[56] G. Cœdès, 'La stèle de Ta-prohm', BEFEO, 6 (1906).

[57] L. A. Sedov, 'On the Problem of the Economic System in Angkor, Cambodia in the IX–XII Centuries', Narody Asii: Afriki, Istoria, Ekonomika, Kul'tura, 6 (1963), estimates that 366.8 tons of rice were supplied by roughly 66,625 villagers, each of the 3140 villages providing roughly 117 kilograms per year to the central temple.

royal temples than about making a local temple economically subordinate to a royal temple.

Endowments to temples at both the state and local level represented the mobilization, organization, and pooling of economic resources (capital, land, labour, and so forth) to support portions of the overall ritual process of the temple—for example, financing a single event in the temple's religious calendar of ritual, the construction of a building in the temple compound, clothing for a temple image, or a subsidy for a temple priest. While this redistribution of economic capital was central to a temple's existence, the mobilization of 'symbolic capital' was also critical, as temple endowments generated one or more ritual contexts in which honours rather than material returns were distributed to and received by donors. In this way economic capital was converted to culturally symbolic capital, honours that enhanced the status of the donor in the minds of his kin and clients.[58]

An endowment permitted the entry and incorporation of Khmer corporate units (e.g., families and kings) into a temple as temple servants (priests, assistants, and so on) or as donors. The donor represented a social, economic, or political unit; the gift was a means by which the group or its leader could formally and publicly receive recognition. While an endowment supported the deity, and often returned some material advantage to the donor, perhaps more important were the symbolic returns of the 'donation'. Rulers—regional élites or Khmer monarchs—were patrons and protectors of temples, ensuring the continuance of a temple's services, resources, and rules. They were not 'rulers' of temples, however, but were servants of the temple's deity, human agents of the lord of the temple—a stone image that could not arbitrate in the real world on its own behalf—who protected and served the deity.

In the Indian tradition a ruler's relationship with a temple represented a symbolic division of sovereignty, whereby the ruler became the greatest servant of the temple's lord, his patronage of the temple's deity sustaining and displaying his rule over men.[59] Yet kings and others who claimed political authority were subject to challenges by those who perceived their shares and rights—a consequence of other individual or group endowments to a temple—to be independently derived from the sovereign deity. An example of the competition to claim the shared sovereignty of the secular (the ruler) and the sacred (the temple) is provided in the Khmer realm, where local élites and kings each patronized temple deities. The issue of who was the ultimate servant of the temple's lord had political significance and explains the attempts by Angkor's monarchs to subordinate the deities of local temples to those of royal temples or to integrate these local deities into royal cults.

The returns from temple donations thus had both economic as well as political implications, and explain the significant flow of economic resources from rulers at various levels to Khmer temples. If an identification

[58] On symbolic gifting see Pierre Bourdieu, *Outline of a Theory of Practice*, Cambridge, UK, 1977.
[59] Arjun Appadurai and Carol Appadurai Breckenridge, 'The South Indian Temple: Authority, Honour, and Redistribution', *Contributions to Indian Sociology*, NS, 10, 2 (1976), point to the role of temples as centres of symbolic redistributions.

with a deity was essential to legitimize rule, as seems to have been the case in the Khmer realm, then instead of material returns upon one's investment symbolic returns must have been equally desirable, especially to Khmer kings who never reaped substantial material benefit from their assignment of local income rights to local temples. The temple's redistributive role was thus critical to issues of sovereignty in both the secular and sacred Khmer world order, and raises questions of how to equate economic and symbolic capital, if it is really possible to quantify this conversion process, and whether there was any attempt to achieve 'equity'—topics beyond the scope of the available historical records.

The redistributive functions of Khmer temples are summarized in Figure 4.1. In this diagram the state's resources flow as donations or dues (gold, land, livestock, food, and labour) from villages and local and regional temples to the state's central temples. Returns may have been in kind, utilizing the temple as a 'bank'. In such instances the donor received a material return (i.e. 'economic capital') upon his 'investment', either directly via a prescribed rate of return or indirectly through the greater productivity achieved regionally as a consequence of the temple's efficient management of land. Returns might also have been 'symbolic capital', which contributed to the legitimacy of various regional and state aristocrats through the performance of temple ceremonies that emphasized the donor's superior spiritual prowess or through the act of recording the gift in an inscription that perpetually honoured the donor's piety.

Thus, in the Khmer realm temples never became independent of those in political authority, whether at the local or state level. Rivalries and tensions developed, rather, among local and state authorities whose power was based on their control over labour, landholdings, and temple administration. There was never a shift of socio-economic power away from secular authorities to a religious order. However, Khmer monarchs were limited by the very nature of their policy of utilizing temples and temple networks as a means of integrating their domains economically and politically. They never developed a centralized bureaucratic order, depending instead upon assignments of land rights and impressive titles to those in royal favour to elicit the loyalty of semi-autonomous regionally based landed élites. Yet there does not appear to have been a lack of ability to finance major royal projects. In the absence of a bureaucratic system for collecting large amounts of income for the state's treasury, temples were viewed as important centres of economic accumulation that could be tapped to finance the king's patronage of religion. Most conspicuous were temple construction and elaborate temple ceremonies and festivals, which provided a pretext under which the state's economic and social resources could be mobilized to achieve the state's political goals. These goals mainly focused on the construction of a state-dominated political system replacing the previous system, which had been built on a series of personal alliances. In this new system temples assumed major roles in the process of political integration.

The Khmer state's centralized temple complex thus related land and population to the king's capital. Temples controlled land, the labour on the land, and the land's productive output. Religious development was

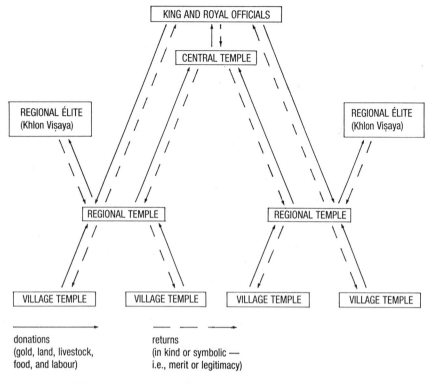

Figure 4.1   The Angkor era temple network.

viewed as an aid to the state's economic development. The extension of
cultivated land in the tenth and eleventh centuries was thereby connected
to the endowment of religious establishments. Rich temples formed economic bases that were tapped for construction projects, the development
of irrigation, rice production, and so on—projects which were healthy for
the economy as a whole and which the central government could not
always cover financially.

BUDDHISM AS AN ECONOMIC FORCE IN PAGAN BURMA

The Burmese state of Pagan, at its height from the eleventh to the
fourteenth centuries, also drew economic support from a temple network.
Early Pagan monarchs had two needs as they established their authority:
economic and ideological bases that substantiated their superiority over
their political rivals. Buddhism provided the answer. The Buddhist *sangha*
was able, as an existing body of literati with at least a primary level of
technological expertise, to assist in the development of hydro-agricultural
systems. In Burma, King Anawrahta (r. 1044–77) resettled skilled and
unskilled labour in central and northern Burma during the eleventh
century, and also 'imported' Theravāda Buddhism from the Thaton region
of southern Burma into the three 'core' agricultural zones (*kharuin*) that

surrounded the Pagan royal centre. The Pagan state 'cores' consisted of Kyaukse *kharuin* north of the capital, Toṅplun to the east, and Maṅbu to the west; eighteen secondary 'frontier' settlements (*tuik*) were agrarian communities adjacent to the mountains west of Pagan; forty-three fortified towns were interspersed up the Irrawaddy River from the 'core' to the border of the neighbouring Nanchao realm in the north.[60] Buddhist monasteries and temples were established in critical locations throughout these zones, and upon receiving allocations of rights to land and labour assumed a leadership role in the development of irrigation networks and wet-rice agriculture in each new population centre.

Pagan-era society was organized into professional communities, which in some instances corresponded with ethnic groups (the Mon populations from the Thaton region in lower Burma were resettled in the Pagan economic core during the eleventh-century reign of Anawrahta and were a categorically distinct group in epigraphic records). During the Pagan age, social and political status was determined by one's birth, occupation, and ethnicity. Hereditary status was enforced by the state and the Buddhist Church. Free society was divided into public and private sectors. Public functionaries (*amhū*) served in the military as supervisors of local irrigation and public granaries, and as tax collectors. Private functionaries (*asañ/athi*) included artisans, merchants, and peasants, all of whom were free from service obligations.

During the Pagan age private workers, as seemingly with others, were subject to intensified specialization and became more and more regimented by occupation into specialist groups. Among the Pagan-era working class, those who worked on temples—notably carpenters, masons, wood-carvers, painters, scribes, clerks, artisans, and metal workers—were of higher status than were musicians, dancers, and other performers, food vendors, cooks, hunters, butchers, milkmen, and keepers of game. All such workers were paid for their services rather than providing their labour as a corvée labour tax to the government or temples. Their normal income included gold, silver, lead, land, horses, elephants, clothes, and produce.

Debt bondsmen and women (*kywan*) also figure prominently in the Pagan socio-economy. They pledged their service to a patron for payment in kind, and normally received a share of income from the land they farmed or the work they performed on their patron's behalf. Bondsmen could be assigned to work on a temple's behalf, or they might be transferred with donated land to serve a temple. In early Burmese history bondsmen could easily redeem themselves from servitude; but during the Pagan era, due to the rising complexity of the Burmese political economy and a growing rigidity in the Burmese social hierarchy, it became very difficult for bondsmen to escape their clientage. This is documented in the transition of the common understanding of the word for 'redemption' (*tolhan*), which during Pagan times changed to 'rebellion'.[61] Increasingly a bondsman's only viable option was to enter a monastery as a full-time monk.

Headmen (*sukrī/thugyi*) exercised personal control rather than territorial

---

[60] Michael Aung-Thwin, *Pagan: The Origins of Modern Burma*, Honolulu, 1985.
[61] Michael Aung-Thwin, 'Kingship, the Sangha, and Society in Pagan' in Hall and Whitmore, *Explorations*, 209.

authority over community occupational groups. They were expected to keep group records, collect and pay revenues to the state, and to enforce hereditary occupation. They pledged their loyalty to a client of the Burmese monarch, who in turn shared locally collected revenues with the king. The king benefited by this regimentation by occupational and ethnic group, and the king and his élite clients provided the linkage among these groups via their sponsorship of monumental architecture, court ceremony, dress that distinguished one group from another, bestowal of titles on loyal subordinates, and the use of a special court language.

Revenue flowed to the centre, and was redistributed as payments and rewards to those favoured by the monarch. However, much local revenue never reached the king or his clients, but instead found its way to the local Buddhist institutions or individual monks as 'in-lieu-of-tax' payments for the upkeep of the *sangha*, but also to finance assorted economic development projects that were co-ordinated by the Church. Workers were hired with endowed funds to work temple fields, build and maintain temples, and to service temples. The expenses of monks were paid from temple endowment funds; wells, tanks, and irrigation canals were dug, and palm trees and gardens were planted. Various performances by theatrical and dance troops, festivals, and feasts were financed from revenue assignments to temples. Thus, reassignments of royal revenue collections provided jobs, extended cultivated lands, and financed religion and entertainment.

In Burma status was defined by how much one gave to the Buddhist Church rather than the wealth one accumulated. Kings received merit and consequent legitimacy in return for their generosity. In Burma *kammatic/karma* Buddhism, which stressed that salvation was due to one's good works, took precedence over belief that salvation accrued via intellectual attainment (*nibbānic/nirvāna* Buddhism).[62] From a Burmese perspective, the intellectual quest for salvation was more appropriate to the overly pious; *kammatic* Buddhism was more practical for the average lay person. *Kamma* could be transferred or shared—the merit of one person could enhance the merit of another (usually deceased)—or it could be redistributed, as a rich man could build a temple for the merit of those who could not afford to do so. The king was, ultimately, the one with the most wealth to share. The more a king donated, the more merit he gained. Pagan era kings were considered to be close to Bodhisattva status. Thus, the dilemma of a king was whether to accumulate material or symbolic capital, to maintain the wealth of his kingdom, while being required to give much of his personal wealth away. The Pagan era political-economy may thus be characterized as being based on three mutually related concerns: (1) salvation was achieved through good works and the sharing of merit; (2) religious endowments were a practical means of achieving one's religious as well as social and political goals; and (3) the political-economy depended upon assorted redistributions of material wealth.[63]

[62] Stanley J. Tambiah, *World Conqueror and World Renouncer: A Study of Buddhism and Polity in Thailand against a Historical Background*, Cambridge, UK, 1976.
[63] Michael Aung-Thwin, 'Divinity, Spirit, and Human: Conceptions of Classical Burmese Kingship' in Lorraine Gesick, ed., *Centers, Symbols, and Hierarchies: Essays on the Classical State of Southeast Asia*, New Haven, 1983.

In the absence of a strong centralized political system, Pagan monarchs drew upon the Buddhist religious order to sanctify their authority; by endowing monasteries and temples with land and people, kings set in motion the legacy of royal patronage. Pagan kings were ultimately the individuals with the most wealth to share; by donating more they gained the greatest merit as the chief patrons of the Church. The king was the *kammarāja*, who achieved status by merit and past deeds (*kamma/karma*) as opposed to the Hindu rulers of other early Southeast Asian states who partook of the divine (*dharmarāja*). This system of patronage, however, posed a serious dilemma. The authority of early rulers among their secular subordinates was especially dependent upon periodic redistributions of wealth to maintain bonds of loyalty. Donations to the *sangha* by the king and his subordinates began to replace previous material redistributions with redistributions of symbolic capital. Royal allies, by their recognition of the Buddhist *sangha* and the king as the chief patron of the *sangha*, became participants in the state-sponsored religious system, and enhanced their own personal status as subordinates to the king's 'sacred sovereignty'.

Potential problems in this system were largely emergent in times of political succession, as bonds of personal loyalty could not easily be transferred at the death of a ruler. While a king reigned, there was usually political stability based upon alliance networks that a monarch constructed during his rise to power. Personal bonds of loyalty—titles, position, and even landholding rights—became subject to review when a king died. In such periods of political transition, the hierarchical social structure, the redistribution-based economy, and *kammatic* Buddhism helped to hold the state together.

The history of Pagan demonstrates the pitfalls of this system of *kammatic* kingship, as the *sangha* ultimately became the state's major holder of economic resources. The *sangha* could, because of the tax-free status of the Church's economic resources, come to control the state's land and labour force. Temple building and religious endowments, initially intended to extend the state's economy and enhance the king's prowess, eventually doomed the monarchy to a status of subservience to the *sangha* when the state's economic base fell under its control. To challenge the *sangha's* control over the state's economic resources would have led to the negation of the state's image as the Church's leading patron.

Buddhist temples and monasteries became secondary redistribution centres for areas outside the Pagan capital-city palace complex. Burmese monarchs attempted to neutralize the flow of wealth to the *sangha*; for example, the king's personal approval was necessary to validate large donations. But the king's authority to restrict donations was neutralized, due to the very nature of Pagan's kingship noted above. As chief patron of religion, the king could not inhibit donations, and, indeed, had to bestow more upon the *sangha* than anyone else. Once it had given them, the state was not entitled to take back its income rights to land. In contrast, income rights to land assigned to secular authorities, including royal military and administrators, could be confiscated. To avoid this, royal subordinates frequently reassigned their income rights to the Buddhist *sangha*—normally to a specific monk or a local temple rather than to the *sangha* in general.

When the monk receiving the income assignment died, property rights reverted to the donor, who could then redonate or retain his property rights, depending on the political climate at that time. Reassignments of income rights to the Church thus were a means by which one could protect personal property from state confiscation.

Overexpansion of the *sangha* was thus a major political problem, since the *sangha* had the institutional capacity to co-ordinate its affairs over the entire realm, while the state could not. The king's one recourse against the Church's wealth and power was the periodic 'purification' of the religious order, by which the king reduced the Burmese *sangha* to small, localized, 'other-worldly' groups with a few material resources, which were under the control of a unified *sangha* élite directly appointed and supervised by the king.[64] Pagan monarchs initiated the purification process by publicly accusing the *sangha* of being 'corrupt', 'lazy', 'worldly', and thus 'impure'. The ideal *sangha* order was one of austerity and asceticism. Thus, to purify the *sangha* was an act of piety by the king. In Buddhist tradition there was the expectation that due to the ultimate vulnerability of monks to material corruption (since they were human rather than divine), kings had to purify the religious order periodically to perpetuate the religion.

Burmese rulers followed their public accusation by sending selected monks to Sri Lanka, which was considered to be the centre of Buddhist piety in that era, to be purified (reordained). When they returned, these monks would in turn lead the reordination and purification of all Burmese monks. While the selected monks were gone, the king built an ordination hall for the reordination ceremony. First the ground was ritually cleansed to release the spiritual ties of the local *nat* spirits that might pollute the ceremony; a moat was dug around the hall so that the water in the moat could insulate the grounds of the ordination hall from impurities and all trees that overhung the grounds were cut to prevent their contamination of the grounds.

According to Buddhist tradition, the quality of one's merit was a product of the piety of the monks one donated to. Thus, newly purified Burmese monks, patronized by the king, had the greatest status. Other monks had to subordinate themselves or risk being cut off from state and public funding. Seniority depended upon the order of reordination; detailed accounts were kept to record the minute of ordination/reordination that could demonstrate one's superiority over others in the Burmese *sangha* hierarchy. In an era of reordination, the highest-ranking monks thus owed their superior rank to the king, who carefully selected the monks to be sent to be reordained in Sri Lanka and also determined the order of reordination in Burma based upon his perception of a monk's personal loyalty. The king appointed a reordination committee who received applications from those wishing to be reordained. To be worthy of reordination, a monk had to give up his worldly possessions—cattle, land, and manpower. Rights to these could not be transferred to a layman but could only pass to the state.

[64] Michael Aung-Thwin, 'The Role of Sasana Reform in Burmese History: Economic Dimensions of a Religious Purification', JAS, 30, 4 (1979).

Those who chose not to give up their material, this-worldly possessions were required to assume lay status, and their property immediately became subject to state tax assessments.

In the Pagan era, strong monarchs were initially capable of instituting periodic purifications of the Burmese *sangha*, and thereby re-establishing their right to collect taxes on the formerly tax-free *sangha* property. In the thirteenth century the interests of the new landed élite, an artisan class who had become wealthy due to their work on the numerous temple construction projects that had been financed by the state and its secular subordinates, and who had reinvested their wages earned on these projects in land, coincided with the 'impure' *sangha*. The large, wealthy *sangha* had more wealth to redistribute than did the state—especially to the artisan class who supervised the construction of temples and monasteries. The economic power of this landed artisan class and the *sangha* was thus pitted against the political power of the state. Because the *sangha* had by that time become closer to this society, its beliefs and its values, than was the old élite, and had also become its economic patrons, there was little public support for the state in its attempts to curb the power of the *sangha*.[65]

The thirteenth-century Church supported peasant uprisings and land disputes against the state. It openly bought and sold land and sponsored lavish feasts to celebrate legal victories, where quantities of cattle, pig, and liquor, items normally considered extremely polluting, were consumed.

Pagan's thirteenth-century rulers no longer monopolized wealth, and were no longer able to subjugate the *sangha* to their authority. With the continued devolution of land and labour to the *sangha*, strong regional socio-economic units rather than a 'unified' state system came to dominate Burma, until fifteenth-century Burmese rulers again found it possible, due to growing public disapproval of an 'impure' and materialistic *sangha*, once more to institute a *sangha*-wide purification. But following a new purification, the state, needing the economic leadership and merit the *sangha* could provide, once again began to make donations of land and labour to the *sangha*, and thereby instituted a new cycle of competition between the *sangha* and the state.

INTERNATIONAL TRADE AND COMMERCIAL EXPANSION ON THE MAINLAND, c. 1100–1300

Expansion of the regional agricultural base allowed the dramatic political expansion of both the Khmer and Burmese states during the tenth and eleventh centuries. By the first half of the eleventh century, Khmer monarchs had pushed their control to the west into the Chao Phraya valley of present-day Thailand and toward the Isthmus of Kra of the Malay peninsula. While tenth-century Khmer political interests had been directed toward the eastern portion of the realm, Sūryavarman I (r. 1002–50) reversed this pattern with his activities in the west.[66] Sūryavarman's

---

[65] Aung-Thwin, *Pagan*. See also G. E. Harvey, *A History of Burma from Earliest Times*, London, 1925.
[66] Hall, *Maritime Trade*, 169–78.

extension of Khmer authority into the Lopburi region had strong economic
implications, for control of the lower Chao Phraya provided access to
international commerce at Tāmbraliṅga (known as *Tan-liu-mei* to the
Chinese), the Chaiya-Suratthani area of southern Thailand, giving the
Khmers a more direct contact with the international trade routes than had
previously been the case.

Sūryavarman appears to have been especially intent upon establishing a
flow of trade from South Indian Cōḷa ports to the Southeast Asian
mainland via the Isthmus of Kra and Suratthani area. Goods could then be
transported north from the isthmus to Lopburi, where they followed the
two exchange networks that evolved in Sūryavarman's reign. The first
entered the royal heartland in the Sisophon area; the second encompassed
the region north of the Dangrek mountain range, with a link to the core at
Prāḥ Vihār and a possible connection to the Mekong River in the east.
Under Sūryavarman's rule the commercial economy of the Khmer state
achieved such importance that the upper Malay peninsula receded from
the patterns of power and trade in the island world and was drawn into
those of the mainland. The contacts of this area came to lie not with the
international trade route but with a more local route that went across
the Bay of Bengal to South India and Sri Lanka. Where previously it had
been the locus for outside contact with the islands and the international
route for the Mons of lower Burma and southern Thailand, now the
isthmus provided a more regional contact for the wet-rice states of Pagan
and Angkor and through them to the northern mountain areas where the
stirrings of the Tai-speaking peoples were becoming ever more important.
This regional trade and communication network rapidly became a path for
the spread of Theravāda Buddhism to the western and central sections of
the Southeast Asian mainland, establishing a cultural relationship of great
significance for later centuries.

As the Khmers were developing commercial contacts with the West, the
Burmans were pushing south into the delta of the Irrawaddy and were also
moving toward the Isthmus of Kra. After establishing a base at Pagan in
the tenth century, the Burmans in an eleventh-century expansion annexed
the Mon kingdoms of Pegu and Thaton in lower Burma. Here the Burmans
established control over the Mon commercial centres. Around 1050 the
Burmans were expanding into the Malay peninsula, where they encountered
little resistance from the Khmers. It would appear that after 1050 internal
disorder prevented a Khmer presence in the Malay peninsula, leaving
the isthmus to the Burmans. The Chams were applying pressure on
the eastern Khmer border, Sūryavarman died, and the centre of Khmer
political power temporarily shifted north into the Mun River valley
beyond the Dangrek mountain range.[67] Angkor-era epigraphy reflects
a corresponding lack of interest in commercial affairs until the late
twelfth century.

Tenth-century disorder in the region the Chinese knew as the Nanchao
region north of the Burman and Khmer realms appears to have blocked

---

[67] Milton Osborne, 'Notes on Early Cambodian Provincial History: Isanapura and Samb-
hupura', *France Asie/Asia*, 20, 4 (1966), 447.

the overland commercial networks connecting the Irrawaddy plains and China, and thus generated Burman interest in opening commercial channels to the south. Before the closing of the northern route, Burma had served as a centre of exchange between northern India and China; overland trade to Bengal via Arakan had been of major economic importance to the Burmese heartland. Commercial centres on the Malay peninsula provided an alternative source of foreign commodities for this Indian trade after the route to China had been closed. Isthmus ports were located well within the range of Mon coastal shipping, but communication between the Pegu coast of lower Burma and the isthmus was disrupted by a Cōḷa raid in 1024–5.

Under Anawrahta, there was new interest in restoring Burmese commercial intercourse with the isthmus. Around 1057, Anawrahta followed his conquest of Thaton by moving his armies south to Mergui. From Mergui, one historian believed, the Burmese forces crossed the isthmus.[68] Burmese military success in this direction is reflected in a request by King Vijayabāhu I (r. 1055–1110) of Sri Lanka for aid against the Cōḷas, to which the Burmese king responded with 'peninsular products', which were used to pay Vijayabāhu's soldiers. The Cōḷas did not look favourably upon this show of support. In 1067, they launched an expedition against 'Kaḍāram' (Takuapa, the west-coast port terminus of the Persian–Arab trade until the mid-eleventh century), in 'aid of its ruler', who had been forced to flee his country and had sought Cōḷa assistance. Cōḷa administrative problems in Sri Lanka made this intervention short, however; by 1069–70, South Indian control over Sri Lanka had been eliminated. The Cūlavaṃsa, the Sri Lankan Buddhist chronicle, records that in 1070, after Vijayabāhu I gained control, many costly treasures were sent to the Pagan king; then in 1075, Buddhist priests from Burma were invited to Sri Lanka to purify the order.[69]

Takuapa's position as the dominant port on the peninsula was dealt a death blow by this second Cōḷa raid; archaeological evidence from the Takuapa area terminates in the second half of the eleventh century, the period corresponding to the raid.[70] The 1025 Cōḷa raid resulted in a loosening of commerce in the straits region, with new ports developing as alternative entrepôts to Śrīvijaya-Palembang. By the late eleventh century the northern Sumatra coast was becoming an important commercial centre. The Kedah coast to the south of Takuapa was more strategically located to be a part of this new pattern of Melaka Straits commerce. A Burmese military presence at Takuapa, followed by the second Cōḷa raid, sealed Takuapa's fate and reinforced the attractiveness of the Kedah coast— Takuapa was no longer a port that could offer security to foreign merchants.

Archaeological remains at Takuapa and Kedah suggest that such a shift occurred, with evidence at Takuapa ceasing and that of Kedah showing a dramatic increase during the second half of the eleventh century. As

[68] G. H. Luce, 'The Career of Htilaing Min (Kyanzittha), the Unifier of Burma A.D. 1084–1113', JRAS (1966), 59.

[69] Wilhelm Geiger, trans., Cūlavaṃsa, Colombo, 1929–1930, 58, 8–9; G. H. Luce, Old Burma—Early Pagan, New York, 1969–70, I. 40.

[70] Alastair Lamb, 'Takuapa: The Probable Site of a Pre-Malaccan Entrepôt in the Malay Peninsula' in John Bastin and R. Roolvink, eds, Malayan and Indonesian Studies, London, 1964.

a consequence of early eleventh-century disorders, the port élites of Takuapa transferred their operations to the new 'preferred port' at Kedah, which explains the Arab geographers' continued use of 'Kalāh' to identify their preferred Malay coastal entrepôt—that is, the Arabs used 'Kalāh' to identify their preferred port wherever it was in the Isthmus of Kra region or the western coast of the Malay peninsula.[71] Similarly, even after Palembang had been replaced by Jambi-Malāyu as the capital of the Śrīvijaya maritime state, the name 'Śrīvijaya' still identified the ports of the southeastern Sumatran coast. It is significant that in 1070 the eastern Isthmus of Kra port of Tāmbraliṅga presented its first tribute to the Chinese court since 1016. This mission may be seen as a response to the events of 1067: while the Cōḷa raid against Takuapa and the shift of Kalāh to the Kedah coast established a new pattern on the west coast, Tāmbraliṅga's mission was sent to reassure the Chinese that its east coast status was unchanged.

After the 1067 Cōḷa raid, the Burmese moved to ensure their external trade connections. The importance of communication networks linking Burma with northern India was recognized by Kyanzittha (r. 1084–1112) in his restoration of the Bodhgāyā shrine in Bengal. An inscription from Bodhgāyā (1105–6) recorded that ships laden with large quantities of jewels had been sent by the Burmese ruler to finance the restoration and the endowment of the Buddhist monument.[72] The fact that this mission was sent by sea is indicative of Pagan's new status as a participant in the regional trade of the Bay of Bengal. An inscription from Pagan records another mission that Kyanzittha sent to either South India or Sri Lanka:

> Then the king wrote of grace of the Buddharatna, Dhammaratna, and Sangharatna [upon a leaf of gold with vermilion ink]. The king sent it to the Chōli prince. The Chōli prince with all his array, hearing of the grace of the Buddha, the Law and the Church, from King Srī Tribhuwanādityadhammarāja's mission . . . he cast off his adherence to fake doctrines, and he adhered straight away to the true doctrine.[73]

Although stated in religious terms, there are strong economic implications in this account. Campaigns that were clearly military in character, and probably economic in purpose, were recorded as religious missions; military campaigns became 'quests for relics'. By triumphantly bringing back relics and sacred treasures, the king could justify the expenses of campaigns whose benefits might remain obscure to the people of the kingdom.

Evidence of such commercial contact is provided in a thirteenth-century Pagan inscription noting that a native of India's Malabar coast made a donation to a temple at Pagan that was connected with an international merchant association based in South India.[74] This thirteenth-century Pagan inscription indicates that the merchants' temple had been present there for

[71] G. R. Tibbetts, *A Study of the Arabic Texts Containing Material on South-East Asia*, Leiden, 1979, 118–228, and passim.
[72] Shwesandaw Pagoda Inscription, *Epigraphia Birmanica* [hereafter EB], l, viii, 163; *Epigraphia Indica* (hereafter EI), 11 (1911–1912) 119.
[73] EB, l, viii, 165, the Shwesandaw Pagoda Inscription.
[74] EI, 7, 197–8. See also Kenneth R. Hall, *Trade and Statecraft in the Age of the Cōḷas*, Delhi, 1980.

some time; the recorded gift provided for the construction of a new shrine (*maṇḍapa*) for the temple compound. Further evidence of a continuing economic relationship between Pagan and South India is reflected in an 1178 Chinese note on the Cōḷas: 'Some say that one can go there by way of the kingdom of P'u-kan [Pagan].'[75]

It thus appears that as Burma came to dominate the Takuapa region and as 'Kalāh' shifted to the Kedah coast, the Burmese empire became a focal point of regional commerce in the late eleventh century. International merchants who were formerly active at Takuapa moved their activities either south to Kedah or north to the regional commercial centres of the Burma coast. In the process the old dominance over international trade enjoyed by Śrīvijaya along the Straits of Melaka was shattered. Java and the northern Sumatra ports drew the major international route south and west, the Burmese drew the regional route of the Bay of Bengal north, and the Isthmus of Kra came to exist essentially as a transition area to the mainland states.

In the following decades, the upper Malay peninsula became the centre of a multipartite interaction among the Sinhalese of Sri Lanka, the Burmese, and the Khmers as the regional trade route developed. Based on his study of Buddhist votive tablets and other evidence, G. H. Luce believed that Pagan controlled the isthmus from 1060 until roughly 1200.[76] Examining the chronicles of Nakhon Sithammarat together with Pāli literature from Sri Lanka, David Wyatt has revised Luce's dating, suggesting that from 1130 to 1176 Tāmbraliṅga was under Sinhalese hegemony.[77] About 1176, King Narapatisithu of Pagan (r. 1174–1211) made an expedition from the Pegu coast into the isthmus and established Pagan's control over the Tāmbraliṅga area 'with the permission of the King of Sri Lanka'.[78]

Burma's twelfth-century influence on the upper peninsula is substantiated by the *Cūlavaṃsa*.[79] When in the 1160s the Burmese refused (or monopolized) the trade in elephants and blocked the way across the peninsula to Angkor, the Sinhalese responded with a retaliatory raid. In this account five ships from Sri Lanka arrived at the port of Bassein in lower Burma. Furthermore, a ship commanded by a government treasurer reached another Mon port, where Sinhalese troops fought their way into the country's interior to the city of Ukkama where they killed the local monarch. This brought the kingdom under Sri Lanka's influence. The people of Burma granted concessions to the Sinhalese and envoys were sent to the community of monks on the island, with the result that the Theravāda monks interceded with the Sri Lankan king on behalf of the Burmese.

Since only six ships reached Burma, this could not have been the record

[75] Hirth and Rockhill, *Chau Ju-kua*, 94, 98.

[76] 'The Early *Syam* in Burma's History: A Supplement', JSS, 47, 1 (1959) 60–1.

[77] 'Mainland Powers on the Malay Peninsula', paper presented at the Third Conference of the International Association of Historians of Asia, Kuala Lumpur, 1968.

[78] 'Episode of the Tooth Relic'. See David K. Wyatt, *The Crystal Sands, Chronicles of Nagara Sri Dharmaraja*, Ithaca, 1975, 26–8, 38–9, 42, 59, 66–71, 72–9; and Wyatt, 'Mainland Powers on the Malay Peninsula', 13–14. The dating of Narapatisithu's reign is based on the research of Aung-Thwin, *Pagan*.

[79] Geiger, *Cūlavaṃsa*, 76, 10–75.

of a large-scale war, but rather of a successful naval raid against lower Burma. Such a plundering expedition was similar to those undertaken by the Cōḷas in the eleventh century, with additional emphasis given to gaining trade concessions. It is unlikely that the raid penetrated to Pagan and killed the Burmese king. Burmese chronicles record that during the reign of Alaungsithu (1113–65) that corresponded with this raid the lower Burma provinces were in a state of 'anarchy' and 'rebellion', suggesting that a local governor had become quite powerful and attempted to assert his independence from Pagan. 'Ukkama', the residence of the 'king' killed by the Sinhalese has been identified as a commercial and administrative centre of lower Burma—possibly Martaban, a later capital of the area—where a local governor could well have been put to death by the raiders. Governors in lower Burma derived considerable income from trade revenues generated by the regional commercial networks. Such an obstruction of commerce may actually have represented an attempt to establish independent control over this lucrative trade. It is notable that one of the attack ships was led by a Sinhalese treasurer, an individual who would have had a great interest in increasing trade revenues. The raid of the Sinhalese on lower Burma can be seen as the high point of the twelfth-century competition for control of the isthmus and is best explained in terms of an interruption and difficulties concerning the patterns of trade and communication in this area.

While the twelfth-century relationship of Sri Lanka and Burma is relatively clear, that between Sri Lanka and the Khmer state is not. As indicated in the *Cūlavaṃsa*, the major reason for the 1160s conflict between Sri Lanka and Burma was Sri Lanka's concern that Burma was preventing free access to the communication channels between Sri Lanka and Angkor. This explanation is indicative of the peninsula's relationship to the Khmer core domain as well. The upper peninsula was significant as the intermediary between Sri Lanka and Angkor, so that it was more important as a source of economic and cultural contact than as an area to be dominated politically. As a result Sri Lanka was willing to risk a war with Burma to preserve the peninsula's neutrality. Of particular interest is the *Cūlavaṃsa's* reference to the interception by the Burmese of a betrothed Sinhalese princess en route to 'Kamboja', a story that is presented as one of the events leading to the 1160s war. This report of a marriage alliance between the Sinhalese and the Khmers suggests that such alliances were a common tool of the Sinhalese royal house. The cross-cousin marriage patterns of the Sinhalese royalty favoured continuing relationships, and to form such an alliance with the Angkor realm would have provided long-range benefits.[80]

Thus, as in the eleventh century, the northern Malay peninsula played an important role in communication between Cambodia and the West. From the other direction, Chinese authors of the Sung period saw the upper east coast of the peninsula as being within the Angkor sphere of influence, and one of them believed that its markets produced some of the best incense available:

[80] Thomas R. Trautmann, 'Consanguineous Marriage in Pali Literature', *Journal of the American Oriental Society*, 93, 2(1973). Such marriage alliances were a common practice of Khmer kings as well. See A. T. Kirsch, 'Kinship, Genealogical Claims, and Societal Integration'.

Beyond the seas the Teng-liu-mei gharuwood ranks next to that of Hainan [where the price of incense had become too high]. It is first rate. Its trees are a thousand years old . . . It is something belonging to the immortal. Light one stick and the whole house is filled with a fragrant mist which is still there after three days. It is priceless and rarely to be seen in this world. Many of the families of the officials in Kuangtung and Kuangsi and families of the great ones use it.[81]

But by the twelfth century Chinese merchants were dealing directly with the sources of supply on the peninsula, Sumatra, and Java, eliminating their earlier need for a dominant port of the Śrīvijaya type. Tāmbraliṅga, a recognized source of forest products on the east coast of the Isthmus of Kra, was one of their trade partners. Another was the western Chen-la (used consistently by the Chinese to designate the Khmer realm) state of Lo-hu (Lavo), which sent a present of elephants to the Chinese court in 1155. This mission indicates that the Chao Phraya valley (Lo-hu) was then free from Khmer control.

The independence of the formerly subordinate western regions of the Khmer realm corresponds in time to the increasing number of military expeditions that Khmer monarchs despatched against their eastern Vietnamese and Cham neighbours. These expeditions assume an important role in Khmer history from the late eleventh century on, and Khmer inscriptions imply that Khmer monarchs, like their Cham neighbours, began to depend more and more on war booty to finance the activities of their court. Khmer inscriptions eulogize successful expeditions of royal 'conquest' and consequent redistributions of booty to Khmer temples. The increasing importance of these plundering expeditions as a source of state revenue demonstrates that Khmer monarchs were unable or unwilling or did not need to increase the state's direct revenue collections from its agrarian base.

As explained above, the Khmer state's 'ritual sovereignty' statecraft depended on endowing production. The success of this system is reflected in Khmer inscriptions that report the widespread prosperity, general stability, and continuous expansion of the state's agrarian base, despite periodic wars of succession and invasions by the Vietnamese and Chams, which also dominate Khmer history from the eleventh century on and must have placed additional financial burdens on the state. It is puzzling, then, that although the Khmer developed a wet-rice agrarian system that was more than capable of supplying the state's needs, Khmer monarchs pursued plunder anyway. Their obsession with war may have been a necessary response to the periodic Vietnamese and Cham incursions; that is, the best defence was a good offence. A second possibility is that these wars represented a quest for the prowess and personal honour that were bestowed upon a Khmer king who led a successful expedition against the Vietnamese and Chams, and thereby fulfilled the Khmer subjects' expectations of their monarchs. If this were the case, the Khmer military, which appears to have been perpetually active, could have lived off its plunder. It

[81] O. W. Wolters, 'Tāmbraliṅga', BSOAS, 21, 3 (1958) 600, translated from the *Ling-wai-tai-ta* (1178).

is also conceivable, thirdly, that, like the Burmese state of Pagan, Khmer monarchs had so lavishly endowed state temples to promote ritual sovereignty that they had to explore alternative sources of income to provide for their personal activities—for example, to initiate new temple construction and ritual and to pay the various troops that participated in Khmer military campaigns—instead of increasing the assessments of their agricultural producers. A fourth possibility is that, even more than revenue, the Khmer monarchs needed manpower to staff the state's ever-active military and administration and as well to meet the labour needs of the expanding agrarian system and their ambitious construction projects.

As was the case of Java, early Southeast Asian state systems that depended upon income from their agrarian sector alone were limited in their development potential. In a river plain state it was only when those claiming sovereignty became actively involved in external economic affairs that the supreme powers of the state vis-à-vis competing élites and institutions became secure. As in Java, economic leadership in the commercial sphere provided a new source of income that Khmer and Burmese monarchs in the tenth and eleventh centuries utilized to enhance their state's political accomplishments.

Although the evidence discussed above indicates more than casual involvement, participation of the Khmer and the Burmese states in the international commercial routes must be regarded as a secondary concern of their monarchs. Khmer and Burmese rulers were committed to developing their agrarian bases around Angkor and Pagan as well as to overcoming their peripheral relationship, geographically speaking, to the major East–West maritime routes. Thus monarchs expanded their economic base by encouraging their subordinates to bring unused land under cultivation, extending political hegemony from their core domains, while also making diplomatic overtures to their neighbours. But after the twelfth century Angkor and Pagan rulers chose to internalize state polity rather than to promote a stronger interaction in the supraregional trade routes. However, their neighbour to the southeast, the Cham state that controlled the southern portion of present-day Vietnam, had a more compelling desire to penetrate these international commercial channels.

CHAMPA'S PLUNDER-BASED POLITICAL-ECONOMY

The Cham state that ruled over the southern region of Vietnam from the second to the fifteenth centuries CE, exemplifies the accomplishments of a culturally integrated yet decentralized polity. Like its contemporary Southeast Asian civilizations, Champa, the name by which the realm of the Cham people was known in its epigraphic records as well as in external sources, left impressive temple complexes and numerous inscriptions (composed in both Sanskrit and the Cham language), which are the main source for early Cham history. On the basis of its archaeological remains, Champa has to be classified as a major early Southeast Asian state. Yet Cham epigraphic records reflect a weakly institutionalized state system that depended upon personal alliance networks to integrate a fragmented population. The Cham realm consisted of scattered communities in river valleys and coastal plains between the South China Sea and the mountains. Chams lived in an environment conducive to a multi-faceted subsistence from agriculture, horticulture, fishing, trade, and piracy. Their capitals were widely separated settlements on different parts of the coast, which took turns assuming hegemony over others—each hegemony was known to the Chinese by a different name. Weakly integrated politically, Cham culture still was highly cosmopolitan and was in constant communication with its neighbours by land and sea to the south and west.[82] A network of lagoons and navigable rivers between Hué and Quang Tri provided protected waterways for internal communication. Cham archaeological remains dot the upriver and highland regions. Cham ruins upriver from Binh-dinh (Vijaya) at Cheo Reo, Yang Prong, and other highland locations especially document Cham presence throughout the Song Ba river network that bends around the Binh-dinh mountains, with mountain pass access beyond the highlands into Laos and Cambodia.[83]

Lowland landholding rights were often shared by several villages, whose leaders co-operated in the control over activities therein. Economic co-ordination between villages included the maintenance of shared water management systems and the provisioning of communal granaries. Cham farmers cultivated paddy fields using relatively sophisticated iron ploughshares and large water wheels for irrigation. Each village had a 'water chief' who organized villagers in the clearance of land and the preparation and maintenance of water channels and dykes. Village chiefs met to co-ordinate overall system maintenance. The Cham realm was especially noted for its 'floating rice', that was quick-growing ('hundred day') and could be grown even under water cover of up to five metres. Cham agricultural settlements were scattered up river valleys and on terraced hillsides and entered an ecological frontier between the highlands and lowlands where wet-rice cultivation was practised in Cham areas, but where swidden shifting (slash-and-burn) cultivation and hunting and gathering predominated among adjacent hill tribes.

Rather than representing shifts from one dynasty's rule to that of another, the periodic movement of the Cham royal centre ('capital') among several river-mouth urban centres bearing Indic titles—Indrapura (Tra-kieu), Vijaya (Binh-dinh), and Kauṭhāra (Nha-trang)—corresponded to transfer of hegemony from the élite of one Cham river valley system to that of another, as one river system's élite became dominant over the other river-mouth urban centres of the Cham coast. As such, the Cham polity was more like the Malay riverine states noted above than its mainland wet-rice plain neighbours to the west and north. Like the rulers of the

---

[82] Paul Mus, *India Seen From the East: Indian and Indigenous Cults of Champa*, trans. I. W. Mabbett and D. P. Chandler, Monash Papers on Southeast Asia no. 3, Clayton, Victoria, 1975; Georges Maspero, *Le Royaume de Champa*, Paris, 1928.
[83] Gerald C. Hickey, *Sons of the Mountains*, New Haven, 1982, 460.
[84] For extended discussion of 'men of prowess', see O. W. Wolters, *History, Culture, and Region in Southeast Asian Perspectives*, Singapore, 1982.

archipelago riverine-based political-economies, the authority of a Cham
monarch was concentrated within his own river-mouth plain; beyond his
river-mouth urban centre base, a Cham monarch's sovereignty depended
on his ability to construct alliance networks with the leaders of the
populations in his upriver hinterland as well as with those of the Cham
coast's other riverine systems.

Despite the periodic spatial transfers of authority from one river-mouth
urban centre to another, there was one constant. The Cham sacred centre
at Mi-son, located on the edge of the highlands and upriver from the Cham
urban centre at Indrapura (Tra-kieu) on the coast, served as the locus of
Cham royal ceremony that promoted a sense of cultural homogeneity
among the disparate populations of the Cham realm. Thus, although Cham
society was weakly linked institutionally, the common values expressed in
Champa's widely distributed inscriptions demonstrate a high level of societal
integration that provided the foundation for a functional Cham polity.

The vocabulary of Cham statecraft as it is portrayed in the inscriptions
places stress on the personal achievements of the Cham monarch. Early
local belief supported the idea that some individuals (especially the Cham
society's leaders) could be superior to others. It was held that there was an
uneven distribution of both secular and spiritual prowess. An individual's
heroic secular accomplishments confirmed his spiritual superiority. Personal achievements in one's lifetime earned an individual ancestor status.

There were strong traditional concerns for the dead. Just as one allied
to those of superior prowess in life, so too one desired a personal bond to
'ancestors of prowess' whom it was believed could bestow material and
spiritual substance on their devotees.[84] Those who achieved greatness in
life were considered to have contact with the ancestors that was greater
than among others of their generation. By establishing a relationship
with a successful leader, the follower confirmed his own bond with the
ancestors; homage to one's overlord was thus a gesture of obedience to
the ancestors.

Subject populations validated their own potential for ancestor status
by sharing in their overlord's continuous achievement. The successful
overlord projected himself as influencing his supporter's stature in life as
well as their hopes for recognition after death. Successful patrons carefully
recognized their clients' achievements and meritorious deeds by bestowing
'gifts'—both material (titles and wealth) and spiritual (ritual and death
status)—on those whose secular performance on their patron's behalf was
noteworthy.

Early Cham society thus rallied behind spiritually endowed leaders who
were supported by a blend of local and Indian cultural symbols and values
that allowed their leaders to mobilize local populations and their resources
for various inter-regional adventures. Specifically, early Cham rulers patronized Śiva, noting his patronage of asceticism and his identification as
the lord of the universe and the abode of the dead; they also had affinity
for Indra, the Vedic god of war, and in various later times equally
identified with Viṣṇu and Buddhist deities.[85] Cham rulers were less

[85] I. W. Mabbett, 'Buddhism in Champa' in Marr and Milner, 289–313.

concerned with developing state institutions, but instead initiated syncretic religious cults that allowed their followers to draw from their leader's spiritual relationship with the ancestors as well as Indian universal divinity.

Ultimately, however, the successful ruler had to generate income for his direct subordinates and secure for his subjects the material well-being that monarchs were expected to provide. With the loss of economic prosperity, serious questions arose regarding the successful magical qualities of the ruler's cults, and the autonomy of regional units soon would be reasserted. Throughout Champa's history, periodic regional autonomy and resistance to the centralizing ambitions of would-be Cham monarchs were coincident with an inability to provide expected economic returns.

While Southeast Asia's early rulers of major wet-rice states based their sovereignty on income derived from a relatively stable agricultural base, the various records of Cham civilization indicate that Cham rulers could not expect a sufficient flow of agricultural surpluses to finance their political ambitions. There is disagreement among historians about the agricultural productivity of the Cham realm. Chinese sources substantiate that the Cham were wet-rice cultivators, and that the Cham territory was especially known to the Chinese as the source of quick-growing 'floating rice' that the Chinese adopted in southern China. But the remaining evidence of Cham civilization, including Chinese sources, does not demonstrate the extensive hinterland agrarian development that is found in the evolving major wet-rice states that were Champa's contemporaries in Cambodia, Burma, Java, and the Red River delta of Vietnam. The comprehensive problem faced by Cham monarchs was that the region between the Mekong delta and Hué where Cham authority was concentrated did not have a broad plain that could serve as a rice bowl to support an elaborate polity.

The king's place, according to Cham inscriptions, was not in managing the day-to-day affairs of his state, but in the battlefield where he protected his subject communities and thereby secured their prosperity. Cham monarchs are never referenced in records of local water management. Nor did Cham monarchs assume a role as supervisors of communal granaries, which in addition to the local water-management networks were the source of unity among local peasant communities. However, Cham monarchs did periodically assign the responsibility for the supervision of new or existing public granaries to newly established temples.

Inscriptions report that, in return for securing his subjects' prosperity, the Cham monarch was entitled to receive one-sixth of local agricultural production. But it is repeatedly proclaimed that due to the ruler's 'benevolence', the state expected to collect only one-tenth. Since such references appear in inscriptions reporting transfers of the ruler's remaining income rights on property to temples (which assume an increasingly significant role as centres for the concentration of economic resources), it can be inferred that the state was either unwilling or unable to collect a share of local production even in its own river system base, and thus assigned its token one-tenth share in the hope that a temple, an institution with local roots, might have better luck making such collections. What was normally assigned were income rights to uncultivated and unpopulated lands, further indication that the state had only limited rights over cultivated lands.

Manpower (war captives or other bondsmen and women) was fre-quently assigned as well to support the extension of agriculture under the direction of a temple and its temple staff. Such consolidation of control over land and existing granaries and their assignment to temples, which in turn promoted the king's sovereignty in their religious cults, might have provided the Cham king with indirect access to local production that was otherwise inaccessible to the state.

The inherent instability of Cham sovereignty is especially revealed in the inconsistency between the epigraphic stress on the ruler's moral and physical prowess, and their conclusion that this prowess was insufficient to guarantee the future security of endowed temples. Cham inscriptions use curses to protect temples rather than threatening physical retribution to offenders. Cham inscriptions glorify the physical capacity and personal heroism of Cham rulers, but normally end with the proclamation that those who plunder temples (which, based on consistent reference, would seem to have been a common occurrence) were subject to divine retribution —normally a shortened and unprosperous life and the promise of hell as one's destiny in the after-life. For example, a typical endowment inscription ends with the following warning:

> Those who protect all these goods of Indrabhadreśvara in the world, will enjoy the delights of heaven along with the gods. Those who carry them away will fall into hell together with their family, and will suffer the sorrows of hell as long as the sun and moon endure. . . . [86]

One may conclude based on the epigraphic evidence that during a king's reign, but especially after his death, his territory and notably his richly endowed temples were subject to pillage by his various political rivals. Thus, inscriptions of Cham monarchs report their restoration of the temples of previous Cham rulers; these temples had been destroyed by demonic 'foreigners', but also by various Cham chiefs who had attempted to acquire the material resources and labour necessary to proclaim their sovereignty. The act of restoration was a statement of legitimacy, and was a proclamation that the new monarch had sufficient resources to guarantee his subjects' future livelihood.

Since Champa possessed an extensive coastline, one alternative source of income for Cham monarchs was the sea. But here, too, there is little evidence that Cham monarchs depended on trade revenues—port cesses or the returns on royal monopolies on the sale of local commodities to international traders—to finance their sovereignty.

Trade on the Cham coast depended upon the summer monsoon winds, which propelled sea traffic north to China. Prevailing autumn to spring winds from the north made the Cham coast a natural landfall for the merchants of the South China Sea, known collectively as *Yueh*, who were headed for the archipelago and beyond. Despite the Cham coast's favourable position relative to the prevailing seasonal winds, Chinese sources always considered Cham ports to be secondary rather than primary centres of

[86] Barth and Bergaigne, ISCC, 226ff.

international commercial exchange. Yet Cham ports did have important products which the Chinese and other international traders desired— notably luxury items such as ivory, rhinoceros horn, tortoiseshell, pearls, peacock and kingfisher feathers, spices, and aromatic woods.[87]

Chinese and Vietnamese sources enumerate the commodities available at Cham coast ports, and demonstrate the importance of the highlands as the source of Cham trade goods. Elephants and their tusks, for example, were desirable and were included among the tribute gifts the Cham monarch sent to the Chinese court on fourteen separate occasions between 414 and 1050 CE. These elephants came from the highland regions upriver from Vijaya (Binh-dinh) and Pāṇḍuranga (Phan-rang). Rhinoceros horns (ground rhinoceros horn is a prized aphrodisiac among the Chinese), cardamon, beeswax, lacquer, resins, and scented woods (sandalwood, camphor wood, and eagle or aloeswood) were also products of the same upriver region.[88] Areca nuts and betel leaves, the chewing of which gave teeth the distinct red colour, were products of the highlands upriver from Indrapura (Tra-kieu); cinnamon was a product of the region upriver from Vijaya, and gold was said to be mined at a mountain of gold some 30 li from modern Hué.[89]

Highland oral histories provide valuable insight into the nature of Cham commercial exchange, which is ignored in all the remaining written sources. In local legend among the highlanders in the Darlac Plateau region near Cheo Reo, the prime source of the highland products enumerated, Cham are reported to have made attempts to integrate highlanders into the Cham political economy by negotiation rather than by force. Highlanders were offered the protection of the Cham armies, as well as the privilege of becoming the trade partners of the Cham.[90] Apparently the most valuable among the trade commodities the Cham offered was salt, which was critical to the highland diet as well as local animal husbandry. In addition to substantiating that the highlands were the source of the trade items enumerated in external sources, highland oral histories report that Cham monarchs were entitled to receive locally woven cloth as tribute.[91]

Among the highland populations in the region north of the Mekong delta the local headmen were said to have organized a band of men to assist the Cham in the search for eaglewood, valued for its fragrance when burned in Cham, Vietnamese, and Chinese ritual. Local tribesmen became Cham vassals and received a Cham sabre, seal, and a title, which roughly translated 'lord/master', that confirmed their leadership status.[92]

[87] Paul Wheatley, 'Geographical Notes on Some Commodities involved in Sung Maritime Trade', JMBRAS, 32, 2 (1959).
[88] Maspero, Champa, 57, 67, 87–8, 99, 120, 133, 138.
[89] The Italian adventurer Nicolo de Conti went to Champa via Java in 1435 and reported that Champa was a major dealer in aloes, camphor, and gold. Nicolo Conti, The Travels of Nicolo Conti in the East in the Early Part of the Fifteenth Century, London, 1857, 8–9.
[90] Hickey, Sons of the Mountains, 116.
[91] Cloth woven from a variety of local fibres by village women, and generally in rich shades of red, blue, and yellow contrasted with black, white, and grey, worked into stripes or geometric patterns, is still a valuable product of highland groups: ibid., 446.
[92] ibid., 117.

An especially close network of cultural dialogue between Champa and Java emerged by the eighth century that included a special trade partnership. During the seventh to the tenth century, there developed what art historians call 'Indo-Javanese architecture' in Champa, which expressed Tantric Mahāyāna Buddhist themes that are similarly depicted in contemporary Javanese art. The reliefs of the temples at the Cham sacred centre at Mi-son are said to resemble those of the Borobudur.[93] There was a unique Śiva-Buddhist syncretism at temples downriver from Mi-son at Dong-duong (Indrapura); here there is an inscription dated 911 CE that records the adventures of the tenth-century Cham courtier Rājadvara. Rājadvara twice travelled to Java to study Buddhist magic science; the word used in the inscription is *siddhayātrā*, the same Tantric term used to describe the magical powers of supernatural prowess contained within Buddhism that were pursued by late seventh-century Śrīvijaya monarchs.[94]

The Italian adventurer Nicolo de Conti visited Champa in 1435 on his way from Java to China in the early fifteenth century. During the fourteenth century the Cham monarch, Jayasiṃhavarman II (r. c. 1307), married a Javanese princess, Tapasī. A short time later Che Nang (r. 1312–18), the Cham puppet ruler set up by the Vietnamese conqueror An Huang, asserted his independence by fleeing to Java—perhaps he was the son of the Java princess.[95] There is also the Javanese legend of Dvāravatī, sister of a Cham king, who married the ruler of Majapahit and then promoted the spread of Islam in Java during the late fourteenth century. Cham sources that document an Islamic economic community resident at Pāṇḍuranga in the late tenth century support Javanese belief that the spread of Islam to Java was attributable to Champa.[96]

Despite this evidence that indicates that international trade on the Cham coast could be an important source of income, dependency on sales of local products to an external marketplace was not an adequate economic base upon which to build a state polity. Periodic fluctuations of the sea trade due to disorders at the route's ends in China and the Middle East meant that, like the leaders of the Malay states to the south, Cham monarchs could not depend upon international commerce as a stable and continuous source of royal redistributions. That Cham rulers did not directly control external trade can be concluded from records of Cham coast commerce. These report that the major centre of international trade was at Pāṇḍuranga, at the extreme southern edge of the Cham political domain. The maritime populations of Pāṇḍuranga must have maintained a good deal of autonomy from Cham political control, judging from a description of the community that appears in an eleventh-century inscription, which characterizes the Pāṇḍuranga population as 'demonic, unrespectful, and always in revolt' against the state's authority.

Based on the total omission of reference to merchants in remaining inscriptions from the Cham heartland, it appears that international trade

[93] B. P. Groslier, *Indochina*, Geneva, 1966, 39, 54, 77.
[94] E. Huber, 'La Stele de Dong-duong', BEFEO, 4 (1904) 85ff., verse BXI; Hall, *Maritime Trade*, 79ff.
[95] Maspero, *Champa*, 189.
[96] Hall, *Maritime Trade*, 183.

was confined to Pāṇḍuraṅga. Here at the extreme southern edge of the Cham realm the 'ferocious' threatening foreigners could be isolated (not unlike China to the north, where seagoing trade with the West was similarly isolated at Canton on the extreme southern edge of the Chinese state). Foreign merchants based at Pāṇḍuraṅga would have received the enumerated products of the Cham hinterland via active coastal and upriver trade networks that were dominated by a seagoing population permanently resident on the Cham coast.

When they could not depend on the normal flow of commerce to supply them with their livelihood, this seagoing population of the Cham coast was likely to turn to piracy. During such periods of ebb rather than flow, these seamen were likely to pillage neighbouring river-mouth urban centres and their temples. Thus, the eighth-century sack of the Po Nagar temple near modern Nha Trang by 'ferocious, pitiless, dark-skinned sea raiders' may be attributed to the Cham seagoing populations rather than 'foreigners'.

The Chinese court was always trying in vain to compel Cham monarchs to assume responsibility for the behaviour of their coastal populations; judging from the frequency of Chinese demands, it would seem that this coastal population was only marginally under the Cham monarch's control. Cham coast piracy was widely known among the international trade community. Voyagers were often warned to avoid the Cham coast when travelling from the Melaka Straits region to China. This weakened the appeal of Cham ports to international traders and further increased the likelihood that Cham monarchs could not regularly depend on trade revenues to finance their political ambitions.

Being thus unable to secure either sufficient revenue income from their subordinate river valley agricultural communities or consistent return from internal or external trade, Cham monarchs had to seek alternative sources to finance the alliance networks that were critical to their sovereignty. Therefore, it was necessary for Cham rulers to seek wealth beyond their own population centres by leading their allies on periodic military expeditions outside the Cham realm. Plundering raids were thus waged on a regular basis against Champa's neighbours—initially rival river-mouth population centres and later Khmer territories to the west and Vietnamese territories to the north.

This dynamic of plunder explains why Cham history is dominated by seemingly consecutive military expeditions. Periodic Cham raids are reported not only in Cham epigraphy but also in Vietnamese chronicles and from the tenth century on in inscriptions from the Khmer realm to the west. Cham military expeditions acquired plunder and labour—Cham ports were widely known as a major source of slaves, i.e. war captives, who were traded there to various international buyers. The proceeds from successful expeditions were subsequently divided among expedition participants. These included the various warriors who figure so prominently in Cham epigraphy as the monarch's principal political allies and/or the coastal populations, whose navigational skills made them useful participants in raids against Vietnamese coastal settlements to the north as well as against Khmer settlements up the Mekong River in the south—

warriors who in return recognized the Cham monarch's sovereignty.

Successful plundering expeditions were also a means by which the Cham monarch's needed cultural image as the source of his subjects' well-being was validated. Warriors and other key participants in a successful expedition were often assigned jurisdiction over land that was either undeveloped or needed redevelopment. Inscriptions record that one of the first acts of these royal supporters was the lavish endowment of temples, whose staffs subsequently assumed supervision of land development projects. Seemingly these warrior élite were donating, or redistributing, a portion of their share of the successful royal expeditions via their reassignment of various objects, money, and labour that made local development possible.[97]

Royal subordinates also sanctified the development projects by instituting lingas and establishing new temples beyond the royal core that honoured the temple's benefactor, but especially proclaimed the glory of past and present Cham monarchs, for whom the temple lingas were named. Such recognition of the monarch through the endowment and consecration of temples promoted local appreciation of the monarch's accomplishments and encouraged their subordination, in the absence of a direct royal administrative presence, to the sovereignty of the Cham state.

The Cham state may thus be understood as a loose and marginally interdependent polity that encompassed a series of river-mouth urban centres and their upriver hinterlands. In the absence of a sufficient resource base to support their political aspirations, Cham kings by necessity depended on periodic military expeditions to acquire plunder that could be redistributed, directly (sharing booty with their warrior allies) or indirectly (via temple endowments), to maintain the loyalty of the inhabitants of the Cham riverine networks. Cham monarchs maintained the subordination of their direct military allies by keeping them 'in the field' on various plunder expeditions. In the absence of a royal bureaucracy that could directly administer the regions of the Cham realm, Cham monarchs instead depended on the willingness of local élites to recognize the monarch's sovereignty via their participation in his expeditions of conquest and/or by their support of religious cults that proclaimed the ruler's superior prowess. There was an inherent instability in this political-economy that ultimately depended upon redistributions of plunder. The fate of the Cham state was sealed, and Vietnamese retaliatory expeditions finally destroyed the Cham realm in the fifteenth century.[98]

THE EMERGENCE OF THE VIETNAMESE POLITICAL-ECONOMY

The early maturation of a Vietnamese economy moved spatially from higher, upland areas of the Red River valley into the delta region, and then south into previous Cham territory. Early Vietnamese society consisted of

[97] e.g., Barth and Bergaigne, ISCC, 218, 275.
[98] Maspero, *Champa*, 237–9. For comparison, see George W. Spencer, 'The Polities of Plunder: The Cholas in Eleventh Century Ceylon', JAS, 35, 4 (1976).

small communal groups who farmed the area above the delta, using the natural ebb and flow of the tides of the Red River system to support local irrigation networks. By the tenth century Vietnamese society was based on villages, and had developed elaborate dyke and drainage systems to control the raging monsoon-fed waters of the Red River delta. Staples of Vietnamese life were fish and rice; twelfth-century Chinese writers report that the Vietnamese grew the special early-ripening strain of rice that had come into Vietnam from Champa, although an indigenous type remained of greater preference.[99]

Early Chinese political interest in Vietnam was a consequence of the desire among China's rulers to secure southern trade routes and to gain access to southern luxury goods, which included pearls, incense, drugs, elephant tusk, rhinoceros horn, tortoiseshell, coral, parrots, kingfishers, peacocks, and 'other rare and abundant treasures enough to satisfy all desires'.[1] Han era outposts in Vietnam at the beginning of the Christian era were primarily commercial centres; the Han did not want to develop an elaborate administrative presence, and Vietnam was viewed as being too remote. In this era Vietnamese Lac lords became 'prefectural and district officials' in a chiefly symbolic Chinese political order. They paid tribute and received 'seals and ribbons' from their Han overlords that legitimized them, and in theory added prestige in the eyes of their peers. This Vietnamese élite was more or less allowed to rule in traditional ways, although there were modifications of their social system that the Chinese found inconsistent with a Chinese sense of morality, notably their disregard for Chinese-style patriarchal marriage and their favouring of the less standard bilateral kinship patterns practised throughout the Southeast Asian region. The Lac lords enjoyed labour, comestibles, and craft goods that were supplied by subject communities. Lac lords were in turn expected to pass on some of their normal collections of local produce, but especially 'rare objects and goods' as tribute payments to their Han overlords.

An influx of Han ruling-class refugees during the Wang Mang first-century interlude (9–23 CE) reinforced Han officials, and new patterns of Chinese rule emerged. Of foremost concern to Chinese administrators was their need to pay for their expanded administration. To do this they began to target development of the local agrarian economy as a stable tax base. Chinese administrators promoted greater productive efficiency as well as the extension of agriculture into previously uncultivated lands. Further, they encouraged movement to a formal patriarchal society as a way to increase the role of men in agricultural production. Hunting and fishing, the main focus of male economic activities, produced no taxable surplus; agriculture was a more stable source of tax revenues. Because of the high degree of male mobility in pursuit of game, Vietnamese society in the early Han era seemed, from the Chinese perspective, to have no stable family system. The male role in agriculture, or the lack thereof, and the apparent female control of cultivation, were difficult for Chinese administrators to

---

[99] John K. Whitmore, 'Elephants Can Actually Swim: Contemporary Chinese Views of Late Ly Dai Viet' in Marr and Milner, 130.
[1] Keith W. Taylor, *The Birth of Vietnam*, Berkeley, 1983, 78, from Hsueh Tsung's early third-century account.

accept. In the first century CE, one Han official tried to combat this by ordering all men aged 20–50 and all women 15–40 to marry; would-be élite were expected to pay for Chinese-style marriage ceremonies. Subsequent registration of new family units made kin groups responsible for tax payments.

Promotion of a stable family unit had further consequences. Unlike some societies that remain settled in one place and have no 'frontier spirit', the Vietnamese developed an intense, culturally supported, desire to hold land—which supported periodic Chinese and Vietnamese government efforts to extend wet-rice cultivation into new territories. In Vietnam possession of land eventually came to be considered synonymous with the well-being of a family, and essential for the perpetuation of the family line. Sons needed to have land to keep the family unit together. Together the family property maintained family ancestor cults. Substantial houses that would endure for generations, rather than makeshift dwellings, become the norm. Ancestors' spirit houses were also constructed, with a central sanctuary honouring ancestors of the patrilineage; this was the centre of family rituals and feasting. Stone tombs, too, were reminders of generations past. Unnourished, ancestral spirits became malevolent errant spirits that ceaselessly wandered in search of offering. Family income had to support ancestors by means of rituals and feasts. Cult lands were farmed by the members of the lineage collectively; guardianship was under the head of the kin group, usually the oldest male. Land thus had social, economic, and religious functions, and the need to hold family land thereby stimulated the migration of the landless.

The Lac lords tried to resist the assertion of Han authority, but were no match for the Han armies. Thereafter Vietnam's Dong-son culture faded. Indigenous landholding patterns, which were initially based on communal usage rather than ownership, were directly assaulted by Chinese bureaucrats. New state-wide revenue systems based on private ownership began to emerge. Han soldiers were settled in newly built 'walled cities' to govern new administrative prefectures and districts. These 'soldier-farmers' supervised the digging of ditches, to irrigate the fields surrounding these new centres that were nearer the Red River delta than the previously developed regions in the upper river plain. Han policy kept soldiers in place, as they settled in and became part of the local social fabric, and thereby removed a potential revenue drain on newly conquered territory (i.e. the resident military was self-sustaining) and further disaffection among the conquered people which additional revenue demands would have brought. Overall, Han rule established a co-ordinated authority over the Giao-chi (as the Vietnam province was then known) irrigation systems, which they helped to extend, and a merging of Chinese and Vietnamese societies began to take place.

Private property rights became important in the areas nearest the urban centres of Han rule. A powerful Han-Viet landlord class came into existence as government tax demands forced peasants to sell land to rich officials and become tenant farmers on their private estates; or, as Han soldiers were given communal lands in return for their service, previous populations who were driven off this newly assigned land began to settle uncultivated lands, based on the same individual holding basis.

This Han-Viet society was based on a clearly defined sense of status and wealth that depended on the private ownership of land. Tomb remains from this era show a material culture of accumulated wealth that was taken to the grave—iron swords, Han coins, glass ornaments, bronze and earthenware vessels, game boards, musical instruments, mirrors, inkstones, and lampstands. There were even model ceramic farms that well illustrate the local agrarian culture—horses, granaries, wells, and kilns (but with the notable absence of ancestor houses) were encompassed with fortress-like compounds. Great families supported a private community of 'guests' that included scholars, technical experts, spies, assassins, and private armies. The élite ruled by virtue of character seals that were applied in the roofs of their houses, replacing Lac era 'seals and ribbons' as symbols of their authority.

The tombs of the élite reflect a cultural intermix between Chinese and Vietnamese. It was normal for Chinese men to take Vietnamese wives. In the first generation Chinese patterns of life were preponderant, but by the third and fourth generations a substantial synthesis with local culture had taken place, and Vietnamese variations predominate.

As the Han dynasty declined in the late second century, the Han-Viet élite became more interested in seaborne trade as an alternative source of income. Commerce in luxury goods became a major preoccupation of local administrators. The Vietnamese coast in general became an international entrepôt during this period that is coincident with the rise of Fu-nan and Lin-yi, which was founded in the Hué coastal region in 192 by a son of a Han-Viet district official, who killed the local Han magistrate. By the fourth century, Lin-yi's rulers were proclaiming themselves to be kings in the Indic Hindu tradition.[2] The Vietnamese north, under the leadership of the Shih family, turned more toward Buddhist influences.

This Vietnamese devotion to Buddhism became associated with commercial wealth and royal authority. Temples were founded for guardian deities of agricultural fertility. Buddhism represented a new 'other-worldly' method of controlling nature for the benefit of local agriculture. Buddhist temples were dedicated to local spiritual manifestations of the monsoon season, which became syncretic incarnations of the Buddha: the Buddha of the Clouds, Rain, Thunder, and Lightning. Local pre-existing values were thus reinforced with the authority of this new international religion. Art historians note that Vietnamese architecture from this period was more like that of the Javanese Borobuḍur than the northwest Indian Gandhāran style favoured in northwestern China. This substantiates Vietnamese participation in the wide-ranging Buddhist communication network that was coincident with the southern seas trade route between China and India, and especially indicates interaction with the straits region to the south.

During the Sui and Tang era the power of the great landowning Han-Viet families that had emerged in the Han age was partially countered by

[2] Taylor, *Vietnam*, 196–9; Hall, *Maritime Trade*, 71–7, 178–9.

the introduction of the Chinese 'equal-field' system. In its ideal form, state bureaucrats assigned all able-bodied adults a certain amount of land (which was in theory all the property of the emperor) for the duration of their lifetimes. This was intended to stabilize the state revenue base by blocking the drift of free, taxpaying farmers off the tax rolls into great private estates. Since the Chinese collected taxes on a per capita basis, farmers who became tenants on great estates were not counted for taxation; they were thereafter encompassed within assessments of the estate, which was better able to neutralize the state's revenue demands. Thus the equal-field system was an attempt to keep farmers in a free, taxpaying status that would enhance the state's tax revenues. In the Tang era the 'equal-field' system acknowledged the special rights of great families by the assignment of perpetual landholding rights, theoretically no more than one hundred times the amount assigned to a free farmer.[3]

Seventh-century Tang rule in Vietnam was coincident with the initial development of the Hanoi area as the first Vietnamese urban centre south of the Hong River. This era was also marked by the extension of the dyking system down the Hong River into the delta lowlands. The Hanoi region emerged as the new power base of Chinese rule outside the traditional provincial heartland where great families and their estates predominated, and was part of a general Tang assault upon the powers of the old élite. The 'equal-field' system was applied to the newly opened delta lands, and free farmers were assigned to initiate cultivation. To counter the power of the great families, these free farmers were provided with military training and were organized into militia units. By the ninth century, however, a new class of great landlords began to emerge in the newly developed territory due to a 'double-tax' reform that was adopted by the Tang in 780, which based tax collection on land ownership rather than the number of cultivators. Further attempts to implement the 'equal-field' system of land distribution were abandoned and there was no longer a legal barrier to the accumulation of land into estates by men of wealth.[4]

A Tang centre of civil administration was rebuilt near modern Hanoi after a sea raid in 767, and defensive ramparts were built, which were repaired and enlarged in the ninth century. To validate this transfer of political authority to the new urban centre, the Tang consecrated the Kai-yuan cult that associated the Chinese emperor Xuanzong (r. 712–56) with a local earth spirit of the Hanoi area; this union symbolically guaranteed local prosperity, and attributed this success to Chinese rule.

Before the Tang, no Chinese dynasty was strong enough to enforce their land systems. The Chinese land system was based on private ownership that was not uniformly applicable to Vietnam, where communal ownership remained strong; and great estates remained largely beyond the effective reach of the imperial revenue-gathering capabilities. The effectiveness of attempted Chinese reforms to landownership and tax collection depended on proximity to an administrative centre. Tax collection was not due to any theory or law, but was a specialized skill developed by Chinese

---

[3] E. O. Reischauer and J. K. Fairbank, *East Asia*, Boston, 1989, 100–2, 118–19.
[4] Taylor, *Vietnam*, 209–15.

bureaucrats to extract revenue in particular circumstances within Vietnamese society. Imperial land taxation in Vietnam was thus unorthodox and underwent constant evolution. Since it depended on the personal skill of the bureaucrat, the system was inherently vulnerable to personal greed and corruption. The Chinese government would on occasion police itself, as for example in the Han era when two officials were executed for extorting bribes and filling a storehouse with improperly seized possessions, which were subsequently redistributed among local court officials.[5]

Due to administrative incapacity, Chinese revenue interest in Vietnam before the seventh century was directed more at the control of lucrative international markets on the Vietnamese coast, which were viewed as an important source of enrichment. Chin officials were said to have normally extorted 20–30 per cent of merchandise value at Vietnamese coast ports.[6] There was a fine line between piracy, corruption, and appropriate state service. In 446, war booty from the plunder of Lin-yi was an 'economic inspiration'.[7] Among the Sui era records is a statement that 'men who go to Giao abandon the thankless task of government for more lucrative occupations of commerce'. This account further notes that 'barbarians of Giao often assemble for plunder'.[8] The Sui, eager to secure the luxuries of the Vietnamese coast, gave special titles to local 'leaders' who helped them collect slaves, pearls, kingfishers, elephant tusks, and rhinoceros horns.[9] In 863, Tang officials confiscated merchant vessels and seized their cargo to finance a war with the Nanchao realm to the north.

Development of the delta environment was important not only for its additional agricultural productivity, but also because of its proximity to the sea. The Dai Viet state that established its independence from Chinese sovereignty in the tenth century, like its Southeast Asian contemporaries, depended on the production of its wet-rice economy. Sung rule in China was a great boon to international commerce, and like the neighbouring mainland wet-rice states to its west, the Dai Viet state became increasingly involved in contacts with the international route. Dai Viet rulers enhanced their resource base by promoting contacts initiated by the lords assigned to rule the outer territories—the delta, the south, and the highlands—to acquire trade goods.

Khmer rulers at Angkor were in diplomatic contact with the new Vietnamese state in the early eleventh century, and these embassies had economic purpose. Increasing commercialization of interstate contacts undoubtedly contributed to rising tensions on the eastern mainland. During the period between 1120 and 1210 Angkor, Champa, and the Dai Viet state were frequently at war. One cause, at least from a Cham point of view, was the emergence of a new trading route across the Gulf of Tonkin to Nghe-an, south of the Red River delta; from there, goods could be transported across the mountains to the Mekong River valley and Angkor

[5] ibid., 59, quoting the *Le Tac*, Hué, 1961, 86.
[6] ibid., 107, from the *Chin shu*, 5, 9b.
[7] ibid., 121, from the *Sung shu*, 5, 14b.
[8] ibid., 148, from the *Ch'en shu*, 34, 24a.
[9] ibid., 167, quoting Katakura Minoru, 'Chūgoku Shihaika no Betonamu', *Rekishigaku Kenkyū*, 381 (February 1972) 31, a study of law and taxation in Vietnam under Chinese rule.

via the Ha-trai Pass, thereby bypassing access to Angkor by the lower Mekong and consequently threatening Cham control of the coastal trade.

The route across the Gulf of Tonkin from China also brought numerous Chinese settlers into the lower Red River delta and the lowland areas south of the delta in Thanh-hoa and Nghe-an.[10] One result of this thriving Chinese community was a flow of labour and copper cash out of China into Dai Viet, which must have helped the local economy to develop rapidly. Zhao Rugua's account of southern ocean commerce in the early thirteenth century demonstrates Dai Viet's role as a source of goods for the international trade, especially metals. Vietnamese gold and silver went to Angkor (probably via Nghe-an and the Mekong), to Kelantan on the east coast of the Malay peninsula, to the Jambi-based Śrīvijaya realm on the east coast of Sumatra, and also to Java. In return, the Vietnamese received spices and other local and international products. Vietnamese dynastic records report that Van-don on the coast east of their capital at Thang-long was the major port during the twelfth to the fourteenth century, and had contact with the area around the Gulf of Thailand as well as parts of the island world, especially Majapahit Java.[11]

Another Chinese source confirms the Dai Viet international trade in precious metals, and also reports that the Vietnamese had seized mountain territory in the south that had been Khmer, and was a rich source of the aromatic woods much desired by international traders. Control of this highland trade in aromatic woods, which had previously been a major export of Cham ports, must have been another source of contention among the Vietnamese, Khmer, and Chams.

Li Cho, ninth-century Tang protector-general of the Vietnamese territory, was said to have changed the terms of trade between the Vietnamese lowlands and the mountain chiefs, who had been bartering horses and cattle for salt. He took control of salt production of villages in the tide-waters, and hoped thereby to obtain a larger number of horses that he could sell to accumulate a fortune. An efficient local official is quoted: 'If we cut off the salt and iron trade on the southern coast [we would] cause the ruination of their market . . . after two years they can be crushed in a single battle.'[12] These sources reflect the importance of Vietnamese expansion into the delta, which gave them access to salt, the key commodity in lowland–highland exchange.

Administratively, the Vietnamese and Chinese were both uninterested in the southern highlands because the upland region lacked sufficient land and water sources to allow paddy farming on a scale necessary for Vietnamese agriculture. Further, there was a Vietnamese traditional antipathy for the highlands since they were thought to be the home of evil spirits, as well as the source of poisoned water that caused malaria. But commercial and revenue needs forced the Vietnamese to re-evaluate their traditional distaste.

[10] Two inscriptions dated 1161 and 1207 report well-to-do Chinese families resident at Thanh-hoa. Whitmore, 'Elephants', 131.
[11] John K. Whitmore, 'Vietnam and the Monetary Flow of Eastern Asia, Thirteenth to Eighteenth Centuries', in J. F. Richards, *Precious Metals in the Late Medieval and Early Modern World*, Durham, N.C., 1983, 374.
[12] Taylor, *Vietnam*, 239–40; 96, from the *Chin shu*, 67, 5a.

To gain control over the highland sources of numerous trade goods, the Vietnamese needed to establish their political presence in the Cham territory to the south, which provided access to the highlands via the river systems of the Cham coast. A nineteenth-century Vietnamese document explains that the highlands had been part of the kingdom of Champa, but after his final victory over the Chams in 1471, Le Thanh Ton (r. 1460–97) resettled this coastal plain with Vietnamese. By the early sixteenth century the highlands had been loosely incorporated into the Vietnamese state; initially a local chief was recognized as being in charge of highland civil administration, although several minor Vietnamese bureaucrats were sent to regulate trade with the highland populations. Commercial agents from the lowlands traded with designated highlanders who held licences to trade; those licensed paid taxes to the commercial agents, who in turn passed a specified amount along to the assigned bureaucrats.[13]

Control of trade products naturally enhanced a state's place in international commerce and the wealth and power that derived therefrom. But the Thanh-long government was caught between its own cultural policy and its economic needs. On the one hand the government believed that the highland barbarians might pollute the superior Vietnamese way of life—the Chams were thought of as only a little better than the highlanders. Yet highland products were necessary to enhance Vietnamese participation in international trade. Thus the Vietnamese government tried to restrict highland contact, and Vietnamese traders, who were themselves described in the Vietnamese records as 'rootless errants', were nevertheless honoured as hardy pioneers who preceded the later 'pacification' and 'social education' of highland people.

The tenth and eleventh centuries were especially critical in the transition to a more externally focused Vietnamese economy, which, significantly, was coincident with the emergence of an independent Vietnamese state. The new Vietnamese court at Hoa-lu, on the southern edge of the Hong River plain, was a market for trade as well as promoting it. It is reported that in 976 merchant boats from different nations beyond the sea arrived and presented the goods of their countries.[14] A new port at Bo-hai, near the mouth of the Hong River, where inland trade met the southbound seaborne trade, grew in importance. Economic reorientation toward the sea routes leading south paralleled the rising power of the Dai Viet state in the southern delta, and an alliance between the two centres of Hoa-lu and Bo-hai, one political and the other commercial, supported the political unification of Vietnamese lands.

The political unity achieved by Dinh Bo Linh, the first Vietnamese emperor, made large regional markets possible. This encouraged commercial expansion and attracted foreign merchants. The Hoa-lu court provided a new market for the luxury goods in which foreign merchants specialized. In an edict of 975 Bo Linh prescribed types of clothing to be worn by civil and military officials at the court. To meet these clothing needs, as well as the other material requirements of the emergent Vietnamese court, foreign trade was a necessity. Envoys were sent to China with many gifts,

[13] Hickey, *Sons of the Mountain*, 155.
[14] Taylor, *Vietnam*, 287–8, from the *Ngo Si Lien Dai Viet su'ky toan thu*, 1, 46.

presumably to proclaim Vietnam as an international marketplace as well as to secure political recognition. The Vietnamese economy was thus transformed to serve the needs of a strong king from a hitherto insignificant place.

Other economic development projects were initiated in the eleventh century. In 1048, Ly Thai Tong (r. 1028–54) revived a China-inspired cult of culture, in which the monarch was the highest officiant. As the symbolic source of fertility, the Vietnamese emperor led springtime rites in which he would plough the first furrows, and he also symbolically assisted in the gathering of rice at harvest. At the south gate of the Hoa-lu capital, offerings were made to bring rain and to guarantee crops at the Esplanade of the Gods of the Soil and Harvest. In 1044, a road construction programme linked the capital and the regions in a realm-wide communication network that would have had a favourable impact on commercial transport. In 1042, 5000 Cham war captives were assigned land and resettled in undeveloped unpopulated areas of the southern Hung Hoa Province, and were allowed to name their new communities after their native Cham settlements.[15]

New villages received names selected by villagers and approved by the emperor, who appointed guardian spirits to watch over the village and bring it prosperity. As the Khmer and Majapahit systems used temple networks to integrate outlying areas into the state, so Vietnamese villages were expected to construct communal temples (*dinh*) as repositories for new imperial documents that named the village guardian spirit. Further, local lands had to be designated to support the temple, which was subject to continuing government regulation to assure proper maintenance and ritual performance; this guaranteed local prosperity, which was the self-proclaimed responsibility of the monarch.

During the thirteenth century great estates (*trang-dien*) began to emerge. In 1266, Emperor Tran Thanh Tong authorized nobles to press vagabonds and those without work into bondage, to have them clear land and to farm unused land. Aristocrats dominated southern expansion that began in earnest during the fifteenth century.[16] Conflict emerged at the local level between new Vietnamese settlers and the old Cham residents in the Amarāvatī region. During the reign of Le Thai To (1428–32) there was an attempted socio-economic reform that included a general land redistribution of the sort intended in the Chinese 'equal-field' system. All were to receive a land share, from high-ranking officials to the elderly and orphans, 'isolated persons' (widows and widowers, i.e., those without families), as well as youths. To prevent the re-emergence of powerful estates, large landholding units were forbidden. Communal lands, normally periodically redistributed according to social ranks, were declared inalienable.

Le Thanh Ton decreed that those convicted of crimes should be sent to remote parts of Quang Binh Province in the south. Under his general economic development programme, there was again a ban on large landholdings. Southern settlement in the Nghe-an and Ha Tinh provinces was encouraged by the establishment of fortifications to protect newly developed

[15] Le Thanh Khoi, *Le Viet-Nam*, Paris, 1955, 164.
[16] ibid., 173.

paddy fields. Land was to be cleared—a decree forbade the waste of any land. Prisoners and criminals were sent to settle the new lands. Military officers in local posts were rewarded with plots of land that would not revert to the state at their death. Bureaus were organized in every province to supervise the digging of dykes and canals. State representatives were also charged to provide information that would improve animal husbandry and the cultivation of mulberry trees. After two years of settlement, officials were to be sent to establish appropriate taxes, and to promote the new patriarchal family-focused Confucian moral code.

At the dawn of the sixteenth century, Vietnamese civilization was in a position to prosper due to the political and economic initiatives taken by Le Thanh Ton. Faced with perpetually contracting tax rolls, the consequence of the repeated devolution of revenue-collection authority from the state to land-based military and aristocratic élite, the Vietnamese state authorities of the past had continuously attempted to extend their economic base. Conquest of the Cham territories in 1471 provided ample opportunity for the future.

Cham plunder raids on Vietnamese territory had challenged the theoretical base of Vietnamese imperial authority, which in its cults of legitimacy proclaimed the emperor's ability to guarantee his subjects' prosperity. These raids also depleted the state of needed resources. While the Vietnamese state had itself benefited economically from its various military expeditions against the Chams over the centuries, such actions had been justified as acts of reciprocity; they were also seen as necessary to initiate the future security of the Vietnamese people. Periodic Cham raids against Vietnamese territory forced the Dai Viet state to fund the elaborate preparations that these 'defensive' acts of reciprocity necessitated; to lose against the 'barbarian' Chams was unthinkable. Final victory against the Chams stabilized the Dai Viet state's wet-rice economy not only by removing this financial drain, but also by supplying prime territory for agricultural expansion, together with some 30,000 Cham prisoners (including the Cham monarch and fifty members of the Cham royal family) to settle it. The victory over Champa also put the Vietnamese state in a position to monopolize the coastal access to the highland products most desired by international traders—although highlanders still had the option of trading overland with their Khmer neighbours to the west instead.

The Vietnamese state leadership could not, like their Cham neighbours, turn to plundering raids as a regular source of state financing. This would have been inconsistent with the developing Vietnamese bureaucratic administration that depended upon its land-based military and aristocratic élite to support a harmonious state system modelled on that of China. Yet, in the late fifteenth and early sixteenth centuries, the Vietnamese state actively pursued participation in and facilitation of the East–West sea trade as an acceptable source of state finances. This was like its fellow rulers of Southeast Asian wet-rice states in that same era, who equally found trade-derived revenues an attractive alternative to squeezing additional tax revenue from the land; as in Dai Viet, the bureaucratic capacity among these states was insufficiently developed to guarantee the regular collection of revenue cesses beyond the court's immediate agrarian core.

THE EARLY SOUTHEAST ASIAN SOCIO-ECONOMY: A CONCLUDING OVERVIEW

It has been posited in the above discussion that major structural changes were taking place in Southeast Asian society during the era from the first century to the fifteenth that were associated with an expanding Southeast Asian socio-economy. Political and economic ties between major 'higher order' centres and their subordinate regions or hinterlands were enhanced during this era, as specifically evinced in inscriptions and other internal and external primary sources that demonstrate the emergence of hierarchical political and economic networks. But was there a change of institutions taking place, characterized by a new administrative capacity eminating from centres of power; or was there a structural change relative to the wider acceptance of new ideas about political and economic activity in general, the creation of a new popularly accepted idiom that made participation in political and economic activities beyond one's immediate locale, and regular interaction with major economic centres, culturally appropriate? Expressed in contemporary anthropological jargon, to define political and economic transition in Southeast Asia one might determine whether early Southeast Asia centres were 'centres of status' or 'centres of power'.[17] Critical to study of this perceived era of change are two parallel questions: (1) how does one define an economic centre ('city') in early Southeast Asia and (2) how does one define an economic network?

In keeping with most contemporary Western understanding of the terms 'city' and 'network', one may study early Southeast Asian history by focusing on administrative institutions that made cities and networks possible. Specifically, one may examine the evolution of religious institutions (temples) and political institutions that could administer the populations of urban centres, and could subsequently utilize this bureaucratic capacity to draw in ('mobilize') the surplus production of their subordinate hinterland populations.[18]

In contrast, the economic development of early Southeast Asia may be equally understood as a consequence of the sequential pooling of economic resources that took place in the process of the establishment of socially recognized cultural centres.[19] Herein economic resources were valuable not for their material content or relative to profit goals as appropriate to a modern economy, but as resources that could enhance the status of an individual or of a ceremonial centre. Cultural centres (or individuals who claimed superior status) drew in the resources of their realm to support culturally significant ceremony, to build impressive buildings (including temples), to accumulate manpower, to finance elaborate gift-giving, or to amass wealth, all in the hopes of impressing surrounding populations into submission rather than in building raw power resources. Such a stockpile of wealth could also finance a centre's participation in external commerce. The centre acted as a societally approved negotiator on behalf of its population vis-à-vis outsiders. In such a role the centre insulated its

---

[17] Geertz, *Negara*.
[18] Wheatley, *Nagara*.
[19] Wolters, *History, Culture, Region*.

followers from the hardships of the outside world, where local cultural requirements were of little concern. In this external realm, personal gain was a foremost goal, in contrast to the local population's preference for cultural and social well-being.

The majority of the early Southeast Asian political-economies gave cultural and social goals precedence. Economic resources flowed by choice of the producer to a cultural centre, and then were redistributed outward (both internally as well as externally to the local system) to benefit the indigenous population through gifting strategies that enhanced the status of the centre. As such an economy expanded or as the cultural centre widened its realm, the centre could begin to mobilize resources at a less personal level, but with the culturally approved goals. In this transition, temples—whether Hindu or Buddhist—assumed enhanced roles as economic centres, and new ritual networks that focused on the centre of royal power provided additional infrastructure that did not exist in earlier kingdoms.

Consequent to this expansion, a movement from a political-economy of 'cultural redistribution' to a political-economy of 'culturally mobilized wealth' could take place. Despite significant bureaucratic initiatives undertaken by the leaders of some states (notably the post-1300 Majapahit and Dai Viet states, which have been characterized in this overview of the pre-1500 era as the most fully integrated among their archipelago and mainland contemporary polities), the gathering of material resources at a centre continued to be justified through reference to traditional symbols and values. Widespread popular opinion still held that such accumulation allowed the centre leadership to accomplish culturally approved goals, but there was increasing personal distance between the centre and its subordinate population. These developing polities continued to depend on voluntary subordination and contributions rather than upon the administrative draw of resources by a bureaucracy based at the centre. The 'mobilizing centre' of each state did not have an effective bureaucratic capacity upon which it could draw, but depended as in the past on the belief that granting legitimacy to centre or leader was important relative to the bestowal of cultural well-being upon subordinate populations.

In these 'mobilizing economies' there were also traditional competitions for power, as land-based rivals continued to pool resources in their attempts to build new cultural centres. Trade was significant in this competitive process as a source of material wealth that could endow the awe-inspiring centres and their leaders, who dispensed power and bestowed economic and psychological well-being on populations that chose to become subordinate to the centre. Such traditional focus thus continued at a higher level of productivity and exchange, but with the ever-present threat that economic activity could become increasingly impersonal, including less sympathetic manipulation and direct control (administration) of a population by the centre. Another possibility was that new coastal centres of commercial activity, whose development was initially encouraged, might break away from the more internally focused and culturally-defined hinterland centres that remained bound to a more personalized agrarian-based order. Yet another option was that the religious institutions that had initially enhanced the centre's power might themselves become a wealthy and popularly supported rival against an increasingly impersonal polity.

Beyond this 'mobilizing political-economy' is a political and economic order in which wealth allowed the development of less personal bureaucratic, military, or religious administrations and networks that managed lands and economic resources. Agricultural areas increasingly interacted with centre-based administrators in contrast to the earlier age in which local contact with the centre was insulated by a locally-based élite. There were more direct centre-based collections of local surplus (as opposed to earlier stress on donations of local production to the centre) as well as more direct centre-based dispersements to the outside and to the lower levels of the socio-economic order. Market networks would be controlled by political élites, or even by merchants—commercial specialists whose behaviour was largely inconsistent with traditional values. Previously, merchants had been forced to transact their affairs in ways subordinate to local cultural norms; but as political systems with stronger administrative centres developed, this might offer consequent mobility to those whose way of life demonstrated less personal commitment to their fellows. In this new order, the merchant could assume a more significant role as the direct mobilizer of surplus production, orchestrating the flow and return of external goods and services to and from the local producer—as the agent of centre-based cultural brokers, of a power-holding monarch, or as a participant in a developing free-trade economy.

It is the view of this essay on the early Southeast Asian economy that this impersonal order was not appropriate to pre-1500 Southeast Asia. While in the Majapahit, Angkor, Pagan, and Dai Viet states there were emergent patterns consistent with this latter characterization, political-economies retained their internally-focused and traditional agrarian-based structures, which were more similar than dissimilar to those of other archipelago and mainland polities in this period before 1500.

BIBLIOGRAPHIC ESSAY

Scholarly interest in Southeast Asia's early economic history has largely been a by-product of the development of interdisciplinary and multi-disciplinary studies since World War II. The pioneering scholarship on Southeast Asia's history in the West was the product of well-trained Dutch, French, and British historians whose research was an extension of their countries' colonial experience. These early twentieth-century scholars tended to highlight the external forces that shaped Southeast Asia, and the court-based religious and political aspects of the epigraphic and literary sources. In this pre-World War II vision, Southeast Asia was viewed as a region of passage for foreign merchants and other travellers, which provided shelter for ships and seamen based in India, West Asia, and China. As an intermediate region, Southeast Asia developed either 'Indianized' or 'Sinicized' civilizations that had their origin outside the region, or were deeply influenced by external elements. This historiography, which provided important reconstructions of dynastic chronologies, is well reflected in the impressive works of G. Cœdès (*The Making of Southeast Asia*, English edition, 1966, and *The Indianized States of Southeast Asia*, ed. Walter Vella, trans. Susan Brown Cowing, Honolulu, 1968), and D. G. E. Hall (*A History of South-East Asia*, 1955).

A new view of the region wherein integrated local state entities existed prior to the coming into contact with foreign cultural elements, and outside ideas were accepted, adapted, and adopted based on local needs, first surfaced in the English translation of the writings of J. C. van Leur (*Indonesian Trade and Society: Essays in Asian Social and Economic History*, 1955). During the 1950s a new generation of scholars arose, notably the Indonesian epigraphers Boechari, L. C. Damais, and J. G. de Casparis (*Prasasti Indonesia*, 1950, 1956); the Indonesian philologist Th. G. Th. Pigeaud (*Java in the Fourteenth Century*, 1960–3); and the historians Paul Wheatley ('Geographical Notes on Some Commodities Involved in Sung Maritime Trade', JMBRAS, 1959; *The Golden Khersonese*, 1961), Wang Gungwu ('The Nanhai Trade', JMBRAS, 1958) and O. W. Wolters ('Tambalinga', BSOAS, 1958); they began to explore the history of early Southeast Asia by expanding their scope beyond the more traditional use of the epigraphic and philological sources. These scholars not only re-examined the old sources with a new set of questions, but they also tested these texts against new archaeological data that were becoming available, and began to define Southeast Asia as a distinct entity apart from the Indic and Sinic worlds.

Representative of the published reports of this archaeological research are Alastair Lamb in FMJ (1961) and Louis Malleret, *L'archeologie du delta du Mekong* (1959–63). Important studies of agricultural and peasant economies were also taking place during the 1950s and early 1960s, among these: D. H. Burger, *Structural Changes in Javanese Society* (1956); Robbins Burling, *Hill Farms and Padi Fields* (1965); Alice Dewey, *Peasant Marketing in Java* (1962); Raymong Firth, *Malay Fishermen* (1966); Clifford Geertz, *Agricultural Involution* (1963); Pierre Gourou, *The Tropical World* (1953); Gerald C. Hickey, *Village in Vietnam* (1964); Karl J. Pelzer, *Pioneer Settlement in the Asiatic Tropics* (1948); and David E. Sopher, *The Sea Nomads* (1965).

By the late 1960s and early 1970s Southeast Asian historians were able to incorporate the developments in the scholarly fields of archaeology, social anthropology, linguistics, art history, and the natural and biological sciences. Their work included Wolters' *Early Indonesian Commerce* (1967) and *The Fall of Srivijaya in Malay History* (1970); Wheatley's 'Satyānṛta in Suvarnadvīpa: From Reciprocity to Redistribution in Ancient Southeast Asia' (1975); L. A. Sedov's 'On the Problem of the Economic System in Angkor, Cambodia in the IX-XII Centuries' (1963); M. C. Ricklefs' 'Land and the Law in the Epigraphy of Tenth Century Cambodia' (1967); Brian Colless' 'Traders of the Pearl' (*Abr Nahrain*, 1970–74); G. H. Luce's *Old Burma—Early Pagan* (1969–70); J. Noorduyn's series of articles in BKI; and Anthony Reid's 'Trade and the Problem of Royal Power in Aceh' (1975); and they began to ask specific questions about early Southeast Asian economic systems. The status of the field, so to speak, was summarized in

R. B. Smith and W. Watson, eds, *Early Southeast Asia: Essays in Archaeology, History and Historical Geography* (1979).

During the 1980s a new generation of historians, most of whom were trained by the aforementioned scholars, carried the new historiography further. As previously noted, the continuing research of Wheatley (*Nagara and Commandery*, 1983) and Wolters (*History, Culture, and Region in Southeast Asian Perspectives*, 1982), established the context for historical inquiry. Among those who responded were Pierre-Yves Manguin, Jan Wisseman-Christie, and Hermann Kulke, who focused on Indonesia's early history; Michael Aung-Thwin on Burma, Keith W. Taylor and John K. Whitmore on Vietnam; Claude Jacques and Michael Vickery on Cambodia; and David K. Wyatt on Thailand. A sample of the work of each of these and others is encompassed in David G. Marr and A. C. Milner, eds, *Southeast Asia in the 9th to 14th Centuries* (1986).

In economic history, which places so much emphasis on statistical analysis, the early Southeast Asianist is too often placed on the defensive. Facing a paucity of sources, the historian of Southeast Asia's early economy must be broadly trained and imaginative. The current task of the Southeast Asian economic historian remains that of bridging the gap between the archaeological and written sources. There are continuing problems of fit where the constantly changing archaeological picture does not quite correspond with the written records. Widening the range of questions asked of these sources, the economic historian must move from the pre-tenth century forward, largely drawing upon archaeological data, while constantly looking backward from post-tenth-century written sources and societies.

The economic historian needs to consider especially how a people lived in a particular time and place, how they viewed the world around them, and how they communicated their ideas. There is a need to know more about the meaning and context of their words as well as their archaeological remains, to understand the environment that produced these artefacts. While most current historical emphasis is on local initiative, there must be care not to underestimate the external. In a region of great cultural diversity, the indigenous needs to be more clearly distinguished from the foreign elements in the integrated cultures that emerged in the early centuries of the Christian era. The economic historian may contribute to this delineation through the study of ecological differences, and through determining distances and proximities of populations from urban centres—as well as coming to terms with what an early urban centre was, and discussing the economic importance of existing kinship structures; the interactive economic role of spiritual beliefs, ritual, and regalia; as well as the level of technology and productivity among the early populations, not only cultivators, but also fishermen, artisans/craftsmen, bondsmen/slaves, and non-village-based producers.

There are problems of periodization—are dates relevant to an under-standing of the region during this era, and is it possible to accept certain dates as universally important? The mapping of economic activity would better identify economic centres and peripheries, the flow of goods and services, the consideration of overland non-maritime communication and connection, and the understanding of eastern edges of the region (including the Philippines)—areas conspicuously absent in the above discussion of Southeast Asia's early economy, in relation to the Southeast Asian world as well as that beyond.

Despite the awareness among Southeast Asia scholars of early regional traditions of economic activity, there has still been little systematic study of the early economic system. Authors of the colonial era, seemingly concerned more with practical issues of their contemporary political-economy, focused on land tenure rather than on regional gastronomy, indigenous systems of product availability, or intra-household exchange. More recent ethnographically inspired literature has considered the 'structure' and 'function' of economic activity within a local community, or changing systems of exchange, rather than address the system in total.

There is need to come to terms more fully with the empirical data currently available, especially in the epigraphic records; there is equally need for new micro and macro studies in which goods 'flow' freely (transform, transvalue, transfigure) within a recognized natural-cultural whole. Economic activity is not static: it is a medium for communication that both reinforces and shapes the local social reality and individual welfare. Economic activity is a socially bonding experience with interpersonal emotions lacing each transaction, yet it is especially a personal expression wherein an individual asserts control over goods and services (what is received or consumed) as a personally responsible act. With this in mind, there are four sets of critical questions for future study:

1. What were the uses and meaning of economic activity to those who participated?
2. Where did goods and services come from and to whom did they go?
3. How did exchange maintain the health and welfare and improve and prolong life?
4. How did societies cope with scarcity and abundance?

Existing 'embedded' description of transactional behaviour needs more fully to evolve into issue-specific discussions of the regional socio-economy in the early age. Wider variables and variations relative to continuing study will require new and different combinations of economic data on classification, categorization, use, and interpretation. Moreover, one may postulate that the study of the past patterns of production, distribution, and consumption will move us to a more comprehensive understanding of early Southeast Asia, and will lead us to become more broadly sensitive to socio-cultural and ethno-historical issues.

CHAPTER

5

RELIGION AND POPULAR BELIEFS OF SOUTHEAST ASIA BEFORE c. 1500

The world of Southeast Asia presents a variegated cultural pattern. Geographically, the area can be divided into mainland and maritime Southeast Asia with the Malay peninsula as the dividing line, the southern part of which belongs to the island world, whereas its northern part is more continental in nature. As to maritime Southeast Asia, the motto of the modern Republic of Indonesia: *Bhinneka Tunggal Ika*, freely translated as Unity in Diversity, can be applied to the area as a whole. For, although numerous different languages are used in this vast area, they all belong to the family of Austronesian languages—apart from small pockets of tribal areas. Culturally, too, there is an underlying concept of unity despite the astounding diversity in almost every aspect. The conception of Indonesia as a 'field of ethnological study', as formulated by Dutch anthropologists, can be applied to the entire area.[1]

As far as religion is concerned, the diversity is less pronounced since Islam strongly predominates in Malaysia, Indonesia, Brunei and the southern Philippines, and Catholic Christianity in the major part of the Philippines. In mainland Southeast Asia, on the other hand, Theravāda Buddhism is the established religion of all states except Vietnam, where both Mahāyāna Buddhism and Confucianism predominate. Yet Hindu-Buddhist religion prevails in Bali, and tribal religions have persisted almost everywhere in the more remote areas. Moreover, the great religions have been influenced by earlier tribal beliefs. It is the task of the historian to describe and, if possible, to elucidate the religious developments in order to enable us to look at the present conditions against their historical background.

The study of religious developments is, however, beset with difficulties. These are essentially of two kinds: the nature of religion in the context of Southeast Asia; and the condition of our sources. In Western societies religion is generally felt to be clearly separated from other fields of social and political life, so that it can be studied for its own sake. This is also the case with modern Southeast Asia. In pre-modern Southeast Asia, however, it is hardly possible to separate religion from other fields of socio-economic and cultural life, with which it is closely interwoven. There is not even a

---

[1] P. E. Josselin de Jong, *Unity in Diversity: Indonesia as a field of Anthropological Study*, Dordrecht, 1964.

real equivalent of our term religion in the pre-modern languages of the area. To study religion one has, as it were, to detach from their social and political contexts those elements that we subsume under religion. These include, for example, various rituals and other forms of the worship of God, of deities or superhuman spirits and powers, as reflected in art and architecture, in literature and inscriptions. These considerations naturally lead us to the second type of difficulty: the nature of our sources.

The sources that have come down to us for the study of religion in Southeast Asia are, on the whole, richer than those available for other aspects of civilization. This is mainly because religious values were considered eternal, so that buildings erected for religious purposes—unlike dwellings for men, including kings—had to be made of durable materials such as stone or brick. Whereas perishable materials could be used for worldly purposes (toys, portraits etc.), effigies of gods and other divine powers required the use of stone or metal. Similarly, texts dealing with religious topics or containing important religious elements were written down for future generations. They were regularly copied as soon as the originals had become difficult to read. Land grants with immunities for the benefit of religious foundations, inalienable 'as long as the sun and the moon illuminate the world', used to be written on stone or bronze. Such documents, classed as inscriptions, are, by and large, the most important sources for the history of religion in Southeast Asia, but, as they are almost always associated with temples or other religious foundations, they are available only for the areas and periods in which such foundations existed. The unequal distribution, rather than the paucity, of sources is indeed one of the most serious problems facing the historian of the ancient period. Thus, the epigraphic sources are rich for Burma from the eleventh century, for Thailand from the thirteenth, for Cambodia and Champa (southern Vietnam) from the fifth, for central Java from the eighth century to the tenth, for eastern Java and Bali from the tenth century; but they are scarce or non-existent for the remaining areas and periods. Thus, nearly all Sumatran inscriptions are either from the end of the seventh or from the end of the thirteenth century to the fifteenth, and the situation is even worse for most of the remaining parts of Southeast Asia.

The literary sources are even more unequally distributed over the area and period. In contrast with the rich literary sources for (northern) Vietnam, written in Chinese, we do not possess a single line of literature from ancient Cambodia, nor from Champa or the Philippines. For eastern Java there is a rich literature in Old Javanese from the tenth century, and in Burma from the twelfth century, written in Pāli, the sacred language of the Buddhists of the Theravāda school. For western Malaysia, Sumatra and Thailand, the literary sources begin just before the end of the period under consideration. No literary sources are available for the remaining parts of Southeast Asia. Their absence is only partly compensated for by some foreign, mainly Chinese, references as well as by archaeological data. This distribution of sources is by no means a coincidence, for important source materials for early religion, whether written or archaeological, can be expected mainly in the principal centres of civilization, which were mostly important political and economic centres as well.

These different types of sources may inform us about different aspects of religious thought and institutions. The Old Javanese texts include not only major poetical works and prose literature, but also religious tracts and treatises. The oldest of these can be dated back to the tenth century. This is a compilation of two or more Mahāyāna texts, called *Sang Hyang Kamahāyānikan*. A number of other texts belong to a somewhat later period, in particular a few Śaiva treatises, such as the *Sewasasana, Wrĕhaspatitattwa, Bhuwanakośa, Bhuwanasaṅkṣepa, Tattwa sang hyang Mahājñāna, Agastyaparwa*, and others. In addition, the *Brahmāṇḍapurāṇa*, an Old Javanese ency-clopaedic text based on an Indian prototype, is important for our knowl-edge of brahmanic Hinduism as known in Java.[2] Among the literary works some have a direct bearing on religion. Foremost among these is the *Nāgarakĕrtāgama*, a long poetical text composed in 1365 by a high official at the court of Majapahit.[3] It is important not only for the history of religious, especially Buddhist, ideas but also for religious institutions. Thus, a few cantos give us lists of different kinds of buildings associated with various religious sects. A somewhat later text, the *Śivarātrikalpa*, supplies much detailed information on Śaiva ritual. Whereas such learned and poetical texts inform us mainly about religious ideas and practices among the classes associated with the royal courts, the inscriptions often allow us glimpses of popular beliefs, especially in the long imprecation formulas found at the end of many Old Javanese inscriptions. These texts nearly always deal with the transfer to religious institutions or to certain persons of fiscal revenues and other emoluments. In the latter case it is usually stipulated that all or part of the revenues shall be used to the benefit of some named religious or charitable institution(s). Some such details may supply valuable information on the nature and socio-economic status of religious foundations.[4]

As to mainland Southeast Asia, Burma has left a considerable number of religious, legal and grammatical texts written in Pāli. The oldest of these, inscribed on gold plates, originates from the neighbourhood of modern Prome and dates back to the seventh century or earlier, but a rich Pāli literature, commentaries on Buddhist texts, lawbooks etc., was written at the court of Pagan, central Burma, from the end of the twelfth century. There, too, the inscriptions inform us about many aspects of religion on which the scholastic texts are silent.

The same type of Theravāda Buddhism, originating from Sri Lanka, also flourished in the area of present Thailand, but our sources supply less

[2] For these and other Old Javanese texts the reader is referred to Theodore G. T. Pigeaud, *Literature of Java*, I–IV, The Hague, 1967–80, cf. in particular the general index in vol. III. Five works deserve particular metion: (1) J. Kats, *Sang Hyang Kamahāyānikan*, The Hague, 1910; (2) J. Gonda, *Het Oud-Javaansche Brahmāṇḍa-Purāṇa. Prozatekst en kakawin*, Bandung, 1932; translation, ibid., Bandung, 1933; (3) Sudarshana Devi, *Wrhaspatitattwa*, Nagpur, 1957; (4) A. Teeuw, S. O. Robson, Th. P. Galestin, P. J. Worsley, and P. J. Zoetmulder, *Śiwarātrikalpa of Mpu Tanakung*, 1969; (5) Haryati Soebadio, *Jñānasiddhānta*, 1971.
[3] Theodore G. T. Pigeaud, *Java in the 14th Century. A Study in Cultural History*, I–V, The Hague, 1960–3.
[4] The most comprehensive collections of Old Javanese inscriptions are J. L. A. Brandes and N. J. Krom, *Oud-Javaansche Oorkonden* (hereafter OJO), 'Batavia'-'s-Hage 1913 (without translations) and H. B. Sarkar, *Corpus of the Inscriptions of Java*, I–II, with translations but only up to 929.

information than on Burma. A considerable number of votive inscriptions from northern and central Thailand, written in Mon, testifies to Buddhist piety in the eleventh century, but long inscriptions, mainly in Thai, start only at the end of the thirteenth century. Buddhist texts in Pāli from the area of present Chiengmai are even considerably later in date, but often supply information on earlier religious history. An example is the *Jinakālamālī*,[5] written in 1516 by the scholar-monk Ratanapañña at Chiengmai. It is, in fact, a kind of Buddhist chronicle comprising pious stories, usually with precise dates. The chronology seems, however, confused: at least we have not yet succeeded in understanding the system that was used. The text mingles facts with legends. For example, it tells the story of a miraculous statue of Buddha brought back from Sri Lanka by king Rocarāja, a name which is, however, unknown from other historical sources. In conjunction with other, roughly contemporary, Buddhist works the story can be placed in the context of turbulent developments in Thailand and Cambodia at the beginning of the eleventh century.[6] For the history of Theravāda Buddhism, rather more valuable information is to be derived from exogenous sources such as the *Mahāvaṃsa*, written in Sri Lanka, which contains a number of references to the religious contacts with Southeast Asia, in particular Burma, or the later *Gandhavaṃsa* (probably seventeenth-century) or the *Sāsanavaṃsa*. More even than for maritime Southeast Asia, Chinese sources, in particular dynastic annals and travel accounts, supply important information on certain periods and areas with which the Chinese came into contact. An example of the first type of sources is the *Liang Shu*, a seventh-century history of the Liang dynasty. Original Chinese travel accounts include the records of Buddhist pilgrims such as Fa Hsien (beginning of the fifth century) and I Ching (seventh century).[7]

A few words should be added on the archaeological sources. In most parts of Southeast Asia there are impressive and beautiful religious monuments of the past, often restored to their pristine glory. The most prestigious monuments can be admired at Pagan (central Burma), Chaiya and Nakhon Sithammarat (southern Thailand), Sukothai and Ayutthaya (central Thailand), Angkor (western Cambodia), central and eastern Java, and Bali. These monuments are visible expressions of piety founded by kings with important contributions by members of the royal families and other court dignitaries, but constructed by compulsory and sometimes voluntary labour of the artisans and of the agricultural masses. This probably explains why the archaeological sources, in contrast to most of the literature, may give us some idea of popular beliefs. These can be expressed in different ways, especially in the iconography and in the reliefs. Thus the reliefs of Borobuḍur in central Java (first half of the ninth

---

[5] A. P. Buddhadatta, *Jinakālamālī*, London: Pali Text Society, 1962.

[6] G. Cœdès, *Les États Hindouisés d'Indochine et d'Indonésie*, 3rd edn, Paris, 1964, 251f.

[7] W. P. Groeneveldt, *Notes on the Malay Archipelago and Malacca, compiled from Chinese Sources*, Batavia, 1876; E. Chavannes, *Mémoire composé à l'époque de la grande dynastie T'ang sur les religieux éminents qui allèrent chercher la loi dans les pays de l'occident*, Paris, 1894; J. Takakusu, *A record of the Buddhist religion as practised in India and the Malay Archipelago (671–695 A.D.) by I-tsing*, Oxford, 1896.

century) and the Bayòn in Angkor (end of the twelfth century) show many scenes that depict aspects of the daily life of different classes of people. The study of such reliefs may supplement the information obtained from texts, inscriptions and foreign notices.

The study of the less spectacular archaeological data of the historical period has hitherto received little attention, except for sherds of Chinese and other (Thai and Vietnamese) ceramics, which may give valuable chronological data. On the other hand, the study of ancient tools, foundations of non-religious buildings, major irrigation works, coins and other material remains may well contribute to a better understanding of different aspects of daily life, including religion.

One other type of source, though not strictly legitimate as evidence for ancient history, may nevertheless give some insights into the character of the ancient local religious traditions as they existed before Indian or Chinese influence, and that is constituted by our knowledge of the religious practices current in recent times among the upland or montagnard tribal peoples of the area. Such communities have preserved distinctive cultural traditions characteristic of those who, like the ancestors of modern Southeast Asians, live in relatively small scattered groups and lack a written language or full-time religious specialists. It must be emphasized, though, that it is the general character rather than the detail of specific myths and rituals that is relevant.

The montagnards or hill peoples of Vietnam, for example, have (or had, when studied by modern scholars) a rich variety of what may in a loose sense be called animistic cults and beliefs. Some cults are addressed to ancestors, others to spirits of various types—of waters, mountains, and fields—as well as to the wandering spirits who may be encountered anywhere. There is no clear dividing line between such spirits and the local gods of the hearth, or of the earth, fire, sky and thunder. Magic energies are believed to be everywhere potential, and an apparatus of magical procedures has evolved, including the use of amulets. Sorcerers conduct rituals to cure illnesses, speed the spirits of the dead to a safe haven, and procure fortune in tribal war. Chiefs have important ritual functions, especially at harvest time when as representatives of their communities they cut the symbolic first sheaves of grain, and such seasonal rituals are accompanied by feasting and celebrations.

Features of particular groups include the *phi* (spirits of forests, mountains and waters) worshipped by the Lao, the ancestral totem dog Pau Hou from whom the Mau believe themselves to be descended, the cult of the Muong common ancestor who is regarded as the inventor of agriculture, the forest spirits with whom individuals ally themselves among the Jarai, and the offerings to Yang Xo'ri, protectress of the crops, made by the Sedang.[8]

It is the task of the historian to try to reconstruct the Southeast Asian past with the help of these different types of sources, which often confirm or supplement each other, but sometimes appear contradictory. In the latter case the historian has to examine the sources very carefully to make a

[8] Le Than Khoi, *Le Viêtnam, histoire et civilisation*, Paris, 1955, 44–51, 87f.

choice on the basis of relative reliability. Thus contemporary documents are generally more reliable than texts written many centuries after the period that they describe. It should, however, be added that by and large these sources are richer for religion than for political or economic history.[9]

THE EARLIEST TIMES

This section is concerned with the transitional period from the beginning of the Christian era to the fifth century, in relation to which we dispose of some written sources both from Southeast Asia itself (a few Sanskrit inscriptions) and from outside the area (mainly Chinese notices). This was a decisive period when the first real kingdoms emerged in conjunction with the first contacts with the more ancient civilizations of India and China. In contrast with Chinese influence, which remained confined to Vietnam, Indian cultural influence gradually spread over many parts of the region. In the absence of any direct data on Indian cultural expansion, historians have formulated different theories as to the causes and the nature of this process, which is often termed Indianization. The disadvantage of this term is that it may suggest a conscious effort on the part of Indians to spread their culture over major parts of Southeast Asia. This was indeed the view expressed by most scholars until about half a century ago and is still occasionally found in works by Indian historians. It was based mainly on analogies with Greek, Roman or Western expansion.[10]

As there is, however, no evidence for Indian conquests in Southeast Asia (apart from an occasional raid in the eleventh century), nor for any large-scale Indian emigration or colonization, it is now generally thought that the influence of Indian civilization, including religion, should mainly be attributed to endeavours by some Southeast Asian élites to assimilate important elements of Indian culture. The eclectic nature of Indian influence is a strong argument in favour of this latter view. This applies to religion as much as to other elements of civilization. By the beginning of the Christian era some parts of the region had already reached a high level

---

[9] No comprehensive history of the religion of Southeast Asia exists. There are, however, many excellent works on specific areas, periods or aspects, for example W. Stöhr and J. Zoetmulder, *Die Religionen Indonesiens*, Stuttgart, 1965, French translation under the title *Les Religions d'Indonésie*, trans. L. Jospin, Paris, 1968. All references given here are to the French edition. Stöhr deals with tribal religions in Indonesia: known only since relatively recent times, they are not directly relevant to this chapter. Zoetmulder's account, on the other hand, is a judicious discussion, based almost entirely on literature, of classical Indonesian religion. The present account owes much to this publication, from which, however, it differs by the inclusion of much archaeological and epigraphic material.

[10] Many accounts tend to overemphasize the importance of these foreign influences on the beginnings of Southeast Asian kingdoms. There can be little doubt that foreign contacts would only have carried significant effects at a time when there already existed ordered societies in Southeast Asia with élites that were capable of assimilating foreign influences and utilizing these to their own advantage. For a discussion of such problems see especially Ina E. Slamet-Velsink, *Emerging hierarchies. Processes of stratification and early state formation in the Indonesian archipelago: prehistory and the ethnographic present*, Leiden, 1986, and C. Higham, *The Archaeology of Mainland Southeast Asia*, Cambridge, UK, 1989, 306–18.

of civilization which enabled local élites to choose, albeit mostly unconsciously, those forms of Indian religion which were consistent with, or
could be adapted to, their own beliefs and practices.

Earlier scholars have often assumed that Indian influence was mainly
confined to the early centuries of the Christian era, when the first contacts
between South and Southeast Asia were established. More recent research
has, however, emphasized the continuous nature of such relations, at least
until the maritime supremacy of the Western powers rendered such
regular contacts more difficult or nearly impossible.

The sources at our disposal mainly reflect the beliefs held by such local
élites, but to understand religious history in its social reality, we need to
step outside the monastery or temple library and look at the didactic bas-
reliefs on the temple walls, shiny from the reverent fondling of the faithful;
at the wayside shrines decked with their little offerings of flowers or
incense; at the stories told to children of the spirits of heroes who lived
long ago; at the whole lore which a community tells itself about the
invisible sacred world that surrounds and contains it.

It is from this perspective that we should view the influence of Indian
religions on Southeast Asia. Yet, although only a small part of the
population was directly influenced by Indian ideas, it should be emphasized that this was the élite which left us ancient literature, architecture
and iconography—in other words, the products of high civilizations
which we still admire. In addition, the court culture was never completely
separated from the rest of the population, and much of it gradually
percolated to the agricultural masses. On the other hand, it was inevitable
that the court was also influenced by the popular culture.

The manner in which Indian ideas blended with ancient cults must have
differed from one area to another. For ancient Champa, a non-Vietnamese
kingdom occupying territory that was later absorbed by the southward
expansion of the Vietnamese, Paul Mus has proposed an analysis of the
way in which Indian cults, notably those of the Hindu god Śiva with the
linga (*liṅga*, a phallic symbol) as his icon, were moulded to the tradition of
prior cults such as those of the earth gods identified with the territory
inhabited by specific communities. In each such cult, the deity was
represented by an icon, often a rough stone (easily replaced by the linga of
Śiva), and could be approached by the prayers of the faithful only through
rituals addressed to this icon. Such rituals were directed especially to the
assurance of fertility; the *yoni* (womb) stone on which the linga stood,
which received the sacral fluid poured over the linga, was especially apt to
symbolize the fertilized earth. Thus a high god of Hinduism was, as
happened also in India, adapted to serve the purpose of primal religion,
becoming in the process part of a particularistic tradition identifying a
community with its territory.[11]

It is possible to see small-scale territorial cults of this sort surviving
beneath the mantle of imported Indian religion in other parts of the region.

---

[11] L. Cadière, 'Croyances et Pratiques Religieuses de Vietnamiens', *Bulletin de la Société des Études Indochinoises*, 33, 1 (1958) 1ff.; P. Mus, *India seen from the East: Indian and Indigenous cults in Champa*, trans. I. W. Mabbett and D. P. Chandler, Monash Papers on Southeast Asia no. 3, Clayton, Vic., 1975, 7.

Cambodian inscriptions of the pre-Angkor period (i.e. before c. 900 CE) include references to many shrines, such as the 'god of the stone pond', which appear to be addressed to local spirits that inhabit or (as Mus argued in the case of the earth god) are identified with features of the landscape. The old Mon states in Burma, which became staunchly Buddhist, had a chthonic cult; kings as representatives of their communities presided over rituals that linked them with their local patron gods, and after their death the rulers would go to join their ancestors in an invisible other-world where they would be united with the earth goddess, a tree or mound serving as the point of contact between the sacred and profane worlds. With the advent of Buddhism, burial mounds turned into Buddhist stupas and the tree spirits, blithely integrated into Buddhist observance, turned into *sotapan*, followers of the Buddhist teaching who were set on the path to salvation.[12] Such practices were in accordance with Buddhist teaching in India, where the oldest stupas were also burial mounds, in which corporeal relics of Lord Buddha or of Buddhist saints were enshrined. Certain trees, including the famous *aśwattha* beneath which Lord Buddha attained Enlightenment, were the abodes of Yakṣas, ferocious giant spirits who became pious protectors of early Buddhism.

The worship of mountains as abodes of gods or of powerful spirits is also well attested in Indian religion where, for example, Śiva is thought to reside on top of mount Kailāsa, identified with one of the highest peaks of the Himalaya, and Mount Mahāmeru or Sumeru (in Pāli Sineru), the mountain of the gods at the centre of the universe, is an important cosmographic motif influential in art and architecture. In Southeast Asia, however, mountain worship developed into important cults. Thus, in Indonesia some volcanoes, conceived of as 'living' mountains, received worship as the abodes of great Hindu gods, such as Śiva, 'Lord of the Mountain(s)' (Girīndra) and Brahmā, who became identified with the (subterranean) fire. One of the most impressive temple complexes in (east) Java, Candi Panataran, which will be briefly discussed later, is devoted to the cult of Śiva Girīndra. The greatest Buddhist monument in Southeast Asia, Borobudur in central Java, is not a temple but a complex of terraces and galleries, richly decorated with narrative reliefs and statues, which encloses a natural hill as a kind of mantle in stone.

In Cambodia, more even than in other Southeast Asian kingdoms, mountain symbolism was embodied in monumental architecture. There, a whole series of monuments of the Angkor period (from c. 900) were constructed as large terraced pyramids. Though they were dedicated to Śiva or Viṣṇu or to a Buddhist Bodhisattva (a being destined to become a Buddha in a future life, and in Mahāyāna, which was the prevalent form of Buddhism in Southeast Asia before the thirteenth century, effectively an object of worship in his own right), the magnificence and obsessiveness of their Mahāmeru symbolism went far beyond any Indian models.

Further, there are many evidences of mountain spirit cults that were not Indian in origin. An early example in Cambodia is the site of Ba Phnom, situated on the Mekong River near the Vietnamese border. Though indeed

[12] H. L. Shorto, 'The *dewatau sotapan*, a Mon prototype of the 37 *nats*', BSOAS, 30 (1967).

the evidence identifying it as a major cult site in pre-Angkor times is equivocal, it does appear to have long been a symbolic centre of the kingdom—hence a Mahāmeru—and the scene of sacrificial rituals addressed to a goddess; according to one view this goddess was a fusion of an aboriginal Me Sa (White Mother) with the Indian Umā Mahiṣāsuramardinī, a demon-slaying embodiment of the spouse of Śiva; sacrifice was conducted at the site as recently as the nineteenth century.[13]

Other kingdoms had their mountain spirit sites, where rituals had to be conducted for the sake of the prosperity of the state. In Pagan, it was Mount Popa. In Sukothai in the thirteenth century, it was at the hill site where the spirit, Phra Kapung, resided beside a spring that issued from a mountain:

> If the prince who is sovereign in Muang Sukothai worships this spirit properly and presents it ritual offerings, then this country will be stable and prosperous; but if he does not present ritual offerings, then the spirit of this hill will no longer protect or respect this country, which will fall into decline.[14]

Origin myths, legitimizing kingdoms and giving their peoples a place in the grand scheme of the universe, were sometimes taken from India but often betray local myths. In Vietnam, for example, the story is told of Lac Long Quan, the Dragon Lord, who first civilized the Vietnamese people; from this spirit's union with queen Ao Co came the line of lords who, according to the tradition, first ruled in the Hong (Red) River area.

Archaeological evidence includes, notably, that of the Dong-son culture, northern Vietnam, which reflects aspects of early religion in the late centuries BC. Richly decorated bronze drums were found all over Southeast Asia, for example in Kuala Terengganu on the east coast of west Malaysia, and on the island of Alor in eastern Indonesia. They show incised designs likely to embody symbols current in myth and ritual.[15] Some scholars have associated the Dong-son culture with a speculatively reconstructed complex of cultures characterized by sky spirits, as opposed to another complex represented by the many megalithic remains in the region and characterized by earth gods. However, it is nowadays widely believed that the megaliths do not in fact attest any one coherent culture.

Funerary rituals normally enclosed elements of indigenous religion. The Indian religions favoured cremation, but a wealth of sources vouches for the survival in historical times of other practices, particularly interment, though this was often only partial: a body was first cremated and its remains were subsequently buried, commonly in an urn. Chinese sources assert that in ancient Champa the great men of the land were dealt with in this way, except that the urns were then committed to the sea or to rivers. The kingdom known as Tun-sun, presumably situated on the eastern coast of the Malay peninsula, was claimed to practise exposure, corpses being

[13] D. P. Chandler, 'Royally sponsored human sacrifices in nineteenth century Cambodia: the cult of nak ta Me Sa (Mahiṣāsuramardinī) at Ba Phnom', JSS, 72 (1974).

[14] Cœdès, États, 377f.; cf. also Cœdès, Recueil des Inscriptions du Siam, 2nd edn, Bangkok, 1961, 44f.

[15] A. J. Bernet Kempers, The kettledrums of Southeast Asia: a bronze age world and its aftermath, Rotterdam, 1988; Higham, Archaeology, 201.

offered up to the birds.[16] The earliest state in Cambodia, known by the Chinese appellation of Fu-nan and flourishing from the second to the sixth century, was said to know four practices: cremation, depositing in the sea, grave burial, and exposure. In Burma, in the later Shan states, the remains of a monk were sometimes buried under a post.

Human sacrifice, attested in remote parts of the area until the recent past, may have been more widespread in the ancient period. This type of practice is likely to have attended the antique cults of territorial gods and spirits of tree, river, and mountain. In each case, it was considered that the spirit, dwelling essentially in a placeless, timeless, sacred world, was inaccessible to the community except through special rituals designed to give him the means of communication. It should, however, be added that there is no real evidence as to the prevalence of human sacrifice in the civilized areas of ancient Southeast Asia.

There are many indications of the importance of the worship of local deities. Just as ancient India had its Yakṣa cults, many areas, villages or even impressive trees and other striking points in nature had their guardian spirits. Thus, the cult of the *nats* in Burma acquired official status and was sanctioned by the Buddhist orthodoxy. The same applies to the cults of the *nāgas* (mythical snakes) in many parts of the region. Thus, a five-headed cobra was the main tutelary spirit of the maritime kingdom of Śrīvijaya, while the founder of the earliest kingdom in Cambodia is said to have married a Nāgī (female cobra), from whom later rulers trace their descent.

Except in Vietnam, where Chinese influence predominated, ancestor worship was not common, except again for the royal dynasties where ancestor cults emphasized the continuity of the state. The same applies to totemism, which does not seem to be observed—at least not in the sense that includes the idea of families or communities descending from certain animals which, for that reason, were considered sacred within such communities.[17]

Some animals seem to have enjoyed a kind of worship. Snakes have already been mentioned in connexion with the *nāga* cult, in which Indian influence probably blended with ancient indigenous snake cults. There are scattered references to other animals but, compared with, for instance, India, animal worship was and is relatively unimportant. In addition, most of the references are in the context of religions of Indian origin, such as the special status of the Garuḍa, a mythical eagle and mount of god Viṣṇu, in Indonesia.

In the areas where the influence of Indian religions was strong, we often see complicated patterns in which outside influence is closely interwoven with ancient Southeast Asian beliefs. In many cases one may discern the

---

[16] P. Wheatley, *The Golden Khersonese: Studies in the Historical Geography of the Malay Peninsula before A.D. 1500*, Kuala Lumpur, 1966; P. Pelliot, 'Le Fou-nan', BEFEO, 3 (1903) 279.

[17] Some scholars, in particular W. H. Rassers and his followers, have found evidence of totemism in Indonesia, but the indications are marginal or unconvincing. Thus, many Javanese authorities during and after the Kaḍiri period (c. 1100–1222 and later) are mentioned by names preceded by a term indicating an animal, such as *macan*, 'tiger', *kĕbo*, 'buffalo', *gajah*, 'elephant', etc., but there are no indications that such names refer to totem animals. It is much more likely that these are warrior names reflecting the animals figuring on their banners, etc.

power of ancient beliefs at the background of apparently Hindu or Buddhist ceremonies. In Pagan, for example, *naga* spirits were regarded as the owners of the site where the palace of King Kyanzittha (c. 1084–1112) was to be built, and had to be propitiated. The rituals involved in the ceremonies attending the dedication of the palace, though accompanied by the recitation of Buddhist texts, were hardly Buddhist.

Amulets, talismans, portents, the whole panoply of apotropaic magic pervaded the religious life of everybody, high or low, monk, ascetic or layman. In mainland Southeast Asia, Buddhist monks, like the ascetics in maritime Southeast Asia, were regarded as a vehicle of a sort of spiritual energy that could operate in the arena of local magic forces. The monks subscribed readily to notions of magic inhering in relics, and impressed laymen with Buddhist miracles. Several such cases belong to Thai tradition; at the shrine of Wat Mahathat in Sukothai, which contained Buddha relics, a neckbone was seen to float out of the stupa.[18] Such prodigies were regarded as signs to the faithful to encourage them to make the pilgrimage to Sri Lanka. It should be added that many of the magic features of Buddhism in Southeast Asia were already inherent in Buddhism before it spread to Southeast Asia, but underwent various forms of adaptation to Southeast Asian beliefs and practices. Similar observations can be made with reference to Śaivism and Vaiṣṇavism in the region, including maritime Southeast Asia. As, however, religious developments in the mainland and in maritime Southeast Asia are quite different in many respects (though agreeing in others), especially during the classical period (from about the fifth to the end of the fifteenth century CE), it is proper to discuss them separately.

RELIGIONS OF INDIAN ORIGIN ON THE MAINLAND

Brahmanism

On the mainland of Southeast Asia, it was ultimately Buddhism that came to dominate, but it is important to recognize that, from early times, Brahmanism and Buddhism were mingled in the cultural legacy bequeathed to all the 'Indianized' states. Just as ancient Southeast Asian traditions mingled freely with the observances of imported religion, so did the lore of different imported religions mingle with each other: the orthodoxy of a state would favour one, each king being free to patronize his own favoured cults and divinities, but others persisted, their representatives dotted about the countryside in temples and monasteries.

Persecutions were rare, but not perhaps quite unknown. The seventh-century Chinese traveller I Ching tells us that Buddhism had been persecuted early in that century in Zhenla (Chen La),[19] a Chinese designation of Cambodia, especially in the pre-Angkor period, i.e. before the end of the

---

[18] Cœdès, *Recueil*, I, 54.
[19] I Ch'ing, *A Record of the Buddhist Religion as practised in India and the Malay Archipelago*, trans. J. Takakusu, Oxford, 1896, 12.

ninth century, and the absence of significant evidence of Buddhism (there is some, but not much) during the reign of Jayavarman I (c. 657–81) may possibly lend some support to the story. Śiva cults, as well as Viṣṇu cults, Mahāyāna Buddhism as well as Hīnayāna, coexisted in most kingdoms during the early centuries, though as time passed a process of polarization gradually skewed the distribution of different sects and schools; after the thirteenth century, and particularly under the influence of the prestige attached to ordination in Sri Lanka, Theravāda Buddhism rapidly rose to prominence in kingdom after kingdom as state orthodoxy. Even then we must not overlook the continuing importance of brahmins in a narrower role: up to the present century, the Buddhist courts have engaged brahmins in astrological and ritual functions.

If such brahmins were Indians (the Indian brahmins are indeed occasionally mentioned in Southeast Asian inscriptions), one wonders how or why they should have left India. This is the more surprising since Indian lawbooks contain prohibitions for brahmins against overseas travel, which was regarded as ritually polluting. These prohibitions may have had little practical effect, and would not have deterred ambitious men lured by the hope of honour and fortune in a distant land. It has been suggested that some learned brahmins were invited by Southeast Asian rulers at a time when commercial relations between Indian and Southeast Asian ports had spread the fame of such brahmins to the courts. It is indeed likely that this happened sometimes, but probably not on a large scale. It is, for example, striking that the Indian *gotra* names, never omitted in Indian inscriptions, are not normally mentioned in Southeast Asia. On the other hand, in the few cases where they are mentioned it is likely that they refer to Indian brahmins. It therefore follows that the great majority of Southeast Asian brahmins would have been Southeast Asians, many of whom had acquired their knowledge of the Sanskrit texts and of brahmanic ritual in Indian ashrams.

Whatever their origin, brahmins had great influence in the Southeast Asian courts in various capacities. As they had access to the sacred texts, the lawbooks and other literature in Sanskrit, they were employed as priests, teachers, ministers and counsellors: the principal advisers of the kings. Government, particularly in early centuries, depended upon such men, who were the chief available sources of literacy and administrative talent and experience. As in the early Indian kingdoms, an important office was that of the *purohita*, a chief priest with ritual and governmental functions. The epigraphic record of the mainland kingdoms demonstrates the powerful influence of *purohitas*, notably in Burma and Cambodia, where they often served under several successive rulers and provided continuity to the government in troubled times. In ninth-century Angkor, for example, Indravarman I had the services of Śivasoma, who was a relative of the earlier king Jayavarman II and was said to have studied in India under the celebrated Vedānta teacher Śaṅkara.[20]

It is noticeable that sacerdotal offices such as that of the *purohita* tend in Cambodia to pass from uncle to nephew in the maternal line. This has

[20] Cœdès, *États*, 205.

often been seen as a persisting influence of indigenous matrilineal social organization. More recently it has been suggested that this type of succession might rather show how a line of kings would seek to ally itself to particular powerful families by marriage, generation after generation; a family thus related would come to have its male members given high office by tradition, which would produce the effect actually observed.[21] Although this was a desirable side-effect, it is unlikely that the kings would have been able to enforce this matrilineal succession unless it was based on tradition among the priestly families.[22]

Not only in the 'Hindu' courts, such as Angkor, but also in the Buddhist courts, such as those of Pagan in Burma and Sukothai in Thailand, the brahmins conducted the great ceremonies, such as the royal consecration, and functioned as ministers and counsellors, but had to share their influence with that of the Buddhist monks. By its very nature Buddhism was concerned with the acquisition of spiritual merit and moral perfection rather than with the rites and ceremonies of a royal court, which were left to the brahmins. The grand ceremonies in Pagan that attended the dedication of Kyanzittha's palace have already been mentioned; they required the services of numerous brahmins, although Theravāda Buddhism was then well established. In Cambodia, as late as the thirteenth century (during the revival of 'Brahmanism' after the extravagant Mahāyāna Buddhism of Jayavarman VII), Jayavarman VIII built a temple for the scholar-priest Jayamaṅgalārtha, and likewise for the brahmin Vidyeśavid, who became court sacrificial priest. The Chinese visitor Chou Ta-kuan refers to the presence of brahmins wearing the traditional sacred thread.[23]

What is shown by the role of such brahmins is that it is appropriate to speak of Brahmanism as distinct from the specific cults of Śiva or Viṣṇu, or any of their innumerable kin: the priests stood for a social order and for the rituals that gave to the political or local community a sense of its unity and its place in the world.

Śaivism

Cults of Śiva were strong in the ancient kingdoms of Cambodia and Champa. Two major roles played by Śiva need to be distinguished: the political and the devotional.

The political role was as the focus of linga cults: the linga, originally the 'phallus', was the emblem of Śiva as god of creation and fertility for his devotees. Such cults were sponsored by rulers at the central shrines that constituted the ritual hub of their kingdoms. State-sponsored linga cults

---

[21] Thomas A. Kirsch, 'Kinship, Genealogical claims and Societal Integration in Ancient Khmer Society: an Interpretation', in C. D. Cowan and O. W. Wolters, eds, *Southeast Asian History and Historiography: Essays presented to D. G. E. Hall*, Ithaca, 1976.

[22] There are interesting parallels suggesting that royal succession could be based on principles different from those followed by other sections of society. This was the case with the old Minangkabau kingdom (Sumatra Barat), where the rulers succeeded one another along patrilineal lines in a society generally based on matrilineal succession. See especially P. E. De Josselin de Jong, *Minangkabau and Negri Sembilan, socio-political structure in Indonesia*, Leiden, 1951, passim.

[23] *Mémoires sur les coutumes du Cambodge de Tcheou Takouan*, trans. P. Pelliot (Oeuvres Posthumes de P. Pelliot, vol. III), Paris, 1951, 14.

were maintained in Cambodia till the twelfth century. In Champa, the royal capital at Mi-son in the fourth century (in Quang Nam district of present central Vietnam) had a royal Śiva cult with a linga called Bhadreśvara (combining the king's name, Bhadravarman, with Iśvara, a title of Śiva) as its principal object of worship; the later king Śambhuvarman endowed a linga called Śambhubhadreśvara. In the eighth century this linga, thought to incorporate the essence of the kingdom, was taken away by 'Javanese' raiders.[24] In the late thirteenth and early fourteenth centuries, Jayasiṃhavarman III established a linga cult down in the south, at the shrine of Po Klaung Garai.

In Cambodia many state monuments had Śiva lingas in their central shrines, often with the iconography of other gods (or even Buddhist divinities) represented in the sculpture of surrounding buildings. The rulers of Cambodia favoured great tiered pyramidal masses that became more elaborate as time went on; many of these had lingas in the central towers that stood at their pinnacles. The *devarāja* (either 'god-king' or 'king of the gods') cult, instituted at the beginning of the ninth century, though its precise nature has been debated,[25] was presumably Śaiva nevertheless, and for a number of kings of Angkor it represented for them the sanctification of their role.

But Śiva was not only an emblem of royalty and power; he was also a god of grace; he is referred to as such, for example in a Cambodian inscription of 624, which identifies him with Brahmā and thus represents a sort of mystic theism. One Śaiva sect, represented in Cambodia, was that of the Pāśupatas, who had a doctrine of union with Śiva as the one god.[26]

This form of devotion has been seen as attesting the Śiva cult as a personal form of religion that stepped aside from social and sectarian divisions. Many inscriptions also embody a type of cult that made of Śiva not a possession of brahmanic ritual but a personal god who had a particular relationship with a divinely inspired ruler. The Śiva cult in Cambodia has thus been interpreted as a means of exalting the king as a vehicle of spiritual energy. A rather similar idea of kingship is attested in the Ly dynasty of Vietnam (c. 1010–1225), though with a quite different cultural vocabulary to express it; the ruler is not a god but has in him a concentration of the spiritual energies of the land.[27]

Vaiṣṇavism

The god Viṣṇu claimed his purlieu from the beginning, though with a few exceptions his dominion was never quite as conspicuous or constant as those of Śiva or of the Buddha. In Cambodia, the inscription of Queen Kulaprabhāvatī, who died in 514, attests that she founded a hermitage and a reservoir for the benefit of brahmins, and the record refers to the

[24] For these 'Javanese' raids see Cœdès, *États*, 173.
[25] For the *devarāja* cult see pages 324–9.
[26] O. W. Wolters, 'Khmer "Hinduism" in the seventh century,' in R. B. Smith and W. Watson, eds, *Early South East Asia: Essays in Archaeology, History and Historical Geography*, London and New York, 1979, 431.
[27] K. W. Taylor, 'Authority and legitimacy in eleventh century Vietnam', in D. G. Marr and A. C. Milner, eds, *Southeast Asia in the 9th to 14th Centuries*, Singapore and Canberra, 1986, 143.

Vaiṣṇava myth of Śeṣa, the cosmic serpent on whom Viṣṇu reclines in rest between the world cycles; iconographically Viṣṇu is thus represented recumbent upon the serpent and with a lotus growing from his navel. The inscription of Guṇavarman, likewise, indicates a devotion to Viṣṇu, for whom an image of his footprints was endowed. (Viṣṇu in the form of the sun god spanned the universe in three strides, and, in a related myth, as the dwarf Vāmana, performed the same feat to gain the promised possession of whatever ground he could cover in three steps; Viṣṇu's footprints are thus evocative of power and dominion.)

The association of Viṣṇu with the sun is an important theme in the history of his cult; it was made early in India and influenced the form of religious art and myth in places where Vaiṣṇavism was practised. There may thus have been a fusion of the Viṣṇu cult with the influence of sun worship from Persia and the dynasties established by Persian conquerors. Some early images of Cambodia, belonging to the so-called 'Fu-nan' period (before the seventh century), represent deities with tunics in a Central Asian style, also found on images of Persia and northwestern India. They have been thought to reflect Iranian influence. Inscriptional references to a 'Śakabrāhmaṇa' may similarly reflect an extension of 'Scythian' influence, as Śaka corresponds to our term Scythian; some have even thought that the Śaka dominions in India, which from the second to the end of the fourth century covered much of western India, may have been a major contributor to the 'Indianization' of much of Southeast Asia.[28] Such inferences, though, are speculative.

In southern Burma, the very name of one of the early cities of the Pyu, an ancient people closely related to the Burmans, viz. Viṣṇupura (modern Beikthano), may emphasize the cosmic aspect of Viṣṇu as the heavenly king of the universe. The religious observance at Śrīkṣetra (modern Hmaw-za near Prome) had a place for images of Viṣṇu and his consort Lakṣmī, goddess of royal majesty and of fortune, and the Kagyun cave site has a relief of a recumbent Viṣṇu. It was only in Burma, incidentally, that we find statues portraying the god standing on his mount, the mythical eagle Garuḍa.[29]

In Pagan, Viṣṇu played an important part in the state ritual if not in private devotion; under Kyanzittha Viṣṇu had his own temple, and the myth of Buddhist prophecy promulgated to glorify the king made of Kyanzittha an incarnation of Viṣṇu. Brahmins associated with the building of the palace may have been custodians of an old Vaiṣṇava cult. Lakṣmī was worshipped at Pagan as Kyak Sri.

In Angkor, several rulers such as Jayavarman III (r. c. 850–77) gave honour to Viṣṇu, but by far the most conspicuous success of Vaiṣṇavism in gaining state support was embodied in the construction of Angkor Wat by king Sūryavarman II (r. c. 1113–50). This, the most famous and the most impressive of all the monuments of Angkor, was built as a series of concentric courtyards surrounding a central pyramidal pile on top of which five towers rose in quincunx to place the Mountain of the Gods

---

[28] K. Bhattacharya, *Les Religions Brahmaniques dans L'Ancien Cambodge*, Paris, 1967, 130.
[29] G. H. Luce, *Old Burma—Early Pagan*, New York, 1969–70, I. 216.

(Mahāmeru) in the centre of the kingdom, and the kingdom in the centre of the universe. The complex measures overall about 1550 by 1800 metres. An outer gallery was decorated with a series of bas-relief carvings over two metres high running in long sections around the complex, extending more than 1600 metres. They depict secular as well as religious scenes, notably including myths of Viṣṇu and his incarnation of Kṛiṣṇa. The ritual and cosmological symbolism of the monument is richly embodied in every detail of Angkor Wat's art and design, but it has also been claimed to represent a devotional form of Viṣṇu worship. Such cults were strongly developed in India (especially that founded by Rāmānuja) and, to some extent, in Java, where most kings of the Kaḍiri period (c. 1100–1222) were considered incarnations of Viṣṇu. On the other hand, it has been pointed out that the Vaiṣṇava character of Angkor Wat was not pronounced— even to the extent that the monument was later adopted by the Buddhists as their own.

The devotional aspect of Vaiṣṇavism found expression from early times, and the Pāñcarātra sect, whose doctrines crystallized in the first two centuries CE, taught devotion (bhakti) to Viṣṇu as the supreme deity. An inscription of the time of Jayavarman I, in seventh-century Cambodia, refers to a Pāñcarātra priest. Ninth- and tenth-century Angkor knew the sect also, displaying a knowledge of metaphysics according to which Viṣṇu had four emanations (vyūha) and lay at the basis of the universe in all its forms, himself being without form.[30] Thus Vaiṣṇavism, like Śaivism, included a significant stream of devotional monistic theism.

Buddhism

Buddha images and votive seals attest the introduction of the Dharma (Buddhist teaching) from early times. The record begins with a number of Buddha statues, found in various parts of Southeast Asia, both on the mainland, especially at Dong-duong (near Danang in central Vietnam), Korat (northeastern Thailand), Vieng-sra (peninsular Thailand), and in the archipelago at Sempaga (south Sulawesi, north of Ujung Pandang), Jěmběr (east Java) and on the Bukit Sěguntang near Palembang (south Sumatra). These Buddhas, usually represented standing and dressed in clinging transparent robes, reflect a style the prototype of which has been found in Amarāvatī, Andhra Pradesh, India, and dated back to the early centuries of the Christian era. It has, however, convincingly been argued that the earliest Southeast Asian Buddhas were not made in or directly inspired by Amarāvatī, but more probably by Anurādhapura in Sri Lanka, which had itself been strongly influenced by Amarāvatī. As a consequence these earliest Buddhas in Southeast Asia must be dated considerably later than had been thought and probably belong to between the fourth and the sixth century CE.[31]

[30] K. Bhattacharya, 96–9; 'The Pāñcarātra sect in ancient Cambodia', Journal of the Greater India Society, 14, 1955, 111–16.

[31] J. Boisselier, in his La Statuaire du Champa, Paris, 1963 (Publications de l'École Française d'Extrême-Orient, vol. 54), dates the Dong-Duong bronze Buddha to a period ending in the early sixth century; cf. P. Dupont, L'Archéologie Mône de Dvāravatī, Paris, EFEO, 1959; L. Malleret, L'Archéologie du Delta du Mékong, II, Paris, EFEO, 1960, 202–208 and pl. LXXXV.

Buddhism, with its universal values, came to be embodied perhaps more than brahmanism in the teachings of pilgrims and wandering scholars. Certainly, in the first seven or eight centuries CE, there was a cosmopolitan oecumene of Buddhist culture disseminated across Asia by travelling monks. Our knowledge of these, like that of the earliest states that grew up along the trading routes, depends a great deal upon Chinese texts, which tell of monks from India and the Buddhist lands of central Asia finding their way by the Silk Road to northern China or by sea through Southeast Asia to destinations often in Kiao-chi (Tonkin) or southern China. In the second and third centuries, the monks who in one way or another reached or passed through Tonkin in the course of their teaching and studying included the Parthian An-shih-kao; Mou Po from China, who was converted to Buddhism there; the Sogdian Kang-seng-hui, child of a merchant in Tonkin; the Indo-Scyth Kalyāṅaruci who translated the Lotus Sūtra; and Mārajīvaka, who went from India to Tonkin and later to Canton at the end of the third century.[32]

Such travels criss-crossed the Buddhist world. Most of the monks were scholarly, actuated by the desire to disseminate the Dharma embodied in holy scriptures, or to find and study such scriptures in foreign lands. From the fifth century, the desire of Chinese Buddhists to refresh and purify their scriptural tradition led numbers to make the hazardous journey to India. Fa-hsien was one, at the beginning of the fifth century, and he gained fame by the account he left of his journey; on the return stretch he took the sea route via Sri Lanka and arrived back in China after an adventurous journey; he suffered shipwreck and was obliged to stay in (probably western) Java for five months waiting for another ship to finish his journey.[33]

Quite a few monks passed that way in the following two centuries, some spending long periods or settling down in places like Fu-nan, the Chinese transcription of the earliest kingdom in Cambodia. Nāgasena was a Buddhist monk sent to China by the ruler of that country. He carried two ivory models of stupas and Chinese references suggest a possible Mahāyāna element in the Buddhism he practised. In the seventh century, the great Chinese Hsuan-tsang went to India and back, but he took the land route both ways. At the end of the century, though, I Ching went to India by sea and spent several years in Southeast Asia, notably in Śrīvijaya at or near present Palembang in south Sumatra. His accounts are of great value, especially for the data they contain about the distribution of Buddhist schools and sects in different countries. Thus, he notes that the Saṃmitīya Nikāya, a sect closely related to the Theravādins of Sri Lanka, was well represented in Champa, while the Sarvāstivādins, asserting the reality of the dharmas (in this context: elements of existence), had followers in other areas.

I Ching wrote a valuable compilation of short biographies of about sixty monks who set off for India in search of the Buddhist teaching, but some of

---

[32] Tran Van Giap, 'Le Bouddhisme en Annam des origines au XIIIe siècle', BEFEO, 32 (1932) 211f.

[33] Fa-Hsien, A Record of Buddhist Kingdoms, trans. J. Legge, New York, 1965 (reprint); also translated by S. Beal in Travels of Fa-hien and Sung-Yun, London, 1964 (reprint).

these died en route.[34] Places in mainland Southeast Asia which they visited include Cambodia and Dvāravatī (in present-day Thailand). At the time of the Tang dynasty (from 618) the Vietnamese were taking an active part in Buddhist traffic; monks such as Mokṣadeva, Khuy Sung, and Hue Diem set off on pilgrimages, and the teacher Van Ki, traditionally supposed to have been a disciple of the Chinese master Hui-ning, brought to Vietnam Buddhist texts translated into Chinese, which was the language of literati in Vietnam until the nineteenth century.

Thus the early stages of Buddhist history in the eastern zone, in 'Indochina', are reasonably well represented in the historical record, even though the rulers of Cambodia and Champa generally favoured Brahmanism for their court cults. Few Chinese sources are, however, available for present-day Burma, then the country of the Mon (especially the coastal areas including the Irawaddy and Salween deltas), the Pyu in south-central Burma, the Burmans in north-central and northern Burma and others. Almost all sources before the eleventh century, inscriptions and monuments, are those of the Pyu with their centres in Srīkṣetra (present Hmaw-za near Prome) and Viṣṇupura (Beikthano). The archaeology of the latter site has suggested to its excavator that Buddhism is represented by undecorated monuments with square bases and drum-shaped superstructures, which are not unlike certain stupas in eastern India; they apparently date back to as early as the second century.[35]

The history, and particularly the architecture, of Srīkṣetra are much better known. Buddhist architecture of Old Prome was technically advanced, and employed the true arch—a feature which, remarkably, occurs only in Burma among the countries of Southeast Asia. Three great pagodas guarded the city; the best preserved of these is the Bawbawgyi, which is fifty metres high.

Inscriptions on gold plates from Maungun near Prome, probably datable to the seventh century, reflect the Pāli tradition and thus represent the earliest Southeast Asian evidence of Theravāda Buddhism, which gradually, especially from the eleventh century, became the prevalent religion of Burma and, a few centuries later, of most of mainland Southeast Asia. On the other hand, there is much evidence for Mahāyāna Buddhism in Pyu art, which includes various representations of the Bodhisattvas (future Buddhas) Avalokiteśvara and Maitreya, as well as of the Buddha Dīpaṅkara, who was thought to calm the waves. The Pyu were familiar with a Sanskrit Buddhist canon, which perhaps came to them from northeastern India.

The seventh-century Chinese pilgrim Hsuan-tsang mentions Srīkṣetra as a Buddhist kingdom, as does I Ching in 675. There are Chinese literary references to Pyu embassies to China in 802 and 807; the notice given of their country claims that in it there were more than a hundred Buddhist monasteries, and all boys and girls would serve for a spell as novices in the order.[36]

---

[34] *Chinese Monks in India*, trans. Latika Lahiri, Delhi, 1986.
[35] Aung Thaw, *Historical Sites in Burma*, Rangoon, 1972; *Report on the Excavations in Beikthano*, Rangoon, 1968.
[36] G. H. Luce, 'The ancient Pyu', JBRS, 27 (1937) 249f.

Thus it is evident that Buddhism was strong among the Pyu; but it was the Mon kingdoms that seem to have become the chief disseminators of Buddhism of the Theravāda school to the later empires which from the eleventh century came to displace them; and the early history of Mon Buddhism is particularly obscure.

It may go back a long way. For example, there is the tantalizing evidence provided by an ivory comb found in Thailand, at Chansen, possibly from the second century, though the radiocarbon datings are discrepant; it bears what appear to be Buddhist symbols.[37] The oldest known Mon Buddhist inscription, near Nakhon Pathom, sixty-five kilometres west of Bangkok, is not much earlier than 600 CE. P. Dupont considered that the influence of the Mon kingdom of Dvāravatī can be seen in the archaeology of Cambodia before the seventh century, but there is no religious sculpture from before the sixth century; when it begins in the following century, it resembles that of Dvāravatī and shows the influence of the Gupta style.[38]

The recent discovery of a Buddhist inscription at Noen Sa Bua in the Prachinburi area of eastern Thailand, dated 761 CE, written in Old Khmer with a quotation of three verses in Pāli,[39] indicates the expansion of Theravāda Buddhism to near the present Thai–Cambodian border in the pre-Angkor period.

The manner in which Buddhism expanded is, however, still far from clear. Dvāravatī may have been no more than a specific Mon kingdom with its heartland in central Thailand and a Buddhist culture quite distinct from that of any of its neighbours, or it may be part of a wider culture that included all the Mon lands of Burma and Thailand and even extended into pre-Angkor Cambodia. The use of Old Khmer in the Prachinburi inscription may be an indication in that direction. Although Indian culture, and Buddhism in particular, seems to have spread predominantly from west to east, the actual pattern may have been much more complicated. The earliest evidence for an Indianized society actually comes from Fu-nan, in particular from the ancient city of Oc-eo on the Gulf of Thailand.[40] On the other hand, little is known of the state of Buddhism among the Mon of present Burma. There, too, the population may have been Buddhist since very early times without leaving any significant traces.

The Buddhism of Dvāravatī is well enough attested, hazy though the political outline of the state may be. Cœdès identified Mon Buddhist sites associated with Dvāravatī culture in the peninsula and in various parts of Thailand, including Haripuñjaya (Lamphun) to the north.[41] The art of Dvāravatī is represented in iconography by a particular style of the Buddha image with a broad face and eyebrows continuing above the nose. Standing

---

[37] Higham, *Archaeology*, 272; E. Lyons, 'Dvāravatī, a consideration of its formative period', in Smith and Watson, 354; see also B. Bronson, 'The late prehistory and early history of central Thailand', ibid., 330f.

[38] Dupont, *L'Archéologie Mône de Dvāravatī*.

[39] Mendis Rohanadeera, 'Telakatāhagāthā in a Thailand Inscription of 761 A.D.', *Vidyodaya Journal of Social Science*, I, 1 (1987) (with thanks to Dr N. Chutiwongs, who kindly drew our attention to this important inscription).

[40] L. Malleret, *L'Archéologie du Delta du Mekong*, I–IV, Paris, EFEO, 1959–63.

[41] *Le Royaume de Dvāravatī*, Bangkok, 1929; 'Les Mons de Dvāravatī', in Ba Shin, J. Boisselier and A. B. Griswold, *Essays offered to G. H. Luce*, Ascona, 1966, I. 112–16.

Buddha statues are often represented with *both* hands in the attitude of protection (*abhayamudrā*). Another particular feature is the representation of the Buddha descending from heaven attended by Indra and Brahmā. Local artists may have been inspired by models from Amarāvatī and Sri Lanka, as well as from Gupta India, but adapted these to their own aesthetic conventions.

Thaton, centre of an ancient Mon state, certainly knew Buddhism by the eleventh century, when it was conquered by king Anawrahta (Aniruddha) of Pagan (r. c. 1044–77). Perhaps it had been recently influenced by Haripuñjaya, but we may perhaps give credence to the tradition which ascribes the advent of Buddhism in the area to the great fifth-century scholar Buddhaghoṣa, who would have spent his last years in Thaton after a fertile career in Sri Lanka. On the other hand, there are indications that the Buddhist tradition which was passed on to the Burmese may have been derived from Kāñcī (Conjeevaram) in South India. There may be some truth in all of these possibilities; one direction of influence does not exclude others.

At all events, the early Mon states bequeathed their Theravāda Buddhism to the various expanding kingdoms that, from the eleventh century onward, overran their territory. The expansion of Angkor under Sūryavarman I (r. c. 1002–50) brought Dvāravatī within the Khmer empire; Pagan, under Anawrahta, absorbed the culture of Thaton; and later on, with the rise of the Thai kingdoms, these too took as part of their cultural legacy a substantial inheritance from the Mon. In Pagan, a major role is ascribed to Anawrahta in doing away with the corrupt old religious practices and purifying the religious establishment with a graft of Mon Theravāda, but this account belongs to a subsequent rewriting of history in the interest of an orthodox establishment; it is likely that, in identifying Buddhist legitimacy with the actions of a strong king regarded as the founder of Pagan's fortunes, it exaggerates the changes made by Anawrahta. Anyhow, the tradition is that he was converted to Theravāda after his conquest of Thaton in 1057, influenced by the Mon teacher Shin Arahan who then became the court teacher for himself and subsequent kings.[42]

Links with Sri Lanka were certainly important. The Sinhalese king Vijayabāhu I (r. c. 1055–1110) was confronted with the task of restoring the Buddhist faith after the depredations of the South Indian Cōḷas, and in 1071 at his request some Burmese monks were sent to help. This initiated a close relationship between Sri Lanka and mainland Southeast Asia. It worked both ways, the Theravāda communities in each helping those of the other, but for most of the time it was the established Mahavihāra order in Sri Lanka that was regarded in the east as the fountainhead of pure religion, and numerous missions were sent across so that Burmese and other monks could take the higher ordination (*upasampadā*) in the Mahavihāra lineage and transmit successive purifying streams of it to their homelands.

Anawrahta was said to have obtained a set of scriptures from Sri Lanka, and a replica of the Tooth Relic of Lord Buddha. The archaeology of his

---

[42] Michael Aung-Thwin, *Pagan: the Origins of Modern Burma*, Honolulu, 1985; and 'Kingship, the sangha and society in Pagan', in K. Hall and J. Whitmore, eds, *Explorations in Early Southeast Asian History: the Origins of Southeast Asian Statecraft*, Ann Arbor, 1976.

reign, more trustworthy than such traditions, demonstrates his piety by a large number of votive seals, inscribed variously in Sanskrit and Pāli.[43] It has been debated how far they show the influence of Mahāyāna Buddhism, but they are certainly not deep-dyed Theravāda; it is altogether likely that the real conquest of Theravāda in Pagan came later, under Kyanzittha, whereas Anawrahta's religious allegiance was more eclectic.

Kyanzittha (r. c. 1084–1112) was certainly an active sponsor of Buddhist foundations and activities (but not exclusively Buddhist as we have seen). He endowed the construction of a number of monuments, the most famous of which is the Ānanda or Nanda temple (*Anantapaññā*, 'Endless Wisdom'), completed probably by 1105 and said to be a miraculously inspired copy of the legendary Nandamūla grotto in the Himalayas. It is decorated with reliefs representing scenes based on the life of Lord Buddha, as well as stories of his earlier incarnations (Jātaka). Kyanzittha also completed the famous Shwezigon, and he sent a mission to India to carry out repairs to the Vajrāsana shrine at Bodhgaya, site of Lord Buddha's Enlightenment. Some scholars have found evidence of Burmese style in some details of the temple.[44] The inscription recording the restoration of the Vajrāsana ends in the well-known wish that the spiritual merit that the king acquired by this pious deed may enable all sentient beings to escape from the cycle of death and rebirth.

Kyanzittha gave special patronage to all forms of the Mon cultural legacy, but like many of his successors, fostered the relations with Sri Lanka. Copies of the Mahavihāra recension of the Scriptures were distributed to monasteries.

Burma was thus the chief power-house in the dissemination of Theravāda Buddhism, which eventually became the dominant orthodoxy in the mainland kingdoms. The status and prestige attached to the spiritual lineages established by the returning monks in their home countries assured a steadily increasing success for the Sīhala (Sinhalese) orders and their offshoots. But we must not allow this Theravāda dominance to obscure the fact that a variety of sects flourished before and even during its ascendancy.

We need to recognize, for example, that Mahāyāna Buddhism long remained influential, and there is evidence of it at many places and times. Bodhisattvas such as Maitreya and Mañjuśrī were popular in Burma before the rise of Pagan. As early as 791 CE an inscription in Cambodia (at Siemreap) refers to an image of Lokeśvara (better known as Avalokiteśvara). Mahāyāna in Angkor has been seen as a continuing thread, whatever the orthodoxies of successive monarchs. Many inscriptions refer to character-istically Mahāyāna doctrines, such as those concerning the Void (*śūnya*), the 'mind-only' (*cittamātra*) and the three bodies of the Buddha. Perhaps most conspicuously, the reign of Jayavarman VII (1181–1218) is a high point of Mahāyāna aspiration.

Under this ruler, Avalokiteśvara was virtually the patron god of the state, in his various forms and associations, including Balaha and the

[43] Than Tun, *History of Buddhism in Burma, A.D. 1000–1300*, Rangoon 1978 (JBRS, 61.1,2, *separatum*), 4f.

[44] Luce, *Old Burma*, I. 62.

personified Perfection of Wisdom, the goddess Prajñāpāramitā. Compassion is the pre-eminent quality of a Bodhisattva in Mahāyāna perception, and Avalokiteśvara was above all a vessel of grace, making possible a rebirth in heaven for the faithful; as an embodiment of this Bodhisattva, the king sought to present himself as a loving guardian and father figure, building hospitals and caring for the welfare of all his subjects on the Aśokan model.

This currency of Mahāyāna Buddhism, between the eighth and the thirteenth centuries, cannot be understood in isolation from developments in India. In the first place, Buddhism was on the retreat in the land of its birth, yielding to the brahmanical orthodoxy over much of the subcontinent but acquiring strongholds in certain kingdoms on the periphery, especially in Bengal where successive rulers gave lavish patronage to the Mahāyāna foundations, and it was Bengal that was the most conspicuous source of religious influence upon Southeast Asia during this period. Cœdès identified three strands in Bengali Buddhism: a tendency to Tantric practices, syncretism with Hinduism, and accommodation to indigenous traditions such as ancestor cults.[45]

In the second place, from the eleventh and especially in the thirteenth century, Muslim invasions may have prompted the flight of many monks as refugees. Tāranātha, the Tibetan historian of Buddhism, refers to monks travelling to various lands in the east, including Cambodia and perhaps Pagan. Another link between Southeast Asia and Bengal is constituted by the career of Atīśa (982–1054), who is supposed to have spent twelve years in 'Suvarṇabhūmi', probably southern Burma, before going to Tibet to reform the Tantric tradition there.

Evidence of Tantric Buddhism is not wanting in Burma in the period when we would expect it. In official Burmese tradition, as embodied in the 'Glass Palace Chronicle' (Hmannan Yazawin), a corrupt Tantric type of religion represented by the 'Ari' sect was practised among the Burmese in the eleventh century, before the creation of a great empire by Anawrahta; with his conversion to Theravāda and the assistance of Shin Arahan to purify the religion, the degenerate practices were stamped out. However, it appears probable that this account owes more to the desire of the proponents of the later Sinhalese orthodoxy for historical legitimacy in association with the great king than to actual historical fact. Actually, the chief substantial evidence of Tantric-style practices belongs to the thirteenth century, two centuries after the reign of Anawrahta. Some temples have decorations such as images of Hayagrīva that are associated with Tantra, and in particular some thirteenth-century inscriptions in the Minnanthu temple southeast of Pagan describe the Samantakuṭṭaka monks who took beef and fermented spirits, heterodox practices suggestive of Tantra.

Who then were the degenerate Aris referred to by the Glass Palace Chronicle, who were supposed to wear 'strong beards and untrimmed hair' and, according to one interpretation of the enigmatic relevant passage, to practise a form of jus primae noctis with maidens about to be married?[46] There has been much debate over the meaning of the term ari, some seeing

45 États, 182.
46 G. H. Luce cites the Hmannan in a review in the JBRS, 9 (1919) 54.

it as representing *āriya*, 'noble' and others as representing *āraññaka*, 'silvan', alluding to the forest monks who meditated in seclusion. The latter interpretation is more generally favoured now. In the thirteenth century, there were inscriptions indicating an araññavāsi ('forest-dwelling') sect headed by one Mahākassapa, who was perhaps the leader of a powerful and well-endowed community that attracted the rivalry of the orthodox Sīhala school. But in 1248 the head of the Sīhalas returned from Sri Lanka and his school regained favour.

At this point it is necessary to look back at the importance of this link with Sri Lanka, for of course it was not Bengal which made the running; from the eleventh century, inspired by the Mon legacy, rulers of Pagan (and eventually of other kingdoms besides) were more and more interested in acquiring the spiritual status conferred by the prestige of a state-established Mahāvihāra order sanctified by the ordination of its teachers in Sri Lanka.

In the twelfth century, a particularly important episode was the mission of 1170 headed by the patriarch Uttarajīva, which returned in 1180; the monk Capaṭa, however, remained a further ten years and returned with five colleagues (enough to constitute a chapter capable of transmitting the sect's lineage) and re-established the Mahāvihāra order in Burma; this new line was known as the Sīhala *saṅgha* (coming from Sri Lanka), while the older one that had been headed by Shin Arahan was the Mrammā *saṅgha*; by the thirteenth century there were four sects as a result of further splits. A Cambodian prince was, incidentally, supposed to have been one of Capaṭa's party. Sinhalese Buddhism speedily became the major recipient of state support in mainland Southeast Asia.

One influential offshoot of the Sinhalese Mahāvihāra was created in Martaban by the monk Anumati, who returned from Sri Lanka in 1331. The spread of his school thereafter owed much to the interest of the rulers of the new Thai kingdoms, especially Sukothai. Under Lü Thai (acc. 1347), the monks Sumana and Anomadassi went to Martaban and took the higher ordination. On returning Sumana was given his own *Vat* (wat); he performed various Buddhist miracles and later went to Chiengmai, which thus, from 1369, became a major centre for the Sīhala school.

A further expedition to Sri Lanka in 1423 saw thirty-nine monks from Chiengmai, Lopburi and Burma going to take the higher ordination; on their return they promoted Sinhalese Buddhism in their own countries. In Chiengmai in particular they received considerable favour, but there is evidence of conflict in that state over the rules of monastic discipline. This suggests rivalry between the newer and older schools.

In Angkor, the wave of Sinhalese Theravāda bore fruit in the thirteenth century, when the ostentatious display of Mahāyāna by Jayavarman VII was followed first by a temporary revival of Hinduism and then by the increasing influence of the saffron-robed Theravādin monks observed late in the century by the Chinese visitor Chou Ta-kuan.[47] The oldest Pāli inscription (after that of 761) dates from 1309. The king Indravarman dedicated a Theravāda monastery and Buddha image; the *Khmer Chronicle*,

---

[47] *Mémoires sur les coutumes de Cambodge*, 14.

which marks a new court tradition wholly influenced by Theravāda, begins its record in the middle of the fourteenth century.

Some have linked the fall of the great Angkorean tradition with Theravāda itself, suggesting that the Sinhalese school, with its emphasis on individual salvation rather than public Bodhisattva worship and with its implied egalitarianism, eroded the ideological foundations of the state. However, there is perhaps no need to appeal to such factors to account for the end of Angkor; economic and social conditions offer less speculative possibilities of interpretation.

In the western part of mainland Southeast Asia, the destruction by the Mongols of Pagan at the end of the thirteenth century did not affect the continued influence of Theravāda Buddhism, for the various successor states continued the tradition of generous patronage of the *sangha*. In particular, the fifteenth century witnessed a revival of the Mon state of Pegu under the pious ruler Dhammaceti. He was a former monk who set about reforming the order. According to a sixteenth-century text he codified the pantheon of thirty-six spirits, thus regulating and accommodating to the official Buddhist cosmology the local *nat*-type spirits, re-identifying them as beings destined for Buddhist salvation, just as had been done in Pagan. Most of these beings were in fact tree spirits at Buddhist sites. Further, the king sent a mission to Sri Lanka. The monks who constituted it took their higher ordination by the Kalyāṇī (Kälani) river, and on their return a religious establishment, called the Kalyāṇī Sīma, was built for them; the Kalyāṇī inscription of 1479 records their pilgrimage.

The declaration by the Kalyāṇī inscription that the Buddhist order was corrupt, lazy and impure, and needed immediate action, demonstrates once more the concern of rulers to regulate the affairs of the *sangha*, and raises the complicated question of the relationship of the monks to state and society. In theory, they had cut themselves off from society and sought no political influence; they were wholly dedicated to the Buddha's teaching. But how far was this theory embodied in reality?

In the Burmese case, kingdoms such as Pegu and Pagan provide evidence on both sides, and scholars have placed the emphasis some on one side, some on the other. It has been argued that, although royal patronage tended to politicize some sects, there were many other patrons; the various claims to secular authority over the monks tended to cancel each other out. The monks anyway had freedom of conscience. The hold of Buddhist devotion over national culture worked to limit the power of a ruler to regulate the order; when kings tried to confiscate large parts of the *sangha's* possessions, popular opinion operated to thwart such attempts.[48]

On the other hand, there is no doubt that monks were in various ways intimately involved in affairs of government and society. Rulers made decisions that governed their concerns. Thus, a revised edition of the Buddhist Pāli canon was written by order of Kyanzittha. In 1154 King Aloncañsu determined that large temple donations would require royal permission. Monks spent time performing ritual functions on behalf of

[48] Than Tun, *History of Buddhism*, 39.

the state, praying for the king and chanting *parittas* for the benefit of royal enterprises. Monks were caught up in the hurly-burly of politics; some were even involved in rebellions. Kings determined which sects or subsects received large endowments and which did not, exploiting all the tendencies to factionalism of a community whose members had plenty of time to sit and think.

Similarly, in Angkor, rulers exercised a preponderating influence upon the economic life of the *saṅgha* by regulating the system of endowments to religious foundations of all sorts; by giving 'royal' status to favoured donations, they effectively bestowed tax exemption privileges upon the donors. By giving or withholding support to Buddhist foundations, they had influence upon the fortunes of the faith. Sūryavarman I (r. c. 1002–50) should not be seen as exclusively a Buddhist ruler, but he gave much emphasis to Buddhism. Jayavarman VII, as already noticed above, gave considerable prominence to the Mahāyāna school.

Conspicuous are the Thai kingdoms which rose on the rubble of Angkor's power. They sent monks on missions to Martaban or Sri Lanka, and provided well-appointed temples for favoured teachers. Ramkamhaeng (r. c. 1280–97),[48] in particular, paid special respect to the *saṅgha*. If his inscription of 1292 is to be given credence, he had a stupa built at Śrī Sajjanālaya (Savankhalok), which took six years to construct, and endowed a number of monasteries.[49] At one, Vat Aranyika, he celebrated *kaṭhina*: the bestowal of robes on monks after the rainy season retreat. Further, the state of Ayutthaya, which succeeded Sukothai as the main Thai power in the fourteenth century, was no less pious. King Paramarāja, for example, built a monastery, the Laṅkārāma, for the benefit of the famous monk Dhammakitti, a Pāli scholar.

Further east, in Champa, the most notable episode of state support for Buddhism is constituted by the Chan Ch'eng kingdom (to use its Chinese name), established at Indrapura in Quang Nam by Indravarman, who made a state shrine to Avalokiteśvara called Lakṣmīndralokeśvara. There was a striking florescence of Buddhist art under this ruler and some of his successors.[50]

In Vietnam, where Buddhism received strong and consistent support—even though this had to be shared with other traditions—the Chinese way of life determined that the influence of the state upon religious organization should be highly regulated by the ruler. Patriarchs of favoured sects were regularly given important advisory positions in the palace, and this inevitably politicized their following.

It is here that we can most appropriately review the influence of Chinese Buddhism upon Vietnam, for the organization is most marked in Chinese tradition.[51] The most influential Chinese sect was the Ch'an (in India,

---

[49] Cœdès, *États*, 360, 377; A. B. Griswold and Prasert na Nagara, 'The inscription of King Rāma Gaṃheṅ of Sukhodaya (1292 A.D.), Epigraphical and Historical Studies No. 9', JSS, 69 (1971).

[50] I. W. Mabbett, 'Buddhism in Champa', in Marr and Milner, 298–303.

[51] On Buddhism in Vietnam, see Tran Van Giap, 'Le Bouddhisme en Annam'; K. W. Taylor, 'Authority and legitimacy in eleventh century Vietnam', in Marr and Milner, 139–76; K. W. Taylor, *The Birth of Vietnam*, Berkeley, 1983; Thich Thien-An, *Buddhism and Zen in Vietnam in relation to the development of Buddhism in Asia*, Los Angeles, Rutland, Vermont, Tokyo, 1975.

Dhyāna, 'meditation'; in Japan, Zen; in Vietnam, Thien). According to Chinese tradition, the first Ch'an patriarch in China was the monk Bodhidharma, about whom legends grew up, and although such a person existed it is difficult to know the true facts about him. He is supposed to have practised 'wall meditation' (sitting meditating in front of a blank wall) for nine years, and to have visited Shao Lin, the monastery which became renowned as the home of various Ch'an practices and martial arts. The line of teachers which he originated was responsible for the dissemination of Ch'an to Vietnam.

Vietnamese tradition codifies and categorizes religious history, identifying a number of specific schools each with its stylized record listing patriarchs and generations of teachers. It is likely that this traditional account makes the pattern seem more organized and institutionalized than it was; there were temples dotted about the settled lands, each largely managing its own affairs under the eye of patrons and benefactors. However, there were certainly lines of teachers acknowledging allegiance to particular schools of Buddhism that traced their origins to a Chinese legitimacy.

The first was the Vinītaruci school (Ty-Ni-Du-Luu-Chi), named after its founder who was supposed to have been an Indian brahmin who went to China in the sixth century and studied under Seng-tsan, third patriarch in the Ch'an school in China. Going to Tonkin, he was installed in the Phap-Van temple, Ha-dong Province. The line of transmission that led from him, proceeding by the Ch'an process of 'mind-seal' (by which the master imprints his spiritual insights upon the disciple), is said to have passed through nineteen generations. Some patriarchs in the school (including, for example, Phap Thuan in the tenth century) were royal counsellors, some were renowned for spiritual attainments, some gained a reputation for scholarship.

The second major Ch'an-derived Vietnamese sect was the Vo Ngon Thong school, which was founded during the T'ang dynasty but found considerable favour from subsequent independent Vietnamese rulers; for example its fourth patriarch Khuong Viet taught at the palace and advised Le Dai-Hanh (980–1005), and the later king Ly Thai Tong was himself a patriarch of the school, representing the symbiosis of dynasty and *sangha*, which was conspicuous under the Ly, a dynasty which was brought to power largely through the work of Buddhist monks.

The third major Buddhist sect identified by Vietnamese tradition was that of Thao Dong, founded by a Chinese monk, Ts'ao-t'ang, in Champa, who was caught up in a war and taken to the Vietnamese court as a captive; there however he was given an important ministerial position as *quoc-su*, a largely secular, partly religious, supervisory post. His teaching was based on the *Amitābhasūtra*, stressing the extinction of the individual self; a famous poem he wrote compares the phenomenal world to a flower in the sky—it is unreal, illusory. The line of patriarchs which directed the fortunes of the school he founded included a number of members of the royal family, notably the emperors Ly Anh Tong and Ly Cao Tong in the twelfth century.

As such examples remind us, the Buddhist communities, like the Brahmanical foundations, could not work in a vacuum; they depended upon, and to a great extent were moulded by, the aspirations of the society in which they lived. Inscriptions are in Southeast Asia the chief sources for our knowledge of their organization, and inscriptions, left by pious rulers and laymen, tell us what were the motives of those who were willing to bear the burden of supporting a large and (at first glance) economically unproductive class.

These motives were partly material, and indeed the function of temples and monasteries in society needs to be seen against the background of that society's economic and political organization. But we need also to take account of the spiritual motives, which were real enough. Consider Pagan, a striking embodiment of religious zeal, where three or four thousand temples were built in an area of sixty-five square kilometres. The inscriptions which record the endowment of many of these foundations usually indicate why the donations were made. In most cases the donors hope to achieve *nirvāṇa* (the extinction of all *karma* and release from rebirth), *sambodhi* (the perfect enlightenment which is a condition of this release), or Buddha-hood. Sometimes they express the ambition to have a future life at the time of Maitreya, the next Buddha; thereby, profiting from his teaching, they can hope to attain enlightenment. Women donors sometimes profess the desire to become males in a later life (thus acquiring better means to progress towards salvation), or even to become Buddhas. Some rulers saw themselves as Bodhisattvas; such was Lu Thai in Sukothai, and it was said when he entered religion and embarked upon his spiritual career, the earth trembled.[52]

Notable is the way in which the doctrine of merit is interpreted. Strictly speaking, the good *karma* of an act of merit such as endowing a religious foundation could accrue (in Theravāda at least) only to the agent himself, but loopholes were found in Theravāda traditions just as in Mahāyāna to make possible the transfer of merit to others; donors of property frequently willed the merit of their actions to the benefit of others (of a widow for her husband, or of a temple endowment for the poor). In Angkor, Jayavarman VII could seek to benefit his mother by virtue of the fact that, as a partial cause of his existence, she was partly responsible for his actions and thereby earned a share in his merit.

But it is clear enough that there could be rewards in life on earth for those who endowed temples and monasteries. They did not altogether relinquish any economic interest in the property they made over; the beneficiaries were like lease-holders in some respects, and there are cases in Pagan of disputes between temple and donor over the nature of the interest retained by the latter. An officially recognized endowment would be declared free of all claims by tax collectors and other royal officers, as in Angkor, even though the family of the donor might be continuing to exploit the donated land to some extent, and its members might be abbots or senior monks. Further, property made over to religion was less liable to future depredations of governments, bandits, or relatives, and would earn social status in the measure of its abundance. Donors who wished to maximize the merit they would gain by this spiritual banking system, as it

---

[52] Cœdès, *Receuil*, I. 111–16 (Inscription palie du bois des manguiers) at 115.

is sometimes called, would seek to emphasize their donations' permanence by solemn imprecations against any who in the future should violate the terms of the endowment. One such imprecation, in Pagan, says: 'Whoever injures these pagoda slaves, may the axe burst his breast! May he fall off a ladder!'[53]

As recipients of so much pious generosity, the religious foundations of places like Pagan or Angkor became more and more prosperous, dotting the landscape everywhere and acquiring a major role in the economic system. Frequently they acquired fresh property by new donations; rarely did they lose property.

The monks, priests and nuns who were supported in them often enjoyed many of the amenities of a comfortable life, with bonded temple servants to look after all their wants. There has been some discussion of the status of such servants, who for many purposes were effectively slaves, and are usually named as such in translations of the sources which refer to them; but we need to take account of the fact that temple 'slavery' could, for some at least, be something of an honour. Not untypical is the case of a queen in Pagan making over three sons as slaves to a monastery, subsequently to be redeemed by a gift of property. Such transactions involve a purely ritual slavery. But plenty of those who toiled on temple lands or looked after the needs of the incumbents were menials descended, quite often, from captives seized from hill tribes.[54]

The riches of the monasteries eventually made them rivals of the royal power of the state. A convincing argument advanced by Michael Aung-Thwin about the role of the wealth of the Buddhist order in the decline of Pagan may apply to other states as well: while land was plentiful, there was room for both state and *saṅgha* to extend their spheres of control and authority, but as time went on available resources became scarcer, and eventually the *saṅgha* became a rival to the state, disposing of abundant land and labour which otherwise should have been available to furnish the economic resources of government. This stage came in the thirteenth century, and prompted rulers to look more and more critically at the possessions of the monasteries, some seeking to 'purify' the Buddhist order—that is, to confiscate its surplus wealth. On one calculation, the *saṅgha* in Pagan came eventually to control 63 per cent of productive land. The attempts at confiscation were not always successful, and the conflict over resources tended to heighten factionalism, for the interest of the monasteries was bound up with that of the great landed families which endowed them, had members in the monkhood, and lived in symbiosis with the monastic estates. Hence centrifugal forces increased and civil war became more likely.[55] It is entirely possible that the same sort of process could be charted for Angkor.

[53] Luce, *Old Burma*, I. 109.
[54] On slavery in Cambodia, see C. Jacques, 'A propos de l'esclavage dans l'ancien Cambodge', in *XXXIXe Congrès International des Orientalistes, Paris, 1973. Proceedings. Asie du Sud-est continentale*; Y. Bongert, 'Note sur l'esclavage en droit khmer ancien', in *Études d'Histoire du Droit Privé Offertes à Pierre Petot*, Paris, 1959; A. K. Chakravarti, 'Sources of slavery in ancient Cambodia', in D. C. Sircar, ed., *Social Life in Ancient India*, Calcutta, 1971.
[55] Aung-Thwin, *Pagan*; and Aung-Thwin, 'Kingship, the sangha and society in Pagan', in Hall and Whitmore, *Explorations*.

In Vietnam, too, there was potential friction between state authority and
the independence of religious orders. Chinese tradition supplied an ideology
that legitimized state authority over all phases of life and justified it in
regulating the affairs of the Buddhist monks to a greater degree than was
generally accepted elsewhere. This ideology was Confucianism.

Of course it is questionable how far Confucianism is a religion, but it
deserves to be considered alongside the other systems since, like them,
it provided a coherent ideology that gave men a view of their place in the
universe, prescribed a code of morality and ethics, and furnished a body of
rituals that gave expression to the sense of community identity.

Confucianism in independent Vietnam was taken over from China as a
form of state orthodoxy, providing a didactic literature that could serve to
shape national culture to a considerable extent. Under the Ly, Confucian
scholars were required to write commentaries on Confucian texts. Statues
of the Duke of Chou and Confucius were set up as icons in a national
shrine. Confucianism was a part of the syllabus for state examinations
alongside the other religions, but it really came into its own in the revival
of the fourteenth and fifteenth centuries, with the sternly political reassertion
of national identity: state cults were promoted and Confucianism benefited
from the rise of state power. Rulers such as Le Thanh Ton (r. 1460–97)
actively promoted Confucianism.[56]

RELIGIONS OF INDIAN ORIGIN IN THE
MARITIME REALM

The religious developments in the island world of Southeast Asia are in
many respects similar to those in the mainland, but there are important
differences. The island world can be divided into two zones separated
by a line running from north to south, west of the Philippines, between
the islands Kalimantan and Sulawesi and east of Sumbawa. Very little is
known of the early history and religion of the eastern zone before the
sixteenth century; our sources are limited to the western zone, or rather
to important parts of this zone, in particular large parts of Sumatra, the
Malay peninsula, central and eastern Java, Bali and small parts of Kalimantan. These are the very areas where Indian influence made itself felt from
the early centuries of the Christian era and where Indian religions were
introduced, especially in circles associated with the royal courts.

The geography of maritime Southeast Asia shows important differences
from that of the mainland, differences which carry historical implications.
Owing to the presence of mountain ranges running mainly north to south,
the mainland is split into at least four sub-zones, each with its own
language and culture; maritime Southeast Asia, in contrast, presents a
much more consistent pattern. Both in language and in culture the islands
have much in common. Apparently, the straits and seas separating the
islands and the Malay peninsula, easily navigable in general, were not

---

[56] K. W. Taylor, 'Authority and legitimacy in eleventh century Vietnam', in Marr and Milner,
153.

barriers like the mountain ranges of the mainland: they linked, rather than separated, the different parts of the region.

When, in the early centuries of the Christian era, Indian influence began to make itself felt, the population of many areas already enjoyed a high level of civilization, enabling their élites to adopt and adapt those elements of Indian civilization that they regarded as valuable or useful. These naturally included religion: in particular Brahmanic Hinduism, including especially Śaivism, and, apparently at a later stage, Mahāyāna Buddhism. Vaiṣṇavism seems to have had a much more limited appeal, whereas Jainism and Theravāda Buddhism left no traces in maritime Southeast Asia. As to Brahmanic Hinduism it should be stated at the very outset that the use of the term 'Hinduism' may be misleading because one of its most important features, the caste system, existed only in theory.[57] As, however, the brahmins and Brahmanic culture (including, for example, the use of Sanskrit, especially at an early stage before the seventh century) formed the chief element of the forms of Hinduism in Southeast Asia, the term 'Brahmanism' is preferable. As it preceded Śaivism and Buddhism, it is proper to discuss it first.

Brahmanism

Old Javanese sources from the eleventh century on regularly mention three religious communities (*tripakṣa*): the Śaivas (worshippers of Śiva as the supreme deity, also called Māheśvaras), the Buddhists (also called Saugatas) and the Rěsis (also called Mahābrāhmaṇas), each under the supervision of a central government official, called *dharmādhikāra* for the first two communities and *mantri er-haji* for the third.[58] The latter, though few in numbers, were by no means unimportant. They included not only different kinds of ascetics but also court brahmins, who were in charge of royal ceremonies, as well as of education.

The oldest inscriptions of the area, those of king Mūlavarman of Kutai in east Kalimantan (end of the fourth century CE) and of Pūrṇavarman of Tārumā (fifth century) are probably non-sectarian. Those of Mūlavarman describe precious gifts to brahmins, including thousands of cattle and large amounts of gold. The terms used for different kinds of gifts are known from the Indian epics and *Purāṇas*, but seem to reflect potlatch ceremonies. Precious gifts to brahmins are also mentioned in Pūrṇavarman's inscriptions, which are, however, of special interest for references to the worship of the footprints of the king and of his elephant. At several sites in west Java we may witness the king's footprints, more than life-size, by the side of his inscriptions, sometimes with curious symbols (such as a spider in front of each of the footprints carved into a large inscribed rock at Ci-aruteun,

---

[57] This is, however, a complicated issue, for the system of four classes (*caturwarṇa*) is occasionally mentioned in Old Javanese texts and inscriptions. There are, however, strong indications that this was a purely theoretical division of society mentioned mainly in stereotyped contexts, without any of the implications of the Indian caste system. See, for example, J. G. de Casparis, 'Pour une Histoire Sociale de l'Ancienne Java, Principalement aux Xème s.', *Archipel*, 21 (1981).

[58] See *Nāgarakěrtāgama* (abbreviated *Nāg.* in the sequel), 81–1–4; Pigeaud, *Java in the Fourteenth Century* IV. 258 and 479–93. Pigeaud uses the term 'the three denominations'.

west of present Bogor). Although the worship of footprints, especially those of Viṣṇu and, much more stylized, of Lord Buddha, is well attested in India and Sri Lanka, there are no examples of the worship of human, let alone elephant, footprints there. In Indonesia, on the other hand, there is good evidence for the worship of footprints of ancestors in some areas, especially on the island of Nias near the west coast of Sumatra. It is therefore likely that in this case, as in the 'potlatch' ceremonies of east Kalimantan, a traditional Austronesian practice was continued in the guise of Sanskrit terms.[59]

Two typically Hindu ceremonies occupied an important place in Indonesian courts: royal consecration (*abhiṣeka*) and funerary rites (*śrāddha*). The term *abhiṣeka* often occurs in Old Javanese sources. Although the oldest epigraphic reference to royal consecration dates back to 1019, the year of Airlangga's *abhiṣeka*, it is likely that the ceremony was performed much earlier, perhaps even at the time of king Pūrṇavarman of Tārumā (fifth century), who dated his Tugu inscription in his twenty-second regnal year. As regnal years are always counted from the year of consecration, this is an implicit indication of the performance of such a ceremony. The use of elaborate Sanskrit names preceded by *śrī*, 'His Majesty', in addition to Old Javanese names and titles in ninth- and tenth-century inscriptions, confirms the performance of consecration ceremonies, since the conferment of such names, usually ending in *uttuṅgadeva*, 'Exalted Majesty' (aptly called *abhiṣekanāma*), has always been an essential part of the ceremony. The 'Calcutta' inscription of King Airlangga (dated 1041) contains the interesting passage *kṛtasaṃskāra pratiṣṭha ring singhāsana*, 'had the consecration ceremony carried out, established on the Lion Throne'. A pilgrimage to Īśānabajra, the shrine dedicated to the memory of King Siṇḍok, Airlangga's great-great-grandfather, and the erection of a rice-pestle (*halu*), symbolizing the king's potency to promote the fertility of the ricefields, completed the ceremony, which was carried out by Buddhist, Śaiva and Brahmanic priests (*mpungku sogata maheśwara mahābrāhmaṇa*, in that order). These details clearly show how much of the ceremony differed from its description in Indian texts.

The second important ceremony is another of the 'rites de passage': the funerary rites, or rather those performed to ensure the liberation of the soul of the deceased. In India such rites are of great importance to all Hindus. According to the texts they involve elaborate ceremonies, which were to take place at regular intervals after death and were performed by six generations in both ascending and descending lines; the presence of a son of the deceased was essential.

In ancient Java, the elaborate description of *śrāddha* in the *Nāgarakĕrtāgama* concerns the purification and liberation of the soul of the 'Rājapatnī' (Spouse of the King), the youngest of the four daughters of King Kĕrtanagara (r. 1268–92), who were also the four queens of King Kĕrtarājasa (r. 1293–1309). She was also grandmother of King Hayam Wuruk (r. 1350–89) and

[59] J. Ph. Vogel, 'The Yūpa inscriptions of king Mūlavarman from Kutei (East Borneo)', BKI, 74 (1918); and 'De Giften van Mūlavarman', ibid., 76 (1920); J. G. de Casparis, 'The Oldest Inscriptions of Indonesia' in C. M. S. Hellwig, and C. D. Grijns, *A Man of Indonesian Letters*, Dordrecht, 1986.

died in the year of her grandson's accession. The great *śrāddha*, performed in 1362, twelve years after her death (which was the usual period in ancient Indonesia), is described in no fewer than seven cantos of the text. This account contains many interesting features, which tend to show that the ceremony differed completely from its description in Sanskrit texts and from contemporary practice in Gaya (Bihar). The participants included not only members of the royal family but also high officials, as well as simple servants with their wives, priests and monks of different denominations, dancers, musicians, story-tellers and others. These details stand in clear contrast to the Indian *śrāddha*, confined to the close relatives of the deceased.[60]

The ceremony itself involved various Tantric rites carried out by both Buddhist monks and by a *purohita*, 'chief court brahmin', all versed in the three Tantras (*Nāg*. 64–3). The centre of veneration was a lion-throne in the middle of a square: the place where the soul of the Rājapatnī was to descend after the completion of the correct rites. If our understanding of the passage is correct, an effigy of the Rājapatnī, made of flowers (*sang hyang puṣpaśarīra, Nāg*. 67–2) had been placed on the throne; subsequently the soul (*swah*) of the Rājapatnī was made to enter the 'flower body'. After seven days of ceremonies (which included ritual meals comparable with the *slamětan* of modern times) the queen was 'deified' as Prajñāpāramitā, 'Supreme Wisdom', conceived of as the mother of all Buddhas in Tantric thought.[61] In addition to food and drink, money and clothes were distributed, which gave the whole ceremony a 'potlatch' aspect in addition to its animistic background. The analysis of the ceremony is therefore quite complicated. Its formal basis was the *śrāddha*, on to which not only Buddhist, but also ancient Austronesian beliefs were grafted. One could, however, just as well describe it as an essentially Austronesian rite embellished by learned elements from both Sanskrit ritual literature and Buddhist thought.

Such a *śrāddha*, performed on the twelfth anniversary of the death of a king or queen, is also mentioned in one of the last known Old Javanese inscriptions. It deals with a sacred domain called Trailokyapurī and is dated 1486.[62] The text includes an order by King Girīndrawardhana dyaḥ Raṇawijaya addressed to a court brahmin, Brahmarāja of the Bhāradvāja *gotra*, presumably an Indian (such *gotra* names tracing back a brahmin's family to a legendary Rishi are usual in India, as we have seen, but do not seem to occur elsewhere in Indonesia), to perform a *śrāddha* for the benefit of the soul of a king deceased at Indranibhawana. Another inscription mentions the worship of the eminent sage Bhāradvāja and of Lord (*bhaṭāra*) Rāma. As to the above-mentioned brahmin, he is said to have been well-versed in the Four Vedas (*caturvedapāraga*), a common epithet in India but

---

[60] Among the numerous publications on ancient Indian royal consecration are P. V. Kane, *History of Dharmaśāstra*, III. 72ff.; J. C. Heesterman, *The ancient Indian royal consecration*, The Hague, 1957; J. Gonda, *Ancient Indian kingship from the religious point of view*, Leiden, 1966, 79–83.

[61] For the *śrāddha* as performed in ancient Java see Pigeaud, *Java*, IV. 171f. Pigeaud rightly compares modern Javanese *ñadran*, 'visiting ancestral tombs in the month of Śaban'.

[62] See the translation of this inscription in Md. Yamin, *Tatanegara Madjapahit*, Jakarta, 1962.

unusual in Java, where even *caturveda* occurs only in Old Javanese texts which are closely based on Indian prototypes. Rāma is well-known in Indonesia, but there are no other examples of a foundation (*pratiṣṭhā*) devoted to Rāma as a deity. In South India, on the other hand, such foundations are not rare. Since we know of a revival of Hinduism in its classical form during the time of the South Indian kingdom of Vijaya-nagara (1336–1565), it is likely that there was a direct relation between the developments in South India and eastern Java at a time when both were confronted with the expansion of Islam.[63]

It should however be emphasized that the influence of Brahmanism is not confined to the earliest or last periods, nor to the performance of certain rituals. In fact, an important feature of the Indian way of life, at least for the higher classes, was the possibility to opt out of ordinary society to choose a life of contemplation—either as a hermit in the forest or as a member of some religious community. Such *āśramas* often became centres of education, since those who had chosen a spiritual vocation were considered to have acquired the wisdom which could attract people from elsewhere.

In some cases there developed a true alternative society. This appears to have happened at the Dieng plateau (*ḍihyang* in the inscriptions) in central Java. Situated at about 2000 metres above sea level on volcanic soil with many solfataras, it breathes an atmosphere of awe in which supernatural forces manifest themselves to mankind. More prosaically, this same atmosphere accounts for the serious weathering of buildings, statues and stone inscriptions. On the basis of important research by Krom, Poerbatjaraka and others, it may be concluded that an archaic form of Brahmanic Hinduism flourished on and around the plateau from early times to at least the eleventh century. There was a community of ascetics and monks with such titles as *pitāmaha*, literally 'grandfather', *guru hyang*, literally 'teacher of the gods' but apparently corresponding to the later term *dewaguru*, 'superior of a religious community'. Some other, more puzzling, titles such as *talahantan* also seem to denote priestly functions.[64]

The most surprising feature of religion as practised there is the worship of a god called Haricandana. This name seems unknown in India as that of a god, but the word itself occurs in the meaning of 'yellow sandalwood'. As Haricandana is often invoked at the beginning of the imprecation formulas in Old Javanese inscriptions, usually in conjunction with the sage Agastya, it has been suggested that Haricandana was an epithet of Agastya indicating an image of the great Rishi made of yellow sandalwood (an Agastya statue made of *black* sandalwood is actually mentioned in the Dinoyo inscription of 760) but this is less likely as we have evidence of a Haricandana cult.[65] Thus a three-yearly and a, probably less elaborate,

[63] J. G. de Casparis, *India and Maritime Southeast Asia: a lasting relationship*, Kuala Lumpur, 1983.
[64] N. J. Krom, 'Over het Çiwaïsme van Midden-Java', *Mededeelingen der Koninklijke Nederland-sche Akademie van Wetenschappen, Afdeling Letterkunde*, 58, serie B, no. 8 (1929).
[65] F. D. K. Bosch, 'De Sanskrit inscriptie op den steen van Dinaja (682 çaka)', TBG, 57 (1916); 'Het Lingga-Heiligdom van Dinaja', ibid., 64 (1924); J. G. de Casparis, 'Nogmaals de Sanskrit-inscriptie op den steen van Dinojo', ibid., 81 (1941).

yearly festival of Haricandana, for which villages had to supply rice and fruits, are mentioned in an inscription of 878. This cult was combined with that of Brahmā, for whom a 'pillar of rice' (*annaliṅga*) had to be prepared.[66] In this connection we also find the archaic Sanskrit term *makha* denoting a sacrifice. A reference to the worship of Haricandana is even found as late as the end of the fifteenth century in the *Tantu Panggĕlaran*, a late Old Javanese text in which brahmins are said to pay homage to this god. Here, as in other cases (such as those concerning Brahmā and Bhaṭāra Guru), we may have examples of ancient Austronesian deities under Indian names, but this remains no more than a plausible hypothesis as long as there is no clue as to the identity of such Austronesian deities.[67]

The imprecation formulas, regularly found at the end of Old Javanese charters, are interesting examples of the manner in which Hinduism was blended with ancient Austronesian beliefs. Sometimes a considerable number of deities are invoked, including the great gods of the Hindu pantheon: Brahmā, Viṣṇu and Mahādeva (or Maheśvara or Śiva, but always in that order), followed by sun and moon, the eight 'elements': earth, water, fire, wind, the sacrificer, ether, time (*kāla*) and death (*mṛtyu*). Subsequently we get a whole list of lower deities, not only the usual kinds (*gaṇa, bhūta, preta* etc.) but also day and night, as well as the two (later three) twilights, the four guardians of the sky, the mysterious *putradewatā* and *rāmadewatā* (may we compare the fifteenth-century reference to Lord Rāma?). The six Vināyakas, forms of Gaṇeśa or deities associated with Gaṇeśa,[68] also figure in these lists, which also includes the eight points of the compass plus below and above (*i sor i ruhur*). Even the goddess Durgā (always as *durggādewī*) occurs among these lower powers. As has been demonstrated by Hariani Santiko, these imprecation formulas mark the beginning of a development leading to the conception of Durgā as a horrific man-eating demon abiding in cemeteries.[69]

The most interesting item in these imprecations is the invocation addressed to the blessed deities (*dewatā prasiddha*) who 'protect the royal residence of the kings in the land of Mataram' (*mangrakṣa kaḍatwan śrī mahārāja ing bhūmi matarām*). This example is taken from the Sugihmanek inscription of King Dakṣa, dated 915—a time when the *kĕraton* was still in central Java. As to these 'blessed deities' there can be no doubt that the royal ancestors, the deified kings of Mataram, are meant, for the corresponding passage in the Mantyasih inscription of 907[70] lists the names and

---

[66] Conical shapes of boiled rice are still commonly used in Javanese *slamĕtan* ceremonies; cf. Clifford Geertz, *The Religion of Java*, London, 1960, 39f.; Pigeaud, *Java*, III. 118 and IV. 178.
[67] Haricandana is well known in India as the name of one of the trees in heaven; the authors have, however, not come across any example of this term indicating a divinity in Indian texts.
[68] For Ṣaḍwināyaka and other terms found in Old Javanese imprecations see Edi Sedyawati, 'Pengarcaan Gaṇeśa masa Keḍiri dan Siṅhasāri', Ph.D. thesis, Universitas Indonesia, 1985. An English edition of this important work is in preparation at the Koninklijk Instituut voor de Taal- Land- en Volkenkunde, Leiden, Netherlands.
[69] Hariani Santiko, 'Kedudukan bhaṭārī Durgā di Jawa pada abad X–XV Masehi', Ph.D. thesis, Universitas Indonesia, 1987, 146ff.: an equally important work of which no English edition is as yet available.
[70] W. F. Stutterheim, 'Een belangrijke inscriptie uit de Kedoe', TBG, 58 (1927), in particular 210.

titles of those preceding kings. As to the Sugihmanek inscription,[71] this text adds the puzzling words *umasuk i śarīra ning wang kabeḥ*, 'entering into the bodies of all people', just after the mention of the 'blessed deities'. Apparently the spirit of those former rulers was thought to pervade the minds of the people and lead them to protect the foundation. Protection was the supreme duty of kings, who were supposed to carry on their beneficial activity after their life on earth by pervading, as it were, the intentions of their subjects. The above passage also illustrates the idea of the deification of kings, on which more details will be given below.

Buddhist powers and concepts never figure in these imprecations; and Śaivism is not prominent. There is mention of Mahādeva or Maheśvara (two names of Śiva) and of Durgā (Durgādevī, at a lower level than would have been expected of Śiva's *śakti*), as well as of Nandīśvara and Mahākāla (two subordinate forms of Śiva acting as doorkeepers, *dwārapāla*). There is also an important reference to the saints of the Pāśupatas and related Śaivite sects in the term *pañcakuśika*, sometimes specified as Kuśika, Garga, Maitri, Kuruṣya and Patañjali.[72]

Some typically Austronesian deities or supernatural powers are a crocodile with the name of Si Pamunguan and another aquatic monster called Taṇḍang Luah, perhaps a river spirit for *luah* = river. The latter's name recalls that of Tandrun Luah, invoked at the beginning of the imprecations in the Śrīvijaya inscriptions of Kota Kapur, Karang Brahi, Tĕlaga Batu and Palang Pasĕmah.[73] This Tandrun Luah probably was a special patron deity of Śrīvijaya, perhaps associated with the river Musi. His unexpected reappearance in central Java more than two centuries later may be an example of inter-island borrowing of potent deities. The example occurs in the above-mentioned inscription of 907.[74] On account of its particular importance many more deities are mentioned than usual. There is a crocodile by the name of Manalu, and there are different snakes (*ulāsarpa*) and different fires (*ñāla* and *apuy*). All these terms and names are preceded by *sang hyang*, always indicating deities, animals and objects considered sacred. There are a sacred axe (*sang hyang wadung*), a sacred heart (*sang hyang tĕas*), presumably the centre of the foundation, and a sacred rice block (*sang hyang kulumpang*).

Some rivers were sacred, such as the Bengawan Solo (*sang hyang bhagawān*), as were some mountains. Thus, the fifteenth-century *Tantu Panggĕlaran* records the myth that the Mahāmeru or Sumeru, abode of the gods, was carried to Java and put down in the east of the island: the present Gunung Sĕmeru. The worship of a still active volcano in its neighbourhood, the Bromo, is attested in the tenth century, where it is considered the abode of god Brahmā, who became identified with fire in ancient Java. A much smaller mountain, the Pĕnanggungan, southwest of

---

[71] See Brandes and Krom, OJO, 30, B-27/28.

[72] First mentioned in the Mathurā inscription of Candra Gupta II (380 CE), published by D. R. Bhandarkar, *Epigraphia Indica* 21 (1921) 8f.; D. C. Sircar, *Select Inscriptions*, 2nd edn, Calcutta, 1965, I. 277–9; R. C. Agrawala, *Journal of the Historical Society of Baroda* 20 (1970) 355f.

[73] G. Cœdès, 'Les inscriptions malaises de Çrīvijaya', BEFEO, 30 (1930); for this term see line 12 on p. 40 and cf. p. 55.

[74] See Brandes and Krom, OJO, 30 line B-28/29.

Surabaya, was worshipped on account of its perfect shape: a central peak surrounded by four lower peaks approximately at the four points of the compass, the supposed shape of the mountain of the gods. Numerous smaller temples, mainly of the fifteenth century, have been discovered on its slopes.[75]

Most of these cults, though probably Austronesian, are in harmony with Brahmanic Hinduism. Worship of mountains as abodes of mighty gods is reflected in mythology: for instance, the Himalaya is the father of Pārvatī, Śiva's spouse. The supreme god himself is often described as 'Lord of the Mountain' (Girīndra or synonyms), and royal dynasties often pay homage to one particular mountain, such as the Rajput dynasties worshipping Mount Abu and the Eastern Gāṅgas of Orissa paying homage to Mount Gokarṇa, 'Cow's Ear'. As to the worship of rivers, not only the names of the Gaṅga (Ganges) and Yamunā (and the place of their confluence at Prayāga near Allahabad), but also those of the Kāvērī (the 'Southern Gaṅgā'), the Sarasvatī, Gomatī (Gumti) and others come to mind. Fire was worshipped in the form of the three sacrificial fires of the brahmins, of the god Agni etc., and snakes were worshipped as *nāgas*. Ancient Indian and Indonesian cults are intertwined to such a degree that it is often impossible to decide whether certain elements of religion in maritime Southeast Asia are Austronesian under an Indian name or Indian influenced by Austronesian tradition.

The development of the great religions, especially Śaivism and, to a lesser extent, Vaiṣṇavism and Buddhism, has to be considered against the background of the cults and ceremonies, as well as the ideas and beliefs, described in this section.

Śaivism and Vaiṣṇavism

The worship of Śiva, as well as the gods and divine symbols associated with Śiva, was the prevalent form of Hindu religion in Java before the sixteenth century. Sects worshipping Viṣṇu as the supreme deity are also mentioned but were less important. (Mahāyāna) Buddhism, on the other hand, strongly prevailed in Sumatra, the Malay peninsula and west Kalimantan. In Java it flourished mainly during the Śailendra period (c.750–850) and again, but by the side of Saivism, during the Singhasari-Majapahit period (c.1250–1450).

In the areas where Śaivism prevailed it was mainly centred on the royal courts from where, however, it radiated to secondary centres and to the countryside. Its influence on the agricultural communities was probably confined to those elements of Śaivism that were consistent with popular beliefs. Despite such limitations, the importance of Śaivism is considerable mainly because it flourished in those parts of maritime Southeast Asia that left most of the great monuments and pre-Muslim literature.

As to literature, not only the didactic texts mentioned at the beginning of this chapter but most of the Old Javanese literature is inspired or

---

[75] V. R. van Romondt, *Peninggalan-peninggalan Purbakala di Gunung Penanggungan*, Dinas Purbakala Republik Indonesia, Jakarta, 1951.

influenced by Śaivism. As to archaeology, numerous Śiva temples have been preserved and restored in central and eastern Java and in Bali. Statues of Śiva and associated deities, especially Durgā, Gaṇeśa and the so-called Guru, abound. Most Śiva images represent the god in his majestic Mahādeva form: four-armed with ascetic hairdress (jaṭāmakuṭa), third eye, characteristic emblems (trident, rosary, sacred thread in the form of a snake, etc.), royal attire and ornaments. Less frequently the god is represented in his demonic form of Kāla or Bhairava: nude, except for garlands of skulls and other horrific attributes, or else as a 'doorkeeper' (dvārapāla): guardian of the entrance to a temple (Nandīśvara, the god together with his mount, the bull, and Mahākāla, as the destructor of the world). In addition to these iconic forms, Śiva was also worshipped in the shape of his main symbol: the linga, originally a phallus but in a stylized representation as a column with a square base, a hexagonal middle part and roundish top, but with many variations. Other forms of Śiva, which were popular in South India, such as the dancing Naṭarāja and composite sculptures such as Somāskanda (Śiva together with his spouse Umā and Skanda, his little son, in between) are not attested in Java.

The typical Śiva temple has either a linga or a standing Śiva statue in its cella, to which the eastern entrance gives access through a small vestibule. On either side of the entrance there is a shallow niche for the above-mentioned guardian statues. Also in the three other main walls of the temple there are niches or, in the larger temples, secondary cellas. On the southern side is a standing figure of a bearded and corpulent deity, two-armed and soberly dressed, carrying a fly-whisk (cāmara) and a water bottle (kamaṇḍalu). At the corresponding place in the western wall there is a four-armed elephant-headed Gaṇeśa and, on the north, a Durgā, another form of Śiva's spouse, as mahiṣamardinī, 'slaying the buffalo-demon'. The goddess, standing on the back of the buffalo and brandishing many different weapons in her eight arms, is on the point of killing the demon while he tries to escape through the wound in the buffalo's neck.[76]

These details are of great interest, especially because this combination of deities is typical of ancient Java, although the individual images correspond to similar representations in India, except for the image in the southern niche. In South Indian temples this niche is usually occupied by a seated figure of Śiva Dakṣiṇāmūrti, the 'Supreme Guru', but this figure wears a conical crown (kirīṭa), is four-armed, carrying various attributes, and is richly decorated. In Java this deity is replaced by the sober figure of a teacher, whose Śaiva association is confined to the presence of a trident. On the analogy with the Dakṣiṇāmūrti, this statue was usually defined as that of the Divine Teacher (Bhaṭāra Guru), but, following R. Ng. Poerbatjaraka,[77] more recent researchers interpret it as a representation of the sage Agastya. It may seem strange that a ṛṣi, however wise and powerful he may have been, should be represented on a par with deities like Durgā and Gaṇeśa, but it is known that Agastya, for whom a temple and an image were made in east Java in 760,[78] enjoyed special veneration in Java.

[76] The iconography of Gaṇeśa and Durgā is discussed in the works mentioned in notes 68 and 69 above. No similar study of Agastya (or Bhaṭāra Guru) is available.
[77] Agastya in den Archipel, Leiden, 1926.

Whichever is the correct interpretation, there is no doubt that the Guru was one of the most popular representations in ancient Java. This may well reflect the particular awe felt for a teacher in Java till recent times.

The two other deities, Durgā and Gaṇeśa, were also very popular, as appears from the comparatively very large number of statues that have come down to us. It is curious that the goddess Durgā, Śiva's spouse, is most often represented in the bellicose stance described above, whereas Gaṇeśa, though carrying weapons, is rather benevolent. As to the group of four deities: Śiva 'surrounded' by the Guru, Gaṇeśa and Durgā, it has been suggested that it symbolizes, on a divine level, the principal actors on the stage of the world: the king, his spiritual guide, his prime minister and his queen.[79] The view of the world as a stage is well-known in Indonesia. It is, for instance, implied in the first verse of the poem *Arjunavivāha* (Arjuna's Wedding) and in the performances of the Javanese shadow theatre (*wayang kulit*).[80]

In addition to belonging to this group of four deities, Durgā and Gaṇeśa also enjoyed worship by themselves. Whereas Durgā became more and more closely associated with cemeteries. Gaṇeśa was worshipped for his ability to move huge obstacles with his boundless force. Gaṇeśa statues were therefore placed at dangerous spots, such as river crossings or mountain passes. We have also at least one instance of a Gaṇeśa image placed by the side of a highway frequented by robbers, as appears from the inscription, dated 891, written on its back.[81] In addition, Gaṇeśa is regularly invoked at the beginning of manuscripts of literary works.

In India Śiva was associated with Brahmā and Viṣṇu in a Hindu Trinity, the Trimūrti, but this term is not attested in Old Javanese literature. The concept was well known,[82] but received little attention. Both Brahmā and Viṣṇu were held in great veneration. Numerous statues of the four-headed Brahmā have come down to us, comparatively many more than in India or in mainland Southeast Asia. A particular feature of Brahmā in ancient Java is the god's association with fire, including the subterranean fire revealing itself through the active volcanoes.[83] His consort Sarasvatī and his mount

---

[78] See note 38 above. The Dinoyo inscription of 760 CE deals with a temple and image of Agastya (actually the replacement by an image of black stone of an earlier sandalwood (*candana*) image.

[79] W. F. Stutterheim, 'De dateering van eenige Oostjavaansche beeldengroepen', TBG, 66 (1936).

[80] J. Zoetmulder, *Kalangwan*, The Hague, 1974, 241f.

[81] OJO XIX and XX; H. Bh. Sarkar, *Corpus of Inscriptions of Java*, I, Calcutta, 1971, nos. LVI and LVII, in particular the latter, lines 10–11. The first part of the text is written on an ordinary type of stone, the second on the back of a Gaṇeśa image. The most interesting passage in this context is: *makaphalā karakṣāna nikanang hawān gĕng*, 'hopefully resulting in the protection of the highway'.

[82] It is, for instance, clearly reflected in the conception of the Loro Jonggrang complex at Prambanan, where the three main temples are devoted to Śiva, Brahmā and Viṣṇu, each with a smaller temple devoted to the cult of their respective mounts (Nandi, Haṃsa and Garuḍa). It should, however, be noted that the central and clearly predominant temple is devoted to Śiva, not to Brahmā. Actually, the worship of 'compound' deities such as Hari-hara or Ardhanārīśvara has never been popular in Indonesia—in contrast to ancient Cambodia where Hari-hara statues are very common.

[83] J. G. de Casparis, 'Oorkonde uit het Singosarische (midden 14e eeuw A.D.)', *Inscr. Ned.-Indië* I (1940). The inscription deals with regulations concerning the worship of the god Brahmā in close association with the volcano Gunung Bromo.

Haṃsa (the Goose) are rarely represented, although a few images show the god seated on this big bird.

The numerous Viṣṇu images raise, however, a different issue. From several sources it is known that there existed in Java a relatively small, but influential, Vaiṣṇava community. The *Nāgarakĕrtāgama*, after devoting two stanzas to the Śaivas, five to the Buddhists and four to the Rĕsis community of ascetics, continues with one verse, half of which gives the names of eight Vaiṣṇava (*Vaṅgśa Viṣṇu*) foundations (78–5). Compared with the thirty-eight Śaiva institutions this is a small number, but the devotees of Viṣṇu may have had considerable influence, especially in the twelfth century, when poetical works (*kĕkawin*) extolling Viṣṇu or one of his incarnations were composed (*Kṛṣṇāyaṇa, Hariwangśa, Bhomakāwya*, and others). In addition, many of the kings of that period were praised as 'partial incarnations' (*angśāwatāra*) of that god. King Jayanagara of Majapahit (r. 1309–21) is said 'to have returned home to Hari's (Viṣṇu's) estate' (*Nāg.* 48–3a) and was worshipped as a Viṣṇu image (*Nāg.* 48–3c).[84]

Statues of the god, easily identifiable by his main emblems, the wheel (*cakra*) and the conch (*śaṅkha*), were quite common in Java. As a divine prototype of kings, especially in his incarnations as Kṛṣṇa and Rāma, his cult was probably closely associated with the royal courts. Viṣṇu's spouse, Lakṣmī or Śrī, not only symbolized royal sovereignty but especially became a rice goddess whose activity promoted the fertility of the ricefields. As such she is still worshipped, in particular in west Java under the name Ni Pohaci Sangyang Sri.[85]

More even than the goddess, Viṣṇu's mount, the heavenly bird Garuḍa, who rescued the immortality drink (*amĕrta*) and devoured dangerous snakes, was quite popular. Either as a bird or, more often, partly anthropomorphic, he is represented not only as Viṣṇu's mount but also by himself. An east Javanese fourteenth-century temple, Caṇḍi Kĕdaton, even has a series of reliefs devoted to the story of Garuḍa (the *Garuḍeya*).[86] In addition, Garuḍa is prominently represented in the coat of arms of the Republic of Indonesia and in the name of its national airline.

Apart from striking differences in emphasis, the worship of Śiva and associated deities shows few significant deviations from Indian tradition. On the other hand, the conceptions lying at the basis of early Indonesian art and architecture were probably quite different. As in India, a temple does not stand by itself but forms part of a group or complex. In Indonesia such complexes may be very large, comprising hundreds of separate buildings. This suggests that the deity to whom the temple complex as a whole is dedicated was conceived of as a heavenly king ruling the cosmos

[84] N. Krom, *Hindoe-Javaansche Geschiedenis*, 2nd edn, The Hague, 1931, 170–5. For the poetical works under discussion see J. Zoetmulder, *Kalangwan*, 283–324. For the statues of King Kĕrtanagara see Pigeaud, *Java*, IV. 141: *arcā* is translated by 'statue' and *pratimā* by 'statuette'. In the *Nāgarakĕrtāgama*, Jayanagara (1309–21) is the only *king* identified with Viṣṇu, but among the princes there were others, for instance Hayam Wuruk's brother-in-law Prince of Wĕngkĕr, who was deified as Viṣṇu.

[85] K. A. H. Hidding, *Nji Pohatji Sangjang Sri*, Leiden, 1929; V. Sukanda Tessier, 'Le triomphe de Srī en pays soundanais', Publications de l'EFEO, 101 (1977).

[86] N. Krom, *Inleiding tot de Hindoe-Javaansche Kunst*, 2nd edn, 1923, II. 223–9; Stutterheim, *Cultuurgeschiedenis van Java in Beeld*, 'Weltevreden', 1926, figs 137–42.

as an earthly king ruled his kingdom (in theory, 'the earth'). In general, the kingdom was conceived of as a *maṇḍala*,[87] consisting of concentric circles with the king as its centre. The innermost circle was reserved for the king and his immediate associates; the middle circle was occupied by dependants and officials considered subordinates of the centre, while the outer part was occupied by (semi-) independent rulers who were obliged to pay homage to the (principal) king. In addition there was a vertical stratification with the king at the apex of a stepped pyramid: the different, hierarchically ordered, groups comprising the society of those times.

In accordance with these ideas, the great Śaiva complex of Roro (Loro) Jonggrang (about twenty-five kilometres east of Yogyakarta) consists of three divisions, each surrounded by its own wall with gateways. In the centre stands the majestic tower-like temple of Śiva; on either side, to the north and the south, are the somewhat lower temples of Viṣṇu and Brahmā. Opposite these main temples there are much smaller temples dedicated to the mounts of the three gods. Finally there are small structures near the gateways giving access to the middle division. The latter consists of about a hundred and fifty small temples arranged in three rows, which were apparently shrines for minor deities. These are again surrounded by a wall enclosing the present site of the monument. There still are, however, traces of a third enclosure, not parallel with the other two. As no remains of buildings have been discovered in the outer section, it is likely that this area was used for dwellings of priests and other temple personnel, schools with dormitories, and perhaps guesthouses.

As to the significance of the many small temples of the middle area, something more may be concluded by analogy with the contemporary Buddhist complex of Plaosan-Lor. There, many of the small temples and stupas surrounding the main building bear small inscriptions with the word *anumoda* followed by a title and name, indicating that the structure was a pious contribution by the authority mentioned there. This suggests that officials or local chiefs in different parts of the kingdom were asked or ordered to contribute to the royal foundation, thus attesting both their piety and their loyalty. Presumably the same applies to Roro Jonggrang, where indeed a few titles, written in black or red paint, have remained vaguely visible. It was probably, as already suggested by Krom,[88] a state temple which mirrored the relationships within the kingdom.

Roro Jonggrang marks a culmination which was followed by more than three centuries without major temple foundations in Java. It has already been mentioned that Buddhism strongly predominated in Sumatra and the Malay peninsula, but there are important exceptions. Thus, the three statues of P'ra Narai (Takuapa, southern Thailand)[89] are Śaiva and so are

---

[87] For the *maṇḍala* concept see the *Arthaśāstra*, ed. R. P. Kangle, Bombay, 1963, 164–7 (text), 364–71 (translation); U. N. Ghoshal, *A History of Political Ideas*, OUP, 1959, 91–9; O. W. Wolters, *History, Culture, and Region in Southeast Asian Perspectives*, Singapore, 1982.

[88] *Hindoe-Javaansche Geschiedenis*, 172; de Casparis, *Prasasti Indonesia*, II (1956) 307ff.; 'Short Inscriptions from Tjandi Plaosan-Lor', *Berita Dinas Purbakala*, no. 4 (1958), especially plate I.

[89] Alastair Lamb, 'Miscellaneous papers on Early Hindu and Buddhist Settlements in Northern Malaya and Southern Thailand', FMJ, N.S. VI (1961); Stanley J. O'Connor, *Hindu Gods of Peninsular Thailand*, Artibus Asiae, Supplementum 28, Ascona, 1972, 52–88 and figs 28–31; M. C. Subhadradis Diskul, *The Art of Śrīvijaya*, Paris, UNESCO, 1980, 23f.

the numerous sites of the Bujang valley, Kedah, Malaysia. In the absence
of iconographic and epigraphic data, the buildings (actually only foundations as the superstructures must have been of perishable materials) are
awkward to date, but stray finds of pottery may point to the end of the
eleventh century or somewhat later.[90]

From the middle of the thirteenth century Śaivism again flourished, as
appears from the numerous sites in east Java and Bali, which can be dated
between c.1250 and 1450. Two sites are of particular importance on
account of their size and beauty: Singhasari and Panataran. The tower
temple (prāsāda) at Singhasari is especially remarkable for its marvellous
sculptures representing gods of the Śaiva pantheon. In addition to Śiva in
his majestic four-armed Maheśvara form, there are statutes of Durgā (as
nearly always in Indonesia, as mahiṣamardinī, 'killing the buffalo-demon'),
of Gaṇeśa and of Guru (or Agastya): the customary Śaiva pantheon. In
addition, however, we find a demonic Bhairava with the inscription
cakracakra as well as statues of Viṣṇu and Brahmā. From the same, or a
closely associated, site a famous image of Prajñāpāramitā, 'Perfect Wisdom',
represented as a seated, two-armed goddess carrying a manuscript,[91] has
been recovered, thus pointing to a close association between Śaivism and
Buddhism.

The great temple complex of Panataran near Blitar, east Java, belongs
mainly to the fourteenth century, the age of Majapahit, during which it
was probably a state sanctuary. Dedicated to Śiva, Lord of the Mountain,
it consists of three courtyards with the main entrance gate on the west and
the main temple in the eastern courtyard. Such a composition differs
fundamentally from those of the central Javanese temple compounds such
as Roro Jonggrang. There the secondary structures are all arranged in rows
around the principal building. The arrangement as seen at Panataran, on
the other hand, reminds one of that of the kraton, the Javanese royal
residence. Thus in the present Yogyakarta kraton one may enter through
the eastern gate and, crossing a number of courts, one would (if it were
permitted) arrive at the king's private quarters. The resemblance is not
fortuitous, for the Kingdom of Heaven is an idealized projection of the
kingdom on earth. It is, however, important to note that such compounds
differ completely from the Indian conception of the Mahāmeru.[92]

As noted earlier, Panataran is devoted to Śiva as Lord of the Moun-
tain(s), in this case especially the Kĕlud. As one of Java's most active
volcanoes it was, like the Bromo, an object of veneration. It seems, indeed,
as though the worship of mountains as abodes of divine power, though
Austronesian in origin, became more common or explicit in the fourteenth

[90] Lamb, 'Misc. Papers', 79–81.
[91] For the Durgā see Stutterheim, Cultuurgeschiedenis, 72, fig. 10. The Prajñāpāramitā of
Singosari is illustrated in all works on Indonesian art, e.g. Karl With, Java, Brahmanische,
Buddhistische und eigenlebige Architectur und Plastik auf Java, Hagen, 1920, plates 138–9.
[92] H. J. J. Winter, 'Science', in A. L. Basham, ed., A Cultural History of India, Oxford, 1975; P. S.
Rawson, 'Early Art and Architecture', ibid., 204. 'Each temple is conceived, as the Buddhist
stūpa was, as "the axis of the world", symbolically transformed into the mythical Mount
Meru, around which are slung, like garlands, the heavens and the earth.' The Buddhist
system of cosmology, as followed in Indonesia, it seems, is set out in detail in such texts as
the Abhidharmakośa, book III.

and fifteenth centuries. Thus, the numerous little sanctuaries discovered on the slopes of the Penanggungan in east Java have already been mentioned, and two large sites of mainly the fifteenth century have been discovered on the slopes of the Lawu, viz. Sukuh and Cĕta. At Sukuh the cult of the linga of Śiva, though always characteristic of Śaivism, was more pronounced than elsewhere. It appears, however, that this cult was primarily associated not with fertility but with the liberation of the soul.

This cult was linked with that of Bhīma, one of the five Pāṇḍava heroes of the *Mahābhārata*, known for his enormous force. There are a number of Bhīma statues from Sukuh and contemporary sites, and also literary works in which Bhīma is represented as a saviour who, like Avalokiteśvara in Buddhism, even goes to hell to redeem sinners. Some late Old Javanese texts, such as the *Nawaruci*, *Dewaruci*, and *Bimasuci*, assign an important role to Bhīma. These texts have a strong mystical flavour. The Bhīma tradition, linked with speculation about death and immortality, has persisted in Bali also in the shadow theatre (*Bhimaswarga*).[93] Another late text, the *Tantu Panggĕlaran*, composed about 1500, describes numerous hermitages and communities of ascetics especially in the mountain areas.[94] When parts of the lowlands had already been Islamized, Brahmanic culture still survived in the mountainous areas of eastern Java for a considerable time.

Buddhism

Buddhism, like Islam and Christianity, but in contrast to Austronesian beliefs, Brahmanism and Śaivism, is a world religion, which can be studied from numerous manuals. This section is therefore mainly confined to aspects which received particular emphasis in maritime Southeast Asia, but also covers the expansion of Buddhism and its place in the history and culture of the area.

The Buddhist doctrines are based on the revelation by Lord Buddha of the Four Noble Truths—the awareness that worldly existence is a form of suffering, that the causes of suffering can be determined, that therefore suffering can be eliminated, and that, finally, there is a Path leading to that end. However, the actual Buddhist doctrines reflect a rational approach. This includes a theory of causation which traces the miseries of existence back to ignorance (*pratītyasamutpāda*),[95] following which all things are linked in a web of cause-and-effect relations containing twelve categories. The suffering that forms part of life stems from ignorance of the true nature of things. Beings are condemned by ignorance to a constant round of rebirth in conditions governed by *karma(n)*—the law by which all morally qualified acts, good or evil, necessarily carry their fruits, sometimes in this life, more often in the next. This belief, closely interwoven with the theory of transmigration of the soul (or of its equivalent) pervades

---

[93] M. Prijohoetomo, *Nawaruci*, Groningen-'Batavia', 1934, 1–139; *Bhīmasuci*, ibid., 140–213; R. Ng. Poerbatjaraka, 'Dewa-Roetji', *Djawa*, XX (1940); H. I. R. Hinzler, *The Bima Swarga in Balinese wayang* in VKI, 90, The Hague, 1981.

[94] Th. G. Th. Pigeaud, *De Tantu Panggĕlaran*, The Hague, 1924.

[95] This twelvefold chain of causes and effects was well-known all over the Buddhist world. In Java it has been found inscribed on a set of gold plates, together with an elaborate commentary; see de Casparis, *Prasasti Indonesia*, II (1956) no. III; Buchari, *Prasasti Koleksi Museum National*, Jakarta, 1985–6, 224–35.

all Indian thought. In the older form of Buddhism, the doctrine of the Elders (Theravāda), the supreme ideal of the pious Buddhist is to achieve a complete cessation of the circle of rebirths to attain *nirvāṇa*. This form of Buddhism is the norm in most of mainland Southeast Asia, as we have seen.

In maritime Southeast Asia, however, there is hardly any evidence of Theravāda, but another form of Buddhism called Mahāyāna (the 'Great Vehicle') emphasizes the gradual rise to the perfection of Buddha-hood through a long succession of existences as a Bodhisattva: a being, not necessarily human, striving for Buddha-hood and following a way of life which may ultimately lead to that end. Some Bodhisattvas, thought to abide on the verge of Buddha-hood, received special veneration, as did the ever-increasing number of Buddhas. Thus a new pantheon developed: it consisted of different kinds of Buddhas, in iconography distinguishable by the position of their hands; many different Bodhisattvas, each recognizable by particular emblems; and their female counterparts (Tārā). Even Hindu gods were incorporated into Mahāyāna, though at a lower stage than the Buddhist deities.

As to the influence of Buddhism in maritime Southeast Asia we have to distinguish between the western part of the area (Sumatra, western Malaysia and west Borneo) and its eastern part (Java, Nusa Tenggara and east Borneo). Whereas Buddhism prevailed in most of its western part until the coming of Islam, it flourished in the eastern zone mainly during certain periods. In Java these are the Śailendra period (c.750–850) and the Singhasari-Majapahit period (especially c.1250–1400). During the intervening period Buddhism continued to have followers, but remained somewhat in the background.

In Java Buddhism was strongly patronized by the Śailendra kings (c.775–860), as reflected in art and architecture. The archaeological sources, which include also a number of inscriptions, give us a fair idea of Buddhism as professed during that period.

The greatest of all Buddhist monuments in the region, Borobudur in central Java, is often described as a gigantic stupa. But, although there are numerous stupas on terraces, which recall the *maluwa* and *pesāwa* of the Sri Lankan stupas,[96] Borobudur is different in that the galleries and terraces predominate, whereas the main stupa functions as a kind of crown. A more satisfactory interpretation is that of a *stūpa-prāsāda*, a term occurring in the *Sang Hyang Kamahāyānikan*. The second part of the compound indicates a building consisting of several storeys or terraces. Borobudur has also, but less successfully, been described as a Tantric *maṇḍala*: a (magical) circle or closed sacred area within which certain rites could be carried out. Although Borobudur may well have been *used* as a huge *maṇḍala*, it is unlikely that this was the intention of its creator(s), for clearly Tantric features are not apparent in Borobudur. Others have seen the monument as a monumental encyclopaedia of Buddhism, a view based on the illustration of numerous types of buildings, including palaces and stupas, many kinds of ships, trees, animals, crowns, etc. Its reliefs depict

[96] R. Silva, *Religious Architecture in Early and Medieval Sri Lanka*, Meppel, 1987, 19–26.

basic Mahāyāna texts with the help of which a keen student could receive excellent instruction under the guidance of a teacher.[97]

On more than one occasion, a name occurring in two inscriptions of 842, Bhūmisaṃbhāra, has been identified with Borobuḍur and it has been concluded from its description as a *kamūlān*, 'place of origin', that the monument marks the 'cradle' of the dynasty of the Śailendras ('Lords of the Mountain'). In this manner the dynasty would emphasize both its piety and its authority. Such an interpretation does not rule out the likelihood that Borobuḍur was also used as an encyclopaedia of Buddhism or, a few centuries later, as a Tantric *maṇḍala*.[98]

The conception of the other two great Buddhist monuments of central Java, Caṇḍi Sewu and Plaosan,[99] is quite different. Caṇḍi Sewu ('A Thousand Temples') at Prambanan, about thirty kilometres east of Yogyakarta, is a vast complex consisting of one large temple in the middle, surrounded by four rows of small temples, about 250 in all. It reflects the conception of a vast Buddhist pantheon with Buddhas, Bodhisattvas and other superior beings, each assigned to its proper place in the sacred hierarchy. Its building may have started in or shortly before 782 and must have continued till well into the ninth century.

The northern complex of Caṇḍi Plaosan, one kilometre distant from Sewu, also comprises numerous structures, but there are important differences. At the centre there are two large, two-storey buildings separated by a wall, with a similar wall separating both from three rows of small temples and stupas. The two main buildings were built at the expense of the king and queen respectively; whereas many of the small structures carry short inscriptions, each indicating the name and title of the dignitary or official who contributed to its foundation.

Like Borobuḍur, these buildings are all inspired by Mahāyāna with strong emphasis on the worship of Bodhisattvas, Tārās, and some Hindu gods such as Kubera, Guardian of the North and associated with wealth.

[97] This is not the right place to discuss the manifold problems of the interpretation of Borobudur—problems which are commensurate with the size and richness of the monument. Actually, most of the interpretations that have been proposed long ago are clearly out of date (though still repeated in some modern publications). The best works at present available are Soekmono, *Chandi Borobudur. A Monument of Mankind*, Amsterdam and Paris: UNESCO, 1976; Jacques Dumarçay, *Borobuḍur*, Kuala Lumpur, 1978; and Jan J. Boeles, *The secret of Borobudur*, Bangkok, 1985.

[98] De Casparis, *Prasasti Indonesia*, 1950, 134–92; De Casparis 'The Dual Nature of Borobuḍur', in Luis Gomez, and Hiram W. Woodward, eds, *Borobudur, History and Significance of a Monument*, Ann Arbor, 1980. As to its interpretation as a Tantric *maṇḍala*, based partly on a passage in the *Nāgarakĕrtāgama*, where Budur (*sic*) is mentioned in a list of buildings of the Vajradhara sect (canto 77, verse 3), as well as on a passage in the *Sang Hyang Kamahāyānikan* (see the bibliographic essay for this chapter), Stutterheim was probably the first to propose the interpretation of Borobudur as the Tantric *maṇḍala*, i.e. primarily an object of meditation. The idea of Borobuḍur being a kind of Encyclopaedia of Buddhism was first proposed by Siwaramamurti. Although both interpretations are correct as Borobuḍur has probably been used as a maṇḍala and as an encyclopaedia providing information on many topics (not only on Buddhism), it is unlikely that either was the original purpose in the mind(s) of its creator(s).

[99] Jacques Dumarçay, *Candi Sewu et l'architecture bouddhique du centre de Java*, Paris, EFEO, 1981; Indonesian edition under the title *Candi Sewu dan Arsitektur Bangunan Agama Buda di Jawa Tengah*, Pusat Penelitian Arkeologi Nasional, Depdikbud, 1986; De Casparis, 'Short Inscriptions from Tjandi Plaosan-Lor', *Berita Dinas Purabakala*, no. 4 (1958).

The Śailendras were outward-looking and in regular contact with other Buddhist kingdoms. Thus, an inscription of 782 mentions a monk from Gauḍa, present (northern) Bangladesh, who consecrated a Mañjuśrī image at or near Caṇḍi Sewu. Ten years later learned monks from Sri Lanka inaugurated a replica of the 'Abhayagiri of the Sinhalese monks', while teachers from Gurjaradeśa, modern Gujerat, took part in the consecration of the main building of Caṇḍi Plaosan. An inscription from Nālandā in Bihar (India) deals with a monastery built there by order of the Śailendra king, presumably on behalf of Indonesian students and pilgrims staying at or visiting Nālandā, one of the greatest centres of Buddhist learning at that time.

At the time of the Nālandā foundation (c. 860) the Śailendras were no longer reigning in Java but had moved to Śrīvijaya in southern Sumatra. Their successors in Java, though by no means hostile to Buddhism, did not patronize it. We have to wait till the second half of the thirteenth century before we witness a revival of Javanese Buddhism.

In Sumatra, on the other hand, Buddhism continued to flourish under the patronage of the kings of Śrīvijaya, but left few great monuments. Sumatra is not so poor in monuments as has sometimes been thought, but they bear no comparison with those of Java, either in number or in splendour. This has been attributed to the mercantile spirit of the empire, but there were probably other factors involved. As the soil of southern Sumatra is generally poor, the country did not produce the dense agricultural population with its reserve of labour necessary for the construction of great monuments. This same Śrīvijaya sponsored, however, great monuments in countries as far away as India and China. Thus, at the turn of the millennium the king of Śrīvijaya had a large monastery constructed on the east coast of South India, as well as a temple in Canton.[1]

In the thirteenth and fourteenth centuries Buddhism again flourished not only in Sumatra but also in Java. King Kĕrtanagara of Singhasari (r. 1268–92) was known, at least after his death, as Śiva-Buddha, but neither his inscriptions nor the long *Nāgarakĕrtāgama* passage dealing with his reign show unambiguous evidence of Śaivism. Both are imbued with the spirit of Tantric Buddhism, in particular Vajrayāna, a sect which attributes superhuman power to the vajra, mentioned earlier. Different rituals in which this symbol played an important part were performed in order to shorten the otherwise long road towards Buddha-hood and Nirvāṇa. The nature of these ceremonies, which are only alluded to in our texts, is difficult to determine since the most important text mentioned in this connexion, the *Subhūtitantra*, has not yet been identified. A late source, the Old Javanese *Pararaton*, attributes to Kĕrtanagara the performance of rituals involving the use of alcoholic drinks and other excesses, but there is no contemporary evidence to prove that such rituals were actually carried out.[2]

[1] G. Cœdès, *The Indianized States of Southeast Asia*, ed. Walter F. Vella, trans. Susan Brown Cowing, Honolulu, 1968, 141f.

[2] ibid., 198f.; but see also *Nāg.* XLIII-1 to 5 with Pigeaud's discussion of these difficult verses in *Java*, IV. 128–34. Cf. also the older interpretations proposed by J. L. Moens, 'Het Buddhisme op Java in zijn laatste bloeiperiode', TBG, 44 (1924), and P. H. Pott, *Yoga and Yantra*, The Hague, 1966, 124f. and 130f.

Buddhism remained important throughout the fourteenth century, as reflected in art and literature. Some of the most important texts composed in that period are Buddhist in character,[3] but the clearest evidence is archaeological. A number of the most important temples are Buddhist. Foremost among these is Caṇḍi Jago (or Tumpang) near present Malang, east Java. Its Buddhist character is clearly reflected not in its architecture or narrative reliefs, but in its statuary, which represents a Buddhist Tantric pantheon. These splendid images can now be studied in different museums. They are carved in a soft style and carry inscriptions in Nāgarī script of a type current in northeastern India, in particular Orissa, in this period. This may also be the strongest indication of an influx from India of new ideas and practices into Buddhism, although Buddhism in India was in serious decline at that time. This was not, however, the case with the entire subcontinent, for Mahāyāna continued to flourish in some areas, in particular coastal Orissa (Ratnagiri, Udayagiri and Lalitagiri). A possible relationship between this region and east Java has never been adequately studied, but it seems likely. From the end of the fourteenth century, however, there are very few, if any, Buddhist remains and this religion seems to have faded away even before the Islamization of Java.

In Sumatra, the kingdom of Śrīvijaya, which had patronized Buddhism for six centuries, declined in the thirteenth century but was succeeded by Malāyu, which had its centre in present Jambi but moved to the west coast by the beginning of the fourteenth century. Unlike Śrīvijaya, Malāyu maintained close relations with Java. In 1284 King Kĕrtanagara sent a curious composite statue, consisting of copies of statues of Caṇḍi Jago in east Java, to the king of Malāyu. It was escorted by a high delegation and received by the Malāyu authorities with great pomp. These details are recorded in the Old Malay inscription carved on the back of the statue.[4]

Sixty years later it changed place again, this time to west Sumatra by order of one of the most fascinating figures on the politico-religious scene of the fourteenth century: King Ādityavarman (r. c. 1347–79). Possibly of partly Javanese descent, he spent his early career in Majapahit but returned to Sumatra before 1347. There he issued a large number of inscriptions in Sanskrit and Old Malay, written in a characteristic local script, and also one in Tamil. These texts are difficult to understand owing to the use of curious ungrammatical forms of Sanskrit and of esoteric Tantric terminology, the precise meaning of which is still imperfectly known. As to the type of Tantrism followed by Ādityavarman there is a statement that the king was 'always concentrated on Hevajra', a demonic form of the Jina Akṣobhya,[5] whose worship involved bloody and erotic rituals, the latter in conjunction with female partners. Eating and drinking, presumably of palm wine, are also mentioned, but it is doubtful whether such excesses regularly took place. In any case, they did not prevent

[3] Such as the *Nāgarakĕrtāgama*, the *Sutasoma* and the *Kuñjarakarna*. For these texts see P. J. Zoetmulder, *Kalangwan. A Survey of Old Javanese Literature*, The Hague, 1974.

[4] N. J. Krom, 'Een Sumatraansche Inscriptie van koning Kṛtanagara', *Versl. Med. Kon. Ak. Wet.*, Afd. Lett. 5, (1916).

[5] Satyawati Suleiman, 'The Archaeology and History of West Sumatra', *Berita Pusat Penelitian Purbakala dan Peninggalan Nasional*, 12 (1977). She correctly read *hewajra* in the last line of one of the Suroaso inscriptions (p. 11).

Ādityavarman from reigning for at least thirty-two years and becoming the spiritual father of the kingdom of Minangkabau. It is curious that not a single temple built by Ādityavarman has hitherto come to light, and only very few images. One of these few is, however, the largest statue discovered in Indonesia: a huge two-armed, horrific Bhairava,[6] a demonic form of Śiva represented nude and brandishing a knife, while standing on a corpse above a pedestal decorated with human skulls.

Finally, attention is called to the important site of Padang Lawas in south Tapanuli. Ruins of at least sixteen brick temples and stupas were found in this arid plain, probably part of the ancient kingdom of Panai, with its capital situated on the river of that name. Originally a dependency of Śrīvijaya, it made itself independent in or before the thirteenth century. Apart from an important set of Buddhist bronzes, dated 1039, most other antiquities seem to belong to the thirteenth century. The brick temples are remarkable for the reliefs depicting dancing Yakṣas and other demons.[7]

Nothing more is heard of Buddhism after Ādityavarman. It is unlikely that the esoteric and demonic form of Buddhism would have appealed to the population as a whole, unlike Theravāda on the mainland which was, and is, a truly popular religion. Already half a century before Ādityavarman a Muslim kingdom had been established at Pasai on the northeast coast of Sumatra. Its first ruler Malik al-Salih died in 1297. Other Muslim kingdoms and sultanates arose in ports of eastern Sumatra during the fifteenth century.

TWO SPECIAL PROBLEMS

Before discussing early Islam in Southeast Asia, it is proper to consider two special problems which have given rise to much discussion. They concern the generally held views that kings were regarded as gods and that there was a considerable degree of religious syncretism. Both views are open to serious doubt.

Historians of ancient India have given much thought to the problem of the kings' divinity. As kingship in Southeast Asia was strongly influenced by Indian ideas, some points have to be made.

First of all it should be emphasized that pre-partition India is a vast subcontinent with a written history that can be traced back to the second millennium BC. Generalizations are therefore often misleading.

Second, one has to be clear about the concept of divinity. In Christianity and Islam, divinity implies perfection and the absolute. Indian thought recognizes different stages or degrees of divinity, whereas the absolute— designated by terms such as *mokṣa*, *nirvāṇa*, *sac-cid-ānanda* according to various creeds—is a state far beyond the mere divine. It is true that kings were generally addressed as *deva*, usually translated as 'god', but this was

---

[6] F. M. Schnitger, *The Archaeology of Hindoo Sumatra*, Leiden, 1937, plates XIII–XVI. The height of the statue is 4.41 m!

[7] Rumbi Mulia, 'The ancient kingdom of Panai and the ruins of Padang Lawas', *Berita Pusat Penelitian Arkeologi Nasional*, 14 (1980).

a formality which would not necessarily imply a belief in the king's divinity. Although some passages in the texts are ambiguous, there is now a large measure of consensus among scholars to the effect that kings were not, as a rule, considered divine, but there were probably exceptions in particular periods or regions, or in the minds of some of the king's subjects.

Third, even if kings were considered to some extent divine, they would have shared this 'divinity' with many other creatures, including some priests and cows, or even snakes and trees.

Finally, there are many passages in texts and inscriptions in which kings are compared with deities in a manner suggesting a close relationship, if not identity, with deities. Thus, as early as the fourth century CE King Samudra Gupta is described as the equal of the Lokapālas (*Dhanada-Varuṇendrāntaka-sama*, 'the equal of Kubera, Varuna, Indra and Yama').[8] Such phrases, which are confined to court poets intent on bestowing exaggerated praise on their patrons, carry little weight as arguments in favour of the king's divinity. On balance it may therefore be concluded that kings were not considered divine in any real sense in ancient India.[9]

By and large, the same applies to Southeast Asia, but the matter is far more complicated. Not surprisingly, as far as the deification of rulers is concerned, there are considerable differences among individual areas of the region, partly due to differences in official religions. Thus, the very idea of deification of kings is contrary to the monotheism of Islam. This is not the case with Theravāda Buddhism, but there the position of the gods (*deva*) is a modest one: they lead a happy life but, although they live very long, they are not immortal. In addition, their world is quite separated from ours. This would not have encouraged kings to seek identification with gods. The same applies to Mahāyāna, but there the multitude of Buddhas and Bodhisattvas provides an opportunity for ambitious rulers to claim the status of one of those superior beings. Their superiority was, however, mainly confined to wisdom and charity rather than to superhuman power. As we shall see, however, these concepts of Mahāyāna may have significant implications for some Buddhist kings. 'Hinduism', on the other hand, in particular Śaivism, provided the kings with opportunities to receive the kind of worship reserved to gods during, or more often after, their life on earth. The survey which follows will therefore mainly be confined to Mahāyāna and Śaivism. Because of the differences among various areas it seems necessary to separate mainland and maritime Southeast Asia.

In mainland Southeast Asia, there was a major religious dimension to kingship, but it is necessary to remember that, whatever it implies for the notion of royal divinity, it did not mean that any ruler once crowned was treated by everybody with awe-filled veneration and unquestioning obedience. The fallible humanity of a king was commemorated by the

---

[8] D. C. Sircar, *Select Inscriptions bearing on Indian History and Civilization*, 2nd edn. Calcutta, 1965, book III, no. 2: Allahabad Pillar Inscription of Samudragupta, pp. 262–8, line 26.

[9] The supposed divinity of ancient Indian kings has long been a point of controversy among Indologists, but the *communis opinio* is perhaps best summarized by A. L. Basham, *The Wonder that was India*, London, 1954 (reprint 1961), 81–8.

constant need to fight enemies abroad, in the provinces, at court and within his own family.

The significance of the idea of divine kingship, then, is not as an instrument of enhanced power. It is, rather, a ritual statement. But this statement, though it may not have worked magic for the political fortunes of rulers, may be important enough in its own way as an expression of cosmological belief about the spiritual forces informing the operation of human society and nature. Further, we must remember that the agrarian societies with which we are dealing lacked the modern idea of an impersonal state commanding a loyalty from its citizens that transcends the claims of individuals in government. In its place, the legitimacy of a ruler required a symbolism that could be supplied by religious categories.

There are various sorts of evidence of the divine sanction for kingship. One is constituted by the Indochinese linga cult, where the lingas were given the names of kings who endowed them in combination with Śiva's title Īśvara. As we have seen, the Chams had such cults at Mi-son, with a Bhadreśvara and subsequently a Śambhubhadreśvara. In Angkor, above all, many lingas and statues of gods were endowed by kings and by members of the royal family and the great men of the land.

A special case in Angkor, which has commonly been treated as an example of the royal linga cult but needs to be considered separately, is the *devarāja* cult instituted by the founder, Jayavarman II, to sanctify the independence and unity of the Khmer kingdom. It is known from only a few inscriptions, which show that the cult was maintained by a number of subsequent kings, and that it had attached to it a specially assigned lineage of priests.

Much has been written about this cult by modern scholars. Cœdès regarded it as more or less identical to the cult of the great 'temple-mountains', the pyramidal monuments which so many rulers built.[10] More recently Kulke has argued against this, identifying the *devarāja* instead as a portable and probably bronze icon which could be installed at different places.[11] The name of the cult, as Filliozat was the first to argue, need not be translated as 'god-king' (comporting the idea of royal divinity); it could refer instead to Śiva as 'King of the Gods'. Filliozat, who argued for a South Indian provenance of the cult, has further proposed that the Śiva cult thus attested was one in which the devotees had a sophisticated theology of Śiva as the supreme deity and unique and universal sovereign. The *devarāja*, therefore, was not confused with the person of the individual king; the divine self of Śiva is eternally pure, and no earthly ruler, even if partaking of divinity to the extent that in his innermost self he comes from Śiva, can possess that purity.[12]

Other aspects of the cult have been explored. Claude Jacques has examined it through the Khmer-language terms used in the inscriptions,

---

[10] Cœdès wrote on the subject in various places. A summary of his views is in *Angkor—an Introduction*, trans. E. F. Gardiner, Hong Kong, 1962, 22ff.

[11] 'Der Devarāja-Kult', *Saeculum*, 25, 1 (1974); trans. I. W. Mabbett, as *The Devarāja Cult*, Cornell University Southeast Asia Program, Data Paper no. 108, Ithaca, 1978.

[12] J. Filliozat, 'Sur le Çivaïsme et le Bouddhisme du Cambodge, à propos de deux livres récents', *BEFEO*, 70 (1981).

and suggested that, instead of the Khmer expression *kamrateń jagat ta rāja* being a translation of the Sanskrit *devarāja*, it may be the other way round—the Sanskrit term may name no Indian god at all but refer to a purely local god of a sort that may be called upon to protect a lineage or, in this case, a royal line.[13]

This reminds us of Paul Mus' view of the evolution from prehistoric cults of earth gods, their icons often consisting of rough stones, to linga cults which took over the same religious meaning that the earth gods had possessed. In one sense, the imported linga cult melted into the local tradition, appealing to the same set of ideas as did the cult of the territorial earth spirit; in another sense, the local tradition evolved into a more sophisticated ritual inspired by the imported myth—both perspectives, in Mus' interpretation, would be legitimate. Either way, a cult such as the *devarāja* should be seen as having signified to its worshippers the king as ritual embodiment of the patron god. Filliozat argued against this identification, asserting that Śiva's transcendence and purity excluded it. Both interpretations could, however, be right—one on the level of theology, the other on that of the sociology of religion.

The idea of royal divinity, however, depends upon more than just the linga cults and divinized statues of royalty. There are, for example, the shrines dedicated to royal ancestors which have as icons statues of gods and goddesses identified with human ancestors. At Angkor, Indravarman I dedicated the Preah Koh to the former king Jayavarman II and his wife, to Indravarman's own parents, and to his maternal grandparents. One can no doubt see in such a practice elements of the tradition indigenous to the soil which, on Mus' reconstruction, saw ancestors—especially ancestors of community chiefs—as merging with community gods. Such a merging is well attested in Chinese indigenous religion, and there are traces of such thinking in Indian ideas about the afterlife entered by ancestors.

But perhaps the most conspicuous sort of evidence is the symbolism implicit in the architecture of many Southeast Asian capital cities and the great monuments which were often constructed in their centres to represent the Mahāmeru, the home of the gods and *axis mundi*. A particularly elaborate example is constituted by Angkor Thom, capital city of Jayavarman VII, and the Mahāyāna Buddhist shrine, the Bayòn, in the centre of it: the whole complex was rich in cosmological meaning, representing on one level the myth of creation by churning the ocean of milk, and the causeways that approached the city walls being assimilated to Indra's rainbow, the ascent to heaven. The king sent twenty-three statues of himself to the provinces, and in return received images of the gods of the localities which were housed in the Bayòn's galleries; thus the Bayòn, as home of the gods, embodied all the spiritual energies of the kingdom.

Vietnam, which inherited the more secular Chinese traditions, was a different case, but there were similar ideas at work: the rulers were not

[13] C. Jacques, 'The Kamraten Jagat in ancient Cambodia', in Karashima Norobu, ed., *Indus Valley to Mekong Delta: explorations in epigraphy*, Madras, 1985.

perhaps seen as gods, but they had spiritual or quasi-divine characteristics often expressed in Buddhist terms. As Keith Taylor has put it, they 'stimulated and aroused the supernatural powers dwelling in the terrain of the Vietnamese realm'.[14]

What one can infer from such evidence of royal divinization is perhaps that in order to understand it we must revise our conceptions of the nature of divinity. In the cultures of monsoon Asia, divinity was a quality of the sacred world that lies unseen and implicit in the things of the world around us, like electromagnetic radiation or gravity. It could make itself accessible and potent through ritual. Kingship was itself a kind of ritual, serving to centre the kingdom on an individual, just as a shrine could centre it on an icon; in each case, the spiritual energy of the gods in the sacred world would be manifested.

Compared with mainland Southeast Asia, we notice many differences in maritime Southeast Asia as far as the divinization of kings is concerned, although there seems to be some agreement in its principal features.

Living kings were not generally regarded as gods. Thus, one of the best-known (semi-)historical texts, the *Pararaton*, tells us how the last king of Kaḍiri in east Java, Kĕrtajaya, wished to be venerated as a deity. When the courtiers were reluctant, the king decided to teach them a lesson. After briefly leaving the audience hall he returned complete with four arms, a third eye in the middle of his forehead and other marks of Śiva. The ministers and courtiers were, however, unimpressed. Suspecting some kind of magical trick, they left the palace to join the insurgents.[15] The anecdote suggests that some kings may have tried to get themselves venerated as gods, but without success.

Of King Kĕrtanagara of Singhasari in east Java it is known that, in 1289, he had himself consecrated as the Jina Akṣobhya, as described in the Sanskrit inscription carved on the lotus cushion of a large Akṣobhya statue, which can therefore be considered an idealized representation of the king.[16] It should, however, be emphasized that Akṣobhya, though endowed with superhuman qualities, is not a god but a transcendental Buddha: a state of perfection which, at least in principle, can be attained by any living being. This did not, however, prevent Kĕrtanagara from being killed in an attack by the subordinate ruler of Kaḍiri.

There is, however, a different conception which seems to have been generally adhered to in maritime Southeast Asia, at least in some areas and periods. It implies that kings were originally divine beings who descended to earth for the benefit of mankind, but returned to heaven as soon as their task was accomplished. This return required, however, the performance by the deceased king's successor of the appropriate rituals. Such rites are

---

[14] 'Authority and legitimacy in eleventh century Vietnam', in Marr and Milner, 143.

[15] Harry J. Benda and John A. Larkin, *The World of Southeast Asia, Selected Historical Readings*, translated from the Dutch by Margaret W. Broekhuysen, New York, Evanston, London, 1967, 38f.

[16] This statue, probably originating from the area around Trowulan, East Java, now stands in a park near Jalan Pemuda at Surabaya. For the inscription see H. Kern, *Verspreide Geschriften*, VII, The Hague, 1917 (originally published in 1910). For important corrections see R. Ng. Poerbatjaraka, 'De inscriptie van het Mahākṣobhya-beeld te Simpang (Soerabaja)', BKI, 78 (1922).

described in Indian texts, in particular the so-called *śrāddha*, which had to be performed by the king's eldest son at regular intervals after death. Indonesian sources mention, however, only a single great *śrāddha* to be carried out twelve years after the death of a royal person. The great *śrāddha* for the benefit of the soul of the Rājapatnī in Majapahit has already been described. We saw that the queen was transformed into Prajñāpāramitā as a result of the ceremony, and was thenceforward worshipped in a temple near present Tulung Agung south of Kaḍiri.[17]

King Jayanagara, the second ruler of Majapahit (1309–21), is said to have been deified as both Viṣṇu and the Jina Amoghasiddhi, and other kings and queens were deified in a similar manner.[18] On the other hand, most kings of Kaḍiri (mainly twelfth century) are described as incarnations of Viṣṇu, or rather of mythical kings who were themselves incarnations of Viṣṇu, such as Rāma, Paraśurāma, Kriṣṇa and Vāmana. Thus, one king is described as *Madhusūdanāvatāra* (incarnation of Viṣṇu as Kriṣṇa, slayer of the demon Madhu) or as *Vamanāvatāra* (incarnation of Viṣṇu as the Dwarf who conquered the world with three steps). Being a second-degree incarnation of the god dilutes the divine element, which is even further watered down by the fact that the king is often described as being merely a partial incarnation (*aṃśavatāra*) of the god (or his incarnation). The king's 'divinity', if this is the right term, was therefore strictly limited.[19]

Whatever their status during life, kings were sometimes worshipped as gods after their death when, as the poet puts it, 'they returned home to the gods' abode' (*Nāg.* 41–4a). This suggests that the king was a deity who temporarily stayed on earth in the guise of a human being but returned 'home' when his task was accomplished. The fact that this 'return' was often brought about by human violence (only one king of the Singhasari dynasty died a natural death) does not seem to have made any difference: while abiding on earth the king naturally behaved like a human being and suffered the consequences of his acts.

As stated above with reference to the Rājapatnī, many kings after the beginning of the second millennium were venerated in the form of a statue of the deity into whom the king had 'returned' after his death on earth. It is thought that many of the extant stone statues of Śiva and Viṣṇu, especially those with unusual attributes and individual facial expression, represent deified rulers or members of the royal family.[20] This is quite likely. It has, however, also been assumed that the temples known to have been dedicated to deceased kings were actually mausoleums in which the mortal remains after a king's cremation were kept in an urn deposited in a pit below the principal cult image. Such pits occur in all Śaiva temples, but their contents have usually been disturbed by treasure-hunters. On the

[17] Pigeaud, *Java*, I and III, cantos LXIII–LIX and IV, 169–211.

[18] For Jayanagara's apotheosis see canto XLVIII of the same publication.

[19] cf. Sanskrit *aṃśāvataraṇa*, title of sections 64–7 of the Indian *Ādiparvan*. The Old Javanese *Ādiparwa* (ed. Juynboll, The Hague, 1906, 47f.) mentions *aṅgsāwatāra*: 'it always seems to mean that only part of the god was incarnated': Stutterheim, 'Some remarks on pre-Hinduistic burial customs on Java', *Studies in Indonesian Archaeology*, 1956 (originally published in 1939), 71 n. 18.

[20] Stutterheim in the preceding article and in 'Een Oud-Javaansche Bhīma-cultus', *Djāwā*, XV (1935).

one hand, in none of the pits discovered intact have any human remains been identified; any ashes found have proved to be of vegetable or animal origin. The idea of the god arising as a Phoenix out of his ashes finds no support in Indonesian religion, in which corporeal remains were generally considered polluting (as in India), to be disposed of as completely as possible. Thus, in present-day Bali the ashes remaining after a cremation are taken to the ocean.[21]

If temples dedicated to the cult of defunct rulers were not mausoleums they could have been cenotaphs, but it is preferable to abandon the funerary association altogether and regard the temples concerned as commemorative monuments devoted to the cult of the deity with whom the essence of the deceased would have merged. With the help of the *Nagarakĕrtāgama* and other texts, it is often possible to determine whether a certain temple is dedicated to the cult of a deified ruler or to a deity as such. Thus, the large Amoghapāśa of Caṇḍi Jago is an effigy of King Viṣṇuvardhana of Singhasari (r. 1248–68) according to the text (*Nāg.*, 41–4), while of King Anuṣapati (r. 1227–47?) it is stated (41–1) that he returned 'home to Girīndra's [Śiva's] abode . . . in the likeness of Śiva, splendid, in the eminent *dharma* [religious domain] in Kidal' (i.e. Caṇḍi Kidal near present Malang).

On the other hand, there are many east Javanese temples without any known association within a defunct ruler. Thus the greatest temple complex of the province, Caṇḍi Panataran, was a state temple devoted to Śiva as Lord of the Mountains. In many cases, however, the sources do not permit us to decide in favour of either alternative.

The second problem concerns the so-called syncretism of Śaivism and Buddhism. Here, too, the issue is more complicated than it may seem at first. Following H. C. Kern and W. H. Rassers,[22] it has long been accepted that the two main religions merged into one from the reign of Kĕrtanagara (1268–92). More recent research has, however, demonstrated that our sources do not warrant such a conclusion. Except perhaps for one or two individual cases, such as that of Kĕrtanagara, known as *sang Śiva-Buddha* after his death (if not during his life), there was no true syncretism but a more complicated and more interesting relationship between those two religions. As early as the eighth century CE the stone inscription of Kĕlurak, central Java, dated 782, writes of the Mañjuśrī image, the erection of which is the main object of the incription, that 'this is the majestic Vajra-bearer (vajrabhṛt), Brahmā, Viṣṇu and Maheśvara', thus suggesting that the Bodhisattva embodies, as it were, Indra and the three main gods of Hinduism. It would, however, be wrong to regard this passage as an expression of syncretism. It is much better explained as an expression of the universality of the image, which embraces these gods but also conceals in its interior (*antargatāñ sthitāḥ*) the Buddha, the Dharma and the *Sangha*.[23]

---

[21] Soekmono, 'Candi: Fungsi dan Pengertiannya', thesis, Universitas Indonesia, 1974. An English edition of this important work is in preparation.
[22] *Çiva dan Buddha. Dua karangan tentang Çiwaïsme dan Buddhisme di Indonesia*, with an introduction by Edi Sedyawati, Jakarta, 1982.
[23] F. D. K. Bosch, 'De inscriptie van Keloerak', TBG, 48 (1928).

Even an 'orthodox' Mahāyāna text such as the *Daśabhūmikasūtra* equates the highest Bodhisattva stages with those of the great Hindu gods.[24]

Most modern scholars, for example J. Gonda, Hariati Soebadio and Soewito Santoso, have rightly rejected the use of the term syncretism. Gonda replaced it by 'coalition', suggesting a close link between the two religions. Soebadio devoted an important section of the introduction to her edition of the *Jñānasiddhānta*, an Old Javanese text of the Majapahit period (?), to this problem. Though accepting Gonda's term, she interpreted it as 'a striving for the same ultimate goal using different ways' and, on the basis of some verses of the probably contemporary *Sutasoma*, compared it with 'climbing a mountain. Different ways are used, but in the end the same peak is reached. Nevertheless the ways that are used are considered different.' In addition, she rightly pointed out that 'many facts plead for a longstanding peaceful coexistence of Buddhism and Śiwaism', perhaps including 'plain borrowing of a Buddhist text by Śaivites, and adapting it for the Śaivite purposes'.[25]

There remains, however, a serious problem concerning Kĕrtanagara. The statement that 'the king as the highest principle in the country quite logically would have been identified also with the highest principles of the religions in his country' is unexceptionable, but it is strange that no other king is ever described as Śiva-Buddha. The compound does not indicate a composite deity such as Hari-hara—half Viṣṇu half Śiva—for no Śiva-Buddha image is known to have existed. It is therefore more likely that the king's memory was worshipped in a temple with both a Śiva and a Buddha image. This agrees with a difficult passage in the *Nāgarakĕrtāgama* (56–2), which describes a temple (Jajawi, i.e. the present Caṇḍi Jawi) having a Śiva statue below (*i sor*) but a statue of the Buddha Akṣobhya above (*i ruhur*). This suggests a two-storey temple with a Śiva image in the lower, and a Buddha image in the upper storey. This is a good illustration of Soebadio's view that Śaivism and Buddhism, though united in one building, are also separated: truly a good example of *Bhinneka Tunggal Ika!*[26]

There are also other contexts in which the term syncretism has been used, probably with better justification. This applies not only to Hari-hara, but also to the absorption of ancient Austronesian deities into the great religions. In the former case, however, the process had already taken place in India; in the latter it is preferable to use other terms, such as acculturation.

In conclusion, it is clear that the term 'syncretism' requires inverted commas, or else it should be avoided. The same applies to other uses of this term, for example, in respect of Islam in Java or of the influence of the Austronesian substratum on the great religions.

---

[24] See also the *Daśabhūmikasūtra*, ed. Rahder, Utrecht-Leuven, 1926, in particular the Seventh Stage. Cf. also Rahder, 'Daśabhūmika-Sūtram. Seventh Stage', *Acta Orientalia*, IV (1926). The most detailed analysis of the Śiwa-Buddha concept is that by Soewito Santoso in his edition of the *Sutasoma. A Study in Javanese Wajrayāna*, Śatapiṭaka Series, vol. 213, New Delhi, 1975, ch. IV, 40–127.

[25] Gonda, 'Śiva in Indonesien', *Wiener Zeitschrift für die Kunde Südasiens*, XIV (1970); Soebadio, *Jñāasiddhānta*, 1971.

[26] cf. also Max Nihom, *Studies in the Buddhist Tantra*, Leiden, 1982, for a different interpretation.

THE BEGINNINGS OF ISLAM

In contrast to the predominance of Theravāda Buddhism on the mainland, Islam became the predominant religion of maritime Southeast Asia except for most of the Philippines. Islam appeared in the area, however at a late stage, more than six centuries after its foundation. The earliest Muslim kingdom arose at Pasai near present Loh Seumawe on the north coast of Aceh, just before the end of the thirteenth century. At about the same time we notice the earliest Muslim tombs in east Java (except for an isolated example in the eleventh century).[27] Islamization was slow at first, mainly owing to the presence of strong Hindu-Buddhist kingdoms. Their decline in the fifteenth century stimulated the expansion of Islam.

The conversion to Islam of the king of Melaka (Malacca), founded around 1400, was a strong incentive to further Muslim expansion, especially after the middle of the fifteenth century, when Melaka had developed into the greatest commercial centre of Southeast Asia.

From there Islam soon spread to other centres in the area, in particular to those with which Melaka had close commercial relations. Muslim kingdoms or principalities, often styled sultanates, arose in such centres and these, in turn, became secondary foci of further expansion. During the fifteenth century Muslim kingdoms emerged on the west coast of the Malay peninsula in Perak and Kedah, as well as in Pahang, Kelantan and Terengganu, where Muslim laws had already been promulgated at the end of the fourteenth century,[28] and also at Pattani in southern Thailand. Similar developments took place in the river ports on the east coast of Sumatra, for example at Siak and Kampar. This 'network' of Muslim states confirmed Melaka's hegemony in the straits until its conquest by the Portuguese in 1511.

In Java, some of the Muslim tombs at Troloyo near ancient Majapahit, about sixty-five kilometres southwest of Surabaya, may belong to the end of the thirteenth century, but the inscribed tombstones have disappeared. We still have, however, a few tombstones with dates in the latter half of the fourteenth century. Such stones, called *maesan* in Javanese, are of a peculiar shape. At Troloyo they carry a date in the Śaka era (starting from 78 CE) and in Old Javanese script on the front within a panel of rich floral decoration. On the back there often is an inscription in Arabic script: a quotation from the Koran (Qur'an) or another holy text. But, strange though it may seem, the names of the deceased are never mentioned. Nevertheless, their proximity to the royal court of Majapahit strongly suggests that the deceased were closely associated with the court. The shape of the *maesan*, their ornamentation, and especially the use of Old Javanese numerals in the Śaka era suggest that the deceased were Indo-

---

[27] For the inscription of Leran, East Java, see J. P. Moquette, 'De oudste Mohammedaanse Inscriptie of Java, m.n. de Grafsteen te Leran', in *Handelingen 1ste Congres voor de Taal-, Land-, en Volkenkunde van Java*, 1919, and Paul Ravaisse, 'L'inscription coufique de Léran à Java', TBG, 45 (1925).

[28] H. S. Paterson, 'An early Malay Inscription from Trĕngganu', JMBRAS, 2 (1924); C. O. Blagden, ibid., 258–63; M. B. Hooker, 'The Trĕngganu Inscription in Malayan Legal History', ibid, 49 (1976); Hooker, *Islamic Law in South-east Asia*, Singapore, 1984.

nesians rather than foreign merchants; it would follow that there were already a considerable number of Muslims among the officials and dignitaries of the court of Majapahit when the empire was still at the height of its power.[29]

A recently discovered, probably apocryphal, text, the so-called *Malay Annals* of Semarang and Cheribon,[30] assigns the main part in the Islamization of Java to Chinese Muslims. Although this text cannot be accepted as evidence, this does not necessarily exclude the possibility of Chinese influence on the progress of Islam. Actually, one of the principal assistants of the Chinese admiral Ch'eng Ho, named Ma-huan, was a Muslim who stayed in Java in 1403. His presence may have strengthened Islam in Java, but the new religion had already taken root before his arrival.

Javanese tradition, on the other hand, attributes the Islamization of the island to nine preachers (*wali-sanga*),[31] the first of whom was a clearly historical figure: Malik Ibrāhīm, whose tomb at Gresik near Surabaya is dated 1419. The tombstone (*nisān*) indicates that the deceased was a trader from Gujerat, but of Persian origin, and mentions no missionary activities. The neighbouring site of Giri, however, soon became an important Muslim centre with the establishment of a dynasty of so-called 'priest-kings'. Their influence on religious, and probably also political, developments in Java and Maluku, at least until the sixteenth century, should not be underrated.

In Javanese tradition the *wali* were associated with particular mystical doctrines. They would also have taken an important part in the construction of the oldest mosque in Java at Demak east of Semarang, at the beginning of the sixteenth century.

This mosque is a typical example of the early Javanese mosque in which pre-Muslim building traditions were adapted to the requirements of Islam. The result is a building that differs considerably from the mosque in India or in the Middle East. The Javanese mosque has a square ground-plan with a pointed roof consisting of up to five storeys. It has a verandah at the entrance and is surrounded by a low wall with a more or less elaborate gateway. It generally stands on the western side of a carefully oriented square (*alun-alun*), as found in all important towns in Java. The absence of statuary is compensated for by the richness in decoration with a profusion of geometric, floral and sometimes even animal motifs. It has been suggested that the prototype of the mosque was the traditional cock-fight arena.[32] In addition to that of Demak the mosques at Mantingan (near Jepara) and Sendang Duwur (on the north coast, north of Lamongan), though substantially rebuilt in later times, still contain sixteenth-century

[29] Louis-Charles Damais, 'Études Javanaises I. Les tombes musulmanes datées de Tràlàyà', BEFEO, 48 (1959), plates I-XXXIV.
[30] H. J. De Graaf, and Th. G. Th. Pigeaud, *Chinese Muslims in Java in the 15th and 16th century*, Monash Papers on Southeast Asia, no. 12, Melbourne, 1984.
[31] Zoetmulder in Stöhr and Zoetmulder, *Les Religions d'Indonésie*, 338–45; H. J. de Graaf and Th. G. Th. Pigeaud, 'De eerste Moslimse vorstendommen op Java', VKI, 69, The Hague, 1969.
[32] H. J. De Graaf, 'The Origin of the Javanese Mosque', SEAH, 4 (1963); G. F. Pijper, 'De Moskeeën van Java' in *Studiën over de geschiedenis van de Islam in Indonesia 1900–1950*, Leiden, 1977, 13–62.

ornamental panels sculpted according to the ancient tradition. In many respects there is no clear break with the pre-Muslim past.

As to the religion itself there is a strong tendency towards mysticism flourishing by the side of orthodox Islam. In north Sumatra (Aceh) this mysticism remains well within the grounds of orthodox Islam, but in Java the influence of pre-Islamic doctrines is undeniable. The classical Brahmanic doctrine prescribes a life of contemplation, preferably in a forest hermitage, for all Hindus of the higher social strata after they had performed their worldly duties. Such a quiet life, far from the turmoil and temptations of the world, would create the right atmosphere for the contemplation of the secrets of being and non-being, of relative and absolute truth and of unification with the universal soul. Some forest hermitages attracted pupils from far away, so that such *āśramas* developed into centres of education. This Indian tradition seems to have been widely followed in ancient Java where, as we have seen, sites such as the Dieng plateau became important educational centres for the élite. In lieu of paying fees, the pupils carried out all required services. They owed absolute obedience to the Guru and worked in fields and gardens reclaimed from the forest. The larger *āśramas* were mainly self-sufficient communities. Similar centres, called *maṇḍalas*, proliferated in the last century of Majapahit and are described in texts like the *Tantu Panggĕlaran.*[33]

After the introduction of Islam such institutions continued as *pesantren* or *pondok*, where pupils study the sacred texts under the guidance of a teacher. One of the most famous centres, Giri, has already been mentioned; it flourished till the middle of the seventeenth century, when Sultan Agung of Mataram conquered the area and made an end to the influence of the priestly 'dynasty' ruling there. About that time, however, another strong Muslim centre emerged at Kajoran, east of Yogyakarta. Little is known of the doctrines preached there, but during a critical period in the third quarter of the seventeenth century the *ulamā* of Kajoran conspired with a rebellious prince of Mataram, as well as with troops from Sulawesi and Madura, to make an end to the reign of Sultan Agung's successor, Amangkurat I (1677), who was considered unorthodox. As often happens in such cases, it is difficult to decide how far religious motives, especially resistance to court ceremonies and practices deemed contrary to strict Islamic teaching, were the principal factor involved. It should not be forgotten that the Muslim foundations, like their earlier Hindu-Buddhist counterparts, had important material interests, especially land and labour, which they enjoyed on a privileged basis in the so-called *pĕrdikan* villages. True religious conflicts have always been rare in Java, but religious factors were often involved in dynastic or agricultural conflicts.

In Java, with its glorious pre-Muslim tradition, Islam had to compromise with long-established attitudes. Already at an early stage there is evidence of speculation about the fundamental identity of the old and new religions. Thus there is a statement ascribed to one of the ancestors of the Mataram dynasty to the effect that 'there is no difference between Buddhism [which

[33] Pigeaud, *De Tantu Panggĕlaran.*

included other religions of Indian origin] and Islam: they are two in form, but only one in essence [literally: name]'.[34]

This tendency to compromise is clearly reflected in the Javanese shadow theatre (*wayang kulit*) with its plots based on the great Indian epics (*Mahābhārata* and *Rāmāyaṇa*), but adapted to Javanese tradition. The characters are represented by flat leather puppets, elaborately carved and painted, which are 'brought to life' by a puppeteer (*ḍalang*), who moves the puppets and makes them talk. The Muslim prohibition against the representation of living beings is avoided by giving the puppets a very peculiar shape. A striking feature is the part played by 'clowns' (*pånåkawan*), such as Sěmar, a retainer of the hero Arjuna, who, despite his funny appearance, often pronounces basic truths in the form of jokes.[35] Though only superficially influenced by Islam, these *wayang* performances often give splendour to Muslim celebrations, for example circumcisions, and are introduced by some pious words.

Other Javanese ceremonies, too, show the strength of ancient tradition. Most of the important occasions, such as those connected with the 'rites de passage', are concluded with a ceremonial meal (*slamětan*).[36] Depending on the nature of the occasion, such as birth, circumcision, commemoration of the death of a relative and many others, the *slamětan* has special features. Though attended by an official of the local mosque and preceded by Muslim prayers, the *slamětan* has a strong traditional character, reminding one of similar ceremonial meals in the ancient period, for example those described in the inscriptions at the inauguration of a sacred foundation. Originally perhaps a purification rite, it has gradually become a means to strengthen friendship and solidarity between the participants.

Indian influence was insignificant outside Java, Sumatra and the Malay peninsula. Islam was generally established there at a late stage, either from Melaka (as in Brunei) or, more often, from Java, especially from the great Muslim centres at Giri (Gresik), Tuban, Surabaya and others. As, however, these developments took place in or after the sixteenth century, they will be considered in another chapter.

On the eve of the Portuguese conquest of Melaka (1511) Islam was firmly established in the main centres in northern Sumatra, west Malaysia, west Kalimantan and on the north coast of Java. The Portuguese and Spanish activities in maritime Southeast Asia not only failed to stem the expansion of Islam, except in the northern and central Philippines and eastern Indonesia, but may, on the contrary, even have intensified it. Islam may have been felt as a strong spiritual force capable of resisting the ruthless encroachment by Western conquerors upon major parts of maritime Southeast Asia.

---

[34] P. J. Zoetmulder, *Pantheisme en Monisme in de Javaansche Soeloek-litteratuur*, Nijmegen, 1935, 346f. My English version is based on the Dutch translation in Zoetmulder's work.

[35] There is much literature on these 'clowns'. See e.g. Ph. Van Akkeren, *Een gedrocht en toch de volmaakte mensch. De Suluk Gatolotjo*, The Hague, 1951; James R. Brandon, *On thrones of Gold. Three Javanese Shadow Plays*, Cambridge, Mass., 1970.

[36] Geertz, *Religion of Java*, 30–85; Zoetmulder in Stöhr and Zoetmulder, *Les Réligions*, 323–5.

BIBLIOGRAPHIC ESSAY

The Mainland

Sources for religion in early periods, primary and secondary alike, tend not to be distinct from sources for other aspects of history—religion pervades them all. Of general works on early history containing information about religion, chief mention must be made of the general summary of the period by a pioneering scholar, G. Cœdès' *Les États Hindouisés d'Indochine et d'Indonésie*, Paris, 1964 (*The Indianized States of Southeast Asia*, ed. Walter Vella, trans. Susan Brown Cowing, Honolulu, 1968). More up-to-date scholarship is to be found in some relatively recent collections of articles such as D. G. Marr and A. C. Milner, eds. *Southeast Asia in the 9th to 14th Centuries*, Singapore and Canberra, 1986, and R. B. Smith and W. Watson, eds. *Early South East Asia: Essays in Archaeology, History and Historical Geography*, New York, 1979. This latter is particularly important for the archaeology of the historical period. A valuable recent synthesis, with implications for our understanding of the evolution of religious cults from prehistoric times, is C. Higham's *The Archaeology of Mainland Southeast Asia*, Cambridge, 1989. Another is E. Slamet-Velsink, *Emerging Hierarchies*, Leiden, 1986.

Not many secondary sources are dedicated to religious history in the early period, though there are relevant sections in K. L. Hazra, *History of Theravada Buddhism in Southeast Asia*, Calcutta, 1982.

Most of the research results, including editions of inscriptions and other primary material, are to be found in the pages of journals. For Indochina these include most notably the *Bulletin de l'École Française d'Extrême-Orient*, Paris, which has appeared since 1901; relevant contributors include L. Finot, E. Huber, P. Dupont, G. Cœdès, and more recently J. Filliozat and C. Jacques.

Among primary sources bearing on the region in general, conspicuous are the accounts by travellers from outside, such as I Ching and Chou Ta-kuan: I Ching, *A Record of the Buddhist Religion as Practised in India and the Malay Archipelago*, trans. J. Takakusu, Oxford, 1896; Chou Ta-kuan, *Mémoires sur les coutumes de Cambodge de Tcheou Takouan*, trans. P. Pelliot (Oeuvres Posthumes de P. Pelliot, vol. 3), Paris, 1951. I Ching also wrote accounts of the travels through the region of other Buddhist pilgrims: I Ching, *Chinese Monks in India*, trans. Latika Lahiri, Delhi, 1986. For the earliest period, a useful collection of primary source material (especially Chinese accounts), analysed and discussed by Paul Wheatley from the point of view of historical geography, is *The Golden Khersonese: Studies in the Historical Geography of the Malay Peninsula before A.D. 1500*, Kuala Lumpur, 1966.

Champa is something of a Cinderella in modern research. Its inscriptions have been studied in articles by E. Huber and others in the BEFEO, and edited by R. C. Majumdar, in vol. I, *Champa*, of his series *Ancient Indian Colonies in the Far East*, Lahore, 1927, though it must be said that there is plenty of room for more work on Cham epigraphy. J. Boisselier's

La Statuaire de Champa, Paris, 1963, contributes to the history of religious art in the period.

Cambodia is comparatively well served. G. Cœdès' *Inscriptions du Cambodge*, Hanoi and Paris 1937–66, 8 vols, incorporates most of the known epigraphy (nearly all of which, of course, is concerned with matters of religion). More recent contributions are by J. Filliozat and C. Jacques and others, especially in the pages of the BEFEO. Important is the work of Kamaleswar Bhattacharya, notably *Les Religions Brahmaniques dans l'Ancien Cambodge*, Paris, 1961; his articles on religious history include for example 'La secte des Pāśupata dans l'ancien Cambodge,' *Journal Asiatique*, 243 (1955).

Further west, in the area of the Mon, Pyu and Burman peoples before the rise of the Thai states, the outlines of history are vague and problematic. G. Cœdès' *Le Royaume de Dvāravatī*, Bangkok, 1929, offers interpretations of Mon religious culture. G. H. Luce worked extensively on the ancient cultures of Burma, and his *Phases of Pre-Pagan Burma, Languages and History*, 2 vols, Oxford, 1985, surveys the early period.

Material available on Burmese archaeology is scant and patchy; tantalizing results of excavations of Pyu sites are reported by Aung Thaw in *Report on the Excavations at Beikthano*, Rangoon: Ministry of Union Culture, 1968, and *Historical Sites in Burma*, Rangoon: Ministry of Union Culture, 1972, with claims for the beginnings of Buddhism.

Pagan is somewhat better served, with a number of relevant inscriptions edited in the series *Epigraphia Birmanica*. Secondary sources include G. H. Luce, *Old Burma—Early Pagan*, 3 vols, New York, 1969–70; Than Tun, *History of Buddhism in Burma, A.D. 1000–1300*, Rangoon, 1978 (JBRS, 61.1,2, *separatum*); and Nihar Ranjan Ray, *Sanskrit Buddhism in Burma*, Calcutta, 1936. Many relevant articles appear in the *Journal of the Burma Research Society*.

The epigraphy of the Thai kingdoms is represented particularly in G. Cœdès, *Reçueil des Inscriptions du Siam*, 2 vols, Bangkok, 1924, and a series of studies of inscriptions by A. B. Griswold and Prasert na Nagara in the *Journal of the Siam Society*, appearing from vol. 56 (1968) to vol. 63 (1975); important is the one on the famous Ramkamhaeng inscription, 'The inscription of King Rama Gamhen of Sukhodaya (1292 A.D.)', JSS, 59, 2 (1971). A. B. Griswold has written extensively on Thai religious art (for example, 'Imported images and the nature of copying in the art of Siam,' in Ba Shin et al., eds, *Essays Offered to G. H. Luce*, Ascona: Artibus Asiae, 1966, II. 37–73). Religious art is also served by J. Boisselier's *La Sculpture en Thailande*, Paris, 1974.

Vietnamese culture is not characterized in the same way as the 'Indianized' states by inscriptions associated with temples, and literary sources are relatively more important. These are exploited for religious history by Tran Van Giap in 'Le Bouddhisme en Annam des origines au XIIIe siècle', BEFEO, 32 (1932). A standard synthesis much used in the past is Le Thanh Khoi's *Le Viet-nam, Histoire et Civilisation*, Paris, 1955, which contains comments on montagnard religious practices. A major recent summary with much on religious history is K. W. Taylor's *The Birth of Vietnam*, Berkeley, 1983.

Maritime Southeast Asia

The sources available for the religion of early maritime Southeast Asia are, on the whole, less easily accessible than those for the mainland. Although many Old Javanese and Old Balinese inscriptions have been published (though not always according to present-day standards), relatively few have been translated, and then mostly into Dutch or Indonesian.

Almost all English translations are those by H. Bh. Sarkar, published in 1971 and 1972 in two volumes as *Corpus of the inscriptions of Java*. As has been noticed above (note 4), this is a useful, almost indispensable, work, which has, however, to be used with caution. The translations are based on old transcriptions by Brandes and Krom, about which a little more is said below; no fresh reading of the originals was possible. Although the author is the foremost Indian scholar of Old Javanese language and literature, he has little experience with the very special idiom of the Old Javanese charters and therefore often gives a wrong or incorrect impression of the purport of a considerable number of these texts. In addition, the inscriptions reproduced and translated in these volumes are only those dated before 929 CE.

The most comprehensive collection of inscriptions is that by Brandes and Krom, mentioned in note 4 above. Like the preceding work, this collection is indispensable, although it is unsatisfactory in several respects. The transcriptions by Brandes were sometimes produced in a final form, more often as provisional drafts, not meant to be published in that form. In the absence of any better transcripts, Krom rightly decided that also the latter ought to be published. Although Krom must often have made his own, more precise, transcriptions, he preferred, no doubt out of piety towards Brandes, to produce the drafts in exactly the form in which they were left by Brandes at his death. Although Krom's feelings deserve full respect, it would have been better for the progress of Old Javanese studies if he had been less conscientious.

Of the later inscriptions there are a number, mainly dated during the fourteenth century, available in English translation by Th. Pigeaud in vol. III of his monumental *Java in the 14th Century: A Study of Cultural History*. As in Sarkar's work the translations are based on existing transcriptions which are generally reliable—partly because they are all on copper plates which are still in an excellent condition. Although Pigeaud was undoubtedly one of the best Western scholars of pre-modern and modern Javanese literature and culture, his translations sometimes suffer from his conviction that Javanese civilization hardly changed during the centuries, so that the ancient texts could be interpreted with the help of his excellent knowledge of more recent forms of the language. There are obvious dangers if this conviction is applied with reference to religion. It is true that the conversion to Islam did not imply a complete break with the past (as argued above, there was some continuity in certain fields), yet Pigeaud has perhaps gone farther in this respect than is warranted by the sources. Moreover, Pigeaud wrongly assumed that ancient Javanese society was 'feudal' in character. As a consequence he translated a number of important Old Javanese terms by equivalents of English feudalism in particular.

The main Old Javanese text discussed by Pigeaud is the *Nāgarakĕrtāgama*, written by a court poet in the middle of the fourteenth century. It is the basic text for our knowledge of Old Javanese religious ideas and institutions in that period, supplemented by a few other Old Javanese texts and inscriptions. It should, however, be emphasized that the *Nāgarakĕrtāgama* belongs to the court circles and only occasionally throws some light on the religious observances of the majority of the population. But this is the case with almost all our sources for ancient Southeast Asia.

The archaeological sources may in some cases offer some materials on popular religion. Although the artisans worked under the supervision of priests and other members of the élite, they themselves belonged to lower strata of the society and it was inevitable that their own ideas were sometimes reflected in the buildings and iconography of ancient Indonesia. Thus, Borobuḍur not only shows us numerous types of buildings associated with Buddhism and, occasionally, other religions but also, especially in the reliefs, examples of the manner in which buildings (such as stupas) were worshipped. Different types of heavens and hells are represented. We also get an impression of the garments and paraphernalia of monks, ascetics and priests of different orders and of their attitudes towards other classes of the population. In this respect the reliefs of the East Javanese period (tenth to fifteenth century) are even more valuable for all the details that are provided.

Also the statuary is important for our knowledge of religion. It should be emphasized that the statues are not only icons that are worshipped for their own sake, but rather function as a means to enable the worshipper to form an idea of the shape that the deity can take. It is difficult to pay homage to a mental idea of the deity. For most of the population it was therefore important that they could have a visible shape of the deity in front of their eyes. Iconography can therefore help us to understand how the pious represented their gods.

Also, other objects used in religious worship have been found in considerable quantity, thus enabling us to visualize some aspects of actual religious rites. Among these I may mention lamps—usually offered to the deity as votive gifts—sacrificial vessels of all kinds, mirrors, sacrificial plates (*talam*), different tools, etc.

As to foreign sources, the accounts by the Chinese pilgrim I Ching have already been discussed in the section on mainland Southeast Asia. The other foreign accounts, whether Chinese or Arabic, are of only minor importance for the study of religion.

Only one of the secondary works is directly concerned with the religions of Indonesia. This is the study by W. Stöhr and J. Zoetmulder mentioned in note 8 above. The section written by Stöhr deals with the tribal beliefs and rituals in Indonesia, which are not discussed in this chapter because they have been known only since recent times. Zoetmulder's section, however, is of direct importance as a supplement to this chapter since it is mainly concerned with religious concepts (Hindu, Buddhist and Muslim), as reflected in literature.

Another important work, mentioned earlier, is Pigeaud's study on fourteenth-century Java. Especially in vol. IV there are important, but somewhat controversial, chapters on religious institutions and practices in the Majapahit empire. Pigeaud's strong conviction of continuity in Javanese religion, also after the coming of Islam, lends a particular colour to his analysis.

As religion is inextricably interwoven with social and political life in ancient maritime Southeast Asia, it is inevitable that all works on the ancient history of the area give some attention to religion. Thus, all the general works mentioned at the beginning of this bibliographical essay discuss various aspects of religious developments in the area.

In addition a few works deserve particular attention. Thus, N. J. Krom's works *Hindoe-Javaansche Geschiedenis*, 2nd edn. The Hague, 1932, *Inleiding tot de Hindoe-Javaansche Kunst*, 2nd edn, The Hague, 1923, and *Barabudur, Archaeological Description*, 2 vols, The Hague, 1927, contain invaluable data and discussions on Buddhism in ancient Java. Some of the most important contributions by W. F. Stutterheim, which often present original views on many aspects of Indonesian (in particular, Javanese) religion, are available in English translation as *Studies in Indonesian Archaeology*, The Hague, 1956. This volume contains, in particular, his study of Borobudur, briefly discussed in this chapter, as well as a very important study on an aspect of ancient Austronesian religion, 'Some remarks on pre-Hinduistic burial customs on Java'. In addition, there are important articles on a ninth-century copper plate with a drawing of a Mother Goddess with a long Sanskrit *mantra* (mystical or magical formula), and on the Javanese Bhima cult, also briefly discussed in this chapter. As nearly all ancient Malaysian, Indonesian and Philippine antiquities were inspired by religion, most publications on archaeology are important for our knowledge of ancient religion in the area. They can be found in e.g. the *Tijdschrift voor de Taal-, Land- en Volkenkunde*, the *Bijdragen tot de Taal- Land- en Volkenkunde*, the *Journal of the Malay Branch of the Royal Asiatic Society*, and many others. The last-mentioned journal and the *Federation Museums Journal* contain some important articles by H. G. Quaritch Wales and Alastair Lamb on the excavations in the state of Kedah.

Among the increasingly numerous and important studies published in Indonesia three Ph.D. theses of the Universitas Indonesia at Jakarta should be mentioned. The work by Soekmono, *Candi, Fungsi dan Pengertiannya*, Jakarta 1974, an English edition of which is in preparation, throws important new light on the meaning and significance of ancient temples and images. The work by Edi Sedyawati, *Pengarcaan Ganesa masa Kadiri dan Sinhasari*, Jakarta, 1985, will also soon appear in English: it deals with the iconography and religious significance of the elephant-headed god Gaṇeśa, who enjoyed much popular worship in ancient Java, Sumatra and Bali. Finally, the no less important thesis by Hariani Santiko, *Kedudukan Bhatari Durga di Java pada Abad X-XV Masehi*, Jakarta, 1987, analyses the significance of this fierce goddess, usually represented victoriously standing on the back of the buffalo demon.

Much has been written on the provenance of early Islam in Malaysia, Indonesia, Brunei, Champa and the southern Philippines (especially Mindanao and the Sulu Archipelago). J. E. Moquette's article on the Muslim tombstones of Pasai and Gresik (*Tijdschrift*, LIV 1912), which traces

Indonesian Islam back to Gujerat, has long been accepted as a convincing argument, but G. E. Marrison, 'The coming of Islam to the East Indies', JMBRAS, 24 (1951), has rightly emphasized the strong arguments in favour of South India, some of which had already been proposed by Van Ronkel, as the area from which Islam spread to Indonesia and Malaysia. The best analysis of this problem, as well as of others connected with early Islam in maritime Southeast Asia, is by S. Q. Fatimi, *Islam Comes to Malaysia*, Singapore, 1963. Unfortunately the author has not used the article by L.-C. Damais, 'Études Javanaises. I. Les Tombes Musalmanes datées de Tralaya' (Troloyo), BEFEO 48 (1956), in which the importance of Islam during the empire of Majapahit is pointed out on the basis of the dated Muslim graves in the immediate vicinity of the royal residence. The earliest dates found on these stones are about contemporary with those on the earliest tombs in the northern Sumatra (Pasai). These data, which are unexceptionable, put the problem of early Islam in Southeast Asia in a new light. Although the role of Melaka in Muslim expansion is beyond doubt, the Troloyo stones prove that Islam was already firmly established in eastern Java by the end of the thirteenth century, more than a century before the foundation of Melaka.

FROM c. 1500 TO c. 1800 CE

The second part of this work covers the period from the late fifteenth century to the late eighteenth and early nineteenth centuries of the Christian era. The opening chapter places the region in an international context, affected by changes of which the advent of the Europeans was only one. The three chapters that follow outline the political, economic and social, and religious changes that Southeast Asia underwent. A fifth chapter surveys the region on the eve of the phase in which it came almost entirely under European political control.

In the period 1500–1800 Indians and Chinese, who had visited Southeast Asia since the early Christian era, came in far greater numbers. In the seventeenth century the Japanese became involved in Southeast Asian trade for the first time. But the latest and most formidable arrivals were the Europeans. Chapter 6 deals with the arrival and establishment of these groups in the region. It also deals with the interaction between the foreign and Southeast Asian communities, and the innovations and adaptations that resulted. These included the establishment of European-controlled cities and the emergence of mestizo communities. The chapter also discusses developments in shipbuilding and firearms technology that had important repercussions for Southeast Asian societies.

This period also saw a slow movement towards larger political groupings, which subsequently were to form the basis of modern nation-states. This is the focus of Chapter 7. Neither increased participation in international trade, nor the incursion of the Europeans, necessarily worked against the fragmentation that characterized the region. By 1600 the basis for future consolidation in Siam, Burma and Vietnam had been laid down, and the Spaniards had established a strong position in Luzon and the Visayas. The existence of small units in the island world helped the Dutch. Even the most potentially cohesive island, Java, was divided into distinct spheres.

Many of the economic changes that characterized the period date back, Chapter 8 argues, to the fifteenth century. This is true of the surge in international commerce that lasted into the early decades of the seventeenth century. Whole communities came to engage in cultivating pepper, cloves, cotton, sugar and benzoin, and became dependent on the international market, and large cosmopolitan port-cities emerged. In a region then short of population, the mobilization of labour was crucial. There were sophisticated methods for investing capital in trade and securing an adequate return. But capital and fixed property in private hands enjoyed less security over against the state than in early modern Europe. The need to counter Dutch pressure added to absolutist trends that in the end might be counter-productive. That pressure, and the reaction to it, are to be seen in the context of the economic crisis that marked the mid-sevententh century in Southeast Asia as elsewhere. From the late seventeenth century, the direct involvement of Southeast Asian states with international commerce diminished. The Chinese communities secured new opportunities.

Chapter 9 takes up the account of religious developments in Southeast Asia from about 1500. European material, particularly from missionary sources, is used to survey indigenous beliefs in areas still in the sixteenth century little touched by world religions. The advance of Islam and Christianity, particularly in the island world, is then discussed. Their adaptation to the local context may be compared with that of Hinduism, Buddhism and Confucianism in the preceding phase. The eighteenth century, a time of disruptive economic and political change, was also a time of renewed religious activity.

Chapter 10 describes the region in the late eighteenth and early nineteenth centuries as it began to be drawn into a new phase of world economic development and of European political aspiration. On the mainland three new dynasties were founded—the Konbaung, the Chakri, and the Nguyen—but their policies and their prospects differed. In Java reaction to growing interference by the Dutch led to the Java War of the 1820s. In the other Indonesian islands their inactivity facilitated British commercial enterprise, in turn stimulating the development of a number of indigenous states, as well as an outbreak of adventurism and marauding. The temporary British occupation of Manila in the 1760s forced the Spaniards to reappraise their policy in the Philippines. The islands were increasingly opened to world trade, and substantial economic and social change resulted.

6

INTERACTIONS WITH THE OUTSIDE WORLD AND ADAPTATION IN SOUTHEAST ASIAN SOCIETY, 1500–1800

Southeast Asia in the period 1500–1800 witnessed important demographic developments which were to have significant consequences in the region. While the Indians and the Chinese had visited Southeast Asia regularly since the early Christian era, they were now coming in far larger numbers than previously. During the early seventeenth century the Japanese, new to the area, became involved in Southeast Asian trade in order to redress internal economic problems faced by the new Tokugawa shogunate. The newest and most formidable of the foreigners were the Europeans, who were determined to acquire a monopoly of the spice trade. The story of the circumstances which brought these foreign groups to the region and the manner in which they became established is an essential part of Southeast Asian history.

Equally important to the history of this period is the interaction between the foreign and Southeast Asian communities which brought innovations and adaptations in local society. The establishment of the European-controlled city, which created a unique mixture of foreign and indigenous elements in its physical structure, government, economic affairs, and inhabitants, was one such innovation in Southeast Asia. With its European administration and large foreign Asian population, the city presented local inhabitants with the opportunity to observe and participate in new economic activities, to adopt and adapt useful novel ideas, and even to establish sexual liaisons with the foreigners which produced the various types of mestizo or mixed racial/ethnic communities. These mestizo communities flourished in the cities and became the ideal intermediaries, helping to bridge the social, economic, cultural, and technological gaps which divided the foreign groups from the Southeast Asians.

The frequent interaction between Southeast Asians and foreign groups also led to transmission of ideas in shipbuilding and firearms technology. The Southeast Asian boat had evolved through contact with traditions of neighbouring lands, and local shipwrights continued to build new types of ships, modify existing ones, or abandon outdated designs in accordance with their needs. The vastly increased presence of European and foreign Asian shipping in Southeast Asian waters in this period provided the Southeast Asian with an ideal opportunity to learn new foreign shipbuilding techniques and to make crucial decisions regarding the feasibility of competing with particular foreign carriers or warships. The decisions taken were to have important repercussions on Southeast Asia's ability to maintain its dominance in both long-distance and regional trade.

The technology of firearms was introduced to Southeast Asia via China, India, and Turkey, but it was Europe which made the greatest impact on local firearms production in this period. While Southeast Asians had learned to manufacture their own cannon, handguns, and gunpowder, they and the rest of the world were left in the wake of the European as a result of a technological revolution in the late seventeenth century which took the European to the forefront in firearms technology. The Southeast Asians on the whole attempted to incorporate the latest ideas, but cultural factors hindered a total adoption of the new technology. An added obstacle was the policy of the European governments in Asia to deny outsiders access to this information, thereby reducing Southeast Asia's ability to maintain the pace of change.

This, then, is a story of certain innovations and adaptations which occurred in Southeast Asia as a result of the interactions between foreign groups and the local inhabitants between 1500 and 1800. The Southeast Asians received foreign groups with their new ideas, and they adopted and adapted those ideas which best suited their purposes. In the past such an approach had always been appropriate, and in this period there was little reason to believe that a selective response would not once again prove successful in strengthening and enriching Southeast Asian society.

THE COMING OF FOREIGN GROUPS

The Asians

Throughout their long trade and cultural relations, China has always regarded Southeast Asia as inferior in status. China was the Middle Kingdom, the Centre of the Universe, the superior and self-sufficient civilization. The non-Chinese 'barbarian' races sought contact with China to receive its beneficence in the form of knowledge and material goods. Objects from the outside world could therefore be regarded only as 'tribute', while reciprocal goods in exchange from the Chinese emperor were seen as 'gifts'. In keeping with this state philosophy, all foreign trade was entrusted to the Ministry of Ritual Affairs (*Li bu*). Chinese imperial governments actively discouraged the movements of their traders to foreign lands and regarded overseas trade as 'tributary trade', a concept which had originally applied to China's relations with its nomadic neighbours but later extended to all foreign groups. Soon after 1433, the date of the last of seven vast overseas expeditions known as the 'Ming voyages', the Ming emperors turned away from the sea and enforced a policy in which 'not even a little plank was allowed to drift to the sea'.[1] The state-initiated expeditions ended, and all overseas trade was placed under a ban, not to be lifted until 1567.

Despite the periodic central government decrees forbidding such trade, the southeastern provinces of Fujian, Guangdong, and Zhejiang were not significantly hampered in their traditional participation in overseas commerce. Fujian had been engaged in this trade since the ninth century and was the first to establish large settled communities in the 'Nanyang' ('Southern Ocean', the term used to refer to Southeast Asia). Quanzhou, the centre for Fujianese maritime enterprises between the ninth and the fifteenth centuries, was supplanted by Yuegang in Zhangzhou prefecture (later renamed Haicheng, as a new administrative seat in 1567) in the late fifteenth century, and in turn was displaced by Amoy (Xiamen) between the mid-seventeenth and the eighteenth centuries. Fujian's prominent role in overseas ventures was due to the availability of capital derived from land and labour from a large lineage organization. Prominent local families with capital from their landed estates usually funded a junk and would hire a relative or servant to become managing 'partner' to undertake the risky overseas journey. While the shipowner held the largest part of the investment on the ship, all the crewmen were also given the opportunity to join the partnership (*gongsi*). Others were consigned space on the ship for their goods in a commenda system. It was commonplace to regard the crew as merchants first and sailors second. Rural poverty, particularly after the mid-sixteenth century, was also a contributing factor in forcing many Fujianese to go abroad, and by the beginning of the seventeenth century they were found in increasing numbers in the Philippines, Japan, and the Indonesian areas. Canton (Guangzhou) in Guangdong province and Ningbo in Zhejiang were two other ports which played an important role in China's overseas trade.

The Eastern (*Dongyang*) and Western (*Xiyang*) Seas trade system was initiated in Fujian in 1567. At Yuegang passes were awarded annually to the overseas trade guild (*yanghang*) that outfitted junks which took one of two routes. The Western Seas route went along the Southeast Asian mainland coast from Vietnam to the Malay peninsula and ended at the entrepôt of Banten in west Java. The Eastern Seas route went via Japan, the Ryukyus, the Philippines, and the Indonesian islands and had its principal terminus in Manila. In the early seventeenth century the system was disrupted by the cruisers of the Vereenigde Oost-Indische Compagnie (VOC, the Dutch East India Company) which made the waters off Manila unsafe, attacked the Fujian coast, and blockaded Banten.

The disturbances created by Dutch activity on the China coast provided the opportunity in 1629 for an ex-pirate Zheng Zhilong to gain the favour of the provincial authorities and eventually control Fujian's overseas

---

[1] Leonard Blussé, 'Chinese commercial networks and state formation in Southeast Asia', paper presented to the Conference on Southeast Asia from the Fifteenth to the Eighteenth Centuries, Lisbon, December 1989, 3.

shipping. When the Manchus began their conquest of China, the south under the dominance of the Zheng, including the famous 'Coxinga' (Zheng Chenggong), remained loyal to the Ming and continued to trade to Southeast Asia. Nevertheless, there was a marked drop in the numbers of junks arriving in the region, which forced the Chinese trade agents already settled in Southeast Asia to adapt to local economic networks in order to survive. Many of those who had settled in Batavia after 1619 were forced to move either to the northern coastal towns of Java to continue their former intermediary functions, or to the interior to become tax farmers.

With the end of Ming resistance in 1683, the new Manchu Qing dynasty adopted a more positive attitude toward overseas trade which lasted for over a century and led to greater co-operation between the merchants and state officials. The desire for security and 'maritime defence' encouraged the Qing dynasty to lift the maritime ban in 1684. They realized that places such as Fujian were dependent on international trade for their livelihood, and maritime security could be jeopardized by discontented coastal provinces. It was this security factor, rather than the ideological reasons of trade with the outside world, which was the reason for the promulgation and the rescinding of bans on overseas activities.

The return of Chinese trade and migration led to the opening of Batavia's Ommelanden where the Chinese became involved in agriculture, especially in the establishment of sugar plantations. Those who had earlier moved to the north Javanese coasts and the interior of Java helped to monetize Java's economy, with the most prominent even becoming part of the nobility in the northern coastal towns. The Fujianese were joined in this period by those from Chaozhou and Quanzhou, with the former becoming involved in the lucrative Siamese rice trade and in building junks in Ayutthaya because of the lack of suitable timber in their home region. Their ships also brought large numbers of Hakka migrants to Southeast Asia. The increased emigration from China was a major factor in the imperial authorities' decision in 1717 to impose yet another ban on overseas trade. But this ban was a failure at the very outset: trade to Vietnam was barely affected and that to the Indonesian islands was resumed after five years. The ban was thus officially withdrawn in 1727. The lifting of the ban saw the resumption of Chinese trade and migration to Southeast Asia and the involvement of Chinese in new ventures. There were those who established gambir plantations in Riau, and others who opened tin mines on Bangka and the Malay peninsula and gold mines in Borneo. With these new enterprises Chinese settlements began to sprout in the interior, as well as in the coastal towns.

After the establishment of Spanish Manila in 1571, it became one of the principal destinations for Chinese migrants, with an estimated 630 junks arriving from southern China in the first thirty years. By 1586 the Chinese population of 10,000 dwarfed the approximately 800 Spaniards and Mexican creoles in the city. The growing disparity in numbers caused the Spanish authorities grave concern and so they created a separate Chinese quarter, known as the Parian, within the Spanish walled city, the Intramuros. After the old Parian was burned down, a new one was built in 1595 outside the walls for security reasons. The numbers of Chinese continued to grow despite massacres in 1603, 1639, 1661 and 1686, and in a number of other 'reprisals'. Attempts by the Spanish authorities after 1603 to limit the numbers of Chinese to 6000 through legislation proved unsuccessful, and by 1750 the Chinese population had risen to 40,000.

Batavia, founded by the Dutch East India Company in 1619, came to harbour another major concentration of overseas Chinese in Southeast Asia. It was the policy of the Company from the outset to attract a large population of Dutch freeburghers and Chinese. The former failed to come in sufficient numbers, and the Chinese were at first brought from coastal areas of China and from the northern Javanese port cities where Chinese communities had been established in earlier centuries. In 1620 junks began to arrive from China depositing hundreds of migrants, and with the resumption of China's official trade to Southeast Asia in 1683, the numbers of junks arriving annually in Batavia's roadstead grew from an average of three or four to about twenty. Many who came were illegal immigrants who were landed on the islands or isolated coastlines near Batavia and eventually found their way to northern Javanese ports. The new Chinese migrants were primarily from Amoy, Canton, Zhenhai, and Ningbo.

While the Dutch found the Chinese to be ideal settlers because of their diligence and ability to fulfil a great variety of tasks, they feared the sizeable Chinese population which dwarfed the European presence. Between 1680 and 1740 the Chinese population in Batavia doubled, with the Chinese accounting for 20 per cent of the total population or 50 per cent of the non-slave population. The office of Kapitan China was created by the Dutch in 1619 to administer the Chinese population, but the spectacular growth of the Chinese population in Batavia eventually led to the creation of other Chinese officials called 'lieutenants' and 'secretaries' to assist the Kapitan. By 1740 there were one captain and six lieutenants holding office in Batavia.

The third major area of Chinese concentration in Southeast Asia was in Siam, in the royal capitals of Ayutthaya, then Thonburi, and finally Bangkok. In the seventeenth century the Chinese lived both within the walls of Ayutthaya and outside. The Chinese quarter was located in the southeast corner of the city, while outside the walls the Chinese were concentrated to the south and the east. Only the Chinese and the Muslim trading communities had any substantial population in the city, and two of the finest streets ran through their quarters. Along these streets were the major public market and more than 100 two-storey houses of stone or brick with tiled roofs, which contrasted sharply with the vast majority of other buildings of bamboo and thatch. The Chinese community was so numerous that unlike the other foreign communities it had two leaders called *kapitan*, or by the Siamese noble title of *nai*. In addition to being traders and merchants, the Chinese were pig-breeders, artisans, physicians, and actors, with a fortunate few even becoming Siamese court officials.

The Chinese had a very favourable position in Siam because they were outside the system by which all freedmen (*phrai*) were registered in a specific district under a lord or noble (*nai*) and thus liable for corvée labour. The Chinese were therefore able to use the Siamese royal capital as a base and move freely throughout the country or go overseas and engage in

trade or become wage-labourers. They came to manage successful commercial enterprises and were employed by the rulers to collect taxes or to
run government enterprises, such as tin-mining and state overseas trade.
Since the bulk of the latter trade was with China, the Siamese court used
Chinese as port officials, captains and navigators of royal junks, and
purchasers and sellers of overseas consignments for the king and the
nobility. In addition to the offical tribute trade, Chinese merchants resident in
Siam and China conducted an 'unofficial' trade by supplying products for
the royal trade to China and assuring the delivery of tribute gifts to the
Siamese court from the Malay vassal kingdoms. The most prominent
Chinese came to serve as court officials in the Sino-Siamese tributary trade
on behalf of the Ayutthaya court. Although such practices were condemned
by the Chinese emperor elsewhere, he tolerated the Chinese serving the
Siamese ruler as *Ratakusa-tibodi* (individuals charged with outfitting
the royal junks for trade), interpreters, shipmerchants, shipmasters, and
crewmen in the tributary trade.

When Taksin, the son of a Teochiu father and a Thai mother, was
formally crowned in Thonburi in 1768, he was assisted by many Chinese
from his father's home area of Chaozhou. Their trade provided the food
and other resources necessary for Taksin to build his new capital at
Thonburi on the Chao Phraya and to overcome the challenges of other
Thai groups for dominance after the fall of Ayutthaya in 1767. Once Taksin
was firmly in control, the Chinese helped to stimulate the local economy
with their gold and silver and through their international trade. In recognition of their role, Taksin created a privileged group known as the *chin
luang*, or 'royal Chinese', whose role was perhaps modelled after the
huangshang or emperor's merchants in China. He relied on them to deal not
only with commercial matters but also with political and military affairs.
Along the Gulf of Thailand and in peninsular Siam, Taksin appointed *chin
luang* as tax farmers, provincial governors, and military commanders.

A great advantage of the Chinese as royal trade agents was their
familiarity with and acceptance into international Chinese commercial
circles. Through their knowledge of the China market, their personal links
with the mercantile groups in southeastern China, and concessions made
by Chinese authorities to Chinese sailors and Chinese-style vessels whatever the ultimate ownership of the ship or the cargo, the Chinese became
indispensable to the Siamese élite for the China trade. Since those Chinese
who served as officials of the state automatically became incorporated into
the Siamese system of ranking based on 'dignity marks' (*sakdina*), the
Chinese provided with the position of 'captain' of a trade vessel or of a tax
farm achieved sufficient marks to be classified as nobility. In the late
eighteenth century Chinese headmen in lower Siam were given clientships
by Rama I with equivalent powers to an autonomous ruler.

While Manila, Batavia, and Ayutthaya-Thonburi-Bangkok became the
three major centres of overseas Chinese populations in Southeast Asia,
Vietnam through propinquity and historical circumstances continued to be
a focus of Chinese activity in this period. The port of Fai-fo (present-day
Hoi An) was a major trading centre in South Vietnam in the early
seventeenth century and consisted of two settlements, one Japanese and

the other Chinese. By 1695 the Chinese were still prominent, serving the ten to twelve Chinese junks which arrived annually from Japan, Canton, Siam, Cambodia, Manila and Batavia. The Japanese, on the other hand, had disappeared from Vietnam and from many other parts of Southeast Asia, ending their short but spectacular involvement in the economic affairs of the region.

Toward the middle of the sixteenth century the continuous civil wars which had wracked Japan were coming to an end, and many of the lords (daimyo) began to devote their energies to overseas trade. The development of the domestic economy and the growth of towns gave birth to a wealthy class of merchants who also began to invest in international commerce. The first Tokugawa shogun, Ieyasu, encouraged foreign trade as a means of strengthening the finances of the shogunate. Japanese ships carrying the shogun's red seal increased in numbers in Southeast Asia, and they were welcomed by local rulers because they bore personal letters and gifts from the shogun himself. Between 1600 and 1635 more than 350 Japanese ships went overseas under the Red Seal permit system. They called into approximately nineteen ports, including Vietnam, Cambodia, the islands in the Malay-Indonesian archipelago, and Luzon in the Philippines. A measure of the importance of this Japanese trade was their export of silver. Between 1615 and 1625 an estimated 130,000–160,000 kilograms of silver was sold, amounting to 30–40 per cent of the total world output outside Japan.[2]

The Japanese were especially prominent in Ayutthaya, and by the late 1620s the trade between Siam and Japan was probably greater than Siam's total trade with other nations. Japanese sources indicate that between 1604 and 1616 some thirty-six Japanese ships issued with the official Red Seal permit were destined for Siam, the highest number authorized for any single country in those years A large colony of Japanese came to settle in Ayutthaya, with 1000--1500 living in the Japanese quarter of the city. King Sontham (r. 1620–8) had a personal Japanese bodyguard, and the Japanese adventurer Yamada came to wield considerable influence in the Siamese court. But in 1632 the new Siamese ruler Prasat Thong (r. 1629–56) massacred many of the Japanese in the city and forced others to flee the country. Thereafter the Chinese regained their dominance in the Siamese trade.

Between 1633 and 1636 the Tokugawa shogunate gradually closed Japan to foreign traders, but the links between Japan and Southeast Asia, especially Siam, remained open. Between 1647 and 1700 some 130 Siamese ships arrived at Nagasaki, and though the Siamese in 1715 were limited to one junk a year, it was a privilege denied many other nations. Other Southeast Asian areas benefited from Tokugawa policy which divided foreigners into three groups: the Chinese (To-jin), the Catholic Europeans, i.e. the Spaniards and Portuguese (Nanban-jin), and the Protestant Dutchmen (Kōmōi-jin, lit. 'red-haired people'). Among the To-jin was a special category for areas of Southeast Asia known as 'inner ports' (Okuminato). Ships

---

[2] Iwao Seiichi, 'Japanese foreign trade in the sixteenth and seventeenth centuries', *Acta Asiatica*, 30 (1976) 10.

from such places as Tonkin, Cambodia, Ayutthaya, Nakhon Sithammarat, Songkhla, Pattani, Melaka, and Batavia were therefore able to maintain trade with Japan.[3] One important consequence of Tokugawa policy forbidding Japanese abroad from returning home was the gradual amalgamation of the Japanese community into Southeast Asian society.

A third important foreign Asian group in Southeast Asia in this period was the Indians. Like their Chinese counterparts, the Indians had been trading to Southeast Asia since the early Christian era and had left a lasting impact on local culture. Indian overseas commercial ventures were mainly in private hands, since Indian states relied on agricultural production and internal commerce for their revenue. Nevertheless, there was considerable individual investment in overseas trade by rulers, administrators, and military officials who were content to leave control in the hands of merchants.

The high cost of building a ship and of obtaining a full cargo, as well as the danger of losing all through shipwreck, discouraged most merchants from purchasing more than one ship. Although an owner-merchant could go with his ship and cargo overseas, he usually appointed an agent to captain the vessel and to undertake all the necessary commercial transactions. The owner-merchant and the captain were allotted the largest cargo space, while the rest of the ship was parcelled out to small traders who accompanied their one or two bales of cotton cloth in the hope of gaining profit overseas. These smaller merchants were able to compete effectively alongside the few wealthier ones because they were satisfied with a lower profit margin and were able to establish their own personal networks in foreign ports. The ubiquity of the Indian trader, which so impressed Tomé Pires and other Portuguese observers in the sixteenth century, was a consequence of the practice of Indian ships bringing large numbers of these small Indian merchants with their goods. The sailors and ship's officers were also provided with space to carry trade goods which were sold abroad to supplement their wretched incomes. Unlike the Chinese, however, the Indians did not settle in large numbers in Southeast Asia in this period.

The vast majority of Indian traders to Southeast Asia came from three regions: the northwest (Gujerat), the south (Malabar and Coromandel), and the northeast (Bengal). In these areas there were a few major emporia serving as collection centres for a large well-developed inland trading system, while small individual ports serviced small specific interior trade networks. The importance of Gujerat lay in the strategic location of its ports lying at the confluence of a number of trading systems. Cambay in the sixteenth, Surat in the seventeenth, and Bombay in the eighteenth century linked the oceanic regional trade of Asia with the coastal and interior trade of India. Through links with the Portuguese ports of Goa and Diu, Gujerat became part of an international trade network which extended to China in the east and Europe in the west.

South India was a second major centre for Indian overseas trade. It was pepper which had made the Malabar coast attractive to international

    [3] Yoneo Ishii, 'Seventeenth Century Japanese Documents about Siam', JSS, 59, 2 (July 1971) 164–5.

traders, and by the beginning of the seventeenth century the ports of Calicut, Travancore, and Cannanore had emerged as commercial centres. However, the Coromandel coast in southeast India proved to be even more successful in international trade than Malabar. Masulipatnam in the northern Coromandel and Nagapattinam in the southern Coromandel were the most prominent trading centres in that region. In the sixteenth century Coromandel Hindu traders, called 'Klings' by the Portuguese, frequented the ports of Portuguese Melaka, Aceh, and Banten where they had factors and agents. From these western ports they then sailed westward to the other islands in the Indonesian archipelago. Coromandel trade suffered from Dutch restrictions in the seventeenth century, but Perak, Kedah, and Johor on the Malay peninsula continued to be major terminal points of the Coromandel trade. In mainland Southeast Asia, the Coromandel merchants were active in Arakan, Ava, and Ayutthaya, with Tenasserim serving as a terminal for Mergui and a transit point to the ports on the Gulf of Thailand and Cambodia. Ayutthaya and its outlying provinces became a major growth sector in the Coromandel trade in the seventeenth century.

The decline in Coromandel's trade began in the final decade of the seventeenth century with the fall of the Qutb Shahs of Golconda. The nobility and the patrician merchants appear to have abandoned overseas commerce, and Masulipatnam in northern Coromandel survived with only a reduced amount of international trade. In southern Coromandel Porto Novo, the successor to Nagapatnam, San Tomé, and Cuddalore became the chief ports of the principal Tamil Muslim traders known as 'Chulias'. They reaffirmed links with the rulers of Kedah, Johor, Arakan and Ayutthaya, which had been forged in earlier centuries.

Bengal was the third major Indian area involved in Southeast Asia. In the sixteenth century Satgaon and Chittagong were the two major ports from which Bengal merchants sailed to the Southeast Asian areas, but in the seventeenth century they were replaced by Hooghly, Pipli and Balasore. Bengal's trade was directed principally to Aceh, the Malay peninsula, and to the Burmese and Thai coasts. The Bengal Muslim merchants who were prominent in this trade in the seventeenth century consisted of influential expatriate merchants from west Asia, and possibly from Surat and Golconda, as well as local Islamic communities who were converts from Hindu seafaring castes. Hindu merchants were also an important part of the Bengal trade, though they were less influential than the Muslims. As in the other areas of India, Bengal witnessed a decline in its overseas trade toward the end of the seventeenth century due to the political and economic chaos in the interior.

The Europeans

In addition to the foreign Asians, the Europeans formed another substantial presence in Southeast Asia between 1500 and 1800. The new European traders had a distinct advantage over their more established and more experienced Asian counterparts because they enjoyed support from their governments. Indeed, the earliest European ventures were those initiated and funded by the Portuguese and Spanish royal houses, with the former the first to undertake a systematic policy of finding a direct sea route between Europe and the spice-producing areas of Asia. Since the fourteenth century Portuguese rulers had encouraged the successful trading families of Italy, Spain and France to settle in Lisbon by granting them special privileges. This policy succeeded in making Portugal the 'wharf between two seas',[4] serving both the northern European and the Mediterranean states. By the end of the century there were an estimated 400–500 ships loading annually in the port of Lisbon. The enclaves of Genoese, Venetians, Florentines, Flemings, French, and Germans established in Portugal provided the expertise and capital which encouraged the Crown to expand its trade links beyond Europe.

A major impetus for overseas expansion was the trade in spices— pepper, cinnamon, and the highly-desired trinity of clove, nutmeg, and mace. In the second half of the fifteenth century, Turkish control of the Levant forced the traditional spice routes to move away from the Persian Gulf to the Red Sea. The desire to escape this dependence on the Muslims (an association which in Portugal had been strictly limited by law and constantly condemned by the Church) and to participate directly in the highly lucrative spice trade were important stimuli in Portugal's gradual search for a sea route to Asia. In the first half of the fifteenth century Prince Henry the Navigator encouraged a systematic programme of discovery, which culminated in Vasco da Gama's successful voyage to the west coast of India in 1498. The arrival in Asia was the culmination of Portugal's 'Glorious Enterprise' which had been motivated by a blend of religious fervour, national pride, and commercial profit. Though the Portuguese had not yet reached the home of the fabled clove, nutmeg, and mace in Maluku, da Gama's cargo of spices 'together with the boughs and leaves of the same' aroused considerable excitement in Portugal. To keep the new route a secret, King Manuel of Portugal decreed in 1504 that, on pain of death, complete secrecy must be maintained with regard to the new discoveries. This ban appeared to have been successful, for not a single book on the new information being collected on Asia by the Portuguese is known to have been published during the first fifty years of the sixteenth century.

Affonso de Albuquerque became the architect of the Portuguese Asian empire, or the *Estado da India*, with its administrative centre at Goa. It was he who conceived of the strategy to control the vital nodes of the spice route. This meant seizing Melaka, the principal collecting port of cloves, nutmeg, mace, and Southeast Asian pepper; controlling maritime traffic along the west coast of India; capturing Hormuz at the mouth of the Persian Gulf; and conquering Aden, which was strategically located at the entrance to the Red Sea. This grand plan nearly succeeded: the island of Goa fell in 1510, to be followed by Melaka in 1511 and Hormuz in 1515. Only Aden successfully resisted a Portuguese attack in 1513 and remained outside direct Portuguese control.

The Portuguese Crown created a unique form of state capitalism. It

---

[4] B. W. Diffie and G. D. Winius, *Foundations of the Portuguese empire 1415–1580*, Minneapolis, 1977, 41.

became the sole entrepreneur investing the state's resources to create a trade monopoly in its overseas territories. The Crown monopoly in spices continued in Melaka until 1533 and in Maluku until 1537. But long before this time, the profitability of Crown capitalism was being questioned, and even the Crown began to realize that a steady fixed income free from the vagaries of the marketplace and the venality of its own people was desirable. Thus began the practice of granting concessions to individuals as rewards to buy and sell certain quantities of spices, with the only requirement being that they resell to the Crown one-third of the cargo at a fixed price. If the goods were transported in state ships, then an additional percentage of the freight had to be paid to the Crown. By the second half of the sixteenth century voyages were made in ships owned by the concessionaries themselves, with no royal expense involved.

The Crown trade, including the concessions awarded to various individuals by the king, was only one part of the Portuguese Asian commercial picture. Portuguese private trade was also able to prosper because it relied on products and exchange networks within the Asian region itself. The Portuguese never succeeded in finding a European product which was in demand in Asia, except for gold and silver and armaments, and they lacked the resources to control the existing production system in Asia. They therefore learned to participate in the Asian trade, quickly identifying Indian cloth as the essential item of exchange in the Southeast Asian area. Like the Asian traders, the Portuguese became involved in the peddling trade; they carried goods from port to port, buying, selling, and reselling, and creating profit in each transaction. The transition to the peddling trade was facilitated and even encouraged by the advice and assistance provided by rich Asian merchants residing in ports under Portuguese control.

Portuguese private trade operated in secondary ports of Southeast Asia and complemented the Crown and concessionary trade located in the major stapling centres of Goa, Melaka, and Macao. Private Portuguese merchants were mentioned in Timor in 1522, north coast Java in 1532, with a further 300 trading between Melaka and China and another 300 based in Pattani. Of the eight or nine Portuguese ships in the mid-sixteenth century sailing annually to Coromandel to purchase cloth, only one belonged to the Crown. By the fourth decade of the sixteenth century, Portuguese trade had to all intents and purposes become a part of the Asian system.

In comparison to that of the Portuguese, the Spanish enterprise in Asia was a modest affair, confined almost exclusively to the Philippines. It was very much in the shadow of the Spanish empire in the Americas, being under the direct jurisdiction of the Viceroyalty of Nueva España (New Spain, present-day Mexico). The earliest Spanish contact with Asia was in March 1521 when Magellan's expedition reached the Philippines. Though Magellan himself was killed at Mactan, his crew continued the journey to Maluku and eventually to Spain in 1522, thereby becoming the first to have successfully circumnavigated the globe. The return of the expedition revived the Spanish rulers' dream of reaching Maluku and monopolizing the lucrative trade in spices. Unfortunately, at the time that the expedition reached the Spice Islands, they learned that the Portuguese had been there since 1512. Despite Spain's attempts to include Maluku in its sphere of influence through the Treaty of Tordesillas of 1494, circumstances in Europe forced it to 'relinquish' its claims to Maluku in return for a payment of 350,000 cruzados by Portugal.

For the remainder of the sixteenth century, Spanish initiatives in Asia originated in the viceregal office in Nueva España and only indirectly from the Spanish Crown. In 1542 an expedition was outfitted from Mexico under the command of Ruy López de Villalobos. It was directed to go to the Islas del Poniente, or the Western Islands, a name which navigators after Magellan had given to the Philippine islands. Magellan himself had christened these islands 'San Lazaro' because he had sighted them on that saint's day, and it was Villalobos who honoured the Crown Prince Felipe of Spain by renaming the islands of Samar and Leyte in the Visayas, Felipinas, or the Philippines, a name which was later applied to the entire archipelago. Villalobos was instructed not to violate the arrangements with Portugal, but to investigate the products of the Western Islands. But this expedition, like those which went before, ended in failure.

In November 1564 another expedition of five ships and more than 400 men under the command of Miguel Lopez de Legazpi set sail from Natividad in Mexico with instructions to occupy the Philippine islands. Legazpi was ordered to

> sail with God's blessings to the Western Islands; not to Maluku . . . which according to existing agreements fall under the jurisdiction of the King of Portugal, but to other islands nearby such as the Philippines which lie within the demarcation of the King and are also rich in spices. The main purposes of this expedition are . . . the conversion of the natives and the discovery of a safe route back to Nueva España, that the kingdom may increase and profit from trade and by other legitimate means.[5]

From the outset of the Philippine venture, the Christianization of the natives was regarded as one of the most important priorities of the Spaniards.

Though the profit motive was still prominent, the economic prospects of the Philippines as a colony appeared to Legazpi to be bleak. The only marketable spice was cinnamon, which grew in the hostile Muslim-dominated island of Mindanao. The amounts available were not sufficient to sustain a Pacific trade with the Americas, and there was only a small quantity of gold. Furthermore, the natives were too poor to provide a ready market for manufactured products. In short, Legazpi informed the Spanish monarch that the Philippine colony could not be sustained by trade. But once the Spanish authorities in the Philippines had time to observe the local and international trade being conducted around them, they realized that there was in fact great potential for Spanish participation in the thriving economic link between these islands and China.

The move of the Spanish government from Cebu to Manila in 1571 was a decisive step in the establishment of direct trade ties between the Spaniards and the Chinese. By 1576 the Chinese were frequenting the port of

---

[5] Rafael Lopez, trans., *The Christianization of the Philippines*, Manila, 1965, document 5, 262.

Manila as they had done in pre-Hispanic times, but this time dealing with the Spaniards rather than with their former local trading partners. It was Legazpi who first suggested that a trade in Chinese silk could perhaps replace the loss of the trade in spices to the Portuguese. Thus began the galleon trade, where merchants from Macao brought Canton silk, cotton cloths, and other wares to waiting merchants from Acapulco, who offered their silver from the American colonies in exchange. So valuable was this Macao–Manila–Acapulco trade that the Spanish merchants from Nueva España settled in Manila in order to be able to supervise operations and assure the proper loading of the Chinese goods on the large Spanish galleons. The best years of the galleon trade were the last decades of the sixteenth and the first decades of the seventeenth century. In the peak year of 1597, the amount of bullion sent from Acapulco to Manila reached a total of twelve million pesos, a figure exceeding the total value of the official trans-Atlantic trade, although the normal value of the trade was still an impressive three to five million pesos. Despite the later restriction of a single galleon leaving annually from each of the two ports, the galleon trade remained a dominant force in the Spanish–Philippine economy until the late eighteenth century and was abandoned only in 1815.

The Philippines never provided Spain with the fabulous riches which it received from the gold and silver mines in America. But it was perhaps because Philip II of Spain was able to rely on a steady source of revenue from the Americas that he was willing to tolerate the losses sustained in the Philippines and magnanimously offer to make it 'the arsenal and warehouse of the faith'.[6] With this pronouncement the religious aspect of the colonization now took indisputable precedence in the Philippines. Restrictions on Spanish travel to the interior, because of the perceived dangers of a hostile population and environment, led the authorities to rely increasingly on the clergy to help govern and prepare the inhabitants in the interior for the acceptance of the 'Spanish' religion and state. Though the numbers of regular and secular clergy were not very high— perhaps some 400 in the whole of the Philippines during the sixteenth and seventeenth centuries—their leadership in both spiritual and secular affairs was a crucial factor in the maintenance of Spanish control.

Neither the Portuguese nor the Spanish economic efforts in Asia had fulfilled the early promise of fabulous riches from the East. Learning from their experience, the northern Europeans came to experiment with a new economic form in the hope of succeeding where the Iberian nations had failed. The seventeenth century was to bring the English and the Dutch into the Asian commercial scene and introduce a highly innovative trading idea: the joint-stock company. It had distinct advantages over other commercial ventures because it could maintain large fixed assets, exist beyond shifting groups of investors, and obtain exclusive trading rights from the state.

The English East India Company (EIC) was organized in 1600, two years before the formation of the United Dutch East India Company. It

6 John Leddy Phelan, *The Hispanization of the Philippines: Spanish aims and Filipino responses, 1565–1700*, Madison, 1967, 14.

embodied the spirit of mercantilism in its manipulation of political power and privileges for commercial goals. Nevertheless, the EIC sought to avoid being dominated by the Crown or the aristocracy, even to the point of refusing to approve the membership of James I in 1624. From the beginning the EIC's policy was dictated by its own concerns, rather than those of the state. In like manner the Company's interests had a low priority for the early Stuart kings.

The first English voyages proceeded with great caution, and only after the safe return of each fleet was another outfitted. By the end of the second voyage (1604–6) the English realized that the English goods would not be profitable in the Malay-Indonesian archipelago, and that there needed to be a greater variety of products from Europe. They also learned through experience and through contact with Portuguese traders that Indian piece-goods were essential for any bartering in Southeast Asia. Thus in the third voyage in 1607 the English had instructions to establish trade with Surat or the Red Sea ports before going on to Southeast Asia. On this and subsequent voyages the EIC sought to develop markets for goods for the Europe-to-Asia trade, while seeking sources of Indian piece-goods for the archipelago.

Up to 1612 the English voyages were separately financed, with shareholders participating in a particular expedition. There was no co-operation among English factors handling different voyages, which resulted in a situation where there existed three rival English lodges in Banten. With the proliferation of trading factories in Asia, the EIC decided in 1615 to centralize its operations by placing all factories 'to the Northwards' (Gujerat westward) under Surat and those 'to the Southwards' (Coromandel eastward) under Banten. On the seventh voyage (1611–15) it founded factories at Masulipatnam, at Ayutthaya, and at Pattani. The Thai ruler was only too willing to allow the English to trade in his kingdom as a counter to the ever-growing strength of the VOC. In eastern Indonesia the EIC had successfully opened a factory in the kingdom of Makassar and gained control of the islands of Run and Nailaka in the Banda islands. By its presence in these sites it had obtained access to the cloves, nutmeg, and mace, thereby imperilling the attempted monopoly of these valued spices by the VOC. In 1623 the chief factor of the EIC and others at the English factory in Ambon were killed by the Dutch, ending for over a century any further English involvement in the Spice Islands.

The situation for the English in Batavia, where they had moved from Banten in 1619, became unbearable. In 1628 they finally received instructions to return to Banten where the sultan was said to be eager to have them back. Although the English factories in the Spice Islands, Ayutthaya, Pattani, and Japan were abandoned, the Banten factory continued to receive pepper from the east-coast ports of Sumatra and spices from Makassar. But the tiny English presence in the archipelago, harassed at every turn by the VOC, had little real chance of success. In 1682 the English were forced to abandon Banten, retaining only a small post in Bengkulen in southwest Sumatra. The EIC in effect retreated to the Indian subcontinent and made India its principal area of activity until the middle of the eighteenth century.

Throughout this early period the EIC was often at a disadvantage compared to other European traders. The English government opposed the export of bullion, even though this was the principal means of obtaining goods in Asia. Furthermore, private English trade was allowed to flourish because it was regarded as being complementary to EIC activities. In practice, however, EIC officials and their wives were able to enrich themselves through private trade at the expense of the Company. Finally, the EIC never exercised the degree of centralization of finances and administration in the seventeenth century which was such a prominent feature of its much more efficient rival, the Dutch East India Company.

The expansion of the Dutch into Asia was part of a commercial and technological revolution which transformed the Low Countries from a colony of Spain into one of the leading European nations in the seventeenth century. This 'Golden Century' of the United Provinces of the Netherlands was the culmination of a long process of capital accumulation dating back to the fourteenth century in the herring trade. From the highly successful fisheries, the Baltic trade, the carrying trade, and the much older river trade, the Lowlands accumulated vast capital resources. In addition, persecution of Calvinists by the Spaniards in the southern Netherlands led to an exodus of wealthy merchants and industrialists from Antwerp, Ghent, Brussels, and other cities who brought their riches and expertise to the north, especially to Amsterdam. It was they, with their long experience in the Portuguese enterprise, who were in the forefront in financing new commercial and trade ventures. The combination of capital and expertise enabled the northern Netherlands to become the centre for the leading European financiers.

The readiness of the Dutch to invest in new ventures to Asia was a natural progression in their growing involvement in world trade. The first Dutch fleet to reach the islands of Indonesia was in 1596 when three ships and a yacht anchored off Banten. There then followed similar voyages sponsored by a number of port towns in the Netherlands. In the six years of the 'Wilde Vaarten' (Free Navigation) of these competing companies, the profits made were less than two or at the most three months' profit in the herring fisheries. Nevertheless, the lure of the riches to be made in the spice trade attracted rival companies which threatened to destroy the profitability of the whole venture. Finally, in 1602, after much bargaining and compromising they were persuaded to amalgamate into the United Netherlands Chartered East India Company (Vereenigde Geoctroyeerde Oost-Indische Compagnie, VOC).

The directors of the Company, the *Heeren XVII* (Seventeen Gentlemen), initially instructed the VOC officials in Batavia to avoid unnecessary wars with native kingdoms, especially in 'the neutral places belonging to free nations, where we find the laws and do not have to bring them'.[7] However, under the powerful Governors-General Jan Pieterszoon Coen (1618–23, 1627–9) and Antonio van Diemen (1636–45), the directives of the *Heeren XVII* were generally ignored. In 1619 Coen seized Jayakatra

---

[7] P. Mijer, 'Punten en artikelen, in vorm van Generale Instructie', 26 April 1650, in *Verzameling van instructiën, ordonnaciën en reglementen voor de Regeering van Nederlandsch-Indië*, Batavia, 1848, 89.

(Jakarta) from Banten and established the city of Batavia, which became the VOC headquarters in Asia. He then removed the English from the Banda islands in 1623; the Portuguese from Maluku in 1605, Negombo and Gale in Sri Lanka in 1640, and Melaka in 1641; and the Spaniards from the northern part of Taiwan by 1643 and Maluku in 1663. Since these successes had helped secure the spice monopoly and contributed to the ousting of the English and Portuguese, the *Heeren XVII* raised few objections. Coen's policy of maintaining VOC power by the establishment of forts, garrisons, and warships was generally upheld. But by the second half of the seventeenth century, they were less tolerant of costly wars to enhance trade.

Learning from Portuguese experience, Coen pleaded with the *Heeren XVII* in 1619 for sufficient ships to enable the VOC to participate in the intra-Asian trade. His aim was not to dismantle the Asian peddling trade but to co-ordinate it to the VOC's advantage by retaining ships and capital within Asia, rather than repatriating them as was then the practice. By not issuing dividends to its stockholders in these early years, the VOC was able to preserve its capital in Asia and to create a fleet and a network of factories to participate in the profitable intra-Asian trade.

In addition to the creation of Asian capital, Coen was also instrumental in introducing a system of intelligence-gathering to assist the VOC against its European and Asian competitors. Economic accounts and local political reports were sent regularly to Batavia from Dutch posts throughout the Asian region. Important trade decisions were thus based on an analysis of economic and political intelligence stretching from Europe to the farthest outpost of the VOC trading empire. The VOC would sustain a loss in one area to eliminate a competitor, while making it up in another area by using crucial information on production shortages or political instability. With the VOC ships also becoming the dominant carriers of Asian trade, many kingdoms were dependent on the goodwill of the VOC to assure the continuing export of their products and the import of valued goods.

By 1640 the total VOC capital circulating in Asia, known as the 'Indies Funds', was as much as eight to ten million guilders, which equalled or exceeded the entire Portuguese investment in the pepper trade at its height. But although the sheer size of its investments, personnel and ships had an influence on the Asian peddling trade, the VOC did not displace this trade but simply operated with it. While the Company's organization was superior to the pedlar, its costs were higher. A shrewd pedlar who was satisfied with a smaller profit margin than the Company could operate successfully alongside the Company.

Through the joint-stock company, both the VOC and EIC were able to penetrate the Asian market and make a far greater impact on the local economies than either the Portuguese or Spanish Crown monopolies. Because of the dominance of the VOC, the English Company was never able to compete effectively in Southeast Asia. The VOC, on the other hand, through its Indies Fund, superior freight capacity, and its unique intelligence-gathering system, permanently altered trading patterns and affected the economic and political future of many Southeast Asian societies. Even though most European activities were confined to the coastal regions, frequent intercourse between the coast and the interior in many

Southeast Asian kingdoms meant that even the interior could not long remain insulated from the new ideas and pressures being introduced by the Europeans.

The principal attraction of Southeast Asia to foreign groups had always been the trade in spices and other exotic products. But in the period between 1500 and 1800, many also came to Southeast Asia driven by the higher ideals of national honour and religion, as well as by the more immediate concerns of security and survival. The search for a safe haven for trade and settlement in Southeast Asia was facilitated by the openness of local rulers to outsiders. The result was the establishment of large permanent foreign settlements in Southeast Asia. Many continued to participate in international trade, while others pursued occupations learned in their own lands or developed new skills to cater to the changing Southeast Asian economic landscape.

Because of the size of the foreign communities, especially in the cities of Melaka, Manila, and Batavia, there arose new foci of power which came to challenge the indigenous states in trade, in political influence, and in terms of loyalty from foreign and local groups. What assisted this process was the establishment of the European-controlled city in Southeast Asia. Within the walls, the protected suburbs, and the roadsteads or harbours of these cities, the Southeast Asian could witness the creation of a new urban form; the symbiotic relationship between the European, the Chinese, the mestizo or mixed ethnic group, and the local inhabitants; and the new shipbuilding and firearms technology of the European and the foreign Asians. These developments foreshadowed the type of colonial society which was to emerge in later centuries from the increasing disparity in resources and strength between the Southeast Asians and the foreign groups.

INNOVATIONS AND ADAPTATIONS IN SOCIETY

The European-Controlled City

Between 1500 and 1800 there were three European-controlled cities which attained great prominence in Southeast Asia: Portuguese (and later Dutch) Melaka, Spanish Manila, and Dutch Batavia. They came to symbolize to the Southeast Asian the new and growing importance not only of the Europeans but also the foreign Asians in the area. Though these cities shared a number of similar features, there were also differences which reflected the role which they had been given in the overall goals of their masters in Europe. Portuguese Melaka and Dutch Batavia were entrepôts serving the economic interests of the Portuguese Crown and the shareholders of the Dutch East India Company, respectively. The Portuguese enterprise had a decided religious thrust as a result of the *Padroado Real*, or the Royal Patronage, in which the Papacy had entrusted the conversion of heathen lands to the Portuguese Crown. Nevertheless, ultimately it was the profits from the spice trade which informed the activities of the Portuguese in their factories and customs houses. For the Dutch the establishment of Batavia had one basic purpose: to create a base and headquarters for the expansion of the Company's economic empire in Asia. Batavia also functioned as an entrepôt, but its principal role was to act as the administrative centre and the symbol of the Company's greatness and power in the Asian world. In marked contrast to the Portuguese in Melaka and the Dutch in Batavia, the economic impetus of Manila was clearly subordinated to cultural-religious imperatives, for imperial Spanish policy saw urban centres as a means of transmitting Spanish language, customs, and religion to the heathen worlds of America and Asia. But whatever the ultimate justification for the establishment and maintenance of the European-controlled cities, they served a useful func- tion in providing the Southeast Asians with the opportunity to observe and learn from the activities of the foreigners resident in their midst.

These European-controlled cities occupied sites which were previously thriving local settlements. When the Portuguese fleet under Vasco da Gama first reached Calicut on the west coast of India in 1498, Melaka was already famous as an international emporium. It was located in the sheltered waters of the Straits of Melaka, a major waterway which linked East Asia to India, the Middle East, and Europe. Moreover, it was at the 'end of the monsoons', the winds which brought the traders from the west on the southwest monsoon, and those from the east on the northeast monsoon (see Map 2.2). The Portuguese thus seized the Malay city in 1511 and rebuilt it on the same site for good reason. Manila was already a thriving Muslim trading settlement of 2000 people located at the mouth of the Pasig River when the Spaniards arrived in 1570. Both Manila and the neighbouring settlement of Tondo were linked through Brunei to the inter- national trade network centred in Melaka. The Spaniards' decision to conquer Manila and to use the site for the development of their own centre was based on Manila's established reputation in the trading world and its access to a rich agricultural interior. Batavia, formerly Jayakatra, was under a provincial lord who acknowledged the overlordship of the sultan of Banten. Its location close to the Sunda Straits, the only other opening through the western half of the archipelago, made it an ideal site for the Dutch who were already using the port extensively for their trading ships. Since the Straits of Melaka were closed off to the Dutch by the Portuguese, the former decided in 1619 to take control of Jayakatra, rebuild it as the main headquarters of the Dutch East India Company, and christen it 'Batavia' after the ancestors of the Dutch people.

By rebuilding on established sites, the Europeans were inheriting excel- lent locations and a trade reputation which they hoped to maintain. At first fortresses and buildings were erected in the native style, using wood, bamboo, and nipa palm thatching. Frequent fires led to a policy of using stone, bricks, and roof-tiles, which resulted in more fire-resistant, durable and imposing edifices. The new physical appearance of the European- controlled cities came to symbolize the strong and seemingly permanent presence of the Europeans in the region. In Manila the Spaniards adopted the grid design which had been used in Mexico City with its well-arranged streets and squares. Around the main plaza (*plaza mayor*) were found the cathedral and the municipal buildings, while in the smaller plaza (*plaza de armas*) were the fort and the royal buildings. The wooden palisades were replaced by a stone fortress at the northwest and southwest corners of the city, and in 1593 the city itself was enclosed by stone walls to form the Intramuros. Within these walls stood the equally grand monuments to the spiritual and secular authorities now ruling in Manila. It was no accident that the stone cathedral in Manila was long the most imposing building in the Philippines, though the sturdy but gracious palaces of the archbishop and the governor-general were also impressive. The hall of the colonial assembly (the *Audiencia*), the monasteries, the churches, and the private homes with their balconies, tiled roofs, inner courts, and iron grilles over windows and entrances, were all testimony to the new power exerting its will over the local landscape.

Batavia, too, underwent physical transformation to satisfy the requirements of security, the comfort of a familiar environment, and a style of architecture which would assert Dutch dominance in the surrounding landscape. The fort built at the mouth of the Ciliwung River was earlier sufficient to house many of the Dutch East India Company's buildings, such as the governor-general's residence, the workshops, the treasury, the garrison, the armoury, the counting houses, the prison, the meeting hall of the Council of the Indies, and the first church. The growth of the Dutch population eventually forced the authorities to create more housing outside the fort. As a result new fortifications were erected in 1645 to enclose the settlements on both the east and west banks of the river. With security ensured, the Dutch undertook to replicate Holland in the East by creating a system of canals (Figure 6.1). The river was straightened to form one large canal, with a number of other smaller canals encircling and criss-crossing the city. Along these canals stood the one- or two-storey brick homes of the more prominent citizens. Among the stone and brick structures, the most impressive was the town hall built in 1710 with its two storeys and large cupola, a fitting tribute to the dominance of the burgher element in the Company and the city.

In Melaka the Portuguese built their stone fortress on the site of the former palace of the exiled Malay sultan and placed a wall around the main centre, forming an Intramuros. Within these walls the large stone fortress dominated the city of mainly wooden and nipa-thatched houses in the first half of the sixteenth century. By the early seventeenth century the city boasted such large stone structures as the cathedral, the churches, the headquarters of the religious orders, the bishop's palace, and the town hall. In the centre was a small hill on which stood the stone church and the towers of St Paul and the Jesuit convent. In Melaka it was the massive fortress which dominated the landscape, an appropriate symbol of Portugal's long and, in the end, fruitless struggle to maintain an official spice monopoly through the use of force. After the VOC conquest of Portuguese Melaka in 1641, Dutch-style buildings were erected next to Portuguese ones, giving Melaka its distinctive atmosphere.

In keeping with the message conveyed by the durable and imposing European architecture, the superiority of the European was reinforced in other ways in these multi-racial cities. The Europeans controlled the guns,

Figure 6.1   One of the principal canals in Batavia along which were built
imposing Dutch brick buildings.

From Johan Nieuhof, *Voyages and Travels to the East Indies, 1653–1670*, Singapore, 1988, opp. p. 266;
reproduced courtesy Oxford University Press, Kuala Lumpur, Oxford in Asia Historical Reprints.

the ships, and a formidable army composed of a core of Europeans and a
majority of native mercenaries who came from the various areas where the
Europeans had posts. A typical example of the mix of the military force in a
European-controlled city was Dutch Melaka in 1756. One battalion consisted
of 240 Europeans, 100 native Christians, 77 Bugis, and a mixed group of
270 Malays, Indians, Portuguese, and Chinese.[8] Batavia, too, relied heavily
on Asian mercenaries, as well as militia units organized into separate
ethnic groups of Dutch, English, Danish, French, Portuguese and other
Christians (presumably the *Mardijkers*, who were Asian slaves who had
been given their freedom by the Portuguese on their becoming Christian).
The division of the fighting forces into separate ethnic and racial groups
was part of a deliberate Dutch policy to forestall any possibility of their
combining against the authorities. In keeping with this policy, each group
was assigned a specific residential district and encouraged to maintain its
own language, dress, religion, and custom. The Spaniards in Manila relied
principally on recruits from the local Filipino communities, their most
famous mercenary force being the Macabebe Pampangans.

---

[8] Barbara Watson Andaya, 'Melaka under the Dutch, 1641–1795', in K. S. Sandhu and Paul
Wheatley, eds., *Melaka: The transformation of a Malay capital c. 1400–1980*, Kuala Lumpur,
1983, I. 210.

The Europeans quickly stamped their authority on the cities. There was some attempt to build upon earlier political structures, but the different needs and aims of the Europeans inevitably led to changes. Melaka no longer had a Malay sultan, but the Portuguese retained the Malay offices of *bendahara, temenggong,* and *syahbandar* and assigned them different functions. The *bendahara* was no longer the chief Malay civil official likened to a prime minister; instead he was now an Indian merchant in charge of the civil and criminal affairs of the Indian population. The *temenggong* retained his former judicial functions of adjudicating in disputes and punishing offenders, but now his jurisdiction was limited only to the Minangkabau subjects living in areas outside Melaka. The office of *syahbandar*, an important position dealing with international trade in the port, was taken completely out of the hands of the Malays and made into a European office. Affairs of the various ethnic groups in the city were regulated by one of their own people appointed by the Portuguese with the title of *kapitan* or captain. In Manila and Batavia nothing of the former native administration was retained, although the Dutch in Batavia and Melaka (after it was seized from the Portuguese in 1641), also adopted the practice of appointing captains of foreign groups.

Portuguese Melaka was headed by a captain and a council, who were assisted by a factor, a judge, scribes, market inspectors and constabulary officials. Melaka's administration was responsible to the Viceroy and the council of state based in Goa, the headquarters of the entire Asian Portuguese enterprise known as the *Estado da India*. In addition to the royal administration, there were two other types of institutions which were regarded as the twin pillars of Portuguese colonial society: the *Senado da Camara* (town or municipal council) and the *Santa Casa de Misericórdia* (Holy House of Mercy). Since Portuguese overseas appointments of governors, bishops, and magistrates were rarely for more than three years, these institutions provided the needed continuity in administration. The tasks of the councils were vast and varied. In Melaka the council controlled the finances of the city, priced all provisions, established correct weights and measures, maintained the fortress and other public facilities, and acted as a court of first instance. The *Misericórdia* was responsible for the sick and needy and maintained hospitals in Portugal's overseas settlements.

In Manila the Governor-General of the Philippines was appointed by the Viceroy of Nueva España and was ultimately responsible to the Council of the Indies in Spain. He was guided by royal orders and edicts known as the *Recopilación*, or the 'Laws of the Indies', which were transmitted through the Council, as well as other laws applied generally throughout the Spanish colonies. In addition to his administrative status, the governor-general wielded vast military, ecclesiastic, and legislative powers in his position as captain-general, viceregal patron under the *Patronato Real*, and president of the Philippine *Audiencia*. The *Audiencia* was created in 1583 to serve as a supreme court of the colony, an advisory body to the governor-general, and as a check on his powers. But the last function was not often exercised since the governor-general had sufficient powers to have the members imprisoned or sent to distant provinces.

Manila's authority extended to the provinces, where a system of *encomiendas* was introduced. The *encomienda* was a quasi-feudal right granted by the king to favoured individuals to obtain tribute or service from inhabitants of a 'pacified' area. In return the *encomendero* was entrusted with the task of assuring the physical and spiritual well-being of his wards. By the end of the sixteenth century the system was replaced by a provincial administrative structure consisting of the *alcaldia-mayor* in pacified areas, and *corregimientos* in unpacified and strategic areas. These provincial governments mirrored the central government in Manila, with the *alcalde-mayor* (governor) exercising executive, judicial, and military powers. Below the provincial governments were the municipal governments which were principally in the hands of native leaders, the *datus*. They were heads of the traditional villages who had been incorporated into the Spanish administrative structure and given the Spanish title of *cabeza*, meaning 'head'. One was then chosen to be the principal head with the Spanish title of *gobernadorcillo* ('little governor').

In 1619 Batavia was developed as the headquarters of VOC activities in Asia. Supreme power was invested in the High Government (*Hoge Regering*), consisting of the governor-general and the Council of the Indies. Batavia appointed the officials and the commanders of garrisons who manned Company posts scattered throughout the region. Each post was a smaller version of Batavia but with relatively fewer Europeans. As we have seen, regular political and economic reports were sent by these outposts to Batavia, which then became the basis for major decisions taken by the governor-general and the Council of the Indies. Batavia was ultimately responsible to the body of directors in Amsterdam, the *Heeren XVII*, which in turn had strong links with the States-General. But, as in Portuguese Melaka and Spanish Manila, the authorities in Batavia exercised considerable initiative and independence because a message and reply between Europe and Asia often took two to three years.

The European governments ruled over cities which were noteworthy for their large foreign Asian population with only a minimum of native inhabitants. Although pre-European cities in Southeast Asia were also renowned for their cosmopolitan nature, these new cities reflected the expansion of the Europeans to all parts of Asia. Groups from China, India, Japan, Persia, and the many different areas in Southeast Asia were all represented. But because these cities had been created at the expense of some local lord, the Europeans initially could not rely upon the support of the inhabitants. The Dutch in Batavia not only forbade any Javanese or Sundanese from entering the city, but also banned the purchase of Javanese slaves because of security risks. In Manila the Spaniards took the precaution of forbidding the local people and foreign Asians from settling within the Intramuros. Before the gates closed at nightfall, all Chinese, Japanese, and Filipinos, except for a handful of municipal employees, retail traders, and household servants, had to leave the city. The Portuguese in Melaka were equally wary of the Malays whose loyalty to their exiled lord, now based in Johor-Riau at the southern end of the Malay peninsula, was still strong.

Because of their distrust of the local inhabitants, the Europeans came to depend increasingly upon the Chinese to develop their cities. Eager to succeed in their new homelands, the Chinese migrants quickly carved a niche for themselves and became the sole suppliers of goods and services to the European cities. In Manila Chinese silver and goldsmiths could faithfully copy any jewellery brought from Spain. Chinese capacity to absorb new skills and to perfect them was evident in the creation of religious art, bookbinding, and even in the making of saddles, bridles, and stirrups, where they soon surpassed their Spanish teachers. In addition they brought other skills from their homeland, where they were bakers, carpenters, druggists, market gardeners, ceramic makers, tobacco dealers, dyers, hatmakers, weavers, locksmiths, tailors, etc. Attempts to remove Spanish dependency on the Chinese by transferring some of the occupations to other groups failed, mainly because there were many in authority who profited from their links with the Chinese and were willing to provide protection and patronage. Some Chinese became established in market gardening in the outskirts of Manila, supplying the city with a reliable source of fresh food. Only in their role as middlemen did the Chinese impinge directly on the local inhabitants. They went directly to the producers in the provinces to exchange silk and cotton goods for food and other products, and then sold them at a considerable profit in the cities. So popular did Chinese cloth become among the Filipinos that the Spanish government feared locally manufactured cloth would disappear.

In Batavia the Chinese performed many of the same functions as in Manila, since they essentially became the retail traders of this cosmopolitan city. But like their counterparts in Manila, they also engaged in agriculture, establishing sugar estates in the city environs. To encourage the Chinese to establish market gardens and other agricultural ventures, the Dutch offered incentives in the form of exemption from poll tax, guaranteed purchase of products by the Company, and the establishment of minimum prices. The Dutch decision to afford legal protection to property was a further incentive to acquire land, leading to the rise of a Chinese property-owning middle class. The Company's hope of developing the agricultural potential of Batavia's surrounding lands led to Dutch possession of more agricultural land, but most of it was then leased to Chinese who worked it with Javanese labour.

While the Spaniards in Manila eventually excluded the Chinese from the Intramuros, the Dutch lived together with them in Batavia. This decision was taken to safeguard the Chinese from hostile local inhabitants and thus ensure a steady flow of income to the Company from Chinese entrepreneurial activity. The Company was always careful not to impose too burdensome a tax on the Chinese, lest they flee and live under a Mataram or Banten lord whose taxes were lower. By the beginning of the eighteenth century the numbers of Chinese in central Java had increased greatly. One contemporary observer remarked that 'there is not a river, harbour, bay or creek navigable for shipping, which does not have a customs post [tollgate], of which the keeper is invariably Chinese'.[9] So important were the Chinese to the economy that both the Javanese and the

---

[9] Peter Carey, 'Changing Javanese perceptions of the Chinese communities in Central Java, 1755–1825', *Indonesia*, 37 (April 1984) 8.

Dutch attempted to protect them through laws. According to Javanese code laws, the fine for killing a Chinese was twice that for killing a Javanese. The Dutch, too, made certain that the Chinese were protected by signing treaties with the Javanese rulers which placed the Chinese under Company jurisdiction. These measures were nevertheless totally ignored when the Company believed its interests were threatened by the Chinese.

In Portuguese Melaka the Chinese were not as prominent in the economic life of the city as in Manila and Batavia. That role was filled by Indians who had the advantage of close ties with the Portuguese both in the Indian subcontinent and in Melaka. The importance of the Indians in Melaka is confirmed by the practice of appointing one of the Indian merchants to be the *bendahara* in the new Portuguese administrative structure. Most influential were the Hindu Tamils from the Coromandel, known as Klings, whose considerable expertise in the Asian trade helped the Portuguese to integrate successfully into the system. After the Dutch seizure of Melaka in 1641, there was a noticeable shift in the influence of foreign Asians in the city. The Indians were suspected of sympathy for the Portuguese and accused of 'smuggling' Indian piece-goods despite Dutch restrictions. Their favoured place was now taken by the Chinese, whom the Dutch always believed to be essential for the prosperity of any city. In 1641 there were only 400 Chinese in Melaka, but by the middle of the next century the number had grown to 2000. Some were involved in masonry and carpentry, but apparently the majority of the Chinese were shop-owners and teahouse proprietors. The Dutch were able to gain substantial revenues by taxing the Chinese for gambling, pig slaughter, and wearing a queue.

In addition to the Chinese, another group which flourished in the European-controlled city was the mestizo communities. Liaisons between foreign men and local women had become more common in this period because of the large established communities of foreign males who rarely brought their womenfolk with them to Southeast Asia. The hybrid nature of the European city encouraged the mixing of groups through formal or informal arrangements, and so the city became a symbol of a development which was spreading throughout Southeast Asia at this time. For the Chinese, Indian, or European private trader, there were advantages in obtaining a Southeast Asian wife in a society where blood ties established trust and facilitated exchange. The women provided their foreign husbands with an entrée into local society which was essential to trade. Moreover, the women themselves often engaged in the negotiations for the purchase of desired products for their husbands.

The process of 'indigenizing' foreign groups could scarcely be avoided because of the types of activity in which these groups were engaged and because of government policies. Chinese and Indians quickly learned that there was more profit in obtaining products at the source, and so made it a practice to go frequently into the countryside. Spanish and Dutch policy of encouraging agricultural activities among the Chinese further contributed to increased Chinese contact with local inhabitants. When the Spaniards offered to grant Chinese who converted to Christianity permission to live outside the Parian, a sizeable number did so and settled in areas near

Manila and closer to local villages. They were exempted from paying an annual tribute to the Spaniards for a period of ten years and allowed to move freely in the interior. Baptismal books from certain Manila churches in mainly Chinese districts in the early seventeenth century indicate that many Chinese males between twenty to forty years old became Christian as a preliminary to marriage with Filipinas. From about 1629 baptisms of infants begin to appear in the registers, almost all of Chinese fathers and Filipino mothers, as the first generation of a Filipino-Chinese *mestizaje* or mestizo community became established. As the population of Manila increased, Spaniards, Chinese, and Japanese came to live in the native *arrabales* or suburbs. The frequent interaction of these groups and the Filipinos eventually led to the mixing of the races and the rise of a distinct group by the mid-seventeenth century.

The Europeans who settled in Southeast Asia rarely returned home and thus became an important source of urban mestizo communities in the cities. Although many high-ranking officials brought their women to Asia, they were the exception. The private trader, the clerk and copyist, and the common soldier were too poorly paid to afford the passage for European women and therefore sought companions from local communities. Other factors prevented the migration of European women to Asia. The Portuguese overseas territories were regarded as a 'frontier land of conquest', and few white women dared venture to the East. Rarely were there more than a dozen women on a ship from Europe carrying between 600 and 800 people.

Because of the difficulty in obtaining white women to help establish Portuguese settlements in Asia, Affonso de Albuquerque encouraged Portuguese to marry Indian women of Aryan origin who had been converted to Christianity. He saw these marriages and the offspring of such unions as a basis of a loyal population which would solve Portugal's chronic shortage of labour in its overseas territories. This policy was condemned by many in the Church and in the government, but the common soldier and lowly official in the Portuguese overseas posts welcomed this ruling, some even regarding it as being too rigid. In defiance of the stated guidelines, they married local woman whatever their status or origin. Those who married in the East were allowed to leave the royal service and become *casados*, or married men. To support themselves the *casados* normally engaged in trade, and it became a common phenomenon of port cities to have quarters inhabited by the *casados*, their Asian wives, and their Eurasian children.

Through their Asian wives, the *casados* tended to become more involved with indigenous society than with their own. Their children came to learn the language and the culture of the mother and, less perfectly, the religion, language and culture of the father. It was this Indo-Portuguese group which came to facilitate commerce between the European and the local population. In the seventeenth century the Dutch relied heavily on them as intermediaries and interpreters, and many Dutchmen chose Indo-Portuguese Christian women as wives. By the seventeenth century this mestizo culture was prevalent in the European-controlled cities and in most Asian trade ports.

The Dutch East India Company faced the same problem as the Portuguese in attempting to bring white women to Asia. In the early years spinsters and girls from orphanages were sent to the East. Some thirty-six white women were sent in 1609 with the hope of establishing permanent Dutch colonies. It soon became apparent, however, that those who came were not the respectable women that the authorities had hoped would immigrate. The unsatisfactory experiment with the early shipments of white women to the East forced the directors of the Company to admit that 'it was of no use for the man in the street and expensive and prejudicial to the interests of the Company to send Dutch women'.[10] By 1652 the Dutch established a policy which remained in force for the next 200 years to restrict the immigration of white women.

The Company was thus forced to adopt the earlier Portuguese practice of creating a loyal corps of individuals from the offsprings of marriages between Dutchmen and Asian women. The men were Company soldiers and officials who had served their five-year tour of duty and wished to remain in the East. Upon swearing an oath of loyalty and obedience to the Company's laws, and upon agreeing to engage only in business activity approved by the Company, these freeburghers were allowed to remain in Asia. In 1617 the *Heeren XVII* decreed that the freeburghers could marry only with the Company's permission and only with Asian or Eurasian women. Permission would be granted on the condition that these women first became Christian, and that their children and slaves 'in so far as possible' be raised as Christians. At first only Maluku was open to the freeburghers and their families, but they were later allowed to go to Batavia, Melaka and a few other places. To keep the freeburghers in Asia and fulfil the original intention of establishing colonies, in 1639 the Company forbade them to return to Europe while still married. As reinforcement of this policy, Asian and Eurasian women were also forbidden to go to Europe. The practice of grooming sons to become members of Dutch society in Asia or Europe, while preparing daughters for life as wives of officials in Asia, reinforced the policy's intention of keeping Eurasian women in Asia.

It is no surprise, therefore, that women and their children in Dutch colonial society exhibited many of the traits of indigenous Southeast Asian society. Even the very few white Dutch women in Batavia who were born and raised in the East preferred to speak a creole form of Portuguese in preference to their halting Dutch. Since many of the Dutch soldiers and a few merchants had also married Indo-Portuguese women, this unique culture was continued in the Dutch settlements. In commenting on the married women in Batavia, a seventeenth-century Dutch observer made no distinction in the behaviour, dress, and demeanour of the Asians, Eurasians, or Europeans:

---

[10] Leonard Blussé, 'Batavia, 1619–1740: The Rise and Fall of a Chinese Colonial Town', JSEAS, 12, 1 (1981) 166; Jean Gelman Taylor, *The Social World of Batavia: European and Eurasian in Dutch Asia*, Madison, 1983, 9, 12.

They adopted—or retained—such Oriental habits as squatting on their hams on the floor, instead of sitting on chairs and they ate their curry with their fingers instead of with spoon and fork. They spoke little or no Dutch among themselves, but only a bastard form of creole Portuguese . . . Whenever they went to church or appeared in public, they were decked out with silks, satins and jewels, and were followed by a train of slaves; but at home they squatted around in their shifts or in the most transparent of underclothes.[11]

At home these women behaved in a Southeast Asian way, but in public they attempted to be European in dress and demeanour.

Children born of foreign males and Southeast Asian women were not a new phenomenon in the region, but it was the size and prominence of such mestizo groups in this period which was noteworthy. The existence of large communities of Chinese and European men in the midst of Southeast Asian society encouraged intermarriage. By contrast to the past, however, children from such marriages were no longer automatically absorbed into Southeast Asian society, especially where the father was an important foreign merchant or official. The fathers now had the alternative of raising their children, but most often their sons, in their own communities. These mestizo children were socially located between the cultures of their foreign fathers and their Southeast Asian mothers, and not totally accepted by either. Yet their very presence half-way between these societies made them ideal intermediaries in trade, diplomacy, and in the transmission of ideas between the two cultures. It was in cities such as Melaka, Manila, and Batavia that these mestizo communities were most prominent and successful in this role.

Aside from the slaves, the lowest rung of the social and economic ladder in the European-controlled city was occupied by the local inhabitants. There were some 12,000 native Filipinos living in Manila's suburbs in 1609, many of whom found employment as craftsmen, small merchants, market gardeners, domestic servants, soldiers, and wage labourers in the city. In a letter to the Crown in 1729, the archbishop of Manila wrote: 'We find in this country many who are skillful and who can practise all the trades and who can supply us with all the necessary supplies but they will never be able to do this as long as there are so many Chinese.'[12] Despite the archbishop's advocacy for greater participation of the local inhabitants in the life of Manila, he was unable to uproot the deeply entrenched Chinese-Spanish interests defending the status quo.

In Batavia there were relatively few Javanese or Sundanese living within the city walls. A population count in 1673 revealed that 2024 were Dutch, 726 Eurasian, 2747 Chinese, 5362 *Mardijkers* (free Portuguese-speaking Indonesian soldiers), 1339 Moors (Indian Muslims) and Javanese, 611 Malays, 981 Balinese, and 13,278 slaves, a total of 27,068.[13] The Company and the Chinese would occasionally recruit both Javanese and Sundanese

---

[11] Comments were made by Nicholas de Graaff and paraphrased by C. R. Boxer in *The Dutch seaborne empire 1600–1800*, London, 1965, 225.

[12] Maria Lourdes Diaz-Trechuelo, 'The role of the Chinese in the Philippine domestic economy' in F. Alfonso, ed., *Chinese in the Philippines*, Manila, 1966, I. 177, 181.

[13] Susan Abeyasekere, *Jakarta: A history*, Singapore, 1987, 19.

through their local lords for seasonal work in the sugar plantations established in the environs in Batavia or for some public building project in the city. But, as the population figures indicate, most of the manual labour in the city was done by slaves brought from various parts of the archipelago and from Dutch posts elsewhere in Asia.

The Malay population of Melaka lived on the coast south of the fort and along the river under their own leaders. Their primary function appears to have been the supplying of rice, fruit, vegetables, and fish to the city, but they were also employed as craftsmen and ordinary labourers in the shipyards, factories, and the various religious and civic bodies in Melaka.

Despite the limited role of the local inhabitants in the European-controlled cities, their daily interaction with foreign groups exposed them to a number of new ideas. Through direct observations and active enquiry, the Southeast Asians assessed foreign objects and techniques and selected those which were the most useful and practical for their purposes. This pragmatic stance, bred of centuries of exposure to outside influence, had been successful in strengthening Southeast Asian society in the past, and it was an attitude which was again adopted in this period. Some of the most far-reaching of these ideas were in the field of shipbuilding and the production of firearms, technological developments which had important implications for the future of Southeast Asia's long-distance trade and warfare.

Ship technology: The carrier and the warship

Southeast Asia's long contact with the Arabs, Indians, and the Chinese was principally by sea, and therefore it was inevitable that many nautical ideas and techniques were transmitted. It must be stressed, however, that the record of shipbuilding techniques before 1800 is sparse, since shipwrights' plans were not written down and the archaeology of shipwrecks has barely begun. The absence of archaeological and other reliable historical evidence makes it difficult to determine the extent of the interaction between the shipbuilding traditions of Southeast Asia and those of its principal trading partners in the Indian Ocean and China. But while there was an exchange of ideas, some of the developments in the Southeast Asian ship were a response to specific environmental features.

As far as is known, Southeast Asia's pre-fourteenth century boatbuilding traditions evolved from the dug-out canoe. Over time, planks lashed with vegetable material were gradually raised higher and higher on both sides of the keel. These sewn-plank boats used a lashed-lug technique, in which the planks are carved out so that pieces of wood, or lugs, protrude on the inner side; holes are drilled in the lugs to take ties which attach the planks to the ribs of the boat. These boats were unique to Asia, although they resemble early Scandinavian boats. Many of these boats in Southeast Asia had a detachable animal or dragon head and tail on their prows to symbolize the *nāga*, the sacred snake which assured the fertility of the land. The use of such boats in warfare was linked with fertility rites, since the shedding of blood was a crucial aspect in the impregnating of the soil with the god's fecundity.

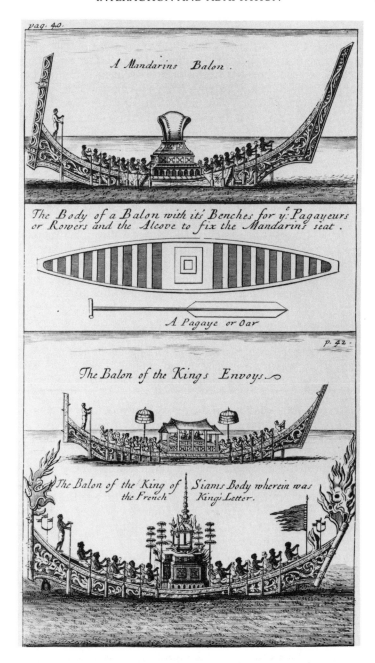

Figure 6.2   Two long-boats from Siam used here for ceremonial purposes.
Similar boats were also used for war, with the sides protected by shields. Note
the use of the dragon or *naga* head at the prow.

From Simon de la Loubere, *The Kingdom of Siam*, London, 1693, reprinted Kuala Lumpur, 1969,
opp. p. 40; reproduced courtesy Oxford University Press, Kuala Lumpur, Oxford in Asia Historical
Reprints.

From the basic dug-out canoe, another common Southeast Asian boat
was developed: the outrigger canoe, known as the *kora-kora* in Maluku
and *caracoa* in the southern Philippines. One of the earliest detailed
descriptions of such a boat is from north Maluku in 1537. The boat was
egg-shaped in the middle with both ends sloping upwards, and it could
sail forwards and backwards. No nails or caulking were used; instead the
keel, ribs, and fore and aft timbers were lashed by the black horsehair-like
fibre (*gamuto*) from a palm, either areng (*Arenga*, Labill.) or sago (*Metrox-
ylon*, Rottb.). Small holes were made through which the cords could pass,
and they were then tied to the grips inside. Planks were joined edge-wise
with wooden dowels and were caulked with the fibre of the *baru* tree
(*Hibiscus tiliaceus*). The Dutch at the end of the sixteenth century noted a
similar practice in Banda in which coir was used for caulking the boat's
seams, and joints were smeared with a lime mixture.

Some 10–12 thwarts or cross-beams extended outward between two and
nine metres on each side, depending on the bulk of the boat. To these
beams were attached two or three rows of floats where additional paddlers
sat. At the very end of the cross-beams were wooden forks to which were
tied other thicker and larger bamboo poles for support against listing.
Platforms of split bamboo with walls and roofs of local material were built
on the outrigger beams, which could be enlarged to carry more passengers
or cargo. As in the long-boat, the prow carried a detachable neck and head
of a serpent with the antlers of a deer. Among the largest of this type of
outrigger canoe was the north Malukan *juanga*, which could have four
banks of fifty paddlers on each side, with another 100 men on the platform
in the boat.

There were some variations in the outrigger canoe. The single outrigger
was favoured by some because of its better performance in the open sea,
and perhaps because it may have served some practical function such as
making it easier to cast a fishing net. Another variation was the replacement of one of the outriggers with another canoe. These large double
canoes and single outriggers with a large platform built over the hulls
using certain types of rigs were still in use at the time of the arrival of the
Europeans in the sixteenth century. A separate development in boatbuilding
traditions was the raft which, along with the dug-out, was the principal
mode of transport in the rivers of Southeast Asia.

When the Dutch first arrived in the busy port of Banten at the close of
the sixteenth century, they noted a number of boats which were common
throughout the region. The first was the *perahu*, a name which was
generally used for a small undecked boat. At Banten the *perahu* had a
house-like structure built over part of the hull to serve as a shelter. It also
had a large mainmast and a foremast with bamboo booms. The sails were
made of a type of palm or rattan matting and sometimes even of woven
palm leaves. Some six men sat in the front of the *perahu* and would row if
necessary, while two men remained in the back to work the two rudders
placed on either side of the boat. There was also a bamboo rudder under
the middle of the *perahu* which was kept in place by a rope. There was
another boat called the *katur* which impressed the Dutch for its speed. It
was a basic dug-out with a round keel, pointed bows, and a double

Figure 6.3   A *kora-kora* or *juanga* from Banda, showing the double outriggers with four banks of rowers on each side, the shelter with other rowers and dignitaries, and the upper deck with the warriors. A swivel-gun is placed prominently at the front of the boat, and a dragon or *naga* head is attached to the prow.

From I. Commelin, *Begin ende Voortgang*, 'Eerste Schip-vaerd der Hollanders', Amsterdam, 1646, I. opp. p. 22; facsimile Uitgaven Nederland N.V., in co-operation with N. V. Het Parool, publishers, Amsterdam; N. Israel, antiquarian and publisher, Amsterdam; and B. de Graaf, antiquarian and publisher, Nieuwkoop, Z.H.

outrigger. It had such a large sail that the Dutch marvelled that it did not overturn in the wind. There was also a trader called a *jong*, which had a bowsprit and in some cases a forked mast, as well as a mainmast and a foremast. There was an enclosed upper deck stretching the whole length of the *jong*, part of which formed a special cabin for the captain. Below the main deck were compartments where the goods were stowed, with access through two openings on either side of the ship. The capacity of the largest *jong* which the Dutch saw in Banten was estimated to be not more than forty tonnes, though they commented that those from China and Pegu were far larger.

The *jong* was a specialized cargo-carrier which appears to have been a descendant of an earlier long-distance ship which the Chinese called *kunlun bo*. It was reported to be the principal carrier of exotic products to China and was also engaged in direct trade to India. From Chinese records of the third and eighth centuries CE and from excavations of two wrecks found in China, one dating from c.1271, the following reconstruction of the features of the *kunlun bo* can be made: its size was usually about fifty metres in length with a carrying capacity of 500–1000 people and a burden of 250–1000 tonnes; absence of iron in fastening; V-shaped hull with a keel;

Figure 6.4   **A.**   A type of *perahu* from Banten with its mat sail and shelter.
B.   An outrigger canoe from Banten known as a *katur*, whose sail was so large
that the Dutch marvelled that it did not overturn in the wind.
C.   A Banten *jong*, showing the opening in the lower deck where goods were
stowed.

From I. Commelin, *Begin ende Voortgang*,'Eerste schip-vaerd der Hollanders', Amsterdam, 1646, I.
opp. p. 78; facsimile Uitgaven Nederland N.V., in co-operation with N. V. Het Parool, publishers,
Amsterdam; N. Israel, antiquarian and publisher, Amsterdam; and B. de Graaf, antiquarian and
publisher, Nieuwkoop, Z.H.

pointed, basically symmetrical stems and sterns; strakes and frames joined
by wooden dowels; several layers of planks; no bulkheads; double, quarter
rudders; rigging with multiple masts and sails; and no outriggers. Carvings on Southeast Asian monuments up to the fourteenth century show
local boats with tripod or bipod masts, quarter rudders, the canted square-
sail and a type of lug-sail, and outriggers. The difference in description
between the Chinese and the Southeast Asian evidence may be due to the
fact that the former is referring to a long-distance carrier, while the latter
depicts a more familiar local boat not meant for the open sea.

All the features of the *kunlun bo* were found in the *jong*, which sixteenth-
century Portuguese sources called a *junco*. They described the *jong* as larger
than the Portuguese ship (which had a burden of 300 to 400 tonnes), very
tall and sheathed with four layers of planks, making it impervious to
Portuguese gunfire. Other contemporary accounts state that the *jong* had
an average burden of 400 to 500 tonnes; used no iron, with the planks of
the hull edge-fastened by the use of wooden dowels inserted into the
seams; and contained multiple sheathing, two lateral rudders, and multiple masts, usually two to four of the canted square-sail and the lug-sail

types, plus a bowsprit. Unfortunately, to date there have been no archaeological finds of *jongs* exactly fitting these historical descriptions.

The size and special requirements of the *jong* demanded access to expertise and materials not available everywhere. Consequently, the *jong* was mainly constructed in three major shipbuilding centres: north coastal Java, especially around Rembang and Cirebon; south coast Borneo (Banjarmasin) and adjacent islands; and Pegu on the Gulf of Martaban. A common feature of these three places was their accessibility to forests of teak (*Tectona grandis*, Linn.); this wood was highly valued as shipbuilding timber because of its resistance to the shipworm. Southern Borneo's supply of teak would have come from north Java, a short journey southward on the Java Sea. For the various types of smaller Southeast Asian boats the different areas had their own boatbuilding villages and traditions, many of which persist to the present day.

There was a new development in shipbuilding techniques as a result of mutual borrowings between the Chinese and Southeast Asians. The Chinese *chuan*, better known in the West as 'junk', evolved from the raft and had a flat or slightly rounded bottom without keel, stern or sternpost; a transom stem and stern; no ribs or internal frames; and solid transverse bulkheads. It used local matting for sails attached to bamboo, a practice which is believed to have originated from Southeast Asia.[14] From a combination of South China's boatbuilding techniques and those of Southeast Asia emerged a hybrid tradition which one scholar has termed the 'South China Sea tradition'. What he argues is that the Chinese techniques, which had proved adequate for their principally riverine and coastal navigation, underwent change as a result of contact with ocean-going vessels of the Southeast Asians. Thus the Chinese created long-distance trade junks, which combined Chinese features (such as partitioned watertight bulkheads, axial rudders, and iron fastening for planks) with those of the *kunlun bo* (V-shaped hulls with keel, rigging of multiple masts and sails, multiple sheathing of hulls, stem and stern posts). The earliest such hybrid ship found in an archaeological site in Southeast Asia is dated sometime in the first half of the fifteenth century.[15] With the increase of the junk trade to Southeast Asia and the practice of having the junks built in the region, there was a natural progression to the amalgamation of characteristics of both the Southeast Asian and the Chinese ship.

The increasing use of the hybrid *chuan* by both Chinese and Southeast Asian traders was encouraged by Chinese imperial policy. In Chinese ports junks and their cargo were taxed at a lower rate than Western and other ships. As long as the specifications of a Chinese junk were met, Chinese officials cared little about the foreign origins and ownership of the vessel. This measure encouraged all merchants to ship goods to China on junks, and in the seventeenth century even the Dutch employed Chinese junks crewed by Chinese in the Batavia–China trade. The Thais

---

[14] Paul Johnstone, *The Sea-Craft of prehistory*, Cambridge, Mass. 1980, 191.
[15] Pierre-Yves Manguin, 'The trading ships of insular Southeast Asia: New evidence from Indonesian archaeological sites', *Proceedings Pertemuan Ilmiah Arkeologi*, 5 (July 1989) 213–16.

were especially encouraged to maintain Chinese-style craft in their trade with China, since fee and tariff concessions were granted to these vessels in both China and Siam. The increasing demand for Chinese-style ships encouraged Southeast Asian shipwrights to build the hybrid *chuan*, a task made easier because of their familiarity with many of the indigenous features of the ship. The hybrid *chuan* was very popular in the seventeenth and eighteenth centuries; it had all the advantages of the *jong* as well as the official encouragement of the Chinese imperial authorities, and this led to the gradual relegation of the *jong* to inter-island trade. The latter's demise was hastened also by the arrival of the specialized carriers and warships of the Europeans.

Three particular European crafts came to make an impression in the Southeast Asian world. The first was the Mediterranean galley, which was adapted by the Spanish and the Portuguese for use in the Philippines and eastern Indonesia. It was long and narrow, with a length of seven or eight times its breadth; the vessel narrowed considerably fore and aft. It had a deck running the whole length of the boat and was propelled by long oars. A special deck was built for the fighting men, and along the whole length of the galley were placed shields to protect the rowers and the soldiers. The Dutch in the late sixteenth century commented on a Banten version of a galley, which had a galley built at the stern. The slave rowers sat confined below deck, while the soldiers stood above deck ready for combat. The Banten galley had two masts and was armed with four small cannon placed at the bow.

The second type of European craft introduced to Southeast Asia was the cargo carrier, especially the Dutch *fluyt* or fly-boat. It measured between thirty and forty metres, had a full section, almost flat bottom, a high proportion of keel length to overall length, and a rounded hull suited to bulk transport. The fly-boat successfully challenged the *jong* and the hybrid *chuan* in the carrying trade of Southeast Asia.

The third type of European vessel was the armed merchant ship, a combination of warship and cargo carrier. It was constructed to carry cargo, but its gundecks and structure were also reinforced to take the weight of heavy artillery and to withstand the tremors which resulted from the recoiling of fifteen to twenty cannons firing simultaneously. The technological breakthrough which had enabled the building of the armed merchantman gave the Europeans a considerable advantage over their competitors. Not only could they absorb protection costs in the carrying trade, but they could simultaneously prevent their competitors from participating in certain areas.

The Southeast Asians were aware of the advantages of European ships, and there was a steady transfer of construction detail from European to Southeast Asian shipwrights. As iron became cheaper, iron fastenings were used; the Western square sterns were borrowed from sixteenth-century Iberian models. Local shipwrights were capable of building European-type ships since they had suitable timber, skilled shipwrights, sufficiently trained artillery personnel, and access to guns through their own foundries or through purchase from foreign sources. Pegu, for example, maintained its shipbuilding reputation well into the late eighteenth century. One of the ships built for the English in 1787 served both as a man-of-war and a merchant ship and was eventually converted to carry convicts to Australia. It was still in operation in 1897 when it made a final voyage from Australia to England and 'surprised everybody and made but little water'.[16]

On the whole, however, Southeast Asians built few larger vessels with European features but continued to rely mainly on Asian prototypes which they adapted for trade or war. The Vietnamese frequently employed junks for these purposes. The Trinh in north Vietnam had 500 large junks each carrying at least three cannon, and one sixteenth-century Jesuit observer regarded these vessels as the equal of any European ship in Asian waters at that time. In the archipelago the various types of two-masted *perahu* were preferred for their lightness and speed, and they could be easily and conveniently adapted for carriage or warfare. The large trade vessels, such as the Malay *gurab* and *pancalang*, and the Bugis-Makassar *padewakan* and *penjajab*, were converted in times of war by installing swivel-guns (*rantaka*). The larger *gurab* had two guns fore and fifteen on each side, while the smaller carried two fore and ten on each side. Even the smallest native craft had at least three swivel-guns on each side. The guns were attached to the bulwarks of the boats and could be turned, lifted, or lowered by means of a wooden handle inserted in a hollow tube in the breech end of the guns. They were intended to injure and kill, much like the traditional arms, rather than to sink enemy boats.

The increasing domination of long-distance trade by the Chinese, Indians, and Europeans did not provide the incentives for further modification of Southeast Asia's own carrier, the *jong*, which had in any case already produced the successful hybrid *chuan*. Moreover, the growing risks associated with the arming of merchant vessels, not only by the Europeans, but now also by the Indians and Chinese, made overseas trade much less attractive. International traffic to Southeast Asia was rising, and attractive profits could be made in local ports free from the hazards and risks of long-distance trade. The *jong* continued to be used, but now it was smaller and involved almost exclusively in trade in the coastal areas of Southeast Asia. In addition various types of *perahu* and 'sampans', a vague term used to describe a whole range of cargo ships adapted from a foreign model, became the major carriers in local trade. The Southeast Asians relinquished their role in long-distance trade; they chose to rely on their superior knowledge of local waters and their small, light, and fast vessels armed with swivel-guns to carry on their regional trade in defiance of the heavier armed but slower European and foreign Asian ships.

Innovations in firearms technology and land warfare

China, the Middle East, and Europe were the three major sources of the new firearms technology which reached Southeast Asia. The evolution of

16 W. H. Coates, *The old 'Country Trade' of the East Indies*, London, 1911, 100.

this technology occurred in China, beginning with the use of incendiaries in Taoist ritual. From incendiaries the technology progressed through the stages of flame-throwing weapons (fire lances), explosives (bombs launched from trebuchets), rockets, and finally barrel guns and cannon. The discovery in the thirteenth century of a fast-burning gunpowder mixture, high in nitrate, of sufficient propellant force to send off a projectile from a narrow metal bore set the stage for the production of cannon and small firearms.

Knowledge of this new technology was brought by the Mongols to India, the Islamic world (Arabs, Turks, Persians), and Europe. The Ottoman Turks perfected the large siege cannon and created muskets in the sixteenth century which were considered the equal of the Spanish musket, then the finest in Europe. The Europeans improved cast-iron cannon in the seventeenth century, and standardized and mass-produced them in the eighteenth. They concentrated on light and mobile artillery, rather than on the large siege cannon which preoccupied the Turks. But it was in handguns that the Europeans excelled. In Germany in the mid-fifteenth century a matchlock mechanism was invented which enabled a continually burning match to ignite the gunpower mixture to fire a bullet from the barrel of a handgun. The matchlock arquebus was the result, an unwieldy gun which required one hand to hold the barrel and another to adjust the match and pull the trigger. But the matchlock mechanism was simple, cheap, and fairly foolproof, and remained the principal handgun until it was replaced by the flintlock in the late seventeenth century.

By the sixteenth century firearms technology was not yet universally or even generally applied in the armies of China, Europe, or the Islamic lands. The new technology still had to demonstrate its superiority over traditional arms and be incorporated in established war tactics in each area. Perhaps the greatest obstacles to the widespread use of firearms was cultural opposition. In China Confucianism was only barely tolerant towards things military, and the Confucian officials believed it beneath them to devote their energies and skills to the development of firearms. In the Islamic lands of the Middle East, the creation of light cavalry armed with recurved bows arose naturally in the nomadic environment. As long as such skills were being produced and the cavalry was effective, there was little reason to adopt the new firearms. In Europe there was initial reluctance to adopt the use of cannon and small firearms because this meant a challenge to the traditional warrior, the armed knight, and a whole way of life. But prior to the greater acceptance of firearms, the introduction of the steel crossbow had already demonstrated the vulnerability of the armed knight and the growing prominence of the unskilled common soldier who, with a powerful weapon, was the equal of or superior to the noble armoured knight on horseback. The European world was thus far less reluctant than the Chinese or the Islamic world to adopt firearms.

Cultural factors do not appear to have prevented the Southeast Asians from expressing keen interest in the new technology. In the sixteenth century they purchased guns from foreigners and enticed or forced gun-founders to remain in their lands to reproduce these new weapons. Gun-foundries in Pegu and Ayutthaya provided some of the firearms found in Melaka when it was taken by the Portuguese in 1511. In Ayutthaya it was the Chinese and in Pegu the Indians who appear to have been the first to establish foundries. The Burmese readily adopted firearms and incorporated special corps of gunners into their armies. After the Burmese capture of the port city of Syriam from Portuguese adventurers in the early seventeenth century, the surviving Europeans were forcibly resettled in villages northwest of Ava in upper Burma and were later joined by a thousand Indian Muslim sailors and gunmen. These captives and their descendants became the backbone of Burma's artillery corps and musketeer forces. To bolster the firepower of its own units, Burma followed a policy of hiring short-term mercenaries for specific campaigns.

Although the figures provided by the Burmese sources seem to be inflated, they provide an indication of the proportion of guns to soldiers. In a Burmese royal order of 1605, a fighting force of 1000 men was to be 'adequately equipped with weapons including guns and cannon'.[17] Another royal order dated 1637 describes a typical armed unit with 1000 men, 10 cannon, 100 guns, and 300 bows. So well-established were gun units within Burma by this time that, in addition to a foreign (feringi) gun group, there were many other local gun units, all of which were given an area of land to inhabit. In the outfitting of one unit of 100 gunners, each man was issued with a gun and all necessary supplies. They were well-trained and encouraged to improve their marksmanship, 'provided they do not practice on live targets'.[18] The division of the Royal Bodyguard of Bayinnaung in the invasion of Ayutthaya in 1568 was said to have 4000 Kala Brin-gyi (Portuguese) gunners and another 4000 Kala Pathi (Muslim Indian) musketeers, figures which may well be exaggerated especially for the 'Portuguese'. So valued were firearms that Burma's port officials were entrusted with the task of procuring foreign guns and gunners. Burma had its own foundries and gunpowder mills, but it preferred to replace its obsolete guns and to obtain European gunpowder through periodic arms purchases at the coast.

The Chinese brought firearms technology to the Thais, but by the sixteenth and seventeenth centuries the latter looked to Europe for the latest developments. A Portuguese from Macao was brought into the service of the ruler of Ayutthaya in the seventeenth century to cast cannon, although the Thais were already capable of producing their own. A treatise on the casting of cannon is believed to have been furnished by a seventeenth-century Dutchman to the governor of Sukothai. It describes the composition of the metal, provides a diagram of the proportions of the weapon, explains the methods of loading and firing, and has sketches of ramrods, cleaning rods, and gun mounts. The pair of cannon sent to Louis XIV by King Narai in the seventeenth century was described by the French as 'six feet long [1.82 metres] made of malleable iron, beaten while cooling . . . inlaid with silver, mounted on carriages also inlaid with silver'.[19] The

---

[17] Than Tun, trans., *The royal orders of Burma, AD 1598–1885*, I, Kyoto, 1983, order dated 16 Feb. 1605, 16.

[18] Ibid., Order dated 24 July 1638, 103.

[19] C. A. Seymour Sewell, 'Notes on some old Siamese guns', JSS, 15, 1 (1922) 5.

French regarded them as well-made, and they were used in the storming of the Bastille on 14 July 1789.

The demand for cannon for the wars against the Burmese could not be met by the foundries in Ayutthaya, and so they were imported, especially from the Europeans, or seized from conquered areas. The paintings on some of the beautiful lacquered bookcases now housed in the Vajiranana Library in Bangkok show Thai soldiers with muskets and cannon in battle against the Burmese. What is distinctive is the sight of cannon attached to a timber tripod and trestle to attain the right elevation. When a cannon was brought into service, a special ceremony was held to inscribe its name on the barrel. Among some of the names bestowed on cannon were: 'The Lao who plays polo', 'The Javanese who performs the kris dance', 'The Annamese who wields the spear', 'The Shan who plays in the vanguard', 'The fierce Farang [foreigner] who shoots straight', 'The Chinese who disembowels', 'The Burman who thrusts with the lance', 'The Makassar who destroys the camp', and 'The Bugis who runs amok'.[20] On each barrel the calibre of the weapon and the amount of gunpowder required were inscribed; it was prudent of the Thais to adopt this measure, since the wrong quantity and mixture of gunpowder in an imperfectly made cannon often caused explosions and the loss of the gunner's life.

The importance of good gunpowder was recognized early by the Thais. A treatise dating back to 1580 prescribes the various mixtures to produce incendiary rockets; to discharge flames to frighten elephants, horses, and footmen; to produce 'murk and darkness'; and to shoot men and animals with soft bullets so as not to kill them. The ability of the Thais to produce these varying strengths of gunpowder demonstrates a good knowledge of its propulsive force. The Thais were equally competent in the production of handguns. In Trailok's laws of 1454 determining civil and military status there are obvious interpolations from perhaps the late sixteenth or the seventeenth century which list occupations such as a corps of artillery with large and small firearms, gunfounders, and gunpowder-makers. The Thais became so well known for their production of firearms and gunpowder that the Japanese shogun Ieyasu, founder of the Tokugawa dynasty, requested muskets from the Ayutthaya ruler in 1606, and muskets and gunpowder in 1608.

A major incentive to the Thais in the production and incorporation of the new weaponry in their armies was the persistent threat from the Burmese between the sixteenth and the early nineteenth centuries. In an attempt to stop the advance of a Burmese invading force in 1760, the ruler of Ayutthaya sent two armies, one by land and another by sea. The land and the sea forces were divided equally into 30,000 men with 2000 guns. The guns in the land force were mounted on carriages and on elephants, while those in the sea force were placed on warboats. When Ayutthaya was finally captured in April 1767, the armoury of the city contained 1000 muskets inlaid with gold and silver tracery and more than 10,000 ordinary muskets; the famous twin cast bronze cannon; 'guns for dismantling city walls; guns for repelling enemy attacks; guns embossed with figures of dragons and seamonsters; guns constructed for mounting on carriages, at the bow of war boats, and on elephants; and breech-loading guns'.[21] In total there were 3550 various sorts of firearms, most of copper or bronze, but some of iron. In addition there were 50,000 shells of various size which were manufactured in China, Laos, Europe, India, Ayutthaya and the Yun country of northern Thailand.

Vietnam was another mainland Southeast Asian state which came to produce and use firearms on a relatively large scale in warfare. By recovering guns from Portuguese, Spanish and Dutch shipwrecks in the sixteenth and seventeenth centuries, and by employing European gunsmiths, the Vietnamese had come to learn about the latest European developments which they then applied to their own foundries. A Portuguese mestizo, João da Cruz, offered his services to the Nguyen family in south Vietnam and established a foundry in Hué to build guns in the European way. The Vietnamese quickly applied the new techniques to their own considerable skills in casting. In the late seventeenth century, they cast two bells of 500 pounds (230 kilograms) for the Christian churches in Ayutthaya at the request of Phaulkon. When the Vietnamese asked the English to send a gunfounder in 1678, it was not to learn about founding but to assess European techniques. They were able to recognize quality workmanship, and in 1689 the Nguyen lord refused to accept from the English two cannon which had certain flaws. At another time only seven of twenty cannon sent by the English were deemed to be of acceptable quality.

The armoury of the Trinh lord in north Vietnam in the seventeenth century contained some fifty to sixty iron cannon from falcons to demiculverins. There were two or three whole culverins or demi-cannon and some iron mortars. The largest weapon was a locally cast bronze cannon of some 3500–4000 kilograms, which was considered by a European observer to be ill-shaped and more for display than combat. Cannon were so highly valued in the north that the Trinh lord had the sole right to purchase them, and guards were posted along rivers and major road intersections to prevent their export. Around the Nguyen court in the south were some 1200 bronze cannon of different calibres. Some bore the Spanish or the Portuguese coat of arms, while others—most likely of local manufacture—were beautifully crafted in the form of dragons, sphinxes, and leopards.

In the archipelago Aceh developed a reputation for the possession and use of large cannon and firearms through its association with Turkey. In the sixteenth century the Ottoman ruler sent 500 Turks, among whom were gunners, gunfounders, and engineers, along with large bombards and ample supples of ammunition, to the ruler of Aceh to assist in an attack on Portuguese Melaka. Although only two ships of the original fleet reached Aceh sometime in 1566 or 1567, this was only the first of a number of shipments of guns which Turkey was to send to Aceh. A Portuguese source in 1585 noted the presence of Turkish bronze cannon of all calibres,

[21] 'Burmese invasions of Siam', translated from the Hmannan Yazawin Dawgyi, compiled under order of Bagyidaw, 1829, *Journal of the Siam Society, Selected Articles*, vol. 5, part 1, Bangkok, 1959, 50.

gunners, naval personnel, and engineers capable of fortifying and besieging fortresses. Among the Turks were those who taught the Acehnese to
make their own guns. The Turks also transmitted to their Acehnese allies
their preoccupation with gun size. One of the cannon founded in Aceh so
impressed the Portuguese by its size that it was sent as a gift to the king of
Spain. By the early seventeenth century Sultan Iskandar Muda of Aceh
boasted an arsenal of possibly 2000 pieces, among which were 1200 bronze
cannon of medium calibre, and 800 other guns such as swivel-guns and
arquebuses. Although Aceh produced its own cannon and guns, its rulers
in the seventeenth century preferred to obtain European firearms, especially those beautifully damasked and bejewelled guns which were brought
as gifts by travellers and traders.

In Java the ancient and respected craft of kris-making provided the
technical skills which were applied to the making of guns. Both cannon
and handguns required special expertise and may have been made by the
same individuals. The craftsman's spiritual power was said to be transmitted to the guns, evoking thereby the same reverence for these new
weapons as for the kris. By the beginning of the seventeenth century the
Javanese in Surabaya were producing their own bronze cannon, and by
mid-century Mataram had the capacity to manufacture some 800 muskets
in a period of three months.

The Bugis and Makassar people of south Sulawesi adapted quickly to the
introduction of firearms because of the frequency of wars between them.
As one Frenchman observed in the early seventeenth century: 'There are
no people in India more nimble in getting on Horseback, to draw a Bow, to
discharge a Fuzil [musket], or to point a Cannon.' He also described
cannon in Makassar which were so big that 'a Man may lie in 'em and not
be seen'. Nevertheless, he believed that these cannon were of little use
since the powder was not of sufficient strength to fire a heavy projectile.[22]
When the Dutch captured the Makassar royal citadel of Sombaopu in 1669,
one of the prizes was the pride of the Makassar armaments, the locally-
made cannon named 'The Child of Makassar' (*Anak Makassar*). Like many
other large cannon in the archipelago, it proved unwieldy and its fire
ineffective because of the lack of good gunpowder. The Dutch also seized
33 large and small bronze and 11 cast-iron cannon, 145 bases (a type of
handgun), 83 breech-loading gun chambers, 60 muskets, 23 arquebuses,
127 musket barrels, and 8483 bullets. Although it is impossible to know the
origin of these armaments, local sources stress that the Makassar people
were already manufacturing muskets sometime in the late sixteenth or
early seventeenth century. By the eighteenth century their neighbours the
Bugis were producing guns of such straight bore and fine inlay work that
they attracted the admiration of Europeans.

The Malays were another ethnic group in the archipelago noted for the
possession and use of firearms. When the Portuguese captured Melaka in
1511, they found a large number of cannon and other firearms among
which were esmerils (small wrought-iron swivel-guns), falconets (cast-

---

[22] N. Gervaise, *An historical description of the kingdom of Macasar in the East Indies*, London,
1701, 72.

bronze swivel-guns larger than the esmeril), and medium sakers (long cannon or culverins between a six and a ten pounder). The Portuguese believed that these captured firearms were not of local manufacture and were probably made in the foundries of Pegu and Ayutthaya, known for their production of small artillery. However, Malay gunfounders were compared favourably with those of Germany, who were then the acknowledged leaders in the manufacture of firearms, and the Malay gun carriages were described as unrivalled by any other land, including Portugal. An Italian participant in the attack mentioned the presence of heavy cannon in Melaka which caused considerable loss of Portuguese lives. Though the Malays were eventually defeated, they were described as 'most valiant men, well trained in war, and copiously supplied with every type of very good weapon'.[23]

Even the Minangkabau from the interior of Sumatra appeared to have manufactured sufficient quantities of firearms to satisfy their own needs and those of their neighbours. Iron and steel were produced in local forges, but by the eighteenth century they became more reliant on the Europeans for their supplies. Their matchlock arquebuses were described in the eighteenth century as having barrels which were 'well-tempered, and of the justest bore'.[24] The barrel was made by rolling a flat bar of iron around a rod and beating the edges together to form the bore. But while the Minangakbaus had mastered the art of manufacturing guns, they were less successful in producing gunpowder. They used the same proportions of charcoal, sulphur, and saltpetre as the Europeans, but often the mixture was improperly corned because of the small quantities made and the haste in the preparation of gunpowder intended for immediate use.

Southeast Asians had known about firearms before the sixteenth century, but it was the arrival of the European and Turkish guns and gunners that showed them the effectiveness of these new weapons. At first Southeast Asians readily purchased or were provided with various types of armaments, from heavy Turkish cannon to smaller hand-held arquebuses. Southeast Asian rulers encouraged foreign gunfounders to establish foundries in their lands so they could learn more about the new technology. Many already possessed translations of foreign manuals explaining the principles and the process of manufacturing firearms and gunpowder. Once the principles were explained, local craftsmen were able to apply their own skills in kris- and sword-making or in the casting of bronze Buddha statues to create their own cannon and small handguns.

Despite the ability of some Southeast Asian gunfounders to supply their own armies and even export to neighbouring lands, they were at a considerable disadvantage in relation to European gunmakers, whose technology quickly outstripped all others by the eighteenth century. In the previous two centuries, it was possible for Southeast Asian rulers to capture European soldiers or seamen or accept 'renegades' to manufacture guns and gunpowder in their kingdoms. With the mass-production of new cast-iron cannon in the late seventeenth century, the relationship

[23] *Lettera di Giovanni Da Empoli*, with introduction and notes by A. Bausani, Rome, 1970, 138.
[24] William Marsden, *A history of Sumatra*, reprint, Kuala Lumpur, 1975, 347.

between the gunner and his gun was no longer one of a special craftsman with his work of art. Fewer people were now required in the manufacture of firearms, and only a few highly-skilled individuals possessed the increasingly complex knowledge necessary to produce the sophisticated arms in the later seventeenth and the eighteenth centuries. It was no longer feasible for Southeast Asian rulers to depend upon captured or even hired European or foreign Asians and expect them to reproduce guns of the same quality as those manufactured in Europe or in European foundries in Asia.

The much more reliable wheel-lock and flintlock mechanisms used in muskets, which were becoming common in seventeenth- and eighteenth-century Europe, appear to have been admired but not reproduced in Southeast Asian foundries. So vast was the gap between the quality of handguns manufactured in Southeast Asia and those in Europe that one English observer in the early nineteenth century remarked that the wheel-locks and flintlocks were a 'complex machinery far beyond their [Southeast Asians'] skill'.[25] With mass production and the rapid changes in technology, the Europeans quickly unloaded obsolete armaments on to Southeast Asians as new and more effective weapons were created. For Southeast Asians, these outdated guns were sufficient for their war requirements, and so there was little incentive to enter into a technological arms race with the Europeans.

Southeast Asians gradually abandoned their efforts to maintain their own independent source of firearms because of the difficulty of obtaining consistent up-to-date knowledge. Although there were always Europeans who were willing to teach the Southeast Asians what they knew, most of those who came to Southeast Asia were not specialist gunsmiths or gunfounders. It is highly unlikely that the occasional 'renegade' who sought safety or employment in a local court would have possessed the skills of the founders in Europe or even of those Europeans and Eurasians in Asia who had made gunfounding a family concern. Excellent bronze guns were being cast at the Indo-Portuguese foundries at Goa and Cochin in India by the master gunfounder, João Vicente, in the first half of the sixteenth century. The Dias and Tavares Bocarro family, the principal cannonmakers in Goa from 1580 to 1680 and perhaps longer, were renowned for their excellent work. Yet the technology which lay so close to Southeast Asia remained out of reach because of the natural tendency for craftsmen to protect their industrial secrets, and because European governments explicitly forbade the transference of knowledge in the production and the use of firearms.

Where the absence of true expertise was sorely evident was in the production of gunpowder. The mixing of the gunpowder ingredients to the right proportion of charcoal, sulphur and saltpetre had taken years of experimentation by the Chinese. The Europeans were able to adopt the successful formula and then adjust the nitrate content to provide the necessary explosive power for the various types of new weaponry. In the sixteenth century the manufacture of good gunpowder was a highly

---

[25] John Crawfurd, *History of the Indian archipelago*, Edinburgh, 1820, I. 191.

respected skill which required a solid understanding of the new guns being developed. Founding techniques were still so imperfect that an overcharge could cause a cannon to burst, while the wrong mixture would not have the propulsive force to send off a ball. The Turks attempted to overcome the problem by engraving on the cannon breech the correct ball size and the weight of powder to fire the projectile, and, as we have seen, this practice was adopted to some extent by the Thais.

For the Southeast Asians newly introduced to the whole firearms technology, the fearsome consequences of an improperly charged cannon made them wary. Southeast Asians continued to maintain their own gunpowder mills, but they preferred to purchase their gunpowder from Europeans. Thus, by the eighteenth century, Southeast Asians had abandoned the attempt to keep pace with new developments in the production of both firearms and gunpowder, and came to rely increasingly on supplies provided by the Europeans.

The new firearms technology did not transform tactics in Southeast Asian warfare. Instead, in many cases the new weapons simply reinforced traditional weapons in established war strategies. In Java massed battles were rare because the main fighting occurred between the vanguards comprising the Javanese headmen and important officials. In this fierce but short combat the death of a few of the leaders was sufficient to send the followers fleeing to safety. Rarely were there many casualties, nor did the battles last longer than two hours. In the battle between leaders the traditional weapons of pikes and krises were used, rather than firearms. Krises were regarded as repositories of spiritual power, and the pitting of one kris-wielding leader against the other was in essence a battle of spiritual potency. Until the musket could achieve the same reverent and exalted status as the kris, it could not replace the latter as an essential weapon of the Javanese prince and nobleman.

Only one-fifth of the number of men brought to the field in a Javanese army consisted of fighting men, the rest being support units. Of these fewer than 10 per cent would normally have a gun. Japara in 1677 had an army of 1576 fighting men and only 79 guns, which were normally kept under guard by the ruler and issued only in times of war. These few firearms were effective against an enemy unaccustomed to the noise and range of the new weaponry. Even more important was the fact that a few firearms in the hands of specialized marksmen could create an immediate advantage by causing the death and wounding of some of the noblemen forming the enemy's vanguard. The fall of a leader was usually sufficient to cause his men to panic and flee. Cannon were less important in Javanese warfare, although on occasion they proved invaluable in creating breaches in heavily fortified stockades. In general, however, sieges were rare, and the skirmishes of small vanguards of special warriors left little place for field artillery.

Among the Bugis-Makassar people, the manner of fighting resembled that of the Javanese. When the king ordered the people to assemble for a war expedition, he distributed clothes, arms, powder and lead. There were some guns available, but those issued with them also carried a sword. After the powder was exhausted, they reverted to their swords and krises

for close combat. Only the principal warriors, who were on the whole
noblemen or princes, wore chainmail armour. The use of iron armour,
believed to have been borrowed from the Portuguese, encouraged local
development of firearms with their superior penetrative power. While the
Bugis-Makassar soldiers continued to rely on the pike, the sword, and
the bow, among the élite troops there was an increasing reliance on
the musket to counter the practice of using chainmail armour. In 1695 of
the assembled army of about 25,000 gathered to pay obeisance to the Bugis
prince Arung Palakka, only his personal bodyguard were fully equipped
with chainmail armour, golden helmets, firelocks (matchlock arquebuses)
and two rounds of ammunition.

In the Malay areas the stockade or *kubu* was an essential component of
warfare. The *kubu* had walls on three sides consisting of rows of palm
trunks filled with earth. The fourth side backed onto a mountain or a
jungle to enable the defenders to escape if the enemy succeeded in
breaching the walls. The *kubu* was not intended to be heavily defended by
guns nor to house a large number of people for long sieges. It provided a
temporary shelter and respite from the fighting and was meant to discourage further action by the enemy. The key element was mobility, and so the
kubu was quickly manned and abandoned as circumstances demanded. This
method of warfare made siege cannon and other heavy guns of little value.

In the archipelago the ambush, the unexpected raid, and the surprise
dawn attack, were established tactics. At times armies were brought
together on the battlefield, but the death of a few leaders and soldiers
appeared to have been sufficient to slake the thirst for blood in compensation for an insult or killing which had caused the war. Even when
'large' Javanese campaigns occurred in the seventeenth and eighteenth
centuries, encouraged by Dutch firepower, the actual casualties caused by
the local people among themselves were often small. A notable exception
occurred in the few sieges of well-populated cities, such as Melaka in 1511
and Makassar in 1669. The presence of guns enabled both defenders and
besiegers to inflict casualties at a distance without the actual confrontation
in battle which appear to have been crucial in the resolution of conflict.

Because of the nature of warfare in the archipelago, only firearms which
contributed to existing tactics were readily adopted. One of the most
common and effective weapons used by maritime kingdoms was the
swivel-gun. It was a light, manoeuvrable cannon ideally suited to the small
stockades. The U-shaped upper part of the swivel-gun held the trunnions
of the gun, while the pointed foot was attached in the walls in the
embrasure of the fort. At the breech end of these guns was a hollow tube
about fifteen centimetres long in which was fitted a wooden spike or
handle for turning, raising, or lowering the muzzle. In *kubu* or stockade
warfare the swivel-gun, known locally as *rentaka* or *lantaka*, merely added a
new weapon to traditional fighting and required little radical change
of tactics. The swivel-gun proved to be especially suited to the design of
Southeast Asian boats and to the requirements of naval combat.

The matchlock arquebus was another weapon which was quickly adopted. Its use was often limited to special corps of foreign mercenaries or a
hand-picked local élite fighting force, usually the personal guards of the

Figure 6.5   **A**.   A Malay brass swivel cannon, called Lela. The barrel was
usually 180 cm long. The finest were made in Brunei.
B.   An ornamental swivel gun with a 'monkey's tail'. All Malay swivel guns
were loaded and fired from the breech. The 'monkey's tail' helped the gunner
to aim.

From Mubin Sheppard, *Taman Indera: A Royal Pleasure Ground*, Kuala Lumpur, 1972; reproduced
courtesy of Oxford University Press, Kuala Lumpur. Originals in the Sarawak Museum.

king. The physical encumbrance of the arquebus, the long delay in
reloading, and its inability to function in wet conditions, quickly outweighed the shock advantage of its noise and penetrative force. An
arquebus was found to be useful only in the first salvo, for the Southeast
Asians do not appear to have adopted the volley technique which employs
several ranks of musketeers firing in turn to maintain a continuous hail of
fire. The lack of sufficient guns and good gunpowder may have been too
great to permit the use of such tactics. Instead, they attached a sharp
pointed object at the end of the arquebus to transform it to a bayonet for
close combat once the single volley had been fired. Swords and daggers
were often issued to arquebusiers for this purpose.

The powerful mainland states, which in this period were engaged in a
struggle for dominance in the region, demonstrated a greater initiative in

Figure 6.6   Three soldiers from Banten armed with the traditional spear, sword
and shield, as well as with a matchlock. The soldier in the middle wears
chainmail armour which consists of iron plates linked together with rings.

From I. Commelin, *Begin ende Voortgang*, 'Eerste Schipvaert der Hollanders', Amsterdam, 1646, I.
opp. p. 72; facsimile Uitgaven Nederland N.V., in co-operation with N. V. Het Parool, publishers,
Amsterdam; N. Israel, antiquarian and publisher, Amsterdam; and B. de Graaf, antiquarian and
publisher, Nieuwkoop, Z.H.

the use of this new weaponry arising out of the necessity to keep abreast
or ahead of their traditional enemies. But even in these states, there is little
evidence that firearms had resulted in new battle techniques which revolutionized established ideas of warfare. In the reign of the Burmese monarch
Bayinnaung in the mid-sixteenth century, guns were successfully integrated into the infantry and elephant units, with musketeers and artillerymen
in a ratio to other troops of 1:2 or 1:3. During the Burmo-Siamese wars of
the sixteenth to the early nineteenth centuries, the Burmese placed heavy
cannons on artifically created mounds or on high towers as siege weapons,
to good effect. In 1564 Ayutthaya quickly surrendered to the besieging
Burmese forces because it had no defence against the array of large-calibre
cannon brought against it.

As a matter of survival against the Burmese, the Thais were as assiduous
as their arch-enemies in adopting firearms in the battlefield. Cannon were
fired at the enemy from a distance and, if the enemy did not panic and
flee, the armies drew closer to each other to fire their muskets and arrows.
One contemporary French account claimed that close combat between the
armies rarely occurred since there was a great reliance on war elephants.
These elephants carried a few guns about one metre long which shot one-
pound (454-gram) balls. Since only the more prominent leaders would
fight on elephants, battles often depended, as in the archipelago, on a

Figure 6.7   Battle between Pegu and Ayutthaya: a duel between princes on
elephants and armies with spears, swords and shields. The outcome of the
duel was often a critical factor in the morale of the opposing armies.

From I. Commelin, *Begin ende Voortgang,* 'Oost-Indische Reyse', Amsterdam, 1646, III. opp. p. 22;
facsimile Uitgaven Nederland N.V., in co-operation with N. V. Het Parool, publishers,
Amsterdam; N. Israel, antiquarian and publisher, Amsterdam; and B. de Graaf, antiquarian and
publisher, Nieuwkoop, Z.H.

duel or a limited skirmish between the princes and noblemen of the
warring armies.

The civil wars in Vietnam encouraged the production and use of
firearms. A Jesuit observer in 1631 commented on the proficiency of the
Vietnamese in handling both cannon and arquebuses:

> The Cochin-Chinese have now become so expert in the managing of them
> [artillery and arquebuses] that they surpass our Europeans; for indeed they did
> little else every day but exercise themselves in shooting at a mark. They are
> so good they could hit with the artillery better than others would with an
> arquebus. And with arquebus, too, they are good. They go daily to the fields
> to practise.[26]

For the field artillery the Vietnamese relied on small cannon which could
be borne on the backs of the soldiers and fire a four-ounce (112-gram) shot.
One man carried the barrel, measuring about 2 metres, while another took

[26] C. R. Boxer, 'Asian potentates and European artillery in the 16th–18th centuries: a footnote
to Gibson-Hill', JMBRAS, 38, 2 (1965) 166.

the carriage, consisting of a round piece of wood about 10 centimetres thick and the same length as the barrel. In action, one end of the carriage was propped up by two legs or by a fork about one metre off the ground, and the cannon was placed on the carriage, lying in an iron socket with a swivel. The gunner could thus control and adjust his aim, aided by a short stock resting against his shoulder. These small cannon were used to clear a pass or to disperse enemy forces waiting to repel a crossing. The soldiers were all taught to make their own gunpowder with little 'engines' to mix the ingredients and to make whatever quantity required. But the Vietnamese suffered the same poor results with their gunpowder as their neighbours. The cause was attributed to the poor corning of the powder which produced unequal lumps.

In the wars between the Nguyen and the Trinh in the seventeenth century, the latter kept ready a force of seventy or eighty thousand men, armed with swords or thick, heavy matchlocks with barrels of 1 to 1.2 metres in length. Soldiers were provided with hollow bamboo to protect the barrel of the gun from dust when it was hanging on a rack in the house, and another larger lacquered bamboo case to protect the entire gun from the elements while on the march. The Vietnamese were considered among the quickest of any nation in the loading and firing of their muskets. In four motions they were able to draw their ramrod, insert the powder and lead, ram the charge down, remove the rod and replace it, and then fire at first sight very successfully. Every soldier carried a leather cartridge box containing small sections of bamboo filled with powder and shot. Each of these sections was sufficient for one charge and could be neatly poured down the barrel of the musket. An Englishman at the same period required some twenty motions to load and fire.

By the middle of the eighteenth century, firearms had become a permanent part of Vietnamese warfare. When the Tayson forces routed the Chinese army sent in aid of the Le emperor in 1789, the leader of the Tayson is described as entering Thang-long (Hanoi) with 'his armour . . . black from the smoke of gunpowder'.[27] Many fleeing Chinese were also killed by mines, demonstrating Vietnamese familiarity with their use.

Despite the varying use of guns in combat, all Southeast Asians were convinced of the spiritual powers which these weapons could bring to battle. Europeans were constantly amazed at the numbers of cannon, large and small, which they found in Southeast Asian arsenals; some were too tiny to be weapons. When the Portuguese seized Melaka in 1511, they claimed to have found some 3000 cannon in the city. Most had never been fired, which elicited disdainful European comments regarding the quality of the locally-produced guns. However, the production of large quantities of guns was often intended for spiritual rather than physical combat. One of the sights which puzzled and amused Europeans was the local practice of dismounting a cannon from its carriage, upending it with its barrel in the air, and then tying it to the pole of a house. These cannon were obviously never fired nor employed as field guns. They became instead representations of the sacred stone of the local deity, a local version

---

[27] Charles B.-Maybon, *Histoire moderne du pays d'Annam (1592–1820)*, Paris 1919, 298.

of the Śiva linga and therefore the repository of powerful protector spirits.

During the final stages of the siege of Ayutthaya by the Burmese in 1767, the ruler of Auytthaya ordered that the great cannon called *Dvaravati*, 'which had been regarded from ancient times as the guardian of the city, should after the customary propitiatory offerings had been made to the presiding spirit',[28] be brought out to be fired at the enemy. When the powder failed to ignite after a number of attempts, the Thais regarded this as a sign of the removal of the protection of the guardian spirit and the end of Ayutthaya. Another greatly revered cannon which had been cast under Narai, and given the name *Phra Phirun* (a rain god), was thrown into the lake after the seizure of Ayutthaya. When Taksin finally reconstituted the Thai state and established his own dynasty, he cast another *Phra Phirun* in 1777 in his capital city of Thonburi 'to be an emblem that the kingdom had recovered from its reverses and had regained its former greatness'.[29] Frequently flowers and incense were placed on these cannon to appease the spirits. Even cannon in use in the field could elicit a similar response among their users. One small three-pounder was especially revered by the Burmese because of its reliability, and so it was sprinkled with fine scents and dressed with beautiful cloth. At one of the battles near Prome in 1755, the Burmese ruler consented to the offer of liquor and meat to the spirit of the *Yan Bon Khwin* cannon.

The Makassar people, too, had their guardian cannon, the *Anak Makassar* (Child of Makassar), whose qualities were praised in a panegyric to the Makassar fighting forces in the war against the Dutch in 1666–9. For the Javanese the effectiveness of the cannon was not measured by its destructive capacity but by its ability to amass spiritual power for the benefit of the community. It is not surprising that among the guns which the Javanese possessed was a wooden cannon which they said had descended from the heavens. The Mataram state cannon, *Guntur Geni*, was fired only to assemble the community, to summon the nobles when the Susuhunan was angry, or to announce the death of a dignitary.

The Southeast Asian decision to adopt firearms for their spiritual potency is in character with the history of the area. The practical value of this new technology on the battlefield was not ignored, but its adoption was not a matter of great concern except perhaps in the warring states of Burma and Siam, and in Vietnam with its own internal wars and its long history of armed conflict with the Chinese. By contrast the spiritual nature of firearms was immediately recognized by all as being in keeping with their perception of the inter-relationship between the material and spiritual spheres of life.

There was, therefore, only a partial adoption of the new firearms technology in Southeast Asia and a tendency to rely on imports rather than on locally-produced guns and gunpowder. But even if Southeast Asians had devoted time to perfecting their understanding of firearms, new advances in Europe would have quickly outstripped the pace of developments in Asia. By the eighteenth century the Europeans had established

---

[28] 'Burmese Invasions of Siam', VI, 46.
[29] Seymour Sewell, 'Notes', 23.

superiority in the production of great quantities of reliable cast-iron cannon and of the much lighter and more reliable flintlock muskets. The close relationship between the producer and the gunner which had characterized earlier centuries no longer held by the eighteenth century. While it may have been possible earlier for Southeast Asian rulers to seize European gunners and expect them to reproduce the armaments which they were using, this was no longer possible by the eighteenth century, as we have seen. The Southeast Asians were now dependent upon the goodwill of the Europeans for their supply of guns and gunpowder. Since the latter were unwilling to provide the Southeast Asians with the means to challenge them, the consequences were predictable. In the early nineteenth century the Burmese arsenal consisted of some 35,000 muskets, most of which were rejects from the English and French armouries. The situation was similar or worse in the other parts of Southeast Asia, signalling the beginning of a European technological monopoly in arms production and supply in the region.

SUMMARY AND CONCLUSION

In the period between 1500 and 1800, local and international circumstances contributed to the arrival in Southeast Asia of an unprecedented number of foreign Asian and European merchants who settled permanently in the region. The new foreign presence differed from that in former centuries by creating economic and political entities outside the control of a Southeast Asian lord. Within these unique urban settlements, the foreign element dominated; only a peripheral role was allotted to the local inhabitants. The partnership forged between the European government and the foreign communities, mainly Chinese, created successful port-city states in Portuguese Melaka, Spanish Manila, and Dutch Batavia which came to challenge the political and economic authority of neighbouring Southeast Asian states.

As in the past, the Southeast Asians regarded the strong foreign presence as an opportunity to exchange ideas and goods which would ultimately benefit the community. In this regard the European cities—with their novel form of government, architecture, technology, and way of life—were a constant source of wonder and a useful model for the local inhabitants. The mestizo communities, being located physically, physiologically, and culturally midway between the European or foreign Asian and the Southeast Asian, proved ideal mediators in the flow of ideas between groups.

As a result of the frequent interaction of the various groups within the European-controlled cities and in smaller outposts, the life of the Southeast Asian was affected. Foreign advances in shipbuilding and firearms production were greatly admired, but the extent to which the Southeast Asians adopted this new technology depended upon their perceived needs. The situation in long-distance trade had changed dramatically with the introduction of new cargo ships and the armed merchantmen of the

Europeans, and with the financial advantages of using Chinese-style junks for the China trade. Furthermore, there were now too many risks in the open sea and too much competition from the government-supported European ventures and from the growing Chinese junk trade. The Southeast Asians therefore concentrated on the commercial traffic within the region and abandoned the long-distance Southeast Asian *jong* for the hybrid *chuan* and for smaller, faster, and more manoeuvrable boats.

A similar pragmatic decision was made with regard to the adaptation of firearms to Southeast Asian warfare. There was a true appreciation of the effectiveness of the new weapons, and the Southeast Asians invested time and effort to develop their own arms and gunpowder. Ultimately, however, the new weapons were used to reinforce traditional ways of fighting rather than to transform the tactics of warfare. In the mainland states there were successful attempts to integrate corps of musketeers and gunners into the armies. Nevertheless, these new guns were employed in traditional war tactics where the war elephant, pikes, swords, and spears were still the dominant weaponry. In the archipelago the new arms technology was admired but used selectively in the traditional battle where the initial skirmish could decide the outcome, and where stockades (*kubu*) were regarded as temporary shelters which could be as easily abandoned as defended. One important use which Southeast Asian rulers had for the new weapons was to harness their spiritual powers for the benefit of the kingdom. This led to the practice of accumulating large numbers of decorative and unuseable guns, and to the tendency to venerate certain cannon as palladia of kingdoms. Southeast Asians were true to their character in regarding both the spiritual and the temporal spheres as being intertwined, hence employing the cannon to fight the enemy on both fronts.

Between 1500 and 1800 Southeast Asians adapted new ideas from the outside world in the same way as they had done in the past. The nature of these adaptations, which involved selective borrowing within an accepted cultural framework, had always been successful in the past. Nevertheless, it was already becoming apparent by the late eighteenth century that this traditional response toward new technological advances in shipbuilding and firearms production was inadequate in face of the threat from the Europeans. The strength of Southeast Asian culture had always been its ability to select outside ideas and to adapt them to accepted practice. But in the nineteenth century this formula proved inadequate to prevent the gradual loss of Southeast Asia's economic and military dominance to foreign groups.

BIBLIOGRAPHIC ESSAY

On foreign groups in Southeast Asia

The Asians
On the Chinese a dated but still useful general work is Victor Purcell, *The Chinese in Southeast Asia*, London, 1965. For a background on the Chinese

traders and migrants who came from Southeastern China, especially from
Amoy, to Southeast Asia in the seventeenth and eighteenth centuries,
see Ng Chin-keong, *Trade and society: the Amoy network on the China coast
1683–1735*, Singapore, 1983. A summary of pre-twentieth-century Chinese
activity in Thailand can be found in chapter one of G. William Skinner's,
Chinese society in Thailand: an analytical history, Ithaca, 1957. Two studies on
the Chinese involvement in Southeast Asia, specifically on the Sino-
Siamese trade, are Jennifer W. Cushman, 'Fields from the Sea: Chinese
Junk Trade with Siam during the Late Eighteenth and Early Nineteenth
Centuries', Ph. D. thesis, Cornell University, 1975; and Sarasin Viraphol's
Tribute and profit: Sino-Siamese trade 1652–1853, Cambridge, Mass., 1977.
One of the few sources on the Chinese in Cambodia is W. E. Willmott,
'History and sociology of the Chinese in Cambodia prior to the French
Protectorate', JSEAS, 7, 1 (March 1966). Leonard Blussé, *Strange Company:
Chinese settlers, mestizo women and the Dutch in VOC Batavia*, Dordrecht,
1986, is a collection of articles on various aspects of Chinese presence
in Batavia and on Java. For a useful periodization of Chinese involvement
in trade to Southeast Asia and Chinese impact on local societies, see
Leonard Blussé, 'Chinese commercial networks and state formation in
Southeast Asia 1600–1800', paper presented to the Conference on Southeast Asia from the Fifteenth to the Eighteenth Centuries, Lisbon, December
1989. See also Peter Carey, 'Changing Javanese perceptions of the Chinese
communities in Central Java, 1755–1825', *Indonesia*, 37 (April 1984). More
spotty in quality is another collection of articles by different authors edited
by Felix Alfonso, Jr, *The Chinese in the Philippines*, Manila, 1968, I: *1570–
1770*; II: *1770–1898*. One particularly interesting article in vol. I of
this collection is Maria Lourdes Diaz-Trechuelo's, 'The Role of the Chinese
in the Philippine Domestic Economy'. A well-researched book on the
Chinese and the Chinese mestizo community in the Philippines is Edgar
Wickberg, *The Chinese in Philippine Life, 1850–1898*, New Haven, 1965.

For the Japanese, see Iwao Seiichi, 'Japanese Foreign Trade in the
Sixteenth and Seventeenth Centuries', *Acta Asiatica*, 30 (1976), for a
summary and discussion on the Japanese trade to Southeast Asia in this
period. A more detailed study is R. L. Innes, 'The door ajar: Japan's
foreign trade in the seventeenth century', Ph.D. thesis, University of
Michigan, 1980. An interesting examination of Japanese sources regarding
Southeast Asian trade, especially with Thailand, is Yoneo Ishii, 'Seventeenth century Japanese documents about Siam', JSS, 59, 2 (July 1971).

For the Indians see M. N. Pearson and Ashin Das Gupta, eds, *India and
the Indian ocean, 1500–1800*, Calcutta, 1987, for articles on the importance
of Southeast Asia in the wider world of Indian trade. See especially
S. Arasaratnam, 'India and the Indian ocean in the seventeenth century',
which provides a discussion on the various arms of the Indian trade and
the role of each region of India in this trade in the seventeenth century. A
similar focus and intent for the sixteenth and eighteenth centuries are
found in this same volume in M. N. Pearson, 'India and the Indian ocean
in the sixteenth century'; and in Ashin Das Gupta, 'India and the Indian
ocean in the eighteenth century'. For an interpretative essay placing India
within the broader canvas of world trade, see K. N. Chaudhuri, *Trade and*

civilizatirn in the Indian ocean: an economic history from the rise of Islam to 1750, Cambridge, UK, 1985. A contemporary account of Indian trading activities in Southeast Asia at the beginning of the sixteenth century can be found in Armando Cortesão, ed. and trans., *The Suma Oriental of Tomé Pires*, 2 vols, London, 1944.

The Europeans
Donald F. Lach's five-volume work entitled *Asia in the making of Europe*, Chicago, 1965–77, focuses on Asian contributions to European civilization and contains English summaries of many obscure European accounts of activities of early explorers and administrators in Asia. Holden Furber, *Rival empires of trade in the Orient, 1600–1800*, Minneapolis, 1976, discusses the individual European trading companies' structures and their trade in Asia in the seventeenth and eighteenth centuries. For a more recent discussion of Asian and European trade in Southeast Asia, consult a collection of articles edited by P.-Y. Manguin and G. Bouchon entitled *Asian trade and civilisation*, Cambridge, 1989.

For the Spanish, there is J. H. Parry's *The Spanish seaborne empire*, London, 1966, which describes Spanish overseas expansion, while J. H. Elliot, *Imperial Spain, 1469–1716*, Harmondsworth, 1963, provides a general background for understanding the motivations and the activities of the Spanish overseas officials. For an account of Spanish explorations to Asia and the Pacific, see O. H. K. Spate, *The Spanish Lake*, Canberra, 1979.

For the Portuguese, B. W. Diffie and G. D. Winius, *Foundations of the Portuguese empire 1415–1580*, Minneapolis, 1977, provides a general account of the Portuguese nation and its efforts to establish an overseas empire. It also contains a detailed discussion of the workings of the *Estado da India* and of Portuguese activities in Asia. C. R. Boxer, *The Portuguese seaborne empire*, London, 1969, complements the previous study in his discussion of the official and unofficial lives and works of the Portuguese and their descendants in Portugal's world-wide empire. For a study of the various Portuguese intra-Asian trade routes and the value of each route in the sixteenth century, see Luis Filipe F. R. Thomaz, 'Les Portugais dans les mers de l'archipel au XVIe siècle', *Archipel*, 18 (1979); P.-Y. Manguin, *Les Portugais sur les côtes du Viet-Nam et du Campá*, Paris, 1972; and George B. Souza, *The survival of empire: Portuguese trade and society in China and the South China Sea, 1630–1754*, Cambridge, UK, 1986.

For the northern Europeans the story of the rise of the Dutch nation as a European maritime power in the sixteenth and seventeenth centuries is discussed in B. Vlekke, *Evolution of the Dutch nation*, New York, 1951; Charles Wilson, *Profit and power*, London, 1957, and Pieter Geyl, *The Netherlands in the seventeenth century, 1609–1648*, 2 vols, New York, 1961. A more recent and stimulating account of Dutch society in the seventeenth century is Simon Schama's *The embarrassment of riches: an interpretation of Dutch culture in the golden age*, London, 1987. C. R. Boxer, *The Dutch seaborne empire*, London, 1965, provides a descriptive account of Dutch society and government overseas, while O. H. K. Spate, *Monopolists and freebooters*, Canberra, 1983, examines the Dutch and English voyages to Asia and the Pacific in the seventeenth and eighteenth centuries. The structure and the economic activities of the English East India Company are documented in K. N. Chaudhuri, *The trading world of Asia and the English East India Company 1660–1760*, Cambridge, UK, 1978. A good collection of articles on the various European East India Companies can be found in L. Blussé and F. Gaastra, eds, *Companies and trade: Essays on overseas trading companies during the Ancien Régime*, London, 1981.

For an account of the intra-Asian trade, the classic study is still M. A. P. Meilink-Roelofsz, *Asian trade and European influence in the Indonesian archipelago between 1500 and about 1630*, The Hague, 1962. Kristof Glamann's *Dutch-Asiatic trade, 1620–1740*, 's-Gravenhage, 1981, 2nd edition, focuses on the products which were sold in Europe in order to reconstruct the relative value of specific items in the Dutch trade with Asia.

On innovations and adaptations in Southeast Asia

The European-controlled city
A readable account of the life of the Portuguese community in Melaka is the article by I. A. Macgregor, 'The Portuguese in Malaya', JMBRAS, 28, 2 (1955). One of the most valuable pictures of Melaka at the time of the Dutch conquest in 1641 is Joost Schouten's report of his visit to Melaka dated 7 September 1641, which forms part of P. A. Leupe's *The siege and capture of Malacca from the Portuguese in 1640–1641*, published in the JMBRAS, 14, 1 (1936). Dutch Melaka is described in a lively style by Barbara Watson Andaya in her 'Melaka under the Dutch, 1641–1795' in K. S. Sandhu and Paul Wheatley, eds, *Melaka: the transformation of a Malay capital c. 1400–1980*, 2 vols, Kuala Lumpur, 1983, I. 195–241. For Batavia the most valuable work remains F. de Haan's *Oud Batavia*, Batavia, 1922. A more recent work which examines the social history of Batavia and present-day Jakarta is Susan Abeyasekere, *Jakarta: a history*, Singapore, 1987. The best single work on Manila is Robert R. Reed, *Colonial Manila: the context of Hispanic urbanism and process of morphogenesis*, Berkeley, 1978.

The mestizo or 'mixed' communities
An interesting study of the mestizo groups in Batavia is Jean Gelman Taylor, *The Social world of Batavia: European and Eurasian in Dutch Asia*, Madison, 1983. It traces the origins and development of the Eurasian population in the Dutch-controlled city of Batavia, with an emphasis on the role of Asian and Eurasian women in the creation of a unique Betawi culture. C. R. Boxer, *The Portuguese seaborne empire*, London, 1969, and *The Dutch seaborne empire*, London, 1965, devote chapters to the special mestizo community which arose from the Portuguese policy to encourage miscegenation in their colonies. Boxer, *Race relations in the Portuguese colonial empire, 1415–1825*, Oxford, 1963, provides a detailed study of the creation of the mestizo communities and the racist issues which arose in Portuguese overseas territories. A recent study of this community is by Ronald Daus, *Portuguese Eurasian communities in Southeast Asia*, Singapore, 1989. Edgar Wickberg, *The Chinese in Philippine life, 1850–1898*, New Haven,

1965, contains excellent sections on the Chinese mestizo. See also Jesus Merino's 'The Chinese Mestizo: general considerations' in Alfonso Felix, Jr, ed., *The Chinese in the Philippines*, Manila, 1968, II: *1770–1898*, 45–66.

Shipping and navigation
For an introduction to early shipbuilding traditions in different parts of the world, see Paul Johnstone, *The sea-craft of prehistory*, Cambridge, Mass., 1980. A reconstruction of the earliest Southeast Asian ship and the type of long-distance ships which the Europeans found in Southeast Asia in the sixteenth century is found in P.-Y. Manguin, 'The Southeast Asian ship: an historical approach', JSEAS, 11, 2 (September 1980). On the latest archaeological finds on Southeast Asian ships, especially of the hybrid 'South China shipbuilding tradition', see P.-Y. Manguin, 'The trading ships of insular South-East Asia: New evidence from Indonesian archaeological sites', *Proceedings Pertemuan Ilmiah Arkeologi*, 5 (July 1989). For a discussion of the more ordinary boats found in the archipelago, see Adrian Horridge, *The perahu: traditional sailing boat of Indonesia*, Singapore, 1985, as well as his *Outrigger canoes of Bali and Madura, Indonesia*, Bishop Museum Special Publication 77, Honolulu, 1987. See Virginia Matheson and Barbara Watson Andaya, *The Precious Gift: Tuhfat al-Nafis*, Kuala Lumpur, 1982, for a list of the types of ships which were used in Malay waters. An excellent discussion of boatbuilding and navigation techniques in the Philippines is William Henry Scott, 'Boat-building and seamanship in classic Philippine society', in Scott, *Cracks in the parchment curtain*, Quezon City, 1982.

Descriptions of other Southeast Asian vessels can be gleaned from reports of contemporary European official documents or travellers' accounts. A short discussion of Maluku boats based on seventeenth-century Dutch archival sources can be found in G. J. Knaap, 'Kruidnagelen en Christenen: De Vereenigde Oost-Indische Companie en de bevolking van Ambon 1656–1696', Ph.D. thesis, Utrecht University, 1985. One especially important collection is I. Commelin, *Begin ende Voortgang van de Vereenigde Nederlandtsche Geoctroyeerde Oost-Indische Compagnie*. 4 vols, Amsterdam, 1646, which provides not only excellent descriptions of various types of boats which the Dutch encountered in Southeast Asian waters at the end of the sixteenth and early seventeenth centuries, but also beautiful illustrations of the different craft.

A general overview of Indian shipping and shipbuilding methods is found in Radha Kumud Mookerji, *Indian shipping: a history of the seaborne trade and maritime activity of the Indians from early times*, Bombay, 1957. K. N. Chaudhuri, *Trade and civilization in the Indian ocean: an economic history from the rise of Islam to 1750*, Cambridge, UK, 1985, contains a more recent discussion on ships and navigation of Indian traders in this period. The type of Indian ships which sailed to Southeast Asia in this period is discussed in Clifford W. Hawkins, *The dhow, an illustrated history of the dhow and its world*, Lymington, 1977.

Regarding the Chinese junks and sampans which were in use in Southeast Asia, see Jennifer W. Cushman, 'Fields from the sea: Chinese junk trade with Siam during the late eighteenth and early nineteenth centuries',

Ph.D. thesis, Cornell University, 1975. On the early development of
Chinese ships and their contribution to the world of shipping and naviga-
tion, see Joseph Needham, *Science and civilisation in China*, IV: *Physics and
Physical Technology*, part 29 'Nautics', Cambridge, UK, 1971, 376–699.

Firearms and warfare
A monumental work on the evolution of gunpowder and various types of
firearms is Joseph Needham's *Science and civilisation in China*, V: *Chemistry
and Chemical Technology*, part 7, 'Military Technology; The Gunpowder
Epic', Cambridge, UK, 1986. From this early beginning, one can trace the
evolution of firearms and battle tactics in Europe, the Muslim lands, and
Asia in the works of Carlo M. Cipolla, *Guns and sails in the early phase
of European expansion 1400–1700*, London, 1965; James D. Lavin, *A history of
Spanish firearms*, London, 1965; John Francis Guilmartin, *Gunpowder and
galleys: changing technology and Mediterranean warfare at sea in the sixteenth
century*, Cambridge, UK, 1974; and Geoffrey Parker, *The military revolution;
military innovation and the rise of the West, 1500–1800*, Cambridge, UK, 1988.
India's contribution to firearms technology can be found in the works
of O. P. Jaggi, *Science and technology in medieval India*, Delhi, 1977; and
Iqtidar Alam Khan, 'Early use of cannon and musket in India, AD 1442–
1526', *Journal of the Economic and Social History of the Orient*, 24, 2 (1981).
A concise account of firearms and battle tactics in Japan, much of which
had relevance to Southeast Asia, is Sugimoto Masayoshi and David L.
Swain, *Science and culture in traditional Japan, AD 600–1854*, Cambridge,
Mass., 1978.
   The material on firearms and battle tactics in Southeast Asia has not
been collected in a compendium, such as those which exist for China,
Japan, and India. One of the more general accounts which attempts to
place Southeast Asian developments in the wider context of firearms
developments in other parts of the world is C. R. Boxer, 'Asian potentates
and European artillery in the sixteenth to the eighteenth centuries: a
footnote to Gibson-Hill', JMBRAS, 38, 2 (1965). Others are much more
specific and often deal only with one group of people, such as Manuel
Godinho de Eredia, 'Description of Malaca, and Meridional India and
Cathay', trans. J. V. Mills, JMBRAS, 8, 1 (1930), on the Malay manner of
warfare and their armaments in the early seventeenth century. On Siam
there is C. A. Seymour Sewell, 'Notes on some old Siamese Guns', JSS, 15
(May 1922), which provides the history and some technical details on guns
and gunpowder-making in Siam. For Burma, despite the lack of material
on the technical aspects on the production of firearms, there are numerous
references to the use of guns and gunpowder in Than Tun, ed and trans.,
The royal orders of Burma, AD 1598–1885, Kyoto, 1983–8. See also Victor B.
Lieberman, 'Europeans, trade, and the unification of Burma, c. 1540–1620',
Oriens Extremus, 27, 2 (1980). Vietnam's early adoption and use of firearms
is documented in Charles B.-Maybon, *Histoire moderne du pays d'Annam
(1592–1820)*, Paris, 1919. A seventeenth-century account of the skills of the
Vietnamese gunners, their training, and the establishment of gun-
foundries is contained in Alexander de Rhodes (trans. Solange Hertz),
Rhodes of Viet Nam. The travels and missions of Father Alexander de Rhodes in

China and other kingdoms of the Orient, Maryland, 1966. For the use of firearms and the making of guns and gunpowder in the archipelago, the information is scattered in a number of works. Luc Nagtegaal's 'Rijden op een Hollandse Tijger: De Noordkust van Java en de V.O.C. 1680–1743', Ph.D. thesis, Utrecht University 1988, discusses Javanese warfare, the production of guns and gunpowder, and the place of firearms in battle tactics. For a similar discussion on Aceh, see Denys Lombard, *Le Sultanat d'Atjeh au temps d'Iskandar Muda, 1607–1636*, Paris, 1967; for the Bugis and Makassar peoples, see Leonard Y. Andaya, *The heritage of Arung Palakka: A History of South Sulawesi (Celebes) in the Seventeenth Century*, The Hague, 1981; for Sulu and Magindanao, see James Warren, *The Sulu zone, 1768–1898: The dynamics of external trade, slavery, and ethnicity in the transformation of a Southeast Asian maritime state*, Singapore, 1981; and for Maluku, see Hubert Jacobs, *A treatise on the Moluccas*, Rome, 1970.

CHAPTER

7

POLITICAL DEVELOPMENT BETWEEN THE SIXTEENTH AND EIGHTEENTH CENTURIES

The immense cultural diversity of Southeast Asia and the linguistic skills required to approach the sources have tended to encourage localized rather than general studies of the region. The yawning gaps in our knowledge, the difficulties in interpreting information and the very real differences within even the larger divisions of 'island' and 'mainland' do not facilitate efforts to draw the Southeast Asian past together. What can the highly literate, Sinicised élite of seventeenth-century Vietnam have in common with the more oral, Muslim courts of the Malay states? Is it possible to conceive of a Shan community in the hills of upper Burma as sharing in any sense the same world as villagers on a small isolated island in eastern Indonesia? At times it seems that the more closely one approaches the material, the more elusive a common history becomes. Yet the longer view may make the task less formidable. From a contemporary vantage-point the most significant development of the pre-modern period is the slow movement towards the larger political groupings which were to form the bases of later nation-states. This movement was by no means irrevocable, nor was it everywhere apparent. But whereas throughout Southeast Asia the 'states' at the beginning of the sixteenth century only generally approximate those we know today, three hundred years later the current shape of Southeast Asia is clearly discernible. It is the process which brought this about which we shall now examine.

THE POLITICAL LANDSCAPE

Reconstruction of early Southeast Asian history has understandably focused on those places which have left tangible evidence in the form of monuments or some kind of documentation. In effect this has encouraged an interpretation of Southeast Asia's past as a progression from one 'great state' to another. But the historical dominance of an Angkor or a Pagan can sometimes lead us to forget that they were a coalescence of local power centres, and that whatever cohesion they attained was at best tenuous. It was the political fragmentation of Southeast Asia which often struck early

European commentators. Marco Polo saw north Sumatra as a place where 'there are eight kingdoms and eight crowned kings . . . every kingdom has a language of its own'; in the same vein a Portuguese, whose country had been under one monarch since the eleventh century, remarked that the Laos appeared to have 'so many kingdoms'.[1]

The 'polycentred' nature of pre-modern Southeast Asia is traceable to a number of factors. First, it is useful to remember that much of the region, even into modern times, has been occupied by peoples who are basically tribal. The essence of a tribal grouping is that it is normally 'not a political organization but rather a socia-cultural-ethnic unity'.[2] Fission into segments, frequently hostile to each other, is common, although these segments can readily act together against any shared threat from outside. But because tribal segments tend to see themselves as equivalent, and because they are often economically and socially self-sustaining units, the normal 'political' condition tends towards disunity rather than towards a permanently organized state.

A second consideration is the potential for division which results from the character of leadership in most Southeast Asian societies. Influence over others can be due to inherited rights, but it more frequently reflects personal standing and exceptional ability, subsumed in the notion that some individuals possessed of extraordinary 'fortune' or 'luck' will be able to control the vagaries of fate. This deep-rooted attitude to leadership coexists with the concept that certain lineages are innately superior because of their descent from some great ancestor. Thus the archetypal Malay hero who had become entrenched in folk legend is known as 'Hang Tuah' (the fortunate lord), while Ramathibodi of Ayutthaya (r. 1491–1529) is described as one of the 'most fortunate kings'. Similarly a Shan chronicle attributes the success of a local *saw-bwa* (tribal head) to his complex but favourable horoscope 'when Lagana was in the realm of Fasuddho . . . and because Venus was together with Lagana'.[3]

Frequently the 'luck' of such a person was made evident to others by the discovery of some unusual object in which was vested a supernatural quality. Javanese *babads* (verse chronicles), for example, relate the story of a coconut owned by a palmwine tapper. Any individual who drank the milk of this coconut was destined to become the founder of a future royal house in Java. The winetapper, however, allowed the future Lord of Mataram to drink the milk in his place, and it was thus that the dynasty which ruled central Java during the seventeenth century was founded. The importance of holding such sacred objects is especially apparent in traditions associated with the Bugis and Makassarese communities of Sulawesi. Here legends describe how the special aspects of the original founder were recognized when he or she came across an item such as a rusty ploughshare, a seed or an unusually shaped stone. These then became the

---

[1] Henry Yule, ed. and trans., *The Book of Ser Marco Polo*, 3rd edn, London, 1926, II. 284; C. R. Boxer, *South China in the Sixteenth Century*, London, 1953, 70.

[2] Marshall D. Sahlins, 'The segmentary lineage: an organization of predatory expansion', in Ronald Cohen and John Middleton, eds, *Comparative Political Systems; Studies in the Politics of Pre-Industrial Societies*, New York: American Museum of Natural History, 94.

[3] Sao Saimong Mangrai, *The Padaeng Chronicle and the Jentung State Chronicle Translated*, Michigan Papers on South and Southeast Asia, no. 19, University of Michigan, 1981, 250.

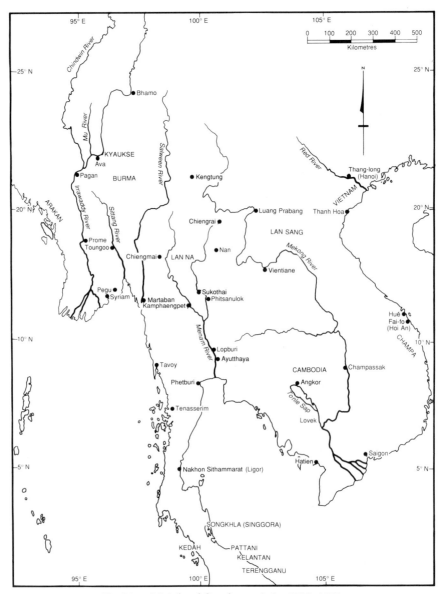

Map 7.1   Mainland Southeast Asia, 1500–1800.

palladium (*gaukang*) of the community and the person who held it the ruler. Throughout Southeast Asia an individual who was successful in obtaining control of these power-laden objects was capable of mounting a formidable challenge to potential rivals.

The proliferation of localized areas of authority was also a reflection of Southeast Asia's geography. The extensive river basins of the mainland and Java may seem conducive to human settlement, but villages were often separated by wide stretches of forest and by hilly ranges, so that few people travelled regularly outside their own district. This social world was even more limited as one moved away from more populated areas. The mountain chains dissecting the highlands, the network of rivers cutting through dense jungle, the inhospitable swamp forests along the coasts, the thousands of islands scattered across the archipelago, all served to encourage the growth of communities which were physically distanced from each other. Styles of dress, social customs and particularly language fostered a local identification with a particular area. In the Philippines today, for instance, eighty languages are still spoken, and on the island of Panay alone there are said to be about forty separate dialects.

The societies which developed naturally from a fragmented environment were infused by attitudes which conceived of the landscape as an array of power-points, each the realm of one or more divinities regarded as manifestations of potent forces within the earth. From Assam to the easternmost islands of the archipelago, clusters of kinship-bonded communities were inextricably linked to ancestor spirits associated with mountains, trees, rivers, caves, rocks and to particular areas under the sway of supernatural deities. As Paul Mus has cogently put it, 'the locality itself is a god'.[4] In some areas this delineation of a 'locality' was clearly determined by landmarks like prominent mountains or watersheds, and the Semai of the Malay peninsula still commonly claim a 'land' that takes its name from a recognized geographical feature such as a small stream. Elsewhere more formalized territorial divisions were established. A royal decree from fourteenth-century Burma, for instance, lays down that 'boundary demarcations are always to be respected', and when the Portuguese first arrived on the island of Ternate in eastern Indonesia they noted that the local people 'keep boundaries and landmarks all over their territories, domains, places, villages and towns'.[5]

Ritual ceremony conducted at sacred spots within these boundaries helped to weld the community together. A missionary travelling in Dai Viet (Vietnam) in the latter part of the seventeenth century described the solemn oath of loyalty taken in each village by the officials. Sworn under the aegis of local guardian spirits, this oath promised the most terrible of punishments for those who broke it. An even more potent means of reiterating communal bonds was the offering of life, either animal or human, to powerful territorial spirits. In the early nineteenth century an

[4] *India Seen from the East: Indian and Indigenous Cults of Champa*, trans. I. W. Mabbett and D. P. Chandler, Monash Papers on Southeast Asia, no. 3, Melbourne, 1973, 13.
[5] Than Tun, trans., *The Royal Orders of Burma, A.D. 1598–1885*, I, Kyoto, Center for Southeast Asian Studies, 1983, 4; A. Galvão, *A Treatise on the Moluccas (c. 1544)*, ed. and trans. Hubert Th. Jacobs, Rome: Jesuit Historical Institute, 1971, 105.

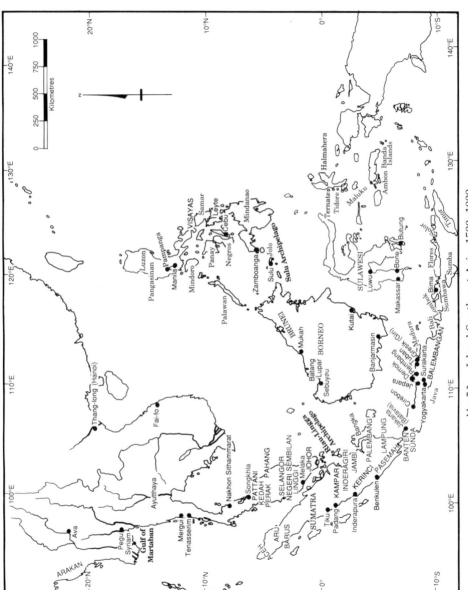

Map 7.2 Island Southeast Asia, 1500–1800.

old ceremony was still practised at Ba Phnom in Cambodia whereby a slave or criminal was sacrificed, the victim's head being impaled and offered to the major cult figure, a fertility goddess, while other parts of the body were offered to gods at other cult sites.

A sense of identification with a particular community was also encouraged by rivalries with neighbouring groups. Usually such feuding occurred because of competition over economic resources, with the aim of gaining control of a strategically placed river junction, a stretch of jungle known to produce certain exotic timbers, or a locality famed for its gold or rubies. In this environment intrusion by one group into an area regarded as properly belonging to another could be a serious crime. Amongst the aboriginal jungle dwellers, the so-called *kubu* of Sumatra, who specialized in collecting valuable forest products, death was the punishment for any individual who trespassed into the territory where he or she had no collecting rights. Slave raiding was another source of inter-communal conflicts. It is probable, for instance, that in early times Cham coastal groups thrived on the slave trade, and the place of such expeditions in Philippine society is suggested by the fact that in all the major languages of the archipelago the word *mangayaw* means 'to raid enemy territory'. Among a number of peoples raiding was also necessary to obtain victims for ritual sacrifice. In Burma, for instance, *myosade* is the name specifically given to a human victim buried alive under the foundations of a great building in order to provide a guardian spirit. Revenge was also a compelling motive for feuding, while among groups such as the Iban of Borneo or the Abung of Sumatra the taking of heads in raids was necessary in order to demonstrate manhood and obtain a wife.

In a discussion of the movement towards greater political entities in Southeast Asia, the potential for friction between communities deserves attention. While such friction could foster the localization of loyalties, it could equally serve as a stimulus for greater co-operation among groups as they sought to withstand attack by a predatory neighbour or themselves prey upon a weaker one. The unity established during these periods might subsequently fall apart, but memories of amicable relations could well be revived. Alliances, even if short-lived, could often allay old rivalries, and legends frequently recall the erection of a boundary stone to symbolize an agreement between two previously hostile communities. Gradually, too, traditions could develop which facilitated the resolution of future grievances. Certain sites such as the graves of ancestors might be designated as places where disputes could be settled by negotiation and discussion, with the decision sealed by an impressive oath. Among numerous archipelago groups it became customary to divert violence into mock battles. Ritual cockfighting, which sanctioned the death of a victim and the letting of blood, could thus serve as a symbolic means of expressing and defusing hostility between opposing factions.

The binding medium in the creation of bonds between communities was always kinship, usually formalized by a ceremony whereby two leaders accepted each other as brothers. The links which this new-found fraternity could bring about are well illustrated by a Shan chronicle's description of an alliance between two brothers, rulers of the Khun (Kengtung) and Lu peoples: 'When heat [mortal danger] comes from the Laos, let the Khun state be the fence, let the Lu state be the roots and yams; when cold [danger] comes from the Chinese, let the Lu state be the fence, let Kengtung state be the roots and yams'. The ancient custom by which two men could become brothers by together drinking each other's blood (called *thwethauk* in Burma) was legitimized in Theravāda Buddhist society by the *dhammathat* law books, and it was the *thwethauk* relationship which frequently bound a Burman overlord to his powerful vassals. The ability of such rituals to transform the most distant stranger into a kinsman is suggested in an early Spanish account of the Philippines when 'the Indian sucked the blood of the Spaniard and vice versa' and they thus became brothers.[6]

The cultural and geographic environment of Southeast Asia had a fundamental influence on the manner in which the polities of the region evolved. Confederations of communities which saw themselves as equivalent were found in many parts of Southeast Asia when the Europeans reached the region at the beginning of the sixteenth century. Relations between leaders and followers mirrored the obligations of kinfolk, and leadership itself was based on the belief that certain individuals were imbued with special qualities and had a relationship with the gods and spirits which enabled them to perform feats beyond the capabilities of ordinary mortals. In areas more exposed to outside influences, most commonly from India or China, this indigenous pattern had been overlaid by one which laid greater stress on hierarchy and which more clearly identified a dominant centre and its subordinate satellites. Yet the analogy of the family was still constantly invoked to explain and justify the resulting overlord–vassal relationships. Like a parent, the overlord should give protection, assistance and occasionally a stern rebuke; in return, the vassal/child should return loyalty, respect and service. The ideal of personal and continuing reciprocity which grew out of concepts of kinship lay at the heart of the Southeast Asian polity, and it could well be argued that whatever 'structure' can be discerned in most early kingdoms was ultimately based on the bonds of family. It was the exchange of women which made these bonds tangible, for the children that resulted from subsequent unions became a living symbol of irrevocable kinship. In the early sixteenth century in Ternate, for instance, the king was surrounded by 'four hundred women' and high ranking chiefs supplied him with sisters, aunts, cousins, nieces, and daughters and 'some are designated for this while they are still in their mothers' wombs'.[7]

A type of authority which resolved potential conflicts through reliance on personal loyalty to a high-ranking elder, chief, ruler or overlord could, at its best, function well. The possibility of fragmentation, however, was always present. The parent–child relationship imposed a clear hierarchy which might in some cases be unacceptable, and ties of kinship could well involve conflicting loyalties. Even the most solemn oath of allegiance could

---

[6] Pedro Chirino, *The Philippines in 1600*, trans. Ramon Echevarria, Manila, 1969, 235; Mangrai, *The Padaeng Chronicle*, 234.

[7] A. Cortasão, ed. and trans., *The Suma Oriental of Tomé Pires*, London, 1944, I. 215; Galvão, *A Treatise*, 89.

not easily be inherited or transferred. The typical Southeast Asian 'kingdom' was a coalescence of localized power centres, ideally bound together not by force but through a complex interweaving of links engendered by blood connections and obligation. Leadership, conceived in personal and ritual terms, required constant reaffirmation. On the death of each ruler, therefore, his successor's authority had to be reconstituted with a renewal of marriage bonds and a vow of loyalty. This was especially true if he had more than one wife. While the women surrounding a leader were an important political statement, they could also yield an abundance of potential heirs, whose claims they could work to support. As states became larger, the liminal period between the death of one king and the installation of the next could often prove to be a time of crisis.

The possibility of retreat from centralized control was the greater because local loyalties remained a feature of all Southeast Asian states, and normally considerable autonomy was retained by regional centres. A prime example is the kingdom of Ayutthaya, which at the end of the fifteenth century dominated the central Menam basin. The territory under Ayutthaya's control, however, was divided into a number of graduated *muang* or settlements, each under its own governor. The latter might acknowledge the overlordship of Ayutthaya and drink the sanctified water of allegiance to show their loyalty, but as royal relatives and *muang* lords their status could be almost equivalent to that of the ruler. The governor of Kamphaengpet, remarked Tomé Pires, was 'like a king' inside his own territory.[8] Independence naturally increased with distance from the centre, and although a law of 1468–9 claims that twenty kings paid Ayutthaya homage, its hold sat lightly on distant Malay Muslim tributaries such as Pahang, Kelantan, Terengganu, and Pattani. These areas essentially acted as autonomous states and as long as appropriate gifts were sent regularly to Ayutthaya there was little interference in their affairs. Similarly loose ties between centre and periphery were found in the kingdoms of the island world, and the sense of independence which this localization of authority encouraged is clearly expressed by the great Malay history, the *Sejarah Melayu*. In the words of a Melaka noble: 'As for us who administer territory, what concern is that of yours? For territory is territory even if it is only the size of a coconut shell. What we think should be done we do, for the ruler is not concerned with the difficulties we adminstrators encounter, he only takes account of the good results we achieve.'[9]

SOUTHEAST ASIA DURING THE SIXTEENTH CENTURY

The sixteenth century saw developments which were to have far-reaching effects on the political evolution of Southeast Asia. One prominent feature of the period is the continuing expansion of international commerce and the consequent rise of new exchange centres. On the mainland, settlements such as Pegu on the Burmese littoral were prime beneficiaries of the

[8] *Suma Oriental*, I. 109.
[9] C. C. Brown, ed. and trans., '*Sejarah Melayu* or Malay Annals', JMBRAS, 25, 2 and 3 (1952) 66.

increased traffic, and a desire for greater participation in seaborne trade may have prompted the shift of the Khmer capital south to Lovek (near modern Phnom Penh) about 1504. It was in the island world, however, where the proliferation of trading centres was most apparent, fuelled by a growing world demand for the region's products. The western archipelago had long been part of a wider commercial world, but now the expanding market for fine spices encouraged Javanese, Malay and Chinese traders to deal directly with sources of supply in the eastern islands. As a result, this previously little-frequented area became integrated into a commercial network which stretched to China, India and into Europe itself.

The rise of new ports was further stimulated by the arrival of Europeans in search of spices and by the Portuguese defeat of Melaka in 1511 which saw the flight of Muslim trade to other centres. It was the patronage of local and foreign Muslims, coupled with the rise of pepper-growing, that led to the emergence of Banten in west Java and of Aceh on the northern tip of Sumatra. Other examples of flourishing settlements which had once been of minor importance come readily to mind. Pattani, on the east coast of the Malay peninsula, was a strategic meeting point for Malay and Chinese vessels; across the sea in Borneo the newly Islamized port of Brunei grew to provide an entrepôt for the southern Philippines and the islands of eastern Indonesia.

Some centres in the western archipelago rose to prominence because Melaka's fall also meant the fragmentation of Southeast Asia's most prestigious maritime state. The refugee Melaka dynasty, located in the Riau-Lingga archipelago or in peninsular Johor, now found it more diffi-cult to maintain its hold over its vassals on the peninsula and the east coast of Sumatra. Though a nineteenth-century Malay account recalls that 'in this period all Malay kings ranked below Johor', the descendants of the Melaka dynasty never completely regained their former status and the sixteenth century saw the breakaway of former dependencies such as Perak on the west coast of the Malay peninsula.

The loosening of ties between overlord and vassal was equally apparent on Java's north coast, where a number of harbours were well placed to benefit from participation in the spice trade and the diversion of Muslims from Melaka. By the early sixteenth century these towns were identifiably Islamic, and their links with the interior Hindu-Buddhist kingdom of Majapahit, their nominal suzerain, were weak. Several coastal lords, like Patih Yunus of Demak, had Chinese blood and had gained their position because of personal ability rather than inherited rights. The lord of Japara was even said to be the son of a slave from Borneo. It was probably around 1527 that a coalition of these ports, led by Demak, defeated Majapahit and established their own independence.

In the political development of Southeast Asia the widening participa-tion in international trade had significant repercussions. For established centres such as Ayutthaya, it brought a confirmation of their dominant position. Already favoured by its geographical site, Ayutthaya had been able to take advantage of growing maritime commerce as a result of admin-istrative reorganization under King Trailok (r. 1448–88). A new ministry, the *Mahatthai*, was established to supervise civil matters and to oversee foreign affairs and trade. In the early sixteenth century some Portuguese ranked Ayutthaya with the most powerful continental empires in Asia, and its prosperity was such that later Thai chroniclers regarded this period as a golden age.

Other ports with more recent origins similarly found that the wealth which came from commerce enhanced their status, raising them well above areas with less access to major maritime routes. On the island of Samar in the eastern Philippines, for instance, cloth could be obtained only through intermittent trading contact with outsiders. When Magellan's ships arrived in 1521 only the chiefs wore cotton, while the clothes of the ordinary people were made of bark cloth. In Brunei, however, Magellan's men found a court where even the servants wore gold and silk. The ostentatious lifestyle there was obviously a major reinforcement to claims by the Brunei ruler to stand as the region's overlord.

On another level the rise of small but thriving exchange centres gave a new impulse towards the development of larger groupings, especially in the Philippines and eastern Indonesia. In these areas there had previously been little need or incentive to move towards the formation of 'kingdoms', but a more commercialized environment made increasingly obvious the value of some form of economic and political co-operation in order to strengthen links with wider trading networks. Perhaps the best illustration of this process is Makassar in southwest Sulawesi: during the sixteenth century it grew from a legendary association of the symbolic 'nine' small communities into the focus of regional commerce. A similar process can be traced in a number of other places, like Manila, where by 1570 several *barangay* or villages had grouped together under the authority of two Muslim *datu* (village leaders), who were themselves linked through kinship ties with the court of Brunei.

To a considerable extent, therefore, the economic climate of the early sixteenth century nurtured the movement towards political consolidation, a movement apparent not only among coastal ports, but among prominent interior centres as well. In the Tai-speaking world Ayutthaya may have dominated the Menam basin but to the north was Lan Na with its important *muang* of Chiengmai and Chiengrai, while eastwards lay Lan Sang which included much of modern day Laos and was focused on two *muang* at Luang Prabang and Vientiane. But throughout Southeast Asia an equally important factor in the centralizing process was the reputation for religious patronage which normally accompanied the rise of a commercial centre. It was in these wealthy and populous places that religious scholars gathered, and where the symbols of spiritual prestige—impressive buildings, saintly graves, sacred relics—were most likely to be found. The leadership of Demak on Java's north coast, for example, was based not only on its trading prosperity but on its fame as a centre for Islamic studies and protector of the venerated mosque associated with the first Muslim teachers on Java. The great Buddha statue which was erected at Luang Prabang in 1512 was a source of pride for local Lao, but it also elevated the *muang's* status in the wider Buddhist world.

To a considerable extent the growth of trade and a common religious heritage promoted links between different centres, providing a basis for closer relationships. It has been argued, indeed, that until the end of the sixteenth century Lovek and Ayutthaya saw themselves not as separate polities but as participants in a shared hybrid culture.[10] In Tai-speaking areas a similarity of dialects encouraged monks to travel between *muang* to preach at leading monasteries, bringing learned scholars from quite distant places together. In 1523 Chiengmai was said to have sent sixty copies of the Tipitaka (the Buddhist canon) and a vulnerable teacher to Lan Sang, while the king of Lan Sang was himself educated by two monks, one of whom came from Nan in eastern Lan Na and the other from Chiengmai. These links were reinforced by the exchange of women between ruling families. In 1546, for example, the king of Lan Sang succeeded in Chiengmai because there was no male heir, but he took the two daughters of the previous ruler as his wives.

In the archipelago, too, the widespread use of Malay and an acceptance of the Islamic faith fostered continuing interaction between many coastal trading centres. The travels of ancestors, heroes, kings and religious teachers between courts which shared basic cultural elements is a recurring theme in local legends. According to Javanese tradition, for instance, the holy man most closely associated with Surabaya came from Champa, while in about 1524 the ruler of Demak received his title of sultan at the hands of a saintly teacher from Sumatra. European sources support the impression that people of ambition and knowledge moved easily between these cosmopolitan ports. The lord of Gresik, said Tomé Pires, was a merchant who was related to the former Melaka king and had himself been born and raised in Melaka. With this kind of exchange it was possible for some Malays to see themselves as part of a culture which extended beyond parochial loyalties. As a noble in the *Sejarah Melayu* remarks, 'Is the Sultan of Pahang or the Sultan of Perak different from [the Sultan of Melaka]? All of them are our masters when all is well.'[11]

Yet despite the similarities which helped to draw many Southeast Asian communities into a mutually beneficial association, competition to attract trade and control resources also fed continuing rivalry between them. The Melaka epic, the *Hikayat Hang Tuah*, even describes Inderapura on the east coast of Sumatra as not truly 'Malay', while Brunei is seen as an 'alien country'. It was often through the emotive language of religion that this rivalry was most clearly articulated. Among Buddhist kings frequent reference was made to the concept of the Universal Monarch, the *cakkavatti*, who has obtained his position because of the great merit he has built up in previous lives and the charismatic glory (*pon*) he has attained in this one. His rule is characterized by the readiness with which other states acknowledge him as king and by his possession of sacred objects such as white elephants, magical horses and women of supernatural power from whom emanate rays of glowing light. A common Buddhist iconography accepted throughout most of the mainland meant 'precious objects' were not now simply of local significance but had a wider value as sources of intense spiritual power. According to a Portuguese observer, the king

---

[10] David Chandler, *A History of Cambodia*, Boulder, 1983, 80.
[11] Brown, '*Sejarah Melayu*', 204.

of Ayutthaya would undergo the 'most severe trials' to acquire as many elephants as possible, and Thai and Burmese chronicles are replete with stories of raids which not only depopulate an entire region but carry off holy images, sacred books and teachers. In an environment where several Buddhist kings aspired to become *cakkavatti*, refusal to surrender a white elephant or a set of the Tipitaka was interpreted as a direct challenge.

In the area covered by contemporary Burma (Myanmar) rivalry between developing religious and political centres was complicated by a heritage of ethnic fragmentation. The revival of Mon strength in the fifteenth century had brought a renewed patronage of Buddhism, enhancing the status of the Mon capital at Pegu. Meanwhile, the locus of Burman prestige, Ava, steadily declined. Previously the dominant centre of the Irrawaddy basin, renowned for its sponsorship of Buddhist scholars and its possession of holy scriptures and white elephants, it was now the target of continuing raids by various Shan tribal groups. The latter had developed more cohesive and hierarchical societies than had most hill peoples, in part because of their wet-rice agriculture, and a number of areas were well known as centres of Buddhist study. In Kengtung, for example, some monasteries are said to date from the mid-fourteenth century. Though called simply *saw-bwa* by Burman rulers, the chiefs of Kengtung were entitled by their own people 'lords of the earth' and were regarded by them as kings. In the process of expansion it was perhaps inevitable that such places should look with envy at the more favourable location of lowland areas, and the early sixteenth century was distinguished in Burmese history by the downward Shan thrust. In a desperate move to hold back Shan raids, the ruler of Ava yielded to them progressively more territorial control, but in vain. By 1527 Ava was in Shan hands. The king was killed and a Shan prince placed on the throne, an event which precipitated the flight of Burman refugees southwards to the relative safety of Toungoo on the Sittang River.

The ethnic fragmentation which characterized Burma is, of course, far more pronounced in the archipelago, and to this was added the economic competition which often undercut the slow trend towards larger political unities. This was especially true when centres were in proximity, produced similar products and drew from the same trading network. The relations between the numerous ports along Java's north coast provide a classic example. For a brief period after Majapahit's defeat, Demak was able to establish its suzerainty over rival harbours and even to expand it across the seas to Palembang in Sumatra and Banjarmasin in Borneo. However, the supremacy of Demak rulers was never completely secured, and by the 1550s their position was already under challenge from neighbouring lords. During the late sixteenth century the remarkable success of the newly emergent Mataram in central Java may have been facilitated because of the inability of the coastal rulers to overcome their rivalry and mount any co-ordinated action.

In island Southeast Asia during the sixteenth century the expression of competition in religious terms was accentuated by the spread of Christianity and the importation of hostilities between Muslims and Christians. In eastern Indonesia, where Portuguese missionaries were most active, some kings readily agreed to baptism in the belief that this would ensure them spiritual power and European assistance against their traditional (Muslim) enemies. Throughout the archipelago the Portuguese goal of winning souls as well as gold meant many Muslims perceived them as a danger to their religion as well as a commercial challenge. At intervals, therefore, attempts were made by Islamic states to invoke *jihad* or holy war and to forge a coalition to drive out the infidels. Portuguese Melaka was a prime target and between 1513 and 1529 alliances involving Johor, Aceh, most of Melaka's former vassals, and even Jepara on Java's north coast unsuccessfully attacked the town twelve times. During the 1560s the anti-Christian mood received some encouragement from Turkey which was involved in its own 'holy war' against Christendom.

Despite the recurring calls for a religious crusade, however, relations between the Christian Portuguese and local Muslim kings were always governed by pragmatism. On the one side, Europeans needed to buy and sell, while for their part native rulers often saw a European connection as an important ingredient in commercial success. During a campaign against unbelievers in the 1580s, for instance, the devout Muslim ruler of Banten in west Java forbade trade by the Portuguese, but it was not long before they were permitted to return. The call to holy war against the Europeans was thus only rarely effective. Far more significant were the entrenched rivalries between centres which had existed long before the European arrival or which had developed as a result of the period's heightened economic activity. Now such rivalries could frequently be justified by calling the enemy's religious beliefs into question. Aceh's hostility was directed as much against the commercial challenge of Johor as against the Portuguese, and a seventeenth-century Acehnese poem depicts the Johor prince as an infidel, a sun worshipper, a follower of the prophet Moses.[12]

This is not to imply, of course, that European influence can be overlooked, but it is important to emphasize that in the pre-modern period the experiences of the mainland and the islands diverged quite markedly. In the first place, European interest in the mainland was limited. It was not seen as a source of spices, and it was the aim of dominating this trade which had brought the Portuguese and Spanish to the region. Second, although Europeans actively frequented ports such as Pegu and Ayutthaya, they never controlled a mainland centre that could be compared with Melaka, and thus never exerted the same influence on established trading patterns. Third, the population and economic resources of the states on the mainland far outweighed those of the Europeans in the region. Occasionally an ambitious Portuguese or Spaniard might propose seizing power in one or another kingdom, but the authorities never considered the dubious gains worth the risks such an enterprise would involve. One scholar has put the case quite forcibly: 'Siam and its continental neighbours remained entirely outside the Portuguese imperial design and charted their own destinies during the sixteenth century.'[13]

[12] G. W. J. Drewes, ed. and trans., *Hikayat Potjut Muhamat: an Achehnese Epic*, The Hague, 1979, 9.
[13] Donald F. Lach, *Asia in the Making of Europe*, Chicago and London, 1965, I. book 2, 571.

The implications of this statement are well illustrated in an examination of developments in Vietnam. Unlike any other Southeast Asian people, the Vietnamese had experienced centuries of Chinese domination which, while infusing their lives with aspects of China's culture, had also enabled them to conceive of themselves as clearly non-Chinese. A close examination of the laws promulgated under the fifteenth-century Le kings has in fact pointed to a greater sense of a nation-state than is apparent in Chinese legal codes of the same period.[14] This sense of a distinct identity may have been encouraged by Vietnam's move south into the Cham areas after 1471, for Chams were commonly regarded by the Vietnamese as morally and culturally inferior, with whom intermarriage was undesirable. Yet the fragile underpinnings of central control in Southeast Asian kingdoms meant that fragmentation was always possible, even in a relatively unified state such as Vietnam. The Chams bitterly resented their subservience, and in 1504–5 there was a major Cham uprising. At the same time less able Le rulers found it impossible to contain the challenge of ambitious individuals. Between 1505 and 1527 eight kings were installed, six of whom were assassinated by rival aspirants to the throne. In 1527 the head of one of the most powerful regional families, the Mac, succeeded in deposing the Le ruler and installing himself instead, but he was confronted with the continuing opposition of other families who pressed for a restoration of the Le. One of these, the Nguyen clan, gained a foothold in the south central area while the Mac remained in control of the delta region. When both sides appealed to the Chinese as mediators, Beijing ruled that the Mac should govern the north and the Le with their protectors the south. By the middle of the sixteenth century, therefore, hints of a future division in Vietnam were already apparent.

Europeans were not directly involved in these hostilities, although Nguyen Kim's son later successfully used Portuguese cannon against his enemies. The exploitation of Western weaponry was more pronounced in the Menam basin, where the movement towards the creation of a single territorial entity under Ayutthaya's domination was already well in train. Indeed, some scholars have already discerned the genesis of the wider cultural-political unity which lies at the heart of the modern Thai state. Three hundred years earlier the terms 'Syam' and 'Tai' may have referred only to the people of Sukothai,[15] but now when outsiders spoke of 'Syam' they clearly meant Ayutthaya and the territory under its control. Local sources, which differentiate between the 'Tai' of Ayutthaya, the 'Tai Yuan' of Lan Na and the Lao of Lan Sang, also point to an emerging 'Siamese' identity, and sixteenth-century Portuguese descriptions make a clear distinction between Lao traders and the Siamese. The European presence in Ayutthaya simply fed into this continuing process of state development, mainly due to the military technology they introduced at a time when Ayutthayan kings were attempting to assert their superiority over often

---

[14] See Nguyen Ngoc Huy and Ta van Tai, *The Le Code, Law in Traditional Vietnam— A Comparative Sino-Vietnamese Legal Study with Historical-Juridical Analysis and Annotations*, Athens, Ohio, 1987.

[15] L. P. Briggs, 'The appearance and historical usage of the terms Tai, Thai, Siamese and Lao', *Journal of the American Oriental Society*, 69 (1949) 62; Wyatt, *Thailand*, 89.

reluctant vassals. In a climate where military organization was receiving closer attention, European weapons were attractive because they could be effectively combined with traditional fighting methods to give the possessor a distinct advantage, even if it was simply to inspire terror through the noise of explosives. Thus a contract made with Ramathibodi in 1518 allowed the Portuguese to trade in Ayutthaya, Ligor, Tenasserim and Pattani in return for guns and war munitions, and a number of Portuguese mercenaries were attached to the Ayutthayan army.

However, it was in Burma where European military technology apparently had its greatest appeal, and may have made a measurable contribution to the resurgence of Burman strength. The founders of a new dynasty originating from Toungoo, Tabinshwehti (r. 1531–50) and his successor Bayinnaung (r. 1551–81), aimed from the outset to recreate a centralized state in the Irrawaddy basin, and the advent of the Europeans was thus timely. Experts in gunnery were recruited into royal service, and during successful attacks on the Mon capital of Pegu in the late 1530s and on Martaban in the 1540s several hundred Portuguese mercenaries were reportedly deployed. While it would be wrong to overestimate the effects of European firearms, local chronicles speak with awe of the 'great guns' by which Tabinshwehti could 'smash the [Shan] *saw-bwas*' warboats to splinters' since they 'had no cannon or large mortars'.[16] By the late 1550s most Shan states had accepted Bayinnaung's overlordship and in 1558 he even defeated Chiengmai, which had successfully resisted the armies of Ayutthaya eleven years earlier. So impressive were his victories that one eminent Thai prince, the viceroy of the northern provinces, was even willing to attach himself to this seemingly invincible conqueror. Besieged by Bayinnaung's army, Ayutthaya fell in August 1569 and by 1574 Vientiane in Lan Sang was also in Burman hands. For the first time in history Burman rulers had been able to subdue the 'great arc of Tai-speaking peoples', and from Chiengmai to Ayutthaya splendid new pagodas built at Bayinnaung's direction proclaimed the power of the king whom the Mons referred to in awe as the 'Victor of the Ten Directions'.[17]

The success of Bayinnaung, however, did not depend solely on military strength. He acted as a model Buddhist king, distributing copies of the Tipitaka, feeding and ordaining monks, and building and repairing monasteries and pagodas. Continued efforts were made to encourage commerce as laws were collated, judicial decisions collected and weights and measures became more standardized. Officials were appointed to supervise merchant shipping and Bayinnaung himself sent out ships to undertake commercial voyages. He also directed his attention to resolving the longstanding Burman–Mon rivalry by bringing Mon princesses into the palace and by taking Mon chiefs as his brothers. Finally, Bayinnaung saw himself as part of a wide diplomatic world, exchanging missions with Bengal, Sri Lanka, Portuguese Goa and China. All these actions were in the tradition of great Burmese kings. What made Bayinnaung's rule

[16] Victor Lieberman, 'Europeans, trade and the unification of Burma, c. 1540–1620', *Oriens Extremus*, 27, 2 (1980) 213.

[17] Victor Lieberman, *Burmese Administrative Cycles. Anarchy and Conquest, c. 1580–1760*, Princeton, 1984, 32–3.

exceptional was the extension of his overlordship hundreds of kilometres from his capital at Pegu into areas like Lan Sang which had never before known Burman control. For the Portuguese in mid-century it was no longer Ayutthaya but Pegu which was 'the most powerfullest monarchy in Asia, except that of China'[18] and it was not lightly that Bayinnaung termed himself the King of Kings.

European involvement in mainland Southeast Asia did not affect the overall direction of political developments during the sixteenth century, although in some cases it may have hastened the movement towards a greater centralization of authority. In island Southeast Asia, however, the impact of the European presence was far greater. In part this was because most 'states' Europeans encountered were smaller than were those on the mainland, and therefore more easily dominated. Even in the larger kingdoms European influence was extensive because of their attempts to gain trading advantages through alliances with local rulers, whom they mistakenly believed had powers similar to kings in Europe. But the notion that a 'state' was a permanent structure controlled by a 'government' to which obedience was automatically due was not shared by many of the societies with which the Portuguese came in contact. When Kampar and Aru, two of Melaka's foremost vassals, asked for friendship with the Portuguese shortly after the conquest of 1511, they were expressing a widely held view of the overlord–vassal relationship. It was essentially a temporary one, and the client state was fully entitled to transfer allegiance should a more desirable patron emerge. In the words of a Bugis text from Sulawesi, 'We are like birds sitting on a tree. When the tree falls we leave it and go in search of a large tree where we can settle.'[19]

The European conception of a state was also inappropriate in much of the archipelago where a type of political entity had evolved which enabled several kingdoms to join together and yet maintain a fundamentally equal status. A prime example of this kind of entity was among the islands of northern Maluku (the Moluccas). Here the myth of an original family of rulers was constantly reshaped in accordance with changing political realities so that the cultural and spiritual unity of the area retained a consistent relevance to the present. In 1522, however, the Portuguese established a fort on the island of Ternate, and in a continuing search for compliant allies they became deeply involved in local affairs, frequently supporting their own candidates in succession disputes or when thrones fell vacant. At the same time they encouraged their royal clients to extend beyond the traditional bounds of the Maluku world and to establish control over places with which Maluku had no historical or cultural bonds. The resulting polities, though far more extensive than their predecessors, were inherently fragile because they had been created in a way which was quite alien to the processes by which 'states' had hitherto developed in this part of Southeast Asia. While the unity of the Maluku islands themselves remained intact, the seventeenth and eighteenth centuries witnessed

---

[18] Ibid.
[19] Leonard Y. Andaya, *The Heritage of Arung Palakka. A History of Southwest Sulawesi (Celebes) in the Seventeenth Century*, The Hague, 1981, 113–14.

increasing reliance on force in order to maintain what were in essence artificial links between the centre and the periphery.

In a sense these developments reflected a growing impatience with the protracted process by which loyalty to an overlord had been built up in the past. Now the ambition to control labour and economic resources inflated the goals of individual chiefs who, with access to greater wealth and military resources, could assert their superiority in a matter of years. In 1512 the ruler of Aceh was simply 'a knightly man among his neighbours', but by the middle of the century the control of his descendants stretched down both coasts of Sumatra, and campaigns in the name of Islam had already been launched against the Bataks of the interior. It appears that the assistance of Turkish mercenaries may have been instrumental in Aceh's success, but contemporary Portuguese writers also felt that they had contributed to the growing dominance of some centres over others. According to the Portuguese chronicler João de Barros, there were once twenty-nine kingdoms along the coasts of Sumatra, 'but since we became involved with these oriental states, favouring some and suppressing others according to the way they received us . . . many have been absorbed to the territory of their most powerful neighbours'.[20] Perhaps the most formidable display of the determination to create a 'state' even in the face of resistance was manifested following the Spanish arrival in the island of Cebu in 1565. Their vision of a united Christian colony owing allegiance to one centre had no precedent in the history of the Philippine archipelago, but it was ultimately to furnish the framework for the modern Philippine state.

While it is already possible to see the implications of the European presence, political development in the island world also had an impulse of its own. In Java, for instance, the Portuguese exerted no influence on the renewed move towards centralization which occurred in the latter part of the sixteenth century. In many ways such a move was predictable, for Java was geographically and culturally more unified than the rest of the archipelago, and even in the fourteenth century the poet Prapanca had extolled the notion that 'the whole expanse of Java-land' should be under the rule of one king. During the 1580s a vague figure known as Senapati moved to establish himself in the interior and expand his control towards the coast. According to later traditions, Senapati had fallen asleep on the Lipura stone, believed to mark Java's centre, where he had received a vision of the dynasty he would found. On a later journey to the bottom of the sea the Princess of the Southern Ocean had even promised him the assistance of all the Javanese spirits. Yet any effort to establish an overlord in Java had to contend with the localization of power and the personal nature of leadership which infused all of Southeast Asian society. Whether the dominance of one centre was achieved by persuasion or force, the kind of state which resulted was fraught with tensions.

---

[20] Mark Dion, 'Sumatra through Portuguese eyes; excerpts from João de Barros', *Decadas da Asia'*, *Indonesia*, 9 (April 1970) 144.

THE CYCLE OF FRAGMENTATION AND UNITY

One of the major reasons for the tendency to fragmentation in all Southeast Asian kingdoms was the difficulty of transferring political power from one generation to another. The potential for conflict was particularly great in larger states where kings were likely to have numerous children by several women and where the rewards for success were high. In theory, succession should be settled harmoniously within the royal clan by an agreed selection. However, the increasing inability to reach a mutually acceptable decision as states became more politically complex necessitated the introduction of laws of succession. According to sixteenth-century reports from Ayutthaya, for example, there had been an attempt two hundred years earlier to regulate succession by providing that on the death of a king his brother should inherit the throne, rather than his son. A practice had also been introduced of appointing a secondary king, who would be regarded as heir. Nonetheless, smooth succession in the Thai as well as the Burmese state was a rarity. Burma had to be forcibly reunited in 1551 after the death of Tabinshwehti, and Bayinnaung was in fact no blood relation to his predecessor, but the husband of Tabinshwehti's sister.

Though Islamic states more clearly identified the elder son as the legitimate heir, disputes between a royal prince and his uncles, younger brothers of the dead ruler, remained common. Complications could arise because of claims and relationships derived from local cultures which were often unrecognized by imported Indian or Muslim law codes. In Bugis-Makassar society the husband of a woman who nursed a royal prince became his *patarana*, and the ties between the two could frequently be stronger than between the child and his true father. Throughout the region, too, a special bond was established between those who as babies had been fed from the same mother. To use the Malay term, they became 'saudara susu' or milk brothers. Tabinshwehti's mother had been Bayinnaung's wet nurse, and in 1688 it was a 'milk brother' of the Ayutthayan king who acted as regent and then succeeded to the throne. Added to these factors was the ever-present possibility of the emergence of the 'extraordinary leader' whose claim to rule could be justified not by royal blood but by his exceptional powers and possession of special objects. A Balinese *babad*, for instance, tells the story of the ancestor of a ruling clan in northern Bali who becomes ruler because he holds a powerful magic kris which not only becomes his adviser and confidant, but enables him to become a *cakkavatti*, a Universal Monarch.

The very personalized nature of royal authority meant that the death of a king or a period of weak rule was often a time of crisis as princely factions and their supporters jockeyed for power. In this process royal women are commonly depicted as playing a crucial role. The *Sejarah Melayu* describes how the dowager queen attempted to poison the Melaka ruler in order to obtain the throne for her grandson, the ruler of Pahang; Thai chronicles attribute the death of Phra Yot Chau (r. 1546?–48?) to the sorcery of his father's concubine who seized the throne for her lover. Women who had

been the initial fulcrum of an alliance between lord and vassal are frequently seen as contributing to its breakdown. Indigenous accounts often
attribute an attack on a neighbouring community not to hopes of acquiring
greater prestige or economic advantage, but to the resentment suffered by
a society over the treatment of one of its high-ranking women. According
to tradition, the *bayin* (independent sovereign) of Ava in the late sixteenth
century revolted against his brother/overlord in Pegu because his daughter, wife of the crown prince, was struck by her husband/cousin, and blood
was drawn. She sent the bloodstained handkerchief to her father, who
promptly rebelled. With minor variations the same story is found in Thai
accounts. Even the offering of a woman can be subsequently interpreted as
a factor in the collapse of a previously flourishing state. Javanese legend
says that Senapati presented a beautiful concubine to his enemy the king
of Madiun, who then neglected the defence of his realm, thus allowing
himself to be overcome by Senapati's forces. Indeed, according to an Old
Javanese text, at the end of the *kaliyuga* (the present age) all women 'long
to be the cause of a dreadful war'.[21]

It was at times of political upheaval that the Southeast Asian state was
particularly vulnerable, because any decline in general prosperity or even
an unusual and unwelcome event was attributed to supernatural anger at
the failings of the ruler. Sickness, an eclipse, late rainfall, a volcanic
eruption, earthquake, the discovery of a deformed elephant—events
which in normal circumstances could be explained away—were now
interpreted as evidence of royal ineptitude. Even kings could share this
view. When no rains fell in Vietnam in 1467, Le Thanh Ton (r.1460–97)
said, 'I am a person without merit . . . I am the father and mother of the
people, sick at heart. If I do not dispense wide grace and generous
forgiveness, then how can genuine blessings reach the people?'[22] In part
Le Thanh Ton's despondency was also due to the popular belief that a king
should be able to foretell and avert disaster, and in Vietnam one of the
tasks of Confucian scholars was to interpret the meaning of occurrences
such as the appearance of a new star. It was no coincidence that during his
reception at the Vietnamese court Alexander of Rhodes 'began talking
about eclipses to pass the time' and his prediction of an eclipse three days
before it happened was greeted with wonder. In the early sixteenth
century in Ternate the king was said to be 'an excellent astrologer', and
according to legend Senapati had told the ruler of Pajang that the appointment of an astrologer was vital to the maintenance of royal power.

The task of such a person was to foretell the future and produce the
magic mantra which would prevent the occurrence of disasters like
drought or famine. The more powerful the kingdom, the more vulnerable
it was to the effects of such events, for the continuing warfare which
maintained a great state placed a heavy burden on peasant society. It was
the peasants who supplied the ranks of the armies, it was their crops and
cattle which were seized for supplies, and it was they who could be carried

---

[21] B. Schrieke, *Indonesian Sociological Studies*, II, The Hague and Bandung, 1955, 72.
[22] Stephen Young, 'The law of property and elite prerogatives during Vietnam's Le dynasty
   1428–1788', *Journal of Asian History*, 10 (1976) 16.

off by opposing armies to be sold as slaves in distant lands or to increase the manpower of rival kings. In Burma the chronicles describe how the ruler of Ava, on hearing of the Shan approach in 1527, devastated the countryside, filling in wells and breaking down irrigation canals to make a barrier between himself and the Shans. In Cambodia Spanish observers of the late sixteenth century remarked that with increasing attacks from the Thai, 'the women work the soil while their husbands make war'.[23] Rarely are peasant voices heard in the sources, but occasionally they found a spokesman. A poem written by a sixteenth-century Vietnamese poet, for instance, tries to depict the distress brought about when people were taken from their villages to swell armies, and were thus unable to maintain their canals and dykes or to plant their crops.

> How monstrous are the great rats
> Which pitilessly deceive and steal
> There is nothing more in the fields but dried up rice germs
> Not another grain in the granaries
> The peasant, bent with weariness, sighs
> The peasant's wife, emaciated, never ceases to weep
> Nothing is more sacred than the life of the people
> But you do it terrible harm.[24]

Given the right leader, most societies were able to justify the argument that an unworthy king should be deposed. An exception, perhaps, was found in the Malay areas where peasant rebellion is comparatively rare. The word *derhaka*, treason against the ruler, is found in Old Malay inscriptions as early as the seventh century and the belief that rebellion would result in the most terrible of punishments was deeply embedded in Malay culture, to be reinforced by later teaching that ultimately Allah himself would punish the wicked king. Unless led by a prince of the royal house, Malays were generally reluctant to oppose the ruler, and it is surely significant that the great folk hero of the Malays, Hang Tuah, is willing to kill his friend rather than be disloyal to his king.

In Java, on the other hand, it has been said that the essential folk hero is the rebel, and rebellion is a favourite theme in both oral and written tradition.[25] A hold on royal power was never guaranteed because the divine effulgence which rulers were believed to possess could leave one individual and pass to another, designating him as the rightful king. This in effect resembles the Sino-Vietnamese concept of the 'mandate of heaven' that in theory at least could pass from the highest in the land to the lowest. In Vietnam rebellion could also be justified because the Confucian classics themselves, while stressing the loyalty which should be given to the emperor, also set high standards for 'benevolent government'. The philosopher Mencius (372–289? BC) even condoned the killing of inept

---

[23] Chandler, *History of Cambodia*, 86.

[24] Cited in Thomas Hodgkin, *Vietnam. The Revolutionary Path*, London, 1981, 73.

[25] Supomo Surohudojo, 'Rebellion in the *kraton* world as seen by the *pujangga*', in J. A. C. Mackie, ed., *Indonesia: the Making of a Nation*, Canberra: Australian National University, Research School of Pacific Studies, 1980, 563–77.

kings who had lost 'the hearts and minds' of their people.[26] During the
first years of the sixteenth century, when the prestige of Le kings reached
its nadir, peasant rebellion was a frequent occurrence. Between 1510 and
1516 there were at least eight uprisings, the most serious in 1516, when
a pagoda keeper declared himself to be a descendant of the Trinh and a
reincarnation of Indra (de Tich). His alleged miracles gained him thousands of followers, and at one point the rebels captured the capital of
Thang-long (Hanoi) and proclaimed their leader king.

Throughout most of Southeast Asia it was this kind of local holy man
who commonly provided the focus of resistance to the ruler. In the
Theravāda Buddhist countries kings could be accused of *acaravipatti*, or
failure of duty, but only a person regarded as possessing abnormal abilities
and sacral power would voice such criticism. The sources yield scattered
evidence of rebellions led by these figures, *weikza* in Burman or *phu mi bun*
in Thai. In 1579 a rebellion broke out among the mountain people of the
extreme south of Lan Sang, led by a holy man who claimed to be a
reincarnation of a previous ruler. He marched on Vientiane with a considerable following and forced the ruler to flee. Two years later another holy
man in the countryside near Ayutthaya led a rebellion in which the
minister of civil affairs, the *Mahatthai*, was slain.

An added impulse to rebellion was the wideheld expectation that the life
of even the mightiest kingdom was dictated by time. Among Javanese it
was commonly believed that some kind of catastrophe, probably the fall of
a dynasty, would occur with the passing of each Javanese century. Similar
beliefs can be found in mainland states. In 1638 in both Ava and Ayutthaya
there was great rejoicing when ruling kings successfully survived the
thousand-year cycle of the Buddhist Era, but a poem written in Ayutthaya
in the late seventeenth century warns that its downfall will inevitably come.

Nonetheless, while crisis years could foster expectations of dynastic
collapse, it still required particular conditions and a leader of considerable
influence to activate actual revolt. For the most part peasants who were
dissatisfied took service under another lord, sought refuge in a monastery
or disappeared into the crowded coastal ports. Southeast Asian historians
have been unanimous in identifying the control of people as a key to the
retention of political control, a view which local sources themselves reflect.
In the words of a Malay *hikayat* (story), 'It is the custom of kings that they
call themselves kings if they have ministers and subjects; if there are no
subjects, who will render homage to the king?'[27]

The ruler's control over people could be crucial in stemming the tendency towards fragmentation because it was ultimately the principal
means of determining the hierarchy between competitors for power,
whether they were royal princes or vassal kings. The language of authority
frequently reflects the value placed on manpower. Seventeenth-century
Filipinos defined the word 'Datu', as 'he who has vassals', and in the Thai
areas military officers were called by the number of people theoretically

---

[26] Alexander Woodside, 'History, structure and revolution in Vietnam', *International Political
Science Review*, 10, 2 (1989) 149.
[27] A Bausani, *Notes on the Structure of the Classical Malay Hikayat*, trans. Lode Brakel, Centre of
Southeast Asian Studies, Monash University, Working Paper no. 16, 20.

under their command, like 'Lord of a Thousand Men' (Kun Pan) and 'Lord of a Hundred Men' (Kun Sen). While death in battle, sometimes on a large scale, was certainly not unknown, a victorious king generally preferred to transport prisoners back to his own territory to augment the population under his control. As long as he could command greater human resources than his rivals he would be able to maintain his superiority. In the words of a Persian visitor to Ayutthaya, 'They have no intention of killing one another or inflicting any great slaughter'.[28] But although the population of defeated states might be carried off, the typical Southeast Asian pattern was to leave tributary kings in power, with the requirement that they send regular gifts and appear at court to make personal obeisance. Despite their conquest by Vietnam, for instance, the Chams retained their own ruler and continued to receive some recognition from Peking well into the sixteenth century. In this type of situation there was no way of preventing a vassal king from increasing the manpower at his command and then mounting a challenge to his overlord.

It was a combination of relative autonomy and demographic recovery which enabled Ayutthaya to cast off Burmese control in the latter half of the sixteenth century. The Burmese left no occupying force in Ayutthaya after the pillage of 1569, and appeared content simply to accept the homage of its kings. They had, however, taken away large numbers of prisoners and for many years Ayutthaya felt the effects of the lack of population. Between 1570 and 1587, for example, the Khmers attacked Ayutthaya six times, no doubt wreaking revenge for earlier Thai invasions. But in 1585 and 1586 the heir to the Ayutthaya throne, Naresuan, was able to rally local forces and declare his independence from Burma. He not only strengthened the city's defences but set in motion reforms which enabled Ayutthaya to retain a tighter hold over its subjects. Expeditions by the Burmese were thrown back, and the defeat of a major offensive in 1593 meant Ayutthaya was once again free.

In a little more than sixty years the balance on the mainland had swung back again in favour of Ayutthaya. Its former rivals, Lan Sang and Lan Na, had suffered considerably at the hands of Bayinnaung and Lan Na was never able to regain its former authority. While Lan Sang, less affected because of its geographical isolation, managed a partial recovery, it too was unable to repeat the challenge it had made to Ayutthaya in the first half of the sixteenth century. Ayutthaya reasserted itself as the dominant Thai state, signalling its new position by a successful attack on the Khmer capital at Lovek in 1594. In desperation, the Cambodian king appealed to the Spanish at Manila, asking for military assistance in exchange for submission to the Spanish Crown. With the failure of this effort there was nothing to stop continued Thai incursions and the eventual enforced submission of Cambodia to Ayutthaya's control.

The triumph of Ayutthaya was a reflection of Burma's fragmentation. Large-scale military expeditions proved impossible to sustain from the capital at Pegu, and there was considerable loss of manpower as villagers fled to escape military service. Regional towns, their populations swollen

---

[28] John O'Kane, trans., *The Ship of Sulaiman*, London, 1972, 90.

by the influx of refugees, were all too ready to assert their independence. Just as serious was the fact that the delicate relationship which Bayinnaung had built up between different ethnic groups began to fall apart. In 1594 an alliance between Mons and Ayutthaya threw back Pegu's forces and the Ayutthayan king Naresuan succeeded in taking the entire southeast coast, even threatening Pegu itself. The final blow to the dynasty came when the *bayin* of Toungoo entered into negotiations with the ruler of Arakan to mount a joint attack on Pegu. By 1600 Burma had once again broken into a number of realms, assuming the 'general appearance of the early sixteenth century before Tabinshwehti started his work of unification'.[29]

In Vietnam, too, internal divisions were becoming more apparent as the compromise mediated by China in the mid-sixteenth century collapsed. The Nguyen were challenged by an even more powerful clan, the Trinh, as both tried to oust the Mac and establish themselves as defenders of the Le. In an effort to maintain his position, the Nguyen leader in 1558 accepted the position of governor of the southern region which bordered on the Cham areas and was thus at the limits of Vietnamese settlement. By 1592 the Trinh had managed to push the Mac back to the mountains on the Chinese border, but this did not lead to greater unity between the Nguyen and Trinh. The latter remained in theory champions of the Le, but it was they who appointed the mandarins, administered revenues and supplied the queens who became mothers of princely heirs. In 1599 the Trinh head assumed the title of *vuong* or prince, and this then became hereditary in his family. The Nguyen simply refused to accept this assertion of supremacy. By 1627 open warfare had broken out between the two families, and it ended only with an uneasy truce in the 1670s.

At the end of the sixteenth century certain clear trends on the mainland can already be seen. Notwithstanding periods of fragmentation, the basis for future consolidation in Siam, Burma and Vietnam had been laid down, and these states had already signalled their potential for domination over the Lao and Khmer. In the island world, however, such trends are not nearly so apparent. In the Straits of Melaka, Johor, Aceh and Portuguese-controlled Melaka remained at odds; Java was divided between the Mataram-dominated interior, Sunda, Hinduized areas like Balambangan in the east, and the Islamicized coastal ports; Brunei was regarded as a leader in the Borneo region; and Balinese forces were sufficiently strong to expand into the neighbouring islands of Lombok and Sumbawa, where they were to clash with the growing strength of Makassar. The presence of the Europeans further complicated the picture. Manila had been confirmed as the Spanish base for their Christianizing effort in the Philippines, and a strong position had already been established in Luzon and the Visayas. In the southern archipelago, however, they faced continued opposition from powerful Muslim centres. It was at this point that new actors appeared on the stage. The English were soon eclipsed by the newly formed Dutch East India Company (Vereenigde Oost-Indische Compagnie, VOC), which in 1605 made apparent its intentions of becoming the pre-eminent European power by capturing the island of Ambon from the Portuguese. In May 1619

---

[29] Lieberman, *Burmese Administrative Cycles*, 45.

the VOC governor-general, Jan Pieterszoon Coen, forcibly seized control of the west Javanese town of Jayakatra, renamed it Batavia and immediately set out to transform it into the hub of the Dutch trading network. The most skilled astrologer would at this point have been hard-pressed to predict future developments. Certain centres in the archipelago could be identified as having more commercial power or greater cultural influence than others, but it was still very much a polycentric world. To a considerable extent the political and economic shifts of the seventeenth and eighteenth centuries were to determine which of these areas would ultimately emerge as leaders in the region.

THE CENTRES OF POWER IN THE
SEVENTEENTH CENTURY

In explaining the rise of the great Southeast Asian kingdoms of the seventeenth century, local chronicles are inclined to attribute the emergence of such states to the 'luck', the prestigious descent and the personal abilities of the ruler. A modern historian, while acknowledging the achievements of individuals, might be more inclined to suggest that the prime factors were geographical. During the seventeenth century the natural advantages enjoyed by some areas became particularly apparent, for increasingly the power of a kingdom came to be determined not merely by commercial wealth but by the ability to marshal large numbers of people who could be supported by the resources of the state itself. In the sixteenth century the kings of Burma had considered the delta town of Pegu as the most desirable site for a capital, but a hundred years later the centre of government was moved back to Ava, which dominated the rice-growing basin of Kyaukse as well as the Mu River irrigation system. In Java, too, the sixteenth century had for a brief time seen the locus of economic power shift to the coast, but after the establishment of Mataram no kings were ever tempted to move away from the fertile regions of the centre. By contrast, the vulnerability of areas dependent on imported food became apparent when the sea lanes were cut. In 1640–1 the VOC laid siege to Melaka and after a blockade of seven months the Portuguese finally surrendered. By this time, however, the inhabitants were so emaciated that mothers were even said to have exhumed their young for food. In this context it can be noted that, despite the rise of Aceh as one of the great Indonesian states during the seventeenth century, its reliance on rice supplies from Minangkabau, Siam and Burma to feed its population has been identified as a possible reason for its later decline.[30]

The correlation between the growing of wet-rice and the development of dominant state structures is not coincidental. First, wet-rice can support a far higher population than the lower-yielding hillside and rain-fed varieties, or the sago and root crops which were a staple diet in most of the eastern Indonesian islands. Second, because wet-rice growers are

[30] Denys Lombard, *Le Sultanate d'Atjeh au Temps d'Iskandar Muda 1607–1636*, Paris, EFEO, 1967, 61.

more sedentary, they are much easier to tie to a central authority. In seventeenth-century Burma it was possible for a royal edict to order the collection of rice 'from over two hundred villages', and in Java a Dutch envoy remarked that 'each family brings ten bundles of padi, every village delivers an amount to the king's receivers'. It is not surprising that the Pampangans in western Luzon, transformed by the Spanish from itinerant traders and fishers to settled rice-growing peasants, became so closely involved with the Spanish, who contrasted their loyalty with the swidden agriculturalists of the forested hills and the roaming 'vagabonds' whose lack of any fixed abode prevented any exaction of tribute. These were views which many Southeast Asian kings would have shared. A Burmese edict of 1598, for example, commands each soldier to remain at the place 'where his ancestors had lived for generations before him' and in Ayutthaya the forests were seen as the home of 'ungoverned' people who should be persuaded to come out and plant rice fields.[31]

For European governors and Southeast Asian rulers alike, large settled populations supported by abundant amounts of food were seen as the key to authority and power. In Ayutthaya, indeed, it was the ownership of rice fields, albeit at times theoretical, that provided the basis for the formal gradings in noble status (*sakdi na*), and in Vietnam rulers had traditionally rewarded their followers by gifts of land. From the centre's point of view, it was important that as much rice as possible was produced. The aim was not only the maintenance of existing fields but their extension. A Burmese regulation of 1643 makes it a requirement for palace guards not on duty to cultivate the fields, while Javanese traditional law specifically laid down that 'a person asking permission to work a wet-rice field [*sawah*] but not carrying out the task so that the field lies fallow must repay the equivalent of the rice harvest of the entire field'. It was the consequent density of population which struck a Dutch envoy to the Mataram court in 1648. He spoke of 'the unbelievably great rice fields which are all around Mataram for a day's travel, and with them innumerable villages'.[32]

Not all states, of course, were able to fulfil the potential which a large population accorded them. Vietnam is a case in point. Here the annual flooding of the Red (Hong) River delta had been controlled since early times by damming and irrigation. The demographic results of this were apparent in a census dating from the fifteenth century which records over three million people living in the delta. Their larger, more organized population had enabled the Vietnamese to overrun the Cham areas, and still in the late seventeenth century an Englishman who had long traded in the region marvelled at the numbers of villages and the push of crowds in the streets of the capital 'even though they are reasonably large'. Internal feuding and the outbreak of war between the Nguyen and Trinh

Than Tun, *Royal Orders*, I. 8; Lorraine M. Gesick, 'Kingship and Political Integration in Traditional Siam, 1767–1824', Ph.D. thesis, Cornell University, 1976, 16.
M. C. Hoadley and B. Hooker, *An Introduction to Javanese Law: A Translation of and Commentary on the Agama*, Tucson, 1981, 174; H. J. de Graaf, *De Vijf Gezantschapreizen van Ryklof van Goens*, The Hague 1956, 52.

in 1627, however, absorbed the energies of the country for nearly four decades, resulting not in the growth of a more settled peasant population but in their dispersal and flight. Even so, the early seventeenth century saw the Nguyen lords effectively taking over control of the Mekong delta as Vietnamese pushed into Khmer-speaking areas and established their own customs house near modern-day Ho Chi Minh City.

The size of the population any centre could command had far-reaching political effects. It was not simply that these places were capable of amassing the economic resources which reinforced their claims to supremacy over their neighbours. They also commanded substantial armies which could compel the obedience of recalcitrant vassals. The point can be made clearly by comparing the armed forces of Johor, the most prestigious of the Malay states but one without any agrarian base, with those of the Trinh. In 1714 the Dutch estimated that Johor could bring to battle 6500 men and 233 vessels of all types. In Vietnam, by contrast, the Nguyen army was tallied at 22,740 men, including 6410 marines and 3280 infantry. The same pattern is apparent in the other rice-producing states. In 1624 the ruler of Mataram was said to have augmented his army by as many as 80,000 soldiers and in 1635 an order was proclaimed in Burma to raise the strength of the armed forces to an unrealistic but presumably ideal figure of 885,000 men. Aceh, which did not have a rice base, is a partial exception, but it drew heavily on its interior peoples to provide manpower, and was able to put to sea galleys which allegedly carried about four hundred men each.[33]

In the seventeenth century these large armies were most commonly deployed to shore up compliance with the hierarchy which the vassal–overlord relationship entailed. In many cases the offer of protection and the prestige of a powerful patron was no longer sufficient recompense for the acceptance of a lower status, since many so-called 'vassals' had considerable standing of their own. The Shan state of Kengtung, for example, was regarded by Ava as a tributary which, though permitted a degree of autonomy, was ultimately subservient to its overlord in the lowlands. Nothing of this, however, emerges in Shan chronicles which describe how Kengtung in its turn acted as protective suzerain to nearby saw-bwas. The ruler of Kengtung 'was possessed of great glory and power without peer, and there was no one, either within or without the state, to rebel against his authority, nor did he go to submit to the ruler of Ava'.[34] In order to incorporate the many centres like Kengtung into larger political systems, the seventeenth century saw a greater reliance on force than ever before. The kind of cultural strains which this could introduce is suggested in a nineteenth-century chronicle which relates how Bayinnaung forbade the 'evil' and 'heathen' practice of burying a Shan saw-bwa's slaves, horses and elephants with him. In so doing, of course, he was condemning his vassals to perpetual poverty in the world beyond death.

[33] Leonard Y. Andaya, *The Kingdom of Johor 1641–1728*, Kuala Lumpur, 1975, 333; Charles Maybon, *Histoire Moderne du Pays Annam (1592–1820)*, Paris, 1920, 111; Schrieke, *Indonesian Sociological Studies*, II. 147; Than Tun, *Royal Orders*, I. 49; Lombard, *Le Sultanat*, 85–6.
[34] Mangrai, *The Padaeng Chronicle*, 185.

A RENEWAL OF THE MOVEMENT TOWARDS
CENTRALIZED CONTROL

By the early seventeenth century, Siam and Burma were reaffirming their
position as the two strongest political and economic powers in the region.
For neither, however, was the path easy. In Ayutthaya Naresuan may
have left behind a relatively strong core but the Thais still felt threatened
by their neighbours. In 1622 the Khmers decisively routed Thai forces, and
Ayutthaya lost four or five thousand men. There were also recurring
rebellions in a number of southern tributary states, sometimes surprisingly
successful. In 1634 Pattani forces were able to defeat those of Ayutthaya,
and it has been suggested that the assertion of Thai control in the
peninsula was accomplished only by recourse to European arms and
military advisers. During the latter part of the century the Thai missions
sent to France by King Narai in 1684 and 1687–8 were apparently directly
aimed at obtaining assistance against insurrections in the south.

In Burma, too, though the process of reunification was quick to take
hold, it entailed nearly a generation of warfare. The son of Bayinnaung by
a minor wife began to attract a following of refugees, and by 1597 he was
extending the areas under his control west towards Pagan and north to
Ava. Repeated military success ensured his standing as a man of *hpon*
(charismatic glory) as he moved against the Shans, and by 1606 his forces
had conquered almost the entire Tai region west of the Salween River. His
son Anaukpetlun (r. 1606–28) completed the process, extending Burmese
sovereignty from Kengtung in the east to Arakan in the west, and from
Bhamo in the north to Tavoy and Chiengmai in the south. According to
stories told a hundred years later, Anaukpetlun's military prowess was
such that he could conquer his enemies simply by laughing, and at news of
his coming 'men, gods, monsters and ghosts' vanished in terror.[35]

From the 1660s, when wars between Ayutthaya and the Burmese were
renewed, there was a continuing rivalry between them for control of
territory and resources. Not only did the demands for tribute from
dependencies grow greater, but there was also far less tolerance of any
signs of disloyalty. The type of semi-autonomy which had characterized
vassal states two or three centuries before could now be sustained only in
the case of considerable geographical separation. The area of modern Laos,
for instance, was ultimately able to survive because it was considerably
removed from the centres of Burmese and Thai control, and was shielded
by its environment. A Genoese traveller remarked on 'the mountains and
inaccessible precipices that surround it on every side like so many ramparts
that none can force their way through and which thus serve as a protection
against the insults of their enemies'.[36] Though in the seventeenth century
it was divided into three separate kingdoms, centred on Vientiane, Luang
Prabang and Champassak, the frequent quarrelling between them did not
destroy the sense of being different from their Thai neighbours to the
south. A long history of regional sponsorship of Buddhism, and the

---

[35] Lieberman, *Burmese Administrative Cycles*, 56.
[36] Cited in Wyatt, *Thailand*, 121.

possession of revered objects like the statue of the Emerald Buddha, also served to reinforce a sense of local pride. Furthermore, it appears that to a significant extent the powerful neighbours of the Lao, the rulers of Vietnam and Ayutthaya, were prepared to recognize its separate identity. Boundaries were set up between Lan Sang and Vietnam with the provision that those who lived on houses on piles were to be regarded as Lao subjects, and those whose houses were on the ground were Vietnamese. In 1670 another frontier marker, sanctified by the consecration of a Buddhist shrine, was set up to reaffirm the borders with Ayutthaya.

Geographical distance thus enabled the Lao kingdoms to survive. The old state of Lan Na (Chiengmai), which had considered itself the equal of both Lan Sang and Ayutthaya in the sixteenth century, was not so fortunate. More accessible from both Ayutthaya and Ava, it became a victim of the increased rivalry on the mainland and the demands of overlords on their vassals. Though subservient to the Burmese and with a governor installed by Ava, Chiengmai did not easily set aside memories of its former independence and was always ready to break away. In 1660, hearing (incorrectly) that Ava had fallen to the Chinese, the governor sent an envoy to Ayutthaya to ask that he be accepted as a vassal. However, when the Siamese took over control (seizing in the process the famed Buddha Sihinga image) they were soon ejected by Burmese forces. By 1664 Chiengmai was again under Ava's suzerainty. But the Burmese, like the Thais, appear to have adopted the policy that 'once a vassal, always a vassal' and the punishment for Chiengmai's defection was harsh. Ava's control was now considerably stricter, with the regular installation of Burmese rather than local governors and frequent calls on local manpower to fill the ranks of Ava's armies.

Though Ava permitted its Tai vassals in the highlands to retain the rank of *pyi* or sovereign state, this was nonetheless a limited autonomy. Between 1613 and 1739 the Burmese launched at least ten campaigns to enforce control in the Tai uplands. But here there was a common religious language, so that patronage of local monasteries and the appointment of learned monks could be used to reinforce the centre's authority. The strains were far greater in areas where cultural and religious links were weak, like those between Ayutthaya and the mixed Malay-Thai culture of the southern isthmus. In the fifteenth century the Malay state of Kedah, along with its neighbours, had been able to pacify two masters by acknowledging the distant overlordship of both Melaka and Ayutthaya. In the changed mood of the seventeenth century, however, the Thai king Prasat Thong (r. 1629–56) demanded that the Raja of Kedah come personally to Ayutthaya and pay him homage. Although the Kedah ruler was excused when he feigned illness, his court was presented with a small image of Prasat Thong and told that homage should be paid to it twice daily, something that would have been anathema to a Muslim king.

The attitude towards the vassal–overlord relationship in the previously lightly governed Malay shadow areas was becoming stricter; a particularly graphic example of this is the case of Songkhla (Singgora). In 1651 the ruler, a Muslim, refused to come to Ayutthaya to swear public allegiance to the Thai king. In one of the many fierce campaigns which followed, a Thai fleet of 120 ships was despatched, each vessel smeared with human blood and hung with human heads to terrify Songkhla into obedience. By 1679 its ruler had finally complied with the order to go to Ayutthaya to pay personal homage. While he was in the Thai capital, however, King Narai (r. 1656–88) ordered almost all Songkhla's inhabitants carried off. Its fate is vividly depicted in a rare eighteenth-century Thai map which shows a deserted city with tigers prowling in the environs.[37] The continuing effort to incorporate these areas into Ayutthaya's cultural ambit is suggested by the fact that in 1689 the viceroy of Ligor, a Malay, was replaced by a Thai.

The greater reliance on force to create new political structures was also evident in the island world, where it had been an integral part of European intrusion into the area. When the Spanish led by Miguel Lopez de Legazpi landed in Cebu in 1565 to find their peaceful overtures rejected, they opened fire on the local settlement. On the island of Luzon, Manila was taken by force, and during an attack in 1570 as many as 500 people may have been killed with 1500 houses burned. In the early years of Spanish colonization natives were often compelled to submit and accept Christianity, with the alternative frequently being death or enslavement. Some Spanish observers noted with distress the degree to which force was used to extract local compliance. 'If no tribute is given', said one commentator in 1573, 'the houses and lodges are burnt with no attention being paid to instructions',[38] and by the 1580s some Filipinos were saying that to be baptized meant to become a slave. The death and impalement of leaders of local rebellions remained a harsh reminder of the Spaniards' military superiority.

In the Indonesian areas the Dutch used even more force to attain their goal of commercial dominance and to provide 'an example' to native kings. With a charter which enabled it to act virtually as a sovereign state, the power of the VOC was made dramatically clear within a few years of its arrival. In 1621 the town of Banda was destroyed because of local resistance to the imposition of a nutmeg monopoly. Thirteen of the leaders were executed, beheaded and quartered and 24 others imprisoned and tortured. Of 15,000 Bandanese only about 1000 were left and Banda itself became a colony settled by Dutch and mestizo concessionaires.

The commercial competition which was a major reason for the European presence also encouraged local states to increase their control over people and resources. Aceh is a foremost example of the manner in which force could be used to compel submission. During the reign of Sultan Iskandar Muda (1607–36) a series of campaigns was launched on neighbouring states along the coasts of Sumatra and on the Malay peninsula. The effective end of Acehnese expansion only came in 1641 when its arch-enemy, Johor, allied with the Dutch in their successful siege of Portuguese Melaka. For nearly thirty years, however, the mere whisper of a possible Acehnese attack had been sufficient to panic whole communities.

What made Aceh particularly feared was recourse to force on a scale never before experienced in the Malay world. During Iskandar's attack on

---

[37] I am indebted to Dr Lorraine Gesick for this reference.
[38] Rosario M. Cortes, *Pangasinan 1572–1800*, Quezon City, 1974, 56.

the peninsular states Kedah was ravaged, the capital demolished, and the remaining inhabitants carried off to Aceh. The following year another five thousand people were taken from Perak. A Frenchman visiting Aceh at the time reckoned that around 22,000 prisoners had been taken away from the areas Iskandar had conquered, but the lack of food in Aceh meant that most of them 'died naked in the streets'. The small kingdoms along the southern Sumatran coasts understandably feared the same fate, and only a promise of protection from both the Dutch and the English was sufficient to dissuade the ruler of Jambi from moving his capital far into the interior.

Other newly emergent centres of archipelago trade, such as Banten in west Java and Makassar in Sulawesi, were also determined to establish their superiority over surrounding states. The territorial expansion of Banten in Java was limited because of the existence of Mataram, but when the Dutch arrived in 1596 its control already extended into the Lampung region of southern Sumatra and it was in the process of attacking Palembang. The Dutch commander, indeed, was promised 'the best' of any booty taken if he would render Banten assistance in this campaign. In after years Banten rulers continued to maintain a tight hold over their vassals, and in 1678 an expedition was sent to punish the lord of one area because he had been so bold as to hold a tournée on a Saturday and 'according to Javanese custom' no one was permitted to sponsor such an occasion except 'emperors, kings and independent princes'.[39] Further east another powerful state, Makassar, drew considerable benefit from Portuguese assistance in building up its military strength. Newly converted to Islam, its ruler found little difficulty in transforming traditional rivalries towards Makassar's Bugis neighbours into a crusade against unbelievers. By the 1640s Makassar was suzerain of all the small states of southwest Sulawesi, and had extended its dominion over the entire island of Sumbawa. During the years of warfare, Bugis and Makassarese soldiers, dressed in their chain-mail armour and carrying muskets which they themselves had made, acquired for themselves a formidable reputation for ferocity and courage which 'surpasses that of all other people in the Eastern Seas'.[40]

Dominating the archipelago, however, was Mataram, where already by 1600 the basis had been laid for future expansion. Under Sultan Agung (r. 1613–46) Mataram extended its power to the northern coast and to the island of Madura, finally defeating its most serious rival Surabaya in 1625. Eastern Java had not been totally subdued, Banten remained independent and successive campaigns against the Dutch in Batavia had failed. Nonetheless, by the time Agung died, Mataram's control had been confirmed over the heartland of central Java and most of the northern ports. For the first half of the seventeenth century Palembang, Jambi and Banjarmasin were also regarded as Javanese vassals, despite treaties made independently with the Dutch East India Company.

Historians have pointed to Agung's reliance on consensus and consultation to maintain the links between Mataram and its vassal states, but should this fail force was the principal means of compelling obedience.

---

[39] J. A. van der Chijs et al., eds, *Dagh Register Gehouden int Casteel Batavia*, 31 vols, 1887–1931, 1678, 629.

[40] William Marsden, *A History of Sumatra*, reprint, Kuala Lumpur, 1966, 209.

When Pajang rebelled in 1617, the city was destroyed and its entire population moved to Mataram. Two years later Tuban was also completely destroyed. The Dutch claimed that after Agung's campaign against Surabaya, 'not more than 500 of its 50–60,000 people were left, the rest having died or gone away because of misery and famine'.[41] While Javanese armies do not appear to have used Western military technology to the same extent as Ava or Makassar, Agung's success reportedly owed much to the recruitment of Portuguese advisers who taught his commanders how to make gunpowder. Certainly Javanese chronicles see military supremacy as a major reason for Mataram's victories. In the words of a *babad* of the early eighteenth century:

> They began to make cannon . . .
> The Adipatis all marched out
> Taking with them the great guns.[42]

Suzerainty of the Javanese interior over the coast was not new. What does appear to be different in the seventeenth century was the degree of force now necessary to maintain this overlordship. A century before, coastal rulers had regarded themselves as the equal of the interior kings; memories of this former independence were not easily forgotten. Even fifty years after the conquest of Surabaya, many coastal regencies saw themselves as merely 'occupied' by the central Javanese. To a casual observer it might seem as if the governors subject to Mataram had considerable autonomy, but in many respects this was illusory, for no longer were the coastal ports able to maintain an essentially separate existence; the chronicles regularly record how regents from areas like Surabaya and Cirebon came to offer personal obeisance, 'offering life and death'. Regardless of the privileges accorded such regents, they were still required to render account to their overlord of all happenings in their domains and to ensure that his orders were carried out. In addition, the marriage ties which so often helped to temper overlord–vassal tensions were increasingly absent in Java because Mataram rulers tended to choose wives from among the ladies of their own court.[43] For the coastal lords the reality of their relationship with Mataram was a constant humiliation and it is significant that when Mataram's superior force declined after Agung's death they were only too ready to defy the centre, necessitating further use of force. The dismissal of regents for some real or imagined crime became a relatively common occurrence, and between 1694 and 1741 at least five coastal lords who had opposed the Mataram ruler were executed.

[41] Schrieke, *Indonesian Sociological Studies*, II. 148.
[42] M. Ricklefs, *Modern Javanese Historical Traditions*, London: School of Oriental and African Studies, University of London, 1978, 36–7.
[43] Luc W. Nagtegaal, 'Rijden op een Hollandse Tijger. De Noordkust van Java en de V.O.C. 1620–1742', Ph.D. thesis, Utrecht University, 1988, 93.

KINGSHIP AND CENTRALIZATION IN THE SEVENTEENTH CENTURY

The death of these lords, killed by their king, points to a continuing question in Southeast Asian statecraft—to what degree should royal power be shared? In most states, accepted attitudes towards the decision-making process had always placed a high value on consensus. The same traditions which allowed any respected individual to contribute to discussion in village debates had been maintained as state structures became more elaborate. In the assemblies of nobles which governed Malay states, for instance, rules for correct behaviour guaranteed speakers a fair hearing: 'When people are talking in the Assembly . . . let no one interrupt a conversation between two persons.' To facilitate joint agreement, all information should ideally be shared: 'The raja must speak of all things, whether good or evil, to his nobles; the nobles should also tell the raja all things.'[44] Even a court like Java, which Europeans saw as autocratic, retained the notion of the free exchange of ideas between king and his advisers.

Popular views of the king's supernatural powers notwithstanding, when he met with his nobles his proverbial relationship (to use Malay imagery) should be that of a tree to its roots, of fire to its fuel, of a captain to his crew. Yet in actuality the ruler was often at loggerheads with both his nobles and his family, and should they oppose him he could easily be outnumbered. Throughout Southeast Asian history there are repeated instances of a cabal of powerful individuals acting against the ruler. In Ayutthaya, for example, Prasat Thong had been made king in 1629 when as *kalahom* (the principal minister) he and his court following took control of the army and seized power. On the *kalahom's* recommendation, the nobles then sentenced the king to be executed. In 1651 it was the Assembly of Nobles of Perak, led by the *bendahara* (chief minister) who quite independently of the king murdered representatives of the Dutch East India Company as they were delivering a letter to court. By 1655, when a boy ruler came to the throne, the *bendahara* and his associates were in complete control. Despite Dutch protests to Perak's overlord, Aceh, he was never brought to justice.

The balance could also be weighted against the ruler because nobles had extensive resources of their own. The twenty-member council or *Hlutdaw* of Ava, for instance, was made up of senior ministers and secretaries who, with additional assistants, supervised most aspects of the country's economy. Court politics were therefore characterized by factional struggles as rulers attempted to align themselves with powerful nobles in order to gain a secure hold on the throne both for themselves and their heirs. It is these struggles that lay behind the succession disputes which occurred in most centres with almost monotonous regularity. In 1631 the son of the Nguyen ruler, though overcoming a challenge from his brother supported by a

---

[44] Cited in B. Andaya, *Perak, the Abode of Grace: A Study of an Eighteenth Century Malay State*, Kuala Lumpur, 1979, 29.

group of Japanese from Fai-fo, felt it necessary to imprison four other half-brothers, sons of royal concubines; in Ayutthaya during 1656 three kings ascended the throne in a little more than two months before Narai was finally installed the following year.

In their efforts to retain power, rulers constantly laboured to increase their own resources vis-à-vis potential rivals, and the course of the seventeenth century thus sees a growing tendency to concentrate trade in the hands of the ruler and his agents. Royal participation in trade not only became commonplace; in many places the ruler's commercial activities completely dominated those of his relatives or nobles. In Ayutthaya in the seventeenth century 72 per cent of all ships mentioned in Dutch sources (excluding foreign vessels) was registered in the king's name. As time went on many rulers, encouraged by the duty European traders were willing to pay, extended the range of royal monopolies. Previously these had covered only rare items like elephant tusks and gems, but they now came to include profitable everyday products such as pepper, rattans and deerhides. Advantageously priced goods, duties and obligatory gifts further swelled the royal treasuries. A Brunei manuscript, for instance, specifies that the sultan should pay only 80 per cent of the ordinary price for any goods he bought, while at the same time receiving 10 per cent toll from all sales in his port. The same text cites the case of a Chinese captain wishing to avoid paying extra duty on his vessel; to do so he had to present the *syahbandar* (head of the port) with a gift of 100 reals, but the ruler received seven times that amount.

It was not only through trade that the wealth of kings grew. It was usual in most states for the property of foreigners or individuals lacking the protection of another noble to revert to the king. When an owner of a house died, a Spanish visitor to Cambodia remarked, 'all that is in it returnest to the king and the wife and children hide what they can and begin to seek a new life'.[45] In Ayutthaya the custom whereby half a man's property was to go to the king after his death was said to have been introduced only in the reign of Ekathotsarat (r. 1605–10). From 1629, during the reign of Prasat Thong, these exactions had increased even further, and now 'when a noble dies, his wife and children are taken into custody'. The same ruler found other means of increasing royal revenues, for he also 'demanded that all subject lands and cities under the Siamese crown list their slaves . . . he had the fruit trees counted everywhere in his kingdom, and placed a tax on each of them'.[46] This tendency to increase impositions from the centre appears to be widespread. In 1663 the ruler of Banten, whose control extended up into the Lampung region in south Sumatra, required all his subjects to plant five hundred pepper vines and bring the crop to Banten.

The growing wealth of kings also helped distance them from the common man. In sixteenth-century Cambodia 'anyone be he ever so simple may speak with the king', and according to tradition the Melaka

---

[45] Chandler, *A History of Cambodia*, 82.
[46] Jeremias Van Vliet, *The Short History of the Kings of Siam*, trans. Leonard Y. Andaya, ed. D. K. Wyatt, Bangkok: Siam Society, 1975, 88, 96.

hero Hang Tuah was shocked when he arrived in Turkey to find he would not be received by the ruler, for 'in the Malay states it is always the custom for a king to receive envoys'.[47] But as the splendour of a ruler increased, he became increasingly less available to his subjects, a tendency which is particularly apparent on the mainland. A Thai decree of 1740 reiterates the king's status as 'the highest in the land, because he is godlike' and like the rulers of Vietnam and Ava, he was rarely seen in public. While kings in the island world may never have assumed the same status as their mainland contemporaries, court hierarchy was still strictly observed and rulers eagerly seized upon the novelty items brought by trade in order to enhance their standing in relation to their peers; now kings wore glasses, ate Dutch bread, drank Spanish wine, wore Japanese brocade and might even, like the ruler of Banten, be entertained by a Portuguese trumpeter. They would have found little surprising in the fact that King Narai of Ayutthaya had an Indian cook and wore Persian clothes, for by this means he was adopting the 'proper manners, fine food and drink and clothing worthy of a mighty ruler'.[48]

In the effort to be seen as a 'mighty ruler', great attention was given to the royal audience. In Mataram, for instance, all coastal lords were required to present themselves at court on specific occasions such as *Garebeg Mulud*, the celebration of the Prophet's birthday, and to absent oneself was regarded as a rebellious act. It was at such times that the king's wealth, his high status and his pre-eminence amongst his kindred and nobles were publicly demonstrated. In these ritual statements a particular place was reserved for the presentation of tribute, the amount and value of which was established by tradition and sometimes carefully prescribed. A text from Brunei thus spells out the products which should be presented by local chiefs—sago from Mukah, padi from Sebuyau, cotton from Batang Lepar, gold from Melanau; in Burma written accounts were kept of the amounts paid in tribute by vassal states, presumably to identify defaulters. In Vietnam missions from Cambodia and the Lao states took the form of 'uncivilized' goods like jungle products, while return gifts from the emperor—paper, porcelain and cloth—were a symbol of his superior standing. Perhaps the most elaborate tribute was that paid to Ayutthaya, where at least from the fifteenth century vassals had been required to present with their gifts two beautifully crafted trees of gold and silver flowers, possibly derived from Hindu-Buddhist legends of magic trees which exist in the golden age of the cycle and which will grant any wish asked of them. The value of such gifts was considerable; according to the *Sejarah Melayu*, one sent from Pasai to Ayutthaya was worth a bahara of gold (about 170 kilograms).

As important as the value and nature of the gifts was the manner of presentation, for the purpose of such occasions was not only the confirmation of the ruler's superior position but the consolidation of ties between overlord and vassal. The ceremony by which vassals affirmed their loyalty

[47] Chandler, *A History of Cambodia*, 81; Kassim Ahmad, ed., *Hikayat Hang Tuah*, Kuala Lumpur: Dewan Bahasa dan Pustaka, 1971, 468.
[48] O'Kane, *Ship of Sulaiman*, 156.

could take various forms. In the Bugis and Makassarese states, for instance, each noble in turn drew his kris and performed a frenzied dance known as the *kanjar*, meanwhile loudly avowing his fidelity. In Vietnam Alexander of Rhodes noted that while swearing their oath of loyalty participants were categorized as to the clarity of their voice, for it was this which determined the length and quality of the robes they would be given. Elsewhere a common practice was to require the ritual drinking of water which had been impregnated with power by the chanting of a special formula or by dipping weapons into the container. Should an oath taken under such conditions be broken, it was believed that a terrible curse would fall on the guilty party. So strong was the belief in the potency of these oaths that during the course of the seventeenth century Ayutthaya consistently pressed independent tributary rulers to drink the water of allegiance, even though in theory they were not required to do so.

The insistence on a public display of subservience which was a feature of the foremost Southeast Asian states in the seventeenth century not surprisingly gave rise to tensions when able princes and ministers were required to humble themselves before an inept or unimpressive king. In a number of cases the recurring conflict between ruler and nobles was fuelled by the introduction of measures intended not only to concentrate more power in royal hands, but to ensure that this power would be passed on to the ruler's chosen successor.

SEVENTEENTH-CENTURY ADMINISTRATIVE REFORMS AND MANPOWER CONTROL

In Ayutthaya the reforming process had begun as early as 1569 following the trauma of the defeat by the Burmese. Naresuan had strengthened the capital at the expense of the provinces, and this trend had continued. Some provincial ruling houses had been almost eliminated, and considerable provincial manpower had been taken under royal control. In every town *yokkrabat* (spies) were appointed as officials of the central government to submit reports on the conduct of the town governor. Another move concerned the position of the ruler's relatives. The royal princes were not, as previously, appointed to govern provincial towns but were required instead to live within the capital city so that they could be more closely controlled.

Considering the close association between Ayutthaya and Burma, it is not surprising to note somewhat similar reforms undertaken by Ava. During the seventeenth century, particularly in the reign of Thalun (r. 1629–48), Burmese kings concentrated princely appanages around the capital, bringing them under much closer supervision. No longer could high-ranking princes rule in virtual independence at a place like Prome or Pegu; now the administration of distant areas was carried out by officers who were clearly appointed by the centre and responsible to it. The king was still cognizant of his kinship obligations, he was still linked by marriage to important officials and territorial leaders, and patronage was still an important tool of government. Nonetheless, the cumulative effects of Thalun's reforms was to reduce the opportunities for princes and nobles to exercise independent power.

Despite the changes which Le Thanh Ton had introduced in fifteenth-century Vietnam in order to increase royal authority, the power which could be wielded by strong Vietnamese nobles had become all too apparent. The battle for supremacy between the Nguyen and Trinh remained unresolved, even though both recruited assistance from Europeans. The Trinh launched massive campaigns against the south in 1643, 1648, 1661 and 1672 but, despite superior forces, they found victory eluded them. The division of Vietnam had already been symbolized by the construction of two great walls north of Hué in 1631, and by the late 1670s an uneasy truce brought the establishment of two separate administrations.

Within these two spheres the assertion of central control remained a preoccupation. Steps had already been taken to try to prevent the crystallization of local power, for Alexander of Rhodes noted that royal relatives were not permitted to hold administrative offices, and no mandarin could govern the province where he had been born. In the seventeenth century it appears that the major challenge to the authority of the Trinh and Nguyen came not so much from nobles as from village leaders whose independence had been nurtured by years of civil war. Successive edicts passed during this period attempted to restrict their activities and bring them more firmly under the state's supervision. Local officials, for instance, were no longer permitted to act as private judges and only the village chief had the power to settle lawsuits. From 1660 taxation and manpower quotas were established for each village, and it was the chief and elders who were required to ensure that these were duly submitted. Similar policies were also followed in the Nguyen-controlled areas, although in a more ethnically mixed population it was harder to discourage Vietnamese from taking on 'undesirable' Khmer customs. The examinations held by the Nguyen also reflected their less traditional environment. While still required to know the Confucian classics, candidates underwent an oral test and were questioned on practical matters as well, including military matters.

In their search for a means of reaffirming the centre's pre-eminence, both Trinh and Nguyen found a ready tool in Confucianism. The support which religion could give to the ruler was as apparent in Vietnam as elsewhere in Southeast Asia, but Confucian ethics had suffered considerably during the years of civil war when military skills had been more highly valued. In the new mood of the seventeenth century, however, district leaders in the north were required to be successful Confucian scholars who could act as models for proper behaviour and provide instruction in Confucian tenets. In 1669 the Trinh declared that the new title of the village leader was henceforth to be *xa quan* (village mandarin) rather than *xa truong* (village chief). A new moral code for village life was issued in 1663 entitled 'The Path for Religious Improvement' which stressed political fealty and the attributes of a good subject.

Underneath the exhortations of the Nguyen and Trinh was the basic desire of all Vietnamese governments to strengthen the centre's hold over manpower. It has been said, indeed, that the legal code of the Le dynasty displays a much greater interest in this aspect of government than does its Chinese counterpart. Reforms in Ayutthaya and Ava reflect the same goal. According to the chronicle given to the VOC official van Vliet, during the early seventeenth century the king of Ayutthaya promulgated laws requiring all commoners (*prai som*) to be registered under a leader (*nai*), who could be either a noble or a royal prince. A tattoo on the wrist identified the *prai som* of any individual *nai*, to whom they owed six months' service. In return, the *nai* would assume general responsibility for their welfare, particularly for any repayment of debt. The king also had servicemen of his own, known as *phrai luang*, and they too were required to undertake service for six months of the year, either in the army or in some other area. Women and monks, though exempt from service, were nonetheless registered so that when a monk returned to the world he would return to the service of his *nai*; registration of women helped determine to which *nai* the children should belong. The problem kings faced was that royal service was regarded as more onerous than service to a *nai*, and there was therefore a constant trickle of *phrai luang* into monasteries or to the protection of nobles and princes. The constant threat that the balance between king and nobles might be upset saw continuing efforts to prevent the erosion of royal manpower. One means, for instance, was to separate the *phrai* from their *nai* by bringing the latter into the capital and keeping his people in the provinces.

A similar concern over control of manpower can be seen in Burma, where the non-slave population was divided into those who were not obligated to provide the king with regular labour (*athi*), and *ahmu-dan* who were required to supply soldiers for the army as well as numerous services for the king, whether as a soldier, a palace servant or a labourer on an irrigation canal. During the first half of the seventeenth century the numbers of *ahmu-dan* in upper Burma rose considerably because large sections of Pegu's population were forcibly moved to the north, being concentrated particularly around the capital. It has been estimated that possibly 40 per cent of the population within a 200-kilometre radius of Ava now owed service to the king. Successive royal decrees appear preoccupied with the compiling of lists of servicemen, incorporating new measures to ensure that they did not change occupations or evade duty 'since it is very easy for a Burmese serviceman to be lost in a Burmese community in this extensive territory under Burmese control'.[49]

The degree of administrative reform which has been traced in the mainland states is far less apparent in the archipelago. Under Iskandar Muda and his son-in-law, Iskandar Thani (1636–41) the privileges of the royal family and nobles in Aceh were substantially curtailed. Royal princes, previously stationed in outlying areas as governors, were replaced by officials responsible to the ruler. These officials, with the title *Panglima*, were appointed every three years. They were required to report annually and were periodically inspected by the ruler's representatives. Punishment for dereliction of duty was severe; the *Panglima* of Tiku, for instance,

---

[49] Than Tun, *Royal Orders*, 69; Lieberman, *Burmese Administrative Cycles*, 96–105.

had his hands and feet cut off when found guilty of charges brought against him. Within Aceh itself Iskandar Muda is credited with laying down the divisions into *mukim* or parishes which were later to be grouped into larger administrative units. But his major concern was a potential challenge from his own nobles, the *orang kaya*, and against them he took strong measures. They were not permitted to build houses which could be used for military defence, nor to keep cannon of their own. A register was kept of firearms, which had to be returned to him and any who dared to oppose him were immediately executed.

The impact of Iskandar Muda's reforms was short-lived. The death of Iskandar Thani brought a restoration of influence for the *orang kaya* who were instrumental in installing queens to rule in Aceh until the end of the century. By the 1680s a Persian visitor described Aceh as a collection of satrapies, where 'every corner shelters a separate king or governor and all the local rulers maintain themselves independently and do not pay tribute to any higher authority'. In the rest of the island world other examples of significant administrative reforms are rare. Amangkurat I of Java (r. 1646–77) did attempt some centralization of royal influence by tightening his control over provincial administration and particularly over the north-coast ports. The most important cities were placed under one or more *syah-bandar*, with several officials called *umbal* given charge over the interior. Japara, for instance, had four *syahbandar* and four *umbal* to supervise the hinterland. These new appointments considerably reduced the power of the coastal lords, making it less possible for them to oppose the king. But to strengthen his position Amangkurat resorted to assassination of large numbers of opponents, including nobles, princes and religious teachers, and the hostility this engendered simply exacerbated the tendency to resist undue intrusion by any central authority.

A number of reasons can be put forward for the slower rate of centralization in the island world and the greater difficulty in controlling populations. Geographic differences provide one obvious contrast. More characteristic of maritime than of mainland Southeast Asia, for instance, is the so-called 'Sumatra-type' polity, typified by a centre at a river-mouth with the areas of production and often of settlement located at a considerable distance upstream. Again, a kingdom made up of a scattering of islands is far less amenable to central control than is the floodplain of a large river basin such as the Irrawaddy or the Menam.

A second problem was the semi-nomadic nature of many societies which was particularly marked in maritime Southeast Asia. Those Javanese living in areas producing wet-rice may have been relatively more settled than peoples in other areas, but movement both internally and to other islands was still common. Javanese lords certainly had a general idea of the numbers of people over which they claimed suzerainty, but the term *cacah*, often translated as 'household', should be seen not as a firm population figure but as a hopeful indication of numbers of families from which tax might be extracted. Traditional *cacah* figures continued to be cited, but they became increasingly unrealistic as villagers moved away to avoid burdensome demands for tribute and labour. In Java as elsewhere most rulers offered rewards to interior groups who captured fleeing subjects or slaves, but in Palembang the Pasemah people had the special status of *sindang*, signifying freedom from corvée and tax, in return for acting as border guards and capturing any royal serviceman (*kapungut*) discovered attempting to escape to the west coast. The kings of Palembang, however, like most other rulers in the archipelago, were heavily dependent on the co-operation of local authorities in the supervision of manpower and organization of corvée. Indeed, the extent to which village elders and family heads were able, in return for royal titles and gifts, to deliver large numbers of people to provide service for the king is remarkable.

Their labour, however, was always conditional. Should the ruler's demands exceed a certain level, he would find his people simply melting away. Nor was it simply a matter of individual flight. Whole communities could move, drawn by more attractive economic conditions or escaping from unwelcome exactions, punishment or sickness. The Suku Pindah (the moving tribe), so called because for generations they had moved back and forth between Palembang and Jambi, were by no means unusual. This kind of 'avoidance protest'[50] is well illustrated in the Philippines as the Spanish administration continued its campaign to move the population into towns where they could be Christianized and made subject to taxes and tribute. In mid-century at least one Spanish observer felt that the 'unconquered' Filipinos, whose numbers were constantly swelled by fugitives from the lowlands, might still exceed Spanish subjects. In addition, many Filipinos, though Christianized, were only nominally pueblo-dwellers. In 1660 a Spanish friar admitted that so-called 'towns' in Negros frequently consisted of only a church and a few huts where the Filipinos stayed when they came to town on a Sunday; they sometimes lived as much as half a day's travel beyond the township. More than a generation later another priest lamented that 'the innate desire of these savages is to live in their caves and their forests'.[51]

But perhaps the most dramatic demonstrations of group flight were the great migrations of Bugis and Makassarese nobles and their followers in the wake of continued disturbances during the course of the century, especially after the Dutch combined with the Bugis leader Arung Palakka (r. 1669–96) to defeat Makassar in 1669. As many as two thousand individuals could be included in one fleet, and because of their reputation as fighters and traders most kings were ready to receive them. In Sumbawa, Flores, Java, Madura, Borneo, Sumatra, the Malay peninsula and even Ayutthaya, refugees from Sulawesi established Bugis and Makassarese communities. Islands such as Kangian off the coast of Java and Siantan in the South China Sea became Bugis-Makassarese strongholds, and in the early eighteenth century Bugis even succeeded in claiming control of the underpopulated region of Selangor, a territory under Johor on the west coast of the Malay peninsula.

As the Bugis diaspora shows, one of the continuing difficulties in controlling manpower in the archipelago was that there were simply so many places where a runaway could find refuge and where he and his

---

[50] The term is used by Michael Adas, 'From footdragging to flight: the evasive history of peasant avoidance in South and Southeast Asia', *Journal of Peasant Studies*, 13, 2 (1981) 65.

[51] Angel M. Cuesta, *History of Negros*, Manila: Historical Conservation Society, 1980, 42, 111.

family would be welcomed. In 1651 Amangkurat I of Java forbade any of his subjects to travel outside Java. Since it would have been impossible to maintain a watch over Java's entire coastline, there is little likelihood that any such measure could have been successful. In the words of the ruler of Palembang in 1747, 'it is very easy for a subject to find a lord, but it is much more difficult for a lord to find a subject'.[52]

A further complication in the Indonesian archipelago was that native states were now competing for manpower and resources with the expanding presence of the VOC. The Dutch took Melaka from the Portuguese in 1641 and during the course of the seventeenth century they effectively eliminated all other European competition, eventually relegating the English to a single post in Benkulen in west Sumatra. In pursuit of their commercial aims, the Dutch became heavily involved in local affairs, especially on Java. Despite a siege in 1628–9, Sultan Agung of Mataram had failed to conquer Batavia. The dynasty's consequent loss of prestige was not restored by the extreme policies adopted by Agung's son Amangkurat I, and omens and dire prophecies of impending collapse were increasingly reported as the end of the Javanese century in 1677 CE approached. In 1670–1 a Madurese prince, Trunajaya, allied with the crown prince, religious figures and Makassarese refugees to launch a full-scale rebellion in east Java. By 1676 he controlled most of the coastal areas. There seems little doubt that had developments been allowed to run their course a new royal house, presumably headed by Trunajaya, would have assumed power. However, at this point the VOC reluctantly decided that its interests would be best served by some form of intervention to support the existing 'legitimate' Mataram line, especially as the rebels had begun to show signs of being anti-Dutch. In 1677 Amangkurat and the VOC concluded a military alliance, and by the end of 1680 Trunajaya was dead, killed by Amangkurat II (r. 1677–1703) himself. Two years later the Dutch also became involved in a succession dispute in Banten, and shortly afterwards its king became a VOC vassal.

Throughout the rest of the archipelago the Dutch were also discovering that it was almost impossible to pursue commercial goals without involvement in regional affairs, an involvement which was made the more likely by the lodges and factories established wherever the VOC saw commercial opportunities. These enclaves, where the Dutch claimed extra-territorial rights, were frequently regarded by local societies as a refuge if the exactions of kings or nobles became too great. But the Dutch also complained of the flight of criminals, debtors and deserters to the shelter of some neighbouring court, and it became common for treaties signed between the VOC and their allies to include a clause on mutual exchange of runaways. In many places long arguments developed over whether the children of a liaison between an Indonesian mother and a Dutch father were local or 'Dutch', and VOC officials were often prepared to engage in drawn-out negotiations to retain authority over their 'subjects'. Another sensitive issue concerned control over foreigners, notably Chinese. Those who had adopted Islam and married Indonesian women were generally

---

[52] VOC 2699, Resident of Palembang to Batavia, 13 March 1747 fo. 51.

regarded as being under local jurisdiction, but the arrival of large numbers of migrants following disturbances in China during the sixteenth and seventeenth centuries meant that in an increasing number of courts the question of 'Dutch' versus 'local' Chinese remained unresolved.

The island world differs further from the mainland in that some cultures actively encouraged their men to leave. The one which comes most readily to mind is that of Minangkabau where the inheritance of land and family goods through the female line impelled young males to leave the village (*merantau*) to make a living. Extensive migration led to a marked increase in Minangkabau settlements in Linggi and Negeri Sembilan on the west coast of the Malay peninsula, and along both coasts of Sumatra. Minangkabau rulers made no effort to summon their people back, but a sense of group identity remained strong and still in the late eighteenth century Minang-kabau communities in the peninsula received their leaders from their original homeland. While its resemblance to great mainland kingdoms such as Ava is slight, the claim of Minangkabau rulers to exercise a vague overlordship over all Sumatra was widely accepted, though never support-ed by resorting to arms. It is difficult to overestimate the extraordinary respect with which the kings and queens of Minangkabau were regarded by the people of the archipelago. Even a text from as far away as Bima accepts the general Sumatran view that they were of the same origin as and equal to the kings of Turkey and China.

THE CREATION OF THE 'EXEMPLARY CENTRE'[53]

By the mid-seventeenth century hundreds of years of exposure to stories of the splendour of great rulers in distant lands had furnished Southeast Asians with a perception of kingship as the epitome of powerful govern-ment. Burmese kings built their religious buildings according to Sinhalese designs and a panegyric commissioned in Aceh in the early seventeenth century was apparently modelled on the *Akbarnama*, a Persian text extoll-ing the reign of the Great Mogul. Powerful though such examples were, however, Southeast Asians could also draw on their own much nearer past. It was in Pagan that Tabinshwehti was crowned king of upper Burma, while an eighteenth-century Vietnamese historian notes that the usurper Mac Dang Dung 'maintained all the Le laws and systems, and did not dare to change or abolish any of them' because he was afraid of possible rebellions from the people 'who were full of memories of the old dynasty'.[54] Nor was the heritage of Angkor lightly laid aside. According to a Portuguese account, the temple complex was 'rediscovered' in the late sixteenth century by a king who was 'filled with admiration' at its splen-dours. Ayutthayan rulers were equally anxious to link themselves with the mixed Thai-Khmer traditions of the period before 1569, and a seventeenth-century chronicle makes Angkor a creation of the first Ayutthayan king.

---

[53] The phrase is from Clifford Geertz, *Islam Observed. Religious Development in Morocco and Indonesia*, New Haven, 1968, 36.
[54] Yu, 'Law and Family', 34.

Prasat Thong even had a plan of Angkor Wat copied to use as the basis for two new buildings, and talked about giving the name of Yasodhara to one of his palaces.[55]

In the western archipelago, memories of Melaka also remained powerful incentives to the restoration of Malay control in the straits long after its conquest by Portugal. A seventeenth-century Malay scribe, copying out the old Melaka law codes, noted wistfully that these were compiled 'in the days when Melaka was still strong'. Johorese expectations of their alliance with the VOC in 1602 are suggested by a popular Malay *hikayat* which depicts Malays and Dutch together defeating the Portuguese and then ruling jointly over a newly emergent Melaka. In Java the passage of time had enhanced Majapahit's reputation as an example of centralized power. Malay sources of the period extol the ruler of Majapahit, whose sovereignty extended from the interior of Java 'to the shores of the southern ocean' and to whom the kings of Banten, Jambi, Palembang, Bugis, Makassar, Johor, Pahang, Champa, Minangkabau, Aceh and Pasai had all allegedly paid homage. In the seventeenth century Javanese sources depict Trunajaya urging Sultan Agung's grandson to move to Majapahit 'so that the whole island of Java may know your Highness has established his court there'.[56]

The collective effect of such potent examples was becoming increasingly apparent by the mid-seventeenth century. It is probable that the number of 'kingless' communities, where government continued to be carried out by councils of elders and heads of clans, far outnumbered the 'kingdoms'. But for the most part these were interior peoples, like the Bisayas of Brunei of whom a Spaniard remarked, 'they have no lord who governs them and whom they obey, although in each settlement there are some important persons'.[57] Only in a few coastal areas had these kingless societies managed to retain power. For example, prior to its destruction by the Dutch, Banda had been ruled by an 'oligarchy of elders' made up of village leaders who met frequently in councils to deal with problems and settle disputes. To a growing extent, however, Southeast Asians themselves were coming to see the lack of kings as a characteristic of lesser peoples. Nandabayin of Pegu (r. 1581–99) was allegedly greatly amused when he heard that Venice was a free state without a king, and English traders in Jambi found they had a powerful argument in their claim that their Dutch rivals had no monarch; VOC officials themselves admitted that for local people, 'this is the point around which the compass turns'.[58]

The identification of several key states as 'power centres' in the seventeenth century is not simply a construct of a modern historian, for in the seventeenth century a number of rulers boasted that they stood high above their neighbours. In Ava the ruler held an elaborate ritual to make himself 'king of kings' in order to subdue 'all the other one hundred kings'; the

[55] Michael Vickery, 'The composition and transition of the Ayudhya and Cambodian chronicles', in A. J. S. Reid and David Marr, eds, *Perceptions of the Past in Southeast Asia*, Singapore, 1979.

[56] M. C. Ricklefs. 'Six Centuries of Islamization on Java' in N. Levitzion, *Conversion to Islam*, New York, 1979, 110.

[57] John S. Carroll, 'Berunai in the Boxer Codex', JMBRAS, 55, 2 (1982) 3.

[58] J. W. J. Wellan, 'Onze Eerste Verstiging in Djambi', BKI, 81(1926) 376.

Thais boasted that since the time of Naresuan 'they had never been subject to any other prince of this world'. A Makassar chronicle sees only Aceh and Mataram as its equals, while the ruler of Aceh considered himself to be 'the most powerful monarch in the world'. In 1667 Amangkurat I of Mataram referred to himself as the one 'to whom all the kings of the Javanese and Malay lands pay homage'.[59]

The hierarchy which these rulers perceived was to a considerable extent accepted by their neighbours. The Khmers, for instance, gradually came to take on the Thai view that they were inferior, and even incorporated into their own histories Ayutthaya's accounts of its victories over Cambodia, accounts which do not mention a Khmer revival in the early seventeenth century. What Khmers remembered was the defeat of Lovek in 1594 and their forced acceptance of Thai overlordship during the eighteenth century. According to legend, Lovek contained two sacred statues inside which were holy books containing special secret knowledge. It was to obtain these that the king of Siam attacked and defeated Cambodia. 'After reading the books, the Thais became superior in knowledge to the Cambodians.'[60]

The assertion of a hierarchy of states within Southeast Asia is matched by a growing tendency to see the centre as 'civilized' and those who live outside this environment as 'wild'. The epithet of 'wild' applied particularly to groups who had not accepted the dominant religious faith and whose lifestyle clearly contrasted with that of the capital culture. The Vietnamese made no sustained effort to spread Confucian customs into the highlands, and the fifteenth-century Le code, while allowing these areas to follow their own laws, had forbidden intermarriage between Vietnamese and hill tribes. Thai and Burman histories also saw Kachins, Karen, Chins, Lahus, Lawas and other illiterate, animist hill peoples as 'barbaric', and talk of country people 'loafing around'. In the Philippines the growth of this attitude can be linked with the separation between Christian and 'pagan', for 'barbarians' were those who lived away from organized communities and who were not amenable to the teachings of the Church. One priest felt that

> the mode of living of these Bisayans . . . appears to oppose all that is rational justice. They make the greatest effort to live like savages, as far as possible from the church, priest, governors and their own *gobernadorcillo* [petty governor] so as to live in freedom without God and without obedience to the king.[61]

The perception of those who do not share the mainstream culture as inferior is also a measure of their irrelevance to the centre. Similar expressions of contempt are far less apparent in those states where minority groups retained an important political or economic role. In the seventeenth century the king of Champa had a wife from the highlands, and in Cambodia when the hill tribes came down to present their tribute, flutes

[59] Than Tun, *Royal Orders*, I. 28; van Vliet, *Short History*, 81; W. Ph. Coolhaas *Generale Missiven van Gouverneurs-Generaal en Raden aan Heren XVII der Verenigde Oostindische Compagnie*, The Hague, 1960–85, I. 103; Schrieke, *Indonesian Sociological Studies*, II. 222.
[60] Chandler, *History of Cambodia*, 84.
[61] Bruce Cruikshank, *Samar 1768–1898*, Manila, 1985, 42.

were played softly and the gifts enumerated as the 'uncles' (the Cambodians) received the willing tribute of their 'nephews' (the hill tribes) and in return presented their chiefs with swords and the titles of Fire King and Water King. Johor and other Malay states continued to rely on the skills of the *orang laut* (the non-Malay sea peoples) for patrols and the collection of ocean products well into the eighteenth century. *Orang laut* leaders therefore retained an influential voice in government. In one Johor chronicle from the early eighteenth century, for example, the head of the *orang laut* is included in conferences concerning delicate matters of state. Whereas the request of a Gwe Karen for an Ayutthayan princess was rejected because he came of 'a race of forest dwellers', Dutch sources from the same period demonstrate how the king of Jambi was related to *orang laut* chiefs through his womenfolk. The gradual displacement of animist groups which occurred through the eighteenth century is a reflection of wider political and economic changes which were to affect the entire region.

THE FRAGMENTATION OF THE EIGHTEENTH CENTURY

None of the great centres of the seventeenth century survived into modern times. By the early 1800s new dynasties ruled in Burma, Siam and Vietnam; in the island world Banten and Makassar had both lost their status as independent entrepôts, Mataram was divided into two, and Aceh had been torn by two generations of civil strife. In tracing the reasons for these developments in mainland Southeast Asia, it could be argued that the very process of centralization contained within itself the seeds of fragmentation. Only a powerful centre could maintain its position in the face of the cumulative tensions induced by continuing efforts to tighten supervision of people and resources. Whenever the dominance of the capital was questioned, it was reflected in the steady seepage of manpower away from royal control. In societies where the king was heavily reliant on his armies to maintain his own standing against potential opposition, this loss of manpower was serious, especially if it coincided with conflicts over succession or the sharing of power.

In Ayutthaya the drift of population from the centre may have begun as far back as the 1630s, and the continuing incorporation of foreigners into royal service reflects the need of successive rulers to strengthen their position in relation to other manpower-controlling groups. At the same time the problem of kingly succession had never been resolved. In 1688 a group of Ayutthaya nobles, apparently alienated by King Narai's patronage of foreigners, acted to remove a Greek adventurer, Constantine Phaulkon, who had been appointed *Mahatthai*. The leader of the cabal, a noble who was Narai's foster brother, was made regent on behalf of the dying king. He quickly moved to have Phaulkon arrested and beheaded and on Narai's death assumed the throne himself. But while the dynasty he founded endured eighty years, it faced undercurrents of opposition. There are several references to village rebellions led by 'holy men', and the succession of King Borommakot (r. 1733–58) was only secured after a battle with rival princes which involved several thousand men. The Malay tributaries grew increasingly restive, and on several occasions it was necessary to despatch armies to subdue the rebellious peninsular states.

Burma was if anything more prey to internal division. Between 1660 and 1715 there were at least eleven attempts to usurp the throne, and as a result the *hlutdaw* came to exert a much greater influence in the selection of rulers. In 1695 an English visitor considered that the two most powerful ministers in fact 'ruled the kingdom', and by the turn of the century the 'royal business' was considered insufficient to warrant a daily meeting between the king and his council. The ruler's failure to resolve a dispute in the Buddhist monkhood over matters of doctrine contributed to the general atmosphere of unease. Not surprisingly, those vassal states that had never willingly accepted Ava's overlordship began to fall away. Chiengmai was lost in 1727, and in 1739 the Shan state of Kengtung drove out a *saw-bwa* appointed by Ava. Added to this was the fact that many royal servicemen were evading their obligations by avoiding registration, commuting their service through payments, entering the monkhood or placing themselves under the protection of other princes or nobles. In Ava the king's militia was seriously under strength as *ahmu-dan* and *athi* alike attempted to be registered as debt slaves in order to escape royal service. Indications of the centre's concern are seen in the periodic checks ordered to ensure that 'undesirables' did not enter monasteries, and a royal decree of 1728 which prohibits menial labourers in the palace from being ordained as Buddhist monks. Those escaping from debts or service could also, however, place themselves under village leaders, rebel monks or bandits who had set up their own centres of localized power in opposition to the centre. Everywhere representatives appointed by the central government were becoming victims of peasant discontent, and between 1727 and 1743 the governors of Martaban, Tavoy, Syriam, Toungoo and Prome were all killed or driven out by local rebels.

The beginning of the end came with the rebellion of Pegu, which had recovered after the devastation of the late seventeenth century but was subjected to a heavy tax burden. In 1740 its leaders declared their independence. Twelve years later, after continuous raiding of the Irrawaddy basin, a southern army which included representatives of several ethnic groups and was led by a prince of Shan descent stood outside the walls of Ava. In early 1752 after two months of siege the city fell, the king fled, and the Toungoo dynasty ended. Just fifteen years later the same fate befell Ayutthaya, where yet another succession dispute had broken out. In 1760 a new ruler in Burma, the founder of the Konbaung dynasty, threw the rejuvenated strength of Burmese might against Ayutthaya, an attack which was renewed by his sons, and Ayutthaya fell in 1767. The Thai capital, however, suffered far more than Ava had done; it was as if the hostilities of the last two centuries had finally found full expression. Its buildings were torched and pillaged, its inhabitants killed or captured. Deprived of a king and a focus of government, Ayutthaya broke up into five separate regions. For the first time in nearly four hundred years the Menam basin was once more politically fragmented.

But it was in Vietnam where the challenge to the existing order was greatest. Efforts by the Trinh to exert greater control over village leaders had been unsuccessful, and many peasants were refusing to be drafted for military service. In 1711 the centre had been forced to allow the village to allot public land within its own jurisdiction, and by the 1730s even the census records were not being maintained properly. The ability of the landed and privileged to escape tax payments meant that the burden was carried by ever fewer people who were at the same time the ones least able to pay. Reforms aimed at taxing private land and widely used items like salt were ineffective, and by 1713 less than one-third of the population under the Trinh were subject to taxation. In 1730 officials were appointed to induce wandering peasants to return home, but only a decade later it was calculated that one-third of the villages were deserted.

The flight of manpower meant both a decline in cultivation and a breakdown in provincial administration. In six provinces in 1721 financial problems compelled the Trinh to abolish the position of the commissioner responsible for checking the growth of undue local power, and as a result the incidence of corruption and oppression in village government markedly increased. Censors reported that 'in the villages the notables, using thousands of tricks, ruling arbitrarily, grabbing other people's property to enrich themselves, oppressing the poor, despising the illiterate, avail themselves of the least opportunity to indict people and bring suits against them'.[62] Lack of food and ineffective officialdom in turn contributed to an increase in peasant rebellion as wandering peasantry organized themselves into bands of local insurgents. Contemporary accounts depict a time of terrible famine, when 'people roamed about, carrying their children in search of some rice, lived on vegetables and herbs, ate rats and snakes'. In this climate the continuing rule of the Trinh was difficult to justify, and in a rebellion in the southern delta peasants carried banners proclaiming 'Restore the Le, destroy the Trinh'. It was not long, however, before some voices were even raised against the Le, whom intermarriage had made simply part of the Trinh clan. As elsewhere in Southeast Asia, people with special qualities, monks, scholars and holy men, emerged to assume leadership of peasant rebels. Some groups succeeded in establishing independent domains where they anulled debts, redistributed land and abolished taxation. One revolt, led by a Confucian scholar and made up of many thousands of peasants, was even able to defeat two Trinh generals.

In the Nguyen-controlled territory, official corruption and the dwindling of foreign trade similarly combined with famines to bring about a collapse of the tax base. Scholar-officials clearly warned the Nguyen that 'the people's misery has reached an extreme degree'. As the century progressed, revolts grew in intensity. In 1771 three brothers from the hamlet of Tayson in south central Vietnam emerged as leaders of what was to become the most effective resistance movement yet seen in Southeast Asia. Despite the fact that the government it established did not last, the Tayson rebellion not only succeeded in reuniting north and south Vietnam but also signalled the end of the old Confucian order.

Much of the island world in the mid-eighteenth century was also in

62 Yu, 'Law and Family', 224.

disarray. It would be easy to attribute this to the influence of the Europeans—on the one hand the Spanish, now suzerain over most of the
Philippines except for the Muslim south, and the VOC, which was not
only overlord of Java, but had built up a network of alliances which linked
it with kingdoms from the north of Sumatra across to the eastern islands.
However, the question of the effects of the European presence must be
approached with caution, for local society retained its own dynamics.
A prime example of an event which had far-reaching implications, but
in which the Dutch played only a minor part, concerns a case of regicide in
Johor in 1699. The nobles, refusing to tolerate any longer the king's
excesses, together plotted his assassination. Although the *bendahara* was
duly installed as ruler, and although Johor quickly recovered economically, Malay society was deeply divided. Many *orang laut*, whose relationship
with the Johor dynasty stretched back to the days of Melaka, simply
refused to serve under the new order. The divisions created by the crime of
derhaka (treason) opened the way for the seizure of the throne in 1718 by a
Minangkabau prince who not only claimed to be the son of the murdered
ruler but brought with him the imprimatur of the queen of Minangkabau.
At this point a large party of Bugis refugees arrived in the area, allied with
the displaced Bendahara, and drove the Minangkabau prince out. As a
result of these events, a new political arrangement came into being in
Johor, whereby the Malay sultan took secondary place to the Bugis raja
muda. In time the trauma associated with the regicide faded, but for many
Malays the new dynasty located on the island of Riau remained a permanent reminder that the Melaka line had ended.

In assessing the impact of the Europeans on political developments in
the archipelago one must also remember that their numbers were never
great. In concluding commercial treaties, VOC officials dealt almost exclusively with the ruler and his court, and this meant that outside Java
comparatively few areas were deeply touched by the Dutch. It is equally
useful to note the limited European presence in the Philippines. As late as
1800 there were almost no Spanish posts at altitudes higher than 150
metres, and except in the central plain of Luzon few Spaniards lived more
than fifteen kilometres from the sea. For most Filipinos in the lowlands,
their only European contact was with the clergy, who were the linchpin of
the Spanish administration, yet their numbers too were small. In Samar in
the western Visayas, a province of more than 13,000 square kilometres
with an official population in 1770 of 33,350, there were only fifteen
priests. While priests acted as local schoolteachers, doctors, archivists,
linguists, and spiritual advisers for town-dwellers, there were many small
communities of baptized Christians who saw a priest only once a year.

Interaction between Spaniard and Filipino was frequently eased because
the Spanish friars, who spent their lives in isolated posts, often developed
a considerable understanding of local society. The same comment also
applies to VOC officials, many of whom had been born in the Indies and
easily adopted local symbols of leadership to enhance their own standing,
employing the kingly insignia of umbrella and betel box and even on
occasion the golden *gelang* (anklets) of Malay royalty. In their correspondence governors-general exploited the terminology of kinship, addressing

rulers as 'son' or 'grandson' and referring to themselves as a 'father'. In the exchange of gifts, the Dutch in many cases acted like an overlord accepting tribute. The small island of Roti in eastern Indonesia, for instance, sent wax, slaves and rice to Batavia, while the governor-general responded with 'civilized' products such as muskets, fine cloth, gold and silver batons, and Dutch gin. During the conclusion of a treaty on Timor, Dutch and Timorese signatories even sealed the treaty by drinking one another's mingled blood.

On the other side, the desire of locals to absorb these outsiders in the way they understood best is suggested by the numbers of Europeans adopted as sons or brothers, accorded high titles and presented with robes of honour. An eighteenth-century Javanese *babad* attempts to bring the Dutch into the fabric of Javanese history by transforming the famed Governor-General Jan Pieterszoon Coen (1619–23, 1627–9) into Mur Jang-kung, son of Baron Sukmul of Spain and a princess from Pajajaran. The latter's flaming genitals mark her as an *ardhanariciwari*, possession of whom can make even the poorest man king. Mur Jangkung vows to wreak revenge when he learns that the Pangeran of Jakarta banished his mother because he could not sleep with her. Loaded with beer, wine, bread and war materials, Mur Jangkung's fleet arrives in Java. He successfully takes Jakarta, thus regaining his birthright and installing his descendants (the Dutch) as the legitimate successors of Pajajaran and the proper rulers of west Java.

Nonetheless, the Dutch could never be just another indigenous power: they were different in the determination with which they pursued their very specific goals, and the assumptions on which they formulated policy were often incomprehensible to local peoples. But while for many archipelago communities the advent of the Dutch had brought hostility and conflict, there were numerous others for whom the VOC was a powerful and protective friend. The Bugis leader Arung Palakka, for instance, assisted the Dutch in the attack on his old enemy Makassar. When the combined Dutch and Bugis forces were successful, Arung Palakka was installed as overlord of all Sulawesi with the title *Torisompae* (the Venerated One) previously held by the Makassar king. In return for Dutch support, he agreed to expel from his lands all other European traders. Now when the Bugis performed the *kanjar* and swore their oath of loyalty, they did so not only before their own king but the Company as well. 'Look at me, Commissaris!' proclaimed one Bugis lord as the drums were beaten and he danced his allegiance, 'let me meet the enemies of the Company and I shall fight them sword in hand!'[63]

Another example of an area where association with the Dutch left memories of a *zaman mas*, a golden age, comes from the Malay peninsula where the state of Perak had long been threatened by outside powers like Aceh and Ayutthaya because of its extensive tin deposits. In 1746 the ruler signed a treaty with the VOC which granted the Dutch a monopoly of all Perak tin in return for protection. Although there were periods of tension,

---

[63] J. Noorduyn, 'The Bugis auxiliaries from Tanete in the Chinese War in Java, 1742–1744', in C. M. S. Hellwig and S. O. Robson, eds, *A Man of Indonesian Letters. Essays in Honour of Professor A. Teeuw*, Dordrecht, 1986, 279.

particularly when the Dutch made attempts to negotiate a lower tin price, the treaty endured until the demise of the Company in 1795.

What these two cases illustrate is the degree to which the Dutch could and did influence the course of local politics in pursuit of trading advantages. For both Arung Palakka and the Perak court, Dutch friendship was crucial; without it, Arung Palakka would not have been able to avenge the humiliation of defeat and regain his homeland; if left to itself, Perak would probably have fallen under the control of a stronger neighbour like Selangor. In the changing relationships between states, and in the power struggles within them, the role of the VOC was often decisive. Lacking support from Dutch forces, for instance, the family which ruled the pepper-producing state of Jambi would have been replaced in the 1690s; the measure of the king's unpopularity is indicated by the extent of population movement away from his jurisdiction and his descent into that anomaly in Southeast Asia, a king with no subjects. Similarly the region of Lampung in the southern part of Sumatra would have fallen under the control of Palembang during the eighteenth century had not the VOC acted to safeguard the interests of its vassal Banten. A converse situation prevailed on the west coast of Sumatra, where the Dutch encouraged the spread of Minangkabau authority following the VOC's successful military expeditions against the Acehnese in 1666 and 1667. In a treaty signed in 1668, Minangkabau was confirmed as the overlord of the west coast from Barus to Manjuta; the Dutch representative at Padang was appointed 'stadthouder' on behalf of the Minangkabau ruler.

Dutch anxiety to ensure that local power structures favoured their presence often meant real shifts in traditional patterns of authority. On a number of islands in eastern Indonesia, for instance, the Dutch passed over ritually superior 'religious' figures when recognizing rulers or regents because they felt such people were not amenable to political control. Instead, they tended to regard as legitimate those figures whom they perceived as 'secular'. By so doing they often elevated individuals who in fact merely held a lower rank in the priestly hierarchy. Another example of the way authority was reshaped comes from Barus, on the west coast of Sumatra. Here jurisdiction was shared between two kings, an 'upstream' and a 'downstream' raja (both of whom actually lived downstream). In order to further their access to camphor supplies in the interior, where both rulers had connections, the VOC played one against the other. In 1694 the Dutch abolished the dual rajaship, although the effective division of authority between upstream and downstream eventually re-emerged with the position of raja rotating between the upstream and downstream families.

The question often arises as to why the Dutch were able to maintain their position in the island world for so long. In part, the reason lies in the profusion of small political units which had always been a feature of the island world and which the VOC helped to perpetuate by working to prevent regional alliances which might form the basis of an anti-Dutch coalition. Furthermore, the Dutch were always able to find one Indonesian group to use against another because local rulers themselves often saw a VOC alliance as a means of gaining an advantage over some long-time enemy. It was thus never possible for any anti-VOC alliance to maintain enough sustained support to ensure success. In the course of the seventeenth and eighteenth centuries various calls were made to rally Muslims against the infidels, but these were insufficient to overcome a tradition which had stressed localized loyalty rather than joint action. A test case came in 1756-7 when Bugis forces from Riau blockaded Melaka. For the better part of a year the town lay helpless, and the siege was only lifted when a fleet arrived from Batavia in mid-1757. Yet neither then nor in 1784, when the Bugis attacked once more, was Malay support against the Dutch forthcoming.

All these permutations of the Dutch presence can be seen in Java after 1680. Though Trunajaya was killed, rebellions against the centre continued. Amangkurat II was able to maintain his position against the challenge of his brother mainly because the Dutch were willing to assist him as the 'legitimate' heir. By doing so they publicly demonstrated that a king who could not rally sufficient popular support to remain upon the throne could yet be maintained by VOC armies. The Dutch continued to shore up their clients through the eighteenth century in the face of continuing unrest. In 1740 a rebellion initially involving Batavian Chinese also turned against the dynasty, and again the court appealed to the Dutch. VOC help, however, had a heavy price. Javanese kings repaid their debt by progressively ceding the coastal areas of Java to the Dutch. Finally in 1749 the entire kingdom of Mataram was signed over, and Pakubuwana II (r. 1726-49) thus became a vassal of the VOC. This new relationship was effectively symbolized when he was installed by the governor-general with the Dutch Resident sitting beside him. An influential faction in the court, however, refused to accept Pakubuwana's authority, and in an effort to prevent continued strife in the royal family the Dutch in 1755 divided central Java between Surakarta and Yogyakarta.

The words put into the mouth of Pakubuwana's rival encapsulate the major problem raised by colonial control:

> My lord, it is not fitting.
> Are you not aware
> that the role of a ruler
> carries the obligation to reign only?[64]

What the VOC wanted was kings and officials who would actually carry out instructions given to them, and would act as executors of the Company's desires. Seduced by titles and emoluments, threatened with exile or dethronement, or simply browbeaten, the indigenous élite became the means by which colonial authority was maintained. To some extent this pressure was felt wherever the Dutch signed a commercial contract, but in some areas the effects were more disruptive than others. In eastern Indonesia, for example, strenuous efforts were made not only to enforce a trading monopoly but also to compel production of particular spices. A great programme of 'extirpation' was set in place, whereby in return for regular payments to a number of kings the VOC acquired the right to

---

[64] M. C. Ricklefs, *Jogjakarta under Sultan Mangkubumi 1749-1792. A History of the Division of Java*, London, 1974, 41.

destroy clove trees on all islands except Ambon and other areas under their control. The VOC requirements for manpower for such expeditions, the infamous *hongitochten*, naturally aroused bitter resentment among local people and placed heavy strains on the loose relationships which had traditionally existed between the Maluku region and culturally separate groups like the Papuans. The same pattern can be traced in Sumatra. When pepper prices fell and people moved to grow cotton instead, the Dutch pressed those kings bound to them by treaty to order the *'extirpatie'* of all cotton bushes. Inevitably kings and local chiefs who agreed to carry out Dutch policies came to be seen as harsh and punitive.

Not surprisingly, it was the peasants of Java and the Philippines who felt the effects of European demands most keenly. In both places villagers were required to grow certain crops and to sell them to the Dutch or Spanish at set prices. A major source of resentment was the labour requirements, which often meant long absences from home and for which minimal compensation, if any, was made. Understandably, resentment was often directed at those seen to be the agents of extortion. In 1726 a Priangan regent was killed by one of his subjects because the price the latter now received for his coffee was so low that he despaired of ever climbing out of debt. The point was, of course, that it was the Dutch who had reduced the amount paid for coffee; the regent was simply passing the reduction on.

In the Philippines the original granting of *encomiendas* (the right to collect tribute) to individual Spaniards had been deemed a failure by the mid-seventeenth century so that by 1721 virtually all had reverted to the Crown. Nonetheless, many of the abuses which had led to criticism of the private *encomienda* persisted. The Spanish administration, constantly in need of funds, leant heavily on Filipinos to supply labour and finance for their national endeavours. In theory workers were supposed to be paid, but this was rare; they were usually supported by stipends of rice from their own villages. Despite government attempts at reform, Filipinos were often drafted for private rather than state labour, or sent to work at places far removed from their village. Still in the 1770s people were fleeing in Samar from the exactions of a governor who asked them to build boats and fortifications without providing adequate rations or time to tend their fields.

Another Filipino grievance was the requirement that certain products be sold to the government, often below the market price, to which was added the collection of tribute and numerous other taxes. The division of the Philippines into parishes administered by religious orders increased the burden carried by ordinary Filipinos, who also supported the clergy by contributing to their stipends and by supplying food and labour. Indeed, the Church often made a healthy profit by selling goods received as alms. In 1704 the *sanctorum* tax to defray the costs of administering the sacraments was imposed over all Spanish-controlled territory. Faced by this array of exactions, the hill people in some areas spoke of an evil spirit called *Tributo* that roamed around the mission towns and ate people up.[65]

---

[65] William Scott, *Cracks in the Parchment Curtain*, Quezon City, 1982, 36.

It was the Spanish-supported élites who were the key to the successful working of this system. Christianized native *barangay* leaders, the *datu* of pre-Spanish times, had been incorporated into the colonial administrative structure and given the title *cabeza*, or head. Members of this largely hereditary élite, termed generally the *principales*, took turns in filling the position of municipal 'little governor' (*gobernadorcillo*), the highest native official in the Spanish bureaucracy. In return for new titles, enhanced status, and privileges, the *principalia* class was expected to help organize labour services and taxation payments. In the process, however, they had to take on the role of buffers between the Spanish régime and the Filipino peasant, and to work closely with the friars in maintaining order; a priest in Samar reported that when a man had failed to come to Mass, 'I sent the Datus to whip him'.[66] The ambiguity of the *principalia* relationship with ordinary Filipinos is particularly evident in the numerous rebellions which broke out against Spanish rule. Sometimes they took on the role of spokesmen for discontented peasants; *principales*, for instance, led a revolt in 1745 which protested against the encroachment of friar estates into peasant land. On the other hand, local élites could be seen as an extension of Spanish government. Diego Silang, who led the uprising of 1762 which followed the British capture of Manila, though himself of *principalia* stock, was opposed to a group whom he saw as the instruments of oppression.

Over a hundred participants in the Diego Silang rebellion were hanged, while others were flogged or imprisoned. Their fate points to a prime reason for the Spanish domination of the Philippines and the successful Dutch manipulation of local politics—the effective and frightening use of force. The inability of the Spanish to subdue the Muslim south is clear evidence that European-led troops were by no means invincible, but their successes remained impressive. It is useful to remember that in Java between 1680 and 1740 the VOC suffered only three defeats, and it had been the hope of harnessing this force which had led many Southeast Asians to seek a greater association with the Europeans. In the *Babad Tanah Jawi* a pretender to the throne is thus advised to call on the Dutch, whose military skills are available in exchange for 'a few promises'. But those who attempted to render Europeans amenable to their wishes were to find that it was like 'riding a tiger'. By their intrusion into the region, Europeans had fundamentally altered the manner in which its history was to develop. Yet in the process they unwittingly provided the basis for the growth of a shared frustration which was ultimately to bring together groups which might otherwise be divided by language or culture or traditional rivalries. As early as 1577, a Filipino had called out to an attacking band of Spaniards, 'What have we done to you, or what did our ancestors owe yours, that you should come to plunder us?' Nearly two hundred years later the same anger was expressed by a group of Demak peasants who pulled a Dutch envoy off his horse, shouting, 'Stop, you Dutch dog, now you will be *our* porter!'[67]

[66] Cruikshank, *Samar*, 37.
[67] Scott, *Cracks in the Parchment Curtain*, 20; Luc W. Nagtegaal, 'The Dutch East India Company and the relations between Kartasura and the Javanese northcoast c. 1680–1740', in J. van Goor, ed., *Trading Companies in Asia 1600–1830*, Utrecht, 1986, 76. The image of the tiger is taken from the title of Dr Nagtegaal's thesis, 'Rijden op een Hollandse Tijger'.

CONCLUSION

While there are identifiable continuities between the sixteenth and eighteenth centuries, a survey of the period also suggests that significant
changes were under way. In the first place, there had been a marked trend
towards a greater centralization of authority, particularly among the mainland states. A combination of prosperity, administrative reform, and
control of labour had enabled a number of centres to confirm their
ascendancy over their neighbours, so that by the eighteenth century the
typical Southeast Asian state was not so much a confederation of nearly
equal communities as a hierarchically organized polity where the component parts paid some kind of allegiance to a dominant centre. An
important aspect of the expansion of political authority was the creation of
a 'capital culture'. Distinctive features of dress, language and custom
which had once been key aspects in a community's separate identity now
came to be seen as variations of the dominant culture which emanated
from the political centre. Even in Burma, where ethnic differences were
more pronounced, the resurgence of the Konbaung dynasty was based at
least in part on a wide acceptance of Burman hegemony and Burman
cultural values. Though some borders were to see adjustment in later
years, in essence the political bases of contemporary Thailand, Burma,
Vietnam, Cambodia and Laos had already been laid down.

In the island world the process of centralization was not nearly so
apparent, facing as it did formidable obstacles of geography and wide
cultural variation. The peoples of the Philippines still thought of themselves very much as 'Cebuanos' or 'Tagalogs', and to these localized
loyalties was added the deeper divide between the Christianized north
and centre and the Muslim south. Nonetheless, significant changes had
taken place. The Spanish administration had helped to impose a degree of
political uniformity, blurring some of the regional differences existing
before the conquest, and their emphasis on the development of Manila
gave it a pre-eminence which has survived to the present day. Nor is it
difficult to point to features of the Malay-Indonesian archipelago which
were to be of critical importance in the creation of contemporary nation-
states. The trading network which had long served to link areas as distant
as Timor and Melaka was not broken, despite VOC efforts, while the
Dutch dependence on Malay as a medium of communication reinforced its
position of lingua franca, and promoted its use in places where it had
previously been little heard. At the same time the dominance of Java had
been enhanced by the concentration of Dutch interests in Batavia, contributing to a polarity between Java and the outer islands that has continued
into modern times.

Despite a foreshadowing of later developments, however, the eighteenth-
century island world appears far more culturally and politically fragmented
than does the mainland. In Vietnam, Siam and Burma the impulse towards
centralization was so strong that within a generation all had recovered
from the fragmentation of the eighteenth century. In the archipelago, on
the other hand, even the most potentially cohesive region, Java, was by

1755 divided into distinct spheres. These differences between island and mainland are reflected in the historiography of Southeast Asia. By the seventeenth century the perception of a 'country' had enabled outsiders visiting mainland states to produce books such as de la Loubère's *Description of the Kingdom of Siam*, and the *History of the Kingdom of Tonkin* by Alexander of Rhodes. The concept of a 'national' history was also developing among indigenous scholars. The first history of Dai Viet had been written under the Tran in 1272; seventeenth-century Thai texts began to divorce Ayutthaya's history from that of Buddhism; in Burma U Kala in 1711 produced an encyclopaedic work aimed at providing a complete account of his country's past. It is rare, however, for chronicles in the island world to look beyond a dynasty or a specific cultural group, and modern scholars still grapple with the problem of writing a broader history that is not biased in favour of one area. While it has proved quite possible to reconstruct the collective past of a particular societies—Pampangans, Javanese, Malays, Toasug—the great difficulty has been to synthesize regional studies on to a larger canvas, particularly given the lack of documents from so many areas. Yet it is important to continue to examine not merely the contrasts but the shared features which ultimately enabled political unities to be created from immense diversity. Only this wider view can assist in the reconstruction of a regional history in which all Southeast Asians are seen as true participants.

BIBLIOGRAPHIC ESSAY

Thailand and Laos

David K. Wyatt's *Thailand. A Short History*, New Haven and London, 1982, is a detailed study by a leading scholar containing material unavailable elsewhere. It is also the only complete analysis in English of Lao history in this period, and contains a helpful guide for further reading. Wyatt lists a number of contemporary European accounts, but of these the most valuable is probably Simon de la Loubère, *The Kingdom of Siam*, ed. D. K. Wyatt, Kuala Lumpur, 1969. Lorraine M. Gesick, 'Kingship and Political Integration in Traditional Siam, 1767–1824', Ph.D. thesis, Cornell University, 1976, discusses the question of tributary relations. A view of Siam from one of its Malay vassals is *Hikayat Patani: The Story of Patani*, ed. A. Teeuw and David K. Wyatt, The Hague, 1970. A seventeenth-century history of Siam based on Thai sources is Jeremias van Vliet, *The Short History of the Kings of Siam*, trans. Leonard Andaya, Bangkok, 1975.

Burma

Burma remains one of the Southeast Asian countries least researched by modern Western scholars, but an important interpretation of the pre-nineteenth-century period has come with the publication of Victor B. Lieberman, *Burmese Administrative Cycles. Anarchy and Conquest, c. 1580–1760*, Princeton, 1984. Although this has superseded all other accounts,

G. E. Harvey's *History of Burma*, London, 1925, can still be read because it
so clearly reflects a chronicle viewpoint. The first three volumes of Than
Tun's translation of the *Royal Orders of Burma, AD 1598–1885*, Kyoto,
Center for Southeast Asian Studies, 1983–8, provide an invaluable source
for the preoccupations of the Burmese court.

Cambodia

Available sources for Cambodian history between the sixteenth and eighteenth century are not numerous, but a good survey is David Chandler,
A History of Cambodia, Boulder, 1983.

Vietnam

Vietnam between the sixteenth and eighteenth centuries has not attracted
much attention among Western scholars. Charles Maybon's *Histoire
Moderne du Pays d'Annam (1592–1820)*, Paris, 1920, is now very dated;
Thomas Hodgkin, *Vietnam. The Revolutionary Path*, London, 1981, has a
clear Marxist standpoint but nonetheless presents a sympathetic and
readable account of this period. A study by Keith W. Taylor, 'The literati
revival in seventeenth century Vietnam', JSEAS, 18, 1 (March 1987), looks
at changes in the bureaucracy. Alexander of Rhodes' account of missionary
work has been translated by Solange Hertz as *Rhodes of Vietnam*, Westminster, Maryland, 1966. The eighteenth century is discussed in Dang Phuong
Nghi, *Les institutions publiques du Vietnam au XVIIIe siècle*, Paris, 1909. Insun
Yu, 'Law and Family in Seventeenth and Eighteenth Century Vietnam',
Ph.D. thesis, University of Michigan, 1978, contains valuable material not
found elsewhere, while Gerald C. Hickey, *Sons of the Mountains: Ethnohis-
tory of the Vietnamese Central Highlands to 1954*, New Haven, 1982, provides
a view of the centre from the 'underside'.

The Philippines

The Spanish move into the Philippines is covered in the still valuable work
by John L. Phelan, *The Hispanization of the Philippines: Spanish Aims and
Filipino Responses 1565–1700*, Madison, 1959, which can be read together
with Nicholas P. Cushner, *Spain in the Philippines: From Conquest to Revolution*, Quezon City: Institute of Philippine Culture, 1970. More stress on the
Filipino reaction is given in Eric A. Anderson, 'Traditions in Conflict.
Filipino Responses and Spanish Colonialism, 1565–1665', Ph.D. thesis,
University of Sydney, 1977. Sources dealing with religious history are
given in the bibliographic essay for Chapter 9, but H. de la Costa, *The
Jesuits in the Philippines 1581–1768*, Cambridge, Mass., 1961, includes
considerable information on political developments. The Philippines is
also well served in the translation of contemporary documents, notably by
E. H. Blair and J. A. Robertson, *The Philippine Islands 1493–1898*, 55 vols,
Cleveland, 1903–9. While there is no recent synthesis of pre-nineteenth-
century Philippine history, a number of local studies have appeared: Angel

Martinez Cuesta, *History of Negros*, Manila, 1980; Rosario Mendoza Cortes, *Pangasinan 1572–1800*, Quezon City, 1974; Bruce Cruikshank, *Samar 1768–1898*, Manila, 1985; Bruce L. Fenner, 'Colonial Cebu: an Economic-Social History, 1521–1896', Ph.D. thesis, Cornell University, 1976; John Larkin, *The Pampangans: Colonial Society in a Philippine Province*, London, 1972; Ana Maria Madrigal, *A Blending of Cultures: the Batanes, 1686–1898*, Manila, 1983. Cesar A. Majul, *Muslims in the Philippines*, Quezon City, 1973, is a full account of Spain's dealings with the Muslims of the south. Dennis Roth, 'The Friar Estates of the Philippines', Ph.D. thesis, University of Oregon, 1974, and David Routledge, *Diego Silang and the Origins of Philippine Nationalism*, Quezon City: Philippine Center for Advanced Studies, 1979, provide the background to major peasant uprisings in the eighteenth century.

Borneo, Sumatra and the Malay World

The most detailed study of Brunei is Donald E. Brown, *Brunei: The Structure and History of a Borneon Malay Sultanate*, Monograph of the Brunei Museum Journal, 2, 2 (1970). Robert Nicholl, *European Sources for the History of the Sultanate of Brunei in the Sixteenth Century*, Brunei, Brunei Museum, 1975, is a collection of translated Spanish and Portuguese documents, while John Carroll, 'Berunai in the Boxer Codex', JMBRAS, 55, 2 (1982), is a most interesting late-sixteenth-century Spanish description of the Brunei court, and Amin Sweeney, ed., 'Silsilah raja-raja Berunai', JMBRAS, 41, 2 (1968), is a genealogical history of its kings.

A survey of Malay history is contained in Barbara Watson Andaya and Leonard Y. Andaya, *A History of Malaysia*, London, 1982. Detailed studies of particular states are Leonard Y. Andaya, *The Kingdom of Johor, 1641–1728*, Kuala Lumpur, 1975; Barbara Watson Andaya, *Perak, The Abode of Grace: A Study of an Eighteenth Century Malay State*, Kuala Lumpur, 1975; R. Bonney, *Kedah, 1771–1821: The Search for Security and Independence*, Kuala Lumpur, 1971. Few of the relevant Malay court chronicles relating to this period have been translated into English. C. C. Brown, '*Sejarah Melayu* or Malay Annals', JMBRAS, 25, 2 and 3 (1952), an account of Melaka up to the early sixteenth century, remains essential reading for anyone interested in understanding Malay culture. A wider study written by a descendant of one of the Bugis migrants to Johor is Raja Ali Haji, *Tuhfat al-Nafis (The Precious Gift)*, Kuala Lumpur, Oxford University Press, 1982 which has been edited and translated by Virginia Matheson and Barbara Watson Andaya.

The most complete study of early seventeenth-century Aceh is Denys Lombard, *Le Sultanat d'Atjeh au Temps d'Iskandar Muda 1607–1636*, Paris, 1967. JSEAS, 10, 3 (Dec. 1969) contains several relevant articles relating to the seventeenth century. For an overview, see J. Kathirithamby-Wells, 'Forces of regional and state integration in the western archipelago, c. 1500–1700', JSEAS, 18, 1 (March 1987). Jane Drakard, *A Malay Frontier. Unity and Duality in a Sumatran Kingdom*, Ithaca: Cornell University Southeast Asia Program, 1990, looks at the previously little researched area of Barus. Christine Dobbin, *Islamic Revivalism in a Changing Peasant Economy.*

Central Sumatra 1784–1847, London and Malmö: Scandinavian Institute of Asian Studies, 1983, is a finely crafted study of Minangkabau society during the eighteenth and early nineteenth century. J. Kathirithamby-Wells, *The British West Sumatran Presidency (1760–85): Problems of Early Colonial Enterprise*, Kuala Lumpur, 1970, considers the situation on the west coast. The best contemporary account of Sumatra, focused on the west coast, is William Marsden, *A History of Sumatra*, reprinted Kuala Lumpur, 1966.

Java

The material for Java is considerable, but has been covered in detail in M. C. Ricklefs, *A History of Modern Indonesia*, London, 1981. He has drawn from his own research, notably *Jogjakarta under Sultan Mangkubumi 1749–1792*, London, 1974, and *Modern Javanese Historical Traditions*, London, 1978, the latter being a translation of a Surakarta chronicle. Earlier work by Dutch scholars has also provided indispensable material for the reconstruction of Java's history. H. J. de Graaf and Th. G. Pigeaud, *De Eerst Moslimse Vorstendommen op Java. Studien over de Staatkundig Geschiedenis van de 15e en 16e eeuw*, The Hague, 1974, is a detailed compilation of all that is known about the northern coastal ports. This should be followed by H. J. de Graaf's important studies—*De Regering van Panembahan Senapati Ingalaga*, The Hague, 1954; *De Regering van Sultan Agong, vorst van Mataram 1613–1645, en die van zijn Voorganger Panembahan Seda-ing-Krapjak, 1601–1613*, The Hague, 1958; *De Regering van Sunan Mangku Rat I Tegal Wangi, Vorst van Mataram, 1646–1677*, 2 vols, The Hague, 1961–2; *De Vijf Gezantschapreizen van Ryklof van Goens naar het hof van Mataram 1648–1654*, The Hague, 1956, which is a valuable account of Mataram by a VOC envoy. B. J. O. Schrieke, *Indonesian Sociological Studies*, 2 vols, The Hague, 1957, touches on a number of important themes in Javanese history which remain to be developed, while Somersaid Moertono examines the nature of Javanese kingship in his *State and Statecraft in Old Java: a Study of the Later Mataram Period, Sixteenth to Nineteenth Century*, Ithaca: Cornell University Southeast Asia Program, 1968. Luc Nagtegaal, 'Rijden op een Hollandse Tijger. De Noordkust van Java en de V.O.C. 1680–1743', Ph.D. thesis, Utrecht University, 1988, examines the relations between the centre and the coast and the way political relationships in Java were affected by the growing Dutch presence.

Eastern Indonesia

The secondary sources for eastern Indonesia are limited. Leonard Y. Andaya, *The Heritage of Arung Palakka: A History of Southwest Sulawesi (Celebes) in the Seventeenth Century*, The Hague, 1981, brings together material relating to Bugis-Makassar history and its implications for the rest of the region. James Fox, *Harvest of the Palm. Ecological Change in Eastern Indonesia*, Cambridge, Mass., 1977, is an anthropological study focusing on

Roti and Savu, but makes frequent use of VOC sources, as does another anthropologist, Ch.F. van Fraassen, 'Ternate, de Molukken en de Indonesische Archipel', Ph.D. thesis, University of Leiden, 1987. An interesting Portuguese account by Antonio Galvão dating from the mid-sixteenth century has been translated by Hubert Th. M. Jacobs as *A Treatise on the Moluccas (c. 1544)*, Rome: Jesuit Historical Institute, 1971. Willard Hanna, *Indonesian Banda. Colonialism and its Aftermath in the Nutmeg Islands*, Philadelphia: Institute for the Study of Human Issues, 1978, is a readable account of the Dutch assumption of control in Banda, while Gerrit Knaap, 'Kruidnagelen en Christenen. De Verenigde Oost Indische Compagnie en de Bevolking van Ambon 1656–1696', Ph.D. thesis, Utrecht University, 1985, examines the way in which the Dutch governed Ambon.

CHAPTER

8

ECONOMIC AND SOCIAL CHANGE,
c. 1400–1800

It has been conventional to assume a new era began in Southeast Asia in 1500 with the arrival of Europeans, if for no better reason than that the sources become much richer and more accessible at this point. If one looked back from the age of high imperialism it was also obvious that the expansion of European empire in Asia began with Vasco da Gama and the discovery of a sea route from Europe to India. If we take our viewpoint from Southeast Asia, on the other hand, it is clear that the rapid social changes transforming the region were already in full flight before 1500, with the upsurge in international commerce of which the arrival of the Portuguese was a consequence, not a cause. The explosion of energy from the new Ming dynasty in China a century earlier is a more appropriate starting point for this new era of economic expansion, since it had some causal relation with a new dynasty in Vietnam, the decline of the 'classical' empires of Angkor and Majapahit, and their replacement by a string of new maritime city-states. Although most evidence about economic and social matters comes from a later period, we will therefore have to go back to 1400 in tracing the reasons for many of the changes.

POPULATION

To understand the impact of the major economic trends in the period it is necessary to have some impression of population levels. Contemporary estimates of population are extremely unreliable, but a combination of the more plausible of them with backward projection from somewhat more reliable and abundant nineteenth-century estimates yields roughly the order of population in 1600 shown in the table on page 463.

One of the characteristics of Southeast Asia before 1750, in contrast to adjacent India and China, was a low population density. Most of the region was still covered with jungle as late as 1800, so that attacks by tigers were not uncommon even on the outskirts of substantial population centres. Although overall density was probably not much above five per square kilometre (in contrast with more than thirty for India and China) most of the 20 to 30 million people of Southeast Asia were concentrated in a dozen trading cities and in the centres of wet-rice agriculture in the Red (Hong) River delta, the Mandalay area of upper Burma, the flood plains of the lower Irrawaddy, Pegu, Salween, Chao Phraya and Mekong rivers, Java (the northern coastal plain and the Mataram area), Bali, and south Sulawesi. Outside these areas a sparse population for the most part practised shifting agriculture in the lower slopes of what seemed a limitless jungle expanse.

The puzzle about pre-modern Southeast Asian population is why it remained so low, in contrast with its neighbours and with its own extremely rapid rise after 1800.[1] The answer does not appear to be wretched health and nutrition. Southeast Asians were relatively fortunate in their secure food-supplies, and they seemed to European and Chinese visitors to be relatively healthy and long-lived. Marriage was virtually universal, and most women appear to have embarked on child-bearing by their late teens. Although divorce was easy and frequent, it presented few barriers to subsequent remarriage. Children were much loved and indulged.

A number of factors may have kept birth-rates low, though none of them can be confirmed confidently from the available evidence. Shifting cultivation typically entails a high female work-load, difficult to combine with more than one child unable to walk. Breast-feeding in Southeast Asia has traditionally continued for two or three years, with resultant lengthening of post-partum amenorrhaea to about twenty-nine months. Abortion appears to have been a normal practice in the pre-Christian Philippines and continued to be so in many other animist areas of Southeast Asia. Belief systems before the acceptance of Islam and Christianity often did not forbid premarital sexual activity, and gonorrhea may in consequence have become endemic in some areas, causing a severe reduction in fertility—as has been the case in some animist areas of the archipelago in this century.[2]

Much the most important factor inhibiting population growth, however, was probably the instability of residence brought about by warfare and raiding, voluntary and forced migration, the pioneering of new cultivation areas, and corvée obligations. Of all the possible factors keeping birth-rates down, it is these that can most readily be seen to have changed in the nineteenth century as wars became less frequent and colonial and other states established zones of relatively stable conditions. Prior to 1750, periods and zones of peace were the exception, and they almost certainly gave rise to rapid population growth both through high birth-rates and immigration.

Southeast Asian warfare was not particularly costly of lives on the battlefield, but it was enormously disruptive of the domestic and agricultural pattern. Because rulers perceived their power in terms of human rather than territorial resources, their object in war was always to capture

---

[1] The best recent discussion of this phenomenon is Norman Owen, 'The Paradox of Population Growth in Nineteenth Century Southeast Asia: Evidence from Java and the Philippines,' JSEAS, 18 (1987).

[2] Anthony Reid, *Southeast Asia in the Age of Commerce, I: The Lands Below the Winds*, New Haven, 1988, 158–62; Norman Owen, 'Population and Society in Southeast Asia before 1900,' unpublished paper, 1988, 3–7.

as many of the enemy as possible, to take home to populate their dominions. Much larger numbers were mobilized for war than in comparable European campaigns—the kings of Burma, Vietnam, Siam and Java might each mobilize over a hundred thousand men—sometimes a majority of the available adult male population. They had to bring their own provisions, or else forage from the enemy territory they traversed. Hunger and disease were inevitably the result of these unwieldy campaigns. If the war went badly, the odds were against the soldiers ever returning to their families. As was said of Burmese–Thai warfare in the sixteenth century, 'these people bring so much damage to their enemies, ravaging all the plain, pillaging or burning all they encounter; but in the end they never return home without leaving half of their people.'[3] For the defenders, a common response to a force which came by sea was to abandon the settlement and flee into the surrounding forest until the attacker had done his plundering and departed. Hence families needed to be able to travel light, with little of their wealth in fixed property and with a minimum of children who could not run on their own.

Some wars of the period were so devastating in the mortality they caused that there can be no question that population declined sharply as a result. The Pegu area of lower Burma, the glittering centre of the vast empire of Bayinnaung (r. 1551–81), was destroyed and depopulated in the 1590s by vengeful Burman kings. Even if Floris' claim that this period 'coste the lyves of many millions of Peguers'[4] is much exaggerated, there is no doubt that the population was not restored for a century or more. In 1757 the Mons of lower Burma suffered another bout of defeat and depopulation by Burman rulers. Siam was twice laid waste by Burman armies, in 1549–69 and again in the 1760s, in each case losing the majority of the population in the immediate vicinity of the capital. When W. A. R. Wood wrote of these events in the 1920s[5] it was widely believed that Siam had barely then regained the population it had had before the onset of the Burmese wars in the 1550s. When Siam did reconstruct its population after these events, it was largely by bringing great numbers of captured Laos, Cambodians, Mons and Malays to central Thailand. Malaya was similarly devastated by the conquests of Sultan Iskander Muda of Aceh in the period 1618–24, with Pahang in particular never recovering its relative prominence after its capital was destroyed and 11,000 men taken captive by the victorious Acehnese. In Java the constant wars of succession between 1675 and 1755 ensured that each revision of the conventional *cacah* figures of households subject to corvée was downward rather than upward.[6]

The pattern of Southeast Asian population before 1750, therefore, was almost certainly one of dramatic ups and downs. Periods of strong rule able to guarantee internal security ensured rapid population growth by

---

[3] Pierre du Jarric, *Histoire des choses plus memorables advenues tant ez Indes Orientales, que autres pais de la descouverte des Portugais*, Bordeaux, 1608–14, I. 620–1.

[4] *Peter Floris, His Voyage to the East Indies in the 'Globe', 1611–1615*, ed. W. H. Moreland, London: Hakluyt Society, 1934, 53. Also du Jarric, *Histoire des choses* I. 618–23; III. 842.

[5] *A History of Siam*, London, 1924, reprinted Bangkok, 1959, 146.

[6] M. C. Ricklefs, 'Some Statistical Evidence on Javanese Social, Economic and Demographic History in the Later Seventeenth and Eighteenth Centuries,' MAS, 20, 1 (1986); Reid, *Age of Commerce*, I. 17–18.

natural causes and by immigration, as happened in fifteenth-century Vietnam, sixteenth-century Burma, seventeenth-century Siam and Laos, Aceh in 1550–1640, Makassar in 1600–60, and Dutch-controlled areas of Java after 1650. Such periods of steady growth were probably almost balanced by terrible setbacks such as those sketched above. Only after 1750 in Java and the Philippines, and after 1820 in most other parts of Southeast Asia, did stability and security begin to appear the norm rather than the exception, so that population increases of more than one per cent a year became general.

Estimated Southeast Asian Population about 1600

Region	Population ('000)	Density (per km²)
Vietnam (north and centre)	4,700	18.0
Cambodia-Champa	1,230	4.5
Laos (both sides of Mekong)	1,500	4.2
Burma	3,100	4.6
Siam (without Northeast)	1,700	4.3
Malaya (incl. Pattani)	500	3.4
Sumatra	2,400	5.7
Java	4,000	30.3
Borneo	670	0.9
Sulawesi	1,200	6.3
Bali	600	79.7
Lesser Sundas	600	9.1
Maluku	160*	2.2
Luzon and Visayas	800	4.0
Mindanao and Sulu	150	1.5
Total Southeast Asia	**23,300**	**5.8**

The basis for these estimates is set out in my *Age of Commerce*, I. 12–14; and in a little more detail in my 'Low Population Growth and Its Causes in Pre-Colonial Southeast Asia', in Norman Owen, ed., *Death and Disease in Southeast Asia*, Singapore, 1987, 33–47. The surprisingly high figure for Laos, not listed in the earlier publications, is based on counts of the corvéable population reportedly taken in 1376 and about 1640, covering a much larger area than the present state. The first yielded 300,000 adult male Lao and 400,000 non-Lao under royal control; the second 500,000 adult male subjects of unspecified ethnicity. David K. Wyatt, *Thailand, A Short History*, New Haven, 1982, 83; G. F. de Marini, *Delle Missioni de Padri della Compagnia de Giesu nella Provincia de Giappone, e particolarmente di quella di Tumkino*, Rome, 1663, 450.
* This figure, lower than my previous estimate, is based on the assumption that the area covered by detailed Dutch population counts in the Ambon and Lease Islands then embraced a quarter of the total Maluku population, as it did at the 1930 census. Gerrit Knaap, *Kruidnagelen en Christenen. De Verenigde Oost-Indische Compagnie en de Bevolking van Ambon 1656–1696*, Dordrecht, 1987, 100–1.

AN ECONOMIC BOOM

Southeast Asia has never been able to isolate itself from international economic forces. It sat athwart the great arteries of world commerce, it produced many of the articles which dominated the global long-distance trade, and it was widely accessible by water. Hence it is not surprising that it shared in some of the notable economic cycles which we know to have affected Europe and China.

The period 1400–1620 was essentially one of boom in both those great markets. Following the trauma of the Black Death throughout Eurasia in the fourteenth century, populations rose steadily in both Europe and China. Prices also rose, almost doubling in England and France during the sixteenth century. This boom was most intense during the period 1570–1620, when new methods of smelting caused a massive increase in the export of silver both by Peru (Potosi) and Japan. In China, Japan, and Europe this relatively well-documented period saw a great expansion of cities and a build-up of the trade networks which gave them life. The same was true in Southeast Asia.

If there is a particular moment for the beginning of this sustained trade boom as it affected Southeast Asia, it should be sought around 1400. China was the largest market for Southeast Asian goods, and the abrupt changes of imperial policy towards foreign trade could have a marked effect in the south. There seems no doubt that the advent of a remarkably stable and prosperous Ming dynasty in 1368, its policy of vigorously encouraging lucrative 'tribute' missions during the subsequent half-century, and especially its exceptional initiative in sending out seven massive state trading expeditions between 1403 and 1433, had an enormous effect in stimulating Southeast Asian trade and commerce. Chinese copper cash became the basic currency of Java, Malaya, and Maluku (the Moluccas) during the fifteenth century. Although small quantities of pepper had been exported from Java in earlier periods, it was around 1400, in response to the great new demand from China, that the Indian pepper vine (*Piper nigrum*) was carried from South India to northern Sumatra, and began its career as the biggest export item of Southeast Asia. During the fifteenth century Indonesian pepper and Siamese sappanwood (used for dye) became for the first time items of mass consumption in China.[7]

Chinese state trading ceased abruptly in 1433, and private Chinese trade remained officially banned, but Southeast Asia's trade to the north remained lively. There were always secluded bays on the South China coast where the imperial ban on trade was ineffective. Furthermore the use of tribute missions to Peking (Beijing) as a way to circumvent the ban was at its peak in the fifteenth century, with Siam sending a total of seventy-eight missions between 1371 and 1503.[8] Finally the island kingdom of Ryukyu, between Japan and Taiwan, became a crucial commercial link between Southeast and Northeast Asia in the period 1430–1512, profiting from its tributary relations with both China and Japan to bring Southeast Asian produce to these theoretically closed kingdoms.

Although the expansion of Chinese demand in the fifteenth and sixteenth centuries was probably the biggest stimulus for Southeast Asian commercial growth, the trade to the west was also increasingly lively. Throughout the European Middle Ages some cloves and nutmeg, grown only in Maluku in eastern Indonesia, had found their way to western Europe, along an arduous trade route that passed by Java, Sumatra,

---

[7] T'ien Ju-kang, 'Chêng Ho's Voyages and the Distribution of Pepper in China,' JRAS, 2 (1981).

[8] Suebsang Promboon, 'Sino-Siamese Tributary Relations 1282–1853,' Ph.D. thesis, University of Michigan, 1971, 106–20.

southern India, the Red Sea and Alexandria (or the Persian Gulf and Beirut) to Venice, Genoa or Barcelona. In the 1390s, however, this trade appears for the first time to have become substantial and predictable. More than twenty tonnes of cloves were then arriving in Italian ports in an average year, and we must assume that the quantities which remained in India were far greater. Although only one small branch of Southeast Asia's export trade, the Maluku spices reaching Europe are the only branch which can be quantified over the whole of our period, and are therefore a precious indicator of overall trade levels. As illustrated for cloves in Figure 8.1, these exports show a rapid expansion in the fifteenth century, a disruption caused by the Portuguese intrusion after 1500, and then a still more rapid growth up till the time when the Dutch East India Company established its monopoly in the 1620s.

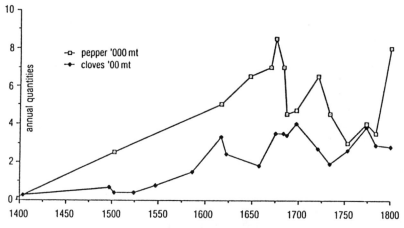

Figure 8.1   Southeast Asian pepper and clove exports, 1400–1800.[9]

[9] The data for cloves (in hundred metric tonnes) after the Dutch monopoly (1650) are based on accurate VOC reports of annual production in Gerrit Knaap, *Kruidnagelen en Christenen: De Verenigde Oost-Indische Compagnie en de bevolking van Ambon 1656–1696*, Dordrecht, 1987, 231, 235, and E. W. A. Ludeking, *Schets van de Residentie Amboina*, The Hague, 1868, 92–3. I have calculated these by decennial averages. Before 1650 what is presented in the graph is not production but my estimate of exports to Europe alone, which represent smaller shares of Moluccan production the earlier period. The pepper line (thousand metric tonnes) is my estimate of total Southeast Asian production, based on reports of amounts carried to Europe and to China, and total production estimated from the sources in notes 10 and 11. The major sources for clove and pepper quantities before 1600 are C. Wake, 'The Changing Pattern of Europe's Pepper and Spice Imports, ca. 1400–1700,' *Journal of European Economic History*, 6 (1979); Vitorino Magalhães-Godinho, *L'economie de l'empire portugais aux XVe et XVIe siècles*, Paris, 1969, 701–4; and Frederick C. Lane, *Venice and History*, Baltimore, 1966, 14. Pepper quantities carried by different agencies after 1600 are recorded in Kristof Glamann, *Dutch-Asiatic Trade 1620–1740*, 1958, 97–101; K. N. Chaudhuri, *The English East India Company, 1600–1640*, London, 1965, 148; G. B. Souza, *The Survival of Empire. Portuguese Trade and Society in China and the South China Sea, 1630–1754*, Cambridge, UK, 1986, 152–3; J. Kathirithamby-Wells, *The British West Sumatran Presidency (1760–85)*, Kuala Lumpur, 1977, 217, 220; J. de Rovere van Breugel, 'Beschrijving van Bantam en de Lampongs,' BKI, 5 (1856), 358–62. The 1800 pepper estimate is that of van Hogendorp, in *Encyclopaedie van Nederlandsch-Indië*. III. 385. For more detail on how the earlier figures were calculated, see Anthony Reid, 'An "Age of Commerce" in Southeast Asian History', MAS, 24, 1 (1990).

Although the exceptional number of hands through which Maluku spices passed on their long journey to the west and north made them far more important than the small quantities might suggest, it was pepper which became the great Southeast Asian cash crop of the sixteenth and seventeenth century. It is not mentioned as a product of Sumatra or Malaya until after 1400, but by 1510 these regions were producing about 2500 tonnes of pepper a year, in contrast to 3600 tonnes exported by the more ancient pepper centres of Kerala in South India.[10] In the course of the sixteenth century Southeast Asian production increased two or threefold—primarily in west, central and south Sumatra, and western Java. Banten (Java) alone exported an average of 2100 tonnes a year in the first two decades of the seventeenth century,[11] and total Southeast Asian production must have been close to 5000 tonnes. The quantities produced continued to increase to a peak of about 8500 tonnes around 1670 before falling off. Prices declined sharply after 1650, though it was another two decades before this was translated into reduced production. In terms of the returns flowing into Southeast Asia, the peak of the pepper boom occurred in the first half of the seventeenth century.

The increase in Southeast Asian production after 1500 almost all went to fill the growing demand in Europe. The initial impact of the Portuguese appearance in the Indian Ocean was to disrupt the existing Muslim-dominated trade routes, though this effect was most damaging for the established pepper-producers of Kerala. Prior to 1500 Indonesian pepper went almost exclusively to China (and other parts of Southeast Asia), but the Portuguese began bringing some to Europe during the first half of the sixteenth century. In the 1550s a major new Muslim trade artery was opened up between Aceh, at the northern tip of Sumatra, and the Red Sea, avoiding the areas of Portuguese strength on the west coast of India. For most of the second half of the century this route carried Sumatran pepper through the Red Sea to Alexandria in quantities at least as large as the Portuguese were taking from India to western Europe.[12] With the arrival of the English and Dutch, Southeast Asia became unquestionably the major source of the world's pepper and therefore the centre of competition between Portuguese, English, Dutch, Chinese and Indian buyers. Pepper, primarily from Sumatra, the Malay peninsula and southern Borneo, provided more than half of the invoice value of both English and Dutch return cargoes from Asia until 1650. Thereafter the proportion dropped sharply as pepper prices in Europe fell and more profitable cargoes were found in Indian cloths and indigo. Pepper had declined to only 10 per cent of the

---

[10] *The Suma Oriental of Tomé Pires*, ed. and trans. Armando Cortesão, London: Hakluyt Society, 1944, 82, 140, 144.

[11] Calculated from M. A. P. Meilink-Roelofsz, *Asian Trade and European Influence in the Indonesian Archipelago between 1500 and about 1630*, The Hague, 1962, 393 n. 80.

[12] Lane, *Venice and History*, 25–34; Fernand Braudel, *The Mediterranean and the Mediterranean World in the Age of Philip II*, trans. S. Reynolds, New York, 1976, 545–51; Charlex Boxer, 'A note on Portuguese Reactions to the Revival of the Red Sea Spice Trade and the Rise of Atjeh, 1540–1600,' JSEAH, 10 (1969).

value of English cargoes by the 1680s, and to 11 per cent of Dutch cargoes by 1700.[13]

These developments for the two Southeast Asian exports about which we know most (because they were the principal articles of European interest in Asia during this period) were paralleled by other indicators of Southeast Asian trade, both local and long-distance. The peak of the boom in Southeast Asia's trade occurred during the period 1580–1630, as a result of the coincidence of exceptional demand from China, Japan, India, and Europe. Price levels were high throughout the world during this period, largely as a result of unprecedented exports of silver from the Americas and Japan, and competition for Southeast Asia's valuable products was intense.

In China this period represented the 'late Ming boom', when trade, urban growth and prosperity were at high levels. In 1567 the emperor Mu-tsung for the first time lifted the Ming ban on private trade to the south. Fifty junks were initially licensed to leave from the southern Chinese ports each year, and this figure grew rapidly to 88 in 1589 and 117 in 1597. A roughly equal number of unlicensed junks appear to have continued the age-old 'smuggling' trade. Roughly half of these junks were licensed for the 'eastern seas', meaning the Philippines and northern Borneo, but especially the flourishing Spanish port of Manila, founded in 1571. Other major destinations for the Chinese ships were western Java (8 ships a year in the 1590s), southern Sumatra (7 ships), the Nguyen-ruled kingdom of what is now central Vietnam (8 ships) and Siam (4 ships).[14] From the records of ship movements kept by the Spanish in Manila and the Dutch in Batavia, it is clear that Chinese shipping to Southeast Asia remained at high levels through the 1630s, but thereafter dropped to only one-third or less until the 1690s.[15]

For Japan the period 1570–1630 was a unique moment when the country was unified, cities prospered as the nuclei of a flourishing internal trade, and exceptional quantities of silver were extracted from the mines to form the basis of a vigorous trade with Southeast Asia. Japanese vessels were still forbidden to trade directly with China, so the exchange of Japanese silver for Chinese silk and other goods had to take place in Southeast Asian ports, notably Manila and Hoi An (known to Westerners as Faifo, central Vietnam). Throughout the period 1604–35 about ten Japanese vessels a year were licensed to trade with the south, the largest numbers going to Vietnam (124 ships during the thirty-one years), the Philippines (56), and Siam (56). In 1635 this activity stopped abruptly when the shogun Iemitsu prohibited Japanese from travelling abroad. Japanese external

[13] K. N. Chaudhuri, *The Trading World of Asia and the English East India Company, 1660–1760*, Cambridge, UK, 1978, 529; J. R. Bruijn, F. S. Gaastra and I. Schöffer, *Dutch-Asiatic Shipping in the 17th and 18th Centuries*, The Hague, 1987, I. 92.

[14] Zhang Xie, *Dong xi yang kao* [Studies on the East and West Oceans, 1617], new edn, Beijing, 1981, 131–3; R. L. Innes, 'The Door Ajar: Japan's Foreign Trade in the seventeenth century,' Ph.D. thesis, University of Michigan, 1980, 52–3.

[15] Pierre Chaunu, *Les Philippines et le Pacifique des Ibériques*, Paris, 1960, 148–75; Leonard Blussé, *Strange Company. Chinese settlers, mestizo women, and the Dutch in VOC Batavia*, Dordrecht, 1986, 115–20.

trade remained high throughout the rest of the century, but only through the tightly controlled Dutch and Chinese trade at Nagasaki.[16]

The enormous increase in output of the silver mines of Spanish America in the 1570s also had its effect on Southeast Asia. Some of this silver was carried directly to Manila from Acapulco, to buy Chinese products and Southeast Asian spices. A larger amount crossed the Atlantic, where first the Portuguese and Venetians, and after 1600 the Dutch, English, Danes and French, carried some of it eastward to buy the precious products of Asia. Magalhães-Godinho has calculated that Europe as a whole was sending precious metals to the equivalent of seventeen tonnes of silver per year to Asia in the 1490s, but that this suffered a 'sensational' drop to only three tonnes in the early 1500s, as a result of Portugal's resort to plunder rather than purchase in the Indian Ocean. The old level was regained by the mid-sixteenth century, as the Portuguese adjusted to more peaceful trade and the Muslim–Venetian route through the Red Sea revived. After 1570 New World silver began pouring into Europe, and the union of Portuguese and Spanish Crowns in 1580 gave the Portuguese ready access to it. Both Portuguese and Venetians were sending unprecedented amounts of silver to the east in the last two decades of the century, when a total treasure equivalent to seventy-two tonnes of silver was being annually shipped to Asia.[17] With the added competition of Dutch, English and French buyers, the amount of silver flowing east from Europe reached a temporary peak in the 1620s. Since Southeast Asian products were then the major goal of the Europeans, by contrast to the situation after 1650, much of this treasure must have served to enrich Southeast Asia during that busy half-century before 1630.

CASH-CROPPING AND COMMERCIALIZATION

Before this long post-1400 boom, most Southeast Asian exports had consisted of the natural products of the forest and the sea—that exotic inventory of medicines, delicacies, perfumes and aromatic woods described in Chinese manuals of the T'ang and the Sung. No doubt there were ups and downs in the trade in such items, but such swings would not have altered the way of life of the majority of Southeast Asians. After 1400 such forest products as camphor, sandalwood and sappanwood were gathered on an increased scale, but they were increasingly dwarfed in importance by cultivated crops grown specifically for export. Whole communities devoted themselves to cultivating pepper, clove, cotton, sugar, and benzoin, and became dependent on the international market for their livelihood. 'This one product with which they abound must furnish them with everything

[16] Iwao Seiichi, *Kaigai Koshoshi no Shiten. 2: Kinsei* [Views on Overseas Contacts, vol. 2: Modern Times], Tokyo, 1976, 300–1. Innes, 'Door Ajar', 51–66. Innes, 376–432, has effectively shown that the overall value of Japan's foreign trade did not fall after 1635, as previously thought. In fact the highest levels were reached in the three periods 1636–8, 1659–62 and 1696–9.
[17] Magalhães-Godinho, *L'economie*, 316, 334–5.

else; this is why . . . these people [of eastern Indonesia] are constrained to keep up continual intercourse with one another, the one supplying what the other wants.'[18]

The spectacular growth of pepper production drew particularly large numbers of people in Sumatra, the Malay peninsula and southern Borneo into this kind of insecure prosperity through cash-cropping. Judging by eighteenth-century calculations that a family pepper farm delivered on average 200 kilograms of pepper a year,[19] the 8500 tonnes of pepper produced at the peak of the boom must have required the labour of 40,000 families or at least 200,000 individuals. These cultivators would have represented about 5 per cent of the total population of Sumatra, Borneo and the Malay peninsula at that time. If we add the people who depend indirectly on this export item as traders, port workers, city-dwellers and dependants of the merchants and officials who drew the largest profit from the trade, the total proportion whose economic livelihood was dependent on cash-cropping would be at least twice as great.

Pepper and the other items in the long-distance trade to Europe and China have left us the best data. They were also crucial in bringing wealth and shipping into the region as a whole and thereby stimulating a vast range of local trade routes which brought provisions and consumer goods to the cash-croppers and the cities. In terms of the overall level of commercialization in the region it was this local and regional trade which was most important, though impossible to quantify. In the sixteenth and seventeenth century the bulk of Southeast Asian cargoes were certainly in foodstuffs, textiles, ceramics and metalware, not the high-value pepper and spices of the long-distance trade.

Cotton was an even more widespread cash crop than pepper, though marketed less far afield and frequently grown alongside rice. Since only those parts of Southeast Asia with a substantial dry season could grow cotton, it was exported around the region both as raw cotton and as cloth. Around 1600 the eastern parts of Java, and Bali, Lombok, Sumbawa and Buton supplied cloth to Maluku, Sulawesi, Borneo and the Malay peninsula. The dry areas of Luzon, Cebu and Panay provided cotton for wetter parts of the Philippines. Cambodia exported cotton as far afield as Pattani on the Malay peninsula. Some Southeast Asian cotton and cloth was even taken back to China by returning traders from ports in Java, Luzon and Vietnam. At least in the eighteenth century, and perhaps for some time earlier, there was a large-scale cotton trade from the dry regions of central Burma up the Irrawaddy and along caravan routes into Yunnan.[20]

Sugarcane, although native to Southeast Asia, was used primarily for chewing as a confection until the seventeenth century, when Chinese refining methods were introduced to Java, Siam, Cambodia and the Quang Nam area of central Vietnam. In Banten around 1630 cultivators were shifting from pepper into sugar, which was more profitable as an export to China. Japan, which grew no sugar of its own, was an even bigger market,

[18] *The Voyage of Francis Pyrard of Laval to the East Indies, the Maldives, the Moluccas and Brazil*, trans. A. Gray, London: Hakluyt Society, 1887–90, II. 169.
[19] Kathirithamby-Wells, 61, 70.
[20] Reid, *Age of Commerce*, I. 90–2.

importing over 2000 tonnes a year in the second half of the century. After Taiwan, the major exporters to Japan were central Vietnam and Siam, each providing several hundred tonnes a year for Chinese and Dutch shippers to take to Nagasaki.[21]

Another important cash crop of the period was benzoin (the resin of the tree *Styrax benzoin*, used for incense), grown wild but also in large plantations in northern Sumatra, Siam, northern Cambodia and Laos. The Mekong valley was exporting 270 tonnes a year through Cambodia in the 1630s, primarily to Asian ports—Persia alone took about 60 tonnes.[22] Tobacco and indigo, on the other hand, were grown primarily for markets within the Southeast Asian region. Seventeenth-century Batavia drew its substantial tobacco needs primarily from the Javanese north coast, but also from Madura, south Sulawesi, Amboina and Mindanao.[23]

Cash-cropping brought wealth, international contacts, and social changes on a considerable scale. Some growers undoubtedly became very wealthy, but the principal beneficiaries were the rulers of the port-cities which marketed these goods, the traders, and the intermediaries who financed the new frontiers of cash-cropping. Since population was scarce relative to land, the key figure in developing new areas was the entrepreneur who could mobilize labour through a sufficient advance of capital and could control access to a market. Those who received an advance of money or goods to set them up as pepper-growers on a new frontier would remain dependent on the financier, and in particular would be obliged to market their harvest through him or her. Sometimes this dependence was akin to slavery, as in the case of the jungle frontier around Banjarmasin (south Borneo), which imported from Makassar and elsewhere 'male and female slaves fitted for labour in the pepper-gardens'.[24] In all cases a large share of the profit would go to this intermediary financier and broker, who might in time become the chief of a small river-system; a percentage would also go as tribute to the ruler of the city-state where the international market was located.[25]

The cash-cropping centres and the cities which they helped to stimulate relied for much of their livelihood on imports. Taking Southeast Asia as a whole, the largest single item of import in the sixteenth and seventeenth century was undoubtedly Indian cloth. Personal adornment and clothing were the principal items of non-essential expenditure for most Southeast Asians, so that any increase in income was likely to show first in expenditure on cloth. As one observer pointed out for the Burmese, they were

[21] Innes, 'Door Ajar', 504–8; Yoneo Ishii, 'Seventeenth Century Japanese Documents about Siam,' JSS, 59, 2 (1971) 170.

[22] W. Ph. Coolhaas, *Generale Missiven van Gouverneurs-Generaal en Raden aan Heren XVII der Verenigde Oostindische Compagnie*, The Hague, 1960–76, I. 592.

[23] Thomas O. Höllman, *Tabak in Südostasien: Ein ethnographisch-historischer Überblick*, Berlin, Dietrich Reimer, 1988, 145–50.

[24] 'De Handelsrelaties van het Makassaarse rijk, volgens de notitie van Cornelis Speelman uit 1670', ed. J. Noorduyn, in *Nederlandse Historische Bronnen*, Amsterdam, 1983, III. 112.

[25] The system of pepper-growing is much better known in the nineteenth century, though these essentials probably remained unchanged. See James Siegel, *The Rope of God*, Berkeley, 1969, 17–21; James Gould, 'Sumatra—America's Pepper-pot, 1784–1873,' *Essex Institute Historical Collections*, 92 (1956).

parsimonious in food and housing, but 'splendid and extravagant in their dress. They have always in their mouths that their dress is seen by everybody; but no one comes into their houses to observe what they eat and how they are lodged.'[26] The conversion of most of the island world to Islam or Christianity in the fifteenth to seventeenth centuries brought new styles of dress using much more cloth, particularly on the upper body. In addition sumptuous cloths were used to decorate houses and public buildings, as a store of wealth, an item of ritual exchange at weddings, and to shroud the dead in burial.

For all these purposes Indian cloth was preferred to the local product because of the much brighter colours Indians could fix in their dyes, the bold designs, and the fine weaving. The boom in Southeast Asian exports was matched by a rapid increase in imports of cloth. The last and wealthiest Malay ruler of Melaka (Malacca), Sultan Mahmud (r. 1488–1511), is credited in the chronicles with sending a mission to south India to acquire forty varieties of rare cloth. The Portuguese who conquered his capital gave estimates of the total value of cloth imports from Bengal, Coromandel (the modern Madras area) and Gujerat which could be conservatively totalled at 460,000 cruzados a year, equivalent to about 19 tonnes of silver.[27] In the period 1620–50, the heyday of Indian cloth exports to Southeast Asia, the Dutch alone carried cloth valued between 10 and 20 tonnes of silver (roughly 1 to 2 million guilders) each year from the Coromandel coast to Batavia.[28] The total Southeast Asian imports of Indian cloth in this period probably peaked at a value of about 50 tonnes of silver, representing more than 20 million square metres of cloth—almost a metre per person per year. Indian cloth was traded not only in the great maritime emporia: it reached the tiny spice-growing islands of eastern Indonesia on the one hand, and the land-locked kingdom of Laos on the other, where at least three months were needed for bullock-carts to haul it from Ayutthaya.

The commercial boom also made it possible for large cities and substantial populations to import their food by sea. The Malay capital of Melaka, without any rice-growing hinterland of its own, was supplied by fifty or sixty shiploads (varying greatly in size, but perhaps averaging 30 tonnes) of rice each year from Java, and about thirty each from Siam and Pegu (lower Burma). Pasai in north Sumatra, and its much larger successor after 1520, Aceh, also imported their rice from Pegu, Tenasserim, and South India, as well as Java. Pattani drew more than half its rice from Songkhla, Nakhon Sithammarat, Siam and Cambodia, and merchants from Pahang, further south, came to the Pattani market to buy their supplies of grain. Banten also imported its foodstuffs by sea from other parts of Java, from Makassar and Sumbawa, until Dutch blockades began to place these supplies in doubt. Other foodstuffs such as vegetables, dried fish and fermented fish-paste, coconut oil, salt, and palm-wine also travelled long distances by sea to feed the flourishing cities. During a two-month period

[26] V. Sangermano, *A Description of the Burmese Empire*, trans. W. Tandy, Rome, 1818, reprinted London, 1966, 159.
[27] *Suma Oriental of Tomé Pires*, 269–72.
[28] Calculated from Tapan Raychaudhuri, *Jan Company in Coromandel 1605–1690*, The Hague: KITLV, 1962, 140–3.

in 1642 the Dutch counted twelve ships arriving in Aceh from Java, carrying 'salt, sugar, peas, beans and other goods'.[29]

In bulk terms rice was the largest single item of trade. The bunded irrigated fields of Java and the flood-plains of Siam, Cambodia and Burma were able to generate large surpluses, which were regularly carried by river or pack-animal to the ports whence the grain was shipped in sacks to urban or rice-deficit areas. In the seventeenth century central Java was usually the largest single exporter, with quantities up to 10,000 tonnes being shipped from Japara in a good year. South Sulawesi under the able chancellor of Makassar, Karaeng Matoaya (r. 1593–1637), was one area where rice cultivation was deliberately expanded for export. Rice barns were built on royal initiative, and regulations framed to ensure that there was always a supply of rice to provide spice traders on their way to Maluku. Even in these circumstances, however, rice cannot be considered a true cash crop. It was grown primarily for local needs, and the surplus only was exported.

URBANIZATION

In Southeast Asia before 1630, maritime cities were probably more dominant over their sparsely-populated hinterlands than they were in most other parts of the world. Unlike the earlier period of Hindu-Buddhist states such as Angkor, Pagan and Majapahit, the capitals of this period were all accessible to ocean shipping. Rulers, and the circle of aristocratic officials around them, drew the bulk of their revenue from trade, participating in it directly as well as taxing it through import dues, gifts and impositions. The maritime capitals did not simply consume wealth from the hinterland and transform it into power: they generated most of the state's wealth through trade, and to a lesser extent manufacture. In most of the languages of Southeast Asia the state and the city were indistinguishable. The power and grandeur of the country essentially resided in its capital, and the ruler's military strength rested on that large proportion of his subjects who could be called to arms in a few hours from within and around it. What Bangkok was for Siam in the nineteenth century, Ayutthaya was to an even greater extent in the sixteenth and seventeenth: 'at once the seat of government, of religion, of foreign commerce, in short of nearly all public life. Bangkok is more to Siam than Paris to France.'[30]

These commercial capitals depended on the vagaries of international trade, and their populations rose and fell accordingly. The seasonality of the monsoons brought foreign traders and seamen who might add to the city's population for six months or more, while festivals and market days brought great crowds in from the hinterland. The Vietnamese capital Thang-long (Hanoi), in particular, became so crowded on the market days at the first and fifteenth days of each lunar month that some observers

---

[29] Reid, *Age of Commerce*, I. 21–31.
[30] Board of Foreign Missions, 1865, cited in L. Sternstein, 'The Growth of the Population of the World's Pre-eminent "Primate City": Bangkok at its Bicentenary', JSEAS, 15, 1 (1984) 49.

thought it then the most populous city in the world, with streets so crowded one could scarcely advance a hundred steps in half an hour.[31] The estimates of contemporary observers, the scale of food imports, and the physical dimensions of city remains, provide the basis for the following tentative estimates of the permanent populations of these Southeast Asian cities at their peak.

The extent of its walls confirms that the population of the Vietnamese capital of Thang-long was in excess of 100,000 throughout the period from the fifteenth to the mid-eighteenth century. Its population was the least dependent on international trade of any Southeast Asian capital, but it was the heart of the region's most centralized and populous state. It was also the major manufacturing centre of the country, with many of its quarters devoted exclusively to a particular craft. The fifteenth century was the golden age of the Vietnamese capital, when the vigorous Le dynasty extended its wall to ten kilometres and built many palaces and temples. Signs of decay were already evident in the seventeenth century.

For two or three decades before its conquest by the Portuguese in 1511, Melaka was the great trade-based city of the Malay world, with a population of around 100,000. It was reduced to about a quarter of that after the Portuguese occupation and the departure of most Muslim traders. In the mid-sixteenth century Ayutthaya and Pegu were probably the two largest cities of the region, until the Siamese capital was devastated by the Burmese in 1569, and Pegu in turn was largely depopulated in 1599. The archipelago cities were then probably somewhat smaller, with Aceh, Brunei (until the Spanish conquest of 1579), Demak and Tuban probably around 50,000 during the latter half of the century.

In the seventeenth century we have more frequent estimates of population, which also show a rapid growth of trade-based cities in step with the peak in the trade boom of 1570–1630. Ayutthaya must have recovered its former population by mid-century, at which point there were probably six Southeast Asian cities in the 100,000 class—Thang-long, Ayutthaya, Aceh, Banten, Makassar and Mataram. Other major cities having about 50,000 were Pattani, Surabaya (until its conquest by Mataram in 1621), the Cambodian capital near the junction of the Mekong and Tonle Sap rivers, the southern (Nguyen) Vietnamese capital at Kim-long, the restored and growing Burmese capital at Ava, and (to judge again from physical dimensions) the Lao capital of Vientiane under its 'sun-king', Soulignavongsa (1654–1712).[32]

Many of these cities were excessively large in relation to their hinterlands if compared with their counterparts in Europe. Numerous observers pointed out that the great Malay port of Melaka was surrounded by little but jungle, and had to import virtually all its rice by sea. Aceh was also dependent on imported rice in the seventeenth century, because it was trade and craft production that occupied the bulk of the population of the

---

[31] Samuel Baron, 'A Description of the Kingdom of Tonqeen,' in *A Collection of Voyages and Travels*, ed. A. and W. Churchill, London, 1703–32, IV. 3. Abbé Richard, *Histoire naturelle, civile et politique du Tonquin*, Paris, 1778, I. 28.

[32] For further details of these estimates see Anthony Reid, 'The Structure of Cities in Southeast Asia: Fifteenth to Seventeenth Centuries', JSEAS, 11, 2 (1980) 237–9; and Reid, *The Age of Commerce*, II. ch. 2.

Aceh river valley. Even in the relatively minor port of Kedah, surrounded by some of the best potential rice-land in the Malay peninsula, the town was said to have 7000 or 8000 inhabitants in 1709, and the whole country only 20,000, filled as it was with 'great forests, where one sees masses of wild buffaloes, elephants, deers and tigers'.[33]

European cities expanded rapidly in the prosperous sixteenth century, but most of them remained in a similar range to the cities above. Only Naples and Paris were in excess of 200,000, with London and Amsterdam rapidly approaching this. Tomé Pires had seen only the modest European cities of the Iberian peninsula when he declared that Melaka had 'no equal in the world', but later observers continued to make such comparisons. The English East India Company in 1617 thought Ayutthaya 'as big a city as London',[34] but it was the capital of a country with only a quarter of England's population. Even in the nineteenth century when the Thai capital was no longer a major international emporium it contained about 10 per cent of the country's population, and Ayutthaya can have had no less a share in the seventeenth century. The Dutch compared Banten in 1597 to 'old Amsterdam'; a French traveller in Burma a century later thought Syriam and Prome were the size of Metz (perhaps 25,000), and compared Pagan with Dijon and Ava with Rheims (both perhaps 40,000).[35] But the agricultural populations these towns served were very much less than those of the Netherlands and France. Their size was made possible by the capability of rice to produce very large surpluses in relation to labour input; by the ease of waterborne transport; by the relative importance of trade in this period; and by the desire of powerful statesmen to have the maximum of their followers around them for military and status purposes.

Southeast Asia in the period 1500–1660 should therefore be seen as highly urban, in relation both to other parts of the world and to its own subsequent experience. The European enclave cities which took over much of the lucrative long-distance trade of the region were much smaller than their predecessors. Portuguese Melaka never rose above 30,000, Dutch Makassar took two centuries to recover its pre-Dutch population, and even Batavia had scarcely 30,000 inhabitants within its walls in the second half of the seventeenth century when it dominated the maritime trade of Asia. The Dutch 'Queen of the East' was still smaller than the economically insignificant Javanese inland capitals in 1812, and Java's de-urbanization continued throughout the nineteenth century.[36] Similarly British Rangoon did not pass the population of the Burmese capital (successively at Ava, Amerapurah and Mandalay) until about 1890, long after it had defeated it economically and militarily. The reason was that these colonial cities discouraged an influx of people from their hinterlands, and played almost no role as political, cultural and religious centres of the regions which they

---

[33] Père Taillandier to Willard, 20 February 1711, in *Lettres édifiantes et curieuses, écrites des missions étrangeres*, new edn, Paris, 1781, II. 409.

[34] Cited John Anderson, *English Intercourse with Siam in the Seventeenth Century*, London, 1890, 69.

[35] P. Goüye, *Observations physique et mathematiques . . . envoyées des Indes et de la Chine à l'Academie Royale des Sciences à Paris, par les Pères Jesuites*, Paris, 1692, 73–4.

[36] Peter Boomgaard, *Children of the Colonial State*, Amsterdam, 1989, 110–11.

dominated economically. Southeast Asian societies themselves had few links with these international and 'modern' cities, and underwent a significant de-urbanization in the eighteenth century, becoming more isolated than before from the cosmopolitan and secular dynamism of city life.

The central features of the Southeast Asian city were the fortified palace or citadel, the mosque or temple, and the market. The citadel contained the residence of the monarch, his consorts and immediate dependants, and it was always surrounded by a high strong wall. This was the city proper, a place of cosmic power and centrality to the realm. Only Vietnamese cities emulated the Chinese model, with a wall around their entirety. In Siam the citadel and the city merged, with most of the important temples and the compounds of ministers contained within the walled and moated citadel, of which the royal palace was only the most important section. Yet even in such vast citadels as Ayutthaya, which embraced the seven square kilometres of an island in the river and contained much empty parkland, the foreigners were kept outside. Consequently much of the commercial life of the city was conducted outside the walled city proper. In Burma, Cambodia, and the Malay world the boundaries of the larger city were even less clear, since it was often only the royal enclosure which had any wall at all. Around this spread village-like assemblages of wooden houses shaded by trees, interspersed with the compounds of rich merchants and officials, the greatest of which replicated the citadel itself with their protective walls (often simply of bamboo, thornbushes, or earth), religious shrines, and accommodation for a large number of dependants.

In the sixteenth and especially the seventeenth century the example (and the threat) of the Europeans and Chinese encouraged more cities to build walls around the whole of the central area which had to be defended. Yet some of the largest cities in the archipelago, including Aceh and Mataram, never built walls except around the royal compound itself. In consequence there was no clear sense of the distinct character or autonomy of the city. Cities spread freely into the countryside, and were not constrained to build dense-packed permanent structures behind their protective walls as in Europe or China. To European visitors it appeared as if even a large Southeast Asian city was 'no more than an aggregate of villages', largely hidden by the profusion of trees.

Given their warm climate and exposure to frequent flooding, it was not surprising that Southeast Asians even in cities preferred to live in light and airy houses constructed on stilts out of temporary materials. There were also political reasons, however, for the scarcity of stone or brick buildings. Europeans were particularly anxious to build in stone, partly to avoid the danger of fire, but chiefly to be able to protect themselves effectively. After the Dutch had succeeded in making themselves impregnable in Jayakatra (Jakarta, which they renamed Batavia) in 1619, Southeast Asian suspicions hardened against this practice. Rulers in the seventeenth century forbade not only Europeans but also their own subjects to build in permanent, defensible materials. The only significant exceptions were the religious buildings which embellished all the cities and towns, and the half-submerged *gudang* (godowns or warehouses) which merchants were permitted to build to contain their flammable cloth and other merchandise.

Fire was a constant threat in these wooden cities. Sudden conflagrations were reported to have consumed 800 houses in Aceh in 1602 and 8000 in 1688; 1260 in Makassar in 1614, and 10,000 in Ayutthaya in 1545, while most of Pattani was burned during a revolt in 1613. For European and Chinese merchants this was a source of endless anxiety, but Southeast Asians appear to have accepted the essential impermanence of their houses, and to have kept what wealth they had in removable gold, jewellery and cloth. After a fire, whole sections of the city would be rebuilt in a matter of three or four days.

THE NATURE OF SOUTHEAST ASIAN COMMERCE

One of the reasons for the relatively large population of Southeast Asian maritime cities was the need of merchants and sailors to spend several months in port selling their wares, buying a return cargo, and awaiting a change of monsoon. The very regular nature of the seasonal winds meant that the most important shipping routes—across the Bay of Bengal, the South China Sea, or the Java Sea—were made at the period of most favourable winds, so that there was at most a single return voyage per year. Chinese and Japanese ships arrived in Southeast Asia in January to March, and returned at the earliest the following August. In many cases they spent a year and a half in the south visiting several ports to gain the best return cargo. Hence the Southeast Asian cities at their peak season were thronged with visiting traders from all over Asia.

The most numerous of these were the sailors and travelling merchants who accompanied their own merchandise. The sailors on Southeast Asian ships were not paid (though some received a food ration), but they were allocated a section of the hold in which they could carry their own trade goods. The officers—the pilot (*malim*), master, boatswains and helmsmen— received a full *petak* (small partition), freemen sailors received half a *petak*, and only slave members of the crew had no share. Since the large trading ships of the region carried 60 to 100 crew members, these allocations could amount to as much as a quarter of the ship's capacity. The travelling merchants, referred to in the Malay Code by the Chinese-derived word *kiwi*, negotiated with the *nakhoda* (supercargo) the number of *petak* they would occupy, and their price.[37]

Because he either owned the ship or represented the owner on shipboard, the *nakhoda* was the key figure on trading voyages and the truest

---

[37] The only discussion of these issues in English is in M. A. P. Meilink-Roelofsz, *Asian Trade and European Influence in the Indonesian Archipelago between 1500 and about 1630*, The Hague, 1962, 36–59, which pioneered the use of the *Undang-undang Laut*—for which see Sir Richard Winstedt, ed., 'The Maritime Laws of Malacca' JMBRAS, 29, 3 (1956). Since her work, important Portuguese sources on Southeast Asian shipping around 1520 have come to light—Luis Filipe Thomaz, *De Malaca a Pegu. Viagens de um feitor Portugues (1512–1515)*, Lisbon, 1966; Geneviève Bouchon, 'Les premiers voyages portugais à Pegou (1515–1520)', *Archipel*, 18 (1979).

Southeast Asian entrepreneur. An excellent picture of his role is provided by the Malay Maritime Code (*Undang-undang Laut*). Drawn up in about 1500 by a group of Melaka *nakhodas* to guide the conduct of business, it naturally underlines the power of the *nakhoda* at sea. The code likened his power to that of the ruler on shore, having the life and death of sailors and passengers in his hands. On arrival at port, when the market was at its most favourable, the *nakhoda* had first right to sell his merchandise, four days before the *kiwis* and six days before the sailors. Besides his own merchandise or that belonging to the ship's owner whom he represented, the *nakhoda* was responsible for the substantial share of the cargo entrusted to him by home-based merchants.

A system of commenda trade was well developed, whereby merchants would send goods in another man's ship, either in the care of some of his agents, travelling as *kiwis*, or entrusted to the *nakhoda* for a fixed return. The system was described for Malay Melaka about 1510 in this way:

> If I am a merchant in Melaka and give you, the owner of the junk, a hundred cruzados of merchandise at the price then ruling in Melaka, assuming the risk myself, on the return [from Java] they give me a hundred and forty and nothing else, and the payment is made, according to the Melaka ordinance, forty-four days after the arrival of the junk in port.[38]

The term 'junk' (Portuguese *juncos*) used here was routinely applied by European, Chinese, Arab or Malay sources to the large Southeast Asian trading ship. The word itself entered European languages from Malay, but its origins probably lie in Javanese. From their arrival soon after 1500 Europeans used this term for a ship of 100 to 600 tonnes, carrying two to three masts and two oar-like rudders on either side of a pointed stern. From modern excavations of wrecks as well as contemporary descriptions we know that a very similar type of ship sailed throughout the waters of Southeast Asia and the South China Sea. In fact it has been suggested that it should be labelled a hybrid 'South China Sea' ship, because its construction by joining the planks of the hull with wooden dowels, and its double rudders, were common to all other types of boatbuilding in Southeast Asia, whereas the ships also used supplementary iron nails and clamps, cargo partitions and other features characteristic of China.[39]

In the fifteenth century, and probably for some time before that, there was sufficient interaction among Chinese, Javanese and Malay shipbuilders and traders to explain such hybrid patterns. Many Chinese took up residence in the ports of Southeast Asia and built their ships there, and even traders based in South China sometimes had ships built in Southeast Asia because of the better and cheaper woods. The busiest shipyards were in the Mon (Pegu) port of Martaban, and Mon traders often sold both ship and cargo in Melaka after a trading voyage from their homeland.

At the time of the Portuguese arrival, these junks of several hundred

---

[38] *Suma Oriental of Tomé Pires*, 284.
[39] Pierre-Yves Manguin, 'Relationship and Cross-influences between Southeast Asian and Chinese Shipbuilding Traditions', *Final Report, SPAFA Consultative Workshop on Maritime Shipping and Trade Networks in Southeast Asia*, Bangkok, 1984, 197–212.

Figure 8.2   Vessels of the Java coast, 1596, as depicted in Willem Lodewycksz's account of the first Dutch voyage to the East Indies. Left: a Javanese junk; right: a Chinese junk; background, a Javanese *prahu*; foreground: a fishing boat.

From Lodewycksz' account of the first Dutch voyage in *De eerste schipvaart der nederlanders naar Oost-Indie*, vol. I, The Hague, Nijhoff for the Linschoten-Vereeniging, 1915.

tonnes dominated Southeast Asian maritime trade, and equalled the Portuguese vessels in size. In the course of the sixteenth century, however, the Portuguese vessels grew larger while the junks grew smaller. At the time of the earliest Dutch descriptions around 1600 only a few of the rice ships taking bulk cargoes from Java to Melaka exceeded 200 tonnes. In most areas the pattern was already established of thousands of small craft of less than 40 tonnes dividing up the cargo. By the middle of the seventeenth century the term 'junk' was no longer being used by either Europeans or Asians for the small Southeast Asian vessels, but only for Chinese vessels which continued to be of several hundred tonnes. The only large vessels remaining in Southeast Asian hands were the few European-rigged ships which the rulers of Siam, Banten and Burma had built for their long-distance trade.

The disappearance of the junk is one of the more spectacular demonstrations of the decline of Southeast Asian involvement with large-scale trade. It is not difficult to understand in light of the havoc the Portuguese wrought in the 1510s amongst these slow-moving vessels. Such large but unwieldy ships were highly profitable in conditions of relative security, but the attacks which Malay and Javanese shipping had to undergo from the Portuguese and later the Dutch made military factors more important. For trade purposes, faster vessels with less capital at stake were preferred. The largest Southeast Asian vessels built after 1640 were the heavily-armed war galleys that played a major part in the military tactics of Aceh, east Indonesia, Borneo, the Philippines, Siam and Vietnam.

It was an age when commerce was far easier by water than by land, and the whole region was remarkably well provided with waterways. All the states of Southeast Asia had access either to the sea or a major river artery. Sailing vessels ascended the Irrawaddy all the way to Ava, while the Red River, the Mekong and the Chao Phraya were navigable as far as the capital cities of Vietnam, Cambodia and Siam respectively. The Khone falls provided a natural frontier between Cambodia and Laos, passable only by disembarking all passengers and cargo, but the several hundred kilometres of navigable river higher up the Mekong provided the essential artery for the kingdom of Laos, centred on Vientiane. By contrast with these river routes, road transport remained extremely slow and dangerous throughout Southeast Asia. The only exceptions were those roads of great military significance to important kingdoms, such as the fine road from Mataram to the sea near Semarang and some strategic routes near the Burmese capital. The most important routes for bullock-carts—from Vientiane to Ayutthaya, from northern Burma and Laos into Yunnan, and across the Malayan peninsula from Tenasserim—had to be travelled in caravans for safety, at the excruciatingly slow pace of the most dilapidated cart.

The financial system of Southeast Asia, as of India, owed much to brokers of Hindu commercial castes—the Gujerati *sharafs* and South Indian *chettiars*—whose networks spread to the major trading cities of the whole Indian Ocean littoral. They had a developed system of saleable letters of credit (*hundi* in Hindi), which could be issued in one city and cashed in another, including such ports as Melaka, Banten, or Aceh. These mercantile caste groups were in the first instance moneychangers, a highly necessary occupation in cities where a score of types of coin might be current, but they also operated as bankers and brokers for merchants. The first Florentine merchant to visit Melaka acknowledged with astonishment that the resident Gujerati merchants there were as capable in every respect as Italian bankers;[40] European merchants in unfamiliar ports generally had to make use of them to avoid being cheated.

In the large international cities of the region there was a reliable money-market, in which the ruler and leading officials often lent their capital to the big merchants. In seventeenth-century Siam, Pattani and Jambi the interest rates were very similar, about 2 per cent per month, while in Iskandar Muda's Aceh interest was reportedly kept by law as low as 12 per cent per annum. Such figures, almost as low as in contemporary European or Indian cities, suggest a dependable and sophisticated money market. However there are also numerous reports of rates of interest as high as 100 per cent per annum or more, suggesting that the lower rates represent a privileged urban network of trusted large-scale borrowers, in which some rulers and the European companies were included.

---

[40] Letter to fra Zuambatista in Florence, 31 January 1513, in Angelo de Gubernatis, *Storia dei Viaggiatori Italiani Nelle Indie Orientali*, Livorno, 1875, 375–7.

Not surprisingly, the Malay word for capital (*modal*) used in the flourishing commercial transactions of the sixteenth century was a Tamil borrowing, while other concepts such as bankruptcy (*muflis*) and usury (*riba*) were taken from the Arabic language and Islamic law. Nevertheless a much older concept of credit and debt was deeply ingrained throughout Southeast Asia, sometimes expressed through the imagery of interest as the flower (Malay *bunga*; Tai *dòk*) and the capital as the plant or tree. The Indian, Chinese and European merchants who found they could invest money in local shipping ventures or advance money against crops, appear to have been less concerned about defaulting than they would have been at home. 'Their laws for debt are so strict that the creditor may take his debtour, his wives, children and slaves, and all that he hath and sell them for his debt.'[41] This was not because of sophisticated financial institutions, but rather the ingrained assumption that debt implied obligation, and particularly the obligation to labour. In every state of Southeast Asia, and even in the stateless tribal societies of the hills, defaulting debtors became the slaves of their creditors, obliged to serve them until the principal was repaid. Such slavery was not viewed as calamitous. On the contrary, every loan taken out already implied some form of obligation to the creditor, whose readiness to issue it implied a readiness to accept the borrower as a dependant. Some debts were contracted deliberately in order to become the dependant of a powerful figure, perhaps thereby escaping some more onerous obligation—for example of corvée due to the king.

The commercialization which undoubtedly marked the sixteenth and seventeenth centuries appears to have accentuated the importance of bondage of this type as the basis of labour obligations. The law codes originating from this period are certainly much concerned with slaves as the most important (and most legally complex) form of property. In the cities in particular, observers wrote as if the majority of the population were slaves and all manual work was done by them. This was true in the sense that there was no free labour market, and those who wanted work done had either to purchase slaves or to hire them from others. Much of the heaviest construction work, building forts, irrigation canals and palaces, was performed by captives regarded as slaves of the victorious king.

On the other hand bondage was not regarded as a pariah status except when it was associated with foreign, 'barbarous' captives, such as newly captured peoples from the hills or the easternmost islands. Even such low-status captives were quickly assimilated into the dominant population, because there was no state-backed legal system that set out to ensure that their slave status was permanent. Although slavery is an inescapable term for those newly captured or bought, because it correctly conveys the fact that they could be transferred without their will to another owner by sale, gift, or inheritance, it must be emphasized that this was an 'open' system of slavery which people moved in and out of almost imperceptibly. As was said of seventeenth-century Aceh: 'neither can a Stranger easily know who

---

[41] E. Scott, 'An exact Discourse . . . of the East Indians', 1606, in *The Voyage of Sir Henry Middleton to the Moluccas 1604–1606*, ed. William Foster, London: Hakluyt Society, 1943, 173.

is a Slave and who not amongst them; for they are all, in a manner, Slaves to one another.'[42]

Since traders from outside the region undoubtedly stimulated the boom in Southeast Asian commerce and contributed much to the life of the mercantile cities, the question may be asked how far commercialization and capitalist forms of exchange and production were simply alien enclaves in Southeast Asia, with as little effect on the surrounding societies as European capital had in the 'dualistic' colonial economies of the nineteenth century. Chinese technology, weights and coins, Indian financial methods, Islamic commercial laws, and European technology and capital, all played a major part in creating the character of Southeast Asian urban and commercial life in this period.

The first point to be made here is that 'foreignness' was an undoubted asset for entrepreneurs in the region. There are numerous examples of the jealousy rulers felt towards their own subjects who became so wealthy that they appeared to pose a threat to the king himself. There were very few institutional curbs on the autocratic power of rulers to confiscate such private wealth. Foreigners were at an advantage in being both outside the local power system and able to move to another port in case of mistreatment from the ruler. Wealthy foreign merchants who remained for a number of years in one port naturally became influential, and might be drawn into the administration of commerce as *syahbandar* (harbourmasters), or even in some cases as virtual prime ministers or chancellors of the realm. In such cases they were useful to the ruler because of their knowledge of foreign merchants, their military skills, and above all their inability, as foreigners, to challenge the position of the king. When such figures or their descendants became so fully enmeshed in court affairs that they were no longer seen as foreign, like the Tamil-descended *bendaharas* in Melaka or the Persian-descended Bunnags in Siam, they were no longer immune from the periodic jealousy or wrath of the king.

However, these 'foreign' traders in any given port always included substantial numbers of Southeast Asians. In Melaka before the Portuguese conquest Javanese and 'Luzons' (Islamized Tagalogs) were among the largest-scale traders and shipowners. After the fall of Melaka its Malayized population of polyglot origins spread around the ports of Southeast Asia, so that 'Malays' (Muslim Malay-speakers) became a major element among the merchants of Banten (and later Dutch Batavia), Makassar, Cambodia and Siam, as well as in Malay ports such as Pattani, Pahang and Brunei. The Mons of Pegu (southern Burma) were shipowners and merchants in many of the ports on the eastern side of the Indian Ocean. The Dutch described the mix of merchants that greeted them in Banten in 1596 as follows:

> The Persians, who are called Khorasans in Java, are those who usually earn their living in [precious] stones and medicines . . . The Arabs and Pegus [Mons] are the ones who mostly conduct their trade by sea, carrying and bringing merchandise from one city to another, and buying up much Chinese

[42] William Dampier, *Voyages and Discoveries*, 1699, reprinted London, 1929, 98.

merchandise, which they exchange against other wares from the surrounding islands, and also pepper, against the time when the Chinese return to buy. The Malays and Klings [South Indians] are merchants who invest money at interest and in voyages and bottomry. The Gujeratis, since they are poor, are usually used as sailors, and are those who take money in bottomry, on which they often make one, two and three times profit.[43]

This picture indicates the importance of internationally-connected minority groups in Southeast Asia, as in Europe, in the early modern period. Not every group filled such roles, to be sure. There is little evidence of ethnic Burmans, Tais, Khmers or Vietnamese doing business outside their own regions, or taking to the sea on trading expeditions. If they did so, they presumably reclassified themselves as Malays, Chinese or Mons and associated with the urban enclaves of these groups. Ethnicity was probably as much a consequence as a cause of entrepreneurial minority status. Every major city had one or more quarters where traders congregated, designated as the 'Javanese', 'Malay', 'Chinese', 'Kling' or 'Portuguese' quarter, but traders who did not seem to qualify in terms of descent were assimilated in functional terms and perhaps eventually in language. When the Dutch arrived at the Cambodian capital to trade in 1636, for example, they were faced with five *syahbandar*, one each to look after the commercial interests of the Portuguese, Malay-Javanese and Japanese quarters, and two for the Chinese quarters. They chose the Japanese *syahbandar* since they were on their way to Japan, and lodged in that quarter.[44]

In considering the ways in which Southeast Asians responded to the commercialization of the 'long sixteenth-century boom', the role of women cannot be ignored. Commerce and marketing were considered predominantly the business of women by all Southeast Asian societies, as to a lesser extent they still are in rural areas. Foreign traders were surprised to find themselves doing business with women, not only in the market-place but also in large-scale transactions. Women frequently travelled on trading ships, to the surprise of Europeans, Chinese and Indians alike. While for males of high status it was considered demeaning to haggle over prices, at least in one's home territory, women had no such inhibitions. The business concerns of powerful men were typically managed by their wives.

For all but the most aristocratic and the most Islamic women, there was also a tolerant attitude towards marriages of convenience with foreign traders. In the busiest ports, therefore, traders in town to await the next monsoon frequently formed a sexual and commercial partnership with a local woman. Sometimes the relationship endured for many years, and many separate voyages by the foreign trader; sometimes it ended with his departure. There was no stigma preventing the woman contracting a subsequent marriage. From the commercial point of view these relationships gave foreign traders an enormous advantage in marketing their goods and obtaining the local knowledge they needed.

---

[43] W. Lodewycksz, 1598, in *De eerste Schipvaart der Nederlanders naar Oost-Indië onder Cornelis de Houtman*, ed. G. P. Rouffaer and J. W. Ijzerman, The Hague, Linschoten-Vereniging, 1915–29, I. 120–1.

[44] Muller, *Oost-Indische Compagnie*, 63–4.

Most part of the Strangers who trade thither [in Pegu], marry a wife for the Term they stay . . . They prove obedient and obliging wives, and take the management of affairs within doors wholly in their own hands. She goes to market for food, and acts the cook in dressing the victuals, takes care of his clothes, in washing and mending them; if their husbands have any goods to sell, they set up a shop and sell them by retail, to a much better account than they could be sold for by wholesale, and some of them carry a cargo of goods to the inland towns, and barter for goods proper for the foreign markets that their husbands are bound to, and generally bring fair accounts of their negotiations.[45]

The local women who made the most advantageous unions of this type occupied very strategic commercial positions. A woman of Mon descent in Ayutthaya, Soet Pegu, was able virtually to monopolize Dutch–Thai trade in the 1640s through her relationships with successive Dutch factors in the city, who in turn could not do without her access to the Thai élite.

In sum, there was a very marked commercialization of Southeast Asian life between the fifteenth and the seventeenth centuries. A large proportion of the population was drawn into the international market economy to some extent, and affected by its ups and downs. There were sophisticated methods for investing capital in trade and securing an adequate return on it. Southeast Asia differed markedly from early modern Europe, however, in its relative lack of legal security for capital and fixed property in private hands, as against the power of the state.

THE STATE AND COMMERCE

With the notable exception of the northern Vietnamese polity under the Le and the Trinh, which deliberately emphasized agriculture at the expense of commerce, all Southeast Asian states sought to woo international trade. As Melaka's illustrious Sultan Mansur wrote in 1468, 'We have learned that to master the blue oceans people must engage in commerce and trade, even if their countries are barren . . . Life has never been so affluent in preceding generations as it is today.'[46] Because no one state could expect to monopolize the countless waterways through which international shipping passed, ports typically competed with each other to attract trade by means of an open-door policy. The arrival of European trading enterprises, much more monolithic in the East than at home and anxious to use their military superiority to secure a monopolistic position in the market, put this free-trading policy under severe strains. Most rulers saw the dangers of succumbing to such pressures, and offered ringing declarations of the freedom of commerce: the ruler of Pidië (north Sumatra) told the Portuguese 'that his port was ever a free one where any man could come and go in safety'; his counterpart in Makassar a century later reproved the Dutch:

[45] Alexander Hamilton, *A New Account of the East Indies*, 1727, new edn, London, 1930, II. 28.
[46] Letter to King of Ryukyu, 1 September 1468, in Atsushi Kobata and Mitsugo Matsuda, *Ryukyuan Relations with Korea and South Sea Countries*, Kyoto, 1969, 111.

'God made the land and the sea; the land he divided among men and the sea he gave in common. It has never been heard that anyone should be forbidden to sail the seas.'

Impositions on trade and traders once they reached port were another matter. Trade offered a rich source of revenue, both public and private, but there was always the danger of squeezing it so hard that it was driven elsewhere. Where formal duties were fixed and regular, they fluctuated between 5 and 10 per cent on both imports and exports. Port officials met incoming ships in the roads and permitted cargo to come ashore only after its value for customs purposes had been determined. Only very occasionally were favoured groups (such as the English in Makassar) exempted from duties in return for some other service to the ruler. In every case, however, gifts had to be made to the king, the chief minister, and the *syahbandar*, as well as to numerous other influential figures in the state and port administration.

It is virtually impossible to assess the extent or even the proportion of revenues flowing to rulers through trade in its various forms. Much state revenue was in kind—the most striking case being the corvée owed to the rulers of Burma and Siam by their male subjects for up to half their total working time. In terms of the more convenient, disposable revenue in money, however, trade in one form or another appears to have provided the bulk of royal revenues in the first half of the seventeenth century except in Vietnam and perhaps Burma. Revenue flowed not only from the customs dues and associated charges. There were also royal monopolies on many of the most lucrative export items, tolls on internal trade, taxes on markets, and the personal trade of the ruler himself aided by his privileged position. Rulers often insisted that traders buy from them at exalted prices before being given access to the market.

It was alleged by indignant European traders that the practice of escheat, whereby the ruler inherited the property of both subjects and foreigners who died without heirs in his dominions, brought untold wealth to covetous rulers. While the practice undoubtedly existed, they probably exaggerated its importance. In Siam, Laos and Burma it appeared to be understood that the king was entitled to reclaim at the death of officials the property they had amassed in official service, but in practice only one-third usually went to the Crown, one-third or more to the heirs, and the rest to funeral expenses. The estates of foreigners dying in sixteenth-century Pegu were divided between the Crown, which took one-third, and the heirs, 'and there hath never been any deceit or fraud used in this matter'.[47] In the Islamic states it was rather a question of whether there were male heirs, without which all the estate could be forfeit. The more autocratic rulers such as Sultan Iskandar Muda of Aceh (r. 1607–36) undoubtedly enriched themselves by executing wealthy traders and subjects and confiscating their assets. Overall, however, this cannot have represented a substantial proportion of royal revenues.

---

[47] 'The Voyage and Travel of M. Caesar Fredericke', in Richard Hakluyt, ed., *The Principal Navigations, Voyages, Traffiques and Discoveries of the English Nation*, London, Everyman's edn, 1907, III. 268.

The cosmopolitan character of Southeast Asian cities meant that a wide array of coins was exchanged in the marketplace, as well as gold and silver by weight. The importance of Chinese demand in stimulating the commercial upturn is indicated by the vast influx of Chinese cash, beginning in the fourteenth century but much accelerating in the fifteenth and sixteenth. These were cheap copper coins with a hole in the middle, designed to be strung together in lots of 200, 600 or 6000 for ease of handling. In the late sixteenth century the outflow of such coins became so great that lead began to be substituted. Around 1500 these Chinese coins were already the principal currency used in the markets of Melaka, Java, Brunei and Maluku. Similar copper coins were minted in northern Vietnam for use there, as tin ones were in fifteenth-century Melaka and lead ones in seventeenth-century Aceh. In Siam and coastal Burma they did not play the same role because cowrie shells were accepted as a convenient low-denomination substitute.

Most rulers also issued their own higher coinage of gold or silver. In the Muslim states of the archipelago the small gold *mas* was the principal coin minted—by the north Sumatran kingdom of Pasai from the fourteenth century, and in the seventeenth by Aceh, Pattani, Makassar and Kedah. It was usually about a thousand cash or a quarter of a Spanish silver real in value. On the mainland silver was more important, in standard weights of a *tikal* (about 14 grams), known locally as a *kyat* in Burma and a *baht* in Siam. In Burma this was simply a standard weight of silver, which in the seventeenth century gradually replaced the previously standard heavy lumps of *ganza*, a copper-lead alloy. In Siam a cylinder of silver was bent into a kidney shape and stamped, halfway to becoming a true coin.

The increasingly complex tasks of government in dealing with the international trade of their ports, the influx of foreign ideas, the adoption of firearms and the need to confront formidable European trading companies, all called for more centralized and co-ordinated state structures. The loosely-integrated states of Southeast Asia had to develop larger and more sophisticated bureaucracies, codified and predictable legal systems, and professional armies, if they were to survive this robust period of competitive expansion. To some extent we can perceive such trends.

The writing of the Melaka legal codes in the reign of Sultan Mahmud (1488–1511), for example, was an explicit response to the needs of a polyglot commercially-oriented population for security of property and predictability of legal decisions in commercial matters. This code was copied and extended during the sixteenth and seventeenth centuries in other Malayo-Muslim centres such as Aceh, Pahang, Pattani and Kedah. In seventeenth-century Aceh there were four distinct courts sitting regularly, one dealing with offences against Islamic law; one with questions of debt and inheritance; one with theft, murder and other disputes; and the fourth with commercial disputes between merchants. The development of such courts in the Muslim sultanates drew on Islamic law not only in religious questions but also in order to deal with many novel problems in the commercial area. The trend towards ever heavier borrowing from Islamic models reached its peak in Aceh during the brief reign of Sultan Iskandar Thani (1637–41), when the ancient practice of trial by ordeal was ended in favour of the witnesses countenanced by Islam. The mid-seventeenth century also marked a high point in the application of Islamic law in Banten and Makassar.

Two contemporary fifteenth-century rulers, Paramatrailokanat in Siam (1448–88) and Le Thanh Ton in Vietnam (1460–97), were energetic centralizers who promulgated or codified laws which sought to assign every stratum of their subjects to their appointed place in a bureaucratically-organized and harmonious polity. Officials were allotted fixed areas of land in accordance with rank, as a remuneration which they lost at dismissal or death. Subsequent kings in both countries allowed centres of personal power to arise again and become hereditary, but both these states retained at least a theory of centralized bureaucratic rule in advance of their neighbours. With the much greater financial and military resources available to King Narai of Ayutthaya (r. 1656–88), the Thai state then impressed even visitors from Louis XIV's France as a model of authoritarian rule:

> All the officials can be made destitute at the pleasure of the prince who established them, he deposes them as he pleases; . . . in the distribution of responsibilities they pay most attention to the merits, the experience and the services that one has given, and not to birth; which ensures that everyone applies himself to earning the favour of the prince.[48]

In the early seventeenth century there were more widespread indications of bureaucratic development. In Burma Anaukpetlun (r. 1606–28) and Thalun (r. 1629–48) replaced princes by lower-ranking *myó-wun* (town governors) as provincial authorities, and also had them watched by centrally appointed military commissioners and 'royal spies'. In Aceh under Iskandar Muda hereditary rulers were replaced by ministeriales, recalled every three years, as governors of outlying districts on the west coast of Sumatra. In seventeenth-century Makassar a hierarchy was developed to supervise the work for military and state purposes of craftsmen of different types, while a unique court diary was begun to record the important decisions and events at the centre of the realm. In a number of states—notably Burma, both north and south Vietnam, Siam, and Aceh— the core of a professional army was established, with regular training and pay.

In fact the early seventeenth century saw a clear trend towards state absolutism, most marked in those Southeast Asian states which survived as vigorous trade centres into the mid-seventeenth century—Ayutthaya, Aceh, Banten, Makassar. Some of the causes of this trend were common to the 'age of absolutism' in other parts of the world, notably the introduction of firearms and heavily-armed ships, usually monopolized by the king, and the new wealth flowing from control of the port. Others were more specific: the aggressive approach to trade of the Europeans, forcing Muslim traders to seek powerful protectors against the Portuguese and Spanish, and all free traders to seek protection against the Verenigde Oost-Indische Compagnie (VOC, the Dutch East India Company); the growing

[48] M. de Bourges, *Relation du Voyage de Monseigneur L'evêque de Beryte*, Paris, 1666, 1581–9.

trend towards monopolistic trading arrangements, largely stimulated by the Dutch; and the use by rulers of the (always ambivalent) influence of the universalist religions to break free of traditional constraints on power.

In the heightened competitiveness of the seventeenth century, it seems as though the needs of trade for security and for freedom proved ultimately irreconcilable. On the one hand those pluralistic societies most congenial to competitive trade were the first to fall before the European onslaught—Melaka to the Portuguese in 1511 and Banda to the Dutch in 1621. On the other hand the more absolutist states which arose in reaction to this pressure sooner or later fell prey to excesses of personal power which destroyed or alienated the important shipowners and capitalists.

The sultanate of Aceh oscillated revealingly between these two dangers, and is especially interesting because it was the most important Southeast Asian port to survive the seventeenth century without major European intervention in its affairs. In the 1580s, if we can believe subsequent French reports, Aceh was dominated by a group of merchant oligarchs, the *orang kaya*, who had 'beautiful, large, solid houses, with cannons at their doors, and a large number of slaves'[49]—a situation not unlike Melaka in 1511 or Banten at the arrival of the Dutch in 1596. The ruler from 1589 to 1604, Sultan Ala'ud-din Ri'ayat Syah al-Mukammil, and his powerful grandson Iskandar Muda, saw these *orang kaya* as a critical danger and suppressed them ruthlessly. The new élite was tightly controlled by the requirement for constant attendance at the palace, a professional praetorian guard composed of foreigners, and a prohibition on building in brick or stone. Even so they continued to be terrorized by the king. In 1634 thirty-four of the leading men were castrated, mutilated or flogged for an alleged breach of palace etiquette. Iskandar Muda had kept the foreign threat at bay, but only by cowing his subjects and concentrating trade in his own hands. Consequently, after his death and that of his short-lived successor and son-in-law, the surviving *orang kaya* opted for a female ruler. Not once but four times in succession, between 1641 and 1699, this 'verandah of Mecca', as the sultanate liked to call itself, put a woman on the throne, as effective power passed progressively to an oligarchy of merchant-officials. Their régime was relatively benign, orderly and encouraging to commerce, but it lost the contest with the Dutch for the control of those former dependencies which produced the pepper and tin on which Acehnese prosperity had been based. In the long run, neither approach was able to prevent a gradual decline.

In Siam, Banten, Makassar, Jambi and Banjarmasin, the third quarter of the seventeenth century saw a steady expansion of royal monopolies, as rulers tried to cope with a less favourable economic climate and constant military threats. Foreign traders were restricted more and more to buying from the king and his agents, at prices above the market rates. Royal fleets were updated with European and Chinese help, and constituted the last challenge to European predominance in the large-scale shipping trade. In Sulawesi the dualism between the twin kingdoms of Gowa and Tallo

[49] Augustin de Beaulieu, 'Memoire du Voyage aux Indes Orientales', 110–11, in M. Thévenot, *Relations de divers voyages curieux*, Paris, 1664–6.

which had been at the heart of Makassar's thriving 'open society' was largely abandoned by Sultan Hasanuddin (1654–69). The pressures of the period were making it very difficult for open societies to continue to flourish, yet the more centralized régimes which replaced them were themselves brittle and full of embittered potential defectors.

A SEVENTEENTH-CENTURY CRISIS

Europeans came to Asia in pursuit of the spices popular in their home markets. They made it their business to use what military advantage they had to try to monopolize this trade. The Portuguese conquered Melaka in 1511 because it seemed to be the single port at which the whole of the Southeast Asian export trade was concentrated. 'The trade and commerce between the different nations for a thousand leagues on every hand must come to Malacca . . . Whoever is lord of Malacca has his hands at the throat of Venice.'[50] Yet the Portuguese incursion did no more than temporarily disrupt and dislocate Southeast Asian trade, dispersing the commerce and the merchants of Melaka to half a dozen different ports. The Portuguese could not in the long run impose a monopoly of any product; they became one more strand in the complex fabric of Southeast Asian commerce.

The Dutch onslaught on the key points of the spice trade was far more sustained and effective. The VOC was one of the most advanced capitalist institutions produced by seventeenth-century Europe, and proved able to operate as the world's first global commercial enterprise, sending six or more ships to the East every year and operating a world-wide trading network based on a number of key strongholds. First among these was Batavia, taken from its Javanese occupants in 1619 and defended definitively against a major Javanese counter-attack in 1629. The Company seized and depopulated Banda in 1621, repeopling this source of the world's nutmeg with slave-owning Dutch planters who delivered all their product to the VOC. The cloves of Maluku were more widely dispersed and took longer to monopolize, but the Dutch had succeeded by 1656 in destroying all the clove trees except those in the Ambon area which they directly controlled. They proceeded to conquer three of the crucial Southeast Asian entrepôts—Portuguese Melaka in 1641, Makassar in 1666–9 and Banten in 1682. Meanwhile Aceh had never recovered militarily from its disastrous failure before Portuguese Melaka in 1629, and the lengthy blockade by the Dutch in the 1650s deprived it of its control of Perak tin and west Sumatran pepper. Most other Indonesian trading cities were forced into monopolistic arrangements with the VOC by 1680. The Japanese decision in 1639 to refuse access to its market and its minerals to any but the Dutch and Chinese gave the Company great advantages in numerous other Asian ports.

---

[50] *Suma Oriental of Tomé Pires*, 286–7.

Figure 8.3   The first Dutch lodge at Banda Nera, to which the Bandanese brought nutmeg for sale. The nutmeg was weighed in units of a *kati* against cloth and other trade goods.

From *De tweede schipvaart der nederlanders naar Oost-Indie*, vol. II, The Hague, Nijhoff for the Linschoten-Vereeniging, 1940.

The retreat of Southeast Asian trade has usually been explained in terms of these military and economic successes of the Dutch. It should also be seen, however, against the background of the crisis facing most of the economically advanced world in the period between 1620 and about 1680. In Europe, Turkey and China, in particular, this period clearly marked the end of the 'long sixteenth-century boom', and was characterized by declining prices, crop failures, a stagnation or decline in population, especially urban population, and a series of major political crises—of which the collapse of the Ming dynasty in China, the religious wars in Germany and the English revolution were the most spectacular.

The most global explanation of this 'general crisis' is also the least understood—that is, the gradual decline in solar activity and in temperatures during the seventeenth century, which reached its nadir in many parts of the northern hemisphere in about 1690 before the modern warming trend began. Evidence has been mounting to link this cooling with reduced rainfall and crop failures in the northern hemisphere, and perhaps therefore with the mid-seventeenth century dip in population.

If this 'little ice age' affected the humid tropics at all, it was by reducing rainfall as a result of the larger share of the planet's water locked up in the polar ice caps, and by increasing the variability of weather. In Southeast Asia the only long-term index of rainfall is Berlage's remarkable series of tree-rings from the teak forests of east-central Java, which provides relative

rainfall levels for every year between 1514 and 1929.[51] This shows the
period 1600–79 to be below the long-term norms for rainfall in Java, and
very markedly the worst substantial period in the whole series. In particular the period 1645–72 has not a single year reaching 'normal' modern
levels of rainfall. If this phenomenon was more widespread than Java, the
effect would have been most dramatic in lengthening the dry season
dangerously in those areas of eastern Indonesia and the Philippines where
survival depends on a delicate balance of wet and dry seasons. There may
also have been crop failures in areas which depended on river flooding for
their annual rice planting.

A number of famines and epidemics were reported in the seventeenth
century, with epidemics killing substantial proportions of the population
in parts of Java in 1625–6 and of Siam in 1659. Probably the worst epidemic
of the century occurred in 1665, affecting many parts of Indonesia extremely
severely. The fact that 1664 and 1665 were the two driest years in the whole
of Berlage's 400-year series of Java tree-rings suggests that climate may
indeed have had a significant effect in increasing mortality, presumably by
a combination of crop failures and inadequate supplies of clean drinking
water.

The only two substantial areas of Southeast Asia for which continuous
population counts are available, the Spanish Philippines and the Dutch-
controlled Ambon area of Maluku, both reveal a very significant drop in
population in the mid-seventeenth century. Spanish counts of *tributos*
in Luzon and the Visayas, from whom they claimed labour and tax,
showed a spectacular drop from 166,900 in 1591 to 108,000 in 1655, before
beginning a rapid rise. In Ambon and the adjacent Lease Islands, which
the Dutch controlled tightly as their centre for clove cultivation, the
population also dropped progressively from 41,000 in 1634 to a minimum
of 34,000 in 1674. While wars and problems of accurate recording have
been advanced to explain each of these population declines, the coincidence of the two series points to the need for a broader climatic or
economic explanation.[52]

If climate was unkind to Southeast Asia in this period, the international
economic environment was even more so. The general decline in prices in
Europe and Asia was reflected in Southeast Asian export products. Pepper,
the largest of these, sold in Indonesian ports for eight or nine reals per
pikul on average throughout the period 1617–50 but then dropped precipitately, so that the Dutch usually paid less than four reals in the 1670s and
1680s. The amount of Japanese and American silver reaching Asia was at a
long-term peak in the 1620s; thereafter the decline was spectacular in the
two sources going directly to Southeast Asia. Japanese silver exports
dropped from as much as 150 tonnes a year in the 1620s to only one-third
of that amount by the 1640s, while the Spanish 'Manila galleons' from
Acapulco in the period 1640–1700 never carried even a half the 23 tonnes of
silver a year they had averaged in the 1620s. Even the Dutch and English,

---

[51] Conveniently set out in H. H. Lamb, *Climate: Present, Past and Future*, London, 1977, II. 603–4.
[52] The climatic and population data are more fully set out in Anthony Reid, 'The Seventeenth
Century Crisis in Southeast Asia', MAS, 24, 4 (1990).

the 'winners' of the seventeenth-century crisis, took somewhat less bullion to the East in the middle of the century than they had in the 1620s.

Although most sections of the world economy faltered in the mid-seventeenth century, Southeast Asia was especially hard hit because its share in world trade dropped markedly. The imports of Manila averaged 564,000 pesos in value per year throughout the peak period 1616–45, but only 218,000 per year in 1651–70.[53] International competition for the products of the region was at its peak in the 1620s, when pepper and Maluku spices accounted for more than half of the value of Dutch, English and Portuguese imports from Asia, while much of the trade between China and Japan also took place in Southeast Asian ports. In the second half of the century Indian cloth and indigo became the most important Asian exports to Europe, and Maluku spices and pepper began to fall in volume as well as price. Most serious of all, the monopoly established by the VOC in Maluku, and its dominance in other major ports of the region, greatly diminished the extent of price competition among buyers. All the profits of handling clove and nutmeg now flowed to the Company, where once they had invigorated a string of Asian ports from Ternate to Suez.

The effect of this reduction in export revenue was apparent in the declining ability to buy imported Indian cloth in the latter part of the century. Although the Dutch gained a steadily increasing share of the Southeast Asian market for Indian cloth, especially through their near-monopoly in many Indonesian ports, the VOC was selling 20 per cent less in Indonesia in 1703 than in 1652.[54] VOC sales to Indonesian vessels visiting Batavia to buy Indian cloth dropped more precipitately, by 43 per cent between 1665–9 and 1679–81, and even more rapidly in the sub-sequent twenty years.[55] Since Gujerati, English and Portuguese trade declined much more drastically after the 1620s, there is no doubt that Southeast Asian consumption of Indian cloth dropped dramatically. This is borne out by the statements of Dutch officials in the last three decades of the seventeenth century, who complained that Southeast Asians were no longer buying the expensive imported cloth because they simply could not afford it. Instead they revived their own cotton-growing and weaving:

> since these countries flourished more formerly than now, most of these peoples sought Coromandel and Surat cloths [for everyday use], not as luxuries, and gave large amounts of money for that . . . Now most of the surrounding [Indonesian] countries are empoverished, and the [Coromandel] Coast and Surat cloths have become limited to the use of the wealthy.[56]

As prices for export products dropped and Dutch military pressures mounted on all who grew spices and pepper, there was also a reaction

---

[53] Calculated from Pierre Chaunu, *Les Philippines et le Pacifique des Ibériques (XVIe, XVIIe, XVIIIe siècles)*, Paris 1960, 78, 82.

[54] I owe this figure to Ruurdje Laarhoven, who has calculated that in 1652–3 the VOC sold 314,039 pieces of Indian cloth in Indonesia, and in 1703–4, 256,458 pieces.

[55] Combining the data in Gabriel Rantoandro, 'Commerce et Navigation dans les Mers de l'Insulinde d'après les *Dagh-Register* de Batavia (1624–1682)', *Archipel*, 35 (1988) 61, and those for Java only in Luc Nagtegaal, 'Rijden op een Hollandse Tijger. De noordkust van Java en de V.O.C. 1680–1743', Ph.D. thesis, Utrecht University, 1988, 181–2.

[56] Governor-General and Council report of 1693, in Coolhaas, *Generale Missiven*, 5. 639.

against cash-cropping. Each time a port was blockaded by the VOC in pursuit of a trade advantage, the inhabitants had no choice but to cultivate rice and other food crops in place of pepper. Where the Dutch succeeded in gaining the upper hand, pepper growers and dealers were forced to deliver at uneconomic prices. Even in some of the court poetry of the late seventeenth and early eighteenth centuries we find evidence of this disenchantment with the instability and ultimate ruin brought about by pepper-cultivation:

> Let people nowhere in this country plant pepper, as is done in Jambi and Palembang. Perhaps those countries grow pepper for the sake of money, in order to grow wealthy. There is no doubt that in the end they will go to ruin.[57]

The most dramatic long-term setback to Southeast Asian commerce cannot be attributed directly to the change in the international commercial or climatic environment, since it occurred at the beginning of the seventeenth century when other indicators were still booming. This was the virtual destruction of the base areas of two of the most dynamic actors in the region's maritime commerce—the Mons of Pegu and the Javanese of the *pasisir* (Java's north coast). Under the disastrous rule of Nandabayin (1581–99), the great wealth of Pegu and its ports in the Bay of Bengal was dissipated in ruinous campaigns to retain the overextended empire of his predecessor, Bayinnaung. In 1599 the city of Pegu finally fell before an alliance of Toungoo and Arakan, and both armies took home all that was moveable of the remaining population and wealth of the coastal region. The king of Arakan left behind one of his Portuguese mercenary captains, Felipe de Brito, to command the most important port of the region at Syriam. De Brito, however, fortified himself in the port and until 1613 held it as an independent city-state with a little help from the Portuguese in Goa. During this period trade with the interior appears to have almost ceased, and the control of the lucrative routes across the peninsula to the Gulf of Thailand to have passed to Siam and its Indian Muslim factors. Mon traders, who had been found in considerable numbers in Melaka, Aceh and Banten in the sixteenth century, ceased to travel significantly by sea.

The thriving ports of Java's north coast had exported Javanese rice and other foodstuffs throughout the archipelago, in exchange for Indian cloth from Aceh and Melaka and spices from Banda and Maluku. The systematic Dutch attempt to cut these commercial arteries to ensure their own dominance in Maluku and the isolation of Portuguese Melaka must have undermined these ports to some extent. In particular the VOC destroyed the shipping of Jepara in 1618 and burned most of the town. However, the major threat to the *pasisir* towns, as to the Mon ports in Burma, came from the interior. Sultan Agung of Mataram (r. 1613–46) was determined to establish a united polity centred on his capital near modern Yogyakarta. He conquered and devastated Lasem in 1616, Tuban in 1619, and the flourishing complex of Surabaya, Gresik and Sedayu in 1623–5. Agung

---

[57] J. J. Ras, *Hikajat Bandjar: A Study in Malay Historiography*, The Hague, 1968, 330.

himself was little interested in trade, except to the extent of monopolizing rice exports through Jepara as a political weapon against the Dutch. His successor, Amangkurat I (r. 1646–77), was bent on the destruction of all commerce not under his own control, since it could lead to potential opposition. Javanese traders of course transferred their operations to other centres such as Banjarmasin, Banten, Palembang, Pattani and Makassar, where they tended to assimilate to the 'Malay' community. In their homeland of east and central Java, however, it was reported in 1677 that the Javanese, 'besides their great ignorance at sea, were now completely lacking in vessels of their own'.[58]

EUROPEANS, CHINESE, AND THE ORIGINS OF DUALISM

The period 1400–1630 was one of economic expansion, in which Southeast Asia became an integral part of a dynamic system of world trade, and changed rapidly to incorporate new commercial techniques and social attitudes. Chinese, Indian and Arab traders married and settled within the maritime kingdoms of the region, and were part of the process of rapid borrowing and innovation which marks this period. To a somewhat lesser extent, even the Portuguese continued this tradition, as the numerous Portuguese or Eurasians who served Pegu, Arakan, Makassar and other states as soldiers, traders and technicians bear witness. The crisis which followed in the middle of the seventeenth century, however, drove a much deeper wedge between Europeans and Chinese on the one side and Southeast Asians on the other.

The Portuguese were in theory servants of their king in a way Asian traders had never been. In practice, however, the Crown could never control or pay all the Portuguese in the East, and still less the varied group of their descendants. In the ports which the Crown tenuously controlled, it badly needed the military support of locally domiciled Portuguese, and therefore encouraged them to marry Asian women, to settle within the walls as *casados*, and to gain their own livelihood through private trade— usually in partnership with Asians.

In the second half of the sixteenth century, therefore, the Portuguese behaved in most Southeast Asian ports very much like Asian traders. By contrast the Spanish in the Philippines, and still more the servants of the VOC everywhere, were relatively carefully controlled and centrally paid. After a tentative experiment in allowing Dutch private trade on the Portuguese model, this was forbidden in 1632 and in numerous subsequent decrees. Of course many Dutchmen married locally and produced a mestizo community of descendants, but these identified with the VOC and very seldom served or inhabited indigenous states. Moreover these states in turn were changing. Outward-looking port-dominated kingdoms like Makassar, Banten, or King Narai's Ayutthaya, where European languages and Arabic were widely spoken and ideas eagerly exchanged, had no successors after they fell in the period between 1669 and 1688. Subsequent

[58] Cited B. Schrieke, *Indonesian Sociological Studies*, The Hague, 1955, I. 79.

régimes were less involved with international exchange, less cosmopolitan, and therefore less in touch with 'modern' developments.

Indian and West Asian traders were among those who lost out in the crisis period. Turks, Persians and Arabs virtually ceased travelling 'below the winds' with the collapse of the spice route from Aceh to the Red Sea in the first two decades of the seventeenth century. Gujeratis continued to bring their cloth to Aceh until about 1700, though in much reduced numbers after the Dutch onslaught on Aceh's tin and pepper resources in the 1650s. Chulia Muslims from the Coromandel coast of Tamil Nadu were the only major group of Asians from 'above the winds' who continued their trade into the eighteenth century, and they too were losing out to European traders during that period. The primary reason was that the reduced amount of Indian cloth being consumed by Southeast Asia in the latter part of the century was now being carried primarily by Europeans, from the factories and fortresses which the Dutch, Portuguese, English, French and Danes established throughout the Indian cloth-exporting regions.

The only sector of the long-distance trade in Asia in which the Europeans failed to establish themselves was that to China. Apart from the Portuguese enclave at Macao, a minor factor in most periods, Europeans were resolutely refused access to the Middle Kingdom to trade. Even when Canton (Guangzhou) was finally opened to them in 1685, discriminatory tariffs against European-rigged ships ensured that Chinese junks continued to carry the overwhelming majority of Chinese trade for another century. In addition, with the closing of Japan to all but Dutch and Chinese shipping in 1635, the junk trade had a great advantage in access to Japanese minerals. For these reasons Chinese trade was largely unaffected by European competition. After a slump in mid-century as a result of the collapse of the Ming and the long struggle by the new Manchu dynasty to gain control of the southern maritime provinces, Chinese trade to Southeast Asia recommenced its rapid upward path in the 1680s.

From about the same period Europeans and Western Asians were almost squeezed out of the trade of Ayutthaya, Cambodia, and the two Vietnamese states. The Siamese 'revolution' of 1688 drove out the previously dominant French, who had earlier replaced Indian Muslims in influential commercial positions. In the Vietnamese states, Burma and Cambodia, the Dutch tried hard to consolidate their trade in the 1630s and 1640s, but towards the end of the century they, along with the English, appear to have found the rewards not worth the restrictions placed on trade by these régimes—particularly once the Europeans gained direct access to China. The international trade of these states was therefore dominated by Chinese throughout the eighteenth century.

Already in the early 1600s Chinese were the largest group of foreign traders in the Vietnamese states, the Philippines, Pattani and Banten. In Ayutthaya they were probably more numerous though less wealthy than the Indian Muslims at the beginning of the century, but by far the biggest foreign group at its end. Contemporaries estimated that there were about 3000 adult Chinese males in Ayutthaya and the same in Banten (Chinese females did not emigrate). In Manila numbers fluctuated in response to official policy, but were often far higher. In the Cochinchina port of Hoi An (near modern Danang) there were perhaps 5000 in the 1640s, and more at the end of the century. Numbers were swelled by those who had support-ed Zheng Chenggong (Coxinga) in his long sea-based resistance to the Manchu régime, and after 1685 by the relative ease of leaving China because of the opening of trade.

As the seventeenth century advanced, these Chinese who stayed behind in the ports of Southeast Asia penetrated further and further into the hinterlands of the great emporia. In Banten around 1600 the Chinese had already begun to buy up pepper in the interior after the harvest, to resell not only to their compatriots but to any other buyers who would pay a good price. By the 1630s the same thing was happening in Jambi and Palembang.

The Europeans initially resented this influence on the market, but quickly came to terms with the Chinese as indispensable middlemen. They increasingly advanced cloth to local Chinese who, aided by their Indo-nesian wives or concubines, carried it into the interior to exchange against pepper. Chinese middlemen were also found far in the interior of Laos and Cambodia in the 1640s, travelling by canoe or ox-cart to buy the local product more cheaply at its source.

In the cities Chinese residents also became highly valued as craftsmen. During the short period at the end of the seventeenth century when they were permitted to trade in Aceh, for example, Dampier described the numerous 'Mechanicks, Carpenters, Joyners, Painters, etc' who came with the Chinese ships and turned the Chinese quarter into the busy heart of the city during the two or three months they were there.[59] Chinese also came to the region as miners and smelters, of silver in northern Burma and copper in northern Vietnam. In the eighteenth century they began to dominate the mining of tin and gold in the Malay world, activities previously the preserve of locals.

Did this input of Chinese skills and energy serve to stimulate or to stifle the indigenous economy? It is a question which cannot be answered categorically, any more than in the case of Europeans. The answer appears to depend very much on the extent of assimilation, or the barriers to it. As shown by the example of the 'South China Sea junk' and by numerous other commercial and technical borrowings of the fifteenth and sixteenth centuries, Southeast Asian urban and commercial culture gained enor-mously from its encounter with emigrant Chinese. As long as Chinese married into the local society and adopted its religious and social norms, their skills became part of the new urban culture being built in Southeast Asia. The greater ease of traffic between China and the Nanyang after 1685, and the rapid increase in numbers of Chinese migrating, necessarily reduced this tendency to assimilate. It also discouraged Southeast Asians from continuing to mine, smelt and work metals which the Chinese could import more cheaply or produce locally more efficiently.

There is much evidence that the establishment of the Spanish in Manila and the Dutch in Batavia helped to make the interaction with outsiders

[59] Dampier, *Voyages and Discoveries*, 94–5.

more dualistic, so that the economic activity of Europeans and Chinese increasingly diverged from that of Southeast Asians. Certainly it is from the Philippines that the earliest European complaints can be heard blaming Chinese industry for the 'laziness' of both Filipinos and Spaniards.[60]

Both Manila and Batavia were dependent on Chinese traders for the import of consumer goods, but also on local Chinese as craftsmen, labourers, market-gardeners, bakers and practically every other productive role. In Batavia the Chinese were allowed to settle inside the city walls, where they represented 39 per cent of the inhabitants (3679 Chinese) in 1699 and 58 per cent in 1739; in Manila they were obliged to concentrate in the Parian outside the walls, where there were already 10,000 in 1586. The Dutch, and even more the Spanish who had experienced Chinese attacks, were profoundly ambivalent about their dependence on the industry of the Chinese colonists. Tensions erupted in horrific anti-Chinese pogroms in both cities (six in Manila, one in 1740 in Batavia). But as Morga noted after 23,000 Chinese had been killed in and around Manila in 1603, 'the city found itself in distress, for since there were no Sangleyes [Chinese] there was nothing to eat and no shoes to wear'.[61] The Europeans knew that their cities could not have been built, their trade maintained, nor their everyday needs supplied, without the Chinese. Chinese had the great merit of being not only industrious but peaceful. Northern Europeans immediately compared their deferential attitude to the proud Southeast Asian aristocracies to that of Jews in Europe—'like Jews, [the Chinese] live crouching under them, but rob them of their wealth and send it to China'.[62]

For the Chinese, the attraction of the European-controlled ports was twofold. As the new centres of international trade they were convenient and lucrative, particularly as sources of the American and Japanese silver which was much needed in China. Second, they provided a relatively stable environment in which a few Chinese could grow very wealthy and influential without ceasing to be Chinese. The Spanish did, unlike the Dutch, expect the leading Chinese to become Christian and cut their hair short, making it difficult for them to return to China. But for both European régimes it was convenient that the Chinese should remain distinct from the majority populations around them, and therefore useful as intermediaries without the danger of becoming leaders of a combined resistance. Batavia, Manila, and their dependencies such as Dutch Melaka, Makassar and Semarang, and Spanish Iloilo and Zamboanga, became centres of extensive Chinese commercial networks, which served to encourage even those Chinese living in Asian-ruled states to maintain their Chinese identity.

The major concentrations of Chinese under indigenous control, in Ayutthaya and Fai-fo, were big enough also to remain culturally distinctive, but their leaders knew that they had to become to some extent Thai or

---

[60] Antonio de Morga, *Sucesos de las Islas Filipinas*, trans. J. S. Cummins, Cambridge, U.K., Hakluyt Society, 1971, 225, Emma H. Blair and James A. Robertson, *The Philippine Islands, 1493–1898*, Cleveland, 1903–9, VI. 270–1; H. de la Costa, *Readings in Philippine History*, Manila, 1965, 41.

[61] de Morga, *Sucesos*, 225.

[62] Scott, 'An exact Discourse', 174.

Vietnamese and take office as court officials in order to protect and develop their interests. The ethnic identification of Chinese with trade and Southeast Asian with office-holding was therefore never so sharp under indigenous rule, but it did slowly take hold nevertheless.

The farming of revenues by Chinese appears to have begun in the Dutch ports, and spread from there to Asian-ruled states. Whereas the *syahbandar* in the previous system was nominally expected to deliver all revenue to the king (though he kept numerous gifts and advantages to himself), the tax-farmer kept the port duties, market tax, or salt, opium and gambling revenues as his own return after having offered in advance to the ruler a fixed sum—often by competitive bidding. The Dutch were familiar with this farming system in Europe, and immediately introduced it in Batavia. It proved a brilliant means to leave the Chinese to their own commercial habits while extracting a heavy tax from them. Within two decades of Batavia's foundation, a system had developed whereby the monopoly right to operate tolls, markets, weigh-houses, gambling-dens, theatres, taverns and numerous other remunerative city services was bid for annually by the leading Chinese. As the Dutch extended their sway to other ports in the archipelago, this system went with them, and the British in due course emulated the practice.

This model of the financial relationship between political authority and Chinese business also offered great advantages to native rulers whose bureaucratic apparatus was even less adequate than the VOC's for levying such taxes directly. Chinese began to carry the system along the north coast of Java at least by the last decades of the seventeenth century. In most ports still under Javanese control, Chinese became not only *syahbandars* but also farmers of the port revenues, the weigh-house, alcohol and gambling, and frequently of particularly lucrative articles of trade. Around 1700 the Javanese rulers began establishing internal toll-gates and farming them out to Chinese, as a further device for raising revenue. In eighteenth-century Siam port revenues, gambling, tin-mining, and even the governor-ships of productive provinces in the south were farmed by Chinese in return for an annual payment to the Crown.

Combined with the retreat of Southeast Asian states from direct involve-ment with trade in the late seventeenth century, this development made it easier for rulers to withdraw entirely from commercial concerns. The Chinese revenue farmers became valued visitors at court, and to that extent had to acquire the dress, language and politenesses acceptable in high society. They were classic cultural brokers who also needed to retain their connections with the Chinese communities in the cities in order to continue their trade. They did not offer a direct threat to indigenous rulers as wealthy and talented members of the local community did. In the long term, however, this development of Chinese revenue farming undoubtedly widened the gulf between the indigenous population and large-scale commerce. It may be significant that the peoples of Southeast Asia among whom the entrepreneurial spirit best survived were those very little affected by Chinese tax farming, either because of remoteness, like the Minangkabaus, Bataks and Torajans, or religious and cultural hostility, like the Acehnese, Bugis and Tausug.

THE TRADE IN NARCOTICS

Narcotics had long been a major trade item within Southeast Asia, but the eighteenth century greatly expanded this trade with the outside world. Chewing a mildly narcotic quid of betel was the age-old social lubricant of the whole region, essential for every ritual and social occasion as well as for coping with hunger and the other hardships of life. The narcotic properties of this quid were obtained by combining a small piece of the nut of the areca palm (*Areca catechu*), a fresh leaf of the betel vine (*Piper betel*), and a pinch of lime. Betel leaves must have been consumed on a vast scale (a Penang consumption estimate of the early nineteenth century[63] amounts to twenty leaves a day for every man, woman and child), but as it had to be fresh it was always grown close to local markets. The areca nut (or betelnut) was traded over much longer distances, Aceh (northern Sumatra) alone exporting about 2500 tonnes to India, China, and Malaya around 1800.[64] It was the newer additives and rivals to this betel quid, however, which had the largest effect on relations between Europeans and Asians.

Gambir, an astringent obtained from the gum of a shrub (*Uncaria gambir*) native to Sumatra, had occasionally been used as another ingredient in the betel chew. This became virtually obligatory in Java and elsewhere in the eighteenth century, and as demand increased a new centre of gambir plantations was opened through a mixture of Bugis and Chinese enterprise in the Riau archipelago (south of Singapore) in the 1740s. As a Malay chronicler put it:

> The Bugis and Malays planted the gambir, establishing several hundred holdings. The labourers who processed it were Chinese from China and with the cultivation of gambir, Riau became even more populous. Trading boats arrived from such eastern areas as Java and the Bugis homeland. Javanese goods were bartered for gambir . . . According to the description of the old people, 'Those days in Riau were good'.[65]

During the following century, gambir cultivation was spread chiefly by Chinese to Singapore and the southern Malayan peninsula. The new market for it was Europe, however, where its remarkable properties in tanning had meanwhile been discovered.

Tobacco was introduced by the Spanish, reaching the Philippines from Mexico in 1575. It spread very quickly, so that in the first decade of the following century the rulers of Java and Aceh were reported to be smoking it in long pipes. By the end of the seventeenth century cheroots of tobacco had become popular among men and women in the Philippines, Maluku, Burma and Siam, and in some parts of the Indonesian archipelago. It grew

---

[63] James Low, *The British Settlement of Penang or Prince of Wales Island*, Singapore, 1836, reprinted Singapore, 1972, 72, 125.

[64] George Bennett, *Wanderings in New South Wales, Batavia, Pedir Coast, Singapore and China*, London, 1834, I. 426–7.

[65] Raja Ali Haji ibn Ahmad, *The Precious Gift (Tuhfat al Nafis)*, trans. Virginia Matheson and Barbara Andaya, Kuala Lumpur, 1982, 90–1.

readily in most parts of the region, and typically was produced in small gardens for local consumption. Much was nevertheless traded by sea. Batavia recorded the entry of forty-four tonnes of Java tobacco in 1659, and in subsequent decades equally large amounts were imported from as far afield as Ternate and Mindanao.

In Europe tobacco was frequently taxed, since it was disapproved of in many quarters and moreover was easy to control. Europeans experimented with the same pattern in the East. In 1624 the Spanish attempted to establish a monopoly of all tobacco and betel supplies to Manila for the benefit of a new seminary, but this project soon fell before popular resistance and the difficulties of control. The Dutch had better success in 1626 in farming out the monopoly of tobacco sales in Batavia to some resident Japanese for a substantial fee. Much the most ambitious attempt in this direction, however, was the Spanish plan to finance the government of the Philippines, after the disaster of the British occupation of Manila in 1762–4, by the establishment of a royal monopoly on all sales of tobacco in the colony. The difficulties of policing the thousands of small tobacco farms seemed initially too great, but in 1782 means were found to place the production of all of central Luzon with a single royal contractor. A factory was built in Manila where 5000 women cut and rolled the tobacco into cigars—probably the largest single manufacturing enterprise in the region. By the 1790s the tobacco monopoly was reckoned to be earning the Crown more than 400,000 pesos per year, almost double the income from the old tribute system. Although Luzon was probably the biggest tobacco producer in Southeast Asia, relatively little was exported legally in the eighteenth century, mainly as a result of the severe Spanish restrictions on trade. The centralized tobacco monopoly nevertheless laid the basis for a major export industry in the nineteenth century.

Opium was a very minor element in the Southeast Asian narcotic scene until the late seventeenth century, when the Dutch and English found it an extraordinarily advantageous way to open up Southeast Asian markets. Southeast Asians no longer had the wealth from pepper and spice sales to buy Indian cloth as they had around 1600, so that the European companies had difficulty selling this ancient staple towards the end of the seventeenth century. Opium provided a substitute, with the added advantages of low transport costs and extraordinary profit margins. Once the Dutch had established control over Java's import trade by the conquest of Banten in 1682, they deliberately set out to make opium a new item of mass consumption in Java. The VOC monopolized its import from Bengal to Batavia, but then sold it at below the previous market price to Chinese dealers who spread it throughout Java. Imports to Batavia (to serve Dutch trade throughout eastern Asia) tripled in the next half-century, reaching seventy tonnes a year on average in the period 1728–38. The amount sold in the Java market rose with particular speed, from 4700 Spanish dollars a year in the 1670s to 83,000 dollars (equivalent to 1404 kilograms of silver) in the 1720s.[66] By the end of the century the quantity sold annually in Java had risen to thirty-five tonnes at a selling price of nearly two million

---

[66] Nagtegaal, 'Hollandse Tijger', 127–8.

Spanish dollars. John Crawfurd reckoned the supply to all the rest of the Indonesian archipelago as another 350 chests or twenty-two tonnes.[67] Poor Javanese sugar-mill workers and dock hands dug into their small earnings to buy a little opium to smoke in a mixture with tobacco. Only wealthier Javanese and Chinese could afford to become real addicts. For the Dutch and British companies who imported the opium, however, the profits were 168 per cent over the Bengal buying price, and 3000 per cent over the Bengal cost price.

EIGHTEENTH-CENTURY TRANSITIONS

By 1700 Southeast Asian entrepôts were no longer the centres of political and cultural life in the region. Two of the last of the great port-centred states, Aceh and Johor, were both thrown into internal chaos in 1699, which drove trade elsewhere. The mainland states least dependent on revenues from trade were the most successful in negotiating the commercial crisis. They achieved a certain stability, and probably increased in population after the terrible disruptions of the seventeenth century: Burma once the kings of Ava had stabilized a much reduced empire around 1634; Vietnam after the north and south wore each other out in wars by 1672; Siam during the relatively peaceful reigns of Thai Sa and Borommakot (1709–58). These mainland states became primarily reliant on Chinese commerce and rightly distrustful of the heavily-armed Europeans.

Even these states, however, were in the long run unable to operate the degree of centralization they had inherited from more prosperous times. In Siam, northern Vietnam and Burma, decrees repeatedly complained that manpower was falling into the hands of officials and monasteries, so that the Crown could not perform its task effectively. The Kyaukse ricebowl of upper Burma suffered increasingly frequent crop failure in the period 1661–1740, as royal authority was no longer sufficient to see that irrigation channels were maintained. In northern Vietnam the same failures of centralized power led to famines, revolts, and what Vietnamese historians consider 'a profound and irremediable crisis' in the eighteenth century.[68] European observers of these states in the period, on the other hand, tended to believe their peoples were kept exceptionally poor by a 'frightful tyranny' which deprived them of the fruits of any initiative.[69]

In short, the mainland states succeeded in retaining their coherence by withdrawing from international commerce and reasserting their bureaucratic control of agriculture. They did not, however, escape impoverishment and eventual collapse under the strain of a bureaucracy more complex than they could maintain without the revenues from trade.

In the archipelago there was also disenchantment with commerce and

---

[67] *History of the Indian Archipelago*, Edinburgh, 1820, 518–20.

[68] Nguyen Khac Vien, *Vietnam: une longue histoire*, Hanoi, 1987, 109. See also Lê Thanh Khoi, *Histoire du Vietnam, des origines à 1858*, Paris, 1987, 303–9.

[69] Most eloquently Pierre Poivre, *Les Mémoires d'un voyageur*, ed. Louis Malleret, Paris: EFEO, 1968, 54–8. Also Dampier, *Voyages*, 32–3; Marcel Le Blanc, *Histoire de la revolution du royaume de Siam, arrivée en l'année 1688*, Lyon, 1692, I. 7–13.

cash-cropping, and an attempt to assert 'traditional' hierarchic values, but it was scarcely possible to cut the troublesome reliance on the sea. Instead, power was diffused to smaller centres and more numerous ports. The VOC, having driven its European rivals from their important bases and helped to destroy the Asian entrepôts, found itself so committed to high administrative and military overheads that it was at a disadvantage in all sectors except where its own monopoly guaranteed a very high profit margin—and these were of dwindling importance. The eighteenth century therefore gave opportunities to a variety of independent traders relatively little beholden to the power centres, European or Asian.

The most successful of these were European and Armenian traders based primarily on the eastern coast of India, but sometimes establishing themselves in Southeast Asian ports such as Aceh, Kedah, Phuket (Junk Ceylon), Tenasserim, Mergui, and Rangoon. They co-operated with Indian merchants and seamen to carry Indian cloth and metals to the smallest Southeast Asian centres, wherever a small profit was to be made. Alongside them, and sometimes sharing cargoes with them, were Chulia Muslims from the Coromandel coast, who often became important figures in these ports. Both elements were active in sectors of the intra-Asian trade which generated less profit than the Dutch or English companies could tolerate. They profited, however, from the flow of English and Indian capital towards the eastern Indian seaboard to feed the enormous European demand for the cottons of this region.

Further east it was locally domiciled Chinese who played the larger role in inter-island trade, as they gained enough capital to own their own small Malay-style vessels to operate out of all the Dutch ports (Batavia, Makassar, Melaka, Semarang, Surabaya, Padang) and also Ayutthaya and Riau. Between 1722 and 1786 Chinese-owned vessels rose from 7 to 39 per cent of all arrivals in Makassar.[70] In 1700 there were still more Malay and Javanese than Chinese vessels in the trade of the north Java coast, but by 1731 Chinese owned 62 per cent of the vessels reaching Batavia from this region.[71] Moreover the direct trade between South China ports and the Nanyang grew ever more intense in the eighteenth century, extending in the 1730s into rice, which became the major Siamese export to China.

Of Southeast Asian traders, the most vigorous beneficiaries of the opportunities for small-scale enterprise were the Bugis of south Sulawesi. The campaign waged by the Dutch and their Bugis allies from Bone against Makassar in 1666–9 was a bitter one, which destroyed the city and drove out most of the merchants who had settled there. Among these were Bugis originating from Wajo, which remained loyal to Makassar to the end and was therefore also severely repressed by the victorious Arung Palakka of Bone. Wajo people fled Sulawesi in their thousands, forming new communities in Java, Sumatra, and especially the eastern coast of Borneo. From these bases they were eventually able to free their homeland from Bone control in 1737. Meanwhile they had become more successful as a commercial diaspora than they had been when operating from their homeland.

---

[70] Information from Heather Sutherland.
[71] Calculated from Nagtegaal, 'Hollandse Tijger'. 47.

They were welcomed into the small Malay ports of the region because they brought trade and wealth, but also because they were hardy warriors, accustomed to modern firearms and chain-mail. They became key factors in the power struggles of the Straits of Melaka area and Borneo. At the same time they occupied a crucial role in inter-island trade, losing out to Chinese in Dutch ports but more than holding their own in all the independent ports of the archipelago. They sailed as far north as Cambodia and Sulu.

Because they generally evaded the port charges imposed by the Dutch, the Bugis were able to operate at even lower profit margins than other independent traders. They had another advantage in the cotton cloths manufactured by the women of south Sulawesi. The decline in Southeast Asian purchasing power from the mid-seventeenth century had reduced sharply the import of Indian cloth, but boosted local production of cotton and cotton cloth. Java began its role as supplier of batik and other cloths to the other islands of Indonesia in this period, but the Bugis were even more successful in filling the gap. Cotton grown in the dry limestone soils of Selayar and the adjacent Sulawesi coast at Bira, or imported from Bali, was woven by the women of Selayar and Wajo into fine checked sarongs which were in demand all over the archipelago. Bugis traders sold these cloths at half the price of the comparable Indian cloths in VOC hands, enabling them to penetrate markets everywhere with very little capital.

VOC profits on its monopoly trade items were never so great in the eighteenth century as in the seventeenth. Where the seventeenth century had seen the Company exploring commercial opportunities in every corner of the world, including Ava and Vientiane far up the great rivers of Southeast Asia, the eighteenth century put it on the defensive as a worldwide trading enterprise. The profitable developments of its second century were in agriculture rather than trade, making use of its increasingly dominant position in Java as well as Maluku.

Sugarcane was already being grown for export in Banten and the Batavia area in the first half of the seventeenth century, mainly by Chinese. Once the VOC had demolished its Banten rival in 1684, it encouraged further planting of sugar by Chinese all along the north coast of Java, which the Company now bought for export to Japan, China and Europe. These Chinese entrepreneurs leased land and labour from the local Javanese authorities in north-central Java. About 1800 labourers were at work in the high season for the thirty-three mills in this area in 1719, effectively performing the corvée they were held to owe the aristocracy. In the environs of Batavia, where the largest number of mills were concentrated, the resident Javanese population had been driven out, and slaves proved too expensive for the task. A system of recruiting landless young labour on a seasonal basis from aristocrats in the eastern Priangan was therefore developed. These workers were not strictly free, but were paid a wage.[72] VOC exports of sugar reached a peak of about 4400 tonnes in 1718–19. For most of the rest of the century the figure was closer to 1000 tonnes,

---

[72] ibid., 134–6.

since slave-grown West Indian sugar could be delivered more cheaply to Europe.

The smaller sugar industries of Siam and Vietnam, though exporting primarily to Japan and China, also encountered problems in the eighteenth century. A dramatic increase began in the last decades of the century, however, partly for local consumption and partly to fill the growing demand in Europe and Japan. By 1800 sugar had probably replaced pepper as the major Southeast Asian export to the rest of the world. Dutch Java and the Spanish Philippines were each exporting about 4000 tonnes at the century's end, though this was but the beginning of a massive growth in the nineteenth century. In addition the smaller Siamese sugar industry was re-established under the new Chakri dynasty at about this time. In all three places the collection and refining of sugar was almost entirely in Chinese hands.

For the Dutch East India Company the other major success was coffee, the new fashion which swept through Europe in the eighteenth century. Prior to 1700 it grew only in the Yemen, and made famous that country's port of Mocha. The VOC introduced it to the Cirebon and Priangan areas of western Java in 1707, and within two decades Java had become the leading world producer. In this case it was not Chinese but Javanese and Sundanese aristocrats who took the initiative in having the trees planted and delivering the crop to the VOC at agreed prices. More than two million trees were planted in the Priangan highlands south of Batavia, and almost as many in the hinterland of Cirebon. But the boom peaked around 1725, oversupply reduced prices in Europe, and the Company lowered its demand to 2000 tonnes a year. Prices were also reduced to a level below that which interested independent cash-croppers, so that quotas were filled only with an element of force.

The experience of the VOC with coffee and sugar, and the Spanish with sugar and tobacco, provided a foretaste of the different quality of economic imperialism which was to dominate the nineteenth century. The VOC had begun buying each of the major Southeast Asian crops—pepper, cloves, nutmeg, sugar, coffee—at a time of commercial boom when prices were high enough to lure growers voluntarily into the international economy. As prices dropped or competition mounted, however, the European companies moved further towards enforcing delivery at prices which were still profitable for the companies, with their high overheads, but not for the growers. Such delivery contracts were always made through the medium of a local élite, for whose subjects it was often presented as a form of corvée. Driven out of Banten by the Dutch victory there in 1682, the British developed the same form of forced delivery of pepper in their new base in Benkulen (southwest Sumatra) as the Dutch were developing through the defeated rulers of Banten and Palembang.

In the eighteenth century these pockets of European-sponsored agricultural activity were marginal to Southeast Asian life. Chinese initiatives such as the gambir cultivation of Riau and Johor, the tin-mining of Bangka and gold-mining of western Borneo were almost equally so. Southeast Asians were not groaning under the effect of Western oppression or Chinese commercial penetration. Their lives were no more squalid, their health no more wretched, their physical stature no worse than those of eighteenth-century Europeans. In some respects they may indeed have been better off as a result of a benign climate, low population density, and sensible diet. Only around 1800, when European prosperity, health and stature began its upward course, did Southeast Asia begin to fall behind in these important measures of well-being.

Nevertheless it was already clear by 1700 that Southeast Asian states were not following the path of European ones. Cosmopolitan urban agglomerations, private concentrations of capital, craft specialization, a curiosity about the scientific world, were all less, not more, central to these states than they had been a century earlier. In order to preserve what they could of cherished values, comfortable lifestyles and familiar hierarchies, Southeast Asian states had disengaged from an intimate encounter with world commerce, and the technology and mind-set which went with it. When this commerce began its restless, almost uninterrupted growth from the late eighteenth century, it of course stimulated numerous new forms of economic life in Southeast Asia. The most vital of these were not the responses of the remaining Asian states, however, but of traders, raiders, cash-croppers, miners and manufacturers at the interstices of the Southeast Asian world. The states which had to confront the new Western onslaught now lacked the technology, the capital, the bureaucratic method, and the national coherence of their opponents, and would be made to pay dearly for it.

BIBLIOGRAPHIC ESSAY

Primary Materials

Although the inscriptions of an earlier period often have useful economic data on temple endowments, freedom from taxation and the like, the manuscript chronicles which dominate the indigenous record of this period are little interested in economic or social conditions, particularly in quantified terms. Surviving Burmese materials provide some exceptions. Many reports from local officials (*sit-tan*) have been translated in F. N. Trager and William J. Koenig, *Burmese Sit-tans 1764–1826*, Tucson, 1979. Than Tun, *The Royal Orders of Burma, A.D. 1598–1885*, 8 vols (Kyoto: Kyoto University Center for Southeast Asian Studies, 1983–8) translates a diverse collection of royal orders, which deal with everyday matters and revenue collection as well as the life of the court. The Vietnamese tradition of local administration also generated land registers and other data of great economic importance. Among texts which have been published but not yet translated, the most important source of pre-1800 economic data is probably the collected work of Le Quy Don, *Toàn Tập*, 3 vols, Hanoi, Nha Xûat Bân Khoa Học Xã Hội, 1977–8.

Chinese records are essential for understanding trade patterns. Among the most important is the 1433 description of Southeast Asia resulting from the Ch'eng Ho expeditions: Ma Yuan, *Ying-yai Sheng-lan: 'The overall survey of the Ocean's Shores'*, trans. J. V. G. Mills, Cambridge, UK: Hakluyt Society,

1970. Much relevant Chinese material is translated in W. P. Groeneveldt, *Historical Notes on Indonesia and Malaysia, Compiled from Chinese Sources*, Batavia, 1880, reprinted Jakarta, 1960, and in the works of Rockhill, Wheatley and Wang Gungwu. Not yet translated is the important work of Zhang Xie, *Dong xi yang kao* [Studies on the East and West Oceans, 1617], new edition, Beijing, 1981. All the Ryukyuan documents pertaining to trade with Southeast Asia in 1425–1638 are translated by Atsushi Kobata and Mitsugu Matsuda in *Ryukyuan Relations with Korea and South Sea Countries. An annotated translation of documents in the 'Rekido Hoan'*, Kyoto, 1969. Many Japanese documents on the Southeast Asian trade are reproduced in two books by Iwao Sei'ichi, *Shuinsen bōekishi no kenkyū* and *Shuinsen to Nihonmachi*, Tokyo, 1958 and 1966. Far richer are the series of reports of the Chinese junks arriving in Nagasaki in the period 1640–1740, the *Kai hentai* [Chinese Metamorphosis], compiled at the time by Hayashi Shunsai and his son Hayashi Hoko. The modern edition is by Ura Ren'ichi, *Kai hentai*, 3 vols, Tokyo, Toyo Bunko, 1958–9.

The standard Portuguese and Spanish chronicles all contain some economic data, though less than one would expect from the commercial interests of their countrymen. By far the best Portuguese source on Southeast Asian trade and economy is *The Suma Oriental of Tomé Pires*, trans. Armando Cortesão, London: Hakluyt Society, 1944.

With the arrival of the Dutch in 1596 there is a dramatic improvement in the quality and quantity of economic reporting. Dutch factors had instructions to report extensively on trade opportunities, shipping movements, prices, and export and import quantities. There is much useful information even in the journals of the early voyages, first collected for publication in *Begin ende Voortgangh van de Vereenigde Neederlandtsche Geoctroyeerde Oost-Indische Compagnie*, ed. I. Commelin (Amsterdam, 1646), and now being progressively edited in a professional manner by the Linschoten-Vereniging. Still more valuable is the systematic reporting of shipping movements in the *Daghregister gehouden in 't Casteel Batavia, 1642–1682*, 31 vols, Batavia and The Hague, 1887–1931. The extraordinarily voluminous correspondence of Jan Pieterszoon Coen, the founder of Dutch fortunes in the East, has been published first by H. T. Colenbrander and finally by W. Ph. Coolhaas as *Jan Pieterszoon Coen: bescheiden omtrent zijn bedrijf in Indie*, 7 vols in 8, The Hague, 1919–53. Although all these series make the period up to 1682 far more accessible than what follows, the most recent of the ambitious Dutch source publications has so far provided edited texts of the regular letters from the VOC Council in Batavia to Amsterdam up to 1735. This is W. Ph. Coolhaas, ed., *Generale Missiven van Gouverneurs-Generaal en Raden aan Heeren XVII der Verenigde Oostindische Compagnie*, 7 vols, The Hague, 1960–76. This series is also particularly rich in data on trade.

Secondary Sources

The biggest debates in this field have revolved around the relationship between the economic systems of the Asian region and the rise of capitalism in Europe. Two Dutch sociologists launched the debate into Indonesian waters before the war, in work which became more widely known in English translation in the 1950s: *Indonesian Sociological Studies: Selected Writings of B. Schrieke*, 2 vols, The Hague, 1955, and J. C. van Leur, *Indonesian Trade and Society: Essays in Social and Economic History*, The Hague, 1955. While Schrieke had pointed to the collapse of Javanese shipping in the seventeenth century, van Leur was more anxious to minimize the impact of the VOC and to argue for a continuity in Asian trade well into the eighteenth century. These themes were examined empirically by M. A. P. Meilink-Roelofsz, *Asian Trade and European Influence in the Indonesian Archipelago between 1500 and about 1630*, The Hague, 1962, who concluded that Asian traders were more varied than van Leur had allowed, and did decline in importance in the seventeenth century, but even at their height lacked critical features of their European counterparts such as the legal protection of property.

Subsequent work has had to become more sophisticated, more quantified, and more global in scope. Because of the nature of the sources and the problems, the best of this work has tended to treat Southeast Asia as part of bigger units. Outstanding examples are Vitorino Magalhães-Godinho, *L'economie de l'empire portugais aux XVe et XVIe siècles*, Paris, 1969; Pierre Chaunu, *Les Philippines et le Pacifique des Ibériques (XVIe, XVIIe, XVIIIe siècles). Introduction methodologique et indices d'activité*, Paris, 1960; K. N. Chaudhuri's two books on the English Company, *The English East India Company. The Study of an Early Joint-Stock Company 1600–1640*, London, 1965, and *The Trading World of Asia and the English East India Company, 1660–1760*, Cambridge, UK, 1978; Niels Steensgaard, *The Asian Trade Revolution of the Seventeenth Century*, Chicago, 1973; Kristof Glamann, *Dutch-Asiatic Trade 1620–1740*, The Hague, 1958; J. R. Bruijn, F. S. Gaastra and I. Schöffer, *Dutch-Asiatic Shipping in the 17th and 18th Centuries*, 3 vols, The Hague, 1979–87; R. L. Innes, 'The Door Ajar: Japan's Foreign Trade in the seventeenth century', Ph.D. thesis, University of Michigan, 1980; and G. B. Souza, *The Survival of Empire. Portuguese Trade and Society in China and the South China Sea, 1630–1754*, Cambridge, UK, 1986.

The interaction between Southeast Asia and the China trade has been well handled by Sarasin Viraphol, *Tribute and Profit: Sino-Siamese Trade, 1652–1853*, Cambridge, Mass., 1977; Wang Gungwu, *Community and Nation: Essays on Southeast Asia and the Chinese*, Singapore, 1981; John E. Wills, *Pepper, Guns and Parleys: The Dutch East India Company and China 1622–1681*, Cambridge, Mass., 1974; Leonard Blussé, *Strange Company. Chinese settlers, mestizo women, and the Dutch in VOC Batavia*, Dordrecht, 1986; and Chingho Chen, *Historical Notes on Hôi-An (Faifo)*, Carbondale: Southern Illinois University Centre for Vietnamese Studies, 1974. There has been even more recent work on the Indian Ocean as a sphere of economic activity, notably K. N. Chaudhuri, *Trade and Civilization in the Indian Ocean. An Economic History from the Rise of Islam to 1750*; S. Arasaratnam, *Merchants, Companies and Commerce on the Coromandel Coast, 1650–1740*, Delhi, 1986; A. Das Gupta and M. Pearson, eds, *India and the Indian Ocean 1500–1800*, Calcutta, 1987; Denys Lombard and Jean Aubin, eds, *Marchands et hommes d'affaires asiatiques dans l'Océan Indien et la Mer de Chine, 13e–20e siécles*, Paris: EHESS, 1988.

Such works have clarified Southeast Asia's interaction with the global economy, and demonstrated a long-term pattern of economic expansion and contraction. To understand the specific economies of the region, however, we must turn to scholars familiar with indigenous literary traditions and informed by field research. Especially useful regarding economic and social change are Victor Lieberman, *Burmese Administrative Cycles: Anarchy and Conquest, c. 1580–1760*, Princeton, 1984, and Nguyen Thanh-Nha, *Tableau économique du Vietnam aux XVIIe et XVIIIe siècles*, Paris, 1970. Some of the most interesting work in this area is being done by the group associated with the journal *Archipel* in Paris, notably Denys Lombard, Claude Guillot and Pierre-Yves Manguin. Important special issues of *Archipel* were devoted to commerce and shipping (no. 18, 1979) and to cities (nos. 36, 1988, and 37, 1989). The problem of slavery is addressed in Anthony Reid, ed., *Slavery, Bondage and Dependency in Southeast Asia*, St Lucia, Queensland, 1983. Finally, the Dutch archives are at last being mined in a number of theses on particular regions, of which the most notable for their economic data are: Gerrit Knaap, *Kruidnagelen en Christenen: De Verenigde Oost-Indische Compagnie en de bevolking van Ambon 1656–1696*, Dordrecht, 1987; Lucas Nagtegaal, 'Rijden op een Hollandse Tijger. De noordkust van Java en de V.O.C. 1680–1743', Ph.D. thesis, Utrecht University, 1988; Ito Takeshi, 'The World of the *Adat Aceh*; A Historical Study of the Sultanate of Aceh', Ph.D. thesis, Australian National University, 1984.

CHAPTER

9

RELIGIOUS DEVELOPMENTS IN
SOUTHEAST ASIA c.1500–1800

The present chapter, which continues the account of religious developments in Southeast Asia from about 1500, is divided into five sections. The
first draws on the European source material that becomes available in the
sixteenth century to survey important features of indigenous beliefs as
they were practised in areas then little touched by the world religions.
An examination of the advance of Islam and Christianity, destined to
have such fundamental effects on the evolution of island Southeast Asia,
makes up the second and third sections. It will become apparent that
the manner in which these newer religions adapted to the local context
in many respects resembles the previous infusion of Hindu, Buddhist
and Confucian ideas already discussed in Chapter 5. The fourth section
therefore takes up several themes common across the region as the world
religions extended and consolidated their position. The chapter closes
with an overview of the eighteenth century, identified as a time when
unprecedented pressures, both internal and external, created new
demands in Southeast Asia's religious environment.

INDIGENOUS BELIEFS

An important contribution to our understanding of indigenous beliefs
comes in the sixteenth and seventeenth centuries as European missionaries began to move into areas of eastern Indonesia and the Philippines
which had to this point been relatively isolated from external religious
ideas. Despite their obvious cultural bias, the accounts missionaries
compiled provide the historian with the first sustained contemporary
descriptions of native religious customs outside a court environment.
   Most striking in these early European sources is not the regional variation in belief which observers noted, but the similarities. All affirm that the
ordinary man and woman conceived of the natural world as animated by a
vast array of deities who inhabited trees, rivers, caves, mountains and who
were capable of great kindness or extraordinary malevolence. Otherwise
inexplicable events such as volcanic eruptions, earthquakes, epidemics, a

failure of the rains, were a sign that the spirits were angry and needed to be appeased with appropriate offerings. In arming themselves against the vagaries of fate, individuals could seek assistance from their ancestors and from past leaders and heroes who, after death, had become powerful spirits in their own right. Often they were believed to have entered the bodies of animals, like the tiger, the crocodile or the pig. In eastern Indonesia such beliefs were especially obvious, and one Portuguese account describes how the people of Maluku (the Moluccas) 'worshipped the celestial bodies, the sun, moon and stars, they made idols to the honour of their fathers and forefathers. These were made of wood and stone with faces of men, dogs, cats and other animals.'[1]

A key factor in communicating with the spirits was propitiation and ritual performed at designated sites like a sacred mountain or at the graves of ancestors. Offerings of food, drink, cloth, and certain symbolic items were most common, but on some occasions the spilling of blood was deemed necessary to allay anger, or ensure the fertility of the soil and the continuance of supernatural favours. After some animal—a goat, pig, or a buffalo—was slaughtered, its head was usually offered to the spirits while the participants ate the rest of the meat in a ceremonial feast. On special occasions a human being might be sacrificed, the victims usually obtained by raids into neighbouring territory or by the purchase of slaves. In the Visayas, for example, the people 'are in the habit of buying some Indios from other provinces to offer them as sacrificial victims to the devil'.[2] Ritual and offering were part of the lives of everyone, especially during the great life crises of birth, marriage and death, but the most elaborate ceremonial was often that associated with funerals. The careful preparation of bodies for burial, the dressing of the corpse, the provision of goods, food, drink, clothing and transport described in several societies, attest to a belief in life after death, where an individual would enjoy a status commensurate with his or her standing while alive.

Although men also assumed high ceremonial positions, early European observers were struck by the prominence of females in religious ritual. When the Spanish first arrived in the Philippines they saw old women (called *babaylan* in the Visayas and *katalonan* in the Tagalog areas) through whom the spirits spoke. Several societies accorded particular respect not only to women but to 'Indians dressed as women', a reference to the transvestites who symbolically combined the regenerative powers of both sexes. To a considerable extent the prestige of such figures was due to their ability to deal with both male and female sacral items and to provide a medium for spirit pronouncements. When they fell into a trance, induced by incantation, dance, and the music of bells, drums and gongs, they became more than human. Shamanistic skills were especially valued in times of illness because this was attributed to non-human agencies. Missionaries in the Philippines described curing sessions in which 'the woman leader can talk to herself with many posturings', anointing the

---

[1] Hubert Th. Th. M. Jacobs, *A Treatise on the Moluccas (c. 1544)*, Rome, 1971, 75.
[2] Cited in Pablo Fernandez, *History of the Church in the Philippines (1521–1898)*, Manila, 1979, 3.

head of the sick person with oil and telling him the *anito* (spirit) would give him strength.

The secret knowledge which set such individuals apart could not be obtained without instruction. In the late seventeenth century in Ceram the Dutch missionary Valentijn described how children were taken into the jungle for months at a time to be inculcated by magic rituals as 'devil priests'. Equipped with these secret skills, the shaman was able to help protect the community against witches and sorcerers who had somehow mastered the magic arts and were ready to use them in harmful designs. Some sorcerers could fly, some could kill without raising a hand, others could cast charms to make the most loving wife reject her husband. In Maluku these alleged 'witches' were called collectively by the Malay word *suangi* (ghost) and were frequently accused by a shaman in trance of having caused illness or other calamities. 'When kings, dukes or ministers fall ill, they order some *suangi* to be killed.'[3] On one occasion missionaries said that over a hundred people were put to death as *suangi* because the ruler had died.[4]

Surrounded by an army of supernatural beings, some kindly but capricious and others simply malevolent, and facing the added danger of hostile elements in human form, the communities depicted by the missionaries placed enormous importance on the possession of amulets and other objects believed to have protective powers. Among the most widely valued weapons against magic were bezoar stones (called by Malays *mestika galiga*), especially from a wild pig and deer. Similar attitudes were attached to other objects such as old spears, krises and cloth, possession of which gave to the owner an extra-human power. In Ambon, for instance, a very rare type of bracelet known as *mamakur*, together with holy stones, Chinese porcelain and clothes worn by deceased ancestors, were carefully preserved to ward off harm. Great credence was also given to dreams and omens, by which messages from the non-human world could be transmitted. If a sneeze on leaving the house was a warning of ill fortune, how much more did the eclipse of the sun or moon presage impending catastrophe? In Ternate, said the Dutch, people believed it was a portent of death, either of their own relatives or the king himself. It was in the hope of appeasing the mighty forces inherent in the heavenly bodies that the people of Makassar kept representations of the sun and moon in their homes long after the court had adopted Islam.

Evidence from this period relating to indigenous religious practices is not as extensive for the rest of Southeast Asia as it is for eastern Indonesia and the Philippines. It is nonetheless apparent that many of the customs described by missionaries in the island world were once common throughout the region. Animal and sometimes human sacrifices to the spirits, for example, could be found in Burma at least into the eighteenth century, despite Buddhist prohibitions against the taking of life. Although some observances have disappeared, students of the modern period will certainly discern much that is familiar in early missionary descriptions of

---

[3] Jacobs, *A Treatise*, 181.

[4] Georg Schurhammer, *Francis Xavier. His Life, His Times*, III, trans. M. Joseph Costelloe, Rome: Jesuit Historical Institute, 1980, 92.

native religions. Indeed, any study of Southeast Asian cultures will stress the tenacity of indigenous beliefs and will point out that for a number of societies they have remained a completely satisfactory means of explaining the world. Such studies will also emphasize that all the world religions which became established in Southeast Asia succeeded because they not only made some accommodation with existing attitudes but elaborated and enhanced them. In Burma, for instance, kings on behalf of their subjects continued to honour the spirits of their forebears before statues covered with gold in the belief that 'proper respect to the ancestors will bring prosperity'.[5] Significantly, these ceremonies came to be held on Buddhist holy days even though propitiation of the spirits of departed relatives receives no canonical sanction in Buddhist teachings. In Vietnam (Dai Viet) by contrast, the classical Chinese works of Confucianism elevated the indigenous veneration for deceased forebears into the central focus of household ritual. 'The piety they display towards the souls of their relatives,' said the Jesuit missionary Alexander of Rhodes, 'surpasses anything we could imagine in Europe. They go to incredible lengths to find suitable places for tombs . . . and spare no trouble or expense to lay out banquets for them after death.'[6]

Well before the arrival of Islam and Christianity, a dominant theme in Southeast Asia's religious development is thus already apparent. The major features of the indigenous belief system survived because for the most part they were able to coexist or to be engrossed by the ritual and teachings associated with the world religions. In a sense an alliance was struck between the new 'deities' and the old. A story found in Burma and the Thai areas describes how the earth goddess, wringing water from her hair, aids the Buddha to victory by flooding the armies of the evil Mara. In Burma this conjoining of indigenous and imported ideas is symbolized by the common depiction of the seated Buddha in the pose of touching the earth with his right hand, the signal to the earth goddess to witness the merit of his previous lives.[7] In much the same way the elaboration of ceremonial and the incorporation of awe-inspiring vocabulary had confirmed the importance of many existing customs. Beneath the formalized Confucian Oath to Heaven carried out in fifteenth-century Vietnam, for instance, can be seen traces of earlier allegiance rituals during which spirits were invoked, animals sacrificed and their blood communally drunk. For Buddhists the notion of *kamma* (*karma*) and the possibility of punishment for wrongful action extending into future lives imbued the oath-taking ceremony with added solemnity. A fourteenth-century inscription from the Thai kingdom of Sukothai thus describes a pact with a neighbouring king calling on the ancestors and guardian spirits of waters and caves to bear witness that all those who broke the oath were destined for hell and would 'never expect to see the Buddha, the Dharma or the

[5] Than Tun, trans., *The Royal Orders of Burma, AD 1598–1885*, Kyoto: Center for Southeast Asian Studies, Kyoto University, 1983–7, IV. 144.
[6] Solange Hertz, trans., *Rhodes of Vietnam*, Westminster, Maryland, 1966, 59.
[7] John Ferguson, 'The symbolic dimensions of the Burmese sangha', Ph.D. thesis, Cornell University, 1975, 24. The emphasis on the earth goddess legend found in Southeast Asia is absent in orthodox Theravāda Buddhist literature from India and Sri Lanka.

Sangha'. Similarly the amulets and talismans which provided such protection against harmful forces became even more effective as they absorbed the potency of beliefs from outside. In the Buddhist states such items were commonly made in the form of the Buddha or a revered monk, and larger Buddha images often became the palladium of the kingdom, special powers being attributed to them.

The persistence of spirits is the primary heritage of indigenous religious beliefs, but increasingly spirits became drawn into a world where the dominant religion was that patronized by the king and his court. In Burma the official abode of a pantheon of 37 *nats* (spirits) was the Shwezigon pagoda at Pagan, but the ruler gave each one a specific fief from whose inhabitants the *nat* received propitiation. In return for this royal patronage and the people's homage, spirits were expected to render service to the king and recognize the moral authority of the court religions. In Vietnam a fourteenth-century Buddhist scholar related how an earth spirit appeared to an earlier king in a dream, promising that his planned attack on Champa would be successful if he sacrificed to her. With the aid of a Buddhist monk the appropriate offerings were made, and subsequently a shrine was established for the 'Imperial Earth Lady' in the capital.

Legends suggest that this process of political and religious integration sometimes met resistance. This same scholar referred to 'depraved divinities' and 'evil demons' who had refused to act as guardians of religion and who were therefore ordered to 'quickly depart to another place'.[8] In Buddhist history across the mainland the subjection of spirits to the authority of Buddhism is a recurrent theme. The *Padaeng Chronicle* from the Shan state of Kengtung recounts how one demon, displeased at the construction of the city, 'went to haunt the golden palace, defying attempts by the ruler to expel him'. Monks were brought in to recite holy scriptures and strengthen the sacred religion. However, the demon 'came to haunt even more, the holy water putrified, the leaves of the magic trees withered, and the Bhikkus were defeated'.[9] The situation was rectified only when a learned monk was brought in to carry out the purification of the Buddha's religion and teaching (*sasana*). In 1527, the king of Lan Sang went so far as to ban spirit worship and order the destruction of all sanctuaries associated with the spirit (*phi*) cult, erecting a Buddhist temple in the capital where the shrine of the guardian spirit had previously stood.

Despite periodic questioning as to the extent to which they should be honoured, spirits never showed any sign of disappearing from Southeast Asia's religious life. The reason appears to lie in the relevance of spirit belief to human existence here on earth. Whereas the great religions were concerned with the future or, in the case of Confucianism, with questions of cosmic significance, the attention of spirits could be drawn to the most mundane matter whether it concerned illness or warfare, a trading venture or childbearing. In the early seventeenth century Tagalog Filipinos gave

---

[8] Keith Taylor, 'Authority and legitimacy in 11th Century Vietnam' in David G. Marr and A. C. Milner, eds, *Southeast Asia in the 9th to the 14th Centuries*, Canberra and Singapore, 1986, 139–76.

[9] Sao Saimong Mangrai, *The Padaeng Chronicle and the Jengtung State Chronicle Translated*, Michigan Papers on South and Southeast Asia, University of Michigan, 1981, 113–14.

Spanish missionaries a clear explanation of the relationship between the lesser *anito* and Bathala, whom they had named as supreme among the pantheon of spirits. 'Bathala', they said, 'was a great lord and no one could speak to him. He lived in the sky, but the *anito*, who was of such a nature that he come down here to talk to men, was to Bathala as a minister and interceded for them.'[10] A not dissimilar view of spirits is expressed in an early nineteenth-century Burmese chronicle which describes how a king of Pagan was once advised by a hermit to worship the Buddha when he looked to the future, but to the *nats* when he looked to the present.[11] The survival of spirit worship is particularly telling in the case of Islam and Christianity, both of which place a primary doctrinal stress on monotheism. These two religions were to become the dominant faiths in island Southeast Asia, and it is to their history that we shall now turn.

THE COMING OF ISLAM

An appreciation of the rapidity of Islam's spread in the sixteenth century necessitates a review of the historical context in which this advance occurred. The nature of the sources, however, makes it impossible to answer the most fundamental questions about the arrival of Islam in the archipelago. In the first place, there is no way of knowing exactly when and where the first significant local conversions occurred. Existing evidence suggests that it was in northern Sumatra, closest to India and the Islamic heartlands, where Islam established its first beach-heads. The evidence for the existence of local Muslim communities does not emerge until the late thirteenth century CE, although they may well have arisen earlier than this. The Venetian traveller Marco Polo mentions Muslims in Perlak in 1292 CE, and in neighbouring Pasai a royal gravestone inscribed with the date 697 AH (1297 CE) and the Muslim title Sultan Malik al-Salih ('the saintly king') has been found. It is apparent, however, that this new faith had not penetrated beyond the coast. A traveller from Morocco, Ibn Batuta, visiting Samudra-Pasai in 1345 on his way from Bengal to China, described it as Muslim in the port, but still 'pagan' in the interior.

The evidence from Java is also sparse. The tombstone of a Muslim woman discovered at Leran (near Surabaya) and dated at 496 or 475 AH (1102 or 1082 CE) is generally believed to mark the grave of a foreign rather than a locally born Muslim. By contrast, the shape, the decorative carving and the Old Javanese script on a number of Muslim gravestone inscriptions situated near the centre of the former kingdom of Majapahit in east Java clearly indicate that those buried there were of local origin. Most are from the fifteenth century, but one stone bears the Śaka date 1290 (1368 CE) while two others are inscribed 1298 and 1302 (1376 and 1380 CE). The proximity of the graves to the site of the Majapahit *kraton* raises the distinct

[10] Emma H. Blair and James A. Robertson, *The Philippine Islands, 1493–1898*, Cleveland, 1903–09, V. 144.
[11] Pe Maung Tin and G. H. Luce, eds and trans, *The Glass Palace Chronicle of the Kings of Burma*, Rangoon, 80–1.

possibility that there were already a number of Muslims in court circles and possibly among the royal family at the time when Majapahit was at the height of its power.

A third important discovery regarding the dating of Islam's arrival was made in Terengganu on the east coast of the Malay peninsula. It consists of a stone, apparently intended as a pillar, which records a royal order to local officials. One side, enjoining them to uphold the Islamic religion and the teachings of the apostle of Allah, has a hijra date which is incomplete because of damage to the stone and which has therefore been read variously between 702 and 789 AH (1303 and 1387 CE). Although the inscribed laws on the remaining three faces cannot be completely deciphered due to surface flaking, several deal with the relationship between creditor and debtor, while others are concerned with punishments for sexual transgressions and perjury.

The available evidence on which to build any argument concerning the date of Islam's first steps into the archipelago is thus hardly extensive. Questions regarding the provenance of Islam are even more difficult to answer, although there are some areas of general agreement. First, it is obvious that Islam spread into Southeast Asia as Muslim traders moved along established maritime trade routes. Later European observers who complained that Islamic 'missionaries' were 'disguising' themselves as traders failed to understand that there is no priestly class as such in Islam, and that the religion itself grew out of a commercial urban environment. Muslim merchants who had become accustomed to conducting their business under the protective umbrella of Muslim law were the most obvious transmitters of Islam's basic beliefs during these early stages.

In the second place, the known strength of the Indian trading presence in Southeast Asian waters at the time when Islam began to move into the region is convincing evidence for the role of Indian Muslims in the diffusion of Islamic ideas. Over the years there has been a sometimes heated debate about which region of India was the most influential in bringing about the conversion of leading courts in the archipelago. Strong arguments have been advanced in favour of Gujerat, Bengal, and the Muslim areas of southern India, all of which had strong trading ties with Southeast Asia. Gujerat came under Muslim rule in 1287 and much of its trade was in Muslim hands. According to Tomé Pires, Bengali traders had long frequented Pasai and in the latter part of the thirteenth century had been responsible for placing 'a Moorish king of the Bengali caste' on the Pasai throne. But later Malay texts from both Pasai and Melaka talk of the coming of the apostle of Islam from Ma'bar, a name frequently given to the Coromandel coast, and to this is added the fact that South Indian Muslims, like Indonesians, are generally adherents to the Shāfi'ī school. These apparently competing sources in fact suggest that one of the reasons why Islam was so attractive in this early period was that influences were coming simultaneously from a number of different areas, for India supplied not only teacher-traders but also acted as a stepping stone for Muslims from other areas of the Islamic world.

Somewhat neglected in this discussion have been other possible sources of contact with Islamic teaching, such as Champa, where two Muslim gravestones dating from the early eleventh century have been located. The Chinese connection may also be significant. Trading contacts with Persia and Central Asia led to the development of Sino-Muslim communities in towns along the southeast coast of China, notably Canton (Guanzhou). The involvement of Muslim Chinese in ocean-going trade in turn fostered the growth of settlements overseas. In 1416, for instance, the Chinese Muslim Ma Huan remarked that most of the Chinese living in Java came from southern China, and that many of them were Muslim. While the dominance of the Hanafi school in China has made scholars reluctant to see Chinese Muslim traders as missionizers, the influence they wielded cannot be discounted. For centuries China had been regarded as the virtual overlord of most of Southeast Asia, and the seal of imperial approval given to Islam by an emperor such as Yung-lo (1402–24) must have aided its cause.

The degree to which Chinese contributed to the spread of Islam in Java remains debatable, although most scholars accept that the founders of several ruling families along the north coast were Chinese Muslims who had married local women. However, Chinese connections for Islam are much clearer elsewhere in the archipelago. In Jolo in the southern Philippines, for example, one of the founders of local Islam is said to have come accompanied by Muslim Chinese, while in about 1590 a Spaniard in Brunei was told that Islam had been brought by a Sultan Yusuf who had come from the Malay lands via China. There he had married a Chinese noblewoman and was confirmed as king of Borneo by the emperor of China 'whom he recognised as a superior king'. It was from this marriage that the rulers of Brunei were descended.[12]

Evidence regarding the arrival of Islam in Southeast Asia and its origins is thus incomplete and at times conflicting. Arabs had known of the region for generations, but only from the thirteenth century is there clear proof of local adoption of the Muslim religion. Even then Islamic influence was confined to scattered ports along coastal trading routes. While India was almost certainly the conduit for Islamic ideas, the first Muslim teacher-traders probably came from various parts of the then Islamic world. Future research may provide a more detailed picture of the way Chinese Muslims contributed to the prestige of the Islamic faith. It is clear, however, that despite continuing Shī'ite influences, it was Sunni Islam which was established in Southeast Asia, together with one of its four schools of law, the Shāfi'ī. We also know that, by the time Islam began to penetrate the region, the central structure of Sunni doctrine had assumed more or less its final form, and the text of the Koran and corpus of traditions relating to the Prophet had been established. Yet in their response to and interpretation of these new teachings, the peoples of the region were able to contribute to a process that was to give Southeast Asian Islam a distinctive character which it has retained to the present day.

---

[12] John S. Carroll, 'Berunai in the Boxer Codex', JMBRAS, 55, 2 (1982) 4.

The Conversion of Melaka

The decision of the ruler of the Malay port of Melaka to adopt Islam is a
milestone in the history of Islam's expansion into Southeast Asia. Apparently founded by a refugee prince from Palembang around the beginning
of the fifteenth century, Melaka grew from a small fishing village into a
trading emporium which became the commercial hub of the archipelago.
The increasing numbers of Muslim traders from India arriving in the
region would also have helped raise Islam's prestige while they themselves conveyed the basic tenets of the faith. Indeed, according to a
well-known Malay epic, Melaka's famed folk hero Hang Tuah was taught
to recite the Koran by a trader from India's Coromandel coast.

Several dates for the conversion of the Melaka ruler, ranging from 1409
to 1436 CE, have been suggested, but the precise year is still subject to
speculation. It is unlikely that the founder of the dynasty was himself
Muslim, and it may have been the third ruler, Sri Maharaja Muhammad
Syah (r. 1425–45) who made the decision to embrace the Islamic faith.[13]
The great Malay description of Melaka, the *Sejarah Melayu*, recognizes the
significance of this event, portraying it in terms of divine revelation, a
formulaic account which is found repeatedly in other local versions of
Islam's arrival. The Prophet himself appears to the ruler of Melaka in a
dream, teaches him the profession of faith (*shahāda*, Indonesian *syahadat*),
gives him the Muslim name of Muhammad and foretells the arrival the
next day of a ship from Jedda. When the king wakes, he discovers that he
has been circumcised. To the amazement of his servants, who believe he is
possessed by a spirit, he continually repeats the confession of faith. That
evening a ship from Jedda duly reaches Melaka carrying an eminent
teacher, a Sayid, one of the Prophet's own descendants. He is received in
honour by the ruler and it is on this occasion that the Melaka chiefs adopt
Islam, while all the people 'whether of high or low degree' are ordered to
do likewise.[14]

In the early sixteenth century Tomé Pires readily accepted the explanation that Islam's success was due to pragmatic rather than spiritual
motives. According to his account the Melaka ruler was aware that Muslim
Pasai owed its commercial vitality largely to the patronage of Indian
Muslim traders. He therefore took active steps to emulate Pasai's success
and himself attract Muslims to Melaka. Muslim merchants were granted
commercial privileges, residences and mosques were built for them, and
they were welcomed at court. Pires goes on to say that under the influence
of Pasai and prominent Muslim merchants and mullahs, both from the
Arab lands and Bengal, the ruler of Melaka adopted Islam at the age of
seventy-two and married the king of Pasai's daughter.

Modern scholars, while accepting the importance of the trading connection, have been more concerned with explaining why Islam had such an
appeal to Malay rulers. It is useful to remember that in the fifteenth

[13] The evidence is conflicting, but has been reviewed in C. H. Wake, 'Malacca's early kings
and the reception of Islam', JSEAH, 5, 2 (1964).
[14] C. C. Brown, ed. and trans., '*Sejarah Melayu*, or Malay Annals', JMBRAS, 25, 2 and 3 (1952)
41–3.

century Muslim traders dominated a commercial network which stretched from Europe to Maluku. The kings of Melaka would clearly have gained by becoming part of a Muslim community that included rulers like those of Cambay or Bengal, Aden and Hormuz. The fifteenth century also saw a resurgence in Islam's temporal power. In 1453 the Ottoman Turks under their new ruler Mehmed II took Constantinople (Istanbul), rebuilding it into a centre of Muslim culture and scholarship. It is highly likely that stories of Mehmed's extensive victories percolated into the region, and certainly local traditions accord the same veneration to the rulers of 'Rum' ('Rome', i.e. Byzantium) as they do to the emperors of China. Furthermore, by this time the influence of Persian notions of kingship, stressing the monarch's sacral nature and elevating him to a place high above ordinary mortals, had spread throughout much of the Islamic world. Already regarded as possessed of supernatural powers, Melaka rulers were now able to assume other new and imposing Persian-style titles. The coins they minted proclaim the ruler as sultan and syah, thus raising him above all other princes in the area who, with the exception of Pasai, bore the simpler title raja. The ruler of Melaka was also termed 'Helper of the World and of the Religion' (*Nāṣir al-dunyā wa'l-dīn*), the deputy of Allah, to whom obedience was due as a religious obligation.[15]

It is therefore not surprising that the promotion of Islam in Melaka was carried out under royal patronage, with rulers themselves actively encouraging teaching and missionary work. Marriages between Muslims and infidels were arranged to attract new converts, and apostasy was forbidden. The performance of the obligatory daily prayers was constantly stressed, and to a considerable extent the legal system began to favour Muslims, especially as witnesses. Successive Melaka rulers also continued to promote Islam in neighbouring states, persuading or compelling their rulers to accept the new religion.

During the course of the fifteenth century, Melaka came to be regarded in the archipelago as a centre for Islamic scholarship, with religious teachers attracted by the patronage of the court and the possibility of acquiring pupils. Since Malay was the language of trade, and since Malay-speaking Melaka was the focus of regional commerce, the spread of Islam outwards along trade routes was a natural development. Indeed, so associated was Islam with Malay culture that in many areas the phrase *masuk melayu* (to become a Malay) came to mean the adoption of Islam. As the vehicle by which instruction in Islam was transmitted, the Malay language acquired a special status. In Bima, for example, the ruler in 1645 ordered that court notebooks should be written in the Malay language 'because this is the writing which has been approved by Allah Almighty'.[16]

Java's Role in the Spread of Islam

The rise of Melaka coincided with other important changes in Java. It appears that Majapahit rulers were aware of the advantages to be obtained from ties with Muslim courts in the region, for several legends mention

---

[15] ibid., 118; A. C. Milner, 'Islam and Malay kingship', JRAS, 1 (1981) 46–70.
[16] Henri Chambert-Loir, *Ceritera Asal Bangsa Jin dan Segala Dewa Dewa*, Bandung, 1985, 11.

high-born Muslim females who are taken into the Majapahit *kraton*. The grave of a Muslim woman found in east Java which dates from 1448 CE is even said to be that of a 'princess' who came from Champa (where leading merchant families were already Muslim) to marry the Majapahit ruler. Firmer evidence for the influence of Islam in the Majapahit court during the fifteenth century is provided by four Muslim graves near the site of the capital which date from between 1407 and 1475. These all bear a carving of the sun which, together with their proximity to the *kraton*, suggests that they mark the burial place of high-ranking nobles or even members of the king's family.

During this period the northern coast of Java, where Muslim communities may date from the last decades of the fourteenth century, was gaining importance economically as trade between Melaka and the Spice Islands of eastern Indonesia expanded. Pires attributes the adoption of Islam by the ruling families of these ports to the missionizing efforts of Sultan Muzafar of Melaka around the middle of the fifteenth century and even suggests that in some cases Muslims forcibly took control. He does not regard these Muslim rulers as Javanese of long standing, but as descendants of Chinese, Indian and Arab traders, many of whom had close links with Melaka. Javanese tradition, on the other hand, had at least by the seventeenth century attributed the coming of Islam to the efforts of 'nine' *walīs* (saints, those acting on behalf of God). At Gresik, which legends claim was with Surabaya the first Javanese port to adopt Islam, is a grave dated 822 AH (1419 CE), popularly believed to mark the burial spot of one of the most famous of these holy men, Malik Ibrahim.

Embedded in the stories of the miraculous deeds of the *walīs* are indications that several had studied or lived in Melaka and were involved in trade, and it was this commercial network which continued to foster Islam's spread. The trading routes from Melaka and north-coast Java brought Muslims naturally to the clove-producing islands of Tidore, Ternate, Makian, Bacan, Jailolo and Motir, where the kings became Muslim about the mid-fifteenth century. By the time the first Europeans arrived in 1512, the ruler of Ternate had established his superiority over his royal neighbours by assuming the title of sultan, and missionaries from Ternate were working to spread the faith in the southern Philippines.

During the fifteenth century, therefore, Islam made significant progress in the region. But while most ports along the major trade routes between Melaka and the Spice Islands had a community of Muslim traders, by no means all coastal rulers had accepted the faith, despite a long exposure to the Muslim presence. Islam's real advance did not occur until the sixteenth and early seventeenth centuries, when a number of factors combined to confirm its position in island Southeast Asia.

The Spread of Islam

There are several reasons for the accelerated pace of Islamization from around 1500 CE. In the first place, the conquest of Melaka by the Portuguese in 1511 closed that port to Muslim traders, who then began to patronize other places where the religious environment was more sympathetic. Aceh, on the northern tip of Sumatra, had apparently adopted Islam in the mid-fourteenth century and quickly developed into a centre for Muslim trade. Acehnese rulers became renowned for their patronage of Islam, and their campaigns carried the faith along both the east and west coasts of Sumatra. Another beneficiary of Melaka's fall was Brunei in northwest Borneo. Its ruler was converted to Islam sometime between 1514 and 1521, and the court soon acquired a reputation for sponsoring Islamic missionary activity, particularly in the Philippine archipelago. The chronology of Islam's advance in the southern Philippines is more difficult to establish, but well before the Spanish arrival in 1565 the courts of Sulu and Magindanao were under Muslim kings, and by this time a Muslim family related to the kings of Brunei had also assumed control in the Manila area.

A second development occurred around 1527 with the defeat of the Hindu-Buddhist kingdom of Majapahit by several north-coast Islamic states under the leadership of Demak. While the defeat of Majapahit does not signify a total break in the continuum of Javanese history, it does mark another stage in Islam's spread. Demak, whose ruler had taken the title of sultan around 1524, was already considered a patron of Islam, and its sacred mosque was regarded with particular veneration. Following the fall of Majapahit, Demak forces took to the field to assert supremacy over neighbouring ports. Under Demak's patronage, Banten in west Java developed into an important Islamic centre, and soon began to push out into the Lampung area of Sumatra. It was also from Demak that Islam spread to south Borneo. By the 1540s Demak's armies were moving into east Java, where Islam had not yet taken hold. Though Demak declined in the 1550s, other Javanese ports continued to foster Muslim missionary efforts. Of particular importance was Gresik, and teachers from here are frequently mentioned in stories of conversion from Lampung, Lombok, Makassar, Kutai and Maluku. In much of eastern Indonesia the 'priest king', the holy man of Giri who lived atop a mountain about half a mile from Gresik was revered as a source of supernatural power who could even bring the dead back to life.

A third milestone was reached with the conversion of the twin kingdoms of Goa-Tallo (better known as Makassar) in Sulawesi. While local chronicles convey an impression of sudden revelation, it is clear that the ruler's decision to adopt Islam was slow and considered. By the early seventeenth century Makassar was one of the few important courts where Islam was not established, despite the patronage given to Muslim traders and the missionary work of teachers from Aceh, Java, Pattani, and elsewhere. A crucial factor in the final decision appears to have been the acceptance of Islam by the ruler of Luwu, the oldest and most prestigious kingdom in Sulawesi, in early 1605. On Friday 9 Jumadilawal 1014 (22 September 1605) the ruler of Tallo, Karaeng Matoaya, recited the confession of faith, and assumed a new Arabic name which meant 'the first of Islam'. At the same time the ruler of Goa took the title Sultan Alauddin.

Makassar's patronage gave Islam a new base for missionary teaching in Sulawesi and eastern Indonesia. In conformity with Islamic custom, Makassar invited surrounding kingdoms to accept Islam. When their rulers refused, a series of campaigns was launched, known locally as the Islam Wars. By 1611 all southwest Sulawesi, including Makassar's Bugis rival Bone, had become Muslim. Only the mountainous area of Toraja did not succumb, primarily because the people here saw Islam as the faith of their traditional enemies. In 1618 Makassar undertook the first of several attacks on the island of Sumbawa to force recalcitrant local rulers to accept Islam. By the 1640s most neighbouring kingdoms had accepted Makassar's overlordship and with it the Muslim faith.

The growing attraction of Islam in the sixteenth century must also be seen in the context of developments in the wider Islamic world. The links with the Islamic heartlands appear to have considerably strengthened in this period, for local and European sources frequently mention the arrival of teachers from Mecca, Egypt and Istanbul. Such men would have brought news of the continuing advance of the Ottoman Turks, who now controlled the holy centres of Mecca, Medina and Jerusalem. Under the leadership of Suleiman the Magnificent (1520–66) Turkish armies proceeded to move into the Balkans, conquering Hungary and transforming the Mediterranean into a Muslim lake. By 1543 Suleiman had defeated the Habsburgs and had established an Ottoman provincial administration in Hungary. Not without reason did he style himself Sultan of Sultans and the Inheritor of the Great Caliphate. Reports of Turkish victories, filtering into Southeast Asia through the trade network, would have impressed local rulers and in about 1548 the ruler of Demak allegedly said that if he succeeded in defeating all Java he would consider himself a 'second Turk'.[17]

In the archipelago the presence of Turkish mercenaries and adventurers helped to reinforce Rum's legendary reputation. Not only were they active traders; in addition, they had particular command of military skills, specifically knowledge of muskets and large siege cannon. Local kings were quick to take advantage of this expertise. Turkish soldiers were incorporated into Aceh's armies and, according to Portuguese sources, were used in Aceh's campaigns against the Batak areas around 1537. They were also incorporated into several attacks launched on Portuguese Melaka by Aceh during the course of the sixteenth century. In the 1560s there were more direct contacts between Aceh and Istanbul as Acehnese rulers despatched missions to try to interest the Ottoman sultan in a military operation against the Christian Portuguese. While Turkey did not become involved on an official level, there were certainly messages of support and valued gifts such as banners and cannon.

Developments in India in the sixteenth century are equally significant, for here too the conquering power of Islam appeared to be amply demonstrated in the creation of a new Muslim dynasty, that of the Mughals (Moguls), in 1526. Gradually over the next fifty years, notably in the reign of Akbar (1556–1605), the Mughals proceeded to establish a kingdom which was to dominate the Indian subcontinent. Despite his eclecticism, Akbar was still formally a Muslim ruler whose incorporation of Hindu and

[17] H. J. de Graaf and Th. G. Th. Pigeaud, *De Eerste Moslimse Vorstendommen op Java*, The Hague, 1974, 76.

Persian traditions help to affirm popular veneration for Islamic kings in India and provides a persuasive example of the power with which Islam was associated. Iskandar Muda of Aceh (r. 1607–36) is thought to have been inspired by the 'Grand Mughal', and the panegyric recounting his deeds, the *Hikayat Aceh*, to have been modelled on the contemporary Indian work, the *Akbarnāma*.

The arrival of the Portuguese and Spaniards, who came determined not only to make Christian converts but to destroy Muslim trading dominance, was paradoxically another stimulus to the spread of Islam in the Indonesian archipelago. Decades of conflict between Christian and Muslim states in Europe and the Middle East had seen frequent recourse to notions of crusade and holy war which were imported into Southeast Asia. Albuquerque, who led the successful attack on Melaka, initially opposed any association with Muslims, and in the aftermath of the conquest the great mosque of Melaka was completely destroyed and all Muslim traders expelled. Local Muslims, for their part, could at times be persuaded that resistance to the Portuguese was enjoined by Allah. Sixteenth-century Javanese texts list obedience to the summons of holy war (*jihad*) as one of the duties prescribed by Islam, and remind Muslims that they should not befriend infidels, 'for this will be recorded against you as a sin in this world and the world to come'.[18] The struggle between Islam and Christianity seemed particularly marked in eastern Indonesia, where Jesuits reported the arrival of 'priests' from Mecca, Aceh, the Malay areas and elsewhere calling for a holy war. Towards the end of the century the atmosphere of confrontation was heightened as the Spanish, newly established in the Philippines, embarked on a push into the Muslim-dominated areas of the south. In 1578 the Brunei mosque was burned and the lord of Magindanao was told that the Spanish aimed to obtain his conversion to Christianity. To some extent, therefore, there was a 'race' between Islam and Christianity, as adherents of each tried to confirm their commercial, political and spiritual hold over particular areas.

While stressing the various stimuli to conversion, however, one should also emphasize the genuine appeal of Islam itself, and particularly the mystical strand known as Sufism (a term probably derived from *suf*, or wool from which the coarse garments of Muslim ascetics were made). Mysticism had been able to maintain a place in the Islamic mainstream because of the teachings of devout Sufis, pre-eminent among whom was one of the greatest Muslim theologians, Abū Ḥāmid al-Ghazālī (450–505 AH, 1058–1111 CE). From about the thirteenth century CE, mystical schools or *ṭarīqa* (Indonesian *tarekat*) had begun to develop, focusing on the teachings of one Sufi leader or *shaykh* which were transmitted to his disciples through a genealogical chain linking pupils and masters to the founder himself. With its willingness in certain forms and traditions to accommodate existing beliefs, Sufism developed into a significant vehicle for the movement of Islam outside the heartlands. Sufi teachers fanned out along trading routes where members of the *ṭarīqa* were often drawn from the commercial community. In India, which had a long tradition of

18 G. W. J. Drewes, ed. and trans., *The Admonitions of Seh Bari*, The Hague, 1969, 69.

veneration for holy men, Sufism found a sympathetic environment. By the end of the fifteenth century a number of orders had gained a footing there, with some of the later but more influential being the Qādiriyya, the Shaṭṭāriyya and the Naqshabandiyya. These three orders also became the most popular in Southeast Asia.

Mystical thought was a part of Southeast Asian Islam from very early times, but not until the sixteenth century are there any contemporary textual sources. The few surviving Javanese mystical works of this period lie firmly within the framework of 'sober' or ascetic mysticism with one referring for its authority to al-Ghazālī's great work, *The Revival of the Religious Sciences* (*Ihyā''ulūm al-dīn*). However, a number of other renowned Sufi teachers are also mentioned, and some of them, like Ibn al-'Arabī (560–638 AH, 1165–1240 CE) held more controversial views. Al-'Arabī is known especially for his formulation of the doctrine of *waḥdatu'l wujūd*, the Unity of Being, from which a myriad of aspects were revealed as the manifold forms of creation, and for his concept of the Perfect Man, the microcosmic figure who represents in himself the perfect attributes of the Divine Being. Ibn al-'Arabī's standing increased considerably during the fifteenth and sixteenth centuries, and Selim I of Turkey even ordered the rebuilding of his mausoleum in Damascus. It is not surprising, therefore, to find his name invoked as an authority in texts of this period. His influence is very clear in the writings of Hamzah Fansuri, a local teacher from Barus in western Sumatra known to have lived in the second half of the sixteenth century and to have been received into the Qādiriyya *ṭarīqa* while visiting Baghdad.

In Southeast Asia the Sufi aim of union with the Absolute blended easily with deep-rooted cultural attitudes that had long conceived of a constant interaction between the world of men and that of spirits. Many of the concepts presented in Sufi teachings thus struck a responsive chord in Southeast Asian societies. As Hamzah Fansuri put it,

> His radiance is a blazing glow
> In all of us
> It is He who is the cup and the *arak*
> Do not look for Him far away, child.

Or again, in the words of a Javanese text,

> there is no difference
> between worshipper and the worshipped
> both are He alone
> as the being of the universe
> cannot be divided.[19]

Southeast Asians would also have been drawn to Sufism because the methods used to achieve an ecstatic sense of unity with the Divine— dancing, singing, music, drumming, meditation, the recitation of *zikir*, 'magic' words in the form of Koranic passages or formulaic prayers—were similar to the religious practices to which they had been accustomed. Sufi

---

[19] *Arak* is rice wine. G. W. J. Drewes and L. F. Brakel, *The Poems of Hamzah Fansuri*, Dordrecht, Holland, and Cinnaminson, U.S.A., 1986, 8; G. W. J. Drewes, 'Javanese poems dealing with or attributed to the Saint of Bonan', BKI, 124, 2 (1968) 225. Professor A. H. Johns suggested a slight change to the original translation.

emphasis on the close relationship between disciple and teacher, which is frequently compared to that of a parent and child or elder and younger brother, would similarly have found ready acceptance in traditional societies like those of Southeast Asia where kinship ties are considered fundamental in human interaction.

Available texts also suggest that an understanding of Sufism in Southeast Asia was facilitated because local teachers, drawing prestige from their links with Pasai, Minangkabau, Melaka, Java or Johor, used familiar images to explain the essence of mystical Islam. 'It is said', wrote one, 'that human sight may be compared to coconut milk, which in the long run will become oil; to an unripe banana, which gradually grows half-ripe . . . gradually human sight is perfected by the lord so that there is no doubt that the eye will behold the essence.'[20] Even so, we have no way of knowing how widely these works were read; one assumes they would have been studied only by the spiritual élite. Despite the obvious appeal of Sufism, its teachings were probably considerably simplified in oral transmission. One text warns against using Sufi terminology without complete understanding and quotes the *hadith* (tradition), 'Tell to the people what they understand; do you want to make God and his Prophet liars?'[21] Furthermore, while there were a number of erudite teachers in the courts, others involved in introducing Islam to the peoples of the archipelago may have had only a general understanding of mystic ideas. In the early seventeenth century, for instance, the Imam of Jambi on the east coast of Sumatra was a trader from Pahang, while in Ambon Javanese traders who could read and write often stayed over for a season to act as religious teachers. The first task of the Islamic schools established in the trading ports would have been to impart basic Muslim ideas, teach the ritual prayers and assist pupils to memorize passages from the Koran rather than to initiate deep discussions about exceedingly complex ideas. While one must be wary of generalizing from the few extant sixteenth-century texts, since they have survived purely by chance, they do provide evidence of this stress on the fundamentals of Islamic practice. Good Muslims should observe the precepts of Islam—perform the ritual prayers (*salat*) five times daily, recite the Koran, pay alms, fast during Ramadan, make the pilgrimage if possible, and respond to any call to join the holy war. Like the later Christian missionaries, Muslim teachers also developed a type of catechism designed to answer some of the most common queries, such as the meaning of unfamiliar words, the nature of paradise, and the fate of those condemned to hell. The condemnation of the pig as unclean received particular attention in eastern Indonesia where this animal had been accorded great veneration and was an important item of food at ritual feasts. In Maluku the Spaniards on Magellan's ships killed all the pigs they carried on board to please the king, 'for when those people happen to see any swine they cover their faces in order that they might not look upon them or catch their odour'.[22]

[20] Drewes, *The Admonitions*, 69.
[21] A. Johns, 'Dakā'ik al-Huruf by 'Abd al-Ra'uf of Singkel', JRAS (1955), 69, 72.
[22] Antonio Pigafetta, *Magellan's Voyage around the World*, ed. James A. Robertson, Cleveland, 1906, II. 29, 81.

At the same time the great triumph of Islam was its ability, within certain limits, to tolerate numerous pre-Muslim beliefs and practices. This was in turn due to the fact that the corpus of Islamic law and tradition, the *shari'a*, allows for some local interpretation. Indeed, the legal codes of Melaka frequently include two penalties for the same crime, one following custom—now subsumed under the Arabic-derived word *adat*—and the other that of 'the law of Allah'. Much of the ritual associated with the great life crises survived, legitimized by Koranic verses and prayers recited by a person considered knowledgeable in the faith. The *Taj us-Salatin*, for instance, declares that after a birth it is the parents' duty to dress the child in proper clothes and then to have the call to prayer (*azan*) recited in the right ear and the following exhortation to prayer (*iqamah*) in the left. A new prominence was also given to circumcision, which was already practised for both sexes in many areas of the archipelago. In Islamic communities, however, it was elevated into an important rite of passage, especially for Muslim males. They and their families gained considerable prestige because the ceremony was performed by respected religious figures, frequently in the mosque itself. Islamic teachers could also be important in curing rites. In Makassar, for instance,

> if the sickness come to be never so little dangerous, they apply themselves no more to the physicians, but go straight to the priests because they do not think it then proceeds from any natural cause; and for that they imagine it is caused by some evil spirit, that is to be expelled by forces of exorcism and prayers.[23]

The new vocabulary offered by Islam, invoking the awe-inspiring authority of a supreme God and his designated spokesman, thus furnished another powerful weapon to defy potentially harmful spirits. In the words of an old incantation from Perak,

> Muhammad my shelter is beside me
> Only if Allah suffer harm
> Can I suffer harm
> Only if His Prophet suffer harm
> Can I suffer harm.[24]

At the same time the introduction of a whole range of angels, prophets and saintly teachers expanded the numbers of heroes and superhuman figures who could be invoked for help, advice and examples of proper conduct. For example, as elsewhere in the Islamic world 'Abd al-Qādir l-Jīlānī (470–561 AH, 1077–1166 CE), the founder of the Qādiriyya order, became an object of particular veneration, in part because of his descent from the Prophet. A manuscript from Banten dating from the early seventeenth century describes him as so pious that as a baby he even refused his mother's breast during the fasting month. This array of Islamic heroes was constantly augmented by the addition of revered locals, like Dato ri Bandang who legend claims brought Islam to Makassar and the surrounding areas, and who is said to have arrived in Kutai riding on a swordfish.

Through this kind of adaptation, Southeast Asian Muslims were already

[23] Gervaise, *An Historical Description*, 140.
[24] Richard Winstedt, *The Malay Magician*, Kuala Lumpur, 1982, 74.

coming to see Islamic beliefs not as imported but as an integral part of their own culture. In the western archipelago it ceased to be associated only with the coastal regions as internal trade and active proselytizing carried Islamic teachings into the interior. A poem written in Aceh in 1679, outlining the creation of the world and the implications of the Day of Judgement, was thus composed in Acehnese rather than Malay because 'few people [presumably in the interior] know the Malay language'.[25] Seventeenth-century chronicles may attribute the introduction of Islam to a holy man from overseas, from Mecca, Pasai, Melaka, Minangkabau or Java, but at the same time the acceptance of the new faith is symbolized by a marriage between this revered teacher and a local woman of high birth. In a number of cases he is associated with cultural features which helped distinguish a society from its neighbours. In Brunei, for instance, Sultan Yusuf was said to have discovered camphor, for which northwest Borneo was renowned; in Java *walīs* such as the great Sunan Kalijaga were often seen as adept in composing certain poetic metres, in kris making, in performing *wayang*—skills which lie at the very heart of Javanese culture.

By the time the Dutch East India Company established its headquarters at Batavia (Jayakatra) in 1619, Islam was clearly the rising faith in island Southeast Asia. The Spaniards themselves acknowledged that, had they not taken Manila in 1571, Islam would have penetrated the entire Philippine archipelago. A comment on the prestige of Islam is the fact that in the seventeenth century at least two mainland rulers converted, probably (like so many of their counterparts in the island world) in the hope of gaining some powerful ally. Some time between 1607 and 1676 the king of Champa, Vietnam's vassal, became Muslim, and Islam here spread to the extent that most Chams were at least nominal Muslims. In Cambodia, where the Thais presented a constant threat, the Muslim Cham and Malay merchant community was instrumental in a successful usurpation of power by a Khmer prince, who around 1643 adopted Islam and underwent circumcision. He took the reign name Sultan Ibrahim, but was called by the people Rama Cul Sas, or 'King Rama who embraced the religion [of Islam]'.

In general, however, Islam made little progress in mainland Southeast Asia, although there were substantial Muslim communities in the major ports. An obvious reason is the entrenched position of Theravāda Buddhism and its widespread integration into local culture, forming an all-encompassing belief system which seriously addressed questions regarding the afterlife as well as the problems of this one. But even in the island world Islam did not carry all before it. Attempts to persuade people to become Muslims not infrequently met with active resistance or simply indifference. The Badui of Sunda provide just one instance of a community which never adopted Islam, despite their proximity to Banten. Islamic ideas were also slow to spread in the scattered islands of eastern Indonesia because of their geographic isolation from trading routes and their very loose links with Muslim centres like Ternate. It is useful to remember that

[25] P. Voorhoeve, 'Three Old Achehnese manuscripts', BSOAS, 14 (1951–2) 337–9.

Islamization in contemporary Indonesia is still continuing and that in a number of societies indigenous beliefs still predominate.

Bali

The most obvious example of a society which was not caught up by Islam's advance is Bali. A glance at the historical background helps explain why this should be so. In Bali the sixteenth century had been a time of political consolidation. Conquest by Majapahit in 1334 had resulted in a union of the entire island, and following Majapahit's decline in the 1520s the tradition of unitary government had been assumed by the kingdom of Gelgel. Under Gelgel's leadership the Balinese extended their control not only over the entire island but into east Java on the one side and as far as Lombok and Sumbawa on the other. During this period the rich heritage of Majapahit was reshaped to create a uniquely Balinese social order characterized by the four basic divisions of the Hindu caste system, now enforced by rules punishing caste infringements. The *brahmana* (brahmins, the priestly caste), *satria* (warrior-kings) and *wesia* (nobles) were known collectively as the *trivangśa*, the three castes, standing apart from the bulk of the population, the *sudras*. There were also important developments in religion. Local temples, which can be seen as elaborated megalithic monuments, cult centres for the invocation of local divinities, the ancestors and the powers of fertility, continued to flourish, but the earlier Buddhism and the veneration of Indra were gradually overshadowed by rituals which stressed the worship of Śiva as manifested by the sun, the making of holy water, the recitation of mantra set down in the sacred scriptures, and ceremonial feasting (*galungan*). Temple priests (*pamangku*) who had survived from previous times were often relegated to commoner status, with the Śiva-worshipping high priests (*padanda*) coming exclusively from the *brahmana* caste and presiding over the ritual central to religious observances.

Bali thus faced the advance of Islam in the sixteenth century strengthened politically and invigorated religiously. In a society which had developed a complex and culturally self-sustaining means of explaining the cosmos and man's place in it, Islam made little headway. Nonetheless, Balinese were not opposed to Islam as such. Balinese who settled in Java tended to become Muslims, and in the eighteenth century Balinese Muslims in Batavia had their own mosque. Active resistance to Islam occurred when it was seen as a tool used by the Javanese or some other rival to lend legitimacy to a Muslim ruler's political ambitions. One tradition, for instance, claims that Balinese lances were smeared with pigfat during conflict between Gelgel and the staunchly Muslim Makassar over control of Lombok. Generally, however, the Balinese treated the new religion as they had done previous Javanese influences, incorporating some elements but merging them with their own culture. Mantras, for example, could include Islamic invocations, while in some areas people refrained from offering port to the gods. Balinese kings showed no opposition to the presence of Muslim communities descended from migrant Makassarese and Malays, as long as traditional customs and caste restrictions in marriage were not flouted. A few Muslim villages grew up at places such as Buleleng in the north, helping to promote a small body of Balinese literature dealing with Islam.

In the early seventeenth century the Balinese state under Gelgel's suzerainty was confident and united. Though Gelgel fell in 1651, the politico-religious base which had evolved over the previous 150 years proved well able to survive the fragmentation of the late seventeenth and eighteenth centuries. Indeed, it has been argued that this proliferation of competing Balinese kingdoms provided new centres of cultural enrichment, and that many of the rituals today associated with Bali in fact developed during this period. The vast array of alternative religious and artistic forms which was thus created has been a major factor in the continuing vitality of Balinese society.

THE ARRIVAL OF CHRISTIANITY

When dealing with the arrival of Christianity, the last world religion to arrive in Southeast Asia, we are on much firmer ground than in the case of Islam and the other major faiths. The motivations behind the spread of Christianity, the time of its arrival and the nature of the doctrine taught, are all well known. Catholic Europe in the late fifteenth and early sixteenth centuries was inspired by a zeal for missionizing which had been encouraged by tensions resulting from the protracted wars with Ottoman Turkey and the challenge of Protestantism, as well as by the excitement of recently discovered 'pagan' lands in Asia and the Americas. Foremost in the new endeavour were the Catholic monarchs of Spain and Portugal, who were strongly influenced by the apostolic idea of Christian kingship so prominent in the Middle Ages. In 1493 Papal Bulls made it an obligation for all Catholic kings to promote the spread of Christianity, and in the following year the Treaty of Tordesillas divided the world into two spiritual jurisdictions. One was assigned to the Portuguese Crown and the other to the Spanish. In actual fact, so little was known about world geography that the dividing line established by the Treaty of Tordesillas could not be satisfactorily identified and became a matter of bitter dispute between Spain and Portugal. Nonetheless, it effectively excluded proselytization by any other Catholic nation until the arrival of the French Société des Missions Étrangères in Vietnam in 1662. The royal patronage granted by the pope to the monarchs of Spain and Portugal made them responsible for the conversion of the 'heathen' and thus for the building of churches and monasteries, for appointing archbishops and lesser religious officials, and for financing the missionary effort. Unlike any other religion which came to the region, therefore, Christianity was shored up by the commitment of a secular government located on the other side of the world.

Under Spanish patronage, the first Christians reached the Philippines in March 1521, when Magellan's decimated fleet arrived in Cebu. There they were welcomed by the chief, Raja Humabon, who, together with his wife and eight hundred of his followers, agreed to accept Christianity. The decisive factor in Humabon's decision appears to have been the assurance that the power of Christianity and the association with the Spanish would help him overcome his enemies and protect him from harm. The new relationship with the Europeans was symbolized not merely by the ritual of holy baptism and the bestowal of Christian names, but by a ceremony in which Magellan and Humabon (now christened Don Carlos) drank each other's blood and thus became brothers.

Southwards, the Portuguese reacted to the Spanish expedition by strengthening their position in Maluku, where the king of Ternate had shown an interest in Christianity as early as 1512. In 1522, claiming that Maluku fell within the territory assigned to them for conversion by the Treaty of Tordesillas, the Portuguese accepted an invitation from the Ternate ruler to erect a fortress in his kingdom. In theory at least the king of Ternate had agreed to allow missionary work, while at the same time himself remaining a patron of Islam. Intent on maintaining their spice monopoly, the Portuguese were willing to live with this anomaly, and the preaching of Christianity was never accorded a high priority. A 'vicar' and a few secular clergy were appointed to the Ternate fortress, but while some baptisms were performed, neophytes received minimal instruction in religious doctrine and the so-called 'Christians' showed a disturbing tendency to apostatize.

The high point in the Portuguese mission in the Indonesian archipelago came in 1546 with the arrival of Francis Xavier, co-founder of the Jesuit order. He spent two years in the Maluku region and was said to have made thousands of 'converts', most of whom were among the Alifuru, the non-Muslim interior tribes. It was still apparent, however, that lack of proficiency in languages native to the eastern archipelago was a continuing obstacle to the explanation of Christian doctrine. Although Francis Xavier had undertaken translation of Christian works into Malay, it was found that this supposed lingua franca was unknown in the interior of many eastern islands. Only after the commitment of Jesuits to the region were efforts made to translate Christian texts and catechisms into local languages such as Ternatan and Siau. But Xavier's missionary efforts did stimulate a wider interest in Christianity, and by 1555 thirty villages on Ambon were considered 'Christian'. Even so, the lack of priests meant that whole communities could find themselves thrown back on their own resources. Furthermore, because the Portuguese never received effective support from the Crown, they were incapable of assisting local kings who had accepted Christianity against their (usually Muslim) enemies. The king of Bacan, for instance, was baptized in 1557 as Dom João, but Christian influence waned when the Portuguese could not protect him from Ternatan attacks. Under pressure from Ternate, Dom João later renounced Christianity and returned to Islam. The same experience was repeated elsewhere. In 1595 it was gloomily estimated that of about 40,000 Ambonese Christians, only 3000 had held to their faith. The situation was considered so hopeless that the Jesuits, who had been working in Maluku since the 1540s, even contemplated abandoning the field.

The mission in Maluku was further weakened after 1605 when the Dutch

East India Company (Vereenigde Oost-Indische Compagnie, VOC) took Ambon and drove the Portuguese from Ternate and Tidore. Surrounding islands fell progressively under VOC influence and the number of Jesuits stationed in the Indies steadily dropped. By 1624 only twelve Jesuits were left in Maluku. The capture of Portuguese Melaka by the Dutch in 1641 and the destruction of its numerous monasteries and churches represented a further blow to the Catholic presence in the Indonesian archipelago. With the departure of the last Spaniard from Ternate and Tidore in 1663, Catholic mission work in eastern Indonesia became confined to Solor, Flores and Timor where the Dominicans had been working since 1562.

The Christian impact on Indonesia was far less than in the Philippines, partly because the Catholic missions there never received a similar level of state support. The VOC domination of the area in the seventeenth and eighteenth centuries brought added changes, for the Dutch never considered conversion to be a goal in itself. Nonetheless, there was some attempt to woo converts away from Catholicism to Protestantism and to eradicate 'pagan' beliefs. In 1622, for example, the VOC governor of Ambon claimed that as many as eight hundred spirit houses had been burned and the offerings confiscated. On a number of occasions edicts were issued threatening the death penalty for anyone in whose garden images of the 'devil' were found. Furthermore, Christians in VOC areas were always favoured over Muslims, a practice which encouraged some conversions among eastern Indonesian groups. The attractions of Christianity were particularly evident after a landmark decision in 1729 when the governor-general laid down that a Christian chief could not be punished by his non-Christian lord. It appears to have been this decision which persuaded the first Rotinese ruler to become Christian, and a little more than a decade later seven hundred people in one area of Roti were said to be awaiting baptism. By the end of the eighteenth century Christianity was well established in many of the eastern islands, and for many groups it had become an important key to ethnic identification. The people of Roti, for example, attribute the advent of Christianity not to European missionaries but to one of their own culture heroes who also brought with him the art of distilling palm syrup, on which their economy is dependent.

The Establishment of Christianity in the Philippines

It was the Spanish colony of the Philippines which was destined to become the great Christian mission field in Southeast Asia. To a far greater extent than the Portuguese, the Spanish came to the archipelago seeing themselves as divinely appointed to spread the gospel among the heathen of the Americas and Asia. Although their encounter with Filipinos in Cebu in 1521 had ended in hostility and Magellan's death, the willingness with which so many people had accepted baptism held out a promise that the Philippines could become a rich source of Christian souls. In 1565, after several abortive attempts, another Spanish force under Miguel Lopez de Legazpi returned to Cebu carrying an Augustinian priest whose task was not only to submit a report on the expedition but 'to preach the Holy Gospel to the inhabitants of those new lands and to baptize those who

accept our faith'.[26] However, during the years which had passed since
Magellan's visit, acquaintance with the Portuguese had made local communities more suspicious of the intentions of white men. Two thousand
Cebuans met Legazpi in full battle array, but their lances, shields, cutlasses
and rope armour failed to sustain their courage when faced by Spanish
musketry. Yet in the burning settlement Legazpi's men found evidence
that the brief glimpse of Christianity offered by Magellan a generation
earlier had not been totally forgotten. Among the charred remains they
came across a statue of the Child Jesus which Magellan had earlier
presented to the chief's wife. For over forty years it had been carefully
preserved and held in veneration because it was a miracle-working *dewata*
(god) of the white men.

In the aftermath of Legazpi's attack, the local community sued for peace.
The legal basis of the Spanish endeavour was the fiction that the Cebuanos
who had received baptism in 1521 had become Spanish subjects. As
'rebels' they were now asked to request pardon for killing Magellan and
'renew' an oath of loyalty to the Spanish Crown. Little missionary work
took place during these early years, however, because the Spaniards were
mostly concerned with survival. Besides, there were not enough priests to
undertake sustained teaching, and it was still uncertain if Spain would in
fact stay in the Philippines. Obviously it would be foolish to embark on a
campaign of conversion if the neophytes were to be abandoned, and in the
five years after the Spanish arrival only about a hundred people were
baptized. But in 1570 Philip II made the important decision to commit
Spain to the colonization and Christianization of the Philippine islands,
despite the fact that they would obviously not yield the great wealth which
had once been expected.

The Spanish capture of Manila in May 1571 marks a new stage in the
spread of Christianity. Having seen his settlement reduced to ashes,
the local chief agreed to a treaty by which he not only accepted Spanish
protection but acknowledged the right of the Spaniards to propagate the
Christian faith. In 1578 fifteen Franciscans arrived in Cavite to join the
Augustinians, followed three years later by the Jesuits, then in 1587 by
the Dominicans and in 1606 by the Recollects. By 1595 there were 134
missionaries working in the Philippines, and it was estimated that 288,000
baptisms had taken place. Each order was assigned to a specific area to
evangelize, the aim being that newly converted areas were to be handed
over to secular priests when the faith was well established. Because of
resistance from the orders, however, the full secularization of parishes
in the Philippines never occurred. During the seventeenth and for much
of the eighteenth century it was thus the religious orders who not
only brought in new converts, but took on the task of maintaining them
as Christians.

The missionizing process in the Philippines followed precedents already
set by the Spaniards in Mexico and South America, whence the orders
drew many of their personnel. One of these precedents was the granting
of *encomiendas*, which were held either by the Crown or by individuals

---

[26] Rafael Lopez, trans., *The Christianisation of the Philippines*, Manila, 1965, 255–6.

designated by the king as *encomenderos*. The latter had the right to collect tribute from a particular area, but in return were responsible for making the people aware of Spanish sovereignty and for giving them some basic knowledge of Christianity. In the Philippines the holding of private *encomiendas* was gradually abandoned, but in the early years the *encomenderos*, often former soldiers, played a significant role in blunting local resistance to the Spanish presence and preparing the way for the missionary orders to move in.

Another important aid to Christianizing was the policy of resettling the native population, which had also been followed in Spanish America. The indigenous Filipino pattern of independent kinship communities or *barangay* was changed to one where there was a main centre (*cabecera*) with a church where the Spanish priest lived, surrounded by a number of outlying hamlets (*visitas*). In these *visitas* small chapels were constructed where the priest periodically celebrated mass, and in his absence suitable Filipinos were sometimes selected to perform important Christian duties, such as baptism and preparing the seriously ill for death. For practical purposes, priests usually tried to combine several hamlets and to persuade people to move closer to the newly established town. But progress in this regard was slow, especially outside the Tagalog areas, and at the end of the seventeenth century there were fewer than twenty centres of more than two thousand people. This meant that priests in sparsely populated areas such as the Visayas had to move constantly between isolated settlements. Yet though some baptized Filipinos might see a priest only once a year, the Spanish commitment meant that Christian communities were very rarely abandoned.

The missionary orders did have their own character and concerns, but they shared many similarities because virtually all those involved were Spanish, because they were under the direction of the Spanish Crown and because they drew heavily on the collective Spanish experience of Christianizing in the Americas. Missionaries there had learnt, for instance, that it was vital to obtain the conversion of chiefs in order to win over their followers. In the Philippines local baptized leaders, grouped together as the *principales*, became the linchpin of the Spanish administration, helping to bring their following under the authority of the Church and the Spanish Crown. The people themselves remarked that 'If the father of them all became a Christian, how could they do otherwise?'[27]

Missionaries in New Spain had long since found that the most effective way of converting local leaders was to teach Christian ideas to their children, giving special attention to the sons of chiefs. In several places in the Philippines the orders established schools to instruct the young in Catholic doctrine, with each class concentrating on a particular topic such as the Hail Mary. When pupils had completed all the classes they were considered ready for baptism. Frequently an entire family was baptized together by using the children to prepare their elders, for priests would not baptize adults unless they could recite the basic prayers from memory and demonstrate some knowledge of the principal obligations of a Christian.

[27] Pedro Chirino, *The Philippines in 1600*, trans. Ramon Echevarria, Manila, 1969, 337.

To achieve this goal, much use was made of music, which had been an integral part of indigenous ritual. It was found that Filipinos, like the peoples of eastern Indonesia and the Americas, quickly learned to chant the Ten Commandments, the Lord's Prayer and other parts of the liturgy when these were translated into their own language and sung. Missionaries noted with delight how the people 'sang the doctrine' in their homes or while working in the fields; one father returning from Mass was amazed to hear a village woman 'singing' the sermon he had just given, which she had rendered into verse and put to a traditional tune. These sermons, which were given in the vernacular following the saying of the Latin Mass, generally dealt with one of four topics—the immortality of the soul; the existence of God; the rewards awaiting Christians in the next life; and purgatory, the place of perpetual pain. Explanations were often assisted by pictures, which were especially useful for priests whose knowledge of a regional language was limited.

An important factor in the success of Christianity was the fact that many aspects of worship struck a familiar chord in Filipino culture. Communion, the partaking of the body and blood of Christ, resonated with echoes of ritual feasting, and Tagalog translations of Christian texts spoke of the Eucharist as a source not only of sanctity but of courage, strength and potency. Another means of obtaining the power of Christianity was baptism. Water had always been an essential part of animist rites, and the holy water of the Christians was widely regarded as a cure for the body as well as for the soul. The priests themselves exploited this belief by deliberately making the baptismal ceremony as solemn an occasion as possible and by using holy water freely, especially in ministering to the sick. The sprinkling of water, the recitation of prayers in Latin, and the sign of the cross provided a compelling alternative to the curing rites of the *babaylan*. Even when Christian sacraments did not bring about recovery, faith in the efficacy of holy water remained. As one man said, 'I know that with the water which the Fathers pour on them [the sick children] will go to heaven.'[28] Baptism had additional advantages on earth, because by this means an individual acquired *compadre* or godparents who were charged with particular responsibility for his spiritual welfare. Filipinos, however, expanded this relationship to link the godparents not only with the child's father and mother, but with the rest of his family as well. Normally godparents of a higher social status were chosen and ritual co-parenthood (*compadrazgo*) thus evolved into a patron–client relationship, with both sides obligated to assist one another.

A further source of power inherent in Christianity was the vast family of holy figures it introduced into a society where the concept of spirit worship was deeply embedded. Saints, especially those to whom a local church was dedicated, came to be viewed as akin to sympathetic and approachable ancestors, whose assistance could be obtained by appropriate gifts and humble petitions and whose names could be invoked as a source of protection. 'Use this weapon [i.e. the names of Jesus and Mary]', says one commentary, 'and do not let it go, so that you may triumph against your

[28] Ana Maria Madrigal Llorente, *A Blending of Cultures: the Batanes, 1686–1898*, Manila, 1983, 60.

enemies.'[29] Blessed by the priest, rosaries, crosses, bibles and holy medals became potent talismans, and the priest's domain—his dwelling, the Christian burial ground nearby, and above all the church—a locus of extraordinary power. In one settlement where the church was moved to higher ground to avoid flooding, the people immediately moved their houses to the new site. The reason, they said, was their dread of the devils who nightly roamed the old town because it now had neither church nor cross.

In the meeting of local culture and Christian teaching there was a considerable degree of compromise. For example, Filipinos gradually came to accept the Christian idea of monogamy and the indissolubility of marriage, although this did cause some tensions in a society where divorce was relatively easy and where wealthy chiefs usually had more than one wife. At the same time, however, there was a steady Filipinization of many aspects of Christian worship. Some Filipinos believed, for instance, that one might not spit, or bathe oneself, or eat meat for three days prior to taking the Eucharist, while the occasion itself became an opportunity for women in particular to display their wealth in dress and jewellery as they had been accustomed to do in traditional *manganito* (spirit propitiation ceremonies) held for a betrothal or the gathering of the harvest. Firecrackers could even be set off during the raising of the host. Holy days in general were marked off for festivities and parties when the people of both sexes and all ages came together after saying the rosary, and observers in Manila noted how people 'diverted themselves by dancing, singing and bold and indecorous games'.[30]

There can be no doubt that this kind of compromise did give the missionaries cause for concern. The Franciscans and Dominicans were especially adamant that non-Christian cultures were the work of the devil, and that tolerance was a betrayal of Christian principles. As in the Americas, priests generally avoided translating key doctrinal concepts in an effort to avoid any confusion with native beliefs. The Spanish word 'Dios', for example, was used for God rather than any local equivalent, and the same principle was applied to other terms such as Trinity, Holy Ghost, grace, sin and hell. Particular efforts were made to root out spirit propitiation. One of the first steps in converting a village community was to insist on the destruction of any 'idols', old altars or places of worship, and when baptized Christians came to confession they were rigorously questioned as to whether they had been treated by sorcerers, or had sworn by dreams, or had made offerings to the spirits. Translated catechisms, like one sixteenth-century Tagalog text, directly addressed the issue of spirit worship: 'Christians, you have been baptized . . . why do you consult the *anito* when you get sick? Can the lifeless give life? Why do you make an offering when you work in the fields? Who else makes the rice grow if not God?'[31] But despite the efforts of the missionaries, the old beliefs

[29] Vincente L. Rafael, *Contracting Colonialism: Translation and Christian Conversion in Tagalog Society under Early Spanish Rule*, Ithaca and London, 1988, 120.

[30] Fernandez, *The Church in the Philippines*, 164.

[31] Antonio M. Rosales, *A Study of a Sixteenth Century Tagalog Manuscript on the Ten Commandments: Its Significance and Implications*, Quezon City, 1984, 35, 39.

remained. Rice seeds might be brought to the priest to be blessed, and the cross might stand guardian in the fields, but planting and harvest times were also the occasion for gatherings when pigs or chickens were presented to the spirits, and deceased ancestors were summoned up through prayers and sacred dances. Like other Southeast Asians, Filipinos continued to make offerings to ensure the co-operation of the supernatural whether they were gathering fruit, cutting wood, or collecting bamboo. In 1731 one friar complained that an accepted method of catching a thief was to place a pair of scissors upright on a screen in the shape of the cross of Saint Andrew, and hang a rosary on it. The name of those suspected was repeated and the shaking of the screen indicated the guilty party.

Caution should naturally be exercised in generalizing about the conversion experience of Filipinos, since cultural attitudes explaining the acceptance of Christian teachings in one area may not necessarily apply in another.[32] Yet regardless of the reasons underlying missionary success, it is clear that by the latter part of the seventeenth century the adaptation process had enabled Christianity to take firm root in the northern half of the Philippines. This in turn had encouraged the Spanish to proceed anew with missionary work in the south. In 1635 a fort was established in Zamboanga, and from this base the Jesuits were able to negotiate peace treaties permitting them to undertake Christian teaching in Muslim areas. But the extent to which force accompanied the Christian missions brought a hardening of Muslim opposition to the Spanish presence. During the 1650s Sultan Qudarat of Magindanao, a powerful centre on Mindanao, declared *jihad*, and his successor is still remembered in *khutba* (sermons given at the Friday prayers) as a ruler who fought the infidel Spaniards. Continuing attacks on Spanish-held areas by the Dutch, the loss of Ternate and Tidore, and the threat of raids on Manila by Koxinga led the Spanish authorities to close the Zamboanga fort in 1663. For half a century the Christian-Muslim division of the Philippine islands was implicitly accepted.

Missionary Work in Vietnam

Christianity had been known in Vietnam since the sixteenth century, for in 1533 there is mention of the religion taught by Ignatius, 'a man of the Ocean', presumably from Melaka. From 1580 representatives of several missionary orders passed through or spent some time in Vietnam. The first church was built in Danang by Father Francis Buzomi who had come from Macao in January 1615 and who in the first year of teaching gained three hundred converts. However, the beginning of the Christianizing effort is properly dated 1624, with the arrival of Alexander of Rhodes and several other Jesuits who had been expelled from Japan. Three years later Father Alexander was sent to the Trinh-ruled north to establish a mission. By the time it was closed three years later by the authorities, it had gained almost seven thousand Vietnamese converts. By 1640 there were said to be 39,000 Christians in the Nguyen territories and 82,000 in the areas under the Trinh.

[32] See Rafael, *Contracting Colonialism*, for a stimulating study of the role of language and textual translation in Tagalog acceptance of Christianity.

The process of 'conversion' in seventeenth-century Vietnam from a local perspective remains to be explored. There are, however, a number of reasons which at least in part explain the initial Christian success. As in the Philippines priests recognized the need to attract the high-born to Christianity, and there was much rejoicing when one of the foremost princesses in the southern Nguyen court was baptized and persuaded others to take the same step. More important, however, was the fact that the Jesuit missionaries, like their counterparts in the island world, placed great importance on learning the local language and preaching directly to the people. Father Alexander's romanization of Vietnamese into a form known as *quoc ngu* made it possible for missionaries to learn Vietnamese more quickly, although Christian material distributed to the faithful was still written in either Chinese characters or *nom* (Vietnamese demotic script). Furthermore in contrast to the Philippines, Jesuit priests in Vietnam argued that a strong native clergy was necessary for the promotion of the religion. By the middle of the century a seminary had been established which had a hundred members. Vietnamese catechists were also given elementary medical instruction and encouraged to move through the Vietnamese countryside spreading Christian teachings. Their rigorous training, understanding of Christian doctrine and religious devotion helped foster Christian conversions despite the very limited number of European priests. During one epidemic, for instance, six Vietnamese catechists supplied by the Jesuits with the weapons of Christianity—the cross, holy water, holy candles, blessed palm leaves and pictures of the Virgin—went to a stricken area to make war on the devil, whom they blamed for the suffering. When the epidemic abated, the local people were so convinced of Christianity's power that the local leader converted.

The growing hostility of both Nguyen and Trinh leaders to Christianity did not dampen missionary fervour; on the contrary, it raised the hope of dying for the faith and thus receiving the martyr's crown. The account given by Alexander of Rhodes on his return to France aroused keen interest there, not only among clerics but among those who hoped to extend French commerce in Asia. In the face of strong Portuguese objections at this incursion into the territory supposedly assigned to them in 1494, the Société des Missions Étrangères was formed in 1658. Some clerics, however, argued that without strong commercial relations evangelization would be unsuccessful. It is no coincidence that in 1664 the Compagnie des Indes et de l'Indochine was chartered to foster French commerce east of the Cape of Good Hope.

The first priests sent out by the Missions Étrangères left France in 1660, establishing a base not in Vietnam but in the more sympathetic environment of Ayutthaya. From here representatives were sent out to Vietnam, Cambodia and Laos. Like the Jesuits, the members of the Missions Étrangères were committed to fostering a native Vietnamese clergy, and in 1666 a seminary was opened in Ayutthaya to give formal training for the priesthood. By 1700 there were forty-five Vietnamese priests, and it was even suggested that in a short time some might be appointed as bishops. In the north a convent was set up for Vietnamese women, aiming to encourage a 'love and esteem for chastity' in this 'kingdom of darkness'.[33]

As elsewhere in Asia, a major concern of the missionaries was the degree of accommodation which should be made with local beliefs. In a foreshadowing of later debates in China, a synod convened by the Missions Étrangères in Fai-fo in 1682 roundly condemned the erection of *than* (private ancestral altars) within the homes of Christians. The synod thus overruled the pleading of Vietnamese catechists, many of whom had been converted by the more tolerant Jesuits. But such disputes were only one of several considerations which made the conversion process in the eighteenth century even more difficult than it had been in the seventeenth. In France sympathy for the missionizing effort was now waning, and without financial resources the Société's work was severely impeded. The situation was not helped by quarrels over religious jurisdiction, and to settle these disputes the Pope finally decided in 1738 that the Jesuits should work in the Trinh areas and the Société in the area under the Nguyen. The decisive factor, however, was the heightened animosity from Vietnamese authorities. Previously missionaries had been able to survive because of the desire of Vietnamese rulers to obtain commercial privileges or to take advantage of European military technology. Periodic persecution had thus been interspersed with liberal intervals when missionaries were well received. In 1682, for example, priests had commented on the freedom with which Christianity could be taught in the Nguyen domains. This was in fact a time when Christians were also welcomed at the Chinese court because of their scientific and technical knowledge. With changes in China missionaries in Vietnam were similarly confronted with a much more intransigent attitude, and in 1750 most were evicted. Though estimates of Christian converts at this time may be exaggerated, the attachment to Christianity found among many Vietnamese survived to re-emerge as a significant factor in the nineteenth century.

RELIGIOUS ISSUES

By the seventeenth century the religious map of Southeast Asia had assumed a shape which modern observers will recognize. Theravāda Buddhism was well established in Burma, Thailand, Laos, and Cambodia, while Islam and Christianity were well entrenched in the island world. In Vietnam a mixture of Mahāyāna Buddhism, Taoism and popular Confucianism continued at the village level, with small pockets of Christianity, while at the élite level there was a renewed emphasis on Confucianism. But although these developments resulted in the division of Southeast Asia into different religious spheres, the process of accommodation and consolidation reveals a range of common preoccupations, an examination of which may go some way towards drawing Southeast Asia's religious history together.

[33] Cited in Georges Taboulet, *La Geste Française en Indochine*, I, Paris, 1955, 35.

The Call to Reform

A feature of Southeast Asian religious history is the periodic call for reform. To an extent this reforming tradition stems from the fact that all the religions which came to the region based their authority on a body of revered texts which could be consulted by experts and invoked to support or refute a particular custom or idea. Added to these texts were the legends attached to sages, prophets, divinities, and scholars which had assumed a standing of their own and were frequently regarded as embodying immutable truths. The intermingling of textual authority and popular tradition meant that there was usually wide scope for debate on most issues, even when questions had theoretically already been resolved by religious scholars generations before. It was therefore possible for a commonly accepted practice to be condemned as contradictory to 'correct' religious interpretation. The recurring cycle of reform was encouraged because all the world religions to a lesser or greater degree shared a belief that society's spiritual and moral life was constantly threatened by declining values. They were also agreed that this process could only be averted or slowed by a return to the unadulterated teachings of the original faith as expressed in the holy texts. It could be argued, furthermore, that the period between 1500 and 1800 was a time of rapid change in Asia generally. In many areas the kinds of changes which occurred fed a belief that society was in a state of decay. In such cases the only remedy was felt to be a purification of religious belief.

The roots of the periodic movements for religious regeneration which occurred in Southeast Asia can thus be traced to a number of causes, and should be seen as a response both to wider developments and to specific events on the local scene. The example of Buddhism is a case in point. For Southeast Asian Buddhists, Sri Lanka (Ceylon) had long stood as the fount of religious orthodoxy and tradition. At various times when the *sasana* (the sum total of Buddhist teaching) was considered in need of restoration, kings despatched monks to Sri Lanka to be reordained into the purer tradition. Through their teachers many Buddhist monks in Southeast Asia were able to trace their spiritual lineage back to some saintly figure renowned in Sri Lanka or India for his wisdom and piety. The links with Sri Lanka were particularly strong in Burma, and were especially fostered by the Mon king Dhammaceti (r. 1472–92). From 1518, however, the maintenance of these links came under pressure as the Portuguese launched repeated attacks on the Sri Lankan coast, looting shrines, turning monasteries into centres of Catholic worship, and converting by highly questionable means. In 1560 they captured the holiest of relics, the Buddha's Tooth, publicly grinding it to powder. The situation was worsened because the Portuguese came to Sri Lanka at a time of internal conflict as rulers of different kingdoms took up arms against each other. By the last quarter of the sixteenth century it was impossible to locate even five properly ordained monks. Although the Buddhist kings of Kandy took up the struggle to unify the country and hold back the Europeans, an army commander could still say in 1630 that 'our religion is fallen'.[34]

---

[34] George Davison Winius, *The Fatal History of Portuguese Ceylon*, Cambridge, Mass., 1971, 28.

The degree to which Southeast Asian Buddhists were aware of the challenges to Buddhism in Sri Lanka is uncertain, although it is known that in 1568 the ruler of Burma, Bayinnaung (r. 1551–81) received a deputation of monks from Sri Lanka, whence he also received a wife. According to later chronicles he even sent some of his best soldiers to assist the prince of Colombo. However, it was the situation in Burma itself which was probably most disturbing.

Burmese chronicles remember the early years of the sixteenth century as a disastrous time, when prolonged warfare between rival groups led to destruction of monasteries and the loss of holy relics. In 1539 a Shan king went so far as to kill 360 monks in the area around Ava. Bayinnaung attempted to restore the strength of Buddhism by initiating the construction of religious buildings, the copying of texts, the collection of relics and the clarification of religious law. Particular attention was paid to the monkhood. While Bayinnaung sponsored mass ordinations, he also commanded that monks be examined to ensure they had an adequate knowledge of religious matters. Missionary work similarly received a high priority. Whenever a hill tribe area was conquered, monks were despatched to 'rectify corruptions' such as animal sacrifice. Though Bayinnaung's edicts show due respect for the *nats*, it is clear that they were expected to lend the king their assistance. In 1569 he called on them to help in 'a quick victory over the Chief of Bangkok, who is an arch enemy of the religion', and even told the principal guardian spirits (including Mahagīri, the 'king' of the *nats*) that if they did not assist him against the Thais, he would burn down their shrines.[35]

The rulers of Burma and Siam may also have felt urgent action was necessary because a critical point in religious history was imminent. Both countries had adopted a common calendar starting in March 638 and the thousandth year of this cycle was due to fall in 1638 CE. Political disruption in both countries towards the end of the sixteenth century may have served to fuel the sense that momentous times were at hand, and this would have increased as the millennium approached. In Ayutthaya, for instance, the end of the world had already been foretold and now disturbing omens were reported; deformed elephants were found, the tower on a famous wat collapsed, and brahmins foretold the king's death.

The ruler of Ayutthaya, Prasat Thong (r. 1629–56) saw a solution to the problem in a reordering of the calendar which would give 1638 a more auspicious name. The chronicles relate that when 'the vile Burman' refused to accede to his proposal, Prasat Thong turned to ritual to rectify time. A great model of the Hindu heavens was built outside the royal palace, depicting Indra and other gods seated atop Mount Mahāmeru. A statue of the Buddha and a copy of the Tipitaka were also placed on the summit: 'At the auspicious moment His Majesty . . . ascended Mount Meru . . . [and] paid obeisance to the three jewels [i.e. the Buddha, the Law and the *Saṅgha*] . . . imploring that his request might be granted. He then raised his hands and erased the writing of the old era.'[36]

---

[35] Than Tun, *Royal Orders*, II. 7–8.

[36] O. Frankfurter, 'A proposed change in the Siamese era Chulasakaraj 1000 (A.D. 1638)', *T'oung Pao*, Second Series 8 (1907) 99–104.

In the Burmese capital of Ava somewhat greater importance appears to have been placed on the purification of Buddhism as part of the administrative reforms being undertaken by Thalun (r. 1629–48). Concerned with the independence of certain monastic groupings and their growing control over property and manpower, Thalun ordered land titles to be registered, and he confiscated religious estates when ownership was unclear. Efforts were made to increase central access to religious revenues and to limit ordination to those who had given evidence of genuine religious leanings. At the same time these reforms may reflect the influence of the prestigious Mahāvihāra sect which had been introduced from Pegu around 1608 and which traced its origins back to the Mahāvihāra (the Great Monastery), the fount of orthodoxy in Sri Lanka. In 1637 orders were given for 'all noxious monks' to be driven from the monkhood, and efforts were made to discourage the involvement of monks in shamanistic activities or in business. There also seems to have been a renewed effort to limit spirit worship. One royal decree for example, notes that a lady could not receive the full merit which should come from the building of a monastery if she had allowed any propitiations to be made to spirits during its construction. All these efforts to purify the *sasana* were rewarded, for in 1638 two footprints of the Buddha were discovered near the capital Ava, a particularly auspicious sign. When Thalun survived the thousandth year he, like Prasat Thong, ordered public rejoicing.[37]

The emphasis on conformity with Islamic law and the strict observance of religious duties which many Europeans noted in the archipelago at the turn of the sixteenth century may also have been partially attributable to calendrical considerations as the millennium of the Prophet's death in 1011 AH (1602–3 CE) approached. In India, some sixteenth-century mystics believed that the Prophet would not remain in his grave longer than a thousand years, and that the coming of the Mahdi (the next Prophet) and the Day of Judgement, when each individual would be held accountable for his religious life, was imminent. Akbar himself is known to have commemorated the thousand-year anniversary of the Prophet's death. If anything, the passing of the millennium brought even greater stress on the need to rejuvenate the faith. The late sixteenth and early seventeenth century gave rise to the reformed Sufism of Shaykh Ahmad Sirhindi (970–1034 AH, 1564–1624 CE), whose call for a return to the *sharī'a* and reform of the Naqshabandiyya *ṭarīqa* earned him the title 'renovator [Mujaddid] of the second millennium'. The task of kings, he said, was to devote their energies towards a restoration of the pristine faith and a promotion of the teachings of the Prophet. Further stimulation to this stress on orthodoxy is given by the accession of the Mughal ruler Aurangzeb in 1658, who swore to bring the lives of his subjects more into accord with the Koran. 'For the first time in their history', one authority has written, 'the Mughals beheld a rigid Muslim in their Emperor.'[38]

Given the long-standing trading links, the sense of living at a momentous time prevalent in India must have penetrated to Southeast Asia. Indeed,

---

[37] Jeremias van Vliet, *A Short History of the Kings of Siam*, trans. Leonard Y. Andaya, ed. D. K. Wyatt, Bangkok: Siam Society, 1975, 96; Than Tun, *Royal Orders*, I and II, passim.
[38] Stanley Lane-Poole, *Mediaeval India under Mohammedan Rule*, Delhi, 1963, 254.

the Koranic stress on Judgement Day had not been ignored by Indonesian teachers. According to a sixteenth-century Javanese text, on this occasion all would be weighed in the scales and Allah would order all those found to have failed in their religious obligations to be bound and thrown into hell fire where they would be gnawed for a hundred years by a great *nāga*. 'Whoever does not believe this is an infidel.'[39] In the late sixteenth century several rulers, like Sultan Baabullah of Ternate, displayed their piety by dressing in Arab clothing, by patronizing religious teachers, by banning pastimes such as cockfighting and by active missionizing. An Englishman in Aceh in 1599 reported that every year the king and his ministers went to the mosque 'to looke if the Messias bee come'.[40]

In Southeast Asia it was in Aceh, in fact, where the reforming mood of the early seventeenth century became most apparent. Here Ibn al-'Arabī's concept of *wujuddiyya*, the grades of being from the Absolute, had been influential in shaping the thinking of Shamsuddin (d. 1630 CE), a teacher from Pasai in north Sumatra who obtained a high position in the Acehnese court during the reign of Sultan Iskandar Muda. However, the monism at the basis of Ibn al-'Arabī's theosophy attracted criticism among mystics like Syaikh Ahmad Sirhindi. With the arrival in 1637 of a Gujerati teacher, Nūr al-Dīn al-Rānīrī, Aceh too felt the impact of these debates. While al-Rānīrī mentions Ibn al-'Arabī's name reverently, he believed that the latter's teaching had been dangerously misrepresented by Shamsuddin and other Acehnese mystics. He therefore proceeded to launch a campaign against those whom he saw as *zindik* (heretics, especially those whose teaching endangers the state). '"I said to them," wrote al-Rānīrī, "you have claimed for yourselves divinity . . . but indeed you are of the unbelieving group [*kafir*]". [When they heard this] their faces betrayed a sour expression and they bowed their heads, for surely they are polytheists.'[41]

For a time al-Rānīrī's condemnation of this tradition of Sufi teaching was apparently supported by the Acehnese ruler, for there was wholesale burning of books, and reportedly executions of those who remained obdurate.[42] Not surprisingly, this campaign alienated many local Muslims, and in 1644 al-Rānīrī abruptly left Aceh, pressured by followers of the school of Shamsuddin at the instigation of Minangkabau.

No such controversy surrounded the return in 1661 of another Acehnese mystic, Abdulrauf (c. 1617–90 CE), who had studied for nineteen years in Mecca. Given authority to propagate the Shattāriyya *tarīqa* in the region, Abdulrauf remains an important figure because he was very aware of the concerns and questions of Southeast Asian Muslims. It was he who produced what is believed to be the first *tafsir* or commentary on the Koran

---

[39] Drewes, *The Admonitions*, 69.
[40] Sayid Alhar Abbas Rizvi, *Muslim Revivalist Movements in Northern India*, Agra University, 1965, 64–78, 262; Samuel Purchas, *Purchas His Pilgrimes*, II, Glasgow, 1905, 323.
[41] Syed Muhammad Naguib al-Attas, *Rānīrī and the Wujūdiyyah of 17th Century Acheh*, Singapore, 1966, 16.
[42] That al-Rānīrī was reflecting Islamic attitudes in India is suggested by an anonymous insertion of a panygyric extolling Aurangzeb into his most famous work, the *Bustan al-Salatin*. See Catherine Grinter, 'Book IV of the Bustan us-Salatin by Nuruddin al-Raniri: A study from the manuscripts of a 17th-century Malay work written in North Sumatra', Ph.D. thesis, University of London, 1979, 27, 51–2.

in Malay (actually a translation of a popular Arabic work), as well as Malay versions of a number of other Arabic texts. Above all, he deplored the accusations of unbelief which had caused such strains in local Islam. 'It is dangerous to accuse another of *kufr* [unbelief],' he wrote. 'If you do so, and it is true, why waste words on it, and if it is not true, the accusation will turn back upon yourself.'[43] Abdulrauf's influence continued long after his death, for one of his pupils, Shaykh Burhanuddin, is said to have brought knowledge of the Shaṭṭāriyya *ṭarīqa* to the west coast of Sumatra, whence it moved up into the Minangkabau interior.

Elsewhere in the archipelago there were other attempts to 'purify' Islam. In Sulawesi, La Maddaremmeng, Sultan of Bone between 1631 and 1644, unsuccessfully tried to apply *sharī'a* law literally, forbidding all superstitious practices, disbanding the *bissu* (indigenous priests, usually transvestites), and freeing slaves. When Alexander of Rhodes arrived in Makassar in 1646, he reported that women there veiled themselves in public. Across the seas in Kedah a formulation of law compiled in 1667 specifically notes that a register should be kept of 'gamblers, cockfighters, opium smokers, drunkards, worshippers of trees and rocks and those not attending the mosque'.[44] In Jambi it was said that the people were 'at present so religious that the ordinary man is half like a pope and the nobles wholly so'. The king himself asked Batavia for some 'clean, unbound books with gold margins on which to write his new laws and daily sermons'.[45]

The changed mood in Jambi probably mirrored that in the court of its overlord, the central Javanese kingdom of Mataram. Here the ruler, Sultan Agung (r. 1613–46), had assumed this Muslim title in 1641. He was described as regularly attending the mosque on Fridays and as a faithful observer of the Muslim fast. In 1633 he had taken the important step of combining the Javanese and Islamic calendar. Even more renowned for its sponsorship of Islamic orthodoxy was Banten, where the ruler received the title of sultan from Mecca in 1638. Sultan Agung of Banten (r. 1651–83) was also invested by Mecca, and his son made the pilgrimage twice. It was common in the court to wear Arab rather than Javanese dress and during religious ceremonies flags from Mecca were carried in processions around the city to cleanse it of evil influences. Sultan Agung forbade the use of opium and the drinking of alcohol, and was reputed to be so pious that he would not even use spices in his food. The strongly religious mood in Banten was enhanced by the arrival of the prestigious Makassar teacher, Shaykh Yusuf, a revered scholar and a vehement opponent of the Dutch. He had gone to Mecca in 1644 as a young man and is reputed to have also studied with Nūr al-Dīn al-Rānīrī. On his return to Sulawesi in 1678 he had been shocked by the extent of opium smoking, offerings to spirits, and other non-Islamic accretions, and after unsuccessful attempts to reform local observances he went to Banten.

[43] Johns, 'Dakai'k al-Huruf', 56.
[44] R. O. Winstedt, *A History of Classical Malay Literature*, Kuala Lumpur, 1969, 169.
[45] P. A. Tiele, *Bouwstoffen voor de Geschiedenis der Nederlanders in den Maleischen Archipel*, II, The Hague, 1890, 458 fn. 2.

The latter part of the seventeenth century also saw reforming tendencies in Vietnam with a revival of emphasis on Confucianism as the state ideology. In the north this was due in part to the desire of the effective ruler, Trinh Thac, to arrogate the symbols of political legitimacy in the face of the Nguyen challenge and to support a group of erudite people as a counter to the powerful warrior clans. The extent to which Trinh leaders were themselves personally committed to Confucianist teachings is not established, but it is apparent that they found in Confucianism a useful tool for government. In this they were supported by those Vietnamese literati who felt that Confucian scholarship had declined during the long years of civil war between the Nguyen and Trinh clans, which had resulted in the partition of the country into two administrative areas. A further source of concern for Confucian scholars was the growing popularity of Buddhism, not only among villagers. Le Thanh Ton, who reigned between 1619 and 1662, was a devout Buddhist. He was also known to be interested in Christianity, and the success of Christian missionaries in Vietnam was another trend which must have caused disquiet among the small circle of Confucian literati.

It is not yet known whether there was any interaction between the Confucian scholarship of China and that of Vietnam in the seventeenth century. Did Vietnamese educated in the classical tradition share the conviction of their Chinese counterparts that the fall of the Ming dynasty in 1644 was due to moral decline? Even if they did, would they have applied this lesson to Vietnam? It is apparent, however, that Vietnamese Confucian scholars saw themselves as part of a reforming process by which the bureaucracy would triumph over the military. In the Trinh-controlled north and to a lesser extent in the new régime which was evolving under the Nguyen, local administration was reorganized, departments were made strictly hierarchical, and the law was systematized in a manner which attempted (largely unsuccessfully) to reinforce Confucian values. Officials were instructed to wear clothing appropriate to their office and all men were urged to discourage their women from extravagant indulgence. There was increasing pressure to discourage villagers from 'bad habits' such as cockfighting, gambling, sorcery, promiscuity and betel chewing. The rulers of Vietnam also attempted to reaffirm their influence over popular religion. Efforts were made to stamp out Christian practices like the wearing of crosses, and Buddhism too became a target for attack. It was customary for local guardian spirits to be 'appointed' by the court; in 1722, for instance, 2511 village deities received royal sanction.

Religious Rivalry

Another issue which became more prominent in this period was religious rivalry. As old enmities resurfaced or new ones were created, the conflicts between different groups were often articulated in religious terms as each attempted to identify itself by delineating the boundaries between 'believers' and 'non-believers'. The most enduring conflicts took place between Christianity and Islam. A century after the fall of Melaka, Christians could still sound the battle cry in the name of religion. In 1634, for instance, the Portuguese epic *Malacca Conquistada* (The Conquest of Malacca) was published, depicting Portugal's conflicts in the archipelago as part of a continuing struggle against those 'hostile to Christ': 'And when the Turk, Persian and Muslim have been defeated, the Golden Age will return to the world.' Suspicion of Muslims had plagued Portuguese dealings with Indonesians; to a considerable extent this was inherited by the northern Europeans who arrived in the archipelago at a time when popular Christianity was imbued with a fear that a resurgence of Islamic strength would herald the end of Christendom. Even in England some astrologers were predicting a Turkish sweep from Germany to Cornwall which would signal the approach of Judgement Day. Certainly the Dutch tended to see their relations with Southeast Asian Muslims in terms of the meeting of two hostile traditions, and though they always presented themselves as simple traders the VOC was itself an outgrowth of a strongly Christian culture. Church ceremonies played a prominent part in the life of even the most isolated Dutch outpost, and any victory over local enemies was publicly celebrated in Batavia as direct proof of the power of the Christian God.

Dutch military strength became apparent in 1628, when Sultan Agung of Mataram launched an unsuccessful attack against Batavia. When his campaigns failed, there was some attempt to persuade Muslim rulers to set aside old enmities and work together against a common enemy. In 1652 influential Muslim teachers persuaded Agung's son, Amangkurat I (r. 1646–77) to abandon his plans for an attack on Banten and to ally instead with Banten and Makassar against the VOC. At approximately the same time a prophecy foretelling the eviction of the Dutch from Java was reported in eastern Indonesia, and some Indonesian states took up the Islamic tradition that any peace between Muslims and Christians could be only temporary. In 1659 the ruler of Banten told the governor-general of an oath he had made to an envoy from Mecca by which he had sworn to wage war against the Christians every ten years. Sultan Amsterdam of Ternate, whose very title had been adopted as a symbol of his close association with the VOC, attempted to organize an Islamic union against the Dutch, telling neighbouring Muslim rulers that they had intended to introduce Christianity into Sulu, Mindanao, and Banten and elsewhere.

These efforts to build up a grand anti-Dutch alliance failed completely. Hostilities between Banten and Mataram began again in 1657, and Makassar was also unable to gain support against the VOC. Throughout the seventeenth century Dutch victories mounted. In 1659 the VOC attacked and defeated Palembang, an important trading port on the east coast of Sumatra; in 1667–8 expeditions quelled Acehnese expansion; 1669 saw the conquest of Makassar, an event which sent shockwaves throughout the archipelago. The ruler of Jambi expressed the feelings of many local Muslims as he wept 'to hear of the terrible defeat of the famed motherland of Islam'. The *Syair Perang Mengkasar* depicts the battle with the Dutch as a holy war, and the poet's greatest condemnation is reserved for the 'heretics', especially the Bugis and Butonese, who fought on the Dutch side against their traditional enemies.

The Christian presence in the archipelago undoubtedly contributed to the heightened consciousness of religious affiliation in the seventeenth century. A similar mood is apparent in Vietnam. The reasons for Christianity's appeal here are not altogether clear, although the dislocation caused by civil war and the resulting neglect of Confucian scholarship may provide part of the answer. The numbers of converts to the new religion concerned many Vietnamese Confucians, who felt these foreign practices would lead to a decline in devotion to the ancestors and neglect of filial piety. This would have serious implications in a state where a subject's relationship to the emperor was equated to that of a son and his father. Furthermore, there were real fears that Christianity might be a pretext for the Europeans to take over Vietnam, as they had done in the Philippines.

Distrust of Christian missionaries, who were often accused of being sorcerers, was present in Vietnam from the outset, but hostility soon extended to those who had chosen to follow the new teaching, despite the conversion of several high-born individuals. The Nguyen and the Trinh both attempted to limit the spread of Christianity by periodically banning missionaries, proscribing preaching, and enacting anti-Christian measures. At first converts were simply forbidden to display their faith by wearing images, crosses and rosaries around their necks, but penalties soon grew more severe. In 1645, for instance, two catechists were executed by the Nguyen.

Notwithstanding their suspicion of Christianity, Vietnamese rulers made it clear that they welcomed commercial exchange with Europeans. They were also eager to acquire technical skills, and Europeans of various nationalities were employed in both courts to advise on the production of arms. The perception of Europeans as bearers of both useful knowledge and a dangerously subversive ideology explains the fluctuating fortunes of the missionaries as recipients of official favours or targets of extreme displeasure. But the effort to detach trade and secular knowledge from other aspects of European culture proved quite impracticable. As we have seen, the Société des Missions Étrangères was supported by commercial interests, and missionaries were often actively involved in trade. In later years Jesuits were frequently accused of disguising themselves as traders in order to exploit the leniency shown toward the commercial presence. Discovery of this kind of subterfuge simply fuelled Trinh hostility towards all Christians, wherever they came from, and in 1712 it was ordered that the words 'student of Dutch religion' be carved on the foreheads of convicted Vietnamese converts.

The growing anti-Christian feeling in Vietnam in the early eighteenth century should also be seen against the background of wider developments in East Asia. In Japan Hideyoshi's 1587 proscription of Christian teaching had been far more rigorously enforced by the Tokugawa, while in China from around 1600 a number of anti-Christian treatises were written. Following the fall of the Ming in 1644 the Chinese court was increasingly suspicious of new ideas, primarily because of the Qing emphasis on neo-Confucian orthodoxy of the Chu Hsi school. In 1724 the imperial edict of toleration was abruptly withdrawn, and Christianity was henceforth considered a heterodox cult. In Vietnam, which received so much intellectual and religious influence from China, distrust of Christianity also gained the upper hand and even covert proselytising proved increasingly impossible. When missionaries were again expelled by the Nguyen in 1750 it was partly because of fears that Europeans, perhaps in conjunction with the Trinh, might be planning an attack. However, according to another account it was also as a result of a letter received from 'a famous Chinese priest' exhorting the Nguyen to emulate the example set by the Emperor of China.[46]

The relationship between Theravāda Buddhism and other major religions in Southeast Asia provides something of a contrast. Bayinnaung, it is true, forbade Muslims to sacrifice animals and wanted them to listen to Buddhist sermons, but observers were generally struck by the relaxed attitudes of Buddhists towards other faiths. In the words of an English sea captain, 'They hold all religions to be good that teacheth men to be good . . . and that the deities are pleased with variety of worship.'[47] Outsiders mistook this tolerance for a lack of commitment to Buddhism and periodically through the sixteenth and seventeenth centuries entertained hopes of converting them to Christianity or Islam. In 1686, for example, there was an abortive rebellion in Ayutthaya led by Makassarese mercenaries who aimed to place the ruler's half-brother on the throne as long as he would accept Islam. But the case of the Cambodian ruler who adopted Islam around 1643 is exceptional. At the end of the sixteenth century Khmer Buddhism appears to have been flourishing, and the first Portuguese missionaries who visited Cambodia in 1555–6 found a well-organized *saṅgha*. Forty years later a Spanish Dominican estimated that there were 1500 Buddhist monks in Phnom Penh alone. However, attacks by the Thais had made Khmer military weakness apparent. The ruler had earlier indicated he might be willing to adopt Christianity in return for assistance, and it is probably in this context that his conversion to Islam should be considered. It is obvious, furthermore, that Khmers had difficulty explaining why the king should have taken this action, and the chronicles attribute it to his overwhelming love for his Malay wife and the spells cast by Malay magic. The consequences, they continue, were serious, for the ruler's failure to carry out his royal duties and protect the *saṅgha* caused Khmer Buddhism to decay. It was only restored when a coup brought about the installation of a Buddhist king once more.

Other Theravāda Buddhist kings might have looked on alien religions with interest and tolerance, but they were never persuaded to set Buddhism aside. A good instance of the environment which fostered this tolerance is found in Ayutthaya, where Catholic missionaries had been permitted to preach since the early sixteenth century. More than a hundred years later Ayutthaya was chosen as the headquarters of the Société des Missions Étrangères, and French records acknowledge with appreciation the provision of building materials by Narai (r. 1656–88) for the construction of a church on the city outskirts. Reference is made to the opening of a seminary and schools where religious instruction was given

[46] Taboulet, *La Geste Française*, 99.
[47] Alexander Hamilton, *A New Account of the East Indies*, ed. William Foster, London, 1930, II. 30.

to 'the children of Cochin Chinese and Tonkinese', while the clergy studied Siamese and Pāli, the scriptural language of Theravāda Buddhism. In 1667 a court official and his wife were baptized.[48] It is even possible that contact with missionaries may have influenced a new type of historical writing in Thai. Known as *phongsawadan*, this is more secular in its orientation than the traditional *tamnan* literature, and depicts the history of kingdoms as part of a universal environment rather than a purely Buddhist one. But such developments should not cloud the fact that the kings of Ayutthaya never doubted Buddhism's superiority to Christianity, whose priests drank wine and condoned the taking of animal life. A ruler like Narai could well take a lively interest in both Christianity and Islam, but any hope of conversion was a chimera.

Religion and Kingship

A third theme which runs through the religious history of Southeast Asia is the relationship between religion and kingship. All the religions which came to Southeast Asia from outside were closely connected with the ruler and the court, and thus became an integral part of the constellations of political power which had emerged by the mid-seventeenth century. Indigenous concepts of a leader as an elder kinsman, whose 'luck', possession of powerful objects, and relationship with supernatural forces set him above his fellows were reinforced by the ideas and the vocabulary of the imported religions. Among Malays, for example, the special power of kings which would punish those guilty of treason, previously subsumed in the Sanskrit word *śakti*, was now conveyed by the Arabic term *daulat*. In Java, too, it was an Arabic-derived word *wahyu*, meaning 'revelation from Allah', which Javanese used to refer to the dazzling light which denotes the legitimate king. In addition the world religions brought with them a formidable body of opinion amassed over centuries concerning the duties of rulers and the criteria by which a 'good' or a 'bad' reign could be judged. While traditions and vocabulary differed, there were underlying similarities. All kings, Christian or Muslim, Buddhist or Confucian, should ideally act not only as supporters of religion but as exemplars of moral and spiritual piety. By so doing they maintained an order in the mundane world and a harmony with the unseen one which merited the loyalty and obedience of their subjects. The Buddha's teachings thus stressed that a king should gain the favour of his subjects 'by the four elements of popularity', which were liberality, affability, justice and impartiality. Throughout his kingdom the religion and the people should be nurtured, no wrongdoing should prevail, and wealth should be given to whomsoever was poor.[49] Southeast Asians were taught that devout rulers who governed wisely would be rewarded, but a king who failed in his duties would ultimately be punished, either by the rejection of his subjects, by reincarnation as a lesser being, or by damnation on Judgement Day. The

---

[48] Adrien Launay, *Histoire de la Mission de Siam 1662–1811*, Documents Historiques, I, Paris, 1920, 17.

[49] Cited in Robert Lester, *Theravada Buddhism in Southeast Asia*, Ann Arbor, 1973, 62–5.

most important religious thinker of medieval Islam, al-Ghazālī, expressed the Muslim view thus: 'The man closest to God is the just Sultan, and the man most hateful and contemptible is the unjust Sultan . . . The harshest torment at the Resurrection Day will be for the unjust Sultan.'[50]

Nevertheless, what amounted to a kind of contractual relationship between ruler and subject was often obscured by the enhanced status assumed by Southeast Asian kings, to which religion itself made a direct contribution. Theravāda Buddhist rulers inherited the politico-religious notion of *cakkavatti* or Universal Monarch who would prepare the world for the coming of the next Buddha. All Burmese kings in the seventeenth century were honoured at their death with the funeral of a Universal Monarch, and the refusal of a ruler to recognize his neighbour's *cakkavatti* claims was often the prelude to prolonged warfare. The reign names assumed by Buddhist rulers also proclaimed them as *dhammarāja* or king of the [Buddhist] law, and they could similarly be compared to Hindu gods such as Śiva, Viṣṇu, and Indra. The 'Three Worlds Cosmology' composed by a Thai prince in the fourteenth century was in no doubt that pious kings 'are called *devata* [divine being] by common agreement'.[51] In a similar mode Muslim kings in Southeast Asia, like Akbar of India, may well have applied to themselves the mystic notion of the Perfect Man, the manifestation of Allah's desire to be known; a poem by Hamzah Fansuri thus speaks of the king of Aceh as 'one of Allah's elect, perfect in communion with Him'. Rulers took a leading role in public worship, and the names of the sultans and a recitation of their deeds were included in sermons during the Friday prayers and on religious holidays. In Vietnam the tendency to attribute special powers to kings may have compensated for the limitations which Confucianism placed on the sacral status assigned to rulers, and for their exclusion from a political role during the shogun-type government of the seventeenth and eighteenth centuries. The devout Buddhist king Le Thanh Ton, for example, was commonly believed to be the reincarnation of a pious Ly ruler who had lived four hundred years earlier.

Language, symbols and ritual derived from religious traditions all formed part of the arsenal of kingly prestige. Sacred texts, religiously potent items like a white elephant, a banner from Mecca, holy water, became part of the royal regalia, and he who possessed them was imbued with supernatural powers. Court ceremonial was in many respects a form of religious ritual. A Dutchman living in Ayutthaya in the seventeenth century described the royal acts of religious piety which reaffirmed the king's legitimacy. 'Once every year . . . the king of Siam shews himself by water and land in state to his people, going to the principal Temple of the Gods, to offer there for the welfare of his Person and Kingdom.'[52] In Burma and Siam a number of the functions previously performed by brahmins were assumed by Buddhist monks; in 1693 a French ambassador referred to an 'Oath of

---

[50] F. R. C. Bagley, trans., *Ghazāli's Book of Counsel for Kings (Naṣīḥat al-Mulūk)*, London, 1964, 14–15.

[51] Frank E. Reynolds and Mani B. Reynolds, trans., *Three Worlds According to King Ruang*, Berkeley, 1982, 217.

[52] Joost Schouten, *A Description of the Government, Might, Religion, Customs, Traffick and other Remarkable Affairs in the Kingdom of Siam*, Bangkok: Siam Society, 1986, 128.

Fidelity' at the Ayutthaya court that consisted 'in swallowing the water, over which the Talapins [i.e. monks] do pronounce some imprecations against him, who is to drink it, in case he fails in the Fidelity which he owes to his King'. In Vietnam a Confucian scholar was similarly responsible for organizing the construction of altars dedicated to ancestral spirits before which the oath of loyalty to the ruler was sworn. *Ulamā*, the learned men of Islam, were equally evident in archipelago courts. An eighteenth-century description of royal Malay *adat*, for example, describes the prominent place given to the *kadi* (cadi, principal Islamic authority) at such ancient rituals as the rocking of the queen's abdomen in the seventh month of pregnancy (*melenggang perut*).

The religious scholars who surrounded the ruler dominated areas of government where literacy was essential. It was they, for instance, who drew up the law codes, adapting Indian, Chinese or Arab models to the local scene and arguing with those who defended traditional custom. The Mons, the Burmans, the Thai, the Lao, the Lan Na Thai and the Khmer all had their version of the *dhammathat*, the Laws of Manu derived from Hinduism, and a Burmese edict of 1607 specifies that judges should consult these when a punishment is to be determined. While functioning *sharī'a* courts in Muslim states may not have been common, a sixteenth-century Javanese text roundly states that 'it is unbelief when people are involved in a lawsuit, and [refuse to] settle the dispute according to the Law of Islam . . . and insist on taking it to an infidel judge'. Specialists in religion were also the major producers of the chronicles which recorded the country's history, tracing its links to the great faraway centres of religion and sometimes to the founder himself. The nineteenth-century Burmese text, the *Glass Palace Chronicle*, thus sees Burma's kings as directly descended from Buddha, and in the same fashion al-Rānīrī's *Bustan al-Salatin* places Aceh firmly within the history of the Islamic world. In these accounts of the past, rulers and their ancestors are depicted as playing a crucial role in the propagation of the religion. In one text from Sulawesi, for instance, it is the king and not his saintly teacher who is favoured by a vision of the Prophet commanding him to 'embrace Islam and bring others to the same faith, and wage war on those who oppose me in this'.[53]

Support from the religious hierarchy gave the ruler practical assistance in the exercise of government. Perhaps the most forthright instance of this alliance is the relationship between Church and state in the Christian areas of the Philippines. The governor in Manila was the ultimate authority of the colony, as the representative of the Spanish king, but the archbishop and the heads of the religious orders were all members of the *Junta de Autoridades*, a committee appointed to advise him. On a number of occasions the archbishop even acted as governor when the position fell vacant. At the provincial level the religious orders worked with the Spanish *alcalde mayor*, while the Filipino *gobernadorcillos* were expected to co-operate with the parish priest. Because relatively few lay Spaniards

---

[53] Cited in Russell Jones, 'Ten conversion myths from Indonesia' in Nehemia Levtzion, *Conversion to Islam*, New York and London, 1979, 150.

lived outside Manila it was the priest who represented the authority of the Spanish Crown. He was the local schoolteacher, he compiled the records and helped collect taxes, supervised the repairs of bridges and roads, drew up grammars, and directed the defence of the town against attacks by hill tribes or by Muslims from the south. But elsewhere in Southeast Asia the religious hierarchy was normally just as supportive of the ruler, who was after all the chief sponsor of religious activity. In the Islamic areas high-ranking Muslim officials, credited with superior knowledge and usually linked to the ruler through marriage, became leading figures in government. In Makassar where there was a special religious council called the *sarat*, Sultan Hasanuddin (r. 1653–69) received the Dutch surrounded by his *ulamā*, and in 1699, when it was decided that a queen could no longer rule in Aceh, it was the son of the *kadi* who succeeded as Sultan. In normal circumstances a king could count on the support of his religious appointees. A Spanish observer in Brunei in the late sixteenth century described how the *kadi besar* (great judge) charged all nobles to obey the heir who would inherit the kingdom, 'being greater than the others'.[54]

In the Buddhist kingdoms rulers similarly relied heavily on the services of monks, who acted as royal teachers, envoys, scribes, and advisers. In return, they were granted various privileges, including exemption from taxes. Royal edicts in Burma also freed the family of a monk from corvée duties, and a French visitor to Ayutthaya in the late seventeenth century remarked that it was favours of this kind that contributed to the large number of men entering the monkhood. The extensive network of monasteries and religious institutions set up by successive kings effectively extended the arm of central government across the country, with monks and novices accorded *sakdina* grades like any other Ayutthayan subject.[55] Royal endowments to religion also acted to reduce the power of regional lords, as in the southern Siamese province of Phattalung where Ayutthayan kings granted a considerable measure of land and people to support ecclesiastical establishments. Religion could equally be used to create or strengthen ties between patron and client. A king of Laos, for instance, anxious to expand his control over settlements distant from the capital, sponsored the ordination ceremonies of the sons of local notables in order to obtain the allegiance of their fathers.

Royal authority in the religious sphere could be further reinforced as rulers were called upon to settle disagreements between different religious groups. This mediating role assumes particular importance in Burma and Siam, where apparently no acknowledged patriarch of the Buddhist monkhood emerged until the eighteenth century. Instead, there seem to have been a number of *saṅgharāja*, or 'rulers of the *saṅgha*', senior monks who apparently had some localized following. Because of the lack of a single religious authority, disputes between (for example) the 'village-dwelling' and 'forest-dwelling' monks regarding practices and behaviour often required royal mediation. In Burma one source mentions a village monk who incited his followers to burn the books of forest dwellers, but was

---

[54] Carroll, 'Berunai in the Boxer Codex', 11.
[55] These *sakdina* grades reflected a theoretical apportioning of rice lands, based on an individual's social distance from the king.

stopped by the king's intervention. Even among the more orthodox 'village' monks, questions as to correct language, dress, deportment, could give rise to deep schisms. In the early seventeenth century one royal edict from Burma refers to further disputes between 'drum-beating monks' and 'lantern-turning monks' as well as arguments over the kind of robe which should be worn. The ruler apparently tried to effect a compromise by stating that monks could wear robes of any style and that as long as they led a good life sects were unimportant.[56]

This normally symbiotic relationship between royal and religious spheres nonetheless contained an inherent tension because as established religions extended their spiritual hold they also acquired control over people and territory. They could therefore be simultaneously co-operating with the ruler and potentially in competition with him. In turn this raised the issue of how far a king's authority extended into the religious domain. At times strains between rulers and the religious leadership could become so acute that they erupted into open confrontation. In such cases the ruler could be accused of neglecting his religious obligations, and the responsibility of the religious to a higher authority or greater principles be evoked. The *Taj us-Salatin*, the seventeenth-century Acehnese text on statecraft, thus argues that the king who does not follow the law of Allah is the enemy of Allah, and it was obligatory to oppose him. Vietnamese Confucian scholars could turn to the writings of the philosopher Mencius (372–289 BC), who insisted that the ruler's task was to provide 'benevolent government' and that if he failed to do so regicide was justified.

While the circumstances underlying each instance of conflict obviously varied greatly, one could argue that the ability of kings to curb the power of religious authorities was particularly problematic in the Islamic areas, where there was no 'priesthood' as such and where local centres of religious activity maintained a strong tradition of autonomy. An extreme case of royal frustration occurred in Mataram in 1648 when Amangkurat I moved to suppress opposition by killing about two thousand Islamic 'popes' who had allied with his younger brother. In so doing, of course, he merely fuelled opposition to himself. In the Buddhist states and in the Philippines, on the other hand, religious establishments were generally more integrated into a network responsive to supralocal authorities. Buddhist rulers, invoking their status as protectors of religion, could thus issue orders for the purification of the *sangha*, enabling them to strip monasteries of land and property, evict senior but uncooperative monks from the order and regain control over lost manpower. In 1684, for example, King Narai ordered that any Ayutthayan monk who could not read a certain Pāli text should be expelled. A few days later a French observer noted 'thousands of men still wearing the robe of the priesthood but working on the land, in the brickyards and bearing the trouble brought upon them through their ignorance'.[57] The Spanish Crown, faced by recurring disputes between church and secular authorities concerning the boundaries of civil and

---

[56] Than Tun, *Royal Orders*, II. 9.
[57] Nicolas Gervaise, *Histoire Naturelle et Politique du Royaume de Siam*, Paris, 1688, reprinted Bangkok 1929, 83.

religious jurisdiction, was able to take even more drastic action. In 1768 the Jesuit order was expelled from all Spanish domains because of suspected disloyalty. Overall, however, the Church in the Philippines proved well able to hold its own against the government, and in 1781 a French visitor commented on the great influence of the clergy. 'These friars are the masters of the country and are more absolute in the Philippines than the king himself.'[58]

Religion and Rebellion

The above remarks lead on to a fourth consideration—the manner in which religion, normally supportive of lay authorities, could also provide the inspiration for popular rebellion against them. In our period significant threats to the ruler's position came not from the formal religious establishment, with whom his ties were usually strong. The real challenge came from individual religious leaders who stood at the periphery of the officially sponsored order, whose status was often derived from indigenous traditions and who at times of social disruption could be seen as an alternative and legitimate authority. Throughout Southeast Asia the belief that even a person of humble origins could acquire extraordinary powers and claim a special relationship with the supernatural could give rise to sudden eruptions of localized religious movements when prophecies, dreams, magic, amulets, claims of invulnerability and secret revelations provided a potent weaponry. Thus in Vietnam at a time of dynastic decline in the early sixteenth century a miracle-working pagoda keeper claiming to be a descendant of the Tran and a reincarnation of Indra led a rebellion involving many thousands of people. So potent was his appeal that he was for a short time able to call himself king of Dai Viet. In 1581, when Ayutthaya had fallen under the overlordship of the Burmese, a holy man led a rebellion which broke out in the nearby countryside. Again, following the 'palace revolution' in Ayutthaya in 1688 a Laotian styling himself a 'man of merit' or *phu mi bun* succeed in convincing the governor of Korat that he was possessed of such magical power that it would be futile to attempt his arrest. According to the royal chronicles, over four thousand men, eighty-four elephants and more than a hundred horses were collected on behalf of the rebel forces before the latter were finally forced to submit.

Such figures could also be nurtured by the Messianic tradition which was found in all the world religions. In Buddhism, for instance, it was believed that the future Buddha, Metteiya, would one day descend to the earth to preach the final sermon, enabling all those who listened to attain *nibbāna* (nirvana) in this life rather than after an infinite number of rebirths. Although Buddhist texts specified that aeons must pass before the Metteya's appearance, there were recurring rumours that this might occur much earlier than originally foretold. The Mahdi, the next Muslim prophet, is most associated with Sh'ia Islam, but popular beliefs among

[58] Cited in Peter Gowing, *Islands under the Cross: the story of the Church in the Philippines*, Manila, 1967, 72.

Sunnī Muslims also incorporated numerous *hadith* which held out the promise of a great religious leader or perhaps a series of leaders who would unite Muslims and revive the faith. In desperate times these hopes were readily attached to individual holy men who predicted the advent of a new age when the tribulations of the present would be at an end.

There are numerous references to rebellions led by 'holy men' in the island world from the late sixteenth century onwards. In part this is a function of the Dutch and Spanish sources, for Europeans were more likely to notice and record such events than were the royal chroniclers. However, it also seems probable that uprisings of this type were in fact more common in maritime Southeast Asia at this time because the arrival of the Europeans had fostered extensive economic and social changes and because the European presence gave popular discontent a new focus. The Philippines, where a sometimes imposed Christianity was linked with other more onerous demands from the colonial government, is the most obvious example. As early as 1574, during an attack by a group of Chinese on Manila, local people turned on a church in the nearby settlement of Tondo, destroying or stealing sacred ornaments, vestments and relics. The practitioners of the ancient beliefs, the *babaylan*, who found themselves the direct target of Christian propaganda, retaliated by leading localized raids on convents and churches, often from places of refuge in the hills. By the 1660s a number of rebellions had already broken out against the Spanish, many of which were led by traditional religious leaders. What is interesting about these movements is the extent to which Christian symbols had been incorporated into the vocabulary of resistance. The leader of one rebellion which broke out in Bohol, for instance, claimed that he too could perform Christ-like miracles, change water into wine, rejuvenate old people, and bring the dead to life. Another uprising in Panay was led by an indigenous transvestite priest, described by the Spanish as 'a noted sorcerer and priest of the demon' who dressed in the clothes of a woman. Claiming that his instructions came from the ancestors, he entitled one of his deputies Son, another the Holy Ghost, and a 'shameless prostitute' (presumably a female shaman) 'Maria Santisima'. His movement had its own apostles, bishops and popes, and he himself took the title 'Eternal Father'.[59]

The goals of these localized rebellions in the Philippines during the seventeenth century were only vaguely articulated but they clearly rejected the payment of tribute, the rendering of corvée labour and subservience to Spain. In effect, their leaders were seeking to turn back the clock, to restore society to what it had been prior to the Spanish arrival. Yet, while attacks might be made on friars and religious buildings as symbols of Spanish rule, there was rarely a rejection of Christianity as such. The leader of a Pangasinan uprising in 1660–1, one of the *principalia* named Don Andres Malong, saw to it that his followers heard Mass and received the sacraments. He said they 'had no desire to abandon the faith of Jesus Christ which they had professed at baptism . . . and would give their lives

---

[59] Eric Anderson, 'Traditions in conflict: Filipino responses to Spanish colonialism, 1565–1665', Ph.D. thesis, University of Sydney, 1977, 146–7.

in its defense, and with the help of God they would be faithful sons of the Church until death'.[60]

One of the reasons behind the failure of this and other rebellions was the lack of co-ordination between neighbouring areas. Malong's revolt coincided with others in Pampanga and Ilocos, but the Pampangans came to terms with the Spanish without his knowledge. Secondly, only extraordinary conditions of hardship and exceptional leadership could maintain effective resistance. The Spanish remarked that the typical rebellion began to fade after less than a month and, as supporters melted away, local *principalia* themselves began to contribute troops to the Spanish forces. When Malong himself was captured, it was with the aid of native spies. The quelling of such movements was therefore not difficult. Several hundred Filipinos might be involved, but a company of Spanish soldiers supported by native levies was sufficient to put down resistance.

Independent movements were usually regarded with suspicion by established religious leaders. In 1681, for instance, two men returned to Ambon from Batavia with a new Islamic teaching focused on the telling of the *tasbih* (rosary), which consisted of two hundred beads each corresponding to a specific Arabic prayer. Devotees were told that by praying in a certain ritually prescribed way they could gain heaven, not only for themselves but for their ancestors. Neophytes had their heads shaved, were given new names, bathed in the river, and were then admitted to the community. But the new movement aroused the ire of local *ulamā*, who declared it to be contrary to Islamic tradition. Supported by village heads, they appealed to the VOC. The Batavian Council considered that the movement's 'undue' stress on prayers imperilled not only ordinary work but the performance of corvée duties. In consequence, it was declared heretical and its leaders banned.

On Java, where the impact of the European presence was strongest, the rebellions of the seventeenth and early eighteenth centuries had far-reaching effects. The long tradition of holy men, ranging from guardians of sacred graves to hermits and wandering teachers, provided a pool of potential leaders of dissent. If they and their followers allied with discontented relatives of the ruler, they could mount a serious challenge to his authority. In 1630, for example, a rebellion broke out in central Java with adherents of local holy figures supported by a branch of the royal family. This uprising, which aimed to replace Sultan Agung, was put down by force, but the growing Dutch influence on Java meant that popular unrest frequently took the form of an 'anti-kafir' movement to which was added specific Javanese ideas, such as the concept of a just king, the Ratu Adil, who would usher in a new age of peace and prosperity.

These factors came together in the 1670s during the rebellion against Amangkurat led by a Madurese prince, Trunajaya, who had allied with Mataram's crown prince. Much of Trunajaya's popular support can be traced to his marriage to a daughter of Panembahan Kajoran, a revered holy man, and to the support he received from the Sunan of Giri, another

[60] Rosario Mendoza Cortes, *Pangasinan, 1572–1800*, Quezon City, 1974, 155.

religious authority from east Java. Prophecies foretold Trunajaya's eventual victory, in accordance with Allah's will, and identified the Dutch as a
principal enemy. Sunan Giri even said Java would not prosper until the
infidels were evicted. The sense of impending crisis was deepened by the
approach of the Javanese year 1600 (1677 CE), for there was a common
belief that the end of a Javanese century would witness major events such
as the fall of a dynasty. Omens, like the eruption of Mount Merapi, were
interpreted as a sign that Judgement Day was at hand, and the crown
prince of Banten, then in Mecca, himself sent back a message to say that
the Javanese war was a sign that the end of the world was near. In this
atmosphere Trunajaya was readily perceived as the harbinger of a new age
at the expected fall of the dynasty, and there can be little doubt that
Amangkurat would have been defeated had it not been for Dutch support.
The succession of Amangkurat II in 1677 did little to resolve popular
opposition to the dynasty, and the following year he was attacked by a
holy man credited with invulnerability, together with forty armed followers.

The sense of crisis infected other areas of the archipelago, although here
protest was more clearly directed against the Dutch than the rulers who
had allied with them. To the west, a Minangkabau 'saint' appeared near
Melaka in 1677 with a force of nearly four thousand men from Rembau,
Naning and other areas. The VOC intercepted several letters here and in
Sumatra calling on all Muslims to take up the sword against the infidel
Dutch and promising that all those who died in the strife would
be immediately transported to heaven. Of more concern was another
Minangkabau-led movement under a Sultan Ahmad Syah, the so-called
Rāja Śakti, a prince who in 1685 claimed he was commissioned by Allah to
expel all Dutchmen. What sets him aside from other holy men is his vision
of an archipelago-wide alliance: letters were sent to Siam, Aceh, west
Sumatra, Borneo, and apparently he also attempted to establish links with
Amangkurat and Surapati, a former Balinese slave himself regarded as a
holy man who between 1686 and 1707 maintained his own independent
domain in eastern Java.

While religion played an important part in the articulation of popular
protest in the Islamic areas of the archipelago, it was never sufficient to
gain undivided support against the Europeans and the local rulers they
supported. The imprisonment or death of a leader could quickly see the
disintegration of his following. Nonetheless, such movements were rarely
taken lightly. An object lesson came in 1735 in Surabaya, where a holy man
called Mangunjaya lived on a hill outside the town with about twenty
followers. Believing he had been given the responsibility to take over
Surabaya and protect Islam, Mangunjaya began to plan an attack on the
VOC officials. Hearing of the conspiracy, the Dutch Resident in alliance
with the Javanese regent of Surabaya ordered Mangunjaya's hilltop residence to be stormed. Nine hundred men were used in the attack, during
which Mangunjaya was killed. So convinced were these Javanese troops of
his invulnerability that his body was stabbed more than a hundred times.[61]

---

[61] Luc Nagtegaal, 'Rijden op een Hollandse tijger. De noordkust van Java en de V.O.C.
1680–1742', Ph.D. thesis, Utrecht University, 1988, 211.

The Status of Women

Yet another consideration which emerges from an examination of religious developments up to 1800 is the retraction of the public role of women. None of the world religions which came to Southeast Asia provided any textual basis for female participation in religious rituals at the highest levels. The Le law codes of Vietnam might have accorded females more rights than did their Tang counterparts, but the legal status of a woman was always below that of a man from the same social class. Thus the Trung sisters, who led a rebellion against the Chinese in 43 CE and were popularly regarded as goddesses with their own temple cults, were in Confucian historiography overshadowed by their husbands. In the Buddhist countries of Southeast Asia it was also accepted that women were inferior to men and must be reborn as males before they could aspire to the higher stages of being. Early Buddhism did allow an active religious role for women, but the tradition of higher female ordination was lost early in the present millennium. In fifteenth-century Burma one of the *sangharāja* was a woman, but two hundred years later observers in Ayutthaya noted that while there were women who led secluded lives and followed a discipline similar to that of monks, they were not full members of the *sangha*.

Christianity had remained true to the Pauline tradition which enjoined submission on women, both because females were created after males and as a punishment for the sin of Eve. While Christian missionaries in Southeast Asia did insist on monogamy as a prerequisite to baptism, they were equally sure that only in paradise would women gain spiritual equality with men. For a devout native woman opportunities to develop a fuller religious life were few, although the first Spanish nuns had arrived in 1621. One initiative in this direction occurred in 1684 in Manila, when a Chinese mestizo founded a *beaterio*, a foundation for pious native women (*beatas*) who wore a religious habit and pursued a devotional life patterned after that of Saint Ignatius of Loyola. Despite a lesser status, it remains clear that female participation made a significant contribution to the evolution of popular Christianity in the Philippines. Missionaries often commented on the piety of Filipinas who took a prominent role in Christian celebrations and church festivals. During the Easter Sunday procession in one parish in Nueva Segovia, for example, it was customary for women to carry the image of the Blessed Virgin. Finding this custom difficult to eradicate, the religious authorities finally specified that at least the devotees should be clothed in a seemly fashion.

Islam too stressed the subordinate position of women. Man had authority over women because Allah had made the one superior to the other, and a wife's duty was therefore to bear children and remain a loyal helpmate to her husband. A Malay manuscript, describing a particularly faithful wife, exhorts its hearers to pattern themselves after her. 'That is how women who love their husbands behave. We women believers should be devoted to our husbands, in the hope that we shall obtain the mercy of Allah the Exalted in the hereafter.'[62] It is certainly true that Muslim women in

---

[62] Russell Jones, ed. and trans., *Hikayat Sultan Ibrahim bin Adham*, Berkeley: Center for South and Southeast Asian Studies, University of California, 1985, 173–5.

Southeast Asia were much freer than their sisters in India or the Arab lands, but the prominence of females in indigenous religious ritual which had caught the attention of early missionaries became progressively less apparent as communal worship came to be dominated by males. Thus in sixteenth-century Brunei, 'the common people go to the mosque and the women never go but it is the men'. In Makassar, where the women had their own mosque, the wife of one of the leading *ulamā* had the effrontery to go to the public prayers on a fast day, but her husband deemed the mosque so profaned that 'he took his wife by the hand and publicly divorced her, as unworthy to be the wife of a priest of the Law'.[63]

The traditional place of women in religious ritual in Southeast Asia was not easily taken away. But increasingly they tended to be relegated to the domain of shamanism and spirit propitiation, while the high positions of the dominant faiths were reserved for males. In the process the status of the shaman, both female and transvestite, declined. Islam and Christianity took strong exception to the homosexuality which was often associated with indigenous religious figures such as the Bugis-Makassar *bissu*, and spirit mediums are among those specifically excluded from the Burmese State Council or *hlutdaw*. An English sea captain in the early eighteenth century described how women and 'hermaphrodites' at a Burmese feast 'danced a dance to the gods of the earth',[64] but there is a significant absence of any *nat kadaw* (*nat* wives) in spirit appeasement at the court level, where brahmins and monks were in charge of ritual. Because women were now the principal practitioners of 'village' as opposed to 'court' magic, they were far more likely to be accused of unacceptable practices such as witchcraft, and a Burmese law of 1785 provides extensive instructions for immersion of a woman in water 'to find out if she is a witch'.[65]

The redefinition of female status had obvious implications for the exercise of political authority. Sparse though the evidence is, the sources suggest that the idea of a male–female duality which comprises the whole had permeated concepts of power in much of early Southeast Asia. Hindu ideas of kingship had in many respects reinforced this notion, and in the early Indianized kingdoms the sexual union of a king and his queen, the bearer of his *śakti*, was regarded as a mystic ritual essential to the fertility of the realm. In a number of early societies it also appears that kingship was seen as properly belonging to the man who gained possession of the community's highest-ranking female, whose body symbolized the land itself. One scholar has been led to speculate that in early Burma 'political power, though held by men, was transmitted through women'.[66] While less common, it was at times possible for a woman (usually a widow or dowager queen) to reign in her own right. During our period this is no longer evident in the mainland states, but in the archipelago a number of seventeenth-century kingdoms, notably Aceh, were under female rulers.

[63] Gervaise, *A Historical Description*, 158–9.
[64] Hamilton, *A New Account of the East Indies*, II. 31.
[65] Than Tun, *Royal Orders*, IV. 102.
[66] J. S. Furnivall, 'Matriarchal vestiges in Burma', *Journal of the Burma Research Society*, 1, 1 (1911) 21.

In Islamic courts this must have led to some criticism from *ulamā* who accepted the prevailing Muslim view that 'women cannot be allowed to assume power, for they are wearers of the veil and have not complete intelligence'.[67] In 1699 the annals of Aceh allege that a *fatwa* arrived from Mecca decreeing that no women should now be permitted to rule, since this was against the law of Allah. Though a historian can still document the continuing influence of women at all levels of Southeast Asian society, it does not appear that their status has been improved by the spread of the major world religions into the region.

THE EIGHTEENTH CENTURY

To some extent periodization is always arbitrary, but there is some argument for regarding the eighteenth century as a time of special interest in the evolution of Southeast Asia's religious history. Disruptive economic changes, civil wars, dynastic collapse, the expanding European presence have contributed to a view that this period is largely one of fragmentation, if not positive decline. Yet an examination of religious developments suggests that Southeast Asians saw in these apparent forces of disintegration a call for renewed religious activity. Accordingly, the eighteenth century witnessed not merely a reaffirmation of the commitments of the past but the formulation of new solutions to deal with unprecedented social and economic pressures.

In Vietnam the Trinh court was steadily losing its hold in the north, and to a lesser extent central government under the Nguyen was also weakening in the south. Throughout the eighteenth century rebellions proliferated. The popularity of Buddhism and Christianity is indicative of peasant dissatisfaction with élite efforts to strengthen Confucianism, and during this period Buddhist temples frequently served as foci of discontent, with monks sometimes organizing their followers into armed militia. Rebels often questioned accepted Confucian values, mocked scholars, abused mandarins and even made fun of the emperor. The educated bureaucracy, however, generally considered that the cause of the prevailing social ills was a collapse of properly ordered human relationships which neo-Confucianism had raised to cosmic principles. Many scholars also felt the only solution was rebellion since, said one, 'for a long time all idea of hierarchy and values has disappeared'.[68] The Tayson brothers who led the great revolt which broke out in 1771, though themselves of peasant background, adopted as their model the ancient sage emperors praised in Confucian writings. Their chief mentor in fact compared himself to Yi Yin, the famous reformer of classical texts who had said he could assist any ruler to become a sage king. In the following century court-sponsored Confucianism flourished anew in Vietnam, yet the Tayson's emphasis on the importance of the people in the functioning of the state and their declaration of the equality of rich and poor alike augured the ultimate end

[67] John A. Williams, *Themes of Islamic Civilization*, Berkeley and London, 1975, 105.
[68] Cited in Thomas Hodgkin, *Vietnam. The Revolutionary Path*, London, 1981, 80.

of the old order. It is significant that of all the imported belief systems it was Confucianism, whose village roots were the most shallow, which was finally to disappear despite hundreds of years of élite patronage.

The eighteenth century was also a critical time in the history of Islam. With the decline of the Ottoman empire the holy cities of Mecca and Medina had reasserted their independence, and their ability to act as the major centres for Islamic study was enhanced. As international shipping expanded, growing numbers of Muslims were able to visit Mecca and Medina, 'the two sanctuaries' (Haramayn), as pilgrims or for longer periods of study. Here they could choose to study under various Haramayn scholars, men from several Muslim countries who were linked by close student–teacher ties and who shared a similar view of religious matters. One of the prime concerns of several Haramayn teachers was to encourage the re-examination of early Islamic sources, rather than merely accepting the judgment of previous scholarship. Like most reformers, they were also especially concerned with purifying society by eliminating accretions not approved by the Koran or Muslim law. Opposing the more monistic forms of mysticism, they were affiliated with *ṭarīqa* known for their commitment to reform of Sufism. Several of the leading teachers in the Haramayn were members of the Naqshabandiyyah, which continued its role as exponent of strict adherence to the *sharī'a*.

The environment of Mecca and Medina clearly had a formative effect on many of the overseas Muslim students who studied with them. A notable example was Shaykh Waliyullah of Delhi (1113–76 AH, 1702–62 CE) who returned from Mecca to continue in the same tradition as Ahmad Sirhind. He condemned the decadence he saw in contemporary Islam, but also envisaged a purifed Sufism which would foster the *sharī'a* as an integral part of Muslim life. In Southeast Asia a strong influence derived from the teachings of the vigorous but puritanical leader from Arabia, Muḥammad ibn 'Abd al-Wahhāb (1115–1201 AH, 1703–87 CE) who had also studied in Mecca. There he became a controversial figure because of his call for a complete social and moral reconstruction of Muslim society, his condemnation of many Sufi teachings and practices such as the worship of saints and veneration for holy graves, and his attack on the unquestioning acceptance of established authority in religious matters. The pristine law was to be the basis of the rejuvenated Muslim faith.

The influence of Wahhābism has been traced in Minangkabau in the early nineteenth century, but the traffic between Southeast Asia and the Islamic heartlands had been steadily growing throughout the eighteenth century. In part this was because of improved communications and shipping connections, but another important factor was the greater number of Arabs now settling in the region. Foremost among these migrants were Sayids from the Hadramaut. Moving out from the arid coastal strip of the Yemen, members of the foremost Sayid families became established from East Africa to Southeast Asia. Since they continued to maintain strong connections with their homeland, they provided links between scholars in many parts of the Islamic world.

The Sayids who found their way to the archipelago had always been received with honour because of their descent from the Prophet, their command of the holy language Arabic, and their assumed expertise in all things Islamic. From the mid-eighteenth century, however, mention of Arab Sayids appears more frequently in the records. Much desired as husbands for high-born women, they quickly acquired an influence which far surpassed their numbers. Now it was Sayids who frequently assumed the position of *kadi* and acted as envoys and royal advisers. By the end of the eighteenth century, most royal families in the western archipelago had some Sayid blood, and Arab communities had grown up in the port towns of Aceh, Kedah, Melaka, Batavia, north-coast Java, Riau, Palembang and in the new British settlement of Penang. In Mempawa, Matan and Pontianak in west Borneo, and in Siak in Sumatra, the founders of dynasties were themselves Sayids.

The growing Sayid presence was to have a considerable effect on the development of Indonesian Islam. While they usually came to the archipelago as traders rather than missionaries, many were recruited as teachers and the strictness with which they observed Islam could not fail to impress. In Melaka, for instance, the Arabs had their own mosque so that they could maintain their own traditions of worship.

A full study of how Indonesia responded to these new influences in the eighteenth century remains to be written. The study of law was always the basis of Islamic education, but by the 1780s it seems that Islamic schools in Minangkabau were giving increased emphasis to the teaching of Muslim law and its application to daily life. During this period another important centre for reformist teaching emerged at Palembang, where a wealthy court sponsored a number of Muslim scholars who expressed concern at what they considered the degeneration of local Islam. Among these the best-known is Abdulsamad, said to be the son of a *shaykh* from the Yemen who had become *mufti* (expert on Muslim law) in Kedah, and a Palembang noblewoman. He went to Mecca as a young man and, although it is not known whether he returned to Palembang, his writings in Malay, summaries of lectures given by Meccan scholars and translations of well-known Arabic works made him an influential figure. It was through Abdulsamad that the Samaniyyah *ṭarīqa* was introduced to the archipelago.

Abdulsamad directed much of his energy towards improving the practice and understanding of Islam among his countrymen. One of the works for which he is most renowned is his Malay rendering of the abridgement of al-Ghazālī's *The Revival of the Religious Sciences*. Another, entitled 'A gift addressed to those desirous of an exposition of the essence of the Muslim faith', devotes considerable attention to a definition of 'faith', reiterating that anything deviating from the Koran or the traditions attached to the Prophet or his Companions is an unacceptable form of *bid'a*, or innovation. He deplores the widespread custom of spirit propitiation, arguing that it is wasteful and of no avail, since there is no evidence that the ancestors are still alive. The authority of old stories, or even the pronouncements of the elders, cannot be taken as proof. Those who claim to be possessed by spirits have simply fallen under the control of evil forces. They should not be called upon in cases of illness, since their 'remedies' have nothing to do with medical treatment. He singles out for particular condemnation those men who wear women's clothes and do women's work, an apparent reference to transvestite groups which had survived from earlier times.

The encroachment of European powers in the Middle East as well as in Southeast Asia probably lies behind the contemporary Muslim interest in the holy war, and Abdulsamad himself produced a tract on this topic in Arabic. By this time central Java had been divided into two kingdoms, Yogyakarta and Surakarta, each a vassal of the VOC. The evidence suggests that the Javanese were themselves trying to resolve the tensions inherent in the deepening association with the VOC. In 1774, at the beginning of a new Javanese century, the crown prince of Yogyakarta composed a poem which sees Javanese culture as eventually absorbing the Dutch who ultimately adopt Islam. Although evidence from the central Javanese courts suggests a self-conscious adherence to accepted Islamic norms, their co-operation with the Dutch had apparently been a source of disappointment to many Muslims. In 1772, in a letter of introduction for two travellers returning to Java, Abdulsamad reminded the sultan of Yogyakarta of the Koranic tradition that those who fall in the holy war are not dead but alive, while the writer of another letter sent at the same time despatched a banner from Mecca which the Sultan could use against his enemies 'and all unbelievers'. A letter from Mecca to Surakarta some years later accuses the ruler of being nothing less than 'the Devil's king' and an apostate. 'Shall the Europeans then indeed be more powerful than Allah?'[69]

The reiteration of the call to holy war sounded by many eighteenth-century reformists aroused a strong response outside Java. The early years of the thirteenth Muslim century, which began in 1785, witnessed a number of serious attacks on Europeans, several of which drew their inspiration from religion. Raja Haji, a Bugis prince from Riau who was regarded even during his lifetime as *keramat*, a living saint, laid siege to Melaka. A Malay text describes how he went into battle reading religious works and, following his death in the fighting, was received into the company of the blessed 'as a martyr . . . in Allah's war'. Six years later, in 1790, a call went out from Penang to 'all Muslims' to drive out the English from Penang, while Malay ships were said to be massing on the east coast for an attack on Dutch Melaka. But it was not only Europeans who were the target of Islamic feeling; at the same time it was reported that several hundred hadjis led by a *shaykh* from Mecca were gathering in Kedah to make war on the infidel Siamese. Growing confrontation was also apparent in the southern Philippines, where enmity between Muslims and Christians had continued throughout the eighteenth century as Spanish priests again tried to push their missionary activities into the southern areas subject to the sultan of Sulu. The more militant mood of Islam combined with Sulu's expanding economy saw an increase in raiding for Christian slaves in the Visayas, adding further fuel to the ongoing Christian–Muslim animosity.

Unlike Islam, Filipino Christianity remained isolated from outside influ-

[69] Ann Kumar, 'Javanese Court Society and Politics in the Late Eighteenth Century: the Record of a Lady Soldier', Part I, *Indonesia*, 29 (April 1980) 69.

ences in the eighteenth century. It was therefore largely untouched by the reformism in Bourbon Spain which had begun to question the superstition and ignorance that had often characterized Spanish Catholicism. The absence of liberalizing trends was also due to the fact that the Spanish clerics who entered the missionary orders during this period generally lacked the commitment and training of their predecessors, and the high purpose of the early years of Christianization was clearly fading. But in addition the Church in the Philippines resisted change because it had flourished in the colonial environment. In the past the friars had often been allied with the Filipinos against government officials, but now their growing acquisition of land, demand for corvée labour and abuse of religious authority meant they were often themselves seen as oppressive. In 1745 an agrarian revolt erupted in the Manila area, notable because it was the first large-scale display of Filipino resentment towards the monastic orders. The revolt was shortlived, but Filipino anger fed into other areas of discontent, primarily that relating to the issue of native ordination. Although the Church had long recognized that one of its major responsibilities was to train a native clergy, no progress had been made in this regard during the seventeenth century. By the 1750s, however, the continuing lack of clergy combined with pressure from the Crown and a few liberal priests compelled the friars to employ some Filipino assistance. Outside the orders, Filipinos had also begun to receive training as secular priests, and by this time there were at least four institutions in Manila training local candidates for the priesthood. Of 569 parishes, 142 were headed by native seculars. But the regular Spanish orders consistently refused to grant full ordination to local priests, partly because of a desire to protect their own positions and partly because of an entrenched conviction that Filipinos were congenitally unfit for full clerical duties. As a result, while the secular priests were almost all Filipinos, the missionary orders remained unrepentantly Spanish. Provincial governors were still unable to act without their co-operation; *principales* needed the support of priests to be confirmed in office; and in numerous cases complaints were received of abuse by the orders of their traditional privileges.

In a climate of growing anti-Spanish feeling, the British capture of Manila in 1762 was hailed by some Filipinos as marking the end of the Spanish era and the hold of the Spanish-controlled Church. People rejoiced, they said, because now there was 'no more king, priest or governor'. Diego Silang, the main figure in the anti-Spanish rebellion which now erupted, had worked for the Spanish authorities and had become convinced that the time was right for the Filipinos to reclaim political control of their country. By the end of 1762 he had established his own government near the town of Vigan and announced a programme which included removal of oppressive officials and freedom from tribute. Initially he attempted to win the friars over to his cause, but the latter regarded Silang as a sorcerer and accused him of condoning the 'pagan' excesses of his allies from the hills. The animosity of the religious was also aroused when Silang claimed to be under the patronage of Jesus of Nazareth with himself as *Cabo Mayor* (Sergeant Major). Furthermore, Silang had his own interpretation of a Christian's duties. He could not be persuaded to confess, for instance, and as far as the Church was concerned could never fully participate in the Mass since he was never in a state of grace. Because of his own attitudes, Diego Silang apparently failed to understand the hold that the friars had over Filipinos, and their ability to use the refusal of communion as a means of enforcing obedience. When he was finally killed in 1762, it was by the orders of a group of friars who had given their appointed assassin a holy relic to ensure the success of his mission.

In 1764 the Treaty of Paris restored the Spanish administration in the Philippines, but the events of 1762–3 in the Philippines did produce some results. From 1767 attempts were made to place native secular priests in charge of parishes formerly controlled by the orders. The experiment, however, was a failure because too many illiterate, untrained Filipinos were suddenly placed in positions of authority. Indeed, at the time Manila wits quipped that there were no oarsmen to be found for the coastal vessels because 'the archbishop had ordained them all'.[70] There were endless complaints from Filipinos themselves about the conduct of the newly appointed clergy—that they favoured their relatives, that they used the rectory for parties, that they exacted large stipends and fees. The most unfortunate result of this venture was its apparent confirmation of the claim that Filipinos did not have a true vocation and could not be permitted to take on greater religious responsibilities. The hardening of Spanish attitudes in turn contributed to a more pronounced hostility among Filipinos towards the Spanish grip on Christianity. A Samarino secular priest in 1775 went so far as to develop his own religion in which he said Indios would be ordained even if they could not read or write, and that the Spanish sacraments would be abandoned. One Spanish friar was ready to regard the Moro raids on Samar as a blessing in disguise, for otherwise, he said, neither royal orders nor warnings from the priests could have persuaded the people to remain settled near the town.

The eighteenth century similarly stands out as a significant period in the Theravāda Buddhist world. In Sri Lanka, the *sangha* had deteriorated during the two hundred years of Portuguese and Dutch occupation, and a lack of proper ordination ceremonies meant that many monks had reverted to virtually lay status. Indeed, it was said that on the entire island only one still knew Pāli. Against this background a Sinhalese revivalist movement developed which emphasized piety, poverty and scriptural knowledge and was led by the *samanera* (senior monk) Valivita Saranamkara. Inspired by the hope of re-establishing the lost tradition of higher ordination (*upasampada*) in Sri Lanka, Valivita Saranamkara persuaded the ruler of Kandy, Kirti Sri Rajasimha (1747–82) to send a mission to Siam.

In itself this decision is a comment on the health of the Thai *sangha*. When Alexander Hamilton visited Siam in 1720 he remarked on the numbers of 'temples and priests', and he reckoned there could be as many as 50,000 'clergymen or Tallapoys' around Ayutthaya. Efforts had even been made to curb the activities of Catholic priests, possibly because Christians were claiming exemption from drinking the water of allegiance.

---

[70] J. L. Phelan, *The Hispanization of the Philippines: Spanish Aims and Filipino Responses, 1565–1700*, Madison, 1956, 84–9.

From 1730 it was at least in theory illegal to write a book on Christianity either in Thai or in the sacred language of Pāli; to preach Christian doctrine to Buddhists or attempt to lure them to conversion; or to criticize Buddhism publicy. The reign of Borommakot (1733–58) is still remembered as a golden age of royal Buddhist sponsorship, and so great was the king's piety that he refused to confer a noble title on someone who had not previously been a monk. The reputation which Ayutthaya had acquired in the Theravāda Buddhist world was clearly demonstrated when, after two abortive attempts, a mission finally left Sri Lanka in 1753 with a request that a chapter of Thai monks be sent to revive the discontinued *upasampada* tradition. One of the Sinhalese ambassadors described the splendour of their reception in Ayutthaya, when they were greeted by the leading monk, Upali Maha Thera, who was borne in a palanquin and accompanied by a procession in which a golden Buddha image was carried, together with flags, music, sacred books and offerings. Subsequently, a party of twenty-five monks headed by Upali Maha Thera was sent to Sri Lanka where they were received with great rejoicing. During his three-year stay, Upali Maha Thera performed seven hundred ordinations for monks and three thousand for novices, and Valivita Saranamkara was himself made Saṅgharāja, the Supreme Patriarch. This mission was followed by another when the Thai monks 'trained the [Sri Lankan] priests in many things relating to the religion, such as abstract meditation' which had been developed by the *saṅgha* in Siam. It was the exchange between Sri Lanka and Siam in the eighteenth century which laid the foundation for the development of the largest order in Sri Lanka today, known as the Siam Nikaya.[71]

However, the rapidity with which even a flourishing religious climate could deteriorate in times of political fragmentation soon became apparent in Ayutthaya. Indeed, it was already evident in Burma, where a divided *saṅgha* had suffered with the decline of the Toungoo dynasty and where contemporaries blamed the ruler's lack of virtue for the country's misfortunes. Inevitably this crisis period saw the rise of a number of charismatic leaders who held out the hope of some extraordinary resolution of mankind's distress. One monk claimed that those who became his followers and accepted his interpretations of Buddhism would automatically become a *sotapanna* (stream winner) with at most only seven reincarnations before reaching the state of *nibbāna*. Such movements were undoubtedly fostered by widely circulating prophecies predicting that a time of chaos would be followed by the rise of a king in Pegu who would usher in an age of utopian prosperity. The Buddha himself was reported to have said that a Bodhisattva would appear by at least 2290 of the Buddhist era (1746 CE), about the middle of the five thousand years predicted for the life of the religion. The emergence of an ex-monk, Smin Dhaw Buddha Kesi, believed to possess 'knowledge of spells, charms, magical incantations and exorcisms' and supernatural powers which gave him invulnerability, was

[71] P. E. Pieris, *Religious Intercourse between Ceylon and Siam in the Eighteenth Century. I. An Account of King Kirti Sri's Embassy to Siam in Saka 1672 (AD 1750)*, Bangkok, 1908, 37–8; Urmila Phadnis, *Religion and Politics in Sri Lanka*, London, 1976, 48; Rev. Siddhartha Buddharakhita Thera, *Syamupadasampada*, printed as *Religious Intercourse between Ceylon and Siam in the Eighteenth Century*, II, Bangkok, 1914, 66–7.

apparently regarded by many as a fulfilment of such prophecies and in 1740 he was proclaimed king of Pegu. His promise of a restoration of religion and a new life of wealth and comfort was for a time sufficient to attract a wide range of followers, but in 1747 he was deposed. Peguan forces, however, continued to apply pressure to Ava, and in 1752 the city fell. Following Ayutthaya's conquest by a rejuvenated Burma in 1767, Siam similarly provided a fertile breeding ground for new religious movements. In Sawangburi, one of the northern provinces, dissident monks led by a certain Phra Fang seized control and rejected some of the fundamental requirements of the *sangha*. Not only did they ignore the *vinaya* and live as laymen; they also adopted military ranks and sought worldly power, even attempting to extend into neighbouring Phitsanulok.

The great leaders who emerged in Siam and Burma in the mid-eighteenth century were a product of this environment. When the founder of the Konbaung dynasty in Burma took the title Alaung Mintayagi or embryo Buddha, and presented himself as a *cakkavatti*, a Universal Ruler, it imbued his campaigns with messianic significance. His wars against Ayutthaya were justified by the claim that the religion there was not 'blossoming nor shining', while his son Bodawpaya (r. 1782–1819) also presented his attack on Arakan as a crusade on behalf of Buddhism. In addition, Bodawpaya attempted to assert himself as the saviour for whom the Burmese had waited. Declaring that the five thousand years allotted for the religion had already passed, he proclaimed that he was not only the Metteyya but a *cakkavatti* as well. Events in Burma may have influenced developments in Siam where Taksin, who reunified the country after 1767, aspired to *cakkavatti* status, expressing a desire to be 'greater than the King of Ava'. In order to attain a more purified state through greater bodily discipline, he embarked on a study of mystical techniques and finally claimed to have reached the status of a 'stream winner', discerning on his own body several marks of the coming Buddha.[72]

Although little is known of developments in Lao and Khmer Buddhism during a period when their countries were increasingly subservient to more powerful neighbours, it appears some Lao princes responded positively to Taksin's vision of himself as the leader of a wider Buddhist community. However, it is clear that demands for the monks to acknowledge him as a spiritually superior being precipitated a major clash with the *sangha*. As a punishment for their refusal to pay him obeisance, Taksin ordered five hundred monks to be flogged and sentenced to menial labour. The hostility Taksin aroused among the religious hierarchy has been seen as instrumental in his downfall in 1782. Some years later, when Bodawpaya presented himself as the Metteya he too faced such opposition from the monkhood that he was largely forced to abandon his claim.

Such developments should not obscure the fact that in most respects these kings all supported Buddhism in traditional ways. Learned monks were honoured, sacred scriptures copied, monasteries built, ordinations

[72] Craig J. Reynolds, 'The Buddhist Monkhood in Nineteenth Century Thailand', Ph.D. thesis, Cornell University, 1973, 32–3. Dr Reynolds' research suggests that Taksin may even have been influenced by mystical Sufi practices learnt from Malay texts, and a monk from the south became his Supreme Patriarch.

sponsored. Alaungpaya attempted to reform Buddhist practice and eliminate deviant sects; he also ordered a revision of the *dhammathat* code which
tried to eradicate hierarchical inequalities before the law and to institute a
more ethical and humane approach in place of the Brahmanic ritualistic
injunctions of its predecessors. Bodawpaya too reaffirmed proscriptions
against gambling and intoxicants, and sent missionary monks out into
marginal areas. Like previous rulers, he was particularly concerned with
the unity of the monkhood. He tried to put an end to the robe controversy
by decreeing in favour of the two-shoulder party while at the same time
reorganizing the *sangha*, appointing monks he favoured to leading monasteries, naming his own teacher as Supreme Patriarch and creating a Council
of Elders to oversee religious affairs. An official was delegated to supervise
and keep records of monastic lands to limit the amount accumulated by
monasteries, and another post was responsible for the maintenance of
monastic discipline. Courses of study with set texts were prescribed for
monks, with monthly examinations to ensure that they were well grounded in knowledge of the *vinaya*. Those who failed were tattooed and
expelled. 'It is not right', declares one edict, 'that monks should remain
doing nothing except keeping away from sins and enjoying free food.'

Bodawpaya's efforts to repair the schisms in the monkhood were only
partially successful. He himself changed his opinion on several issues, and
does not seem to have provided the leadership necessary to overcome a
history of *sangha* factionalism. On occasion he was forced to expel quite
senior monks from the order. The restlessness in Burmese Buddhism is
suggested by the apparent blossoming of radical Buddhist sects during this
period. One such group was known as the Zawti: they rejected the
veneration of Buddha's statues and monks, denied reincarnation and
preached the existence of one supreme deity, the world creator. Though
the leaders were arrested, other sects continued to emerge at the village
level. In the early nineteenth century, faced by peasant discontent and
military setbacks, Bodawpaya appears to have become involved with
another lay group, the Paramat, which stressed meditation and a speculative philosophy more akin to Mahāyāna Buddhism. But despite, or perhaps because of, this proliferation of different groups, Burma maintained
its reputation as a centre for Buddhist activity, and when people of low
caste were forbidden by the ruler of Kandy, the patron of the Siam Nikaya,
from entering the Sinhalese monkhood they sought ordination at the
Burmese capital of Amarapura.

Siam, on the other hand, provides something of a contrast, and Bodawpaya's contemporary, Rama I (r. 1782–1809), stands out as possibly the
greatest Buddhist reformer of the century. Convinced that moral degeneration had led to Ayutthaya's destruction, he reaffirmed the religious
duties of the laity, promoting Thai translations of important Pāli works
such as 'The Questions of Milinda' for lay Buddhists unable to read the
originals. Even more important was the restoration of monastic discipline.
A school of monks was opened at the royal temple of the Emerald Buddha,
with learned men from the Department of Royal Pundits as instructors. In
1801, 128 corrupt monks were disrobed, tattooed and put to hard labour as
punishment for deficiencies in conduct and knowledge. Another key

concern was to restrict the development of fringe groups. Laws were passed aiming at the control of wandering holy men and individuals who 'extolled supernatural power' in attempts to take the throne. Every monk was required to obtain a certificate bearing his name, monastery, and rank, and if he wished to travel to another principality for instruction he had to present this document as proof that he had been properly ordained. Rama I also addressed the potentially divisive issue of royal involvement in monastic disputes. Even though his ecclesiastical laws demonstrate continuing concern for the health of the *sangha*, he was clearly unwilling to become involved in questions of doctrinal interpretation. Accordingly, he decreed that the king should not intervene in religious disputes until the matter had been extensively discussed by the highest-ranking monks. In state ceremonies Rama I sought to emphasize the Buddhist aspects of ritual rather than Brahmanical and animistic ones, warning officials that, while they should pay due respect to the spirits, they should not place them above Buddhism. During the oath of allegiance, evidence of Buddhist devotion should always take precedence over homage to guardian spirits and past rulers. The worship of lingas, on the other hand, was not sanctioned in the scriptures and they should be destroyed.

A further measure sponsored by Rama I was the convening of a great Buddhist Council in order to produce a full revision of the Pāli Tipitaka, the Buddhist canon. The task was carried out in 1788–9 under the supervision of leading monks and with the financial support and active involvement of the king, royal family and court officials. The significance of this event can best be appreciated if it is realized that the last such Council had been held in Chiengmai in 1475, and that the texts which resulted from Rama I's endeavours are still among the standard works of Thai Buddhism. Added prestige came with the completion of a new rendering of the fourteenth-century *Traiphum*, the Three Worlds Cosmology, a version which gave an unprecedented prominence to mankind and the role of kings, placing the merit-making Universal Monarch 'at the apex of the world'.

Spanning a period of nearly thirty years, these refinements of the traditional order infused Rama I's reign with a sense of religious purpose, and imbued Thai Buddhism with a strength which has endured into modern times. Greater monastic unity and a more amicable relationship between rulers and monks meant that the Siamese *sangha* was less subject to internal divisions than its Burmese counterpart. It has been argued, moreover, that the religious reforms of this period are distinguished because they were not simply an attempt to return to the 'pure' traditions of the past. The greater stress on human rationality, the unprecedented exercise of critical faculties, and the re-examination of humanity's relationship to the universe represented a real intellectual shift, a 'subtle revolution' which provided a solid basis for the challenges that Thai society was to face in the nineteenth century.[73]

[73] David K. Wyatt, 'The "Subtle Revolution" of King Rama I of Siam', in David K. Wyatt and Alexander Woodside, eds, *Moral Order and the Question of Change: Essays on Southeast Asian Thought*, New Haven: Yale University Southeast Asia Studies Monograph no. 24, 1982.

CONCLUSION

The three hundred years surveyed in this chapter were a time of considerable change in Southeast Asia's religious development. The increase in source material, both European and indigenous, allows many of these developments to be discussed in greater detail than is possible for earlier periods. Missionary accounts, for example, make an important contribution to our understanding of indigenous beliefs, feeding into other sources from both mainland and island areas to throw light on the process by which the world faiths adapted to the local environment. The arrival of Islam predates our period, but for a number of reasons it was only in the sixteenth century that its expansion into the archipelago gathered pace. This coincided with the coming of Christianity, the last of the world religions to reach the region and the major challenge to Islam's penetration of the island world.

Despite their doctrinal differences, the imported beliefs were all caught up by similar concerns, several of which have been discussed here—the maintenance of basic religious principles in the face of continuing accommodation with indigenous customs, the relationship with other major faiths, the connection between religion and authority, the role which women should play. None of these questions could be fully resolved, and from time to time they still emerge as matters for debate. What the events of the eighteenth century demonstrate, however, is the capacity of Southeast Asian peoples to draw on inspiration from both inside and outside the region in order to formulate their own responses to contemporary challenge.

BIBLIOGRAPHIC ESSAY

There are numerous studies of religious developments in Southeast Asia in more recent times, but relatively few are specifically concerned with the period between 1500 and 1800. A good deal of relevant information is contained in the political histories of the period, for which the reader is referred to the bibliography for Chapter 7. We have given below a selected list of books and articles which expand material discussed above, but reference should also be made to the bibliographies for Chapter 4, and (in Volume II) for Chapters 4 and 9.

Christianity

It should be noted that the early missionary accounts also contain the most detailed descriptions of indigenous customs and beliefs. There is as yet no complete study in English of Portuguese missionary efforts in Indonesia. The basic contemporary source is Artur Basilio de Sá, ed., *Documentação para a história das missões do Padroado portugês do Oriente*, 5 vols, Lisbon, 1955–8. A general study of the western archipelago is Fr Manuel Teixeira, *The Portuguese Missions in Malacca and Singapore (1511–1958)*, 3 vols, Lisbon,

1961–3. The third volume of Georg Schurhammer, *Francis Xavier. His life, His Times*, trans. M. Joseph Costelloe, Rome: Jesuit Historical Institute, 1980, provides detailed material on the Jesuit founder's time in Indonesia. The Franciscan mission is described in Fr Achilles Meersman, *The Franciscans in the Indonesian Archipelago*, Louvain, 1967. See also C. Wessels, *De Geschiedenis der R. K. missie in Amboina vanaf haar stichting door den H. Franciscus Xaverius tot haar vernietiging door de O.I.Compagnie 1546–1605*, Nijmegen-Utrecht, 1926, and B. J. J. Visser, *Onder Portuguese-Spaansche Vlag: De Katholieke Missie van Indonesië 1511–1605* Amsterdam, 1925. J. Fox, *The Harvest of the Palm*, Cambridge, Mass., 1977, gives useful material on Christianity in eastern Indonesia in the VOC period, as does Gerrit Knaap, 'Kruidnagelen en Christenen. De Vereenigde Oost-Indische Compagnie en de Bevolking van Ambon 1656–1696', Ph.D. thesis, Utrecht University, 1985.

For the Philippines the secondary literature is extensive, although of variable quality. The best source of primary material for indigenous beliefs as well as for the missionizing process is E. H. Blair and J. A. Robertson, *The Philippine Islands, 1493–1898*, 55 vols, Cleveland, 1903–9. General studies are Peter Gowing, *Islands under the Cross. The Story of the Church in the Philippines*, Manila, 1967; Nicholas Cushner, *Spain in the Philippines. From Conquest to Revolution*, Quezon City: Ateneo de Manila University, 1971; Miguel A. Bernad, *The Christianization of the Philippines. Problems and Perspectives*, Manila, 1972; H. de la Costa, *Church and State: The Philippine Experience*, Manila, 1978; Pablo Fernandez, *History of the Church in the Philippines (1521–1898)*, Manila, 1979. Gerald Anderson, ed., *Studies on Philippines Church History*, Ithaca and London, 1968, contains several articles on specific issues. H. de la Costa, *The Jesuits in the Philippines 1581–1768*, Cambridge, Mass., 1961, is an extremely detailed study of one of the major orders. Eric Anderson, 'Traditions in Conflict. Filipino responses to Spanish colonialism, 1565–1665', Ph.D. thesis, University of Sydney, 1977, contains interesting material on early rebellions which adopted Christian symbolism. Dennis Roth, 'The Friar Estates of the Philippines', Ph.D. thesis, University of Oregon, 1974, examines the background to the 1745 rebellion, and David Routledge, *Diego Silang and the Origins of Philippines Nationalism*, Quezon City, 1979, considers the relationship between Silang and Church authorities. An intriguing analysis of the vocabulary of conversion is Vincente Rafael, *Contracting Colonialism. Translation and Christian Conversion in Tagalog Society under Early Spanish Rule*, Ithaca and London, 1988. Antonio Rosales, *A Study of a Sixteenth Century Tagalog Manuscript on the Ten Commandments; its Significance and Implications*, Quezon City, 1984, provides a commentary on one translated document.

A useful contemporary account of Christianity in Vietnam is contained in the work of Alexander of Rhodes. See, for example, *Rhodes of Vietnam*, trans. Solange Herz, Westminster, Maryland, 1960. A selection of useful documents and commentary is Georges Taboulet, ed., *La Geste Française en Indochine*, Paris, 1955. See also Adrien Launay, *Histoire de la Mission de Cochinchine 1658–1823*, 3 vols, Paris, 1923–5, and *Histoire de la Mission du Tonkin*, Paris, 1927. His *Histoire de la Mission de Siam, 1662–1881*, 2 vols, Paris, 1920, covers Christian mission work in Thailand.

Confucianism

Much remains to be done in understanding the intellectual climate of Vietnam in this period. An important start has been made by Keith Taylor, 'The literati revival in seventeenth century Vietnam', JSEAS, 18, 1 (1987). Useful discussions of the interaction between China and Vietnam are found in Edgar Wickberg, ed., *Historical Interaction of China and Vietnam: Institutional and Cultural Themes*, Lawrence: Center for East Asian Studies, University of Kansas, 1969, and in Alexander Woodside, 'History, structure and revolution in Vietnam', *International Political Science Review*, 10, 2 (1989).

Islam

An indispensable reference book in several volumes and still in progress is H. A. R. Gibb, C. E. Bosworth et al., eds, The *Encyclopaedia of Islam*, new edn, Leiden and London, 1960– , which provides a ready source of specialized articles on virtually every topic and individual connected with Islam.

As far as Southeast Asia is concerned, there has been considerable debate about the nature and timing of Islam's arrival in the archipelago. A thoughtful synthesis of current views is in M. C. Ricklefs *A History of Modern Indonesia*, London, 1981. See also G. W. J. Drewes, 'New light on the coming of Islam to Indonesia?', BKI 124, 4 (1968), and S. O. Robson, 'Java at the crossroads; aspects of Javanese cultural history in the 14th and 15th centuries', BKI 137, 2 and 3 (1981). A general survey of the premodern period can be found in P. M. Holt et al., eds, *The Cambridge History of Islam*, II, Cambridge, UK, 1970. Raphael Israeli and Anthony H. Johns, eds, *Islam in Asia*, II, Jerusalem, 1984, contains useful essays on the region, as does M. B. Hooker, eds., *Islam in Southeast Asia*, Leiden, 1983. A number of valuable articles, including Merle Ricklefs, 'Six centuries of Islamization in Java' and A. C. Milner, 'Islam and Malay Kingship' are reprinted in Ahmad Ibrahim et al., eds, *Readings on Islam in Southeast Asia*, Singapore: Institute of Southeast Asian Studies, 1985.

The basic work on Sufism in the Indonesian archipelago is A. H. Johns, 'Malay Sufism as illustrated in an anonymous collection of 17th century tracts', JMBRAS, 30, 2 (1957). His publications over the last two decades cover numerous topics but have contributed particularly to our knowledge of the connections between Southeast Asia and the Middle East. See, for example, 'Islam in Southeast Asia; reflections and new directions', *Indonesia*, 19 (April 1975). G. W. J. Drewes has edited several early mystical Muslim texts which provide an insight into sixteenth-century teaching. See *Een Javaanse Primbon uit de Zestiende Eeuw*, Leiden, 1954; *The Admonitions of Seh Bari; a 16th century Javanese Muslim text attributed to the Saint of Bonan*, The Hague, 1969; *An Early Javanese Code of Muslim Ethics*, The Hague, 1978.

Islamic scholars in early seventeenth-century Aceh have been the subject of a number of studies. G. W. J. Drewes and L. F. Brakel, *The Poems of Hamzah Fansuri*, Dordrecht, Holland, and Cinnaminson, USA, 1986; C. A. O van Nieuwenhuize, *Samsu'l-din van Pasai, Bijdrage tot de Kennis der*

Sumatranaasche Mystiek, Leiden, 1945; Syed Muhammad Naguib al Attas, *Rānīrī and the Wujūdiyyah of 17th century Acheh*, Singapore, 1966, rejects al-Rānīrī's criticism of local mystics; A. H. Johns, 'Daḳā'ik al-Huruf by 'Abd al-Ra'uf of Singkel', JRAS (1955) 55–73, 139–158, and P. Riddell, ''Abd al-Ra'uf's *Tarjuman al-mustafid*', Ph.D. thesis, Australian National University, 1984, consider the work of a leading Malay scholar of the period.

The Islamization process in Sulawesi has also been well studied. See J. Noorduyn, 'De Islamisering van Makasar', BKI, 112, 3 (1956); Leonard Andaya, 'Kingship-*Adat* Rivalry and the role of Islam in south Sulawesi', JSEAS, 15, 1 (1984); Henri Chambert-Loir, 'Dato ri Bandang. Legendes de l'islamisation de la région de Célébes-Sud', *Archipel*, 29, 1 (1985); Christian Pelras, 'Religion, Tradition and the Dynamics of Islamization in South Sulawesi', *Archipel*, 29, 1 (1985).

For Minangkabau, especially in the eighteenth century, see Christine Dobbin, *Islamic Revivalism in a Changing Peasant Economy, 1784–1847*, London and Malmö: Scandinavian Institute of Asian Studies, 1983. J. Kathirithamby-Wells, 'Ahmad Shah ibn Iskandar and the late 17th century "holy war" in Indonesia', JMBRAS, 43, 1 (1970), provides a case study of one holy man, as does Ann Kumar, *Surapati. Man and Legend*, Leiden, 1976.

A discussion of the environment in eighteenth-century Palembang is found in G. W. J. Drewes, *Directions for Travellers on the Mystic Path*, BKI, 81, The Hague, 1977. See also his 'Further data concerning 'Abd al-Samad al-Palimbani', BKI, 132, 2 and 3 (1976).

The most comprehensive book on the history of Islam in the Philippines is Cesar A. Majul, *Muslims in the Philippines*, Quezon City, 1973. On Champa, see Pierre Yves Manguin, 'The Introduction of Islam into Champa', JMBRAS, 58, 1 (1985).

Developments in eighteenth-century Islam are discussed in Thomas Naff and Roger Owen, eds, *Studies in Eighteenth Century Islamic History*, Carbondale and Edwardsville, 1977, and John O. Voll, *Islam: Continuity and Change in the Modern World*, Boulder, 1982.

Bali

For recent historical work on Balinese culture, see Adrian Vickers, *Bali: A Paradise Created*, Melbourne, 1989, and also his 'Hinduism and Islam in Indonesia. Bali and the Pasisir World', *Indonesia*, 43 (October 1987). To this should be added David Stuart-Fox, 'Pura Besakih: a study of Balinese religion and society', Ph.D. thesis, Australian National University, 1987.

Buddhism

There is considerable material on contemporary Theravāda Buddhism in Southeast Asia, but the selection below emphasizes works which include material directly relating to the period discussed in this chapter. Robert E. Lester, *Theravada Buddhism in Southeast Asia*, Ann Arbor, 1973, provides a concise but thoughtful introduction. Bardwell L. Smith, *Religion and Legitimation of Power in Thailand, Laos and Burma*, Chambersburg, 1978, contains a number of relevant essays. Milford E. Spiro, *Burmese Supernaturalism*, Philadelphia: Institute for the Study of Human Issues, 1967, is a wide-ranging introduction to spirit worship and its relationship to Burmese Buddhism, while Miharranjan Ray, *An Introduction to the Study of Theravada Buddhism in Burma*, University of Calcutta, 1946, is still a basic reference. E. Michael Mendelson, *Sangha and State in Burma: A Study of Monastic Sectarianism and Leadership*, Ithaca, 1975; Donald E. Smith, *Religion and Politics in Burma*, Princeton, 1965; John Palmer Ferguson, 'The symbolic dimensions of the Burmese sangha', Ph.D. thesis, Cornell University, 1975, can be consulted together to convey a sense of the evolving position of the monkhood in Burma. To these can be added the stimulating arguments advanced by E. Sarkisyanz, *Buddhist Backgrounds of the Burmese Revolution*, The Hague, 1965. On the periodic reforms of the monkhood, see Michael Aung-Thwin, 'The role of *sasana* reform in Burmese history: economic dimensions of a religious purification', JAS, 38 (1979), and the response by Victor Lieberman, 'The political significance of religious wealth in Burmese history: some further thoughts', JAS, 39 (1980). There are only a limited number of historical studies of Thai Buddhism devoted to the pre-nineteenth-century period. Yoneo Ishii, *Sangha, State and Society: Thai Buddhism in History*, Kyoto, Center for Southeast Asian Studies, 1986, offers a broad introduction. Prince Dhani Nivat's booklet, *A History of Buddhism in Siam*, Bangkok: Siam Society, 1969, gives a lucid picture of the evolution of Thai Buddhism, having been written for the as yet unfinished *Encyclopaedia of Buddhism*. Developments in the eighteenth century are discussed in depth by Craig J. Reynolds, 'The Buddhist monkhood in nineteenth century Thailand', Ph.D. thesis, Cornell University, 1972. The exchange of religious missions between Siam and Ceylon (Sri Lanka) in the mid-eighteenth century is the subject of P. E. Pieris, *Religious intercourse between Ceylon and Siam in the eighteenth century*, I: *An account of King Kirti Sri's Embassy to Siam in Saka 1672 (A.D. 1750)*, Bangkok, 1908, and II: *The adoption of the Siamese order of priesthood in Ceylon, Saka Era 1673 (A.D. 1751)*, Bangkok, 1914. The phenomenon of holy men is discussed by Charles F. Keyes, 'Millennialism and Theravada Buddhism', JAS, 26, 2 (1977), and Yoneo Ishii, 'A note on Buddhistic millenarian revolts in northeastern Siam', JSEAS, 6, 2 (1975).

10

THE AGE OF TRANSITION: THE MID-EIGHTEENTH TO THE EARLY NINETEENTH CENTURIES

STATE RIVALRY AND CYCLICITY

Geographical, cultural and ethnic diversity renders any overview of Southeast Asia's history a difficult task. The same problems of diversity are met even in the study of individual components of the region, given, for example, the differences between Shan and Mon in Burma, Vietnamese and Khmer in the Indochinese peninsula, Tagalog and Moro in the Philippines, and coastal Malay and hill Batak in north Sumatra. What cultural and historical identity obtained between or within particular segments was, to a large extent, the dictate of geography. A Confucianist Vietnam and a Christian Philippines on Southeast Asia's fringes confirm the significance of geographical location. Beneath the striking overlay of differences, Southeast Asian societies shared a substratum of distinct traditions of lineage patterns, social structuring and belief systems which were related to the overarching concern over resource management within their particular environment. In time, the accommodation of these features with varying degrees of external influences added a second dimension to the identity of pre-modern societies. Burmese and Thai responses to Theravāda Buddhism were different, as were the responses to Islam in Java and in the Malay world. The European element added a third dimension to the evolution of these societies. European penetration has, in fact, been considered a watershed, with its earlier inroads into the maritime regions constituting a further distancing between developments there and the mainland. To what extent was this dichotomy between colonial and indigenous administrations real in terms of social impact?

From the mid-eighteenth century, Southeast Asian political régimes were strengthened by the vigour of new dynasties on the mainland and in central Java, and the increased pace of activity in the maritime region by the Dutch and Spanish colonial administrations. The new age was universally one of growth and expansion. The concomitant expansion of territorial frontiers, administrative control and economic activity was unprecedented. During the process, the rough outlines and the cultural and ethnic structuring of the future nation-states were imperceptibly settled. Simultaneously, the colonial territories and, uniquely among the independent powers, Siam, were brought within the mainstream of international economic developments. But internal social affairs in these territories were not necessarily different from those prevalent under indigenous despotism. The preoccupation of both indigenous and colonial authorities was primarily with the procurement of security and the management of scarce material and manpower resources for increased productivity and profit. Fulfilment of these aims was through the diverse methods of armed control, ideology, administrative ordering and improved communication. In the process, the Southeast Asian community moved into a period of transition leading into the modern era.

In island Southeast Asia, Western influence directly and indirectly stimulated development in the prosperous maritime centres before the end of the eighteenth century. Relative to these events, the forces which determined the cycles of change on the mainland remained, as yet, internal. The seventeenth-century dalliance of Toungoo Burma, Ayutthaya and Le Vietnam with merchant adventurers, commercial companies and missionary educators had, soon after the mid-century, provoked suspicion and caution, resisting Western involvement. This meant that just as indigenous power in the archipelago reached a point of overall stasis or decline about the mid-eighteenth century, the momentum of cyclic reintegration began to gain full force on the mainland. The new burst of energy was propelled by a complex array of forces. The cumulative impact of population growth and movement, with the related problems of resource mobilization and economic competition, the maturing and leavening of religious and political ideology and the importation of Western arms, launched mainland Southeast Asia into the most spectacular and expansive era of indigenous statehood and centralization.

During the decades straddling the foundation of the last autonomous dynasties—the Konbaung (1752–1885), the Chakri (1782–), and the Nguyen (1802–1945)—the inherent forces of integration and authority were stretched to their maximum limits of growth and geographical expansion. The push from within the Irrawaddy, the Chao Phraya and the Red (Hong) River valleys laid the ground for conflict among the kingdoms of Burma, Siam and Vietnam for political integration, involving expansion along roughly north–south valley and coastal orientations. Wedged between these geographically determined political configurations were the land-locked Lao principalities and Cambodia, suffering the humiliation and loss brought by shrinking borders and the perpetual insecurity of buffer status. The problems of inter-state conflicts were exacerbated and never permanently resolved due to the nature of Southeast Asian political authority, at the apex of a hierarchy of power based on patron–client relations. As power was fluid, the fortunes of the polity fluctuated with the expansion and contraction of its territories. In the absence of fixed boundaries, influence shaded out with distance from the centre. Loyalties in the peripheral areas were less secure than elsewhere, though during the period under survey they were drawn closer to the main centres of power than at any other time before. In the main, regional, economic and

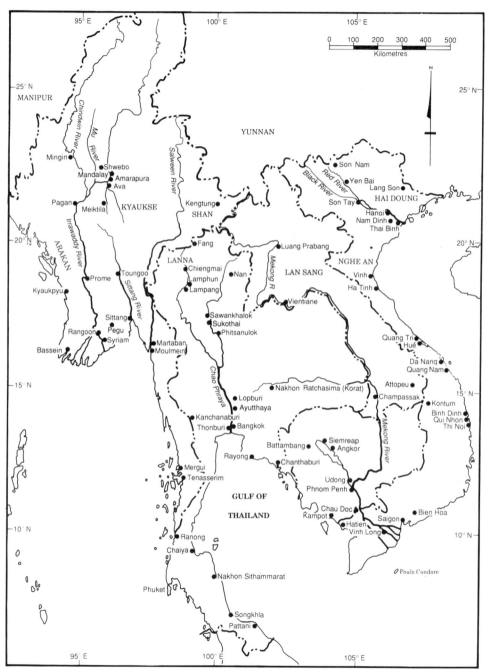

Map 10.1   Mainland Southeast Asia during the early nineteenth century.

religious integration which came with territorial expansion superseded ethnic divisions such as those between Shan, Burman and Mon, or between Thai, Khmer and Lao. Here loyalty and vassalage were elicited more successfully than in the cultural and religious interface between Thai and Malay or Khmer and Vietnamese. The foundation of the three new dynasties of the mainland saw the primary contours of the region take shape, leaving the firming of boundaries to the approaching era of European imperialism.

FORCES OF INTEGRATION: RELIGION, CHARISMA AND RESOURCE CONTROL

Much as in island Southeast Asia, geo-economic and religious factors were essential ingredients for territorial expansion and integration in the Theravāda-influenced Irrawaddy-Salween and Chao Phraya valleys, from indeed at least the time of Pagan and Ayutthaya. This process of expansion and integration marked the gradual establishment of Burmese and Thai hegemony in the respective regions.

The essence of political authority lay in the ruler's effective control and utilization of resources at the centre. The Theravāda Buddhist ruler's role as the fountain of justice and power was idealized in the concepts of *dhammarāja* and *cakkavatti*. It was the duty of the ruler to enhance his *karma* (merit) through charitable acts (*dana*) and by instituting the laws of *dhamma* (Buddhist teachings). But intensification and extension of this function within a larger community of people obliged him to assume the role of *cakkavatti* or Universal Monarch. Within the framework of this philosophy, the Theravāda Buddhist rulers of the mainland managed the manpower and material resources of their environment. A successful interrelation of the spiritual and secular roles was an essential aspect of the ruler's charisma.

Given the ruler's central role in resource management, the recurrent economic calamities during the reigns of Pindale (1648–61) and Pyè (1661–72) in Burma were a logical outcome of diminished royal authority and administrative efficiency and, specifically, the neglect of agriculture. The downward spiralling persisted during the reign of their successors, culminating in the 1752 Mon conquest of Ava.[1] Simultaneously, Ayutthaya showed a clear but less dramatic downward slide in its internal politics. King Borommakot (r. 1733–58) was unable to check the loss of royal manpower (*phrai luang*), as against the growth of private manpower (*phrai som*) amongst the princes and ministers. This undermined the strength of the ruler and laid the court open to political intrigues.[2] Weakness at the capital unleashed centrifugal forces favouring diffuse centres of power and the assertion of subregional and provincial interests. Towards the mid-eighteenth century Ava was plagued by Manipuri and Shan raids, while

[1] V. B. Lieberman, *Burmese Administrative Cycles: Anarchy and Conquest, c.1580–1760*, Princeton, 1984, 142–55, 176–7.

[2] Akin Rabibhadana, 'The Organization of Thai Society in the Early Bangkok Period, 1782–1873', Data Paper no. 74, Southeast Asian Program, Cornell University, 1969, 36–9.

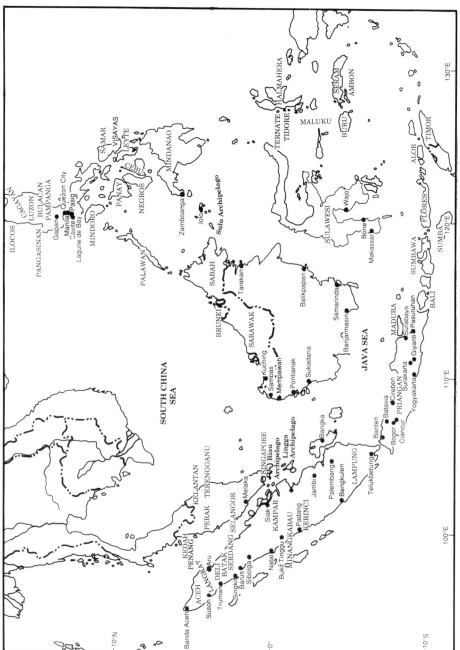

Map 10.2   Island Southeast Asia during the early nineteenth century.

Mon power achieved brief ascendancy in the south, centred on Pegu (1740–52). In Ayutthaya similar fragmentation of power befell the kingdom on the failure of King Suriyamarin (r. 1758–67) to defend his capital successfully against Burma's cataclysmic invasion. It resulted in the decentralization of power at Phitsanulok, Sawankhalok, Nakhon Sithammarat, Phimai and Chanthaburi.

Abandonment of *dhamma*, the universal laws of righteousness, justice and morality enshrined in the teachings of Buddha, was believed to bring dynasties to an end. Conversely, manifestation of the principle became the cardinal qualification for the initiators of new lines of kingship. In Burma and Siam no clear rules of succession were fixed in terms of pedigree or precedence of rank and seniority within the royal house; but male offspring of royal mothers or concubines had preference under normal conditions. When the dynasty's loss of credibility provoked challenge, however, there was provision for tapping new sources of leadership, setting aside ethnic and class boundaries. In Burma, the southern Mon reaction against Ava's decline was led by Smin Dhaw, a man of Gwei-Karen origins, with a polyglot following, who was acclaimed ruler at Pegu in 1740.[3] He was succeeded by the Shan elephanteer, Binnya Dala (r. 1747–57) who was ousted by Maung Aung Zeya, headman of the obscure village of Mok-hso-bo (Shwebo). The latter, as Alaungpaya (r. 1752–60), founded the Konbaung dynasty at Ava. In Siam, Phraya Taksin, the man who rose to power after Ayutthaya's fall in 1767 and founded a new capital at Thonburi, was the son of a wealthy and influential Chinese merchant. His successor, Rama I (r. 1782–1809), who moved the capital to the opposite east bank of Chao Phraya to Bangkok and founded the Chakri dynasty, shared similar ties with the important Chinese merchant élite originating from Ayutthayan times, through his mother Dan Ruang.[4] The Chakri dynasty's links with the foreign merchant community were reinforced through the mother of Rama II (r. 1809–24), Queen Amarin, a member of the prominent Bunnag family of Persian merchant origin.

While the physical prowess of Binnya Dala and Alaungpaya and the royal military commissions of Phraya Taksin and Phraya Chakri were important passports to leadership, enhancement of it through personal charisma was imperative for the mobilization of manpower and realization of the status of *cakkavatti*. It was said that heavenly signs at the time of his birth portended Alaungpaya's future greatness and, just before Ava's fall, in 1752, he was rumoured to have 'the smell of a king about him'.[5]

In the establishment of monarchical power, control over the nuclear resource base was a paramount consideration for the process of legitimization. Preceding Alaungpaya's rise, decline of the agricultural core region in the Kyaukse basin, through the neglect of irrigation and famine, had

[3] N. Brailey, 'A Re-investigation of the Gwe of Eighteenth Century Burma', JSEAS, 1, 2 (1970); Lieberman, *Burmese Administrative Cycles*, 217.

[4] K. Wenk, *The Restoration of Thailand Under Rama I, 1782–1809*, Tucson: Association of Asian Studies, University of Arizona, 1968, 1–2; D. K. Wyatt, *Thailand, A Short History*, New Haven, 1982, 161–2.

[5] Arthur P. Phayre, *History of Burma . . . from the Earliest Times to the End of the First War with British India*, 1883, reprinted New York, 1969, 149–50; Lieberman, *Burmese Administrative Cycles*, 235.

driven population to the south and to Arakan. It was therefore at Shwebo, within the focus of the resource base in the Mu region, that the new ruler established his capital. Not until the unification with lower Burma and the return of relative stability was the prosperity of the traditional Burmese heartland at Kyaukse restored, motivating Ava's resurgence as the capital under Hsinbiyushin (r. 1763–76).

Similar considerations of resource control influenced the political reorganization and consolidation under the rulers of Siam. Faced with the devastation of Ayutthaya by the Burmese in 1767 and the depletion of the population through thousands being carried away as captives, Taksin sought to lay a stable resource base in Teochiu Chinese activity in the south. Labour shortage and a significant upturn in the trade with China since the decline of European commercial influence at the turn of the previous century led Taksin to cultivate the Chinese community on the opposite bank of Thonburi, having already established contacts with them in Rayong, on the Gulf of Thailand. They provided the labour force for draining the marshy region and for laying out new areas of cultivation, together with the skills for carpentry and building construction. The shifting of the capital by Rama I to the more strategic location on the east bank at Bangkok contributed immensely to immigration and trade, and an expanded market for Chinese bricks and tiles. A desperate shortage of rice at the start of the Bangkok era had made supplies from the Malay peninsula imperative. But by the 1780s Siam's double cropping enabled it to resume exports to China, with the Ch'eng-hai merchants assuming a dominant role in this sector of trade.[6]

In Burma, in the course of attempting a valley-wide integration of the Irrawaddy, Alaungpaya did not underestimate the importance of the delta region, the point of ingress for the two essential ingredients for consolidation—Theravāda Buddhism and Western arms. The delta was, moreover, the focus of Mon resistance. In founding the delta entrepôt at the holy city of Dagon, which he renamed Rangoon in 1755, he envisaged effectively undermining Mon power at Pegu and gaining ready access to Western arms at Syriam. Unsuccessful overtures to the British for cannons left Alaungpaya with no option but to fall back on manpower resources, drawn from among the loyal Burmans in the north, to subdue the Mons. Given the river silting which had closed off Pegu and was beginning to affect Syriam, Alaungpaya's move to shift the port to Rangoon was timely and pragmatic.[7] A simultaneous shift of capital to the south remained, nonetheless, out of the question. The delta continued to serve as an important frontier outlet for the dry zone; but economic incentives were insufficient to offset the ravages of malaria and political instability. Despite Burmese attempts at acculturation, Mon hostility remained evident in no less than six rebellions during Konbaung rule. Strategically as well, a centrally located capital in the northern plains was of prime importance.

[6] Hong Lysa, *Thailand in the Nineteenth Century, Evolution of the Economy and Society*, Singapore: Institute of Southeast Asian Studies, 1984, 47; Sarasin Viraphol, *Tribute and Profit: Sino-Siamese Trade, 1652–1853*, Cambridge, Mass.: Council of East Asian Studies, 1977, 109.

[7] B. R. Pearn, *A History of Rangoon*, Rangoon, 1939, 41–8.

Manipuri raids and symptoms of restlessness amongst the Shans did, in fact, force Alaungpaya to break off the expedition to the south in order to return to the north. Moreover, the capital's proximity to the important trade route to Yunnan and access to rice granaries—those of the Kyaukse and Mu valleys in the vicinity as well as Prome in the south—militated against a transfer to the coast.

The isolation from the coast of the Burmese core region in the north, except for a brief period during the reigns of Bayinnaung (1551–81) and his son Nandabayin (1581–99) when the capital was at Pegu, sharply contrasted with the Chakri dynasty's integration of its rice economy with external trade. The main disincentives to the early expansion of the rice economy in the delta would appear to have been the prohibition of rice exports and the diversion of supplies, collected as tax, to the northern dry zone where the escalation of war under the early Konbaung rulers effected a heavy depletion of manpower and food supplies. The lack of economic incentive, combined with the hazards of malaria in newly opened areas, limited rice acreage to clusters of settlements. By 1830 the total area under rice cultivation in lower Burma was no more than 260,000 hectares, as against 1 million hectares in the northern dry zone.[8] But, despite the contrast between coast and interior, there was effective valley-wide economic integration, evident in increased commercialization. Hence, during the period 1750–1830, about 97 per cent of the land sales were made exclusively in silver.[9] By the last decades preceding the British conquest in 1852, the economic disparity between coast and interior was less significant. There was considerable economic growth in the delta which emerged as the chief granary of the Konbaung dynasty.[10]

BUDDHIST IMPERIALISM

The imperial policies of Burma during this period, often challenging any economic and political rationale, were grounded in the philosophy that it was the ultimate end of the Buddhist state, through the ruler as its chief instrument, to extend the *dhamma*, if necessary by forceful conquest. While such acts of humanity as the respective efforts of Alaungpaya and Taksin at the beginning of their reigns to relieve hunger and the ravages of war had won wide loyalty, their later insensitivity and claims to Bodhisattva status alienated the *sangha* and the populace.[11] Standing before the gates of Ayutthaya, Alaungpaya made an appeal for surrender, claiming he was

[8] V. Lieberman, 'Secular Trends in Burmese Economic History, c. 1350–1830', paper presented to the Conference on Southeast Asia in the Fifteenth to Eighteenth Centuries, organized by the Social Science Research Council and Universidate Nova de Lisboa, December 1989, 7.

[9] ibid., 16.

[10] M. Adas, *The Burmese Delta: Economic Development and Social Change on an Asian Rice Frontier, 1852–1941*, Madison, 1974, 20–2.

[11] C. J. Reynolds, 'The Buddhist Monkhood in Nineteenth-Century Thailand', Ph.D. thesis, Cornell University, 1973, 32–4; J. G. Koenig, 'Journal of a Voyage from India to Siam and Malacca in 1779', *Journal of the Straits Branch of the Royal Asiatic Society*, XXVI (1894) 164–5; B. J. Terwiel, *A History of Modern Thailand 1767–1942*, St Lucia, Queensland, 1983, 56–7.

the *arimittiya* or the future Buddha, that brought ridicule and the loss of credibility in the eyes of the Thais.[12]

Quite apart from the need to quell border tribes, it could be argued that the military exploits of the early Konbaung rulers were aimed at securing submission and loyalty; but expeditions beyond the valley complex drained Burmese resources. The economic importance of the wet-rice Shan states and their contribution of manpower for the pacification of the Mons was a strong factor in favour of their reduction to vassalage. Similarly, the capture of Chiengmai in 1762 gave the Burmese the advantage of additional forces for the victorious assault on Ayutthaya in 1767. As it proved, the price that Burma paid for entanglement in the northeast was heavy. Interference with the Shan and Lao states brought the Burmese right up to the borders of China, culminating in friction with the Chinese viceroy over the status of Kengtung. The Burmese under Hsinbiyushin fought off four Chinese invasions, each larger than the last, and secured the Shan states. These events, however, interrupted the lucrative overland trade with Yunnan involving the exchange largely of cotton for silks. The conflict was also a heavy drain on resources, not least with investment in thousands of gold and silver images at the shrines at Shwezigon (Pagan) and Shwedagon (Rangoon) in order to avert the heavenly vengeance portended by the occurrence of earthquake at the time of the Chinese threat.[13] The ruler's control over manpower and natural resources during this period was attested in Hsinbiyushin's boast, recorded in a 1768 inscription at Shwezigon, that he could rebuild the royal city of Ava in 106 days.[14]

After the brief respite from war during the reign of the passive Singu (1776–82) who took refuge in religion, the government of Bodawpaya (r. 1782–1819) marked the high point of imperialist ambitions. Arakanese incursions were countered by conquest in 1784. But, by extending Burma's borders close to British India, Bodawpaya opened the way for later external intervention. At the termination of the war an estimated 20,000 captives were deported, transporting the gigantic Mahamuni image via the Arakan Pass. These barely compensated for casualties incurred by military expeditions. Of an estimated 200,000 men conscripted for the 1785 and 1786 expeditions against Siam, for example, about 40 per cent were lost to disease or desertion.[15] Regardless of the disruption to economic activity brought by war and the general population drain, forced labour was pressed from the Shans, Mons and the Burmese to satisfy the spiritual ambitions of the ruler. He commemorated his claim to future Buddhahood by the construction at Mingun of a bell, smaller only than that in the Kremlin, and an unfinished pagoda of fifty metres—one-third of the proposed height. The effects of labour mobilization reached crisis point in

---

[12] Maung Htin Aung, *A History of Burma*, New York, 1967, 169; J. P. Ferguson, 'The Symbolic Dimensions of the Burmese Sangha', Ph.D. thesis, Cornell University, 1975, 183–4.

[13] Phayre, 198.

[14] Ma Yi Yi, 'A Bibliographical Essay on the Burmese Sources for the History of the Konbaung Period, 1752–1885', paper presented to the First International Conference of Southeast Asian Historians, Singapore, 1961, 4.

[15] F. N. Trager and W. J. Koenig, *Burmese Sit-Tàns, 1764–1826: Records of Rural Life and Administration*, Association of Asian Studies Monograph, no. XXXVI, Tucson, 1979, 29–30.

1795 with a major expansion of the Meiktila tank and irrigation system which affected virtually the entire kingdom. Agriculture was seriously disrupted and, with successive seasons of drought, a prolonged famine set in during 1805 which lasted nearly a decade.[16] In 1809, at the height of widespread hunger, flight and banditry, Bodawpaya launched his five-pronged attack on Siam, the largest he ever mounted. It was largely a failure, apart from securing the ports of Mergui and Tenasserim against Rama I's attempts to continue in possession of them, and it brought Burmese imperialist efforts to a halt through the sheer drain of resources.

In converting the state into a vast war machine, Bodawpaya instituted more efficient collection of revenue through checking irregularities in the functioning of the *hlutdaw* administrative and judicial council. Towards the same end, surveys of population, boundaries and productivity were conducted during his reign.[17] The *sasana* reform, or purification of the *sangha*, also contributed towards increasing royal revenues by checking tax evasions where private property was held under the guise of glebe lands.[18] Military victories earned with the blood of the people were commemorated with architectural excesses executed with even more labour impressed from them. The burdens of labour, aggravated by the rapacity of local officials, drove the Arakanese to rebellion in 1794 and the flight of thousands to Chittagong, precipitating British diplomatic reaction. Others sought refuge in Thai and Shan areas. The opportunities for wage labour at Rangoon, from timber-felling for the growing shipbuilding industry in Calcutta, provided additional outlets for the disgruntled.

Bodawpaya's absolutism alienated him from other sectors of the community as well. It put Burma clearly on the path of decline from which it was unable to recover under more enlightened rulers like Mindon Min (r. 1853–78). Harsh measures were taken against restive commanders and unorthodox clergy alike. As part of the programme of religious purification, Bodawpaya put an end to the longstanding 'shoulder wrapping' controversy pertaining to the dress of monks, in favour of the 'two-shoulder' faction. The office of primate which Alaungpaya had created was modified so that the incumbent acted in consultation with a newly constituted ecclesiastical council. Bodawpaya's merit-making act of feeding thousands of monks, his construction of pagodas in about 250 towns, and his ascetic practices did little to absolve him from negligence of economic affairs. His sternest critics were a reformist lay group who postulated the revolutionary concept of de-emphasizing the material aspects of merit-making. They were punished, but Bodawpaya had no way of forcing the *sangha* to acknowledge his claims for divinity.[19]

Despite many points of similarity in their institutional foundations, and the comparable achievements of the contemporaneous Bodawpaya

---

[16] W. J. Koenig, 'The Early Kón-Baung Polity, 1752–1819: A Study of Politics, Administration and Social Organization in Burma', Ph.D. thesis, University of London, 1978, 87–8.

[17] Trager and Koenig, 53.

[18] M. Aung-Thwin, 'The Role of *Sasana* Reform in Burmese History; Economic Dimensions of a Religious Purification', JAS, 38, 4 (1979) 674; V. B. Lieberman, 'The Political Significance of Religious Wealth in Burmese History: Some Further Thoughts', JAS, 39, 4 (1980) 768.

[19] Ferguson, 202–4.

and Rama I in pushing the boundaries of their respective empires to their fullest limits, Burma and Siam were on different paths. The programme of Burmese expansion, along the finger-like valley and coastal configuration, as well as across Shan and Lao territories, found no natural focus in Ava. In contrast, Thai military activity fanned out from Bangkok with greater facility up the Chao Phraya and down the Gulf of Thailand to the isthmus. Unlike the Burmese who faced Mon challenge, the Thais had the further advantage of the absence of major ethnic conflict within the nuclear zone. Perhaps with a fresh memory of the unfortunate end to which Taksin's spiritual presumptions had led him, the Chakri rulers were content with a more modest interpretation of their role as *cakkavatti* than their Burmese counterparts. Their military initiatives, provoked largely by Burmese and Vietnamese expansion on the outer flanks, involved bringing under their vassalage the Laotian states of the north and northeast, Cambodia in the southeast and the northern Malay states.

Thai territorial expansion followed a systematic policy of consolidation, which was generally not the case in Burma. Begun by Taksin, who achieved integration of the core region by eliminating his rivals at Phitsanulok and Fang, a programme of pacification helped build up a complete circle of border provinces with strong administrative ties with the centre. The importance of Chinese economic activity in the Gulf of Thailand drew Taksin's attention first to the south where Nakhon Sithammarat and Songkhla were brought under Thai vassalage and were maintained as quasi-independent provinces, the latter headed by a Chinese governor.[20] In the north and northwest, the suspension of Burmese military activity during the reign of Singu allowed the Thais the opportunity to gain control over Chiengmai in 1776. Though seriously depopulated and depleted by frequent Thai–Burmese conflicts, it was to emerge during the reign of Rama I as the most influential *müang* (province), supervising the northern tributaries, as Nakhon Sithammarat and Songkhla supervised those in the south.[21] Bangkok appointed the provincial governors, whose sons, in their capacity as royal pages at the capital, were virtually political hostages.

Beyond the circle of the outer provinces, Champassak and Vientiane in the northeast and Siemreap and Attopeu in the southeast formed a buffer zone with local rulers under Thai vassalage. Vientiane and Luang Prabang, the strongest of the Lao states, were not wholly submissive, but their mutual rivalries were used to good effect by Siam. Luang Prabang terminated relations with Burma in 1778 and, as well as offering tribute to China, sent the 'silver and gold tree' to Bangkok. In 1791–2, suspicion of its loyalty caused Siam to reduce it to complete submission, using Vientiane forces. In 1797, 1799 and 1803 Vientiane provided Siam with support also against Burmese attempts to recapture the northern Lao states. Vientiane's buffer status, with expanding Vietnamese power on its eastern flank, led to its adoption of dual allegiance, much in the Cambodian

[20] Chenglo A. Cheng, 'Mac Thien Tu and Phrayataksin, A Survey on their political stand, conflicts and background', *Proceedings of the Seventh Conference of the International Association of the Historians of Asia*, Bangkok, 1977, 1538.
[21] L. M. Gresick, 'Kingship and Political Integration in Traditional Siam, 1767–1824', Ph.D. thesis, Cornell University, 1976, 126–7, 129.

manner. It allied with the Nguyen leader, Gia-long, against the Tayson and, between 1804–17, sent a triennial tribute of elephants, horses, rhinoceros horn, ivory and cinnamon.[22] The termination of Vientiane's tribute after this period could have been due to the preoccupation of the ruler, Chao Anu (Anuvong), with consolidating his power in the face of Thai domination and attempts at assimilation, such as the policy of tattooing enacted in 1824.[23]

Relations between Siam and Vientiane soon reached a crisis. Rebuffed by failure to secure the appointment of his son as ruler of Champassak, as reward for earlier assistance against the northern Lao principalities, Anu prepared for revolt. His audacious march against Bangkok in 1827 was calculated to coincide with an ill-founded rumour of a British attack on the capital. The fierce Thai retaliation that followed dealt a deadly blow to Laotian power. It depopulated virtually the whole left bank of the Mekong through massacre and mass transportation of captives. This episode, encompassing the destruction and abolition of Vientiane, became in time the major trauma of Lao nationalist memory. On the isthmus end of Siam's outer fringe, religious and cultural differences exacerbated the independent spirit of the distant vassals. Terengganu, Perak and Kedah paid tribute only under duress, and recalcitrant Pattani was subdued in 1791.

Excluding the outer rim of independent and semi-independent tributary states (*prathetsarat* or *müang khun*), Thai administration was based on manpower control. The size of provincial units was determined roughly in inverse proportion to the density of population, which decreased overall from the centre to the fringes.[24] Under Rama I, the territories were neatly classified in accordance with the degree of administrative power exercised over them by Bangkok. The tributary peninsular states on the peripheries of the kingdom, with Cambodia, enjoyed the maximum independence, holding the status of first-class *müang*. The remaining provinces were divided into second- third- and fourth-class *müang*. Songkhla, Nakhon Sithammarat and Battambang-Siemreap, as border capitals, enjoyed the status of second-class *müang*. The principalities of Chiengmai, Vientiane, Champassak and Pattani fell within the purview of the third-class *müang*. They owed tribute, manpower and military obligations and could expect arbitrary Thai interference in their internal affairs. The remaining core provinces of the original Ayutthayan kingdom, within the direct control of the capital, constituted the fourth-class *müang*. The degree of territorial integration achieved was evident, for example, in the demotion of Phitsanulok and Nakhon Sithammarat to the status of third- and second-class respectively, from being first-class *müang* during Ayutthayan times.[25] The administrative ordering of the kingdom, imperative for stability, ensured at the same time the mechanics for mobilizing resources. Enhanced centralization allowed for the systematic exploitation of proportionately increased

[22] D. K. Wyatt, 'Siam and Laos, 1767–1827', JSEAH, 4, 2 (1963) 27.
[23] B. Terwiel, 'Tattooing in Thailand's History', JRAS, (1979) 158; Mayoury and Pheuiphanh Ngaosyvathn, 'Lao Historiography and Historians: Case Study of the War between Bangkok and Lao in 1827', JSEAS, 20, 1 (1989) 58–9.
[24] L. Sternstein, 'The Distribution of Thai Centres at Mid-nineteenth Century', JSEAH, 7, 1 (1966) 66–72.
[25] Gesick, 25–6; Wyatt, *Thailand*, 158.

sources of wealth and manpower from the outer circle to the centre, committing the directly administered provinces to greater economic obligations than the vassal territories beyond them. Reinforcement of loyalties to the capital was institutionalized in the annual 'water of allegiance' ceremony for *müang* within the Siamese proper, while vassal states were additionally obliged to send, periodically, the 'gold and silver tree'.[26] Loyalties secured by force, rather than voluntary submission, were then carefully nurtured through military assistance and protection in times of crisis. Where conciliation failed coercion was inevitable, as frequently in the case of the northern Malay states.

BUFFER STATUS AND DOUBLE ALLEGIANCE

Shared affinities with a glorious Khmer past and Theravāda Buddhism accounted for Thai paternalism towards a weak Cambodia as the Vietnamese push into the Mekong gained momentum at the beginning of the eighteenth century. Thai influence at the Khmer capital at Udong had waned after the fall of Ayutthaya but was soon renewed with the diversion of Vietnamese attentions away from Cambodian affairs on the outbreak of the Tayson rebellion (1771–1802) (see page 588). By offering refuge to Prince Ang Eng, fleeing civil war in Cambodia, and the Nguyen prince, Nguyen Anh, who had escaped the Tayson rebels, Rama I won the allegiance of both. Ang Eng provided Rama I the means to restore Thai patronage in Cambodia. The ruler regarded the young prince as 'a priceless jewel' and raised him 'as his own adopted son', installing him at Udong when he came of age (r. 1794–7). In the meantime, backed by supplies and arms from Rama I for resistance against the Tayson, Nguyen Anh established himself in Saigon in 1788. He faithfully acknowledged vassalage with the sending of the 'gold and silver tree' in 1788, 1790, 1795, 1797 and 1801, which the Thai ruler reciprocated with rich gifts of silks, horses, saddles and gongs; this ceased abruptly, however, on his elevation to the throne at Hué in 1802 as Emperor Gia-long. He continued to show his deep gratitude to Rama I, sending lavish presents of gold and silver ingots to the Thai court. But these were in lieu of the 'gold and silver tree', a symbol of vassalage, which he was no longer prepared to offer. Gia-long's claim to equal status with the Thai ruler was evident in the advice he despatched to his former patron about the desirability of appointing a new heir apparent at Bangkok, following the death of the incumbent in 1804.[27]

The instability of Thai influence in Cambodia during the early nineteenth century demonstrated the fragility of tributary relations. In the political upheavals which followed the end of each reign in Cambodia, the military intervention of the suzerain power often established a semblance of stability. The peace was disrupted in time by internal forces of dissent, initiating a new cycle of change. Cambodian leaders lacked the economic options available to the Chakri and Nguyen rulers for rebuilding

[26] Gesick, 37–8.
[27] Chaophraya Thiphakorawong, *The Dynastic Chronicles, Bangkok Era, The First Reign*, ed. and trans. Thadeus and Chadin Flood, Tokyo, 1978, I. 272–3.

independent power. The region's commercial potential was seriously undermined by loss of the coast, south of Phnom Penh, to the Vietnamese. Its chief port, Kampot, was described during the mid-nineteenth century as totally lacking life and bustle, 'with only 300 houses at most'.[28] Cambodia, with its sparse population, was dependent largely on a subsistence economy without the necessary manpower, wealth and arms for effective central-ized authority. Though more tolerant perhaps of the Thais with whom they shared cultural affinities, the Cambodians were resentful of the patronizing 'brother' image and civilizing mission of the Vietnamese in their attempt to impose a Confucianist model government. Vietnamese interference in Cambodian affairs, which had abated during the Tayson rebellion, came to a head with the powerful thrust southward under Emperor Gia-long. Caught between two poles of influence, Cambodia adopted a policy of dual allegiance or the image of the 'double-headed' bird, though its gaze fell more readily on Bangkok. Cambodia's leanings towards the Thai capital, by contrast to its uneasy feelings towards Hué, were succinctly expressed in the informal annual tribute to the one and the formal triennial missions to the other.[29]

The depth of anti-Vietnamese feeling found expression in the 1820 uprising led by a monk named Kai from Ba Phnom, which closely paralleled the anti-colonial revolts in contemporary Philippines and Java, spurred by forced labour and economic repression (see pages 597–8). The Kai rebel-lion had its origins in the recruitment of about a thousand Cambodians out of a total workforce of 50,000 for employment in the construction of the Vinh Te Canal, running some 40 kilometres from Hatien to the city of Chau Doc (Chau Phu). The exploitation of Cambodian labour by a powerful neighbour was not, however, without precedent. Thai chronicles of 1783 report the conscription of ten times as many Cambodians for the construc-tion of the Ropkrung canal to the east side of Bangkok.[30] This would suggest that the Vietnamese recruitment of labour for the Vinh Te canal provided the occasion rather than the cause for the ensuing rebellion. Despite the wide following the movement attracted, Kai's eventual defeat was rationalized by a Cambodian narrative poem of 1869 for popular recitation in typically Southeast Asian terms, as resulting from the loss of merit and charisma.[31]

[A]lthough his people still saw him as a refuge, the misdeeds they all had done were inescapable. In the same way Kai, when he had become a monk, had gained a large amount of merit. After what he had done, the merit had faded away, and now he had no special powers; he had become an ordinary man. His honour was no longer great; his skills were ineffective . . . [T]his time, when the enemy drew near, there was no merit to his blessings. His followers were unable to attack or fire their weapons . . .

[28] H. Mouhot, *Travels in Siam, Cambodia and Laos, 1858–60*, London, 1864, repr. Singapore, 1989, I. 180.
[29] D. P. Chandler, 'Cambodia Before the French: Politics in a Tributary Kingdom, 1794–1848', Ph.D. thesis, Michigan University, 1973, 64–8.
[30] D. P. Chandler, *A History of Cambodia*, Boulder, 1983, 120–1; Thiphakorawong, I. 58.
[31] D. P. Chandler, 'An Anti-Vietnamese Rebellion in Early Nineteenth Century Cambodia: Pre-colonial Imperialism and Pre-Nationalist Response', JSEAS, 6, 1 (1975) 21.

It, nonetheless, left an indelible memory in Cambodian folklore of Vietnamese misrule.[32]

Local reaction was again brought to a head in 1840 following the introduction of census and cadastral surveys aimed at more efficient taxation and
military mobilization. These and other measures of Vietnamization were
viewed as a threat to Cambodian kingship, Buddhism and social structure.
The initiators of the popular anti-Vietnamese rebellion were the *okya* or
high-ranking officials, who viewed themselves as the guardians of Khmer
tradition. Vietnamese reforms relating to taxation and the maintenance of
efficient records, including those pertaining to grain stocks, made heavy
demands on the *okya* who administered the *sruk* (districts). Within the
unchanging Cambodian context of political patronage, the withdrawal of
Vietnamese interference in 1847 followed by the resumption of allegiance
to Siam by Ang Duong, provided only a compromise for the messianic
hopes of the peasantry and the apprehensions of the traditional élite. The
installation of Ang Duong (r. 1848–60) by Thai ceremonial investiture at
Udong and with a seal of authorization from Hué returned Cambodia,
nominally, to dual allegiance, ushering in a brief 'golden era'.[33]

ECONOMIC AND CULTURAL CRISIS

Vietnamese economic and political exploits in Cambodia were a direct
symptom of the agrarian crisis within Vietnam stemming from problems of
land distribution, political instability and institutional weakness. Population growth and pressure on land were aggravated by the creation of
latifundia and socio-economic instability stemming from civil war and
resistance to the burdens of taxation; as of the fifteenth century, this
combination of factors accelerated the push towards Cham and Khmer
territories. Factionalism amongst rival clans and Trinh domination of
the Le court at Hanoi led to Nguyen separatism in 1626 and the Nguyen
bid to find an outlet for their ambitions in the frontier territories to
the south. Establishing their capital in Hué, they supported the southern
expansion through founding military colonies (*don dien*). By the eighteenth
century the environmental constraints of the narrow Annamite coastal
plain brought the focus of migration to the Mekong delta.[34] By 1760, six
delta provinces came under Nguyen lords. Economic problems were
evidently less severe in the south, where greater opportunities existed for
opening up new lands and for commercial activity at Qui Nhon and delta
towns such as Hatien and Vinh Long. Nonetheless, the burdens of
seigniorial authority in the form of taxes, levies, serfdom and encroachment on communal lands were common to both Trinh and Nguyen
territories. These grievances repeatedly fuelled peasant resistance, whether to internal oppression or Chinese domination, contributing to the
overarching theme of liberation in Vietnamese history.

[32] Chandler, 'Cambodia Before the French', 103.
[33] Chandler, *History of Cambodia*, 128–36.
[34] M. Cotter, 'Towards a Social History of the Vietnamese Southward Movement', JSEAH, 9, 1
(1968) 14–15, 18–19.

Evasion was the universal means of avoiding tax burdens, and the 1725 census survey for more efficient collection of taxes resulted in a major insurrection. Oppressive taxes, neglect of irrigation, and natural calamities culminated in famine some ten years later, with the drift and dispersal of population and widespread mortality.[35] There was increased awareness of the ineffectiveness and decadence of seigniorial rule and the corruption of the bureaucracy, brought about by the purchase of offices by the mandarins. This fostered a new spirit of questioning and re-evaluation of traditional values. A succinct and cynical comment on Confucianist-mandarin ideology found expression in the poem, 'Passing by the Shrine of Ch'in', by Nguyen Du (1765–1820).[36]

> A tattered sheepskin on his back,
> he trudged and lugged his bundle home.
> His woman would not leave the loom.
> His sister would not cook for him.
> His parents gave him not one glance,
> treating him like a passerby.
> When fortune disregards a man,
> his flesh and blood ignore him, too.
> But then Su Ch'in's big moment came.
> Six seals of office jingled on his sash.
> Pairs of jade rings, ingots of gold—by tons
> his coaches carried them to his old door.
> His parents met him at the village gate.
> His wife, awestruck, admired him with shy eyes.
> His sister greeted him on bended knees.
> His lifetime's ambition he'd achieved.
> 'You all respect me now—why not before?' . . .

The emergence of new values based on Vietnamese, as opposed to a Chinese identity, was apparent in the use of the *nom* Vietnamese script for prose and poetry and a critical reassessment of human relationships, hitherto viewed from a Confucianist perspective. The assertion of female identity within Vietnamese society, for example, is evident in the eighteenth-century lament by the poetess, Ho Xuang Huong, on 'Husband Sharing':[37]

> One rolls in warm blankets,
> The other freezes:
> Down with this husband-sharing!
> You're lucky ever to have him,
> He comes perhaps twice a month,
> Or less.
> Ah—to fight for—this!
> Turned to a half-servant, an unpaid maid!
> Had I known
> I would have stayed single.

[35] J. Chesneaux, *Contribution à l'histoire de la Nation Vietnamienne*, Paris, 1955, 49; Thomas Hodgkin, *Vietnam: The Revolutionary Path*, New York, 1981, 79.
[36] Huỳnh Sanh Thông, ed. and trans., *The Heritage of Vietnamese Poetry*, New Haven, 1979, 53–4.
[37] Nguyen Ngoc Bich, ed. and trans., *A Thousand Years of Vietnamese Poetry*, New York, 1975, 118.

The quest for self-expression and a national identity accrued from the general socio-economic unrest which prevailed for nearly four decades (1730s–1760s). Localized but powerful insurrections broke out in the areas worst affected by poverty, in the heart of the Red River delta, in the provinces of Son Tay, Hai Duong and Son Nam. Disillusionment spread even among the non-peasant classes. The scholar Nguyen Huu Cau, for instance, led the rebellion in 1743 in Hai Duong. Merchant and minority communities swelled the tide of discontent due to the impositions on trade by the Trinh.[38] These included indirect taxes on minerals, salt, charcoal and saltpetre—commodities essential for local industries—and a direct tax on exports, which affected the production of lacquer and silk.[39]

Significantly, anti-mandarin sentiments coalesced in the central location at Tayson which serviced the areca-nut trade between Qui Nhon on the coast and Kontum in the region of the Muong and Bahnar minorities. The three Nguyen brothers who led the rebellion were, like the bulk of their following, men of diverse experience and different talents. The eldest, Nhac, a betel-nut trader, had previously been a tax collector, while the youngest, Lu, was a bonze. But it was Hue, the second, who was the military genius and charismatic figure, 'with a voice musical as a bell and a look bright as lightning'.[40] With its wide support, the rebellion soon gained momentum, undermining Nguyen power enfeebled by the maladministration of Chua Vo Vuong and the succession dispute following his death in 1765.[41] By 1778 the Tayson took effective control over the south, including Saigon. But victory was incomplete in that Nguyen Anh, a grandson of Chua Vo Vuong, escaped and laid the ground for a counter-revolutionary movement.

In the north a succession dispute amongst the Trinh, and an economic crisis aggravated by famine, won Nguyen Hue an easy victory in 1766. After almost two centuries of division Vietnam was effectively reunited, with the exception of some southern localities which still held out under Nguyen Anh. In 1788 Nguyen Hue repulsed a Chinese attempt in 1788 to take Hanoi on behalf of the Trinh before proclaiming himself emperor with the title of Quang-trung (r. 1788–92). Resumption of tributary relations with China was characteristic of Tayson reluctance to break completely with the past while seeking reform within the framework of existing traditions. Agrarian reforms were attempted through conventional land redistribution and by bringing fallow lands into cultivation. At the same time, communal registers were introduced in order to induce the large floating population to settle.[42] A compromise was attempted between tradition and the assertion of a new indigenous identity. Vietnamese manners, including betel-chewing and the wearing of long hair and local dress, were officially permitted except at court. Similarly, the traditional mandarin examination system was retained, but proficiency was required in the composition of prose and verse in *nom*.

[38] Chesneaux, 49; Hodgkin, 82–4.
[39] Hodgkin, 79; Le Thanh Khoi, *Le Viêt-Nam, Histoire et Civilisation*, Paris, 1955, 254–6.
[40] Hodgkin, 85.
[41] Le Thanh Khoi, 296–7.
[42] Hodgkin, 91.

An important aspect of Tayson reform was the liberation of commerce and industry. To facilitate trade, a unified currency system was introduced. Symptomatic of the increased circulation of cash and the development towards a monetary system was the growth of wage labour in the main commercial centres of Hanoi, Fai-fo (Quang Nam), Binh Hoa and Saigon, well in advance of parallel developments in Burma and Siam. Mining was activated and shipbuilding, military workshops, paper and printing-works established. These developments, in combination with the abolition or the reduction of taxes on local produce, as well as the liberation of the frontier and maritime trade with China, rendered the thirty-year régime of the Tayson an era of important commercial growth, with the emergence of a pre-capitalist merchant community.[43] Impressed by the scene of change and activity, the poet Nguyen Huy Luong wrote in 1802:[44]

> The smoke of the lime-kilns of Thach Khoi climbs in thick spirals.
> On the rapids of the Nhat Thieu the waves roll roaring on.
> Floating at the rim of the bar of Duoi Nheo the sails of merchant junks are
>   pressed close, like the wings of butterflies . . .
> In the village of Yen Thai the night mist throbs with the sound of pestles
>   pounding paper . . .

Despite the impressive beginnings of reform under Quang-trung, there was no radical restructuring of society so as to resolve the perennial agrarian problems. Trade and merchant activity were still in their infancy, and fundamental problems of agriculture remained. The lack of strong leadership after the death of Quang-trung, at the age of thirty-nine, in 1792, contributed to the success of Nguyen Anh's counter-revolutionary movement. Nguyen Anh gained his initial victories, however, with help from Chinese pirates and Cambodian mercenaries. Then, after the capture of Saigon in 1788, he was backed by French mercantile interests under the influence of the Catholic priest Pierre Pigneau de Behaine, Bishop of Adran. Qui Nhon was captured in 1799 and the Tayson capital, at Hué, in 1801.

To symbolize the unification of north and south for the first time under the name of Vietnam, Nguyen Anh took the title of Gia-long, derived from a combination of Gia Dinh (Saigon) and Thang-long (Hanoi). In terms of policy, the Nguyen administration represented a swing in the pendulum towards the reinstatement of the aristocracy and landed bureaucratic classes, on the Confucianist model, as supports for monarchical power. The resulting royal absolutism of Gia-long (r. 1802–20) and his successor Minh-mang (r. 1820–41) involved centralization to a much greater degree than in China. Under Gia-long two regional overlords, one in Hanoi and another in the person of the powerful Le Van Duyet at Saigon, wielded unrestrained local influence; but under Minh-mang the power of these overlords was removed. To increase the effectiveness of the administration, the country, with a population of about eight million, was divided into 31 centrally controlled provinces (*tinh*) and 283 districts (*huyen*). There

---

[43] Chesneaux, 61–2.
[44] Quoted Hodgkin, 91.

were provincial governors (*tuan phu*) who each supervised the administration of two or three provinces. In comparison with this extensive administrative machinery, Ching China, with roughly 350 million people, had an estimated 1500 districts.[45]

Though the Vietnamese were inspired by the Chinese model, resentment of Chinese domination was evident in their refusal to model themselves on any particular dynasty. Instead, the Nguyen administrative system was derived from an adaptation of those Chinese institutions which most contributed to monarchical power and centralization.[46] In reaction to the Tayson régime and the heterogeneous religious culture it had patronized, neo-Confucianism was central to the Nguyen administrative structure. Gia-long's edicts, in fact, stipulated severe punishment for Taoist and Buddhist practices.[47] The adoption of Chinese architectural styles for the royal palace complex and the building of Vauban-type citadels further insulated the ruling classes from the peasantry.

With the exception of the major cities and ports, the administrative centres did not develop into commercial urban centres, and a large amount of trade continued to be conducted at river confluences.[48] There were impediments to trade in the form of royal monopolies on high-value produce such as ivory, stag-horns, cinnamon, cardamom and gold-dust, raised mainly as tribute from the mountain people.[49] A similar royal monopoly affected the production of silk and bronze. The pervasiveness of the bureaucracy resulted in close government control over guilds and artisans, putting many out of business. Equally detrimental to private enterprise was the direction of skills and raw materials to the imperial workshop at Hué. These conditions, as well as the restrictive commercial taxes and licences for the export of rice, salt and metals, put a brake on earlier beginnings towards commercial development.[50] Mines were the monopoly of the state and were leased to favoured mandarins and Chinese entrepreneurs. The latter, estimated at around 40,000 in the 1820s,[51] continued to dominate the important trade with China. Indigenous merchants were confined to the less profitable internal trade.

In agriculture as well the lot of the masses remained unimproved. Despite Nguyen introduction of salaries and pensions to nobles and officials in lieu of land and taxation rights,[52] the problem of landlessness remained. The meticulous land registers (*dia bo*) and census records (*dinh ba*), compiled annually since 1807 as part of the administrative reforms, provided an important tax base. But the complex computation of taxation

[45] A. B. Woodside, *Vietnam and the Chinese Model: A Comparative Study of Nguyên and Ch'ing Civil Government in the First Half of the Nineteenth Century*, Cambridge, Mass., 1971, 23, 84–5, 142–6.

[46] D. G. Marr, *Vietnamese Anticolonialism, 1885–1925*, Berkeley, 1971, 19–20.

[47] Truong Buu Lam, *New Lamps for Old*, Institute of Southeast Asian Studies Occasional Paper no. 66, Singapore, 1982, 4–5; Hodgkin, 108.

[48] Chesneaux, 77–8.

[49] J. White, *A Voyage to Cochin China*, London, 1824; reprinted with an introduction by M. Osborne, Kuala Lumpur, 1972, 249–50; Chesneaux, 78.

[50] Hodgkin, 113; A. Lamb, 'Crawfurd's Report on the State of the Annamese Empire', *The Mandarin Road to Old Hué*, London, 1970, 263.

[51] Woodside, 31–2, 272–3; Lamb, 257.

[52] J. Buttinger, *Vietnam: A Dragon Embattled*, New York, 1967, 279–80.

on the Chinese model was not commensurate with the significantly smaller population and size of the Vietnamese hamlet.[53] Furthermore, increased revenues from more efficient taxation merely paid for the upkeep of the larger bureaucratic machinery. Greater bureaucratic efficiency augmented corvée and poll-tax demands, from which the nobility and mandarins were exempted, shifting the burden to the peasantry. Sixty days or more per head were taken up annually, involving roughly one-third of the male population.[54] The system was probably more exacting than that system in contemporary Siam, accounting for the conspicuous participation of women in all sectors of private enterprise, including cultivation, industry and commerce.[55]

Corvée labour, apart from being engaged for the building and maintenance of public works, served the important military programme of the Nguyen, involving the building of fortifications, warships and arsenals. Nguyen methods of military recruitment and technology were conservative. The traditional method of conscription for the army and navy, which took the peasantry away from cultivation and fishing, proved detrimental to the economy; it also denied the defence sector its professionalism—a prerequisite for modernization. There was no lack of interest on the part of Gia-long and Minh-mang in Western technology. Gia-long's large fleet at Hué consisted of some square-rigged galleys constructed in European style and mounted with guns. Minh-mang displayed a passion for steamships which led him to set up a factory to copy a Western model. The venture failed, exposing the inadaptability of a conservative Confucianist tradition of education geared to conditions and needs long outmoded. The Nguyen military was impressive, 'dressed, equipped and disciplined after the European manner', and so were its fortifications.[56] But tactically and technologically the Vietnamese were antiquated compared to contemporary Western armies. Their generals believed 'in static defence at a time when European gunnery technology was advancing by quantum degrees in terms of increased power, range and mobility . . .'[57] Military and technological developments were intended mostly to defend against internal opposition and to suppress peasant uprisings.

Within barely two decades of Nguyen rule Vietnam re-entered the inherent cycle of mass discontent, sparked off by famine and epidemic resulting from floods, drought and the ravages of locusts. The total of 73 uprisings during Gia-long's reign escalated to some 234 during Minh-mang's rule.[58] Internally insecure and aware of the country's incapacity to resist Western pressure, Minh-mang turned his back on the Europeans, rejecting the earlier French connections. By the reign of Thieu-tri (1841–7), when French imperialism had joined forces with the Catholic Church, Vietnam's plight contrasted sharply with Siam's security, initiated by the 'subtle revolution' of Rama I. The shortcomings of the Confucianist examination system, apparent to Minh-mang himself, precluded adaptation to

[53] Woodside, 163–4.
[54] Lamb, 266.
[55] ibid., 270; White, 215–16, 245.
[56] Lamb, 267–8.
[57] Marr, 23.
[58] Hodgkin, 114.

changing needs and growing challenges. As Nguyen Truong To, the Catholic priest from Nghe-an, observed in the 1860s:[59]

> Look at Japan and Korea . . . If, instead of directing our efforts and time to polishing our style or to embellishing our calligraphy, we were to study current affairs—battle plans, for example, or the methods of building citadels and firing cannons—we should probably be in a position to resist our enemy.

INTELLECTUAL REFORM AND MODERNIZATION

In striking contrast to Vietnam, the important period of intellectual re-orientation under Rama I has been described by one scholar as 'a sort of Buddhist "Reformation"', though in Siam, unlike Europe, the religious reform involved no institutional conflicts.[60] The problem of restoring the moral decay, believed to have brought the downfall of Ayutthaya, was shared by Taksin and Rama I, as the great elect or *mahāsammata* inherent in the role of a Buddhist ruler. Where Taksin in his attempt to fulfil this regal function transgressed traditional concepts of kingship by his claim to sanctity, Rama I successfully strengthened the spiritual role of the monarch by establishing rational ties with the Buddhist community at large. Within the context of a fast-changing world, Rama I secured the co-operation of the *sangha*, the custodians of education within Buddhist society, for casting aside aberrations in favour of the meaningful applica-tion of religious precepts. It was not unusual for Buddhist rulers, such as Alaungpaya and Taksin, to undertake the compilation of scriptures and religious laws. In the case of Rama I, it involved the critical appraisal and revision of the Tipitaka or Buddhist texts by 218 monks and 32 learned laymen at the Nipphanaram temple in the palace grounds. Also under-taken through his initiative was the compilation of a completely new *Traiphūm* or *Traibhūmi* (the Three Worlds), the Siamese cosmological trea-tise. There was also a complete rewriting of the *Rāmāyana* as the *Rāmākian*, an adaptation of the Indian epic meaningful to the Thai environment. It is the subtle mental revolution initiated by Rama I which laid the ground for the impressive adaptation to Western influence undertaken later, by Prince Mongkut, during the reign of Rama III (1824–51). Mongkut, with the princely élite, took to the study of Western languages and sciences, while Buddhist scholars pioneered the critical appraisal of orthodox Buddhism in consort with Sinhalese Buddhists. The two streams of schol-arship were painlessly reconciled in the new Dhammayut sect, within the traditional *sangha* framework of Buddhist scholarship and education. With the aim of restoring Buddhism to its universalism, channels were inadvert-ently opened to the absorbing of Western scientific knowledge and ration-alism without sacrificing indigenous culture and tradition. Investigation into Western religion and science, involving dialectical exchanges with

---

[59] Quoted Hodgkin, 120.
[60] D. K. Wyatt, 'The "Subtle Revolution" of King Rama I of Siam', in A. B. Woodside and D. K. Wyatt, eds, *Moral Order and the Question of Change: Essays on Southeast Asian Thought*, New Haven: Yale University Southeast Asia Studies Monograph no. 24, 1982, 40, 42–3.

Westerners as recorded in the first Siamese printed book, the *Kitchanukit* (The Book Explaining Various Things), constituted an integral part of the intellectual transition.[61]

The importance of a stable political and economic environment for a resolution of the contemporary intellectual dilemma faced by Southeast Asian states was borne out clearly in the less successful attempts at reform by King Mindon Min (r. 1853–78) of Burma. With a background in monkhood similar to Mongkut's, the Burmese ruler strove to strengthen Theravāda Buddhist institutions. At the same time, he encouraged Western learning and technological innovation with the introduction of river-steamers, gun-boats and telegraph lines, at roughly the same pace as in Siam. But he failed to weld the programme of modernization to a reformation of Buddhist mentality. Mindon's intellectual gifts were limited compared to Mongkut's; he was also severely handicapped by circumstances. Among the important factors was the need for closer association between the official class and the nobility which would have allowed for the development, as in Siam, of a strong élite community. Further, lack of commercialization amongst the élite, with insecurity of tenure for officials, resulted in the precarious dependence of both upon the favour of the reigning monarch. This fostered perpetual intrigue and political instability. No less important were the mounting British threat and Anglo-Burmese diplomatic fiascos. Mindon's loss of control over fast-developing lower Burma and Rangoon and his own physical isolation in Mandalay stood in contrast to the spectacular achievements of the early Chakri rulers in the valley of the Chao Phraya.

The economic foundations laid by Taksin and Rama I were strengthened by Rama II (r. 1809–24) and fully developed under Rama III (r. 1824–51). The taxes and commercial restrictions laid by the former on European commercial activity allowed Chinese trade to develop to its fullest potential. Within the framework of the tributary trade, Siam augmented its exchange of rice, sappanwood, rosewood, tin, pepper, cardamom, gamboge, rhinoceros horn and beeswax for silks, porcelain, paper, tea and saltpetre. Simultaneously, by the introduction of cash crops, Siam kept pace with colonial economic developments in the Philippines and Indonesia. The production of sugarcane and pepper was expanded respectively to an estimated 35,000 and 40,000 piculs collected in 1822 as royal monopolies.[62] The newly introduced tobacco cultivation soon exceeded home consumption, allowing for export to Cambodia and Cochinchina.[63] In addition, sugar-milling and iron-smelting industries were developed. These activities, as well as tin-mining, were based on the enterprise of the Chinese, whose immigration was encouraged. Exemption from corvée and conscription, and the payment of an annual poll-tax, much less than the sum payable in lieu of corvée by Thai males,[64] allowed the Chinese the

[61] C. J. Reynolds, 'Buddhist Cosmography in Thai History, with Special Reference to Nineteenth-Century Cultural Change', JAS, 35, 2 (1976) 209–10, 214–15.
[62] J. Crawfurd, *Journal of an Embassy to the Courts of Siam and Cochin China*, London, 1828; reprinted with an introduction by D. K. Wyatt, Kuala Lumpur, 1967, 381.
[63] J. Crawfurd, *The Crawfurd Papers*, Bangkok, 1915, 112.
[64] Terweil, *History of Modern Thailand*, 116.

necessary freedom of movement and activity for cash-cropping and business enterprise. In the meantime, the addition to the Chinese trade of bulk
goods such as pepper and sugar, besides rice, boosted the shipbuilding
industry. Some eight to ten teak vessels were built annually; in size they
were up to 1000 tonnes, nearly twice the size of the vessels which had been
built a century earlier.[65] Though a substantial proportion of the produce
that accrued from the new economic activities went to traditional markets
in China, Cambodia and other neighbouring territories, an increasingly
large amount of sugar, in particular, found its way into the world market
through Singapore.

In addition to the recruitment of Chinese wage labour for reclamation,
building projects and a variety of craft-oriented occupations, measures
were taken to encourage the growth of a free labour market through
modifying the traditional corvée system. The corvée obligation of free men
or *phrai* was reduced from six to three months and this, with the government preference for payment in specie or produce in lieu of labour,
loosened clientage.[66] On the foundation laid by his predecessors, Rama III
built the superstructure of a modern economy by creating a merchant fleet
and introducing larger square-rigged vessels. These changes signalled the
demise of the Chinese junk trade and the gradual tailing off of tributary
trade in favour of alternate lines of modern international commerce.[67] The
new branch of trade with Singapore (founded 1819), stimulated by the
need for Western arms and other factors of economic growth, contributed
to increased monetization. By the mid-nineteenth century, Siam had the
semblance of a modern state concerned with the efficient extraction of cash
revenues. In contrast to Burma, where Mindon had a substantial hold on
commerce, royal monopolies were gradually abolished in favour of tax
farms leased to Thai officials and Chinese. These covered exports of all
luxury goods and cash crops, internal trade, gambling and the consumption of arrack.[68]

Along with the growth of commerce came as well a crucial restructuring
of society. Rama I's policy of encouraging royalty and the official class to
supplement income with trade was given further encouragement by his
successor, Rama II. Prince Chetsadabodin (later Rama III), in his capacity
as *Phrakhlang* or minister in charge of foreign affairs, in partnership with
the prominent Dit Bunnag, played a significant part in the development of
trade with China, for official as well as personal profit.[69] Apart from
reducing the burdens of maintaining the monarchy, such participation
brought the court into the mainstream of the newly emerging commercial
élite, whose influence was no longer derived solely from manpower but

[65] *Crawfurd Papers*, 117–18; Viraphol, 181, 323 n. 5.
[66] Akin Rabibhadana, 'Clientship and Class Structure in the Early Bangkok period', in G. W.
    Skinner and A. T. Kirsch, eds. *Change and Persistence in Thai Society: Essays in Honour of
    Lauriston Sharp*, Ithaca, 1975, 117–18; W. Vella, *Siam Under Rama III, 1824–1851*, New York:
    Association for Asian Studies, 1957, 19–21.
[67] Viraphol, 186–7, 229–30.
[68] Viraphol, 204–5, 207, 215–19, 234–5; Joseph P. L. Jiang, 'The Chinese in Thailand: Past and
    Present', JSEAH, 7, 1 (1966) 43–4; C. L. Keeton 3rd, *King Thebaw and the Ecological Rape of
    Burma*, Delhi, 1974, 7–8.
[69] Viraphol, 192.

also from wealth.[70] By the reign of Rama III the Chinese gained equal opportunity with the Thais for the purchase of land, property and vessels. They became, in the process, part of a settled community. Many inter-married with the Thais and found access to official positions, some rising to governorships.[71] Siam's steady entry into the modern economy was evident in the 1848 population census conducted for the regulation and more efficient extraction, not of services, but of cash revenues. The essence of Ayutthayan glory, drawn from a synthesis of tradition and change, was imaginatively recreated by the Chakri rulers within the context of a new age.

DECLINE OF TRADITIONAL AUTHORITY

In the Dutch-administered territories of Indonesia where the colonial economy was based on the export of produce mainly for the European market, the introduction of coffee as a monopoly at the beginning of the eighteenth century saw the extension of forced cultivation. In Java, the cession by the dying Pakubuwana II (r. 1726–49) of the sovereignty of Mataram in 1749 gave the Vereenigde Oost-Indische Compagnie (VOC, the Dutch East India Company) opportunity to increase coffee, timber, indigo and rice supplies in the form of contingencies and forced deliveries, utilizing the influence of the regents. Besides the low price paid for coffee, the VOC tried to cope with the vicissitudes of the coffee market through a policy of alternate extension and extirpation. This proved economically disruptive. Evasion of forced cultivation constituted an important reason for a drift of population to the urban centres of the north coast to engage in small-scale commercial activity, smuggling and wage labour such as timber-felling. Population movement away from the war-torn west and interior would, nonetheless, appear to have abated with the relative peace which prevailed between 1757 and 1825.[72] The Javanese rulers paid a heavy price for the termination of war. The *mancanagara*, or the outer districts of the Mataram kingdom, were ceded to direct Dutch control. What remained of the inner core, constituting the princely states or *kejawen*, was divided by the 1755 Treaty of Giyanti between Yogyakarta and Surakarta, with a further division later, entailing the creation of the subsidiary courts of Mangkunegara (1757) and Pakualaman (1813).

Although under the influence of the VOC the Javanese economy of the north coast quickly adapted to cash-crop cultivation for the world market, traditional links between the coast and the interior remained crucial to the resolution of political and economic rivalries. The challenge which Sultan Agung (r. 1613–46) had faced from the regents of the prosperous commer-cial ports of the *pasisir* (north coast) was superseded during the reign of Amangkurat I (1646–77) by VOC attempts to seize control over them. The cession of commercial rights by Amangkurat II (r. 1676–1703) to the

[70] Rabibhadana, 'Clientship and Class Structure', 117–19.
[71] G. W. Skinner, *Chinese Society in Thailand, An Analytical History*, Ithaca, 1957, 19, 21–2.
[72] M. C. Ricklefs, 'Some Statistical Evidence on Javanese Social, Economic and Demographic History in the Later Seventeenth and Eighteenth Centuries', MAS, 20, 1 (1986) 29–30.

VOC, in exchange for political alliance, marked the beginning of a new cycle of internal conflicts in Mataram in the form of the Java succession wars, revolving around the question of Mataram's territorial integrity. Ironically, Mangkubumi, the man opposed to the leasing by his brother, Pakabuwana II (r. 1726–49), of the north coast to the VOC, shared in this partition of the old kingdom to become Sultan Hamengkubuwana I (r. 1749–92) of Yogyakarta.

The new sultanates, particularly Yogyakarta, enjoyed progress and prosperity, and problems arising from the division of territory, pertaining to boundaries, laws and jurisdiction, were gradually resolved. The adoption of a regular succession procedure ensured the general stability of the courts, but rivalries amongst them precluded any possibility of a reunification. At the same time, ideological acceptance of a permanent division of the kingdom, under Dutch protection, proved difficult. It was in the court of Hamengkubuwana I that the resolution of this crisis was attempted through the familiar method of literary myth. While earlier the Mataram court had initiated a mythological accommodation to the beginning of Dutch relations with Java through the Sĕrat Baron Sakendher text, the Sĕrat Surya Raja, written in 1774 by the crown prince of Yogyakarta (later Hamengkubuwana II, r. 1792–1810, 1811–12, 1826–8), professed the reunification of the kingdom and the conversion of the Dutch to Islam.[73] Neither Javanese text acknowledged submission to the Dutch. The Sĕrat Surya Raja's prediction of Yogyakarta's conflict with them, backed by the spiritual forces of Islam and Kangjeng Ratu Kidul or Nyai Lara Kidul, the Goddess of the Southern Sea, was uncannily prescient of the impending Java War (1825–30).

Despite the difficulty in accommodating to the changes brought by Dutch intervention, the termination of wars promoted productivity and population growth. In Java and Madura, the population is estimated to have tripled from 1.5 million during the mid-eighteenth century to 4.6 million in 1815.[74] This far exceeded the figure of 3 million for roughly the same period for Siam,[75] and 2.5 million for Burma, and was exceeded only by Vietnam, which had an estimated population of 7–8 million, but in at least twice the area of Java.[76]

---

[73] T. G. Th. Pigeaud, The Literature of Java, The Hague: Koninklijk Instituut voor Taal-, Land- en Volkenkunde van Nederlandsch-Indië, 1967, I. 162–3; M. C. Ricklefs, Jogjakarta Under Sultan Mangkubumi, 1749–1792, Oxford, 1974, 188–211; A History of Modern Indonesia, London, 1981, 97.

[74] M. C. Ricklefs, 'The Javanese in the Eighteenth and Nineteenth Centuries', in D. G. E. Hall, A History of South-East Asia, London, 1981, 509; Sir Stamford Raffles, A History of Java, London, 1817, reprinted with an introduction by J. Bastin, Kuala Lumpur, 1965, I. 63.

[75] Jiang, 41.

[76] H. Burney, 'On the Population of the Burmese Empire', Journal of the Burma Research Society, 31 (1941), reprinted 1977, 343; Koenig, 'The Early Kón-Baung Polity', 97–8; Lieberman, Burmese Administrative Cycles, 20–1; Woodside, Vietnam and the Chinese Model, 158–9. According to Widjojo Nitisastro, Population Trends in Indonesia, Ithaca, 1970, Raffles' figures though more accurate than others were 'a gross underestimate'. For 1820, much higher figures of 4.6 million for Thailand and 13.7 million for Indonesia have been estimated by Kees van der Meer. See 'A Comparison of Factors Influencing Economic Development in Thailand and Indonesia, 1870–1940', in A. Maddison and Gé Prince, eds, Economic Growth in Indonesia, 1820–1940, Verhandelingen van het Koninklijk Instituut voor Taal-, Land- en Volkenkunde, 137 (Dordrecht-Holland, 1989) 280.

FORCED CULTIVATION

Force contributed in no small measure to increased productivity in Java. Compulsory cultivation introduced by the VOC to counter the lack of incentives for cultivation was in itself not a new idea. Such a system, requiring every adult male or nuclear family to cultivate a stipulated number of pepper vines, was enforced by the rulers of Banten during the second half of the seventeenth century. Surveillance of cultivation and punishment for noncompliance, as well as the collection of and payment for produce, were vested in the indigenous administrative hierarchy. This provided the model for the forced cash-crop cultivation introduced during the eighteenth century by the Dutch in Java and by their British rivals in Benkulen. The imposition of European supervision through inspection surveys, conducted by Company officials, increased the efficiency of the indigenous mechanism but, at the same time, removed the customary safeguards against oppression. West Sumatra, Lampung and Banten, areas originally under swidden agriculture and a subsistence economy, were brought within the ambit of international market exchange, resulting in serious socio-economic dislocations. The cultivation of cash crops for the purchase of imports, such as cloth and salt, and the rotation of *ladang*, or hill-paddy, became increasingly difficult under forced cultivation which obliged many to settle permanently. Cultivation of cash crops, by and large, boosted rice production and population increase in those areas suited to *sawah*. However, in areas with poorer soils unsuited to *sawah*, such as west Java and British west Sumatra, the population came to depend more heavily on rice purchased with the meagre returns earned from cash-cropping for the Company. In these areas indebtedness and the flight of population were more common. In Java, as a whole, rice production did not keep pace with the increase in population and export crops during the periods 1795–1810 and 1830–50. Despite the extension of *sawah* cultivation in the principalities (see page 601), and the overall increase in rice production per unit, *sawah* acreage per household and consumption per capita actually decreased.[77]

Contrasting with the simple tribal socio-economic structure found in west and south Sumatra, which came under the protection of the British and Dutch respectively, the indigenous state authority for the extraction of produce and services that existed in Java contributed to the creation of a more efficient colonial machinery on that island. Nonetheless, at all stages of indigenous development in the past, patron–client relations had guarded individual rights and social cohesiveness. These ties of interdependence between *kaula* (servant) and *gusti* (master) in Java, and *anak buah* (dependant) and *ketua* (chief) in the Malay world were gradually undermined as indigenous chiefs and officials became agents of European control. The weakening of these traditional ties was in proportion to the increased extraction of services by the chiefs on behalf of the Company. It is calculated, for example, that at the beginning of the nineteenth century

[77] P. Boomgaard, 'Java's Agricultural Production, 1775–1875', in *Economic Growth in Indonesia*, 109–17.

in the district of Pasuruhan in east Java, one-fifth of the manpower which
was committed to coffee cultivation was engaged in public service. The
latter included the threshing of rice for Company supplies, police and
postal duties, and personal services to an entire hierarchy of Javanese
officials.[78] The Javanese, who initially had found coffee production
lucrative, soon discovered it to be a burden which they bore with resentment. Attitude to the Company monopoly was no different in the British-
administered territories in west Sumatra. Transportation of pepper either
manually over rough terrain, or by raft down hazardous rivers, was
generally unprofitable to cultivators. These hardships were aggravated by
the engrossment of the internal trade in provisions by Company officials,
with consequent indebtedness and, in Java, by the penetration of the
Chinese into the new economic infrastructure.

In Siam the Chinese were accommodated socially; by contrast, in Java
religious difference, and Dutch efforts to use them as apolitical agents in
substitution for the traditional agents of commerce, encouraged their
development as an alien community. Chinese ascendancy in the inter-
island and internal trade under VOC patronage laid the ground to some
extent for the problems of economic disparity and ethnicity which have
continued into the present century. The commercial capital which they
accumulated found investment in a major share of the lands leased out by
the Dutch administration in west and north Java, with a labour force
necessary for the planting and processing of sugar and the cultivation of
coffee. The trade involved in supplying the needs of this workforce
became the virtual monopoly of the Chinese, who were in universal
control also of toll-gates and tax, opium and gambling farms. The Dutch
officials, the Chinese and the Javanese *priyayi* (officials) were partners
within the hierarchy of exploitation, with the indigenous chiefs placed last
in the pecking order.[79]

Movement of population to areas where conditions were relatively
easier—for example, in the Buitenzorg district which offered better communication and warehouse facilities—or where soil conditions were
superior, was not uncommon. In times of severe distress, originating from
oppression or the outbreak of disease such as smallpox, mass flight was
customary. Cultivators working under the European forced cultivation
system in west Sumatra and Java often sought refuge in the economically
precarious interior, awaiting improved conditions. Kerinci was a common
place for flight from the British-administered Benkulen districts. In 1840
Eduard Douwes Dekker, who then served in west Java, noted refugees
from the notoriously oppressive Lebak district in the Priangan region of
west Java.[80] With the expansion of cultivation and the dramatic rise in
Java's population by the end of the eighteenth century, however, recourse
to flight became less practical.

---

[78] Raffles, I. 150–1.
[79] James R. Rush, 'Social Control and Influence in Nineteenth-Century Indonesia: Opium
Farms and the Chinese of Java', *Indonesia*, 35 (1983) 53–61.
[80] Multatuli, *Max Havelaar*, New York, 1927, reprinted with a foreword by J. Kathirithamby-
Wells, Kuala Lumpur, 1984, 133.

THE AGE OF TRANSITION 599

FAILURE OF REFORM: REBELLION AND WAR

Directors of both the Dutch and English East India Companies were not unaware of the corruption in the system of forced cultivation, and its debilitating effects on peasant enterprise. Injunctions from the respective metropolitan powers to improve the system of payments through the adoption of greater honesty and regularity went, in the main, unheeded. The efforts of Governor-General G. W. Baron van Imhoff (1743–50) at regulating payment and reducing exploitation were, in the long term, as ineffective as the more rigorous attempts at reform during the 1770s in the Benkulen presidency. In Java it was the Napoleonic Wars which provided the occasion and a new conceptual framework for serious attempts at reform. But, whether amongst administrators in the East or liberal thinkers in Europe, the new humanitarian concerns were viewed strictly in terms of increased productivity and profit. In line with this objective, the provision of suitable incentives for greater industry was advocated by Dirk van Hogendorp, as member of the 1803 commission for reform. It became, in effect, the cardinal principle of nineteenth-century reformers such as Sir Thomas Stamford Raffles, when he was Lieutenant Governor of Java (1811–16), and W. R. Baron van Hoëvell who spearheaded the move in the Netherlands, some fifty years later, to abolish the *cultuurstelsel*. The freedom of cultivation and sale of produce, which lay at the crux of the liberal policy, pointed to radical socio-administrative changes and financial risks which colonial officials could ill afford to commit themselves to. A compromise struck by the reform commission under S. C. Nederburgh and, later, by Governor-General Herman Willem Daendels (1808–11) was the attempt to eradicate abuses in the system of forced cultivation. For Daendels, a strongly military man, the new policy meant stricter supervision through direct administration and improved communications, assisted by the construction of a coast road from Anjer in the west to Pasuruhan in the east. In the end, the seemingly different ideologies of Daendels, the pragmatist, and Raffles, the visionary, found common ground in the maintenance of forced deliveries, the sale and lease of lands to Europeans and Chinese, and interference in traditional institutions through reducing the power of the regents.[81]

Policies to increase revenue were a natural concomitant of territorial expansion and consolidation whether in European-administered or independent territories in Southeast Asia. The turn of the century witnessed census and cadastral surveys conducted by governments as disparate as the *ancien régime* of Bodawpaya in Burma and the centre for liberal economic experimentation spearheaded by Batavia. Though the latter, under Raffles, attempted to achieve a fair assessment of tax obligations, the practical difficulties involved were probably common to both. Raffles'

---

[81] J. Bastin, *The Native Policies of Sir Stamford Raffles in Java and Sumatra*, Oxford, 1957, 39–40, 63; *Raffles' Ideas on the Land Rent System in Java and the Mackenzie Land Tenure Commission*, Verhandelingen van het Koninklijk Instituut voor Taal-, Land- en Volkenkunde, XIV, The Hague, 1954, 74–92; H. R. C. Wright, *East-Indian Economic Problems of the Age of Cornwallis and Raffles*, London, 1961, 71, 81, 86–7.

policy of individual settlement with the cultivators, through the *desa* (village) chiefs was, in fact, as alien to traditional practices as the efficiency of taxation imposed by the Nguyen in Cambodia. In eliminating opportunities for corruption, the regents were dissociated, in principle, from revenue collection and were compensated with land and salaries. In practice, the 'defeudalization' process proved less practicable than contemporaneous Nguyen attempts at converting the mandarins into salaried officials.[82]

It is ironical that the residuum of French revolutionary zeal which to a degree infected European administration in Java, resulted in the perpetuation and, in some cases, the increase of forced cultivation and labour. This was exactly at the same time that corvée obligation, the basis of the traditional economy, was halved in Siam in favour of paid labour. The construction of the Puncak Pass between Bogor and Cianjur, in Java, is estimated to have taken a toll of 500 lives from a single district,[83] and the heavy labour services extracted for teak-felling on the north coast is calculated to have increased from 1600 males in 1776 to 5050 in 1809.[84] These conditions bear some comparison with the forced labour pressed by Bodawpaya from the Shans, Mons and Arakanese for the construction of the pagoda at Mingun. The end of the Napoleonic Wars and resuscitation of markets for tropical produce saw the restoration by the Dutch colonial government of the economic structure inherited from the VOC. But the foundations for direct rule laid by Daendels and Raffles provided for government interests to be pursued with greater vigour and thoroughness. It was only a matter of time before sporadic protest and rebellion against interference by an external agency in political and economic affairs escalated into the last major war in Java.

Succession disputes, an inherent feature of Southeast Asian politics, arising from the lack of clear rules of primogeniture, had among other factors facilitated Dutch ascendancy in Java. The political manipulations of the Dutch and the military support they afforded local allies provided for greater stability, but economic exploitation gave rise to new sources of discontent, which gradually gained momentum. In areas such as Banten and Cirebon, worst affected by compulsory cultivation, the forces of social and political dissatisfaction brought the variegated strands of society into a voluntary alliance earlier than elsewhere. Discontent against the Company ally, Ratu Sarifa, in Banten caused commoner and élite alike to take up the banner of rebellion under the religious leader, Kiai Tapa. The movement was crushed in 1751, but discontent spread to Lampung and to the Batavian highlands where European plantations were destroyed. The introduction of the forced cultivation of coffee, in lieu of pepper which the Bantenese were long accustomed to planting, and the heavy corvée services demanded by Daendels, brought another revolt culminating in

[82] Woodside, *Vietnam and the Chinese Model*, 79–80.
[83] E. S. de Klerck, *History of the Netherlands East Indies*, Rotterdam, 1938, reprinted Amsterdam, 1975, II. 25.
[84] P. Boomgaard, 'Forest Management and Exploitation in Colonial Java', *Journal of Forest History*, in press.

the sultan's abdication in 1813.[85] In Cirebon, problems of maladministration were compounded during the second half of the eighteenth century by recurrent epidemics, with resulting depopulation at a time of unprecedented upswing in the island's population as a whole. In 1800, the disgruntled peasantry joined forces with a disinherited local prince. Later, in 1811, they were led to revolt by an aristocrat, Bagus Rangin, venting their anger specifically on European and Chinese plantation owners.

In the Javanese principalities, as a whole, there was initial prosperity, particularly under the enlightened rule of Sultan Hamengkubuwana I. The area shared the island's overall population increase, accounting for roughly one-third of the total number of inhabitants during the second half of the eighteenth century. Given demographic growth and central Java's traditional role as the island's chief granary, cultivation expanded at an unprecedented rate. It is calculated that during the ten years between 1796 and 1806, *sawah* cultivation expanded by about 25 per cent around Yogyakarta.[86] It was not long, however, before these developments were countered by burdens of taxation and corvée. Apart from the heavy labour demands for his extensive building projects, in 1802, Hamengkubuwana II took measures to increase revenues by reducing the unit measure of land, or *caca*, allowed per family, without a proportionate reduction in taxes. Daendels' annexation of the north coast in 1811 and the resulting loss of Company rent paid since 1746 created the ruler's need for alternate sources of revenue. Many dignitaries similarly lost their income from appanages with the appropriation of *mancanagara* (outer-territory) lands by Raffles.

A more general problem, arising from the efforts of both the European and Javanese authorities to boost their respective share of revenue earnings, was the proliferation of Chinese-controlled toll-gates and tax farms. Internal trade was affected, with resulting price inflation. A poor harvest in 1821 and contemporaneous outbreak of cholera—originating from India and affecting equally Siam, Cambodia, some Lao states and Cochinchina[87]—brought the agrarian crisis to a head. Governor-General G. A. G. Ph. van der Capellen's efforts to end the abuses connected with the private leasing of land in central Java, and the consequent loss of revenue and burdens of indemnification this brought to the aristocratic landlords, only widened disaffection. Adding to the general instability was the weakness of the two courts, through moral corruption and political intrigues in which the Dutch had no small part. The eye of the impending storm settled on Yogyakarta. Here, a prince of the court, Dipanagara, rose to champion the cause of justice and the return to the ideals of tradition and religious virtue.

Succession wars in agrarian societies often had their origins in peasant unrest, where the emergent leadership assumed a charismatic mantle woven out of popular myth and religious beliefs. In the Java war, Dipanagara, who drew amply from the spiritual forces of Javanese mythology, was conceived as the *ratu paneteg panatagawa* or royal protector of religion,

[85] Raffles, II. 241–3; de Klerck, I. 381–4; II. 15–17, 44.
[86] P. B. R. Carey, *Babad Dipanagara, An Account of the Outbreak of the Java War (1825–30)*, Monograph 9, Malaysian Branch of the Royal Asiatic Society, Kuala Lumpur, 1981, xxxviii.
[87] Crawfurd, *Embassy*, 455.

and won the support of the *santri* (religious élite), under the leadership of Kiai Maja. Increased contacts with Arabia during the early nineteenth century brought Java, much as the rest of the Muslim world, under the reformist Wahhābi movement, turning the Java war into a *jihad* (holy war), aimed equally at the Dutch and *murtad* or apostate Javanese. It was five years before Dutch military power and strategy outdistanced the spiritual strength of the rebellion. With the introduction of the 'Cultivation System' at the end of the war in 1830, unenlightened Dutch economic policies in Java entered their final phase. In the meanwhile, in the highlands of Minangkabau, still free of Dutch control, the voices of social and religious discontent found expression in the Padri movement of the early nineteenth century.

COMMERCE, POLITICAL FRAGMENTATION AND MORAL DILEMMA

If in Java unrestrained interference by the Dutch had forced a reaction in the form of the Java War, their inactivity elsewhere allowed penetration by British commercial enterprise producing, curiously, conditions for a comparable social reaction. Since the English East India Company's expulsion from Banten in 1682, its activities in the archipelago had been confined to Benkulen and the west Sumatran coast. At the same time, British private trade and the Country Trade, of which Company servants in Madras and Benkulen had a considerable share, maintained a substantial presence in the commerce of the region, mainly in the importation of Indian piece-goods in exchange for spices, tin and pepper. The expansion of the China trade and the availability, after the victory at Plassey in 1760, of Bengal opium for barter for archipelago produce such as tin, pepper, birds'-nests and trepang (sea-cucumbers or holothurians) suitable for Canton, brought the Country Trade into increased prominence. Riau and Terengganu in the west and Sulu in the east of the archipelago were conveniently located on the route to China. They rose and prospered on the basis of this trade, stimulating internal lines of commerce with the Malays and the Bugis. In addition to the distribution of piece-goods and opium, there was an important trade in arms, particularly with Sulu, where it supported the slave-raiding activities of the Iranun seeking labour for the collection of sea-produce. The extent of the growth of this trade is evident in a single order made at Jolo for arms and ammunition in the 1780s, which included one dozen swivel guns and cannons, 600 muskets, 100 pistols and one thousand 25-pound (11-kilogram) kegs of gunpowder. Equally impressive was the rise in the importation of opium, from six chests per annum at the beginning of the nineteenth century, to some thirty-five after a period of only two decades.[88]

In the face of Dutch monopoly restrictions and Malay–Bugis dissensions in the Malay peninsula, the upsurge in the activities of the English Country Traders provided a new impetus for indigenous powers in the

---

[88] J. F. Warren, *The Sulu Zone, 1768–1898*, Singapore, 1981, 48–9.

western archipelago. Like Sulu, Riau and Terengganu were brought to
the peak of commercial growth through their role in servicing the Country
Trade. Piece-goods and opium imported by the Country Traders at Riau
were exchanged for Bangka and peninsular tin, Sumatran pepper and
forest produce, as well as gambir cultivated locally. Aceh, Selangor and
Kedah were other ports which benefited from the Country Trade. In
1767, for example, a total of about 500 chests of opium was distributed in
the Straits of Melaka at Aceh, Kuala Selangor and Riau by private traders
operating mainly from Calcutta.[89] As opposed to the free trade fostered at
Riau, trade in the hinterland and outlying regions was often engrossed by
European syndicates operating in collusion with local rulers. In Aceh,
commerce in the 1770s is alleged to have been the monopoly of the sultan
in partnership with the Madras syndicate of Gowan Horrop. It was with
the hope of winning for the Company this lucrative trade that the search
began for a British settlement, resulting in the founding of Penang in 1786
by Francis Light, a leading Country Trader. Following the Dutch take-over
of Riau two years earlier, Penang stepped in to fill the role of chief
distributor of Company opium consumed in the archipelago, amounting to
some 1000 chests at the beginning of the nineteenth century.[90] Like the
west Sumatran ports of Natal and Tapanuli which served as lucrative
centres for English private trade and Company servants at Benkulen,
Penang became the focus of innumerable commercial-cum-political part-
nerships between British traders acting as Company representatives—
such as Francis Light—on the one hand, and local rulers with their native
and European agents on the other.

To furnish the Country Trade, Terengganu's pepper cultivation was
greatly expanded and by the 1780s the state produced between 13,000 and
17,000 piculs annually, for which the main commodity of exchange was
opium.[91] Due to the importance of commercial contracts for revenue
and the supply of arms for security, the local rulers valued their contacts
with the Country Traders who had influential links with the Bengal
government. Faced with insecurity because of the Thai threat from the
north, deep-seated Malay–Bugis rivalry and Dutch monopoly restrictions
in the straits, local rulers quickly began to view the British as potential
allies. It became increasingly apparent, as with the Sultan of Kedah's
appeal for protection against Siam, that the British would not be forthcoming with military assistance. But their growing commerce, particularly with
the founding of Singapore in 1819, bolstered fragmented Malay power in
the peninsula and east Sumatra.

For the east Sumatran states—particularly Siak, Inderagiri and Kampar—
Penang and Singapore provided attractive outlets for produce from the
Minangkabau interior, evading Dutch monopoly controls at Padang. So
attractive, in fact, was this trade that it stimulated the cultivation of coffee

---

[89] J. Kathirithamby-Wells, *The British West Sumatran Presidency, 1760–85: Problems of Early Colonial Enterprise*, Kuala Lumpur, 1977, 145–6.

[90] Wright, 170.

[91] Shaharil Talib, 'The Port and Polity of Terengganu during the Eighteenth and Nineteenth Centuries: Realizing its Potential', in J. Kathirithamby-Wells and J. Villiers, eds, *The Southeast Asian Port and Polity: Rise and Demise*, Singapore, 1989, 215.

and gambier in the hill regions of Agam and Limapuluh Kota, as well as the expansion of pepper cultivation on the east Sumatran coast, between Langkat and Asahan and, on the west coast, from Susoh to Singkel. These coastal areas were under the nominal authority, respectively, of the sultans of Siak and Aceh; but the weakness of royal authority and the new commercial opportunities unleashed a rash of political adventurism, supported by European capital, arms and vessels. Enterprising local chiefs opened up new plantations, attracting Minangkabau and Batak populations from the interior to the east coast, and there was a parallel movement of Acehnese migrants from further north to the west coast.

The lucrative trade involved purchase of cash crops and sale of cloth, opium and other provisions for the plantations; it provided British private trade with a vested interest in maintaining the independence of coastal ports and their chiefs in defiance of central authority. An outstanding case was Leubè Dapa, the Acehnese chief at Singkil and Truman, and his collusion with the British Resident at Natal, John Prince, a partner of the wealthy Calcutta merchant, John Palmer.[92] Shortly after the founding of Singapore, there was actually an attempt by the Acehnese territorial chiefs or *ulèëbalang*, in league with a Penang merchant faction, to depose Sultan Jauhar al-Alam (r. 1819–23) in favour of Syed Alam, son of Syed Hussein, a wealthy local merchant. The plan miscarried, but it spoke amply of the bankruptcy of indigenous sovereignty.

Dissolution of Malay political authority with the Dutch capture of Riau in 1784 threw up opportunities for merchant and entrepreneurial activities on an unprecedented scale. But the many petty rajas, and the pepper kings who rose from amongst them, secured their profits and their status at great risk through management of dubious contacts and alliances. In the absence of legitimized armed power, the *orang laut* (sea people) reverted to marauding activities. They preyed on vessels and the isolated communities of cash-croppers on the Sumatran coasts and at Banjarmasin and the tin mines of Sambas and Bangka, taking captives whom they sold as slaves. The *orang laut* formed an important political force in the interplay of local rivalries, the significance and magnitude of their activities enhanced by alliances with displaced princes or *anak raja*. Political instability at Siak, arising from succession disputes as of the mid-eighteenth century, afford-ed opportunity for intrigue and marauding, sometimes in partnership with Arab political adventurers. In 1787, to avenge humiliation by the Dutch, Sultan Mahmud of Riau turned to the Iranun for assistance, just as four years later the hapless Sultan Abdullah of Kedah sought their aid in taking revenge against the British in Penang.

The innumerable European trading vessels which ran the gamut of archipelago ports were better armed and therefore at less risk than the small native vessels; they thrived on insecurity. They found ready oppor-tunities for cultivating the friendship and alliance of local chiefs and the heads of piratical lairs for profitable commerce, including the exchange of arms for slaves. Illicit trade, developed largely to escape Dutch monopoly

---

[92] Lee Kam Hing, 'Acheh's Relations with the British, 1760–1819', M.A. thesis, University of Malaya, 1969, 80–7.

restrictions, became the life-blood of Penang's contraband trade with the pirates of Lingga.

Regulation of trade and suppression of piracy, which Raffles began to advocate, ushered in a whole new order, based on fuller commitment of British official interest in the region. For the Dutch, Java, Sumatra and Bangka continued to remain the main areas of endeavour. The territories beyond, which suffered political fragmentation and internecine rivalry, posed no serious challenge to Dutch interests; but the inroads there of rival European activity and freebooting, in defiance of monopoly restrictions, claimed Batavia's attentions. Residual centres of local power in Bali, Borneo (Pontianak, Mempawa, and Sambas), south Sulawesi, Palembang and Jambi were accordingly brought under Dutch rule.

In the absence of strong indigenous authority outside the areas of direct Dutch control, the multitude of thriving chiefdoms proved ideally suited to the commercial adventurism of the period. Despite the marauding of coastal settlements and shipping, the decline of royal monopolies created unprecedented opportunities for private enterprise. The pepper plantations of the east Sumatran coasts and the coffee and gambier estates of the Minangkabau interior became new sources of wealth. Quite apart from those who prospered from the smuggling of tin from Bangka, the development of the plantation economy created a significant merchant community involved in the transportation of produce to Penang and Singapore. The attendant prosperity, enjoyed by cultivators and merchants, was double-edged. The increased circulation of wealth brought dependence on a market economy dominated by the indiscriminate sale of opium and arms with piece-goods and other provisions. The availability of cash and the erosion of traditional values had widespread social implications. These rendered the migrant population of plantation workers and itinerant traders susceptible to corrupting influences: the many urban centres servicing the plantations offered gambling and opium-smoking.

As traditionally, increased international trade opened up the mental vistas of the religious élite within Malay society. Greater wealth and the steady inroads of the *sayid* of Hadramaut brought the Arab world closer to the archipelago. For all his dabbling in the opium trade, the ruler of Selangor, for instance, was keen on doing his bit for religion by finding passage on English vessels for Muslim *ulamā* set on the pilgrimage.[93] A belief that moral corruption was affecting the Malay world gained poignancy under the reformist Wahhabi influence which currently swept the Muslim world. The Acehnese poem, *Hikayat Ranto*, for example, lamented the loss of Islamic values among the pepper-growers of the coastal regions.[94]

> Though engaged in trade many pious people practice usury.
> They traffic in opium and in money, so that they always
>   make a profit.

[93] W. Marsden, *A Grammar of the Malayan Language*, London, 1812, 150–1.
[94] G. W. J. Drewes, *Two Achehnese Poems: Hikajat Ranto and Hikajat Teungku Di Meukĕ'*, Biblio- theca Indonesica, 20, Koniklijk Instituut voor Taal-, Land- en Volkenkunde, The Hague, 1980, 15.

> Though having a security in hand, they take interest,
>   and this is usury, my brother.
> They cut off a part of the opium they already weighed
>   out, and this is a great sin.
> Among the shopkeepers there is much breaking of
>   the law. All the world has gone astray . . .
> Once arrived at the *ranto* they neglect the ritual
>   prayer and completely forsake the Lord.

There was an increasing awareness amongst the Malays of their role within the Islamic community at large. The Padri movement, which began in 1803, was a fully-fledged attempt at social reform. It advocated the eradication of gambling, cockfighting, opium-smoking, the consumption of alcohol, betel-nut and tobacco, and even banned the wearing of gold ornaments. Quite unlike the Buddhist reforms successfully engineered by Prince Mongkut which achieved a reconciliation of Thai religious beliefs with Western rationalism, Padri orthodoxy was opposed to any compromise. Through alienating the ruling house and lineage heads or *penghulu* at Tanah Datar, the Padri inadvertently facilitated Dutch intervention which led, at the termination of the war (1821–38), to the introduction of indirect rule in the interests of a coffee monopoly.[95] The Java and the Padri wars left indigenous forces enfeebled and their moral dilemmas as yet unresolved. Just as the remnants of Java's traditional policy sought refuge in an internalized cultural renaissance, the residuum of Malay political culture at Riau indulged in a recreation of the old order of *adat* and Islam.[96]

ECONOMIC DUALISM

The Philippines was affected just as profoundly as the rest of Southeast Asia by the socio-economic changes of the 'era of transition'. These important decades witnessed the gradual erosion of its isolation from the mainstream of developments in the region. Up till this time, any identity which the Philippines and Dutch Indonesia had shared as colonies was more superficial than real. Spain's commitment to the Philippines, like that of the Dutch in Java and eastern Indonesia, was adapted to the siphoning of profits to the metropolitan power in Europe. There was the important difference, however, that while Dutch profits were drawn predominantly from the organization and export of monopoly produce, Spanish preoccupation in the Philippines was from 1565 almost exclusively with the Acapulco–Manila trade. This left the internal economy isolated and undeveloped.[97] It is calculated that over two hundred years preceding the final collapse of the galleon trade at the beginning of the nineteenth century, no

[95] C. Dobbin, *Islamic Revivalism in a Changing Peasant Economy: Central Sumatra, 1784–1847*, Scandinavian Institute of Asian Studies, no. 47, London and Malmö, 1983, 136–7, 228.
[96] B. Andaya and V. Matheson, 'Islamic Thought and Malay Tradition: The Writings of Raja Ali Haji of Riau (1809–c. 1870)', in A. Reid and D. Marr, eds, *Perceptions of the Past in Southeast Asia*, Kuala Lumpur, 1979, 121–3.
[97] W. L. Schurz, *The Manila Galleon*, New York, 1939, reprinted 1959, 38–43.

more than five or six Spaniards owned landed estates (*haciendas*) at any one time.[98] A greater similarity with Dutch-administered territories became evident only with the move in Spain, at the turn of the century, for economic reforms in the colonies. The new policy was impelled partly by the revolutionary spirit in Europe, and partly by financial exigencies which made for economic reorientation.

The dichotomy between the growth of external commerce and internal economic stagnation in the Philippines emanated from the nature of the galleon trade. It was concerned exclusively with the exchange in Manila of Mexican silver for Chinese silks, porcelain, combs and bric-à-brac destined for markets in New Spain and Europe, with the addition of only a small amount of local gold, cotton and wax.[99] While the Chinese controlled the Canton–Manila arm of the trade, the Manila–Acapulco sector was the privilege of the Spanish official class (*peninsulares*) resident in Manila. Under this structure the Philippines had no direct part in international commerce.

Outside the capital, affairs were left in the hands of the *alcaldes mayores* or provincial governors, and the Christianizing endeavour of Spanish ecclesiastical agents, mainly in the form of 'regulars' or friar curates. Large tracts of communal or *barangay* land had been sold by Christianized village chiefs (*datu*) and their relatives (*principales*) to the clergy. These were absorbed into *encomienda*, the original territorial leases made as reward for service to the Spanish Crown. Conversion brought the guarantee for the *datu* of hereditary status and exemption from tax, in return for holding the loyalty of the *barangay*. Inhabitants of the *barangay*, in turn, paid tribute usually in the form of food and provisions, and rendered labour services in exchange, ostensibly, for protection and spiritual ministration by *encomienda* holders. The system of labour and tribute extraction generally resembled that which subsisted in traditionally administered areas in other parts of Southeast Asia. There was a difference, however, in the absence under Spanish rule of reciprocal relations between patron and client for the protection of mutual interests as, traditionally, between *datu* and members of the *barangay*. The *alcaldes mayores*, though entrusted with the overall supervision of the provinces and enjoying virtual autonomy, were unsympathetic to local interests. Involved in the political and commercial affairs of Manila and the Iberian world at large, they were oblivious to internal corruption in the provinces. From the late sixteenth century the sale of communal lands to Chinese mestizos and private Spaniards aggravated problems. The excesses of tribute and corvée extractions, as well as the high interest charged on monetary loans, were comparable to the burdens suffered by the peasantry under Dutch rule in Java.

Resentment against encroachment on Tagalog lands came to a head in a violent revolt in 1745 in the Augustinian estate of Meysapan, north of Laguna de Bay. Spreading to Cavite, Tondo and Bulacan, it involved over 6000 armed men in a bid to secure the restoration of communal lands

[98] D. M. Roth, 'The Friar Estates of the Philippines', Ph.D. thesis, University of Oregon, 1974, 33.
[99] C. Benitez, 'Philippine Progress Prior to 1898', with Tomas De Comyn, *State of the Philippines in 1810*, trans. W. Walton, Filipiniana Book Guild, XV, Manila, 1969, 183.

which they considered ancestral property. In negotiating for a settlement, the sympathy shown to Tagalog demands by Pedro Calderón Henríquez, a judge of the *Audiencia* of Manila, showed the validity of the rebel cause. The inevitable forces of economic change which followed after the mid-century, nonetheless, were to aggravate rather than alleviate the problems of the peasantry.[1]

ECONOMIC REORIENTATION

Ironically, though external influence and direct rule went much deeper in the Philippines than in Dutch-administered regions, the internal economy could not have been less related to Spain's commercial development. The British occupation of Manila (1762–4) and the capture of the outward-bound *Santisima Trinidad*, carrying about three million pesos,[2] exposed the vulnerability of an economy which rested entirely on the annual arrival and departure of no more than a couple of galleons. The opening of Manila to foreign trade during this period did, on the other hand, demonstrate the potential for the development of local exports.[3] The British occupation, in addition, gave release to a long-simmering peasant resentment of corruption, monopoly and perfidy amongst the Spanish official class and of the apathy and insensitivity of the clergy in the provinces. *Indio* rebellions broke out in about ten provinces, the most serious led by Diego Silang in Ilocos.[4] Damaging Spanish prestige, it forced a reappraisal of policy in order to ensure a successful restoration of power. The reforms were anticipated by Governor Don Pedro Manuel de Arandia (1754–9), with the backing of Charles III (r. 1757–88) and his enlightened mercantilist philosophy.

The two important reforms singled out by the Spanish government were the reduction of the powers of the friar curates and greater economic self-reliance of the islands. The first was vigorously championed by Governor Don Simón de Anda y Salazar (1762–4, 1770–6) and resulted in the indictment of the friars for oppression and neglect of spiritual duties and educational responsibilities, including the teaching of Spanish to the *indios*. These reforms were in tune with the anti-clerical sentiments of Charles III. In 1767 he expelled Jesuits from the entire Spanish empire.[5] The lack of sufficient priests from other orders gave rise to a policy of secularization. By 1770 nearly half the parishes were in secular hands.[6] Swiftly promoted *indio* and mestizo clerics, who were ill prepared for their tasks, offered no improvement over their predecessors. The prejudices this created contributed to a gradually increasing gulf between the *indio* and

---

[1] N. P. Cushner, *Landed Estates in the Colonial Philippines*, New Haven: Yale University Southeast Asian Studies Monograph no. 20, 1976, 59–66; Roth, 118–21.

[2] Schurz, 189.

[3] K. Lightfoot, *The Philippines*, London, 1973, 84.

[4] E. H. Blair and J. A. Robertson, *The Philippine Islands, 1493–1898*, Cleveland, 1907, XLIX. 300–5; G. F. Zaide, *Philippine Political and Cultural History*, Manila, 1957, II. 13, 16.

[5] Blair and Robertson, L. 269–77.

[6] Roth, 56.

Spanish clergy which had serious political overtones, especially after 1826 when Ferdinand VII returned most of the parishes to friar control.

In the economic sphere, loss of the galleon trade dictated a policy that constituted a cleaner break with the past than in the ecclesiastical field. As of the beginning of the eighteenth century the galleon trade was already showing signs of weakening. This was brought about partly by the increasing popularity of English and Indian cottons and a proportionate decrease in the demand for Chinese silks, which had hitherto constituted a major item of trade. To improve the climate of trade, Governor José Basco y Vargas (1778–87) established a corporation of merchants (*consulado*) to supervise all commerce. In 1785 the *Real Compania da Filipinas* (Royal Company of the Philippines) was based on the recommendations made twenty years earlier by Francisco Leandro de Viana. Its aim was to develop the economic potential of the Philippines and foster direct commercial links with Spain. Liberalization of trade met firm resistance from the Manila merchants. The Royal Company was excluded from the Acapulco–Manila trade, and the opening of Manila between 1789 to 1794 to foreign ships was restricted to those carrying Asian goods.[7] It was the Mexican revolution in 1820 that dealt the *coup de grâce* to the ailing Manila–Acapulco trade, the Philippines being opened fully to world commerce in 1834.

Crucial to the improvement of the internal economy was agricultural reform. As a basis for this the agricultural society founded by Governor Basco in 1781 disseminated information on agronomy and offered incentives for distributing seed, farm implements, and spinning machines. It fostered the cultivation of cash-crops, such as indigo and pepper, and the production of silk and hemp. By the investment of capital the Royal Company of the Philippines gave further encouragement to the large-scale production of cash-crops, particularly sugar, and to infant industries such as textile manufacture. Revocation of the ban on Chinese immigration in 1778, admitting those who were a source of potential labour, did much to help the expansion of agriculture. Between 1786 and 1800 more than 240,000 piculs of sugar were exported. Cultivation, though concentrated in Pampanga and Pangasinan, continued to expand elsewhere and, in 1854, exports rose to 762,643 piculs.[8]

Surveillance of the Chinese population by the Spanish government, allowing privileges of free movement, lower poll-tax and land leases only to those who embraced Christianity, had encouraged the emergence of a substantial mestizo community. Culturally it had no parallel in Dutch Indonesia and was comparable perhaps only to the large community of Thais of Chinese descent in Siam. A shared religion and Hispanic culture gave the mestizos a shared identity with the *indios*, though their economic status set them apart. Unlike the Chinese whose residence was restricted to Manila where they engaged in commerce, retail trading and various crafts, the mestizos utilized their privileges for extending their commercial enterprise beyond the main city into the provinces. They leased lands for

---

[7] Benitez, 190–2.

[8] N. P. Cushner, *Spain in the Philippines: From Conquest to Revolution*, Quezon City, 1970, 192, 201.

agriculture, mainly rice, sugar and indigo in the central Luzon provinces of
Tondo, Bulacan and Pampanga, either subletting them to *indios* or cultivating them under the *kasamahan* system in which the tiller was allowed a
percentage of the crop.[9] Money-lending to *indio* for seed, machinery and
labour to tide over the period between planting and harvesting, brought
ready opportunities for acquisition of land through confiscation of property for unsettled debts. The mestizos also played a major role in the
purchase and transportation of crops to the capital, successfully competing
in this line of trade with the provincial governors.[10] Apart from gaining a
monopoly of the gaming and opium farms, they locked into the developing international capitalist economy, involving American and British
investment in the plantation enterprise.

British commercial interests in the Philippines had been given a head
start in the late seventeenth century when Country Traders began the
importation into Manila of Coromandel cottons, using the cover of Asian
trade in order to avoid Spanish restrictions.[11] From the mid-nineteenth
century, agricultural entrepreneurs such as Nicholas Loney of Ker and
Company provided advances for crops and machinery for the production
of sugar, copra, coffee and hemp. The financial facilities they offered in the
form of monetary advances for wholesale business aided mestizo commercial activity involving the purchase, transportation and distribution of
goods between Manila and the provinces. The Spanish government's
persistently anti-foreign policies—such as the edict passed in 1828, prohib-
iting foreign merchants from the provinces—were thereby circumvented.
Mestizo and European commercial entrepreneurs enacted complementary
rather than competitive roles, with the latter gaining pre-eminence in
banking and international commerce. By 1859 there were fifteen foreign
firms in Manila, including seven British and three American.

Successful private enterprise brought the Filipinos little benefit. Capitalist exploitation in the privately managed plantations, with compulsory
cultivation for the government, contributed to widespread economic distress among the peasantry. A system of forced cultivation, introduced in
the Cagayan valley, Gapan in the province of Pampanga and the island of
Marinduque, supported a Spanish tobacco monopoly, so lucrative that by
the mid-nineteenth century it rendered the Philippines financially independent. Under this system each family was required to raise 40,000 plants
annually, for sale exclusively to the government. Shortfalls were subject to
a fine, while anything in excess of the stipulated quota was systematically
destroyed. Government inspections ensured that no part of the crop was
held back, even for personal consumption. Pilfering from the homes of
cultivators while conducting searches for concealed tobacco, and substitution for cash payment of promissory notes which were never honoured,
were commonplace. Poor returns to the cultivators from tobacco, and also
production of *vino y nipa* (toddy) for the government monopoly established
in 1786, with reliance on staples purchased on the open market, contribut-

[9] E. Wickberg, *The Chinese in Philippine Life, 1850–98*, New Haven, 1965, 23–30.
[10] ibid., 29–30; J. Larkin, *The Pampangans, Colonial Society in a Philippine Province*, Berkeley,
    1972, 51–4.
[11] H. Furber, *Rival Empires of Trade in the Orient, 1600–1800*, Minneapolis, 1976, 217–20.

ed to smuggling and black marketeering. Many took flight, mainly to Manila, in search of wage labour.[12]

Life was not vastly different even for *indios* outside the forced cultivation system. Under Spanish administration, each family was liable to payment of a tribute or poll-tax, collected in produce, and the system was open to many abuses. In Pampanga, until the early nineteenth century when sugar gained dominance, the tax was paid in the form of rice, supplied to Manila. Incentives for peasant agriculture, in general, were poor due to the *vandala* system which obliged cultivators to sell produce for token payments and promissory notes, as well as render *polo* or corvée services. Periodic floods and the ravages of locusts which destroyed the paddy were other factors that affected peasant welfare.[13]

EVOLUTION OF A 'NATIONAL' IDENTITY

Economic discontent went much further than peasant grievances. The arrival of many *peninsulares* or Iberian-born Spaniards expelled from Latin America, and their failure in large-scale European entrepreneurial activity, set them in competition with the *indio* and mestizo populations. The latter had traditionally staffed the lower echelons of the bureaucracy, but found themselves displaced by the *peninsulares*, who considered themselves socially superior. Similar friction developed between the friar community taking refuge in the Philippines from an anti-clerical Spain and the local clergy bidding for equality with their Spanish counterparts. Tensions increased within the broadening stratum of educated mestizos and *indios*, who evolved a new élite group, the *ilustrado*, claiming equal opportunity with the Spanish. Dissatisfaction pervaded the entire realm of life amongst the indigenous communities, including the army, and spearheaded anti-foreign sentiments. The smallpox epidemic of 1820 in Manila, which was particularly severe in the Pasig River valley, triggered a backlash aimed largely at the life and property of the Chinese.[14] In 1841, the powerful rebellion led by Apolinario de la Cruz, thwarted in his ambition of entering a monastic order, also bore a racial complexion.[15]

The articulation of discontent and the fostering of a new Filipino identity by the small but influential class of *ilustrados* gained momentum during the latter part of the century. This element, more than any, lent new cohesion to a society plagued by divisive economic forces which separated the moneyed and landed, of various origins, from the mass of poorer *indios*. The socio-economic ferment which grew out of Spanish rule—by contrast to the more effective control of colonial affairs by the Dutch in Indonesia—contributed to the early development of a popular movement based on a

[12] Blair and Robertson, LVII. 118–19; Comyn, *State of the Philippines*, 55–63.
[13] Lafond de Lurcy, 'An Economic Plan, from "Quinze Ans de Voyages autour du Monde"', in *Travel Accounts of the Islands, 1832–58*, Filipiniana Book Guild, XXII, Manila, 1974, 28, 32.
[14] Blair and Robertson, LI. 39.
[15] ibid., LII. 92–3 n. 37, 101.

shared Filipinized Hispanic culture. The importance of this cultural phenomenon is made particularly clear in the exclusion of the Moro, by way of
their different religious and economic orientations, from the same historic
process.

CONCLUSION

By the early decades of the nineteenth century Southeast Asia stood on
the brink of the final phase of the European onslaught; indigenous
forces were far from subdued and, in some cases, were actually stronger
than during the initial encounter with the West. On the mainland, the
assertion of Burman, Thai and Vietnamese cultures and their territorial
expansion achieved a modicum of administrative centralization and cultural
unification through the fostering of religious and cultural ideology.
Though assisted to an extent by Western arms, this was achieved largely
through local initiatives and the culmination of internal growth. With the
political maturing and the evolution of statehood towards nation status, an
awareness grew amongst the rulers of Burma, Thailand and Vietnam of
rapidly accelerating change in the external world. Internal developments
and external policies were determined, to a large degree, by rulers concerned about the nature of their own responses. Thai accommodation and
adaptation and Vietnamese mistrust of the West were positive reactions.
Burma under Mindon faltered between isolation and ineffectual efforts at
modernization, while Cambodia and the Lao states found little room for
initiative and were forced into isolation by their powerful neighbours.

In island Southeast Asia, Javanese and Balinese power, emasculated by
the Dutch, adopted introversion and myth-making epitomized in the
grand ideal of the 'theatre state'. In areas such as the Javanese *mancanegara*
and the Philippines which had long been under colonial rule and had
suffered the rigours of its monopoly systems, economic burdens gave new
meaning to religious and cultural identities, ushering in an age of protest,
rebellion and war. At the same time, it was the insular areas close to the
main lines of commerce that witnessed the emergence of the new spirit of
merchant enterprise, its flowering aborted by factors internal as well as
external. Each component part of the region, for better or worse, clearly
articulated a response to the inevitable forces of modernization and Western
encroachment.

BIBLIOGRAPHIC ESSAY

Burma

The importance in Burma of clientage, bondage and taxation, both crown
and glebe, makes M. Aung-Thwin's 'Hierarchy and Order in Pre-Colonial
Burma', JSEAS, 15, 2 (1984), essential reading for an understanding of the
interrelation between politics and socio-economic affairs. Comparison of
the ideas and institutions of bondage in Burma and Thailand are found in

F. K. Lehman, 'Freedom and Bondage in traditional Burma and Thailand', JSEAS, 15, 2 (1984). A detailed account of the organization and influence of the monastic order is found in J. P. Ferguson, 'The Symbolic Dimensions of the Burmese Sanga', Ph.D. thesis, Cornell University, 1975. Problems relating to the administration of the *saṅgha* are discussed in Aung-Thwin, 'The Role of *Sasana* Reform in Burmese History: Economic Dimensions of a Religious Purification', JAS, 38, 4 (1979), and V. B. Lieberman, 'The Political Significance of Religious Wealth in Burmese History: Some Further Thoughts', JAS, 39, 4 (1980).

A general history of the period with an economic emphasis is found in W. J. Koenig, 'The Early Kón-Baung Polity, 1752–1819: A Study of Politics, Administration and Social Organisation', Ph.D. thesis, University of London, 1978. In respect of much of Southeast Asia the lack of hard data from indigenous sources has impeded detailed studies of administrative and economic systems of the pre-colonial period, but the Burmese administrative records or *si-tàn* are an important exception. These have been made accessible in the English translation found in F. N. Trager and W. J. Koenig, eds, *Burmese Si-Tàns, 1764–1826, Records of Rural Life and Administration*, Tucson, 1979. The significance of Mon–Burmese rivalry with reference to population and economic disparities is imaginatively interpreted in M. Adas, 'Imperialistic Rhetoric and Modern Historiography: The study of Lower Burma before and after conquest', JSEAS, 3, 2 (1972).

Thailand

Studies of the socio-economic organization of Siam for this period are found in A. Rabibhadana, 'Organisation of Thai Society in the Early Bangkok Period, 1782–1873', Data Paper, no. 74, Cornell Southeast Asia Program. A more concise statement is 'Clientship and Class Structure in the Early Bangkok period', in G. W. Skinner and A. T. Kirsch, eds, *Change and Persistence in Thai Society, Essays in Honour of L. Sharp*, Ithaca, 1975. A more recent intepretation is B. Terwiel, 'Bondage and Slavery in Nineteenth Century Siam', in *Slavery, Bondage and Dependency in Southeast Asia*, ed. A. Reid, St Lucia, Queensland, 1983.

The subject of fundamental reform within the *saṅgha* as a prelude to modernization is discussed in C. J. Reynolds, 'Buddhist Cosmography in Thai History, with special reference to nineteenth century cultural change', JAS, 15, 2 (1976), and D. K. Wyatt, 'The "Subtle Revolution" of King Rama I of Siam', in *Moral Order and the Question of Change*, A. Woodside and D. K. Wyatt, eds, New Haven: Yale University Southeast Asia Studies Monograph no. 24, 1982.

Studies of individual reigns are found in K. Wenk, *The Restoration of Thailand under Rama I, 1782–1809*, Tucson: Association of Asian Studies, 1968, and W. F. Vella, *Siam Under Rama III, 1824–1851*, New York: Monograph for the Association of Asian Studies, no. 4, 1957. An in-depth study of the structure and workings of Thai monarchy as an administrative institution during the period under survey is L. Gesick, 'Kingship and Political Integration in Traditional Siam, 1767–1824', Ph.D. thesis, Cornell University, 1976.

The standard work on the Chinese in Thailand is G. W. Skinner, *Chinese Society in Thailand: An Analytical History*, Ithaca, 1957. In addition, J. Jiang concerns himself with the role of the Chinese in Thai economy in 'The Chinese in Thailand: Past and Present', JSEAH, 7, 1 (1966), complementing S. Viraphol's definitive study, *Tribute and Profit: Sino-Siamese Trade, 1652–1853*, Cambridge, Mass., 1977, and J. Cushman's 'Fields From The Sea: Chinese Junk Trade with Siam during the late eighteenth and early nineteenth centuries', Ph.D. thesis, Cornell University, 1975. Of the European travel accounts for the period, there is considerable information on the commerce and economy of Thailand in *The Crawfurd Papers*, published by the Vajirañāṇa National Library, Bangkok, 1915, and the same author's *Journal of an Embassy to the Courts of Siam and Cochin China*, London, 1828, reprinted Kuala Lumpur, 1967. A more reliable source for tax and revenue figures is E. Roberts, *Embassy to the Eastern Courts of Cochin China, Siam and Muscat during the years 1832–34*, New York, 1837. A critical appraisal of these early sources is found in B. J. Terwiel, *A History of Modern Thailand, 1767–1942*, St Lucia, Queensland, 1983. Hong Lysa, *Thailand in the Nineteenth Century: Evolution of the Economy and Society*, Singapore: Institute of Southeast Asian Studies, 1984, uses Thai sources to present a comprehensive account of the important economic changes of the early Bangkok period involving the expansion of trade, the increased circulation of currency and the evolution of a new tax and revenue structure.

The best account of Siam's relations with vassal states during the first half of the nineteenth century is W. F. Vella, *Siam Under Rama III, 1824–51*, New York, 1957. An invaluable Thai perspective on politics and interstate relations is presented in Chaophraya Thiphakorawong, *The Dynastic Chronicles, Bangkok Era, The First Reign*, trans. and ed. Thadeus and Chadin Flood, I, Tokyo: Center of East Asian Studies, 1978. For an account of Thai–Lao relations leading to the destruction of Vientiane, see D. K. Wyatt, 'Siam and Laos, 1767–1827', JSEAH, 4, 2 (1963). The latter episode receives a nationalistic perspective in a recent study, Mayoury and Pheuiphanh Ngaosyvathn, 'Lao Historiography and Historians: Case Study of the War between Bangkok and Lao in 1827', JSEAS, 20, 1 (1989).

Cambodia

D. Chandler, *A History of Cambodia*, Boulder, 1983, provides the standard work. There is a more detailed analysis of the period under review in the same author's 'Cambodia Before the French: Politics in a Tributary Kingdom, 1794–1848', Ph.D. thesis, University of Michigan, 1973, and 'An Anti-Vietnamese Rebellion in Early Nineteenth Century Cambodia', JSEAS, 6, 1 (1975).

Vietnam

J. Chesneaux, *Contribution à l'histoire de la Nation Vietnamienne*, Paris, 1955, Le Thanh Khoi, *Viet-Nam, Histoire et Civilisation*, Paris, 1955, and Nguyen Khac Vien, *Histoire Du Vietnam*, Paris, 1974, provide good basic reading.

T. Hodgkin, *Vietnam: the Revolutionary Path*, New York, 1981, offers a more modern account with peasant sympathies. A. Woodside, *Vietnam and the Chinese Model*, Cambridge, Mass., 1971, is a scholarly analysis of Chinese bureaucratic and cultural influence on Vietnam.

As a result of the increased pace of British interest in the mainland during the beginning of the nineteenth century, journals and reports of missions provide rich eye-witness accounts of commerce and society. A handy compilation of these reports is found in A. Lamb, *The Mandarin Road to Old Hué*, London, 1970. The articulation of popular feelings on politics and social problems in verse lends ready access to the Vietnamese perceptions. Huynh Sanh Thong, *The Heritage of Vietnamese Poetry*, New Haven: 1979, provides a good annotated anthology in English.

The Philippines

An integrated history of socio-economic developments during the eighteenth and nineteenth centuries remains to be written. A good account of the administrative history of the period is E. G. Robles, *The Philippines in the 19th Century*, Quezon City, 1969. W. L. Schurz, *The Manila Galleon*, New York, 1939, reprinted 1959, still offers the most vivid and detailed description of the Manila–Acapulco trade. A statistical account of its decline is found in W. E. Cheong, 'The Decline of Manila as a Spanish Entrepôt in the Far East. 1785–1826: Its Impact on the Pattern of Southeast Asian Trade', JSEAS, 2, 2 (1971).

On the agrarian front, the friar estates and the related problems of the peasantry, leading up to the 1745 revolt, are discussed in D. M. Roth, 'Friar Estates of the Philippines', Ph.D. thesis, Oregon University, 1974. N. P. Cushner, *Landed Estates in the Colonial Philippines*, New Haven, 1976, focuses on the problems relating to the province of Tondo. Studies of agrarian problems in another area are found in J. A. Larkin, *The Pampangans: Colonial Society in a Philippine Province*, Berkeley, 1972. For an account of the organization of the government tobacco monopoly see E. C. de Jesus, *The Tobacco Monopoly in the Philippines: Bureaucratic Enterprise and Social Change 1766–1880*, Quezon City, 1980.

Documentary sources in E. H. Blair and J. A. Robertson, *The Philippine Islands, 1493–1898*, 55 vols, Cleveland, 1903–9, lend interesting insights into key events. Travel accounts include translations from the French and Spanish published by the Manila Filipiniana Book Guild (FBG). The most relevant for the period are Tomas de Comyn, *State of the Philippines in 1810*, FBG, XV, Manila, 1969; J. Bowring, *A Visit to the Philippine Islands*, London, 1859, and relevant sections from J. White, *A Voyage to Cochin China*, London, 1824, reprinted Kuala Lumpur, 1972.

The early phase of Chinese penetration into the Philippines is traced in E. K. Wickberg, 'The Chinese Mestizo in Philippine History', JSEAH, 5, 1 (1964); M. C. Guerrero, 'The Political Background', M. L. Diaz-Trechuelo, 'The Economic Background', both published in *The Chinese in the Philippines 1770–1893*, ed. A. Felix, Manila: Historical Conservation Society, XVI, 1969. For a later period a more substantial account is found in E. Wickberg, *The Chinese in Philippine Life, 1850–98*, New Haven, 1965.

Java and Madura

Sir Stamford Raffles, *History of Java*, London, 1817, reprinted Kuala Lumpur, 1965, 2 vols, and J. S. Furnivall, *Netherlands India: A Study of Plural Economy*, Cambridge, UK, 1939, reprinted 1967, are standard references for this period. Representative of modern scholarship are the overviews of M. C. Ricklefs in 'The Javanese in the Eighteenth and Nineteenth Centuries', published in D. G. E. Hall, *History of Southeast Asia*, London, 1981, and chapters 9 and 10 in the same author's *A History of Modern Indonesia*, London, 1981. A more detailed study is his monograph, *Jogjakarta under Sultan Mangkubumi, 1749–1792*, London, 1974. Surveys of socio-cultural aspects are available in the stimulating writings of D. H. Burger, *Sociologisch-Economische Geschiedenis van Indonesia*, intro. J. S. Wigboldus, 2 vols, Amsterdam, 1975; *Structural Changes in Javanese Society: The Village Sphere/The Supra-Village Sphere*, trans. L. Palmier, Ithaca: Cornell Indonesia Project, 1956–7; and the controversial work of C. Geertz, *Agricultural Involution: The Processes of Ecological Change in Indonesia*, Berkeley, 1963.

For the British period the main ground is covered in J. Bastin, *The Native Policies of Stamford Raffles in Java and Sumatra*, Oxford, 1957; 'Raffles' ideas on the land-rent system in Java and the Mackenzie Land tenure commission', VKI, 14 (1954); and H. R. C. Wright, *East-Indian Economic Problems of the Age of Cornwallis and Raffles*, London, 1961.

The mass of Dutch literature on the Java War (1825–30) has been meticulously researched in the modern studies of P. B. R. Carey. See 'The Origins of the Java War', *English Historical Review*, vol. XCI, no. 358; 'The Cultural Ecology of Early Nineteenth Century Java: Pangeran Dipanagara, a case study', Occasional Paper, no. 24, Institute of Southeast Asian Studies, Singapore, 1979; and *Babad Dipanagara: An account of the Outbreak of the Java War (1825–1830)*, MBRAS Monograph, no. 9, Kuala Lumpur, 1981.

Early studies of the culture system have been superseded by C. Fasseur, *Kultuurstelsel en Koloniale Baten: De Nederlandse exploitatie van Java 1840–60*, Leiden, 1975; Robert Van Niel, 'Measurement of Change under the Cultivation System in Java, 1837–51', *Indonesia*, 14 (1972), and 'The Effect of Export Cultivation in Nineteenth Century Java', MAS, 15, 1, (1981). For studies of specific areas see R. E. Elson, *Javanese Peasants and the Colonial Sugar Industry: Impact and Change in an East Javanese Residency, 1830–40*, Singapore, 1984, and C. Fasseur, 'Organisatie en sociaal-economische betekenis van de gouvernements-suikerkultuur in enkele residenties op Java omstreeks 1850', BKI, 133, 2–3 (1977). *Indonesian Economics: The Concept of Dualism in Theory and Practice*, The Hague, 1960, is concerned with the debates on the theory of 'dual economy'. For a recent statistical reassessment of production and a re-evaluation of some aspects of Geertz's theory of 'agricultural involution' see Peter Boomgaard, 'Java's Agricultural Production, 1775–1875', in *Economic Growth in Indonesia, 1820–1940*, VKI, 137, Dordrecht, 1989. *Changing Economy in Indonesia, I: Indonesia's Export Crops, 1816–1940*, initiated by W. M. F. Mansvelt, re-edited and continued by P. Creutzberg, The Hague, 1975, provides statistical information on Java's exports.

For accounts of Chinese enterprise in Java see J. Bastin, 'The Chinese Estates in East-Java during the British Administration', *Indonesië*, 7 (1954); Onghokham, 'The Peranakan Officers' Families in Nineteenth-Century Java', in *Papers of the Dutch-Indonesian Historical Conference, Lage Vuursche, The Netherlands, June 1980*, Leiden and Jakarta, 1982, and J. R. Rush, 'Social Control and Influence in Nineteenth Century Indonesia: Opium Farms and the Chinese in Java', *Indonesia*, 35 (1983).

Sumatra and the Malay World

J. Marsden, *History of Sumatra*, London, 1811, reprinted Kuala Lumpur, 1966, and E. M. Loeb, *Sumatra, Its History and People*, Vienna, 1935, provide important ethno-histories. Most modern studies are concerned largely with European political and commercial activity on the island. These include J. Kathirithamby-Wells, *The British West Sumatran Presidency (1760– 85): Problems of Early Colonial Enterprise*, Kuala Lumpur, 1977; J. Bastin, 'Palembang in 1811 and 1812', in *Essays on Indonesian and Malaysian History*, Singapore, 1961; Lee Kam Hing, 'Acheh's Relations with the British, 1760– 1819', M.A. thesis, University of Malaya, Kuala Lumpur; and J. W. Gould, *Americans in Sumatra*, The Hague, 1961.

C. Dobbin strikes a new path in her admirable study of the Padri War: *Islamic Revivalism in a Changing Peasant Economy, Central Sumatra, 1784– 1847*, London and Malmö, 1983. Her seminal article, 'Economic Change in Minangkabau as a Factor in the Rise of the Padri Movement, 1784–1830', *Indonesia*, 23 (1977), traces the revived commercial links between central and east Sumatra and the Malay peninsula. For an account of early Minangkabau migrations see T. Kato, *Matriliny and Migration: Evolving Minangkabau Traditions in Indonesia*, Ithaca, 1982. E. Graves, *The Minangkabau Response to Dutch Colonial Rule in the Nineteenth Century*, Cornell University Modern Indonesian Project, Monograph Series, no. 60, Ithaca, 1981, is an account of the impact of early colonial rule on Minangkabau society.

Compared to those on Aceh and the Minangkabau, historical writings on other areas of Sumatra are few. There is a good contemporaneous account of east Sumatra in J. Anderson, *Mission to the East Coast of Sumatra*, reprinted Kuala Lumpur, 1971. A. C. Milner, *Kerajaan: Malay Political Culture on the Eve of Colonial Rule*, Tucson, 1982, is also relevant. L. Castles, 'Statelessness and Stateforming tendencies among the Bataks before Colonial Rule', in *Pre-Colonial State Systems in Southeast Asia*, ed. A. J. S. Reid and L. Castles, MBRAS Monograph, no. 6, Kuala Lumpur, 1975, is a discussion of socio-political organization. There is little on Lampung apart from mid-nineteenth century accounts of *adat* and administrative structure in W. R. van Hoëvell, 'De Lampoengsche distrikten op het Eiland Sumatra', *Tijdschrift voor Neerlands-Indië*, 14, 1 (1852), and H. D. Canne, 'Bijdrage tot de Geschiedenis der Lampongs', TBG, 11 (1862). Interest in 'ship cloth' has in recent years attracted the attention of scholars to this area and southwest Sumatra. See Tos van Dijk and Nico de Jonge, *Ship*

Cloths of the Lampung, South Sumatra, Amsterdam, 1980, and M. Gittinger, 'A Study of Ship Cloths of South Sumatra', Ph.D. thesis, Columbia University, 1972.

Tuhfat-al-Nafis, ed. V. Matheson and B. Andaya, Kuala Lumpur, 1982, is indispensable for the history of the Malay world centred at Johor-Riau. Apart from this, the publication in recent years of a number of Malay verse chronicles on Sumatra are of relevance. These include M. O. Woelders, 'Het Sultanaat Palembang, 1811–1825', VKI, 72 (1975); G. W. J. Drewes, ed. and trans., *Hikajat Potjut Muhamat: An Achehnese Epic*, Bibliotheca Indonesica, 19, The Hague 1979; *Two Achehnese Poems: Hikajat Ranto and Hikajat Teungku Di Meuké'*, Bibliotheca Indonesica, 20, The Hague, 1980; J. Kathirithamby-Wells and Muhammad Yusoff Hashim, ed. and trans., *The Syair Mukomuko: Some historical aspects of a nineteenth century Sumatran court chronicle*, MBRAS Monograph no. 13, Kuala Lumpur, 1985; and D. J. Goudie, ed. and trans., *Syair Perang Siak*, MBRAS, Monograph no. 17, Kuala Lumpur, 1989.

For the growth of commerce and piracy in the Malay world N. Tarling, *Piracy and Politics in the Malay World*, Melbourne, 1963, provides a good general background. D. K. Bassett, 'Anglo-Malay Relations, 1786–1795', JMBRAS, 38, 2 (1965); 'British Commercial and Strategic Interest in the Malay Peninsula during the late eighteenth century', *Malaysian and Indonesian Studies*, Oxford, 1964; and D. Lewis, 'The Growth of the Country Trade to the Straits of Malacca, 1760–1777', JMBRAS, 43, 2 (1970), point to the importance of British trade in the area. H. R. C. Wright, 'Tin, Trade and Dominion', in *East-Indian Economic Problems of the Age of Cornwallis and Raffles*, London, 1961, offers interesting insights which remain to be fully explored.

Histories of individual Malay states referred to in the bibliographic essay for Chapter 7 emphasize their growing political insecurity and fragmentation, except at the important commercial nodules of Terengganu and Riau where Malay socio-cultural forces converged. See Shaharil Talib, 'The Port and Polity of Terengganu during the eighteenth and nineteenth centuries', in *The Southeast Asian Port and Polity: Rise and Demise*, ed. J. Kathirithamby-Wells and J. Villiers, Singapore, 1990; E. Netscher, *De Nederlanders in Djohor en Siak, 1602 tot 1865*, Batavia, 1870; 'Bijdragen tot de Geschiedenis van het Rijk van Lingga en Riouw', TBG, IV (1855); V. Matheson, 'Mahmud, Sultan of Riau and Lingga (1823–64)', *Indonesia*, 13 (1972), and B. W. Andaya and V. Matheson, 'Islamic Thought and Malay Tradition: The Writings of Raja Ali Haji of Riau (c. 1809–1870)', in A. J. S. Reid and D. Marr, eds, *Perceptions of the Past in Southeast Asia*, Singapore, 1979. C. Trocki, *Prince of Pirates: The Temenggongs and the Development of Johor and Singapore, 1784–1885*, Singapore, 1979, provides a useful account of early Chinese enterprise in Johor.

The Eastern Archipelago

E. S. de Klerck, *History of the Netherlands East Indies*, Rotterdam, 1938, reprinted Amsterdam, 1975, gives fair attention to the 'Outer Islands', focusing on the eastern half in chapter XIV, though from a colonial viewpoint. For a conceptualization of the area as part of the Indonesian cultural entity see G. J. Resink, *Indonesia's History between the Myths: Essays on Legal History and Historical Theory*, The Hague, 1968. T. Forrest, *A Voyage to New Guinea, and the Moluccas, from Balambangan . . . 1774–1776*, London, 1779, reprinted Kuala Lumpur, 1969, and H. T. Fry, *Alexander Dalrymple (1737–1808) and the Expansion of British Trade*, London, 1970, provide contemporary views of the region.

For modern studies of west Borneo see J. Jackson, *Chinese in the West Borneo Gold Fields: A Study in Cultural Geography*, Occasional Papers in Geography, no. 15, University of Hull, 1970; Wang Tai Peng, 'The Origins of the Chinese *Kongsi* with special reference to West Borneo', M.A. thesis, Australian National University, 1977; and J. van Goor, 'Seapower, Trade and State-Formation: Pontianak and the Dutch', in *Trading Companies in Asia, 1600–1800*, ed. J. van Goor, Amsterdam, 1986. Knowledge of Sulu has been greatly enhanced by the fascinating study by J. Warren, *The Sulu Zone, 1768–1898*, Singapore, 1981. Other modern studies of individual components of the region include H. J. de Graaf, *De Geschiedenis van Ambon en de Zuid-Molukken*, Franeker, 1977; J. Fox, *Harvest of the Palm: Ecological Change in Eastern Indonesia*, London, 1977; and C. Geertz, *Negara: The Theatre State in Nineteenth Century Bali*, Princeton, 1980.

INDEX

gambling, 220, 263, 368, 497, 533, 541–2, 565, 594, 598, 605–6
gamboge, 593
gaming farms, 610
Gandhavamsa, 279
Ganga (Ganges), 311
Gansu corridor, 196
Gansu Province (China), 116
Gapan, 610
Garnier, Francis, 11
Garuda, 285, 314
Gauda (present north Bangladesh), 320
Gaya (Bihar), 307
Geertz, Clifford, 21, 32–3, 39, 204
Geldern, Robert Heine, *see* Heine-Geldern, Robert
Gelgel kingdom, 526–7
Germany, 385
Gia Dinh, *see* Saigon
Gia-long, 583–5, 588–91
Giao-chi, *see* Vietnam
Giap, Tran Van, 10
Gilimanuk (Bali), 121, 133–4
Giri, 331–3, 519
Glamann, Kristof, 21
glass, 132–5, 263
Glass Palace Chronicle, 297, 548
Go Chien Vay, 125
Go Mun phase, 121
Goa, 352, 355, 365, 386, 416, 519
Golconda, 353
gold:
    archaeological records, 134, 199, 207;
    as commodity, 226, 411, 607;
    dust, 590;
    ingots, 584;
    jewellery, 580;
    as legal tender, 212, 214–15, 226, 266, 305, 350, 355, 435, 485;
    mining, 135, 257, 348, 356, 495, 503;
    Siberian, 186;
    see also bullion; money
Goloubew, Victor, 122
Gomatī (Gumti), 311
Gonda, J., 329
gongs, *see* musical instruments
gonorrhea, 461
Goreng Gareng, 210
Gowa, 487
graves, *see* burial
Great Nicobar, 79
Gresik, 190, 412, 492, 518–19
Gua Cha (Malaysia), 87, 101–2
Gua Lawa (Java), 89
Guangdong region (China), 96, 104, 347
Gujerat (India), 352, 471, 491, 494, 514
Gulf of Martaban, 377
Gulf of Thailand, 158, 192, 266, 582
Gulf of Tonkin, 265
gunpowder, 346, 380–2, 384–7, 392, 394–5, 432;
    see also firearms
Gunung Sĕmeru, 310

Gupta period, 295

Ha Tinh province, 268
Habsburg dynasty, 520
hadjis, *see* Muslims, pilgrimage to Mecca
Hadramaut, 558, 605
Hai Duong, 588
hair, 588
Hakkas, 348
Hall, D. G. E., 1–2, 18
Hamengkubuwana I, 596, 601
Hamengkubuwana II, 596, 601
Hamilton, Alexander, 562
hamlets, 215, 531, 591;
    see also village communities
Hammer, Ellen J., 20
Hamzah Fansuri, 522, 547
Han empire, 121, 125, 137, 154, 195–6, 261–3, 265
Hanafi sect, 515
Hang Gon, 131
Hang Tuah, 421, 435, 516
Hangzhou, 211, 217
Hanoi, 137, 139, 588–9;
    see also Thang-long
Hanoi region, 264
Haramayn, 558;
    see also Mecca; Medina
Haripuñjaya kingdom, 169, 294–5
Hariwangśa, 314
Harshavarman III, 161
Hartley, L. P., 45
Harvey, G. H., 6
Hasanuddin, sultan, 549
Hatien, 585–6
Ha-trai Pass, 266
Hayam Wuruk, 306
health, 461;
    see also disease; epidemics; *specific countries*
Heine-Geldern, Robert, 32
hemp, 609–10
Hemudu (China), 92
Henríquez, Pedro Calderón, 608
Henry, the Navigator, 354
Hideyoshi, 544
Higham, C., 97, 99, 120
Hikayat Aceh, 521
Hikayat Hang Tuah, 412
Hikayat Ranto, 605–6
Himalaya, 311
Hindu caste system, 526–7
Hindu gods, 157, 282, 318;
    Brahmā, 283, 295, 309, 313, 315–16, 328;
    Durgā, 312–13, 316;
    Gaņeśa, 312–13, 316;
    Guru, 309, 312–13, 316;
    Haricandana, 308–9;
    Indra, 254, 295, 526, 538, 547, 551;
    Krişna, 291, 314, 327;
    lower gods, 283, 313–14, 316, 319, 324, 327–9;
    Mahādeva, 309–10;

Paramésvara, 175–6
Pararaton, The, 4, 320, 326
Paris, 472, 474
Parkinson, C. N., 21
Parmentier, H., 5
Pasai, 190, 322, 443, 471, 485, 513–14, 516, 523, 525
Pasangan River, 228
Pasemah Plateau (Sumatra), 132, 199
Pasig River valley, 611
Pasuruhan district, 598–9
Patih Yunus, 410
Pattani:
    commerce and trade, 355, 358, 410, 416, 469, 479, 492;
    currency, 485;
    English in, 358;
    fires, 476;
    food supplies, 471;
    history, 409, 428, 583;
    Islam, 330, 519;
    legal system, 485;
    minority groups, 481, 493–4;
    population, 473;
    Portuguese in, 355, 416
Pavie, Auguste, 11
Pe Maung Tin, U., 5
Pea Sim Sim (Sumatra), 106
peasant uprisings, 245, 268, 421–2, 446–7, 453, 601;
    see also specific countries and uprisings
Pegu:
    Buddhism, 539, 563–4;
    commerce, 167, 409, 414, 471;
    firearm industry, 380–1, 385;
    history, 416–17, 420, 423–5, 436, 438, 446, 492–3, 577–9;
    population, 473;
    shipbuilding, 375, 377–9, 477;
    taxation, 446
Peinan (Taiwan), 103–4
Penang, 559, 603–5
Penanggungan, 310–11
pensions, 590
pepper, *see* spices
Perak (Malaysia), 131, 330, 353, 410, 431, 433, 449–50, 488
Perbatjaraka, R. Ng., 10
Perlak, 513
Perning, 67–8
Persia and Persians, 247, 290, 470, 494, 515
Peru, 464
Peruvia, 91
Phap Thuan, 301
Phap-Van temple, 301
Phattalung, 549
Phaulkon, Constantine, 383, 445
Phayre, Sir Arthur, 11
Phetchabun Range, 120
Philip II of Spain, 357, 530
Philippines:
    administrative and commercial structure, 607–11;

agriculture, 79, 102–4, 609–11;
archaeological records, 83, 85, 88, 102–6, 127, 129–30, 134–5;
British commercial interests, 610;
cash-crops, 609–10;
Catholic clergy's role, 357, 448, 452–3, 539–41, 551, 607–9, 611;
Christianity, 276, 356, 424, 448, 453–4, 521, 525, 529–31, 552, 560–1, 607, 609;
Christian–Muslim division, 534, 612;
civil service and bureaucracy, 608, 611;
compared with Dutch Indonesia, 606–9, 611;
corruption, 608;
corvée labour, 552–3, 561, 607, 611;
culture, 532–4, 609, 611–12;
ecological setting, 57, 64, 490;
economic and religious reforms, 608–9;
economy, 357, 411, 452, 593, 606–11;
Filipino grievances and rebellions, 452–3, 552–3, 561–2, 585, 607–8, 610–12;
forced cultivation, 610–11;
history, 135, 218, 418, 454, 530;
human ancestry, 56, 73–4, 76–7, 79;
in mid-eighteenth–early nineteenth centuries, 593, 606–12;
Islam, 276, 330, 333, 448, 453–4, 519, 521, 525, 612;
languages, 405;
mestizo community, 368–9, 371, 607–11;
name change, 356;
peninsulares, 611;
popular beliefs, 509–10, 532–4;
population, 463, 490, 494, 496, 531, 607–9;
principalia class, 453, 531, 552–3, 561;
religion and supralocal authorities, 550–1, 561;
ships and shipbuilding, 479;
Spanish rule, 344, 355–6, 418–503 *passim*, 521, 525, 561, 562, 606–12;
sugar industry, 503, 609;
taxation, 452–3, 530–1, 607, 609, 611;
textile manufacture, 609;
trade, 357, 467–8, 469, 490, 606–11;
see also Catholic Church; Luzon; Manila
Phimai, 577
Phitsanulok, 564, 577, 582
Phnom Kulen, 231
Phnom Penh, 163, 545
Phra Fang, 564
Phra Yot Chau, 419
Phraya Chakri, 577
Phraya Taksin, 577
Phu Hoa, 131
Phu Lon (Thailand), 118
Phuket, 501
Phung Nguyen culture, 96
Pidie, 483
Pietrusewsky, M., 98

INDEX

650   INDEX

stone industries and implements:
  adzes, knives and scrapers, 72, 85–6,
    88–9, 92, 96–7, 99–100, 102, 104,
    127;
  arrows and spears, 89, 102–3;
  Bacsonian tools, 87;
  edge-ground axes and handaxes, 71–2,
    83–4, 89;
  Hoabinhian stone tool industries, 81,
    85–7, 103;
  local variations, 83, 85–7;
  pebble and flake industry, 71–3, 78, 81,
    83–5, 87–9, 128;
  points, 83, 87, 89, 102, 105, 127;
  Sonviian industry, 83;
  Sumatraliths, 87
  'Tampanian' pebble and flake tools, 72;
  technology, 71, 81, 83–5, 87–9, 92, 94,
    98, 100–3, 128;
  Toalin industry, 89;
  transition to agriculture and, 85–9
Straits Asiatic Society, *see* Royal Asiatic
  Society
Straits of Melaka (Malacca), 159–216
  passim, 227, 247, 249, 362, 424, 502
Stutterheim, W. F., 5
Sufism, 521–3, 539–40, 558
sugar:
  cultivation, 55, 91, 94, 112–13, 343, 348,
    367, 468, 593, 598, 609–11;
  labour force, 500, 502;
  local consumption, 220, 503;
  slave-grown West Indian sugar, 503;
  processing, 224, 469, 500, 502–3, 593,
    598;
  source of, 189, 469, 502;
  trade, 469–70, 472, 502–3, 593–4, 609
Sui dynasty, 137, 263, 265
Sukothai, 169–70, 172, 175, 279, 298, 381,
  415, 511
Sukuh, 317
Sulawesi:
  archaeological and epigraphic records,
    83, 88–9, 106, 127, 132, 135;
  Dutch rule, 605;
  ecological setting, 57, 61, 65, 75, 89;
  firearms, 384;
  history and politics, 431, 440, 487–8,
    501;
  Islam, 519–20, 541, 548;
  kingship and religion, 548;
  manufacturing, 502;
  population, 463;
  rice economy, 472;
  tobacco cultivation, 470;
  trade, 469
Suleiman the Magnificent, 520
Sulu, 463, 502, 519, 543, 560, 602–3
Sumana, 298
Sumatra:
  agriculture, 105–6, 114;
  archaeological and epigraphic records,
    88, 132, 199, 277;

Buddhism, 54, 311, 315, 318, 320–1;
Bugis migration to, 440;
cash crops, 452, 469–70, 597, 604;
China and, 217, 227;
coffee cultivation, 603–5;
corruption, 598;
Dutch rule, 605;
ecological setting, 57, 64–5, 75, 80,
  86–7, 89, 105–6, 198;
English administration, 358, 441, 466,
  597–8, 602–4;
forced cultivation, 597–8;
gambir cultivation, 604–5;
history, 207, 217, 227–8, 304;
human ancestry, 79;
in mid-eighteenth–early nineteenth
  centuries, 597–8, 602–5;
Islam, 54, 227–9, 330, 332–3, 513, 519,
  541;
military technology, 385;
Minangkabau settlements, 442;
palynological records, 105–6, 114;
political fragmentation, 403, 418;
population, 463, 469, 501;
socio-economic structure, 597;
spice resources and trade, 198, 227–9,
  358, 452, 466–7, 469, 488, 598,
  602–5;
trade, 198–9, 217, 227, 249, 251, 320,
  597, 602–4;
traditional cults, 407
Sumbawa Island, 424, 431, 440, 469, 471,
  520, 526
Sunan Giri, 553–4
Sunan Kalijaga, 525
Sunda Strait, 173, 186, 198, 209, 424
Sunda-Banda volcanic arc, 57, 59
Sundaland (Sunda Shelf), 57, 61–4, 78,
  80, 84
Sung dynasty, 144–7, 199, 211, 215, 250,
  265
Sun-Moon Lake (Taiwan), 103
Sunnites, 515, 552
Suphanburi, 170
Surabaya:
  archaeological records, 210;
  history, 431–2, 473, 492;
  Islam, 333, 412, 518;
  location, 210–11, 217;
  military technology, 384;
  population, 219, 473, 501;
  religion and rebellions, 554;
  shipping, 219, 501
Surakarta, 451, 560, 595
Surat (India), 352–3, 358, 491
Suriyamarin, 577
Sūryavarman I, 160–2, 165, 234–5, 245–6,
  295, 300
Sūryavarman II, 161–2, 290
Susoh, 604
Sutherland, Heather, 39
Suvanna Banlang, 172
swamps, 80, 93, 99, 578